2016

Administrative Law

Eighth Edition

2016

Administrative Law

Eighth Edition

Paul Craig, MA, (Oxon)
BCL, QC (Hon), FBA
Professor of English Law St John's College, Oxford

SWEET & MAXWELL

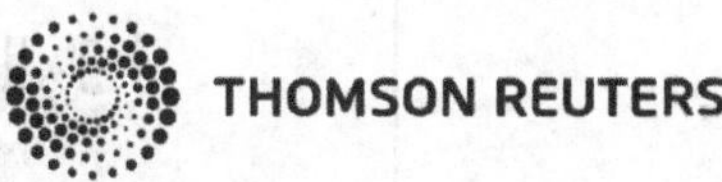

First Edition 1983 by Professor Paul Craig
Second Edition 1989 by Professor Paul Craig
Third Edition 1994 by Professor Paul Craig
Fourth Edition 1999 by Professor Paul Craig
Fifth Edition 2003 by Professor Paul Craig
Sixth Edition 2008 by Professor Paul Craig
Seventh Edition 2012 by Professor Paul Craig
Eighth Edition 2016 by Professor Paul Craig

Published in 2016 by Thomson Reuters (Professional) UK Limited, trading as Sweet & Maxwell, Friars House, 160 Blackfriars Road, London, SE1 8EZ (Registered in England & Wales, Company No.1679046. Registered Office and address for service: 2nd floor, 1 Mark Square, Leonard Street, London, EC2A 4EG).

For further information on our products and services, visit *www.sweetandmaxwell.co.uk*

Typeset by Letterpart Limited, Caterham on the Hill, Surrey, CR3 5XL.

Printed and bound in Great Britain by CPI Group (UK) Ltd, Croydon, CR0 4YY.

No natural forests were destroyed to make this product: only farmed timber was used and re-planted.

A CIP catalogue record of this book is available from the British Library.

ISBN: 978-0-414-05568-1

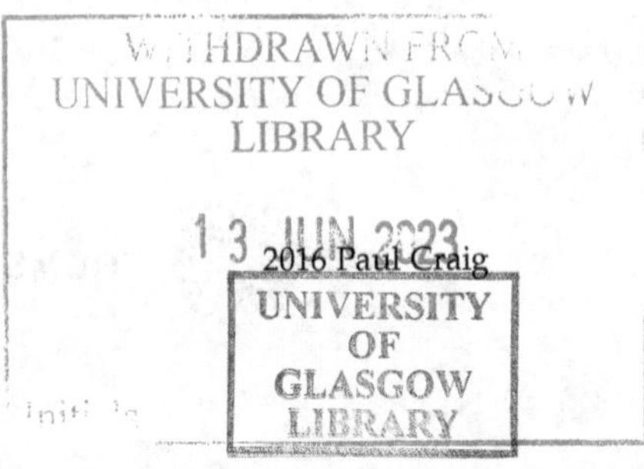

To the Memory of my Parents

Preface

There have been considerable developments in administrative law over the last four years. There has been legislation on a range of matters pertaining to administrative law. The important statutes include the Justice and Security Act 2013, Local Audit and Accountability Act 2014, Wales Act 2014, House of Lords Reform Act 2014, Deregulation Act 2015, Criminal Justice and Courts Act 2015, Scotland Act 2016, and the Cities and Local Authorities Devolution Act 2016. The courts have continued to be active and there have been significant new judicial decisions. Case law is discussed and analysed in detail, important examples being *Kennedy*, *Bank Mellat*, *Pham*, *Jones*, and *Carlile*. The Human Rights Act 1998 has, not surprisingly, generated a large amount of case law, as the courts have grappled with many of the key issues under this new statute. There has been much interesting secondary literature.

I have sought to incorporate all these changes, and to give a balanced account of the subject, which will be of equal use to those who are interested in the administrative system and those whose primary interest lies in judicial review. All chapters of the book have been revised to take account of the new developments, and several chapters have been substantially re-written. The format of the chapters includes a section on central issues at the beginning of each chapter, which provides a structured overview of the principal points raised in each chapter. There are in addition summaries in the course of some chapters, which are designed to aid students in their understanding of complex issues.

There are significant uncertainties concerning events, and/or the timing thereof, that impact on the subject matter of the book. The Conservative government seems committed to some reform of the HRA, and there are the implications of Brexit. There are also possible issues concerning the future of Scotland's place in the UK. Finding a window of opportunity for a new edition is especially difficult in such circumstances. This edition has been written on the basis of the law as it currently stands, including the HRA and the fact that EU law is binding on the UK until we leave the Union. When change occurs on these important matters it will be dealt with in a new edition of the book.

I would like to thank Nicola Thurlow, Krysia Domaszewicz and all those at Sweet & Maxwell who have provided great support in the production process with the book. I would also like to thank Anita for her help and understanding when work on the book impinged on family time.

Paul Craig
St John's College
Oxford

TABLE OF CONTENTS

8. INFORMATION, STANDARDS AND COMPLAINTS

12. NATURAL JUSTICE: HEARINGS

13. NATURAL JUSTICE: HEARINGS, PUBLIC INTEREST IMMUNITY AND CLOSED MATERIAL PROCEDURE

14. NATURAL JUSTICE: BIAS AND INDEPENDENCE

15. RULE-MAKING

17. ERROR OF FACT

18. FAILURE TO EXERCISE DISCRETION

19. ABUSE OF DISCRETION

20. HUMAN RIGHTS ACT

21. RATIONALITY AND PROPORTIONALITY

22. LEGITIMATE EXPECTATIONS

25. REMEDIES: STANDING

26. JUDICIAL REMEDIES

27. REMEDIES AND REFORM

TABLE OF CASES

56 Denton Road, Twickenham, Re; sub nom. War Damage Act 1943, Re [1953] Ch. 51; [1952] 2 All E.R. 799 Ch D 22–028, 22–029
A Local Authority (Inquiry: Restraint on Publication), Re; sub nom. Local Authority v Health Authority (Disclosure: Restriction on Publication) [2003] EWHC 2746 (Fam); [2004] Fam. 96; [2004] 2 W.L.R. 926 20–036
A v B (Investigatory Powers Tribunal: Jurisdiction) [2009] EWCA Civ 24; [2009] 3 W.L.R. 717; [2009] 3 All E.R. 416 . . . . . 5–054, 20–037
A v Essex CC [2003] EWCA Civ 1848; [2004] 1 W.L.R. 1881; [2004] 1 F.L.R. 749 30–018
A v HM Treasury [2010] UKSC 2; [2010] 2 A.C. 534; [2010] 2 W.L.R. 378 . . . . . 15–029, 19–024
A v Secretary of State for the Home Department [2003] EWCA Civ 175; [2003] I.N.L.R. 249; (2003) 147 S.J.L.B. 114 . . . . . 17–003, 17–035
A v Secretary of State for the Home Department [2013] EWHC 1272 (Admin) 9–028, 16–028
A v Secretary of State for the Home Department; sub nom. X v Secretary of State for the Home Department [2004] UKHL 56; [2005] 2 A.C. 68; [2005] 2 W.L.R. 87 . 13–016, 20–014, 23–004, 23–017
A v United Kingdom (3455/05) February 19, 2009 13–017
Abbott v Sullivan [1952] 1 K.B. 189; [1952] 1 All E.R. 226 CA 24–027
ABC v St George's Healthcare NHS Foundation Trust [2015] EWHC 1394 (QB); [2015] P.I.Q.R. P18; [2015] Med. L.R. 307 30–018
Abdulaziz v United Kingdom (A/94); Cabales v United Kingdom (9473/81); Balkandali v United Kingdom (9474/81) (1985) 7 E.H.R.R. 471 ECHR 23–009, 25–029
Abramova v Oxford Institute of Legal Practice [2011] EWHC 613 (QB); [2011] E.L.R. 385 30–018
Ackerley v Parkinson, 105 E.R. 665; (1815) 3 M. & S. 411 KB 16–018
ACT Construction Co Ltd v Customs and Excise Commissioners [1981] 1 W.L.R. 1542; [1982] 1 All E.R. 8 HL 9–021, 16–030, 16–023
Adami v Ethical Standards Officer of the Standards Board for England; sub nom. R. (Adami) v Ethical Standards Officer of the Standards Board for England [2005] EWCA Civ 1754; [2006] B.L.G.R. 397; [2007] L.L.R. 1 12–039
Adams v Adams [1971] P. 188; [1970] 3 W.L.R. 934 PDAD 24–009
Adams v Lord Advocate. See Adams v Scottish Ministers
Adams v Naylor [1946] A.C. 543; [1946] 2 All E.R. 241 HL 29–012
Adams v Scottish Ministers; sub nom. Adams v Advocate General for Scotland; Adams, Petitioner; Adams v Lord Advocate, 2004 S.C. 665; 2004 G.W.D. 18–384 IH (2 Div) 7–009, 25–030
Adams v War Office [1955] 1 W.L.R. 1116; [1955] 3 All E.R. 245 QBD 29–013
Adan (Hassan Hussein) v Secretary of State for the Home Department; sub nom. Secretary of State for the Home Department v Adan (Hassan Hussein); R. v Secretary of State for the Home Department Ex p. Adan (Hassan Hussein) [1999] 1 A.C. 293; [1998] 2 W.L.R. 702 HL 17–002
Adesina v Nursing and Midwifery Council Baines v Nursing and Midwifery Council; sub nom. R. (Adesina) v Nursing and Midwifery Council [2013] EWCA Civ 818; [2013] 1 W.L.R. 3156; (2013) 133 B.M.L.R. 196 20–014
Agricultural, Horticultural and Forestry Industry Training Board v Aylesbury Mushrooms [1972] 1 W.L.R. 190; [1972] 1 All E.R. 280 QBD 12–032
AH v Secretary of State for the Home Department [2011] EWCA Civ 787 13–018
Air Canada v Secretary of State for Trade (No.2) [1983] 2 A.C. 394; [1983] 2 W.L.R. 494 HL 13–008, 13–009, 13–011, 27–006, 27–053
Aklagaren v Fransson (C-617/10) Aklagaren v Akerberg Fransson (C-617/10) [2013] S.T.C. 1905; [2013] 2 C.M.L.R. 46 ECJ (Third Chamber) 20–070, 23–028
AL (Serbia) v Secretary of State for the Home Department [2006] EWCA Civ 1619; [2007] H.R.L.R. 7; [2007] U.K.H.R.R. 564 . . . . . 23–011, 23–017
Al Fawwaz v Secretary of State for the Home Department [2015] EWHC 468 (Admin); [2015] A.C.D. 80 13–022

TABLE OF LEGISLATION

Statutes

Statutory Instruments

TABLE OF EUROPEAN TREATIES & CONVENTIONS

Treaties

Conventions

CHAPTER 1

THE NATURE AND PURPOSE OF ADMINISTRATIVE LAW

1. CENTRAL ISSUES

i. There is considerable diversity of opinion concerning the nature and purpose of administrative law.[1] Description and prescription are not easily separated. For some, it is the law relating to the control of government power. Others place greater emphasis on rules designed to ensure that the administration effectively performs the tasks assigned to it. Yet others see the principal objective of administrative law as ensuring governmental accountability, and fostering participation by interested parties in the decision-making process. **1–001**

ii. None of these are right or wrong in some absolute sense. They are however, incomplete. An understanding of the nature and purpose of administrative law requires us to probe further into the way in which our society is ordered. It requires the articulation of the type of democratic society in which we live and some vision of the political theory which that society espouses. The role of more particular legal topics that constitute administrative law, such as natural justice and judicial review, can only be adequately assessed within such a framework.

iii. Concepts such as accountability, participation and rights do not possess only one meaning, which can be discerned by a purely "factual" inquiry. Nor can the place of such ideas be understood by pointing to their general connections with a democratic society. The meaning and importance of such concepts will differ depending on the type of democratic regime within which they subsist. Or to put the same point in a different way, every democratic society will have some ideas of rights, participation and accountability, but these will differ depending on the nature of that society. An attempt to discuss particular topics without considering these background ideas evidences a series of implicit assumptions about such ideas that are concealed and untested.

iv. The legislature and the courts are both important in determining the nature and shape of administrative law. The legislature enacts the policies that are directly constitutive of the administrative state. The legislature chooses whether these policies should be imbued with, for example, a market-oriented neoliberal philosophy, or with one which is more social democratic in its orientation. In this sense, the shape of administrative law is affected by the philosophy that underlies government policy. The courts

[1] Footnotes have been kept to a minimum within this chapter.

also have a major influence on the nature of the subject. They decide what particular constraints to impose on administrative action, and more generally on the overall purpose of judicial review. Administrative law, when viewed in this way, is always a combination of the political world, combined with the reactions of the judiciary.

v. This chapter begins by considering the Diceyan underpinnings of the traditional model of administrative law based on unitary democracy and the ultra vires model. The implications of this model for central tenets of judicial review are revealed, as are the deficiencies of the model, and there is an overview of the debate concerning the foundations of judicial review. The discussion then turns to rights-based conceptions of administrative law. The meaning of this conception is analysed, and the conceptual foundation for this vision of administrative law is considered. It has not gone unchallenged. The views of critics are explained and there is a response to these critiques. The remainder of the chapter is devoted to showing how different background conceptions of society can have a marked impact on the shape and nature of administrative law.

2. DICEY, UNITARY DEMOCRACY AND THE ULTRA VIRES PRINCIPLE

A. Basis of the Model

i. Unitary democracy

1–002 It is commonplace among administrative lawyers that Dicey is responsible for the subject having a "bad name" in this country. This is brought home to most law students early in their legal career when tackling the rule of law. Dicey's dislike of administrative law is readily apparent from the *Law of the Constitution*.

It is nonetheless very important to recognise that UK administrative law existed for over 300 years prior to Dicey, developing in earnest from the late 16th century onwards.[2] It did not conform to the stereotype depicted by Dicey, or the Diceyan heritage. The reality was that Parliament over four centuries enacted a very great deal of social and economic legislation that was regarded as valuable, subject to normal political contestation as to the desirable direction of policy. It readily used a plethora of institutions to discharge policy. Those charged with administration would normally discharge their task with care, but things could and did go wrong, hence the need for mechanisms of accountability, which were an admixture of political, administrative and legal. The legal contribution was predicated on the normative assumption that constraints were warranted to control such public power. There was, however, nothing specific about public law in this respect, since control was also central to many rules of private law. The legal contribution was not premised on the assumption that administration was something dangerous in the manner conveyed by red-light theory, nor does the evidence support the conclusion that courts generally ignored the social value of

[2] P. Craig, *UK, EU and Global Administrative Law: Foundations and Challenges* (Cambridge: Cambridge University Press, 2015), Ch.1.

the regulatory legislation that they were interpreting. To the contrary, they were mindful of this, and sought to effectuate it. The courts could of course err, being an imperfect institution like all others. It is true that some judges evinced a preference for the common law over legislation, but this was in relation to areas that had been developed by the common law. The courts did not by way of contrast feel that they should be devising broad regulatory scheme relating to the poor, land use, trade regulation, tax and the like. Nor did the courts regard such regulatory legislation in terms akin to being engulfed by some unnatural administrative leviathan. To the contrary, this was the ordinary nature of things in the world they inhabited, the existence of such measures being the norm from the fifteenth century onwards, although their incidence would perforce vary over time.

Dicey did not therefore capture the historical reality of UK administrative law, but his views did colour its later development. He based his view of administrative law on a certain view of democracy, which can be termed unitary. This is not a difficult idea and can be explained as follows.

First, all students are aware of the sovereignty of Parliament in the sense that Parliament is *omnicompetent*. It can in theory ban smoking in Paris, or repeal the grant of independence to former colonies. Less well known is an equally important aspect of sovereignty, which can be termed *parliamentary monopoly*: all governmental power should be channelled through Parliament for legitimation and oversight by the Commons. Dicey believed that the Commons controlled the executive, and that all public power should be subject to legislative oversight.[3] This democratic system was also "self-correcting", in that Dicey believed that the Commons accurately reflected the will of the people and controlled the executive. The all-powerful Parliament would not therefore enact legislation contrary to the wishes of the electorate.

Second, Dicey used the rule of law to reinforce sovereignty in the sense of parliamentary monopoly.[4] The Diceyan rule of law had both a descriptive and a normative content. In descriptive terms it was assumed that the regular law predominated, that broad discretionary power was absent and that all people were subject to the ordinary law. In normative terms it was assumed that this was a better system than that in France, where special rules and a distinct regime existed for public law matters. Thus for Dicey, democracy was unitary, in the sense that all public power was channelled through Parliament.

ii. Unitary democracy, the ultra vires principle and administrative law

This conception of democracy provided the framework for administrative law. **1–003**
Dicey did not provide extensive discussion of this, because he misconceived the scope of administrative power that existed when he wrote.[5] Notwithstanding this

[3] A.V. Dicey, *Introduction to the Study of the Law of the Constitution*, 10th edn (London: Macmillan, 1959), pp.73, 83, 84 and 433.

[4] Dicey, *Introduction to the Study of the Law of the Constitution* (1959), pp.188 and 193.

[5] Craig, *UK, EU and Global Administrative Law: Foundations and Challenges* (2015), Ch.1.

error, it was unitary democracy, buttressed by the rule of law, which provided the foundation for the judicial power of the courts. The connection can be expressed as follows.

It is readily apparent that legislation may grant discretionary power to a minister or agency. Parliament may not be able to foresee all eventualities and flexibility may be required to implement the legislation. The legislature will grant power, subject to conditions. For example, if a house is unfit for habitation a minister may order its demolition. Judicial intervention was designed to ensure that those to whom power was granted did not transgress the will of Parliament. If authority had been delegated to a minister to perform certain tasks on certain conditions, the courts' function was to check that only those tasks were performed and only where the conditions were present. The less well known face of sovereignty, that of parliamentary monopoly, thus demanded an institution to police the boundaries Parliament had stipulated.

The ultra vires principle was the doctrinal tool used to achieve this end. In a narrow sense, it captured the idea that the agency must have legal capacity to act on that subject matter: an institution given power by Parliament to adjudicate on employment should not take jurisdiction over non-employment issues. In a broader sense, the ultra vires principle provided the justification for constraints on the way in which the power was exercised. The agency must comply with rules of fair procedure, it must exercise its discretion to attain only proper and not improper purposes, it must act on relevant and not irrelevant considerations and it must not act unreasonably.

It would be mistaken to assume that the judiciary originally conceived of intervention in these terms. The origins of judicial review are complex and are interwoven with the intricacies of the prerogative writs.[6] The motivation behind early judicial review resided principally in the desire to ensure the predominance of the High Court over "inferior jurisdictions", and to provide remedies to those whom the established judiciary felt had been unjustly or illegally treated by such authorities. In striving to attain these objectives the court could indeed often come into direct conflict with the legislative will.

Notwithstanding this continuing tension, the rationale for judicial review was slowly transformed in the 19th century. The twin rationales for early judicial review continued to exist. They were, however, supplemented by a growing tendency to relate the exercise of judicial power to the will of Parliament. The ultra vires principle became the justification for judicial intervention, and set the boundaries for that intervention. It did so in two distinct, albeit related, ways.

On the one hand, the judiciary began to justify the exercise of jurisdictional control more explicitly in terms of ensuring that the tribunal did not extend the area over which the legislature granted it jurisdiction. Conflicting cases were reconciled by reasoning that the legislature intended differing agencies to possess

[6] S.A. de Smith, "The Prerogative Writs" (1951) 11 C.L.J. 40, and "Wrongs and Remedies in Administrative Law" (1952) M.L.R. 189; L. Jaffe and E. Henderson, "Judicial Review and the Rule of Law: Historical Origins" (1956) 72 L.Q.R. 345; E. Henderson, *Foundations of English Administrative Law* (Cambridge: Harvard University Press, 1963); A. Rubinstein, *Jurisdiction and Illegality* (Oxford: Oxford University Press, 1975); P. Craig, "*Ultra Vires* and the Foundations of Judicial Review" (1998) 57 C.L.J. 63.

different amounts of power.[7] This explanation was unconvincing, since reference to the particular statutes in the conflicting cases gave no indication that the results could be reconciled by differences in legislative intent. The questionable nature of the reasoning did not destroy the utility of the conceptual tool. The courts would simply police the boundaries made manifest by the particular legislative grant of authority, preventing the agency from entering areas where Parliament had forbidden it to tread. The courts acquired a malleable tool through which to justify intervention with administrative behaviour.

On the other hand, the courts became more aware of the limits to the exercise of judicial power. If the administrative agency was within its assigned area, then it was performing tasks allocated to it by the legislature. It was not contravening the legislative monopoly possessed by Parliament. The courts should therefore be wary of substituting their view for that of the chosen agency, and many of the judicial limits on discretion were justified as applications of statutory intent.[8]

The connection between this judicial approach and Dicey's rule of law was a natural one. The flexibility inherent in the idea of legislative intent preserved the veneer that the courts were simply applying the legislative mandate when controlling "inferior" jurisdictions. Dicey's rule of law added respectability by entrenching the idea that it was natural, right and a matter of constitutional principle that the ordinary courts should be supreme and that the ordinary law should be all pervasive. The consequences of this model will now be assessed.

B. Implications of the Ultra Vires Model

i. *Ultra vires: form of judicial intervention*

The model outlined above shaped the form of judicial intervention in the following way. There is a distinction between appeal and review. The former is concerned with the merits of the case; the appeal court can substitute its opinion for that of the initial decision-maker; appeals can lie on fact and law, or simply on law; and appeal rights are statutory, the courts having no inherent appellate jurisdiction. Review is, at least in theory, different from this being concerned not with the merits of the decision, but with its "validity"; and judicial review is not based upon statute, but on an inherent jurisdiction within the superior courts. **1–004**

This inherent power was by no means novel, and the texts of early administrative cases were replete with the language of review and jurisdiction. The original rationale for this inherent jurisdiction was linked to the rationale for judicial review: judicial desire to control inferior agencies and to protect the individual from illegalities committed by them. Nonetheless the development of the traditional model in the 19th century strengthened the rationale for this inherent jurisdiction, and reinforced the division between review and appeal.

It achieved the former by linking the basis for intervention to the enforcement of the legislative will. All grants of power by Parliament can be expressed in the following terms: if X exists, you may or shall do Y. For example, if an employee

[7] See Ch.16.
[8] See Ch.19.

is injured at work a tribunal may or shall grant compensation. The inherent jurisdiction of the court was therefore strengthened by the insistence that it was simply deciding whether X existed, and what considerations could be taken into account when determining Y. The courts, it could now be argued, must possess this inherent jurisdiction to safeguard the legislative monopoly of Parliament.

It achieved the latter by insisting that when the court was enforcing the legislative will it was only undertaking review and not appeal. The court was simply determining the "validity" of agency behaviour. The merits were for the agency, which had been assigned the task by Parliament. This may all appear to be conceptually neat, if not elegant. It however produced a host of problems, which will be examined more fully below.

ii. *Ultra vires: shape and scope of judicial intervention*

1–005 The traditional model had a profound effect on the shape and scope of judicial intervention in three distinct ways.

First, it accorded centre stage to control by the courts of administrative agencies. This was regarded as the main purpose of administrative law. The vigorous assertion of the supremacy of the ordinary law was directed towards controlling or containing the bureaucratic organs of the state. Such agencies were viewed with implicit distrust, and judicial control was the principal means of containing agency power.[9]

A second consequence of the traditional model was to foster a generalist as opposed to a functionalist approach to administrative law, with a reluctance to admit of special regimes. The legacy of the rule of law was that all rules of the legal system should be equally applicable to all.

A third consequence was to foster judicial activism in the following sense. The basic thrust behind this approach was that the ordinary courts and the ordinary law were superior, and that these would safeguard the legislative monopoly of Parliament by policing the boundaries of legislative intent through the ultra vires principle. Where there was a difference of opinion between the courts and an agency as to the meaning of a legislative condition, the opinion of the reviewing court would be preferred. The distinction between "validity" and the "merits" is an elusive one. Almost any scope of judicial intervention can be formally reconciled with the idea that the courts are thereby effectuating the intent of the legislature and simply intervening to determine the validity of the agency's decision.

iii. *The range of protected interests: natural justice and standing*

1–006 The traditional ultra vires model also had an impact on the range of interests within the ambit of administrative law. Administrative law has certain "gateways", methods of getting into the system. Thus, the rules of natural justice specify who should be heard before an agency makes its decision, and the rules of standing stipulate who can complain to the court that an agency overstepped its

---

[9] See also C. Harlow and R. Rawlings, *Law and Administration*, 2nd edn (London: Butterworths, 1997), Ch.1.

powers. A notable feature of administrative law was the insistence that only those with private rights in the sense of a cause of action in contract or tort, etc. were allowed into the system. The gateways were barred to those who did not possess such rights.[10]

The common law preoccupation with traditional rights is a partial explanation of this phenomenon. However, the judicial attitude fitted well with the traditional model. The judicial function was to police the boundaries of legislative intent through the ultra vires principle, with the consequence that the individual's private autonomy was protected by confining the public body to its assigned area. The only types of private autonomy which the courts would recognise were, however, rights derived from contract, tort, etc. The idea that the ordinary law was being applied by the ordinary courts strengthened the belief that the court was doing no more than applying standard notions of contract or tort to cases where the defendant happened to be a public body.

There was, however, a tension inherent in the traditional model, which explains much of the complex case law on natural justice and standing: the twin objectives of policing the frontiers of legislative intent and protecting only traditional private rights could conflict. Legislation relating to matters such as licensing might not affect rights in the traditional sense. A disappointed applicant could not construct a case in contract or tort, etc. The court might, however, be eager to fulfil its policing role. Something has to give. Either the court gives up its policing role in this area, or it relaxes the definition of "right" and thereby widens the gateways for the citizen. The courts sometimes did one and sometimes the other, hence the resulting complexity in the case law.[11]

iv. Type of procedural protection

The traditional model also influenced the meaning of "procedural rights". The **1–007**
twin elements of natural justice are a right to be heard and a right to an unbiased hearing. They assume a method of decision-making which lawyers call adversarial adjudication. The parties present their arguments to the relevant agency, which adjudicates on the matter.

The traditional model shaped this notion of process rights in the following way. If we assume, as the traditional model does, that the ordinary law is being applied by the ordinary courts to cases involving administrative agencies, then it becomes natural to assume that the process rights which such agencies should have to follow will be the same as those used by the ordinary courts. The procedure in the courts is adversarial adjudication. Barristers present their arguments and do battle with their adversaries before an unbiased judge. Agencies should therefore have to comply with the same type of procedure. Three consequences follow from this reasoning.

First, it helps to explain the distinction between "administrative" and "judicial" proceedings in some mid-20th century case law.[12] If the agency

[10] See Ch.25.

[11] See Ch.25.

[12] See Ch.12.

procedure was to be adversarial adjudication then certain courts felt that this was only suitable if the agency was itself in some sense "judging" a matter between two opposing litigants.

Second, the traditional model helps to explain the judicial unwillingness to grant process rights in "legislative" contexts. Courts have been reluctant to interfere when an agency is making a rule of a generalised nature rather than engaging in individualised adjudication. The flaws in this reasoning will be examined later. The judicial response did, however, fit the "logic" of the traditional model. This was because it might be difficult to apply process rights designed for "judging", to a situation when someone was "legislating". It was also because to accept that process rights might be necessary challenged the unitary vision of democracy, which was premised on the assumption that Parliament was the sole body that legislated. The public participated through the vote and then indirectly and vicariously through their MP. To admit that agencies made rules of a legislative nature, and that people should be given process rights to participate in their formation, challenged the idea that democracy really was unitary. It would be to accept that bodies outside Parliament legislated, and that the ordinary parliamentary processes could not adequately control such norms.

The third consequence of modelling procedural rights after those of the ordinary courts was to constrict experimentation with other types of process right.[13] If the courts insist that agency process rights are mirrored on those of ordinary courts even if in a modified way, then it follows that the agency is presumed to be in some way "judging" between two sides. The type of decision-making is adjudication and the species of process rights reflects this. We might, however, decide that certain types of agency decision-making should not take the form of judging, but should rather, for example, be like arbitration, resort to chance or managerial discretion. Distinctive process rights which protect and reflect these types of decision-making will be required. The traditional model impeded such experimentation.

v. *Tort, contract and public bodies*

1–008 The traditional model reinforced the demand that the ordinary principles of tort and contract should be applied to public bodies. Dicey attacked the French system for the way in which he perceived it as giving advantageous treatment to public officials who committed a wrong. The situation in England was different, since the ordinary law applied to all and special regimes did not exist. The Diceyan legacy forestalled reasoned discussion as to how far ordinary principles of tortious or contractual liability ought to be modified when dealing with public bodies by insisting that any such distinct regime would be contrary to the rule of law. When such discourse did surface in the case law it assumed a defensive, almost apologetic air. This has changed recently as the courts have become more willing to articulate and assess what the justifiable, distinct needs of the public body might in fact be.[14]

---

[13] See Ch.12.

[14] See Ch.30.

C. Deficiencies of the Ultra vires Model

1–009 Certain deficiencies of the traditional model have been touched on above. A more structured survey of these difficulties is nonetheless warranted. The traditional view was flawed because the premises about the way in which democratic society operated were false. The idea of unitary democracy and legislative monopoly, in which all public power was channelled through Parliament, and in which Parliament controlled the executive, was flawed. There was a growing awareness that the legislature did not in fact control the executive but vice versa. Legislation became the prerogative of the executive and parliamentary acquiescence was ensured by the managers of the party machine. There was an increasing realisation that Parliament did not wield all public power, and that many other institutions exercised some species of public authority. These themes will be developed more fully later. Let us now consider their general implications for the traditional model.

i. *Mistake avoidance and distrust of the administrative state*

1–010 The growth of administrative law was intimately connected with extension of governmental functions relating to the poor, the unemployed, trade regulation and the like. Those who disliked such social intervention, including Dicey, tended to view the agencies applying such laws with suspicion. The predominance accorded to the "ordinary law" applied by the "ordinary courts" was a means of controlling these agencies, and of supervising their substantive policies.

It is important to understand that this Diceyan legacy did not reflect the conception of administrative law as it developed from the late 16th century onwards. Administrative law during this period developed in part to ensure that the administration was properly accountable for its action, but the courts were also mindful of the social value of the regulatory policies enacted by the legislature and sought to ensure that they were efficaciously applied.[15] This historic theme was picked up by later writers who, like their earlier counterparts, perceived the value of the social policies applied by the administration. A more positive desire that the agency should fulfil its policy mandate became the focus of discussion, as it had been in the past, and the courts were perceived as but one factor in fulfilling this objective. Robson approached the study of administrative justice without

> "… any ready-made assumption that every tribunal which does not at the moment form part of the recognised system of judicature must necessarily and inevitably be arbitrary, incompetent, unsatisfactory, injurious to the freedom of the citizen and to the welfare of society".[16]

---

[15] Craig, *UK, EU and Global Administrative Law: Foundations and Challenges* (2015), Ch.1.

[16] W. Robson, *Justice and Administrative Law, A Study of the British Constitution* (Macmillan,1928), XV.

ii. Form and scope of intervention: indeterminacy of the ultra vires principle

1–011 The basis of the traditional model was that the courts would preserve the legislative monopoly of Parliament by ensuring that the agency remained within the area assigned to it by the legislature, and that the courts would achieve this through the ultra vires principle. Five problems can be identified, all of which relate to the indeterminacy of legislative intent.

The *first* problem is the difficulty of defining the scope of an institution's designated area. The flexibility inherent in the ultra vires concept preserved the veneer that the courts were simply obeying the legislative mandate, but this very flexibility ultimately robbed the reasoning of conviction. Consider a simple statute stipulating that if an employee is injured at work then he or she shall receive compensation. In one obvious sense all these legislative conditions define the scope of the agency's power. There must be "an employee", "who is injured", "at work", before the agency can give any compensation. However, to allow the reviewing court to substitute its opinion on all such matters would mean that the agency then only had power when the court agreed with the agency's findings, not otherwise. Courts have been aware of this conundrum and have defined jurisdictional error in differing ways, some broad, some narrow.[17] The reality is that almost any such justification can be formally reconciled with legislative intent. It can always, for example, be argued that Parliament intended all questions of law to reside with the ordinary courts, or by way of contrast, that Parliament intended that only certain "preliminary" conditions be judicially reviewed. Legislative intent could legitimate almost all types of judicial control, and therefore lost its potency to legitimate any particular one. This malleability of the ultra vires principle led Sir John Laws to the conclusion that it was merely a tautology. The principle did not itself indicate what was to count as a want of power, and thus its invocation amounted to saying no more than that the court would strike down what it chose to strike down.[18] He noted that the ultra vires principle was in reality a fig-leaf, enabling the courts to intervene in decisions without an assertion of judicial power which too nakedly confronted the established authority of the executive or other public bodies.

A *second* problem is that the model came under particular strain when the legislation attempted to preclude judicial interference, as it did when, for example, it said that the minister's determination of the relevant issue should be conclusive or final. If the courts are enforcing legislative intent through the ultra vires principle, then their role should be limited in such instances. If they persist with review then the traditional model must be modified to accommodate the idea that the judiciary are not simply "implementing" legislative intent, but were also

---

[17] See Ch.16.

[18] Sir John Laws, "Illegality: The Problem of Jurisdiction", in M. Supperstone and J. Goudie (eds), *Judicial Review*, 2nd edn (London: Butterworths, 1997), Ch.4.

"supplementing" it, through the existence of certain judicially developed principles, which would be implicitly read into any legislation. This idea has considerable historical lineage.[19]

The *third* difficulty with the ultra vires principle relates to the development of the law across time. Control over, for example, discretion has not remained static. New controls have been added to the list. If, for example, the courts recognise proportionality as an independent head of review in 2018 this will not be because legislative intent suddenly signalled in some miraculous fashion that this should be so. It will be because the courts decide that it should be added to existing heads of review. The result can be expressed through the language of ultra vires. It can, in formal terms be stated that it will henceforth be ultra vires for an agency to exercise its discretion in a disproportionate manner. Any head of review can be rationalised in this manner. This should not conceal the obvious fact that it is the courts which decide on the appropriate heads of review.

The *fourth* difficulty concerns the relationship between direct and collateral attack. Claimants can challenge agency decisions either directly through judicial review, or collaterally through a defence to, for example, a criminal prosecution in which the validity of the order on which the prosecution is based is contested. It would be possible in theory for the courts to determine the incidence of collateral attack by reference to legislative intent. This is, however, difficult since the legislation normally provides no sure guidance on the matter. The courts' approach has been to decide on the availability of collateral challenge by considering issues of first principle concerning, for example, the injustice which could follow if the individual were not able to challenge a decision or order collaterally.[20]

A *final* difficulty relates to the changing nature of the legislation that the courts interpret. The growth of the welfare state led to the use of more open-textured legislation and the grant of wide discretionary powers. The task of interpreting legislative intent became correspondingly more difficult.[21] If statutes require the courts to interpret phrases such as "public interest" and "individual need", then legislative intent may provide scant guidance as to how these broadly framed discretionary powers should be interpreted, with the consequence that the courts form their own view as to what considerations should be deemed to be relevant and what purposes can legitimately be pursued by the agency.

iii. Ambit of public law: straining of the ultra vires principle

A further difficulty with the ultra vires principle concerns the range of institutions and subject matter that are susceptible to judicial review.[22] The ultra vires principle is most readily applicable to statutory powers wielded by traditional public bodies, although there are real problems with applying the doctrine even in 1–012

---

[19] Thus, the rationale for natural justice was sometimes expressed as the application of implied legislative intent, and sometimes as the courts supplying the omission of the legislature.

[20] See Ch.24.

[21] R. Unger, *Law in Modern Society* (New York: Free Press, 1976), pp.192–203.

[22] D. Oliver, "Is the *Ultra vires* Rule the Basis of Judicial Review?" [1987] P.L. 543.

this context. The courts have, however, as will be seen below,[23] expanded the scope of public law in a number of ways, which place the ultra vires principle under further strain.

The courts have applied the principles of judicial review to *non-statutory exercises of power by public bodies*. These principles have been held to be applicable to the prerogative and to certain forms of common law contracting power exercised by such public bodies. It is difficult to apply the ultra vires principle in these instances, because the power is not delineated in the same way as statutory grants of authority, and it is more difficult to characterise the courts' role as demarcating the ambit of parliamentary intent.

The courts have also applied principles of a public law nature to *exercises of power by institutions which are not public bodies in the traditional sense, in circumstances where these bodies do not derive their power from statute*. This has become more marked because of the reforms in the law of remedies,[24] but it is not a recent development. The courts have applied these principles to such bodies ever since the time when it became meaningful to speak of judicial review and public law principles at all. Trade associations, trade unions and corporations with de facto monopoly power have, for example, been subject to some principles that are applied to public bodies *stricto sensu*. These bodies do not derive their power from statute and therefore judicial control cannot be rationalised through the idea that the courts are delineating the ambit of Parliament's intent. The principles of judicial review are regarded as of generalised application to institutions that wield a certain degree of power, and the principles are then read into the governing document under which the body operates.

iv. Defects in the private rights theme

1–013 A characteristic of the traditional model was that the gateways to administrative law were only open to those with private rights in contract, tort, etc. This aspect of the traditional model has three related defects.

We have already touched on the first difficulty with this approach. If the private rights theme were to be taken literally it would mean that the courts could not police or monitor the boundaries of legislative intent, unless such rights were present. There are many areas where legislation is passed that does not accord rights in contract, tort, etc. to the affected parties. Courts have in such instances often ignored the need for private rights, or defined "rights" more expansively in their desire to exercise their policing role over such legislation.

Second, even if traditional private rights are present, it is mistaken to suppose that the case is simply a private dispute, which an individual has with a public body. Imagine that a public body made a compulsory purchase order on John's property. John believes that the order is invalid. If he is correct there will be a trespass action, his private rights will be affected and he comes within the gateways of administrative law. However, the case is not simply "about" John's private rights. If John wins his private rights will be vindicated. Whether he wins will however, depend on the validity of the compulsory purchase order. When

[23] See Ch.27.
[24] See Ch.27.

contesting this issue, John will be concerned with the scope of the planning legislation. The case is not just about John's private rights. It is about the legitimate ambit of the regulatory legislation in that area.[25]

Third, interests that are not rights may nonetheless be extremely important and should properly be the subject of administrative law. Legislation on social welfare, race relations, sexual equality, licensing and trade regulation, may seriously affect people even if the legislation does not accord them rights.

D. Debate about the Ultra vires Principle

The challenge to the ultra vires principle has not gone unanswered. There was a lively debate[26] between defenders of the principle,[27] and those who believe that it cannot provide the real foundation for judicial review.[28] Limits of space preclude detailed examination of the contending arguments. The following will suffice for present purposes. 1–014

First, "ultra vires" is indicative of action that is beyond power. The phrase does not tell us whether an act is beyond power because the legislature intended to place certain limits on an agency, or whether the limits are more properly regarded as a common law creation of the courts. It is this issue which divides the two camps in the debate about the foundations of judicial review.

Second, the traditional ultra vires model, or specific legislative intent model, was based on the assumption that judicial review was legitimated because the courts were applying the intent of the legislature. The ultra vires principle was

---

[25] See Ch.25.

[26] T.R.S. Allan, "The Constitutional Foundations of Judicial Review: Constitutional Conundrum or Interpretative Inquiry" (2002) 61 C.L.J. 87, doubted the utility of the debate, for a response see P. Craig, "Constitutional Foundations, the Rule of Law and Supremacy" [2003] P.L. 92.

[27] Sir William Wade and C. Forsyth, *Administrative Law*, 10th edn (Oxford: Oxford University Press, 2009); C. Forsyth, "Of Fig Leaves and Fairy Tales: The *Ultra vires* Doctrine, the Sovereignty of Parliament and Judicial Review" [1996] C.L.J. 122; M. Elliott, "The Demise of Parliamentary Sovereignty? The Implications for Justifying Judicial Review" (1999) 115 L.Q.R. 119; M. Elliott, "The *Ultra vires* Doctrine in a Constitutional Setting: Still the Central Principle of Administrative Law" (1999) 58 C.L.J. 129; C. Forsyth, "Heat and Light: A Plea for Reconciliation", in C. Forsyth (ed.), *Judicial Review and the Constitution* (Oxford: Hart Publishing, 2000), Ch.18; M. Elliott, *The Constitutional Foundations of Judicial Review* (Oxford: Hart Publishing, 2001); C. Forsyth and M. Elliott, "The Legitimacy of Judicial Review" [2003] P.L. 286.

[28] Oliver, "Is the *Ultra vires* Rule the Basis of Judicial Review?" [1987] P.L. 543; *De Smith's Judicial Review*, 6th edn (London: Sweet & Maxwell, 2007); Laws, "Illegality: The Problem of Jurisdiction", in Supperstone and Goudie (eds), *Judicial Review* (1997); P. Craig, "*Ultra Vires* and the Foundations of Judicial Review" (1998) 57 C.L.J. 63; D. Dyzenhaus, "Reuniting the Brain: The Democratic Basis of Judicial Review" (1998) 9 Pub. Law Rev. 98; P. Craig, "Competing Models of Judicial Review" [1999] P.L. 428; N. Bamforth, "*Ultra Vires* and Institutional Independence", in C. Forsyth (ed.), *Judicial Review and the Constitution* (Oxford: Hart Publishing, 2000), Ch.6; D. Oliver, "Review of Non-Statutory Discretions", in Forsyth (ed.), *Judicial Review and the Constitution* (2000), Ch.14; J. Jowell, "Of Vires and Vacuums: The Constitutional Context of Judicial Review", in Forsyth (ed.), *Judicial Review and the Constitution* (2000), Ch.15; N. Barber, "The Academic Mythologians" (2001) 22 O.J.L.S. 369; P. Craig and N. Bamforth, "Constitutional Analysis, Constitutional Principle and Judicial Review" [2001] P.L. 763; P. Joseph, "The Demise of *Ultra Vires*—Judicial Review in the New Zealand Courts" [2001] P.L. 354; Craig, "Constitutional Foundations, the Rule of Law and Supremacy" [2003] P.L. 92; Craig, *UK, EU and Global Administrative Law: Foundations and Challenges* (2015), pp.125–153.

regarded as both a necessary and sufficient basis for judicial intervention. It was necessary in the sense that any head of judicial review had to be fitted into the ultra vires doctrine. It was sufficient in the sense that if such a ground of review could be fitted into the ultra vires principle it obviated the need for further inquiry. On this view, the doctrines of administrative law derived their legitimacy and content from the fact that the legislature intended them to apply in a particular way in a particular statutory context.

Third, advocates of the common law model of illegality challenged these assumptions. They argued that the ultra vires principle was indeterminate, unrealistic, beset by internal tensions, and unable to explain the application of public law principles to bodies that did not derive their power from statute. Critics of the ultra vires principle are of course concerned to keep bodies within their assigned spheres. It is moreover self-evident that the enabling legislation must be considered when determining the ambit of a body's powers. This is not, however, the same thing as saying that the heads of review, their meaning or the intensity with which they are applied can be justified by legislative intent.

Fourth, proponents of the common law model argued that the principles of judicial review were in reality developed by the courts, and were the creation of the common law. The legislature rarely provided indication as to the content and limits of what constitutes judicial review. The courts imposed the controls they believed were normatively justified on the grounds of justice, the rule of law, etc. They decided on the appropriate procedural and substantive principles of judicial review applicable to statutory and non-statutory bodies alike. If Parliament did not like these controls then it could make this clear and the courts would adhere to such dictates. If, moreover, Parliament manifested a specific intent as to the grounds of review the courts would apply this, in the same way as they would obey such intent in other areas where the primary obligations are the creation of the common law. There is, therefore, nothing odd or strange about principles derived from the common law, which are then supplemented or complemented by specific legislative intent if and when this is to be found. This is indeed the paradigm in areas such as contract, tort, restitution, and trusts.

Fifth, there is also a modified ultra vires model, or general legislative intent model. Supporters of the ultra vires doctrine accepted some criticisms from proponents of the common law model. They maintain, however, that ultra vires must still be the central principle of judicial review. It is argued that legislative intent *must* be found in order to vindicate judicial review, since to discard the ultra vires principle would entail a strong challenge to parliamentary sovereignty. They further maintain that legislative intent *can* be found to legitimate the exercise of judicial power. They argue in terms of general legislative intent. Parliament is taken to intend that its legislation conforms to the basic principles of fairness and justice which operate in a constitutional democracy. However, because Parliament itself cannot realistically work out the precise ramifications of this general idea it leaves or delegates power to the courts, which fashion the more particular application of this idea in accordance with the rule of law.

Sixth, the claim that judicial review *must* be grounded in legislative intent, since to do otherwise would entail a strong challenge to the sovereignty of Parliament, is unfounded. It is premised on misconceptions as to the meaning of parliamentary sovereignty.[29] It is also predicated on an analytical argument to the effect that what an all-powerful Parliament did not prohibit, it must be taken to authorise either expressly or impliedly. From this it was said to follow that all elements of judicial review must be cloaked with legislative intent, since if this were not so the assumption would be that Parliament did not intend the constraints on statutory power to exist, with the consequence that the judicial imposition of such limits would amount to a strong challenge to parliamentary sovereignty. This argument is, however, doubly problematic.[30] It is misconceived in its own terms and if it were correct it would mean that legislative intent must equally be regarded as the foundation for all bodies of law, including contract, tort, trusts, property, restitution and the like, where common law principles are read into legislation. The analytical claim is also problematic because it contains an inherent contradiction, which renders the need for general legislative intent otiose. If the analytical argument were correct, then it would mean that Parliament must be taken to have a specific legislative intent as to the application of the principles of judicial review, with the consequence that there would be no need for any modified ultra vires theory based on general legislative intent; if the argument is inapplicable in some particular instance, such that Parliament does not have any such intent as to the application of judicial review, then the modified ultra vires theory is equally otiose since the courts could choose between any of the possible tests for judicial review without fear of infringing parliamentary sovereignty.

Finally, the claim that general legislative intent to comply with the rule of law *can* be found does not show that this is the foundation for the principles of judicial review. There is no more or less reason to say that the legislature believes in basic precepts of justice in contract or tort, the details of which will be worked out by the common law courts through a delegation of power by the legislature, which is unable to make detailed provision for such matters itself. The same exercise could be applied to all areas of private law, and indeed to criminal law. If the empirical argument as to general legislative intent suffices for the conclusion that such intent is foundational for public law, then the same must be true for all areas of the law where statute exists.[31]

3. RIGHTS, LEGALITY AND ABUSE OF POWER

A. Nature of the Model

The defects of the traditional model of public law have been presented above. A prevalent approach is to argue for a rights-based conception of public law. It is based on the imposition of standards of legality to prevent abuse of power by public bodies *stricto sensu*, and by other quasi-public or private bodies with a certain degree of power. Judicial intervention is no longer premised on the idea that the courts are simply applying the legislative will. Their role is to articulate principles that guide administrative action and interpret legislation in the light of **1–015**

[29] Craig, *UK, EU and Global Administrative Law: Foundations and Challenges* (2015), pp.148–153.

[30] Craig, *UK, EU and Global Administrative Law: Foundations and Challenges* (2015), pp.139–145.

[31] Craig, *UK, EU and Global Administrative Law: Foundations and Challenges* (2015), pp.145–147.

these principles. It is, however, necessary to press further and inquire as to the meaning of this approach, and the standards of legality to be applied.

B. Rights-Based Approach

i. *Protection of fundamental rights*

1–016 A common element of a rights-based approach is that the courts should whenever possible interpret legislation and administrative discretion to be in conformity with fundamental rights. This can be achieved through judicial presumptions that legislation is not intended to interfere with these rights, combined with intensive scrutiny demanding greater justification of discretionary decisions that impinge on such important interests. The courts have taken important steps in this direction,[32] and the Human Rights Act 1998 provides a more secure foundation for this approach.[33]

This approach requires some choice as to what are to count as fundamental rights, and their more particular meaning. This is unavoidable. Any democracy will have some conception of liberty and equality interests. If, however, we delve beneath the surface of phrases such as "liberty" and "equality" then significant differences become apparent, even amongst those who subscribe to some version of liberalism. This leaves out of account the issue as to how far social and economic interests ought to be protected. It also fails to take account of other visions of democracy, of a communitarian rather than liberal nature, which might well interpret the civil/political rights and the social/economic rights differently.[34]

ii. *A rights-based view of law and adjudication*

1–017 A second possible meaning of a rights-based approach to public law draws on a particular theory of law and adjudication. Any view of public law must be based upon some view, explicitly or implicitly, of law and the adjudicative process.[35] Dworkin articulates a rights-based view of law and adjudication.[36] His theory is based on law as integrity, according to which,

> "... propositions of law are true if they figure in or follow from the principles of justice, fairness and procedural due process that provide the best constructive interpretation of the community's legal practice".[37]

It is integral to the Dworkinian approach that, subject to questions of fit, the court should choose between

---

[32] See Ch.19.

[33] See Ch.20.

[34] P. Craig, *Public Law and Democracy in the United Kingdom and the United States of America* (Oxford: Oxford University Press, 1990); W. Kymlicka, *Contemporary Political Philosophy: An Introduction*, 2nd edn (Oxford: Oxford University Press, 2002).

[35] Craig, "Constitutional Foundations, the Rule of Law and Supremacy" [2003] P.L. 92.

[36] R. Dworkin, *Taking Rights Seriously* (Cambridge: Harvard University Press, 1977), and R. Dworkin, *Law's Empire* (Cambridge: Harvard University Press, 1988).

[37] Dworkin, *Law's Empire* (1988), p.225.

> "... eligible interpretations by asking which shows the community's structure of institutions as a whole in a better light from the stand-point of political morality".[38]

An individual has a right to the legal answer forthcoming from the above test.

C. Principles of Good Administration

This second model of judicial review not only protects fundamental rights, but also procedural and substantive principles of good administration, such as: legality, procedural propriety, participation, openness, rationality, relevance, propriety of purpose, reasonableness, legitimate expectations, legal certainty and proportionality. The creativity involved in this exercise should be recognised. Ideas such as legality are just as malleable as those they replace. The existence of legality as a principle of good administration does not dictate its sphere of application. It does not determine whether the courts should always substitute their view on issues of law for that of the administration, the scope of review for fact or how intensively the court should review discretion.[39] 1–018

D. Justifications for this Approach

i. *Courts, legislature and constitutional democracy*

The constitution assigns a role to the courts as well as the legislator and this was perceived by those who laid the foundations for review.[40] In a constitutional democracy it is both right and proper for the courts to impose limits on the way in which power is exercised. This was indeed the traditional approach to the constraints imposed on public power in the seminal case law that laid the foundations for judicial review. The courts imposed limits that were felt to be normatively justified. Coke, Heath, Holt and Mansfield based judicial review on the capacity of the common law to control public power.[41] The principles of judicial review are therefore properly developed by the courts in accord with the common law model set out above. 1–019

The courts impose the controls they believe are normatively justified on the grounds of justice, the rule of law, etc. If the omnipotent Parliament does not like these controls then it can make this unequivocally clear. If it does so the courts will adhere to such dictates. If Parliament manifests a specific intent as to the grounds of review the courts will also obey this, in the same way as in other areas where the primary obligations are the creation of the common law. Rationalisations cast in terms of legislative intent of the kind embodied in the ultra vires

---

[38] Dworkin, *Law's Empire* (1988), p.256.

[39] The only way in which the mere invocation of a term such as legality could provide such answers is if it were taken to incorporate the answers to these difficult issues concerning the respective competence of agencies and courts. This would, however, simply conceal the issues, or treat their resolution in a way thought to be self-evident, even though it manifestly is not.

[40] Sir Stephen Sedley, "Human Rights: A Twenty-First Century Agenda" [1995] P.L. 386; P. Craig, "Public Law, Political Theory and Legal Theory" [2000] P.L. 211.

[41] Craig, "*Ultra Vires* and the Foundations of Judicial Review" (1998) 57 C.L.J. 63, 79–85.

principle came much later. The fact that the legislature can ultimately limit review, given traditional notions of sovereignty, does not mean that the institution of review has to be legitimated by reference to legislative intent in the absence of any such limits being imposed.

Which limits on public power are normatively justified is an inherently controversial issue, to which we shall return in due course. However, invocation of the ultra vires principle never obviated this inquiry, precisely because its content was indeterminate. It merely brushed the inquiry under the carpet with the pretence that the answer was to be found in some elusive legislative intent.

ii. The rule of law

1–020 Justification for some form of a rights-based approach might be founded on the rule of law. This, however, depends on the meaning given to this constitutional concept.[42]

In one sense the rule of law is primarily a *formal* concept. It demands that there should be lawful authority for the exercise of power, and that individuals should be able to plan their lives on the basis of clear, open and general laws. These dictates can be met by non-democratic societies.[43] On this view the rule of law cannot provide the foundation for particular substantive rights. The reason for restricting the concept has been articulated by Raz: if the rule of law is to be taken to demand certain substantive rights then it becomes tantamount to propounding a complete social and political philosophy and the concept would then no longer have a useful role independent of that political philosophy. Adherents to the formal model believe that individuals ought to have certain substantive rights, but argue that these rights should be articulated separately in their own terms.

A second sense of the rule of law is *substantive*. The clearest formulation is in Dworkin's work. He recognises that those who adhere to a formal conception of the rule of law care about the content of the law,[44] "but they say that this is matter of substantive justice, and that substantive justice is an independent ideal, in no sense part of the ideal of the rule of law".[45]

His preferred version is what he terms the rights conception. This conception of the rule of law does not distinguish, as does the formal conception, between the rule of law and substantive justice, "on the contrary it requires, as part of the ideal of law, that the rules in the book capture and enforce moral rights".[46] This version of the rule of law directs us to the best theory of justice. My preference is for this second sense of the rule of law.[47]

There is a third sense of the rule of law. Advocates of this view are unhappy with the purely formal version of the rule of law, but are also mindful of the

---

42 P. Craig, "Formal and Analytical Conceptions of the Rule of Law: An Analytical Framework" [1997] P.L. 467; Lord Bingham, *The Rule of Law* (London: Penguin, 2011); European Commission for Democracy through Law, Report on the Rule of Law, CDL-AD(2011)003 rev.

43 J. Raz, "The Rule of Law and its Virtue" (1977) 93 L.Q.R. 195.

44 R. Dworkin, *A Matter of Principle* (Cambridge: Harvard University Press, 1985), pp.11–12.

45 Dworkin, *A Matter of Principle* (1985), p.11.

46 Dworkin, *A Matter of Principle* (1985), pp.11–12.

47 Craig, "Constitutional Foundations, the Rule of Law and Supremacy" [2003] P.L. 92.

dangers of making the rule of law synonymous with some particular vision of substantive justice. They seek, therefore, to incorporate within the rule of law some substantive rights, while at the same time trying to avoid tying these too closely to any specific conception of justice.[48] It is, however, very difficult to specify particular rights, and not others, that would be agreed to by proponents of differing conceptions of liberalism or democracy. The chosen list reflects the principles which would be agreed to by those who subscribe to a particular version of liberalism, and does not include principles which advocates of other conceptions of liberalism, or other political theories, would regard as equally, or more, important.[49]

A fourth sense of the rule of law is a process-based conception of the rule of law, which accords pre-eminence to the values of accountability and participation. The focus is on public rational justification and on the "citizen as active participant in the legal order and not on the substance incorporated into law".[50] It is clear that any theory of justice will entail some notion of participation and accountability. The meaning accorded to participation and accountability will, however, vary depending on the democratic theory, or theory of justice, being espoused. It is moreover equally clear that process and substance interact. The idea that the rule of law can be explicated principally or solely in terms of participation and accountability is untenable because the meaning accorded to such ideas is dependent on, and resonates with, substantive principles.[51]

iii. Human Rights Act 1998

Justification for a rights-based approach to administrative law can also be grounded on the Human Rights Act 1998 (HRA), which came into force on 2 October 2000. The HRA brought many rights contained in the European Convention on Human Rights (ECHR) into domestic law, so that they can be pleaded directly before national courts.[52] **1–021**

The HRA has implications for administrative law in empirical terms, because a significant number of judicial review cases are now pleaded on HRA grounds. The HRA also has implications for administrative law in conceptual terms. It requires courts to read legislation in so far as is possible to be compliant with Convention rights, and provides for the issuance of a declaration of incompatibility where this is not possible. In this sense, the HRA instantiates a novel relationship between courts and legislature, based on respect for human rights, albeit one that builds on principles developed prior to the HRA. The HRA has therefore had a significant impact on the nature of judicial review by the

[48] T.R.S. Allan, *Law, Liberty and Justice* (Oxford: Oxford University Press, 1993), Ch.2; T.R.S. Allan, "The Rule of Law as the Rule of Reason: Consent and Constitutionalism" (1999) 115 L.Q.R. 221 and T.R.S. Allan, *Constitutional Justice, A Liberal Theory of the Rule of Law* (Oxford: Oxford University Press, 2001).

[49] Craig, "Constitutional Foundations, the Rule of Law and Supremacy" [2003] P.L. 92, 96–102.

[50] D. Dyzenhaus, "Form and Substance in the Rule of Law: A Democratic Justification for Judicial Review", in Forsyth (ed.), *Judicial Review and the Constitution* (2000), p.171.

[51] L. Tribe, "The Puzzling Persistence of Process-Based Constitutional Theories" (1980) 89 Yale L.J. 1063; P. Brest, "The Substance of Process" (1981) 42 Ohio St L.J. 131; R. Dworkin, "The Forum of Principle" (1981) 56 N.Y.U.L. Rev. 469.

[52] See Ch.20.

emphasis thereby given to what has been termed the culture of justification.[53] This requires the primary decision-maker not merely to explain the challenged decision, but to proffer a reasoned argument, which the courts scrutinise within the framework of proportionality to determine whether the limitation of the right was normatively justified.

E. A Critique

1–022 The rights-based vision of public law has been challenged by scholars who fall broadly in the camp of political constitutionalism. Limits of space preclude consideration of all aspects of this vibrant debate.[54] The present discussion will therefore focus on Poole's critique.[55] He assigns the generic label common law constitutionalism (CLC), to capture the views of a range of theorists, including Sir John Laws, Allan, Oliver, Jowell and the present author.

Poole discerns a number of related propositions that constitute CLC. These are that: a political community is ordered according to a set of fundamental values; political decision-making is or ought to be a matter of discovering what fundamental values require in particular cases; the common law is the primary repository of the fundamental values of the political community; ordinary politics does not necessarily connect with fundamental values; public law therefore consists of a set of higher-order principles and rights; and decision-making in judicial review is or ought to be value oriented.

The essence of his critique is as follows. Poole maintains that the nature and practice of judicial review does not fit with the vision of public law advanced by common law constitutionalists. Thus, he maintains that participation within adjudication is perforce limited and is ill-adapted to consideration of a range of competing views; that judicial review is ill-suited to consideration of polycentric disputes; that the arguments in judicial review cases are relatively Spartan when compared to ordinary political debate; that judicial review even in cases concerned with rights does not typically involve considerations about fundamental values, but is more commonly concerned with second order considerations concerning matters such as the intensity of review.

His preferred vision of public law is one that focuses on legitimacy. In instrumental terms, this is said to connote the idea that judicial review is justified

[53] D. Dyzenhaus, "The Politics of Deference: Judicial Review and Democracy", in M. Taggart (ed.), *The Province of Administrative Law* (London: Hart Publishing, 1997), Ch.13; M. Taggart, "The Tub of Public Law", in D. Dyzenhaus (ed.), *The Unity of Public Law* (London: Hart Publishing, 2004), Ch.17.

[54] A. Tomkins, *Our Republican Constitution* (London: Hart Publishing, 2005); P. Craig, "Political Constitutionalism and Judicial Review" (2010) SSRN 1503505, the first half of this paper is available in C. Forsyth, M. Elliott, S. Jhaveri, A. Scully-Hill, M. Ramsden (eds), *Effective Judicial Review: A Cornerstone of Good Governance* (Oxford: Oxford University Press, 2010); A Tomkins, "The Role of the Courts in the Political Constitution" (2010) 60 U.T.L.J. 1; P. Craig, "Political Constitutionalism and the Judicial Role: A Response" (2011) 9 I-CON 112; Craig, *UK, EU and Global Administrative Law: Foundations and Challenges* (2015), pp.166–199.

[55] T. Poole, "Back to the Future? Unearthing the Theory of Common Law Constitutionalism" (2003) 23 O.J.L.S. 453; "Questioning Common Law Constitutionalism" (2005) 25 L.S. 142; T. Poole, "Legitimacy, Rights and Judicial Review" (2005) 25 O.J.L.S. 697.

because of the fallibility in government decision-making. In non-instrumental terms, it is said to capture the idea of trust in government.

F. A Response

It is perfectly right for there to be debate, and the issues that Poole raises should be taken seriously. It is nonetheless important to be mindful of a methodological concern. Poole's argument is presented by drawing selectively from a number of writers, the assumption being that all within the "CLC camp" agree with all the precepts that Poole advances as being integral to CLC. This is certainly not true in the case of the present author, and I doubt whether it is true of the others listed. 1–023

i. The nature of CLC

The depiction of CLC is central to the critique thereof. A number of points can be made in this respect. 1–024

First, the picture painted of the authors who subscribe to CLC is incomplete, since there is no mention of concern with accountability and legitimacy quite independently of judicial review. This is clear from the work of Jowell, Oliver and Craig. These authors do not just mention such matters, and then pass on to judicial review. They examine them in detail.[56] There is no sense in which they think that judicial review and the common law courts are the only relevant players when thinking about constitutionalism. There is no inconsistency in having a view about the role of judicial review and the common law courts as a component in the search for accountability and legitimacy, while at the same time being aware of other important aspects of accountability and legitimacy that flow from institutional design, political controls, and internal agency organisation. This is not a zero sum game whereby attention being focused on judicial review implies lack of concern with other mechanisms for accountability and legitimacy.

Second, we need to think carefully about the role of fundamental values, legality and rights within public law, and to do so in the light of the role of courts in any area of the law. When the courts develop the common law of, for example, crime, contract, tort, and restitution they do so by articulating doctrine that is premised on certain assumptions about the important values that should be applicable within such areas. They make choices within the law of tort that are reflective of commitments to corrective or distributive justice; they develop doctrine within criminal law that is premised on conceptions of moral responsibility and justifiable excuse; and they mould contract law by considerations relating to matters such as consent, autonomy, bargain and the like. It is

[56] J. Jowell, *Law and Bureaucracy, Administrative Discretion and the Limits of Legal Action* (New York: Dunellen, 1975); D. Oliver, *Government in the United Kingdom: The Search for Accountability, Effectiveness and Citizenship* (Open University Press, 1991); D. Oliver, *Constitutional Reform in the UK* (Oxford: Oxford University Press, 2003); D. Oliver and G. Drewry, *Public Service Reforms: Issues of Accountability and Public Law* (Pinter Publishers, 1996); J. Jowell and D. Oliver (eds), *The Changing Constitution*, 7th edn (Oxford: Oxford University Press, 2011); P. Craig, *Administrative Law*, 8th edn (London: Sweet & Maxwell, 2016), Chs 2–11; P. Craig, *EU Administrative Law*, 2nd edn (Oxford: Oxford University Press, 2012), Chs 1–8.

indeed difficult to imagine how such doctrine could otherwise be developed. It should therefore not be taken as somehow aberrant or unnatural for commentators to argue that a similar approach should infuse public law.

Third, the interrelationship between values and established doctrine within public law is not novel. It has been a consistent theme within public law ever since its inception, and this is true irrespective of whether one chooses to try and rationalise this in terms of legislative intent or not.[57] This is readily apparent if one reflects on standard features of public law doctrine. Thus, for example, the law concerning natural justice is premised on the instrumental and non-instrumental values that serve to explain why according a right to be heard before a decision is taken is so important; the law relating to nullity is grounded on the fundamental precept that where a public body takes a decision that is ultra vires it should, in principle, be retrospectively void; and development of the law relating to remedies in the 18th and 19th centuries was based on the value that relief should be granted where power was abused without too close an inquiry as to whether the defendant came within pre-existing categories of those subject to public law. The relationship between value and doctrine will often be piecemeal, and will also be evolutionary, in the sense that courts may well alter doctrine over time in the light of altered perceptions of the values that provide the foundation for that doctrine.

Fourth, what values should be regarded as fundamental, what rights should be protected or what should be included within the rubric of legality, will be contestable. This is however endemic to all areas of the law. Public law is not special or exceptional in this respect. This is attested to by the vibrant debates about theory in contract, tort, restitution, crime and just about any other area of the law, where commentators discuss the values that do and should underpin the respective subjects. I do not believe that the values in public law are wholly self-evident, or axiomatic. Even if people agree on abstract concepts such as liberty, equality, property, security, citizenship and the like they may well have differing conceptions of such rights or values in particular contexts. Insofar as this separates me from some of the others regarded as being within the CLC camp so be it. My adherence to a conception of public law based broadly on rights, legality and abuse of power is not therefore premised on the pretence that the meaning ascribed to these concepts is uncontroversial.

Finally, commitment to a conception of public law based broadly on rights, legality and abuse of power does not resolve important issues about the relationship between courts and legislature, and courts and executive in a constitutional democracy. It does not mean that courts are always right and the political branch wrong. It does not entail any "Whig reading of history", whereby the common law courts always get it "right". It does not "make the case" for US style constitutional review, whereby courts can invalidate legislation. Nor does it resolve the issue as to the extent to which courts should show some measure of deference or respect to legislative or executive choices.[58] The very fact that the interpretation of rights and values can be contestable, and that the legislature or

[57] Craig, "Political Constitutionalism and Judicial Review" (2010) SSRN 1503505; Craig, "Political Constitutionalism and the Judicial Role: A Response" (2011) 9 I-CON 112.

[58] See Ch.20.

executive may have a reasonable considered view, is I believe a relevant consideration in this respect. Some others within the CLC camp may disagree, and if that is so we differ.

ii. *CLC and judicial review: participation*

Poole argues that judicial review is essentially adjudicative and bipolar, and hence is ill-adapted to considering a range of competing points of view. It cannot therefore be a central forum for deliberating about matters relating to fundamental values and cannot match the republican model of active citizenship. There are three related points in this respect. **1–025**

First, this argument elides the issue of participation in the initial agency decision, with judicial review before the court. CLC authors, or at least some of them, favour the development of participatory rights before the initial agency, especially in the context of rule-making, because it enhances the republican ideal of deliberative discourse. They do not claim that this is the present law, but there is no reason in principle why such development should not occur, and indeed participatory initiatives have been developed by the political branch of government.[59]

Second, most CLC authors do not claim that judicial review before the court itself presently comports with a model of republican discourse. It is true that Allan has said something to this effect, but his general line is against the idea of broadening standing rights, because he believes this is inconsistent with the nature of the judicial process. Other CLC authors disagree. They argue that standing and intervention rights should be broadly construed. They do not claim that this position is perfectly embodied in the present law. Nor do they claim that even if it were that it would thereby reflect some perfect model of deliberative discourse. They accept that adjudication imposes limits. What some CLC authors maintain is that broadened participatory and intervention rights before the initial decision-maker, combined with relatively liberal standing and intervention rights before the courts, will enhance the deliberative, republican aspects of decision-making, albeit within the parameters imposed by being within a judicial forum.

Third, Poole's argument is in any event premised upon a vision as to how decisions are made within the political forum, the premise being full consideration of the competing views on which the contested decision is made. Some decisions may be made in this manner, but many are not. Many rules made by the administration or statutory instruments receive little by way of scrutiny, and little in the way of consideration of competing views. It is even more difficult to generalise about individualised decisions made by agencies, ministers, prison governors and the like, especially when, as will often be the case, the contested decision is actually made by an official.

---

[59] See Ch.15.

iii. *CLC and judicial review: polycentricity and the focus of judicial review*

1–026 Poole argues that judicial review properly focuses on a particular issue, and is unsuited to the resolution of polycentric disputes, which will often better be considered in political terms. Three brief comments are warranted.

First, the authors associated with CLC accept that there are certain issues which are polycentric in nature and that courts are limited in their capacity to deal with these issues. The courts have recognised this too in certain cases.[60]

Second, having said this, there is an emerging sophisticated body of work elaborating the types of factor that should be taken into account in deciding on the appropriate intensity of review in cases concerned with resource allocation and social and economic rights.[61] The fact that a dispute is in some way polycentric does not therefore signal that it is or should be a no go area for the courts.[62]

Third, it should not be assumed that the political process conforms to some perfect deliberative ideal when such matters are considered. There is a wealth of literature about how bureaucratic decision-making works, which emphasises its incremental nature and the limited capacity for general overview of issues. This is quite apart from the general literature on the political process at Westminster, with executive domination of the legislature.

iv. *CLC and judicial review: the nature of argument in judicial review*

1–027 Poole argues that the style of argument in judicial review is relatively Spartan as compared to the richness of political debate, that it is restricted to certain well-established categories, and that it cannot therefore conform to a deliberative ideal. Two brief comments are in order.

First, it can be accepted that there are differences between judicial review and normal political argument. The former will be constrained by the need for the argument to be fitted within an established head of review, and by the fact that the grounds of review are premised on assumptions about the relationship between courts and primary decision-makers, such as the injunction against substitution of judgment on matters of discretion that have been assigned to the primary decision-maker.

Second, this should not however lead us to assume that consideration of the particular issue before the court will necessarily be less searching or less rich than when the same issue was considered in the political process. Thus, when

60 *R. v Cambridge Health Authority Ex p. B* [1995] 2 All E.R. 129, CA (Civ Div).

61 S. Fredman, "Social, Economic and Cultural Rights", in D. Feldman (ed.), *English Public Law* (Oxford: Oxford University Press, 2004), Ch.10; K. Syrett, "Opening Eyes to the Reality of Scarce Health Care Resources?" [2006] P.L. 664; J. King, "The Justiciability of Resource Allocation" (2007) 70 M.L.R. 197; A. Pillay "Courts, Variable Standards of Review and Resource Allocation: Developing a Model for the Enforcement of Social and Economic Rights" [2007] E.H.R.L.R. 616; C. Newdick, "Judicial Review: Low-Priority Treatment and Exceptional Case Review" [2007] Med. L.R. 236; E. Palmer, *Judicial Review, Socio-Economic Rights and the Human Rights Act* (London: Hart Publishing, 2007); J. King, *Judging Social Rights* (Cambridge: Cambridge University Press, 2012).

62 J. King, "The Pervasiveness of Polycentricity" [2008] P.L. 101.

legislation is passed there may well have been scant consideration as to whether a particular provision thereof conflicts with Convention rights, or some other precept of public law. Similarly when an executive decision is made that differentiates between groups the extent to which this has been preceded by searching analysis of the justification for the differential treatment may well vary. If such issues are adjudicated before the courts this may offer the opportunity for more in depth scrutiny of the reasons and justificatory arguments for the contested provision than occurred within the normal political process.

v. CLC and judicial review: limited relevance of fundamental values

Poole argues that judges decide cases not by reflecting what fundamental values or rights require, but that even in cases concerned with rights the focus will often be on second-order considerations relating to the intensity or standard of judicial review. This is said to undermine the CLC claim that public law should be conceived in terms of fundamental values. **1–028**

It is unclear as to why Poole regards this as a difficulty for CLC authors of whatever persuasion. The inarticulate premise to his argument is that consideration of matters such as the appropriate intensity of review constitutes a diminution in some way of the precepts on which the CLC model is founded. The argument appears to be that any departure from substitution of judgment by the reviewing court compromises adherence to a rights-based model of review, such that when courts engage in consideration of the appropriate meaning to be given to rationality or proportionality, or when they consider the extent to which they should accord deference to the primary decision-maker, this is somehow at odds with or diminishes the CLC view.

There is no foundation for this. It is true that different authors broadly associated with CLC take different views as to when, for example, deference should be accorded to the primary decision-maker.[63] This does not however mean that judicial engagement with this issue is contrary to the precepts on which the CLC model is based. It is, to the contrary, natural within a regime of judicial review for the courts to focus on issues relating to the standard of review, as well as the meaning of the contested right or value, since the former may be a condition precedent to determination of the latter. Discourse concerning the appropriate standard of review is central in a regime of judicial review committed to rights, legality and the abuse of power, or rights and fundamental values. The answer, whatsoever it may be, encapsulates important values indicative of the relationship between courts and the initial decision-maker.

We shall see below that in many instances the courts do substitute judgment on the meaning of speech, assembly, deprivation of liberty or the like, in which cases the focus will be squarely on the meaning of the contested right. In other instances, notably where the public body raises a defence that the limitation of the right came within grounds allowed by the ECHR, the courts also engage in debate about the proper limits of their control in relation to the political branch of government, which often occurs within the proportionality inquiry, although the courts in such cases will also make determinations about the meaning of the

[63] See Ch.20.

contested right. Both aspects of the inquiry are properly regarded as important within a model of review based on rights, legality and abuse of power, or rights and fundamental values.

vi. Legitimacy and judicial review

1–029 Poole's preferred foundation for public law is cast in terms of legitimacy. In instrumental terms, this is said to connote the idea that judicial review is justified because of the fallibility in government decision-making. In non-instrumental terms, it is said to capture the idea of trust in government. Detailed comment on this can be found elsewhere.[64] Suffice it to say the following for the present. This conception of legitimacy captures a similar idea to that expressed earlier: in a constitutional democracy it is both right and proper for the courts to impose limits on the way in which power is exercised in order to prevent abuse of that power.

4. PARTICULAR IMPLICATIONS OF THE MODEL I: TRADITIONAL PLURALISM

1–030 Divergent background conceptions of democracy can have a marked impact on our subject, both directly and indirectly. They can lead to distinct interpretations of rights, and of many of other ideas, such as participation, rationality, control of power, and the proper scope for judicial review. It would be impossible within this chapter to consider how this occurs in relation to all such background conceptions. The strategy is therefore to elucidate the point through two contrasting visions of pluralism and their impact on administrative law.

A. Intellectual Foundations

1–031 We have already seen that the traditional vision of administrative law was premised on a particular view as to how our democracy functioned. This was termed unitary democracy, to express the idea that all public power was and should be channelled through Parliament, which body possessed a legislative monopoly. When practical necessity required the delegation of power to a minister or agency, the purpose of administrative law was to ensure that the agency remained within its assigned area and therefore did not trespass on the legislative monopoly of Parliament by exercising power outside of this sphere. This Diceyan view of administrative and constitutional law was challenged on the grounds that his vision of unitary democracy was both descriptively flawed and prescriptively questionable. Three strands of this challenge should be distinguished.

[64] Craig, "Political Constitutionalism and Judicial Review" (2010) SSRN 1503505; Craig, "Political Constitutionalism and the Judicial Role: A Response" (2011) 9 I-CON 112.

i. Pluralist critique of the unitary thesis

The first strand of the critique was advanced by writers in the late 19th and early 20th centuries who adopted a pluralist vision of democracy to replace the unitary view espoused by Dicey.[65] Their views differed, but central themes of their argument can nonetheless be delineated. They revealed the historical foundations of the unitary view of the state. The idea that sovereignty was indivisible appeared initially in the writings of, among others, Hobbes, as a defence against anarchy. The state must be all powerful to prevent a breakdown in society. This political justification for the unitary state was unsurprising given the turmoil that occurred in the English civil war. This reasoning was reinforced in the 19th century by jurists like Austin who argued that it was simply not possible to have a sovereign whose power was limited. Dicey built on Austin. In a democracy where the people elected MPs who represented their views and controlled the executive, it was "right" that this central power should be all-embracing. **1–032**

The pluralists challenged the unitary view in descriptive and prescriptive terms. In descriptive terms, they contested the idea that all public power was wielded by the state, pointing to pressure groups that shaped state action, and religious, economic and social associations that exercised authority. In prescriptive terms, group power was applauded rather than condemned. The all-powerful unitary state was dangerous. Liberty was best preserved by the presence of groups within the state to which the individual could owe allegiance. Decentralisation and the preservation of group autonomy were to be valued. This vision of political pluralism was complemented by a concern with the social and economic conditions within the state. There was a strong belief that political liberty was closely linked with social and economic equality.

ii. Limited effectiveness of parliamentary controls

A second strand of the challenge to the unitary vision of democracy was implicitly, rather than explicitly, pluralist. It was argued that the unitary vision of democracy was flawed not just because public power was exercised by groups outside the parliamentary process. It was also misleading because even rules formally legitimated by Parliament were not properly scrutinised. Pressures of time, and executive dominance of the legislature, combined to ensure that legislative control over, for example, secondary legislation was minimal. Moreover, departmental policy choices made pursuant to the implementation of legislation might be inadequately thought through.[66] **1–033**

If Parliament could not effectively control such matters then there should be other ways in which to legitimate and control the use of public power in society, such as citizen participation in the process of making agency rules. Whereas the unitary vision of democracy saw all public power as being legitimated through

[65] H. Laski, *Studies in the Problem of Sovereignty* (New Haven: Yale University Press, 1917), *Authority in the Modern State* (New Haven: Yale University Press, 1919), and *Foundations of Sovereignty* (London: Allen & Unwin, 1921); J. Figgis, *Churches in the Modern State* (London, 1913); E. Barker, *Reflections on Government* (Oxford: Oxford University Press, 1942).

[66] I. Harden and N. Lewis, *The Noble Lie, The British Constitution and the Rule of Law* (London: Hutchinson, 1986).

participation by MPs in Parliament, the pluralist vision was premised on the idea that power could be legitimated and constrained in more diverse ways, such as by citizen participation. It was therefore unsurprising that consultation rights were important for the early pluralists.

iii. Corporatist challenge

1–034 A third strand in the challenge to the unitary state was "corporatism".[67] Pluralism depicted the political process as one in which a relatively wide range of groups affected political decision-making. In corporatist theory a particular group would be accorded a privileged representational status with the government, which would "license" it to represent the interests of other less powerful groups within the same area. The privileged status accorded to the dominant group carried a "price", in the sense that such a group accepted certain constraints on the demands it advanced. The modern state was required to undertake a wide range of activities in order to correct problems arising from the capitalist system. This necessitated discussion and collaboration with major interest groups. The government perceived benefits in dealing with one bargaining agent. A relationship of trust could be built up, and an assuredness that the organisation would promote an agreed policy among the relevant "constituency".

Corporatism undermined the unitary thesis by postulating groups that wielded public power outside the normal parliamentary process, and explained how the alliance between such groups and the executive could bypass Parliament. A policy might be agreed between a dominant group and the executive, which was then forced through Parliament. Or the executive and the relevant group might arrive at an understanding that never saw the parliamentary light of day at all, but remained in a non-statutory form.

B. Implications for Administrative Law

i. Accountability and the scope of administrative law

1–035 The traditional model encapsulated a vision of accountability of the administrative state. The premise, which was explicit in Dicey's work, was that Parliament controlled the executive, and was itself controlled by the electorate. Judicial control through the ordinary law ensured that agencies remained within their designated area, and was all that was required to render the administrative state accountable. The pluralist model undermined this notion of accountability in two ways.

First, a natural corollary of the traditional notion of accountability was that administrative law was essentially only concerned with those bodies to which statutory or prerogative power had been given. It was only where such bodies

[67] P. Schmitter and G. Lehmbruch (eds), *Trends Toward Corporatist Intermediation* (London: Sage, 1979); P. Schmitter and G. Lehmbruch (eds), *Patterns of Corporatist Policymaking* (London: Sage, 1982); A. Cawson, *Corporatism and Welfare* (London: Heinemann, 1982); R. Harrison (ed.), *Corporatism and the Welfare State* (London: Allen & Unwin, 1984); P. Birkinshaw, I. Harden and N. Lewis, *Government by Moonlight: The Hybrid Parts of the State* (London: Unwin Hyman, 1990).

exercised delegated power that there was a danger of encroachment on the legislative monopoly of Parliament. The pluralist model undermined this presupposition by its very insistence that other institutions exercised public power. Any realistic vision of administrative law would therefore have to decide how to treat such institutions.

Second, the pluralist model also undermined the idea that the traditional approach was sufficient to ensure accountability even within those areas where an agency had been given statutory power. Traditional theory, with its assumptions of electoral control over the legislature and legislative control over the executive, could comfortably reach the conclusion that keeping an agency within the area designated by legislative intent would ensure that the will of the people expressed through their elected representatives would triumph. This vision was challenged by the pluralist model, which recognised the power of the executive over the legislature, and the fact that policy often emerged through accommodation between pressure groups and the executive.

ii. Gateways to administrative law: natural justice, standing and intervention

We have already seen why the traditional model tended to construe the "gateways" to administrative law narrowly. Supporters of the pluralist model would argue that the existing gateways should be broadened, and that new types of gateway should be opened up. **1–036**

The rationale for broadening the gateways is easy to understand. The law relating to standing can be taken as an example. Standing determines the range of people who can seek judicial review of agency action. The traditional model tended towards a narrow construction of standing. The public body exercised delegated power from Parliament and was the arbiter of the public interest. An individual could only challenge an agency decision, or so some cases held, where strict private rights were at stake. In such cases, the individual was simply settling a private dispute in contract or tort with the public body.

The pluralist model undermined this narrow construction. The public body might still be conceived as the arbiter of the public interest. It was, however, recognised that other private groups could wield "public" power and exercised influence over agency decisions. The thrust behind the pluralist argument was therefore that a third party should be able to come to court, even if no traditional private rights were affected, and ask the court to determine whether the result reached by the agency, in the light of representations from a particular group, really was in accord with the intent of the legislation.

The pluralist model would also suggest that the other principal gateway, natural justice, should be given a broader interpretation than under the traditional model. Natural justice should not be limited to those with private rights, because pluralists stressed the interconnection between economic and political liberty, and thus believed that recipients of, for example, social welfare benefits should be accorded process rights. The pluralist model also favoured procedural rights in the form of consultation where an agency made rules of a legislative nature. The gateway of natural justice would have to be broadened to accommodate such a development.

1–037 The pluralist model would also indicate that there should be new gateways to administrative law, such as a right to intervene. There may be circumstances in which an interested group wishes to intervene in existing adjudicative proceedings before the agency. The gateways, as traditionally conceived, provided little assistance. Public law adjudication often has far-reaching implications, which are not confined to the nominal plaintiff and defendant. A group may wish to intervene because it feels that the parties to the action are not putting all the relevant arguments, or that they have reached an accommodation with the agency and that this does not reflect the public interest.

iii. Process rights: fostering participation

1–038 An important implication from the pluralist model might be that we should foster participation to a greater extent than at present. Rules made by agencies may be secondary legislation, or simply emerge from the process of bureaucratic decision-making. Traditional theory tells us that rules of a legislative nature should be legitimated through parliamentary scrutiny. This is, however, not very effective, and there are many administrative rules which do not see the parliamentary light of day at all because they are not classified as statutory instruments.[68]

The pluralist model suggests that participation in the making of such rules by interested parties can help to secure their legitimacy. Our democracy is representative primarily because problems of time and scale preclude more direct forms of democracy in the complex modern world. However, representative democracy may be unable adequately to control all rules of a legislative nature. Direct input from the "bottom", in the form of citizen participation in the administrative process, can therefore help by making rule-making more directly democratic and hence accountable. The pluralist model provides support for this idea in a double sense.

In descriptive terms, proponents of this model acknowledge that some participation from external pressure groups already exists. The degree of such participation may, however, be uneven, and the participatory process may be dominated by powerful groups, who have favoured relationships with the public body. Pluralists may well therefore advocate more formal participatory rights in order that a wider variety of groups can be involved in the administrative process. In prescriptive terms, the pluralist model assumes that the decentralisation of public power fostered through consultative rights is a "good thing". Liberty is best preserved by such dispersion of power, and the state is rendered more accountable by allowing an element of direct democracy within the administrative process.

68 See Ch.15.

iv. Scope of judicial review

The pluralist model is more sympathetic to a functionalist approach towards judicial review, with the precepts being tailored to the needs and nature of the particular area being reviewed. The intensity of judicial review will be influenced by the need to ensure that participation rights are taken seriously. The basic premise is that the court should not simply substitute its view for that of the agency. There must, however, be some meaningful review because we have to ensure that the agency does not just go through the motions of listening to people. The courts should play a role in forcing the agency to be rigorous in its reasoning process, and ensure that the views of interested parties are adequately considered. **1–039**

v. Remedies and the ambit of administrative law

The traditional model focused on bodies that derived power from statute, since only such bodies threatened the legislative monopoly of Parliament. Provided that they were kept within the ambit of their power this monopoly would be preserved. The pluralist model undermined this complacency. Parliament did not have a monopoly of public power, which was also exercised by others, including interest groups on both the capital and labour sides of the market. The courts were therefore forced to make difficult determinations as to whether a particular body was sufficiently public to be subject to the principles of judicial review. **1–040**

5. PARTICULAR IMPLICATIONS OF THE MODEL II: MARKET-ORIENTED PLURALISM

A. Intellectual Foundations

Pluralism has both descriptive and prescriptive elements. The descriptive aspect of pluralism helps us to understand how governmental decisions are made within society and the role of non-elected groups in this process. The prescriptive aspect of pluralism seeks to delineate an appropriate role for the state in the light of these "facts". Writers have drawn radically different conclusions from these facts, as evident in contrasting visions of pluralism. **1–041**

There was the pluralism of those who in the early twentieth century reacted against the unitary state postulated by Dicey. These pluralists were generally left of centre politically. Their vision stressed the existence of group power, group rights and obligations, decentralisation and the interconnection between economic and political liberty, the latter requiring governmental intervention to secure such liberties for the individual. There was always an inner tension between the desire for decentralisation, and the existence of the requisite central authority to enable the desired economic objectives to be fulfilled.

There was a more market-based conception of pluralist democracy, manifest in governmental policy within the late 1970s and 1980s, which was closer to pluralism as understood in the USA.[69] The existence of group power that shapes governmental action is acknowledged. The prescriptive role for the state was conceived very differently from the earlier pluralist model. The market was viewed as the best "arbitrator" of many issues. Governmental regulation was necessary only when there was market failure narrowly defined. There were, however, also tensions within this model, since in certain respects it produced a more powerful centralised role for the government. Fulfilment of the free market vision required a strong central government, and there was also a more overtly authoritarian element present within this philosophy.[70]

B. Implications for Administrative Law

1–042 An understanding of these two very different pluralist visions has implications for administrative law. The full ramifications of these differences cannot be examined here. The object is to demonstrate how concepts such as rights, citizenship, participation, and rationality, which constitute the newer model of administrative law, can assume very different meanings depending upon the background ideas against which they are read.

i. *Rights, citizenship and society*

1–043 Citizenship connotes the civil, political, social and economic rights individuals possess, or ought to possess, within society. The rights that individuals presently have will be affected by the particular theory of law and adjudication adopted. A positivist might give one answer to this question, based on the existing corpus of statutory and common law materials. A follower of Dworkin might give a different answer if it is warranted by the application of that theory of law and adjudication. Which rights citizens ought to have has been a major pre-occupation of political theory for at least 2,000 years.

The conceptions of citizenship employed by the major political parties have differed significantly. The Conservative's document did not deal with traditional civil and political rights at all, and emphasised the rights which consumers of services ought to have as against the service provider.[71] The documents from the Liberal Democrats[72] and the Labour party[73] in the early 1990s addressed a wider range of issues, which were political, social and economic in nature.

Differences in the conception of citizenship will affect the interpretation accorded to a model of public law based upon rights, legality and the abuse of power. It will influence the particular construction given to a concept which all would agree should be part of the protected sphere of rights. It will also have a

[69] P. Craig, *Public Law in the United Kingdom and the United States of America* (Oxford: Oxford University Press, 1990), Chs 3 and 4.

[70] R. Levitas (ed.), *The Ideology of the New Right* (Cambridge: Polity Press, 1986); R. Skidelsky (ed.), *Thatcherism* (London: Chatto & Windus, 1988); B. Jessop, K. Bonnett, S. Bromley and T. Ling, *Thatcherism* (Cambridge: Polity Press, 1988); S. Jenkins, *Accountable to None, The Tory Nationalization of Britain* (London: Penguin, 1995).

[71] The Citizen's Charter: Raising the Standard, Cm.1599 (1991).

[72] Citizens' Britain: Liberal Democrat Policies for a People's Charter (1991).

[73] Citizen's Charter: Labour's Deal for Consumers and Citizens (1991).

marked impact on which rights are recognised at all. Thus, for example, all would agree that equality should feature within a list of protected rights, and should preclude differential treatment on the grounds of race, gender and the like. Disagreement centres on the particular conception of equality that should be applied. Traditional pluralists tended to favour a conception of equality and distributive justice, which entailed state intervention to promote greater equality in the resources held by individual citizens. The more market based species of pluralism had a very different conception of distributive justice, which, on some versions, regarded existing property rights as sacrosanct holdings that should not be redistributed by the state.

The same theme is apparent when we consider which rights should fall within the protected sphere at all. Employment can be taken by way of example. Traditional pluralists, such as Laski, argued that society existed for citizens to realise their lives in the best possible manner. They saw a prominent connection between political and economic liberty.[74] A citizen should have the right to work, and certain rights while in work, including adequate wages and the ability to participate in the government of industry. Citizenship should not therefore stop at the factory gates, both because economic well-being was regarded as essential to political participation, and also because "ideas of political citizenship are as relevant in the economic as in the political arena".[75] The market oriented pluralist adopted a very different view of the employment relationship. Market forces should be left to govern the employment field with little in the way of rights to minimum terms or conditions of service; worker participation in the governance of the industry was not encouraged; and the collective rights of unions were closely circumscribed and subordinated in certain respects to the rights of the citizen as consumer.

ii. *Process rights and participation*

The two models also produced differing conclusions concerning both the incidence and objective of participation in agency decision-making. **1–044**

The *incidence* of participation is affected because both models find it necessary to place constraints on groups opposed to the basic philosophy on which the model is based. Thus, constraints were placed on local authorities opposed to the market-oriented philosophy of the conservative government. The earlier pluralists imposed constraints on private property. The participatory role of those with property rights had to be diminished, because it jeopardised the philosophy which underpinned the aims of the pluralists.

The *objective* of granting participatory rights under the two models may also differ. The market-oriented pluralist granted such rights to those involved, with the object of ensuring efficiency. Accountability was seen in market terms and granting participatory rights to "consumers" of the activity was justified on this basis. The early pluralists viewed the objectives of participation rights more

[74] Craig, *Public Law in the United Kingdom and the United States of America* (1990), Chs 5 and 6.
[75] K. Ewing, "Citizenship and Employment", in R. Blackburn (ed.), *Rights of Citizenship* (London: Mansell, 1993), p.117.

broadly. They were to enable the individual to participate in the process of government, and to foster the full development of the individual within society.

iii. Ambit of public law

1–045 The earlier pluralists required government intervention to secure the conditions of economic equality for attainment of political liberty. Nationalisation of industry, direct regulation of other aspects of economic life and economic redistribution of wealth were the consequences of this approach. Proponents of the market-oriented model viewed the connection between economic and political liberty very differently. Deregulation and privatisation were the consequences of this approach. Even where continuing regulation of a privatised industry was required, the aim was coloured by the market-oriented vision. The purpose was often to prevent an industry with monopolistic power from abusing its dominant position.

This still leaves open the range of bodies that should be subject to public law principles. Some would restrict this to bodies with a connection to the state. Others would include any institution with power over the lives of others, irrespective of whether there is any connection with the state or not. Yet others adopt an intermediate position, to the effect that bodies with some monopoly power should be within the ambit of public law. There is moreover a further issue concerning the nature of the principles that should be applied to those bodies deemed to be part of public law. It might well be natural to apply procedural principles, but it may be more difficult to apply all substantive principles of public law, to, for example, private undertakings with monopoly power.

6. CONCLUSION

1–046 The point made at the outset to the previous section should be stressed again here. There are many other background conceptions of democracy and social ordering in addition to those considered above. It might be argued that we should espouse a Third Way, which is distinct from both versions of pluralism considered above.[76] It might alternatively be argued that we should foster a participatory democracy, meaning some version of republicanism[77] or communitarianism. These are specific democratic visions, which embody views of the relationship of citizen and state. They have implications for rights, socio-economic conditions within society and for distributive justice. The virtues of rival theories will always be contested, as will the degree to which they are consonant with the way in which society is currently ordered.

---

[76] A. Giddens, *The Third Way, The Renewal of Social Democracy* (Cambridge: Polity Press, 1998); A. Giddens, *The Third Way and its Critics* (Cambridge: Polity Press, 2000).

[77] Tomkins, *Our Republican Constitution* (London: Hart Publishing, 2005).

CHAPTER 2

THE ADMINISTRATIVE SYSTEM: A HISTORICAL PERSPECTIVE

1. CENTRAL ISSUES

i. The institutions subject to administrative law include the executive, agencies, local authorities, tribunals, inquiries and inferior courts. This list is not exhaustive. The discussion that follows is not an exhaustive historical analysis of each institution, but rather a sketch of the main themes in their development. Details as to the workings of government, agencies, local authorities and the like will be considered in subsequent chapters. **2–001**

ii. An understanding of the antecedents of our administrative institutions is important. It enables us to comprehend how existing institutions have developed. It acts as a counterweight to the assumption that current difficulties are novel. The 20th century produced some new problems. Nevertheless, there is an underlying continuity in the difficulties of administrative organisation, which can be appreciated from an historical perspective. There is, moreover, something faintly absurd about discussing administrative law with only the vaguest idea how its subject-matter evolved.

iii. There was very considerable regulation, which spurred the development of UK administrative law, from the 15th century onwards. Space precludes detailed consideration of this development, which can be found elsewhere.[1] This chapter therefore focuses on the nature and evolution of administrative organisation in the 19th and 20th centuries, and links this to broader social and political developments during this period.

2. THE 19TH CENTURY

A. Industrialisation and the Growth of Central Regulation

We have always had a somewhat messy system of administrative institutions. Bodies were created to deal with problems as they arose, with little thought given to rational allocation of decision-making. Many administrative functions from the 15th century onwards were performed by the local justices of the peace, while others were undertaken by institutions such as the Commissioners of Sewers, or Turnpike Trustees.[2] The limited size of central government in the 19th century **2–002**

[1] P. Craig, *UK, EU and Global Administrative Law: Foundations and Challenges* (Cambridge: Cambridge University Press, 2015), Ch.1.

[2] Craig, *UK, EU and Global Administrative Law: Foundations and Challenges* (2015), Ch.1.

must be appreciated. In 1833 the central departments of government employed 21,305 civilian officials, and most worked in the Revenue departments. The Home Office had a staff of 29, the Foreign Office 39, and the Board of Trade 25.[3] Political parties and pressure groups, albeit for differing reasons, favoured the limitation of central government.[4]

The Tories disliked expansion of central government, since this would often impinge upon the autonomy possessed by local squires and magistrates. Nor was this jealousy of local interests confined to the countryside. In areas controlled by the Whigs, there was a similar dislike of central influence encroaching upon local power. The Radicals wished central government to remain limited, since it was seen as the vehicle for new sinecures and monetary waste. Ricardo and Adam Smith expounded laissez-faire economics in contrast to the mercantilism of the 18th century, and the new industrialists used such theories to resist governmental encroachment on private property, whether through factory legislation limiting hours and conditions of work, or in schemes for improving health.

Despite this opposition there was a considerable expansion in the functions performed by central government between 1830–1850. There was increased central regulation in four main areas: factories, the Poor Law, railways and public health.[5] The advocates of these reforms had different objectives, but the reforms were all the result of growing industrialisation in the 19th century. It gave rise to forms of administrative control, and debates over the appropriateness of public institutions, which are still very much current today. A word about the reforms themselves is, therefore, necessary in order that the institutional question can be better understood.

2–003 Factory reform was the result of the efforts of Oastler, Ashley and Sadler. Oastler was the agent for a landowner in Yorkshire whose humanitarian instincts were severely shocked after witnessing the conditions in Bradford's textile mills. This prompted him to write a letter to the Leeds Mercury comparing the lot of the textile worker with that of the African slave. Oastler's tone is fierce[6]:

> "[T]he very streets which receive droppings of an 'Anti-Slavery Society' are every morning wet by the tears of innocent victims of the accursed shrine of avarice, who are compelled (not by the coach-whip of the negro slave driver) but by the dread of the equally appalling throng or strap of the overlooker, to hasten, half-dressed, but not half-fed, to those magazines of British infantile slavery—the worsted mills in the town and neighbourhood of Bradford!!!"

[3] D. Roberts, *Victorian Origins of the British Welfare State* (New Haven: Yale University Press, 1960), pp.14–16.

[4] Roberts, *Victorian Origins of the British Welfare State* (1960), pp.22–34. See also W. Lubenow, *The Politics of Government Growth: Early Victorian Attitudes toward State Intervention 1833–1848* (Newton Abbott: David & Charles, 1971); Sir D.N. Chester, *The English Administrative System 1780–1870* (Oxford: Oxford University Press, 1981).

[5] Roberts, *Victorian Origins of the British Welfare State* (1960), Chs 2–3; Lubenow, *The Politics of Government Growth: Early Victorian Attitudes toward State Intervention 1833–1848* (1971), Chs 2–5; D. Fraser, *Evolution of the British Welfare State: A History of Social Policy since the Industrial Revolution* (London: Macmillan, 1973), Chs 1–4.

[6] Fraser, *Evolution of the British Welfare State: A History of Social Policy since the Industrial Revolution* (1973), p.233.

Oastler was an Evangelical. So was Thomas Sadler who took up Oastler's cry in the House. Opposition to legislation on children in factories came from a variety of sources. The factory owners were averse to the scheme and sought support from the economic literature. Sadler was unmoved by such "scientific" reasoning, but his attempts to enact legislation were cut short by defeat in a Leeds election in 1832. Ashley took up the banner of reform. His own Bill failed in 1832 but as a consequence of a report by Sadler and the report of a subsequent commission headed by Edwin Chadwick, the Whig government produced its own measure, which was enacted as the Factory Act 1833.

While opposition to the factory legislation had been strong, it did not equal the passions roused by debate over the Poor Law. Prior to the 19th century the Poor Law was governed by the Poor Relief Act 1601. This legislation had been designed to deal differently with the aged or lunatic, the able-bodied unemployed and the able-bodied who had absconded from their own area. The idea was that the first group would be looked after, the second would be set to work and the third group would be punished. Administration was to be through the justices of the peace, who were authorised to appoint overseers of the poor. The latter would levy a rate on property in their area, which fund would then be used to carry out the functions connected with the three different groups. The system came under pressure, because of unemployment in the late 18th century, combined with bad harvests and rising prices, the result being that the wages of employed were insufficient to meet basic needs.

The early decades of the 19th century witnessed increasing dissatisfaction with the old Poor Law. Two general themes lay behind the disquiet. The first was the cost. In the years 1817–1819 the Poor Law cost £8 million, or 12s per head of the population; by 1831 it was still £7 million or in excess of 10s per head. Moreover, the cost had not yielded the benefits of social stability.[7] The second pressure for reform came from those who believed that the old Poor Law was simply wrong, particularly the allowance system of which Speenhamland was an example. This was the age of Malthus and Ricardo. The former with his dire predictions about population growth exceeding food supplies gave ammunition to those who saw the Poor Law as encouraging hasty marriages and providing support for their numerous offspring. Ricardo authored the wage fund theory under which only a fixed percentage of national wealth could be expended on wages. It was argued that the sums expended on poor relief could not be spent on wages, thereby creating an inexorable downward spiral in wages with more and more people being forced to become paupers.

The new Poor Law was born out of the Poor Law Report 1834, the work of Edwin Chadwick and Nassau Senior. The workhouse test which emerged from the Report was to provide much material for later Victorian literature. For Chadwick, however, the logic of the argument was unassailable. The old Poor Law, and particularly the allowance system, had encouraged idlers who could have worked. Poor relief had to be rendered less attractive than any other option. The workhouse test, the idea that relief would only be available in a workhouse, was an adjunct of this philosophy. The Poor Law should not be concerned with **2–004**

[7] Fraser, *Evolution of the British Welfare State: A History of Social Policy since the Industrial Revolution* (1973), p.38.

poverty as reflected in low wages, but with destitution.[8] It should be a deterrent to pauperism. The idea that there could be workers who through no fault of their own were rendered unemployed was recognised by the authors, but it was treated as an exception, an extreme to be dealt with by private charity and not by government intervention. The Poor Law Amendment Act was passed in 1834.

Health was a third area subject to governmental intervention. Growing industrialisation brought an increasing realisation of the health hazards of large groups of people with inadequate sanitary facilities. The organising genius of Chadwick provided the main impetus for reform. During his time as Secretary of the Poor Law Commission Chadwick became aware that a certain proportion of expenditure on poor relief was being devoted to the widows and offspring of those struck down by disease. For Chadwick the realisation of this connection demanded prophylactic measures to stem the root cause of disease.[9] His belief in the necessity for sanitary improvement found its most complete expression in the 1842 Report on the Sanitary Condition of the Labouring Population of Great Britain, which showed the clear correlation between living conditions and disease. The Chadwick Report was followed by the appointment in 1843 of a Royal Commission under the Duke of Buccleuch. The study undertaken by the Royal Commission confirmed many of the findings of the Chadwick Report, but went further in detailed and systematic investigation.

There was nonetheless opposition to change, which rendered the Public Health Act 1848 much less effective than its advocates had hoped. Some objected to the cost involved. These concerns were overlaid by disagreement as to the correct division of function between central and local government. The spectre of a London based bureaucracy dictating how much expenditure local areas should incur was not pleasing to the bastions of the reformed municipal boroughs. The 1848 Act emerged as a shadow of the original proposals. The legislation suffered from being generally permissive rather than obligatory in character. It was to take another 30 years before the Public Health Acts 1872 and 1875 introduced obligations to be fulfilled by sanitary authorities across the nation.

2–005 Pressures for governmental action did not come solely from considerations of health or welfare. New technology, such as railways, produced novel problems. The motives for state intervention were eclectic.[10] A principal reason was the fear of monopoly and excessive prices. The competitive process would be expected to break down monopolistic dominance and restore competitive equilibrium. The magic wand of market forces was however less than effective, in part because one company commonly served one route, and in part because of price fixing between rival companies. Gladstone was certainly less than sanguine as to the efficacy of the competitive process[11]:

[8] Fraser, *Evolution of the British Welfare State: A History of Social Policy since the Industrial Revolution* (1973), pp.41–42.

[9] S. Finer, *The Life and Times of Edwin Chadwick* (London: Methuen, 1952), p.155.

[10] H. Parris, *Government and the Railways in Nineteenth Century Britain* (London: Routledge and Kegan Paul, 1965); Lubenow, *The Politics of Government Growth: Early Victorian Attitudes toward State Intervention 1833–1848* (1971), Ch.4.

[11] Quoted in Lubenow, *The Politics of Government Growth: Early Victorian Attitudes toward State Intervention 1833–1848* (1971), p.129.

> "It was said, let matters … be allowed to go on as at present, and let the country trust to the effects of competition. Now, for his part, he would rather give his confidence to a Gracchus, when speaking on the subject of sedition, than give his confidence to a Railway Director, when speaking to the public of the effects of competition."

Safety was another factor prompting state intervention. Braking power, for example, was not the strong point of early railway transportation. Nor were track or signalling anywhere near pristine condition. There was in addition the problem of over-speculation. The railway mania of the 1840s brought forth a rash of projects and speculation. Companies were often underfunded and exceeded their statutory borrowing limit. The result was the passage of legislation in the 1840s and thereafter regulating railways.

Factory legislation, health, the Poor Law and railways represent four of the main areas in which the state intervened. They do not represent the totality of legislative intervention. A glance through Holdsworth[12] indicates the range and diversity of regulatory enactments passed during the 19th century. There was legislation on mining, chimney sweeps, contagious animals, and building to name but a few. Trades such as chemists, doctors, peddlers and public houses were subject to increasing regulation.

B. The Machinery of Administration

i. *The Board system*

It was common, until relatively recently, to think of new governmental functions being assigned to ministries. The term ministry is used here to denote a department of state, where the power is vested in a single person who sits in one of the Houses of Parliament and is responsible to Parliament for departmental action. However, ministerial government was not the standard procedure in the 19th century, or at least not in the first half thereof. The more common form of administration in the 18th and 19th centuries was the Board system. The precise structure and powers of Boards differed from area to area. What they possessed in common was a degree of independence from direct parliamentary control, although a minister might be answerable for part of their business.[13] **2–006**

The Board system was an integral and accepted part of the machinery of government. A number of factors contributed towards its use.[14] For the Crown, the Board pattern possessed advantages over ministers, who could be too strong or too weak. Positions on Boards could be a useful source of patronage. They allowed greater continuity of policy, being less affected by the ebbs and flows of

---

[12] Sir Willian Searle Holdsworth, *A History of English Law* (London: Methuen, 1965) Vol.15, 6–93.

[13] F. Willson, "Ministries and Boards: Some Aspects of Administrative Development since 1832" (1955) 33 Pub Adm 43, 44.

[14] Roberts, *Victorian Origins of the British Welfare State* (1960), Ch.4; Willson, "Ministries and Boards: Some Aspects of Administrative Development since 1832" (1955) 33 Pub. Adm. 43, 44; H. Parris, *Constitutional Bureaucracy: The Development of British Central Administration since the Eighteenth Century* (London: Allen & Unwin, 1968), Ch.3.

political change, and they were more flexible to the particular needs of decentralised administration. Thus, as Roberts states[15]:

> "The Victorians' experiments in semi-independent, non-political boards reflected their fear that administrative decision would be made the hand-maid of party bias or be caught in the maelstrom of factional politics. The Poor Law Commission was the classic and tragic example of such an attempt."

Developments within the constitutional balance of power, however, placed strain on the Board system. This led to the gradual replacement of Boards by ministries. Parris captures the nature of this strain[16]:

> "The system worked well so long as boards were responsible in fact as well as in name to the King. But once the executive became primarily responsible to parliament, the system came under strain. The result was a decline in the board pattern of administration and its supersession to a large degree by a ministerial pattern."

Parliament wished to control government action. This required someone answerable in the House, who was responsible for the Board. When the Poor Law Commission was created in 1834 none of the Board members could sit in Parliament. Communication was extremely difficult. Parliament became frustrated due to the absence of a person who could be rendered directly answerable. The Commissioners suffered through having no direct way of defending themselves against personal attack or vilification. The Commission was replaced by a ministry in 1847. The experience sent shock waves through other areas.

2–007 A middle way was tried, of having one or more Board members with a seat in Parliament. This was adopted for the Board of Woods, Forests and Land Revenues, to be followed for the General Board of Health. The experiment was not a noted success, because the relationship of the parliamentary member to the rest of the Board and the relationship with Parliament remained unclear.

Dissatisfaction with this constitutional no man's land led to one of two results. The Board was either converted into a formal ministry, or a minister was made directly responsible for the Board. The paradigm of the modern ministry gradually evolved: a minister running a department, and responsible to Parliament. The corollary was civil service anonymity, which only really developed in the mid-19th century. It was quite common, prior to that time, for civil servants to voice their views. This was not surprising when placed within the overall context of the Board system. It was the growth of individual ministerial responsibility for departmental policy that led the bureaucracy to develop its protective cloak.

ii. Powers of Boards

2–008 Generalisation concerning the powers of Boards is difficult. They were established to deal with diverse problems and their powers reflected that

---

[15] Roberts, *Victorian Origins of the British Welfare State* (1960), p.133.

[16] Parris, *Constitutional Bureaucracy: The Development of British Central Administration since the Eighteenth Century* (1968), p.83; G. Le May, *The Victorian Constitution: Conventions, Usages and Contingencies* (London: Duckworth, 1979).

divergence. The wide range of powers possessed by the Poor Law Commission, which could make rules and adjudicate, led Roberts to state that it was the "prototype for the administrative bureaus of the future" with discretionary power to legislate and grant aid.[17] While the precise ambit of a Board or department's powers differed, they nevertheless possessed certain features in common. Speaking of the 16 new departments with nation-wide responsibilities which existed in 1854, Roberts states[18]:

> "All ... could inspect local authorities and publish reports on them. Most could order prosecutions if local officials or industrialists violated those laws established for their regulation. Three of the central agencies could draw up and enforce their own rules and regulations, and nine of them could confirm the rules and regulations drawn up by local officials ... Ten of the departments could hold hearings and pass judgments on matters in dispute, and three could license or certify local institutions, such as hospitals for the insane and prison cells for the criminal. Only three agencies enjoyed the power of dispensing grants of money to local authorities. Six could insist that local authorities keep registers of pertinent information and almost all could demand that local authorities send in periodical releases on their activities."

Even where an addition to the administrative machinery was not a Board, but a sub-department of for example the Home Office, there was often nonetheless a good deal of independence in the administration of the policy in that area. The classic example of this is the working of the Home Office inspectorates. Factory, prison, mining and burial inspectors all came under the aegis of the Home Office.[19] Nineteenth-century papers of successive Home Secretaries are, however, replete with statements concerning the impossibility of the workload that this thereby thrust upon them. Even the tireless Palmerston despaired of ever reading the prison inspectors' reports.

C. The Rationale for Administrative Growth

Historians differ on the rationale for administrative growth in the 19th century. Some regard talk of an age of laissez-faire as misleading. For Holdsworth it possessed only peripheral relevance in matters of trade,[20] and Kitson Clark believed that talk of a period of "laissez-faire" was unhelpful.[21] Whether it is meaningful to talk of an age of laissez-faire is something which continues to divide authorities on the subject.[22] Inextricably linked with this is the relationship between Benthamite utilitarianism, laissez-faire and state intervention. For Dicey **2–009**

---

[17] Roberts, *Victorian Origins of the British Welfare State* (1960), pp.110–111.

[18] Roberts, *Victorian Origins of the British Welfare State* (1960), p.106. The 16 departments of which Roberts speaks are the Prison Inspectorate, the Mining Inspectorate, the Factory Inspectorate, the Anatomy Inspectorate, the Burial Inspectorate, the Poor Law Board, the General Board of Health, the Charity Commission, the Lunacy Commission, the Railway Department, the Merchant Marine Department, the Emigration Office, the Tithe, Inclosure and Copyhold Commission, the Department of Science and Art, the Ecclesiastical Commission, and the Education Committee.

[19] Roberts, *Victorian Origins of the British Welfare State* (1960), pp.93–95.

[20] *A History of English Law* (Methuen, 1965) Vol.15, 6–93.

[21] G. Kitson Clark, *An Expanding Society: Britain 1830-1900* (Cambridge University Press, 1967), p.162.

[22] For a balanced account of the contending arguments see, A. Taylor, *Laissez-faire and State Intervention in Nineteenth-Century Britain* (London: Macmillan, 1972).

the utilitarian ideal of the greatest happiness of the greatest number was to be achieved by laissez-faire policies. This verdict has been stood on its head by subsequent authors, some of whom see Benthamite theory as a direct catalyst of state intervention.[23] Others followed Halévy's[24] lead in distinguishing between economic affairs, in which utilitarianism presupposed a laissez-faire ideology, and social policy in which state intervention was necessary to secure the requisite harmony of interests.

The Halévy approach presumes that one can see a reflection of his view in the reforms adopted in the mid-19th century. Yet while the Poor Law, factory inspection and public health had clear social implications, they also had economic reverberations. Maintenance of the social-economic dichotomy is even more problematic when viewed against the background of price regulation of common carriers and public utilities. The polar opposite conclusions reached by Dicey and Brebner also appear too extreme. While Bentham's economic writings may have been based on laissez-faire principles, he admitted exceptions, as indeed did the classical economists. For Bentham while the basic premise might have been that the greatest good of the greatest number could be best attained without legislative meddling, this was not in the nature of an a priori truth, but more in the form of an empirical hypothesis. With the growing evils of industrialisation, state intervention could well be necessary to attain the utilitarian aim.

There is an unspoken premise underlying the preceding discussion, which is that utilitarian ideology played a significant role in administrative growth in the 19th century. This premise has been challenged by two different views, each of which ascribes minimal importance to utilitarianism.

2–010 MacDonagh[25] sees the expansion of government in more functional and less ideological terms. He developed a model of governmental growth. A social evil was exposed, leading to the demand for government intervention, but opposition rendered the legislation less efficacious than its original proponents had hoped. The realisation that the original legislation was ineffective led to the grant of additional powers, the provision of summary legal procedures and an inspectorate to supervise administration of the legislation. This in turn led to additional information becoming available, demands for further legislation to close gaps that had been revealed, and pressure towards a stronger, more centralised bureaucracy. The administrators however came to recognise that the "problems" with which they were dealing could not be solved once and for all. Administration ceased to be a static concept and developed into a dynamic process.

The MacDonagh thesis has not gone unchallenged. Parris[26] tested the MacDonagh thesis against various types of administrative growth in the 19th

---

[23] J.B. Brebner, "Laissez-faire and State Intervention in Nineteenth-Century Britain" (1948) 8 *Journal of Economic History* 61.

[24] *The Growth of Philosophical Radicalism* (London: Faber & Gwyer, 1928).

[25] O. MacDonagh, "The Nineteenth-Century Revolution in Government: A Reappraisal" (1958) 1 *Historical Journal* 52; O. MacDonagh, *A Pattern of Government Growth: The Passenger Acts and Their Enforcement, 1800–60* (London: MacGibbon & Kee, 1961).

[26] Parris, "The Nineteenth-Century Revolution in Government: A Reappraisal Reappraised" (1960) 3 *Historical Journal* 17.

century and found that the facts did not fit the model. He also disagreed with the role or lack of it that MacDonagh accorded to Benthamite ideology. As Parris noted, it is indeed difficult to discern how many people knew or were influenced by utilitarian thought. He argued moreover that MacDonagh overemphasised the anti-collective strain within Benthamism: the application of the principle of utility could lead to laissez-faire or state intervention depending upon the subject matter. For Parris, therefore, 19th-century government development should be seen as a function both of organic change and contemporary political and ideological thought, one of the main currents of which was Benthamism.

As with most such revolutions the rationale for its occurrence was probably eclectic, as both Parris[27] and Fraser assert.[28] Administrative momentum, political ideology, laissez-faire and Utilitarianism all had their role to play, as did more fortuitous factors such as the political personalities comprising the government of the day and the presence of figures such as Chadwick and Simon.

D. Local Government

> "A fundamental antithesis between centralisation and 'autonomous' decentralisation runs through the whole history of English government and its organisation. It is an antithesis that underlies every polity, but especially that of England, where the origin and building up of the nation give it an unparalleled importance. Indeed, among the primary causes which have governed the process of differentiating the early legal notions and institutions of the nation this conflict plays a leading part."[29] 2–011

We have already seen how the balance between central and local administration affected the shape and pattern of 19th-century reform. Thus far, we have considered this development primarily from the perspective of the central government. The 19th century also witnessed reform of local government. Many administrative functions were performed at local level. A closer look at the transformation of local government is therefore integral to an understanding of the overall pattern of administration.

The balance between central and local administration runs throughout our history. It is evident far earlier than the 19th century. The centralising tendencies of the Norman administration were offset to some extent by the creation of the office of justice of the peace under Edward III. These were appointees of the Crown drawn from the county or town over which they had jurisdiction. Originally their main role was to preserve the peace, but this was augmented by later legislation. An increasing range of regulatory activities were committed to their charge, such as the statutes of labourers and the supervision of the Poor Law.

The precise degree of control exercised by the central authority varied. Powers of appointment and dismissal of justices of the peace could be used to exert Crown influence. It was, however, the Tudors who attempted to extend central

---

[27] Parris, "The Nineteenth-Century Revolution in Government: A Reappraisal Reappraised" (1960) 3 *Historical Journal* 17.

[28] Fraser, *Evolution of the British Welfare State* (1973), Ch.5.

[29] J. Redlich and F. Hirst, *The History of Local Government in England*, 2nd edn (London: Macmillan, 1970), p.12. The book was originally printed in 1903. The second edition, with an introduction and epilogue by Keith-Lucas contains only Book I from the original work.

influence most forcefully. Privy Council supervision over the justices was increased, particularly by the Star Chamber. The traditional machinery of local administration was threatened by the creation of new local machinery more directly under the aegis of the centre, such as the Councils of the North. The grant of municipal charters of incorporation came to be used as a device through which the Crown exercised control over those in Parliament. In the 16th century a large number of charters were granted to a narrow select body of the town. This was supposed to personify the burgesses, but in fact the main group of such burgesses was excluded from participation in government.[30] The select body could perpetuate itself by co-opting new members and thus began the reign of the narrow oligarchy in municipal life that was to persist until the 19th century. For the Crown the benefit resided in the greater ease with which the municipalities could be bribed or bullied into electing representatives to Parliament who would be subservient to the Crown.

2–012 Local autonomy increased in the 18th century. The events of the 17th century had profound effects upon the balance between central and local administration. The Star Chamber was abolished, the Bill of Rights (1689) was passed, parliamentary authority was increased and local power augmented. The legacy of earlier abuses however, lived on. While the fate of Charles I, Charles II and James II added to the power of Parliament and reduced the central administration's hold on local authority, the corrupt nature of local politics continued unaltered. As Redlich and Hirst observe[31]:

> "Town franchises were preserved with all their anomalies and confusion. After two centuries of growth Select Bodies received Parliamentary recognition, and the municipal was confirmed by the political oligarchy. The reason is not far to seek. The ruling classes having conquered, as they thought the King, had no wish to see the basis upon which their own rule rested extended, or the balance of constitutional power again altered. They had come into a King's inheritance and they intended to enjoy it."

It was to be over 100 years before they were forced to share their legacy. The catalyst for change in municipal government was reform of the parliamentary franchise in the Reform Act 1832. The legislation was not radical in its immediate effects. Even after its passage less than 5 per cent of the populace could vote. Its main short-term effect was to bring the better off within the towns under the parliamentary franchise, by allowing the vote to the £10 householder. In the long term its impact was far greater. The old system of parliamentary franchise may have been illogical and unjust, but it was strengthened by the very weight of history. The post-1832 system was based on no real principle at all. It was difficult to think of reasons of principle why the £5 householder should not be admitted to the vote too.

2–013 Extension of the franchise had ramifications for municipal government which came to fruition in the Municipal Corporations Act 1835. In 1833 a Royal Commission was appointed to investigate defects in municipal corporations. The ills of municipal government were related with vigour. Inefficiency was added to

[30] Redlich and Hirst, *The History of Local Government in England* (1970), pp.28–29.
[31] Redlich and Hirst, *The History of Local Government in England* (1970), p.37.

peculation. Because so many municipal corporations were poorly administered, independent boards had developed to provide particular services. This produced divided authority, jealousy and squabbling between the different bodies. Inefficiency in the provision of services at a local level might have been tolerated by central government. Local disorder would not. Considerable disquiet was voiced at the inability of the local authorities to prevent riots and preserve the peace.

It would, however, be mistaken to see the passage of the 1835 Act as solely derived from Whig desires to end corruption. The Municipal Corporations Act 1835 was at least as much concerned with party advantage. As Fraser explains[32]:

> "Since the freemen and other ancient rights voters were to retain the Parliamentary vote for their lifetimes, and since the majority of corporate towns were still to return MPs, this left in the hands of the corporations considerable electoral power which, if past experience was followed, they were likely to use extensively and in a corrupt manner for the Tory interest in Parliamentary elections … The preservation of this electoral power would thus have frustrated the aims of the 1832 reform, and as The Times explained in 1833, 'the fact is that Parliamentary reform, if it were not to include Corporation reform likewise, would have been literally a dead letter'."

The Municipal Corporations Act 1835 extended the vote to all those who had resided and paid rates in the borough for three years. One quarter of the council was comprised of aldermen who were elected by the council. Towns that were not yet incorporated could petition the Crown for a charter of incorporation. The effect of doing so was to render the 1835 Act applicable. In conjunction with the Reform Act 1832, the Municipal Corporations Act 1835 laid the foundations for urban middle class involvement in the political life of the country. **2–014**

For the Whigs there was the hope of extending their power base, both through an alliance between the landed gentry and urban middle class, and through the removal of the old municipal corporations most of which were Tory. From the Tories there was a mixed response. Peel in the Commons presented little opposition to the 1835 Act. This was the Peel of the Tamworth manifesto, accepting the need to reform flagrant abuses. Lord Lyndhurst, leading the Tories in the House of Lords, was more strident, fearing that the removal of the old corporate bastions would herald the advent of democracy. For the Radicals it was hoped that the 1835 Act would be but the first step. Joseph Parkes, the Secretary to the Royal Commission, speaking of the recent reforms in the parliamentary and municipal franchises, puts the matter in apocalyptic terms[33]:

> "The Tories are burked, no resurrection for them. The Whigs … are an unnatural party standing between the People and the Tory aristocracy chiefly for the pecuniary value of the offices and the vanity of power. Their hearse is ordered."

The limits of the 1835 reform must, however, be borne in mind. The counties remained untouched, to be ruled by the squirearchy for another 50 years. Even after the reform of municipal corporations there was still considerable diversity in the bodies which would impinge upon local life. The previous inefficiency of the

[32] D. Fraser, *Power and Authority in the Victorian City* (London: Blackwell, 1979), p.5.

[33] Quoted in Fraser, *Power and Authority in the Victorian City* (1979), p.16.

unreformed boroughs meant that municipal functions from paving to lighting, and from cleaning to the supply of water, had been undertaken by other bodies, such as improvement commissioners. The 1835 Act did not unify these duties within the reformed corporations. It simply enabled the corporations to take over such jobs.

2–015 Reform of the counties was longer in coming. Attempts at reform in the 1840s came to nothing. The justice of the peace continued as the main administrative and judicial organ. As the number of duties imposed upon the justices expanded, so also did the sphere of their summary jurisdiction. The counties could not, however, remain unreformed forever. Legislation in 1867 and 1884 had extended the parliamentary franchise. The former conferred household suffrage on the inhabitants of parliamentary boroughs and rid the voting system of many anomalies. The latter broadened the borough franchise by the addition of a service vote and extended to the counties the household suffrage that already existed in the boroughs.

The Local Government Act 1888 was the early vehicle for county reform and by the turn of the century the pattern of local government had taken on the following form. The metropolis had a two-tier system with the London County Council at the top and metropolitan boroughs providing the second tier. County boroughs, the larger towns, were single purpose authorities. The counties were slightly more complex. The county council was the main authority for the area. Beneath it there were three types of institution: non-county boroughs; urban districts; and rural districts. The last of these could have parish councils within its area, thereby providing a third tier of authority. This system was to remain until 1972.

While the local franchise had been considerably widened the actual powers possessed by the local authorities were never clearly spelled out. We have already seen how the Municipal Corporations Act 1835 merely empowered the borough to take over functions performed by other institutions. As Fraser states[34]:

> "The lack of a clear legal prescription for corporate activity is the most important single factor to weigh against the Webbs' notion of a municipal revolution in 1835. Without adequate powers the councils were unable to fulfil the promise of municipal reform."

Those powers were obtained either by use of the empowering provisions of general legislation, or through passage of local legislation. By the end of the 19th century, Parliament was dealing with over 300 such acts per year.[35] Underlying the vagueness as to the ambit of the local authorities' powers was the recurring theme of the balance between the centre and the parts. A desire to demonstrate that central control was not needed played a part in the welter of local acts secured during this period.[36]

---

[34] Fraser, *Power and Authority in the Victorian City* (1979), p.164.

[35] Fraser, *Power and Authority in the Victorian City* (1979), p.165.

[36] Fraser, *Power and Authority in the Victorian City* (1979), pp.165–166.

E. The Evolution of Statutory Inquiries

While the emergence of statutory inquiries can be traced earlier, it is during the 19th century that it really developed. The agricultural and industrial revolutions increased the occasion for conflict between individual and individual, or individual and government. The inquiry procedure was a mechanism for resolving this conflict.[37] **2–016**

An early example of its use is to be found in relation to inclosures.[38] Inclosure of land was normally achieved by the passage of a private Act of Parliament. Inclosure Commissioners would be appointed to consider the facts of a particular scheme, and objections thereto. The Inclosure Act 1801 provided for the appointment of an ad hoc commission of inquiry. The meetings of the commission were to be advertised and the public could make objections to the scheme or parts of it. The normal private Bill procedure was modified by the General Inclosure Act 1845. This provided for an expedited form of procedure. Normally a private Bill would have to be considered by a Committee of each House. The provisional order procedure enshrined in the 1845 Act provided for an inquiry by a person who could investigate the matter at its actual physical location. The application for the provisional order was made to the appropriate government department which would appoint the inspector. Normally, a public inquiry would be held before a provisional order was made.[39] Much time could be saved by this procedure.

Inquiries were used in other areas besides that of inclosure, such as local government. The Public Health Act 1875 empowered the Local Government Board to hold such inquiries as they thought fit in relation to any matters concerning the public health in any place, or any matter in respect of which their sanction was required by the Act.[40] The inquiry was also used for other purposes, such as investigation of railway, mining and factory accidents. It was, however, expansion of governmental control over land use that provided the main impetus for the expansion of inquiries in the 20th century.

3. THE 20TH CENTURY

A. The Birth of the Welfare State and the Development of the Tribunal System

In 1906 the Liberal landslide produced a majority of 356. The next five years witnessed a range of measures often regarded as the basis for the Welfare State.[41] Protection of children was enshrined in the Children's Act 1908, to be followed **2–017**

[37] R. Wraith and G. Lamb, *Public Inquiries as an Instrument of Government* (London: Allen & Unwin, 1971), Ch.2.

[38] Wraith and Lamb, *Public Inquiries as an Instrument of Government* (1971), pp.17–21.

[39] Under the General Inclosure Act 1845, the procedure was somewhat different. The Assistant Commissioner would hold a meeting to hear objections, the Provisional Order would be made, and then a second meeting would be held for considering objections.

[40] Wraith and Lamb, *Public Inquiries as an Instrument of Government* (1971), pp.23–25.

[41] J. Hay, *The Origins of the Liberal Welfare Reforms 1906–1914* (London: Macmillan, 1975); Fraser, *Evolution of the British Welfare State* (1973), Ch.7.

closely by the introduction of old age pensions in the same year. It was, however, the National Insurance Act 1911 that was most significant in the long term.

It was through the combined energies of Lloyd George and Winston Churchill that this measure made its way on to the statute book. There was no shortage of ideas as to the path which reform ought to take. The Royal Commission on the Poor Law, which sat from 1905–1909, contained a plethora of opinion. Representatives of the Local Government Board wished for a reversion to the principles of 1834, that relief should be based upon less eligibility. While the Majority Report of the Commission did not accept this draconian view, the signatories believed that a remodelled Poor Law could be the basis for future development. Although the terms "Poor Law" and "guardian" were dropped for those of public assistance and public assistance committees, the essential idea that poverty was primarily a personal or moral, as opposed to a social or an economic problem, was adhered to. Beatrice Webb's Minority Report advocated, by way of contrast, the scrapping of the Poor Law entirely and its replacement by a strong Ministry of Labour and the expenditure of public money in times of cyclical depression.

Lloyd George adopted neither view, and had strong ideas of his own. Insurance was the key to Lloyd George's scheme and the means of "dishing the Webbs". Like Bismarck before him, Lloyd George and the Liberals saw a social insurance scheme as the method of reducing the socialist threat. An insurance scheme possessed other advantages. It would reduce the financial burden placed on the state as compared with a completely non-contributory plan. It would be more acceptable to the people, since it would be based on contribution and hence entitlement. The moral stigma attached to the reluctant grant of relief that characterised the Poor Law had become deeply etched upon the country's mentality. Part I of the National Insurance Act 1911 established the foundations of health insurance with contributions from the state, employer and employee.

While Lloyd George was piloting the passage of the health and sickness provisions, Churchill and the young Beveridge were working on unemployment. The Labour Exchanges Act 1909 was intended as one half of a two-pronged attack on the problem, the other half being insurance. This was encapsulated in Pt II of the National Insurance Act 1911, which provided for tripartite contributions from employer, employee and the state. Little controversy attended the passage of this part of the Act as compared with the health provisions contained in Pt I. This was ironic, since it was the unemployment provisions that came under most strain in the ensuing years.

This new legislation required administration. It is in the Liberal enactments of this period that the modern tribunal system has its real roots. Individual tribunals had existed earlier than this. However, the reforms necessitated the development of an administrative and adjudicative mechanism on a scale different from that which had gone before. A variety of machinery was established, the constant theme being that the ordinary courts were kept in the background, for a number of reasons. The cost of using the ordinary courts would often be disproportionate to the amounts involved and the number of potential disputes would simply overburden them. There was also the feeling that the courts were not the appropriate mechanism.[42] Certain judicial decisions on the early factory legislation, concerning hours of work for children, had emasculated the legislative intent by upholding the legality of the relay system. The judiciary had not been happy with their role as arbiters of the reasonableness of railway charges, while experience of appellate involvement in the Workmen's Compensation Acts 1897 and 1906 had been far from successful. Trade union feeling that the ordinary courts were unsympathetic to their position, as evidenced by a series of decisions in the early 1900s, also militated against their use. The Liberal measures were therefore designed to avoid using the ordinary courts.

Reforms continued during the inter-war years. The Ministry of Health was created in 1919 and extension of state involvement in education was enshrined in the Education Act 1918. It was, however, the problem of unemployment and depression that increasingly concerned governments during the 1920s and 1930s. The theme during this period was the de facto modification of the insurance principle that underpinned the 1911 legislation. While this was extended in scope by the Unemployment Insurance Act 1920 the insurance principle came under strain. Rising unemployment caused the quid pro quo of contribution for entitlement to become warped. Increasingly the insurance fund came to bear the weight intended to be borne by the Poor Law. Further inroads into the insurance principle were made as a result of the Blanesburgh Report of 1927. The effect of its recommendations was to dilute the balance between contribution and entitlement. Benefits were no longer to be limited in time. They were no longer realistically seen as the equivalent of contributions. Provided some contributions had been made, benefits could be drawn on the basis of need.[43] The dichotomy between insurance based and non-insurance based assistance was however, partially restored by the Unemployment Act 1934. **2–018**

War brought further changes in its train, exemplified by the publication of the Beveridge Report in 1942. This became a major document for social reform. Insurance was set in the wider context of the eradication of the five evils: Want, Disease, Ignorance, Squalor and Illness. To this end the idea was to have a single weekly contribution which would provide cover for sickness, medical needs, unemployment, widows, orphans, old-age, maternity, funeral benefits and industrial injury. Contributions and benefits were both to be flat rate and not earnings-related. Subsistence was all that was to be guaranteed. Herein lay the seeds of future difficulty, since post-war Britain did not think simply of avoiding starvation, but of maintaining accustomed living standards when earnings were interrupted.[44]

What emerged from the post-war Labour government was a scheme which reflected the essentials of the Beveridge proposals, although the details of contribution levels differed. Industrial injuries were treated separately in the National Insurance (Industrial Injuries) Act 1946, the main difference being that benefits were earnings related. Other benefits were dealt with in the National Insurance Act 1946. Contributions and benefits were both to be flat rate. Why on

[42] B. Abel-Smith and R. Stevens, *Lawyers and the Courts: A Sociological Study of the English Legal System 1750–1965* (London: Heinemann, 1967), pp.111–121.

[43] Fraser, *Evolution of the British Welfare State* (1973), pp.171–174.

[44] Fraser, *Evolution of the British Welfare State* (1973), p.202.

moral grounds, work based injury should be treated differently from that resulting from other causes is something which has puzzled many for a long time. Alongside the insurance system was the National Assistance Board designed to provide a non-contributory sum for those who had used up their insurance entitlement, or who had never qualified for any.

2–019 The emergence and generalisation of the social insurance and assistance principles brought with it a corresponding growth in the tribunal system, since it was by this mechanism that disputes concerning entitlement were to be resolved. Developments in welfare policy were not, however, the only reasons for growth of our administrative system. The government enacted regulatory legislation in many areas, which was enforced outside the traditional court system. Rent and transport tribunals provide but two examples. Tribunals were established to provide protection for the citizen, such as the Mental Health Review Tribunal, while others enforced legislation affecting a large group of people, such as the industrial tribunals. Yet others were concerned with the competitive process such as the Monopolies and Mergers Commission. The list could be considerably extended.

The growth of tribunals was not the only developing part of our administrative system. There was expansion of the inquiry procedure flowing from increase in state control over land use, planning and development. There was also increase in the use of quangos or agencies. A realisation that we were reverting to something approximating to the Board system did not escape all commentators. Willson, writing in 1955, noted that many of the newer regulatory functions undertaken by the state were given to such bodies.[45] An idea of the range and number of such institutions can be grasped by glancing through the appendices of the 1980 *Report on Non-Departmental Public Bodies*.[46] The reasons for the growth of agencies will be discussed later.[47]

As a background to this discussion the reactions of government to the growth of administration will be considered through an examination of four of the major studies completed this century. The details of these reports are not of direct relevance. The interest lies rather in their perception of the problems to be solved, and the government's reaction.

B. Donoughmore, Franks, the 1980 Report and the 1988 Justice Report

2–020 The Committee on Ministers' Powers,[48] known as the Donoughmore Committee, produced a report that reflected the rationale for its establishment. The Committee had been constituted to look at two specific areas, which reflected concern at the extent of ministerial power.[49] These were delegated legislation and the making of judicial or quasi-judicial decisions by a minister or those under his

[45] F. Willson, "Ministries and Boards: Some Aspects of Administrative Development since 1832" (1955) 33 Pub Adm 43, 55.

[46] Sir L. Pliatzky, *Report on Non-Departmental Public Bodies* (1980), Cmnd.7797.

[47] See Ch.4.

[48] *Committee on Ministers' Powers Report* (1932), Cmd.4060.

[49] See Lord Hewart, *The New Despotism* (London: Ernest Benn, 1929).

control. Increasing use of broad delegations of power resulted in the acquisition of both legislative and adjudicative functions by the Executive. A powerful Committee[50] produced a report which contained suggestions for reform in both areas.

Just over 30 years later there appeared the *Report of the Committee on Administrative Tribunals and Enquiries*,[51] known as the Franks Report. The terms of reference were drawn quite specifically. The Committee examined tribunals and inquiries. This put beyond the Committee's purview the broad area of decision-making where no formal procedure had been prescribed, a fact emphasised by the Committee itself.[52] The Committee made a series of recommendations as to the constitution and working of tribunals and inquiries, many of which were enacted in the Tribunals and Inquiries Act 1958. These were valuable reforms. It is the more general premises from which the Committee reasoned, which are of interest here. It reasoned from the premise that tribunals should be seen as part of the machinery of adjudication.[53] There was nothing wrong with this in itself. It was speaking about tribunals against the background of its terms of reference. Many, though not all of tribunals can properly be regarded as part of the machinery of adjudication, involving formal statutory procedures for the resolution of social welfare claims, or rent disputes. However, an indirect result of this categorisation was the implicit assumption that all of our administrative institutions could be fitted into the pigeon-holes "inquiry" or "tribunal", with those terms bearing their Franksian meaning.

The 1980 *Report on Non-Departmental Public Bodies*[54] contained useful factual information, combined with short summaries of the difficulties surrounding agencies and the like. The importance of this aspect of administrative law was increased by developments in governmental policy. Privatisation and deregulation have added to the number of such institutions. The desire to reduce the size of the central civil service, and to administer policy through a variety of executive agencies, has had an important impact in the same direction.[55]

The Justice-All Souls Report[56] contained important recommendations on particular topics, such as the duty to give reasons and the operation of tribunals. It was, however, limited in its scope and in its approach. Thus, for example, the problems generated by agencies were barely touched on; there was no real discussion of how administrative agencies "operated", or of their relationship with government; and the significance of participation within administrative decision-making was not considered.

We can now examine in more detail the principal institutions responsible for making decisions that come within the purview of administrative law. Subsequent

---

[50] It contained Laski, Holdsworth, Scott and Anderson to name but a few.

[51] *Report of the Committee on Administrative Tribunals and Enquiries* (1957), Cmnd.218 (the Franks Report).

[52] The Franks Report, paras 9–15.

[53] The Franks Report, para.40.

[54] Sir L. Pliatzky, *Report on Non-Departmental Public Bodies*.

[55] See Ch.4.

[56] *Administrative Justice, Some Necessary Reforms* (Oxford University Press, 1988). Report of the Committee of the Justice, *All Souls Review of Administrative Law in the United Kingdom*.

chapters will therefore examine the government, agencies, contracting out, tribunals and inquiries, local authorities and devolution.

CHAPTER 3

PARLIAMENT AND THE EXECUTIVE

1. CENTRAL ISSUES

i. The definition of government has always been somewhat problematic, but these problems have been exacerbated by changes in the pattern of administration. The creation of executive agencies, contracting-out, privatisation, and the private financing of public projects have all served to make the definition of "government" more uncertain and to blur the line between the public and the private sector. **3–001**

ii. This chapter is concerned with Westminster, and the relationship between the House of Commons and the Executive. It will be followed by chapters on agencies, service provision and contracting out. There will be analysis of governmental structures outside Whitehall, with separate chapters on devolution, local government and the European Union. The discussion of the administrative system will also focus on principles that are fundamental to good governance, including freedom of information, standards in public life and adequate complaints machinery. Tribunals and inquiries receive separate treatment. The analysis of the administrative system concludes with a case study of competition and regulation.

iii. This chapter examines some of the core features of the relationship between Parliament and the Executive. It begins by considering the foundations for executive power. It will be seen that the expansion of the franchise and the increase in the areas over which government accepted responsibility were intimately connected. This in turn increased executive power in relation to the legislature, since the government had to be able to deliver the broadened range of promises that had led to its election. This led to centralisation of the legislative initiative in the hands of the government and a tighter party system.

iv. The discussion then turns to the role of the legislature in relation to the scrutiny of government policy, and in relation to the legislative process.

v. The principal mechanism for scrutiny of governmental policy is through departmental select committees. Such committees have a relatively long history, but the modern system dates from 1979 when the current system of departmental select committees was established. The limits of such scrutiny, and the achievements of such committees, are considered in the chapter, as are recent reform initiatives.

vi. The role of the legislature in the legislative process is then considered. The House of Commons has battled to preserve and strengthen its role in the passage of legislation. There are tensions between this laudable aim and the adversarial party system that still dominates Westminster politics. The difficulties of securing a greater role for the legislature are explained, as is the success of certain recent reform initiatives.

2. FOUNDATIONS OF EXECUTIVE POWER

3–002 What follows does not purport to summarise central government.[1] It does not attempt to set out systematically the method by which legislation is enacted, the role of the civil service or the various ways in which the Prime Minister can impose his or her will. Detailed exposition of such matters would be a work in itself. Some knowledge of the realities of central government is, however, vital for understanding administrative law.

This is in part because ministerial decisions have often been challenged in the courts. An understanding of the relationship between the Executive and the legislature is necessary to comprehend how such decisions are made. It is in part because the issue of whether administrative functions should be performed within traditional departments of government, or whether they should be "hived off" to an agency, has been much debated. This debate has been fuelled by governmental initiatives to reduce the size of the central civil service, and assign more tasks to agencies. This raises, as we shall see,[2] problems concerning accountability.

However, it should not be assumed that such problems are absent when decision-making is undertaken within traditional governmental departments. An understanding of the interrelationship of the Executive and the legislature enables us to appreciate the problems of accountability that exist even when decisions are made by "ordinary" governmental departments. We must therefore ensure that when we compare different institutional options we do so against a realistic rather than idealistic background. In the debate over agencies, their accountability must be juxtaposed to constitutional reality, not some paradigm long since disappeared.

---

[1] P. Norton, *The Commons in Perspective* (Oxford: Martin Robertson, 1981); P. Norton, *The Constitution in Flux* (Oxford: Blackwell, 1982); D. Kavanagh, *Thatcherism and British Politics: The End of Consensus?* (Oxford: Oxford University Press, 1987); R. Rose, *Politics in England: Change and Persistence*, 5th edn (London: Macmillan, 1989); J. Griffith and M. Ryle, *Parliament, Functions, Practice and Procedure* (London: Sweet & Maxwell, 1989); P. Norton, *Does Parliament Matter?* (Harvester/Wheatsheaf, 1993); R. Rhodes and P. Dunleavy (eds), *Prime Minister, Cabinet and Core Executive* (Macmillan, 1995); C. Foster and F. Plowden, *The State under Stress: Can the Hollow State be Good Government?* (Buckingham: Open University Press, 1996); D. Oliver and G. Drewry (eds), *The Law and Parliament* (London: Butterworths, 1998); R. Brazier, *Constitutional Practice, the Foundations of British Government*, 3rd edn (Oxford: Oxford University Press, 1999); R. Hazell (ed), *Constitutional Futures, A History of the Next Ten Years* (Oxford: Oxford University Press, 1999); P. Dunleavy, A. Gamble, R. Heffernan, I. Holliday, and G. Peele (eds), *Developments in British Politics 6* (Basingstoke: Palgrave, 2002); P. Norton, *Parliament in British Politics*, 2nd edn (Basingstoke: Palgrave, 2005); D. Kavanagh, *British Politics*, 5th edn (Oxford: Oxford University Press, 2006); B. Jones, D. Kavanagh, M. Moran, and P. Norton, *Politics UK*, 7th edn (Harlow: Pearson Education, 2010); R. Heffernan, P. Cowley and C Hay, *Developments in British Politics 9* (Basingstoke: Palgrave, 2011); P. Norton, *The British Polity* (London: Longman, 2011); M. Moran, *Politics and Governance in the UK*, 2nd edn (Basingstoke: Palgrave, 2011).

[2] See Chs 4–5.

A. Expansion of the Franchise and Increase in Governmental Responsibility

> "In the British Cabinet today is concentrated all political power, all initiative in legislation and administration, and finally all public authority for carrying out the laws in kingdom and empire. In the sixteenth century and down to the middle of the seventeenth this wealth of authority was united in the hands of the Crown and its privy council; in the eighteenth century and the first half of the nineteenth, Parliament was the dominant central organ from which proceeded the most powerful stimulus to action and all decisive acts of policy, legislation and administration; the second half of the last century saw the gradual transfer from Crown and Parliament into the hands of the Cabinet of one after another of the elements of authority and political power. This process took place side by side and in organic connection with the passing of political sovereignty into the hands of the House of Commons, supported as it now was by an electorate comprising all sections of the population." **3–003**

This quotation, modern although it may sound, is taken from Josef Redlich writing in 1905.[3] In the early 19th century the Executive was principally concerned with the maintenance of order, the raising of revenue and the conduct of foreign affairs. The idea that the government had an obligation to carry out a set of domestic policies was not yet acknowledged, although there was nonetheless much regulatory legislation enacted in earlier centuries.[4] Domestic legislation would normally receive its stimulus from private members. The government might be persuaded to take up a particular measure, as with certain of the Factory Acts, but it was normally after a private member had provided the catalyst. It was often the adventitious discovery of an "evil", shocking the nation, which produced the impetus for reform. Early 19th century legislation was not therefore generally devised and controlled by government.[5]

The reverse side of the same coin was the relative weakness of the party system when it came to voting. Divisions were not along rigid party lines. Labels such as Tory, Whig, Radical and Liberal contained a spectrum of divergent views. Social and economic legislation of the early 19th century would receive its support from those with widely differing views. The beliefs of those ranged in opposition were similarly broad. Measures could be promoted by the government. Party based domestic legislation was not, however, the norm during this period.

It was, as Redlich observed, the expansion of the suffrage that was a main cause of the altered constitutional balance of power. As the electorate increased in size so it became necessary for governments to appeal to a wider cross section of the population. The Liberal government's social welfare legislation of 1906–1911 was prompted in part by the perceived need to offer the "people" some tangible benefits. There were other reasons leading to its passage, including developing social ideas, the desire to cut the ground from under the feet of the Fabians, and a real wish to cope with the problems of sickness, old age and unemployment.

---

[3] A. Constable, *The Procedure of the House of Commons: A Study of Its History and Present Form* (1908), i, 20, quoted in S. Walkland (ed.), *The House of Commons in the Twentieth Century* (Oxford: Clarendon, 1979), p.247.

[4] P. Craig, *UK, EU and Global Administrative Law: Foundations and Challenges* (Cambridge: Cambridge University Press, 2015), Ch.1.

[5] A wider range of functions was undertaken by various commissions and boards, particularly at the local level, see Ch.2.

There was nonetheless an understandably distinct political motive, namely that many of those who would benefit could vote.

Herein lays the organic connection between the passing of political sovereignty into the hands of the House of Commons, and the passing of real power into the hands of the Executive, of which Redlich spoke. The legitimacy of the House of Commons was strengthened by the extension of the suffrage. Somewhat paradoxically, this strengthened the Executive. The need to appeal to the expanded electorate was a powerful reason for the Executive to bring within its purview a broader range of tasks than hitherto.

3–004 Political change is seldom a one-dimensional process. Factors affecting such development overlap and feed off each other. The fact that the government began to play an increasing role in the initiation, shaping and promulgation of legislation helped to create, and was itself influenced by, a growing expectation that government could be looked on to remedy social and economic evils. The aspirations of the populace were continually increasing. Not only was government seen as having a social responsibility, but the nature of that responsibility was altering. In the realm of social policy, for example, the idea that the government had fulfilled its obligations by providing subsistence benefits was, by the middle of the 20th century, fast becoming outdated. As the fear of destitution diminished, so the aim became one of preserving living standards in times of hardship caused by sickness, death or unemployment. A positive social role for government was apparent in other areas too, such as increases in educational opportunity and improved health standards. The Executive also played an increasing role in management of the economy. The macro-economic theories of Keynes indicated a positive role for government to rectify economic imbalances.

The increase in Executive involvement in an ever-broadening range of domestic policy was attended by changes in the party system and the methods of legislation. If the government of the day was to secure the passage of its policies, then it had to control the legislative process and its own supporters more vigorously than it had done previously. It is to these developments that we should now turn.

B. Centralisation of Legislative Initiative

3–005 Speaking of the change in the pattern of legislation during the late 19th and early 20th centuries, Walkland states[6]:

> "In the case of the legislative process, this period essentially saw a nationalisation and centralisation of legislative initiative in the hands of the government, a massive supplementation of Private Bill procedure by government-introduced Public General Acts, and a marked diminution in the opportunities for private Members to legislate."

[6] "Government Legislation in the House of Commons", in Walkland, *The House of Commons in the Twentieth Century* (1979), p.247.

Three principal causes of this centralisation of legislative initiative were the development of standing committees, increased discussion of legislation in cabinet committees, and the growth of delegated legislation.

Standing committees were used on limited occasions in the late 19th century,[7] but were viewed with suspicion. It was felt that the government should defend its measures, even as to points of detail, in a Committee of the Whole House. This was indeed the norm. Attempts to take the committee stage in standing committee were regarded as devices by which the government sought to escape criticism. This dislike of standing committees was fuelled by the oft-repeated sentiment that wholesale use of such committees would turn the Commons into a legislative machine, grinding out the maximum amount in the shortest possible time.[8] Despite these objections standing committees became the normal way of considering the detail of legislation. Not surprisingly, increase in their use corresponded with periods in which the government had a large legislative programme. The two key periods were 1906 and 1945.

In 1906 a Procedure Committee recommended that all Bills, except finance, consolidated fund, and appropriation Bills, and Bills for confirming provisional orders, should be sent to a standing committee after second reading unless the House otherwise ordered. The government supported these recommendations. Many backbenchers opposed them. It was to take four days of debate, during which the government stood out against demands for amendment, before the recommendations of the 1906 Committee were accepted. Despite assurances by the government that such committees would not be used for controversial measures, the ensuing years witnessed the sending of such minor matters as the National Insurance Act 1911 to a standing committee rather than a Committee of the Whole House.[9]

The use of standing committees received a significant boost as a result of the Select Committee on Procedure, which was established in 1945. As in 1906, the **3–006**
principal reason for expediting parliamentary business was the size of the government's legislative programme. The Labour government in 1945 wished to implement measures, the technical complexity of which exceeded that of normal legislation. If this were to be possible the flow of parliamentary business had to be speeded up. The Select Committee's main brief was to consider how the passage of public Bills could be accelerated. The government accepted the Report. The Committee recommended standing committees on all Bills, except those of major constitutional importance, increase in the number of such committees and the utilisation of the guillotine within the committees in order that the government could be sure that its measures would not be unduly delayed.[10]

If the development of standing committees expedited the passage of business on the floor of the House, the centralisation of the legislative initiative within the Executive was also affected by the increased sophistication of cabinet legislative

---

[7] Walkland, *The House of Commons in the Twentieth Century* (1979), p.255.

[8] Walkland, *The House of Commons in the Twentieth Century* (1979), p.253.

[9] The existence of such committees did however benefit private Members' legislation, see Walkland, *The House of Commons in the Twentieth Century* (1979), p.25.

[10] Walkland, *The House of Commons in the Twentieth Century* (1979), pp.265–268.

planning. *Cabinet committees* were used by Liberal governments to settle the details of legislative proposals.[11] It was, however, the Second World War and its aftermath that saw the growing systematisation of legislative planning at cabinet level. A distinct Legislative Committee of the Cabinet with responsibility for planning a legislative programme existed in 1940. This idea was built on by the post-war Labour government. The planning of the general legislative programme was assigned to a future legislation committee, with a distinct Legislation Committee, which would advise on the more technical aspects concerning the form of the legislation.[12] Bills could well go through several drafts before being presented to the House of Commons. It became rare for an amendment to be forced on a government against its will, whether in committee or elsewhere.[13] Cabinet committees, together with the Prime Minister's Office and the Cabinet Office, are at the heart of executive policy formation in the modern day.[14] Many of the central initiatives relating to service delivery, regulatory reform and the like are directed from these offices.[15] There has, moreover, been increased recourse to what are termed "bilaterals", that is meetings between the Prime Minister and individual ministers, in which policy in a particular area is developed.[16]

The growth of *delegated legislation* has centralised the legislative initiative within the Executive in a rather different way from either standing committees or cabinet oversight. Delegated legislation is not a new phenomenon. The passage of a large volume of social and economic legislation nonetheless led to increase in delegated legislation. This centralised legislative initiative within the Executive as a whole. It is the government, albeit acting through individual ministers, which decides when and whether to initiate such legislation and effective legislative control is problematic.[17]

C. Development of the Party System

3–007 The power of the Executive was also markedly increased by the development of the party system and the consequential control wielded by government over its supporters in the House of Commons.

Parties are not a new phenomenon. They emerged in the late 18th and early 19th centuries. Even early parliamentary party organisation was designed to

[11] Walkland, *The House of Commons in the Twentieth Century* (1979), pp.251–252.

[12] Walkland, *The House of Commons in the Twentieth Century* (1979), pp.265–266.

[13] How rare is a matter of some debate, see Walkland, *The House of Commons in the Twentieth Century* (1979), pp.287–288; J. Griffith, *Parliamentary Scrutiny of Government Bills* (1975).

[14] I. Holliday, "Executives and Administrations", in Dunleavy, Gamble, Heffernan, Holliday, and Peele, *Developments in British Politics 6* (2002), Ch.6; M. Burch and I. Holliday, *The British Cabinet System* (Prentice Hall/Harvester Wheatsheaf, 1996); M. Burch and I. Holliday, "An Executive Office in All But Name: The Prime Minister's and Cabinet Offices in the UK" (1999) 52 *Parliamentary Affairs* 32; Select Committee on the Constitution, *Fourth Report: The Cabinet Office and the Centre of Government*, HL Paper No.30 (Session 2009–10).

[15] Chs 4, 5 and 11.

[16] Kavanagh, *British Politics: Continuities and Change* (2006), Ch.11.

[17] Ch.15.

ensure that members adhered to the party line laid down by the party leaders.[18] The very existence of parties provided an avenue for the channelling of power from the legislature to the Executive. It was, however, a combination of the extended suffrage and the expanded role of the state, which sowed the seeds of more rigid party discipline.

The expansion of the franchise in 1832 and in 1867 changed the nature of politics. Voters could not simply be bought. There were too many. An organisation outside Parliament was required to persuade voters into using their newly acquired rights for the benefit of a particular party. Promises for reform provided the carrot. But promises have, in theory, to be kept. A necessary if not sufficient condition for doing so was greater Executive control within Parliament to ensure the passage of the requisite legislation. The point is put neatly by Norton[19]:

> "Parties certainly had a profound impact upon Parliament: voters not only had to be contacted, they had to be promised something if their votes were to be forthcoming, and party promises could only be fulfilled if party nominees were returned in sufficient number to, and displayed voting cohesion in, the House of Commons; the consequence of this development was to be party government, with the parliamentary parties acting as a conduit for the transfer of power from Parliament to the executive."

The transition from the 19th to the 20th century exacerbated the problem. The role of the state developed partly because of the extension of the franchise. This broadened range of functions placed increasing strain upon parliamentary time. One response was reform of legislative procedures. Another was to tighten party discipline, to ensure the passage of the expanded governmental programme. It should not be thought that MPs are continually being harassed by harridans called Whips. This would be to misrepresent reality. Whips perform valuable functions of communication and management as well as discipline. The government, nevertheless, maintains a carefully calculated legislative programme, the Whip system is applied to standing committees, the guillotine is used to maintain impetus, and there is pressure on a member not to vote against the government, especially on an important issue where the difference in numbers between government and opposition is finely balanced.

The party system not only centralised initiative in the Executive as manifested in **3–008** party voting cohesion, but also in the process of policy formation. As Johnson has noted,[20] policy is normally laid down by the Executive when the party is in office, although on occasion the official leadership may defer to a particular powerful group because the Executive fears to oppose them.

---

[18] P. Norton, "The Organisation of Parliamentary Parties", in Walkland, *The House of Commons in the Twentieth Century* (1979), p.9; R. Rose, *Do Parties Make a Difference?*, 2nd edn (London: Macmillan, 1984); P. Norton, *Dissension in the House of Commons 1945–1974* (London: Macmillan, 1975).

[19] P. Norton, "The Organisation of Parliamentary Parties", in Walkland, *The House of Commons in the Twentieth Century* (1979), p.8.

[20] N. Johnson, *In Search of the Constitution, Reflections on State and Society in Britain* (Oxford: Pergamon, 1977), p.47.

To this process of policy formulation may be added the impact of powerful interest groups outside Parliament. There is nothing wrong with extra-parliamentary groups having an effect on legislative programmes. It happens in all countries. What causes disquiet is the extent of this influence, and the way in which it serves to weaken further the power of the legislature over legislation.

3. ROLE OF THE LEGISLATURE

3–009 Whether we should be dismayed by the preceding developments depends on one's view as the role of the House of Commons. It could be argued that the legislature should primarily be a critic, a body to scrutinise the government rather than one that controls the legislative process. It might alternatively be thought that the House of Commons should have a legislative role, which should be buttressed and strengthened. The two views are not antithetical. They do, however, judge the effectiveness of the House of Commons from different perspectives.[21]

A. The Commons and Scrutiny

3–010 Control or influence over the substance of legislation is, says Ryle,[22] necessarily minimal, since the government can ensure in most instances that its policies become law in much the way that it desires. The picture of the Commons as critic is put forcefully by Ryle[23]:

> "Thus much of the criticism of Parliament and particularly of the House of Commons today, flows, I believe, from this fundamental mistake in their perceived functions. Parliament is wrongly blamed for bad government because Parliament does not govern. To put it baldly: the government governs; Parliament is the forum where the exercise of government is publicly displayed and is open to scrutiny and criticism. And the Commons does not control the executive—not in any real sense; rather the executive control the Commons through the exercise of their party majority power."

This view of the House of Commons' role is essentially pragmatic: little control is possible over the content of legislation, and therefore the value of the Commons must lie elsewhere. There is no doubt that critical scrutiny is a valuable function for a legislature, and select committees are the most important instrument in this respect.

---

[21] P. Norton, "Parliamentary Oversight", in P. Dunleavy, A. Gamble, I. Holliday, and G. Peele (eds), *Developments in British Politics 5* (London: Macmillan, 1997), Ch 8.

[22] "The Commons in the Seventies—A General Survey", in S. Walkland and M. Ryle (eds), *The Commons in the Seventies* (Fontana, 1977), pp.13–14.

[23] "The Commons in the Seventies—A General Survey", in Walkland and Ryle (eds), *The Commons in the Seventies* (1977), p.12.

i. *Select committees: origins and development*

Prior to 1914 such committees were used for a variety of purposes. Johnson lists four[24]: the investigation of alleged abuses, inquiries into areas of public policy when action was demanded, consideration of Bills, and scrutiny of financial rectitude through the Public Accounts Committee established in 1861. The use of such committees declined during the inter-war years, but they were utilised more often after the Second World War. Four main committees carried on investigative work: the Public Accounts Committee, the Estimates Committee,[25] the Select Committee on Nationalised Industry[26] and the Statutory Instruments Committee. **3–011**

The development of select committees received two further boosts, the first in the mid-1960s and the second in the late 1970s. A number of select committees were established in the late 1960s, partly as a result of the Report of the Procedure Committee of 1964–1965, and partly as a consequence of the feeling that the balance between the legislature and the Executive needed redressing. The government's approach was, however, ad hoc and no common theme runs through the committees that were established. Some dealt with a particular subject matter; others were based around the work of a department. Dissatisfaction with the disorganised pattern of select committees, coupled with the belief that greater coverage was required, led the Select Committee on Procedure to recommend extension of select committees along departmental lines.[27] These recommendations were put into effect in 1979, the result being that such committees now cover all major aspects of government.

ii. *Select committees: early assessments*

The effectiveness of such committees depends in part upon one's expectations. The strong argument for select committees was that their investigative and critical functions would enable Parliament to reassert real control over the government. A less ambitious view saw select committees as relatively impartial generators of advice and information, hoping to influence government because of their non-partisan approach.[28] It is doubtful whether the committees have played the stronger of these two roles. This is so for a number of reasons.[29] **3–012**

First, the committees did not have a role in the process by which the government framed its legislation. In this sense, they were ancillary to the

---

[24] "Select Committees and Administration", in Walkland, *The House of Commons in the Twentieth Century* (1979), p.432.

[25] N. Johnson, *Parliament and Administration: The Estimates Committee 1945–65* (London: Allen & Unwin, 1966).

[26] D. Coombes, *The Member of Parliament and the Administration: The Case of the Select Committee on Nationalised Industries* (London: Allen & Unwin, 1966).

[27] Select Committee on Procedure, *First Report*, HC Paper No.588 (Session 1977–78).

[28] N. Johnson, "Select Committees as Tools of Parliamentary Reform: Some Further Reflections", in Walkland and Ryle, *The Commons in the Seventies* (1977), p.195.

[29] G. Drewry (ed.), *The New Select Committees, A Study of the 1979 Reforms* (Oxford: Oxford University Press, 1985); D. Englefield (ed.), *Commons Select Committees: Catalysts for Progress?* (London: Longman, 1984).

principal work of the House, though some select committees attempted to circumvent this limitation by examining matters that were likely to lead to legislation in the near future.[30]

Second, the committees did not have adequate resources, and operated with minimal support staff and a small budget.[31]

Third, it was inappropriate to conceive of the new committees as a "system", since they had different perceptions of their own function.[32] Thus, some committees shied away from involvement with fundamental policy issues; others acted as advocates for particular pressure groups; and yet others engaged in more searching scrutiny of long term governmental objectives.

Fourth, the Memorandum for Guidance of Officials who appeared before the committees limited the information which civil servants should provide. Thus, officials were instructed not to meet requests for information irrespective of the cost; not to disclose advice given to ministers, nor information concerning interdepartmental exchanges on policy issues; not to reveal discussions in Cabinet committees; and to confine their evidence, so far as possible, to questions of fact relating to existing governmental policy, and not to discuss alternative strategies.[33]

Fifth, the opportunities to debate the findings of select committees on the floor of the House were limited. Between 1979 and 1988 only 25 per cent of the reports were debated, and only 13 out of 500 reports were the subject of any substantive motion, although some form of government response was often forthcoming.[34]

Finally, there was concern over the limited scrutiny of financial matters. Scrutiny of expenditure in the Commons was severely limited.[35] The select committee structure replaced the Expenditure committee, the idea being that each committee scrutinised expenditure in its subject-matter area. Robinson argued that this impeded the development of a systematic critical approach to scrutiny of public expenditure.[36] Drewry echoed these sentiments.[37] Some increase in legislative control over money expended was, however, provided by the National Audit Act 1983. The Comptroller and Auditor-General is an officer of the Commons, and can investigate the economy, efficiency and effectiveness with

---

30 A. Adonis, *Parliament Today*, 2nd edn (Manchester: Manchester University Press, 1993), p.166.

31 Adonis, *Parliament Today*, (1993), p.165.

32 P. Giddings, "What Has Been Achieved", in Drewry, *The New Select Committees, A Study of the 1979 Reforms* (1985), p.368; Sir D. Wass, "Checks and Balances in Public Policy Making" [1987] P.L. 181, 183, 192–193.

33 G. Drewry, "Parliament", in P. Dunleavy, A. Gamble, I. Holliday, and G. Peele (eds), *Developments in British Politics 4* (London: Macmillan, 1993), pp.160–161.

34 Adonis, *Parliament Today*, (1993) p.167.

35 A. Robinson, "The House of Commons and Public Expenditure", in Walkland and Ryle (eds), *The Commons in the Seventies* (1977), pp.129–130; A. Robinson, *Parliament and Public Spending* (London: Heinemann, 1978).

36 "The Financial Work of the Select Committees", in Drewry, *The New Select Committees, A Study of the 1979 Reforms* (1985), pp.307–308.

37 Drewry, "Parliament", in Dunleavy, Gamble, Holliday, and Peele (eds), *Developments in British Politics 4* (1993), p.158.

which departments and certain other public authorities discharge their functions.[38] There have, moreover, been initiatives designed to enhance financial scrutiny by Parliament over government budgets.[39]

3–013 While there was therefore little evidence to support the strong role which it was hoped that select committees would play in reasserting parliamentary control over government, they nonetheless had an impact: they could affect government policy on certain issues before it became too fixed; their existence led departments to be more rigorous in justifying policy choices;[40] civil service anonymity was "dented";[41] and they provided a forum for debate on policies.[42]

That there are limitations on the scrutiny function of Parliament is not surprising. They should be seen in the context of a more general problem underlying the concept of an effective critical role for Parliament. Changes in procedure are often thought of as "technical" alterations, which do not have any wider significance. It is assumed that alterations can be made without substantive modification in the balance of power within the political system. A moment's reflection will show that this is not possible.[43] Our political system has been characterised by two major themes: the dominance of the Executive, and an adversarial approach to politics. It is one in which government and opposition face each other in a partisan, gladiatorial combat each backed by its own legions.

Select committees run counter to both of these tenets. They seek to strengthen the power of Parliament as against the Executive, and to proceed by a less partisan approach. A strengthening of Parliament entails a weakening of the Executive's power for relatively untrammelled action, and a less partisan approach to politics in committees presumes either a dichotomy between policy and administration which is so elusive, or a distinction between the approach to politics on the floor of the House and that in committee. Some commentators believe that such a distinction may be emerging, with the committees operating more by way of consensus, with the members not unthinkingly accepting the party whips, with the prime aim being the objective scrutiny of governmental action rather than "the knee-jerk reflexes of Government and Opposition".[44]

iii. Select committees: reform initiatives

3–014 There is little doubt that the committees have increased the Commons' scrutiny of the Executive as compared to the position prior to 1979. A survey of their work

---

[38] G. Drewry, "The National Audit Act—Half a Loaf" [1983] P.L. 531.

[39] Select Committee on Liaison, *Second Report: Financial Scrutiny: Parliamentary Control over Government Budgets*, HC Paper No.804 (Session 2008–09).

[40] Giddings, "What Has Been Achieved", in Drewry, *The New Select Committees, A Study of the 1979 Reforms* (1985), pp.370–371, 374, 377.

[41] Drewry, "The 1979 Reforms—New Labels on Old Bottles?", in Drewry, *The New Select Committees, A Study of the 1979 Reforms* (1985), pp.388–389.

[42] Giddings, "What Has Been Achieved", in Drewry, *The New Select Committees, A Study of the 1979 Reforms* (1985), pp.378–379.

[43] Johnson, *Parliament and Administration: The Estimates Committee 1945–65* (1966), pp.444–445.

[44] Adonis, *Parliament Today* (1993), p.172.

carried out by the Select Committee on Procedure[45] concluded that the system provided an improved framework for the sustained scrutiny of government departments.

There have been important reform initiatives in this area. The Select Committee on Liaison published a valuable Report in 1997[46] on select committees, in which it identified areas where reform would increase their effectiveness. The Report was premised on the assumption that scrutiny of the Executive is one of the most important activities of a democratic Parliament, and that in our legislature this could only be effectively carried out through select committees.[47] Many suggestions were designed to redress the problems outlined earlier. Thus, it recommended that such committees should have power to compel the attendance of any MP, including a minister, and that relevant documentation should be laid before the select committee.[48] There should be a presumption that ministers accept requests from committees that civil servants give evidence to them.[49] Departments should be under a duty to furnish documentation relevant to an inquiry without waiting for a specific request.[50] There should be provision for the recruitment of extra staff by a committee.[51] The work of Executive Agencies should be fully investigated by the committees, and the Heads of such agencies should be allowed to give evidence when invited to do so.[52] When draft Bills are published the Department responsible should send them to the relevant committee.[53] The select committees should intensify their scrutiny of financial matters relating to the relevant department.[54]

These themes were reiterated in Reports from the Select Committee on Modernisation,[55] and the Select Committee on Liaison.[56] Their principal recommendations were that nomination of members of departmental select committees should be independent, and should be entrusted to a Committee of Nomination; departmental Select Committees should be accorded more resources to enable them to function effectively; and there should be a list of core tasks undertaken by such committees.

---

[45] Select Committee on Procedure, *The Working of the Select Committee System*, HC Paper No.19 (Session 1989–90); D. Judge, "The Effectiveness of the Post-1979 Select Committee System: the Verdict of the 1990 Procedure Committee" (1992) 63 Pol. Q. 1.

[46] Select Committee on Liaison, *First Report*, HC Paper No.323-I (Session 1996–97).

[47] Select Committee on Liaison, *First Report*, para.40.

[48] Select Committee on Liaison, *First Report*, paras 11 and 12.

[49] Select Committee on Liaison, *First Report*, para.13.

[50] Select Committee on Liaison, *First Report*, para.14.

[51] Select Committee on Liaison, *First Report*, para.23.

[52] Select Committee on Liaison, *First Report*, para.29 and Appendix 20.

[53] Select Committee on Liaison, *First Report*, para.32.

[54] Select Committee on Liaison, *First Report*, paras 34–36.

[55] Select Committee on Modernisation, *First Report*, HC Paper No.224-I (Session 2002–03).

[56] Select Committee on Liaison, *First Report*, HC Paper No.692 (Session 2001–02).

iv. *Select committees: recent developments*

A number of these reform initiatives were taken forward, in particular the elaboration of core tasks to be undertaken by select committees.[57] This is evident from the Report of the Select Committee on Liaison for 2005–06.[58] Ten such core tasks were elaborated, divided into four groups. **3–015**

Objective A is to consider and comment on departmental policy. The four tasks included within this section are: to examine policy proposals from the UK government and the European Commission; to identify and examine areas of emerging policy, or where existing policy is deficient, and make proposals; to conduct scrutiny of any published draft Bill within the Committee's responsibilities; and to examine specific output from the department expressed in documents or other decisions. Objective B involves one task, which is the examination of expenditure by departments, agencies and non-departmental public bodies. Objective C is to consider administration by the department, and entails four tasks: examination of the department's Public Service Agreements, the associated targets and the statistical measurements employed; to monitor the work of the department's Executive Agencies, non-departmental public bodies and other associated public bodies; to scrutinise major appointments made by the department[59]; and to examine the implementation of legislation and major policy initiatives. Objective D involves one task, which is the provision of reports that are suitable for debate in the House, Westminster Hall or relevant committees.

Select committees are coming of age, and scrutiny of expenditure has become more effective. This has been facilitated by the systematisation of the select committee's tasks, which now include some post-legislative scrutiny.[60] The chairs of select committees are now elected by Parliament.[61] **3–016**

It is equally clear that there are still some difficulties with select committees fulfilling their assigned tasks. Thus, the Select Committee on Liaison was, for example, critical of the government's failure to publish many Bills in draft, thereby preventing pre-legislative scrutiny by the relevant select committee,[62] although figures have improved in this respect.[63] The Select Committee on Liaison also expressed concern that some departments delayed their response to a select committee report in order to avoid a debate on the report in the House or Westminster Hall; and it expressed regret that the number of debates on

[57] A. Brazier and R. Fox, "Reviewing Select Committee Tasks and Modes of Operation" (2011) 64 Parl. Affairs 354.

[58] Select Committee on Liaison, *First Report*, HC Paper No.406 (Session 2007–08).

[59] Select Committee on Liaison, *First Report: Select Committees and Public Appointments*, HC Paper No.1230 (2011).

[60] Select Committee on Liaison, *First Report*, HC Paper No.406, para.105.

[61] Select Committee on the Reform of the House of Commons, *First Report: Rebuilding the House*, HC Paper No.1117 (Session 2008–09); Select Committee on Liaison, *First Report: Rebuilding the House: Select Committee Issues*, HC Paper No. 272 (Session 2009–10); Procedure Committee, *Fifth Report: Elections for Positions in the House*, HC Paper No.1573 (Session 2010–12); Select Committee on Liaison, *Legacy Report*, HC Paper No. 954 (Session 2014-15); M. Russell, "'Never Allow a Crisis to go to Waste': The Wright Committee Reforms to Strengthen the House of Commons" (2011) 64 Parl. Affairs 612.

[62] Select Committee on Liaison, *First Report*, HC Paper No.406, paras 14–17.

[63] Select Committee on Liaison, *Legacy Report*, paras 65-66.

committee reports had dropped from the two-thirds target recommended by the Modernisation Committee.[64] More recent Liaison Committee reports have however attested to the impact of departmental select committees.[65]

B. The Commons and Legislation

3–017 Not all commentators accept that the legislative role of Parliament should be consigned to history. While recognising that the golden age of Parliament cannot be recaptured, proposals have been forthcoming for ways in which Parliament's impact on the legislative process could be strengthened. The proposals are designed to allow more critical input from the floor of the House.[66] A number of reports have addressed this issue.[67]

i. Rippon Commission

3–018 The Rippon Commission[68] made interesting proposals for improving Parliament's role in the legislative process. The initial assumption was that Parliament did not "make the law" as such. This was done by the government. Parliament should nonetheless have proper facilities for scrutinising legislative change.[69] A number of more specific proposals were made to enhance Parliament's role in this respect.

Pre-legislative proceedings could be improved by making use of departmental select committees, which could comment on White Papers and other consultative documents. When a fuller inquiry into proposed legislation was merited then a select committee could be appointed specially for this purpose.[70]

Scrutiny of the actual Bill by the House should be divided into two stages. The first would be a *preliminary briefing stage*, which would operate after the Bill's first reading for more complex or important measures. This would be undertaken by a specially appointed select committee, "first reading committee", which should be free of ministers and opposition shadow ministers. It was hoped that such committees might work by the more consensual approach characteristic of departmental select committees. They would have the power to take evidence from civil servants, outside experts and the wider public. The committees would

[64] Select Committee on Liaison, *First Report*, HC Paper No.406, paras 55–56.

[65] Select Committee on Liaison, *Legacy Report*; Select Committee on Liaison, *Select Committee, Effectiveness, Resources and Powers*, HC Paper No.697 (Session 2012–13).

[66] P. Cowley, "Legislatures and Assemblies", in Dunleavy, Gamble, Heffernan, Holliday, and Peele, *Developments in British Politics 6*, Ch.7; P. Norton, "Parliament in Transition", in R. Pyper (ed.), *British Government under Blair* (London: Macmillan, 1999).

[67] Select Committee on Procedure, *Second Report*, HC Paper No.49 (Session 1984–85); Select Committee on Procedure, *Second Report*, HC Paper No.324 (Session 1985–86); Select Committee on Procedure, *Second Report*, HC Paper No.19-I (Session 1989–90); Select Committee on the Reform of the House of Commons, *First Report: Rebuilding the House*.

[68] *Making the Law, The Report of the Hansard Society Commission on the Legislative Process* (1992).

[69] *Making the Law, The Report of the Hansard Society Commission on the Legislative Process* (1992), para.310.

[70] *Making the Law, The Report of the Hansard Society Commission on the Legislative Process* (1992), paras 322–323.

produce a report, drawing attention "to ambiguities in purpose or meaning, apparent problems in the application or implementation of the legislation, possible consequences of the proposed policies and other practical, technical or drafting points that have emerged".[71]

The second part of parliamentary scrutiny of a Bill would be the *formal committee* stage, which would continue to be undertaken by standing committees. The Rippon Commission noted the widespread dissatisfaction with the standing committee procedures: many MPs regarded the work of such committees to be a waste of time under the current arrangements; and the Opposition was frustrated because it could make so little impact on the Bill.[72] The Commission suggested that the norm should be for Bills to be referred to a *special standing committee*. These would examine witnesses and publish evidence at the beginning of their examination of a Bill, before turning to the more formal debate and party discipline for the decision-taking processes on proposed amendments to the Bill.[73] Membership should include, wherever possible, those who were on the first reading committee, and those who were on a relevant departmental select committee. The special standing committees should carry out detailed scrutiny of the Bill, looking at practical problems of implementation and at matters where the Bill was unclear.[74] It should not, by way of contrast, be the function of these committees to debate major issues of policy, which had been dealt with on the floor of the House during the second reading, or could be raised during the Report stage after the committee, had done its work. 3–019

ii. Select Committee on Modernisation

These issues were also addressed in Reports of the Select Committee on Modernisation of the House of Commons. 3–020

The *1997 Report of the Select Committee* contained a wide-ranging examination of the legislative process,[75] and the Liaison Committee generally supported its conclusions.[76] The Report was premised on the assumption that legislation was a principal function of the House of Commons, and not the exclusive preserve of the Executive.[77] It acknowledged the defects of the legislative regime. These included the absence of consultation with MPs prior to the introduction of a Bill, the patchy quality of consultation with outside interests,

[71] *Making the Law, The Report of the Hansard Society Commission on the Legislative Process* (1992), para.337.

[72] *Making the Law, The Report of the Hansard Society Commission on the Legislative Process* (1992), para.345. See also, J. Griffith and M. Ryle, *Parliament* (London: Sweet & Maxwell, 1989), pp.315–317.

[73] *Making the Law, The Report of the Hansard Society Commission on the Legislative Process* (1992), para.349.

[74] *Making the Law, The Report of the Hansard Society Commission on the Legislative Process* (1992), para.351.

[75] Select Committee on Modernisation of the House of Commons, *First Report: The Legislative Process*, HC Paper No.190 (Session 1997–98).

[76] Select Committee on Modernisation of the House of Commons, *First Report: The Parliamentary Calendar*, HC Paper No.60 (Session 1998–99), Appendix 4.

[77] Select Committee on Modernisation of the House of Commons, *First Report: The Legislative Process*, para.1.

the Whitehall culture which measured legislative success by getting a Bill through Parliament unchanged, the adversarial and ineffective nature of standing committees, and the imbalance of legislative activity at different times of the year.[78]

The Report set out essential criteria for reform.[79] These were that the government should be assured of getting its legislation through in a reasonable time; the opposition and MPs should have a full opportunity to discuss and seek to change provisions; all parts of a Bill should be properly considered; the time and expertise of MPs should be used to better effect; there should be full explanations on the meaning of the legislation; there should be greater accessibility for the public; there should be balance throughout the legislative year; and that monitoring of legislation already enacted should be a vital part of Parliament's role. Many of the detailed issues considered were similar to those analysed by the Rippon Commission.

3–021 Thus, the Select Committee on Modernisation recognised that in principle *pre-legislative scrutiny* of Bills published in draft form was desirable, since it facilitated input from MPs before a measure had become concretised into a formal Bill.[80] There were four possible institutional forms through which such scrutiny could occur: the existing departmental select committees; a new permanent structure of legislative committees; an ad hoc select committee; a joint committee of both Houses.[81]

The Select Committee's Report also followed the suggestion of the Rippon Commission that it should be possible to "refer some Bills to a committee for examination after the First Reading, but before the Second Reading".[82] This would be particularly useful for those Bills that were not subject to pre-legislative scrutiny. In such instances, more especially where the Bill was complex, a reference to a committee after the first reading would have the advantage that a minister would be more likely to be receptive to suggestions for change at this stage. The choice of committee to perform this task was the same as that for pre-legislative scrutiny.

There was much discussion of the *committee stage of a Bill.* It was acknowledged that greater use could be made of ad hoc select committees, and special standing committees.[83] It was nonetheless regarded as inevitable that most Bills would have to be routed through the existing Standing Committee

---

[78] Select Committee on Modernisation of the House of Commons, *First Report: The Legislative Process*, paras 4–12; J. Griffith, "Standing Committees in the House of Commons", in Walkland and Ryle, *The Commons in the Seventies*, p.107; Wass, "Checks and Balances in Public Policy Making" [1987] P.L. 181, 193–194.

[79] Select Committee on Modernisation of the House of Commons, *First Report: The Legislative Process*, para.14.

[80] Select Committee on Modernisation of the House of Commons, *First Report: The Legislative Process*, paras 20 and 91.

[81] Select Committee on Modernisation of the House of Commons, *First Report: The Legislative Process*, paras 19–29.

[82] Select Committee on Modernisation of the House of Commons, *First Report: The Legislative Process*, paras 32–93.

[83] Select Committee on Modernisation of the House of Commons, *First Report: The Legislative Process*, paras 42–46.

procedure.[84] The Report accepted that many of the criticisms of such committees could only be properly addressed by a change of culture by those in the system, particularly ministers. A number of more technical changes were proposed to improve matters.[85]

The Select Committee's Report also adverted to *post-legislative scrutiny*. An "essential criterion of any effective legislative scrutiny system was a proper method of monitoring legislation which has come into force".[86] This task, which is already carried out in relation to some legislation, could properly be assigned to departmental select committees.

The *Select Committee on Modernisation's 2002 Report*[87] reiterated and developed many of the themes in the 1997 Report. The 2002 Report endorsed the importance of *pre-legislative scrutiny* of draft Bills, with this work normally being undertaken by a departmental select committee. Where it was not possible to produce a complete legal text the government should submit proposals for pre-legislative scrutiny based on a detailed statement of policy.[88] There should be consultations with other parties as to the broad shape of the *legislative agenda for that year*.[89] It should moreover be possible *to carry over a Bill* from one session to the next, thereby obviating more detailed scrutiny and avoiding the wastage of parliamentary resources. This would allow more Bills to be considered by a Special Standing Committee.[90] The 2002 Report also contained recommendations for the timing of the working day. The House of Commons approved the Select Committee's Report.[91] **3–022**

The preceding recommendations were reinforced in the *Select Committee on Modernisation's 2006 Report*.[92] It reiterated its belief in the value of pre-legislative scrutiny and like the Liaison Committee criticised the reduction in the number of draft Bills that had been considered in this manner. It also made important recommendations concerning the committee stage for public Bills. The Committee proposed that: special standing committees should be the norm for consideration of public Bills, with the power to take evidence; that special standing committees and standing committees should be renamed Public Bill Committees; and that Public Bill Committees should be one type of general committee.

---

[84] Select Committee on Modernisation of the House of Commons, *First Report: The Legislative Process*, paras 47–49.

[85] Select Committee on Modernisation of the House of Commons, *First Report: The Legislative Process*, paras 48, 95–98.

[86] Select Committee on Modernisation of the House of Commons, *First Report: The Legislative Process*, para.54.

[87] Select Committee on Modernisation, *Second Report: A Reform Programme*, HC Paper No.1168-I (Session 2001–02).

[88] Select Committee on Modernisation, *Second Report: A Reform Programme*, paras 29–34.

[89] Select Committee on Modernisation, *Second Report: A Reform Programme*, para.44.

[90] Select Committee on Modernisation, *Second Report: A Reform Programme*, para.38.

[91] HC Deb., col.801 (29 October, 2002).

[92] Select Committee on Modernisation, *First Report: The Legislative Process*, HC Paper No.1097 (Session 2005–06).

iii. Continuity and change

3–023 It is readily apparent that efforts to increase the effectiveness of Parliament's role in the legislative process have been continuing for some time. The continued pressure for change has borne fruit in certain respects. Thus, the principle of pre-legislative scrutiny has been conceded by government, even if the number of times that it has been used has been disappointing.[93] A number of the Select Committee's recommendations concerning the committee stage have now been enshrined in the relevant standing orders.[94] Thus, the nomenclature has changed to Public Bill Committee, which is one type of general committee. A Bill will, subject to limited exceptions, be referred to a public Bill committee, which will normally have power to take evidence, and see papers and records.[95] These changes have had a positive effect on scrutiny of legislation.[96]

There have moreover been other developments designed to enhance the role of Parliament. Thus, use has been made of Westminster Hall, to facilitate debate on issues for which there is insufficient time on the floor of the main House. It has been adjudged a modest success.[97] There has been consideration of the role of backbench MPs so as to revitalise the House of Commons.[98]

To be counterbalanced against the above is the empirical evidence from the first decade of the new millennium that, while Public Bill Committees are working harder than ever before, their impact on legislation as judged by amendments to the Bill, and by ministerial assurances that proposed changes will be taken into account by ministers, have fallen as compared with study undertaken 25 years earlier.[99]

4. REFORM OF THE HOUSE OF LORDS

3–024 This is not the place for a detailed exegesis on the history of the House of Lords in its legislative capacity, nor of the varying attempts made at reform over the years. The focus is on current reforms, which could significantly alter the nature of the second chamber.

---

93 A. Kennon, "Pre-legislative Scrutiny of Draft Bills" [2004] P.L. 477; J. Smookler, "Making a Difference? The Effectiveness of Pre-legislative Scrutiny" (2006) 59 *Parliamentary Affairs* 522.

94 Standing Orders of the House of Commons (2015), available at: *http://www.publications.parliament.uk/pa/cm/cmstords.htm* [accessed 24 June 2015].

95 Standing Orders 63, 84A.

96 J. Levy, "Public Bill Committees: An Assessment Sought; Scrutiny Gained" (2010) 63 Parl. Affairs 534.

97 Select Committee on Modernisation, *Fourth Report: Sittings in Westminster Hall*, HC Paper No.906 (Session 1999–2000); Select Committee on Modernisation, *Second Report: A Reform Programme*, paras 97–99.

98 Select Committee on Modernisation, *First Report: Revitalising the Chamber, The Role of the Back Bench Member*, HC Paper No.337 (Session 2006–07); *The Governance of Britain* (2007), Cm.7170; Select Committee on Modernisation, *First Report: Scrutiny of the Draft Legislative Programme*, HC Paper No.81 (Session 2007–08).

99 L. Thompson, "More of the Same, or a Period of Change? The Impact of Public Bill Committees in the Twenty-First Century House of Commons" (2013) 66 Parl. Affairs 459.

The Labour manifesto contained a commitment to reform the House of Lords and to abolish the right of hereditary peers to sit and vote.[100] It proposed that this would be the first stage of reform to make the Lords more democratic and representative. The idea, as represented in the manifesto, was that the appointment of life peers would also be reviewed so as more accurately to reflect the proportion of votes cast at the previous election. Much has happened on this issue since Labour's first election victory,[101] but on the general point of principle, that hereditary peers should not be entitled to sit and vote, the government remained firm. Thus, Tony Blair stated that,[102] "it cannot possibly be right that people sit as legislators in the Houses of Parliament on the basis that their birth makes them hereditary peers", and that "it is an absolute democratic scandal that hereditary Conservative peers outnumber the peers of the elected government of the day by three to one", thereby ensuring an in-built Tory majority in perpetuity.

The House of Lords Act 1999 implemented this aspect of the government's policy. It provides in s.1 that "no-one shall be a member of the House of Lords by virtue of hereditary peerage". This is subject to an exception contained in s.2, which allows 92 hereditary peers to remain. Section 3 removed disqualifications from hereditary peers, so that they can vote at elections for the Commons and be elected to that House. **3–025**

This legislation was the first stage of the government's programme for reform of the Lords. A Royal Commission was established under Lord Wakeham to consider more comprehensive reform.[103] It recommended that the second chamber should bring a range of different perspectives to bear on the development of public policy; that it should be broadly representative; that it should act as one of the checks and balances in the constitution; and should provide a voice for the different parts of the United Kingdom. The Wakeham Commission recommended that the House of Lords should retain its existing powers under the Parliament Acts 1911 and 1949. A new Constitutional Committee should be established to consider the constitutional implications of legislation, and keep the operation of the constitution under review, and a new Human Rights Committee should be set up to scrutinise the human rights' implications of legislation. The composition of the reformed second chamber was the most difficult issue addressed by the Commission. It rejected the view that the second chamber should be wholly or largely directly elected, or that it should be indirectly elected. It rejected also random selection and co-option. It recommended that a significant minority of members should be "regional", that others should be appointed by an Independent Appointments Commission, and that this same Commission should ensure that the politically affiliated members reflected an overall political balance of the country as expressed in voting at the most recent election.

[100] *New Labour: Because Britain Deserves Better* (1997), pp.32–33.

[101] House of Commons Research Paper 98/85, *House of Lords Reform: Developments since the General Election* (August 1998).

[102] HC Deb., Vol.313, col.366 (3 June 1998).

[103] Royal Commission on the Reform of the House of Lords, *A House for the Future* (2000), Cm.4534.

The balance between elected and non-elected members of the second chamber continues to be the most controversial aspect of the reforms.[104] A White Paper on House of Lords' reform in 2007 proposed that the chamber should be 50 per cent elected and 50 per cent appointed.[105] Reaction to this suggestion was mixed, and in a subsequent free vote the Commons voted by a large majority for a wholly elected House of Lords, and also by a lesser margin supported a second chamber that was 80 per cent elected and 20 per cent appointed. The Coalition government brought forward the House of Lords Reform Bill 2012–13, which proposed a largely elected second chamber, but the Bill was dropped in 2012 after opposition, principally from Conservative MPs.[106] Legislation has however been enacted in the form of the House of Lords Reform Act 2014. It does not herald change in the composition of the Lords, but rather makes provision for peers to resign from the House of Lords, or to cease to be a member as a result of non-attendance, or conviction of a serious criminal offence.

5. CONCLUSION

3–026 The tensions between the Executive and Parliament will not magically disappear. They were manifest in the Arms to Iraq saga, and in the limited political consequences that followed from publication of the Scott Report.[107] They are evident in the claims that ministers have willingly received leaked reports from select committees in advance of their publication in order the better to prepare their response. The tensions are apparent in the government's reaction to reports from departmental select committees.

There is nonetheless a sense that the scrutiny and legislative functions of Parliament should be and can be reinforced. There is an underlying connection between the proposals made concerning Parliament and scrutiny of government action, and Parliament and the legislative process. This is the desire to enhance Parliament's role and reduce the extent to which the political system works in an adversarial manner dominated by the Executive. The desire for some less party-based scrutiny of governmental action and legislative proposals is a recurrent theme.

This is a laudable objective. Whether it is realisable is another matter. It might be argued that in the absence of a major catalyst prompting a realignment of power between the Executive and the legislature any change is bound to be

---

[104] Constitution Unit, *Reform of the House of Lords* (1996); Constitution Unit, *Rebalancing the Lords: The Numbers* (1998); R. Hazell, "Reforming the House of Lords: A Step by Step Guide", *Constitutional Reform in the United Kingdom: Practice and Principles* (University of Cambridge, Centre for Public Law, 1998), Ch.15; I. Richard and D. Welfare, *Unfinished Business: Reforming the House of Lords* (London: Vintage, 1999).

[105] White Paper, *The House of Lords: Reform* (2007), Cm.7027.

[106] House of Lords Reform Draft Bill (2011) Cm.8077; The House of Lords Reform Bill 2012–13.

[107] *Report of the Inquiry into the Export of Defence Equipment and Dual-Use Goods to Iraq and Related Prosecutions*, HC Paper No.115 (Session 1995–96); I. Leigh and L. Lustgarten, "Five Volumes in Search of Accountability: The Scott Report" (1996) 59 M.L.R. 695; D. Oliver, "The Scott Report" [1996] P.L. 357; A. Tomkins, "Government Information and Parliament: Misleading by Design or by Default?" [1996] P.L. 472; N. Lewis and D. Longley, "Ministerial Responsibility: The Next Steps" [1996] P.L. 490.

marginal. Electoral reform that breaks the dominance of the two major parties might be such a catalyst,[108] but it is unlikely that this will be introduced by one of the two major parties, more especially after the recent referendum rejecting modest change in the voting rules. The very fact that backbench MPs have, in relative terms, been more willing recently to voice and vote their disapproval of government measures is, however, a positive development.

[108] P. Dunleavy, "The Constitution", in Dunleavy, Gamble, Holliday and Peele (eds), *Developments in British Politics 5* (1997), Ch.1.

CHAPTER 4

AGENCIES AND NON-DEPARTMENTAL PUBLIC BODIES

1. CENTRAL ISSUES

i. The complex nature of "government" was noted earlier. The nature of this administrative diversity will be analysed in this chapter and that which follows. The last 40 years have seen the most significant reorganisation of central government since the latter part of the 19th century. A plethora of agencies and non-departmental public bodies has been created. **4–001**

ii. Boards or agencies were, as we have seen,[1] common in earlier centuries. They were, however, gradually taken into government departments because Parliament desired accountability via direct ministerial responsibility. This pattern of administrative organisation persisted for much of the 20th century.

iii. Change came in the 1980s, the result of re-thinking of what functions government should be undertaking. The conclusion was that many activities should be hived off from core government departments, and that some should be undertaken by public bodies outside the normal departmental structure.

iv. The period thereafter witnessed the rapid expansion of public bodies outside the strict confines of government. Classification of these bodies was no easy task, and various terminology was used to describe the institutions that inhabited the administrative landscape. The principal division is however between what are termed executive agencies and Non-Departmental Public Bodies (NDPBs).

v. Executive agencies are part of the Crown. They do not usually have their own legal identity, but operate under powers delegated from ministers and departments. They do not normally have statutory foundation. They have a Chief Executive, who reports to the minister. Most such agencies receive funding from their parent department, although some executive agencies have become Trading Funds, and generate resources from their commercial business. Their functions and responsibilities are set out in Framework documents.

vi. There are various kinds of NDPBs. The most important are termed executive NDPBs. They have separate legal identity and will normally be based on statute, or on occasion the prerogative. Most executive NDPBs require legislation. Most do not have Crown status. The legislation will normally state the composition and powers of such bodies. Where the body

[1] Ch.2.

is created by legislation it will usually be incorporated as a body corporate. The staff of public bodies that have separate legal personality and do not have Crown status are not civil servants.

vii. Executive agencies and NDPBs pose challenges for public administration and administrative law. They raise important issues concerning appointments, control and accountability and effectiveness.

viii. The Coalition government brought further change. It reviewed the number of NDPBs and related bodies with a view to enhancing accountability by considering whether a function really should be performed outside the normal departmental/accountability structure. The number of NDPBs hitherto significantly exceeded that of executive agencies. However, the Coalition government policy was to contract the number of NDPBs by abolishing some, merging others, or transforming them into executive agencies. The reasons that have driven this initiative will be considered later.

ix. The picture of government in 2015 is as follows.[2] There are 24 ministerial departments; 22 non-ministerial departments; 361 agencies and other public bodies, including both executive agencies and NDPBs; 72 high profile groups; 11 public corporations; and 3 devolved administrations

2. EVOLUTION OF EXECUTIVE AGENCIES AND NON-DEPARTMENTAL PUBLIC BODIES

A. Fulton, Hiving Off and Agencies

4–002 Until recently the civil service was still cast in the mould set by the Northcote–Trevelyan reforms of the mid-19th century. It was a unified and uniform service in theory at least, and in most instances in reality too. Governmental functions were organised in and through departments. This was in contrast with the pattern of administration in the earlier part of the 19th century, when public functions were often undertaken by boards, which operated outside departments.[3] The latter part of the 19th century witnessed the decline in such institutions and the emergence of ministerial responsibility, with the corollary of civil service anonymity.

By the 1960s strains had begun to appear in this organisational structure. These became apparent in the Report of the Fulton Committee.[4] It stressed the need for improved efficiency in traditional departments. The Report pressed for reassessment of the activities undertaken directly within the department. Many activities might work better if they were "hived off" and run by bodies outside the departmental framework, albeit subject to overall ministerial guidance.

4–003 The Fulton Committee was one catalyst for the hiving off of functions to newly created agencies. The Civil Aviation Authority was formed from the Department of Trade and Industry in 1971; the Manpower Services Commission, the

[2] *https://www.gov.uk/government/organisations#cabinet-office* [accessed 30 August 2015].

[3] See Ch.2.

[4] *Report of the Committee on the Civil Service 1966–68* (1968), Cmnd.3638.

Advisory and Conciliation and Arbitration Service (ACAS) and the Health and Safety Commission were split from the Department of Employment in 1974. These agencies were regulatory in nature. The general reasons for creating such agencies is neatly summarised in one study as follows[5]:

> "First, there is the 'buffer' theory which sees them as a way of protecting certain activities from political interference. Second, there is the 'escape' theory which sees them as escaping known weaknesses of traditional government departments. Third, the 'corson' theory, following Mr John Corson sees them as used to 'put the activity where the talent was', which might be outside government departments. Fourth, there is the participation or 'pluralistic' theory which thinks it desirable to spread power. Fifth, there is the 'back double' theory. This is based on the analogy with a taxi-driver who finds the main streets too busy and therefore uses back streets—what are known to taxi drivers as 'back doubles'. The back double theory is that if governments, local authorities or other bodies find that they cannot do the things they want within the existing structure, they set up new organisations which make it possible to do them. Sixth, the 'too many bureaucrats' view, mainly an American one, suggests that if the public thinks a country has too many civil servants it can set up quasi-non-governmental organisations whose employees are not classified as civil servants."

These reasons were echoed in a consultation paper *Opening up Quangos*[6] by the Labour government. It listed the following reasons for quangos: the need for bodies at arm's length from the government to carry out certain activities; the provision of expert guidance; the bringing of ordinary people into public life; the ability to respond quickly to matters which are of public concern; and the fact that such bodies facilitate a partnership between government and other interests.

B. Rayner, Ibbs and Executive Agencies

Various attempts at improving civil service efficiency followed the Fulton Committee Report. It was, however, the establishment of the Rayner Unit in 1979, later known as the Efficiency Unit, by the Prime Minister that sowed the seeds for major reform. Lord Rayner had run Marks & Spencer and was brought in by Mrs Thatcher to improve efficiency within the civil service. Rayner headed a small team that subjected government departments to efficiency scrutiny, operating through the medium of the laser beam rather than the arc light.[7] 4–004

The scrutiny produced savings, and acted as a catalyst for further change in the system. Thus, it was a Rayner scrutiny of the Department of Employment that was the impetus for the establishment of MINIS, or Management Information Systems, designed to enable the minister to explore "who does what, why and

[5] D. Hague, W. Mackenzie and A. Barker (eds), *Public Policy and Private Interests: The Institutions of Compromise* (London: Macmillan, 1975), p.362. See also, *Report on Non-Departmental Public Bodies* (1980), Cmnd.7797, paras 10–16; R. Baldwin and C. McCrudden, *Regulation and Public Law* (London: Weidenfeld & Nicolson, 1987), Ch.1; T. Christensen and P. Laegreid (eds), *Autonomy and Regulation: Coping with Agencies in the Modern State* (Cheltenham: Edward Elgar, 2006); M. Flinders, *Delegated Governance and the British State: Walking Without Order* (Oxford: Oxford University Press, 2008). An additional reason for the creation of agencies is that government can immunise itself from criticism in certain politically sensitive areas. In the public mind it will often be the "X commission" which receives the brunt of public disquiet.

[6] Cabinet Office, *Opening up Quangos* (November 1997), Ch.2.

[7] P. Hennessy, *Whitehall* (London: Fontana, 1990), Ch.14; O. McDonald, *The Future of Whitehall* (London: Weidenfeld & Nicolson, 1991), Ch.1.

what does it cost?"[8] The Efficiency Unit under Rayner also conceived what became known as FMI, Financial Management Initiative, made operational by the Financial Management Unit.[9] As Hennessy notes,[10] the FMI was meant to be "fast breeder reactor which would achieve a permanent self-sustaining reaction the length and breadth of every Civil Service chain of command". Managers were to have a clear view of their objectives, well-defined responsibility for making best use of their resources, and the information and expertise necessary to exercise their responsibilities effectively.

4–005 Sir Robin Ibbs succeeded Lord Rayner as head of the Efficiency Unit. He assessed the achievements of the Rayner scrutiny,[11] which was followed by a more radical study culminating in the *"Next Steps" Report*.[12] The radical nature of its proposals led to it being concealed until after the 1987 election. The general conclusions of the study are aptly summarised by Hennessy[13]:

> "Despite the real achievements of the Rayner years, it showed how little in the way of *real* financial and management responsibility had been devolved down the line; how meddlesome the Treasury and Cabinet Office remained; how dominant was the Whitehall culture of caution; how great was the premium on a safe pair of hands; and how rarely were proven managerial skills perceived as the way to reach the top of the bureaucratic tree."

The *"Next Steps" Report* proposed two fundamental changes, which shaped the structure of the bureaucracy. There should be a split between service delivery and the making of policy, with real devolution of power to executive agencies for service delivery, which would cover approximately 95 per cent of civil service activity. There should also be an end to the fiction that the minister was responsible for everything done by officials in his or her own name.

The Report was acted on in 1988–1989. A project manager, Peter Kemp, carried forward the proposals for creation of executive agencies responsible for service delivery. Government departments were required to review their activities and to consider five possibilities: abolition, privatisation, contracting-out, creating an agency and preservation of the status quo. If the agency route was chosen this would be taken forward by a Project Executive, with representatives from Kemp's project team, the Treasury, the Efficiency Unit and the sponsoring department. The Labour government continued the policy of what are now termed executive agencies.[14]

---

[8] G. Drewry and T. Butcher, *The Civil Service Today*, 2nd edn (Oxford: Blackwell, 1991), pp.203–206.

[9] Efficiency Unit, *Financial Management in Government Departments* (1983), Cmnd.9058; Gray, Jenkins, Flynn and Rutherford, "The Management of Change in Whitehall: The Experience of the FMI" (1991) 69 Pub. Adm. 41.

[10] Hennessy, *Whitehall* (London: Fontana, 1990), p.606.

[11] Efficiency Unit, *Making Things Happen: A Report on the Implication of Government Efficiency Scrutinies* (1985).

[12] Efficiency Unit, *Improving Management in Government: The Next Steps* (1988); D. Goldsworthy, *Setting Up Next Steps: A Short Account of the Origins, Launch, and Implementation of the Next Steps Project in the British Civil Service* (1991).

[13] Hennessy, *Whitehall* (1990), p.620. Italics in the original.

[14] Cabinet Office, *Next Steps Report 1997* (1998), Cm.3889.

Large parts of the civil service have been hived off and have agency status. Examples of executive agencies include the: Driver and Vehicle Licensing Agency; Planning Inspectorate; Highways England; HM Courts and Tribunal Service; UK Visas and Immigration; Intellectual Property Office; Occupational Health Service; Treasury Solicitor's department; Pension Service; Meteorological Office; Passport Office; HM Prison Service; and many others. **4–006**

The mechanism for creation of an executive agency is as follows.[15] If following a business review the sponsor department considers that an executive agency is the most appropriate delivery agent, the departmental minister makes a submission to Cabinet Office and the Treasury seeking agreement to the proposals. The "launch project" will address matters such as: the appointment of the Chief Executive, which is normally by open competition; the preparation of the Framework Document, the content of which is described in more detail below; and the preparation of an initial business plan, including key targets. However, proposals to set up new agencies must be supported by "a robust and fully costed business case",[16] and be approved by Cabinet Office and HM Treasury ministers.

C. Non-Departmental Public Bodies

There are also many public bodies that are not executive agencies. *Public Bodies 2014*[17] lists those public bodies that are not part of a government department, and carry out functions to a greater or lesser extent at arm's length from central government. Ministers are ultimately responsible to Parliament for the public bodies sponsored by their department. Departments are responsible for funding and ensuring good governance of their public bodies. **4–007**

There are four types of NDPBs, which denote different funding arrangements, functions and kinds of activity.[18] There are *executive NDPBs*, which are established by statute and carry out administrative, regulatory and commercial functions. They employ their own staff and are allocated their own budgets. *Advisory NDPBs* provide independent and expert advice to ministers on particular topics. They may have their own staff or may be supported by staff from their sponsoring department. They do not usually have their own budget, as costs incurred come within the department's expenditure. *Tribunal NDPBs* have jurisdiction in a specialised field of law. They are usually supported by staff from their sponsoring department and do not have their own budgets. *Independent Monitoring Boards* were formerly known as "Boards of Visitors" of the prison system. Their duty is to satisfy themselves as to the state of the prison premises, their administration and the treatment of prisoners. The sponsoring department meets the costs.

Examples of important executive NDPBs are the: Equality and Human Rights Commission; Health and Safety Executive; Environment Agency; Gambling Commission; Ofcom; Office for Budget Responsibility; Legal Services Board;

[15] Cabinet Office, *Executive Agencies, A Guide for Departments* (2006).
[16] Cabinet Office, *Public Bodies* (2009).
[17] Cabinet Office, *Public Bodies 2014* (2014), p.7.
[18] Cabinet Office, *Public Bodies 2014* (2014), p.16.

Parole Board; Information Commissioner's Office; Independent Police Complaints Commission; Arts Council England; British Museum; Higher Education Funding Council; Security Commission; Judicial Appointments Commission; Advisory Conciliation and Arbitration Service; Economic and Social Research Council; and the Pensions Regulator.

D. Government Reform

4–008 The Coalition government headed by David Cameron signalled the biggest re-think of the NDPB model since the 1980s. It has been driven in part by the need to cut costs in the wake of the financial crisis, and in part by normative precepts. Thus, the Coalition government's starting point was that if a public function was needed it should be undertaken by a body that is democratically accountable at national or local level.[19] The corollary was that a body should only exist at arm's length from government if it met one of three tests: does it perform a technical function; do its activities require political impartiality; or does it need to act independently to establish facts?

To this end the government reviewed 904 bodies to determine whether their functions were still required, and if so whether they should continue to be undertaken by a NDPB or some related body.[20] The initial assessment identified over 200 bodies that did not need to be at arm's length, and over 170 bodies that had overlapping functions that could be merged down to fewer than 70.[21] The remaining NDPBs have been retained because they satisfy one of the three tests set out above, and there were in March 2014 154 executive NDPBs.

The reforms have been carried out via the Public Bodies Act 2011. This legislation confers power on ministers to change the status of the listed public bodies in the following ways. The minister can abolish a public body, merge it with another, modify its constitutional arrangements, modify its funding arrangements, or modify or transfer its functions. The bodies in relation to which the minister can exercise such powers are listed in the Schedules to the Act. The power is exercised through a ministerial order, which is secondary legislation, and is subject to the affirmative resolution procedure. There is a duty to consult before making such an order. The Act provides that an order can only be made if the minister considers that it improves the exercise of public functions, having regard to efficiency, effectiveness, economy, and securing appropriate accountability to ministers. An order cannot be made if the minister considers that it removes any necessary protection, and prevents any person from continuing to exercise any right or freedom which that person might reasonably expect to continue to exercise.

---

[19] See *https://www.gov.uk/guidance/public-bodies-reform* [accessed 30 August 2015]; K. Dommett and M. Flinders, "The Centre Strikes Back: Meta-Governance, Delegation and the Core Executive in the United Kingdom, 2010–14" (2015) 93 Pub. Adm. 1.

[20] Cabinet Office, *Public Bodies Reform—Proposals for Change* (2011); Cabinet Office, *Public Bodies 2014* (2014), p.3.

[21] Cabinet Office, *Public Bodies 2014* (2014), pp.3-4.

The reforms introduced by the government had a rough ride. The Public Administration Select Committee was highly critical of the reform exercise.[22] The Committee concluded that the review was poorly managed; the consultation was inadequate; the three tests to determine if a function should continue to be undertaken by a NDPB were not clearly defined; there was no "fit" between these tests and the criteria in the Public Bodies Act; it was unclear whether the primary concern was accountability or value for money; the size of any cost savings was unclear; and that it was uncertain whether bringing functions back to parent departments would enhance accountability. **4–009**

The Select Committee was also critical of the Public Bodies Bill, echoing the concerns of House of Lords Committees[23] that the Bill encapsulated a very broad Henry VIII clause, whereby primary legislation could be modified by secondary legislation in the form of ministerial orders. The Public Administration Select Committee felt that more use should be made of executive agencies, which provided a clearly identifiable organisation for stakeholders to engage with, while leaving ultimate responsibility with the minister.

The government's response was robust. It rejected many of the criticisms voiced by the Select Committee. The government however accepted that more use could be made of executive agencies, and that the Cabinet Office should provide more guidance to departments as to implementation of the reforms. The cumulative estimated savings since 2010 are approximately £2.6 billion.[24]

E. Terminology

The names of the institutions that have been hived off from central government vary enormously: commission, directorate, agency, inspectorate, authority, service and office are all to be found. Nothing technical normally turns upon these differences. Various labels have been used to describe in more general terms the bodies discussed within this chapter. The term "quango", quasi-autonomous non-governmental organisation, was used in the past. It is however not the most useful term that could be devised, since many of these bodies are non-departmental, rather than non-governmental.[25] **4–010**

The government now distinguishes between *non-ministerial departments*, *executive agencies* and *non-departmental public body* (NDPB),[26] although it admits that classification is not always easy.[27] Non-ministerial departments are government departments in their own right, but do not have their own minister.

---

[22] Public Administration Select Committee, *Smaller Government: Shrinking the Quango State, 5th Report of Session* 2010–11, HC Paper No.537 (Session 2010–11).

[23] House of Lords Constitution Committee, *Public Bodies Reform Bill [HL], Sixth Report of the Session 2009–10*, HL Paper No.51 (Session 2009–10), para.13; House of Lords Delegated Powers and Regulatory Reform Committee, *Public Bodies Reform Bill [HL], Fifth Report of the Session 2010–11*, HL Paper No.57 (Session 2010–11), para.1.

[24] Cabinet Office, *Public Bodies 2014* (2014), p.3.

[25] *Report on Non-Departmental Public Bodies* (1980), Cmnd.7797, para.17; A. Barker, "Quango: A Word and a Campaign", in A. Barker (ed.), *Quangos in Britain* (London: MacMillan, 1982), pp.219–225.

[26] See *https://www.gov.uk/government/organisations#cabinet-office* [accessed 30 August 2015].

[27] Cabinet Office, *Classification of Public Bodies* (2011).

Executive agencies are those bodies created pursuant to the "Next Steps" initiative. They do not usually have their own legal identity, but operate under powers delegated from ministers and departments. They have a chief executive who reports to the minister against specific targets. NDPBs are, as we have seen, those bodies which have a role in the processes of national government, but are not a government department or part of one, and operate to a greater or lesser extent at arm's length from ministers.

It should nonetheless be recognised that many of the issues concerning accountability, transparency and the like are relevant to both sets of organisations.[28] Moreover, some NDPBs have the name "agency", and many other NDPBs or public corporations that perform regulatory functions would be regarded as agencies in other political systems, irrespective of their precise nomenclature.[29]

F. Conclusion

4–011 The developments from Fulton to Rayner to Ibbs did not follow a series of logically inevitable steps. Few changes in the pattern of administration can be viewed in this manner. Yet they are not unconnected either. Once the drive for efficiency was on, and once the existing departmental structure had been challenged, it became natural to consider whether the activity should continue to be performed by government at all; whether it should be undertaken by an executive agency or non-departmental public body, rather than in-house; or whether it should be done outside the department on a contracting-out basis. It is for this reason that our administrative landscape has become more complex, and is still changing, as evidenced most notably in the Coalition government's reforms considered above.

There are connections between these administrative changes and what has been termed "New Public Management" (NPM). The doctrinal components of NPM include[30]: hands-on professional management in the public sector; standards of performance; output controls; the break-up of large bureaucratic structures; greater public sector competition; and greater discipline in resource use.

These developments pose new challenges for public law, relating to accountability, susceptibility to judicial review, and the appropriate procedural and substantive norms to be applied to such bodies. It is to these issues which we must now turn.

[28] Cabinet Office, *Opening up Quangos, A Consultation Paper* (November 1997), Ch.1, paras 2–4.

[29] See, e.g. Civil Aviation Authority, Gambling Commission, Ofcom, Equality and Human Rights Commission, Health and Safety Executive.

[30] C. Hood, "A Public Management for All Seasons?" (1991) 69 Pub. Adm. 3, 4–5.

3. LEGAL STATUS AND ORGANISATIONAL FRAMEWORK

It is, nonetheless, important to distinguish between non-ministerial departments, NDPBs and executive agencies because the legal and organisational framework is different. 4–012

A. Non-Ministerial Departments

Non-ministerial departments (NMDs) are government departments, but do not have their own minister.[31] They are usually headed by a statutory board, and are accountable to Parliament through the minister of the sponsoring department. Their powers are normally derived from statute, and they are staffed by civil servants. There are, however, some NMDs that operate along agency lines, while remaining a separate government department. Prominent NMDs are the UK Statistics Authority, Charity Commission, Serious Fraud Office, Food Standards Agency, Government Legal Department, and HM Revenue and Customs.[32] 4–013

B. Executive Agencies

Executive agencies[33] are part of the Crown. They do not usually have their own legal identity, but operate under powers delegated by ministers and departments. They have a chief executive who reports to the minister against specific targets. Most such agencies receive funding from their parent department and, although they are required to publish and lay before Parliament separate accounts, these are part of their parent department's accounts. Some executive agencies have become Trading Funds, and generate the cash they need to operate from their commercial business.[34] Executive agencies carry out executive functions within government, with the emphasis on delivery of specific outputs within an accountability framework laid down in the published Framework Document. 4–014

While the details of such Framework Documents vary, the Cabinet Office recommends that they should contain[35]: a foreword by the minister; details of the agency's size, location and functions; the agency's aim and objectives; key target areas; the relationship between the minister, the agency chief executive and senior officials in the parent department; the relations with the department accounting officer; the relationship with other bodies; arrangements for dealing with Parliamentary Questions and letters from MPs; the customer complaints procedure and arrangements for handling Parliamentary Commissioner for Administration cases; the financial regime for the agency; the machinery for accounting, audit, monitoring and reporting, both within government and externally; the arrangements for producing accounts; the business and corporate

[31] Cabinet Office, *Classification of Public Bodies*, p.6; Cabinet Office, *Public Bodies 2014* (2014), p.17.

[32] *https://www.gov.uk/government/organisations#cabinet-office* [accessed 31 August 2015].

[33] Cabinet Office, *Executive Agencies*; Cabinet Office, *Classification of Public Bodies*; Cabinet Office, *Public Bodies 2014* (2014), p.17.

[34] Government Trading Act 1990.

[35] Cabinet Office, *Executive Agencies*, Annex A.

planning framework; the arrangements for recruitment and pay; the method of recruitment and the basis of remuneration for the chief executive; appearance before the Public Accounts Committee and departmental select committees; the arrangements for risk management; and the arrangements for changing the Framework Document.

Executive agencies do not normally have separate legal status,[36] and thus legal actions are brought against the relevant minister under whose aegis the agency functions. If an executive agency abuses its powers it will be the relevant minister who will appear in any such action. The agency will simply be regarded as part of the parent department.[37]

C. NDPBs

4–015 Executive NDPBs have separate legal identity and will normally be based on statute or, on occasion, the prerogative.[38] Most executive NDPBs require legislation to confer functions on the body, and also for reasons of government accounting.[39] The empowering legislation will normally state the composition and powers of such bodies. Where the body is created by legislation it will usually be incorporated as a body corporate. The staff of public bodies that have separate legal personality and do not have Crown status are not normally civil servants.

Advisory NDPBs are, by way of contrast, normally set up by administrative action. Legislation is however, required if the activity involves continuing government funding for which parliamentary authority is needed. It is open to departments to decide if they wish to establish the body as part of the Crown, or as an unincorporated/incorporated body with a separate legal personality.

Tribunal NDPBs are normally statutory bodies, which are established to adjudicate on specific subject matter. While tribunals exercise their functions entirely independently, a government department will normally be responsible for providing administrative support.

4–016 The legislation or instrument creating the public body will commonly specify its functions and funding. It is common for the legislation to specify the power to: appoint staff, pay salaries, make pension provision, raise money by levies or charges, borrow and lend, take enforcement action, and acquire property. The legislation or instrument will normally impose obligations on the public body to make external audit arrangements, to report annually to Parliament, to be subject to the Parliamentary Commissioner for Administration, and to set fees and charges for services.

---

[36] Cabinet Office, *Classification of Public Bodies*, p.7; I. Harden, *The Contracting State* (Open University Press, 1992), pp.44, 46.

[37] *R. v Secretary of State for Social Services Ex p. Sherwin* [1996] 32 B.M.L.R. 1; *Castle v Crown Prosecution Service* [2014] EWHC 587 (Admin).

[38] Cabinet Office, *Public Bodies: A Guide for Departments*, Ch.3.

[39] Public Bodies with their own legal personality do not generally enjoy Crown status. The exceptions are the Health and Safety Executive, the Child Maintenance and Enforcement Commission, and the Advisory, Conciliation and Arbitration Service, which are Crown bodies.

The legislation or instrument creating the NDPB will also indicate the role of the minister within the particular area. Thus, the Cabinet Office Guidance to Departments when creating a public body states that departments should strike the balance between enabling the minister to fulfil his or her responsibilities to Parliament, and giving the public body the desired degree of independence. The precise balance will depend on the nature of the public body's functions and the reasons for distancing these from government.[40] It will be common for the legislation to accord the minister power over appointment and dismissal of the chairman and board members. The legislation may also allow the minister to give statutory directions to the agency, or ministerial approval may be required before certain courses of action can be taken, or before borrowing above a certain limit is allowed.[41] Control may be exercised through non-legislative techniques, such as through conditions attached to the issue of grant-in-aid, or in a formal agreement between the department and the body.[42]

An action for judicial review will normally be brought against the public body in its own name, if an individual feels that the agency has exceeded its powers. The relevant minister may also be a party to an action if the applicant claims that ministerial powers under the legislation have been exceeded.[43]

4. EXECUTIVE AGENCIES: STAFFING, ACCOUNTABILITY AND EFFICIENCY

The existence of bodies outside the normal departmental framework gives rise to a number of problems. Executive agencies and NDPBs are treated separately in this respect by government.[44] **4–017**

An important review of executive agencies was undertaken in 2002. The Report[45] made it clear that executive agencies were here to stay and had generally been a success. It nonetheless perceived areas in which further improvement could be made. The recommendations were acted on and are integrated into the subsequent discussion.

A. Staffing

These agencies are staffed by civil servants, and approximately 70 per cent of civil servants now work in such agencies. Agency Chief Executives are, however, recruited through open competition. The official response when executive agencies were created was to talk of a unified, but not uniform civil service, the message being that the structural diversity resulting from agencies would have **4–018**

---

40 Cabinet Office, *Public Bodies: A Guide for Departments*, Ch.3, para.3.1.

41 Cabinet Office, *Public Bodies: A Guide for Departments*, Ch.3, para.5.

42 Cabinet Office, *Public Bodies: A Guide for Departments*, Ch.3, para.3.3.

43 Baldwin and McCrudden, *Regulation and Public Law* (1987).

44 See *https://www.gov.uk/government/publications/public-bodies-information-and-guidance* [accessed 31 August 2015]; Cabinet Office, *Opening up Quangos, A Consultation Paper* (November 1997); Cabinet Office, *Quangos: Opening the Doors* (1998); Cabinet Office, *Quangos: Opening up Public Appointments* (1998).

45 HM Treasury and Office of Public Services Reform, *Better Government Services, Executive Agencies in the 21st Century* (2002).

ramifications for uniform conditions of pay and conditions of service, which were the norm hitherto. HMSO, for example, introduced a new pay and grading structure tailored to meet its business needs, and more flexibility in terms and conditions of service is very much the order of the day.[46] The passage of the Civil Service (Management Functions) Act 1992 facilitated agency autonomy with respect to pay bargaining and conditions of service.

The 2002 Report[47] favoured flexibility that would enable agencies to recruit, pay and promote staff in the light of local needs and labour markets. It also recommended that more executive agencies explore the possibility of gaining trading fund status, since this would help them to generate income. This recommendation was taken up in the Cabinet Office, *Guide on Executive Agencies*, which provides that matters concerning agency pay, terms and conditions of service and the like are normally delegated to the agency's chief executive, and that such matters should be allowed to vary in accord with local employment conditions.[48]

These ramifications may well be greater than initially envisaged. The more that chief executives are encouraged to develop pay structures which suit their own agency, the less easy will it be for there to be a regular interchange between the agency and the department itself. This is particularly so if agency pay is determined in part by commercial criteria while that at the centre is held in check by political considerations.[49] It should nonetheless be recognised that there has been a general change in the way that pay and service are determined throughout Whitehall. The Treasury has delegated pay bargaining to departments, many of which have further delegated this power to agencies within their purview. Departments also have considerable freedom in relation to recruitment to all grades below the senior civil service, and once again will often give the same power to agencies. The financial crisis and subsequent curb on government spending has however led to more centralised Treasury control.

B. Control and Accountability

i. Control

4–019 The degree of ministerial control will be largely dependent on the specificity of the framework agreement, which varies from area to area.[50] The difficulty of sustaining the divide between policy consideration, undertaken by the core department, and service delivery, done by the agency, should be acknowledged. It is not simply that the two can naturally overlap. It is also that past experience with nationalised industries, where a similar functional divide was meant to operate, is salutary. It taught us that governments often meddled with day-to-day operations, while staunchly resisting answering questions on the topic by

46 *Robertson v Department for the Environment, Food and Rural Affairs* [2005] I.C.R. 750 CA (Civ Div).

47 HM Treasury and Office of Public Services Reform, *Better Government Services*.

48 Cabinet Office, *Executive Agencies*, Annex A, para.28.

49 Drewry and Butcher, *The Civil Service Today* (1991), pp.234–237.

50 McDonald, *The Future of Whitehall* (1991), pp.54–55.

claiming that such matters were not within its purview, while governmental guidance on policy was often not forthcoming, or was subject to frequent revision.[51]

ii. *Accountability*

The problems of accountability have occupied more attention. The issue is put succinctly by Drewry and Butcher.[52] **4–020**

> "The basic problem is quite simply stated but not at all easily resolved. How can ministers credibly cling to their virtual monopoly of accountability to Parliament, via traditional models of ministerial responsibility that (according to Mrs Thatcher) were to remain unaltered by the *Next Steps*, in respect of agencies whose chief executives are expected to take managerial initiatives at arm's length from ministerial control?"

The Treasury and Civil Service Committee expressed analogous concerns, but the government indicated that no change in the basic constitutional arrangements was required.[53] It is nonetheless clear that some modification in the traditional conception of ministerial accountability has been accepted.[54]

Agency chief executives are accountable to ministers.[55] The relevant minister is responsible for the policy framework within which the agency operates; for determining its strategic objectives; for setting its annual key financial and performance targets; and for approving business plans. There should be at least one meeting per year between the chief executive and the minister. A senior member of staff within the department will normally act as a sponsor for the agency. The sponsor is a key link between the agency and the department. The sponsor will: advise ministers on the strategic direction of the agency in the context of wider departmental objectives; agree a framework for strategic performance management; advise ministers on their response to strategic performance information; and ensure that the agency has the power to carry out its tasks. This regime was developed to meet concerns in the 2002 Report.[56]

The agency chief executive is responsible for the day to day management of the agency. MPs are encouraged to deal directly with the chief executive on such matters, subject to the caveat that the minister retains the "right to intervene in the operations of the agency if public or parliamentary concerns justify it".[57] The chief executive will normally represent the executive agency before select committees on matters of day-to-day operations.[58] **4–021**

This compromise, reflecting traditional British pragmatism, may be no bad thing. The minister is still there and responsible for matters of principle or general policy. The chief executive is, however, visible and the agency's objectives are publicly known. The existence of a person who can be called to account for

[51] T. Prosser, *Nationalised Industries and Public Control* (Oxford: Blackwell, 1986).
[52] Drewry and Butcher, *The Civil Service Today* (1991), p.228.
[53] Government Reply (1988), Cm.524.
[54] Cabinet Office, *Executive Agencies*, Annex A.
[55] Cabinet Office, *Executive Agencies*, Annex A, paras 11 and 12.
[56] HM Treasury and Office of Public Services Reform, *Better Government Services*.
[57] Cabinet Office, *Executive Agencies*, Annex A, para.17.
[58] Cabinet Office, *Executive Agencies*, Annex A, para.32.

operational agency failure is to be welcomed, more especially so because under the traditional regime prior to executive agencies it was often difficult to determine detailed departmental goals, and who was responsible for them[59]:

> "Next Steps has enhanced accountability to Parliament through its requirements for Agencies to publish their framework documents, annual targets, annual reports and accounts and, where appropriate, their corporate and business plans. Agency Chief Executives are accounting officers and, as such, are answerable to the Public Accounts Committee for the use of the resources allocated to them."

There is nonetheless an interesting contrast between the approach to accountability of executive agencies and NDPBs. The approach taken to the accountability of NDPBs was laudable. The paper on *Quangos: Opening the Doors* and the subsequent *Public Bodies: A Guide for Departments* recognised that accountability had to be viewed in the round. It acknowledged that there was an overtly political dimension to accountability, which was to be secured both from the top, through oversight by select committee and the like, and from the bottom, by facilitating participation, openness, and transparency. This was complemented by an economic dimension, manifest in target setting, benchmarking and efficiency evaluation.

4–022 The approach taken to executive agencies has been subtly different. They are subject to separate guidance, primarily because they are regarded as part of central government.[60] There are, however, limits to this rationale, since the central reason for their establishment is the desire for agencies outside the traditional departmental norm, with considerable autonomy for operational aspects of service delivery. It is true that such agencies are still under the minister's aegis, but this is also true in certain respects of NDPBs. The continued distinction between the two types of agency may well have been the unwillingness to open Pandora's Box. Executive agencies were established on the premise that it was constitutional business as usual. The recognition that they generated new constitutional and political concerns would have run counter to this. If it were accepted that the broader concerns voiced about the political accountability of NDPBs applied also to executive agencies then the original premise behind the establishment of the latter would have been undermined. The incentive to treat NDPBs and executive agencies differently becomes more readily explicable when viewed in this way.

The consequence of this differential treatment is that it led in the case of executive agencies to a concentration on the economic dimension of accountability, and a downplaying of the more overtly political dimension.[61] It was assumed that the political dimension was adequately taken care of through traditional ministerial responsibility, combined with the Framework Documents. Insofar as Charter initiatives addressed concerns relating to consultation and the like they did so from the perspective of the market citizen, rather than directly from the political perspective. It is almost as if this was regarded as the acceptable way to

[59] *Next Steps, Briefing Note* (1992), para.20.

[60] Cabinet Office, *Executive Report on Non-Departmental Public Bodies 1998* (1998), Cm.4157, p.2.

[61] Cabinet Office, *Next Steps Report 1997* (1998), Cm.3889; K. Burgess, C. Burton and G. Parston, *Accountability for Results* (Public Services Productivity Panel, 2002).

introduce such matters in relation to executive agencies, since it could be done without thereby directly confronting change in the constitutional arrangements as a result of the "Next Steps" initiative.

There are, however, signs that the political dimension of accountability is becoming more openly acknowledged in relation to executive agencies. Thus, the documentation concerning target setting by executive agencies emphasises that transparency and accountability are fundamental elements of the government's approach to delivering better public services, and that targets and performance measurement are essential in this respect.[62] There is also considerable emphasis on consultation with delivery staff and those affected by the targets, and this is seen as part of a continuing relationship in which the organisation monitors the experience and satisfaction of customers and their changing needs.[63] This is to be welcomed, since the broader political concerns addressed in relation to NDPBs are equally relevant to many executive agencies.

4–023 The accountability of executive agencies is of increased importance given the government's preference for such agencies over NDPBs. This preference is, as we have seen, predicated on the assumption that because executive agencies remain part of the sponsoring department for which the minister is responsible this thereby alleviates issues of accountability.[64] There is some force in this, but the "curative effect" in terms of accountability of converting NDPBs into executive agencies should not be pressed too far for the very reasons given above. There is still a tension with executive agencies between operational independence and ministerial responsibility, and between front line responsibility that resides with agencies and policy choice that remains with the department. The reality in any event is that change to NDPBs has more often led to the function being folded back into a government department than in creation of a new executive agency.[65]

iii. Effectiveness

4–024 Measuring institutional effectiveness is always difficult, irrespective of whether the task is performed in-house or through an executive agency. It requires statistical evidence and criteria by which to use it. Statistical evidence may however be unreliable, either because there is not enough data, or because the variables to be "computed" are too speculative. The process of determining whether given objectives are being pursued effectively is even more difficult. The enabling legislation may be unclear as to what those objectives are, or they may co-exist in tension. There may be a choice as to the means to achieve the given end and what the "best choice" is may not be readily apparent. It may be inherently difficult to decide how far the given end has been successfully attained.

---

62 HM Treasury, Cabinet Office, National Audit Office, *Setting Key Targets for Executive Agencies: A Guide* (2003), p.3.

63 HM Treasury, Cabinet Office, National Audit Office, *Setting Key Targets for Executive Agencies: A Guide* (2003), pp.12–13.

64 Cabinet Office, *Public Bodies 2014* (2014), p.11.

65 Cabinet Office, *Public Bodies 2014* (2014), pp.11-12.

The government perceived a link between executive agencies and attainment of objectives in the Citizen's Charter, although the Charter has had a lower profile in more recent years.[66] The Charter established a number of principles for governmental service delivery[67]: *standards* for service delivery; *openness* as to how the services are run; *consultation* with service users; *choice* where possible as to the available services; *value for money*; and *remedies*. Executive agencies are often in the front line of service delivery and hence, the government attached weight to Charter goals in this area. Official documents bore testimony to the zeal for demonstrating cost savings and better delivery of services.[68] The Labour government renewed the Charter ideals in 1998. Its paper on *Service First, the New Charter Programme*[69] set out nine principles for public service delivery: set standards of service; openness and provision of information; consult and involve; encourage access and choice; treat all fairly; remedies; use resources effectively; innovate and improve; and work with other providers.

Things have now moved on. The government is still concerned with targets and the measurement of performance, but this is less linked to Charter initiatives than hitherto. The new strategy will be explained more fully in the following chapter, and it has been markedly influenced by the need to reduce public spending in the wake of the 2008 financial crisis.[70]

The recommendations contained in the 2002 Report must be seen in the light of these developments.[71] Strategic performance monitoring was felt to be lacking in focus. There should be greater alignment between departmental and agency target setting. The government acted on these recommendations. Landscape and business reviews were conducted in relation to executive agencies, and the government published detailed guidance on target-setting, designed to ensure greater alignment between the Public Service Agreement made by the department and the targets set by the executive agency.[72]

---

[66] G. Drewry, "Whatever Happened to the Citizen's Charter" [2002] P.L. 9.

[67] The Citizen's Charter, *Raising the Standard* (1991) Cm.1599.

[68] *Improving Management in Government: The Next Steps Agencies* (1991), Cm.1760; *Improving Management in Government: The Next Steps Agencies* (1992), Cm.2111; *Next Steps, Briefing Notes* (1992–1998); *Next Steps Report 1997* (1998), Cm.3889.

[69] Cabinet Office, *Service First, the New Charter Programme* (1998).

[70] Cabinet Office, *Open Public Services 2013* (2013); Cabinet Office, *Choice Charter* (2013).

[71] HM Treasury and Office of Public Services Reform, *Better Government Services*; See also, Report by the Comptroller and Auditor General, *Measuring the Performance of Government Departments*, HC Paper No.301 (Session 2000–01).

[72] HM Treasury, Cabinet Office, National Audit Office, *Setting Key Targets for Executive Agencies: A Guide*; National Audit Office, *Improving Service Delivery – The Role of Executive Agencies* (2003).

5. NDPBS: APPOINTMENTS, ACCOUNTABILITY AND EFFICIENCY

A. Appointments

There has in the past been concern about the process by which people are appointed to the NDPBs, and the power this gives the minister in the sponsoring department. The Labour government recognised these concerns,[73] and reforms were implemented. The appointment process is now highly regulated to ensure fairness and openness. **4–025**

There is a Commissioner for Public Appointments,[74] as a result of the First Nolan Report.[75] The Commissioner's role is to regulate, monitor, report and advise on appointments made by UK ministers and by members of the National Assembly for Wales to the boards of national and regional public bodies. Government departments are required to follow the Commissioner for Public Appointments Code of Practice when making ministerial appointments to the boards of public bodies.

The principles contained in the Code are that[76]: the ultimate responsibility for appointments is with ministers; selection should be based on merit, be fair and open; there should be a departmental panel to oversee the appointments process; members of the CPA's team, known as public appointments assessors, must in general chair panels overseeing appointment of all Chairs of public bodies and statutory office holders; the selection process should be considered and agreed at the outset; appointments should comply with legislation, such as that on equal opportunities; and appointees must be committed to the values of public service and perform their duties with integrity. Prospective appointees to key positions on NDPBs are also subject to scrutiny by departmental select committees.[77]

The Cabinet Office publishes guidance on public appointments, which builds on that of the Commissioner.[78] The Cabinet Office in addition provides advice to departments about the arrangements for staffing of NDPBs, including a model code for staff of executive NDPBs and a model code for contracts of employment for those in senior posts.[79]

B. Control and Accountability

Control and accountability have been major concerns in relation to NDPBs. Control refers to the way in which the parent department may influence or direct an agency. Accountability is concerned with the answerability of that institution to the public, either through Parliament or through some more direct means of **4–026**

---

[73] Cabinet Office, *Opening up Quangos, A Consultation Paper* (1997), Ch.1, para.8i–j.

[74] *http://publicappointmentscommissioner.independent.gov.uk/* [accessed 31 August 2015].

[75] Committee on Standards in Public Life, *First Report* (1995) Cm.2850-I.

[76] Office of the Commissioner for Public Appointments, *The Commissioner for Public Appointments Code of Practice for Ministerial Appointments to Public Bodies* (2012).

[77] Cabinet Office, *Pre-Appointment Hearings by Select Committees: Guidance for Departments* (2013).

[78] Cabinet Office, *Public Appointments: Guidance to Departments* (2015).

[79] Cabinet Office, *Public Bodies: A Guide for Departments*, Ch.5.

public participation.[80] Control and accountability need not go hand in hand. It may be desirable for the agency to have significant independence in its decision-making. While this would indicate relatively little direct control, it does not follow that accountability should be minimal.[81]

It is not, however, difficult to perceive why the term accountability has been used to cover both control and the narrower sense of accountability mentioned here. The traditional notions of ministerial responsibility see accountability as existing by and through normal departmental mechanisms to the minister and hence to Parliament. It is presumed that what the minister is answerable for he or she also controls, or should do at least in theory. In the case of agencies this presumption cannot always be maintained.

i. Control

4–027 Control can take two principal forms. It may be *ex ante*. This will be a function of *the degree of precision laid down in the enabling legislation* as to what is to be done, how it is to be achieved,[82] and the *type of relationship between the institution and the department responsible for it*. A wide discretion may be accorded to the organisation, because the problem is novel, or because the subject matter makes it difficult not to delegate broad discretion. As the Cabinet Office states, "the nature of the controls will depend both on the NDPB's functions, and on the closeness of supervision which ministers wish to exercise".[83]

This is developed further in the Cabinet Office guidance to departments concerning NDPBs.[84] It states that departments should identify whether ministers need to retain control over aspects of the NDPB's activities. This includes matters such as whether questions of policy can be left to the NDPB acting in accordance with responsibilities conferred by the governing instrument, or whether ministers must be able to direct or modify policy; whether the NDPB should be subject to guidance from the minister; whether the minister should have powers of direction; whether decisions in individual cases can be left to the NDPB, subject to appeal to the courts or a tribunal, or whether appeal to ministers is needed on some matters; whether the minister needs to retain control over the fees charged by the NDPB; and whether the exercise of financial powers should be subject to ministerial approval or consent.

Control may also be exercised by *monitoring* the decisions reached by the institution. It is difficult to assess how closely departments exercise this type of control. It will be partly dependent on the composition of the particular organisation and the subject matter it is dealing with. Johnson concludes that executive control is blurred and spasmodic,[85] but points out that diffuse control is

[80] M. Bovens, "Analyzing and Assessing Public Accountability: A Conceptual Framework" (2007) 13 E.L.J. 447.

[81] D. Keeling, "Beyond Ministerial Departments: Mapping the Administrative Terrain 1. Quasi-Governmental Agencies" (1976) 54 Pub. Adm. 161, 169.

[82] Hague, Mackenzie and Barker, *Public Policy and Private Interests: The Institutions of Compromise* (1975), pp.363–364.

[83] Cabinet Office, *Public Bodies: A Guide for Departments*, Ch.3, para.5.3.

[84] Cabinet Office, *Public Bodies: A Guide for Departments*, Ch.2, para.6; Ch.3, para.5.

[85] "Editorial: Quangos and the Structure of British Government" (1979) 57 Pub. Adm. 379, 388–389.

not necessarily a bad thing. Organisational theory indicates that there may be institutions that function better where restraint is diffuse as opposed to a more rigid form of internal management control.

ii. *Accountability*

Most public disquiet has been focused on the traditional realm of accountability. The discussion of administrative machinery in the 19th century revealed the strains placed on the Board system by Parliament's desire to have a person directly answerable in the House for its activities.[86] The resurgence of NDPBs raised this problem in a more acute form, since we have become accustomed to the idea of ministerial responsibility as the "constitutional norm". Government policy to NDPBs since 2010 has, as we have seen, been predicated in part on the desire to enhance accountability. It has favoured bodies with a closer link to democratic accountability through Parliament. Thus, while many NDPBs have been preserved, others have been abolished, converted into executive agencies, or in many instances the activities have been folded back into the department.[87] **4–028**

Accountability can operate in a number of ways. The rules are a blend of accountability from the top, accountability from the bottom via public participation, and increased transparency.

The NDPB is *accountable to the minister, with the latter being responsible to Parliament*. Government practice is as follows. If a parliamentary question raises issues as to the day to day operation of a NDPB then the relevant minister refers it to the chief executive officer of the NDPB for a reply, which will be printed. Where however the queries raised on a particular issue are numerous, or the subject of the query sufficiently sensitive and/or high profile, then a ministerial response will be more appropriate.[88] Similar principles apply in relation to correspondence from MPs: ministers will answer correspondence relating to policies about sponsored bodies and the frameworks within such bodies operate, but issues concerning their day to day operation will normally be passed on to the chief executive of the NDPB. Each NDPB is also subject to a wide-ranging triennial review of its function and effectiveness.[89]

Accountability may be secured from the top through *select committees*.[90] Departmental select committees can examine the expenditure, administration and policy of the "associated public bodies" of the departments concerned, which is interpreted broadly to include those instances where there is a significant degree of ministerial responsibility for the body concerned.[91] The chief executive, as accounting officer, may also be summoned to the Public Accounts Committee. It **4–029**

---

[86] Ch.2.

[87] Cabinet Office, *Public Bodies 2014* (2014), p.11.

[88] Cabinet Office, *Public Bodies: A Guide for Departments*, Ch.8, para.5.1; Cabinet Office, *Guidance on Reviews of Non-departmental Public Bodies* (2011), pp.18–36.

[89] Cabinet Office, *Public Bodies 2014* (2014), p.12; Cabinet Office, *Triennial Reviews: Guidance on Reviews of Non-Departmental Public Bodies* (2014).

[90] *Report on Non-Departmental Public Bodies* (1980), Cmnd.7797, paras 81–85; Cabinet Office, *Quangos: Opening the Doors*, para.6.

[91] Cabinet Office, *Public Bodies: A Guide for Departments*, Ch.8, para.5.3.

is, however, questionable whether select committees are capable of comprehensive oversight of agencies, as opposed to having a more targeted impact upon particular issues.[92] Research on select committees would appear to substantiate these reservations.[93]

Accountability can also be enhanced from the bottom, *through public participation* and the like. This is accepted by the government. The Cabinet Office guide states that, "departments and public bodies should aim to consult their users and stakeholders on a wide range of issues by means of questionnaires, public meetings or other forms of consultation"[94] to ensure that they are responsive to the needs of their customers. The government's Code of Practice on Consultation is to be followed in all cases.[95] The Cabinet Office guide also enjoins NDPBs to establish complaints procedures.[96]

Accountability is fostered by *greater transparency*. A number of initiatives addressed this issue. Agencies were encouraged to hold open annual meetings,[97] to make reports available to the public[98] and to provide summary reports of their meetings.[99] Much of this is now reproduced in the Cabinet Office guidance to public bodies,[100] and NDPBs also come within the remit of the Freedom of Information Act 2000.

The *Parliamentary Commissioner for Administration* (PCA) can also help to ensure accountability. A number of agencies have been brought within the PCA's jurisdiction.[101] While the PCA cannot provide systematic scrutiny of agency action, this reform is nonetheless to be welcomed.[102]

C. Efficiency and Effectiveness

4–030 The efficiency and effectiveness of NDPBs is closely monitored, although the way in which this is done has altered.[103] The principal mechanism used to be quinquennial or financial management and policy reviews. This then changed to a regime of "landscape" and "business" review. The system has altered once again, and now reflects the government's desire to question the need for NDPBs. The reviews take place every three years. They are designed to challenge the continuing need for individual NDPBs, and to review governance arrangements

---

92 N. Johnson, "Editorial" (1979) 57 Pub. Adm. 379, 390; N. Johnson, "Accountability, Control and Complexity; Moving Beyond Ministerial Responsibility", in Barker (ed.), *Quangos in Britain* (1982), Ch.12.

93 See above, Ch.3.

94 Cabinet Office, *Public Bodies: A Guide for Departments*, Ch.8, para.4.1.1.

95 Cabinet Office, *Public Bodies: A Guide for Departments*, for discussion of the Code, see below Ch.15.

96 Cabinet Office, *Public Bodies: A Guide for Departments*, Ch.8, para.4.2.

97 Cabinet Office, *Quangos: Opening the Doors*, para.20.

98 Cabinet Office, *Quangos: Opening the Doors*, para.16.

99 Cabinet Office, *Quangos: Opening the Doors*, para.23.

100 Cabinet Office, *Public Bodies: A Guide for Departments*, Ch.8, para.3; Cabinet Office, *Public Bodies 2014* (2014), pp.7-10.

101 Cabinet Office, *Sweeping Extension of the Parliamentary Ombudsman's Jurisdiction* (February 1999).

102 Cabinet Office, *Public Bodies: A Guide for Departments*, Ch.8, para.4.3.

103 Cabinet Office, *Guidance on Reviews of Non-departmental Public Bodies*.

to ensure that the public body is complying with recognised principles of good corporate governance.[104] There are two stages to the review process that reflect these two principal aims.

The first stage of the review examines the key functions of the NDPB, and whether they are still needed. The review considers a wide range of delivery options. This includes whether the function can be delivered by local government, the voluntary or private sectors, the sponsoring department, by a new or existing executive agency or by another existing central government body. Government policy is that NDPBs should only "be set up, and remain in existence, where the NDPB model can be clearly evidenced as the most appropriate and cost-effective model for delivering the function in question'".[105]

The NDPB option must be assessed against the three tests mentioned earlier: is this a technical function, which needs external expertise to deliver; is this a function which needs to be, and be seen to be, delivered with absolute political impartiality; or is this a function which needs to be delivered independently of ministers to establish facts and/or figures with integrity?

The second stage is predicated on the assumption that the NDPB is to remain in existence. The review is then concerned with the control and governance arrangements to ensure that the public body is operating in line with recognised principles of good corporate governance, including openness, transparency and accountability.

6. AGENCIES: INSTITUTIONAL DESIGN AND LEGAL PRINCIPLE

Agencies raise a number of important issues of institutional design and legal principle. These issues are approached initially through study of different agencies to determine the legal problems they pose.[106] Some more general conclusions will be drawn thereafter. **4–031**

[104] Cabinet Office, *Public Bodies 2014* (2014), p.12; Cabinet Office, *Triennial Reviews: Guidance on Reviews of Non-Departmental Public Bodies* (2014).

[105] Cabinet Office, *Triennial Reviews: Guidance on Reviews of Non-Departmental Public Bodies* (2014), para.4.6.

[106] Hague, Mackenzie and Barker, *Public Policy and Private Interests: The Institutions of Compromise* (1975); Baldwin and McCrudden, *Regulation and Public Law* (1987); F. Ridley and D. Wilson (eds), *The Quango Debate* (Oxford: Oxford University Press, 1995); C. Foster and F. Plowden, *The State under Stress* (Open University Press, 1996); N. Lewis, "IBA Programme Contract Awards" [1975] P.L. 317; D. Bradley and R. Wilkie, "The Arts Council: The Case for an Organisational Enquiry" (1975) 53 Pub. Adm. 67; P. Giddings, "Parliament, Boards and Autonomy: The Case of Agricultural Marketing Boards" (1975) 53 Pub. Adm. 383; R. Baldwin, "A British Independent Regulatory Agency and the "Skytrain" Decision" [1978] P.L. 57; M. Purdue, "The Implications of the Constitution and Function of Regional Water Authorities" [1979] P.L. 119; R. Baldwin, "A Quango Unleashed: The Abolition of Policy Guidance in Civil Aviation Licensing" (1980) 58 Pub. Adm. 287; G. Tyrrell, "The Politics of a Hived Off Board: The Advisory, Conciliation and Arbitration Service" (1980) 58 Pub. Adm. 225; F. Gains, "Implementing Privatization Policies in "Next Steps" Agencies" (1999) 77 Pub. Adm. 713; F. Gains, "Hardware, Software or Network Connection? Theorizing Crises in the UK Next Steps Agencies" (2004) 82 Pub. Adm. 547.

A. The Civil Aviation Authority

4–032 Baldwin has shown how the CAA, which is now a public corporation, evolved as a result of dissatisfaction with its predecessor the Air Transport Licensing Board.[107] The ATLB operated like a traditional tribunal and suffered from three related defects: it failed to develop a working relationship with the minister; it was unable to produce durable policies to guide its licensing decisions; and it lacked expertise. These criticisms were echoed by the Edwards' Committee on "Air transport in the seventies", which advocated replacement of the ATLB by an agency, combining economic and safety regulation, air traffic control and the negotiation of traffic rights. Departmental licensing was rejected as an alternative because independent airline operators were unsure that they would obtain fair treatment from the government.[108] To circumvent the constitutional problems flowing from the creation of an independent agency to control air transport licensing, it was proposed that the CAA be subject to guidance by the minister by way of written policy statements.

With some modification what emerged as the Civil Aviation Act 1971 followed the main thrust of the Edwards' Committee Report. The Secretary of State for Trade was empowered to give guidance on policy.[109] The CAA had an impact on this policy through reports and consultation. In addition to such policy guidance from the department, the CAA structured its discretion through announcements and consultation.

The CAA was not the first regulatory agency to be given broad powers. The Poor Law Commission possessed a broad spectrum of powers, but Parliament's desire for more direct control and the controversial nature of the subject matter led to its downfall.[110] The CAA was based on appreciation of the benefits of administration outside the departmental norm. There was nonetheless a desire to maintain some political control over the agency, to enable a minister to give it a clearer idea as to the manner in which its broad discretion should be exercised. The system of policy guidance was intended to achieve this end.

4–033 A result of the ministerial guidance indicating no competition on long haul routes was that the Laker "Skytrain" was told that it would not be allowed to operate. This was unfortunate because Laker had invested nearly £7 million on the strength of government representations that he would be granted the route. Laker took the government to court. He argued that the policy guidance that led to the withdrawal of Laker Airways from the North American route was ultra vires. The Court of Appeal agreed.[111] It held that "guidance" had a limited role. The secretary of state's power to give such guidance was contained in s.3(2) of the Civil Aviation Act 1971. The preceding subs.(1), set out four basic objectives that

---

[107] R. Baldwin, *Regulating the Airlines, Administrative Justice and Agency Discretion* (Oxford: Oxford University Press, 1985) and "Civil Aviation Regulation: From Tribunal to Regulatory Agency", in Baldwin and McCrudden, *Regulation and Public Law* (1987), Ch.8. See also Baldwin, [1978] P.L. 57 and (1980) 58 Pub. Adm. 287.

[108] "Civil Aviation Regulation", in Baldwin and McCrudden, *Regulation and Public Law* (1987), pp.164–165.

[109] Civil Aviation Act 1971 s.3(2).

[110] Ch.2.

[111] *Laker Airways Ltd v Department of Trade* [1977] Q.B. 643.

the CAA was to pursue. Guidance given pursuant to s.3(2) could not contradict the general statutory objectives laid down in s.3(1).[112] The secretary of state's policy guidance was, said the Court of Appeal, attempting to do just that. It was therefore ultra vires.

The case raised a number of important legal issues. The precise way in which the policy guidance contradicted the statutory objectives was never made quite clear.[113] It is however, the broader issue as to the relationship of the CAA and the secretary of state that is relevant here. Baldwin argued persuasively that the court misconceived the role of the CAA[114] They treated it as if it were a traditional body with quasi-judicial functions, which should be "protected" from executive interference, failing to perceive that it was a multi-faceted agency that was not intended to be independent of government.

The aftermath of the *Laker* decision is of interest.[115] The limitations placed on the secretary of state's power to issue policy guidance resulted in an increased structuring of discretion by the CAA itself. There is no reason why the CAA should not be able to structure its discretion in this way.[116] This does not, however, touch the issue of principle, which is whether it is preferable to have some broad political control exercised through the mechanism of policy guidance. The debates on the Civil Aviation Bill 1979 reflected the two opposing views. The government decided to drop the notion of policy guidance, the argument being that if an area was to be hived off it should be truly independent: "both hands should be taken off the wheel", with political control maintained by alterations in the list of statutory criteria. The opposition saw this as an abdication of legislative responsibility to a largely unaccountable body. Refining the list of statutory objectives would not solve the problem. Such criteria were often in conflict and had to be balanced.[117] It is nonetheless instructive that s.6 of the Civil Aviation Act 1982 continues to accord the secretary of state with power to give directions to the CAA on a wide range of issues concerning the national interest. **4–034**

What the foregoing discussion of the CAA demonstrates is that issues of legal principle concerning decision-making by agencies can assume many forms. They can involve questions as to the proper levels of procedural constraint, or the scope of substantive review. Challenges framed in terms of ultra vires can, however, also raise fundamental questions as to the institutional structure of a particular agency. While such organisations cannot be forced into the traditional framework of ministerial responsibility for measures carried out within a department, this does not necessarily lead to a "both hands off the wheel" approach.

---

[112] The Court of Appeal was influenced in reaching this conclusion by the power to give directions contained in s.4 of the 1971 Act which would override the objectives set out in s.3(1).

[113] Baldwin, "A British Independent Regulatory Agency and the "Skytrain" Decision" [1978] P.L. 57, 78–79.

[114] Baldwin, "A British Independent Regulatory Agency and the "Skytrain" Decision" [1978] P.L. 57, 78.

[115] Baldwin, "A Quango Unleashed" (1980) 58 Pub. Adm. 287.

[116] See below, Ch.18.

[117] Baldwin, "A Quango Unleashed: The Abolition of Policy Guidance in Civil Aviation Licensing" (1980) 58 Pub. Adm. 287, 293–294.

B. Nationalisation and the Public Corporation[118]

4–035 Public corporations have been the principal vehicle used in the nationalisation of industry. The reasons for nationalisation have varied. They include the belief that certain functions are vital to the nation and should not be left in the hands of private enterprise; a desire to provide services which the market would not sustain; a belief that natural monopolies should be run by the state; and a political belief that the people should own the industrial assets of the nation, or at least a proportion of them.

The principal institutional form to realise these objectives was the public corporation.[119] The precise details of nationalisation statutes varied, but certain common features were evident.[120] The general theme was that the industry should be autonomous in its day-to-day administration, but that ministers should have power to determine overall policy. This theme manifested itself in a number of ways: ministers possessed the power of appointment to the boards of the industries; they could issue general directions to these boards; ministerial sanction was required for major development programmes and ministers exercised specific powers over financial matters.

The ideal of day-to-day autonomy coupled with ministerial control over long term planning was not a success. It was undermined from both sides. Successive governments used nationalised industry to respond to short term pressures. Long term planning was upset by ministerial pressure, often covert, to buy British, to resist wage increases, or to curtail a capital investment programme. Governments were also notably lacking in the broad policy directive envisioned by the enabling legislation.

4–036 There was, moreover, uncertainty as to the role that such industries should play in the economy. Some saw them primarily as commercial enterprises, balancing revenue and expenditure. Others perceived their commercial role as secondary to their function as an arm of government, to prevent regional unemployment, or to help implement governmental policy. This did not make life easy for those running the major corporations. Pushed from pillar to post they were lambasted for poor commercial returns, while being cajoled by government to achieve ends that ordinary commercial judgment would reject.

This uncertainty enabled successive ministers to use the formal statutory scheme as a sword and a shield. Ministers used it as a sword to exercise influence over the industry. They used it as a shield to protect them from embarrassing questions in Parliament. Such unwelcome interrogatories were commonly met by the response that day-to-day administration was outside the minister's responsibility. The uncertainty as to the role such industries should play can be

---

118 R. Robson, *Nationalised Industry and Public Ownership*, 2nd edn (London: Allen & Unwin, 1962); W. Friedmann and J. Garner (eds), *Government Enterprise* (London: Stevens, 1970); W. Friedmann, *The State and the Rule of Law in a Mixed Economy* (London: Stevens, 1971); W. Friedmann (ed.), *Public and Private Enterprise in Mixed Economies* (London: Stevens, 1974); D. Coombes, *State Enterprise: Politics or Business?* (London: Allen & Unwin, 1971); T. Prosser, *Nationalised Industries and Public Control* (Oxford: Blackwell, 1986).

119 Other techniques include the government taking a shareholding in an existing company.

120 Coal Industry Nationalisation Act 1946; Civil Aviation Act 1946; Transport Act 1946; Gas Act 1948; Iron and Steel Act 1949.

demonstrated by considering the answers given concerning the relationship between these industries and government.

The initial idea which permeated Labour thinking from 1945–1950 was that the change of ownership from private to public would remove the profit motive and enable nationalised industries to act as "high custodians of the public interest". The shift from private to public ownership did not however resolve the task of defining the public interest. The imprecision in this phrase could enable managers and politicians alike to pursue their own objectives under the guise of acting in the national interest: "wolfish self-interest is all too easily cloaked in the public interest sheepskin".[121] **4–037**

A second approach was evident in the White Papers of 1961 and 1967.[122] The latter advocated marginal cost pricing, set criteria for investment decisions, and proposed that non-commercial activities should be accounted for separately, with the government deciding whether to support such activities on cost-benefit criteria. This approach while reflecting a coherent policy proved to be of little effect. There "was no attempt to develop an adequate structure of incentives to encourage managers to act in the desired ways",[123] and consequently many ignored the pricing and investment guidelines. Moreover, the problem of ministers seeking to attain goals other than those stipulated in the White Paper was left unresolved. Not surprisingly they continued to do so.

A third approach was apparent in the 1978 White Paper and in Conservative policy subsequent thereto.[124] Financial target setting became the principal form of control, supplemented by performance indicators to enable sponsoring departments to assess efficiency.[125] The post-1978 framework of control relied most heavily on external financing limits (EFL), which placed constraints on the annual change of the net indebtedness of public corporations to the government. This served to restrict the difference between revenue and expenditure. The use of EFLs highlighted the difficult situation of public corporations. EFLs were accorded such prominence principally because of governmental concern over macro-economic issues, such as the existence of fiscal deficit and the corresponding desire to control public sector borrowing. The tension between exercise of commercial freedom, and utilisation of public corporations as part of a broader governmental strategy was apparent once again.

[121] J. Vickers and G. Yarrow, *Privatization, An Economic Analysis* (Cambridge, MA: MIT Press, 1988), p.130.

[122] White Paper, *Financial and Economic Obligations of the Nationalised Industries* (1961), Cmnd.1337; White Paper, *Nationalised Industries: A Review of Economic and Financial Objectives* (1967), Cmnd.3437.

[123] Vickers and Yarrow, *Privatization, An Economic Analysis* (1988), p.132.

[124] White Paper, *The Nationalised Industries* (1978), Cmnd.7131; Vickers and Yarrow, *Privatization, An Economic Analysis* (1988), pp.133–135; Prosser, *Nationalised Industries and Public Control* (1986), pp.44–47, 54–74.

[125] Compare these themes to the policy espoused by the NEDO study of 1976, Prosser, *Nationalised Industries and Public Control* (1986), pp.41–43.

C. Privatisation and Regulatory Control

4–038 A fuller analysis of the problems of regulating market power will be considered in a subsequent chapter.[126] It is, however, useful to consider here the agency structure established to oversee telecommunications privatisation.

The reasons for privatisation are, like those for nationalisation, eclectic.[127] They include the following: improving efficiency, reducing government involvement in industrial decision-making, widening share ownership, encouraging share ownership by employees, alleviating problems of public sector pay determination, reducing the public sector borrowing requirement and enhancement of economic freedom.

The cogency of these reasons has been challenged.[128] The argument that privatisation will enhance economic freedom has been criticised because it assumes that a private monopoly will be less threatening to such freedom than a statutory monopoly. It has also been criticised because it defines "freedom" in a limited way to mean the absence of government intervention in the market, thereby foreclosing a more active role for the state that might enhance economic liberty. Moreover, the argument that privatisation augments economic freedom must be qualified, because some privatised industries require regulatory control.

4–039 The contention that privatisation will improve efficiency has also been questioned.[129] The "conclusion" that nationalised industry performed inefficiently is contested. It is dependent upon analysis of complex performance data, which must then take account of the managerial difficulties experienced by public corporations stemming from lack of clarity as to their objectives. Furthermore, even if it is accepted that a change in ownership rights can have an effect upon incentives, behaviour and efficiency, by sharpening corporate incentives, the realisation of these benefits will "depend crucially upon the framework of competition and regulation in which the privatized firm is to operate".[130]

The problems posed by privatisation vary, but it is important to keep distinct two different situations. There has been the privatisation of large companies, which do not possess undue market power. Firms such as British Aerospace, Britoil, and Cable and Wireless, operate in reasonably competitive industries. When privatised, these corporations are of no greater concern to public law than other large companies that have never been within public ownership.[131] These firms do not possess the market power to necessitate a regulatory regime to

[126] Ch.11.

[127] Vickers and Yarrow, *Privatization, An Economic Analysis* (1988), pp.157–160; J. Kay, C. Mayer and D. Thompson (eds), *Privatization and Regulation—the UK Experience* (Oxford: Oxford University Press, 1986), Chs 3 and 4; C. Foster, *Privatization, Public Ownership and the Regulation of Natural Monopoly* (Oxford: Blackwell, 1992), Ch.4; T. Prosser, *Law and the Regulators* (Oxford: Oxford University Press, 1997), Ch.3.

[128] D. Heald and D. Steel, "Privatising Public Enterprises: An Analysis of the Government's Case", in Kay, Mayer and Thompson (eds), *Privatization and Regulation—the UK Experience* (1986), Ch.2.

[129] Kay, Mayer and Thompson, *Privatization and Regulation—the UK Experience* (1986), Chs 5 and 6.

[130] Vickers and Yarrow, *Privatization, An Economic Analysis* (1988), pp.7–44 and 157–159.

[131] This leaves open the more general issue as to how far corporate power generally should be the concern of public law.

control their prices. Such privatised companies may, nonetheless, have "special features" distinct from the normal corporation. The government may possess shareholdings in the company, there may be government directors and the articles of association may be structured to allow the government to prevent undesirable takeovers or changes in control.[132]

The alternative scenario is where the privatised corporation has significant market power, and this requires some regulatory regime to oversee it. The end result is a privatised firm or firms, which are controlled by an agency. The telecommunications industry can be taken as an example.

The Telecommunications Act 1984 brought about the first privatisation of a major public utility in this country. From 1912 until 1981 telecommunications were the responsibility of the Post Office, a state-owned monopoly. Legislation in 1981 separated telecommunications from postal services and established British Telecom as a public corporation.[133] The 1984 Act privatised BT and created a regulatory framework to oversee the industry. **4–040**

Section 1 of the 1984 Act created the Director General of Telecommunications (DGT), who was appointed by the secretary of state and s.2 abolished BT's exclusive privilege of running telecommunications systems. The duties of the secretary of state and the DGT were set out in s.3. They were to act in the manner best calculated to secure the provision of telecommunications services. Eight broad guidelines structured fulfilment of these duties. They included the promotion of: the interests of consumers, effective competition, efficiency and economy, research and development and the international competitiveness of UK firms supplying telecommunications services.

Section 5 required operators of telecommunications systems to possess a licence. The DGT and the secretary of state granted these under s.7.[134] Under s.12 the DGT could modify licence conditions, and s.13 empowered him to refer a matter to the Monopolies and Mergers Commission (MMC), which could decide whether it operated against the public interest. The DGT was empowered, by s.16, to make an order requiring compliance by the licensee. This could be enforced either by the DGT,[135] or by an action for breach of statutory duty.[136] The DGT also had other duties and powers, which included[137]: the investigation of complaints, and the publication of information to consumers. The DGT could exercise the powers of the Director General of Fair Trading to investigate anti-competitive practices or abuses of market power.[138] A number of comments on this system are warranted.

---

[132] C. Graham and T. Prosser, "Privatising Nationalised Industries: Constitutional Issues and New Legal Techniques" (1987) 50 M.L.R. 16; C. Graham and T. Prosser, *Privatizing Public Enterprises, Constitutions, the State, and Regulation in Comparative Perspective* (Oxford: Oxford University Press, 1991).

[133] British Telecommunications Act 1981 (1981 Act).

[134] See also 1981 Act s.9, which created the separate category of public telecommunications systems. Such systems have the conditions of s.8 attached, which include a duty not to discriminate and required the operator of such a system to permit interconnection with other systems.

[135] 1981 Act s.18(8).

[136] 1981 Act s.18(6).

[137] 1981 Act Pt III.

[138] 1981 Act s.50. See now the Competition Act 1998 s.54 and Sch.10.

4–041 First, removing a firm from public ownership does not provide the answer as to the type of new regime that is to be established. If a privatised firm has significant market power then this can be addressed either structurally, or through regulation.[139] The former entails the breaking-up of the large firm. The latter involves monitoring the conduct of the dominant firm, with the added theme of introducing competitors via the issuing of new licences. The United Kingdom adopted the latter approach, the effectiveness of which depends upon two crucial issues, the criteria for regulation and the attitude of the regulator.

Second, the most important of the regulatory criteria relate to the price which the regulated industry can charge for its services. This will determine whether it is being "fair" to consumers. Deciding upon the correct formula is a complex issue.[140] Claims that privatisation would necessarily produce efficiency were crucially dependent on the correct resolution of such issues.

Third, the success of the scheme is also dependent upon the energy, attitude and resources of the DGT. The DGT ran an agency called the Office of Telecommunications (Oftel). The breadth of the main empowering provisions of the legislation and the guidelines contained therein, gave the DGT considerable latitude. The DGT and Oftel were not "captured" by the firms being regulated, and pursued a fairly vigorous pro-competitive strategy.[141] However the effectiveness of Oftel was circumscribed by a number of factors. Regulatory control was dependent on adequate information being available to the regulator, and the DGT complained that this was not forthcoming from BT on a regular basis. It was not clear initially that Oftel possessed the requisite resources to discharge its functions adequately. Decisions by the MMC pursuant to a reference by the DGT allowed BT to acquire other companies subject to conditions that were difficult to enforce. There is more evidence that BT "captured" the government rather than Oftel.[142] The government devised the privatisation "package". The change from public to private ownership was the principal concern, the promotion of competition being a secondary objective. The government made several policy decisions that favoured BT, including the choice of the pricing formula, and the limit upon licensees.

4–042 Fourth, it was partly in response to these problems, and partly because of the spirit of the Citizen's Charter, that the regulatory powers were increased by the Competition and Service (Utilities) Act 1992. The 1992 Act modified s.27 of the Telecommunications Act 1984. It empowered the DGT to make regulations prescribing the standards of performance that ought to apply in individual cases, with provision for the award of compensation if these were not met.[143] The DGT could, moreover, determine standards of overall performance in connection with the provision of the relevant services.[144] The 1992 Act also contained additional powers with respect to the information that the DGT could demand as to the

---

[139] Vickers and Yarrow, *Privatization, An Economic Analysis* (1988), p.212.

[140] Vickers and Yarrow, *Privatization, An Economic Analysis* (1988), pp.213–216; Prosser, *Law and the Regulators* (1997), pp.66–71.

[141] Vickers and Yarrow, *Privatization, An Economic Analysis* (1988), pp.217–241; Prosser, *Law and the Regulators* (1997), pp.63–65.

[142] Vickers and Yarrow, *Privatization, An Economic Analysis* (1988), pp.210–211 and 235–236.

[143] Telecommunications Act 1984 s.27(A).

[144] Telecommunications Act 1984 s.27B.

levels of individual and overall performance.[145] Customers were to be given information about overall performance,[146] and complaints' procedures were to be established by the telecommunications operators.[147] Specific provisions governed matters such as discriminatory pricing and billing disputes.[148]

Fifth, the regulatory system became increasingly complex as a result of a number of factors. There were EU initiatives in relation to telecommunications.[149] There was a growing emphasis on the role of the DGT as a specialist competition authority,[150] which was enhanced by the passage of the Competition Act 1998.[151] There was also greater attention to social aspects of regulation, such as measures to facilitate universal access, this being defined as affordable access to basic telecommunications services for all those reasonably requiring it regardless of where they live.[152]

Finally, while the regulatory regime has become more complex as a result of the factors mentioned above, the Communications Act 2003 has brought some greater measure of order into this area, at least insofar as the regulatory structure is concerned. The functions of the DGT, and other bodies concerned with telecommunications, have been transferred to Ofcom, the Office of Communications, which has overall regulatory responsibility for this area. The Communications Act 2003 has largely superseded previous legislation in this area.[153]

7. A CONSTITUTIONAL AND LEGAL FRAMEWORK FOR AGENCIES

While the diversity of institutions makes statements of principle difficult, consideration of constitutional and legal principle is nonetheless important. Similar problems recur in differing organisations. This is not to say that such bodies should be forced into some administrative straitjacket. There is, however, a significant spectrum running between the pure ad hoc and institutional rigidity. **4–043**

The first issue concerns the divide between executive agencies and NDPBs. It may well be the case that we should simply accept these differences. They do, to some extent, reflect differing philosophies as to how far agencies should be independent from the traditional departmental structure: executive agencies have no separate legal foundation, having been created by administrative reorganisation, unlike NDPBs. There are however tensions in relation to executive agencies, between the desire to foster agency autonomy and the preservation of departmental responsibility. This tension will not disappear. It is evident that current arrangements for executive agencies and NDPBs are not regarded as writ

[145] Telecommunications Act 1984 s.27C.
[146] Telecommunications Act 1984 s.27D.
[147] Telecommunications Act 1984 s.27E.
[148] Competition and Service (Utilities) Act 1992 ss.5, 6.
[149] Prosser, *Law and the Regulators* (1997), pp.60–61.
[150] Prosser, *Law and the Regulators* (1997), pp.76–78.
[151] Competition Act 1998 s.54 and Sch.10.
[152] Prosser, *Law and the Regulators* (1997), pp.78–83.
[153] The Telecommunications Act 1984 has been largely superseded by the Communications Act 2003. The provisions of the Competition and Service (Utilities) Act 1992 concerning telecommunications have been superseded by the Communications Act 2003.

in stone, as witnessed by the fact that other ways of providing the relevant service, such as privatisation or contracting-out, are kept under review.[154]

Second, it is important that there should be some general overseeing institution. The reality is that the Cabinet Office performs this role, with input from the Treasury and the National Audit Office. It is beneficial for oversight of executive agencies and NDPBs to be undertaken by the same body. It is equally important that the body entrusted with this task has some real power within government. The implementation of reforms on NDPBs was the more likely given that the proposals emanated from a body operating in the heart of government, rather than one, such as the Council on Tribunals, which exists on the periphery. There are potential dangers with this oversight strategy, since an institution such as the Cabinet Office may feel constrained as to what it can propose because of its very centrality in government. The Cabinet Office has, however, shown willingness to respond to suggestions as to how Executive Agencies and NDPBs could be improved, as exemplified by the fact that it adopted the great majority of the suggestions contained in the 2002 Report on Executive Agencies.[155]

The third stage in the framework concerns the relationship of any such organisation with the parent department and Parliament. In the case of executive agencies, the relationship is defined by the Framework Document. The general aim is to foster agency autonomy for policy implementation, although initiatives have stressed the need for co-ordination between the agency and its sponsoring department. The issue of ministerial power over agencies is also present in relation to NDPBs. The enabling legislation should make it as clear as possible what degree of insulation the agency should have from the minister. The last stage in the framework is control. This can have three meanings. The extent of legislative control should be answered by the terms of reference on which the institution was established. The extent of ministerial control will depend on the area over which the agency exercises power: what is suitable for competition policy will not be the same as for funding of the Arts. Control may mean quality control, supervision over the effectiveness of the internal institutional structure and study as to how far agency aims are being fulfilled. Control may also connote judicial review, which will be considered below. A general point about procedural and substantive review can, however, be made at this stage.

The procedural constraints imposed will reflect the purposes of the particular scheme. If, for example, it is felt that a high premium should be placed upon public participation then this may be reflected in rules as to notice and standing, and produce a procedure more akin to consultation than the adversary process. Trade-offs will, however, have to be made between the degree of participation and the time that this involves. The Citizen's Charter had some impact on this, with its emphasis on consultation with users of services, and the impetus it gave to the making of Charters for particular areas. The Citizen's Charter also provided

---

154 Cabinet Office, *Executive Agencies*, paras 20–22; Cabinet Office, *Guidance on Reviews of Non-departmental Public Bodies*.

155 HM Treasury and Office of Public Services Reform, *Better Government Services*.

the conceptual foundation for statutory changes to increase the openness of the process, to improve citizen access to information and to enhance reasoned decision-making.[156]

Substantive judicial review should be sensitive to the nature of the organisation in question. If, for example, the institutional form makes it clear that the minister is intended to retain control over the general direction of policy then this should be respected. Judicial decisions should not operate from an inarticulate premise of organisational "independence" and "ministerial interference", which does not reflect the true division of roles between agency and minister. Where procedures have been designed for a specific body they should not be struck down merely because they do not conform to the adversary model which characterises adjudication in the ordinary courts.

[156] Competition and Service (Utilities) Act 1992.

CHAPTER 5

CONTRACT AND SERVICE PROVISION

1. CENTRAL ISSUES

i. Contract is of increasing relevance for governance.[1] The topic is significant, and the boundaries are contested. Contract and contractual language have been used in areas as diverse as public procurement, service provision, contracting-out, the private finance initiative, concordats between branches of government, public service agreements, framework agreements between departments and executive agencies, the control of deviance, unemployment services, and education. There are various taxonomies that might be used. **5–001**

ii. A criterion might be whether the contract is legally binding.[2] Thus, in terms of the subject matter in the previous paragraph, in some instances the contracts are legally binding, in others they are not. This is a significant distinguishing factor, although even in the latter instance the contracts or agreements frame the obligations of the respective parties and may be backed by sanctions that are real, notwithstanding the fact that the contract is not legally binding.

iii. An alternative suggested criterion is to distinguish between public procurement, government by agreement and new public contracting, the last of which is used to characterise delegation of powers to public agencies in contractual arrangements whereby central government preserves control and power of intervention.[3] The choice of subject matter for inclusion within each of these categories may, however, be contentious.

iv. It is not possible within the confines of this chapter to consider all instances in which contract or contractual language has been used. Contract is relevant at varying points in administrative law. Thus, for example, the use

---

[1] H. Street, *Governmental Liability* (Cambridge: Cambridge University Press, 1953), Ch.3; J.D.B. Mitchell, *Contracts of Public Authorities* (LSE, 1954); C. Turpin, *Government Procurement and Contracts* (London: Longman, 1989); S. Arrowsmith, *Civil Liability and Public Authorities* (Earlsgate Press, 1992); I. Harden, *The Contracting State* (Open University Press, 1992); A.C.L. Davies, *Accountability: A Public Law Analysis of Government by Contract* (Oxford: Oxford University Press, 2001); P. Vincent-Jones, *The New Public Contracting: Regulation, Responsiveness, Relationality* (Oxford: Oxford University Press, 2006); A.C.L. Davies, *The Public Laws of Government Contracts* (Oxford: Oxford University Press, 2008); R. Noguellou and U. Stelkens (eds), *Comparative Law on Public Contracts* (Brussels: Bruylant, 2010); S. Arrowsmith, *The Law of Public and Utilities Procurement: Regulation in the UK and the EU,* 3rd edn (London: Sweet & Maxwell, 2014).

[2] Davies, *Accountability: A Public Law Analysis of Government by Contract* (2001), Ch.1.

[3] Vincent-Jones, *The New Public Contracting: Regulation, Responsiveness, Relationality* (2006), Ch.1.

of framework agreements in the context of executive agencies has been considered in the previous chapter,[4] while the susceptibility of contracts to judicial review,[5] and the extent to which contracts can be a fetter on the exercise of administrative discretion, will be considered within the appropriate sections of the book.[6]

v. The present chapter will focus on certain important aspects of contract and governance. The discussion begins with the way in which procurement policy is framed. There is analysis of the institutions that frame procurement policy, the guidelines they produce and the range of procurement options they can use.

vi. This is followed by analysis of contract and service provision by central government. The discussion begins with consideration of the increasing use of contracting-out in the provision of public services. The policy of the Conservative government in the 1980s and subsequent governments is explained and analysed. This leads naturally to legal issues concerning contracting-out and to the policy arguments for and against this mode of service delivery. The focus then shifts to service provision by central government through the Private Finance Initiative, which is an innovative tool for financing public projects.

vii. There is then analysis of contract and service provision by local government. This area has become more highly regulated in the last 40 years, as attested to by the number of statutes that address the issue. The policies of the Conservative, Labour and Coalition governments to contract and service provision are explained, as is the role played by the Private Finance Initiative at local level.

viii. The focus then shifts to a more general consideration of contract as a tool of government policy. The chapter concludes with detailed consideration of the legal rules governing the making of contracts, including constraints imposed by EU law.

2. TOWARDS "BETTER PROCUREMENT": THE FRAMING OF GOVERNMENT PROCUREMENT POLICY

5–002 Central government spends a very large sum of money on procuring goods and services. The principal purchasers have included the Ministry of Defence, the Property Services Agency, HMSO and the Department of Health. We shall consider the institutions that shape procurement policy, their guidelines and the range of procurement options at the government's disposal.

[4] See above, 4–014.

[5] See para.27–027 to 27–028.

[6] See paras 18–024 to 18–030.

A. Institutional Responsibility

A number of institutions have played a role in shaping procurement policy. The institutional structure of procurement altered as a result of a government review considered below. **5–003**

Traditionally it was the Treasury that exercised direct, overall responsibility for public procurement. This was not surprising given that department's role in the management of public expenditure. It was the Treasury which would "distil and promulgate agreed principles",[7] and conduct negotiations with the European Union and industry. The Treasury principles would often take the form of guidance to departments on matters such as tendering procedures, the conditions to be included in the contract and project management.[8] Treasury guidance on procurement was focused around the Procurement Group (PG). The Cabinet Office was also involved with procurement through the Buying Agency, an executive agency that provided support for large-scale procurement through contract negotiation and facilities management.[9] Individual departments had a section responsible for procurement, and there was often a dialogue between them and the Treasury.

Institutional responsibility for procurement was reorganised as a result of the Gershon review in 1999.[10] The review found that procurement strategy was fragmented across different government departments and agencies. This resulted in the centre lacking the "clout" that it should have. The review recommended the creation of a central body with overall responsibility for procurement. This led to creation of the Office of Government Commerce (OGC) in 1999, which was an independent office in the Treasury, with its own chief executive.[11]

The present reality is that responsibility for procurement is divided between the Cabinet Office and the Treasury. In 2010, the OGC was folded into the Efficiency and Reform Group within the Cabinet Office, and in 2011 the government appointed a chief procurement officer to cut waste across government.[12] The Treasury is, however, still very much involved, which is scarcely surprising given the sums at stake. It was the Treasury that authored the 2007 Report on *Transforming Government Procurement*.[13] A key element in the Report was the emphasis on review of major projects, to ensure that they were subject to scrutiny and review at key stages. The Cabinet Office and Treasury have taken forward this commitment.[14] **5–004**

---

[7] Turpin, *Government Procurement and Contracts* (1989), p.62.

[8] Turpin, *Government Procurement and Contracts* (1989), p.64.

[9] Buying Agency, *Pathfinder Guides you through the Procurement Maze* (1998).

[10] P. Gershon, *Review of Civil Procurement in Central Government* (1999).

[11] See *https://www.gov.uk/government/publications/best-management-practice-portfolio/about-the-office-of-government-commerce* [accessed 4 January 2016].

[12] See *http://www.cabinetoffice.gov.uk/news/government-appoints-chief-procurement-officer-cut-waste* [accessed 4 January 2016].

[13] HM Treasury, *Transforming Government Procurement* (2007).

[14] See *http://www.cabinetoffice.gov.uk/content/major-projects-authority* [accessed 4 January 2016]; HM Treasury and Cabinet Office, Major Project Approval and Assurance Guidance (2011), *http://www.hm-treasury.gov.uk/psr_major_projects.htm* [accessed 4 January 2016].

There is a Major Projects Authority (MPA), which was located in the Efficiency and Reform Group of the Cabinet Office,[15] but was merged to form the Infrastructure and Projects Authority on 1 January 2016.[16] The MPA constitutes a partnership between the Treasury and the Cabinet Office. There are four principal components to the new arrangements.[17] There is a Government Major Project Portfolio (GMPP), which consists of all central Government funded programmes that require Treasury approval. The second component is known as the Integrated Assurance and Approval Plan, to ensure in the most efficient manner that the project is delivered in a timely manner. For projects that are problematic this is then supplemented by what is known as Consequential Assurance and Intervention. The final component is Transparent Reporting, which includes publication of project contracts on line, and an annual report on progress of Government's Major Projects. Government departments must engage in a Starting Gate review, or its equivalent, to assess the deliverability of all major new projects before project delivery gets underway. It will be for the Treasury to assess affordability before any contract awards are made.

B. Guidelines on Procurement

5–005 The institutions responsible for procurement have always published guidelines to aid departments in the procurement process.

There are *general guidelines*, as exemplified by the *Procurement Policy Guidelines* produced by the Procurement Policy Unit.[18] The Labour government's general strategy was to focus on "Better Procurement". The general guiding principle was value for money with due regard for propriety and regularity.[19] The Coalition government published a series of papers with detailed guidance on its general strategy for major projects.[20]

There has been guidance in relation to *specific types of procurement*. This is exemplified by the guidance provided by the Procurement Group in relation to construction projects.[21] Value for money was the guiding theme.[22] There were "approval gateways" at various stages of the project, the object being to ensure that the value for money approach could be confirmed by people independently

[15] Available at: *http://www.cabinetoffice.gov.uk/resource-library/major-projects-authority-general-information* [accessed 4 January 2016].

[16] Available at: *https://www.gov.uk/government/news/new-government-body-to-help-manage-and-deliver-major-projects-for-uk-economy* [accessed 4 January 2016].

[17] HM Treasury and Cabinet Office, *Major Project Approval and Assurance Guidance* (2011), *http://www.hm-treasury.gov.uk/psr_major_projects.htm* [accessed 4 January 2016].

[18] Procurement Policy Unit, *Procurement Policy Guidelines* (November 1998).

[19] Procurement Policy Unit, *Procurement Policy Guidelines*, para.1.1.

[20] Cabinet Office, *Major Project Approval and Assurance Guidance* (2011); Cabinet Office, *MPA Starting Gate Guidance for Departments* (2011); Cabinet Office, *Integrated Assurance and Approval Strategy and Integrated Assurance and Approval Plans* (2011), see *http://www.cabinetoffice.gov.uk/resource-library/major-projects-authority-assurance-toolkit* [accessed 4 January 2016].

[21] HM Treasury Procurement Group, *No.1: Essential Requirements for Construction Procurement* (1997); *No.2: Value for Money in Construction Procurement* (1997); *No.3: Appointment of Consultants and Contractors* (1997); *No.4: Teamworking, Partnering and Incentives* (1997); *No.5: Procurement Strategies* (1997).

[22] *Value for Money*, para.3.1.

of those managing the project.[23] There was detailed guidance on matters such as risk management, value management, project assessment and the like.[24] The government in addition provides guidance on the UK and EU procurement rules.[25]

There are also *Model Conditions of Contract*. The Central Unit on Procurement, as it then was, produced detailed model conditions for procurement contracts.[26] It was not mandatory for departments to use such conditions, but they were strongly advised to incorporate them in their purchasing and supply manuals. The model conditions spanned over 40 pages and went into great detail. They covered all matters relating to a procurement contract, including: the nature of the contract; the contract period; its commencement; service provision and payment; liabilities; compliance with legal obligations; control of the contract; default, breach and termination; and dispute resolution. The degree to which contracts made by public bodies involve standard conditions will obviously differ depending on the type of public authority involved, but standardised forms of contract have predominated in relation to contracts made by the government itself.[27] **5–006**

From 1999–2010 the OGC had, as we have seen, central responsibility for procurement. It developed many of the guides published by institutions that had responsibility for procurement hitherto. Thus, the Procurement Policy Guidelines were updated,[28] and guidelines on best practice, successful delivery, project management and property and construction were published. The OGC also had responsibility for best management practice. These functions are now undertaken by the Cabinet Office.[29]

C. Range of Procurement Options

The government has a range of procurement options at its disposal. Traditional procurement took the form of the government buying in the services it required. The activity would be run in-house, by a government department. The last 30 years witnessed the proliferation of procurement strategies. **5–007**

In institutional terms, the restructuring of government departments has meant that the procuring body may well be an agency rather than a central department of state. In strategic terms, there has been increased emphasis on contracting-out service provision. In financial terms, new ways have been developed to finance government services. The government emphasises the most effective procurement strategy for the project at hand. Thus, the guidance on construction

[23] *Value for Money*, para.5.

[24] *Value for Money*, Appendix A.

[25] See *http://www.cabinetoffice.gov.uk/resource-library/policy-and-standards-framework-%E2%80%93-legal-framework* [accessed 4 January 2016].

[26] HM Treasury Central Unit on Procurement, *No.59D: Documentation: Model Conditions of Contract* (July 1997); P. Craig and M. Tyrbus, "England and Wales", in Noguellou and Stelkens (eds), *Comparative Law on Public Contracts* (2010), pp.338–366.

[27] Turpin, *Government Procurement and Contracts* (1989), pp.105–111.

[28] Office of Government Commerce, *Procurement Policy Guidelines* (2001).

[29] See *http://www.cabinetoffice.gov.uk/resource-library/best-management-practice-bmp-portfolio* [accessed 4 January 2016].

procurement listed the procurement strategies that could be used in this context. These included the Private Finance Initiative, a Private Developer Scheme, a Leased Building, Crown build, new build and refurbishment.[30]

D. Contract and Government Contracts

5–008 The eclectic nature of government contract principles is peculiarly English. The unwillingness to codify reflects our dislike of the rigidity that can be attendant upon such reform. There are clearly advantages in the flexibility of the present system. However, standard terms can save costs. They can, moreover, be easily reviewed to take account of changing circumstances, or the needs of a particular contract. The ordinary principles of contract play only a limited role in this area, and solutions will normally be decided pursuant to standard government contract terms.[31]

Street[32] suggested nonetheless that certain issues central to the contract such as agency, building, appropriations, supervision, direction and power to amend, should be enshrined in a Governments Contracts Act. Other less immutable terms should be applied to a contract by delegated legislation, thereby preserving a balance between flexibility, certainty and accessibility. Davies has also called for codification of the contracting power.[33]

Turpin, on the other hand, contended that the present system was not less satisfactory than those in other countries, which formally recognise a separate body of government contract law.[34] He did, however, suggest that the revision of standard forms should only be undertaken after proper consultation with representative organisations of contractors, and that more substantial changes in the regime of government contracting should be open to wider public scrutiny.[35] This reflects the fact that "contract … is a kind of treaty by which the conditions of a relationship of interdependence between government and its suppliers are established" and this is "something of legitimate concern to the public".[36] Thus, while internal management systems are necessary to oversee the operation of government contracts, these must be supplemented by "arrangements for external political accountability that are proper to governmental functions in a parliamentary democracy".[37]

---

30 HM Treasury Procurement Group, *No.1: Essential Requirements for Construction Procurement* (1997), p.20 and *No.5: Procurement Strategies* (1997); OGC, *Procurement and Contract Strategies, Achieving Excellence in Construction Procurement Guide* (2007).

31 Craig and Trybus, "England and Wales", in Noguellou and Stelkens (eds), *Comparative Law on Public Contracts* (2010).

32 Street, *Governmental Liability* (1953), pp.104–105.

33 A. Davies, "Ultra Vires Problems in Government Contracts" (2006) 122 L.Q.R. 98, 104.

34 Turpin, *Government Procurement and Contracts* (1989), p.114.

35 Turpin, *Government Procurement and Contracts* (1989), p.114.

36 Turpin, *Government Procurement and Contracts* (1989), p.258.

37 Turpin, *Government Procurement and Contracts* (1989), p.260.

3. TOWARDS "BETTER GOVERNMENT": CONTRACT AND SERVICE PROVISION BY CENTRAL GOVERNMENT

5–009 The government has always made contracts to purchase goods and services. There has, however, been increased use of contractual language over a broader area in the last 30 years.[38] We have already seen how contractual ideas influenced the relationship between executive agencies and their sponsoring departments, even though there is no real contract because the agency possesses no separate legal personality. Contractual themes have also had a marked impact upon other areas such as the Health Service.[39] The principal concern here is the use of contracting-out as a method of providing public services, and the links between this and the regime for executive agencies.

A. Contracting-Out: Initial Conservative Policy

5–010 The connection between the present topic and the previous chapter should be made clear at the outset. The Conservative government's approach to institutional reform included not only the hiving-off of functions to agencies, but also contracting-out. When a department reviewed its existing activities it considered five options. The activity could be abolished, privatised, contracted-out, given to a Next Steps agency or the status quo could be maintained. Market Testing[40] was a key criterion for deciding between these options.[41] The previous chapter discussed the implications of choosing the agency route. This chapter focuses on the consequences of adopting the contracting-out option.

It should however be made clear that the contracting-out option applied to activities performed in-house and to those for which agencies were responsible. The five choices mentioned above applied to a *general* sphere of activity. It might, for example, be decided to create an agency for the payment of social welfare benefits. It might be decided to preserve some of the more general policy matters in the social welfare field in-house. Contracting-out as an option was considered for more *particular* activities *irrespective* of whether they were done by the agency or the department itself.

The *reasons for* contracting-out are said to be that[42]: public sector "in-house" monopolies are inefficient, with low productivity; there is "open-ended" financial commitment to public sector "in-house" units and such units do not take sufficient account of costs; competition generates new ideas, techniques, etc. and contractors can be penalised for defective performance and late delivery.

The *reasons against* contracting-out are said to be that: private contractors are unreliable, and may well default; contractors use low bids to eliminate the

---

[38] M. Freedland, "Government by Contract and Private Law" [1994] P.L. 86.

[39] D. Longley, *Public Law and Health Service Accountability* (Open University Press, 1992); Harden, *The Contracting State* (1992); Davies, *Accountability: A Public Law Analysis of Government by Contract* (2001).

[40] The Citizen's Charter, *First Report* (1992), Cm.2101, pp.60–64.

[41] *The Government's Guide to Market Testing* (1993).

[42] K. Hartley and M. Huby, "Contracting-Out Policy: Theory and Evidence", in J. Kay, C. Mayer and D. Thompson (eds), *Privatization and Regulation—The UK Experience* (Oxford: Oxford University Press, 1986), p.289.

in-house capacity, thereby making the public body dependent on a private monopoly; competitive tendering entails monitoring costs; and private contractors in areas such as the Health Service can place patients at risk.

B. Contracting-Out: Labour Strategy

5–011 A consistent theme in the Blair/Brown Labour government strategy for service delivery was the search for "better" government, or "better" quality in the provision of services. While the Labour government distanced itself from the more extreme implications of the previous government's market-oriented strategy, it adopted much of the same general strategic thinking.

This is exemplified by its approach towards service delivery at the central level, which was set out in its document on *Better Quality Services, Guidance for Senior Managers*.[43] The objective was said to be "better" government. Competition was not the only option, and value for money meant better quality services at optimal cost.[44] Twelve guiding principles were laid down, which were to be used when market testing and contracting-out. The most important of these were: development of modern, high quality, efficient, responsive and customer-focused central government services; partnerships with the private sector were encouraged; market testing and contracting-out were to be used when they offered better value for money; ministers should remain accountable for services contracted-out to the private sector; and staff were trained to carry out market testing, contracting-out, benchmarking, and restructuring. Each department had to review its activities within a five-year period,[45] to decide which of the five options to pursue[46]: the service could be abolished; it could be restructured internally after benchmarking; the service could be contracted-out, after competition between external bidders; there could be market testing, which involved an in-house team bidding against external bidders; or the service could be privatised if it did not need to be undertaken by the government.

5–012 The Labour government's strategy for service delivery moved on in its second term in office. Service delivery in key areas such as health and education was central to the government's aims. This was reflected in the creation of the Office of Public Services Reform (OPSR) and the Delivery Unit within the Prime Minister's Office. The strategy for service delivery was informed by four principles.[47] There were to be *national standards* with targets for schools, hospitals, the police and local government. There was to be *devolution and delegation* to front line professionals to achieve these targets. The service providers were to have *flexibility* as to the manner in which to improve services. Consumers were afforded choice as to the type of public services delivered. In Labour's third term of office, the work of the OPSR was taken forward by the Cabinet Office.

---

[43] Cabinet Office, *Better Quality Services, Guidance for Senior Managers* (1998).

[44] Cabinet Office, *Better Quality Services, Guidance for Senior Managers*, paras 2–3.

[45] Cabinet Office, *Better Quality Services, Guidance for Senior Managers*, para.7.

[46] Cabinet Office, *Better Quality Services, Guidance for Senior Managers*, para.9.

[47] Office of Public Services Reform, *Reforming our Public Services, Principles into Practice* (2002).

The Treasury was also integral to the attainment of service delivery goals. It administered Public Service Agreements (PSAs), which set out commitments on what the public could expect for their money, and which minister was responsible for delivery of the relevant target. PSAs were underpinned by Delivery Agreements (DAs), in which government departments explained how they would achieve the targets in the PSAs.

C. Contracting-Out: Coalition and Conservative Government Strategy

The 2010–15 Coalition government's approach to contracting-out and service provision differed yet again. It was strongly influenced by the need to save money in the light of the financial crisis, as exemplified by the focus on the Green Efficiency Review.[48] The approach to public service delivery has however also been driven by more general policy beliefs of the Coalition government. **5–013**

This is readily apparent in the 2011 White Paper on *Open Public Services*.[49] The policy on public service delivery was predicated on the "failure" of centralised control. Five principles were central to Coalition government thinking: increase choice wherever possible; public services should be decentralised to the lowest appropriate level; public services should be open to a range of providers; fair access to public services; and public services should be accountable to users and to taxpayers. The White Paper applied these principles to three types of public service: individual services, such as adult social care and childcare, used by people on an individual basis; neighbourhood services provided locally on a collective, rather than an individual basis, such as leisure and recreation facilities; and commissioned services, which are local and national services that cannot be devolved to individuals or communities, such as tax collection, prisons, emergency healthcare or welfare to work.

Contracting-out in the broad sense of the term is still central to attainment of the government's strategy.[50] Thus, the White Paper made clear that just because commissioned services must be decided by government did not mean that the principles of choice, decentralisation, diversity, fairness and accountability should not apply. To the contrary, the principles of open public services "will switch the default from one where the state provides the service itself to one where the state commissions the service from a range of diverse providers".[51] This purchaser/provider split encourages "new, innovative providers to compete for contracts". The general principle in the White Paper is that apart from those public services where the government has a special reason to operate a monopoly, such as the military, "every public service should be open so that, in line with

[48] Sir Philip Green, *Efficiency Review* (2010), available at: *http://www.cabinetoffice.gov.uk/sites/default/files/resources/sirphilipgreenreview.pdf* [accessed 4 January 2016].

[49] White Paper, *Open Public Services* (2011), Cm.8145, available at *http://www.openpublicservices.cabinetoffice.gov.uk/* [accessed 4 January 2016].

[50] See *https://www.gov.uk/government/organisations/open-public-services/about* [accessed 4 January 2016].

[51] White Paper, *Open Public Services*, para.5.2. See also, *Open Public Services 2014*, available at *https://www.gov.uk/government/publications/open-public-services-2014-progress-report/open-public-services-2014* [accessed 4 January 2016].

people's demands, services can be delivered by a diverse range of providers".[52] The list of providers includes the public sector, the voluntary and community sector, and the private sector.

D. Contracting-Out: Problems and Concerns

5–014 An appropriate place to begin is with the *issue of principle*: are there activities that should not be contracted-out? Should certain types of service only be run by the state *stricto sensu*? If so, which services would be placed within this category, the police, adjudication, prisons? The latter have in fact already been contracted-out to some degree. So too have some aspects of the court process, such as the movement of prisoners.

If an activity is contracted-out are there problems of *accountability*? The answer is both yes and no. Clearly the very fact that the activity has been contracted-out, rather than being privatised, means that the state has responsibility for its provision. There is however a danger that a contractor, who was intended only to "execute" a chosen policy, may influence the policy itself. It can nonetheless be argued that these very contracts, like the framework documents used in agency creation, sharpen accountability by defining goals, setting targets and monitoring performance. This does not mean that we should be complacent about accountability in this context. Techniques have to be fashioned to fit the new order. An interesting suggestion has been to distinguish between three senses of accountability: programme, process and fiscal.[53] These techniques of control are not, however, self-executing. They require positive input from the government side. In order that programmes can be made accountable, government must be as clear as possible in the terms of the contract as to what it requires of the contractor. Management within government must also be capable of assessing the completed work. Where the preceding techniques of control operate effectively contract can be a beneficial way of structuring administrative discretion. As Harden states[54]:

> "Although contract is not a panacea for the problem of discretion, it does offer an opportunity to make real progress towards greater accountability by clearly identifying who is responsible for a policy, what it is, whether it is being carried out in practice and if not, why not."

At a more practical level there are *organisational* concerns. Can contracting-out function with sufficient *flexibility*, given that the demand for certain public services may fluctuate either due to market factors, or because of shifts in governmental policy? How far does contracting-out produce problems of *integration*: are there difficulties of ensuring a coherent, integrated service when some parts of the whole are operated by private undertakings, while others are performed in-house? As Harden notes[55]:

---

[52] White Paper, *Open Public Services*, para.6.1.

[53] A. Robinson, "Government Contracting for Academic Research: Accountability in the American Experience", in B. Smith and D. Hague (eds), *The Dilemma of Accountability in Modern Government* (London: Macmillan, 1971), Ch.3.

[54] Harden, *The Contracting State* (1992), p.71.

[55] Harden, *The Contracting State* (1992), p.33.

> "The public interest-i.e. the overall functioning of the public service in question-is not the responsibility of a single unitary organization, but instead emerges from the process of agreement between separate organizations, none of which has responsibility for the public interest as a whole."

Closely related to the organisational concerns are those relating to *personnel*. There are a number of different dimensions to this problem. There are the complexities involved with the Transfer of Undertakings Regulations where employees are transferred to a private firm. There is concern about the morale of those within the department who fear for their jobs. There is concern about the impact of contracting-out on the broader work ethic of the public service. When work is contracted-out to private firms they will not normally have a "public service ethos", but will be principally concerned with the interests of their shareholders.[56]

E. Contracting-Out: Contract Formation and Legal Principle

The agreements made as a result of contracting-out are legal contracts. There is a legally binding obligation between two entities with separate legal status. This raises important issues of legal principle. **5–015**

i. Contracting-out: contract creation

The first relates to the creation of the contract. This is subject to the EU law regime on public procurement, which was extended to cover services.[57] There are provisions relating to the competitive process, and the criterion for choosing to whom the contract should be awarded. Transparency is safeguarded by requirements as to publicity and reasoned decision-making. There will be more detailed examination of these rules below.[58] **5–016**

ii. Contracting-out: legal foundations

It is important to consider the legal foundation for contracting-out. Part II of the Deregulation and Contracting-out Act 1994 makes provision for the contracting-out of certain functions by government to bodies which will normally be private. Government departments have frequently contracted-out functions independently of this Act. The statute was passed in order to enable the body to which the power has been contracted-out to operate in the name of the minister, by analogy with the *Carltona* principle.[59] **5–017**

Section 69 enables functions which, by virtue of any enactment or rule of law, can be performed by an officer of a minister, to be contracted-out to an authorised party, and s.70 contains an analogous provision for contracting-out by local

[56] D. Faulkner, "Public Services, Citizenship, and the State—The British Experience 1967–97", in M. Freedland and S. Sciarra (eds), *Public Services and Citizenship in European Law, Public and Labour Law Perspectives* (Oxford: Oxford University Press, 1998), pp.42–44.

[57] Council Directive 92/50.

[58] See below, 5-033 to 5–037.

[59] Ch.18.

authorities.[60] Section 69(5)(c) makes it clear that the minister may still exercise the function to which the authorisation relates. Section 71 imposes limits on the functions that can be contracted-out. Section 72(2) is designed to render the minister ultimately responsible for action taken by the body to which the power has been contracted-out, although the meaning of this particular section is not free from doubt. It is clear from s.72(3)(b) that s.72(2) does not apply in respect of any criminal proceedings brought against the person to whom the power has been contracted-out. The precise import of s.72(3)(a) is far less clear.[61] This states that s.72(2) does not apply "for the purposes of so much of the contract made between the authorised person and the Minister, office-holder or local authority as relates to the exercise of the function".

We are therefore faced with an increasingly complex picture in relation to contracting-out as a whole. Contracting-out has been a feature of governmental policy for some time, and has often been undertaken without any statutory foundation. The Deregulation and Contracting-out Act is facultative not mandatory: a minister *may* provide for a function to be contracted-out using the provisions of the Act. There are therefore at least two tracks a department can follow if it wishes to contract-out. It can do so independently of the Act, or it can do so by promoting an order under the Act. The picture is rendered more complex by the existence of particular provisions for contracting-out in other legislation, which contain rules on contracting-out for specific services, such as prisons.

iii. Contracting-out: application of public law principles

5–018 It is also important to consider whether public law principles are applicable to contracted-out activities. If the department or agency is fulfilling a statutory function, then it will be subject to public law principles. If it chooses to fulfil part of that statutory remit by contracting-out to a private undertaking it would be contrary to principle for the citizens' protections to be reduced through this organisational choice. While the department or agency may still be subject to public law, it may be difficult to show that it has broken such principles where the activity has been contracted-out.[62] It is therefore important to decide whether the private party to whom the activity has been contracted-out is subject to public law. The courts have however been reluctant to hold that such private parties are subject to the Human Rights Act 1998,[63] or to the procedures for judicial review.[64] This is regrettable,[65] and the courts' reasoning will be examined below.[66]

---

[60] *De Winter Heald v Brent LBC* [2010] 1 W.L.R. 990.

[61] See below, 18-006 to 18–010.

[62] *R. v Servite Houses and the London Borough of Wandsworth Council Ex p. Goldsmith and Chatting* (2000) 2 L.G.L.R. 997.

[63] *Poplar Housing and Regeneration Community Association Ltd v Donoghue* [2002] Q.B. 48; *R. v Leonard Cheshire Foundation (A Charity)* [2002] 2 All E.R. 936; *YL v Birmingham City Council* [2007] 3 W.L.R. 112.

[64] *Servite* (2000) 2 L.G.L.R. 997.

[65] P. Craig, "Contracting-Out, the Human Rights Act and the Scope of Judicial Review" (2002) 118 L.Q.R. 551.

[66] See 27–025 to 27–028.

iv. *Contracting-out: legal responsibility*

There is in addition the issue of ascription of *legal responsibility* for activities that have been contracted-out. If a tort is committed against an individual by a prison officer who works in a prison, the running of which has been contracted-out to a private firm, the prison officer would be individually liable and the private employer would be subject to vicarious liability. It is less clear whether an action could be maintained against the department that had contracted-out the work. This will be important if the private firm is insolvent. **5–019**

A court might interpret the governing statute as imposing a duty, the legal responsibility for which could not ultimately be delegated to another. Thus, the department could contract-out the activity if it wished to do so as a matter of organisational choice, but this would not divest it of legal responsibility. It might alternatively decide that the department satisfied its legal responsibility if it took due care in the appointment of the independent contractor.[67]

4. PUBLIC PRIVATE PARTNERSHIPS, THE PRIVATE FINANCE INITIATIVE AND PF2: CONTRACT AND SERVICE PROVISION BY CENTRAL GOVERNMENT

The discussion thus far has focused on the way in which services are delivered by central government, and governmental approaches to contracting-out. The discussion of service delivery would be incomplete if it did not address Public Private Partnerships (PPPs) and the Private Finance Initiative (PFI).[68] Lest anybody should doubt the importance of this topic it is salutary to realise that in March 2006 the capital value of PFI agreements in the pipeline was in excess of £26 billion[69] and £35 billion in 2011–12. **5–020**

In terms of *history*, PFI dates back to 1992 and statements of the Chancellor of the Exchequer, which were designed to encourage the provision of public services through the use of private capital funding. The PFI was fully embraced by the Labour government.[70] When it took office in May 1997 it launched a review of PFI, the Bates Review. It recommended a streamlined procedure, which was accepted by the government. There was a further review to improve the use of private sector finance in relation to public projects.[71] The Labour government reaffirmed its commitment to PFI in 2006.[72] It would be used only where it could demonstrate value for money and was likely to continue to comprise around 10–15 per cent of total investment in public services.[73]

---

[67] *Quaquah v Group 4 Securities Ltd (No.2)* [2001] Prison L.R. 318. The case did not however involve contracting out pursuant to the 1994 Act.

[68] HM Treasury, *The Private Finance Initiative—Breaking New Ground* (1993); HM Treasury, *Private Opportunity, Public Benefit—Progressing the Private Finance Initiative* (1995).

[69] HM Treasury, *PFI: Strengthening Long Term Partnerships* (2006).

[70] Treasury Taskforce, *Partnerships for Prosperity—The Private Finance Initiative* (1997).

[71] Treasury Task Force, *Geoffrey Robinson Unveils Second Significant Projects List* (1998); Treasury Task Force, *Geoffrey Robinson Announces Second Review for the Private Finance Initiative* (November 1998).

[72] HM Treasury, *PFI: Strengthening Long Term Partnerships*, p.1.

[73] HM Treasury, *PFI: Meeting the Investment Challenge* (2003).

The current government has continued to use PPPs, with the Treasury in overall control. The PPP policy team was located in Infrastructure UK within the Treasury,[74] which became the Infrastructure and Major Projects Authority on January 1 2016.[75]

It is important to be clear about *the meaning of PPPs and PFI*. PPPs are a key element in the government's strategy for delivery of high quality public services.[76] They cover a range of business structures and partnership arrangements, from PFI to sale of equity stakes in state-owned businesses. PFI is therefore one species of PPP. The idea is that the government decides between competing objectives, defines the standards required and safeguards the wider public interest.[77] The private sector brings the discipline of the market place, a focus on customer requirements, management expertise and innovation.[78]

5–021 Freedland helpfully identified *three main species of PPPs*.[79] The first is where the private sector provides capital assets the use of which is then paid for by the public sector. This is exemplified by the private sector funding the building of a prison, offices, classrooms and the like, which are then rented by a public body. The second is where a public service such as a bridge or a road is built by the private sector, which then is entitled to the tolls from users. Much public infrastructure in the nineteenth century was run in this fashion. There can, thirdly, be areas where the asset provided by the private sector will be paid for partly by rent from the public body and partly by payments from the public. The more particular form of PPPs will vary depending upon the type of project in question.

There are *two rationales* underlying PPPs and PFI. In micro-economic terms,

> "governments which are in general enthusiastic about privatisation and liberalisation of public services see advantage in private finance contracting because they believe that public services can in general be provided more efficiently by means of such contracting than by means of direct provision by public authorities".[80]

In macro-economic terms, "such governments also perceive private finance contracting as a way of minimising or deferring immediate apparent public spending or borrowing requirements",[81] in much the same way that a private person will take a mortgage rather than pay cash for the house now. This is all the more attractive for government given that PFI deals augment public sector investment and stand alongside conventionally funded capital spending.

---

[74] See *http://webarchive.nationalarchives.gov.uk/20130129110402/http://www.hm-treasury.gov.uk/ppp_policy_team.htm* [accessed 4 January 2016].

[75] See *https://www.gov.uk/government/news/new-government-body-to-help-manage-and-deliver-major-projects-for-uk-economy* [accessed 4 January 2016].

[76] HM Treasury, *Public Private Partnerships: The Government's Approach* (2000).

[77] HM Treasury, *Public Private Partnerships: The Government's Approach*, pp.10–11.

[78] HM Treasury, *Public Private Partnerships: The Government's Approach*, pp.11–12.

[79] M. Freedland, "Public Law and Private Finance—Placing the Private Finance Initiative in a Public Law Frame" [1998] P.L. 288, 290–291.

[80] Freedland, "Public Law and Private Finance—Placing the Private Finance Initiative in a Public Law Frame" [1998] P.L. 288, 298–299.

[81] Freedland, "Public Law and Private Finance—Placing the Private Finance Initiative in a Public Law Frame" [1998] P.L. 288, 299.

The *administration of PPPs and PFI* is shared. Most major government departments will have a group responsible for PPP projects coming within its remit. The Treasury provides the overall direction on policy in this area. It was assisted by Partnerships UK, which was itself a form of PPP, but it was closed down in 2011. HM Revenue and Customs also provide input.[82]

PFI agreements are real contracts, the terms of which are set out in considerable detail. There is a standardised form of PFI contract.[83] The objectives are to promote a common understanding of the risks in a standard PFI project; to engender consistency across similar projects; and to reduce the time and costs of negotiation. The standardised contract addresses a whole range of issues that are central to PFI agreements. Guidance is provided on: the duration of the agreement; its commencement; incentives to timely service commencement; delay; service availability; service maintenance; performance monitoring; payment mechanisms; the effect of change in the law; the possibility of price variation; and termination of the agreement. **5–022**

There were *reforms to the PPP regime in 2012-13.* Freedland had rightly noted the danger of private contractors "acquiring large commercial interests in the way that those decision-making powers are exercised, even though those powers remain, nominally at least, in the hands of the public authorities".[84] There were also concerns as to the financial value of the deals that were made. This led to a wide-ranging review in 2012, in which the Treasury noted the shortcomings of the PFI regime, which included windfall gains for investors, failure to deliver value for money, excessive risk borne by government and lack of transparency. While the government remains committed to making use of private sector finance, the review led to revisions of the PPP regime and the birth of what is termed PF2, a central feature of which is that the government acts as a minority equity co-investor in future projects.[85]

---

[82] See *http://www.hmrc.gov.uk/thelibrary/manuals.htm* [accessed 4 January 2016].

[83] HM Treasury, *Standardisation of PFI Contracts*, Version 4 (2007), available at: *http://webarchive.nationalarchives.gov.uk/20130129110402/http://www.hm-treasury.gov.uk/ppp_standardised_contracts.htm* [accessed 4 January 2016].

[84] Freedland, "Public Law and Private Finance—Placing the Private Finance Initiative in a Public Law Frame" [1998] P.L. 288, 307.

[85] HM Treasury, *A New Approach to Public-Private Partnerships* (2012); Infrastructure UK, *PF2: A User Guide* (2012); HM Treasury, *Standardisation of PF2 Contracts* (2012), available at: *https://www.gov.uk/government/publications/private-finance-2-pf2*; *https://www.gov.uk/government/consultations/a-new-approach-to-public-private-partnerships-consultation-on-the-terms-of-public-sector-equity-participation-in-pf2-projects* [accessed 4 January 2016].

5. TOWARDS "BEST VALUE": CONTRACT AND SERVICE PROVISION BY LOCAL GOVERNMENT

A. Provision of Local Services: The Market and the Conservative Government's Approach

5–023 The Conservative government's approach to the provision of local services was, not surprisingly, imbued with the same market ethos that it applied to service provision by central government.[86] This was overlaid by measures designed to restrict local financial autonomy. This strategy was implemented in three main ways.

i. *Competitive procedures*

5–024 Local authorities had an obligation to employ competitive procedures in the award of their contracts. The Local Government Act 1972 s.135 requires such authorities to promulgate standing orders which make provision for competitive procedures when contracts are awarded. There are financial thresholds for the obligation to bite. The objectives are to ensure value for money and to help to prevent the improper allocation of valuable contracts.

ii. *Exclusion of non-commercial considerations*

5–025 The Conservative government enacted legislation aimed at preventing local authorities from taking non-commercial considerations into account when awarding contracts. Section 17 of the Local Government Act 1988 prevented public authorities from taking into account non-commercial matters when exercising their power to make contracts. The secretary of state could however make an order that a matter should cease to be a non-commercial consideration for these purposes.[87]

Non-commercial matters are defined in s.17(5). A public authority cannot take account of any of the following matters: the terms and conditions of employment by contractors of their workers; whether the terms on which contractors contract with their sub-contractors constitute, in the case of contracts with individuals, contracts for the provision by them as self-employed persons of their services only; any involvement of the business activities of contractors with irrelevant fields of government policy; the conduct of contractors or their workers in industrial disputes; the country or territory or origin of supplies to, or the location in any country of the business activities of contractors; any political, industrial or sectarian affiliations of contractors or employees; the fact of financial support given to or withheld from an institution to which the public authority gives or withholds support; and use or non-use by contractors of technical or professional services provided by the authority under certain building legislation.

---

[86] I. Leigh, *Law, Politics and Local Democracy* (Oxford: Oxford University Press, 2000), Ch.10.

[87] Local Government Act 1999 s.19; Local Government Best Value (Exclusion of Non-commercial Considerations) Order 2001 (SI 909/2001).

The legislation is fierce in respect of enforcement. If a public authority asks any question relating to a non-commercial matter, or includes such a matter in a draft contract, it will be deemed to have made its decisions on that forbidden ground. It cannot, moreover, escape s.17 merely by "keeping quiet" and basing its decision on a non-commercial ground, because the disappointed contractor has a right to a reasoned decision as to why it was not chosen.[88] It may be difficult to formulate such reasons without revealing a "forbidden" consideration. The aggrieved contractor can seek judicial review of the public authority's decision, and also damages. The damages remedy is limited to reliance type losses: expenditure reasonably incurred for the purpose of submitting the tender.

The legislation was part of the more general Conservative ethos that the "market" should govern allocative decisions wherever possible. The principal difficulty with applying the legislation arises from the breadth of the non-commercial considerations. It is easy to envisage situations in which a public authority may wish to ask a question concerning a precluded matter because it believes that it will affect the commercial viability of the tender submitted. If, for example, a contractor obtains supplies from, or is located in, a country that is politically unstable this will affect its ability to deliver the goods on schedule. Such an inquiry is, however, precluded by the legislation.[89] 5–026

The courts are faced with a difficult choice. They can apply s.17(5) "formalistically" with the consequence that the authority will be prevented from choosing the bid that really was the best in commercial terms. They can, alternatively, hear such arguments, with the consequence that the peremptory force of s.17(5) will be weakened. Public authorities will then be able to argue that they are considering s.17(5) matters only in so far as they relate to the commercial viability of the tender.

The arguments *in favour of such legislation* are as follows. The ability to award contracts gives considerable power to public authorities and should not be used for improper purposes. If there were no restrictions on an authority's contracting power it could pursue a policy that might have no legislative sanction, which might be unrelated to the objective for which the contracting power was granted. To allow authorities unrestricted freedom could also lead to regional variations in the criteria applied for contract awards, and these criteria might not be known to prospective contractors. Covert blacklists might exist. Central legislation which establishes contracting criteria facilitates the judicial task of deciding whether the conditions employed by a particular authority are valid or not, rather than leaving the matter to be dealt with through ad hoc applications of tests such as improper purposes or unreasonableness.[90]

The arguments *against such legislation*, or against legislation as broad as s.17(5), are as follows. Contracts made by public bodies should not be viewed solely as commercial bargains. The power to grant contracts should be able to be used to advance socially desirable objectives, because such authorities cannot and should not be politically neutral towards such matters. It may not always be possible to 5–027

[88] Local Government Act 1988 s.20.

[89] Local Government Act 1988 s.17(5)(e).

[90] *R. v Lewisham LBC, Ex p. Shell UK Ltd* [1988] 1 All E.R. 938.

pass legislation that enshrines such objectives,[91] and even where this has been done, contracting power may be an effective method of enforcing such legislative norms.[92] The existence of some regional variations in contracting criteria is on this view a natural corollary of local autonomy, which should be respected. This should be upheld against the centralising tendencies of government legislation that establishes criteria to be applied by all public authorities. This second view does not deny the need for some constraints on contracting power. It would clearly be wrong to blacklist a contractor because it held different political views from that of the authority. Subject to such constraints it should, however, be open to an authority to decide, for example, to employ a local firm which will give employment to the area even if it does not submit the lowest tender. The line between pursuit of acceptable and unacceptable policies would then have to be determined upon an ad hoc basis through techniques such as propriety of purpose or unreasonableness. It is however noteworthy that s.17(11) has been added by the Public Services (Social Value) Act 2012, the effect of which is to require a local authority to consider how what is proposed to be procured might improve the economic, social and environmental well-being of the relevant area; and how, in conducting the procurement process, it might act with a view to securing that improvement.

iii. Contracting-out and compulsory competitive tendering

5–028 The Conservative market-oriented strategy stretched beyond the commitment to ensuring that procurement was based on commercial considerations. It extended to the decision whether a service should be performed "in house", or whether it should be "contracted-out" to a private undertaking. The objective was to further market-based practices in order to ensure that the activity was undertaken most efficiently, whether in-house or through a private firm.

The Local Government Planning and Land Act 1980 Pt III, made compulsory tendering a requirement for local authorities. The regime was extended by the Local Government Act 1988, the Local Government Act 1992 and secondary legislation. The 1988 Act s.2, imposed contracting-out obligations in relation to matters such as refuse collection, street cleaning, vehicle maintenance and some aspects of catering. This list was augmented as a result of powers exercised by the secretary of state, who could act against authorities that did not comply with the CCT competition rules. The exercise of this power was subject to judicial review, but the courts interpreted the secretary of state's discretionary powers broadly.[93]

[91] T. Daintith, "The Executive Power Today: Bargaining and Economic Control", in J. Jowell and D. Oliver (eds), *The Changing Constitution* (Oxford: Oxford University Press, 1985), Ch.8.

[92] See Religious and Political Discrimination and Equality of Opportunity in Northern Ireland, *Report on Fair Employment* (1987), Cm.237.

[93] *R. v Secretary of State for the Environment, Ex p. London Borough of Haringey* [1994] C.O.D. 518.

B. Provision of Local Services: "Best Value" and the Labour Government's Approach

The Labour government moved away from CCT and towards service provision based on "Best Value",[94] as developed in *Modernising Local Government: Improving Local Services through Best Value*.[95] The Best Value strategy was designed to secure the efficient and effective provision of local services, while preserving greater local autonomy and choice. The CCT regime was abolished because it led to the neglect of service quality; the efficiency gains were uneven; it was inflexible; and because the compulsion which underpinned the system bred antagonism.[96] 5–029

The Local Government Act 1999 enshrined the central elements of this strategy. Compulsory Competitive Tendering was abolished,[97] and replaced by the concept of best value. Local authorities and a number of other public bodies are best value authorities.[98] A best value authority (BVA) must make arrangements to improve the way in which its functions are exercised, having regard to economy, efficiency and effectiveness.[99] The 1999 Act provided for performance indicators set by the secretary of state by reference to which a BVA's performance could be measured and for performance standards to be met by BVAs.[100] It stipulated that BVAs should conduct best value reviews in accordance with an order made by the secretary of state specifying the matters to be taken into account.[101] The BVAs were in addition obliged to prepare a best value performance plan for each financial year, subject to guidance or an order made by the secretary of state.[102]

The best value regime was modified and "softened" in later legislation. The Local Government and Public Involvement in Health Act 2007[103] removed certain obligations in the 1999 Act from English local authorities. The secretary of state's power to specify performance indicators and standards for best value authorities and the duties of such local authorities to prepare best value reviews and performance plans, have been abolished. The rationale for these changes was to reduce the regulatory burden that the 1999 Act imposed on local authorities.[104]

---

[94] P. Vincent-Jones, *The New Public Contracting: Regulation, Responsiveness, Relationality* (2006); P. Vincent-Jones, "Responsive Law and Governance in Public Services Provision: A Future for the Local Contracting State" (1998) 61 M.L.R. 362, and "Central–Local Relations under the Local Government Act 1999: A New Consensus" (2000) 63 M.L.R. 84.

[95] Department of the Environment, Transport and the Regions, *Modernising Local Government: Improving Local Services through Best Value* (1997).

[96] Department of the Environment, Transport and the Regions, *Modernising Local Government: Improving Local Services through Best Value*, para.1.5.

[97] Local Government Act 1999 s.21.

[98] Local Government Act 1999 s.1.

[99] Local Government Act 1999 s.3(1).

[100] Local Government Act 1999 s.4.

[101] Local Government Act 1999 s.5(1).

[102] Local Government Act 1999 s.6(1).

[103] Local Government and Public Involvement in Health Act 2007 ss.139–140.

[104] Department for Communities and Local Government, Strong and Prosperous Communities, *The Local Government White Paper Implementation Plan: One Year On* (2007), paras 22 and 26–27.

5–030 The schema in the Local Government Act 1999 was but part of the overall strategy for improved service delivery by local authorities. There were other parts of this strategy, such as Local Area Agreements (LAAs), whereby performance targets were agreed between central and local government on all outcomes delivered by local government alone or in partnership. The Local Government and Public Involvement in Health Act 2007 placed LAAs on a statutory footing.[105] It imposed a duty on all upper tier authorities to prepare an LAA. There was also the Beacon Council Scheme, whereby local authorities could apply for recognition as beacon councils, in recognition of their excellence in relation to service delivery. The regime for service delivery contained in addition provision for Local Public Service Agreements,[106] whereby a local authority committed itself to targets that required performance over and beyond what would otherwise have been expected, for which it received financial reward. The final element in the schema was the Comprehensive Performance Assessment (CPA), which rated local authorities in terms of their quality of service delivery.[107]

C. Provision of Local Services: Beyond "Best Value", the Coalition and Conservative Governments

5–031 The 2010-2015 Coalition government's approach was a blend of continuity and change, and this remains so for the Conservative government. The Local Government Act 1999 remains in force, as does some of the Local Government and Public Involvement in Health Act 2007, although the duty to prepare LAAs has been repealed as part of the drive to lift regulatory burdens from society.[108] The efficiency-driven tools from the 1999 and 2007 legislation have not surprisingly been retained, because of the need to cut costs in the light of the financial crisis.

There are nonetheless differences in government thinking about local service delivery from that existing hitherto. This is apparent from the White Paper on *Open Public Services*,[109] read together with the Localism Act 2011. It is clear that the five principles from the White Paper apply just as much to delivery of services at local level, as they do when services are provided by central government. The substance of the White Paper is certainly as relevant to the local as to the central level. Thus, the focus of the discussion on neighbourhood services is on ways in which the five principles in the White Paper can empower local communities through, for example, the community right to purchase assets,

---

[105] Local Government and Public Involvement in Health Act 2007 ss.103–114.

[106] Department of Transport, Local Government and the Regions, *Local Public Service Agreements, New Challenges* (2001); Office of the Deputy Prime Minister, *Building on Success, A Guide to the Second Generation of Local Public Service Agreements* (2003).

[107] Department of Transport, Local Government and the Regions, *Strong Local Leadership—Quality Public Services* (2001), Cm.5327, Ch 3; Audit Commission, *CPA—The Harder Test Framework for 2007* (2007).

[108] Deregulation Act 2015 s.101.

[109] White Paper, *Open Public Services*.

the community right to build and the right given to local/voluntary groups to take over the running of certain local services. These are rights enshrined in, or dealt with by, the Localism Act 2011.

6. THE PRIVATE FINANCE INITIATIVE: CONTRACT AND SERVICE PROVISION BY LOCAL GOVERNMENT

The discussion of the provision of services by central government revealed the interplay between the search for "better government" and the PFI. The same interplay is apparent at the local level. While the Treasury has the principal oversight role in relation to PFI the initiative was carried forward in relation to local authorities by the Department of the Environment, Transport and the Regions (DETR), by the Office of the Deputy Prime Minister and by the Department of Communities and Local Government.[110] The Office of the Deputy Prime Minister published a paper on *Local Government and the Private Finance Initiative*,[111] which set out government thinking in this respect. The reform in PFI, noted above,[112] and the advent of the modified PF2 regime, can also impact on local authorities. **5–032**

Partnerships between the public and the private sectors were said to be central to the government's aims of establishing first-class public services and infrastructure, and promoting economic growth and regeneration.[113] What was required was a system that made the best use of both sectors in effective public/private partnerships (PPPs). The PFI was regarded as integral to such a system by facilitating access to private capital to fund facilities such as schools, roads, stations, museums, police stations and leisure centres. These were commonly known as DBFO schemes, Design, Build, Finance and Operate, where the risks relating to the funding and operation of a capital asset were transferred to the private sector.

The precise nature of the PFI agreement varies depending upon the project. However, as in the case of central government, there is a broad distinction to be drawn between those schemes where the private sector supplier undertakes a capital project which the local authority then pays for the use of, and those schemes where the private supplier is in effect granted a concession and recoups its money direct from charges to the public.[114]

The administration of PFI reflects the general interplay between central and local government in relation to finance. Many of the local projects that might be suited for PFI will only be viable if the local authority can secure additional revenue support from central government. Such support is intended to assist local

---

110 See *http://webarchive.nationalarchives.gov.uk/20120919132719/http://www.communities.gov.uk/localgovernment/localgovernmentfinance/pupprivatepartnership/* [accessed 4 January 2016].

111 Office of the Deputy Prime Minister, *Local Government and the Private Finance Initiative* (1998).

112 5–022.

113 Office of the Deputy Prime Minister, *Local Government and the Private Finance Initiative*, Preface 1.

114 See *https://www.gov.uk/government/publications/private-finance-initiative-pfi-2015-to-2016-indicative-allocations*; *https://www.gov.uk/government/publications/procurement-and-contract-management* [accessed 4 January 2016].

authorities in meeting the service costs of the PFI agreement.[115] The promise of central government support was given in the form of a letter, which set out a level of "PFI credits" issued for that project.

7. PUBLIC PROCUREMENT AND THE EU: CONTRACT AND SERVICE PROVISION BY GOVERNMENT

5–033 The principles considered thus far are those found in domestic law or policy. There are, in addition, EU rules, which stipulate how certain types of contract should be advertised and made.[116] The rules are complex. They are, however, of great practical importance, and also raise interesting conceptual issues. An outline of the main provisions will, therefore, be provided within this section.

A. Object of the EU Rules

5–034 A principal objective of the European Union is to create a single market. Many of the Treaty articles are directed towards this, by prohibiting, for example, trade barriers, tariffs, and quantitative restrictions on the free movement of goods within the European Union. These provisions by themselves are not, however, sufficient to achieve the desired goal. Member States may inhibit free movement by more subtle means than tariff barriers.

They may, for example, discriminate against companies from other Member States that wish to tender for a contract, by favouring their own domestic firms. This may be a particular problem during a recession when a country's instinct may be to put its own industry first, and perhaps second and third, at the expense of more EU-minded goals. This is of economic significance because public procurement accounts for approximately 15 per cent of the gross domestic product of the European Union. If discrimination is not eradicated from this area then the hope of attaining a single market will always remain partially unfulfilled. With this in mind the EU institutions have applied Treaty norms to cases involving public procurement, and have passed directives which address the issue more specifically. These will be considered in turn.

B. Application of the Treaty

5–035 The Treaty articles will be applied to cases involving public procurement where relevant. Thus, in *Commission v Ireland*[117] a water company called for tenders for a project, and specified an Irish national standard for pipes that was met by only

[115] Local Government PFI Annuity Grant Determination (No.1) 2011 [No.31/1934]; *http://webarchive.nationalarchives.gov.uk/20120919132719/http://www.communities.gov.uk/localgovernment/localgovernmentfinance/pupprivatepartnership/centralgovernment/* [accessed 4 January 2016].

[116] Turpin, *Government Procurement and Contracts* (1989); Arrowsmith, *Civil Liability and Public Authorities* (1992), Ch.3 and Arrowsmith, *The Law of Public and Utilities Procurement: Regulation in the UK and the EU* (2014).

[117] *Commission v Ireland* (45/87) [1988] E.C.R. 4929.

one firm, which was also Irish. This was held to be prima facie in breach of what is now art.34 TFEU. This article prohibits quantitative restrictions on the free movement of goods or measures which have an equivalent effect. A different specification of pipe might have been just as good for the job at hand and therefore the requirement in the tender document impeded free movement. The ECJ, in the *Du Pont* case,[118] invalidated a requirement of national legislation that obliged local authorities to obtain a minimum proportion of their supplies from a particular region. Articles 49 and 56 TFEU, which relate to freedom of establishment and freedom to provide services, can also be used in this context. Thus, in *Commission v Italy*[119] it was held that a national rule, whereby only those companies which had a majority of shares owned by the state could tender for certain government contracts, was in breach of these articles.

C. Directives on Public Procurement

i. EU Directives

Notwithstanding the application of the Treaty provisions it has long been acknowledged that more detailed regulation of these areas was needed. To this end the EU enacted directives on Public Works and Public Supplies, which have been in force in the United Kingdom since 1973 and 1978 respectively. These directives were later strengthened: Directive 93/37 for Public Works,[120] Directive 93/36 for Public Supplies,[121] Directive 92/50 for Public Services,[122] Directive 89/665 for Public Sector Remedies,[123] and Directive 93/38 governs Utilities.[124] The current regulatory regime is embodied in two Directives dating from 2004,[125] the first of which relates to public works contracts, public supply contracts, and public service contracts,[126] while the second Directive deals with contracts made by utilities.[127] **5–036**

[118] *Du Pont de Nemours Italiana SpA v Unita Sanitaria Locale, No.2 di Carrara* (21/88) [1990] E.C.R. I–889.

[119] *Commission v Italy* (3/88) [1989] E.C.R. 4035.

[120] [1993] OJ L199/54.

[121] [1993] OJ L199/1.

[122] [1992] OJ L209/1.

[123] [1989] OJ L395/33.

[124] [1993] OJ L199/84.

[125] R. Williams, "The New Procurement Directives of the European Union" (2004) 13 P.P.L.R. 153; S. Arrowsmith, "Implementation of the New EC Procurement Directives and the *Alcatel* Ruling in England and Wales and Northern Ireland: A Review of the New Legislation and Guidance" (2006) 15 P.P.L.R. 86.

[126] Directive 2004/18 of the European Parliament and of the Council of March 31, 2004 on the coordination of procedures for the award of public works contracts, public supply contracts and public service contracts, [2004] OJ L234/114.

[127] Directive 2004/17 of the European Parliament and of the Council of March 31, 2004 coordinating the procurement procedures of entities operating in the water, energy, transport and postal services sectors, [2004] OJ L134/1.

ii. Application in the UK

5–037 Directives dictate the ends that must be reached, while leaving the means to the Member States.[128] The EU directives on public procurement have been given effect in the United Kingdom through secondary legislation, as exemplified by the Public Contracts Regulations 2015,[129] and the Utilities Contracts Regulations 2006.[130] This legislation will, in line with the *Von Colson*[131] principle, have to be construed so as to effectuate the objects of the directives. Space precludes a detailed examination of the entirety of this legislation. The main provisions of the Public Contracts Regulations 2015 will be taken by way of example.

The principal objectives of the EU rules are: to ensure that public contracts above a certain value are advertised, thereby enabling all those in the European Union who are interested to tender for them; to prohibit the use of technical specifications in the contract documents which could favour domestic firms; to mandate procedures for the award of the contract; and to stipulate the substantive criteria for award of the contract itself.

The Public Contracts Regulations apply to *contracting authorities*, which means: the State, regional or local authorities, bodies governed by public law or associations formed by one or more such authorities or one or more such bodies governed by public law, and includes central government authorities, but does not include Her Majesty in her private capacity.[132]

A *public contract* is held to cover[133] public works contracts, public supply contracts and public service contracts. The regulation then defines each type of contract. It only applies if the contract is worth more than a certain amount,[134] but there are provisions designed to prevent the contracting authority from dividing contracts in order to avoid the bite of the regulatory scheme. Subject to this threshold, the regulations pertain whenever a contracting authority offers a public contract other than one which is expressly excluded from the operation of the regulations.

5–038 There are detailed rules which relate to the *technical specifications* permitted in the tender document, the object being to avoid discrimination against non-domestic companies by the specification of standards which can be more easily met by the domestic operator.[135]

A central part of the regulation concerns *procedures*. There are four principal procedures.[136] Under the *open procedure* any interested party can submit a bid; under the *restricted procedure* only those selected by the contracting party can do so; under the *negotiated procedure* the authority negotiates the terms of the contract with one or more persons who are selected by it; while under the *competitive dialogue procedure* a limited number of parties are invited to engage

128 See below, Ch.10.
129 The Public Contracts Regulations 2015 (SI 102/2015).
130 The Utilities Contracts Regulations 2006 (SI 6/2006).
131 *Von Colson & Kamaan v Land Nordrhein-Westfalen* (14/83) [1984] E.C.R. 1891.
132 SI 102/2015 reg.3.
133 SI 102/2015 reg.2.
134 SI 102/2015 regs 5–6.
135 SI 102/2015 reg.47.
136 SI 102/2015 regs 27–30.

in the competitive dialogue, which is used for complex contracts. The open and restricted procedures are regarded as the norm, and there are limits as to when the other two procedures can be used. Notice of intent to seek offers in relation to public works must be publicised in the Official Journal. There are detailed rules which specify when a contractor may be excluded from the tendering process, such as in the event of bankruptcy. The contracting authority is entitled to consider the economic and financial standing of the contractor.

The regulation designates the criteria to be used when *awarding* the contract. This must be on the basis either of the tender which offers the lowest price, or the offer which is the most economically advantageous, taking account of considerations of price, period for completion, running costs, environmental considerations, functional and aesthetic considerations, profitability and technical merit.[137] If the contracting authority intends to apply the economically advantageous test all the criteria must be stated in the contract documentation. It may be lawful to specify a policy objective the contractor should comply with, provided that this is compatible with EU law. But compliance with such an objective is not relevant to the assessment of that contractor's technical capacity to do the work, nor is it part of the actual criteria for deciding upon the award of the contract.[138]

When the contract has been awarded the regulations impose a duty to provide *reasons* as to why a particular contractor has been chosen.[139] This duty is owed to any unsuccessful contractor who requests a reasoned explanation. There is, in addition, an obligation to furnish a more general dossier, which indicates the procedure adopted, the successful applicant, and the reasons for this choice.

A defect of earlier provisions on public procurement was the lack of effective *remedies*. This problem was addressed by Directive 89/665, the Remedies or Compliance Directive, which was amended in 2007. Provisions to effectuate these obligations were incorporated in the relevant UK regulations.[140] There is an action for breach of duty, presumably breach of statutory duty, in civil law. The aggrieved contractor must first tell the contracting authority of the apprehended breach of duty and the intention to bring the action. The court has a number of options: it may issue an interim order, which, in effect, halts the contract award procedure; it may set aside the decision by the contracting authority and it can award damages to the contractor.[141] The choice of remedies can be dependent on whether the contract has been entered into.[142] There are a range of issues concerning the measure of damages.[143] The remedies set out are without **5–039**

[137] SI 102/2015 regs 56, 58, 67–69.

[138] *Gebroeders Beentjers BV v State of the Netherlands* (31/87) [1988] E.C.R. 4635.

[139] SI 102/2015 reg.55.

[140] SI 102/2015 regs 85–104.

[141] *Harmon CFEM Facades (UK) Ltd v Corporate Officer of the House of Commons* (2000) 2 L.G.L.R. 372 QBD.

[142] SI 102/2015 regs 97–98.

[143] S. Arrowsmith, "Enforcing the EC Public Procurement Rules: The Remedies System in England and Wales" (1992) 1 P.P.L.R. 92; *Chaplin v Hicks* [1911] 2 K.B. 786; *Hotson v East Berkshire Health Authority* [1987] 1 A.C. 750; H. Leffler, "Damages Liability for Breach of EC Procurement Law:

prejudice to any other powers of the court. This leaves open the possibility of an application for judicial review,[144] and a damages action for breach of the Treaty or norms made there under.

8. CONTRACT, SERVICE PROVISION AND GOVERNANCE

5–040 The discussion thus far has been concerned with the framing of government procurement policy and the way in which this operates at the central and local level. It is now appropriate to stand back and consider in more general terms the implications of these developments for governance.

A. Contract as an Instrument of Policy

5–041 Governments and public bodies disburse extremely large sums through contracts, and have in the past used such power to attain policy goals other than the provision of goods or services. The power to award contracts has been used to further the Fair Wages Resolution,[145] and policies such as "Buy British". Bargaining has been a not uncommon feature in the planning context, and the award of contracts has been used as a device to secure compliance with anti-inflation policy.[146] The general policy is that procurement power should not be used in this manner, since it would in many instances violate EU law.

The legality of such action has always been debatable. Judicial review may be applied in certain circumstances to the exercise of public contractual power. The precise metes and bounds of judicial review in this context will be considered below.[147] Statute imposes constraints on the considerations that public bodies can take into account when awarding contracts. There are, in addition, EU controls over public procurement. The Treaty imposes constraints on the types of policies which governments can pursue through their contracting power. It is clear, for example, that "Buy British" policies are illegal under EU law, as an impediment to the free movement of goods.[148] The directives, which apply to a wide range of bodies concerned with the award of contracts for works, supply and services, have further restricted the degree to which contracting power can be used to attain other socio-political goals.

Governing Principles and Practical Solutions" (2003) 12 P.P.L.R. 151; M. Bowsher and P. Moser, "Damages for Breach of the EC Public Procurement Rules in the United Kingdom" (2006) 15 P.P.L.R. 195.

144 See, however, *Cookson & Clegg v Ministry of Defence* [2005] EWCA Civ 811; S.H. Bailey, "Judicial Review and Public Procurement Regulations" (2005) 14 P.P.L.R. 291.

145 O. Kahn-Freund, "Legislation through Adjudication, The Legal Aspect of Fair Wages Clauses and Recognised Conditions" (1948) 11 M.L.R. 269, 429.

146 J. Jowell, "Bargaining in Development Control" (1977) J.P.L. 414 and "Limits of Law in Urban Planning" (1977) C.L.P. 63; R. Ferguson and A. Page, "Pay Restraint; The Legal Constraints" (1978) 128 N.L.J 515; T. Daintith, "Regulation by Contract: The New Prerogative" (1979) C.L.P. 41; T. Daintith, "Legal Analysis of Economic Policy" (1982) 9 Jnl. Law & Soc. 191; A. Page, "Public Law and Economic Policy: The United Kingdom Experience" (1982) 9 Jnl. Law & Soc. 225.

147 See Ch.28.

148 *Commission v Ireland* (249/81) [1982] E.C.R. 4005.

The preceding principles are however qualified by the Public Services (Social Value) Act 2012, which requires contracting authorities to consider the economic, environmental and social well-being of their area during the pre-procurement stage of awarding a contract for services. They must consider how what is proposed to be procured might improve the economic, social and environmental well-being of the relevant area; and how, in conducting the procurement process, it might act with a view to securing that improvement. Failure to comply with the duties under this legislation does not however affect the validity of things done to comply with the Public Contracts Regulations.

B. Source and Nature of Executive Power

Daintith[149] distinguished two ways in which government could attain its goals.[150] **5–042** It could do so through what he termed imperium, which was manifest in the ordinary command of law. It could also do so through dominium, which was the use made by government of its power to disburse benefits to those who complied with governmental objectives. There can be limitations and disadvantages in seeking to pursue objectives through the use of imperium. It may be impracticable to draft the necessary legislation, which may be lengthy, complex and uncertain in its impact. Pursuit of objectives through dominium can, by way of contrast, have positive attractions. Where expenditure requires statutory authorisation the legislation will often leave broad discretion to the implementing body. Dominium power can also be used in other ways, such as bargaining and informal agreement. This can facilitate short-term experimentation with policy choices and obviate the need for legislative authorisation. Daintith acknowledged that constitutional problems could occur through use of dominium power, such as when third parties were affected by agreements of which they had no knowledge, or where an individual had no real choice as to whether to enter such an agreement.[151]

There is no single legal response to the many instances in which dominium power is used as opposed to the more formal exercise of governmental power through imperium.[152] There are a number of options at our disposal. These could include process rights for third parties, and for those more directly involved in the bargaining. There could be an obligation to make the transactions more transparent, open and public to those affected by them. There could, as a matter of principle, also be intervention designed to safeguard the legislative process itself, by stipulating that if the executive wishes to achieve certain policy objectives then it must obtain specific legislative authorisation. This is not as strange as it might appear, since much of the history of judicial control over

[149] "The Techniques of Government", in J. Jowell and D. Oliver (eds), *The Changing Constitution*, 3rd edn (Oxford: Oxford University Press, 1994); "Regulation by Contract: The New Prerogative" (1979) C.L.P. 41; "Legal Analysis of Economic Policy" (1982) 9 Jnl. Law & Soc. 191.

[150] "The Techniques of Government", in Jowell and Oliver (eds), *The Changing Constitution* (1994), pp.213–219.

[151] "The Techniques of Government", in Jowell and Oliver (eds), *The Changing Constitution* (1994), pp.228–229.

[152] "The Techniques of Government", in Jowell and Oliver (eds), *The Changing Constitution* (1994), p.236.

prerogative power has been concerned with just this issue: placing limits on the policies the Executive can pursue without Parliamentary authority. The options at our disposal are, therefore, varied. Their suitability will depend on the more particular type of dominium power that is at stake. The importance of the issue should not, however, be doubted.

C. Blurring of the Public/Private Divide and the Responsibility for Policy Formation

5–043 The preceding discussion has shown how the public/private divide has become blurred as a result of initiatives concerning service provision. The line between policy formation and policy execution is always fragile, and becomes even more so as a result of financing methods which consciously lay emphasis on public-private partnerships and the like. There have been developments that have constrained the use of dominium as a technique of government policy.[153]

It is, however, equally the case that the increased emphasis on innovative financing of service provision means that what "government" delivers by way of services is increasingly dependent on what the market is willing provide. It also raises broader issues about the ethics of public service, and how these are being transformed as a result of these developments.[154]

9. MAKING THE CONTRACT: GENERAL PRINCIPLES

A. Capacity to Contract

i. Crown

5–044 Ministers are often granted a power to conclude contracts by a statute, but in addition the Crown possesses a common law power to contract.[155] It is debatable whether this power should be seen as part of the prerogative.[156] Whatever label is attached, the Crown's contracting power is unconstrained by restrictions as to subject-matter or person.[157]

ii. Ministers of the Crown

5–045 The contractual *capacity* of Ministers of the Crown, and other Crown agents, requires separate treatment. A Minister will normally possess the *authority* to

---

153 "The Techniques of Government", in Jowell and Oliver (eds), *The Changing Constitution* (1994), pp.229–235.

154 Faulkner, "Public Services, Citizenship, and the State – The British Experience 1967–97", in Freedland and Sciarra (eds), *Public Services and Citizenship in European Law, Public and Labour Law Perspectives* (1998); N. Lewis and D. Longley, "Ethics and the Public Service" [1994] P.L. 596.

155 *Bankers Case* (1700) 90 E.R. 270, Turpin; *Government Procurement and Contracts* (1989), pp.83–84; Arrowsmith, *Civil Liability and Public Authorities* (1992), pp.53–54.

156 Daintith, "Regulation by Contract: The New Prerogative" (1979) C.L.P. 41, 42–43.

157 Compare *New South Wales v Bardolph* (1934) 52 C.L.R. 455 at 496.

make a contract on behalf of the Crown. This will be examined below. What is relevant here is whether a minister possesses *capacity* to make contracts in his or her own name.

It could either be argued that such agents have no independent contractual capacity, in the sense that the Crown is the only entity which is a party to the contract, or that while the primary liability rests with the Crown, the minister may also be a party to the contract. It might alternatively be argued that ministers have an independent contractual capacity within their area of responsibility, in the same way as any other artificial legal entity. Thus on this view, while they can contract on behalf of the Crown, they can also choose to make a contract to which the Crown is not a party, and for which the Crown bears no liability.[158]

There is some authority that a minister or other Crown agent can choose to contract in his or her own name, even in relation to those functions which are carried out on behalf of the Crown, and that whether this has occurred depends on the intent of the parties.[159] The principal motivation behind these cases was, however, to allow plaintiffs to sue without the necessity of using the Petition of Right procedure, since this procedure was only necessary in actions against the Crown, not when suits were brought against individual ministers.

A different approach has been adopted in other cases. In *Town Investments*,[160] rent legislation only gave protection from rent increases where the tenant and the occupier were the same person. The Department of the Environment (DOE) organised accommodation for other departments and had negotiated a lease, but the building was occupied by a different department. The landlord argued that the tenant and occupier were not the same, that the DOE had power to make the lease in its own name and hence that the protective rent legislation did not apply. The House of Lords rejected the argument. Acts of government done by ministers were acts done by the Crown, and the Crown was to be treated as one entity. Although there are ambiguities in the judgments, the general thrust is that ministers do not possess independent contractual capacity. **5–046**

A ministerial office may be created at common law or by statute. If the minister's office is one which exists at common law then the minister will, it seems, possess the contractual capacity of the Crown. Thus, a contract made will be valid even if it is outside the specific terms of a statute, unless a court construes the statute as imposing a limit on contractual power in the area covered by the enabling instrument. Where a minister is a purely statutory creation the argument for restricting the contracting power by the ultra vires principle is, in theory, stronger. However, as seen above, the effect of *Town Investments*[161] appears to be that the contractual capacity and authority of a specific minister merges with that of the Crown. It is unclear whether this will always be the case, but certain dicta suggest an affirmative answer.[162] Thus, on this view any contract made by the minister in a public capacity will bind the Crown, and it would also

[158] Arrowsmith, *Civil Liability and Public Authorities* (1992), pp.56–59.

[159] *Graham v Public Works Commissioners* [1901] 2 K.B. 781; *International Railway Co v Niagara Parks Commission* [1941] A.C. 328.

[160] *Town Investments v Department of the Environment* [1978] A.C. 359 HL. See however, *R. (BAPIO Action Ltd) v Secretary of State for the Home Department* [2008] 1 A.C. 1003 HL at [28].

[161] *Town Investments* [1978] A.C. 359.

[162] *Town Investments* [1978] A.C. 359 at 380–382, 400.

seem to be the case that the minister has no separate contractual capacity as such, unless this is specifically conferred by statute. Other jurisdictions have, however, not adopted this approach,[163] nor as will be seen below, does it sit easily with the approach of our own courts in other areas. Three comments may be made on the foregoing.

5–047 First, it is doubtful whether anything should turn on whether the minister's office existed at common law or was the creation of a statute. There is no reason in principle why there should be any difference in their respective contractual capacities.

Second, the argument for saying that the minister possesses the contractual capacity of the Crown is that the Crown in its governmental capacity operates through individual ministers or other Crown servants. It has to do so. It is, therefore, thought to be unrealistic to speak of the Crown in a governmental sense that is divorced from those servants. However, our courts have recognised that ministers and departments can be regarded as separate from the Crown. This is commonly acknowledged in judicial review proceedings where the orthodox view is that the prerogative orders will not lie against the Crown itself, but will lie against individual ministers.[164] Thus, in the context of such proceedings, it has been recognised that ministers can act in an *official* capacity separate from the Crown itself. The statute will be construed as giving powers to a particular minister to be exercised in his or her own name as *persona designata*, and not as agent for the Crown.[165] The "logic" of merging the capacity of the minister with that of the Crown is not pursued remorselessly in this context.[166] It is clear, therefore, that on some occasions our courts have chosen to regard the Crown and its ministers as one and indivisible, while on others they have accepted that they can be treated as separate entities for many important purposes.[167] It has indeed been persuasively argued that the way in which the law treats the Crown differs significantly as between administrative law and contract, such that in the former there is a tendency to disaggregate the powers of different ministers, whereas in the latter the tendency has been to aggregate government into a unified whole.[168]

Third, given that this is so, a preference for one of these theories should not be allowed to dictate an unacceptable conclusion. For example, even if one subscribes to the *Town Investments'* approach, and believes that the contractual capacity of the minister merges with that of the Crown, this should not enable clear delimitations of a minister's contracting power in a statute to be circumvented by reliance on some more general contractual power of the Crown. Where such a limit is clearly expressed or can be implied then, by analogy with the case law on the royal prerogative, such a limit should be respected and enforced.[169]

---

[163] *JE Verrault & Fils v Quebec* [1971] S.C.R. 41; *Meates v Attorney General* [1979] 1 N.Z.L.R. 415.

[164] Whether this orthodoxy is correct is questionable, see Ch.29.

[165] *M v Home Office* [1994] 1 A.C. 377, HL.

[166] Many statutes such as the Ministers of the Crown Act 1975 are, however, premised on the hypothesis that a minister accepts rights and obligations in his or her own name.

[167] See also, *Department for Environment Food and Rural Affairs v Robertson* [2005] I.C.R. 750, CA (Civ Div).

[168] J. McLean, "The Crown in Contract and Administrative Law" (2004) 24 O.J.L.S. 129.

[169] *Attorney General v De Keyser's Royal Hotel Ltd* [1920] A.C. 508, HL.

iii. *Statutory bodies*

Authorities which are not Crown agents and which derive their powers from statute are subject to the limitations imposed by the legislation. Thus, a contract that is beyond the limits imposed by the statute will be ultra vires.[170] This is exemplified by the decision in *Hazell*.[171] A local authority was held to have no power to enter into speculative interest rate swap transactions, which would result in profits or losses depending upon movements in interest rates. The public body's contractual capacity will, therefore, be dependent on the construction of the relevant statute. However, many such bodies are granted broad powers to facilitate the carrying out of their tasks. Thus, for example, the Local Government Act 1972 s.111, empowers local authorities to do anything which is calculated to facilitate the discharge of any of its functions, or is incidental thereto; the Localism Act 2011 s.1, accords local authorities the power to do anything that an individual can do, subject to certain exceptions; and the Local Government Act 2000 s.2, accords to local authorities the power to do anything they consider is likely to achieve the promotion or improvement of the economic, social or environmental well-being of their area. Moreover, the courts have held that a power to contract may be implied as an incidence of other powers the particular body has been given.[172] **5–048**

B. Authority of an Agent

The public body must have capacity to make the contract, and the agent must have been authorised to do so. Special problems can occur when such an agent purports to act on behalf of a public authority. **5–049**

i. *Extent of the agent's authority: general*

In a contract made between two private parties an agent can bind the principal if the agent has authority, actual or ostensible.[173] There are, however, difficulties in applying these principles to the situation where a public body makes a contract through an agent. These problems will be considered in the discussion of representations.[174] The principles can be briefly reiterated here. **5–050**

Actual authority may be given by the terms of a statute, and it may be excluded where the legislation stipulates that an individual cannot bind the authority in a certain transaction. The fact that the authority has purported to delegate to a particular officer will not legitimate the contract if the statute is clear that the function must be performed by a different party. Ostensible authority exists where a representation is made by the principal that the agent has authority to deal with a certain type of transaction, or perhaps where an agent in

[170] *Attorney General v Manchester Corporation* [1906] 1 Ch. 643; *Attorney General v Fulham Corp* [1921] 1 Ch. 44, CA.

[171] *Hazell v Hammersmith and Fulham LBC* [1992] 2 A.C. 1, HL.

[172] *Attorney General v Great Eastern Railway* (1880) 5 App. Cas. 473 at 478.

[173] *Bowstead and Reynolds on Agency*, 20th edn (London: Sweet & Maxwell, 2014).

[174] See Ch.22.

that position would normally do so. However, ostensible authority cannot validate a transaction that is ultra vires the public body, nor can it validate a delegation of authority to an agent where this is prohibited by the relevant statute. The harsh results of this doctrine will be considered below, and the reforms suggested there are equally apposite here.[175]

These principles apply in general to Crown servants and agents. Thus, it will normally have to be shown that a minister possesses actual or ostensible authority to enter into a contract of the type in question. These principles have been applied to servants of the Crown who are not ministers.[176] The only difference between such servants and ministers of the Crown is that the latter are likely to have a broader remit of authority than the former.[177]

ii. Breach of warranty of authority

5–051 In normal circumstances if an agent is duly authorised to make a contract then the principal will be liable but the agent will not. Where, however, the agent possesses no authority he or she can be sued for breach of warranty of authority. There is some case law indicating that this action will not lie against a servant who makes a contract on behalf of the Crown. Thus, in *Dunn*[178] the plaintiff was engaged for three years by the defendant on behalf of the Crown. He was dismissed prior to the end of his term and claimed breach of an implied warranty of authority by the defendant. The action failed, but the case is not conclusive authority that such an action could never succeed. The reasons given for the decision differed. Charles J. believed that such an action would be against public policy,[179] while the Court of Appeal preferred to rest its decision on the fact that there had been no breach.[180] The reasoning based upon public policy is unconvincing. It is difficult to see why the agent acting on behalf of the Crown should be in any better position than any other agent.[181]

C. Parliamentary Appropriation

5–052 Given the breadth of the Crown's power to contract, the legislature must have power to refuse an appropriation to pay for a contract of which it disapproves that has been made by the Executive.[182] It was at one time thought that unless an express appropriation of money had been made the contract would be invalid and

---

175 See Ch.22..

176 *Attorney General for Ceylon v AD Silva* [1953] A.C. 461.

177 Unless one were to read the *Town Investments* case to mean that ministers always had the authority of the Crown generally, but this would be an extreme application of the merger theory applied in that case.

178 *Dunn v MacDonald* [1897] 1 Q.B. 401 QBD at 555.

179 *Dunn* [1897] 1 Q.B. 401 at 404–406.

180 *Dunn* [1897] 1 Q.B. 401 at 556–558.

181 Street, *Governmental Liability* (1953), p.93 makes the further points that the representation may well have been one of law rather than fact and that the plaintiff may not, on the facts, have relied upon it.

182 Street, *Governmental Liability* (1953), pp.93, 84–90.

null. This belief was derived from dicta by Shee J.,[183] and Viscount Haldane.[184] However, it is clear from later cases that Viscount Haldane regarded the absence of the requisite appropriation as making the contract unenforceable, as there was nothing against which to enforce it, rather than making the contract null.[185] The view that the absence of appropriation goes to enforceability and not validity is supported by fully reasoned authority in Australia,[186] which also establishes that the appropriation does not have to be specifically directed towards a particular contractual expense.

The meaning of "enforceability" is not entirely clear. It is unclear what the result is if the necessary funds are not appropriated. In *Bardolph*, Evatt J stated that failure to vote the funds would relieve the Crown from performance, the voting being an implied condition of the contract.[187] This comes perilously close to regarding appropriation as a condition of validity by the backdoor. On appeal, the High Court disagreed with this part of Evatt J's judgment, finding that the lack of appropriation did not relieve the Crown from its obligation to perform.[188]

Enforceability could have one of two other meanings. It has been suggested that it should bear the same interpretation as in the Statute of Frauds.[189] There are, however, difficulties in transferring the meaning of unenforceable from a statute concerned with ensuring written evidence for certain transactions, to the different context of the absence of the requisite parliamentary appropriation. Another suggestion is that enforceability is best seen as a condition to the satisfaction of judgment, rather than as to the enforceability of the claim. The difficulty with this view is that it amounts simply to saying there is no legal right to execute judgment against Crown property, which is the general rule for judgments against the Crown. Appropriation Acts are, in any event, drawn broadly at present and thus the above problems are unlikely to occur.

D. Proceedings against the Crown

In claims against public authorities they can be sued in their own name. Where the defendant is the Crown the position is different. The petition of right developed as a mechanism whereby actions, including those for breach of contract, could be brought against the Crown.[190] **5–053**

The Crown Proceedings Act 1947 abolished the petition of right and certain other forms of procedure. Under s.1 any claim against the Crown which could have been enforced, albeit subject to fiat, by petition of right, or under any of the more specialised statutory liabilities prior to the Act, can now be enforced without the fiat, as of right. The defendant is either the appropriate government

[183] *Churchward v R.* (1865) L.R. 1 Q.B. 173 at 209, Cockburn CJ was of a different opinion at 200 and 201.

[184] *Commercial Cable Co v Government of Newfoundland* [1916] 2 A.C. 610 at 617.

[185] *Commonwealth of Australia v Kidman* [1926] 32 A.L.R. 1 at 2 and 3; *Attorney General v Great Southern and Western Ry. Co of Ireland* [1925] A.C. 754.

[186] *New South Wales v Bardolph* (1934) 52 C.L.R. 455.

[187] *Bardolph* (1934) 52 C.L.R. 455 at 483–484.

[188] *Bardolph* (1934) 52 C.L.R. 455 at 497–498 and 508–510.

[189] Street, *Governmental Liability* (1953), pp.91–92.

[190] See Ch.29.

department or the Attorney General. The areas covered by the old petition of right still determine the scope of actions that can be brought against the Crown. However, apart from actions in tort and salvage the coverage of the petition of right appears to be comprehensive. Two qualifications are necessary.

First, the Act is only applicable in relation to the UK government.[191] A plaintiff seeking redress against the Crown in relation to other areas is dependent on the petition of right procedure. It has been held that even this pre-1947 procedure is unavailable and that the repeal of the Petitions of Right Act 1860 is total. This conclusion is debatable.[192] Secondly, it is unclear whether the Crown can be sued personally. It was, prior to 1947, possible to bring a petition of right but this, as stated, has been abolished and s.40(1) states that nothing in the 1947 Act shall apply to proceedings by or against the sovereign in his private capacity. It may, however, be that the petition of right survives to the extent of allowing such actions.

E. Crown Service

i. Existence of a contract

5–054 There are special problems with the law relating to Crown service, which has been much criticised.[193] An initial issue is whether Crown servants have a contract of service.

The argument that Crown servants do not have a contract of service is based, in part, on the fact that they can be dismissed at will. However, as noted by Lord Atkin in *Reilly*,[194] the existence of a power to dismiss such servants at will is not inconsistent with the existence of a contract prior to that dismissal. In *Bruce*,[195] May L.J. held that there was nothing unconstitutional about civil servants being employed by the Crown pursuant to a contract of service, and that is consistent with the modern view of civil servants vis-a-vis the Crown. However, he went on to hold that prior to 1985 the Crown did not intend that civil servants should have such contracts. The point arose once again in *McClaren*,[196] where a prison officer claimed that the introduction of a new shift system constituted a breach of contract, or of his conditions of service. It was held that it was at least arguable that the relationship between the Home Office and prison officers was contractual. The willingness to think of Crown servants as having a contract of service is also apparent in *Nangle*,[197] where the court affirmed the view in *Bruce*

[191] Crown Proceedings Act 1947 s.40(2)(b) and (c).

[192] *Franklin v Attorney General* [1974] Q.B. 185 QBD at 201. The 1947 Act states that nothing in it shall affect proceedings against the Crown relating to non-UK claims. This saving should, in this respect, preserve the 1860 Act.

[193] S. Fredman and G. Morris, *The State as Employer, Labour Law in the Public Services* (Mansell, 1989).

[194] *Reilly v King* [1934] A.C. 176 at 180.

[195] *R. v Civil Service Appeals Board, Ex p. Bruce* [1988] I.C.R. 649 QBD. The point was not taken before the Court of Appeal, [1989] I.C.R. 171.

[196] *McClaren v Home Office* [1990] I.C.R. 824, CA (Civ Div).

[197] *R. v Lord Chancellor's Department, Ex p. Nangle* [1991] I.C.R. 743 QBD, but not for members of the armed forces, *Quinn v Ministry of Defence* [1997] P.I.Q.R. P387.

that the Crown has capacity to make a contract with its staff. It went on to hold that a contract had been created on the facts, and that there was a strong presumption in favour of an intention to create legal relations. This was followed in *British Telecommunications*.[198]

These decisions are to be welcomed. The regime has in the past been based on the assumption that no such contract existed.[199] There is no sound reason in the modern day why civil servants should not be employed under a contract of service. Statutory protections have been extended to Crown servants,[200] and management of the civil service has been placed on a statutory foundation.[201] The recognition that Crown servants have a contract of employment would, nonetheless, go some way to demystifying the relationship between the Crown and its employees, and to undermining the idea that such employees should be treated very differently from others. This does not, however, necessarily mean that they should be treated in the identical manner as those in private employment, as the following extract from Fredman and Morris demonstrates.[202]

> "We would argue that the major difference is that, while private employers are free to act unless constrained by the law, public employers derive their authority from prerogative or statute. There is a 'public' dimension to the way in which the civil service and the rest of the public services are administered, which means that the State owes duties to the general public as well as its workforce. It is necessary to find a balance between these interests. To declare that civil servants have no contract is to give too little emphasis to the rights of the individual employee; but simply to reverse this and declare that they do have contracts is to ignore the public duties of the Crown."

ii. *Dismissal of Crown servants*

Crown employees have been at a disadvantage in relation to dismissal. In **5–055**
Dunn,[203] a consular agent was appointed for three years and dismissed before the end of that period. His claim for damages for wrongful dismissal was denied, the court stating that Dunn's office was held at pleasure. This rule was applied by analogy with the dismissibility of military servants, the policy being the necessity for the Crown to be able to rid itself of a servant who might act detrimentally to the state. There are obvious flaws in this reasoning. While some Crown servants in senior positions might represent a danger of this type, it is difficult to envisage this being so for the majority. More important is the fact that this reasoning only goes to preclude specific performance of the contract, not to the award of damages.

The rule of dismissibility at pleasure can be excluded by statute.[204] It is less clear whether it can be excluded by the terms of the contract itself, and if so what

---

[198] *British Telecommunications Plc v Royal Mail Group Ltd* [2010] EWHC 8; *A v B (Investigatory Powers Tribunal: Jurisdiction)* [2009] EWCA Civ 24 at [25].

[199] Fredman and Morris, *The State as Employer, Labour Law in the Public Services* (1989), pp.61–70.

[200] Equal Pay Act 1970 s.1(8); Sex Discrimination Act 1975 s.85(2); Race Relations Act 1976 ss.75 and 76; Disability Discrimination Act 1995 s.64.

[201] Constitutional Reform and Governance Act 2010 Pt I.

[202] Fredman and Morris, *The State as Employer, Labour Law in the Public Services* (1989), p.66.

[203] *Dunn v Queen* [1896] 1 Q.B. 116, CA.

[204] *Gould v Stuart* [1896] A.C. 575.

terms are capable of doing so.[205] In a sequel to the *Dunn* case the Court of Appeal found that a provision for a fixed term would not in itself prevent dismissibility at pleasure.[206] There are, however, indications in the case law that appropriate terms in the contract can exclude the general rule,[207] for example, where there is provision for a fixed term and for power to determine for cause.[208] However, other cases support the conclusion that dismissibility at pleasure can only be excluded by statute, and that any contractual term purporting to exclude this rule will be disregarded.[209] The reasoning in these latter cases is not convincing,[210] but they have not been overruled.

iii. *Arrears of pay*

5–056 Until 1943 it was believed that a civil servant would be entitled to salary accrued at the date of dismissal.[211] The point had not, however, been fully argued and in *Lucas* Pilcher J.[212] reached the opposite conclusion. The reasoning is unconvincing. Starting from the premise that a Crown servant is dismissible at pleasure, Pilcher J. reached the conclusion that therefore arrears of pay were irrecoverable, which is a non sequitur. As Lord Atkin stated in *Reilly*, a right to terminate the contract at will is not inconsistent with the existence of a contract prior to termination.[213] The decision in *Lucas* has been cogently criticised by the Privy Council,[214] which refused to follow it. It is to be hoped that other courts will adopt the same approach.[215]

iv. *Statutory protection*

5–057 In the context of Crown service the maxim that the common law will supply the omission of the legislature has been reversed: it is statute which has provided protection. The common law has not been overruled, but rendered less important by legislation concerning unfair dismissal.[216] The legislation, now contained in the Employment Rights Act 1996, provides that an employee has the right not to be unfairly dismissed[217] and the legislation sets out what constitutes dismissal. Remedies for unfair dismissal are either a monetary award, or an order for

---

[205] G. Nettheim, "*Dunn v The Queen* Revisited" [1975] C.L.J. 253.

[206] *Dunn v Macdonald* [1897] 1 Q.B. 401 QBD at 555.

[207] *Shenton v Smith* [1895] A.C. 229.

[208] *Reilly v King* [1934] A.C. 176; *Robertson v Minister of Pensions* [1949] 1 K.B. 227.

[209] *Rodwell v Thomas* [1944] K.B. 596 KBD; *Riordan v War Office* [1959] 1 W.L.R. 104; [1961] 1 W.L.R. 210 QBD.

[210] In neither case are the authorities relied on convincing for establishing the propositions laid down As pointed out above, the provision for a fixed term in the *Dunn* case appears to have been held not to be inconsistent with a power to dismiss at pleasure, rather than a clog upon such power. See also, *Terrell v Secretary of State for the Colonies* [1953] 2 Q.B. 482.

[211] *R. v Doutré* (1884) 9 App. Cas. 745; *Sutton v Attorney General* (1923) 39 T.L.R. 294.

[212] *Lucas v Lucas* [1943] P. 68; *Mulvenna v The Admiralty* 1926 S.C. 842; D. Logan, "A Civil Servant and his Pay" (1945) 61 L.Q.R. 26.

[213] *Reilly* [1934] A.C. 176.

[214] *Kodeeswaran v Attorney General of Ceylon* [1970] A.C. 1111 at 1123.

[215] Compare Crown Proceedings Act 1947 s.27.

[216] Employment Protection (Consolidation Act) 1978 Pt V.

[217] Employment Rights Act 1996 s.94.

reinstatement or re-engagement. The general scheme of the legislation relating to unfair dismissal applies to Crown employment,[218] which means employment under or for the purposes of a government department, or any officer or body exercising on behalf of the Crown functions conferred by any enactment. The most important general exception, apart from the military, is for national security.[219]

F. Effect of an Unlawful Contract

The precise effects of a contract that is beyond the capacity of the relevant body are not entirely clear. The common law rule was that the unlawful contract was unenforceable against the corporation that made it.[220] The principal rationale was to prevent corporate funds from being disbursed for an unauthorised purpose, to the detriment of the shareholders and creditors of the company. The common law position has been amended by statute, which, in general, allows such agreements to be enforced against the company. **5–058**

Whether the common law rule applies to unlawful contracts entered into by a public body is not entirely clear. If they are unenforceable then this can cause real hardship to the contractor who may lose any profits on the transaction, and may be unable to recover expenses incurred in preparing to perform the contract.

Credit Suisse[221] is the leading authority. The defendant local authority established a company to assist with the financing of a leisure pool complex, with the intention that the company could obtain finance outside the statutory controls imposed on local authority borrowing. The plaintiff bank loaned the company £6 million and the local authority entered into a contract of guarantee to repay the money in the event that the company was wound up. The company failed, and the bank sought to enforce the guarantee. The local authority resisted the claim on the ground that it lacked the statutory power to make the contract. The Court of Appeal recognised the unfairness of the local authority relying on its own illegality to evade its contractual obligations,[222] but held that the contract was void and unenforceable since the local authority had no power to make it.

Neill L.J. pointed to the distinction drawn in company law between acts beyond the capacity of the company, which were wholly void, and those which were within the capacity of the company but involved a misuse of power. In the latter instance the enforceability of the transaction would depend upon whether the third party had notice of the excess of power.[223] He considered whether a similar distinction could apply in relation to acts done by public authorities. Neill L.J. recognised that the concept of ultra vires had been expanded in *Anisminic*, but acknowledged that in public law cases the courts exercised a broad discretion as to whether a remedy should lie even though an ultra vires act had occurred.

---

218 Employment Rights Act 1996 s.191. See also, Public Interest Disclosure Act 1998 s.10.

219 Employment Rights Act 1996 s.193, as amended by Employment Relations Act 1999 Sch.8.

220 *Ashbury Carriage and Iron Co v Riche* (1875) L.R. 7 H.L. 653.

221 *Credit Suisse v Allerdale BC* [1997] Q.B. 306; *Credit Suisse v Waltham Forest LBC* [1997] Q.B. 362; *National Transport Co-operative Society Ltd v Attorney General of Jamaica* [2009] UKPC 48.

222 This was also recognised in *Stretch v West Dorset DC* (2000) 2 L.G.L.R. 140 CA (Civ Div).

223 *Rolled Steel Products (Holdings) Ltd v British Steel Corporation* [1986] Ch. 246 CA (Civ Div) at 302.

The bank argued that the courts should exercise a similar discretion where the decision was ultra vires not for lack of statutory capacity, but for some other reason, and drew on the analogies from company law. Neill L.J. rejected the argument. The ultra vires decisions of local authorities could not be classified into categories of invalidity and any error in the *Anisminic* list resulted in the decision being void. This conclusion is open to question. The bank was not seeking to argue that there should be different categories of invalidity, but whether, *assuming that the act was invalid*, there could be any discretion as to the granting of the remedy.

5–059 The approach of Hobhouse L.J. was somewhat different. He held that public law was only relevant for determining the ambit of the local authority's powers. When it was decided that the local authority had no power, the effect of that lack of capacity was dealt with by private law, and the broad remedial discretion exercised by courts in judicial review actions was irrelevant. This line of argument is also open to question. The reasoning assumes that it is meaningful to categorise the case along the public law-private divide in this manner.

The central issue is the extent to which a public body that lacks the power to contract, or which has used it for an improper purpose, should be bound by the contract it has made. The resolution of this issue is not easy, since we wish to protect citizens against illegal government action and also to protect the public purse from the effects of illegal government conduct.[224]

In *Charles Terence Estates*[225] the Court of Appeal distinguished *Credit Suisse*, holding that the ability of the local authority to rely on its own illegality to avoid a contract was limited to cases of pure ultra vires, where there was a lack of legal capacity. This is to be welcomed and it should also be noted that reliance by a public body on the ultra vires nature of its own action may constitute a breach of Convention rights, more particularly the right to property.[226]

5–060 We should moreover accept that the courts possess remedial discretion in such cases. To deny the existence of such discretion by rigid demarcations between public law, where such discretion exists, and private law, where it does not, is unhelpful, although the courts may be less minded to exercise such discretion so as to enforce a contract where the invalidity goes to the contractual capacity of the public body. The extent to which the other contracting party had notice that the public body lacked contractual capacity should be a factor affecting the exercise of this discretion.[227]

These problems will be less likely to occur as a result of the Local Government (Contracts) Act 1997. The Act was passed to allay fears about the *Credit Suisse* judgment and the inhibiting effect that this was having on bank

[224] P. Cane, "Do Banks Dare to Lend to Local Authorities?" (1994) 110 L.Q.R. 514.

[225] *Charles Terence Estates Ltd v Cornwall CC* [2012] EWCA Civ 1439 at [30]-[37]. See also *National Transport Co-operative Society Ltd v Attorney General of Jamaica* [2009] UKPC 48, where the contractual error to which *Credit Suisse* was applied was a lack of legal capacity.

[226] *Stretch v United Kingdom* (2004) 38 E.H.R.R. 12.

[227] See also, Arrowsmith, *Civil Liability and Public Authorities* (1992), pp.64–65. For detailed consideration of the problems surrounding recovery in the *Hazell* case [1992] 2 A.C. 1, M. Loughlin, "Innovative Financing in Local Government: The Limits of Legal Instrumentalism-Pt II" [1991] P.L. 568.

lending to local authorities. The banks were unwilling to do so if they might be unable to recoup the loan in the event that the contract was found to be ultra vires.[228]

Section 1(1) provides that every statutory provision conferring or imposing a function on a local authority confers power on the local authority to enter a contract with another person for the provision of assets or services, for the purposes of discharging that function. Section 1(2) in effect empowers the local authority to make financial arrangements with a bank that has loaned money to a party other than the local authority itself, as exemplified by the facts of *Credit Suisse*.

Section 2 makes provision for the certification of a contract. The certification signifies that the local authority had power to make the contract, and the certificate is not invalidated by anything in the certificate that is inaccurate or untrue.[229] The certification protects the contract from challenge in private law proceedings.

It is, however, still possible to argue that the contract was ultra vires in proceedings for judicial review and audit review.[230] Where the court finds that the contract was ultra vires it is empowered to find that the contract should nonetheless have effect, having regard to the consequences for the financial position of the local authority, and for the provision of services to the public.[231] The enforceability of contract discharge terms is preserved in the event that the contract is found to be ultra vires.[232] Where the contract has been found to be of no effect, but there are no discharge terms, there is provision for a damages remedy for a sum equivalent to that which would be given where there was a repudiatory breach by the local authority.[233]

---

228 A. Davies, "Ultra Vires Problems in Government Contracts" (2006) 122 L.Q.R. 98, 115–122, makes a number of valuable suggestions for improvements to the legislation.

229 Local Government (Contracts) Act 1997 s.4.

230 Local Government (Contracts) Act 1997 s.5.

231 Local Government (Contracts) Act 1997 s.5(3).

232 Local Government (Contracts) Act 1997 s.6.

233 Local Government (Contracts) Act 1997 s.7.

CHAPTER 6

LOCAL GOVERNMENT

1. CENTRAL ISSUES

i. The development of local authorities in the 19th century has already been charted. There will be no attempt to provide a comprehensive legal guide to these authorities within the discussion that follows. This is a specialist field with a wealth of literature.[1] 6–001

ii. An understanding of local government is, however, essential, since such authorities are among the principal decision-makers in the public law sphere. Their powers have been transformed, which means that it is no longer possible to define *local government* merely by describing the present pattern of *local authorities* and their respective powers.

iii. Many of their traditional responsibilities have been transferred to *agencies*, which are often subject to central control, while others have been *contracted-out* to private contractors. This development has led some

---

[1] J. Griffith, *Central Departments and Local Authorities* (London: Allen & Unwin, 1966); D. Hill, *Democratic Theory and Local Government* (London: Allen & Unwin, 1974); A. Alexander, *Local Government in Britain since Reorganisation* (London: Allen & Unwin, 1982); M. Elliott, *The Role of Law in Central–Local Relations* (1981); G. Jones (ed.), *New Approaches to the Study of Central–Local Government Relationships* (Aldershot: Gower, 1980); M. Loughlin, D. Gelfand and K. Young (eds), *Half a Century of Municipal Decline 1935–1985* (London: Allen & Unwin, 1985); G. Jones and J. Stewart, *The Case for Local Government*, 2nd edn (London: Allen & Unwin, 1985); M. Goldsmith, *New Research in Central–Local Relations* (Aldershot: Gower, 1986); M. Loughlin, *Local Government in the Modern State* (London: Sweet & Maxwell, 1986); D. King and J. Pierre (eds), *Challenges to Local Government* (London: Sage, 1990); G. Stoker, *The Politics of Local Government*, 2nd edn (London: Macmillan, 1991); M. Loughlin, *Legality and Locality, The Role of Law in Central–Local Government Relations* (Oxford: Oxford University Press, 1996); D. King and G. Stoker (eds), *Rethinking Local Democracy* (London: Macmillan, 1996); I. Leigh, *Law, Politics and Local Democracy* (Oxford: Oxford University Press, 2000); S. Bailey, *Cross on Principles of Local Government Law*, 3rd edn (London: Sweet & Maxwell, 2004); C. Needham, *The Reform of Public Services under New Labour: Narratives of Consumerism* (London: Palgrave Macmillan, 2007); A. Arden, C. Baker, J. Manning, *Local Government Constitutional and Administrative* Law, 2nd edn (London: Sweet & Maxwell, 2008); D. Wilson and C. Game, *Local Government in the United Kingdom*, 5th edn (London: Palgrave Macmillan, 2011).

commentators to distinguish between formal and informal local government,[2] while others speak in terms of a shift from local government to local governance.[3]

iv. The following section will, therefore, chart the powers of local authorities, and the other bodies with local responsibilities will be considered thereafter. The final section will consider more generally the issue of central–local relations and democracy, in the light of legislative initiatives.

2. LOCAL AUTHORITIES: STRUCTURE, ORGANISATION, POWERS AND FINANCE

A. Structure

6–002 The pattern of local authorities established by the end of the 19th century continued largely unchanged until 1972. In the period after the Second World War there was, however, increasing disquiet. The shape of local government was felt to be outdated and ill-adapted to the demographic and technological development that occurred in the post-war period. This sentiment was voiced most strongly by Richard Crossman in 1965, who was then Minister of Housing and Local Government. In 1966 a Royal Commission was established under the chairmanship of Lord Redcliffe-Maud.[4] The Report of the Royal Commission identified a number of key problems: the division between town and country, that between boroughs and counties, the allocation of responsibility within counties, the small size of some local authorities, and the relationships between local authority and the public, and local authority and government.

The response of the Royal Commission to these difficulties was to reverse conventional thinking about local decision-making. The traditional pattern was based on the assumption that single-tier authorities would be suited to the larger urban areas and that a two-tier structure was required in other contexts. This thinking was directly challenged. For the future the Redcliffe-Maud Report proposed that unitary authorities should be the norm. These would cover urban and rural areas, normally focused around the main towns. The unitary principle would be departed from only in those large urban conurbations where, to adhere rigidly to the single-tier principle, would make the authority unwieldy and remote from the community. In such conurbations a two-tier structure was recommended.

The Labour government was largely in favour of the Royal Commission's proposals and accepted the unitary concept.[5] The Conservative Party was,

---

[2] D. King, "Government Beyond Whitehall: Local Government and Urban Politics", in P. Dunleavy, A. Gamble, I. Holliday and G. Peele (eds), *Developments in British Politics 4* (London: Macmillan, 1993).

[3] P. John, "Local Governance", in P. Dunleavy, A. Gamble, I. Holliday and G. Peele (eds), *Developments in British Politics 5* (London: Macmillan, 1997), Ch 13; G. Stoker, "Introduction: Normative Theories of Local Government and Democracy", in King and Stoker (eds), *Rethinking Local Democracy* (1996), Ch 1.

[4] Royal Commission, *Local Government in England 1966–1969*, Cmnd.4040 (1969) (the Redcliffe-Maud Report).

[5] Royal Commission, *Reform of Local Government in England*, Cmnd.4276 (1970).

however, in favour of the two-tier principle. Its return to government in 1970 ensured the demise of the Redcliffe-Maud proposals. It reverted to the two-tier principle,[6] which was embodied in the Local Government Act 1972.[7]

There were four different types of local government. The first was the metropolitan county of which there were six, divided into 36 metropolitan districts. Second, there were 39 non-metropolitan counties with 296 districts. Both types of county could have parishes beneath the districts. Third, in London there was the Greater London Council, under which existed 32 London boroughs. Fourth, Wales had eight counties, 37 districts, and communities below these. Boundary Commissions, one for England and one for Wales, were constituted by the 1972 Act. Both Commissions have the duty to review district and county areas within 10 to 15 years or otherwise as the secretary of state may direct. **6–003**

This pattern of local authority organisation was radically revised, with the abolition of the metropolitan county councils (MCCs) and the Greater London Council (GLC). The Conservative government argued that such authorities should be abolished because they had limited operational responsibilities, their expenditure had been excessive, and they sought to establish a role that was not really required. It was argued that reform would "streamline" the cities, save money, and provide a simpler system. The cogency of these arguments was challenged by studies commissioned by the MCCs. Evidence as to likely cost savings was not readily apparent, and the argument concerning simplicity was undermined by the institutional changes that were to replace the MCCs and the GLC. The Local Government Act 1985 abolished the MCCs and the GLC. Some of their functions were transferred to district or borough councils. Others were assigned to new joint authorities composed primarily of members from the relevant district or borough councils. The decision to abolish the MCCs and the GLC was motivated more by the desire to dismantle large authorities that had been predominantly Labour, rather than by the objective of improving local government in large conurbations.[8]

The present structure of local authorities varies from area to area. In some there are two layers or tiers, a district council and a county council; in others there is just one, a unitary authority. In London each borough is a unitary authority, with the Greater London Authority, the Mayor and Assembly, providing strategic, city-wide government.[9] There can in addition be a town or parish council, covering a much smaller area.

Structural reviews have been used to decide whether or not a single, all-purpose council, rather than two councils, would better reflect the interests of local communities and lead to more effective local government. These reviews were undertaken by the Local Government Commission (LGC) established under the Local Government Act 1992. The LGC was replaced by Boundary Committees. The Boundary Committee for England was established in April 2002, but it was **6–004**

[6] *Local Government in England*, Cmnd.4584 (1971).

[7] It did not take effect until 1 April 1974.

[8] S. Leach and C. Game, "English Metropolitan Government since Abolition: An Evaluation of the Abolition of the English Metropolitan County Councils"' (1991) 69 Pub. Adm. 141.

[9] *A Mayor and Assembly for London: The Government's Proposals for Modernising the Governance of London* (1998); Greater London Authority Act 1999; Greater London Authority Act 2007.

replaced by the Local Government Boundary Commission, LGBC, in 2010. The LGBC can recommend the creation of one or more new unitary authorities, or the division of an existing authority into one or more new authorities.[10]

The detailed provisions by which an area where there are two-tiers of local government can be reorganised so that there is a single tier of local government, and the process by which the boundaries of local government areas can be altered, are regulated by the Local Government and Public Involvement in Health Act 2007.[11] There is also statutory provision for combined local authorities, which exercise certain powers.[12]

B. Internal Organisation

6–005 The internal structure of local authorities changed as a result of new initiatives contained in the DETR's[13] White Paper on *Modern Local Government, In Touch with the People*.[14] The traditional committee structures used by most councils was said to lead to "inefficient and opaque decision making", with significant decisions being taken behind closed doors by political groups, or by a small group within the majority group.[15] Councillors were felt to be unproductive, since they spent too much time in meetings when decisions had already been taken elsewhere.[16] Leadership was said to be lacking, and people often did not know who was taking the decisions.[17] The cure for this malaise was the separation of roles as between the local authority executive and the backbench councillors. This separation was said to enhance efficiency, transparency and accountability.[18] The executive should propose the policy framework and implement policies within the agreed framework. The backbench councillors should represent their constituents, share in the policy and budget decisions of the full council, suggest policy improvements and scrutinise the executive.[19]

These ideas were enshrined in the Local Government Act 2000,[20] as amended by the Local Government and Public Involvement in Health Act 2007 and the Localism Act 2011. The following analysis deals with local authorities in England. There are two principal ways in which this new division of roles can be introduced for local authorities in England, although it is open to the secretary of state to prescribe, within certain limits, other forms of executive organisation.[21] A local authority must submit proposals to the secretary of state as to which type of executive arrangement it wishes to adopt. The local authority must consult the

---

[10] See *https://www.lgbce.org.uk/current-reviews* [accessed 6 January 2016].

[11] Local Government and Public Involvement in Health Act 2007 ss.1–23. See, however, Local Government Act 2010.

[12] Local Democracy, Economic Development and Construction Act 2009 ss.103–113D.

[13] Department of the Environment, Transport and the Regions.

[14] White Paper, *Modern Local Government, In Touch with the People* (1998), Cm.4014.

[15] White Paper, *Modern Local Government, In Touch with the People*, para.3.4.

[16] White Paper, *Modern Local Government, In Touch with the People*, para.3.5.

[17] White Paper, *Modern Local Government, In Touch with the People*, paras 3.6–3.7.

[18] White Paper, *Modern Local Government, In Touch with the People*, para.3.14.

[19] White Paper, *Modern Local Government, In Touch with the People*, paras 3.13, 3.39, 3.41–3.44.

[20] Leigh, *Law, Politics and Local Democracy* (2000), pp.230–246.

[21] Local Government Act 2000 s.9BA.

local electors and other interested persons. Detailed guidance has been published as to the workings of this regime.[22] The Secretary of State has power to make regulations concerning the governance arrangements of local authorities.[23]

There can be a *directly elected mayor plus a cabinet*.[24] The mayor is elected by the whole electorate and then forms a cabinet from among the councillors. The mayor acts as the political leader for the community, proposing policy for approval by the council and steering implementation by the cabinet through council officers. The default assumption is that all executive functions can be undertaken by the mayor. The Local Government Act 2000 has been amended by the Localism Act 2011 to allow the government to trigger a referendum in large cities outside London to decide whether they wish to have an elected mayor.[25] **6–006**

The second option is to have a *leader and cabinet executive*.[26] A councillor is elected leader of the executive by the local authority. Two or more councillors are appointed to the executive by the executive leader. The executive arrangements can make provision for the allocation of any executive function to the executive, any member of the executive, any committee of the executive, and any officer of the executive.[27]

There is also provision for the *local authority executive to take such form as may be prescribed by the secretary of state in regulations*, subject to criteria specified in the Act itself.[28] There are detailed provisions concerning the variation of executive arrangements by local authorities.[29]

The Local Government Act 2000 makes provision for overview and scrutiny committees. These committees can review and scrutinise decisions taken by the executive, and they can require members of the executive to appear before them to answer questions.[30] The Act contains provisions as to which meetings of the executive are held in public and which in private.[31] Local authorities are required to have a constitution,[32] containing such information as the secretary of state may direct. The secretary of state has said that the constitution should describe clearly the way in which the local authority conducts its business and should be readily available to the public.[33]

The provisions for London are in the same vein with a directly elected mayor and a directly elected assembly.[34] They are enshrined in the Greater London

---

22 Department for Communities and Local Government, *New Council Constitutions, Guidance to English Authorities* (2006).

23 Cities and Local Authorities Devolution Act 2016 ss.15–16.

24 Local Government Act 2000 ss.9C, 9H–9HE. See also, Local Democracy, Economic Development and Construction Act 2009 ss.107A–107F.

25 Local Government Act 2000 s.9N.

26 Local Government Act 2000 s.9C.

27 Local Government Act 2000 ss.9E–9EB.

28 Local Government Act 2000 s.9BA.

29 Local Government Act 2000 ss.9K–9MG.

30 Local Government Act 2000 ss.9F–9FE.

31 Local Government Act 2000 ss.9G, 9GA.

32 Local Government Act 2000 s.9P.

33 Local Government Act 2000 (Constitutions) (England) Direction 2000; New Council Constitutions.

34 White Paper, *A Mayor and Assembly for London: The Government's Proposals for Modernising the Governance of London*, Cm.3897 (1998).

Authority Act 1999.[35] The mayor has the main executive responsibility, and is responsible for general planning, the establishment of the budget, the running of new transport and economic development bodies, and improvements to the environment. It is for the Assembly to question the Mayor on his or her actions, and to agree or suggest changes to the mayor's overall budget and plans. In general terms, the GLA has responsibility, in varying degrees, for transport, economic development, the environment, planning, the police, fire authorities, culture and health.

It is clear that the government regarded these as more than mere organisational changes. They were designed to reinvigorate local democracy by providing for more efficient, accountable and transparent local government. The broader impact of these initiatives will be considered below.

C. Functions and Powers

6–007 The functions of local government have altered considerably over the last 100 years. Five periods can be broadly identified.

i. Industrialisation and urbanisation

6–008 The modern role of local authorities has its origins in the problems attendant upon industrialisation and urbanisation in the 19th century. This necessitated collective action to provide a variety of goods and services, and local authorities were perceived as well placed to undertake this task.[36] Some of these services were "public goods", which the market would not provide, or would do so inefficiently. Others were trading services, which the private market could provide, but only with the attendant risk of private monopoly profit. Yet other services were redistributive, being designed to benefit certain groups within society, such as by the provision of social welfare.[37]

ii. Trading and redistribution

6–009 The second period is characterised by the relative decline in the importance of trading services and the relative increase in the importance of providing redistributive services. In 1885 the latter accounted for only 23 per cent of local authority expenditure, whereas by 1975 this had risen to 65 per cent.[38]

iii. Market forces and local authority services: Conservative policy 1970s–1990s

6–010 The third period was characterised by changing perceptions as to the proper functions of local authorities as a result of Conservative policy in the late 1970s

[35] See also Greater London Authority Act 2007.
[36] Loughlin, *Local Government in the Modern State* (1986), p.4.
[37] Loughlin, *Local Government in the Modern State* (1986), pp.4–5.
[38] Loughlin, *Local Government in the Modern State* (1986), p.6.

and 1980s. The general theme was that the functions of local authorities should be opened up to market forces, and judged by the criteria of market efficiency. Local authority services should be provided in accordance with what are essentially individualistic principles for action rather than any overriding conception of collective good.[39] A range of devices was employed to this end. These included direct competition with private industry for service provision, contracting-out service provision, the sale of local authority assets, and the encouragement of market accountability to consumers.[40]

Thus, legislation such as the Local Government Act 1988 specified services which local authorities were required to put out to competitive tendering. The Housing and Building Control Act 1984 extended the policy of selling off council houses to tenants. The Education Reform Act 1988 reduced local authority control over schooling. The Local Government Act 1992 empowered the Audit Commission to require local authorities to supply information to enable it to make comparisons based on cost, economy, efficiency and effectiveness, between the standards of performance of different bodies. Other legislative initiatives were aimed at forcing local authorities to privatise further areas, such as municipal airports, and to sell off other municipal property. King brings out the change in the role of local authorities[41]:

> "Instead of envisaging local government as an institution representing a local community and its local tradition, it is to be designed as an institution responsible for overseeing service provision. Local government is thought of as an enabling institution and not one of direct service delivery ... This new role maximises efficiency and profit criteria in local government. It treats citizens as customers of government services. Furthermore, local authorities are viewed as purchasers rather than providers of services."

iv. Market forces and local authority services: Labour policy 1990s–2000s

The fourth period covers local authorities' functions as seen in the light of the Labour government's approach to this area. The White Paper on *Modern Local Government, In Touch with the People*,[42] should be read in conjunction with the papers on *Modernising Local Government: Improving Local Services through Best Value*[43] and *Local Government and the Private Finance Initiative*.[44] The latter two papers were considered in the chapter on service provision.[45] The general approach to local authority services was maintained in the 2006 White Paper *Strong and Prosperous Communities*.[46] The essence of the overall approach can be set out here. **6–011**

[39] Loughlin, *Local Government in the Modern State* (1986), p.170.

[40] Loughlin, *Local Government in the Modern State* (1986), pp.167–171.

[41] King, "Government Beyond Whitehall: Local Government and Urban Politics", in Dunleavy, Gamble, Holliday and Peele (eds), *Developments in British Politics 4* (1993), p.204.

[42] White Paper, *Modern Local Government, In Touch with the People*, Cm.4014 (July 1998).

[43] *Local Government and the Private Finance Initiative* (1997).

[44] *Local Government and the Private Finance Initiative* (September 1998).

[45] Ch.5.

[46] Department of Communities and Local Government, *Strong and Prosperous Communities* (October, 2006), available at: *http://www.communities.gov.uk/publications/localgovernment/strongprosperous2* [accessed 3 June 2012].

The Labour strategy for the powers of local authorities was less doctrinaire than that of the previous Conservative government. The market was not always perceived as the best way to secure service provision. However, while the Conservative strategy was toned down, and while the Labour approach was designed to be less confrontational, it was also clear that the Labour government accepted that service provision should be by the "most effective, economic and efficient means available".[47] The Best Value strategy, enshrined in the Local Government Act 1999, as amended by the Local Government and Public Involvement in Health Act 2007, was designed to secure the efficient and effective provision of local services, while preserving greater local autonomy and choice. Efficient and effective public services were seen as an essential part of a healthy democracy.[48]

The attainment of Best Value was seen as being about quality as well as efficiency. There was no presumption that services must be privatised, nor was there any compulsion to put services out to tender, but there was no reason to provide services in-house if other more efficient means were available. Competition was only one tool in assessing Best Value, but it was an important one. Partnerships between the public and the private sectors were central to the government's aims of establishing first-class public services and infrastructure, and promoting economic growth and regeneration. The Private Finance Initiative, which is designed to facilitate such partnerships, was applied vigorously at local level.

v. Market forces and local authority services: Coalition and Conservative government policy post-2010

6–012 There is much in the preceding schema that has been retained, but it has been modified in certain respects by the Localism Act 2011, which is shaped by background ideals of the "Big Society". The most salient features of the 2011 Act for present purposes are as follows.

It gives local authorities a general competence to act, subject to certain limitations. Thus, such authorities have the same power to act that an individual generally has, and the power may be used in innovative ways to do things unlike anything that a local authority has done before, or may currently do.[49] The Act enables Ministers to transfer local public functions from central government and quangos to local authorities, combined authorities and economic prosperity boards, in order to improve local accountability or promote economic growth.[50] The Localism Act 2011 thus empowers local authorities.

It also empowers individuals and citizens as against the local authority. Thus, the Act requires a relevant authority to consider an expression of interest submitted by a voluntary or community body, charity, parish council, or employees of the authority in relation to providing or assisting in providing a

---

[47] White Paper, *Modern Local Government, In Touch with the People*, para.7.1.
[48] White Paper, *Modern Local Government, In Touch with the People*, para.1.2.
[49] Localism Act 2011 s.1.
[50] Localism Act 2011 ss.15–18.

service provided by or on behalf of the local authority.[51] The local authority must consider such requests, accept them or reject them on grounds specified by the secretary of state.[52] The Localism Act 2011 also requires local authorities to maintain a list of assets of community value which have been nominated by the local community. When listed assets come up for sale, the Act gives community groups the opportunity to bid and buy the asset when it comes on the open market.[53]

D. Finances

The system of local authority finances is complex and only a general outline can be provided here. **6–013**

i. Resources

Local authorities do not have their own source of revenue derived from local income tax. The traditional basis of local authority revenue was the rates, which were levied upon property owners,[54] combined with income from charges and fees. These sources of revenue were supplemented by grants from central government. **6–014**

A radical change was brought about by the Local Government Finance Act 1988, which replaced the rating system with the community charge/poll tax. The objective was to increase the financial accountability of local authorities. The rating system imposed the financial burden on property owners. It was argued that many who lived in an area could support expensive local policies, secure in the knowledge that they would not have to bear the financial burden if they were not liable to pay rates. The poll tax was to be levied on all those who lived in an area, subject to certain exceptions, at a flat rate.

The political debacle caused by the poll tax is well known. The poll tax was replaced by the council tax in the Local Government Finance Act 1992. The tax is made up of a personal and a property element, although each household only receives one bill. Properties are valued through a banding system, so those houses in the same band should receive the same bill. An obvious problem of any system based upon property values is that the financial returns are susceptible to fluctuation with movements in the value of property. The Localism Act 2011 amended the 1992 Act to include novel provisions concerning the determination as to whether a council tax rise is excessive and to require a local referendum on such tax increases.[55]

---

[51] Localism Act 2011 s.81.

[52] Localism Act 2011 ss.83–84.

[53] Localism Act 2011 ss.87, 95–98.

[54] Rating and Valuation Act 1925; Local Government Act 1948; Rating and Valuation Act 1961; Local Government Act 1966.

[55] Local Government Finance Act 1992 ss.52ZB–52ZI.

ii. Grants and curbs on spending: history

6–015 Local authorities only ever derived part of their funds from rates, the poll tax or the council tax. Grants from central government provide approximately 80 per cent of their funds. It is important to understand a little history of this area.

In historical terms the basic grant was the Rate Support Grant (RSG),[56] the main objective of which was to provide some degree of equalisation between the financial resources and expenditure requirements of different local authorities. The method of calculating the RSG was felt to be complex and prone to encourage higher spending by local authorities. A new mechanism for calculating the grant was therefore introduced in 1980.[57] The technique for calculating the grant is complex, and cannot be examined here. The essential idea was to provide a simpler, more equal system of grant allocation, which removed incentives for "excessive spending". Expenditure above the level of the grant would have to be funded from rates. It was argued that such expenditure would indicate that the local authority was seeking to provide a higher level of service than was necessary, or that it was being inefficient. These arguments are of questionable validity, as is the claim that the new method of calculation is simpler.[58]

This attempt to curb local expenditure proved relatively ineffective because many local authorities chose not to cut the provision of services, but to raise the additional revenue from rates.[59] This led to the Rates Act 1984, which empowered the secretary of state to limit the rating level of local authorities. The Act gave broad discretionary power to the secretary of state,[60] and this was used to "rate-cap" a number of authorities. Local authorities used creative accounting to enhance financial independence, and to make ends meet. The best known of these devices was the "swaps" transaction, which was held to be ultra vires by the House of Lords.[61]

The rationale for such controls over local authority current expenditure was questionable. The main foundation of the government's argument was that it was necessary for the success of its macro-economic strategy, which entailed control of public expenditure and hence local authority expenditure. Whether this justified the measures adopted is however contested.[62]

iii. Grants and curbs on spending: current position

6–016 The present position is as follows.[63] The Spending Review determines the total level of grant to local authorities. The annual Local Government Finance

[56] Local Government Act 1974.

[57] Local Government, Planning and Land Act 1980 ss.54–62; Local Government Finance Act 1987 ss.1–5.

[58] Loughlin, *Local Government in the Modern State* (1986), pp.25–35, 38–39.

[59] Loughlin, *Local Government in the Modern State* (1986), pp.38–49.

[60] Rates Act 1984 s.2; Local Government Finance Act 1987 ss.6, 7, 8.

[61] *Hazell v Hammersmith and Fulham LBC* [1992] 2 A.C. 1; M. Loughlin, "Innovative Financing in Local Government: The Limits of Legal Instrumentalism" [1990] P.L. 372; [1991] P.L. 568.

[62] Loughlin, *Local Government in the Modern State* (1986), pp.20–22.

[63] Department for Communities and Local Government, *A Guide to the Local Government Financial Settlement in England* (2013), available at: *https://www.gov.uk/government/publications/a-guide-to-the-local-government-finance-settlement* [accessed 7 January 2016].

Settlement is concerned with the distribution of Formula Grant, which is made up of Revenue Support Grant, redistributed business rates and the Police Grant. Councils also fund their spending by raising Council Tax. The Formula Grant is distributed by formula through the Local Government Finance Settlement.[64] There are no restrictions on what local government can spend it on. Specific grants are distributed outside the main settlement. Some of these are known as ring-fenced grants, which control council spending. These usually fund particular services or initiatives that are a national priority.

The Labour government signalled a shift in thinking about curbs on local authority expenditure.[65] It acknowledged that central government has a strong interest in local government's taxation and spending decisions, because of its desire to ensure best value and because a significant proportion of local spending is financed by the national taxpayer.[66] Labour's strategy was based on a balance between local financial accountability, and the existence of reserve powers for central government to intervene where necessary. It abolished what it regarded as "crude and universal capping".[67] The central government's reserve powers were structured more flexibly.[68] The repeal of the previous capping legislation and introduction of a more discriminating system to regulate local authority expenditure were key features of the Local Government Act 1999.[69] The Coalition and Conservative government's approach to local authority grants has been strongly influenced by the need to reduce such expenditure as part of the more general drive for savings in the light of the financial crisis.

Government also exercises control over capital expenditure. Prior to 1980 local authorities required loan sanction from central government for specific projects. Before the Labour government took office the trend was towards an increasing use of allocations for restricted purposes, with a corresponding reduction in block allocations that could be used flexibly to meet a range of spending priorities.[70] The Labour government introduced the idea of a single capital pot. The single capital pot constituted a cross-service allocation for the bulk of central government capital support to councils. The idea was to allow councils to take greater responsibility for the internal allocation of their resources among services.[71] This must now be seen in the light of the Local Government Act 2003, which allows local authorities to raise finance for capital expenditure, without government consent, where they can afford to service the debt without government support, subject to certain reserve powers for government to set limits on borrowing and credit.

The financial controls considered above, which aim to control and limit expenditure in advance, are supplemented by audit, which reviews past

---

[64] Available at: *https://www.gov.uk/government/collections/final-local-government-finance-settlement-england-2014-to-2015* [accessed 7 January 2016].

[65] White Paper, *Modern Local Government, In Touch with the People*, Ch.5.

[66] White Paper, *Modern Local Government, In Touch with the People*, para.5.3.

[67] White Paper, *Modern Local Government, In Touch with the People*, para.5.7.

[68] White Paper, *Modern Local Government, In Touch with the People*, para.5.11.

[69] Local Government Act 1999 Sch.1, introducing a new Pt IVA to the Local Government Finance Act 1992.

[70] White Paper, *Modern Local Government, In Touch with the People*, para.9.6.

[71] White Paper, *Modern Local Government, In Touch with the People*, para.9.7.

expenditure decisions. This is now undertaken by local auditors pursuant to the Local Audit and Accountability Act 2014.

3. LOCAL GOVERNANCE: AGENCIES AND SERVICE DELIVERY

6–017 The statutory changes introduced by the Conservative government in the 1980s, combined with an increasing emphasis on contracting-out and the like, led to the creation of a variety of agencies that are responsible for certain important functions which affect the local community.

Thus John, writing in 1997, provided the following list of bodies with responsibility for service provision at the local level[72]: companies/management buyouts supplying contracted-out services such as waste collection; private or semi-public bodies providing services purchased by local authorities, such as nursing homes; hospital trusts; central government agencies administering new or formerly local government functions, such as urban development corporations and Housing Action Trusts; partnership organisations such as Business Links; micro-agencies formerly under the umbrella of the local authority, such as schools running their own budgets, or schools which opted out of local authority control; existing public agencies that were given an enhanced new role, such as housing associations; regional officers of central government reorganized into government offices for the regions in 1995 (GORs); decentralised offices of Next Steps Agencies; voluntary associations; revitalised business organisations, such as larger Chambers of Commerce; large private sector companies with a renewed interest in local public decisions; privatised public utilities; and new or rejuvenated regional organisations.

The proliferation of such bodies led to attention being focused on local governance as opposed to local government, the former capturing the idea that local services were being provided by a range of bodies over and beyond local authorities. This remains true today, although some were abolished pursuant to the Public Bodies Act 2011, while others have been altered following organizational changes. The Localism Act 2011, which seeks to empower community groups in the provision of local services in the name of the Big Society project, is also relevant in this context.

4. CENTRAL–LOCAL RELATIONS AND DEMOCRACY

6–018 The previous discussion indicated how much influence central government wields over local authorities. How much influence it should wield is another matter. The debate on central–local relations can only be touched upon here. It involves fundamental issues, such as the balance between efficiency and democracy, between uniformity of standard and diversity, and the meaning to be attached participation. In historical terms there have been two opposing views of central–local relations, that which sees the latter as a mere agent of the former, and that which accords the two a more equal or autonomous status.

[72] John, "Local Governance", in Dunleavy, Gamble, Holliday and Peele (eds), *Developments in British Politics 5* (1997), pp.255–256.

The agency view was adopted by some Utilitarians. For Chadwick the prime consideration was efficiency with a presumption of uniformity. This was reflected in the administrative structure of the Poor Law, and public health. A strong central authority was desired and concessions to local autonomy were grudgingly accepted. The utilitarian approach must also be seen in its temporal setting. Municipal corporations were only just being reformed. Little faith could be placed in the corrupt oligarchies, which had not yet come to conceive of themselves as trustees of public funds. Most municipal functions were still performed independently of the municipal corporation by improvement commissioners and the like. It is unsurprising that Chadwick was wary of local power.

The modern heirs of the agency view add notions of equality and pragmatism to that of efficiency.[73] Divergent treatment of the same problem in different areas is regarded as unjust. Benefits and services should not depend upon the fortuity of where one lives, more especially because poorer areas will be those with greater needs and smaller sources of independent revenue from the rates. Pragmatism is used to buttress arguments from equality. The major sums involved in local authority financing necessitate centralised control in the form of loan sanctions, government grants and the like. A coherent economic policy would be impossible without such restraints.

6–019 The structural expression of the agency view tended towards relatively large unitary authorities. Fewer authorities providing the combined services a local community requires with the maximum economies of scale, was thought to be the ideal. While admitting the benefits of local democracy and participation, the proposals of the Redcliffe-Maud Report[74] reflected a preference for the unitary model. More modern advocates of the agency view have, however, to some extent moved away from the preference for large unitary authorities. This is in part because of the "dangers" that large power structures outside of central government were felt to pose, and in part because of the very desire to remove functions from local authorities and place them with a plethora of other institutions, either in the public or private sector.

The agency concept also manifests itself in the types of power that are left with local authorities. These may well be diminished if it can be shown to be preferable for functions to be administered from the centre, or by an institution separate from the traditional local authority.

The agency view was vehemently opposed in the 19th century by Toulmin Smith, for whom the parish was sacred. Opponents of the agency view do not however have to rely solely upon the Victorian sentimentality of a Toulmin Smith. The argument for more equal treatment between the centre and the local authorities can stand on stronger ground than that. This second view of central–local relations challenges certain key tenets of the agency approach. Notions of representative democracy may provide no sure guide as to the degree of freedom to be accorded to different levels of government, both of which have been duly elected.[75] It has, however, been argued that a strong democratic case can be made for local government as compared with the alternative, which is

[73] D. Hill, *Democratic Theory and Local Government* (London: Allen & Unwin, 1974), Ch.5.

[74] Redcliffe-Maud Report, Cmnd.4040 (1969).

[75] Griffith, *Central Departments and Local Authorities* (1966), pp.507–508.

local administration accountable upwards to an elected minister, and downwards to customers.[76] When criteria such as accountability, responsiveness and representativeness are applied to these two modes of governance a system of local democracy is clearly to be preferred.

6–020 The argument from equality is founded on a contentious premise. It can be argued that if a duly elected local authority chooses to administer benefits and services differently from another authority then that choice should within bounds be respected. What those bounds are is the focus of debate. The agency view tends to set narrow limits reflecting a predisposition for centrally determined standards uniformly applied. The alternative view would allow greater latitude to the local body, although subject to some constraints. While central government would ensure that minimum standards for a particular service were adhered to, greater choice over and beyond this would remain with the local authority than that allowed by advocates of the agency view.

Opponents of the agency model have also taken a different view as to the structure of local authorities and the ambit of their powers. Large unitary authorities were opposed because of the distancing effect that this produced. People no longer perceived of such authorities as "local", but as simply another arm of government with its seat appearing remote from the community. Two-tier authorities were preferred. Greater community participation was advocated and found expression in neighbourhood councils. Involvement of the local populace in community decision-making was encouraged. This could take the form of co-option of local people onto council committees dealing with particular matters. It could, more radically, become allied with movements for tenants' rights and social welfare pressure groups.

The distinction between the two views of central–local relations has no doubt been presented in an overly black and white fashion. Shades of grey clearly exist. It should not, moreover, be thought that the two views discussed here represent the only perspectives on central–local relations. Theories abound. Some argue that the relationship is more accurately characterised as one of exchange, in which the central and the local authorities bargain with each other to maximise their respective positions. Others articulate a more complex model, which denies a straightforward dichotomy between central and local authorities. They emphasise the fact that the centre is a collection of different units, as are the local authorities. Yet other approaches seek to advance the debate by placing it within a more general conceptual frame.[77] Each of these theories focuses upon distinct facts. They place varying weights on the sum total of facts that constitute the central–local relationship.[78]

6–021 It is, however, readily apparent from the preceding discussion that central control over local authorities increased considerably under the Thatcher government, and that this changed the way in which the two spheres of government interrelated. Local authorities were perceived as agents of central government. Their

[76] D. Beetham, "Theorising Democracy and Local Government", in King and Stoker (eds), *Rethinking Local Democracy* (1996), Ch.2.

[77] King and Stoker, *Rethinking Local Democracy* (1996).

[78] R. Rhodes, *Beyond Westminster and Whitehall, The Sub-Central Governments of Britain* (London: Routledge, 1988).

expenditure was controlled by the executive. The manner in which they conducted their operations was imbued with the central government's market-based perspective. Their powers were curtailed and given to the private sector or local agencies. Participation in local authority decision-making was not perceived as being beneficial in the sense of facilitating the development of the individual, or as being an integral aspect of partaking in civic life. When people participated they did so in a "market-role" as "consumers" of local services.

This strategy had an effect on the legal dimension of central–local relations. Traditionally the statutes that empowered local authorities were phrased in broad, open-textured terms. There might well be central supervisory powers to prescribe standards, control through an inspectorate, or default powers, which enabled a minister to take over the functions of a failing local authority.[79] Notwithstanding this framework, central–local relations were generally governed by bargain, negotiation and administrative practice, rather than resort to formal legal machinery.[80] The latter provided the framework for the bargain rather than being determinative of the particular outcome.[81]

The Conservative government's legislation in the late 1970s through to the mid-1990s changed this approach. It placed an increasingly large number of specific duties on local authorities and sought to curb expenditure by local government. The result was that central–local relations became more politicised, in the sense that a previous general mutuality as to objectives was questioned. The relations also became more juridified, in the sense that the law assumed a more significant role in defining the boundaries of central–local power, and in resolving conflicts between the two levels of government.[82] The role of law was transformed from that of providing a facilitative framework, into one where it operated as a tighter regulatory regime whereby central control over local authorities was imposed.[83] The earlier facilitative legislation was designed to provide "a flexible structure enabling norms to emerge through working practices",[84] whereas the regulatory mode of legislating had as its object the specification of the norms which would regulate the central–local relationship. This transformation required the passage of an increasing amount of detailed legislation. It forced the courts to adjudicate on a range of issues which had not

---

[79] Griffith, *Central Departments and Local Authorities* (1966).

[80] Loughlin, *Legality and Locality, The Role of Law in Central–Local Government Relations* (Oxford: Oxford University Press, 1996), p.365.

[81] R. Rhodes, *Control and Power in Central–Local Government Relations* (Gower, 1981).

[82] Loughlin, *Local Government in the Modern State* (1986) Ch.9; J. Gyford, "The Politicization of Local Government", in Loughlin, Gelfand and Young (eds), *Half a Century of Municipal Decline 1935–1985* (1985), Ch.4.

[83] Loughlin, *Legality and Locality, The Role of Law in Central–Local Government Relations* (1996), p.367.

[84] Loughlin, *Legality and Locality, The Role of Law in Central–Local Government Relations* (1996), p.381.

hitherto been felt suitable for legal resolution,[85] while being hampered by limitations of judicial review concerning fact finding, discovery and cross-examination.[86]

6–022 The Labour government's initiatives signalled a shift away from much that characterised the Conservative government's approach to central–local relations. This is apparent from the paper *Modern Local Government, In Touch with the People*,[87] and other documents. The general approach was to revitalise local government and enhance local democracy. There will be those who take issue with the suggestions made to achieve this end. This should not, however, serve to mask the general objective, which found expression in the Local Government Act 2000, the Local Government Act 2003, the 2001 White Paper on *Strong Local Leadership, Quality Public Services*,[88] and the 2006 White Paper on *Strong and Prosperous Communities*.[89]

The changes in the organisational pattern of local government, as expressed through the division between the executive and legislative arm thereof, were designed to foster accountability, transparency and efficiency.[90] There was increased emphasis on empowerment of local communities, involving greater choice for local communities in the way local services were designed and delivered, combined with increased duties on local authorities to inform and consult.[91] London has a central governing authority once again. A new ethical framework was devised for those in local politics.[92] Financial controls from the centre continued to exist, but the controls were more discriminating.[93] The general principle underlying service provision was Best Value, which was considered earlier in this Chapter.[94] The Best Value approach could result in services being provided by agencies, firms or organisations outside of local government. The market was, however, viewed in less doctrinaire terms than under the previous Conservative government. The Compulsory Competitive Tendering regime was abolished because it led to the neglect of service quality; the efficiency gains were uneven; it was inflexible; and because the compulsion which underpinned the system bred antagonism. The Local Government Act 1999, which gave effect to the Best Value regime, allowed local authorities more leeway, while still preserving the possibility of central intervention, and the local area agreements, LAAs, were designed to enhance flexibility and choice in relation to service provision.

---

[85] Loughlin, *Legality and Locality, The Role of Law in Central–Local Government Relations* (1996), p.368.

[86] Loughlin, *Legality and Locality, The Role of Law in Central–Local Government Relations* (1996), pp.405–407.

[87] White Paper, *Modern Local Government, In Touch with the People*.

[88] Office of the Deputy Prime Minister, *Strong Local Leadership, Quality Public Services* (2001).

[89] Department of Communities and Local Government, *Strong and Prosperous Communities* (October, 2006).

[90] White Paper, *Modern Local Government, In Touch with the People*, para.3.14.

[91] Department of Communities and Local Government, *Strong and Prosperous Communities* (October, 2006).

[92] Local Government Act 2000 Pt III.

[93] Local Government Act 1999 Sch.1.

[94] Local Government Act 1999 Pt I.

Time will tell how far these and other changes reinvigorated local government. There is clearly still more to be done in terms of reinvigorating local communities, increasing their freedom as to how to deploy resources and improving their accountability, as recognised by the Lyons Inquiry.[95] These themes continue to be relevant to government policy. Commentators will hold differing views about the Big Society project that provided the background thinking for the Localism Act 2011. This legislation does nonetheless seek to empower local authorities and community/voluntary groups therein, although it also repealed provisions in the Local Democracy, Economic Development and Construction Act 2009 that had not been brought into force, which imposed duties on local authorities to promote understanding of the functions and democratic arrangements of local authorities, and how members of the public could take part in those functions.

[95] Lyons Inquiry into Local Government, *Place-Shaping: A Shared Ambition for the Future of Local Government* (2007).

CHAPTER 7

DEVOLUTION

1. CENTRAL ISSUES

i. The Blair Labour government's programme of constitutional reform included important devolution settlements. This chapter focuses on the devolution regimes that apply to Scotland and Wales. Limits of space preclude treatment of Northern Ireland. 7–001

ii. The Government of Wales Act 1998 and the Scotland Act 1998 brought major changes in the pattern of government for the United Kingdom. Taken together with devolution of power in Northern Ireland and reforms in the pattern of local government, they constitute a significant change in the structure of political authority for the United Kingdom.[1]

iii. There are various ways in which a devolution settlement can be structured, but two forms predominate. The parent legislature may retain all power other than that given to the devolved legislature. The parent legislature may alternatively give all power to the devolved legislature other than that which it expressly retains. It should not be assumed that one schema is necessarily more or less empowering for the devolved legislature, since much depends on the extent to which power is given or retained by the parent legislature, and on the detail with which the distribution of power is specified in the enabling legislation.

iv. The "demand" for some form of devolution was greatest in relation to Scotland. It was given expression in the Scotland Act 1998. The legislation established a Scottish Executive, now known as the Scottish Government, and a Scottish Parliament. The 1998 Act gives the Scottish Parliament plenary power to legislate, except in relation to a long list of reserved matters set out in the legislation. The subsequent analysis will examine the legislative and executive powers accorded to Scotland, the constraints placed on those powers through the list of reserved matters, and the way in which the courts have interpreted these constraints on Scottish legislative and executive power. We shall also consider the future prospects for the devolution settlement.

v. The "demand" for some form of devolution was weaker in Wales, and this was reflected in the terms of the Government of Wales Act 1998. It embodied a devolution settlement for Wales, but the powers accorded to the

[1] The reports pursuant to the Devolution Monitoring Programme run by the Constitution Unit provide an invaluable picture of the reality of devolution, available at: *http://www.ucl.ac.uk/constitution-unit/research/devolution* [accessed 27 January 2016].

Welsh authorities were considerably less than those given to Scotland. The 1998 Act established a form of executive devolution and the Welsh institutions were largely confined to passage of subordinate legislation in areas devolved to them. The limited nature of the powers accorded to Wales prompted calls for reform and this led to the Government of Wales Act 2006. It significantly increased the powers of the Welsh institutions, more especially so after a referendum triggered the coming into effect in 2011 of provisions of the 2006 Act allowing the National Assembly to enact Assembly Acts.

2. SCOTLAND

A. Background

7–002 The history of Scottish nationalist and separatist sentiment is too rich and diverse to be captured here, and no attempt will be made to do so.[2] This brief background will, therefore, simply provide a chronology of some important developments relating to the governance of Scotland.

A Secretaryship for Scotland and a Scottish Office were established in 1885 with responsibility for a number of areas, including education, health, the Poor Law, local government, police, prisons, roads and public works. The following year the all-party Scottish Home Rule Association was set up. The Scottish Secretary became a full secretary of state in 1926, and in 1939 responsibility for Scottish affairs of a number of departments was vested in him.

It was the upsurge in the fortunes of the Scottish National Party in the late 1960s, combined with economic factors such as the discovery of North Sea oil, which placed the future shape of the United Kingdom on the political agenda. There was a growing sense that the Westminster Parliament did not adequately address the concerns of those in Scotland. We shall see in the discussion of Wales the impact this had on the setting up of the Royal Commission on the Constitution. The Labour government of 1974–1979 enacted the Scotland Act 1978, which provided for devolution of power. The referendum in Scotland was in favour of the measure, but not by the majority required for the Act to become effective. The Act was then repealed by the Conservative government on taking power in 1979.

[2] H. Drucker and J. Gordon Brown, *The Politics of Nationalism and Devolution* (London: Longman, 1980); C. Harvie, *Scotland and Nationalism: Scottish Society and Politics 1707–1994* (London: Routledge, 1994); J. Mitchell, *Strategies for Self-Government* (Edinburgh: Polygon, 1996); V. Bogdanor, *Devolution in the United Kingdom*, (Oxford: Oxford University Press, 1999), Ch.4; N. Walker, "Beyond the Unitary Conception of the United Kingdom Constitution?" [2000] P.L. 384; N. Burrows, *Devolution* (London: Sweet & Maxwell, 2000); R. Hazell and R. Rawlings (eds), *Devolution, Law Making and the Constitution* (Exeter: Imprint Academic, 2005); A. Trench (ed.), *The Dynamics of Devolution: The State of the Nations 2005* (Exeter: Imprint Academic, 2005); A. Trench, *Devolution and Power in the United Kingdom* (Manchester University Press, 2007); R. Hazell, *Constitutional Futures Revisited: Britain's Constitution to 2020* (London: Palgrave Macmillan, 2008); M. Keating, *The Independence of Scotland: Self-Government and the Shifting Politics of Union* (Oxford: Oxford University Press, 2009); G. Lodge and K. Schmueker (eds), *Devolution in Practice 2010* (London: IPPR, 2010).

The Conservative government under Margaret Thatcher had no interest in devolution. When the Conservatives were re-elected in 1987 the Campaign for a Scottish Assembly created a group to draw up plans for a constitutional convention. The committee published a report in 1988, entitled, *A Claim of Right for Scotland*, which recommended that a scheme should be drawn up for a Scottish Assembly. These plans gained further support because of a growing sense of Scottish alienation, since the Conservatives who dominated Westminster politics had a steadily declining share of the Scottish vote. The Scottish Constitutional Convention (SCC) held its first meeting in 1989. All parties were invited to attend, but the Conservatives declined, and the SNP, after taking part in the preparations for the Convention then withdrew. When the Conservatives were re-elected in 1992 the SCC established a Scottish Constitutional Commission to work out the details of their proposals. The Commission reported in 1994, and its work was incorporated in the SCC's report presented in 1995. The document, *Scotland's Parliament, Scotland's Right*, contained detailed proposals for a Scottish Parliament. The return of a Labour government in 1996 brought the possibility of devolution on to the Westminster political agenda.[3]

B. Composition of the Scottish Parliament

Section 1 of the Scotland Act 1998 (SA)[4] establishes the Scottish Parliament, elections for which were held on 6 May 1999, with the Parliament and the Executive, now known as the Scottish Government, taking up their powers on 1 July 1999. Ordinary general elections for the Scottish Parliament are held every four years.[5] The Scotland Act 2016 amended the Scotland Act 1998 through addition of s.63A, which provides that the Scottish Parliament and Government are permanent features of the UK's constitutional arrangements, and can only be abolished by a referendum of the people of Scotland. **7–003**

A member is returned for each constituency under the simple majority system,[6] and the constituencies are the parliamentary constituencies that operate for elections to the Westminster Parliament, plus the Orkney Islands and the Shetland Islands.[7] MSPs are also elected from regions under the additional member system of proportional representation.[8] There are eight regions, which are those used for elections to the European Parliament, and seven members are returned for each region.[9] Electors will therefore vote for both a constituency member and regional members.[10]

---

[3] N. Walker, "Constitutional Reform in a Cold Climate: Reflections on the White Paper & Referendum on Scotland's Parliament", in A. Tomkins (ed.), *Devolution and the British Constitution* (London: Key Haven, 1998), Ch.6.

[4] C. Himsworth and C. Munro, *The Scotland Act 1998*, 2nd edn (London: Sweet & Maxwell, 2000); C. Himsworth and C. O'Neill, *Scotland's Constitution: Law and Practice*, 3rd edn (Haywards Heath: Bloomsbury Professional, 2009).

[5] Scotland Act 1998 (SA) s.2(2).

[6] SA s.1(2).

[7] SA Sch.1 para.1.

[8] SA s.1(3).

[9] SA Sch.1 para.2.

[10] SA s.6.

Entitlement to vote is based on those who would be entitled to vote as electors in local government elections in an electoral area which falls wholly or partly within the constituency, provided that the person is registered in the register of local government electors at an address within the constituency.[11]

C. Formal Operation of the Scottish Parliament

7–004 We shall consider below how the Scottish Parliament and Executive have fared in practice.[12] The present discussion concentrates on the formal allocation of powers and offices.

A Presiding Officer of the Scottish Parliament plus two deputies are appointed from the elected members.[13] There is also a Clerk for the Parliament appointed by the Scottish Parliamentary Corporate Body.[14] This Corporate Body is composed of the Presiding Officer and four MSPs.[15] The Corporation provides the Parliament with the property, services and staff required for the Parliament's purposes,[16] and it has power to do anything it considers necessary or expedient for the discharge of its functions.[17]

The proceedings of the Parliament are regulated by standing orders,[18] which may or must make provision for a range of matters, including[19]: preserving order in the Parliament; withdrawal of members' rights and privileges; the reporting of parliamentary proceedings; and the way in which committees function. Proceedings of the Parliament are to be held in public, except so far as the standing orders dictate otherwise.[20] There is a Register of Members' Interests, which is to be open for public inspection.[21]

The Scottish Government at it is now known[22] is composed of the First Minister, such ministers as he or she appoints, and the Lord Advocate and Solicitor General for Scotland.[23] They are known collectively as the Scottish ministers,[24] they can hold property,[25] and appoint persons to be members of the Scottish Administration.[26] The First Minister is appointed by Her Majesty from among the members of the Scottish Parliament,[27] but the nomination for the

[11] SA s.11(1).
[12] See paras 7–025 to 7–027.
[13] SA s.19.
[14] SA s.20.
[15] SA s.21(2).
[16] SA s.21(3).
[17] SA Sch.2 para.4(1).
[18] SA s.22(1); Standing Orders of the Scottish Parliament (2011), available at: *http://www.scottish.parliament.uk/help/17797.aspx* [accessed 27 January 2016].
[19] SA Sch.3.
[20] SA Sch.3 para.3(1).
[21] SA s.39.
[22] Scotland Act 2012 s.12.
[23] SA s.44(1).
[24] SA s.44(2).
[25] SA s.59.
[26] SA s.51.
[27] SA s.45.

position comes from the Parliament itself.[28] Ministerial appointments made by the First Minister must also be approved by Her Majesty, but the First Minister must secure the agreement of Parliament before tendering names.[29]

D. Powers of the Scottish Parliament: Legislative Powers

i. Devolution strategies

The Scottish Parliament has been given power to make primary laws. Before examining its legislative powers it may be helpful to say something more general about techniques for the devolution of legislative power. There are in essence two approaches that can be adopted. Central government can devolve all its power to the other body, with the exception of reserved matters. It can, alternatively, devolve specified matters, with the corollary that all other matters remain within the power of the central authority. Both strategies have been employed in the United Kingdom. The Government of Ireland Act 1920 adopted the first of these approaches, the Scotland Act 1978 the second. **7–005**

It is tempting to think that the first approach will be more generous to the body to which power is devolved. There is no necessary reason why this should be so. The method used is in this sense neutral,[30] although there may well be symbolic differences between the two approaches. This is because, even if the first approach is adopted, so much turns on the list of reserved matters, as is apparent by comparison of the list of such matters in the Government of Ireland Act 1920 and the Scotland Act 1998. The list of reserved powers contained in the former Act is relatively short, and relatively general. The list contained in the Scotland Act 1998 is very long, contains general reservations and a plethora of much more detailed specific reservations.

Where the list of devolved or retained powers is long and complex it is difficult for the lay person to know for certain whether action really is within the power of the body to which authority has been devolved. The Scotland Act 1978 adopted the second strategy of providing a very detailed, complex list of devolved powers, on the assumption that all else remained with the central authority. It provoked the following comment from MacCormick.[31] When reading the material that follows it would be well to reflect on whether this same sentiment might not apply to the Scotland Act 1998.[32]

> "One fears that only lawyers and civil servants, but by no means all of them, will be able to work out or give reliable advice on the full meaning of the affirmations as qualified by the

---

[28] SA s.46(1).

[29] SA s.47(1)–(2). The same regime applies for the appointment of Scottish Law Officers: s.48.

[30] Constitution Unit, Scotland's Parliament, Fundamentals for New Scotland Act (1996).

[31] N. MacCormick "Constitutional Points'", in D. Mackay (ed.), *Scotland: The Framework for Change* (Harris, 1979), pp.53–54.

[32] See, however, the more positive tone of N. MacCormick, "Sovereignty or Subsidiarity? Some Comments on Scottish Devolution", in A. Tomkins (ed.), *Devolution and the British Constitution* (1998), Ch.1.

negations. Beyond doubt, this complexity and difficulty of comprehension is a defect of the Act. It infringes the principle of intelligibility of law, a principle most to be prized in constitutional enactments."

ii. Legislative powers: sections 28 and 29(1)

7–006 With these thoughts in mind we can now turn to the 1998 Act and consider the legislative powers it accords. The Scottish Parliament is given the power by s.28 SA to make primary laws, which are known as Acts of the Scottish Parliament. Standing orders must make provision for general debate on a Bill. There must be an opportunity for MSPs to vote on its general principles; to consider and vote on the details of a Bill; and for a final stage at which a Bill can be passed or rejected.[33] The Parliament's legislative capacity is presumptively general. It is however qualified in three ways.

First, s.28 does not affect the power of the Westminster Parliament to make laws for Scotland,[34] but it has been established by what is known as the Sewel Convention that the Westminster Parliament will not legislate on devolved matters without the consent of the Scottish Parliament. The Sewel Convention has been embodied in the Scotland Act 1998[35] as a result of the Scotland Act 2016.

Second, the legislative competence of the Scottish Parliament is bounded, and s.29(1) provides that an "Act of the Scottish Parliament is not law so far as any provision of the Act is outside the legislative competence of the Parliament". The meaning of this section is not beyond doubt. It could be interpreted to mean that if any provision of the challenged Act is outside the Parliament's legislative competence then the Act itself is not law. This would be very draconian. It is also not the most natural reading of the relevant words.[36] The better interpretation of s.29(1) is that the challenged Scottish Act is only not law so far as the provisions are ultra vires. The remainder of the Act that is untainted remains good law. There may however be occasions where the invalidity of certain provisions of an Act prevents the remainder from being viable legislation.

Third, the Scotland Act was amended in 2016 to require a two thirds majority relating to protected subject matter, which means any Bill that modifies, or confers power to modify: the persons entitled to vote as electors for the Scottish Parliament; the system by which members of the Parliament are returned; the number of constituencies, regions or any equivalent electoral area; and the number of members to be returned for each constituency, region or equivalent electoral area.[37]

---

33 SA s.36(1).

34 SA s.28(7).

35 SA s.28(8).

36 I. Jamieson, "Challenging the Validity of an Act of the Scottish Parliament: Some Aspects of *A v Scottish Ministers*" [2002] S.L.T. 71.

37 SA s.31(2A), (4), (5), and s.31A.

iii. Limits to legislative power: section 29(2)

Section 29(2) defines the bounds of the Scottish Parliament's competence. The member of the Scottish Government who is in charge of a Bill must, on or before the introduction of the Bill in the Parliament, state that in his or her view the provisions of the Bill would be within the legislative competence of the Parliament.[38] The Presiding Officer must also do so.[39] Section 29(2) states that a provision is outside the Parliament's competence if[40]: 7–007

> "(a) it would form part of the law of a country or territory other than Scotland, or confer or remove functions exercisable otherwise than in or as regards Scotland,
> (b) it relates to reserved matters,
> (c) it is in breach of the restrictions in Schedule 4,
> (d) it is incompatible with any Convention rights or with EU law,
> (e) it would remove the Lord Advocate from his position as head of the systems of criminal prosecution and investigation of deaths in Scotland."

iv. Limits to legislative power: section 29(2)(b) and Schedule 5

Section 29(2)(b) requires further explanation because it leads to the list of reserved matters, which is set out in Sch.5. This Schedule, which is divided into three parts, is very lengthy and therefore only the broad outlines of its provisions can be described here. Section 29(2)(b) states that a matter is outside the competence of the Scottish Parliament if it "relates" to reserved matters. Whether a provision of an Act of the Scottish Parliament relates to a reserved matter is to be determined by reference to the purpose of the provision having regard to its effects in all the circumstances.[41] 7–008

Part I of Sch.5 deals with General Reservations and lists a number of matters that are outside the competence of the Scottish Parliament. Important aspects of the *Constitution* are one such category[42]: the Crown, including succession to the Crown and a regency; the Union of the Kingdoms of Scotland and England; the Parliament of the United Kingdom; the continued existence of the High Court of Justiciary as a criminal court of first instance and of appeal; and the continued existence of the Court of Session as a civil court of first instance and of appeal. The prerogative and other executive functions are not, however, reserved matters.[43] A second general reservation relates to the *registration and funding of political parties*.[44] The *conduct of foreign affairs*, including relations with the European Union, other international organisations, and the regulation of

---

[38] SA s.31(1).

[39] SA s.31(2).

[40] SA s.29(2).

[41] SA s.29(3); *Imperial Tobacco Ltd v Lord Advocate* [2012] UKSC 61. See also s.29(4) which touches on the this same issue.

[42] SA Sch.5 Pt I para.1.

[43] SA Sch.5 Pt I para.2(1).

[44] SA Sch.5 Pt I para.6.

international trade, is not surprisingly another reserved matter.[45] The other general reservations relate to, *the public service, defence and treason*.[46]

Part II of Sch.5 deals with Specific Reservations.[47] A glance at this part of the Act makes one realise that it will be difficult for the Scottish Parliament to determine with certainty whether it has legislative competence or not. This may lead to legal challenge to test the correctness of the Parliament's judgment on these matters.

Part II contains a large number of reserved heads, which are listed as "Head A—Financial and Economic Matters", "Head B—Home Affairs", "Head C—Trade and Industry" and so on, there being 11 such heads in total.[48] Each of these Heads is then sub-divided into a number of sections labelled in the case of, for example Trade and Industry, which is Head C, from C1–C15. The list of the sub-divisions which apply for Trade and Industry relate to: business associations; insolvency; competition; intellectual property; import and export control; sea fishing; consumer protection; product standards, safety and liability; weights and measures; telecommunications and wireless telegraphy; Post Office, posts and postal services; Research Councils; designation of assisted areas; Industrial Development Advisory Board; and the protection of trading and economic interests.

The legal advisor's task of indicating whether the Scottish Parliament has competence or not is made more difficult by the style of drafting used in Pt II. On some occasions the reserved heads are set out at a high level of generality, without mentioning any existing statute. On other occasions the reserved heads will specify a particular section of a particular statute which is off-limits for the Scottish Parliament. On yet other occasions it will stipulate that the subject matter dealt with by an entire statute is outside the legislative competence of the Scottish Parliament. The format of Pt II is further complicated by the fact that these styles are often accompanied by exceptions, which allow the Scottish Parliament to legislate within the area thus stipulated, by interpretive statements designed to clarify the reach of the reserved head, and by illustrations aimed at clarifying the meaning of generally worded statements. These differing techniques will not infrequently be used within the same sub-division.[49]

Part III of Sch.5 has a more institutional focus. This is somewhat strange given that the Schedule is about "Reserved Matters": it is difficult to see how an institution as such can be a reserved matter. The gist of this Part of the Schedule is nonetheless to reserve certain bodies, or to clarify which bodies are not reserved. Thus, for example, a body mentioned by name in Pt II of Sch.5 is a reserved body, as is the Commission for Racial Equality, the Equal Opportunities Commission and the Disability Rights Commission.[50] The effect of being

[45] SA Sch.5 Pt I para.7(1). The implementation of international obligations, including those flowing from EU law and the ECHR, is not a reserved matter, Sch.5 para.7(2).

[46] SA Sch.5 Pt I paras 8–10.

[47] It is also the case that SA Sch.4 para.1 prevents the Scottish Parliament from modifying certain legislative provisions including, inter alia, the Human Rights Act 1998.

[48] The other Heads are: Energy, Transport, Social Security, Regulation of the Professions, Employment, Health and Medicines, Media and Culture and Miscellaneous.

[49] See, e.g. SA Sch.5 Pt II, ss.D1, E1, E3 and F1.

[50] SA Sch.5 Pt III para.3.

denoted as such a body is to reserve its constitution and its functions. Thus, it is outside the bounds of the Scottish Parliament's power to pass legislation that would interfere with the constitution or functions of these bodies.

Section 29(2)(b) and Sch.5 are reinforced by s.29(2)(c). This latter section brings Sch.4 into play, para.2(1) of which states that an Act of the Scottish Parliament cannot modify, or confer power by subordinate legislation to modify, the law on reserved matters. It is clear that the "law on reserved matters" covers any enactment whose subject matter is reserved, which is comprised in an Act of Parliament or subordinate legislation made there under. It also covers any rule of law that is not contained in an enactment where the subject matter is a reserved matter.[51] There is an exception where the modification is incidental to a provision that does not relate to the reserved matter, provided that the modification does not have a greater effect on reserved matters than is necessary to give effect to the purpose of the provision.[52] The Scottish Parliament can, however, restate the law.[53]

v. *Limits to legislative power: legal challenges and judicial approach*

The majority of legal challenges have been on the ground that Scottish legislation is incompatible with Convention rights. The courts have generally interpreted the compatibility of such Scottish legislation with Convention rights in the same way as when faced by an analogous challenge to UK legislation.[54] **7–009**

The judicial approach to Schs 4 and 5 has been cautious. Lord Hope in the *DS* case[55] stated that an attempt by the Scottish Parliament to widen the scope of its legislative competence as defined in those Schedules would be met by the requirement that any provision that could be read in such a way as to be outside competence must be read as narrowly as was required for it to be within competence. Lord Hope in *Martin*[56] adopted the rule evolved in commonwealth federal adjudication to the effect that the court would consider the pith and substance of the challenged legislation, or its true nature and character, to decide whether it fell within a prohibited or permitted sphere.

---

51 SA Sch.4 para.2(2).

52 SA Sch.4 para.3(1).

53 SA Sch.4 para.7(1).

54 *Starrs v Ruxton* 2000 S.L.T. 42; *Adams v Scottish Ministers* [2002] UKHRR 1179; *Anderson v Scottish Ministers* [2003] 2 A.C. 602; *Brown v Stott* [2003] 1 A.C. 681; *HM Advocate v McIntosh (Robert) (No.1)* [2003] 1 A.C. 1078; *Montgomery v HM Advocate* [2003] 1 A.C. 641; *Mills (Kenneth Anthony) v HM Advocate (No.2)* [2004] 1 A.C. 441; *HM Advocate v R* [2004] 1 A.C. 462; *Flynn (Patrick Anthony) v HM Advocate (No.1)* [2004] H.R.L.R. 17; *DS v HM Advocate* [2007] H.R.L.R. 28; *Friend v Lord Advocate* [2007] UKHL 53; *Somerville v Scottish Ministers* [2007] UKHL 44; *AXA General Insurance Ltd v HM Advocate* [2011] UKSC 46; *S v L* 2011 S.L.T 1204; *HM Advocate v Murtagh* [2011] 1 A.C. 731; *Ambrose v Harris* [2011] UKSC 43; *Moohan v Lord Advocate* [2014] UKSC 67.

55 *DS* [2007] H.R.L.R. 28 at [23].

56 *Martin v HM Advocate* [2010] UKSC 10.

It has not been easy for claimants to convince the courts that Scottish legislation should be invalidated for breach of s.29 and Schs 4 and 5.[57] The courts have striven to interpret the reservations so as allow the contested Scottish legislation to be regarded as valid,[58] although there have been instances where legislation has been caught by the reservations.[59]

The Supreme Court in *AXA*[60] made it clear that while Scottish legislation, emanating from a non-sovereign body, was subject to the supervisory jurisdiction of the UK courts, it was nonetheless made by a body with plenary authority over its assigned area, subject to the limits in s.29. The consequence was the legislation did not have to be made for a specific purpose, or with regard to particular considerations, and accountability lay primarily to the electorate rather than the courts. A further consequence was that common law tools of judicial review such as irrationality, developed for review of administrative bodies, were constitutionally inappropriate when reviewing Scottish legislation, although the Supreme Court did reserve the right to review on grounds other than those in s.29 in exceptional instances where the challenged legislation abrogated fundamental rights or the rule of law.

E. Powers of the Scottish Parliament: Executive Powers

7–010 The Scottish ministers that comprise the Scottish Government are accorded power in four ways by the Scotland Act.

First, specific statutory functions can be conferred on the Scottish ministers by name through any enactment.[61] Such statutory functions are to be exercisable on behalf of Her Majesty, and can be exercised by any member of the Scottish Government.[62]

Second, the SA makes a general transfer to the Scottish ministers of functions hitherto exercised by a minister of the Crown.[63] The functions transferred are[64]: those prerogative and other executive functions which are exercisable on behalf of her Majesty by a minister of the Crown; other functions conferred on a minister of the Crown by a prerogative instrument; and functions conferred on a minister of the Crown by any pre-commencement enactment.[65] The Scottish ministers are therefore prima facie given the powers exercised by ministers of the Crown in relation to Scotland. Subordinate legislation can adapt the functions previously exercised by a minister of the Crown in order to facilitate the

57 A. Poole, "Recent Legislative Competence Challenges" [2011] S.L.T. 127; C. Himsworth, "Nothing Special about that? Martin v HM Advocate in the Supreme Court" (2010) 14 Edin. L.R. 487.

58 *Martin* [2010] UKSC 10; *Imperial Tobacco Ltd v Lord Advocate* [2012] UKSC 61.

59 *Henderson v HM Advocate* 2011 S.L.T. 488; *Whaley v Lord Watson of Invergowrie* 2000 S.L.T. 475; *Salvesen v Riddell* [2013] UKSC 22.

60 *AXA General Insurance* [2011] UKSC 46.

61 SA ss.52(1) and 52(7).

62 SA s.52(1)–(3).

63 SA s.53(1).

64 SA s.53(2).

65 This provision, s.53(2)(c), is subject to Sch.4 paras 12–14.

transfer.[66] These functions are, however, only transferred in so far as they are exercisable within "devolved competence".[67] The exercise of a function will be outside a devolved competence if it would be outside the legislative competence of the Scottish Parliament itself.[68] What this means is that the Scottish Government cannot act so as to circumvent the limits placed on the legislative competence of the Parliament,[69] and that Scottish ministers cannot act incompatibly with Convention rights or EU law.[70] This is entirely logical given the general scheme of the SA. It follows that the difficulties in interpreting the boundaries of legislative competence charted above will apply whenever the executive seeks to act, irrespective of the form the act takes.

Third, notwithstanding the generality of the transfer of functions described in the preceding paragraph, the SA stipulates that the functions under certain statutes are to be exercisable by a minister of the Crown as well as the Scottish ministers.[71] There is, moreover, a power to make an Order in Council which would provide for a function that had been transferred to the Scottish Government to be exercised by a minister of the Crown instead, or a by a minister of the Crown concurrently with a member of the Scottish Government, or by a member of the Scottish Executive only with the agreement, or after consultation with, a minister of the Crown.[72]

Finally, an Order in Council can be passed providing for the transfer of additional functions to Scottish Ministers.[73]

F. Powers of the Scottish Parliament: Subordinate Legislation

The discussion thus far has concentrated on the making of Acts of the Scottish Parliament and the powers of the Government. The SA also makes provision for subordinate legislation. **7–011**

i. *Subordinate legislation and earlier enactments: the scope of the power*

The position here is clear. Where any pre-commencement enactment, prerogative instrument or other instrument or document contain references to a minister of the Crown these are to be read as including references to the Scottish ministers.[74] The power of the Scottish ministers to make such legislation is premised on the assumption that it is within their devolved competence.[75] **7–012**

66 SA s.106.
67 SA s.53(1).
68 SA ss.54(2)–(3).
69 *Somerville* [2007] UKHL 44 at [14].
70 SA s.57(2).
71 SA ss.56–57; *Somerville* [2007] UKHL 44; *Napier v Scottish Ministers* [2004] U.K.H.R.R. 881; *Potter v Scottish Prison Service* [2007] C.S.I.H. 67; *X v Scottish Ministers* [2007] C.S.I.H. 45; *B, Petitioner* [2007] C.S.O.H. 73.
72 SA s.108.
73 SA s.63.
74 SA s.117.
75 SA s.118(1).

ii. Subordinate legislation made under the Scotland Act: the scope of the power

7–013 The Scotland Act gives extensive power to make subordinate legislation in a wide variety of circumstances. Four situations are of particular importance.

First, as we have already seen, the Act provides for both specific and general transfer of functions to Scottish ministers that were previously exercised by a minister of the Crown, and these functions clearly include the making of subordinate legislation.[76]

Second, s.104 allows subordinate legislation to make such provision as the person making it considers necessary or expedient in consequence of any provision made by or under any Act of the Scottish Parliament.

Third, s.105 provides that subordinate legislation may modify any pre-commencement enactment, prerogative instrument, or any other instrument or document, as appears necessary or expedient to the person making the legislation in consequence of the SA. It seems clear from the definition of "pre-commencement enactment"[77] that this term includes primary legislation passed before the SA. This therefore means that s.105 constitutes a broad "Henry VIII" clause allowing earlier primary legislation to be modified by secondary legislation.[78] The subordinate legislation made under s.105 is, however, subject to scrutiny by the Westminster Parliament.[79]

Finally, a further important "Henry VIII" power is to be found in s.107. This in effect allows subordinate legislation to be used to cure defects in an Act of the Scottish Parliament, or exercise of power by the Scottish Government, which has been found to be ultra vires. The "curative" subordinate legislation, if made without a draft having been approved by resolution of each House of Parliament, is subject to annulment pursuant to a resolution of either House.[80]

---

[76] SA ss.52–54.

[77] SA s.53(3). The matter is not entirely free from doubt for two reasons First, although the definition of pre-commencement enactment given in s.53(3) is stated to be a definition for the purposes of the Act, the context of s.53(3) is in relation to the transfer of power to the Scottish ministers, which is different from the modification of earlier legislation. Second, the definition of "enactment" in s.126 may be narrower. This definition is itself problematic. We are told that the term "enactment" includes, inter alia, "an enactment comprised in, or in subordinate legislation under, an Act of Parliament whenever passed or made". It is not clear whether the phrase "an enactment comprised in an Act of Parliament" is intended to mean a section of such legislation, or whether it has some other meaning. In any event the use of the same word, enactment, to describe both legislation, such as an Act of the Scottish Parliament, and a section of an Act of the Westminster Parliament is confusing to say the very least.

[78] See, e.g. Scotland Act 1998 (Consequential Modifications) (No.2) Order (SI 1820/1999); Scotland Act 1998 (Consequential Modifications) Order (SI 2040/2000); Scotland Act 1998 (Consequential Modifications) Order (SI 1400/2001).

[79] SA Sch.7 paras 1(2) and 2, applying the Type G procedure to such subordinate legislation.

[80] SA Sch.7 para.1(2).

iii. *Subordinate legislation made under the Scotland Act: exercise of the power*

The SA therefore gives extensive powers to make subordinate legislation. Section 112 states that if no other provision is made as to the person by whom the power is exercisable, it shall be exercisable by Her Majesty by Order in Council or by a Minister of the Crown by order. This is not problematic in relation to the specific or general transfer of functions to Scottish ministers, since the relevant sections of the Act clearly authorise them to make subordinate legislation. However, other sections of the SA which authorise the making of subordinate legislation, such as ss.104, 105 and 107, do not provide any further definition as to who can exercise the power, and therefore s.112 is operative in such instances. The key issue is whether the Scottish ministers can exercise these powers. **7–014**

It might be argued that Scottish ministers are ministers of the Crown and therefore come within s.112(1). The arguments in favour of this approach are as follows. The Scottish ministers are appointed by, and hold office at, Her Majesty's pleasure.[81] Section 117 provides that any pre-commencement enactment, or prerogative instrument, *and any other instrument or document*, shall be read as if references to a minister of the Crown were, or included, references to the Scottish ministers. It might be argued that the italicised words resolve the matter. This would be so if these words could be read so as to include the Scotland Act itself. Scottish ministers come within the definition provided in the general legislation on this issue.[82] The reference to "Her Majesty's Government" within this definition might be read as excluding other parts of Her Majesty's possessions (such as the remaining dependencies), but it is taken to include Northern Ireland.[83] Given that this is so, there is no reason why it should not also include Scotland. The Scottish ministers, moreover, fit the summary of minister of the Crown provided in the academic literature.[84]

There are, however, arguments the other way, which suggest that Scottish ministers are not regarded as ministers of the Crown. Most important in this respect is the fact that the Act, at a number of relevant points, expressly treats ministers of the Crown and Scottish ministers separately.[85] The very breadth of the subordinate legislative powers contained in ss.104–107 also indicates that only a minister from the Westminster Parliament should exercise them. This view is supported by *Hansard*.[86]

The reality in practice is that statutory instruments made pursuant to ss.104–105 SA are signed by the relevant Whitehall minister, who is normally the Secretary of State for Scotland or an Under Secretary of State. The statutory instruments will commonly deal with modifications to Westminster legislation consequent on Scottish Acts of Parliament. This does in itself preclude Scottish

---

[81] SA ss.45 and 47.

[82] Ministers of the Crown Act 1975 s.8(1) which provides that: "In this Act … 'Minister of the Crown' means the holder of an office in Her Majesty's Government in the United Kingdom, and includes the Treasury, the Board of Trade and the Defence Council".

[83] R. Brazier, *Ministers of the Crown* (Oxford: Oxford University Press, 1996), p.24.

[84] Brazier, *Ministers of the Crown* (1996), pp.30–31.

[85] See, e.g. SA ss.52(6), 53(1), 60(1), 106(1), 108(1) and 112(5).

[86] *Hansard*, HL Vol.593, col.592 (8 October 1998).

ministers seeking to promote an Order in Council, which is the other option mentioned in s.112(1); the Scottish minister would be the person who drafted and presented the subordinate legislation for approval to Her Majesty by Order in Council.[87]

iv. Subordinate legislation made pursuant to the Scotland Act: the procedure

7–015 The procedural rules applicable to the making of subordinate legislation are complex, and only an outline can be provided here. It is important to distinguish broadly between two types of situation.

First, there is the situation where a function has been transferred to a Scottish minister, and this includes the power to make subordinate legislation. The Scotland Act provides that where the making of subordinate legislation under the pre-commencement enactment required the laying of the measure before the Westminster Parliament, and for the annulment or approval of it by resolution of either or both Houses of Parliament, then the reference to the Westminster Parliament is to be taken to be a reference to the Scottish Parliament.[88] In essence therefore the mode of approving such legislation which applied when it was made at Westminster is carried across to Scotland.

Second, there are many situations where the Scotland Act allows subordinate legislation to be made in relation to powers conferred by the Act itself. Detailed rules are stipulated as to the procedure for the passing of such legislation. Schedule 7 sets out 11 different procedures that can apply to the making of subordinate legislation under the SA. It then dictates which procedure is to apply to each of the stated sections of the Act. The procedures vary considerably as to what is required. The common theme is, however, that approval in some form must be gained from the Westminster Parliament as well as from the Scottish Parliament. The procedures in Sch.7 therefore apply to subordinate legislation that is of some real importance, and such legislation requires the approval of each House of Parliament, or is subject to annulment in pursuance of a resolution of either House.[89]

G. Political Challenge to the Competence of the Scottish Parliament

7–016 The Scotland Act contains provisions enabling the secretary of state to intervene in certain cases. Two sections of the Act are of particular importance in this respect.

Section 35 allows the secretary of state to make an order prohibiting the Presiding Officer from submitting a Bill for Royal Assent if it contains provisions which he or she has reasonable grounds to believe would be incompatible with

[87] The standard practice is for statutory Orders in Council to be drafted by the relevant government department, which would, of course normally be a Whitehall department, Sir C. Allen, *Law and Orders*, 3rd edn (London: Stevens, 1965), pp.90–91.

[88] SA s.118(2).

[89] SA Sch.7 para.1, applying the Type G procedure in such instances.

any international obligations, or the interests of defence or national security. The secretary of state can also make such an order where the Bill has provisions which modify the law as it applies to reserved matters, and which he or she has reasonable grounds to believe would have an adverse effect on the operation of the law as it applies to reserved matters. Reasons must be given for making such an order.

Section 58 contains a parallel power for the secretary of state to intervene on the same grounds in relation to subordinate legislation made by the Scottish Government.[90] In such instances the secretary of state may by order actually revoke the legislation. This section also empowers the secretary of state to direct that action proposed to be taken by the Scottish Government, which would be incompatible with international obligations, is not taken, or to direct that such action is taken where that is required to give effect to an international obligation.[91]

H. Judicial Challenge to the Competence of the Scottish Parliament

The SA places significant limitations on the legal competence of the Scottish Parliament. The corollary is the need for legal rules that indicate when a challenge can be made.[92] Schedule 6, which is made operative by s.98, is central in this respect. It defines "devolution issue" to mean[93]: **7–017**

> "(a) a question whether an Act of the Scottish Parliament or any provision of an Act of the Scottish Parliament is within the legislative competence of the Parliament,
> (b) a question whether any function (being a function which any person has purported, or is proposing, to exercise) is a function of the Scottish Ministers, the First Minister or the Lord Advocate,
> (c) a question whether the purported or proposed exercise of a function by a member of the Scottish Government is, or would be, within devolved competence,
> (d) a question whether a purported or proposed exercise of a function by a member of the Scottish Government is, or would be, incompatible with any of the Convention rights or with EU law,
> (e) a question whether a failure to act by a member of the Scottish Government is incompatible with any of the Convention rights or with EU law,
> (f) any other question about whether a function is exercisable within devolved competence or in or as regards Scotland and any other question arising by virtue of this Act about reserved matters.
>
> But a question arising in criminal proceedings in Scotland that would, apart from this paragraph, be a devolution issue is not a devolution issue if (however formulated) it relates to the compatibility with any of the Convention rights or with EU law of (a) an Act of the Scottish Parliament or any provision of an Act of the Scottish Parliament, (b) a function, (c) the purported or proposed exercise of a function, (d) a failure to act."

Section 101 provides important guidance for courts faced with devolution issues. The effect is to impose an interpretive obligation on courts to try and read Acts and Bills of the Scottish Parliament, and subordinate legislation, as being

90 SA s.58(4).
91 SA ss.58(1)–(2).
92 *Martin* [2010] UKSC 10
93 SA Sch.6 para.1.

intra vires rather than ultra vires. Where any provision of such a measure could be read so as to be ultra vires, s.101(2) states that it is to be read as narrowly as possible as is required for it to be within competence,[94] if such a reading is possible.[95] The SA contains detailed rules as to the different types of legal challenge.

i. *Resolution of devolution issues: direct reference to the Supreme Court*

7–018 A devolution issue may be resolved through direct reference to the Supreme Court. There are three types of case where this can occur.

First, there can be *pre-enactment scrutiny*. The Advocate General, the Lord Advocate or the Attorney General may refer the question, whether a Bill or any provision of a Bill would be within the legislative competence of the Parliament to the Supreme Court for a decision.[96] The Presiding Officer must not submit a Bill for Royal Assent at any time when such a law officer is entitled to make a reference, or where the reference has been made, but the Supreme Court has not yet disposed of the matter.[97] If the Supreme Court decides that the Bill is ultra vires then the Presiding Officer cannot submit it for Royal Assent in its unamended form.[98] Special provision is made for cases which might be referred by the Supreme Court to the Court of Justice of the European Union, CJEU.[99] Pre-enactment scrutiny by the Supreme Court now also covers contestation as to whether a Bill falls within protected subject matter and thus requires a two-thirds majority.[100]

Second, there is the possibility of a direct reference to the Supreme Court *from existing proceedings*. Law officers must be notified of a devolution issue which arises in particular proceedings, and they are entitled to take part in the proceedings so far as they relate to the devolution issue.[101] The Lord Advocate, the Advocate General, the Attorney General and the Attorney General for Northern Ireland may require the court or tribunal to refer the devolution issue to the Supreme Court.[102]

Third, there can be a direct reference of a devolution issue *which is not the subject of existing proceedings*. The same law officers can exercise this power.[103]

---

[94] "Competence" is defined in relation to an Act of the Scottish Parliament, or a Bill, to mean the legislative competence of the Parliament; in relation to subordinate legislation it is defined to mean the powers conferred by the SA s.101(3).

[95] *Somerville* [2007] UKHL 44.

[96] SA s.33(1). Such a reference can be made within four weeks beginning with the passing of the Bill, and any period of four weeks beginning with the subsequent approval of the Bill in accordance with standing orders which are made, s.33(2).

[97] SA s.32(2).

[98] SA s.32(3).

[99] SA s.34.

[100] SA s.32A.

[101] SA Sch.6 paras 5–6, 16–17, 26–27. Which Law officers must be notified depends on where the proceedings initially arise, Scotland, England and Wales or Northern Ireland.

[102] SA Sch.6 para.33.

[103] SA Sch.6 paras 34–35.

ii. Resolution of devolution issues: institution of proceedings by a law officer

The SA allows the relevant law officer to institute proceedings for the determination of a devolution issue. The Lord Advocate will normally be the defendant in such actions.[104] The law officers have the power to require the devolution issue to be referred to the Supreme Court, as described above, but may choose not to exercise this power. **7–019**

iii. Resolution of devolution issues: reference to other courts

The discussion thus far, has focused on the role of the law officers in enforcing the limits to the Scottish Parliament's power. Devolution issues may, however, arise in the course of proceedings involving individuals, or between an individual and a public body. The Act contemplates such actions.[105] It makes provision in such instances for the referral of devolution issues from one court to another. Proceedings which raise devolution issues may occur in Scotland itself, in England and Wales or in Northern Ireland. The SA establishes a reference system for all three jurisdictions. The description which follows applies in relation to England and Wales. **7–020**

In non-criminal proceedings, magistrates' courts can refer devolution issues to the High Court.[106] Other courts cases may refer such issues to the Court of Appeal.[107] In criminal cases, a court, other than the Court of Appeal or the Supreme Court, can refer a devolution issue to the High Court, in the case of summary proceedings, or the Court of Appeal in the case of proceedings on indictment.[108] Tribunals from which there is no appeal must refer to the Court of Appeal, and may make a reference in other instances.[109] The Court of Appeal can refer any devolution issue which comes before it, other than on a reference as described above, to the Supreme Court.[110]

Appeals from the High Court or the Court of Appeal on devolution issues lie to the Supreme Court. Permission is required for such an appeal from the High Court or Court of Appeal, or from the Supreme Court.[111]

iv. Resolution of devolution issues: decision made by the court immediately seized of the matter

The court immediately seized of the matter has the power to refer the matter in the manner described above. It does not have the duty to do so, subject to being compelled to make a reference by the intervention of a law officer. **7–021**

---

104 SA Sch.6 paras 4, 15, 25.

105 SA Sch.6 paras 4(3), 15(3) and 25(3).

106 SA Sch.6 para.18.

107 SA Sch.6 para.19, with the exception of magistrates' courts, the Court of Appeal or the Supreme Court, or the High Court where acting under para.18.

108 SA Sch.6 para.21.

109 SA Sch.6 para.20.

110 SA Sch.6 para.22.

111 SA Sch.6 para.23.

v. Devolution issues which "arise": relevance of the general law on collateral challenge

7–022 The Scotland Act is framed in terms of devolution issues "arising".[112] The paradigm case is one of direct challenge, but devolution issues may also arise indirectly. There will be collateral challenges where, for example, the Assembly is enforcing a piece of subordinate legislation and the applicant claims that it is ultra vires, and should not therefore be enforced. Recent decisions of the courts have been more liberal in allowing collateral challenge, although there are still some uncertainties.[113] This raises the interesting question as to how far the general rules concerning collateral challenge and vires issues will apply in this context. The courts' more liberal attitude to collateral challenge should mean that if the general legal rules on collateral challenge are applied, claimants will normally be able to raise vires issues indirectly as well as directly.

vi. Result of finding that the Scottish Parliament acted outside its competence

7–023 The SA makes provision as to what should occur if an Act of the Scottish Parliament, or subordinate legislation, is found to be ultra vires.

In political terms, the SA contains a "Henry VIII" clause allowing the passage of subordinate legislation to amend an Act of the Scottish Parliament, or other subordinate legislation, which has been found to be ultra vires.[114] The subordinate legislation which performs this corrective function is, however, subject to scrutiny by the Westminster Parliament.[115]

In legal terms, the SA empowers a court or tribunal which has decided that an Act of the Scottish Parliament, or subordinate legislation, is ultra vires, to make an order removing or limiting any retrospective effect of that decision, or suspending the effect of that decision for any period and on any conditions to allow the defect to be corrected.[116] The court, in deciding whether to make such an order, must take into account the extent to which persons who are not party to the proceedings would otherwise be adversely affected.[117] The appropriate law officer must be given intimation that such an order might be made, and can then join the proceedings for this issue.[118] The power to limit the retrospective effect applies only to legislation, and not to a decision of the Scottish Government that is ultra vires.[119]

---

[112] SA Sch.6.
[113] Ch.27.
[114] SA s.107.
[115] SA Sch.7 para.1(2).
[116] SA s.102(2).
[117] SA s.102(3).
[118] SA s.102(4).
[119] *Cadder v HM Advocate* [2010] UKSC 43.

I. Scottish Devolution: Some Reflections

Time will tell whether devolution to Scotland weakens separatist claims, or whether it proves to be but the first step towards a more formal separation from the rest of the United Kingdom. Political, legal, and inter-governmental considerations are important in this respect. **7–024**

i. Political considerations

In political terms, the Scottish Parliament was initially run by a coalition between the Scottish Labour Party and the Scottish Liberal Democrat Party. However, 2007 saw the SNP take office, albeit as a minority government, together with the election of a nationalist First Minister, Alex Salmond. The Scottish Executive was rebranded in September 2007 as the Scottish Government, and this is now also the legal appellation. It remains to be seen whether Scottish devolution is a "motorway without exit to an independent state". These were the evocative words of Tam Dalyell,[120] although experience from other countries demonstrates that the grant of autonomy may invigorate an existing union, and not lead to its destruction.[121] **7–025**

The SNP Scottish government published a White Paper on constitutional reform, *Choosing Scotland's Future: A National Conversation*,[122] in which it canvassed three choices: retention of the devolution scheme in the Scotland Act 1998, with the possibility of further evolution of these powers; redesigning devolution by adopting a specific range of extensions to the current powers of the Scottish Parliament and Scottish government, possibly involving fiscal autonomy, but short of progress to full independence; extending the powers of the Scottish Parliament and Scottish Government to the point of independence.

The SNP Scottish Government was, not surprisingly, in favour of the third option, which would involve repeal of the 1707 Anglo-Scottish Union. Much of the White Paper was nonetheless devoted to discussion of the powers that could be devolved to Edinburgh without thereby dissolving the United Kingdom. It advocated transfer of further powers in areas such as economic and fiscal policy, employment and trade union law, social security and pensions, broadcasting, anti-terrorism and firearms law, energy and climate change policy. The opposition parties were vocal in their condemnation of the nationalist agenda, but were willing to engage in debate about the best way for devolution to develop.[123]

The SNP was returned as the dominant party in 2011, and a referendum on independence was held in 2014, in which the voters rejected the idea of an

---

[120] R. Hazell and B. O'Leary, "A Rolling Programme of Devolution: Slippery Slope or Safeguard of the Union?", in Hazell (ed.), *Constitutional Futures, A History of the Next Ten Years* (1999), p.23.

[121] Hazell and O'Leary, "A Rolling Programme of Devolution: Slippery Slope or Safeguard of the Union?", in Hazell (ed.), *Constitutional Futures, A History of the Next Ten Years* (1999), pp.23–26.

[122] Choosing Scotland's Future: A National Conversation. Independence and Responsibility in the Modern World (August 2007), available at: *http://www.gov.scot/Publications/2007/08/13103747/0* [accessed 29 January 2016].

[123] Jack McConnell, Annabel Goldie and Nicol Stephen, "Statement on Independence" (August 13, 2007), available at: *http://news.bbc.co.uk/1/hi/scotland/6944185.stm* [accessed 17 April 2012].

independent Scotland.[124] However, notwithstanding the SNP's failure to secure independence, it had very marked electoral success in the UK general elections 2015. Although there is no set date for a further Scottish referendum the result of the Brexit referendum is significant in this respect. There were was a majority in the UK for exiting the EU, but there was also a significant majority in Scotland for remaining. Nicola Sturgeon, the First Minister, stated that this provided the rationale for another Scottish referendum on independence. Whether and when it is held remains to be seen.

ii. Legal considerations

7–026 The Scotland Act 2012 amended the Scotland Act 1998: it made some changes to the list of devolved matters; formally changed the nomenclature from Scottish Executive to Scottish Government, thus making legal form catch up with political reality; modified the powers of the Lord Advocate; and extended s.102 SA to allow the courts to limit the retrospective effect of ultra vires decisions of the Scottish Government. The most important change made by the legislation was, however, to increase Scotland's financial autonomy, pursuant to recommendations from the Calman Commission,[125] such that the Scottish Parliament can set its own rate of income tax, and gain revenue from certain other taxes, dealing with land transactions and waste disposal, which are devolved to Scotland.

The political parties opposed to independence in the 2014 referendum promised devolution of further powers if Scotland remained within the UK. The cross-party Smith Commission was set up after the referendum in order to carry this promise forward. The Scotland Act 2016, which amends the Scotland Act 1998, implements recommendations from the Smith Commission.

Its principal provisions stipulate that the Scottish Parliament and the Scottish Government are considered permanent parts of the UK's constitutional arrangements and will not be abolished without a decision of the Scottish people of Scotland; that the UK Parliament will not normally legislate in relation to devolved matters without the consent of the Scottish Parliament, while retaining the sovereignty to do so; it gives increased autonomy to the Scottish Parliament and the Scottish Ministers in relation to the operation of Scottish Parliament and local government elections in Scotland; it gives increased autonomy to the Scottish Parliament to amend sections of the Scotland Act 1998 which relate to the operation of the Scottish Parliament and the Scottish Government within the United Kingdom; it increases the financial accountability of the Scottish Parliament; it devolves further welfare powers to Scotland; and also augments the Scottish Parliament's powers over areas such as energy.

Much will still turn on the way in which the courts treat challenges to the competence of the Scottish Parliament. The law officers will be wary of using their power to refer to the Supreme Court where a clash between an Act of the Scottish Parliament and a reserved matter is not relatively clear. This is borne out by the Memorandum of Understanding, which states that a reference to the Supreme Court on a vires issue will be seen "very much as a matter of last

[124] Scotland's Referendum, available at *http://www.scotreferendum.com/* [accessed 28 January 2016].
[125] *Serving Scotland Better: Scotland and the UK in the 21st Century* (2009).

resort".[126] The emphasis is squarely placed on resolving problems through discussion. The very fact that the matter being challenged is an Act of the Scottish Parliament is, moreover, likely to make the courts wary of finding that its provisions are ultra vires. This is all the more so given the presence of the interpretative obligation contained in the SA, encouraging the courts to give a narrow reading to a provision in Scottish legislation in order to render it legal.[127]

The Scottish Parliament will, nonetheless, have to be aware of the "judge over its shoulders" when framing legislation. The Parliament's legal advisers will have to scrutinise Scottish Bills carefully to ensure that they do not impinge on reserved matters. This is equally true of actions of the Scottish Government.[128] The fact that the member of the Scottish Government in charge of the Bill states that, in his view, it is within the competence of the Scottish Parliament, and that this is affirmed by the Presiding Office, are mere statements of opinion, which do not bind the courts.[129]

iii. Intergovernmental considerations

The relationship between Scotland, Wales and Westminster is ordered through a Memorandum of Understanding (MOU),[130] and accompanying Concordats. The MOU is not legally binding,[131] but it is of central importance for relations between the bodies to whom power has been devolved and Westminster. The MOU provides for communication and consultation between the different administrations, co-operation on areas of mutual interest, and exchange of information. A Joint Ministerial Committee (JMC) was established to consider non-devolved matters that impinge on devolved responsibilities, and vice-versa, the respective treatment of devolved matters in different parts of the United Kingdom, and disputes between the administrations. The JMC meets in plenary session once a year, and in sectoral areas, dealing with Europe, Health, the Knowledge Economy and the European Union. **7–027**

The MOU is supplemented by individual Concordats between the Scottish government and UK government departments,[132] and between the National Assembly for Wales and such departments. There are also Concordats on issues that cut across particular departments, such as EU Policy,[133] and International

[126] *Memorandum of Understanding and Supplementary Agreements between the United Kingdom Government, Scottish Ministers, the Cabinet of the National Assembly for Wales and the Northern Ireland Executive Committee* (2001), Cm.5240, para.26; *Memorandum of Understanding and Supplementary Agreements between the United Kingdom Government, the Scottish Ministers, the Welsh Ministers and the Northern Ireland Committee Executive* (2010), para.27.

[127] See *Martin v HM Advocate* [2010] UKSC 10; *AXA General Insurance* [2011] UKSC 46.

[128] S. Tierney, "Convention Rights and the Scotland Act: Re-defining Judicial Roles" [2001] P.L. 38; B. Winetrobe, "Scottish Devolved Legislation and the Courts" [2002] P.L. 31.

[129] *Anderson* [2003] 2 A.C. 602 at [7].

[130] *Memorandum of Understanding*, para.27.

[131] *Memorandum of Understanding*, para.2.

[132] A list of such concordats is available at: *http://www.scotland.gov.uk/About/concordats* [accessed 27 January 2016].

[133] G. Clark, "Scottish Devolution and the European Union" [1999] P.L. 504.

Relations. Inter-governmental mechanisms for resolving conflict and co-ordinating policy are essential in the new order,[134] and similar mechanisms exist in other countries.[135]

3. WALES

A. Background

7–028 Proposals for devolution to Wales are not new, but go back for approximately 100 years.[136] While Gladstone could claim that the distinction between England and Wales was unknown to our constitution, it was during his period in office that the issue of home rule for Wales began to emerge. It was no coincidence that this occurred when the franchise was extended in 1867 and 1884, since this brought politics to many in Wales for the first time. By the early 1890s Lloyd George was urging home rule for Wales. This early initiative failed because the Welsh liberals were divided on the issue, because these divisions grew with the industrialisation of South Wales, and because this very industrialisation led to the collapse of the Liberal Party.[137]

The post-war years saw the growing recognition of Wales as a separate area of concern within central government. In 1951 a Minister for Welsh Affairs was established, in 1957 a separate Minister of State was appointed as the first full-time Minister for Wales, and in 1964 this post was upgraded to secretary of state, with the holder being given a place in the Cabinet.

The attitude of the Labour Party during the 1960s and 1970s was mixed. It derived considerable support from Wales, which inclined it to take Welsh concerns seriously, but it also had a strong belief in the need for nationalisation and economic planning, both of which inclined it towards centralisation. A catalyst for central action during this period was the success of the SNP, which had achieved this largely at the expense of the Labour Party.

A Royal Commission on the Constitution was established, initially under Lord Crowther, and then under Lord Kilbrandon.[138] The Commission reported in 1973, shortly before Labour returned to power in 1974. There was a good deal of disagreement among the members of the Commission, although they were united in rejecting separation, federalism or the status quo. A number of different devolution options were suggested.

7–029 The response of the Labour government was to opt for a minimal form of devolution for Wales. The proposed Assembly was to have executive powers only, with no power to raise revenue. This model was the basis of the Wales Act 1978. The entry into force of the Act was, however, predicated on approval in a

---

[134] R. Cornes, "Intergovernmental Relations in a Devolved United Kingdom: Making Devolution Work", in Hazell (ed.), *Constitutional Futures, A History of the Next Ten Years* (1999), Ch.9; R. Rawlings, "Concordats of the Constitution" (2000) 116 L.Q.R. 257.

[135] J. Poirier, "The Functions of Intergovernmental Agreements: Post-Devolution Concordats in a Comparative Perspective" [2001] P.L. 134.

[136] Constitution Unit, *An Assembly for Wales* (1996).

[137] Constitution Unit, *An Assembly for Wales* (1996), para.6.

[138] *Report of the Royal Commission on the Constitution, 1969–1973*, Cmnd.5460 (1973).

referendum by 40 per cent of those who were eligible to vote. This approval was never forthcoming. The voters rejected the idea of a Welsh Assembly by four to one.

Labour returned to power in 1996 after 17 years of Conservative rule. The Labour Party was committed to devolution as part of its project of constitutional reform. Devolution to Wales was enshrined in the Government of Wales Act 1998.[139] A referendum was held in 1997, and on this occasion the voters were in favour of a Welsh Assembly. The margin was, nonetheless, perilously thin. It turned on approximately 7,000 votes out of 1,100,000. The yes vote was 50.3 per cent, the no vote 49.7 per cent, and the turn out a meagre 50.1 per cent.

The GWA 1998 only provided for executive devolution. The National Assembly for Wales in effect assumed the responsibilities hitherto exercised by the Secretary of State for Wales. In 2002 those exercising executive powers on behalf of the National Assembly adopted the title "Welsh Assembly Government", and appointed a Commission under the chairmanship of Lord Richard to review the operation of devolution in Wales. The Richard Report recommended that the Assembly should be able to make primary legislation for Wales.[140] This was the catalyst for the White Paper on *Better Governance for Wales*,[141] which laid the foundations for the Government of Wales Act 2006 (GWA 2006). This legislation, as amended by the Wales Act 2014, now provides the framework for Welsh devolution. Relations between the Welsh Assembly, the Welsh Government, and the UK government continue to be regulated through the Memorandum of Understanding considered above.[142]

B. The Assembly

i. Composition

Section 1 of the GWA 2006 established the National Assembly for Wales. **7–030**
Ordinary elections for the return of the Assembly normally take place every fifth year.[143] The Assembly consists of one member for each Assembly constituency, and members for each Assembly electoral region.[144] Voters have two votes.[145]

---

[139] For a valuable account of the early operation of the 1998 Act, R. Rawlings, "The New Model Wales" (1998) 25 J.L.S. 461; R. Rawlings, *Delineating Wales: Constitutional, Legal and Administrative Aspects of National Devolution* (University of Wales Press, 2003).

[140] Richard Commission, *Report on the Powers and Electoral Arrangements of the National Assembly for Wales* (2004); R. Rawlings, *Say Not the Struggle Naught Availeth: The Richard Commission and after* (Centre for Welsh Legal Affairs, University of Wales, 2004); T. Jones and J. Williams, "The Legislative Future of Wales" (2005) 68 M.L.R. 642.

[141] White Paper, *Better Governance for Wales* (2005), Cm.6582; R. Rawlings, "Hastening Slowly: The Next Phase of Welsh Devolution" [2005] P.L. 824.

[142] *Memorandum of Understanding and Supplementary Agreements between the United Kingdom Government, Scottish Ministers, the Cabinet of the National Assembly for Wales and the Northern Ireland Executive Committee* (2001), Cm.5240, para.26; *Memorandum of Understanding and Supplementary Agreements between the United Kingdom Government, the Scottish Ministers, the Welsh Ministers and the Northern Ireland Committee Executive* (2010), para.27.

[143] GWA 2006 s.3(1).

[144] GWA 2006 s.1(2).

[145] GWA 2006 s.6.

The constituency vote is given for the candidate for an Assembly constituency and the election is based on the simple majority system.[146] The electoral region vote is given for a registered political party that has submitted a list of candidates for the electoral region in which the Assembly constituency is included, or an individual who is a candidate to be an Assembly member for that region.[147] There are five electoral regions, each of which returns four members.[148] Voting for electoral regions is based on the additional member system of proportional representation.[149] The result is an Assembly of 60 members, 40 of whom are elected from Assembly constituencies, the other 20 from regions.

ii. Operation

7–031 The procedure of the Assembly is regulated by standing orders.[150] The GWA 2006 mandates important procedural and substantive principles as to the operation of the Assembly. Thus, for example, the English and Welsh languages are to be treated equally,[151] and the Assembly is instructed, when conducting its business, to have due regard to the principle that there should be equality of opportunity for all people.[152] Proceedings of the Assembly are to be held in public.[153] There is an Ombudsman to investigate complaints. There has to be a register of interests of Assembly members, which is open to the public.[154]

The Assembly elects from among its members a Presiding Officer and a Deputy Presiding Officer, who cannot in general be from the same party.[155] There is also a Clerk of the Assembly,[156] and an Assembly Commission, the latter being responsible for ensuring that the Assembly has the requisite staff, services and property.[157] Provision is made for Assembly committees.[158]

---

146 GWA 2006 s.6(4).
147 GWA 2006 s.6(3).
148 GWA 2006 s.2(2) and (4).
149 GWA 2006 s.6(5).
150 GWA 2006 s.31; Standing Orders of the National Assembly of Wales, available at: *http://www.assembly.wales/NAfW%20Documents/Assembly%20Business%20section%20documents/Standing_Orders/Clean_SOs.eng.pdf* [accessed 29 January 2016].
151 GWA 2006 s.35(1).
152 GWA 2006 s.35(2).
153 GWA 2006 s.31(5).
154 GWA 2006 s.36.
155 GWA 2006 s.25.
156 GWA 2006 s.26.
157 GWA 2006 s.27.
158 GWA 2006 ss.28–30.

C. The Executive

i. Composition

The GWA 2006 differs from the GWA 1998 in relation to executive power. The scheme in the GWA 1998 was in effect that the executive was constituted as a committee of the Assembly,[159] although there was much to suggest that it acted like a cabinet. **7–032**

The GWA 2006 by way of contrast makes distinct provision for what is now formally called the Welsh Government. The government consists of the First Minister, Welsh Ministers, Deputy Welsh Ministers and the Counsel General to the Welsh Assembly.[160] The First Minister, who must be a member of the Assembly, is appointed by the Queen, after being nominated by the Assembly,[161] and holds office at Her Majesty's pleasure.[162] It is then for the First Minister to appoint the Welsh Ministers from among the Assembly members,[163] with an upper limit of 12 such appointments.[164]

ii. Functions

The GWA 2006 specifies distinct functions for the Welsh Government. Thus, Welsh ministers have those functions conferred on them by the 2006 Act itself, or by any other enactment or prerogative instrument.[165] Many such functions were transferred to the National Assembly for Wales under the GWA 1998, and were effectively exercised by the members of the executive.[166] Under the GWA 2006 executive functions are transferred directly to the Welsh government. **7–033**

When a function is conferred on Welsh ministers it can be exercised by any of the ministers.[167] There is a mechanism for the transfer to the Welsh ministers, or specifically to the First Minister or to the Counsel General, of functions in relation to Wales which are exercisable by a minister of the Crown, or for the concurrent exercise of those functions by Welsh ministers and the minister of the Crown.[168] Welsh ministers can be designated under s.2(2) of the European Communities Act 1972 to implement EU obligations.[169] The Welsh ministers are moreover accorded a broad power to do anything which they consider is appropriate to achieve the promotion of the economic, social or environmental

[159] GWA 1998 ss.53–56.
[160] GWA 2006 s.45.
[161] GWA 2006 s.47(1).
[162] GWA 2006 s.46.
[163] GWA 2006 s.48. The appointment of the Counsel General and Deputy Welsh Ministers are dealt with in ss.49–50.
[164] GWA 2006 s.51.
[165] GWA 2006 s.56.
[166] The first TFO transferred UK Minister of the Crown functions to the National Assembly for Wales under some 350 Acts and 32 Statutory Instruments, The National Assembly for Wales (Transfer of Functions) Order 1999 (SI 672/1999).
[167] GWA 2006 s.57.
[168] GWA 2006 s.58.
[169] GWA 2006 s.59.

well-being of Wales,[170] and power to take appropriate action in relation to culture, such as buildings of historical or architectural interest.[171] The GWA 2006 also makes provision for liaison mechanisms between the Welsh Government and local authorities, the voluntary sector and business interests in Wales.[172]

The GWA 2006 imposes obligations as well as powers on the Welsh Assembly Government. Thus, it is enjoined to: create a code for regulatory impact assessments; to make arrangements to ensure that their functions are exercised with due regard for equality of opportunity for all people; to adopt a strategy for how it is to promote the Welsh language; and to make a scheme for sustainable development.[173] The Welsh ministers are also obliged to comply with EU law,[174] and cannot exercise any of their powers if they violate Convention rights.[175] There is further provision dealing with compliance with international obligations.[176]

D. Powers

7–034 The GWA 2006 has enhanced the lawmaking powers of the Assembly, but these still fall short of those accorded to the Scottish Parliament. The schema in the GWA 2006 is as follows.

i. Assembly measures

7–035 Under the GWA 2006 Pt 3, the Assembly was given power to make laws, which were termed Measures of the National Assembly for Wales,[177] although this did not affect the power of the UK Parliament to make laws for Wales.[178] An Assembly Measure could, in principle, make any provision that could be made by an Act of Parliament.[179] An Assembly Measure was not law so far as any of its provisions fell outside the Assembly's legislative competence.[180] A provision of an Assembly Measure was within the Assembly's legislative competence in two types of case.

First, the provision of an Assembly Measure had to relate to one or more of the matters specified in Pt 1 of Sch.5, and not apply outside Wales.[181] Second, a provision of an Assembly Measure could alternatively fall within the Assembly's competence if it provided for the enforcement of a provision that was within the

---

170 GWA 2006 s.60.
171 GWA 2006 s.61.
172 GWA 2006 ss.72–75.
173 GWA 2006 ss.76–79.
174 GWA 2006 s.80.
175 GWA 2006 s.81.
176 GWA 2006 s.82.
177 GWA 2006 s.93.
178 GWA 2006 s.93(5).
179 GWA 2006 s.94(1).
180 GWA 2006 s.94(2).
181 GWA 2006 s.94(4).

Assembly's competence, or it was otherwise appropriate for making such a provision effective, or it was otherwise incidental to, or consequential on, such a provision.[182]

A provision which satisfied one of the two preceding conditions would nonetheless fall outside the Assembly's legislative competence if: it breached any of the restrictions in Pt 2 of Sch.5, subject to exceptions in Pt 3 of that Schedule; it extended otherwise than only to England and Wales; or it was incompatible with Convention rights or with EU law.[183]

Part 3 of the GWA 2006 that deals with Assembly measures was, however, repealed when the new provisions concerning Assembly Acts came into force in 2011.[184] The repeal does not affect the validity of Assembly measures in force.

ii. Assembly Acts

The GWA 2006 Pt 4 makes provision for the Assembly to have primary legislative powers across the broad range of the subjects in Pt 1 of Sch.7, without the need for further recourse to Parliament. Thus, when Pt 4 of the 2006 GWA became operative there was no need to seek authorisation for a particular exercise of legislative competence in the manner described above in relation to Assembly Measures. Part 4 of the GWA 2006 became operational on 5 May 2011, after a positive vote in a referendum.[185] The Assembly now has legislative powers to make law on all subjects within its devolved fields, as delineated in Sch.7, subject to the conditions listed in ss.107–108 GWA 2006. **7–036**

However, by way of contrast to the Scotland Act 1998, the GWA 2006 defines the scope of the Assembly's legislative powers after a referendum by listing the subjects in relation to which the Assembly can make law, rather than only listing those areas outside its legislative competence. Assembly legislation made in exercise of this "primary" legislative power is known as Acts of the National Assembly for Wales.[186]

iii. Subordinate legislation

We should also consider powers in relation to subordinate legislation. Many functions were transferred to the National Assembly pursuant to Transfer of Functions Orders. The GWA 1998 provided for the transfer of functions of the minister of the Crown in relation to Wales to the Assembly.[187] The GWA 2006 now accords the power to make such subordinate legislation to the Welsh ministers and there are transitional provisions specifying that Assembly functions over such legislation are transferred to the Welsh ministers.[188] The subordinate legislation will normally be subject to either the affirmative procedure, requiring **7–037**

[182] GWA 2006 s.94(5).
[183] GWA 2006 s.94(6).
[184] GWA 2006 s.106(1).
[185] Government of Wales Act 2006 (Commencement of Assembly Act Provisions, Transitional and Saving Provisions and Modifications) Order (SI 1011/2011).
[186] GWA 2006 ss.107–108.
[187] GWA 1998 s.22.
[188] GWA 2006 Sch.11 para.30, subject to para.31.

Assembly approval before it takes effect, or the negative procedure, requiring the Assembly to active steps to annul the measure. The scrutiny is undertaken by the Subordinate Legislation Committee.

E. Judicial Challenge

7–038 The Assembly and Welsh government have limited powers and the GWA 2006 makes provision for legal challenge to ensure that they do not stray beyond their respective powers.[189] The rules are contained in Sch.9 para.1(1) of which defines the phrase "devolution issue" to mean:

> "(a) a question whether an Assembly Measure or Act of the Assembly, or any provision of an Assembly Measure or Act of the Assembly, is within the Assembly's legislative competence,
>
> (b) a question whether any function (being a function which any person has purported, or is proposing, to exercise) is exercisable by the Welsh Ministers, the First Minister or the Counsel General,
>
> (c) a question whether the purported or proposed exercise of a function by the Welsh Ministers, the First Minister or the Counsel General is, or would be, within the powers of the Welsh Ministers, the First Minister or the Counsel General (including a question whether a purported or proposed exercise of a function is, or would be, outside those powers by virtue of section 80(8) or 81(1)),
>
> (d) a question whether there has been any failure to comply with a duty imposed on the Welsh Ministers, the First Minister or the Counsel General (including any obligation imposed by virtue of section 80(1) or (7)), or
>
> (e) a question of whether a failure to act by the Welsh Ministers, the First Minister or the Counsel General is incompatible with any of the Convention rights."

It is possible that there will be attempts to challenge competence where there is no real foundation for the argument. The GWA 2006 makes provision for this eventuality by providing that a devolution issue shall not be taken to arise in any proceedings merely because it is raised by one of the parties. The court or tribunal can disregard the issue if the claim is frivolous or vexatious.[190]

A devolution issue may arise in proceedings that are begun in England and Wales, Scotland, or Northern Ireland. The GWA makes provision for all these jurisdictional possibilities. The discussion will concentrate on the rules that apply where a devolution issue arises in England and Wales. The applicable rules where the case is heard in Scotland or Northern Ireland are not different in principle. There are a number of different ways in which devolution issues can come before the courts.

i. Direct reference to the Supreme Court

7–039 A devolution issue can be resolved by direct reference of the matter to the Supreme Court. This can occur in three types of case.

First, there is the possibility of *pre-enactment challenge and scrutiny.* The Attorney General or the Counsel General may, pursuant to Sch.9 para.30(1), refer

---

[189] For discussion of analogous provisions under the GWA 1998, P. Craig and M. Walters, "The Courts, Devolution and Judicial Review" [1999] P.L. 274.

[190] GWA 2006 Sch.9 para.2.

to the Supreme Court any devolution issue which is not the subject of civil or criminal proceedings. Paragraph 30(2) states that where a reference is made under para.30(1) by the Attorney General in relation to a devolution issue which relates to the proposed exercise of a function by the Welsh ministers, the First Minister or the Counsel General, the Attorney General must notify the Counsel General of that fact, and the function must not be exercised by the Welsh ministers, the First Minister or the Counsel General in the manner proposed during the period beginning with the receipt of the notification and ending with the reference being decided or otherwise disposed of.

Second, there can be *post-enactment challenge even where the devolution issue has not arisen in independent proceedings*. This follows from the wording of para.30(1). Thus, the Assembly may have passed certain subordinate legislation, which is later felt to have exceeded the bounds of its powers under a Transfer of Functions Order. The matter can be referred to the Supreme Court by the Attorney General or Counsel General, even though the subordinate legislation has not been contested in any other proceedings.

Third, it is open to the *Attorney General or Counsel General to require a court or tribunal to transfer a case to the Supreme Court*. Paragraph 29(1) of Sch.9 authorises the Attorney General or Counsel General to require any court or tribunal to refer to the Supreme Court any devolution issue which has arisen in any proceedings before it to which he is a party. Courts and tribunals are under an obligation to give notice of devolution issues that arise in any proceedings to the Attorney General and the Counsel General.[191] The person or body given notice is entitled to take part in the proceedings so far as they relate to the devolution issue.[192]

ii. Institution of proceedings by a law officer

The GWA allows the Attorney General or Counsel General to institute proceedings for the determination of a devolution issue.[193] The law officer has the power to require the devolution issue to be referred to the Supreme Court, as described above, but may choose not to exercise this power. **7–040**

iii. Reference through other courts

A devolution issue can also arise before a court that is empowered by the GWA to refer the matter on to another court. The relevant rules distinguish between civil and criminal proceedings. The rules discussed within this section relate to referral. It is the devolution issue that is referred to the higher court. Once this matter has been decided the case returns to the lower court for final resolution of the case. There will, however, be cases where the resolution of the devolution issue will be conclusive for the entire dispute. **7–041**

---

191 GWA 2006 Sch.9 para.5(1).

192 GWA 2006 Sch.9 para.5(2).

193 GWA 2006 Sch.9 para.4.

The rules on civil proceedings are that a magistrate's court may refer a devolution issue to the High Court.[194] A court may refer a devolution issue that arises in civil proceedings to the Court of Appeal,[195] but this does not apply to a magistrates' court, the Court of Appeal or the Supreme Court, nor to the High Court taking a reference from a magistrates' court pursuant to para.6.[196] Civil proceedings are defined by the Act to mean any proceedings other than criminal proceedings.[197] It therefore includes proceedings for judicial review.

If the devolution issue arises in criminal proceedings then a court, other than the Court of Appeal or the Supreme Court, may refer the issue to the High Court in the case of summary proceedings or to the Court of Appeal if the proceedings are on indictment.[198]

7–042 It is open to the Court of Appeal to refer a devolution issue that has come before it other than by way of reference from a lower court on to the Supreme Court.[199] This option will be open to it where the devolution issue emerges in proceedings before the Court of Appeal itself.

The discussion thus far, has concentrated on courts. Tribunals are treated somewhat differently. A tribunal from which there is no appeal must refer the devolution issue to the Court of Appeal. Where there is an appeal from the tribunal's findings it has discretion to refer, but does not have a duty to do so.[200]

Provision is made for an appeal against a determination of a devolution issue by the High Court or the Court of Appeal when a reference has been made to those courts in the manner described above. The appeal lies to the Supreme Court, but only with the permission of the court concerned, or failing such permission, with special permission from the Supreme Court.[201]

iv. Decisions made by the court immediately seized of the matter

7–043 The provisions described above give courts discretion whether to refer a devolution issue. They do not have the duty to do so. The court before which the issue is raised is therefore entitled, subject to the discussion below, to decide the case for itself. Thus, the High Court exercising its judicial review jurisdiction may well feel able to resolve devolution issues,[202] and be wary, moreover, of overburdening the Court of Appeal through too ready an exercise of the referral power. The discretion of the court seized of the matter to hear the case is qualified to the extent that the Attorney General or Counsel General may, as discussed above, require the case to be referred to the Supreme Court.

---

194 GWA 2006 Sch.9 para.6.
195 GWA 2006 Sch.9 para.7(1).
196 GWA 2006 Sch.9 para.7(2).
197 GWA 2006 Sch.9 para.1(2).
198 GWA 2006 Sch.9 para.9.
199 GWA 2006 Sch.9 para.10.
200 GWA 2006 Sch.9 para.8.
201 GWA 2006 Sch.9 para.11.
202 See, e.g. *South Wales Sea Fisheries Committee v National Assembly for Wales* [2001] EWHC Admin 1162.

v. *The relevance of the general law on collateral challenge*

Schedule 9 GWA 2006 is framed in terms of devolution issues "arising" before a particular court. It is clear that such issues may arise directly, as in the context of a judicial review action. There will, subject to the normal rules on such actions, be no difficulty about raising the vires of action by the Assembly or Welsh government in this manner. **7–044**

Devolution issues may also arise indirectly. There will be collateral challenges where, for example, the applicant claims that subordinate legislation being applied against him is ultra vires, and should not therefore be enforced. Recent decisions of the courts have been more liberal in allowing collateral challenge, although there are still some uncertainties.[203] The courts' more liberal attitude to collateral challenge should mean that if the general legal rules on collateral challenge are applied, claimants will normally be able to raise vires issues indirectly as well as directly.

vi. *The effect of a finding that the Assembly or Welsh government lacked power*

The Supreme Court has held that despite its constitutional significance, the GWA 2006 had to be interpreted in the same way as any other Act. However, any difficulties of interpretation were to be resolved by bearing in mind that its purpose was to define, in fairly abstract terms, permitted or prohibited areas of legislative activity with the aim of achieving a constitutional settlement.[204] In that sense it will, therefore, try to interpret Welsh legislation to be intra rather than ultra vires, although the Supreme Court has also found an Assembly measure to be ultra vires.[205] **7–045**

The GWA 2006 deals with acts of the Assembly or the Welsh government that are ultra vires in a number of ways. The secretary of state has broad powers to initiate the making of a statutory instrument, which can modify any enactment or instrument that lies beyond the legislative competence of the Assembly.[206] There is a further broad power to remedy ultra vires acts by Order in Council.[207]

The GWA 2006 also makes provision for what is to happen if a court or a tribunal decides that the Assembly or Welsh government did not have the power to make the relevant measure. The basic assumption behind s.153 is that the effect of the judicial decision finding the lack of power is that the measure is retrospectively null. Section 153(2) empowers the court or tribunal to make an order removing or limiting any retrospective effect of the decision, or suspending the effect of the decision for any period and on any conditions to allow the defect to be corrected. In deciding whether to make such an order the court or tribunal is to have regard to the extent to which persons who are not parties to the

---

[203] Ch.27.

[204] *Attorney General v National Assembly for Wales Commission* [2012] UKSC 53; *Attorney General for England and Wales v Counsel General for Wales* [2014] UKSC 43.

[205] *Recovery of Medical Costs for Asbestos Diseases (Wales) Bill, Re* [2015] UKSC 3.

[206] GWA 2006 s.150.

[207] GWA 2006 s.151.

proceedings would otherwise be adversely affected by the decision.[208] When considering making such an order the court, etc. must give notice of that fact to the relevant law officer, unless they are already party to the proceedings. They can join the proceedings so far as they relate to the making of the order.[209]

F. Welsh Devolution: Some Reflections

7–046 It is clear that Welsh devolution has evolved since 1998, and that the foundations of the 2006 legislation differ from those of the GWA 1998.

The GWA 1998 conferred formal powers on the Assembly, and not on the individual members of the Executive Committee.[210] Notwithstanding this, the GWA inclined strongly towards a cabinet model, with the executive role being taken by the Executive Committee. The provisions of the Act were premised on this Committee taking such a role, and the extensive powers to delegate authority to it served to reinforce this. The cabinet image of the Executive Committee was fostered by the National Assembly Advisory Group (NAAG), the recommendations of which fostered the image of the Executive Committee as Assembly cabinet.[211] The standing orders reinforced the cabinet model.[212] Rawlings captures the shift of power when speaking of the rapid emergence of a "virtual parliament" in Wales and the de facto development inside the corporate body of a divide between the Executive in the guise of the Welsh Assembly Government and the representative institution as a whole.[213] He notes moreover that when viewed in this way the architectural proposals in the White Paper that set the ground for the 2006 GWA were largely derivative in nature, "whereby London plays catch up with, as well as usefully building on, the institutional dynamics in Cardiff, so giving them formal legal recognition".[214]

The 2006 GWA represents a step forward in terms of Welsh devolution. The Assembly and the Welsh Government are formally separated. The Assembly was accorded law-making power via the technique of Assembly Measures described above, and more recently through competence to pass Assembly Acts. The Welsh Government assumes in formal terms many of the traditional executive functions within a devolved body, and is accorded power over subordinate legislation, subject to scrutiny by the Assembly.

There were a number of legislative competence orders completed during the 2007–2011 Assembly session.[215] When such an order was approved the Assembly then had legislative competence to pass Assembly Measures on that

---

[208] GWA 2006 s.153(3).

[209] GWA 2006 ss.153(4)–(6).

[210] GWA 1998 s.22.

[211] National Assembly Advisory Group, *Report to the Secretary of State for Wales* (August 1998), section 2, paras 7, 19, 21 and 32.

[212] Standing Orders of the National Assembly of Wales (2011).

[213] R Rawlings, "Law Making in a Virtual Parliament", in R Hazell and R Rawlings (eds), *Devolution, Law Making and the Constitution* (Imprint Academic, 2005).

[214] Rawlings "The Next Phase" [2005] P.L. 824, at 825.

[215] See *http://www.assembly.wales/en/bus-home/bus-third-assembly/bus-legislation-third-assembly/bus-legislation-progress-lcos-measures/Pages/bus-legislation-progress-lcos-measures.aspx* [accessed 30 January 2016].

topic thereafter, and in that sense each LCO approved by the Assembly and by the Westminster Parliament augmented the overall area in which the Assembly could legislate. It should also be noted that Westminster legislation fleshed out Sch.5, specifying "matters" within fields such as education and local authorities over which the Assembly could then enact Assembly Measures.[216]

The impact of any particular LCO in expanding the legislative competence of the Assembly was markedly affected by the breadth of definition of the "matters" that were brought within the Assembly's competence. These could be broadly or narrowly defined. An example of relatively broad definition was the LCO on vulnerable children,[217] which specified eight "matters" to come within the general field of social welfare. These were: safeguarding children from harm and neglect; fostering and adoption; social care for children and the persons who care for them; social care for young persons; co-operation between those who look after vulnerable children; strategic planning by local authorities in relation to the well-being of children and young persons; continuance, dissolution or creation of, and conferral of functions on, an office or body concerned with safeguarding and promoting the well-being of children or young persons; and the promotion of equality between children and young persons in relation to their well-being. A further example of relatively broad definition of "matters" over which the Assembly can then enact Assembly Measures is to be found in relation to local authorities.[218] **7–047**

The Fourth Assembly has the enhanced powers to pass Assembly Acts, pursuant to Pt 4 of the GWA 2006. A considerable number of Assembly Acts were passed during the Fourth Assembly.[219] The powers of the Assembly were, moreover, augmented by amendments to the Government of Wales Act 2006,[220] which have given it new taxation powers. The provisions are however not yet in force at the time of writing.[221]

---

[216] See, e.g. Local Government and Public Involvement in Health Act 2007 s.235 and Sch.17; Further Education and Training Act 2007 s.27.

[217] The National Assembly for Wales (Legislative Competence) (Social Welfare and Other Fields) Order (SI 3132/2008).

[218] Local Government and Public Involvement in Health Act 2007 s.235 and Sch.17.

[219] See *http://www.assembly.wales/en/bus-home/bus-legislation/Pages/assembly_acts.aspx* [accessed 30 January 2016].

[220] Wales Act 2014 s.6.

[221] GWA 2006 Pt.4A.

CHAPTER 8

INFORMATION, STANDARDS AND COMPLAINTS

1. CENTRAL ISSUES

i. The flourishing of a healthy democracy, in which governmental organs are accountable for their actions, depends on a range of factors. There are nonetheless certain factors that generally enhance accountability, irrespective of the specific nature of the institution in question. **8–001**

ii. This chapter examines three such matters: access to information, standards in public life and complaints machinery, principally in the form of the Ombudsman model. These issues are central to the relationship between government and governed.

iii. Access to information is vital if there is to be an informed public, which can participate in public life and hold the government to account.

iv. Standards of propriety are equally essential, since if they are not adhered to public trust in the soundness of governmental policy will suffer.

v. Mechanisms whereby individuals can voice complaints outside of the traditional court system now play an increasingly important role in monitoring the administration of government policy.

vi. There is a micro- and macro-perspective to the issues addressed in this chapter. The former focuses primarily on the position of the specific individual, whether this is as seeker of information, target of a complaint of breach of standards, or applicant who seeks redress for maladministration.

vii. The macro-perspective looks to more systemic concerns. In the context of access to information, this may be the desire to combat a culture of secrecy and to foster citizen participation in public life. In relation to standards of government, it will be apparent in initiatives designed to imbue an ethical code among those in power, and to structure appointments so as to maximise transparency and opportunity. In the context of complaints machinery, it becomes apparent in the debate as to whether the Parliamentary Commissioner for Administration should be able to conduct more general administrative audits, as well as being able to respond to individual applicants.

2. Freedom of Information: Rationale and Background

A. Rationale for Freedom of Information

8–002 Access to information and openness is crucially important in ensuring the accountability of government. We have not until recently had any general freedom of information legislation such as exists within many other countries.[1] It is important to consider both the reasons for such legislation, and its effectiveness.

The most prominent *reasons* for freedom of information legislation are as follows. First, access to information concerning governmental decision-making is central to the idea of a democratic society. Government should be accountable for its action, and this is difficult if it has a "monopoly" over the available information. Second, individual citizens should be able to know the information held about them in order to check its correctness and the uses to which it is put. Third, public disclosure of information will, it is hoped, improve decision-making.

The *effectiveness* of any such legislation is dependent on a number of variables. We need to consider the range of *exceptions* contained in the legislation, and the way in which these are interpreted. The effectiveness of such legislation will also be dependent on the *way it is administered*. Thus, the original American legislation was modified in 1974 to meet problems arising from agency delay in responding to requests for documents. The amended legislation set time limits within which the documents must be produced, and subjected officials who arbitrarily withheld information to disciplinary proceedings. The cost of using the system, and the way in which the material is presented to the individual, will also be important in determining the utility of the scheme.

B. Freedom of Information Legislation in the UK

8–003 Legislation to ensure freedom of information was long overdue in this country.[2] Specific statutes had some impact,[3] but these were no substitute for more general legislation of the kind that exists in many countries.[4] The Campaign for Freedom of Information published a draft Bill designed to provide general access to information.[5] Various arguments were nonetheless advanced against a Freedom

[1] P. Birkinshaw, *Freedom of Information, The Law, the Practice and the Ideal*, 4th edn (Cambridge University Press, 2010); P. Birkinshaw, *Government and Information: The Law Relating to Access, Disclosure and Their Regulation*, 3rd edn (Tottel, 2005).

[2] Birkinshaw, *Freedom of Information, The Law, the Practice and the Ideal* (2010).

[3] Data Protection Act 1984; R. Austin, "The Data Protection Act 1984: The Public Law Implications" [1984] P.L. 618; Local Government (Access to Information) Act 1985; P. Birkinshaw, *Open Government, Freedom of Information and Local Government* (Local Government Legal Society Trust, 1986); Access to Personal Files Act (1987); Data Protection Act 1998.

[4] The extent to which a government employee can reveal information obtained in confidence cannot be examined here. See Y. Cripps, "Disclosure in the Public Interest; The Predicament of the Public Sector Employee" [1983] P.L. 600; *Attorney General v Guardian Newspapers Ltd (No.2)* [1990] 1 A.C. 109; Constitutional Reform and Governance Act 2010 s.9.

[5] M. Frankel, *A Freedom of Information Act for Britain* (1991).

of Information Act. It was argued that such legislation was unnecessary; that it would interfere with the effectiveness of government; that it would somehow subvert the ordinary democratic process; and that it would be too costly.[6] These arguments were unconvincing. For example, in relation to the contention that such legislation would interfere with the efficiency of government, Birkinshaw states[7]:

> "Quite frankly, this argument has no support from the evidence of those countries where FOI operates. Organizing sections of the administration to facilitate responses to requests from citizens for information about their government and its operations is a small price to pay for treating citizens as citizens and not as subjects."

The Conservative government evinced some concern for greater openness and transparency, as exemplified by the Citizen's Charter, which had openness as a central principle.[8] This theme was taken up in the White Paper on *Open Government*,[9] which built on the Charter initiatives.[10] It established a Code of Practice on Access to Government Information,[11] which was applicable to all departments, agencies and authorities within the jurisdiction of the Parliamentary Commissioner for Administration (PCA). It allowed access to facts and analysis which the government considered relevant when framing major policy proposals and decisions; explanatory material on departments' dealings with the public, including rules and procedures; the reasons for decisions; and information relating to the running of the public services. This access was qualified by exceptions relating to matters such as defence, security and international relations, internal policy discussion, and effective management of the public service. The Parliamentary Commissioner for Administration adjudicated on complaints relating to breach of the Code. The Code did not, however, establish any general legal right to access to government information.

3. THE FREEDOM OF INFORMATION ACT 2000

The Labour government came to power committed to legislation on freedom of information, and published a White Paper.[12] The legislation took longer to emerge than was initially thought, and it was vigorously criticised for taking a more limited view of freedom of information than the White Paper. Different sections of the Act come into force at different times. 8–004

[6] P. Birkinshaw, "Citizenship and Privacy", in R. Blackburn (ed.), *Rights of Citizenship* (Mansell, 1993), pp.43–47; P. Birkinshaw, *Freedom of Information, The Law, the Practice and the Ideal* (2010), Chs 1 and 3.

[7] P. Birkinshaw, "Citizenship and Privacy", in R. Blackburn (ed.), *Rights of Citizenship* (1993), p.46.

[8] The Citizen's Charter, *Raising the Standard* (1991) Cm.1599, p.5.

[9] White Paper, *Open Government* (1993), Cm.2290.

[10] P. Birkinshaw, "'I only ask for information'—The White Paper on Open Government" [1993] P.L. 557.

[11] Home Office, Open Government, *Code of Practice on Access to Government Information*, 2nd edn (1997).

[12] White Paper, *Your Right to Know, The Government's Proposals for a Freedom of Information Act* (1997), Cm.3818.

A. Freedom of Information Act 2000: The Basic Right

8–005 Section 1(1) of the Freedom of Information Act 2000 (FOIA) established the basic right. It provides that any person making a request for information to a public authority is entitled to be informed in writing by the public authority whether it holds information of the description specified in the request, and if that is the case to have that information communicated to him.[13] This is termed the duty to confirm or deny. The public authority must comply with the request promptly and in any event, subject to exceptions, within 20 days from the date of the request.[14] The basic right is however qualified by other provisions of the FOIA.

Thus, s.1(3) states that where a public authority reasonably requires further information to identify and locate the information, and has told the applicant of that requirement, the authority is not obliged to comply with s.1(1) unless it is supplied with that information. The basic right is further qualified by s.2. This, in effect, excludes it in relation to the exempted categories listed in Pt II of the FOIA. This is so either where a provision of Pt II confers absolute exemption, or where, in all the circumstances of the case, the public interest in maintaining the exemption outweighs the public interest in disclosing whether the public authority holds the information, or in disclosing that information.[15] The force of the basic right is further limited by the fact that a fee may be charged,[16] and the public authority may refuse to supply information where the cost of compliance would exceed the "appropriate limit".[17] There are also provisions dealing with vexatious or repeated requests.[18]

B. Freedom of Information Act 2000: Public Authorities

8–006 The FOIA applies to public authorities, s.3. The term public authority is broadly defined.[19] It covers any body listed in Sch.1, or designated by an order made under s.5. The list is extensive, and can be amended by the secretary of state. The term public authority also covers publicly-owned companies. It is also possible for a public authority to be listed in Sch.1 only in relation to certain specified information.[20]

---

[13] *Independent Parliamentary Standards Authority v Information Commissioner* [2015] EWCA Civ 388, [2015] 1 W.L.R. 2879.

[14] Freedom of Information Act 2000 s.10.

[15] Information Commissioner's Office, *The Public Interest Test, Freedom of Information Act, https://ico.org.uk/for-organisations/guidance-index/freedom-of-information-and-environmental-information-regulations/* [accessed 11 August 2015].

[16] Freedom of Information Act 2000 s.9.

[17] Freedom of Information Act 2000 s.12; the basic figure is £600, Freedom of Information and Data Protection (Appropriate Limit and Fees) Regulations 2004 (SI 3244/2004) reg.3.

[18] Freedom of Information Act 2000 s.14.

[19] *BBC v Sugar* [2009] 1 W.L.R. 430, HL; *University and Colleges Admissions Service v Information Commissioner* [2014] UKUT 557 (AAC).

[20] Freedom of Information Act 2000 s.7.

C. Freedom of Information Act 2000: Publication Schemes

Public authorities have a duty to maintain publication schemes, which must be approved by the Information Commissioner.[21] The duty requires public authorities to adopt and maintain a scheme relating to the publication of information by that authority. The scheme must specify classes of information that the authority publishes, the manner in which this is to be done, and whether a fee is to be charged. The Information Commissioner may approve model publication schemes.[22] **8–007**

D. Freedom of Information Act 2000: Exempt Information

Part II of the FOIA specifies the categories of exempt information, thereby qualifying the basic right in s.1. Information that is reasonably accessible by other means is exempted, as is information intended for future publication.[23] There are exemptions for information held by security bodies, and information required for the purposes of safeguarding national security.[24] There are other exemptions dealing, inter alia, with defence, international relations, relations within the UK, the economy, investigations conducted by public authorities, law enforcement, court functions, audit functions, parliamentary privilege, the formulation of government policy, and the disclosure of information that would be prejudicial to the effective conduct of public affairs, personal information and information given in confidence. **8–008**

It is readily apparent that the efficacy of any scheme for freedom of information will depend in part on the range of exemptions. The list of exemptions contained in the FOIA is long. Issues concerning exemptions have come before the courts on a number of occasions.[25] A number of the exemptions, such as that dealing with the formulation of government policy, are very broad. Moreover, the general formula used in the FOIA is that information can be withheld if its disclosure would, or would be likely to, prejudice the interest specified in the exempt category. This is by way of contrast to earlier formulations, where the criterion had been "substantial prejudice". The breadth of the exemptions is compounded by the "enforcement override" that the Act accords to certain public bodies.

---

[21] Freedom of Information Act 2000 s.19.

[22] Freedom of Information Act 2000 s.20.

[23] Freedom of Information Act 2000 ss.21–22.

[24] Freedom of Information Act 2000 ss.23–24.

[25] *Corporate Officer of the House of Commons v Information Commissioner* [2008] EWHC 1084 (Admin); *Department for Business, Enterprise and Regulatory Reform v O'Brien* [2009] EWHC 164 (Admin); *HM Treasury v Information Commissioner* [2009] EWHC 1811 (Admin); *BBC v Sugar* [2012] UKSC 4, [2012] 1 W.L.R. 439; *Kennedy v Information Commissioner* [2014] UKSC 20, [2015] A.C. 455.

E. Freedom of Information Act 2000: Administration

8–009 The freedom of information scheme is administered by the Information Commissioner (IC),[26] and a tribunal in the General Regulatory Chamber.[27] The Ministry of Justice has overall responsibility for policy in this area. The IC has a number of general duties to promote the observance by public authorities of the requirements of the FOIA.[28] The IC also has more specific enforcement functions. The IC, having received a complaint, can decide that a public authority has not complied with its duty under s.1.[29] Where this is so, the IC can serve an enforcement notice on the public authority,[30] which can be further enforced through contempt proceedings in the High Court.[31] There are provisions for appeals from the IC to the tribunal.[32]

The IC's enforcement power is subject to an important limitation. It is open to certain bodies, including government departments, to override the IC. An accountable person within such a body can attest that in relation to the provision of exempt information, he has reasonable grounds to believe that there was no breach of s.1.[33] This means that the IC's assessment of whether the disclosure of information in an exempt category would be prejudicial to the relevant interest is subject to departmental override. In *Evans* the Supreme Court however held that s.53 did not entitle an accountable person to issue a certificate to override a court's decision that information should be disclosed simply because he disagreed with its conclusion. Thus the Attorney General had not been entitled to issue a certificate to override an Upper Tribunal decision that communications between the Prince of Wales and government departments should be disclosed.[34]

4. STANDARDS OF CONDUCT IN PUBLIC LIFE

A. Cash, Sleaze and Concerns: The Development of the Administrative Machinery

8–010 Over the last 20 years administrative institutions have been designed to regulate the standards of conduct in public life. The origin of this machinery is interesting.[35] In 1994 the Committee of Privileges published a Report on what became known as cash for questions, the practice whereby an MP would table a question in the House of Commons in return for payment. The Committee, not

---

[26] See *https://ico.org.uk/* [accessed 11 August 2015]; Freedom of Information Act 2000 s.18.

[27] See *https://www.gov.uk/information-rights-appeal-against-the-commissioners-decision* [accessed 11 August 2015].

[28] Freedom of Information Act 2000 ss.47–49.

[29] Freedom of Information Act 2000 ss.50–51.

[30] Freedom of Information Act 2000 s.52.

[31] Freedom of Information Act 2000 s.54.

[32] Freedom of Information Act 2000 ss.57–61.

[33] Freedom of Information Act 2000 s.53.

[34] *R. (Evans) v Attorney General* [2015] UKSC 21, [2015] 2 W.L.R. 813.

[35] D. Oliver, "Standards of Conduct in Public Life—What Standards?" [1995] P.L. 497.

surprisingly, took a dim view of this practice.[36] Concerns over standards of conduct in public life were further fuelled by other issues that occurred at this time. There was the dubious practice whereby a MP would table amendments to Bills before the House in the name of other MPs without their consent. There was the general sense that "sleaze" had infected government, and there was a feeling that ministers and civil servants had not always behaved with due propriety in the Matrix Churchill affair that led to the Scott Inquiry.

These concerns led to the establishment in 1994 of the Committee on Standards in Public Life under the chairmanship of Lord Nolan, a Law Lord. This is a standing committee of the House of Commons the work of which will be examined below. Suffice it to say for the present that it developed a programme for inquiry into standards in public life, but the Committee did not look into individual cases. The first report from the Nolan Committee contained a number of recommendations relating to the conduct of MPs and the like. It was the catalyst for the House of Commons to establish a Select Committee on Standards in Public Life to consider the Nolan Report. The House of Commons accepted most recommendations from the Select Committee. This in turn led to the creation of a new Select Committee on Standards and Privileges, which took over the role of the Select Committee on Privileges and Members' Interests. It also led to the establishment of a Parliamentary Commissioner for Standards (PCS), and a Commissioner for Public Appointments (CPA).

The regulation of standards in public life is now to be found in the work of the Committee on Standards in Public Life, the Select Committee on Standards, which was separated from the Committee on Standards and Privileges in 2012, the PCS and the CPA. The interrelationship between these bodies is interesting. The Committee on Standards in Public Life focuses on standards at the macro-level, and does not consider individual cases. The PCS and the select committee consider issues at the macro-level, but they also investigate specific allegations of a breach of standards.

B. Committee on Standards in Public Life

There has always been much in the constitutional life of the UK that has been regulated not by statute, but by convention, practice and the rules of the game. The work of the Committee on Standards exemplifies this tradition.[37] Its original terms of reference in 1994 were to examine concerns about standards of conduct of all holders of public office, including arrangements relating to financial and commercial activities. It was to make recommendations as to changes that might **8–011**

[36] Committee of Privileges, *Complaint Concerning an Article in the "Sunday Times" of July 10, 1994 relating to the Conduct of Members*, HC Paper No.351 (Session 1994–95).

[37] See *https://www.gov.uk/government/organisations/the-committee-on-standards-in-public-life/about* [accessed 11 August 2015].

be required to ensure the highest standards of propriety in public life. The Committee is now an independent advisory non-departmental public body, which is sponsored by the Cabinet Office.[38]

The Committee's First Report[39] was wide-ranging. It began by identifying "seven principles of public life", which were to apply to all those who worked in the public sphere: selflessness, integrity, objectivity, accountability, openness, honesty and leadership.[40] It recommended that there should be Codes of Conduct drawn up by public bodies, which incorporated these principles, and that such internal systems for the maintenance of standards should be supported by external scrutiny. It felt also that more should be done by way of education to inculcate standards of conduct in public bodies. These recommendations were complemented by detailed proposals relating to parts of government.

In relation to MPs, the proposals were directed principally at the probity of contacts between MPs and those outside the House. The Report recommended that there should be full disclosure by MPs of their consultancy agreements and payments, and that the Register of Members' Interests should be more informative. A Parliamentary Commissioner for Standards should be appointed, who would have responsibility for advising and guiding MPs on their conduct.

In relation to ministers, the Report recommended that allegations of misconduct made against a particular minister should be investigated promptly. A minister should not, on leaving office, take up a position with a company for a period of time if there had been official dealings with that company while he was in office.

8–012 There were numerous recommendations related to quangos or executive non-departmental public bodies. These were directed principally at the need for appointments to be made on merit, the importance of propriety for those who worked in such bodies and greater transparency.

Jaundiced political observers might have expected that the Report would have been left to gather dust like many other such initiatives. The reality proved otherwise, and many of the proposals were acted on. To be sure this was because the government was willing to accept them. This is, in a reductionist sense, a condition of almost any change within our political system. It should not mask the difficulty the government would have faced if it had tried to reject the proposals. Nor should it mask the astuteness of those who framed the Report. Each recommendation had a mark, A, B or C, attached thereto. These signified respectively recommendations that the Committee believed could be implemented immediately, those which should be implemented by the end of the year, and those on which progress would be re-examined in the latter part of the following year. The strategy of including "timed action points" made it more difficult for the government to resist.

8–013 Most of the recommendations that related to MPs and the House of Commons were accepted. A new Select Committee on Standards and Privileges was

[38] Committee on Standards in Public Life, *Annual Report 2014–15, https://www.gov.uk/government/uploads/system/uploads/attachment_data/file/447604/CSPL_Annual_Report_2015.pdf* [accessed 11 August 2015].

[39] Committee on Standards in Public Life, *First Report* (1995), Cm.2850.

[40] Committee on Standards in Public Life, *Sixth Report: Reinforcing Standards* (2000), Cm.4557.

established, the PCS was created, there was a new Code of Conduct[41] and the Register of Interests was revitalised. The government also accepted, albeit with some modifications, the principles which applied to ministers.[42] It acknowledged that ministers should behave according to the highest standards; that they should ensure that there was no conflict between their public duties and their private interests; and that public resources should not be used for party political purposes.

The recommendations from the Nolan Committee also had an impact on other governmental initiatives. The comments made in the Committee's First Report were a catalyst for reform of quangos.[43] A later Report from the Committee[44] on standards of conduct in local government provided the foundation for the government's proposals for a new ethical framework within local politics.[45]

The terms of reference of the Committee on Standards in Public Life were extended in November 1997 so as to enable it to review the funding of political parties. The Committee produced a valuable Report on the funding of political parties,[46] which led to the Political Parties, Elections and Referendums Act 2000. Later reports from the Committee have dealt with important topics such as the boundaries between ministers, special advisers and civil servants,[47] review of the Electoral Commission,[48] MPs expenses,[49] political party finance,[50] and police accountability.[51]

C. Parliamentary Commissioner for Standards and the Select Committee on Standards

The office of Parliamentary Commissioner for Standards (PCS)[52] was created in 1995 as a result of recommendations from the Committee of Standards. The principal responsibilities of the office are: overseeing the Register of Members' **8–014**

---

41 Select Committee on Standards and Privileges, *The Code of Conduct together with the Guide to the Rules Relating to the Conduct of Members*, HC Paper No.688 (1995–96).

42 *The Government's Response to the First Report from the Committee on Standards in Public Life* (1995), Cm.2931.

43 Cabinet Office, *Opening up Quangos: A Consultation Paper* (1997).

44 Committee on Standards in Public Life, *Third Report: Standards of Conduct in Local Government in England, Scotland and Wales* (1997), Cm.3702.

45 Department of the Environment, Transport and the Regions, Modern Local Government, *In Touch with the People* (1998), Cm 4014, Ch.6.

46 Committee on Standards in Public Life, *Fifth Report: The Funding of Political Parties in the United Kingdom* (1998), Cm.4057.

47 Committee on Standards in Public Life, *Ninth Report: Defining the Boundaries within the Executive, Ministers, Special Advisers and the Permanent Civil Service* (2003), Cm.5775.

48 Committee on Standards in Public Life, *Eleventh Report: Review of the Electoral Commission* (2007), Cm.7006.

49 Committee on Standards in Public Life, *Twelfth Report: MPs' Expenses and Allowances, Supporting Parliament, Safeguarding the Taxpayer* (2009), Cm.7724.

50 Committee on Standards in Public Life, *Thirteenth Report, Political Party Finance, Ending the Big Donor Culture* (2011), Cm.8208.

51 Committee on Standards in Public Life, *Fifteenth Report, Tone from the Top- Leadership, Ethics and Accountability in Policing* (2015), Cm 9057.

52 See *http://www.parliament.uk/mps-lords-and-offices/standards-and-interests/pcfs/* [accessed 11 August 2015].

Interests; providing confidential advice to individual MPs and the Select Committee on Standards about the interpretation of the Code of Conduct and Guide to the Rules relating to the Conduct of Members[53]; preparing guidance and providing training for MPs on matters of conduct, propriety and ethics; monitoring the operation of the Code of Conduct and Guide to the Rules and, where appropriate, proposing possible modifications to the Committee; receiving and investigating complaints about members who are allegedly in breach of the Code of Conduct and Guide to the Rules, and reporting the findings to the Committee. A valuable summary of the work of the first PCS, Sir Gordon Downey, is to be found in an Appendix to a Report of the Select Committee.[54]

The Select Committee on Standards has a number of functions.[55] It is to oversee the work of the PCS, including arrangements proposed by the PCS in relation to the register of members' interests.[56] The Select Committee also considers any matter relating to the conduct of MPs which is drawn to its attention by the PCS, including specific complaints about alleged breach of any applicable Code of Conduct, and it can make any recommendation as may be necessary for modification of the Code.[57]

The nature of the relationship between the PCS and the Select Committee has given rise to debate, particularly with respect to appeal procedures. The Select Committee produced a Report that attempted to clear the ground.[58] In most cases, the PCS will investigate a complaint and report the findings to the Select Committee. The Select Committee then reviews the PCS's procedures and evidence, reaches a conclusion as to whether the rules have been broken, assesses the gravity of the breach and recommends what penalty should be imposed.[59] The imposition of any penalty is then a matter for the House itself.

8–015 The initial investigation is undertaken by the PCS. If the PCS is of the opinion that there is no case to answer then this will normally be upheld by the Committee, which will not report the matter to the House.[60] If the PCS finds that there is a case to answer it will be considered by the Committee. This does not usually give rise to difficulty, but there are instances where issues of fact may be seriously in dispute. The Select Committee rejected the suggestion that in such instances a sub-committee of the Select Committee should investigate the matter.

---

[53] *The Code of Conduct together with the Guide to the Rules Relating to the Conduct of Members*, HC Paper No.1076 (2015), available at: *http://www.publications.parliament.uk/pa/cm201516/cmcode/1076/1076.pdf* [accessed 11 August 2015].

[54] Select Committee on Standards and Privileges, *Nineteenth Report: Retirement of the Parliamentary Commissioner*, HC Paper No.1147 (1998).

[55] *http://www.parliament.uk/business/committees/committees-a-z/commons-select/standards/role/* [accessed 11 August 2015].

[56] Committee on Standards and Privileges, *Ninth Report: Select Public Access to Registers of Interest*, HC Paper No.437 (1997).

[57] Select Committee on Standards and Privileges, *Nineteenth Report: Review of the Code of Conduct*, HC Paper No.1579 (2011).

[58] Select Committee on Standards and Privileges, *Twenty-First Report: Appeal Procedures*, HC Paper No.1191 (1998).

[59] Select Committee on Standards and Privileges, *Twenty-First Report: Appeal Procedures*, para.5.

[60] Select Committee on Standards and Privileges, *Twenty-First Report: Appeal Procedures*, para.10.

It felt that in serious cases the PCS might invite the Committee to appoint a legally qualified assessor who would assist in the investigation and share responsibility for its findings.[61]

The Select Committee then considered what appellate procedures should apply in cases where there were disputes as to the facts. It felt that the PCS should inform the subject of the complaint of the factual findings in sufficient detail for the latter to decide whether to appeal on this ground.[62] The nature of the appeal before the Select Committee was contested. Some were in favour of the Committee exercising a limited review on grounds akin to those in judicial review cases. Others advocated a full re-hearing by the Committee. The Committee itself felt that the nature of the appeal should be determined by it according to the circumstances of the case, and accepted that there would be some instances where a re-hearing was appropriate.[63] There were also differences of view expressed as to whether the Committee or some other body should hear any appeal. The Select Committee concluded that it depended on the nature of the appeal. If this was akin to a judicial review then it felt that the Committee itself could undertake the task. Where, however, the appeal was more in the nature of a re-hearing it believed that the appointment of an ad hoc tribunal was the best solution.[64]

This Report of the Select Committee raises important issues. The existing regime is premised on internal self-regulation by the House. There is, however, clearly a tension between this and the need to ensure procedural rectitude. The Select Committee was mindful of the need to comply with procedural fairness, but was wary lest this led to the over-judicialisation of the process and the surrender of ultimate competence to an external body. It was for this reason that on the key issues relating to appeal procedures and the choice of an internal or an external appellate body the Committee ended up treading such a fine line. A later Report by the Committee broadly endorsed the procedures used by the Committee.[65]

D. Independent Parliamentary Standards Authority

The scandal concerning MPs' expenses led to the Parliamentary Standards Act 2009 and the creation of the Independent Parliamentary Standards Authority (IPSA).[66] It has two principal roles: to administer and reimburse MPs' expenses and pay MPs' and their staff members' salaries; and to regulate MPs' expenses. Parliament subsequently passed legislation creating a Compliance Officer for IPSA and making provision for IPSA to take on responsibility for determining MPs' pay and pensions in the future. In relation to expenses, IPSA sets the **8–016**

---

[61] Select Committee on Standards and Privileges, *Twenty-First Report: Appeal Procedures*, para.16.
[62] Select Committee on Standards and Privileges, *Twenty-First Report: Appeal Procedures*, para.19.
[63] Select Committee on Standards and Privileges, *Twenty-First Report: Appeal Procedures*, para.24.
[64] Select Committee on Standards and Privileges, *Twenty-First Report: Appeal Procedures*, paras 25–32.
[65] Select Committee on Standards, *Sixth Report, The Standards System in the House of Commons*, HC 383 (2014–15), paras 135–157; *Hoon v United Kingdom* (Application 14832/11).
[66] See *http://parliamentarystandards.org.uk/Pages/default.aspx* [accessed 11 August 2015].

expenses rules, manages submitted expenses, verifies expense claims, reviews claim determinations and publishes details of MPs' expense claims.

5. THE PARLIAMENTARY COMMISSIONER FOR ADMINISTRATION

A. General

8–017 In the late 1950s there was increasing concern over administration. The Crichel Down affair, which was a catalyst for the Franks Committee, proved to be outside its terms of reference. In 1961, Justice[67] published a report, which made two suggestions. There were recommendations for a General Tribunal to deal with a miscellaneous group of appeals. This suggestion was not adopted. The report also considered the possibility of machinery to deal with maladministration. While the courts could tackle some such instances, others might not be reviewable, or such control might be inappropriate. The inspiration for the subsequent proposals was the Ombudsman in Scandinavian countries, an independent and impartial person who would investigate complaints of maladministration made by members of the public.

Largely as a result of these recommendations the Parliamentary Commissioner Act 1967 was passed, appointing a Parliamentary Commissioner for Administration[68] (PCA).[69] The PCA is appointed by the Crown and holds office for the period for which he or she is appointed, which cannot be more than seven years. The incumbent may be removed from office as a result of an address from both Houses of Parliament.

The idea of having an Ombudsman to provide a check on maladministration has taken hold in other areas. The work of the Health Service Commissioner and the Local Government Commissioners will be considered below.[70] There is a PCA for Northern Ireland,[71] and provision has been made for investigative machinery in relation to the Scottish Parliament and the Welsh Assembly.[72] There

---

[67] The Whyatt Report, *The Citizen and the Administration: the Redress of Grievances* (1961).

[68] F. Stacey, *The British Ombudsman* (Oxford: Clarendon, 1971); R. Gregory and P. Hutchesson, *The Parliamentary Ombudsman* (London: Allen & Unwin, 1975); F. Stacey, *Ombudsmen Compared* (Oxford: Oxford University Press, 1978); M. Seneviratne, *Ombudsmen in the Public Sector* (Open University Press, 1994); G. Drewry, "The Ombudsman: Parochial Stopgap or Global Panacea?", in P. Leyland and T. Woods (eds), *Administrative Law Facing the Future: Old Constraints & New Horizons* (Oxford: Blackstone, 1997), Ch.4.

[69] See *http://www.ombudsman.org.uk/* [accessed 11 August 2015].

[70] See paras 8–042 to 8–043.

[71] Parliamentary Commissioner (Northern Ireland) Act 1969; *http://www.ni-ombudsman.org.uk/* [accessed 11 August 2015].

[72] Scotland Act 1998 s.91; Public Services Ombudsman (Wales) Act 2005, as amended by the Government of Wales Act 2006.

is now an Ombudsman in important areas such as[73]: Pensions,[74] Financial Services,[75] Energy Supply,[76] Estate Agents,[77] Prisons and Probation,[78] and Legal Services.[79]

B. Who can be Investigated

8–018 The PCA is empowered to investigate complaints relating to any action, subject to the limitations mentioned below, which is taken by or on behalf of a government department or other authority to which the Act applies, where the action taken is in the exercise of administrative functions of that department or authority.[80]

The departments and other authorities to which the Act applies are listed in Sch.2, which can be altered by Order in Council.[81] Reference to a department or other authority is taken to include a reference also to the ministers, members or officers of the department.[82] The list of bodies within the PCA's jurisdiction has been expanded, and includes many agencies and non-departmental public bodies.

Agencies created independently of the "Next Steps" initiative will normally have to be added to Sch.2 to be within the PCA's remit. Executive agencies are part of the parent department and do not have formal separate identity. Given that this is so they come within the PCA's ambit of authority by virtue of his jurisdiction over the department itself.

Somewhat more difficult is the position of firms to whom work has been contracted out. The 1967 Act is framed in terms of administrative functions being carried out by or *on behalf of* departments.[83] Firms to whom work has been contracted out are acting on behalf of the department and should therefore be regarded as within the 1967 Act. This is the view taken by the PCA, and it is surely correct as a matter of principle.[84]

---

[73] For a full list, see: *http://www.ombudsman.org.uk/make-a-complaint/if-we-cant-help/useful-links#otherombudsmen* [accessed 11 August 2015].

[74] See *http://www.pensions-ombudsman.org.uk/* [accessed 11 August 2015].

[75] See *http://www.financial-ombudsman.org.uk/* [accessed 11 August 2015]; R. James and M. Seneviratne, "The Building Societies Ombudsman Scheme" (1992) 11 C.J.Q. 157; A. Mowbray, "Ombudsmen: the Private Sector Dimension", in W. Finnie, C. Himsworth and N. Walker (eds), *Edinburgh Essays in Public Law* (Edinburgh University Press, 1991), pp.315–334.

[76] See *http://www.energy-ombudsman.org.uk/links/index.php* [accessed 11 August 2015].

[77] See *http://www.oea.co.uk/* [accessed 11 August 2015].

[78] See *http://www.ppo.gov.uk/* [accessed 11 August 2015].

[79] Courts and Legal Services Act 1990; R. James and R. Seneviratne, "The Legal Services Ombudsman: Form versus Function?" (1995) 58 M.L.R. 187; Legal Services Act 2007 ss.114–115 and 159; See *http://www.legalservicesboard.org.uk/index.htm*; *http://www.legalombudsman.org.uk/* [both accessed 11 August 2015].

[80] Parliamentary Commissioner Act 1967 ss.4(1), 5(1); *http://www.ombudsman.org.uk/about-us/who-we-are/how-to-complain/government-departments-and-other-public-bodies-which-the-ombudsman-can-investigate* [accessed 11 August 2015].

[81] See *http://www.ombudsman.org.uk/make-a-complaint/how-to-complain/government-departments-and-other-public-bodies-which-the-ombudsman-can-investigate* [accessed 11 August 2015].

[82] Parliamentary Commissioner Act 1967 s.4(8).

[83] Parliamentary Commissioner Act 1967 s.5(1).

[84] Parliamentary Commissioner for Administration, *Annual Report 1992*, p.2.

C. What can be Investigated

i. Administrative, legislative and judicial functions

8–019 The complaint must relate to action taken in the exercise of administrative functions of that department, body or agency. This could be said to exclude judicial or legislative functions. Thus, the question arises as to whether, for example, the making of delegated legislation is within the PCA's jurisdiction. The Attorney General, in evidence before the Select Committee,[85] expressed the view that the making of a statutory instrument is a legislative process and hence outside the PCA's jurisdiction, and that this applied equally to the preliminary stages of the making of the instrument. When the instrument has been made, the Attorney General felt that the PCA could receive complaints about its operation and ensure that the relevant department was keeping the matter under review, but that the actual content of the rules could not be questioned. This appears to be the position adopted by the PCA. Where a statutory order is not a statutory instrument, the PCA's powers appear to be wider, allowing an investigation of maladministration in the administrative process leading to the actual making of the order.

Judicial functions in the sense of the work of tribunals or courts are not within the PCA's powers. This will not exclude any matter with a judicial flavour. Public inquiries have, for example, been the subject of the PCA's attention.

ii. Administrative functions and maladministration

8–020 Provided that the action is taken by a body listed in the Act, and the action is taken in the exercise of administrative functions, the PCA is empowered to investigate claims of injustice resulting from maladministration, which have been referred by a Member of Parliament.[86]

The term maladministration is not defined in the Act.[87] A sense of what the legislature intended is to be derived from the Crossman catalogue which included bias, neglect, inattention, delay, incompetence, ineptitude, arbitrariness and the like. The PCA has defined maladministration to mean poor administration or the wrong application of rules.[88] Examples include: avoidable delay; faulty procedures or failure to follow correct procedures; not telling the individual about appeal rights; unfairness, bias or prejudice; giving misleading or inadequate advice; refusing to answer reasonable questions; discourtesy; mistakes in handling claims; and not offering an adequate remedy where one is due.[89]

In reality the defects most commonly found are failing to provide information, misapplication of departmental rules, misleading advice, unjustifiable delay and

[85] Select Committee on the Parliamentary Commissioner for Administration, *Report*, HC Paper No.385 (Session 1968–1969).

[86] Parliamentary Commissioner Act 1967 s.5(1).

[87] G. Marshall, "Maladministration" [1973] P.L. 32.

[88] Parliamentary Commissioner for Administration, *About the Ombudsman* (1998).

[89] See also, *R. v Parliamentary Commissioner for Administration, Ex p. Balchin* [1997] C.O.D. 146 QBD, where Sedley J held that maladministration included bias, neglect, inattention, delay, incompetence, ineptitude, perversity, turpitude and arbitrariness.

inconsiderate behaviour. The PCA criticises discretionary administrative action most often because a relevant consideration has not been taken into account, or the evidence has not been properly collated prior to making the decision.

iii. Administrative functions, maladministration and principles of good administration

The PCA has more recently published *Principles of Good Administration.*[90] These principles are intimately linked with a finding of maladministration. Six such principles are elaborated. The first such principle is termed "*getting it right*", which embraces the following: acting in accordance with the law and with due regard for the rights of those concerned; acting in accordance with the public body's policy and guidance (published or internal); taking proper account of established good practice; providing effective services, using appropriately trained and competent staff; and taking reasonable decisions, based on all relevant considerations. **8–021**

The second principle is "*being customer focused*", which covers: ensuring that people can access services easily; informing customers what they can expect and what the public body expects of them; keeping to its commitments, including any published service standards; dealing with people helpfully, promptly and sensitively, bearing in mind their individual circumstances; and responding to customers' needs flexibly, including, where appropriate, co-ordinating a response with other service providers.

The third principle of good administration is "*being open and accountable*". This demands that the relevant public body should be: open and clear about policies and procedures, ensuring that information, and any advice provided, is clear, accurate and complete; state its criteria for decision making and giving reasons for decisions; handle information properly and appropriately; keep proper and appropriate records; and take responsibility for its actions.

The fourth such principle requires that the public body should act "*fairly and proportionately*". This entails: treating people impartially, with respect and courtesy; treating people without unlawful discrimination or prejudice, and ensuring no conflict of interests; dealing with people and issues objectively and consistently; and ensuring that decisions and actions are proportionate, appropriate and fair. **8–022**

The penultimate principle is "*putting things right*". Thus, the public body should: acknowledge mistakes and apologise where appropriate; put mistakes right quickly and effectively; provide clear and timely information on how and when to appeal or complain; and operate an effective complaints procedure, which includes offering a fair and appropriate remedy when a complaint is upheld.

The final principle is entitled "*seeking continuous improvement*", which requires that the relevant body should: review policies and procedures regularly to ensure that they are effective; ask for feedback and use it to improve services

[90] Parliamentary and Health Service Ombudsman, *Principles of Good Administration* (2009), *http://www.ombudsman.org.uk/improving-public-service/ombudsmansprinciples/principles-of-good-administration* [accessed 11 August 2015].

and performance; and ensure that the public body learns lessons from complaints and uses these to improve services and performance.

iv. *Administrative functions, maladministration and the merits*

8–023 The PCA is not authorised to question the merits of a decision taken without maladministration by a government department or other authority in the exercise of discretion.[91] The purpose of this provision is not entirely clear. It seems merely to restate the requirement from s.5(1), that maladministration is a condition precedent to the exercise of the PCA's jurisdiction.

It might, however, be taken to indicate that the maladministration must reside in the procedure by which the decision was made. This interpretation was adopted by the first PCA. He drew a distinction between the procedure leading to a decision and the decision itself. The latter he regarded as outside his competence, even if it resulted in manifest hardship to the complainant. The Select Committee regarded this interpretation as over-restrictive,[92] and the PCA subsequently broadened his perspective.

A similar caution initially constrained the PCA in relation to departmental rules and regulations. The Select Committee, once again, encouraged a broader interpretation,[93] enabling the PCA to consider the effect of statutory instruments and the action taken to review their operation, with a wider jurisdiction in relation to rules that were not statutory instruments.

Complaints about the content of government policy or legislation are, however, not within the PCA's remit: the former is for the government, the latter for Parliament.[94]

v. *Maladministration and political response*

8–024 The decision in *Bradley*[95] casts light on the relationship between a finding of maladministration by the PCA and the subsequent political response. A number of people had lost all or part of their final salary pensions when their occupational pension schemes were wound up. The PCA made various findings of maladministration by the secretary of state, who rejected all but one. The claimant sought judicial review of the secretary of state's decision to reject the PCA's findings. The first of the PCA's findings of maladministration related to whether official information concerning the security that members of final salary schemes could expect was inaccurate and misleading.

---

[91] Parliamentary Commissioner Act 1967 s.12(3).

[92] Select Committee on the Parliamentary Commissioner for Administration, *Second Report*, HC Paper No.350 (Session 1967–1968), para.14.

[93] Select Committee on the Parliamentary Commissioner for Administration, *Report*, HC Paper No.385 (Session 1968–1969), para.11; Parliamentary Commissioner for Administration, *First Report*, HC Paper No.49 (Session 1974–1975), para.63.

[94] Parliamentary Commissioner for Administration, *About the Ombudsman* (1998).

[95] *R. (Bradley) v Secretary of State for Work and Pensions* [2008] EWCA Civ 36; *R. (Evans) v Attorney General* [2015] UKSC 21, [2015] 2 W.L.R. 813 SC. Compare *R. (Equitable Members Action Group) v HM Treasury* [2009] EWHC 2495 (Admin).

The Court of Appeal held that the 1967 Act did not require the body investigated to accept the findings of maladministration. The secretary of state, acting rationally, was therefore entitled to reject a finding of maladministration and prefer his own view. However, the decision to reject the PCA's findings in favour of his own view was itself subject to rationality review by the courts. The secretary of state had to have a reason for rejecting the PCA's findings and the secretary of state was not entitled to reject those findings merely because he preferred another view which could not be characterised as irrational. The court concluded that it was irrational for the secretary of state to reject the PCA's finding that the official information was incomplete and potentially misleading, and quashed the secretary of state's decision in that respect.

D. Matters Excluded from the PCA's Jurisdiction

i. Section 5(2): PCA and courts

Section 5(2) prevents the PCA from investigating any action in respect of which the person aggrieved has or had a right of appeal, reference, or review to, or before, a tribunal constituted by, or under, any enactment or by prerogative, and any action in respect of which the person aggrieved has or had a remedy by way of proceedings in any court of law. This prohibition is subject to an exception where the PCA is satisfied that it would not be reasonable to expect the claimant to resort to such a remedy.[96] Section 5(2) raises issues of general interest as to the PCA's role, which will be considered in the next section. For the present, it is sufficient to say that there has, despite s.5(2), been overlap between the courts' jurisdiction and that of the PCA. This is particularly so as the courts have expanded the ambit of judicial review. **8–025**

ii. Section 5(3) and Schedule 3: excluded matters

The second type of exclusion is contained in s.5(3). This prevents the PCA from investigating any action or matter described in Sch.3 of the Act. This Schedule covers a wide range of matters, including: **8–026**

1. Actions certified by a minister to affect relations between the UK government and any other government or international organisation.
2. Subject to limited exceptions, action taken, in any country or territory outside the UK, by or on behalf of any officer representing or acting under the authority of Her Majesty in respect of the UK, or any other officer of the UK government.
3. Action taken in connection with the administration of the government of any country or territory outside the UK, which forms part of Her Majesty's dominions or in which Her Majesty has jurisdiction.
4. Action taken under the Extradition Act 2003.

[96] D. Foulkes, "Discretionary Provisions of the Parliamentary Commissioner Act" (1971) 34 M.L.R. 377.

5. Action taken by or with the authority of the secretary of state for the purposes of investigating crime or of protecting the security of the State, including action so taken with respect to passports.
6. The commencement or conduct of civil or criminal proceedings before any court of law in the UK, or proceedings before any international court or tribunal, or under relevant legislation concerning the armed forces.
7. Action taken by any person appointed by the Lord Chancellor as a member of the administrative staff of any court or tribunal, so far as that action is taken at the direction, or on the authority (whether express or implied), of any person acting in a judicial capacity or in his capacity as a member of the tribunal.
8. Action taken by any member of the administrative staff of a relevant tribunal, so far as that action is taken at the direction, or on the authority (whether express or implied), of any person acting in his capacity as a member of the tribunal.
9. Any exercise of the prerogative of mercy.
10. Action taken on behalf of the minister by certain health authorities.
11. Action relating to contractual and commercial transactions, whether in the UK or elsewhere, other than the acquisition of land whether compulsorily or by agreement, and the disposal of surplus land thus acquired.
12. Personnel matters, which encompasses both civil and military services, and cases where the government has power to take, determine or approve action.
13. The grant of honours, awards or privileges by the Crown.

The two areas where there has been most pressure for reform have been the exemptions for contractual/commercial matters and personnel. The existence of other machinery for scrutiny of these areas, and the idea that the PCA is concerned with the relationship of the government and the governed and not with the government as employer or trader, are the main arguments against reform. Neither of these reasons is convincing.[97]

iii. Matters within the remit of devolved jurisdictions

8–027 The Parliamentary Commissioner Act 1967 has been amended[98] so as to ensure that the PCA does not investigate matters that fall within the remit of the devolved administrations in Scotland and Wales, both of which have their own Ombudsmen regimes.

[97] Sir C. Clothier, "The Value of an Ombudsman" [1986] P.L. 204, 210–211.
[98] Parliamentary Commissioner Act 1967 ss.4(3A), (3B), 5(5A) and (5B).

E. Complainant and Procedure

i. Who can complain

Section 6(1) spells out who can complain. In essence, it provides that complaints can be made by any individual or body of persons, whether incorporated or unincorporated. Complaints cannot, however, be made by local authorities, nationalised industries, or other bodies appointed by a minister or a government department. These exclusions are designed to emphasise the PCA as someone who arbitrates between the government and the governed, but who does not hear complaints by one department against another. The complaint must be made by the person aggrieved, or a personal representative. It must be submitted to an MP within 12 months from the date on which the person aggrieved first had notice of the matters alleged in the complaint, but the PCA has discretion to allow a claim to proceed outside that time limit.[99] The complainant must either be resident in the UK, or the complaint must relate to action taken while he or she was present in the UK.[100] **8–028**

ii. MP filter

The complaint must be addressed initially to an MP.[101] This is in contrast to the position in other countries where the individual is allowed direct access to the Ombudsman. This has always been rejected in the UK. The PCA is viewed as an adjunct to Parliament, who aids Parliament in the performance of its traditional function of protecting the citizen, but is not intended to be an independent citizen protector. The argument against allowing direct access has been bolstered by more practical considerations. It is felt that in a country with a large population direct access would place an impossible burden upon the PCA. The disadvantages in not allowing direct access have partly been overcome by a system whereby the PCA passes to the relevant MP a complaint received directly from the public, stating that he is willing to consider the case should the MP wish him to do so. This allows the MP to function as a filter, but avoids the necessity of outright rejection of the claim by the PCA. It would nonetheless be preferable if individuals could have direct access to the PCA.[102] The Public Administration Select Committee recommended removal of the MP filter, but the government rejected the recommendation.[103] **8–029**

---

[99] Parliamentary Commissioner Act 1967 s.6(3).

[100] Parliamentary Commissioner Act 1967 s.6(4), subject to the qualifications in s.6(5). See also, Parliamentary Commissioner (Consular Complaints) Act 1981.

[101] Parliamentary Commissioner Act 1967 s.5(1); L. Cohen, "The Parliamentary Commissioner and the 'M.P. Filter'" [1972] P.L. 204.

[102] Justice, *Our Fettered Ombudsman* (1977), paras 24–31; Justice/All Souls Review, *Administrative Justice—Some Necessary Reforms* (Oxford University Press, 1988), p.90.

[103] Public Administration Select Committee, *Tenth Report*: *Parliament and the Ombudsman*, HC Paper No.471 (Session 2009–2010).

iii. Investigation

8–030 The PCA has considerable choice as to whether to investigate,[104] the method of investigation and possesses wide powers to obtain evidence. There is in effect a three-stage procedure, which is divided into screening, investigation and report.[105]

Screening serves principally to remove those cases where the PCA lacks jurisdiction. Where the PCA proposes to investigate she must afford the principal officer of the department or authority concerned, and any other person alleged to have taken or authorised the action complained of, an opportunity to comment on the allegations. Investigations are conducted in private, but the PCA has a broad discretion as to the type of information required, the persons who are questioned, and whether any person may be represented by counsel, solicitor or otherwise in the investigation.[106] Provision is made for the payment of expenses to the complainant, or to a person involved in the investigation.[107] An investigation by the PCA does not, however, invalidate or suspend action taken by an authority.[108]

The PCA can require the minister, or any other person with information relevant to the investigation, to furnish it. The PCA has the same powers as a court with respect to the attendance of witnesses, including the administration of oaths, and the production of documents.[109] No obligation to maintain secrecy, whether derived from any enactment or any rule of law, applies to the disclosure of information for the purposes of an investigation under the Act, nor can the Crown claim Crown privilege in respect of such documents.[110] Information related to the Cabinet or Cabinet committees cannot, however, be furnished. A certificate issued by the Secretary of the Cabinet with the approval of the Prime Minister certifying that any document does so relate is conclusive of the matter.[111]

The PCA must furnish a number of reports at various stages of the investigatory procedure. A report must be sent to the MP who requested the investigation, stating the result, or the reasons why the investigation cannot be undertaken.[112] Where an investigation is conducted a report is also sent to the principal officer of the department concerned.[113] If, having made a report finding maladministration, it appears to the PCA that the injustice will not be remedied,

---

[104] Parliamentary Commissioner Act 1967 s.5(5); *Re Fletcher's Application* [1970] 2 All E.R. 527; *R. (Sharma) v Parliamentary and Health Service Ombudsman* [2011] EWHC 2609 (Admin).

[105] Cabinet Office, *The Ombudsman in Your Files* (1996).

[106] Parliamentary Commissioner Act 1967 s.7(1) and (2).

[107] Parliamentary Commissioner Act 1967 s.7(3).

[108] Parliamentary Commissioner Act 1967 s.7(4). Except in so far as the person aggrieved has been removed from the UK, he must, if the PCA so directs, be brought back to the UK, subject to such conditions as the secretary of state may direct, for the purposes of the investigation.

[109] Parliamentary Commissioner Act 1967 s.8(1) and (2).

[110] Parliamentary Commissioner Act 1967 s.8(3). There are however provisions to prevent the PCA disclosing information to any person where it would be contrary to interests of the state. This does not prevent the PCA from seeking such documents, s.11(3).

[111] Parliamentary Commissioner Act 1967 s.8(4).

[112] Parliamentary Commissioner Act 1967 s.10(1).

[113] Parliamentary Commissioner Act 1967 s.10(2), and to any other person who is alleged to have taken or authorised the action complained of.

he may lay before each House of Parliament a special report on the case.[114] An annual general report must be laid before each House, and the PCA may submit other reports if he thinks fit.[115]

F. Remedies

i. Remedial awards and compliance

The PCA has no formal power to award a remedy. The investigation will in general not even have a suspensory effect on the action under investigation.[116] If the recommendations are not complied with a special report can be submitted to Parliament,[117] and there is the possibility of judicial review to challenge rejection of the PCA's findings.[118] The PCA's reports have, however, led to a wide range of remedies. This is apparent from any of the annual reports. **8–031**

Thus, the Annual Report for 2010–11 states that over 99 per cent of all recommendations made during the year were accepted,[119] and the performance for 2013–14 was also very good.[120] The nature of the "remedy" varied. In some instances, it took the form of an apology. In others it took the form of action to prevent recurrence of the problem, by, for example, a review of or changes to procedures, staff training or change in departmental practice. In yet others it took the form of action to remedy the failure identified, or reconsideration of the decision. In many instances the recommendation was for financial compensation for loss, inconvenience or distress.

The PCA has also had an impact on certain more high profile cases. The Sachsenhausen case[121] concerned the distribution of money provided by the German government to compensate those who had been victims in the Sachsenhausen concentration camp. The sum was distributed by the UK government, but money was withheld from 12 people who claimed that they fell within the relevant criteria. The PCA found maladministration. The government gave compensation even though the original sum given by the German government had already been distributed.

Another example of a high profile case is the Barlow Clowes affair.[122] The Barlow Clowes investment business collapsed in 1988 leaving many investors with substantial losses. The business had been licensed by the Department of Trade and Industry. The PCA found maladministration by the DTI, and although

---

[114] Parliamentary Commissioner Act 1967 s.10(3).

[115] Parliamentary Commissioner Act 1967 s.10(4).

[116] Parliamentary Commissioner Act 1967 s.7(4).

[117] Parliamentary Commissioner Act 1967 s.10(4).

[118] *Bradley* [2008] EWCA Civ 36.

[119] Parliamentary and Health Service Ombudsman, *Annual Report 2010–11, A Service for Everyone* (HC Paper No.1404; Session 2010–2011), p.7.

[120] Parliamentary and Health Service Ombudsman, *Annual Report 2013–14*, pp.13–14.

[121] Parliamentary Commissioner for Administration, *Third Report* (HC Paper No.54; Session 1967–68).

[122] R. Gregory and G. Drewry, "Barlow Clowes and the Ombudsman—Part I" [1991] P.L. 192; "Barlow Clowes and the Ombudsman—Part II" [1991] P.L. 408.

the government did not accept these findings it provided ex gratia compensation for up to 90 per cent of the losses. The PCA will not, however, always be successful in such high profile cases.

ii. Remedial principles

8–032 The PCA has developed remedial principles, which are intended to guide government departments and public bodies.[123] The underlying principle is that the service provider restores the complainants to the position they would have been in if the maladministration or poor service had not occurred. If that is not possible, the service provider should provide appropriate compensation.

Thus, "*getting it right*" entails putting right cases of maladministration or poor service that have led to injustice, and considering all relevant factors when deciding the appropriate remedy. The principle of "*being customer focused*" means apologising for and explaining the maladministration or poor service, understanding people's expectations and needs, dealing with people professionally and sensitively, and providing remedies that take account of people's individual circumstances. The ideal of being "*open and accountable*" requires the relevant body to be open and clear about how it decides remedies, to operate a proper system of accountability and delegation in providing remedies, and to keep a clear record of what it has decided in relation to remedies.

The injunction to "*act fairly and proportionately*" means offering remedies that are fair and proportionate to the complainant's injustice or hardship, providing remedies to others who have suffered injustice or hardship as a result of the same maladministration or poor service, where appropriate, and treating people without bias, unlawful discrimination or prejudice. The principle of "*putting things right*" requires that the complainant and, where appropriate, others who have suffered similar injustice or hardship, should where possible be returned to the position they would have been in if the maladministration or poor service had not occurred. If that is not possible, there should be compensation. The final principle, which entailed "*seeking continuous improvement*", meant that lessons should be learned from complaints to ensure that maladministration or poor service did not recur, and that information concerning complaints should be used to improve services.

G. Workload

8–033 An overview of the current workload of the PCA can be gleaned from the Annual Reports. In 2010–11[124] the following picture emerged. Before the PCA takes a case for investigation it ensured that the complaint was within its remit; that the body complained about had not been able to resolve it; that there was evidence of maladministration leading to unremedied injustice; and that there was a

[123] Parliamentary and Health Service Ombudsman, *Principles for Remedy* (2009), available at: *http://www.ombudsman.org.uk/improving-public-service/ombudsmansprinciples/principles-for-remedy* [accessed 12 August 2015].

[124] Parliamentary and Health Service Ombudsman, *Annual Report 2010–11, A Service for Everyone.*

reasonable prospect of a worthwhile outcome to the investigation. The PCA dealt with 23,657 enquiries during the year, 605 cases were resolved informally, and 404 cases required formal investigation.

In 2013–14 the PCA received 27,566 enquiries, and there was a six-fold increase in the number of cases investigated, which was the result of a considered shift in policy. Previously, the PCA would only investigate if it was likely that the complaint would be upheld; the current policy is to investigate if there is a case to answer.[125]

H. Select Committee on the PCA

The Public Administration Select Committee examines the PCA's reports laid before the House. It provides a focal point for parliamentary attention on the work of the PCA. The Select Committee has encouraged the PCA to adopt a broad view of his powers, and exerted political pressure to ensure departmental compliance with the PCA's recommendations.[126] **8–034**

In 1993 the Select Committee conducted a wider inquiry into the powers, work and jurisdiction of the PCA.[127] It recommended that: the legislation should be amended so as to specify exclusions from, rather than inclusions within, the PCA's jurisdiction; the retention of the MP filter; speedier handling of complaints; examples from the PCA's reports should be distributed to government departments in order to provide guidance as to good administrative practice; and that the PCA should on occasion be able to conduct a broader ranging administrative audit of a particular body. The government was supportive of some of these recommendations, but rejected others, such as that regarding the conduct of broader ranging administrative audits.[128]

In 2009 the Select Committee recommended removal of the MP filter and that there should be a guaranteed debate on the floor of the House where the PCA reported that the government had failed to remedy maladministration. The government however rejected both recommendations.[129] In 2013 it produced, as will be seen below, a more far-reaching report on reform of the Ombudsman regime.[130]

---

125 Parliamentary and Health Service Ombudsman, *Annual Report 2013–14, A Voice for Change* (HC Paper No.536; 2014), p.13.

126 R. Gregory, "The Select Committee on the Parliamentary Commissioner for Administration 1967–1980" [1982] P.L. 49; Public Administration Select Committee, *The Ombudsman in Question: The Ombudsman's Report on Pensions and its Constitutional Implications* (HC Paper No.1081; Session 2005–06).

127 Select Committee, *First Report* (HC Paper No.333; Session 1993–94).

128 P. Giddings and R. Gregory, "Auditing the Auditors: The Select Committee Review of the Powers, Work and Jurisdiction of the Ombudsman 1993" [1994] P.L. 207; P. Giddings, R. Gregory and V. Moore, "Auditing the Auditors: Responses to the Committee's Review of the United Kingdom Ombudsman System 1993" [1995] P.L. 45.

129 Select Committee on Public Administration, *Fourth Report*: *Parliament and the Ombudsman* (HC Paper No. 107; Session 2009–10); Select Committee on Public Administration, *Tenth Report*: *Parliament and the Ombudsman, Further Report* (HC Paper No. 471; Session 2009-10).

130 See para.8–046.

I. Judicial Review and the PCA

8–035 The PCA is subject to judicial review in relation to decisions made concerning matters which are appropriate for investigation, and the proper manner of the investigation. The court will not readily be persuaded to interfere with the PCA's exercise of discretion, more especially given the broad terms in which this discretion is cast by ss.5(5) and 7(2) of the Act.[131] Controls based on for example, reasons and relevancy are nonetheless applied to determinations made by the PCA.[132]

J. Role of the PCA

8–036 The role of the ombudsman has developed considerably since the office was first introduced. The scope of bodies within the PCA's jurisdiction has been expanded, and Commissioners for health and local government have been established. The idea of an ombudsman has taken hold more generally. The role of the PCA is still however a matter for debate.[133] There are at least three ways in which the PCA can be viewed.

i. The PCA and remedying of individual grievances

8–037 The first is to see the PCA's main task as the remedying of individual grievances caused by neglect, bias, or inattention within the administration. In performing this role, the PCA operates as an adjunct to Parliament, aiding that body in the protection of the individual. The MP filter, the absence of the power to award remedies, and the duty to report to Parliament, all reinforce this perspective.

This picture of the PCA sees the job as primarily concerned with the avoidance of mistakes. The jurisdictional divide between the courts and the PCA serves to emphasise this. Each is responsible for ensuring the avoidance of mistakes within its sphere of responsibility, and this is so even accepting that there is some overlap. There is no doubt that correction of individual grievances is an important aspect of the PCA's work.[134]

ii. The PCA, enhanced remedial power, and Small Claims Administrative Court

8–038 A second way in which the PCA could be viewed preserves the mistake avoidance approach, but seeks to expand the existing jurisdiction. There are suggestions that citizens should have direct access to the PCA, and that the

[131] *R. v Parliamentary Commissioner for Administration, Ex p. Dyer* [1994] 1 W.L.R. 621 DC.

[132] *R. v Parliamentary Commissioner for Administration, Ex p. Balchin* [1997] C.O.D. 146 QBD; *R. v Parliamentary Commissioner for Administration, Ex p. Balchin (No.2)* [2000] 2 L.G.L.R. 87 QBD; *R. (Balchin) v Parliamentary Commissioner for Administration (No.3)* [2002] EWHC 1876 (Admin); *In the matter of an application by JR55 for Judicial Review (Northern Ireland)* [2016] UKSC 22.

[133] C. Harlow and R. Rawlings, *Law and Administration*, 2nd edn (Butterworths, 1997), Ch.13.

[134] R. Gregory and J. Pearson, "The Parliamentary Ombudsman after Twenty-Five Years" (1992) 70 Pub. Adm. 469, 492–496.

discretion to take cases that are within the jurisdiction of the ordinary courts should be generously exercised. There are also suggestions that the PCA should have remedial power, directly or indirectly. The PCA would be able to give remedies, or apply to the court for the grant of relief. The image of the PCA as a small claims administrative court emerges.

The attractions of this second approach are obvious, but it is problematic. The suggestion that the PCA should be a form of small claims court would involve a significant re-orientation of the PCA's original role. It would transform the PCA into a judicial figure with a bureaucratic hierarchy. Benefits of the present system, such as informality of procedure and negotiated settlement, would be lost or placed in jeopardy. There would be a tendency for the process to become adversarial. Procedures would become more rigid. These comments apply with equal force to suggestions that the PCA should have the power to award a remedy, since this is bound to generate demands for more formal hearings before being condemned, the right to representation, and other safeguards associated with judicial proceedings.[135]

The suggestion that the PCA should liberally exercise the discretion to hear complaints that are within the courts' purview[136] also has important ramifications. There is bound to be some overlap between the PCA and the courts. The nature of administrative law precludes rigid statements that a matter is or is not within the purview of the courts. The reason for caution is the danger of there being two inconsistent views on the same topic, or the application of the same view in an inconsistent manner.

There is a link between this point and the possibility of the PCA applying to a court for the award of a remedy. If the PCA had this power and also liberally interpreted the discretion to take cases that could come before the court, we would be faced with the following conundrum. Let us assume that in some cases the PCA might reach a result inconsistent either with the judicial principle applied in an area or, while consistent with the principle, applied it in a way in which a court would not. The PCA approaches the court claiming maladministration. Either the court accepts the claim and grants the remedy, in which case the dual system of jurisprudence would be a reality, or the court would look to the substance of the claim and reassess whether maladministration had taken place. If the court re-examined the matter and found that the action should not be deemed maladministration because, for example, estoppel should not bind the Crown, then the dual system of jurisprudence would be avoided, but a cumbersome and partial form of review would have taken its place. **8–039**

It might be argued that these fears are misconceived because the courts and the PCA are doing different things. The courts are concerned with the limits of jurisdiction and the principles on which discretion should be exercised, while the PCA focuses on principles of good administration. We are in danger of allowing form to blind us from substance. Whether, for example, a representation should bind is the substantive question. To imagine that there is no conflict if the conclusions are reached under different labels called ultra vires or good

[135] Clothier, "The Value of an Ombudsman" [1986] P.L. 204, 210.

[136] A. Bradley, "The Role of the Ombudsman in Relation to the Protection of Citizen's Rights" [1980] C.L.J. 304, 331–332.

administration is short-sighted. We are back once again with a dual system of jurisprudence, or a dual set of values being applied to the same problem.

iii. The PCA, remedying of individual grievances and improved administration

8–040 If this second view of the PCA is felt to be problematic, the office could still be expanded in a third direction. Proponents of this view accept the mistake avoidance role of the PCA, outlined as the first view, but advocate expansion of the jurisdiction in a different direction. This is to ask the PCA to draw attention to lessons that should be learned from individual cases in order to improve administrative practice generally.[137] This would not mean neglect of individual cases. It would be an additional task. The investigation of individual cases would be, as Harlow says,[138] a catalyst for discovering more general administrative deficiencies. This could be particularly helpful given that MPs do not at present seem to pay undue regard to the PCA's role in addressing individual grievances.[139]

It is clear that the PCA already fulfils this general function to some degree, as a glance at the annual reports confirms. Problems in individual cases lead to the discovery of a more general concern, and result in recommendations for changing the administrative practice that gave rise to the problem.[140] The Select Committee has emphasised that the PCA may have a role in assessing whether an agency's performance matched up to the standards laid down in the Citizen's Charter.[141] It has, moreover, been accepted that reports of good administrative practice should be circulated to departments, and that departments should provide a response to a finding of maladministration, indicating the steps taken to rectify the situation.[142]

8–041 The publication in 2007 of the *Principles of Good Administration* and the *Principles for Remedy* fit well with this vision of the PCA. They are designed, as we have seen, to provide general guidance to individual departments and bodies concerning good administrative practice, with the hope that adherence to these precepts will reduce the incidence of administrative deficiency and individual error. The PCA has moreover signalled that more attention will be given to the ways in which public services can be improved by learning from individual complaints.[143]

---

137 C. Harlow, "Ombudsmen in Search of a Role" (1978) 41 M.L.R. 446.

138 Harlow, "Ombudsmen in Search of a Role" (1978) 41 M.L.R. 446, 452.

139 G. Drewry and C. Harlow, "A Cutting Edge? The Parliamentary Commissioner and MPs" (1990) 53 M.L.R. 745; A. Bradley, "Sachsenhausen, Barlow Clowes—And Then?" [1992] P.L. 353.

140 Gregory and Pearson, "The Parliamentary Ombudsman after Twenty-Five Years" (1992) 70 Pub. Adm. 469, 480–484; Parliamentary and Health Service Ombudsman, *Annual Report 2013–14, A Voice for Change* (HC Paper No.536; 2014), pp.19–23.

141 Select Committee on the PCA, *Second Report: The Implications of the Citizen's Charter for the Work of the PCA* (HC Paper No.158; Session 1991–92).

142 Giddings, Gregory and Moore, "Auditing the Auditors: Responses to the Committee's Review of the United Kingdom Ombudsman System 1993" [1995] P.L. 45, 47.

143 See *http://www.ombudsman.org.uk/improving-public-service* [accessed 12 August 2015].

The breadth of any formal PCA report will nonetheless be limited by the nature of the complaint made.[144] Governments have, moreover, not accepted that the PCA should be able to carry out administrative audits, and have rejected such suggestions made by the Select Committee.[145] The rationale for the government's attitude was in part that other bodies already undertake this type of task. The principal reason for rejecting this suggestion was however that the PCA's independence when conducting individual investigations could be compromised where the complaint related to a department which the PCA had approved in such an audit.[146] This reasoning is questionable. The fact that the PCA had, for example, given a clean bill of health to the general procedures applied by a particular department would not necessarily imply that the department was incapable of maladministration in a specific case. There is nothing inconsistent between sound standard operating procedures and mistakes in the application of such procedures in a particular instance.

K. Health

The National Health Service Reorganisation Act 1973 created two Health Service Commissioners, one for England and the other for Wales. The PCA holds the office for England, as well as the office created by the 1967 Act. Scotland was provided with a Commissioner by the Health Service (Scotland) Act 1972. The Health Service Commissioner (HSC) can investigate certain health authorities[147] and persons therein.[148] The matters that can be investigated are an alleged failure in a service provided by the authority, an alleged failure by an authority to provide a service that it was meant to provide, and maladministration connected with any other action taken by or on behalf of an authority. The complainant must allege that injustice or hardship has been suffered.[149] Maladministration in this context connotes avoidable delay, not following proper procedures, rudeness or discourtesy, not explaining decisions, or not answering complaints fully or properly. The Commissioner can also investigate complaints about the exercise of clinical judgment, although cannot investigate the merits of decisions taken without maladministration. The matters excluded from the jurisdiction of the HSC are similar to those excluded from the general jurisdiction of the PCA. **8–042**

A difference between the PCA's jurisdiction under the 1967 Act and the legislation relating to health is that direct access is allowed under the latter legislation. The reason is that MPs do not occupy the same constitutional position

144 *R. (Cavanagh) v Health Service Commissioner* [2006] 1 W.L.R. 1229.

145 Select Committee, *Review of Access and Jurisdiction* (HC Paper No.615; Session 1977–78). The Select Committee argued that the PCA should have some capacity to undertake audits where investigation of individual complaints revealed a more general problem. This was not accepted by the government, *Observations by the Government on Review of Access and Jurisdiction*, Cmnd.7449 (Session 1977–78); Select Committee, *First Report* (HC Paper No.33; Session 1993–94); Select Committee, *Fifth Report* (HC Paper No.619; Session 1993–94).

146 Giddings, Gregory and Moore, "Auditing the Auditors: Responses to the Committee's Review of the United Kingdom Ombudsman System 1993" [1995] P.L. 45, 48.

147 Health Service Commissioners Act 1993 s.2.

148 Health Service Commissioners Act 1993 s.2A.

149 Health Service Commissioners Act 1993 s.3.

with respect to the health service as they do in connection with ordinary departments. A condition precedent to direct access is, however, that the complainant first brings the matter to the notice of the health authority or relevant practitioner, which must be allowed a reasonable opportunity to respond to the complaint.

6. LOCAL COMMISSIONERS

A. Scope of Authority

8–043 The 1967 Act did not include complaints against local authorities. This was remedied by the Local Government Act 1974.[150] Two Commissions for local administration were established, one for England and one for Wales.[151] The work is done by local commissioners, who are appointed by the Crown. There are now three commissioners for England who deal with complaints from different parts of the country. The local commissioners can investigate complaints against local authorities and this includes committees, members and officers.[152] Access to the local commissioner was originally indirect, the complaint being referred initially to a member of the local authority. Since 1988 individuals have been given a right of direct access to the local commissioner,[153] but a complaint can be referred to the local commissioner by a member of a local authority with the consent of the complainant.[154]

The complainant must allege that injustice has been suffered as a consequence of maladministration and allow the local authority a reasonable opportunity to investigate and reply to the complaint.[155] Exclusions exist similar to those governing the jurisdiction of the PCA. Thus, cases where there is a remedy before a court or tribunal are excluded, as are cases subject to an appeal to a minister.[156] There is a discretionary exception to this prohibition, which is the same as that in the 1967 Act.[157] There are important exclusions for cases where the complaint affects all or most of the inhabitants of the authority's area,[158] and for certain other types of case.[159]

The procedure for investigation is similar in certain respects to that of the PCA.[160] Copies of the report must be sent to the complainant, the local authority

---

[150] See *http://www.lgo.org.uk/* [accessed 12 August 2015].

[151] Scotland has its own system.

[152] Local Government Act 1974 ss.25 and 34(1).

[153] Local Government Act 1988 s.29 Sch.3 para.5.

[154] Local Government Act 1974 s.26C.

[155] Local Government Act 1974 s.26(5); *R. v Local Commissioner for Administration, Ex p. Bradford MBC* [1979] Q.B. 287, CA (Civ Div); *R. v Commissioner for Local Administration, Ex p. Eastleigh BC* [1988] Q.B. 855, CA (Civ Div); M. Jones, "The Local Ombudsmen and Judicial Review' [1988] P.L. 608.

[156] *R. v Commissioner for Local Administration, Ex p. H* [1999] C.O.D. 382 QBD.

[157] Local Government Act 1974 s.26(6); *R. v Commissioner for Local Administration, Ex p. Croydon London Borough Council* [1989] 1 All E.R. 1033 QBD.

[158] Local Government Act 1974 s.26(7). Other exclusions are investigation or prevention of crime, contractual or commercial transactions, personnel matters, educational matters.

[159] Local Government Act 1974 s.26(8) and Sch.5.

[160] Local Government Act 1974 ss.28–30.

and the member who originally referred it. The report must be made available for public inspection.[161] The procedural powers of the local commissioners were reinforced in 1989.[162] When an adverse report has been made the local authority is under a duty to respond to it. If no such action is forthcoming in three months, or the commissioner is not satisfied with the proposed course of action, the local commissioner must make a further report setting out the facts and making recommendations about remedying the injustice. If the local authority still proves recalcitrant, or has not taken the necessary action, then it can be forced to issue a statement in the press containing the local commissioner's proposals and any reasons why it has not taken action.

B. Commissioners, Internal Complaints Procedures and General Advice to Local Authorities

A complainant will have only to resort to the local ombudsman if the local authority does not redress a grievance. We should therefore focus not only on the local commissioner, but also on internal grievance procedures used by local authorities. **8–044**

Valuable work on this was done by Lewis and others at Sheffield.[163] They found that less than 50 per cent of local authorities had general complaints procedures, that those with such procedures did not advertise their existence and that few systematically monitored complaints with a view to checking on service quality. Their recommendations included a statutory duty to have a complaints procedure, the appointment of a complaints officer, and the adoption of a code of good administrative practice. Other studies, such as that by the Public Law project, also cast doubt on the efficacy of local complaints procedures.[164]

The Commission for Local Administration published guidance on this issue. Its paper on *Running a Complaints System*[165] emphasised the virtue of a good complaints system, and provided practical guidance on the principles for its effectiveness. The current guidance from the Local Government Ombudsman on *Running a Complaints System*[166] emphasises accessibility, communication, timeliness, fairness, credibility and accountability.

The Sheffield study also contained interesting suggestions about the role of the local commissioners. Some of these, such as direct access, have been implemented. Other recommendations included: modification of the jurisdictional limits; allowing the local commissioners to investigate on their own initiative, rather than waiting for a complaint; enabling them to comment on issues where many people are affected; shifting away from the concern with **8–045**

---

161 Local Government Act 1974 s.30.

162 Local Government and Housing Act 1989 s.26, amending s.31 of the Local Government Act 1974.

163 N. Lewis, M. Seneviratne and S. Cracknell, *Complaints Procedures in Local Government* (Centre for Criminological and Socio-Legal Studies, University of Sheffield, 1987); C. Crawford, "Complaints, Codes and Ombudsmen in Local Government" [1988] P.L. 246.

164 Public Law Project, *Review of the Local Government Ombudsman* (1996), p.14.

165 Commission for Local Government in England, *Guidance on Good Practice* (2002), p.1.

166 Local Government Ombudsman, *Guidance on Running a Complaints System http://www.lgo.org.uk/publications/advice-and-guidance#guidance* [accessed 12 August 2015].

maladministration to allow the local ombudsmen to investigate more general failure in the administrative system. The study did not, however, favour judicial enforcement in the event that a local authority did not comply with the commissioner's recommendations. This role for the courts has been advocated,[167] but such a change would render the investigative process more formal. If local authorities know that a report of the local commissioner could produce legal liability, even indirectly, they are likely to demand more extensive rights to controvert his findings.[168]

The Local Government Ombudsman published a number of papers to provide more general guidance to local authorities on a range of matters.[169] Statutory provisions reinforce this aspect of the CLA's role, by encouraging the giving of general advice on good administrative practice.[170] Most notable in this respect are the papers on good administrative practice, remedies and devising a complaints system.

The paper on *Good Administrative Practice*[171] extrapolates from the commissioners' work in individual cases and sets out 42 principles or axioms of good administration. Some of the principles reflect legal requirements, such as keeping within the allowable legal limits, not acting for improper purposes, taking account of relevant considerations, giving reasons and the like. Other principles may not be formally required by the law, but are desirable in the interests of good administration, such as the formulation of policies that set the general criteria for decision making in a particular area, and communication of these policies to customers. Yet other principles are designed to ensure that the internal administrative process within the local authority is structured in the optimum manner, as exemplified by the maintenance of adequate records and the monitoring of progress in dealing with a problem.

The paper on *Remedies*[172] provides a helpful overview about the commissioners' thinking on this issue. The guiding principle is, as is the case with the PCA, that the remedy should place the complainant in the position he would have been in had the maladministration not occurred.[173] It is clear that practical action to redress the grievance, such as repairs to a council house, or the provision of special educational needs, is regarded as the first line of attack.[174] Financial compensation becomes of greater relevance where the practical action is not possible, where loss has been suffered in the interim, or where the very essence of the complaint is a failure to pay money.[175] The paper provides detailed guidance on provision of remedies for complaints about different subject matter.[176] The

---

167 *Administrative Justice, Some Necessary Reforms* (Oxford University Press, 1988), pp.128–129.

168 *Administrative Justice, Some Necessary Reforms* (1988), pp.127–128; Sheffield study, *Complaints Procedures in Local Government* (1987), p.39; C. Himsworth, "Parliamentary Teeth for Local Government Ombudsmen" [1986] P.L. 546; G. Marshall, "Ombudsmanaging Local Government" [1990] P.L. 449.

169 See *http://www.lgo.org.uk/publications/advice-and-guidance#special* [accessed 12 August 2015].

170 Local Government Act 1974 s.23(12A).

171 Commission for Local Administration, *Guidance on Good Practice 2* (2001).

172 Local Government Ombudsman, *Guidance on Good Practice: Remedies* (2015).

173 Local Government Ombudsman, *Guidance on Good Practice: Remedies*, para.2.

174 Local Government Ombudsman, *Guidance on Good Practice: Remedies*, para.7.

175 Local Government Ombudsman, *Guidance on Good Practice: Remedies*, paras 8–9.

176 Local Government Ombudsman, *Guidance on Good Practice: Remedies*, pp.13–103.

Local Government Ombudsman currently provides a range of training manuals concerning complaints procedures and the effective handling of complaints.[177]

7. OMBUDSMAN: LOOKING TO THE FUTURE

The PCA and the Local Commissioners have argued for overhaul of the existing system. They advocated a modern, unified Ombudsman scheme dealing with central and local government and health. The Cabinet Office undertook a review in 2000.[178] It proposed a major overhaul of the present system, the creation of an integrated system for the ombudsmen sector in England, and the removal of the MP filter. A further consultation took place in 2005, albeit narrower in scope.[179] The latter consultation led to passage of a Regulatory Reform Order, which facilitates collaboration and joint investigation between the PCA, HSC and Local Commissioners where the subject matter of the complaint falls within the remit of more than one jurisdictional area.[180] **8–046**

The government now appears committed to change. The Public Administration Select Committee had recommended that there should be consultation on the creation of a single Ombudsman service,[181] and this was duly undertaken in the light of a review by Robert Gordon commissioned by the Cabinet Office. The Gordon Review[182] advocated creation of a single Ombudsman service that would bring together the ombudsmen responsible for parliament, health, local government and housing. This approach was endorsed by the Cabinet Office in its consultation,[183] and has been supported by the current PCA.[184] Legislation to make this a reality was included in the Queen's speech in 2015, and the expectation is therefore that a Bill will be brought forward by the Cabinet Office.

---

177 See *http://www.lgo.org.uk/training-councils/good-complaint-handling–gch-/* [accessed 12 August 2015].

178 Cabinet Office, *Review of the Public Sector Ombudsmen in England* (2000); M. Seneviratne, "'Joining Up' the Ombudsmen—The Review of the Public Sector Ombudsmen in England" [2000] P.L. 582.

179 Cabinet Office, *Reform of Public Sector Ombudsmen Services in England* (2005).

180 The Regulatory Reform (Collaboration etc. between Ombudsmen) Order 2007 (SI 1889/2007).

181 Public Administration Select Committee, *Fourteenth Report, Time for a People's Ombudsman Service* (HC Paper No.655; Session 2013–14).

182 R. Gordon, *Better to Serve the Public: Proposals to Restructure, Reform, Renew and Reinvigorate Public Sector Ombudsmen* (2014), *https://www.gov.uk/government/consultations/public-service-ombudsman* [accessed 12 August 2015].

183 Cabinet Office, *A Public Service Ombudsman, A Consultation* (2015), *https://www.gov.uk/government/consultations/public-service-ombudsman* [accessed 12 August 2015].

184 *http://www.ombudsman.org.uk/about-us/news-centre/press-releases/2015/julie-mellor-to-stand-aside-as-chair-of-phso-when-public-services-ombudsman-bill-receives-royal-assent* [accessed 12 August 2015].

CHAPTER 9

TRIBUNALS AND INQUIRIES

1. CENTRAL ISSUES

i. Tribunals and inquiries have been part of our administrative landscape for some considerable time.[1] They constitute an important part of the machinery for the discharge of public functions in the modern state. 9–001

ii. The operation of tribunals has been affected by general and specific legislation. The Tribunals and Inquiries Act 1958 made significant changes in the legal rules governing both tribunals and inquiries.

iii. There was a more radical overhaul of tribunals in the Tribunals, Courts and Enforcement Act 2007, which produced far-reaching changes in the organisation of tribunals and the way in which they function.

iv. Inquiries are central to certain areas of administration, most notably planning. They are also used more generally to investigate matters of public concern, and this aspect is now governed by the Inquiries Act 2005.

v. The detailed rules for the operation of inquiries in areas such as planning also embody and reflect different ideologies concerning the purposes served by legal regulation in this area, as will be apparent from the subsequent discussion.

2. TRIBUNALS: RATIONALE AND NATURE

A. Reasons for their Creation

The reasons for the creation of tribunals were considered in the historical discussion.[2] A word or two more is warranted at this juncture. Three principal arguments have been used to justify assigning tasks to tribunals. 9–002

First, tribunals are often preferred to courts because they have the advantages of speed, cheapness, informality and expertise. These advantages are of particular importance in areas involving mass administrative justice, such as social welfare. It would, moreover, be extremely difficult for the ordinary courts to cope with the case load if these matters were assigned to the ordinary judicial process.

[1] R. Wraith and P. Hutchesson, *Administrative Tribunals* (London: Allen & Unwin, 1973); J. Farmer, *Tribunals and Government* (London: Weidenfeld & Nicolson, 1974); P. Birkinshaw, *Grievances, Remedies and the State*, 2nd edn (London: Sweet & Maxwell, 1994); R. Rawlings, *Grievance Procedure and Administrative Justice. A Review of Socio-Legal Research* (1987).

[2] See Ch.2.

Tribunals can also alleviate problems for the courts, which can become inundated by judicial review applications within a particular area.[3]

Second, a rather different type of argument was that the ordinary courts might not be sympathetic to the protection of the substantive interests contained in the legislation that laid the foundation of the welfare state at the turn of the century, and that therefore the matter should be assigned to a tribunal instead.

A third and more radical argument sees the creation of some tribunals as a symbolic means of giving the appearance of legality in a particular area in order to render more palatable unpopular changes in the substantive benefits to which individuals were entitled. Thus, Prosser[4] has argued that appeals machinery introduced in the Unemployment Assistance Act 1934 was designed to defuse opposition to cuts in benefits by directing it into channels where it could be controlled and have a minimal effect.

9–003 These reasons may well have force in different contexts. What is readily apparent is that tribunals have been set up in many areas. There are, for example, tribunals dealing with industrial matters, financial services, mental health, immigration, social security, revenue and child support to name but a few, and new tribunals are often created. The government classifies tribunals as non-departmental public bodies (NDPBs), and the 2006 Report on Public Bodies listed 40 Tribunal NDPBs, counted on the basis of tribunal systems, rather than individual panels.[5]

B. The Nature of Tribunals

9–004 The definition of what constitutes a tribunal is no easy matter. The name is not conclusive. The Council of Tribunals supervised bodies called authorities, commissions and committees, as well as tribunals. We must look beyond the label attached, and have regard to the nature of the body. It is possible to articulate a number of "properties" that a tribunal should possess, and then test to see how many do in fact possess them.[6] These properties could be: the ability to make final, legally enforceable decisions, subject to review and appeal; independence from any department of government; the holding of a public hearing that is judicial in nature; the possession of expertise; a requirement to give reasons; and the provision of appeal to the High Court on points of law. However, few of the tribunals listed in the Tribunals and Inquiries Act 1992 possessed all of these features.[7]

The Tribunals, Courts and Enforcement Act 2007 has had a marked impact on this issue. The Act provides for the establishment of a First-tier Tribunal and an Upper Tribunal. The functions previously performed by most central government

---

[3] Sir Harry Woolf, "Judicial Review: A Possible Programme for Reform" [1992] P.L. 221, 228.

[4] T. Prosser, "Poverty, Ideology and Legality: Supplementary Benefit Appeal Tribunals and their Predecessors" (1977) 4 British Jnl. of Law and Soc. 44; L. Bridges, "Legality and Immigration Control" (1975) 2 British Jnl. of Law and Soc. 221, 224.

[5] Cabinet Office, *Public Bodies 2006* (2006), p.ii.

[6] Farmer, *Tribunals and Government* (1974), pp.185–186.

[7] Farmer, *Tribunals and Government* (1974), pp.186–187.

tribunals have been transferred to the newly created tribunals under the 2007 Act, thereby reducing the number of separate tribunal jurisdictions that existed hitherto.

It should in any event be recognised that while tribunals may differ from the courts in the way in which they operate, the difference is one of degree rather than kind.[8] Studies have shown[9] that, for example, while not bound by precedent in the same way as the superior courts, tribunals will often follow and build on past decisions.[10] Nor is this necessarily something to be deprecated. Consistency of treatment and rational development of principles are important.

3. TRIBUNAL REFORM: FRANKS AND LEGGATT

A. The Franks Report

i. The Committee's remit

In the 1950s there was growing concern as to the diversity of tribunals, uncertainty as to the procedures they followed, and worry over the lack of cohesion and supervision. The catalyst for the establishment of the Franks Committee[11] was however the Crichel Down affair. This received wide publicity, but as it was an example of ad hoc high-handed administrative behaviour it was not within the brief given to the Franks Committee. **9–005**

This brief was limited in two important ways. The Committee was not to consider decisions made in the ordinary courts. It was only to discuss those areas in which a decision was reached after a formal statutory procedure had been followed, thereby excluding the "one-off" high-handed administrative action, and informal decision-making.

ii. Recommendations

The Franks Committee proceeded on the assumption that tribunals should be regarded as part of the machinery of adjudication, and not as part of the machinery of the administration,[12] and that tribunal procedure should be open, fair and impartial.[13] **9–006**

---

[8] K. Whitesides and G. Hawker, *Industrial Tribunals* (London: Sweet & Maxwell, 1975); J. Evans, *Immigration Law*, 2nd edn (London: Sweet & Maxwell, 1983); L. Dickens et al., *Dismissed: A Study of Fair Dismissal and the Industrial Tribunal System* (Oxford: Blackwell, 1985); J. Peay, *Tribunals on Trial: A Study of Decision-Making under the Mental Health Act 1983* (Oxford: Clarendon, 1989); J. Baldwin, N. Wikeley and R. Young, *Judging Social Security: The Adjudication of Claims for Benefit in Britain* (Oxford: Clarendon, 1992).

[9] Wraith and Hutchesson, *Administrative Tribunals* (1973), Ch.10; Farmer, *Tribunals and Government* (1974), Ch.7.

[10] T. Buck, "Precedent in Tribunals and the Development of Principles" (2006) 25 C.J.Q. 458.

[11] *Report of the Committee on Administrative Tribunals and Enquiries* (1957), Cmnd.218 (the Franks Report).

[12] The Franks Report, para.40.

[13] The Franks Report, para.42.

> "In the field of tribunals openness appears to us to require the publicity of proceedings and knowledge of the essential reasoning underlying the decisions; fairness to require the adoption of a clear procedure which enables parties to know their rights, to present their case fully and to know the case which they have to meet; and impartiality to require the freedom of tribunals from the influence, real or apparent, of departments concerned with the subject matter of their decisions."

The Franks Report contained valuable recommendations concerning the *constitution* and *procedure* of tribunals.[14] As to *constitution*, the Committee stated that the Lord Chancellor should appoint chairmen of tribunals, and the Council on Tribunals should appoint other members. Chairmen should normally have legal qualifications and should always do so in the case of appellate tribunals.

Detailed recommendations were made concerning *procedure*. The Council on Tribunals should formulate procedure for particular tribunals, the aim being to combine orderly procedure with an informal atmosphere. The citizen should be aware of the right to apply to a tribunal and should know in good time before the hearing the case to be met. Tribunal hearings should be public except where there were considerations of public security, intimate personal or financial circumstances had to be disclosed, or the hearing was a preliminary investigation of a case involving professional reputation. Legal representation before tribunals should normally be allowed. Tribunals should be empowered to award costs, to take evidence on oath and to subpoena witnesses. Decisions should be as fully reasoned as possible, and a written notice of the decision should be sent to the parties as soon as possible after the hearing. Final appellate tribunals should publish selected decisions and circulate them to lower tribunals.

The Report also contained recommendations on *appeal* and *judicial review*. As to the former, the Committee advocated an appeal on fact, law and merits from a first instance tribunal to an appellate tribunal, except where the tribunal of first instance was particularly well qualified. There should not, on principle, be an appeal from a tribunal to a minister. As to review, the Committee recommended that no statute should contain words purporting to oust the remedies of certiorari, prohibition and mandamus.

In addition to judicial control by review and appeal, the Committee urged that bodies called the Council on Tribunals for England and Wales and the Scottish Council be established. Their main functions would be to advise on the detailed application to tribunals of the general principles contained in the Franks Report.

iii. *Implementation*

9–007 Many recommendations of the Franks Committee were enacted in the Tribunals and Inquiries Act 1958, replaced by the Tribunals and Inquiries Act 1992, while others were implemented by changes in administrative practice.

The Council on Tribunals was established with a membership of not more than 15 and not less than 10.[15] Its functions were advisory, and it was instructed to keep under review the constitution and working of the tribunals listed in a

[14] The recommendations are summarised in The Franks Report, Ch.31.

[15] Tribunals and Inquiries Act 1992 ss.1–2. There is provision for a Scottish Committee of the Council.

Schedule to the Act. In addition it could report on any matter referred to it by the government. It had power to make general recommendations concerning the membership of those tribunals listed in the Schedule, and it had to be consulted prior to enactment of any new procedural rules pertaining to them.[16]

Other recommendations enacted were the right to a reasoned decision, subject to the condition that it was requested on or before the giving or notification of the decision,[17] and the restrictive construction to be placed on clauses that purported to exclude judicial review.[18] The list of tribunals subject to the legislation could be augmented by ministerial order, as was done.

In some areas less was achieved than advocated by the Franks Committee. Appeals to the High Court were limited to questions of law, excluding questions of fact and the merits,[19] and the procedure for the appointment of chairmen and members of tribunals diverged from that recommended by the Franks Committee.

B. The Leggatt Report

In May 2000 the Lord Chancellor appointed Sir Andrew Leggatt to undertake a review of tribunals. The Leggatt Report, *Tribunals for Users—One System, One Service*,[20] is the most important since the Franks Report, and its recommendations were far-reaching. **9–008**

i. The Tribunals Service

The Leggatt Report recommended the creation of a Tribunals Service, which should be an executive agency of the Lord Chancellor's Department.[21] This should be a national organisation with a strong local presence, structured along regional lines. The Tribunals Service should set out in a Charter the standards of service that users can expect, as well as indicating what should occur if those standards have not been met. **9–010**

ii. The tribunals system

The recommendations made in relation to the tribunal system were equally important. The reality is that we did not have anything that could be called a tribunal "system", notwithstanding the fact that they shared some procedural rules, and some organisational features. The Leggatt Report sought to remedy this. **9–011**

[16] Tribunals and Inquiries Act 1992 s.8.

[17] Tribunals and Inquiries Act 1992 s.10.

[18] Tribunals and Inquiries Act 1992 s.12.

[19] Tribunals and Inquiries Act 1992 s.11.

[20] Report of the Review of Tribunals by Sir Andrew Leggatt, *Tribunals for Users—One System, One Service*, 16 August 2001, *http://webarchive.nationalarchives.gov.uk/+/http://www.tribunals-review.org.uk/* [accessed 2 November 2015].

[21] Report of the Review of Tribunals by Sir Andrew Leggatt, *Tribunals for Users—One System, One Service*, paras 5.3–5.4.

It proposed that the Tribunals System should be divided into subject-matter divisions, with new tribunals allocated to Divisions by Practice Direction.[22] First-tier tribunals should be grouped into eight divisions to deal with disputes between citizen and state, and one to deal with disputes between parties. There should be a single route of appeal for all tribunals, to a single appellate division. First-tier tribunals would consider each case on its merits and their decisions would not create binding precedent. Appellate tribunals could, following the practice of the Social Security Commissioners, designate binding cases. The Presidential system should be generalised. There would be a Senior President for the Tribunals System, who would be a High Court judge. There would also be Presidents for the appellate divisions, and for the nine first-tier divisions. The Tribunals System should be directed by a Tribunals Board.

There should be a right of appeal on law, by permission, from first to second-tier tribunals, and from the latter to the Court of Appeal. The appellate body would have power to quash the original determination, remit it for reconsideration, grant declaratory relief, or decline to grant relief where there was no substantial prejudice.

The establishment of this comprehensive system of appeals led the Leggatt Report to recommend the exclusion of judicial review in relation to decisions of first-tier tribunals, if the rights of appeal had not been exhausted. The Leggatt Report also recommended that the decisions of second-tier tribunals should be excluded from the supervisory jurisdiction of the High Court, in part because such tribunals would often be headed by a High Court judge, who would develop expertise, and thus it was felt to be inappropriate to subject such decisions to review by another judge of equal status. It was in part because there would, in any event, be a right of appeal on a point of law to the Court of Appeal.

iii. Operation of the tribunals system

9–012 The Leggatt Report contained a wealth of important recommendations as to how the tribunal system should operate. The tribunal system should be *independent*, in the sense that there should be separation between the ministers and other authorities whose decisions were tested by tribunals, and the minister who appointed them. The tribunal system should be *coherent*, in the sense that the citizen should be presented with a single, overarching structure, which gave access to all tribunals. The system should be *user friendly*, with ready access to information about how to bring a case before a tribunal.

---

[22] Report of the Review of Tribunals by Sir Andrew Leggatt, *Tribunals for Users—One System, One Service*, paras 6.3–6.4.

4. TRIBUNALS: TRIBUNALS, COURTS AND ENFORCEMENT ACT 2007

The Leggatt Report was the most important document published about tribunals. It led to a government White Paper,[23] and many of the Leggatt recommendations were incorporated in the Tribunals, Courts and Enforcement Act 2007 (TCE Act).[24] **9–013**

A. Senior President of Tribunals

The TCE Act s.2 creates the office of Senior President of Tribunals, who is appointed on the recommendation of the Lord Chancellor.[25] The Senior President has a range of powers and duties. **9–014**

1. The Senior President's concurrence is required in relation to the chambers structure for the First-tier Tribunal and the Upper Tribunal (and any change in it), s.7(1).
2. The Senior President may, with the concurrence of the Lord Chancellor, make provision for the allocation of functions between chambers, s. 7(9).
3. A duty to report to the Lord Chancellor on matters which the Senior President wishes to bring to the attention of the Lord Chancellor and matters which the Lord Chancellor has asked the Senior President to cover, s.43.
4. Power to make practice directions, s.23.
5. The right to be consulted on the making of fees orders, s.42(5).
6. The concurrence of the Senior President is required in relation to the making of orders prescribing the qualifications required for appointment of members of the First-tier Tribunal, Sch.2 para.2(2) and the Upper Tribunal, Sch.3 para.2(2).
7. The Senior President has power to request a judge of the First-tier Tribunal or the Upper Tribunal to act as a judge of those tribunals, Sch.2 para.6(2), Sch.3 para.6(2).
8. The duty to maintain appropriate arrangements for training, welfare and guidance of judges and other members, Sch.2 para.8, Sch.3 para.9.

There is power to delegate most of these functions.[26] The Senior President of Tribunals must, in carrying out these functions, have regard to the need for tribunals to be accessible, for proceedings before tribunals to be fair, to be handled quickly and efficiently, and for members of tribunals to be experts in the subject-matter of the relevant area. The Senior President of Tribunals should also have regard to the need to develop innovative methods of resolving disputes.[27]

[23] White Paper, *Transforming Public Services: Complaints, Redress and Tribunals* (2004) Cm.6243.
[24] The provisions of the TCE Act 2007 came into effect at different times, The Tribunals, Courts and Enforcement Act (Commencement No.1) Order 2007 (SI 2709/2007).
[25] The details of the appointment process are set out in TCE Act 2007 Sch.1.
[26] TCE Act 2007 s.8.
[27] TCE Act 2007 s.2(3).

B. First-Tier Tribunal and Upper Tribunal

9–015 The government's response to the Leggatt recommendation for a single tribunal system was to create two new, generic tribunals, the First-tier Tribunal and the Upper Tribunal, into which existing tribunal jurisdictions could be transferred.

Thus the TCE Act s.3 provides for the creation of a First-tier Tribunal and an Upper Tribunal, each consisting of judges and other members, and presided over by the Senior President of Tribunals.[28] The Upper Tribunal is primarily, but not exclusively, an appellate tribunal from the First-tier Tribunal. The intent is that not only existing, but new tribunal jurisdictions will be fitted into this framework, such that in the future, when Parliament creates a new appeal right or jurisdiction, it will not have to create a new tribunal to administer it. The Upper Tribunal is a superior court of record, like the High Court and the Employment Appeal Tribunal. The TCE Act makes detailed provision for appointment of judges and other members of the First-tier Tribunal and Upper Tribunal.[29] The First-tier and Upper Tribunals are empowered to appoint assessors,[30] award costs and expenses,[31] and monetary awards made by the Tribunals are enforceable through the courts.[32]

The Act also provides for the establishment of "chambers" within the two tribunals so that the many jurisdictions transferred into the new system can be grouped together appropriately. Each chamber is headed by a Chamber President.[33] There are now 12 chambers within the First-tier Tribunal, which are: Asylum Support; Care Standards; Criminal Injuries Compensation; General Regulatory Chamber; Immigration and Asylum Chamber; Mental Health; Primary Health Lists; Property Chamber; Social Security and Child Support; Special Educational Needs and Disability; Tax Chamber; and War Pensions and Armed Forces Compensation. There are four chambers within the Upper Tribunal: Administrative Appeals Chamber; Immigration and Asylum Chamber; Lands Chamber; and the Tax and Chancery Chamber.[34]

C. Transfer of Functions to First-tier Tribunal and Upper Tribunal

9–016 The transfer of jurisdictions to the First-tier Tribunal and the Upper Tribunal is central to the regime of the TCE Act. The new tribunals exercise the jurisdictions hitherto exercised by the tribunals listed in the TCE Act Sch.6 Pts 1–4. This constitutes most of the tribunal jurisdictions administered by central government. Government policy is that when a new tribunal jurisdiction is required it will be given to these new tribunals. The Lord Chancellor is given power, subject to

28 They can sit anywhere in the UK, TCE Act 2007 s.26.
29 TCE Act 2007 ss.4–5 and Schs 2–3.
30 TCE Act 2007 s.28.
31 TCE Act 2007 s.29.
32 TCE Act 2007 s.27.
33 TCE Act 2007 s.7 and Sch.4.
34 34 See *https://www.gov.uk/government/organisations/hm-courts-and-tribunals-service/about* [accessed 2 November 2015].

certain constraints, to amend the list of tribunals in Sch.6.[35] Some tribunals have been excluded from the new structures because of their specialist nature, and tribunals run by local government have been excluded for the present because of their different funding and sponsorship arrangements.

The detailed provisions for the transfer of functions are set out in TCE Act s.30. The Lord Chancellor is empowered to provide that a function of a tribunal listed in Sch.6 should be transferred to the First-tier tribunal, the Upper Tribunal, the employment tribunals or the Employment Appeal Tribunal.[36]

The Lord Chancellor is given supplementary powers consequent on the transfer of function. Thus, the Lord Chancellor can, for example, provide by order for the abolition of a tribunal whose functions have been transferred under TCE Act s.30,[37] and he can provide for members of the "old" tribunal who are judicial office holders to have a new office within either the First-tier Tribunal or the Upper Tribunal.[38] The TCE Act also provides for the transfer to the Lord Chancellor of the administrative functions of other ministers in relation to tribunals listed in Sch.6.[39] This theme is further reinforced by s.36 of the TCE Act, which enables the Lord Chancellor by order to transfer power to make procedural rules for certain tribunals to himself or to the Tribunal Procedure Committee.

The courts will in any event protect the independence of tribunals. Thus, in the *Brent* case,[40] the court held that where Parliament had created an arm's length relationship between a department/local authority and a tribunal it was unacceptable for the former to collapse the distinction between administration and adjudication by the use of ministerial guidance.

D. First-Tier Tribunal and Upper Tribunal: Self-Review, Appeal and Judicial Review

The TCE Act contains an interesting array of mechanisms for checking decisions made by the First-tier Tribunal and the Upper Tribunal. 9–017

i. Self-review

The speedy and efficient discharge of tribunal business is central to the TCE Act 2007. This serves to explain the powers contained in ss.9 and 10 to allow the First-tier Tribunal and the Upper Tribunal to review their own decisions. 9–018

Thus s.9 of the TCE Act empowers the First-tier Tribunal to review a decision made by it, unless it is an excluded decision,[41] and subject to limits laid down in

[35] TCE Act 2007 s.37.

[36] Functions that are within the sphere of devolved administrations are, subject to certain exceptions, not transferred, TCE Act s.30(5)–(8). However, the TCE Act ss.32–34, provides for the possibility of appeal to the Upper Tribunal in relation to Wales, Scotland and Northern Ireland, when the relevant function has not been transferred to the First-tier Tribunal.

[37] TCE Act s.31(1).

[38] TCE Act s.31(2).

[39] TCE Act s.35.

[40] *R. (S (a child)) v Brent LBC* [2002] EWCA Civ 693; [2002] A.C.D. 90.

[41] TCE Act 2007 s.11(5).

Tribunal Procedure Rules. The First-tier Tribunal's power is exercisable of its own initiative, or by a person who has a right of appeal in respect of the decision. When the power of review is exercised the First-tier Tribunal can correct accidental errors in the decision or in a record of the decision; amend reasons given for the decision; or set the decision aside.[42] If the First-tier Tribunal sets a decision aside, it must either re-decide the matter, or refer it to the Upper Tribunal. If the latter occurs, the Upper Tribunal can make any decision which the First-tier Tribunal could make if the First-tier Tribunal were deciding the matter. A decision of the First-tier Tribunal cannot be reviewed more than once, and if the Tribunal has decided that an earlier decision should not be reviewed under s.9(1) it may not then change its mind.

The Upper Tribunal has held that the power of self-review by the First-tier Tribunal should only be used in cases where the original decision was clearly wrong in law, the rationale being that if it was used more widely then it would in effect remove rights of appeal from the First-tier to the Upper Tribunal in cases where the point of law was contentious.[43]

The TCE Act s.10 contains analogous provisions, which empower the Upper Tribunal to review its own decisions. The only salient difference is of course that if the Upper Tribunal decides to set aside its own earlier decision, then it must re-decide the matter itself.

ii. *Appeal of First-tier Tribunal decisions to the Upper Tribunal*

9–019 A party to a case generally has a right of appeal on a point of law from the First-tier Tribunal to the Upper Tribunal.[44] The right of appeal is subject to permission being given, by either the First-tier Tribunal or the Upper Tribunal. There is, however, no right of appeal against a decision which is "excluded", and the list of "excluded decisions" is set out in TCE Act s.11(5). The Lord Chancellor is empowered to specify who may or may not be treated as being a party to a case for the purposes of making an appeal from the First-tier Tribunal to the Upper Tribunal.

The effect of the TCE Act is therefore that appeal rights in general remain as they are now when jurisdictions transfer to the new tribunal. Thus, where there is a right of appeal, it will also exist after transfer. Where decisions could not be appealed, the transfer of the jurisdiction to the First-tier Tribunal will give rise to new rights of appeal, unless an order excluding such rights is made under s.11(5)(f), which empowers the Lord Chancellor to characterise a decision of a First-tier Tribunal as an excluded decision.[45]

The TCE Act s.12 specifies the powers of the Upper Tribunal when it decides that an error of law has been made by the First-tier Tribunal. The TCE Act s.12(2) states that the Upper Tribunal may "but need not" set aside the decision of the First-tier Tribunal. Thus if the Upper Tribunal decides that the error of law does not invalidate the decision of the First-tier Tribunal it can let that decision stand.

---

[42] *Essex CC v TB* [2014] UKUT 559 (AAC).

[43] *R. (RB) v First-tier Tribunal (Review)* [2010] UKUT 160 (AAC); [2010] UKUT 160.

[44] TCE Act 2007 s.11.

[45] The Lord Chancellor's power in this respect is limited by TCE Act 2007 s.11(6).

If it does set aside the decision the Upper Tribunal then has two options. It can remit the case back to the First-tier Tribunal with directions for its reconsideration, and the Upper Tribunal may direct that a different panel reconsiders the case, and give procedural directions in relation to the case.[46] The alternative option is for the Upper Tribunal to make the decision which it considers should have been made, and in doing so it can take any decision that could have been taken if the First-tier Tribunal were remaking the decision. The Upper Tribunal can also make findings of fact.

iii. Appeal of Upper Tribunal decisions to the Court of Appeal and Supreme Court

The TCE Act s.13 provides for a right of appeal to the relevant appellate court[47] on any point of law arising from a decision made by the Upper Tribunal, other than an excluded decision.[48] The right is subject to permission being granted by the Upper Tribunal, or the relevant appellate court on an application by the party. The time limits within which such appeals can be made are specified in rules of court made by the Civil Procedure Rules Committee. **9–020**

The Lord Chancellor may by order make provision for a person to be treated as being, or to be treated as not being, a party to a case for the purposes of the right to appeal. It is also open to the Lord Chancellor by order[49] to restrict appeals to the relevant appellate court to cases where the Court of Appeal or the Upper Tribunal considers that the proposed appeal would raise some important point of principle or practice, or that there is some other compelling reason for the appeal to be heard.[50] This restriction of second appeals applies where the prospective appellant has already had the case considered by both the First-tier Tribunal and the Upper Tribunal.[51]

The TCE Act s.14 specifies the powers of the relevant appeal court in deciding an appeal under s.13. If the appeal court finds an error on a point of law it may "but need not"[52] set aside the decision of the Upper Tribunal. This is analogous to the power of the Upper Tribunal when hearing appeals from the First-tier Tribunal. If the appeal court does set aside the decision it has two options.[53]

It can remit the case to the Upper Tribunal with directions for its reconsideration.[54] It can stipulate that the reconsideration should be undertaken by persons **9–021**

[46] See, e.g. *Worcestershire CC v JJ* [2014] UKUT 406 (AAC); *MM (Sudan) v Home Secretary* [2014] UKUT 105 (IAC); *LW v Norfolk CC* [2015] UKUT 65 (AAC).

[47] TCE Act 2007 s.13(12), which may be the Court of Appeal for England and Wales, the Court of Session for Scotland or the Court of Appeal for Northern Ireland.

[48] TCE Act 2007 s.13(8).

[49] TCE Act 2007 s.13(6). The exercise of the power under the subsection is subject to the affirmative resolution procedure, s.49; Appeals from the Upper Tribunal to the Court of Appeal Order 2008 (SI 2834/2008).

[50] *JD (Congo) v Secretary of State for the Home Department* [2012] EWCA Civ 327.

[51] TCE Act 2007 s.13(7).

[52] TCE Act 2007 s.14(2).

[53] *Sandhu v Secretary of State for Work and Pensions* [2010] EWCA Civ 962.

[54] TCE Act 2007 s.14(2)(b)(i), or, where the decision of the Upper Tribunal was on an appeal or reference from another tribunal or some other person, to the Upper Tribunal or that other tribunal or person, with directions for its reconsideration.

other than those who made the decision subject to appeal, and it can give procedural directions for the handling of the case. If the case remitted to the Upper Tribunal concerns an appeal that it heard from, for example, the First-tier Tribunal, as will commonly be so, then it is open to the Upper Tribunal to remit the case to the First-tier Tribunal for reconsideration in accord with the directions given by the appeal court.[55]

The appeal court can alternatively re-make the decision itself. If it does so it can make any decision which the Upper Tribunal could make if the Upper Tribunal were re-making the decision, and may make such findings of fact as it considers appropriate.

The TCE Act s.14A–C makes provision for appeals to the Supreme Court in limited circumstances, although it is not in force at the time of writing. It applies where there is a point of law concerning the interpretation of a statute or statutory instrument, or a point of law where the Upper Tribunal is bound by a decision of the appeal court or Supreme Court. The point of law must be of general public importance, and the Upper Tribunal must be satisfied that a hearing by the Supreme Court is justified and outweighs such a hearing by the Court of Appeal.

iv. *Appeal and the meaning of "law"*

9–022 The appeal rights considered above are dependent upon there being a question of law.[56] The existing jurisprudence on the meaning of "law" for the purposes of appeal will therefore still be relevant.

There has been considerable discussion of the *analytical distinction* between law and fact. Distinctions can be made between primary facts, what people saw, heard, did, etc. and the application of a statutory term to these facts, which is a question of law. Numerous cases avowedly support this division.[57] It is, however, unclear whether the meaning of any statutory term is itself a question of law and hence susceptible to appeal. Denning LJ held that where a layman, albeit one instructed on the relevant legal principles, could declare the inferences from the primary facts, the conclusion reached would be one of fact. Where however to reach a correct conclusion from the primary facts required a thoroughgoing legal knowledge then that conclusion would be one of law.[58]

The distinction between law and fact has also been affected by *functional or pragmatic considerations*, as manifested by the desire of the court to intervene or not. The difficulty of analytically separating law from fact will allow the courts to apply the label which best fits their aim of intervention or not, as the case may be.

It is moreover important to distinguish two issues that can arise in this area: whether the alleged error involves a question of law, and the test the courts use to

---

[55] TCE Act 2007 s.14(5).

[56] *Sandhu v Secretary of State for Work and Pensions* [2010] EWCA Civ 962; *SA (Sri Lanka) v Secretary of State for the Home Department* [2014] EWCA Civ 683.

[57] *Farmer v Cotton's Trustees* [1915] A.C. 922, HL at 932; *British Launderers' Research Association v Hendon Rating Authority* [1949] 1 K.B. 462, CA at 471; *Woodhouse v Peter Brotherhood Ltd* [1972] 2 Q.B. 520, CA (Civ Div) at 536; *R. v Barnet LBC, Ex p. Nilish Shah* [1983] 2 W.L.R. 16, HL at 24; *ACT Construction Ltd v Customs and Excise Commissioners* [1981] 1 W.L.R. 49, CA (Civ Div); [1981] 1 W.L.R. 1542.

[58] *British Launderers* [1949] 1 K.B. 462 at 471–472.

determine whether there has been an erroneous construction of the legal term. The courts may simply substitute their view as to what the meaning ought to be.[59] They may alternatively apply a less rigorous standard, which demands only that the construction was reasonable and based on some evidence.

The choice in this respect is evident in *Edwards v Bairstow*.[60] Bairstow alleged that the General Commissioners for income tax had made an error of law in finding that a transaction to which he was a party was not "an adventure in the nature of trade" for tax purposes. Lord Radcliffe began by stating that the disputed phrase involved a question of law, the meaning of which had to be interpreted by the courts. The law did not however, give a precise meaning to that phrase. It was clearly susceptible to a range of meanings[61]: **9–023**

> "[T]he field so marked out is a wide one and there are many combinations of circumstances in which it could not be said to be wrong to arrive at a conclusion one way or the other. If the facts of any particular case are fairly capable of being so described, it seems to me that it necessarily follows that the determination of the Commissioners … to the effect that trade does or does not exist is not 'erroneous in point of law'."

Thus far, Lord Radcliffe's reasoning demonstrated the distinction highlighted above. The meaning of trade was a legal question, but there might be no error of law given the standard applied in the above quotation. The role of the court was, in his Lordship's own terms, to lay down the limits within which it would be permissible to say that a trade existed in the meaning of the legislation.

What followed was more difficult, since Lord Radcliffe labelled cases in which the facts warranted a determination either way as questions of degree, and therefore as questions of fact. This was, with respect, a confusing label to apply. A legal issue does not cease to be such because it is open to a range of possible meanings. The reason for denying an appeal where these conditions are present is to say that there is an issue of law, but that there has been no error in construction, and therefore the appeal fails.

Lord Radcliffe's judgment was, nonetheless, based on the assumption that the courts did not necessarily have to substitute judgment. The court would, said his Lordship, intervene if there were anything ex facie which was bad law and which affected the determination. There would also be an error of law if, in the absence of any misconception appearing ex facie, the facts found were such that no person acting judicially and properly instructed to the relevant law could have reached the determination under appeal. Such a case should best be described as one in which the true and only conclusion contradicted the determination actually made.[62] The decision made by the Commissioners was overturned for this reason. A number of cases have followed this approach.[63]

---

[59] *Woodhouse v Peter Brotherhood Ltd* [1972] 2 Q.B. 520, CA (Civ Div); *Instrumatic Ltd v Supabrase Ltd* [1969] 1 W.L.R. 519, CA (Civ Div); *British Railways Board v Customs and Excise Commissioners* [1977] 1 W.L.R. 588, CA (Civ Div); *Farmer* [1915] A.C. 922; *ACT Construction* [1981] 1 W.L.R. 49.

[60] *Edwards v Bairstow* [1956] A.C. 14, HL pp.33–36.

[61] *Edwards v Bairstow* [1956] A.C. 14, HL at p.33.

[62] *Edwards v Bairstow* [1956] A.C. 14 at 36.

[63] *Marriott v Oxford and District Co-operative Society Ltd (No.2)* [1969] 1 W.L.R. 254 QBD; *Global Plant Ltd v Secretary of State for Social Services* [1972] 1 Q.B. 139 QBD; *Central Electricity*

9–024 Where matters of technical legality or broad principle[64] are involved the courts have tended to veer towards substitution of judgment. They will be influenced by the comparative qualifications of the courts and the tribunal for resolving the question posed, and also by the need to provide a uniform answer in an area where tribunals may interpret the same term differently. There is, by way of contrast, a significant area between technical legality and broad principle in which the court is content to allow the decision-maker the degree of latitude provided by Lord Radcliffe's test in the *Edwards*[65] case.

The Supreme Court in *Jones*[66] lent further authority to this less intensive standard of review for tribunals. It held that where the interpretation and application of a specialised statutory scheme was entrusted by Parliament to the new tribunal system, an important function of the Upper Tribunal was to develop structured guidance on the use of expressions that were central to the scheme, thereby reducing the risk of inconsistent results by different First-tier panels. The interpretation of the expression "crime of violence" within the statutory scheme was a task primarily for the tribunals, not the appellate courts. A pragmatic approach should therefore be taken to the dividing line between law and fact, so that the expertise of tribunals at the First-tier and that of the Upper Tribunal could be used to best effect. An appeal court should not venture too readily into this area by classifying as issues of law issues that were best left for determination by the specialist appellate tribunals.

v. *Judicial review by the Upper Tribunal*

9–025 The inherent powers of judicial review are vested in the High Court. The TCE Act is, however, innovative in that it vested judicial review powers in the Upper Tribunal.

The TCE Act s.15(1) empowers the Upper Tribunal to grant mandatory, prohibiting and quashing orders, and a declaration and an injunction. The Upper Tribunal can also grant restitution or monetary relief, if satisfied that the High Court would have done so.[67] The relief granted by the Upper Tribunal has the same effect as that granted by the High Court on an application for judicial review. The Upper Tribunal must apply the principles of judicial review developed by the High Court. Applications under s.15 are subject to the same hurdles as judicial review applications before the High Court. Thus, permission is

---

Generating Board v Clywd CC [1976] 1 W.L.R. 151 Ch D at 160; *O'Kelly v Trusthouse Forte Plc* [1984] Q.B. 90, CA (Civ Div); *Shaw (Inspector of Taxes) v Vicky Construction Ltd* [2002] S.T.C. 1544 Ch D; *New Fashions (London) Ltd v Revenue and Customs Commissioners* [2006] S.T.C. 175 Ch D; *Salaried Persons Postal Loans Ltd v Revenue and Customs Commissioners* [2006] S.T.C. 1315 Ch D; *Wood v Holden (Inspector of Taxes)* [2006] 1 W.L.R. 1393, CA (Civ Div); *Zurich Insurance Co v Revenue and Customs Commissioners* [2007] EWCA Civ 218; *Boots Co Plc v Revenue and Customs Commissioners* [2009] EWCA Civ 1396; *Revenue and Customs Commissioners v Kearney* [2010] EWCA Civ 288; *Thomson v Revenue and Customs Commissioners* [2014] UKUT 360 (TCC); *Why Pay More For Cars Ltd v Revenue and Customs Commissioners* [2015] UKUT 468 (TCC).

[64] *Ransom v Higgs* [1974] 1 W.L.R. 1594, HL at 1610–1611.

[65] *Edwards* [1956] A.C. 14 at 36.

[66] *R. (Jones) v First-tier Tribunal (Social Entitlement Chamber)* [2013] UKSC 19, [2013] 2 A.C. 48.

[67] TCE Act 2007 s.16(6).

required,[68] the applicant must have a sufficient interest in the matter to which the application relates, and there are provisions concerning undue delay.[69]

The circumstances in which the Upper Tribunal can exercise powers of judicial review are set out in TCE Act s.18, which specifies four conditions. The first condition[70] is that the application does not seek anything other than the relief that the Upper Tribunal is able to grant under s.15(1), a monetary award under s.16(6), interest and costs. The second condition[71] is that the application does not call into question anything done by the Crown Court, the rationale being that it would be anomalous for a tribunal, a superior court of record, to have supervisory powers over another superior court of record. The third condition[72] is that the application falls within a class specified for the purposes of s.18(6) in a direction given in accordance with the Constitutional Reform Act 2005.[73] The direction is made by or on behalf of the Lord Chief Justice with the concurrence of the Lord Chancellor. The final condition[74] relates to the status of judge presiding at the hearing of the application.[75]

A Practice Direction was made specifying two classes of case for the purpose of the third condition in s.18(6).[76] These are any decision of the First-tier Tribunal on an appeal made in the exercise of a right conferred by the Criminal Injuries Compensation Scheme in compliance with the Criminal Injuries Compensation Act 1995 s.5(1); and any decision of the First-tier Tribunal made under Tribunal Procedure Rules or s.9 of the TCE Act 2007 where there is no right of appeal to the Upper Tribunal and where that decision was not an excluded decision within s.11(5)(b), (5)(c), (5)(f) of the 2007 Act. The Practice Direction does not have effect where the application sought, whether alone or not, a declaration of incompatibility under the Human Rights Act 1998 s.4. A later Practice Direction specified certain immigration and asylum cases as falling within the Upper Tribunal's remit of judicial review.[77] **9–026**

If the conditions in s.18 are not met the judicial review application is transferred to the High Court.[78] If all four conditions are met then an application for judicial review made to the High Court must be transferred to the Upper Tribunal.[79] If all conditions are met apart from the third, the High Court may nonetheless decide to transfer the case to the Upper Tribunal if it appears just and

---

[68] Refusal of permission by the Upper Tribunal can be appealed to the Court of Appeal, TCE Act 2007 s.16(8).

[69] TCE Act 2007 s.16.

[70] TCE Act 2007 s.18(4).

[71] TCE Act 2007 s.18(5).

[72] TCE Act 2007 s.18(6).

[73] Constitutional Reform Act 2005 Sch.2 Pt 1.

[74] TCE Act 2007 s.18(8).

[75] He or she must be either a judge of the High Court or the Court of Appeal in England and Wales or Northern Ireland, or a judge of the Court of Session, or such other persons as may be agreed from time to time between the Lord Chief Justice, the Lord President, or the Lord Chief Justice of Northern Ireland, as the case may be, and the Senior President of Tribunals.

[76] Practice Direction (Upper Tribunal: Judicial Review Jurisdiction) [2009] 1 W.L.R. 327; *KF v Birmingham and Solihull Mental Health NHS Foundation Trust* [2010] UKUT 185 (AAC).

[77] Practice Direction (Upper Tribunal: Judicial Review Jurisdiction) [2012] 1 W.L.R. 16.

[78] TCE Act 2007 s.18(3) and (9).

[79] TCE Act 2007 s.19, inserting a new s.31(A) into the Senior Courts Act 1981.

convenient to do so. Thus even if the case does not fall with a class of case designated for the Upper Tribunal by a direction, the High Court has a discretion to transfer it to the Upper Tribunal, subject to the caveat that this does not apply to matters concerning immigration and nationality. There are separate provisions dealing with Scotland.[80]

If the Upper Tribunal makes a quashing order it can in addition remit the matter to the court, tribunal or authority that made the decision, with a direction to reconsider the matter and reach a decision in accordance with the findings of the Upper Tribunal. It can alternatively substitute its own decision for the decision in question, provided that the decision was made by a court or tribunal, the decision was quashed for error of law, and without the error, there would have been only one decision that the court or tribunal could have reached.[81]

vi. *Judicial review of First-tier Tribunal*

9–027 The discussion thus far has been concerned with the new statutory regime established by the TCE Act 2007. This will have implications for traditional judicial review by the High Court.

First, a claimant may seek judicial review of a decision made by the First-tier Tribunal before the High Court. Such a claim will fail if the matter is one which satisfies all the conditions for the Upper Tribunal to exercise judicial review, since it must then be transferred to the Upper Tribunal. It will also fail where the High Court decides that even if the third condition is not met that it is just and convenient for the judicial review application to be heard by the Upper Tribunal.

Second, a claimant who seeks judicial review of a decision by a First-tier Tribunal before the High Court may also be rejected because the High Court decides that the claimant should exercise the statutory appeal rights to the Upper Tribunal.[82] There is extensive case law on the circumstances in which statutory appeal rights must be used rather than judicial review.[83] The High Court's strong preference is for the claimant to use the statutory appeal from the First-tier to the Upper Tribunal and thence onward to the Court of Appeal.[84] This is likely to be so even where the case does not fall within the judicial review jurisdiction of the Upper Tribunal, since it may still come within its general statutory jurisdiction to hear appeals on points of law from the First-tier Tribunal.

vii. *Judicial review of Upper Tribunal*

9–028 A claimant may also seek to challenge a decision made by the Upper Tribunal. It is important to distinguish two scenarios in this regard.

First, the policy of the TCE Act is, as seen above, that subject to an order made by the Lord Chancellor an onward appeal should be to the Court of Appeal, and then only where the Court of Appeal or the Upper Tribunal considers that the

---

[80] TCE Act 2007 ss.20–21.

[81] TCE Act 2007 s.17.

[82] TCE Act 2007 s.11.

[83] See paras 27–062 to 27–064.

[84] *R. (Great Yarmouth Port Co Ltd) v Marine Management Organisation* [2013] EWHC 3052 (Admin).

proposed appeal would raise some important point of principle or practice, or there is some other compelling reason for the appeal to be heard.[85]

Second, there are, however, limited circumstances in which there is no appeal from the Upper Tribunal, in which case judicial review is the only option. *Cart* is the leading decision on this point.[86] C and R failed in appeals to the social security and child support and the immigration and asylum chambers of the First-tier Tribunal respectively and were refused permission to appeal to the Upper Tribunal by both the First-tier Tribunal and Upper Tribunal. They could not appeal this refusal to the Court of Appeal, because the refusal of permission to appeal by the Upper Tribunal was an "excluded decision" for the purposes of the TCE Act, which signified that it was not amenable to further onward appeal.[87] They therefore sought judicial review by the Divisional Court of the refusal of permission by the Upper Tribunal.

The government initially argued that the Upper Tribunal was immune from judicial review, because it was a "superior court of record".[88] This argument was rejected by Laws LJ in the Divisional Court on the ground that designation of a body as a superior court of record did not suffice to exclude judicial review. The Supreme Court endorsed this reasoning. It held, moreover, that the TCE Act 2007 did not contain the clear words necessary to oust or exclude judicial review of unappealable decisions of the Upper Tribunal. The scope of judicial review was, said the Supreme Court, an artefact of the common law, the object being to ensure that insofar as possible decisions were taken in accordance with the law, and in particular the governing statute in the particular area. The Supreme Court acknowledged that neither tribunals nor courts were infallible and a judge at any level might be wrong in law. It concluded that there should be the possibility that a second judge, who should always be someone with more experience or expertise than the judge who first heard the case, could check for errors in the case. **9–029**

If the decision of the Upper Tribunal to refuse permission to appeal to itself was never amenable to judicial review, there was, said the Supreme Court, a real risk of the Upper Tribunal becoming the final arbiter of the law, even when it was wrong in law, so that errors of law of real significance could be perpetuated. There had therefore to be some possibility of judicial review. The Supreme Court was nonetheless mindful of the status of the new tribunal regime. This was reflected in the "restrained" test adopted as to when the ordinary courts would review the Upper Tribunal. The Supreme Court reasoned by analogy from s.13(6) of the 2007 Act, which limits the circumstances in which there can be a second-tier appeal: it is for the claimant to show that the proposed appeal raised some important point of principle or practice, or there was some other compelling reason for the appellate court to hear the appeal. This was adopted as the criterion for judicial review. Thus, judicial review of the Upper Tribunal is available, but

[85] TCE Act 2007 s.13(6)–(7).

[86] *R. (Cart) v Upper Tribunal* [2011] UKSC 28.

[87] TCE Act 2007 ss.13(1) and 13(8)(c).

[88] TCE Act 2007 s.3(5).

only when the claimant can come within the preceding test.[89] The broader implications of *Cart* for judicial review will be considered below.[90]

E. Tribunal Procedure Rules

i. The position prior to the TCE Act

9–030 Tribunals have traditionally had their own procedural rules, and rule-making normally vested in the Lord Chancellor or secretary of state, subject to consultation with the Council on Tribunals.[91] The Council sought to balance uniformity with the need to design procedures for a particular tribunal.[92] Thus pre-2007 there were procedural codes for different subject matter areas, which drew on the guide produced by the Council on Tribunals. These procedural codes were formally binding and enshrined in statutory instruments. They applied to diverse areas from regulation of estate agents to mental health, from tax to social welfare, from lands disputes to asylum and from employment to financial services.[93]

Procedural protection prior to the TCE Act 2007 was an admixture of the tribunal procedural rules, statutory rules requiring the provision of reasons[94] and the common law rules of natural justice, which specified when a hearing was required and the content of the procedural protection.[95]

ii. The position under the TCE Act

9–031 The TCE Act s.22 is intended to produce greater consistency in the development of procedure. Tribunal Procedure Rules are made by the Tribunal Procedure Committee.[96] It is to exercise this power with a view to securing the objectives specified in the TCE Act s.22(4) that: justice is done; the tribunal system is accessible and fair; proceedings are handled quickly and efficiently; the rules are both simple and simply expressed; and that the rules where appropriate confer on members of the First-tier Tribunal, or Upper Tribunal, responsibility for ensuring that proceedings before the tribunal are handled quickly and efficiently. The

[89] See, e.g., *Phillips v Upper Tribunal (Tax and Chancery Chamber)* [2013] EWHC 2934 (Admin); *A v Secretary of State for the Home Department* [2013] EWHC 1272 (Admin).

[90] See Ch.16.

[91] Tribunals and Inquiries Act 1992 s.8.

[92] Council on Tribunals, *Model Rules of Procedure for Tribunals* (1991) Cm.1434. The Model Rules of Procedure were revised in 1999 to take account of the Human Rights Act 1998; N. Brown, "Tribunal Adjudication in Britain: Model Rules of Procedure" (1993) Special Number ERPL 287.

[93] P. Craig, "Perspectives on Process: Common Law, Statutory and Political" [2010] P.L. 275, 288–289.

[94] Tribunals and Inquiries Act 1992 s.10.

[95] Chs 12–14.

[96] See *https://www.gov.uk/government/organisations/tribunal-procedure-committee* [accessed 3 November 2015].

Senior President of Tribunals is also empowered to make Practice Directions concerning practice and procedure of the First-tier Tribunal and the Upper Tribunal.[97]

The details concerning the making of procedural rules are set out in the TCE Act Sch.5. Part 1 makes provision for what the tribunal procedural rules may contain, relating to time limits, the extent to which matters may be decided without a hearing and whether a hearing may be public or private, proceedings without prior notice, representation, evidence and witnesses, use of information, and arbitration. Schedule 5 Pt 2 is concerned with the creation of the Tribunal Procedure Committee, and Pt 3 with the process by which the procedural rules are made. The Committee is required to consult before rules are made. The Lord Chancellor's powers are limited. He can allow or disallow the rules, and can specify a purpose that the rules must attain. Schedule 5 Pt 4 gives the Lord Chancellor power to amend, repeal or revoke any Act in pursuance of a rule change, this being based analogously on the provisions in the Civil Procedure Act 1997. An order exercising this power is subject to the affirmative resolution procedure.

The Tribunal Procedure Committee has produced greater consistency in procedural rules, more especially because the number of separate tribunals has been reduced as a result of the TCE Act. Insofar as there is a need for different procedural rules for different subject matter areas this is accommodated by tailoring procedural rules to the specific chambers.

The rules of natural justice continue to be applicable under the TCE Act. The procedural rules devised by the Tribunal Procedure Committee can be tested for conformity with the guiding principles set out in TCE Act s.22(4), and with the principles of natural justice. **9–032**

Detailed procedural rules have now been made pursuant to the powers in s.22.[98] The rules are tailored to the needs of the specific subject matter dealt with by the Chamber. They constitute what are in effect procedural codes for the relevant area and the quality is high. They reveal a willingness to draw on both adversarial and inquisitorial models of procedure when devising the procedural rules. We are strongly wedded to the adversarial system in this country, which forms the basis for adjudication in the superior courts, and is the norm for the tribunal system. The assumptions that underlie the adversarial system may nonetheless be absent in certain areas. An implicit premise behind the adversary system is that the two opponents are equal, save for natural inequalities of intellect and experience. This premise may not be sustainable in relation to certain types of tribunals, such as those concerned with social welfare and immigration. The very fact that the adversarial system tends to see parties in the position of "plaintiff" and "defendant" may well be inappropriate in some areas.

---

[97] TCE Act 2007 s.23.

[98] See *https://www.gov.uk/government/organisations/tribunal-procedure-committee* [accessed 3 November 2015]; Craig, "Perspectives on Process: Common Law, Statutory and Political" [2010] P.L. 275, 290–292.

Public law litigation will, moreover, often raise a wider public interest, over and beyond that of the particular parties before the tribunal.[99]

It may well, therefore, be appropriate for tribunals to take a more "active" role.[100] Some tribunals have power to require the attendance of witnesses or the production of documents,[101] while others, particularly those dealing with land and property, have powers of inspection and examination. Care should be taken to ensure that this does not develop into what has been termed accusatory inquisition,[102] where the individual feels under attack from the tribunal itself. We should nonetheless be willing to fashion procedures that draw on the best from the adversarial and inquisitorial systems, and be willing also to consider the virtues of what has been termed active adjudication.[103] The blanket rejection of anything that savours of an inquisitorial role for any tribunal is unwarranted. The idea that better justice can never be achieved by a procedure adopted by a large number of civilised jurisdictions smacks of the parochial and insular.

9–033 When fashioning procedures a balance should also be struck between formality and informality. The site of the hearing, the absence of the accoutrements of judicial office, and the presence of lay members on the adjudicating panel, all tend to produce a less formal, more relaxed atmosphere than in an ordinary court. There are, nonetheless, limits to informality as Genn has shown.[104] She identified four factors that constrain the degree of informality of the proceedings. The *complexity of the subject matter* may militate against an approach that is too informal. Many issues in, for example, social welfare cases, are complex because of the statutory material. *Procedural informality should not be confused with substantive informality*. The fact that the procedure itself is informal may lead the claimant to believe that the substantive outcome is to be decided on a similarly informal basis. This will often not be so where the statute prescribes specific criteria if the claimant is to succeed. *Unrepresented applicants are often at a disadvantage in tribunal proceedings*, notwithstanding the efforts of the tribunal to put the person at their ease. The disadvantage is often a consequence of the applicant believing that the whole matter could be dealt with by a quiet chat, tailoring any solution to the applicant's own personal circumstance, and not realising the constraints which the legislation place upon the tribunal's discretion. Finally, the *tribunal may be less able to assist an unrepresented claimant than has been commonly thought in the past.* The standard picture is of a tribunal composed of those with expertise in the area who are capable of aiding the individual, particularly if he or she is unrepresented. Such assistance may be less

---

[99] A. Chayes, "The Role of the Judge in Public Law Litigation" (1976) 89 Harv. L.R. 1281; L. Fuller, "The Forms and Limits of Adjudication" (1978) 92 Harv. L.R. 353, 382–384.

[100] For the limits of a tribunal's obligation to assist an unrepresented applicant see, *Chilton Saga Holidays Plc* [1986] 1 All E.R. 841; *R. v Criminal Injuries Compensation Board, Ex p. Pearce* [1994] C.O.D. 235; *R. v Criminal Injuries Compensation Board, Ex p. Milton* [1996] C.O.D. 264.

[101] G. Ganz, *Administrative Procedures* (London: Sweet & Maxwell, 1974), pp.31–32; Wraith and Hutchesson, *Administrative Tribunals* (1973), pp.146–147.

[102] Ganz, *Administrative Procedures* (1974), p.35.

[103] S. Green and L. Sossin, "Administrative Justice and Innovation: Beyond the Adversarial/Inquisitorial Dichotomy", in S. Begley and L. Jacobs (eds), *The Nature of Inquisitional Processes in Administrative Regimes: Global Perspectives* (University of Toronto Press, 2011).

[104] Genn, "Tribunals and Informal Justice" (1993) M.L.R. 393.

forthcoming, because of constraints of time, because the tribunal may not know what questions would best help the applicant, and because the more adversarial are the proceedings the more reluctant are tribunal members to get involved on one side of the case.

The duty to give reasons contained in the Tribunals and Inquiries Act 1992 s.10 was not repealed by the TCE Act. It applies to the tribunals listed in that legislation, it is dependent on the claimant requesting the provision of reasons and there are exceptions to the duty. It is nonetheless likely that some of the case law concerning the duty to give reasons developed under the 1992 legislation will inform the interpretation of reason-giving under the procedural rules made pursuant to the 2007 legislation. Thus, where the obligation to give reasons applies, the court has made it clear that the reasons must deal with the substantial points that have been raised, and must not be too vague.[105] Lord Brown in the *Porter* case summarised the matter as follows[106]:

> "The reasons for a decision must be intelligible and they must be adequate. They must enable the reader to understand why the matter was decided as it was and what conclusions were reached on the 'principal important controversial issues', disclosing how any issue of law or fact was resolved. Reasons can be briefly stated, the degree of particularity required depending entirely on the nature of the issues falling for decision. The reasoning must not give rise to a substantial doubt as to whether the decision-maker erred in law, for example by misunderstanding some relevant policy or some other important matter or by failing to reach a rational decision on relevant grounds. But such adverse inference will not readily be drawn. The reasons need refer only to the main issues in the dispute, not to every material consideration."

The legal consequence of failure to provide the required reasons under the 1992 legislation is not entirely clear. Some authorities have held that such a failure itself constitutes an error of law,[107] while others have held that inadequate reasons do not per se constitute an error of law, and will lead to invalidity only if they furnish evidence of such an error.[108] Sedley J signalled that this issue should be reconsidered, so that the law in this respect could be brought into line with that on judicial review.[109] However, Lord Brown in *Porter*[110] held that a "reasons challenge will only succeed if the party aggrieved can satisfy the court that he has genuinely been substantially prejudiced by the failure to provide an adequately reasoned decision".

---

105 *Poyser and Mills' Arbitration, Re* [1964] 2 Q.B. 467 QBD. They can, however, be brief, *Westminster City Council v Great Portland Estates* [1985] A.C. 661, HL.

106 *South Buckinghamshire DC v Porter (No.2)* [2004] 1 W.L.R. 1953 QBD at [36].

107 *Poyser* [1964] 2 Q.B. 467; *Givaudan v Minister of Housing and Local Government* [1967] 1 W.L.R. 250 QBD.

108 *Mountview Court Properties Ltd v Devlin* (1970) 21 P. & C.R. 689 QBD; *Crake v Supplementary Benefits Commission* [1982] 1 All E.R. 498 QBD; *S (A Minor) v Special Educational Needs Tribunal* [1996] 1 All E.R. 171 QBD; *Yeoman's Row Management Ltd v London Rent Assessment Committee* [2002] EWHC 835; G. Richardson, "The Duty to Give Reasons: Potential and Practice" [1986] P.L. 437, 450–457.

109 *R. v Northamptonshire CC, Ex p. Marshall* [1998] C.O.D. 457 QBD at 458.

110 *Porter* [2004] 1 W.L.R. 1953 at [36].

F. Mediation and Alternative Dispute Resolution

9–034 It is increasingly common for mediation and other forms of alternative dispute resolution to be used in the justice system. The TCE Act s.24 provides the statutory basis for mediation. It enables staff appointed for the First-tier and Upper Tribunals to act as mediators in relation to disputed matters in proceedings before the First-tier or Upper Tribunal. It is however made clear by s.24(1) that mediation is to take place only by agreement between the parties, and that where they fail to mediate, or where mediation between the parties fails to resolve disputed matters, the failure is not to affect the outcome of the proceedings.

G. The Courts and Tribunals Service, Administrative Support and Staffing

9–035 The TCE Act s.39 imposes an obligation on the Lord Chancellor to ensure that there is an efficient and effective system of tribunal administration. This duty applies to the First-tier Tribunal, the Upper Tribunal, employment tribunals, the Employment Appeal Tribunal and the Asylum and Immigration Tribunal.

This duty is complemented by the TCE Act s.40, which empowers the Lord Chancellor to provide staff, services and accommodation for tribunals. Civil servants can be employed as tribunal staff. Certain functions can be contracted-out, but not those that involve making judicial decisions or exercising any judicial discretion, and even the contracting-out of administrative functions has to be legitimated by an order authorising the Lord Chancellor to do so.

Following the recommendations of the Leggatt Report, a Tribunals Service was created in 2006. This was replaced in 2011 by the Courts and Tribunals Service, an agency of the Ministry of Justice that integrates the support service for courts and tribunals.[111] Its objectives are to: provide the supporting administration for a fair, efficient and accessible courts and tribunal system; support an independent judiciary in the administration of justice; drive continuous improvement of performance and efficiency across all aspects of the administration of the courts and tribunals; collaborate effectively with other justice organisations and agencies, including the legal professions, to improve access to justice; and work with government departments and agencies, as appropriate, to improve the quality and timeliness of their decision making in order to reduce the number of cases coming before tribunals and courts.[112]

---

[111] See *https://www.gov.uk/government/organisations/hm-courts-and-tribunals-service/about* [accessed 3 November 2015].

[112] *Her Majesty's Courts and Tribunals Service Framework Document* (2011), Cm.8043, para.2.3.

H. Oversight

The TCE Act s.44 established the Administrative Justice and Tribunals Council (AJTC),[113] to oversee the system of tribunals and inquiries, and s.45 abolished the Council on Tribunals, which previously performed the oversight role. However, as will be seen below the AJTC was abolished in 2013. **9–036**

i. The Council on Tribunals

The establishment of an institution to keep tribunals under review developed out of the Franks Committee. It proposed two councils, one for England and Wales, the other for Scotland.[114] They were to be concerned with the procedure, constitution, and organisation of tribunals; they should be consulted prior to the creation of any new tribunal; and they should have responsibility for the appointment of lay members. What emerged in the subsequent legislation was more limited. There was only one Council, albeit with provision for a Scottish Committee, appointment of lay members remained with departments, and the Council's role in the procedural area was reduced. The Franks' Committee proposed that the Council would formulate procedural rules, but the legislation accorded it only a consultative role. The Council was thus an advisory as opposed to executive body, although its advisory role encompassed keeping under review the working of the tribunals brought within the legislation.[115] **9–037**

The effectiveness of the Council was questioned. It made a real contribution to procedural rules where it was consulted,[116] produced a valuable set of model procedural rules for tribunals,[117] and made important recommendations concerning the organisation and independence of tribunals.[118] Success in other fields was more limited. The government was under no statutory obligation to consult the Council about proposed legislation creating or affecting tribunals. The Council was often not consulted adequately; it was often dissatisfied with the reaction to its suggestions; and there was dissatisfaction with its powers.

ii. The Administrative Justice and Tribunals Council

The detailed workings of the new AJTC, which was a non-departmental public body, were set out in the TCE Act Sch.7. The AJTC was instructed[119] to keep the administrative justice system under review; consider ways to make the system accessible, fair and efficient; advise on the development of the system; refer proposals for change to the Lord Chancellor and others; and make proposals for **9–038**

[113] See *http://www.ajtc.gov.uk/index.htm* [accessed 3 November 2015].

[114] The Franks Report, paras 131–134.

[115] D. Foulkes, "The Council on Tribunals: Visits, Policy and Practice" [1994] P.L. 564.

[116] The Annual Reports 1999/2000 and 2000/2001 contain representative examples of the work of the Council.

[117] Council on Tribunals, *Model Rules of Procedure for Tribunals*. The Model Rules of Procedure were revised in 1999 to take account of the Human Rights Act 1998; Brown, "Tribunal Adjudication in Britain: Model Rules of Procedure" (1993) Special Number ERPL 287.

[118] Council on Tribunals, *Tribunals, Their Organisation and Independence* (1997) Cm.3744.

[119] TCE Act 2007 Sch.7 para.13(1)–(2).

research into the system. The "administrative justice system" was defined to cover the overall system by which decisions of an administrative or executive nature are made in relation to particular persons, including the procedures for making such decisions; the law under which such decisions were made; and the systems for resolving disputes and airing grievances in relation to such decisions.[120]

The AJTC's responsibility in relation to tribunals was as follows.[121] It was to keep listed tribunals under review and report on those tribunals, and also on any matter that the AJTC thought was of special importance, or referred to it by the Lord Chancellor, Scottish Ministers and Welsh Ministers. It could also scrutinise and comment on existing or proposed legislation, including procedural rules, relating to tribunals. The AJTC also had responsibility for statutory inquiries.[122] The expanded jurisdiction accorded to the AJTC by way of comparison to the Council on Tribunals was welcomed, as exemplified by its paper listing seven principles for administrative justice.[123]

It was, however, abolished in 2013 as a result of the government's austerity programme.[124] The Public Bodies Act 2011 empowers a minister, subject to certain conditions, to abolish certain bodies, including the AJTC.[125] The AJTC published a report in 2011[126] in which it charted the risks for administrative justice as a result of its possible demise. The report challenged the government to recognise the scale of poor decision-making, and the unnecessary cost, generated through poorly drafted laws in some areas of administrative justice. The AJTC was nonetheless abolished, which was a most regrettable step. The overall cost of the AJTC was relatively small, and it almost certainly saved the government more than it cost because its reports helped to avoid administrative error.

iii. The Administrative Justice Forum

9–039 Any savings flowing from the demise of the AJTC must be balanced against the costs of its successor, the Administrative Justice Forum, which is an advisory body reporting to the Ministry of Justice.[127] The aims of the AJF are to gauge how the administrative justice and tribunals system is working, identify any areas of concern or good practice, and provide for early, informal, testing of policy initiatives. It is scheduled to meet approximately twice a year, and this will perforce limit its impact.

---

[120] TCE Act 2007 Sch.7 para.13(4).

[121] TCE Act 2007 Sch.7 para.14.

[122] TCE Act 2007 Sch.7 para.15.

[123] Administrative Justice and Tribunals Council, *Principles for Administrative Justice* (2010).

[124] Public Bodies Act 2011; Public Bodies (Abolition of Administrative Justice and Tribunals Council) Order 2013/2042.

[125] Public Bodies Act 2011 s.1, Sch.1.

[126] Administrative Justice and Tribunals Council, *Securing Fairness and Redress: Administrative Justice at Risk?* (2011).

[127] See *https://www.gov.uk/government/groups/administrative-justice-advisory-group* [accessed 3 November 2015].

It is clear that the government wishes to bring policy development and oversight of the administrative justice system within the Ministry of Justice.[128] It argues that the independence of the tribunals system administered as it is by the Courts and Tribunals Service suffices to ensure that tribunal members and their administrative support systems are sufficiently removed from decision makers to diminish the case for a standing body to oversee tribunals.[129]

This argument is however contestable. The danger is not direct challenge to the independence of tribunal members, which is safeguarded by the legislation and the Courts and Tribunals Service. The danger is rather that removal of an independent body such as the AJTC, with statutory foundation and defined duties, will perforce weaken oversight of administrative justice broadly conceived. There is scant if any foundation for the claim that the "work" of the AJTC was "done", and concern that the protection it provided will be weakened moving forward.

5. STATUTORY INQUIRIES

A. The Background

The historical antecedents of the inquiry procedure have already been related.[130] It was, however, the 20th century that saw expansion in the use of inquiries, most particularly in the context of land and housing. A variety of purposes are served by the inquiry procedure, the two most important of which are as a mechanism of appeal and as a means for airing objections. An example of the former is the system of appeal against the refusal of planning permission by a local authority, while objections to the siting of a road or building exemplify the latter. Inquiries may also be used as a form of post-mortem to investigate an accident, or a breach of governmental secrecy, or as a method of preliminary investigation into the viability of a proposal.[131] **9–040**

Inquiries collate information, and/or resolve conflicts. Insofar as they serve the latter function they are often used where it is felt desirable that political control be maintained by vesting the ultimate decision in a minister. Decisions concerning the siting of a new town, the approval of a slum clearance order, or the confirmation of a road building scheme, involve considerations of policy, which should be decided by those who are politically accountable. It will not be the minister who makes the initial decision and very often officials will render decisions in the minister's name. The process of government would grind to a halt were it to be otherwise. The minister will, however, make the final choice in circumstances that are especially contentious or important.

[128] Ministry of Justice, Administrative Justice and Tribunals, A Strategic Work Programme 2013–2016 (December 2012), para.34.

[129] Ministry of Justice, Administrative Justice and Tribunals, paras 35–40.

[130] See Ch.2.

[131] R. Wraith and G. Lamb, *Public Inquiries as an Instrument of Government* (London: Allen & Unwin, 1971), pp.14–15, 305–306; J. Beer (ed.), *Public Inquiries* (Oxford: Oxford University Press, 2011), Ch.1.

B. The Franks Committee

i. The recommendations

9–041 Prior to 1957 there was increasing public disquiet not just with tribunals, but also with inquiries. Issues concerning cost and delay were overlaid by frustration at the secrecy of the procedure. The report of the inspector who held the inquiry would normally not be made public, and there was a feeling that the administration was just "going through the motions".

Witnesses who gave evidence before the Committee were divided as to the role of inquiries. One group saw inquiries as part of the process of administration, as an extension of departmental decision-making in specific areas, which should be relatively free from controls other than those imposed by Parliament. A different view was expressed by those who saw the inquiry as akin to a judicial process, in which the inspector who undertook the hearing was in the position of a judge. The corollary of this latter approach was that the inquiry procedures should be modelled on the judicial process.[132] The Franks Committee rejected both positions[133]:

> "Our general conclusion is that those procedures cannot be classified as purely administrative or purely judicial. They are not purely administrative because of the provision for a special procedure preliminary to the decision—a feature not to be found in the ordinary course of administration—and because this procedure, as we have shown, involves the testing of an issue, often partly in public. They are not on the other hand purely judicial, because the final decision cannot be reached by the application of rules and must allow the exercise of wide discretion in the balancing of public and private interest. Neither view at its extreme is tenable, nor should either be emphasized at the expense of the other."

Instead of attempting to model the inquiry procedures on either of the preceding views the Franks Committee drew up recommendations which attempted to balance the conflicting interests. What emerged were proposals concerning the pre-inquiry stage, the procedure at the inquiry, and post-inquiry practice.[134]

9–042 As to the practice *before the inquiry*, the Committee recommended that the public authority should be required to make available in good time a written statement giving full particulars of its case. The minister who had the ultimate power of decision should whenever possible provide a statement of the policy relevant to the particular case, but should be free to direct that the statements be wholly or partly excluded from discussion of the inquiry. Where this policy changed after the inquiry the letter conveying the ministerial decision should explain the change and its relation to the decision.

As to procedure *at the inquiry*, it was recommended that the initiating authority should be required to explain its proposals fully and support them by oral evidence, and that in principle the procedure should be public. A code of procedure should be formulated by the Council on Tribunals, which should be

[132] The Franks Report, paras 263–264.

[133] The Franks Report, para.272.

[134] These are summarised at paras 96–98 of the Franks Committee Report.

made statutory; rules of evidence should be relaxed; the inspector should have power to subpoena witnesses and should have a wide discretion in controlling the proceedings.

Post-inquiry procedure was mainly concerned with the inspector's report and the consequent ministerial decision. It was proposed that the inspector's report be divided into two parts comprising a summary of the evidence, finding of facts and inferences of fact on the one hand, and reasoning from those facts, including application of policy on the other. The whole report should then accompany the minister's letter of decision, and there should be provision for a person to suggest corrections of fact. When the minister made the final decision he or she should be required to submit to the parties concerned any factual evidence obtained after the inquiry, while the decision itself should set out in full the findings and inferences of fact and the reasons for the decision.

Apart from proposals concerning procedure there was also an important recommendation that the main body of inspectors should be placed under the control of the Lord Chancellor, while being allowed to be kept in contact with policy developments in the departments responsible for inquiries.

ii. *Implementation*

The Franks Committee Report was warmly received. Some proposals were taken **9–043** up rapidly by the government and the Tribunal and Inquiries Bill duly appeared before Parliament. What, however, became apparent at the Committee stage was that the Bill said very little about inquiries. It was mainly concerned with tribunals. As a result of pressure in the House of Lords, the Government introduced a new sub-paragraph, which became s.1(1)(c) of the Tribunals and Inquiries Act 1958. This provided that the Council on Tribunals was to consider and report on such matters as might be referred to it, or as the Council itself should determine to be of special importance, with respect to administrative procedure involving an inquiry. The Council's powers with respect to inquiries were therefore somewhat different to those concerning tribunals. While it had no power to keep such inquiries under review, as it did with tribunals, it did have power to intervene on its own initiative in more specific terms than in connection with tribunals. The Council's powers were, however, advisory rather than executive.

Despite the extension of the Council's role in relation to inquiries as a result of the Committee stage of the Bill, many changes advocated by the Franks Committee were implemented by administrative practice and not by statute. Most recommendations were put into effect, but two proposals were rejected by the government: those related to placing the inspectorate under the Lord Chancellor, and the requirement that the minister should make available a statement of policy prior to the inquiry. The procedure that now applies is a mixture of law and administrative practice. The precise details differ in different areas, but the general principles are the same. It is to these that we must now turn.

C. Inquiries: Practice and Procedure[135]

i. *Procedure before the Inquiry*

9–044 A number of statutory instruments have been enacted, drafted by the Lord Chancellor's office pursuant to the Tribunals and Inquiries Act 1992 s.9.[136] These will normally be drafted in conjunction with the appropriate department. Others have emanated directly from, for example, a government department. The details of the rules differ, but there is also much commonality. Thus, there are provisions concerned with procedure prior to the inquiry covering both the length of notice that must be given of the holding of the inquiry, and also a statement of reasons of the case to be met. The precise length of notice varies: in some areas it is 21 days; in others 28 days; and in yet others 42 days. There will in addition be rules requiring, for example, an acquiring authority acting under compulsory purchase legislation to provide facilities for the inspection of relevant documents and plans.

ii. *Procedure at the inquiry*

9–045 The procedure at the inquiry is, as recommended by the Franks Committee, very much left in the hands of the inspector,[137] subject to the rules of natural justice.[138] Ordinary legal rules of evidence do not, for example, apply[139] and the inspector is often given power to enforce the attendance of persons and the production of documents. The inspector will also have the power to take evidence on oath.

Bushell demonstrates the breadth of the discretion accorded to the decision-maker.[140] A public local inquiry was held to consider objections to a road building scheme. At the time of the inquiry procedural rules concerning highway inquiries had not yet come into force. A key element in the department's case for the new motorways was projected traffic flow, the statistical basis of which was derived from a publication known as the "Red Book". Objectors at the inquiry sought to challenge the accuracy of the Red Book's predictions, but the inspector refused to allow them to cross-examine the Department's witnesses as to the reliability of the Red Book. He did, however, allow the objectors to call their own evidence as to the need for motorways. The objectors sought to quash the decision of the minister confirming the scheme, on the ground that the denial by the inspector of a right to cross-examine was in breach of natural justice. The House of Lords found for the minister.

135 J. Beer, "Evidence and Procedure", in *Public Inquiries* (2011), Ch.5.

136 See, e.g. Town and Country Planning (Inquiries Procedure) (England) Rules 2000 (SI 1624/2000); Town and Country Planning (Hearings Procedure) (England) Rules 2000 (SI 1626/2000); Town and Country Planning (Enforcement) (Hearings Procedure) (England) Rules 2002 (SI 2684/2002); Compulsory Purchase (Inquiries Procedure) Rules 2007 (SI 3617/2007); Town and Country Planning (Hearings and Inquiries Procedure) (England) (Amendment and Revocation) Rules 2015 (SI 316/2015).

137 SI 1626/2000 r.11.

138 *Edwards v Environment Agency* [2006] EWCA Civ 877; [2007] Env. L.R. 9.

139 *Miller (TA) Ltd v Minister of Housing and Local Government* [1968] 1 W.L.R. 992, CA (Civ Div).

140 *Bushell v Secretary of State for the Environment* [1981] A.C. 75, HL.

The majority decided that in the absence of statutory rules prescribing the conduct of the inquiry, the procedure to be followed was a matter for the discretion of the minister and inspector. This was subject to the general safeguard that the procedure be fair to all concerned, including the general public and supporters of the scheme. In deciding what was a fair procedure the court should not be tied to the ordinary model of civil litigation between private parties. Lord Diplock put this point most strongly[141]:

> "To 'over-judicialise' the inquiry by insisting on observance of the procedures of a court of justice which professional lawyers alone are competent to operate effectively in the interests of their clients would not be fair. It would, in my view, be quite fallacious to suppose that at an inquiry of this kind the only fair way of ascertaining matters of fact and expert opinion is by the oral testimony of witnesses who are subjected to cross-examination on behalf of parties who disagree with what they have said. Such procedure is peculiar to litigation conducted in courts that follow the common law system of procedure; it plays no part in the procedure of courts of justice under legal systems based upon the civil law … So refusal by an inspector to allow a party to cross-examine orally at a local inquiry a person who has made statements of facts or has expressed expert opinions is not unfair *per se*."

Whether refusal to allow cross-examination was unfair depended on all the circumstances. These included the nature of the topic on which the opinion was expressed, and the forensic competence of the proposed cross-examiner. The court would also consider the inspector's view as to whether the cross-examination would enable him to make a report more useful to the minister than it otherwise would have been, and that this justified the extra cost in time thereby expended.

The most important of these factors for the majority was the nature of the topic. **9–046** The majority distinguished between general government policy, which would clearly not be suitable for discussion at a local inquiry, an example being the desirability of having a nation-wide set of motorways, and a matter such as the exact line that a road should follow, which would be amenable to local discussion.[142] Midway between these there was a "grey area" in which the suitability of a point for cross-examination could well be debatable. The validity of the Red Book's methodology was treated as akin to a matter of government policy and therefore not suitable for local discussion and cross-examination. It was not that the majority saw these technical matters as of the same order as the decision to have a nation-wide set of motorways. Rather that the techniques for determining traffic need involved a wider range of issues than could appropriately be considered at a local inquiry.

The rules governing procedure in any particular area will also delineate those who have a right to appear. In general, such a right is only accorded to those who have some legal interest at stake, while allowing the inspector discretion to admit others.[143] This discretion is normally exercised liberally, but such third parties may nevertheless be placed at a disadvantage as compared with those who do

---

[141] *Bushell* [1981] A.C. 75 at 97. See also, *R. (Great Yarmouth Port Co Ltd) v Marine Management Organisation* [2014] EWHC 833 (Admin).

[142] *Bushell* [1981] A.C. 75 at 97–98, 108–109, 121–123; *R. v Secretary of State for Transport, Ex p. Gwent County Council* [1987] 2 W.L.R. 961, CA (Civ Div); *R.(on the application of Bonhoeffer) v General Medical Council* [2011] EWHC 1585 (Admin).

[143] See, e.g. SI 1626/2000 r.9.

have a right to appear. They may not, for example, have a right to see a statement of the authority's case, nor does evidence obtained outside of the inquiry have to be disclosed to them. It was, however, held in *Hamsher* that a person admitted at the discretion of the inspector was entitled to a fair hearing and that this entailed being enabled to know the nature of the opposing party's case,[144] while in *Jory* it was held that fairness required that such a party should be informed of proposed amendments to planning conditions in the same way as other parties to the case.[145]

iii. Procedure after the inquiry: inspectors' reports

9–047 Procedure after the inquiry raises a number of important issues, one of the most controversial of which has been whether the inspector's report ought to be published or not. An inspector will be appointed to conduct a wide range of inquiries. Typically, the situation will be one in which a local authority proposes to acquire land, to clear an area of slums. Having passed a resolution to that effect it will advertise the matter in the local press, as well as informing those whose property rights are affected so that they have an opportunity to object. If such objections are forthcoming then the minister will be obliged to establish an inquiry presided over by an inspector. It is this report which will then be confirmed or not by the minister.

The Franks Committee received much evidence on the publication of these reports.[146] The arguments for publication were primarily fairness and acceptability. A main cause of public dissatisfaction had been the secrecy shrouding the inquiry procedure, a sense which publication of the reports would have done much to dispel. Greater knowledge would bring a greater acceptance, since the public would be more aware of the policies underlying the decisions being made. A number of arguments were put against publication. It was argued that the inspector's report was but one consideration that the minister should take into account, and that to publish it alone would be to accord it an unwarranted primacy, creating a misguided impression as to its relative importance. In addition, it was felt that inspectors would be less frank if their reports were published and that there was not in fact a widespread demand to see the reports.

The Franks Committee came down firmly in favour of publication,[147] and this has been the general practice since 1958. In some instances the statutory instruments make provision for this,[148] in others publication is dependent on departmental practice. None of the fears voiced by those opposed to publication appear to have transpired and public confidence in the inquiry procedure has undoubtedly been increased by this reform.

---

144 *R. (Hamsher) v First Secretary of State* [2004] EWHC 2299 (Admin) at [20]–[21]; *Local Government Board v Arlidge* [1915] A.C. 120, HL at 147; *Wednesbury Corporation v Ministry of Housing and Local Government (No.2)* [1966] 2 Q.B. 275, CA at 302.

145 *Jory v Secretary of State for Transport, Local Government and the Regions* [2002] EWHC 2724 (Admin).

146 The Franks Report, paras 327–346.

147 The Franks Report, para.344.

148 See, e.g. Town and Country Planning Appeals (Determination by Inspectors) (Inquiries Procedure) (England) Rules 2000 (SI 1625/2000) r.19.

iv. *Procedure after the inquiry: extrinsic evidence*

We have seen that an argument against publication of the inspectors' reports was that they were but one source relied on by the minister when reaching a decision. What types of extrinsic evidence the minister does and should be enabled to take into account is a difficult problem, as exemplified by the *Essex Chalkpit* case of 1961. **9–048**

A company had been refused planning permission to dig and work chalk, this decision being upheld by an inspector, on the basis that the proposed development would injuriously affect neighbouring landowners. The company appealed to the minister who consulted the Ministry of Agriculture, experts from which stated that the development of the land could take place without any injurious effect on the neighbours, provided that an appropriate process was used. On receipt of this evidence the minister upheld the appeal, even though the objectors to the scheme had had no opportunity for comment on the new evidence.

An appeal to the courts having failed,[149] the objectors complained to the Council on Tribunals. The Council criticised the way in which the case had been handled. It recommended that if a minister differed from an inspector on a finding of fact, because of fresh evidence, or because a new issue had arisen which was not one of government policy, then the parties should be notified and be allowed to comment thereon. This has become the established practice and is enshrined in some of the statutory instruments governing procedure at inquiries.[150] Difficulties can, however, still arise when distinguishing between findings of fact and matters of opinion.[151]

Natural justice will also impose limits upon the receipt of extrinsic evidence. Thus, in the *Bushell*[152] case it was accepted that the minister could not, after the close of the inquiry, hear one side rather than the other, or receive evidence from third parties without allowing comments thereon. There is, however, a distinction between evidence from such sources and advice from within the department itself. **9–049**

In the *Bushell* case a further ground of complaint was that after the close of the inquiry, but before the report was made, the department revised their methods of computing traffic needs, the result being a prediction of slower traffic growth than originally forecast. The objectors asked the minister to reopen the inquiry but he declined, saying that he would look at their representations as part of his continuous consideration of the department's proposals. In his decision the minister stated that, despite the change in the criteria for traffic need, he still felt that the inspector's recommendation should be upheld. The House of Lords rejected the argument that the minister had acted wrongfully by confirming the inspector's report without allowing the objectors an opportunity to comment on

---

[149] *Buxton v Minister of Housing and Local Government* [1961] 1 Q.B. 278 QBD.

[150] See, e.g. SI 1626/2000 r.13.

[151] *Luke (Lord) v Minister of Housing and Local Government* [1968] 1 Q.B. 172, CA (Civ Div); *Murphy and Sons Ltd v Secretary of State for the Environment* [1973] 1 W.L.R. 560 QBD; *Darlassis v Minister of Education* (1954) 52 L.G.R. 304.

[152] *Bushell* [1981] A.C. 75 at 102.

undisclosed information. The minister was, said Lord Diplock,[153] "perfectly in order in consulting his own department for advice on whether to confirm the recommendations. He did not have to disclose this advice to objectors, nor did he have to allow them to comment thereon." Viscount Dilhorne and Lord Lane placed the matter rather more generally on the ground that such consultation involved no breach of natural justice in the circumstances of the case.[154]

v. *Procedure after the inquiry: reasons*

9–050 An obligation to provide reasons is imposed by s.10(1)(b) of the Tribunals and Inquiries Act 1992. The section provides for the giving of reasons where the minister notifies any decision taken by him after the holding by him or on his behalf of a statutory inquiry, or taken by him in a case in which a person concerned could (whether by objecting or otherwise) have required the holding of such a statutory inquiry, where an individual requests the reasons for the decision, on or before the giving or notification of the decision. The provisions of the Act operate in the same way and subject to the same qualifications as in the case of tribunals. A decision will be quashed if the reasons given are obscure, too vague, or confused.[155]

vi. *Inquiry rules of procedure: an example*

9–051 We have already seen that the Lord Chancellor can enact procedural rules, pursuant to s.9 of the Tribunals and Inquiries Act 1992. Some aspects of these rules have been touched upon in the previous discussion. It is nonetheless helpful to consider such rules as they have been made in a specific area. Planning appeals will be taken by way of example.[156] The Planning Inspectorate was an executive agency under the Department of Communities and Local Government (DCLG), but is now a joint venture between DCLG and a private company.[157]

The procedure begins with a *notice* from the secretary of state addressed to the local planning authority that an inquiry is to be held in connection with an appeal

---

153 *Bushell* [1981] A.C. 75 at 102–103.

154 *Bushell* [1981] A.C. 75 at 110 and 123–124. See also, *Steele v Minister of Housing and Local Government* (1956) 6 P. & C.R. 386, CA at 392. Compare however *Edwards* [2007] Env. L.R. 9.

155 *Iveagh (Earl) v Minister of Housing and Local Government* [1964] 1 Q.B. 395, CA; *Givaudan & Co Ltd v Minister of Housing and Local Government* [1967] 1 W.L.R. 250 QBD; *French Kier Developments Ltd v Secretary of State for the Environment* [1977] 1 All E.R. 296 QBD; *Barnham v Secretary of State for the Environment* (1985) 52 P. & C.R. 10; *Reading BC v Secretary of State for the Environment* (1985) 52 P. & C.R. 385.

156 The Town and Country Planning (Inquiries Procedure) (England) Rules 2000 (SI 1624/2000), govern certain planning applications and appeals decided by the Secretary of State; The Town and Country Planning Appeals (Determination by Inspectors) (Inquiries Procedure) (England) Rules 2000 (SI 1625/2000), govern certain appeals decided by an inspector appointed by the Secretary of State where the inspector makes the decision in the name of the minister; Town and Country Planning (Hearings Procedure) (England) Rules 2000 (SI 1626/2000). Most appeals are decided by an inspector, Sir D. Heap, *An Outline of Planning Law*, 11th edn (London: Sweet & Maxwell, 1996), Ch.13; R. Duxbury, *Telling and Duxbury's Planning Law and Procedure*, 15th edn (Oxford: Oxford University Press, 2012); V. Moore, *A Practical Approach to Planning Law*, 13th edn (Oxford: Oxford University Press, 2014).

157 See *http://www.planningportal.gov.uk/general/aboutus/legal/* [accessed 4 November 2015].

made to the secretary of state. The local planning authority must then tell the secretary of state the name of any statutory party who has made representations about the matter under appeal. A similar obligation lies on the secretary of state. The date for the inquiry will then be fixed, and the secretary of state will identify the inspector who will handle the matter.

The local planning authority and the appellant must then serve their respective *statements of case* on each other, the secretary of state and other statutory parties. The statement of case will contain the principal submissions to be made at the inquiry.

There will generally be a *pre-inquiry* meeting in order to facilitate the efficient and expeditious resolution of the problem, where the inquiry is expected to last for eight days or more, and such an inquiry can be held in respect of shorter inquiries where it is felt to be necessary.

Those who are *entitled to appear* at the inquiry itself are: the appellant, the local planning authority, any other local authority in whose area the land is situated, any person who, in effect, claims proprietary rights over the land in question, and any other person who has served a statement of case under the relevant rules. Other parties are allowed to appear at the discretion of the inspector. A lawyer can represent those who are entitled or permitted to appear.

The *procedure at the inquiry* is determined by the inspector who will have **9–052** discretion as to matters such as the calling of evidence and cross-examination. However, the appellant, the local planning authority and certain other parties entitled to appear as of right, have the right to call evidence. The inspector may receive written representations from any person before the inquiry, provided that disclosure is made at the inquiry itself.

The *procedure after the inquiry* is that the inspector will make the decision. This will be given in writing and be supported by reasons. The report must be given to all those entitled to appear at the inquiry, who did appear, and also to those who, having appeared at the inquiry, then asked to be notified of the inspector's decision. The report will go to the minister, who may disagree with the inspector's report either because he takes a different view on a matter of fact, or because of fresh evidence which is not a matter of government policy. If the former occurs those taking part in the inquiry are to be afforded an opportunity of making written representations within 21 days. If the latter takes place then those who participated in the inquiry can either make written representations or request that the inquiry should be re-opened within the 21-day period.

vii. Limitations: discretionary inquiries

An important limitation on the scope of the legislation on tribunals and inquiries **9–053** is that the term "statutory inquiry" was originally defined to include only those inquiries held in pursuance of a statutory duty. This excluded inquiries the holding of which was at the discretion of the minister, such as inquiries held under the general powers of the Education Act 1944[158] and the Highways Act

[158] Education Act 1944 s.93.

1980.[159] The Tribunals and Inquiries Act 1966 dealt with this unsatisfactory situation by empowering the Lord Chancellor to make orders designating certain groups of inquiries as subject to the Tribunals and Inquiries Act 1958.[160] Designating orders have been made pursuant to this power.[161]

viii. Related types of decision-making: decisions by appointed persons and written representations

9–054 An inquiry conducted by an inspector who sends proposals to the minister is the "standard" or "normal" method of proceeding. There are, however, a number of related procedures, which have the central theme of preserving decision-making in the hands of those who are politically accountable, while allowing some degree of public participation.

These techniques are designed to expedite the process of reaching a decision as compared with the full panoply of an inquiry. Serious delays over planning appeals led to legislation empowering the secretary of state to designate certain classes of appeal that could be heard and decided by a person whom he had appointed. Flexibility in procedure was increased by making statutory provision for such appeals to be decided on written representations if both parties agreed.[162] Even within areas in which the final decision resides with the secretary of state the parties may agree to have their case settled on the basis of purely written representations.[163] Pressures of time have rendered the written representation procedure an attractive one for the parties, and over 80 per cent of all planning appeals are decided in this way. The main disadvantage of this procedure was that third parties had no opportunity to participate,[164] but the current regulations afford such parties the opportunity to take part in the appeal process.[165]

ix. Related types of decision-making: Planning Inquiry Commissions

9–055 If the increase in the number of decisions reached by written representation reflects one development in the planning sphere, the Planning Inquiry Commission reflects another. While the former is a response to the demand for quicker and cheaper decisions, the latter demonstrates the need for planning machinery to consider problems on a level which the previous institutions did not allow.

---

159 Highways Act 1980 s.302.

160 Tribunals and Inquiries Act 1992 s.16(1)(b) and 16(2) makes the designated inquiries subject to the Act. The provisions concerning the giving of reasons do not, however, apply unless the designating order specifically so directs, s.10(4).

161 See, e.g. SI 451/1967; SI 1379/1975; SI 1287/1983.

162 Town and Country Planning Act 1990 ss.78, 319A and Sch.6; Town and Country Planning (Appeals) (Written Representations Procedure) (England) Regulations 2009 (SI 452/2009).

163 M. Purdue, *Cases and Materials on Planning Law* (London: Sweet & Maxwell, 1977), pp.218–221; Wraith and Lamb *Public Inquiries* (2011), pp.198–200.

164 Council on Tribunals, *Annual Report 1966*, paras 89–91; Heap, *An Outline of Planning Law* (1996), pp.204–205.

165 SI 452/2009 rr.6 and 13.

Under the Town and Country Planning Act 1990 s.101 a planning inquiry commission can be established. It will be used in circumstances where there are considerations of regional or national importance demanding a special inquiry, or where novel technical or scientific questions are involved that cannot adequately be resolved without some such mechanism. The Commission will proceed in two stages, the first being a general investigation, the second a local inquiry conducted by one member of the Commission. The former will be in the nature of a roving, unrestricted investigation, comparable to a Royal Commission, to be used in circumstances such as the development of a new airport.[166]

D. The Inquiries Act 2005

i. The position pre-2005

Inquiries have in the past been ordered on a variety of issues, such as the first inquiry into the expansion of Stansted airport, and the inquiry into the "Arms to Iraq" affair.[167] A number of these inquiries did not have a statutory base. They were used for a variety of purposes,[168] including the Crichel Down affair,[169] which was a catalyst for the establishment of the Franks Committee, though paradoxically the type of behaviour in this case was not within the Committee's terms of reference. **9–056**

There were also inquiries made pursuant to the Tribunals of Inquiry (Evidence) Act 1921, which was passed to provide a procedure for investigating allegations of improper behaviour by officials in connection with armaments contracts.[170] It was used mainly to investigate similar allegations of misconduct by ministers, civil servants or other organs of government. Thus, the leaking of budget secrets[171] and the bribing of a junior minister were both the subject of such an inquiry,[172] as were the circumstances surrounding the spying activities of Vassall.[173] The powers possessed by such tribunals of inquiry came to the forefront of the public eye during the Vassall inquiry, the catalyst being the imprisoning of three journalists for contempt of court[174] after failing to disclose the sources of stories which they had written about the Vassall affair.

In 1966 a Royal Commission was established to review the operation of such inquiries.[175] It made 50 recommendations designed to safeguard the operation of such inquiries, focusing in particular on the absence of procedural checks.

166 Town and Country Planning Act 1990 Sch.8.

167 House of Commons, *Inquiry into the Export of Defence Equipment and Dual-Use Goods to Iraq and Related Prosecutions*, HC Paper No.115 (Session 1995–96).

168 Wraith and Lamb, *Public Inquiries as an Instrument of Government* (1971), pp.202–212; Beer, *Public Inquiries* (2011), paras 1.19–1.36.

169 Sir Andrew Clarke QC, *Report of the Inquiry* (1954), Cmd.9176.

170 Wraith and Lamb, *Public Inquiries as an Instrument of Government* (1971), pp.212–217.

171 (1936) Cmd.5184.

172 (1948) Cmd.7616.

173 (1962) Cmnd.2009.

174 The Tribunal of Inquiry could not itself punish for contempt, but it did certify the journalists before the High Court.

175 Royal Commission, *Report on Tribunals of Inquiry* (1966), Cmnd.3121; Beer, *Public Inquiries* (2011), paras 1.37–1.50.

ii. *The Inquiries Act 2005*

9–057 More recently in 2004 the government published a consultation paper on inquiries and this was the catalyst for the passage of the Inquiries Act 2005 and the consequent repeal of the Tribunals of Inquiry (Evidence) Act 1921.

The Inquiries Act 2005 is intended to provide a comprehensive statutory framework for inquiries set up by ministers to look into matters of public concern. A minister may cause an inquiry to be held where it appears to him that particular events have caused, or are capable of causing, public concern, or there is public concern that particular events may have occurred.[176] There is power to convert actual or pending inquiries created independently of the 2005 Act into inquiries that come within its remit.[177] An inquiry panel is not to rule on, and has no power to determine, any person's civil or criminal liability, but it is not to be inhibited in the discharge of its functions by any likelihood of liability being inferred from facts that it determines or recommendations that it makes.[178]

Appointment to the inquiry panel is made by the relevant minister, and the Act requires those appointed to be suitable, possess the requisite expertise and that they should be impartial.[179] It is for the minister to set out the terms of reference of the inquiry, which may be amended. The terms of reference cover: the matters to which the inquiry relates; any particular matters where the inquiry panel is to determine the facts; whether the inquiry panel is to make recommendations; and any other matters relating to the scope of the inquiry specified by the minister.[180]

9–058 The chairman of the inquiry has control over its procedure and conduct, subject to provisions of the 2005 Act or rules made there under.[181] In making any decision as to the procedure or conduct of an inquiry, the chairman must act with fairness and with regard to the need to avoid unnecessary cost, whether to public funds, witnesses or others. The chairman may take evidence on oath, and administer oaths. The inquiry has the power to compel production of evidence.[182] The inquiry chairman must report its conclusions to the minister,[183] and subject to certain qualifications the report is published and laid before Parliament.[184]

The default position is that members of the public should be able to attend, and obtain or view a record of evidence put before the inquiry.[185] Restrictions can however be placed on public access where this is required by any statutory provision, enforceable EU obligation or rule of law. Restrictions can also be placed on public access where the minister or chairman considers this conducive to the inquiry fulfilling its terms of reference or to be necessary in the public interest. In making such a determination the minister or chairman must have

---

176 Inquiries Act 2005 s.1; *R. (Litvinenko) v Secretary of State for the Home Department* [2014] EWHC 194 (Admin).

177 Inquiries Act 2005 s.15.

178 Inquiries Act 2005 s.2.

179 Inquiries Act 2005 ss.8–9.

180 Inquiries Act 2005 s.5.

181 Inquiries Act 2005 s.17.

182 Inquiries Act 2005 s.21.

183 Inquiries Act 2005 s.24.

184 Inquiries Act 2005 ss.25–26.

185 Inquiries Act 2005 s.18.

regard to: the extent to which any restriction on attendance, disclosure or publication might inhibit the allaying of public concern; any risk of harm or damage that could be avoided or reduced by any such restriction; any conditions as to confidentiality subject to which a person acquired information that he is to give, or has given, to the inquiry; and the extent to which not imposing any particular restriction would be likely to cause delay or to impair the efficiency or effectiveness of the inquiry, or otherwise to result in additional cost, whether to public funds, witnesses or others.[186]

The Inquiries Act 2005 is to be welcomed insofar as it introduces regularity into the conduct of inquiries set up as a result of public concern about a particular matter. The government intends that the Act should be the mechanism for holding such inquiries and this too is to be welcomed. It remains to be seen how chairmen of inquiries exercise their power to set inquiry procedure, although such decisions would be subject to judicial review for compliance with the precepts of natural justice. It will also be important to monitor the way in which the rules allowing restriction on public access are interpreted and applied.

E. Supervision

Inquiries are subject to judicial review. More general supervision was exercised by the Council on Tribunals. The Tribunals and Inquiries Act 1992 s.1(1)(c) gave the Council on Tribunals power to consider and report on such matters as were referred to them, or as the Council deemed to be of special importance. The Council also had to be consulted by the Lord Chancellor when the latter made procedural rules for inquiries, an obligation which did not attach to procedural rules made by other ministers. The Council's powers were therefore advisory and not executive. It was nonetheless of value in a number of ways, by receiving complaints from individuals concerning specific problems encountered at inquiries, by publication of special reports on aspects of tribunal procedure, and through its comments on draft legislation concerning inquiries.[187] **9–059**

The Tribunals, Courts and Enforcement Act 2007 abolished the Council on Tribunals and replaced it with the Administrative Justice and Tribunals Council.[188] The AJTC had responsibility for statutory inquiries.[189] It was to keep under review, and report on, the constitution and working of statutory inquiries, both generally and in relation to any particular statutory inquiry or type of inquiry; it was to consider and report on any other matter that related to statutory inquiries in general, to statutory inquiries of a particular description or to any particular statutory inquiry, which the AJTC determined to be of special importance; and it was to report on any particular matter referred to it concerning such inquiries referred to it by the Lord Chancellor, the Welsh ministers and the

[186] Inquiries Act 2005 s.19; *Officer L, Re* (2007) 1 W.L.R. 2135; *R. (E) v Chairman of the Inquiry into the Death of Azelle Rodney Inquiry* [2012] EWHC 563 (Admin); *R. (Associated Newspapers Ltd) v Leveson* [2012] EWHC 57 (Admin).

[187] Wraith and Lamb, *Public Inquiries as an Instrument of Government* (1971), pp.140 and 236.

[188] TCE Act 2007 ss.44–45.

[189] TCE Act 2007 Sch.7 para.15.

Scottish ministers.[190] The AJTC has, however, been abolished as noted in the earlier discussion,[191] and it is unclear whether and how far the Administrative Justice Forum will focus on inquiries.

The Parliamentary Commissioner was a member of the Council on Tribunals,[192] and was a member of the AJTC.[193] In his own capacity, when investigating complaints of maladministration, he has had occasion to examine matters arising from public inquiries such as delay and cost. This overlap between the Council/AJTC and the Commissioner was not neat, but was beneficial given the more extensive powers of investigation possessed by the latter.

F. Planning Inquiries, the Government and the Public

9–060 Lawyers tend to have a limited interest in inquiries, once they are satisfied that the procedures are fair. To some extent this is because inquiries present the lawyer with less familiar issues, as compared to those that arise in relation to tribunals. The uncertainties as to inquiry procedure are reflected in the way in which we consider the fundamental questions that arise in this area. What rights should third parties have at inquiries? How much time should be expended on consultation with interested parties? To what extent should we allow discussion of policy at inquiries? How costly are these procedures and what do we mean when we speak of an efficient process of decision-making? The answers will be based upon the perceived aim of the law in this area. There is nothing surprising about this. Indeed it would be odd if the situation were otherwise. What is less obvious is that, in determining what those purposes are, we may have to make value judgments, the implications of which go over and beyond the particular area in question.

That this is so is brought out by McAuslan's study of planning law.[194] The author identified three different ideologies, which shaped the law in this area. The first saw the aim of the law as to protect private property, which was termed the traditional common law approach to the legal role. The second conceived the purpose of the law as to advance the public interest, even as against traditional property rights. This was called the orthodox public administration approach to the legal role. The third ideology was that the function of the law was to aid the cause of public participation in decision-making, which might be in opposition to the other two approaches. This ideology was labelled the populist approach.[195] Which approach predominated could affect the answers to the central questions posed above.

---

190 TCE Act 2007 Sch.7 para.16.

191 See para.9–038.

192 Parliamentary Commissioner Act 1967 s.1(5).

193 TCE Act 2007 Sch.7 para.1(1).

194 P. McAuslan, *The Ideologies of Planning Law* (Oxford: Pergamon Press, 1980). On planning law in general see Heap, *An Outline of Planning Law* (1996); P. McAuslan, *Land, Law and Planning* (London: Weidenfeld and Nicolson, 1975); Purdue , *Cases and Materials on Planning Law* (1977); M. Grant, *Urban Planning Law* (London: Sweet & Maxwell, 1983); Duxbury, *Telling and Duxbury's Planning Law and Procedure* (2012); Moore, *A Practical Approach to Planning Law* (2014).

195 McAuslan, *The Ideologies of Planning Law* (1980), p.2.

This is readily apparent by looking further at McAuslan's study. The essence of the argument was that the first two approaches towards planning were dominant, albeit in varying degrees, that participation was much genuflected to in theory, but pushed into third place in practice. The author demonstrated this in a number of areas,[196] two of which may be taken as examples.

The relevant legislation on planning was, until 2005,[197] contained in the Town and Country Planning Act 1990, which imposed an obligation on the local planning authority to make a survey of its area, including size, composition and distribution of the population, and the principal physical and economic features of the area.[198] The survey was then forwarded to the secretary of state, together with what was known as a unitary development plan for metropolitan areas and a structure plan for non-metropolitan areas. These plans consisted of a written statement which formulated the local planning authority's policy and general proposals for development and other use of the land in that area, together with a statement as to how that development related to development in neighbouring areas.[199] Local plans were designed to fill in the details of the wider ranging policies considered in the structure plan.[200] Public participation takes place both before and after submission of the plans to the secretary of state.[201] **9–061**

In 1966 the Skeffington Committee had been established specifically to consider and report on the best method of ensuring publicity for and public participation in the formative stages of drawing up plans for an area. The Committee reported in 1968.[202] It recommended that there should be pauses in the plan-making process to enable the public to comment, and that the local planning authority should arrange meetings for local groups to consider planning issues. Alternative choices should be put forward and community involvement with the project should be encouraged. These recommendations must, however, be seen in the light of the Committee's conclusion that responsibility for the making of the plan lay with the elected representatives and that their role should not be diminished.

It was three years before the government responded to the proposals of the Skeffington Committee. A circular was sent to the local authorities setting out the government's attitude.[203] The general impression left by this document was that discretion should remain with local authorities as to implementation of the Committee's proposals. Juxtaposed to this general theme were warnings about the time and cost that participation could entail, which were particularly evident

[196] McAuslan, *The Ideologies of Planning Law* (1980), Chs 1–2. I am indebted to McAuslan's study for the material which appears in this example. See also, C. Harlow and R. Rawlings, *Law and Administration* (London: Weidenfeld and Nicolson, 1984), Chs 14 and 15.

[197] Planning and Compulsory Purchase Act 2004; Planning Act 2008.

[198] Town and Country Planning Act 1990 s.11 applied to metropolitan areas, s.30 to non-metropolitan areas.

[199] Town and Country Planning Act 1990 ss.12 and 31.

[200] Town and Country Planning Act 1990 s.36.

[201] Town and Country Planning Act 1990 ss.13, 20, 33, 35 and 39–42.

[202] People and Planning, *Report of the Committee on Public Participation in Planning* (1969).

[203] Department of the Environment, Circular No.52/72.

in the way in which the circular addressed the Skeffington proposals concerning stages of participation. As McAuslan states[204]:

> "The overall impression given by the circular is that the Skeffington Committee had been a little over enthusiastic … and that the hard headed realism and discipline of costs and time, very much administrative concerns, were to be determining factors in public participation in plan-making. Only by placing the organisation and implementation of participation firmly under the jurisdiction of local authorities and reminding them of their statutory obligations, as opposed to the Report's recommendations, were these overriding concerns likely to be met."

9–062 Consultation prior to the submission of the unitary development or structure plan to the minister was intended to be but part of the participation by the public. It was to be complemented by examination of the plan before it was approved by the secretary of state.[205] The nature and degree of any such participation was, however, firmly placed in the hands of the secretary of state. The legislation left no doubt that the scope of any examination into the structure plan would be decided upon by the secretary of state. There was no general duty to consult or to consider the views of interested parties.[206] This reflection of the public interest ideology of planning, with that interest being decided on by the government of the day, was further reinforced by the non-statutory code of practice, which provided guidance as to the nature of the examination. The code made it clear that the conduct of the examination would be kept firmly in the hands of the secretary of state, who would choose which matters would be considered at the examination, and who would be entitled to take part in the discussion.

The second example of the conflicting ideologies underlying the planning sphere can be seen in the public local inquiry pursuant to a refusal of planning permission. The very idea of, or necessity for, an inquiry prior to the refusal of planning permission[207] was a natural outgrowth of the common law's protection of private property. If property belonged to you and someone wished to prevent you using it as you chose an appeal should be provided.[208] Despite this the inquiry procedure prior to the Franks Committee reflected the predominance of the public interest perspective: the absence of procedural rules, the secrecy surrounding inspector's reports, and the closed nature of the government policy all contributed towards this. With the reforms of the Franks Committee came a shift in the ideology underlying the inquiry. The pendulum was realigned to take greater account of private property rights through the grant of procedural safeguards prior to, at, and after the inquiry. These provisions that were originally enacted to protect the interests of property owners have been used by third parties to widen the scope of the inquiry. The inspector, who has discretion over inquiry procedure, can and often will admit those without a legal right to attend. Interest groups will use the inquiry to advance arguments over and beyond the facts of the particular case, and once admitted to the inquiry such third parties may for some

---

[204] McAuslan, *The Ideologies of Planning Law* (1980), p.23.

[205] McAuslan, *The Ideologies of Planning Law* (1980), pp.39–45.

[206] 1990 Act ss.20 and 35.

[207] McAuslan, *The Ideologies of Planning Law* (1980), pp.45–55; Wraith and Lamb, *Public Inquiries as an Instrument of Government*, pp.253–264.

[208] Town and Country Planning Act 1990 Pt III.

purposes at least be in as good a position as those with legal rights.[209] Notwithstanding these advances of the public participation ideology, third parties still stand in a somewhat uneven position.[210]

The preceding two examples may be supplemented by a third drawn from developments in planning. Partnership between the public and the private sector in land development was fostered, and there were moves to expedite the planning process, to enable such joint schemes to proceed more rapidly.[211] Local authorities were encouraged by central government to "play the roles of facilitator and underwriter of the profitability of private development proposals".[212] Bargains could be negotiated in secret to facilitate particular developments, with the consequence that "public participation is squeezed out, and policy conflict internalized within the local authority".[213]

What these examples show is that the type of procedure at the inquiry, the very type of inquiry itself, and the substantive rights accorded to participants will depend on the prevailing ideology in the particular area. We cannot resolve questions as to third party rights, or the inquisitorial as opposed to adversarial method of investigation, without implicitly if not explicitly adopting one of these perspectives. **9–063**

Thus, the private property approach to planning would tend to favour an adversarial procedure akin in broad nature to the common law model of adjudication, with its rules of examination and cross-examination. Substantive rights would be restricted to the property owner being affected, and the issues that could be raised at an inquiry would be confined to the case at hand.

The public interest approach to planning would gravitate towards a less formal, more inquisitorial style of procedure. The government of the day is regarded as the embodiment and guardian of the public interest, and should be relatively free to pursue the procedures of its choosing, subject to certain elementary concepts of fairness. This view finds expression in *Bushell*,[214] and especially the judgment of Lord Diplock. The substantive rights accorded are limited, as the example of the structure plan shows. Policy is retained firmly in the hands of the government, and the public interest as thereby defined takes prominence over private property and the views of those participating in the decision-making.

The public participation ideology would require more modifications to our institutional mechanisms. The inquiry procedure would be modified to enable a wider variety of views to be taken into account at the formative stages of, for example, a structure plan or unitary development plan. Consultation would be a

---

209 *Turner v Secretary of State for the Environment* (1973) 28 P. & C.R. 123.

210 Report of the Council on Tribunals on the position of third parties at planning appeal inquiries (1962), Cmnd.1787.

211 Enterprise zones, Local Government, Planning and Land Act 1980 s.179, and Town and Country Planning Act 1990 ss.88–90; simplified planning zones, Town and Country Planning Act 1990 ss.82–87.

212 M. Loughlin, *Local Government in the Modern State* (London: Sweet & Maxwell, 1986), p.157.

213 M. Grant and P. Healey, "The Rise and Fall of Planning", in M. Loughlin, M. Gelfand and K. Young (eds), *Half a Century of Municipal Decline 1935–1985* (London: Allen & Unwin, 1985), p.185.

214 *Bushell* [1981] A.C. 75 at 92–104.

continuing process and would take place after the plan has been submitted to the secretary of state. As seen both pre- and post-submission consultation has taken place, but the reins are kept firmly in hand by local and central government. A real commitment to the public participation ideology would entail an increase in the rights of the participator and a corresponding diminution in the control and discretion of the government. In some areas the procedure would cease to be either inquisitorial or adversarial, but be more in the nature of consultation, discussion, with broader community involvement.

The portrayal of these different ideologies is of course somewhat stark. A system of planning may well be a balance between them. This does not however deny the formative influence that each can have on the type of procedures adopted and the nature of the rights granted to those entitled to participate. It is not therefore surprising that lawyers find inquiries involving them in territory with which they are less familiar. Answers to apparently more straightforward issues such as those of costs and delay, let alone those of third party rights and the questioning of government policy, cannot be formulated without addressing our minds to these complex problems.[215]

---

215 See M. Purdue, R. Kemp and T. O'Riordan, "The Government at the Sizewell B Inquiry" [1985] P.L. 475, and "The Layfield Report on the Sizewell B Inquiry" [1987] P.L. 162, for an interesting account of the problems presented by the large public inquiry.

CHAPTER 10

EUROPEAN UNION

1. CENTRAL ISSUES

i. The discussion thus far has focused upon the principal domestic institutions relevant for administrative law. To stop there would, however, be to give a misleading picture, since many important "public" decisions are now made not in Whitehall, but in Brussels.[1] 10–001

ii. This chapter examines the European Union and its significance for administrative law.

iii. The basic structure and powers of the Council, the Commission, the European Parliament, the European Council and the Court of Justice of the European Union (CJEU) will be described here.

iv. There will then be an analysis of the main EU legal doctrines that are of relevance. Subsequent chapters of the book include more detailed discussion of particular points of EU law doctrine that are relevant for UK administrative law.

v. The Brexit referendum resulted in a vote to leave the EU. The UK government will negotiate the withdrawal of the UK from the EU. If and when this occurs, the principles propounded in this chapter will no longer be applicable to the UK, but the UK remains subject to all rights and obligations under EU law prior to withdrawal.

2. THE INSTITUTIONS

A. Council

Article 16(2) TEU states that the Council shall consist of a representative of each Member State at ministerial level, who is authorised to commit the government of that State. The members of the Council are, therefore, politicians as opposed to civil servants, but the politician can be a member of a regional government. The Council meets when convened by the President of the Council, at the request of a member, or at the request of the Commission. Council meetings are arranged by subject matter with different ministers attending from the Member States, and are regulated by the Council's Rules of Procedure. There are at present ten such 10–002

[1] Wyatt and Dashwood's *European Union Law*, 6th edn (London: Hart, 2011); D. Chalmers, G. Davies and G. Monti, *European Union Law Text and Materials*, 3rd edn (Cambridge University Press, 2014); P. Craig and G. de Búrca, *EU Law, Text, Cases and Materials*, 6th edn (Oxford: Oxford University Press, 2015).

Council configurations, having been reduced from the 22 that prevailed in the 1990s: General Affairs Council; Foreign Affairs Council; Economics and Finance Council (Ecofin); Justice and Home Affairs Council; Transport, Telecommunications and Energy; Employment, Social Policy, Health and Consumer Affairs; Agriculture and Fisheries; Competitiveness; Environment; and Education, Youth, Culture and Sport. The ministers responsible for these matters within the Member States will attend such meetings. They will be supported by their own delegations of national officials with expertise in the relevant area. The Commission attends Council meetings and has a particular role in relation to the GAC.[2]

The Lisbon Treaty provides that the work of the Council is to be prepared by the Committee of Permanent Representatives (Coreper), and that it shall carry out the tasks assigned to it by the Council.[3] Coreper is staffed by senior national officials and operates at two levels. Coreper II is the more important and consists of permanent representatives of ambassadorial rank. It deals with the more contentious matters such as economic and financial affairs, and external relations. It also performs an important liaison role with the national governments. Coreper I is composed of deputy permanent representatives and is responsible for issues such as the environment, social affairs, the internal market, and transport. Coreper plays an important part in EU decision-making,[4] because it considers draft legislative proposals that emanate from the Commission, and helps to set the agenda for Council meetings. A large number of working groups, approximately 150, feed into Coreper. They are the lifeblood of the Council, and examine legislative proposals from the Commission. They are composed of national experts from the Member States or from the Permanent Representations.

The Lisbon Treaty provides scant guidance as to the powers of the Council. Article 16(1) TEU merely provides that:

> "The Council shall, jointly with the European Parliament, exercise legislative and budgetary functions. It shall carry out policy-making and coordinating functions as laid down in the Treaties."

A simple reading of this provision does little to convey the reality of the Council's powers. The Council exercises an important role in the decision-making process in numerous ways: it has to vote its approval of virtually all Commission legislative initiatives before they become law; the Council has become more proactive in the legislative process and can in effect suggest to the Commission that the latter develop particular legislative initiatives; the Council can delegate power to the Commission, enabling the latter to pass further regulations within a particular area; the Council, together with the EP, plays a major role in relation to the European Union's budget; the Council concludes agreements on behalf of the European Union with third states or international organisations; and the Council has significant powers in relation to the Common Foreign and Security Policy (CFSP).

---

[2] TEU art.16(6).

[3] TEU art.16(7), TFEU art.240(1).

[4] J. Lewis, "The Methods of Community in EU Decision-Making and Administrative Rivalry in the Council's Infrastructure" (2000) 7 J.E.P.P. 261; D. Bostock, "Coreper Revisited" (2002) 40 J.C.M.S. 215.

B. Commission

While the Council represents the interests of the Member States, the Commissioners must be completely independent in the performance of their duties, and can neither seek nor take instructions from a government or any other body.[5] Thus, while Commissioners come from the Member States they do not represent their own state. 10–003

The Lisbon Treaty provided that the Commission would, until 31 October 2014, consist of one national from each Member State, including the President and the High Representative for Foreign Affairs.[6] After that date the Commission was to consist of members, including the President and the High Representative for Foreign Affairs, which correspond to two thirds of the Member States, unless the European Council, acting unanimously, decides to alter this number. The European Council could therefore vote to retain one Commissioner per Member State post-2014, and it made this commitment to Ireland prior to its second referendum.[7] The commitment was honoured through a European Council decision in 2013, which provided that one Commissioner per Member State would continue.[8] Prospective Commissioners are commonly subject to scrutiny by the relevant parliamentary committee before approval by the European Parliament. Commissioners hold office for five years, and this term is renewable.[9]

The permanent officials who work in the Commission, and who form the Brussels bureaucracy, are organised into Directorates General (DGs), which cover the major internal areas over which the Commission has responsibility. The Commissioners will in addition have their personal staffs (or cabinets), consisting partly of national and partly of EU officials. There will be approximately 15 officials in these teams.

The powers of the Commission are set out in art.17(1) TEU. It states that: the Commission shall promote the general interest of the Union and take appropriate initiatives to that end; ensure the application of the Treaties, and of measures adopted by the institutions pursuant to them; oversee the application of Union law under the control of the ECJ; execute the budget and manage programmes; exercise coordinating, executive and management functions, as laid down in the Treaties; ensure the Union's external representation, with the exception of the common foreign and security policy; and shall initiate the Union's annual and multiannual programming with a view to achieving inter-institutional agreements. 10–004

It is important to realise that the Commission has an array of powers, which are judicial, administrative, executive and legislative in nature. The EU institutional structure is not characterised by a rigid doctrine of separation of

---

[5] TEU art.17(3).

[6] TEU art.17(4).

[7] Brussels European Council, 10 July 2009 [I.2].

[8] 2013/272/EU: European Council Decision of 22 May 2013 concerning the number of members of the European Commission [2013] OJ L165/98.

[9] TEU art.17(3).

powers, and the Commission is at the heart of many EU initiatives. The Commission is central to the legislative process and has the right to initiate EU legislation.[10]

C. European Parliament

10–005 The European Parliament has been transformed since the inception of the Community. It was originally known as the Assembly, and the change of name was brought about by the Single European Act (SEA), which was signed in 1986 and ratified in 1987. The European Parliament was originally indirectly elected from national parliaments, and direct elections occurred in 1979. The powers of the European Parliament have, moreover, been continually increased in subsequent revisions of the original Treaty. The number of seats per country ranges from 99 for Germany to 5 for Malta. The Parliament's term is five years, like that of the Commission.[11] MEPs sit according to political grouping, rather than nationality. These groupings correspond to those to be found within the states, including Conservatives/Christian Democrats, Labour/Socialist and more centrist parties.

The European Parliament (EP) has three different types of power: budgetary, legislative and supervisory. The EP plays an important role in the budgetary process within the European Union. The legislative powers of the EP have increased significantly over the last 30 years. Prior to the Single European Act 1986 the general rule was that the EP only had a right to be consulted on legislation where the particular Treaty article so specified. The SEA introduced the co-operation procedure, which brought the EP into the legislative process more fully than hitherto. The co-decision procedure was introduced by the Maastricht Treaty, and in effect made the EP a co-equal partner, or something close thereto, with the Council in the areas where it applied.[12] It has been renamed the ordinary legislative procedure in the Lisbon Treaty[13] and its remit has been extended to approximately 40 further areas. The co-equal status of the EP and Council is affirmed in art.14(1) TEU, which now states that the EP shall, jointly with the Council, exercise legislative and budgetary functions. There are a number of ways in which the EP exercises supervisory control: it can establish a temporary Committee of Inquiry; EU citizens can petition the Parliament; and provision is made for an Ombudsman to investigate maladministration.

[10] TEU art.17(2).
[11] TEU art.14(3).
[12] art.251 EC.
[13] TFEU arts 289 and 294.

D. European Council

The European Council consists of the Heads of State or Governments of the Member States, together with the President of the Commission. It came into existence in 1974, and regular meetings have been held ever since. Formal recognition was accorded by art.2 of the SEA. The governing provision is now art.15 TEU: 10–006

> "1. The European Council shall provide the Union with the necessary impetus for its development and shall define the general political directions and priorities thereof. It shall not exercise legislative functions.
> 2. The European Council shall consist of the Heads of State or Government of the Member States, together with its President and the President of the Commission. The High Representative of the Union for Foreign Affairs and Security Policy shall take part in its work.
> 3. The European Council shall meet twice every six months, convened by its President. When the agenda so requires, the members of the European Council may decide each to be assisted by a minister and, in the case of the President of the Commission, by a member of the Commission. When the situation so requires, the President shall convene a special meeting of the European Council.
> 4. Except where the Treaties provide otherwise, decisions of the European Council shall be taken by consensus."

The European Council emerged to deal with important problems that could only be resolved at the highest governmental level, such as crises over Member States' budgetary contributions, the consequences of the collapse of Communism in Eastern Europe, or the timetable for the European Union's development, such as the steps towards economic and monetary union. The reality is that nothing important happens in the European Union without the approval of the European Council. Its decisions are, therefore, of considerable consequence for the speed and direction of EU change.

E. Court of Justice of the European Union

The Court of Justice of the European Union, (CJEU), hitherto known as the European Court of Justice, (ECJ), has played a vital role in the development of the European Union. There is one judge from each Member State, and they are appointed for six years renewable. The judges elect a President for a period of three years, and the post is renewable. The CJEU can decide cases either in plenary session or in Chambers. 10–007

The CJEU is assisted by Advocates General. The post has no real analogy within the common law system. After the parties have submitted their arguments, and before the court delivers its judgment, the Advocate General will present an Opinion on fact and law to the court. It is not formally binding on the court, but will often be influential.

In addition to the CJEU there is now a General Court, previously known as the Court of First Instance, which was established by the SEA. It was created to relieve the ECJ's workload. More recently judicial panels have been created on specific topics, such as staff disputes.

3. THE LEGAL ORDER: SUPREMACY AND DIRECT EFFECT

10–008 The ECJ has had a marked impact on the development of the European Union and has been a major force in securing greater EU integration. Two of its most important contributions have been supremacy and direct effect.

A. Supremacy

10–009 There will inevitably be clashes between EU law and national law. These will often be inadvertent, simply the result of an "absence of fit" between complex EU and national provisions. More intentional recalcitrance by Member States is less common, though not unknown. Some rules must exist for such cases. Not surprisingly, the ECJ held that EU law is supreme in the event of any such conflict.

This principle was first enunciated in *Costa v ENEL*[14] where the ECJ responded to an argument that its preliminary ruling would be irrelevant, because the Italian courts would be bound to follow national law. It held:

> "By creating a Community of unlimited duration, having … powers stemming from a limitation of sovereignty, or a transfer of powers from the States to the Community, the Member States have limited their sovereign rights, albeit within limited fields, and thus have created a body of law which binds both their nationals and themselves."

The European Union's supremacy was given added force by the *Simmenthal* case,[15] where the court made it clear that Community law would take precedence even over national legislation adopted after the EU law. The existence of EU rules rendered automatically inapplicable any contrary provision of national law, *and* precluded the valid adoption of any new national law in conflict with the EU provisions.[16]

> "It follows from the foregoing that every national court must, in a case within its jurisdiction, apply Community law in its entirety and protect rights which the latter confers on individuals and must accordingly set aside any provision of national law which may conflict with it, whether prior or subsequent to the Community rule."

10–010 The supremacy of EU law was felt to pose particular problems for our legal system, which is wedded to Parliamentary sovereignty. The leading decision is *Factortame.*[17] The applicants were companies incorporated under UK law, but the majority of the directors and shareholders were Spanish. The companies did sea fishing and their vessels were registered as British under the Merchant Shipping Act 1894. The statutory regime governing sea fishing was altered by the Merchant Shipping Act 1988. Vessels that had been registered under the 1894 Act had to register once again under the new legislation, 95 vessels failed to meet the criteria in the new legislation, and they argued that the relevant parts of the 1988 Act were incompatible with what were arts 7, 52, 58, and 221 of the EC Treaty.

---

14 *Costa v ENEL* (6/64) [1964] E.C.R. 585 at 593.

15 *Amministrazione delle Finanze dello Stato v Simmenthal Spa* (106/77) [1978] E.C.R. 629.

16 *Simmenthal Spa* [1978] E.C.R. 629 at [21].

17 *R. v Secretary of State for Transport, Ex p. Factortame Ltd* [1990] 2 A.C. 85, HL.

The question in the first *Factortame* case concerned the status of the 1988 Act pending the decision on the substantive issue by the ECJ. This decision might not be forthcoming for some time and if the applicants could not fish in this period they might go out of business. The applicants sought therefore either for the 1988 Act to be "disapplied" pending the ECJ's substantive decision. Or if the Act remained in force to prevent them from fishing, then the government should give an undertaking to provide compensation if the ECJ's ultimate decision was in the applicants' favour. Lord Bridge gave the judgment of the House of Lords. He rejected the applicant's argument that the 1988 Act should be disapplied pending the final determination by the ECJ, and decided that there was no jurisdiction under English law to grant interim injunctions against the Crown.[18] He then sought a preliminary ruling from the ECJ as to whether the absence of any interim relief against the Crown was itself a violation of EU law. The ECJ was therefore being asked to rule on whether a "gap" in the availability of administrative law remedies in UK law was itself a breach of EU law.

The ECJ decided for the applicants,[19] and reasoned from the earlier judgment in *Simmenthal*.[20] In that case the ECJ held that provisions of EU law rendered "automatically inapplicable" any conflicting provision of national law. The *Simmenthal* decision had given a broad construction to the idea of a "conflicting provision" of national law, interpreting it to cover any legislative, administrative or judicial practice that might impair the effectiveness of Community law.[21] With this foundation the ECJ in *Factortame* concluded that[22]:

> "[T]he full effectiveness of Community law would be just as much impaired if a rule of national law could prevent a court seised of a dispute governed by Community law from granting interim relief in order to ensure the full effectiveness of the judgment to be given on the existence of the rights claimed under Community law. It follows that a court which in those circumstances would grant interim relief, if it were not for a rule of national law is obliged to set aside that rule."

The case then returned to the House of Lords to be reconsidered in the light of the ECJ's preliminary ruling, *Factortame Ltd (No.2)*.[23] Their Lordships accepted that, at least in the area covered by EU law, interim relief would be available against the Crown.[24] The present discussion focuses upon the House of Lords' approach to sovereignty and the European Union.

Factortame (No.2) contains dicta by their Lordships on the more general issue of sovereignty. The substantive decision in the case involved a potential clash between the EC Treaty, combined with rules on the common fisheries policy, and a *later* Act of the UK Parliament, the Merchant Shipping Act 1988. The traditional UK idea of sovereignty has been that if there is a clash between a later statutory norm and an earlier legal provision, the former takes precedence. The **10–011**

---

[18] See Ch.29.

[19] *R. v Secretary of State for Transport, Ex p. Factortame Ltd* (213/89) [1990] E.C.R. I-2433.

[20] *Simmenthal Spa* [1978] E.C.R. 629.

[21] *Simmenthal Spa* [1978] E.C.R. 629 at [22]–[23].

[22] *Factortame* [1990] E.C.R. I-2433 at [21].

[23] *R. v Secretary of State for Transport, Ex p. Factortame Ltd (No.2)* [1991] 1 A.C. 603, HL.

[24] See Ch.29.

strict application of this idea in the context of the European Union could be problematic, since the ECJ has held that EU law must take precedence in the event of a clash with national law.

Earlier UK cases had taken various approaches to clashes between the two legal systems. Some authorities appeared to stick to the traditional orthodoxy of giving precedence to national law.[25] Others applied a rule of construction, under which it would be assumed that Parliament had not intended there to be any inconsistency between UK law and EU law, unless Parliament had expressly stated its intent to derogate from EU law. The dicta of the House of Lords in *Factortame (No.2)* are therefore clearly of importance. Lord Bridge had this to say[26]:

> "Some public comments on the decision of the Court of Justice, affirming the jurisdiction of the courts of the member states to override national legislation if necessary to enable interim relief to be granted in protection of rights under Community law, have suggested that this was a novel and dangerous invasion by a Community institution of the sovereignty of the United Kingdom Parliament. But such comments are based on a misconception. If the supremacy within the European Community of Community law over the national law of member states was not always inherent in the EEC Treaty it was certainly well established in the jurisprudence of the Court of Justice long before the United Kingdom joined the Community. Thus, whatever limitation of its sovereignty Parliament accepted when it enacted the European Communities Act 1972 was entirely voluntary. Under the terms of the 1972 Act it has always been clear that it was the duty of a United Kingdom court, when delivering final judgment, to override any rule of national law found to be in conflict with any directly enforceable rule of Community law. Similarly, when decisions of the Court of Justice have exposed areas of United Kingdom statute law which failed to implement Council Directives, Parliament has always loyally accepted the obligation to make appropriate and prompt amendments. Thus there is nothing in any way novel in according supremacy to rules of Community law in areas to which they apply and to insist that, in the protection of rights under Community law, national courts must not be prohibited by rules of national law from granting interim relief in appropriate cases is no more than a logical recognition of that supremacy."

Lord Bridge's dictum is a general statement concerning the priority of EU law over national law in the event of a clash. The reasoning is essentially contractarian: the United Kingdom knew when it joined the European Union that priority should be accorded to EU law, and it must be taken to have contracted on those terms. If, therefore, "blame" was to be cast for a loss of sovereignty then this should be laid at the feet of Parliament and not the courts. Space precludes detailed analysis of *Factortame (No.2)* on the traditional concept of sovereignty.[27] It is clear that our courts are now willing to disapply even a primary statute where it comes into conflict with EU law.[28] The *Factortame* decision means that the concept of implied repeal, under which inconsistencies between later and earlier norms were resolved in favour of the former, will no longer apply to clashes

[25] P. Craig, "Sovereignty of the United Kingdom Parliament after Factortame" (1991) 11 Y.B.E.L. 221, 240–243.

[26] *Factortame (No.2)* [1991] 1 A.C. 603 at 658–659.

[27] Craig, "Sovereignty of the United Kingdom Parliament after Factortame" (1991) 11 Y.B.E.L. 221; Sir William Wade, "Sovereignty—Revolution or Evolution?" (1996) 112 L.Q.R. 568; T.R.S. Allan, "Parliamentary Sovereignty: Law, Politics and Revolution" (1997) 113 L.Q.R. 443; N. MacCormick, *Questioning Sovereignty, Law, State and Practical Reason* (Oxford: Oxford University Press, 1999), Ch.6; P. Craig, "Britain in the European Union", in J. Jowell, D. Oliver and C. O'Cinneide (eds), *The Changing Constitution*, 8th edn (Oxford: Oxford University Press, 2015), Ch.4.

[28] *Equal Opportunities Commission v Secretary of State for Employment* [1994] 1 W.L.R. 409.

concerning EU and national law. If Parliament wishes to derogate from its EU obligations then it must do so expressly and unequivocally. Whether our national courts would then choose to follow the latest will of Parliament, or whether they would argue that it is not open to our legislature to pick and choose which obligations to subscribe to while still remaining within the European Union remains to be seen.

Factortame must however now be seen in the light of the decision in *HS2*, where the Supreme Court made clear that the relationship between EU law and national law was to be determined by UK constitutional law, and that it could not be assumed that Parliament had intended to accord priority to EU law over UK constitutional statutes.[29] **10–012**

B. Direct Effect

The doctrine of EU law supremacy has been a cornerstone of the Union legal order. The ECJ's other principal contribution has been direct effect. In order to appreciate its importance, it is necessary to understand why it was introduced. **10–013**

i. The limits of public enforcement

The concept of direct effect allows individuals to bring actions in their own names within national courts to vindicate Treaty rights. It is in this sense a species of *private enforcement*. Whether the framers of the original EEC Treaty intended individuals to be able to bring such actions is debatable. It is nonetheless clear that the Treaty obligations have to be enforced in some manner, and the principal mechanism for doing so was through *public enforcement*, art.258 TFEU. A principal rationale for the introduction of direct effect was to supplement public enforcement of EU law with private enforcement, because of the weaknesses of the former. Under art.258 the Commission has the responsibility of bringing Member States who fail to comply with the Treaty before the ECJ. There are six principal limits to this manner of enforcing EU norms, each of which is cured, or at the least alleviated by, the development of direct effect. **10–014**

The first, and most obvious, difficulty created by this approach is that it thereby effectively places the entire burden of policing EU law on the Commission, since one Member State will rarely sue another. This entails a considerable *workload* for the Commission, which has many other responsibilities quite separate from that of "prosecutor". Private actions, rendered possible by direct effect, complement the enforcement role of the Commission by sanctioning claims brought by individuals in their own capacity.

A second difficulty with public enforcement is closely related to the first. *Knowledge* of the existence of a breach is a condition precedent for an enforcement action. This knowledge could be acquired by the Commission, but this would be difficult given the size of the Treaty and the volume of EU legislation. This is so even though individuals can inform the Commission of a

[29] *R. (HS2 Action Alliance Ltd) v Secretary of State for Transport* [2014] UKSC 3; P. Craig, "Constitutionalising Constitutional Law" [2014] P.L. 373.

possible Treaty violation. Direct effect alleviates this problem. An individual who believes that a Member State has violated the EU Treaty is in the optimal position to know the facts to which the alleged violation relates, and has a strong incentive to take steps to have the matter tested.

10–015 The third limit of public enforcement is that it is *only available against a Member State*. While an individual may wish to assert rights against the state, there may be many instances where the appropriate defendant is another individual or a corporation, such as actions involving, for example, competition law or discrimination. Direct effect imposes obligations on private parties, subject to the limits mentioned below, and allows such actions to be brought before the national courts.

The fourth difficulty with relying on public enforcement per se is the *conflict of interest* problem. The Commission has a wide range of powers, legislative as well as judicial. This can lead to tension. An important legislative initiative may be under consideration in the Council, with the consequence that the Commission may be wary of pursuing an action against a Member State lest the latter should manifest its displeasure by rendering the passage of the legislation more protracted. If the legislation is important, and the wrongdoing is of less significance, the temptation to ignore the latter, or to pursue it less vigorously, may be great, even though the breach may be important to the particular group affected by it. It is difficult to determine how often the Commission has been placed in this conundrum. A system that relies exclusively on public enforcement, and in which the "prosecutor" also exercises legislative powers, will be prone to this tension. Direct effect eases this tension, since the individual brings the action and cannot be subject to the same pressures as the Commission.

The fifth shortcoming with the regime of public enforcement concerns *remedies*. Article 258 TFEU as originally formulated stipulated that a Member State found in breach of the Treaty should take the necessary measures to comply with the ECJ's judgment. If the state should continue to prove recalcitrant there was, until the Maastricht Treaty, little more that could realistically be done, short of bringing a further action. The ECJ now has the power to fine a Member State pursuant to art.258. Notwithstanding this, direct effect provides a particularly effective way to secure a remedy. This is because the action begins and ends in the national courts, and national governments are more likely to adhere to a judgment given directly from within their own system. The impact of direct effect at the remedial level is, however, more significant than this. The ECJ, while leaving some choice of remedy to the national courts, has made it clear that the remedy must provide an effective protection for the right in question.[30] The more precise implications of this depend on the nature of the issue. At the most general level the ECJ has demanded that national courts should, in effect, treat as done what ought to be done. Thus if, for example, a state has imposed a tariff that is inconsistent with EU law and has levied money pursuant thereto, then the national court should treat the tariff as invalid and return the money.

The final stumbling block with public enforcement is of a more symbolic nature. The approach in art.258 produces a *public relations problem*. The

[30] For a detailed discussion of EU jurisdiction in relation to remedies, see Craig and de Búrca, *EU Law, Text, Cases and Materials* (2015), Ch.7.

preamble to the Treaty spoke of laying the foundations "of an ever closer union among the peoples of Europe". This theme has always been close to the heart of the federalist-minded Commission. Vigorous enforcement of existing Treaty norms against Member States is not formally inconsistent with this long term goal. It does nonetheless not look "quite right" that a European Union which is meant to be moving closer should have countless cases in which one organ of the European Union is continually suing its constituent members. Direct effect therefore possessed a significant symbolic advantage. EU norms could be enforced without there being endless cases in which the Commission was directly suing the states. The reality was, as reality is, unchanged. Actions brought by individuals were still about states whose compliance with EU law was imperfect. However, the concept of direct effect served to ensure that this did not appear as a direct confrontation between the Commission and the Member States.

ii. Direct effect and empowerment of the individual

10–016 The discussion thus far has concentrated on the way in which direct effect alleviated the problem attendant upon public enforcement of EU norms. The discussion would, however, be incomplete if it were to rest there. Direct effect made a positive contribution to EU law independently of this. Granting rights to individuals, which they can enforce in their own name, transformed the very nature of the EU treaty. No longer would the Treaty be viewed solely as the business of nation states in the manner of many other international treaties.

It was to be a form of social ordering in which individuals were involved in their own capacity. They were no longer to be passive receptors that had to await action taken on their behalf by other organs of the European Union. They were now accorded rights that they could enforce in their own name. This was a necessary step in the transformation of the European Union from a compact between states, which was principally economic in nature, to that vision glimpsed at in the preamble of the Treaty "a closer union among the peoples of Europe".

iii. Van Gend en Loos

10–017 The seminal case in the development of direct effect was *Van Gend en Loos*.[31] Dutch importers challenged the rate of duty imposed on a chemical imported from Germany. They argued that a reclassification of the product under a different heading of the Dutch tariff legislation had led to an increase in the duty and that this was prohibited under art.12 EEC, which prohibits the imposition of any new customs duties on imports and any increase in existing rates. The Dutch court asked the ECJ whether art.12 gave rise to rights which could be invoked by individuals before their national courts.

The details of the arguments advanced by Holland, Germany and Belgium differed, but their general tenor was the same. The major theme was that EC law was to be enforced through what are now arts 258 and 259 TFEU. This theme was complemented by a second, which was that the Treaty was simply a compact between states, to be policed in the manner dictated by the Treaty. If a Member

[31] *Van Gend en Loos v Nederlandse Administratie der Belastingen* (26/62) [1963] E.C.R. 1.

State was in breach of the Treaty then it should face the consequences at the hands of another state, or the Commission. To afford individuals the right to initiate actions within national courts would be to alter the nature of the obligations accepted by the signatories.

10–018 Three strands of reasoning are apparent in the ECJ's judgment. The first demonstrates the use of a purposive and teleological approach that has become a characteristic of the ECJ's jurisprudence. The judgment opens with reference to the general aims and spirit of the Treaty, the objective being to deny the very basis of the Member States' reasoning. The European Union was *not* simply to be viewed as a compact between nations. The "interested parties" included the people, a fact which was affirmed by the preamble and by the existence of institutions charged with the duty of making provisions for those individuals. This laid the foundation for the now famous passage from the judgment. The ECJ depicted the European Union as a new legal order for the benefit of which states limited their sovereign rights, with the consequence that individuals had rights and could be regarded as subjects of the European Union.

The second strand in the ECJ's judgment was designed to buttress the first by drawing upon the Treaty to substantiate the conclusion that individuals could proceed before national courts. The ECJ used art.177 (now art.267 TFEU), which is concerned with the reference of questions on EU law by national courts to the ECJ. This provision was said to indicate that the states acknowledged that EU law had an authority which could be invoked by nationals before national courts.

The third aspect of the ECJ's reasoning focused on the particular Treaty articles in the case. The argument sought to show that art.12 was a natural candidate for enforcement in this manner. Thus, the ECJ stressed the *negative* nature of the obligation, the fact that it was *unconditional*, and that its *implementation was not dependent on any further measures* before being effective under national law. It was thereby able to conclude that the very nature of this prohibition made it ideally suited to produce direct effects in the legal relationship between Member States and their subjects.

iv. Expansion of direct effect: Treaty articles

10–019 The years following *Van Gend en Loos* witnessed the application of the concept to a growing range of Treaty articles. The court itself was keen to expand the concept given its advantages. In applying direct effect to other Treaty articles the ECJ began to relax the conditions for its application. Direct effect was applied in circumstances where it could not be said that the Treaty article in question created a negative obligation which was legally perfect, in the sense that no further action was required by the European Union or the Member States, and no real residue of discretion existed. The concept was applied to Treaty articles dealing with broad areas of regulatory policy, which were as much social as economic.

The *Reyners* case[32] provides a simple example. The plaintiff was a Dutch national educated in Belgium, who obtained a Belgian legal qualification. He was, however, unable to practice because of a Belgian law which restricted this

[32] *Reyners v Belgian State* (2/74) [1974] E.C.R. 631.

right to those of Belgian nationality. Dispensation from the nationality condition could be granted, but the plaintiff had been unsuccessful in such applications. He therefore sought to argue that Belgian law was inconsistent with art.52 EEC on freedom of establishment.

A number of Member States contended that this article could not have direct effect because it represented a statement of general principle, which had not yet been fleshed out by the secondary legislation in the manner envisaged by the Treaty. The European Union and the Member States were required to take further action before this part of the Treaty fulfilled the conditions for direct effect. It was not therefore for "the courts to exercise a discretionary power reserved to the legislative institutions of the Community and the Member States".[33]

The ECJ did not accept this argument. It based its reasoning on interpretation of the relevant chapter taken as a whole. Viewed in this light primacy of position was accorded to the prohibition of discrimination contained in art.52 itself. The further legislation was perceived as a way of effectuating this goal, but its absence could not impede a fundamental legal provision of the European Union.

The ECJ may well have been correct in deciding that art.52 should have direct effect even in the absence of the regulations/directives being promulgated. This should not however blind us to the fact that the original conditions for direct effect were modified and that this was necessitated by the difference in the type of Treaty article in question. Article 52, when placed within the relevant chapter of the Treaty, could not be regarded as complete and legally perfect in the same sense in which this phrase was used in relation to, for example, art.12. This is so even if one accepts the analysis of the ECJ. **10–020**

Article 52, and the provisions on freedom of establishment, expressly contemplated further action by the legislative organs of the European Union and by the Member States in order to effectuate the social and economic aims of this part of the Treaty. The very regime of freedom of establishment involves a complex array of legislative norms in order that these aims can be achieved.

The requisite EU legislation pursuant to art.52 had not been enacted in large part because Member States were unwilling to make the compromises to allow this to happen. The choice was clear. Either these spheres of policy could be left unfulfilled. Or the ECJ, through direct effect, could ensure that the basic principles within these areas should be enforced and developed through the judicial process.[34]

The same theme is evident in other important ECJ decisions, such as the seminal *Defrenne* case.[35] Sabena employed Defrenne as an air hostess. Her contract stated that she should retire at 40. She sought to argue that the conditions of her employment were discriminatory and contrary to art.119 EEC insofar as they were less favourable than those applicable to male stewards who performed the same task. The fact that the tasks performed by female hostesses and male stewards were identical was not disputed. **10–021**

---

[33] *Reyners* [1974] E.C.R. 631 at 648–649.

[34] J. Weiler, "The Community System: The Dual Character of Supranationalism" (1981) 1 Y.B.E.L. 267; P. Craig, "Once Upon a Time in the West: Direct Effect and the Federalization of EEC Law" (1992) 12 O.J.L.S. 453.

[35] *Defrenne v Sabena* (43/75) [1976] E.C.R. 455.

The ECJ acknowledged the central importance of art.119 from an economic and a social perspective. It recognised that the complete implementation of the article might well involve "the elaboration of criteria whose implementation necessitates the taking of appropriate measures at Community and national level".[36] This was not, however, to be a bar to giving direct effect to the article. Direct and overt discrimination could be identified solely through art.119 itself. Direct effect could operate in relation to such forms of discrimination, even if the proscription of more indirect forms of discrimination could only be identified by reference to explicit implementing provisions of a European Union or national character.

Article 119 EEC like art.52, provided the general aim for a complex sphere of regulatory social and economic policy. It could not be regarded as complete and legally perfect in the same manner as, for example art.12, without radically distorting the meaning of that phrase. It was clear that art.119 required, as the court recognised, further measures at both European Union and national level in order for the aims to be fulfilled. Not all the requisite measures had been promulgated in the stipulated time. As with *Reyners*, the ECJ introduced direct effect to provide an alternative method through which the principles of equal pay could be furthered, at least in the area of direct discrimination.

v. *Expansion of direct effect: regulations*

10–022 The discussion thus far has concentrated on the application of direct effect to Treaty provisions. The ECJ, however, also made it clear that the concept could apply to legislation enacted pursuant to the Treaty itself, such as regulations. Article 288 TFEU states: "A regulation shall have general application. It shall be binding in its entirety and directly applicable in all Member States".

In *Leonosio v Italian Ministry of Agriculture and Forestry*,[37] (known affectionately as *Slaughtered Cow*), the applicant sought to rely on two regulations under which she was entitled to receive a premium if she slaughtered a dairy cow. The relevant Italian authority was awaiting the necessary allocation of funds before it could pay over the money. The ECJ held that the regulation conferred rights on individuals, which they could use in national courts, and that the absence of the requisite allocation of funds was no excuse.

It is moreover clear that the Member State cannot alter the content of the EU norm. Thus, in *Amsterdam Bulb*[38] the ECJ held that the direct application of an EU regulation meant that its entry into force was "independent of any measure of transformation into national law",[39] and that states were precluded from adopting "any measure which would conceal the Community nature and effects of any legal provision from the persons to whom it applies".[40]

---

36 *Defrenne* [1976] E.C.R. 455 at 473.

37 *Leonosio v Italian Ministry of Agriculture and Forestry* (93/71) [1973] C.M.L.R. 343.

38 *Amsterdam Bulb v Produktschap voor Siergewassen* (50/76) [1977] E.C.R. 137.

39 *Amsterdam Bulb* [1977] E.C.R. 137 at 146.

40 *Amsterdam Bulb* [1977] E.C.R. 137 at 146.

vi. Expansion of direct effect: Directives

According to art.288 TFEU Directives are binding as to the result to be achieved while leaving the choice of form and methods to the Member States. Moreover, while regulations are binding on all states, Directives are only binding on the specific Member States to whom they are addressed. **10–023**

Directives have proved to be a particularly useful device for legislating in an enlarged European Union. Many areas of EU policy concern complex topics ranging from products liability to the environment and from the harmonisation of company law to the free movement of capital. The "normal" methods of legislating are ill-suited to these spheres. Regulations are intended to be directly applicable in the Member States without being transformed into national laws. This requires that the legislation be written with sufficient clarity and specificity to pass into national systems without more ado. It also requires that the norm is capable of so entering many different legal systems, some of which have a common law foundation, others of which have a civil law base. Directives are therefore invaluable because without this doctrinal form it would be more difficult to legislate in many important areas.

The application of direct effect to Directives has proven more controversial than in the context of regulations. This is because Directives require further action by the Member States, and because they leave the states with some discretion as to methods of implementation. The reluctance to admit that Directives can have direct effect is also because art.288 states that regulations are directly applicable, while not using this phraseology in relation to Directives. The ECJ nonetheless held that Directives are capable of having direct effect. The court used three arguments to justify this conclusion.

First, there was an argument from *general principle*, the essence of which was that it would be inconsistent with the binding effect of Directives to exclude the possibility that they could confer rights. The mere fact that regulations were deemed to be directly applicable, and hence capable of conferring rights, should not be taken to mean that other EU norms could never have the same effect.[41] **10–024**

The second argument was derived from *art.267*. This article allows questions concerning the interpretation and validity of EU law to be referred by national courts to the ECJ. The court concluded that questions relating to Directives can therefore be raised by individuals before national courts.[42]

The third reason for according direct effect to Directives was the *estoppel* argument. Given that the peremptory force of Directives would be weakened if individuals could not rely on them before national courts, a Member State which had not implemented the Directive could "not rely, as against individuals, on its own failure to perform the obligations which the directive entails".[43]

Provided, therefore, that the Directive is sufficiently precise, that the basic obligation is unconditional and that the period for implementation has passed, an individual can derive enforceable rights from a Directive. The decision in *Van*

[41] *Van Duyn v Home Office* (41/74) [1974] E.C.R. 1337 at [12].

[42] *Van Duyn* [1974] E.C.R. 1337 at [12].

[43] *Pubblico Ministero v Ratti* (148/78) [1979] E.C.R. 1629 at [22].

Duyn[44] provides an apt example. The applicant was a Dutch woman who wished to take up employment with the Church of Scientology. Article 48 EEC protected the free movement of workers within the European Union, subject to exceptions based upon public policy. The United Kingdom sought to exclude the applicant on the ground that it believed that the Church was socially undesirable, even though it did not prevent its own nationals from working there. The ECJ considered whether an individual could rely on Directive 64/221, which specified in greater detail the circumstances in which foreign nationals could be excluded on grounds of public policy, public security or public health. More specifically, the applicant sought an interpretation of art.3(1) of the Directive, which provided that exclusionary measures must be based solely on the personal conduct of the individual concerned. The ECJ held that this provision had direct effect.

vii Directives: horizontal and vertical direct effect

10–025 While the ECJ has been willing to give direct effect to Directives it has, however, held that they only have vertical as opposed to horizontal direct effect. Treaty articles and regulations give individuals rights enforceable both against the state, vertical direct effect, and against private parties, horizontal direct effect. Directives only have vertical direct effect.

The seminal case is *Marshall*.[45] The Southampton Area Health Authority operated different retirement ages for men and women, and the applicant claimed that this was in breach of Directive 76/207 on equal treatment. The ECJ reiterated its previous holding that Directives were capable of having direct effect. It held that a Directive could not, however, impose obligations on individuals, but only on the state, either as state or as employer. It reached this conclusion because of the wording of what is now art.288: the binding nature of the Directive existed only in relation to "each Member State to which it is addressed".

There are differing opinions on the correctness of, and rationale for, this ruling. The arguments cannot be fully explored here.[46] It is doubtful whether the argument advanced by the ECJ is correct. It is true that art.288 talks of Directives being binding on the state to which they are addressed. To infer from this that they cannot impose duties on individuals is more questionable. The relevant wording of art.288 is simply expressive of the fact that states are the primary addressees of the obligation contained in the Directive. It is they who have the duty to take the requisite measures to effectuate the ends stipulated therein. This does not necessarily mean that individuals should not be under an obligation flowing from a Directive. A similar argument was rejected in the *Defrenne* case.[47]

10–026 If there is a more meaningful argument against giving Directives horizontal direct effect then it is based on legal certainty. The essence of the argument is that

---

[44] *Van Duyn* [1974] E.C.R. 1337.

[45] *Marshall v Southampton & South West Hampshire Area Health Authority (Teaching)* (Case 152/84) [1986] E.C.R. 723; *Faccini Dori v Recreb Srl* (C-91/92) [1994] E.C.R. I-3325.

[46] See, e.g. Advocate General Reischl in *Ratti* [1979] E.C.R. 1629 at 1650; Advocate General Slynn in *Becker v Finanzamt Munster-Innenstadt* (8/81) [1982] E.C.R. 53 at 81; P. Craig, "The Legal Effect of Directives: Policy, Rules and Exceptions" (2009) 34 E.L. Rev. 349.

[47] *Defrenne* [1976] E.C.R. 455.

private individuals should not be placed in unreasonable doubt concerning the nature of their obligations. Given that Directives require national implementing legislation this uncertainty might occur if individuals were required to scrutinise differing texts at national and EU level to find out what the law was. There are, however, two limits to this argument.

On the one hand, the articles of many Directives are suited to application between private parties, without leading to problems of legal certainty. Directive 76/207 on equal treatment can be taken as an example. Article 3(1) of the Directive prohibited discrimination on grounds of sex in relation to access to employment, and art.5 banned such discrimination in relation to working conditions. The state was instructed to take a range of measures to implement the Directive. These included measures to ensure that terms in contracts of employment which were contrary to the Directive would be declared null and void. Even if the state had not taken these measures there is no reason not to impose duties on individuals. The obligations contained in the Directive were clear. An employer who continued to discriminate on these grounds should not be allowed to shelter behind the fact the state has been tardy in fulfilling its duties to implement the Directive.

On the other hand, it is not obvious why the objection based upon legal certainty is thought to be relevant in the context of Directives when no such objection is raised in the context of the primary Treaty provisions themselves. Many such articles have been interpreted expansively by the ECJ. These articles have horizontal direct effect, and no one has raised the objection of legal certainty. This is so even though there are often conflicting national laws on the same issue, and even though it may not be easy for an individual to know in advance whether there will be a clash between EU law and national law.

Even though Directives only have vertical direct effect the force of this limitation has been weakened in four ways: by an expansive definition of the state, by the development of the doctrine of indirect effect, by the creation of what has been termed "incidental" horizontal direct effect, and by damages actions against the state for loss caused by non-implementation of a Directive. The first three of these will be examined within the remainder of this section, the fourth in the section which follows.[48]

viii Directives: the scope of vertical direct effect

Given that Directives only have vertical and not horizontal direct effect it is clearly important to define the ambit of the state for these purposes. The ECJ has given an expansive interpretation to this concept. **10–027**

In *Foster*[49] the applicant wished to rely upon the Equal Treatment Directive 76/207, because she had been compulsorily retired earlier than male employees. The defendant was British Gas, and the question was whether it was to be treated as part of the state for these purposes. The ECJ held that the Directive could be relied upon against any institution, whatever its legal form, which has been made

[48] The ECJ has in addition held that general principles of law can in certain instances have horizontal direct effect, *Mangold v Helm* (C-144/04) [2005] E.C.R. I-9981.

[49] *Foster v British Gas* (C-188/89) [1990] E.C.R. I-3133.

responsible, pursuant to a measure adopted by the state, for providing a public service under the control of the state, and has for that purpose special powers over and beyond those which normally apply as between individuals.[50]

The correctness of this expansive definition may be questioned. It may well be accepted that bodies such as British Gas should be treated as part of the state for certain purposes, given the nature of its powers and the service which it is providing. What is less obvious is whether it should be so treated for this purpose, *given* the reasoning in *Marshall* itself. The premise underlying *Marshall* must be that the state as the addressee of the Directive is meant to implement it. Yet bodies such as British Gas plainly have no powers in this respect, nor can estoppel-type arguments meaningfully apply against such institutions. It will often only be central government which has the authority to execute the Directive. It is, of course, true that other bodies may well be in a position to abide by a Directive or not as the case may be. But this is equally true for purely private parties as it is for bodies such as British Gas. There is no more or less reason to apply a Directive against such bodies than against any other corporation. It is difficult to escape the conclusion that the expansive definition of the state given in *Foster* is an indirect way of circumventing the holding in *Marshall* itself.

ix. Directives: indirect effect

10–028 The other way in which the force of the *Marshall* limitation has been blunted has been through the development of the doctrine known as indirect effect. The concept is associated with *Von Colson*.[51] The applicants relied upon the provision of a Directive in order to argue that the quantum of relief provided by German law in cases of discrimination was too small. The ECJ held that these provisions were not sufficiently precise to have direct effect. It went on, however, to hold that national courts had an obligation to interpret national law so as to be in conformity with the Directive. The purpose of the Directive was to provide an effective remedy in cases of discrimination, and if states chose to fulfil this through the provision of compensation then this should be adequate in relation to the damage suffered. National courts should, therefore, construe their own national law with this in mind.

This principle of construction was extended in *Marleasing*.[52] The case was concerned with Council Directive 68/151, which contained rules on safeguards for the establishment of companies within the European Union. The plaintiff claimed that one of the defendant companies had been established "without cause" and that it was established to perpetrate a fraud. The plaintiff sought a declaration that the contract establishing the defendant corporation should be held void, and sought to found this claim on a provision of Spanish law. The defendant resisted the claim on the ground that art.11 of Directive 68/151, which listed the grounds on which the nullity of a company could be ordered, did not include lack

---

[50] D. Curtin, "The Province of Government: Delimiting the Direct Effect of Directives in the Common Law Context" (1990) 15 E.L. Rev. 195.

[51] *Von Colson and Kamann v Land Nordrhein-Westfalen* (14/83) [1984] E.C.R. 1891.

[52] *Marleasing SA v La Commercial International De Alimentation SA* (C-106/89) [1990] E.C.R. I-4135.

of cause among these grounds. The Directive had not yet been implemented in Spain, but the Spanish court asked the ECJ whether art.11 could be said to be directly applicable, so as to preclude a declaration of nullity of a public company on a ground other than one set out in that article.

The action was between private corporations, and the ECJ reiterated the holding that a Directive could not, in itself, impose obligations on individuals, citing the *Marshall* case as authority.[53] However, the ECJ qualified this by drawing on *Von Colson*. It held that the authorities of the Member States have an obligation to effectuate the ends stipulated in a Directive, and that this obligation is binding on all authorities in the state, including the courts. It followed that in applying national law, whether *passed before or after* the Directive, a national court was required to interpret national law *in every way possible* so as to be in conformity with the Directive. From this it followed that the Spanish court should so interpret their national law so as not to order the nullity of a company on a ground not listed in art.11 of the Directive.

While the ruling of the ECJ preserved its previous position, that there is no horizontal direct effect for Directives, its findings on the interpretive duties of the national courts go a considerable way to according Directives a measure of "indirect" direct effect. Thus, although an individual cannot derive rights from a Directive in an action against another individual, it is possible to plead the Directive in such an action. When the Directive has been placed before the national court, then the interpretive obligation derived from *Von Colson/ Marleasing* comes into operation. Where the Directive encapsulates precise obligations, and where the national court is minded to interpret national law in the required fashion, this "indirect" species of enforcement of a Directive as between individuals will have the same results as if the Directive had been accorded horizontal direct effect. **10–029**

There is little doubt that indirect effect offers a way to circumvent the holding in *Marshall*, or to reach similar results in many instances, albeit by a different route. There is also little doubt that the interpretative obligation creates real problems of its own.[54]

It places national courts in some difficulty in deciding how far they can go in reconciling national legislation with EU law while still remaining within the realm of interpreting, as opposed to rewriting or overruling national norms. It also raises questions of legal certainty for individuals which are more problematic than if Directives had been given horizontal direct effect. Individuals will have to guess how far their national courts might feel able to go in reconciling national law with differently worded EU legislation. If Directives did have horizontal direct effect then at least the individual would know that in the event of any inconsistency between the two norms EU law would trump national law.

UK courts have, on the whole, shown themselves to be willing to construe national law in the light of the Directive in the event of any inconsistency between the two,[55] particularly where the national law was passed to effectuate

[53] *Marleasing SA* [1990] E.C.R. I–4135 at [6].
[54] G. de Búrca, "Giving Effect to European Community Directives" (1992) 55 M.L.R. 215.
[55] *Webb v EMO Cargo* [1995] 4 All E.R. 577, HL.

the Directive.[56] The courts have shown more ambivalence where the relevant national law was not promulgated to carry out the Directive.[57]

x. Directives: "incidental" horizontal direct effect

10–030 The jurisprudence in this area has become even more complex as a result of cases in which the ECJ has been willing to accord some measure of effect to a Directive in actions between private individuals.

This is exemplified by the *CIA Security* case.[58] CIA Security claimed that the defendants had libelled it by asserting that its alarm systems had not been approved, as required by Belgian legislation. CIA accepted that it had not sought approval under the national legislation, but argued that this legislation was itself in breach of art.30 EEC. This was because the Belgian legislation had not been notified to the Commission as required by Directive 83/189, which imposed an obligation on states to notify the Commission of any new national provision which could limit the free movement of goods. The ECJ held that failure to comply with the Directive meant that the non-notified national legislation could not be enforced against individuals.

C. Direct Effect: Rights and Remedies

10–031 The discussion thus far has focused on the extent to which EU law creates rights that are enforceable by individuals in their own national courts. Rights demand remedies. How far EU law has an impact upon the remedies that are available at the national level is a complex topic. A brief outline will be given here.[59]

The ECJ's early stance is exemplified by *Rewe v Hauptzollamt Kiel*,[60] where it was held that, while national courts were under an obligation to use all available national remedies to aid the enforcement of EU law, they were not bound to create new remedies for this purpose. However, in *San Giorgio*[61] the court held that a Member State could not render claims for the repayment of charges, which were levied in breach of EU law, subject to procedural requirements which made that recovery virtually impossible.

The reconciliation of these two authorities was by no means easy. It was felt that a litigant could only claim a form of relief in aid of EU law rights if national law allowed that relief to be granted between the parties in proceedings before the court in question. If it did not do so then recourse was to be had to the legislature to fill the gap. However, if national law allowed the relief to be granted between the parties by the court before which the proceedings were instituted, it was the duty of that court to make that relief available in aid of EU law, and to disregard

[56] *Litster v Forth Dry Dock* [1990] 1 A.C. 546, HL. See however *White v White* [2001] 2 All E.R. 43 HL.

[57] *Duke v GEC Reliance* [1988] 1 A.C. 618.

[58] *CIA Security International SA v Signalson SA and Securitel SPRL* (C-194/94) [1996] E.C.R. I-2201; *Criminal Proceedings against Rafael Ruiz Bernaldez* (C-129/94) [1996] E.C.R. I-1829; *Panagis Pafitis v Trapeza Kentrikis Ellados AE* (C-441/93) [1996] E.C.R. I-1347.

[59] Craig and de Búrca, *EU Law, Text, Cases and Materials* (2015), Ch.8.

[60] *Rewe v Hauptzollamt Kiel* (158/80) [1981] E.C.R. 1805 at 1838.

[61] *Amministrazione delle Finanze dello Stato v San Giorgio* (199/82) [1983] E.C.R. 3595.

any substantive restrictions or procedural conditions of national law which are either discriminatory, or deprive the Community right of useful effect.

10–032 Indications that EU law might well require greater modifications in the regime of national remedies are to be found in the *Factortame* litigation. Prior to the House of Lords' decision in the second *Factortame* case,[62] UK law did not allow interim injunctive relief against the Crown. The ECJ in *Factortame*[63] nonetheless held that such relief should be available in principle, and that its absence was itself a breach of EU law. The requirements of EU law as to the national remedies for the protection of EU rights were, therefore, more stringent than had previously been thought.

The principle underlying the *Factortame* litigation was that provided the type of relief sought by the applicant is recognised by national law, in this instance the injunction, the fact that it was not previously available against the Crown would be regarded as an example of ineffective protection of Community rights, with the consequence that the national law must be changed. There are other ECJ decisions that evince the same concern that the remedy provided by the Member State must constitute effective relief for breach of the right in issue.[64] Later ECJ jurisprudence has, however, been somewhat less interventionist and allowed greater room for national remedial rules to continue to apply.[65]

The case law considered thus far was concerned primarily with the extent to which EU law would intervene in relation to the adequacy of the remedies currently provided by Member States for breach of Union law. In the *Francovich* case[66] the ECJ, however, created a remedy in damages for breach of EU law. This was conceived as an EU remedy in its own right, and not simply as an option which a particular Member State might or might not choose to embrace. The applicant claimed damages from the Italian government for losses suffered as a result of the non-implementation of a Directive designed to safeguard workers when a firm became insolvent. The ECJ held that the principle of state liability for harm caused to individuals by breach of EU law for which the state was responsible was inherent in the system of the Treaty. The full effectiveness of EU rights would be impaired if no such right to compensation existed.[67] This argument from first principle was buttressed by reference to what is now art.4(3) TEU, which requires Member States to take all appropriate measures to ensure

---

[62] *Factortame (No.2)* [1991] 1 A.C. 603.

[63] *Factortame* [1990] E.C.R. I-2433.

[64] *Cotter and McDermott v Minister for Social Welfare and Attorney General* (C-377/89) [1991] E.C.R. I-1155; *Marshall v Southampton and South West Area Health Authority (No.2)* (C-271/91) [1993] E.C.R. I-4367.

[65] *Steenhorst-Neerings v Bestuur van de Bedrijfsvereniging voor Detailhandel, Ambachten en Huisvrouwen* (C-338/91) [1993] E.C.R. I-5475; *R. v Secretary of State for Social Security, Ex p. Sutton* (C-66/95) [1997] E.C.R. I-2163.

[66] *Francovich v Italian Republic, Bonifaci v Italian Republic* (C-6 & 9/90) [1991] E.C.R. I-5357; M. Ross, "Beyond Francovich" (1993) 56 M.L.R. 55; D. Curtin, "State Liability under Private Law: A New Remedy for Private Parties" [1992] I.L.J. 74; J. Steiner, "From Direct Effects to Francovich" (1993) 18 E.L. Rev. 3; P. Craig, "Francovich, Remedies and the Scope of Damages Liability" (1993) 109 L.Q.R. 595.

[67] *Francovich* [1991] E.C.R. I-5357 at [32]–[35].

fulfilment of Union obligations. This included the obligation to nullify the unlawful consequence of a breach of EU law.[68]

The ruling in *Francovich* left open numerous issues concerning the nature of the damages remedy. Many of these were clarified in *Brasserie du Pecheur* and *Factortame*.[69] The principle of state liability in damages was held to be general in nature and existed irrespective of whether the EU norm which had been broken was directly effective or not. Liability could be imposed irrespective of which organ of the state was responsible for the breach, the legislature, the executive or the judiciary. The ECJ set out the criteria to determine when the state could incur liability. Where a Member State acted in an area in which it had some measure of discretion, comparable to that of the EU institutions when implementing Union policies, the conditions for liability in damages must, said the ECJ, be the same as those applying to the European Union itself. The right to damages was dependent upon three conditions: the rule of law infringed must have been intended to confer rights on individuals; the breach of this rule of law must have been sufficiently serious; and there must have been a direct causal link between the breach of the obligation imposed on the state and the damage which was sustained by the injured parties.

4. THE IMPACT OF EU LAW

10–033 There will be numerous cases concerned with the application of EU law principles at national level. National agencies and institutions are under a duty to apply the principles laid down in the Treaty and the norms made pursuant thereto. If they do not do so then an action can be maintained. This will be brought either by way of the public law procedures, or an ordinary action will be used. In reading the materials in this book one should, moreover, be aware of the fact that EU law can have an impact in four different ways.

First and most obviously, are the instances in which EU law dictates the result in a particular area, and takes precedence over national law.

Second, there are instances where EU law has a "spillover" effect for the resolution of analogous domestic problems. Thus, the fact that interim injunctive relief had to be available against the Crown in the EU law context, was a catalyst for the rethinking of this issue within domestic law, in part at least because it looked odd for the remedy to be available in the one context but not the other.

Third, EU law can be a spur for more general doctrinal development in our regime of public law. The development, for example, of proportionality as a ground for review is due, in no small measure, to the fact that it exists as such within EU law.

Finally, the existence of the European Union has had the effect of bringing the public law systems of the differing European countries closer together. This is due in part to the fact that EU law draws its inspiration from the laws of the Member States. It is due also to the fact that the very existence of the European Union has fostered a growing awareness of the mutual dependence of its

[68] *Francovich* [1991] E.C.R. I-5357 at [36].

[69] *Brasserie du Pecheur SA v Germany, R. v Secretary of State for Transport, Ex p. Factortame Ltd* (C-46 & 48/93) [1996] E.C.R. I-1029.

component parts. This has led to an increased interest in understanding the ways in which civilian and common law systems tackle the same problem.

CHAPTER 11

A CASE STUDY: COMPETITION AND REGULATION

1. CENTRAL ISSUES

i. The institutions directly covered by administrative law have been considered in the previous chapters. It is, however, helpful to consider the operation of the administrative process in more detail, and this chapter will do so in relation to competition policy and the regulation of utilities and market power. 11–001

ii. These areas are well-suited to such an analysis. They demonstrate how the choice of regulatory machinery has been affected by political considerations. They exemplify many of the procedural and substantive issues with which administrative law has to grapple. They are also areas of importance given the market-based approach to regulation.

iii. There are three central issues that have to be addressed in any instance where the state is thinking of engaging in regulation.

iv. The first is whether to regulate at all and if so why. In some instances the answer is obvious. The state may seek to regulate an area in order to prevent, for example, the production of drugs that might be injurious to health. In other instances the rationale for intervention is more debatable.

v. The second issue concerns the choice of the regulator. This may be relatively obvious in certain areas. The reality is however that there is often a relatively wide choice as to the regulatory authority for a particular area. It might for example, be decided that it is best to regulate the area through a department of central government, through a governmental agency outside the normal departmental structure or through a more formal tribunal. This chapter will examine the factors that shape the choice as between these options.

vi. The third issue is concerned with how to regulate. This is perhaps the most complex of all, in the sense that it entails the greatest range of choices to be made. Suffice it to say for the present that if it is decided to regulate a particular area there will inevitably be a range of more detailed matters to be resolved concerning the objectives of the regulatory schema and how they are to be attained in a particular area.

2. COMPETITION: WHETHER TO REGULATE

11–002 Competition policy is concerned with controlling firms in order that they do not harm the competitive process. Central examples of such behaviour are cartels and monopolies. Cartels are agreements by rival companies to fix prices or divide the market, with the consequence that fewer goods are available to consumers at a higher price than if normal market conditions prevailed. Monopoly power can enable a company to raise price and restrict output with the consequence that it can reap "abnormal" profits. It may also enable the monopolist to drive other firms from the market or prevent their initial entry.

The common law exercised some control over these areas, but this was, by the end of the 19th century, not very effective in promoting competition. The interpretation of the restraint of trade doctrine meant that preservation of competition was not the prime objective. Reluctance to interfere with a bargain even if the direct consequence was to injure the economic interest of another reached its high point in the case law on conspiracy. A price-fixing and market-allocation scheme, backed up by exclusionary tactics employed against those unwilling to submit, was held not to be an illegal conspiracy at common law.[1] The 19th century did, however, see some statutory regulation of monopoly power. Thus, it was common for utility services to be regulated by the Board of Trade, which would oversee the rates to be charged. It was nonetheless some considerable time before Parliament attempted any more comprehensive control of market power.[2] The reasons for the absence of intervention were eclectic.

First, it was felt that there was no urgent case for legislation dealing with market power.[3] Second, the First World War had fostered a climate of co-operation between firms, which was regarded as beneficial.[4] Third, the failure of post-war prosperity, the depression, business failure and unemployment, brought forth cries of "ruinous competition". There was a feeling that the market mechanism had failed and that collusion was "good". This was fostered by the idea of rationalisation, one tenet of which was that large firms were more efficient and therefore should be encouraged.

The eventual passage of legislation after the Second World War owed its origins partly to a change in attitude towards competition, and partly to other governmental policies canvassed during this period. Thus, some within government began to feel that industry would have to become more efficient, and that cartels were an impediment to this development. This view was given added force by the White Paper on employment policy.[5] It was argued that the object of securing full employment could be jeopardised by monopoly power and cartels, both of which could lead to higher prices and restricted output, thereby hampering employment prospects.[6]

---

[1] *Mogul SS Co Ltd v McGregor Gow* [1892] A.C. 25, HL; *Sorrell v Smith* [1925] A.C. 700, HL.

[2] Some governmental initiatives occurred after the First World War, e.g. *Committee on Trusts* (1918), Cmd.9236.

[3] *Committee on Trade and Industry* (1929), Cmd.3282.

[4] L. Hannah, *The Rise of the Corporate Economy* (London: Methuen, 1979), pp.32–33.

[5] 5 White Paper, *Employment Policy* (1944), Cmd 6527.

[6] G. Allen, *Monopoly and Restrictive Practices* (London: Allen & Unwin, 1968), p.62.

3. Competition: Who Should Regulate

The first modern legislation was the Monopolies and Restrictive Practices (Inquiry and Control) Act 1948. The choice of regulatory institution is often influenced as much by short-term political arguments as by any attempt to devise an optimum administrative strategy. The choice of regulatory institutions for competition policy exemplifies this. Five stages can be identified. **11–003**

The initial allocation of regulatory power was to an agency, the Monopolies and Restrictive Practices Commission (MRPC). It was felt that a body outside the normal departmental framework would be better suited to the investigatory work, and this institutional choice facilitated the involvement of non-civil servants with specialist expertise. These are common reasons for establishing an agency.[7] **11–004**

The second stage came in 1956. The Restrictive Trade Practices Act 1956 was passed to deal specifically with the problems of cartels, and the Restrictive Practices Court (RPC) was established to adjudicate on the area. The shift from a system of discretionary administration via an agency, to a judicial regime that purported to apply "black-letter" legal rules, is particularly interesting. It was motivated principally because of industry's dissatisfaction with the MRPC. The selection of an industry for investigation was regarded as arbitrary, firms which appeared before the MRPC felt themselves to be on trial, and corporations said that they had little idea as to which types of behaviour were suspect. The legislators responded by enacting a statute framed in formalistic legal terms, which purported to clarify the type of proscribed behaviour. A court was created to adjudicate on the matter, as opposed to a court-substitute tribunal, because it was thought that such a body would gain the respect of industry more easily.

The third stage saw expansion of the functions of the Monopolies Commission. This body was retained to investigate issues concerning monopoly power after 1956. Its powers were augmented by two major legislative developments. The Monopolies and Mergers Act 1965 added merger regulation to its jurisdiction, and the body was henceforth called the Monopolies and Mergers Commission (MMC). The Competition Act 1980 gave the MMC power to investigate certain anti-competitive practices, which were defined in broad, open textured terms. In exercising its powers in relation to monopolies, mergers or anti-competitive practices, the MMC worked with the Office of Fair Trading (OFT). It was the Director General of Fair Trading (DGFT) who made[8] a monopoly reference to the MMC, or a reference concerning an anti-competitive practice.[9] Merger references were dealt with differently, and the DGFT advised the secretary of state as to whether a reference should be made to the MMC.[10] The OFT was an agency with responsibilities for consumer protection as well as competition policy.[11]

---

[7] See Ch.4.

[8] Fair Trading Act 1973 s.50. A government minister could also refer, s.51.

[9] Competition Act 1980 s.5.

[10] Fair Trading Act 1973 s.76.

[11] I. Ramsay, "The Office of Fair Trading: Policing the Consumer Market-Place", in R. Baldwin and C. McCrudden (eds), *Regulation and Public Law* (London: Weidenfeld & Nicolson, 1987), Ch.9.

The fourth stage in the choice of institutions to administer competition policy was the rejection of a composite, single authority to oversee the area. The division between cartel policy, regulated by the OFT and the RPC, and the remainder of competition policy which was within the jurisdiction of the OFT and the MMC, was always questionable. The inability of one authority to consider all anti-competitive aspects of a problem made little sense. The division of authority also produced a large volume of complex legislation dealing with these distinct areas. The issue came to a head during the discussion that led to the Competition Act 1980. It was unclear whether this new area should be assigned to the MMC or the RPC, or whether there should be a new authority with jurisdiction over all areas of competition policy.[12] In the end the new powers were assigned to the MMC, and plans for a single competition authority were not pursued. The reasons for rejecting this bolder option were not convincing,[13] and the result was the continuance of an administrative strategy that was over-complex and outdated.

The fifth stage saw the acceptance of the bolder option. The Competition Act 1998 radically revised the United Kingdom's approach to competition policy. The specific legislation on restrictive trade practices ceased to have effect,[14] as did certain provisions of the legislation concerning anti-competitive practices.[15] The basic institutional structure now is that decision-making is shared between the Competition and Markets Authority (CMA) and the Competition Appeal Tribunal.[16] It is the CMA that makes the initial decision as to whether there has been a breach of the rules relating to agreements, and whether there has been an abuse of a dominant position.[17] This decision is subject to appeal to the Competition Appeal Tribunal, which was created by the Enterprise Act 2002.[18] This is a much more rational decision-making structure than that which previously existed. The force of this change will be even more apparent when we consider the criteria that apply to determine whether there has been a competition violation.

4. COMPETITION: HOW TO REGULATE

A. Effectiveness and the Choice of the Legislative Criterion

11–005 Any legal system that regulates competition has to decide whether to frame its legislation in terms of legal form or economic effects. The essence of this choice is easily explained. There are many types of cartels. They can be agreements to

---

[12] Green Paper, *Review of Restrictive Trade Practices Policy* (1979), Cmnd.7512.

[13] P. Craig, "The Monopolies and Mergers Commission: Competition and Administrative Rationality", in Baldwin and McCrudden (eds), *Regulation and Public Law* (1987), Ch.10. A later government report indirectly undermined much of the reasoning contained in the earlier report: Green Paper, *Review of Restrictive Trade Practices Policy* (1988), Cm.331.

[14] Restrictive Trade Practices Acts 1976 and 1977, Restrictive Practices Court Act 1976 and the Resale Prices Act 1976. See, Competition Act 1998 s.1.

[15] Competition Act 1980 ss.2–10. See, Competition Act 1998 s.17.

[16] Enterprise and Regulatory Reform Act 2013 ss. 25-26.

[17] Competition Act 1998 s.25.

[18] See *http://www.catribunal.org.uk/* [accessed 2 November 2015].

fix price, divide the market, share information or boycott third parties. They can be contracts under which one party will accept a certain type of product, such as beer or petrol, only from a particular supplier, as in the case of contracts covered by the restraint of trade doctrine.[19]

An approach based upon legal form attempts to set out in black-letter legal terms the types of agreement to be caught. This was the strategy in the initial legislation on cartels.[20] There are two difficulties with this approach. It was introduced, as we have seen, partly under pressure from industry, which wished to have a more "certain" system than that which had preceded it. Legal form was intended to provide this. There are, however, certain key terms within such legislation, such as whether activity "restricts" competition, which are very difficult to define purely "legally". An economic analysis is required. The other difficulty is that companies making illegal agreements will attempt to conceal the fact that they are dividing the market by, for example, an elaborate exchange of information about production. Legislation based on legal form encourages such "escape" devices.[21]

An approach based upon economic effects uses economic criteria to determine whether the legislation will "bite". Such legislation tends to be shorter, and focuses on the economic effects of an agreement irrespective of the way in which it is "dressed up" by the parties. This is the approach used in the European Union and the United States, and it was exemplified by the Competition Act 1980 in this country.

We have already seen that a central issue when assessing regulatory agencies is their effectiveness. If legislation does not use the most appropriate criterion there is little hope that the regulatory scheme will be successful. There was increasing consensus that form-based legislation did not work,[22] and that it was not sensible to base one part of the regulatory strategy on a criterion of legal form, and another on economic effect. **11–006**

The Competition Act 1998 marked a major shift in policy by using a general criterion of economic effect. The approach based on legal form, which dominated thinking in relation to restrictive agreements, has gone. The basic rationale behind the legislation is to bring the criteria for domestic competition policy into line with that in the European Union. Articles 101 and 102 TFEU govern anti-competitive agreements and abuse of a dominant position respectively. The wording of these articles is the basis for domestic law. Thus, s.2(1) of the 1998 Act borrows directly from art.101, while s.18 of the 1998 Act adopts the language of art.102.

---

[19] *Esso Petroleum Co Ltd v Harper's Garage (Stourport) Ltd* [1968] A.C. 269, HL.

[20] Restrictive Trade Practices Act 1976.

[21] *Re Cadbury Schweppes Ltd and J Lyons & Co Ltd's Agreement* [1975] 1 W.L.R. 1018 Ch D.

[22] A later government report was more favourable to an effects system: Green Paper, *Review of Restrictive Trade Practices Policy*.

B. Procedure and Procedural Rights

11–007 The earlier discussion touched upon the choice between adversarial and inquisitorial procedures that an agency might adopt.[23] Competition policy provides an apt illustration of these differing approaches.

The procedure before the RPC was essentially adversarial. Cartels within the ambit of the legislation had to register, and the DGFT then had a duty to take proceedings before the RPC.[24] In the subsequent trial the RPC heard arguments from the DGFT and the firms concerned as to whether the agreement should be allowed to stand because it was claimed to be beneficial to the public interest.[25]

The procedure before the MMC was more inquisitorial and investigative in nature. When the MMC received a monopoly reference from the DGFT it would collect information concerning the industry. An oral hearing might be held to ascertain the facts. It would then consider the impact of the monopoly upon the public interest. The firms involved would be sent a "public interest letter", and they could make representations to the MMC about it. A public interest hearing would then be held at which the firms could present their arguments. It was clear that the MMC had to comply with natural justice.[26] It was also clear that its procedure did not fit the traditional adversarial mould. The MMC did not sit as an "umpire" to hear the arguments from opposing sides. It carried out investigative work of its own, it possessed technical staff to assess financial evidence, it had its own view as to what constituted the public interest in a particular area, and it had considerable latitude in devising its procedures.[27]

11–008 The procedures under the Competition Act 1998 represent an interesting blend of the inquisitorial and the adversarial. It is common for those who make agreements which they know or think might be in breach of s.2 to conceal them. If the legislation is to be effective there must therefore be adequate investigative powers. The CMA's powers are modelled on those of the European Commission, which makes the initial determination of a competition violation in the European Union. The CMA is given extensive powers to investigate to see whether there is an anti-competitive agreement or an abuse of a dominant position.[28] The CMA's decisions can then be appealed to the Competition Appeal Tribunal[29] with a further appeal on limited grounds to the Court of Appeal.[30] The procedure before the appeal tribunals will be more traditionally adversarial, although even here there is discretion as to the way in which the hearing is conducted.[31]

---

[23] See Ch.9.
[24] Restrictive Trade Practices Act 1976 s.1(2)(c), subject to s.21.
[25] Restrictive Trade Practices Act 1976 ss.10 and 19.
[26] *Hoffmann-La Roche & Co v Secretary of State for Trade and Industry* [1975] A.C. 295, HL.
[27] Fair Trading Act 1973 s.81(2).
[28] Competition Act 1998 ss.25–31.
[29] Competition Act 1998 s.46.
[30] Competition Act 1998 s.49.
[31] Competition Act 1998 Sch.8 para.9.

C. Defining the Public Interest: Rule-making and Discretion

The question whether regulatory agencies should proceed through the application of rules/policy guidelines, or through the exercise of ad hoc discretion, is of particular interest to administrative lawyers.[32] **11–009**

Competition policy provides an interesting example of this general problem. The legislation allowed the MMC to take into account a wide variety of factors in determining the public interest including[33]: maintaining effective competition; promoting the interests of consumers; reducing costs; developing new products; maintaining the balanced distribution of industry and employment in the UK; and encouraging overseas competitiveness. This broad list seemed to dictate that the MMC should proceed by way of ad hoc discretion and this was indeed generally the case.

It was, however, argued that a more rule-based system should be applied to mergers for the following reason.[34] Economic analysis might indicate that mergers could produce welfare benefits, in terms of economies of scale. These could in theory be balanced against the disadvantages from having a larger firm as the result of the merger, which would have more market power and greater ability to raise price and restrict output. Such cost-benefit analysis is, however, difficult and time consuming, and the necessary data is often not available. It was argued that the best approach was therefore to proceed by way of rules, rather than through ad hoc discretion. A rule might, for example, prohibit all mergers leading to a market share in excess of 50 per cent.

The preceding argument was nevertheless based upon an important implicit premise. If the reduction of competition was regarded as the principal factor within the public interest analysis, then it might well be possible to devise rules accordingly. Where the range of factors felt to be relevant was broader, then the problems of rule definition became more intractable. Thus, if the effects of a merger on unemployment, the balance of payments, regional policy and the like are felt to be of integral importance, then the possibility of formulating appropriate "rules", while still yielding predictability of result is questionable.[35] **11–010**

The balance between rules and discretion can be relevant in a number of other areas within competition policy. This is readily apparent by considering the Competition Act 1998. In substantive terms, there is, for example, the device of the block exemption. Agreements that are prima facie caught by s.2 can be exempted if certain conditions are present. The grant of individual discretionary exemptions is however time consuming for the competition authorities and can lead to uncertainty for the parties. The approach taken in the European Union has been to promulgate block exemptions, which are designed to exempt categories

[32] See Ch.18.

[33] Fair Trading Act 1973 s.84.

[34] Crew and Rowley, "Antitrust Policy: Economics versus Management Science" (Autumn 1970) *Moorgate and Wall Street*; Howe, "Antitrust Policy: Rules or Discretionary Intervention" (Spring 1971) *Moorgate and Wall Street*; Crew and Rowley, "Antitrust Policy: The Application of Rules" (Autumn 1971) *Moorgate and Wall Street*.

[35] The 1969 and 1978 Merger Guidelines took a broad range of factors into account, but how much "guidance" they actually provided is debatable.

of agreements that fulfil certain criteria. This option is open under the 1998 Act.[36] The balance between rules and discretion can also be of relevance on the procedural level. Thus the CMA is given power to make a wide variety of rules relating to matters such as the procedure to be followed when dealing with an application, the documents to be provided and the way in which agreements should be notified.[37]

D. Defining the Public Interest: Politics, Policy and Justiciability

11–011 Governments have differed as to the way in which the public interest "list" ought to be interpreted. These differences had a considerable impact on the operation of the OFT and the MMC, because the secretary of state had power both in the initiation of references to the MMC, and at the remedial level. Two views of the "public interest" can be contrasted.

The Labour Party of the 1970s believed that, for example, merger policy should be based upon a relatively thorough consideration of the list of public interest factors mentioned in the legislation. The MMC should weigh the economic costs and benefits to competition, industrial efficiency, and the balance of payments, against the wider social costs and benefits to workers and consumers in each merger reference. Such an assessment had to be qualitative as well as quantitative.

The Conservative Party's attitude differed. Their market-based philosophy meant that they attached prime importance to competition within the public interest list. Other factors, such as the possible effects upon employment, were not regarded as the principal concerns of the OFT and MMC.[38] This approach also favoured quicker investigative mechanisms in order to determine whether behaviour was in fact injurious to competition.[39]

11–012 It would be wrong to assume that the government could in a literal sense dictate to the MMC the type of view it should adopt on the meaning of the "public interest". It would also be wrong to assume that the fact that the government exercised power in this respect was "wrong". The legislation upon competition was structured to leave discretion and ultimate control in the hands of the minister. Competition, like planning, was regarded as an area that should not be completely divorced from political considerations and one where some executive control was required. No conclusion can be reached about the effectiveness of a regulatory institution without some prior idea as its purpose. The object of competition policy has been crucially bound up with the political question concerning the meaning of the public interest. Indeed attempts to divorce such matters more thoroughly from the political arena have produced arguments that they are not readily justiciable.

This was a recurring theme in the operation of the RPC, which had to consider whether a cartel should be exempted under the "gateways". These were broad. It

[36] Competition Act 1998 ss.6, 7–11.

[37] Competition Act 1998 s.51 and Sch.9.

[38] *Charter Consolidated Ltd, Anderson Strathclyde Ltd* (1982), Cmnd.8771; *R. v Secretary of State for Trade, Ex p. Anderson Strathclyde Plc* [1983] 2 All E.R. 233 QBD.

[39] Competition Act 1980.

could, for example, be argued that removal of the restrictive agreement would deny specific and substantial benefits to users of goods. It was doubtful whether a court was best suited to resolving such issues, and questionable whether they should be divorced from the political arena.[40]

E. Enforcement

If a regulatory strategy is to be successful then it must be enforced. The choice of enforcement mechanisms will often throw considerable light on the regulatory regime. Two features have characterised the enforcement process in this area: the emphasis on negotiation, and on public as opposed to private enforcement. These will be considered in turn. **11–013**

Regulatory systems often have formal enforcement powers that mask a more informal process of negotiation between the parties. Competition policy placed negotiation at the forefront of its regulatory strategy. The DGFT was instructed to seek undertakings pursuant to an adverse report from the MMC under the Fair Trading Act 1973.[41] Under the Competition Act 1980 the emphasis was on negotiation between the DGFT and the firm under investigation.[42] More formal powers existed should the negotiating strategy prove unsuccessful,[43] but they were regarded as a long stop. This same theme is apparent in the Competition Act 1998. The CMA has significant formal enforcement powers, including the ability to impose interim measures and to fine.[44] The legislation nonetheless places much emphasis on reaching a solution without recourse to such formal measures. Thus the first step in the "enforcement process" will be directions issued by the CMA as to how the infringement can be brought to an end by, for example, modifying an agreement or conduct.[45] The importance given to the "negotiated solution" reflects the belief that this will be more effective than a formal legal sanction.

Competition policy in the United Kingdom has traditionally evinced a strong preference for public as opposed to private enforcement. With few exceptions, the enforcement process has been concentrated in the hands of the DGFT/CMA and the secretary of state. Individuals have had little role to play. They may serve as a catalyst for the initiation of an investigation, but they are not generally viewed as a separate means of enforcement in their own right.

This stands in stark contrast to competition policy in, for example, the European Union and the United States where private actions assume a more prominent role.[46] Changes to the EU competition regime have, however, accorded national courts and national competition authorities a more prominent role in enforcement in this area, with consequential implications for private enforcement.

---

[40] R. Stevens and B. Yamey, *The Restrictive Practices Court* (London: Weidenfeld & Nicolson, 1965); A. Hunter, *Competition and the Law* (London: Allen & Unwin, 1966).

[41] Fair Trading Act 1973 s.88.

[42] Competition Act 1980 ss.4, 8, 9 and 10.

[43] Fair Trading Act 1973 ss.56 and 73.

[44] Competition Act 1998 ss.35–36.

[45] Competition Act 1998 ss.32–33.

[46] K. Elzinga and W. Breit, *The Antitrust Penalties* (New Haven: Yale University Press, 1976).

F. Accountability and Control

11–014 The general concern over the accountability and control of agencies has been considered above.[47] Two aspects of this problem can be considered here: ministerial control and judicial control.

Ministerial control is evident at varying points within the system. Under the Fair Trading Act 1973 the relevant minister possessed powers to initiate a reference to the MMC. Such consent was necessary before any merger reference could take place. The minister could stop certain types of reference from being considered further. It was the minister who had the power to order formal sanctions where negotiation failed. He could also exert more general influence over the pattern of competition policy dependent upon the political party's interpretation of the public interest. Ministerial influence continues to be present under the Competition Act 1998. Thus, the secretary of state may modify the list of agreements excluded from the Act,[48] and similar powers exist in relation to abusive conduct.[49] The CMA has to secure the secretary of state's approval for a block exemption.[50] How far such control is warranted is a contentious issue. The fact that decisions concerning the public interest may be felt to warrant some political oversight does not immunise particular ministerial decisions from criticism.

Judicial review has generally played a limited role in this area. This may seem surprising: given that companies have no continuing "client" relationship with the competition authorities, there would be no risk of upsetting future relations by seeking judicial review. The explanation lies principally in the broad discretion possessed by the CMA, both in the decision whether to investigate, and also in determining whether behaviour is in the public interest. There are, however, instances where the actions of the competition authorities have been challenged.[51]

G. The Importance of Competition Policy

11–015 The effectiveness of competition policy has become increasingly important as a result of the privatisation programme. The privatisation of utilities led to the creation of new regulatory bodies to oversee such industries. Sectoral regulators run these new regulatory structures. Two important consequences flow from these developments.

First, the degree of prominence given to the promotion of competition by the different sectoral regulators may well differ. They are given a duty framed in broad terms, which is then "guided" by a wide range of factors, including the promotion of consumer interests, effective competition, and the encouragement of research and development. The prominence they accord to the promotion of

[47] See Ch.4.

[48] Competition Act 1998 s.3.

[49] Competition Act 1998 s.19.

[50] Competition Act 1998 s.6.

[51] See, e.g., *R. v Monopolies and Mergers Commission, Ex p. Elders IXL Ltd* [1987] 1 W.L.R. 1121; *R. v Monopolies and Mergers Commission, Ex p. Mathew Brown Plc* [1987] 1 W.L.R. 1235; *R. v Secretary of State for Trade and Industry, Ex p. Lonrho Plc* [1989] 1 W.L.R. 525.

effective competition may therefore differ. Second, the extra burdens these developments have placed upon the CMA means that there is an even greater need to ensure that its resources are properly used.

5. UTILITIES AND MARKET POWER: WHETHER TO REGULATE

There are many activities that are regulated in varying ways. The focus of the ensuing analysis will be on the regulation of utilities, but it is important at the outset to have some idea of the more general rationales for regulation. The literature identifies two broad rationales for regulation. **11–016**

A. The Public Interest Rationale for Regulation

On one view regulation in certain areas is justified on public interest grounds.[52] The market will decide the incidence of many activities in capitalist societies. This is the default position. Individual consumer choice will determine the demand and supply of goods, and the prices at which they are sold. Markets allow individuals to express their preferences for certain products, and in this sense enhance individual autonomy. The ordinary competitive process also enhances allocative efficiency within society. A standard rationale for regulation is where there is market failure, and this can occur in a number of different ways. **11–017**

A classic example of market failure is the *natural monopoly*. The market model is premised on competition. If this cannot operate then the assumptions underlying the model cannot be fulfilled. Impairment of the competitive process can be dealt with by the competition authorities, through their power to control cartels and monopoly power. Regulatory regimes can also be established to control privatised firms with market power.[53] This regulatory control can subsist in addition to that provided under competition law. There may be a desire to regulate the pricing policy of the monopolist and the terms on which it deals with its customers. There may be concern over the way in which it can hinder new entry into the industry. There may be fears over the quality of service provided by the dominant firm. This is particularly so in relation to natural monopolies where it is less costly for production to be carried out by one firm rather than many. As Breyer has stated[54]:

> "The most traditional and persistent rationale for governmental regulation of a firm's prices and profits is the existence of a 'natural monopoly'. Some industries, it is claimed, cannot efficiently support more than one firm. Electricity producers or local telephone companies find it progressively cheaper (up to a point) to supply extra units of electricity or telephone service. These 'economies of scale' are sufficiently great so that unit costs of service would rise significantly if more than one firm supplied service in a particular area. Rather than have three

---

[52] A. Ogus, *Regulation, Legal Form and Economic Theory* (Oxford: Oxford University Press, 1994), Ch.3; B. Morgan and K. Yeung, *An Introduction to Law and Regulation, Text and Materials* (Cambridge: Cambridge University Press, 2007), Ch.2.

[53] See Ch.4.

[54] S. Breyer, *Regulation and its Reform* (Cambridge, MA: Harvard University Press, 1982), p.15. The validity of the traditional economic rationale for regulating such forms of monopoly power has, however, been questioned, pp.16–19.

connecting phone companies laying separate cables where one would do, it may be more efficient to grant one firm a monopoly subject to governmental regulation of its prices and profits."

A second example of market failure arises in relation to what are known as *public goods*. Such goods have two characteristics[55]: consumption by one person does not leave less for others to consume, and it is impossible or too costly for the supplier to exclude those who do not pay for the service. National defence is an oft-cited example of a public good. There are also "impure" public goods, which may well be bought in the market, but which require regulatory intervention in order to correct a degree of market failure. Thus, while the primary beneficiary of education is the immediate recipient, it is generally acknowledged that others within society benefit from having a better-educated workforce.[56]

11–018 A third public interest rationale for regulatory intervention exists where an activity creates *externalities* for others. The classic example is the firm that pollutes a river when making its product. There are strong arguments for making the firm internalise its costs, including the harm caused to the river. Private law, in the form of nuisance actions and the like, may well help to achieve this, as can regulation in the form of, for example, environmental standards.[57] The existence of such externalities may also impact beyond state boundaries. A strong theme running through the literature on integration is that the European Union developed in part to meet the problems caused by such international externalities.[58]

A fourth important reason for regulatory intervention is *to correct information deficits* or to address circumstances where there is a strong asymmetry in information. This idea is captured by Ogus[59]:

> "The market system of allocation is fuelled by an infinite number of expressions of … preferences. However, the assertion that observed market behaviour in the form of expressed preferences leads to allocative efficiency depends crucially on two fundamental assumptions: that decision-makers have adequate information on the set of alternatives available, including the consequences to them of exercising choice in different ways; and that they are capable of processing that information and of 'rationally' behaving in a way that maximizes their expected utility. A significant failure of either assumption may set up a prima facie case for regulatory intervention."

B. The Private Interest Rationale for Regulation

11–019 The idea that regulation is intended to serve the public interest has been contested.[60] It has been argued by those within the public choice literature that much regulation is designed to serve the private interests of certain groups within society.

---

[55] Ogus, *Regulation, Legal Form and Economic Theory* (1994), p.33.

[56] Ogus, *Regulation, Legal Form and Economic Theory* (1994), pp.34–35.

[57] Ogus, *Regulation, Legal Form and Economic Theory* (1994), pp.35–38.

[58] P. Craig, "Integration, Democracy and Legitimacy", in P. Craig and G. de Búrca (eds), *The Evolution of EU Law*, 2nd edn (Oxford: Oxford University Press, 2011), Ch.2.

[59] Ogus, *Regulation, Legal Form and Economic Theory* (1994), p.38.

[60] Ogus, *Regulation, Legal Form and Economic Theory* (1994), Ch.4; Morgan and Yeung, *An Introduction to Law and Regulation, Text and Materials* (2007), Ch.2.

The intellectual ancestors of public choice were pluralists, who emphasised the group nature of politics and stressed that the public interest was nothing more than the outcome of the current group exchange. Public choice theorists brought more finely tuned tools of economic analysis to the political forum to explain the behaviour of political markets, but agreed on many points with the conclusions of earlier pluralist writers.[61] The public choice theorists based their analysis on methodological individualism,[62] and while they were willing to accept that individuals could have selfish or altruistic preferences, they also believed that there was no conception of the public interest separate from the results of individual choice.[63] Collective action was a means of reducing the costs of purely private or voluntary action. Individuals would engage in such action where the costs thereby saved outweighed the transaction costs, combined with the costs of loss of autonomy, in the sense of the consequential risk that the individual might have to accept a decision which he or she disliked. The fact that collective political decisions took place over time generated vote-trading, with each individual's vote possessing an economic value for which a market would develop in the same way as with any other commodity.

Regulation was seen as a function of the demands of interest groups which would benefit from the measure, coupled with the responses of those, normally politicians, who had power to deliver the measure. Proponents of this thesis argued that producer groups would normally be stronger, more coherent and better financed than other groups, and that therefore most regulation could be expected to benefit industry directly or indirectly.[64]

Public choice theorists believed that the role of the state should be narrowly confined for a number of reasons. They felt that private markets were better at reaching optimal decisions than political markets. They argued strongly that much regulatory legislation was a front to mask wealth-transfer and rent-seeking behaviour by particular interest groups. Rent in this context is the difference between the revenue from producing a product and the cost of production. The very process of competition will eliminate the rent. Public choice theorists contended that regulation, such as that limiting entry into a profession, was often designed to protect the existing incumbents from competition, allowing them to retain monopoly rents rather than passing them on to the consumer. Public choice theorists also disapproved of regulation because they felt that governmental intervention via redistributive policies was illegitimate, since it offended against **11–020**

[61] J. Buchanan and G. Tullock, *The Calculus of Consent* (Ann Arbor: University of Michigan Press, 1962); J. Buchanan, *The Limits of Liberty: Between Anarchy and Leviathan* (Chicago: University of Chicago Press, 1975); J. Buchanan, *Freedom in Constitutional Contract* (College Station: Texas A & M, 1978); J. Buchanan, *Liberty, Market and State: Political Economy in the 1980s* (Brighton: Wheatsheaf Books, 1986); G. Brennan and J. Buchnanan, *The Reason of Rules* (Cambridge: Cambridge University Press, 1985); I. McLean, *Public Choice: An Introduction* (Oxford: Blackwell, 1987); D. Mueller, *Public Choice* (Cambridge: Cambridge University Press, 1979).

[62] Although they fully accepted that individuals would be likely to operate through pressure groups because of the gains in terms of power which individuals could attain by so grouping together, Buchanan and Tullock, *The Calculus of Consent* (1962), pp.286–287.

[63] Buchanan and Tullock, *The Calculus of Consent* (1962), pp.32, 122–124, 125–130 and 209.

[64] G. Stigler, "The Theory of Economic Regulation" (1971) 2 Bell Jnl. Econ. 3; R. Posner, "Theories of Economic Regulation" (1974) 5 Bell Jnl. Econ. 335; S. Peltzman, "Towards a More General Theory of Regulation" (1976) 19 Jnl. Law & Econ. 211.

individual entitlements.[65] The descriptive and normative assumptions that underlie public choice have been contested.

In descriptive terms, it has, for example, been argued that the equation between individual behaviour in the marketplace and the political arena is not self-evidently correct. Even if the assumption is accepted it still leaves open the issue of how market-place behaviour itself should be perceived. At one extreme is the view that elected officials and individuals seek to maximise a specific wealth function. At the other is the non-falsifiable view that seeks to incorporate all ideological and other variables within an individual's utility function. On this latter view behaviour and motivation are flattened and reduced to an economic calculus, which often amounts to little more than the tautological observation that people who understand the consequences of their actions "will do things that make them as well off as they can be".[66]

The normative aspect of public choice has proven to be equally contentious.[67] The methodology is self-avowedly contractarian, but there are crucial differences in the use of this methodology when compared to the work of Rawls. It is highly debatable whether a vision of politics that seeks to legitimate legislation on the basis of group bargain is consistent in normative terms with the theory of justice postulated by public choice theorists. The norms which public choice theorists regard as emerging from their contractarian foundations are questionable. Their arguments for the restriction of wealth transfers on the ground that they offend entitlements are weak.

C. Natural Monopoly: Regulation or Structural Adjustment

11–021 The preceding discussion has revealed why some form of regulation of natural monopoly has been felt necessary. It might be argued that the monopoly should simply be broken up, with a corresponding increase in competition. This is an option, but it is not always the most desirable one. Breaking up the monopoly may not lead to greater efficiency. The monopoly may possess economies of scale, which would not be available to smaller units. It may, moreover, be more efficient to organise a particular economic activity within one corporate unit rather than through a number of smaller firms.[68] While it would be theoretically possible for all economic activity to be undertaken by individuals who contract with one another, this may not be efficient because the individuals may not have the knowledge through which to make the rational calculation as to the best course of action in all circumstances. As Foster notes[69]:

---

[65] Brennan and Buchanan, *The Reason of Rules* (1985), Chs 6–8; Buchanan, *Liberty, Market and State: Political Economy in the 1980s* (1986), Chs 12, 13, 15, 22 and 23; Buchanan, *The Limits of Liberty: Between Anarchy and Leviathan* (1975).

[66] M. Kelman, "On Democracy Bashing: A Skeptical Look at the Theoretical and Empirical Practice of the Public Choice Movement" (1988) 74 Virg. L. Rev. 199, 206.

[67] P. Craig, *Public Law and Democracy in the United Kingdom and the United States of America* (Oxford: Oxford University Press, 1990), pp.84–90.

[68] O. Williamson, *Markets and Hierarchies* (New York: Free Press, 1975).

[69] Foster, *Privatization, Public Ownership and the Regulation of Natural Monopoly* (Oxford: Blackwell, 1992), p.147.

> "It is because of lack of information and bounded rationality—that is an inability to weigh all factors relevant to making a rational decision between all feasible alternatives—that firms develop as alternative ways of completing a set of transactions."

It is not therefore surprising that when a firm is experiencing difficulties in devising satisfactory contracts it may well take on the activity itself.[70] The reverse side of the same coin is the problem encountered if the monopoly is broken up: how far can the transactions, which were previously internalised, be undertaken "contractually between the divorced parties?"[71]

If the break-up of a monopoly is not always the most desirable solution it is then necessary to decide what the regulator should try to do when regulating the firm. Some economists argue that regulation is in fact unnecessary even in the absence of competition. They contend that natural monopolies can be kept efficient by ensuring that there is free entry into the particular market. Others disagree. They believe that regulation of such markets is both necessary and desirable to prevent predatory behaviour,[72] control excess monopoly profits and detect organisational inefficiency in firms with monopoly power. There is, moreover, the aim of fostering competition by allowing other firms to use the distribution network of the monopolist, or what is known as competition through interconnection.[73] These rationales for regulatory intervention have been the subject of vigorous debate between economists,[74] but the existence of regulatory regimes to oversee the privatised industries indicates that governments in the United Kingdom have accepted some of these arguments.

D. Whether to Regulate: The Government's Approach to Regulation

An understanding of the economic theory behind regulation is important. It is equally important to understand the government's approach to regulation. Responsibility for regulatory matters now lies with the Department for Business, Innovation and Skills (BIS),[75] which deals with Business Regulation,[76] and houses the Better Regulation Delivery Office,[77] and the Better Regulation Executive, the latter being a directorate within BIS that takes the lead on the regulatory reform agenda. 11–022

---

[70] Foster, *Privatization, Public Ownership and the Regulation of Natural Monopoly* (1992), p.148.

[71] Foster, *Privatization, Public Ownership and the Regulation of Natural Monopoly* (1992), p.150.

[72] This is, in essence, behaviour designed to drive would-be competitors out of the market in order to preserve the monopolist's power.

[73] Foster, *Privatization, Public Ownership and the Regulation of Natural Monopoly* (1992), pp.1–13 and Ch.5.

[74] There is considerable disagreement as to whether predation is in reality a problem at all, and as to whether the difficulties of defining it render regulatory cure worse than the disease. Compare, R. Bork, *The Antitrust Paradox* (New York: Basic Books, 1978), Ch.7, with Foster, *Privatization, Public Ownership and the Regulation of Natural Monopoly* (1992), pp.163–167.

[75] See *https://www.gov.uk/government/organisations/department-for-business-innovation-skills* [accessed 2 November 2015].

[76] See *https://www.gov.uk/government/policies/business-regulation* [accessed 2 November 2015].

[77] See *https://www.gov.uk/government/organisations/better-regulation-delivery-office* [accessed 2 November 2015].

The government's approach to regulation is evident from the Better Regulation Framework Manual 2015.[78] The guiding principles are that: regulation will only be used where there is no satisfactory alternative; that it will only be used where analysis of costs and benefits demonstrates that the regulatory approach is superior by a clear margin to alternative, self-regulatory or non-regulatory approaches; and where the regulation and enforcement framework can be implemented in a fashion which is proportionate, accountable, consistent, transparent and targeted.

The regulatory approach also includes the "One-in, Two-out rule", which in effect requires each department to assess the net cost to business (IN) of complying with any proposed regulation, ensure that the net cost to business is validated by the independent Regulatory Policy Committee (RPC); and find a deregulatory measure or measures (OUT), which relieve business of twice the cost as any IN. The BRF also places considerable emphasis on sunset clauses in new regulations, whereby policy-makers have to review regulations after five years to determine whether they are still relevant. This is complemented by the "Red Tape Challenge", whereby the public can have their say and help reduce unnecessary and obsolete regulations in our country. European Regulation is to be applied faithfully, but there is to be no "gold-plating" of such regulations, which are to be copied out and transposed into domestic law.

Larger proposed regulatory measures are subject to an Impact Assessment (IA), through which costs and benefits of the regulation can be calculated. The IA requires that the purpose and effect of the measure be specified, that the options listed above have been considered, that the benefits of the measure be identified, that the costs for business and other bodies be estimated, and that there should be consultation with those affected.

11–023 The emphasis placed on assessing whether regulation is warranted and on regulatory simplification[79] has been carried over into legislation. The Deregulation and Contracting Out Act 1994 gave the government broad powers to dispense with, or amend, any provision that had the effect of imposing a burden on business, where it would be possible, without removing any necessary protection, to remove or reduce the burden. This was replaced by the Regulatory Reform Act 2001, and it has now been overtaken by the Legislative and Regulatory Reform Act 2006.

The LRRA 2006 includes two order-making powers which a minister can use to amend primary legislation. The first allows a minister to make a Legislative Reform Order (LRO), for the purpose of removing or reducing burdens. The second allows a minister by LRO to ensure that regulatory functions are exercised so as to comply with the five principles of good regulation. These mandate that regulatory activities should be carried out in a way that is transparent, accountable, proportionate, consistent, and targeted only at cases in which action is needed. The 2006 Act allows LROs to amend primary legislation,

---

[78] See *https://www.gov.uk/government/uploads/system/uploads/attachment_data/file/468831/bis-13-1038-Better-regulation-framework-manual.pdf* [accessed 2 November 2015].

[79] Cabinet Office, *Administrative Burdens—Routes to Reduction* (2006); Department for Business, Enterprise & Regulatory Reform, *Next Steps on Regulatory Reform* (2007).

and in that sense it contains a "Henry VIII" clause.[80] The Act proved to be controversial because of the breadth of these powers, notwithstanding the fact that such statutory instruments are subject to a special procedure.[81]

E. Utilities Regulation: Political, Economic and Social Considerations

The remainder of the analysis will focus on the regulation of utilities. The earlier discussion might have given the impression that the only force at work in this area was economics. This would be mistaken, both in relation to the initial privatisation process, and in relation to the way in which the utility regulators operate. **11–024**

If we consider the *privatisation process itself*, it should not be assumed that the privatised industries in the United Kingdom, such as British Telecom and Gas, were necessarily preserved as monopolies because of their potential for enhanced efficiency. When these public corporations were privatised it would have been possible to enhance competition by the "structural remedy" of breaking up, for example BT, rather than opting for the "regulatory remedy" which was chosen.[82] The preference for the latter appears to have had more to do with political strategy than with alleged benefits of enhanced efficiency which might follow from the preservation of a monopoly. As Vickers and Yarrow state[83]:

> "The objective of promoting the well-being of B.T. was favoured by those in Government wishing to maximise the proceeds from the sale of B.T. shares, their merchant bank advisers, and of course the management of B.T. Especially in view of the Government's evident desire to privatize B.T. speedily, good relations with B.T. management were imperative, and they came to have considerable influence."

The interplay between different forces is equally marked when we consider the general way in which the *regulators supervising the utilities operate*. It has been argued forcefully by Prosser[84] that the enabling legislation that governs the privatised utilities, and the way in which this has been interpreted by the relevant regulatory authorities, shows that three different tasks are being performed in this area.

The first is the regulation of monopoly itself, which is most evident in the constraints imposed by the regulator on the prices that can be charged by the regulated entity. The second is what is termed regulation for competition. This is designed to create the conditions for competition to exist and ensure that it continues to exist. This is exemplified by the grant of licenses to firms other than the dominant firm in the area, and the fixing of conditions for the interconnection of competing but interdependent systems. The third task undertaken by the regulator is social regulation. Here the regulatory rationale is not primarily economic, but social, and is linked to concepts of public service. It is exemplified

---

[80] See Ch.15.

[81] See Ch.15.

[82] Foster, *Privatization, Public Ownership and the Regulation of Natural Monopoly* (1992), p.121.

[83] Vickers and Yarrow, *Privatization, An Economic Analysis* (1988), pp.235–236.

[84] Prosser, *Law and the Regulators* (Oxford: Oxford University Press, 1997), Ch.1.

by provisions made for the securing of universal service by some utilities. The regulatory principles applied by the regulators are therefore "not limited to those concerned with the maximization of economic efficiency … but include those based on more egalitarian or rights-based arguments".[85] This development has been fuelled in part by EU law, which requires Member States to impose universal service obligations on certain service providers.[86] We shall return to these arguments in the ensuing analysis.

F. Utilities Regulation: The Broader Context

11–025 The discussion in the previous section leads naturally to the broader context within which the privatisation of utilities occurred. It is important to recall the earlier discussion about the changing nature of the public–private divide.[87] The privatisation of utilities has been but part of a broader development.

This led to the creation of what Freedland has termed a public-service sector,[88] which is distinct from the purely public and the purely private sectors. The essential characteristic of the public-service sector is that the state no longer assumes direct responsibility for the provision of certain services, but nonetheless retains certain secondary responsibility in these areas. This secondary responsibility is manifested through, for example, the creation of regulatory regimes to oversee the activities of the privatised utilities.

An equally important feature of the public-service sector is that the citizen has a relationship both with the service provider, who has the primary responsibility for the delivery of the service, and the state itself, which retains a secondary responsibility within the relevant area. The relationship therefore becomes trilateral rather than bilateral.

6. UTILITIES AND MARKET POWER: WHO SHOULD REGULATE

11–026 The choice of "regulator" for market power has altered considerably over the last 400 years. Five differing institutions have undertaken the regulatory mantle.

A. The Common Law and the Courts

11–027 The common law has exercised influence over corporations with monopoly power. Two areas are of principal interest, one which is well known, the other far less so.

The area that is relatively well known is the law of monopolies stricto sensu. Somewhat paradoxically, this was the less important of the two areas in which the

---

[85] Prosser, *Law and the Regulators* (1997), pp.30–31.

[86] See, e.g. Communications Act 2003 ss.65–72; T. Prosser, *The Limits of Competition Law, Markets and Public Services* (Oxford: Oxford University Press, 2005).

[87] See Ch.4.

[88] Freedland, "Law, Public Services, and Citizenship—New Domains, New Regimes", in M. Freedland and S. Sciarra (eds), *Public Services and Citizenship in European Law, Public and Labour Law Perspectives* (Oxford: Oxford University Press, 1998), Ch.1.

common law courts exercised control over market power. Such control existed, but the leading cases had as much to do with other issues as they did with the adverse economic effect of market power. Thus in *Darcy v Allen*[89] it was held that a royal grant of a patent to manufacture and import playing cards was void if it created a monopoly. Two main themes pervade the court's judgment: the desire to protect the right to work which would be weakened should the patent be allowed to stand, and the desire not to allow the Crown prerogative powers of this novel form. It would therefore be mistaken to allow such cases on the law of monopolies to create the impression that the common law courts were zealous in their control of market power per se; nor should one believe that the right to work precluded the existence of any monopoly power. As Letwin states[90]:

> "The common-law right to work was predicated on an economic system that would protect the established trades from competition, whether from foreign workmen, improperly qualified English workmen, overly aggressive guilds, or domestic monopolists. The right to work was protected by giving each guild a monopoly, and Darcy's grant was condemned not because it was a monopoly and therefore necessarily bad, but because it was a bad monopoly."

The other area in which the common law courts exercised influence is less well known. It was almost forgotten, but it is of considerable importance. The courts held that the common law imposed an obligation on those who had market power to charge no more than a reasonable price for their goods. The courts were in effect imposing a common law based species of price regulation on those who wielded monopoly power, and they reasoned through the rationale for doing so from first principles.

In *Allnutt*[91] the question was whether the London Dock Company, which by licence from Parliament possessed a monopoly to receive certain wines, could lawfully exclude from the docks a cargo owner who refused to pay their schedule of charges. Lord Ellenborough reasoned as follows.[92] While a man could fix his own price for the use of his property, he could not do so where the public had a right to resort to the premises and to make use of them. Where a person had the benefit of a monopoly this entailed a correlative responsibility, the consequence of which was that he could charge no more than a reasonable price for the service offered. The monopoly itself could be either "legal" or "factual": it could result from the grant of an exclusive licence from Parliament, or it could exist because, on the facts, the provider of the service controlled the entirety of the space available for the warehousing of the goods. The statute, which required that the goods be warehoused in the Dock Company's premises, was not passed solely for the benefit of the Company, but also for the benefit of trade and the public. The latter purposes could be defeated if the Dock Company was at liberty to charge any price it chose.

---

[89] *Darcy v Allen* (1602) 11 Co. Rep. 84 (*The Case of Monopolies*).

[90] W. Letwin, *Law and Economic Policy in America: The Evolution of the Sherman Antitrust Act* (New York Random House, 1965), pp.28–29. The court in *Darcy v Allen* did, however, take note of the potential for monopoly power to lead to price increases.

[91] *Allnutt v Inglis* (1810) 12 East 527 KBD.

[92] *Allnutt* (1810) 12 East 527 at 538–539. See also, *Bolt v Stennett* (1800) 8 T.R. 606 KBD.

11–028 Similar reasoning is evident in other areas where monopoly power existed. In *Pawlett*[93] the corporation possessed the right to hold two fairs each year. It customarily received a "toll" of 2d on the sale of certain items at the fair. The defendant refused to pay the toll. The court held that where the word toll was found in a charter it should be taken to mean reasonable toll. It was not open to the King to allow a corporation to charge an unreasonable toll, and any such excess charge could be recovered in a legal action. The principle underlying such cases is the same as that expounded above. The grantee of rights to a market or fair was the holder of an exclusive privilege. The grant was not merely for his benefit, but for the benefit of the public and the trade. It could be defeated if any price whatsoever could be charged.[94]

This reasoning receives further support from that used in the context of common callings. There is abundant authority for the proposition that those who exercise a common calling can charge only a reasonable price for their services.[95] The history of common callings is complex and cannot be fully developed here. The origin of the term common calling was simply one that was available to the public generally, "a holding out". There could therefore be common carriers, common innkeepers, and common millers. Those who exercised a common calling had a duty to serve at a reasonable price. Historically this obligation appears to have evolved due to economic and social conditions. In times of social hardship, such as the period following the Black Death, it could be possible for surviving tradesmen to exact "any price they pleased".[96] The obligation to serve at reasonable rates was intended to counteract this potential for abuse of market power. As the law developed the types of industry that retained the label "common" tended to be those with a monopoly character, such as railways and public utilities.

It would therefore be mistaken to regard the common law as having had no regulatory role within this area. There is moreover a link between common law regulation by the courts and departmental regulation: the two formed an intersecting web as will be apparent from the subsequent discussion.

B. Departmental Regulation

11–029 The pattern of administrative development in the 19th century has already been reviewed and one aspect is of particular relevance here.[97] Many administrative functions during this period were undertaken neither by central nor local

---

[93] *Corporation of Stamford v Pawlett* (1830) 1 C. & J. 57 at 400.

[94] See also, *Gard v Callard* (1817) 6 M. & S. 69; *Wright v Bruister* (1832) 4 B. & Ald. 116; *Attorney General v Horner* (1912) 107 L.T. 547; *Duke of Newcastle v Worksop Urban DC* [1902] 2 Ch. 145 at 161; *Nyali v Attorney General* [1955] 1 All E.R. 646, CA at 651; [1956] 2 All E.R. 689 at 694; B. McAllister, "Lord Hale and Business Affected with a Public Interest" (1929–30) 43 Harv. L. Rev. 759; P. Craig, "Constitutions, Property and Regulation" [1991] P.L. 538.

[95] *Harris v Packwood* (1810) 3 Taunt 263; *Thompson v Lacy* (1820) 3 B. & Ald. 283 KBD; *Ashmole v Wainwright* (1842) 2 Q.B. 837 QBD at 845; *Peek v North Staffs Ry. Co* (1862) 11 H.L.C. 473; *Great Western Railway v Sutton* (1869) L.R. 4 HL 226 at 237–238.

[96] N. Arterburn, "The Origin and First Test of Public Callings" (1926–27) 75 Univ. of Penn L. Rev. 411, 421.

[97] See Ch.2.

government. They were often performed by corporations, which had special statutory authority insofar as this was necessary to enable them to carry out their tasks. The provision of most utilities, such as water, lighting, canals, railways and roads, was carried on in this way even after the reform of the municipal corporations. Moreover, such bodies normally possessed a large degree of market power. A considerable amount of time was spent in the Commons on the legislation that empowered the statutory undertakings to perform these tasks. For example, in 1844 there were 248 Railway Bills, which necessitated a system of Commons' committees in order to oversee their passage. It also led to the introduction of certain "Model Bills" concerned with issues such as the compulsory purchase of land, and railway development, which were intended to ensure greater uniformity in the measures which emerged.[98] The growing need to pave roads in order to render them suitable for increased use by heavier wheeled traffic was the motivation behind the turnpike trusts, and by 1830 there were 1,100 in existence.[99] Once again, each such turnpike trust derived its power from a local Act of Parliament, subject to supervision pursuant to more general Turnpike Acts. Improvement Commissioners, who derived their authority from a local Act of Parliament, often undertook the provision of municipal lighting and cleansing.

The rates to be charged for services by those who possessed a degree of monopoly power granted to them by statute had to be regulated. A common technique was for direct departmental supervision of the "tariff" which the statutory undertaking proposed to charge. This was used, for example, in relation to roads and canals. The trustees or commissioners would forward to the Board of Trade a detailed list of the prices they intended to levy, specifying, for example, that the toll to be charged for a wagon of certain size and weight which journeyed from Oxford to Woodstock would be Xd. The Board of Trade had to approve such charges before they could be lawfully levied. Direct departmental price regulation in areas of market power was, therefore, quite common.

We can now understand the link between common law and departmental price regulation. The former was utilised particularly in those circumstances where direct departmental price regulation was absent. This could be for one of two reasons: either the area might be one over which no such departmental supervision had yet been established; or it might be an area where it was difficult to exercise departmental supervision. This normally operated through a relatively fixed series of possible charges: so much per mile, per weight, etc. There could be areas where this type of advance delineation of charges might not be possible, principally because the variables that could affect the price were more complex. It was such areas in which the common law proscription that "unreasonable charges" should not be levied remained of particular relevance.[100]

---

[98] Sir N. Chester, *The English Administrative System 1780–1870* (Oxford: Oxford University Press, 1981), pp.118–119.

[99] Chester, *The English Administrative System 1780–1870* (1981), p.326.

[100] The common law insistence upon the reasonableness of prices charged by public utilities has been of particular importance in the USA, see W. McCurdy, "The Power of a Public Utility to Fix Its Rates in the Absence of Regulatory Legislation" (1924–25) 38 Harv. L Rev. 202; *Smyth v Ames* 169 US 466 (1898); *Texas & Pacific Ry v Abilene Cotton Oil Co* 204 US 426 (1906). The common law authorities were also of seminal importance in determining the constitutionality of later attempts at statutory

C. Regulation by Tribunal or Board

11–030 The importance of Boards within the 19th-century administrative landscape was considered above.[101] They provided a further institutional technique through which to regulate entrepreneurial behaviour. Railway regulation within the last century can be examined by way of a brief example.[102]

Prior to 1840 the main regulatory body was the Railway Commission. Although its formal powers were limited it had the authority to certify that a railway was "complete" before it could commence operations. It could attach conditions to its certificate, and was willing to use this as a mechanism for requiring minimum standards of service by the railways. Failure to abide by the conditions of the certificate led to its revocation, and the Commission published criteria for judging applications.[103] From the 1840s significant responsibility was transferred to the railway department of the Board of Trade.[104] The department, however, suffered a political set-back in 1844–1845 and this combined with concern over railway speculation led to the establishment of an independent Railway Commission in 1846.[105] This body was to be short-lived: the railway boom collapsed, the Commission was dissolved and its powers reassigned to the Board of Trade.

Experimentation with differing institutional devices to regulate railways continued in the 1850s with the assignment of responsibility to the common law courts, where "it languished for almost twenty years, hostage to the notion that all adjudication is properly the business of the courts".[106] A further turn of the institutional wheel occurred in 1873. A new Railway and Canal Commission was established with a range of activities including the fixing of tolls, fares and routes. The Commission was also meant to ensure that the public could use the facilities with as much ease as possible.[107] The commissioners had power to inspect property, require the production of documents and the giving of testimony, and could use assessors with technical knowledge.[108] Notwithstanding these powers the Commission established in 1873 was not a noted success, with one critic observing that it had "the power enough to annoy the railroads, and not power enough to help the public efficiently".[109] A new Railway and Canal Commission was set up in 1888, and although it enjoyed some early success, it,

---

regulation of price, *Munn v Illinois* 94 US 113 (1877); M. Finkelstein, "From *Munn v Illinois* to *Tyson v Banton*, A Study in the Judicial Process" (1927) 27 Col. L. Rev. 769.

[101] See Ch.2.

[102] H. Parris, *Government and the Railways in Nineteenth Century Britain* (London: Routledge, 1965); Foster, *Privatization, Public Ownership and the Regulation of Natural Monopoly* (1992), Chs 1 and 2.

[103] H. Arthurs, *'Without the Law,' Administrative Justice and Legal Pluralism in Nineteenth Century England* (University of Toronto Press, 1985), pp.120 and 124.

[104] Railways Regulation Act 1840.

[105] Commissioners of Railways Act 1846.

[106] Arthurs, *'Without the Law,' Administrative Justice and Legal Pluralism in Nineteenth Century England* (1985), p.126.

[107] Regulation of Railways Act 1873.

[108] Arthurs, *'Without the Law,' Administrative Justice and Legal Pluralism in Nineteenth Century England* (1985), p.128.

[109] Arthurs, *'Without the Law,' Administrative Justice and Legal Pluralism in Nineteenth Century England* (1985), p.129.

like its predecessors, turned out to be an ineffective regulatory mechanism. Control over the rates charged by railways was assigned to the Railway Rates Tribunal in 1921, and in 1947 the railways were nationalised.

D. Public Ownership

The nationalisation of the railways provides a suitable transition to the option of public ownership. Earlier discussion has revealed how the choice of regulatory institution has been influenced by the political beliefs of those who operate the system. Thus, the very demise of the board system was caused by the growing insistence that there should be a member of the executive directly answerable in the Commons for major spheres of administrative activity.[110] Certain changes in the institutions to regulate the railways were motivated by the wish for more direct legislative control. 11–031

The shift towards public ownership provides a further exemplification of this theme. While the reasons for nationalisation were eclectic, one prominent rationale was that major repositories of market power should be within state ownership in order that excess profits should not be left in private hands, and in order to ensure that the industry operated in the public interest. The general difficulties that beset the nationalised industries were considered above.[111] What is relevant here is the fact that public ownership of a firm with market power does not, in and of itself, mean that the firm will necessarily be operated so as to further the public interest.[112] This point can be understood by considering the gas industry prior to privatisation.

The industry was nationalised by the Gas Act 1948, and there were 12 area boards that were largely autonomous as regards the manufacture and supply of gas. Operations were later centralised[113] with a single public corporation assuming responsibility for the activities covered by the 12 boards. As Vickers and Yarrow state[114]:

> "By the 1970's the policy framework for the industry had been brought into line with that pertaining in telecommunications and electricity generation: there was a single national firm, protected from competition by statutory entry barriers and regulated by a department of central government. The underlying rationale for this approach was the familiar argument that the core activities of gas transmission and distribution constituted a natural monopoly, and that the operation of more than one firm in the market would therefore lead to cost inefficiencies. To protect consumers from the effects of the resulting market power, it was considered desirable that the industry should be publicly owned and controlled."

The transfer of the industry to public ownership did not, however, necessarily serve to ensure that the consumers really were protected. Important aspects of the operation of the British Gas Corporation were open to serious question. Thus British Gas was granted sole rights to purchase gas from other producers. The ostensible reason was to prevent the accumulation of excessive profits by such 11–032

---

110 Ch.2.

111 See Ch.4.

112 Foster, *Privatization, Public Ownership and the Regulation of Natural Monopoly* (1992), Ch.3.

113 Gas Act 1972.

114 Vickers and Yarrow, *Privatization, An Economic Analysis* (1988), p.255.

producers, but it is highly questionable whether the award of this privileged position to British Gas was the optimum method of achieving this goal.[115] Moreover, research indicates that British Gas was selling its product at too low a price.[116] Consumers can be harmed by paying too little as well as by being overcharged. If the former occurs the product is rendered "artificially" attractive as compared with other possible fuels. Too much is consumed at the artificially low price, with the consequence that resources within society are allocated inefficiently. Irrespective therefore of the problems caused by ad hoc governmental interference with public corporations, the retention of ownership in public hands did not always lead to the accrual of public benefit.

E. Privatisation and Agencies

11–033 If the move towards public ownership was motivated by the political beliefs of its advocates, this was equally true of the shift towards privatisation. The general reasons for this shift have been considered above, as have the difficulties that face the regulatory organisations.[117]

The decision as to "who" should regulate market power has come down firmly in favour of agencies. This strategy bears some analogy to the regimes which existed in the 19th century, where a private firm with market power would be regulated by a commission or board.[118] Experience from this period also indicates that the efficacy of such regulatory devices will depend crucially on the degree of market power wielded by the private firm, and the range of regulatory powers granted to the board or commission. These two factors are central to the analysis that follows. This will be concerned with "how" market power is controlled under the present regime of privatised industry plus regulatory agency.

7. UTILITIES AND MARKET POWER: HOW TO REGULATE

A. Selling State Assets: Constitutional Implications

11–034 The privatisation programme entailed the sale of assets that had been in public ownership in the form of nationalised industries.[119] This is a trite proposition, but it is important nonetheless. The fact that the assets were public raises a legitimate public interest in seeing that they were disposed of on beneficial economic terms, or at the very least that the public coffers did not end up being under-compensated on the sale of public property.

The government used two main methods for the sale of public assets, offers for sale and tender offers. The former involved offering shares to the public at a price fixed in advance of the sale. The latter entailed inviting bids at or above a stated minimum price; the final price was then established when all bids had been

[115] This statutory privilege was terminated by the Oil and Gas (Enterprise) Act 1982.
[116] Vickers and Yarrow, *Privatization, An Economic Analysis* (1988), pp.256–257.
[117] See Ch.4.
[118] See Ch.2.
[119] T. Daintith and M. Sah, "Privatisation and the Economic Neutrality of the Constitution" [1993] P.L. 465.

received. Offers for sale were used more widely than tender offers, largely because they were simpler to operate. The latter are, however, probably more accurate economically, since they do not require a precise estimate of the value of the firm to be made prior to the sale itself. This is advantageous because most assets sold to the public did not have a previously quoted value, and there was therefore a relative scarcity of information on which to base estimates of value. The tender offer procedure which "permits the market to establish the valuation therefore has substantial appeal".[120]

Whether the proceeds from the sales would have been significantly improved by greater reliance on tender offers may be debatable. However, few would argue that the public coffers received the real value of the assets sold. As Mayer and Meadowcroft state[121]:

> "Whatever one's views about the desirability of a programme of privatization, considerable concern must be felt about the techniques that have been employed in implementing the programme to date. As set out at the beginning of this article there are three primary considerations that may have influenced the form of the asset sales: extent of ownership, costs of sale, and disruption to markets. Certainly on the first two there is little evidence that objectives have been met: costs have been high, primarily as a consequence of underpricing of assets, and large personal shareholdings have only been maintained for very short periods. Furthermore, there would appear to be a simple way of avoiding high costs by staggering sales, which would also diminish financing disruptions to equity markets."

It might be felt that this under-valuation of state assets was "unfortunate", but that it did not have constitutional or legal implications. This assumption bears testimony to the limited nature of our constitutional constructs. Let us imagine the converse situation in which the state is nationalising assets held by private individuals. If those assets were "forcibly" acquired at a value significantly less than that determined by the market, lawyers would immediately talk of interference with private rights, expropriation without proper compensation and infringement of private autonomy.[122] The situation in which the state decides to sell public property, and does so at a price which is too low, prompts no such automatic legal response. No conception of "public property rights" comes readily to hand.

The distinctive manner in which we respond to these similar situations provides a good example of Daintith's thesis concerning the exercise of dominium powers.[123] The legal response where the government can be said to "own" something, whether money or other assets, is far more muted than it is where the government operates so as to command others to do something with their **11–035**

[120] C. Mayer and S. Meadowcroft, "Selling Public Assets: Techniques and Financial Implications", in J. Kay, C. Mayer and D. Thompson (eds), *Privatization and Regulation—the U.K. Experience* (Oxford: Oxford University Press, 1986), p.325.

[121] Mayer and Meadowcroft, "Selling Public Assets: Techniques and Financial Implications", in Kay, Mayer and Thompson (eds), *Privatization and Regulation—the U.K. Experience* (1986), p.339.

[122] Whether an effective legal remedy could be provided would depend upon the form of the governmental action: the sovereignty of parliament would serve to protect such governmental action if it was enshrined in a statute. It would now be possible to make a challenge under the Human Rights Act 1998 and secure a declaration of incompatibility under ss.3–4.

[123] Daintith, "Legal Analysis of Economic Policy" (1982) 9 Jnl. Law & Soc. 191.

property. In the former situation the government is implicitly treated like a private individual and can dispose of "its" property on the terms it thinks best. If the bargain is bad so be it.

The very fact that we draw a "legal blank" where the government undervalues state assets is reflective of the limited nature of our constitutional concepts. It is clear that such concepts can be utilised in the context of privatisation, as experience from France indicates. The Conseil Constitutionnel applied constitutional provisions to the sale of state holdings. While it held that the basic law on privatisation did not infringe the Constitution it attached a number of important conditions to the privatisation process. As Prosser states[124]:

> "A central issue was the pricing of the enterprises to be privatized. The deputies had argued that it would be unconstitutional to sell enterprises below their true value as this would breach constitutional principles of equality and would give vendors an unfair advantage; indeed it was argued that the obligation to sell by 1991 could have precisely this effect, and could also lead to transfers to foreigners threatening national independence. The Conseil accepted that both the Constitutional principle of equality and the protection for rights of property in the Declaration of the Rights of Man prohibited the sale of public goods to private parties at a price below their value; these principles applied to the property of the state as well as to that of private individuals."

The French government anticipated this response of the court and proposed that an independent body of experts should undertake the valuation work. A Privatisation Commission was established that valued the assets to be sold. The minister established the actual sale price, but it could not be below that recommended by the Commission.[125]

The absence of a written constitution, combined with the characterisation of public assets as government property, to be disposed of like an ordinary private sale, renders it difficult to reach the same conclusion in this country. There are, however, threads of legal reasoning which point in a more interventionist direction. Thus, the courts have, for example, held that local authorities owe a fiduciary duty towards their ratepayers in the way in which they manage local funds.[126] The application of this concept has been criticised. However, if such a concept exists it is difficult on principle to see why an analogous idea should not apply to central government's duties towards taxpayers. A sensible and sensitive use of such a concept could provide the basis for the development of public property rights better suited to the needs of the age.

---

[124] *The Privatization of Public Enterprises in France and Great Britain, The State, Constitutions and Public Policy*, EUI Working Paper No.88/364 (1988), p.37; C. Graham and T. Prosser, *Privatizing Public Enterprises, Constitutions, the State and Regulation in Comparative Perspective* (Oxford: Oxford University Press, 1991).

[125] *The Privatization of Public Enterprises in France and Great Britain, The State, Constitutions and Public Policy*, pp.38–39.

[126] See Ch.19.

B. The Regulatory Regime: Legal Powers and Legal Constraints, the Initial Regime for Gas

The law both empowers and constrains. This, like the proposition that began the previous section, is trite. It is also important, and particularly so in the context of the regulatory mechanisms. The success of regulatory machinery will be crucially dependent on the degree of monopoly power that resides with the privatised firm, and the powers accorded to the regulator. The greater the degree of monopoly power statutorily preserved to the privatised company, the more necessary it is for the regulator to have effective supervisory powers, since the firm will be relatively immune from the discipline of the market. The legal structure under which the firm is privatised will therefore be of considerable importance. The legal rules will both empower and constrain the privatised corporation, and will also empower and constrain the regulatory agency. The effectiveness of the new scheme will be dependent upon these respective powers. This is evident from the earlier discussion of the telecommunications industry,[127] and can be demonstrated by considering privatisation of the gas industry. **11–036**

Historically, the major activities of the gas industry were[128]: the production of natural gas; transmissions of gas to landing points; transmission of the gas to regional take-off points; local distribution of gas to customers' premises; the sale of gas; and the sale and installation of gas appliances. Prior to privatisation the British Gas Corporation had a monopoly in the third, fourth and fifth of these tasks, and also enjoyed a statutory exclusive right to buy gas produced by other companies.

The industry was fully privatised by the Gas Act 1986. Section 1 empowered the secretary of state to appoint the Director General of Gas Supply, who headed the Office of Gas Supply (Ofgas). The Gas Consumers' Council, a watch-dog body for consumers, was established by s.2. British Gas's monopoly privilege in relation to the supply of gas through pipes was abolished by s.3, and this opened the possibility for alternative suppliers to sell their product to customers. Section 4 established guidelines for the DGGS and the secretary of state in pursuit of their functions; these included: protecting the interests of consumers in relation to the prices charged and the other terms of supply; promoting efficiency by gas suppliers and users; preventing dangers which can arise from gas transmission; and enabling persons to compete effectively in the supply of gas which, in relation to any premises, exceeds 25,000 therms a year. Section 7 empowered the secretary of state to authorise a "public gas supplier" to supply the product to any premises within a designated area, but s.7(9) precluded such an authorisation in any area that was within 25 yards from the main of another public gas supplier. Given that British Gas is an authorised public gas supplier, this had the effect of preventing a new gas supplier from emerging to challenge British Gas in the ordinary domestic sales market. Section 8 did, however, allow the secretary of state to authorise other persons to supply gas where the supply was expected to exceed 25,000 therms per annum. The effect of this was to allow competition in the provision of gas to large commercial customers. Subsequent legislation

[127] See Ch.4.

[128] Vickers and Yarrow, *Privatization, An Economic Analysis* (1988), p.248.

empowered the secretary of state to modify or remove the 25,000 therm condition.[129] Section 19 empowered the DGGS to grant an applicant the right to use a pipeline owned by a public gas supplier.

11–037 The legal powers and constraints applied to British Gas and the DGGS left little doubt that the former emerged in a strong position as a result of the original legislation. This can be understood by reflecting on their respective powers and duties. British Gas was empowered in three important ways by the 1986 legislation.

First, the law sanctified the continued existence of British Gas as a single corporation post-privatisation. The assets of the previously nationalised industry were transferred to a successor corporation.[130] The possibility of restructuring the industry prior to privatisation was therefore not pursued. Such a course would have been feasible, and could have been achieved by the creation of 12 separate regional gas companies, together with an enterprise that would operate the transmission system.[131] This restructuring would have increased competition within the system.[132] It would have lowered the barriers to entry and facilitated the task of other gas producers who wished to become direct sellers of gas to, for example, large industrial concerns. It would have reduced the exclusive purchasing power of British Gas, since each of the regional companies would have had to compete in the purchase of supplies from other gas producers. It would have improved regulatory control, for although each distribution company would still have had monopoly power within its own region, Ofgas "would have been able to draw on information from several independent sources, opening up the possibility of yardstick competition".[133]

The failure to pursue such a policy of regionalisation, despite its competitive advantages, was the result of political factors.[134] A restructuring of the industry would have slowed down the privatisation process, with the consequence that the receipts from the sale would have accrued to the revenue authorities at a date that was less advantageous to the government, given its concerns over the public sector borrowing targets. The management of the British Gas Corporation was hostile to any such restructuring. It was possible that short-term gas prices would have increased to the consumer, which was disadvantageous in electoral terms, even though restructuring the industry and installing greater competition would have yielded greater medium and long term efficiency. The decision not to reorganise the industry has been termed a response to interest group pressure from management and consumers in which short-term electoral considerations took precedence over longer-term economic efficiency.[135] There is no doubt that this decision coloured the privatisation process, and that the dominance of the privatised corporation was augmented by other legal powers it was accorded. It is to these that we now turn.

---

129 Competition and Service (Utilities) Act 1992 s.37.

130 Gas Act 1986 ss.49–61.

131 E. Hammond, D. Helm and D. Thompson, "British Gas: Options for Privatization", in Kay, Mayer and Thompson (eds), *Privatization and Regulation—the U.K. Experience* (1986), Ch.13.

132 Vickers and Yarrow, *Privatization, An Economic Analysis* (1988), pp.268–269.

133 Vickers and Yarrow, *Privatization, An Economic Analysis* (1988), p.269

134 Vickers and Yarrow, *Privatization, An Economic Analysis* (1988), pp.270–271.

135 Vickers and Yarrow, *Privatization, An Economic Analysis* (1988), p.271.

Second, the original legal regime established by the Gas Act 1986 insulated the dominant privatised firm from new competitors. As noted above, s.7(9) effectively precluded new entrants into the market for the domestic sale of gas, although, as seen, later legislation modified this. There were, moreover, significant difficulties to be faced by the new entrant who attempted to supply to larger industrial concerns. British Gas had access to low price gas and could probably undercut potential new entrants, or even engage in disguised "predatory pricing" to deter a new competitor. Furthermore, control over the pipeline network provided British Gas with certain tactical advantages. New entrants had to negotiate for the transfer of their gas, "thus providing the incumbent with advance notice of its rival's intentions and giving the former time to offer more favourable terms to the targeted customer".[136] This was all the more important given that the proscriptions in the legislation on giving undue preference to any person did not it seems apply to sales to industrial concerns. British Gas could therefore price as it chose in relation to these concerns.[137] **11–038**

Third, given that the privatised industry was not restructured, and given the difficulties faced by new entrants into the industry, the pricing formula for gas supplies to tariff customers[138] was of particular importance. The details of the formula were complex and cannot be examined here, but one detailed study concluded that the "pricing constraints imposed on British Gas can hardly be described as stringent".[139]

The powers given to the DGGS and to Ofgas were not strong when juxtaposed to those of British Gas. The DGGS could impose conditions on the grant of authorisation to a public gas supplier.[140] These conditions could then be modified either by agreement with the supplier,[141] or the DGGS could make a reference to the Monopolies and Mergers Commission. The MMC could specify the ways in which modification of the authorisation could remedy any possible harmful effects on the public interest that was caused by the gas supplier.[142] The DGGS also had power to secure compliance with the authorisation conditions,[143] and to investigate complaints made to him by the Gas Consumers' Council and certain interested parties.[144] He had to keep under review the general provision of gas supplies and could publish information and advice to customers.[145] Notwithstanding this array of legal powers, the original regulatory mechanism was relatively weak for the following reasons. **11–039**

[136] Vickers and Yarrow, *Privatization, An Economic Analysis* (1988), p.275.

[137] The obligation not to show undue preference was contained in Gas Act 1986 s.9(2), but only applied to the supply of gas "to persons entitled to a supply". The effect of s.10(5) was that a public gas supplier was under no obligation as such to supply gas to any premises in excess of 25,000 therms per year, which effectively removed the force of s.9(2) from sales to major gas users such as large industry. The only limit on this freedom was the general provisions of competition law.

[138] Tariff customers are, in essence, those within the market who receive less than 25,000 therms per year, Gas Act 1986 s.14. Large industrial concerns are therefore not included.

[139] Vickers and Yarrow, *Privatization, An Economic Analysis* (1988), p.265.

[140] Gas Act 1986 s.7(7).

[141] Gas Act 1986 s.23.

[142] Gas Act 1986 ss.24 and 26.

[143] Gas Act 1986 ss.28, 29 and 30.

[144] Gas Act 1986 s.31.

[145] Gas Act 1986 ss.34–35.

The DGGS could not alter the legal structure of the 1986 Act itself and this placed British Gas in a strong monopolistic position which, for the reasons given above, it was difficult for competitors to assail. An important factor in determining the effectiveness of the DGGS was the degree of access to information concerning costs, etc. from British Gas. The DGGS had statutory power to require information,[146] but the provisions of the authorisation granted to British Gas concerning its accounting did not place the DGGS in a strong position. The company had to prepare separate accounts for its gas supply business, but this was defined very broadly and covered the bulk of its activities. It was therefore

> "... difficult to assess whether or not British Gas is willing to make its transmission grid available to third party suppliers on reasonable terms, since there is no requirement to treat the transmission system as a separate cost centre".[147]

It was also difficult more generally to monitor the efficiency of the firm. The relationship between the initial DGGS and the industry was adversarial,[148] and the general conclusion reached by Vickers and Yarrow was not encouraging[149]:

> "We conclude that the most fundamental weaknesses of U.K. regulatory policy are associated with an excessively short-term view of the underlying economic issues. The Government has been content to focus upon the initial post-privatization period, leaving many fundamental issues unresolved ... What has happened is that one of the major deficiencies of the U.K. control system for nationalized industries—preoccupation with short-term political issues—has been duplicated in the policy framework set for the regulated privately owned gas industry."

C. The Regulatory Regime: Legal Powers and Legal Constraints, the Modified Regime for Gas

11–040 The regulation of the gas industry has moved on since the initial legislation. The adversarial relationship between the regulator and British Gas led to references to the MMC. The MMC review laid the groundwork for later government proposals concerning the increase in competition in the domestic market for gas. The MMC proposed the divestment by British Gas of its trading business by 1997, to be followed by the opening up of the domestic market over a five-year period.[150] The government decided that it would be sufficient if the trading business was separated from its other activities, but decided also that competition in the domestic market should be introduced more rapidly. Meanwhile, British Gas came to the conclusion that it would separate into two companies, TransCo International dealing with transport and production, and British Gas Energy dealing with supply, retail and service.

The Gas Act 1995 was passed to facilitate these changes. The Utilities Act 2000 amended the Gas Act 1986. The separate regulatory authorities for gas and

146 Gas Act 1986 s.38.
147 Vickers and Yarrow, *Privatization, An Economic Analysis* (1988), p.263.
148 Prosser, *Law and the Regulators* (1997), pp.95–96.
149 Vickers and Yarrow, *Privatization, An Economic Analysis* (1988), p.278.
150 *Gas* (1993), Cm.2314.

electricity were replaced by Ofgem,[151] which protects consumer interests by promoting competition and regulating monopoly. It must have regard to the need to secure that all reasonable demands for gas are met, and must have regard to the interests of those who are disabled or chronically sick, those who are of pensionable age, those with low incomes, and those who live in rural areas. Ofgem and the secretary of state must carry out their respective functions in the manner best calculated to promote efficiency and economy on the part of the gas companies. They must promote the efficient use of gas, secure viable long-term energy supply, and protect the public from the dangers arising from gas. The secretary of state is required to issue guidance on social and environmental matters, which Ofgem must take into account when discharging its duties.

It is clear that the emphasis has shifted to what Prosser termed regulation for competition.[152] This is evident in the emphasis placed on the protection of consumers through competition wherever this is appropriate.[153] It is apparent in the fact that the areas held by persons holding gas transportation licences are not exclusive,[154] and by the duty imposed on gas transporters to facilitate competition in the supply of gas.[155]

The regime also contains elements of social regulation. The scheme introduced in 1995 brought new issues of social regulation to the fore, most notably provisions designed to prevent "cherry-picking". The licence conditions issued to gas suppliers were structured so as to minimise any attempt to restrict supply to the most profitable customers within a particular area, or to exclude supply from those who are old, disabled or of pensionable age.[156]

Thus, as Prosser states,[157] the "regulation of suppliers to enforce licence requirements concerning social obligations is likely to become more, not less important" over time. This has been borne out by the obligation to have regard to the position of the disabled, old, etc. and the obligation to give guidance on social and environmental matters, contained in the Utilities Act 2000.

D. The Regulatory Regime: Institutional Design

The discussion thus far has focused on the regulatory regime established for the gas and the telecommunications industries.[158] It is now necessary to stand back from the detail of these areas and consider some more general pre-conditions for effective regulatory control. 11–041

An appropriate starting point is the importance of *information*. As Foster notes,

[151] See *https://www.ofgem.gov.uk/home* [accessed 2 November 2015].
[152] Prosser, *Law and the Regulators* (1997), pp.104–106.
[153] Gas Act 1986 s.4AA.
[154] Gas Act 1986 s.7.
[155] Gas Act 1986 s.9.
[156] Prosser, *Law and the Regulators* (1997), pp.108–110.
[157] Prosser, *Law and the Regulators* (1997), pp.109–110.
[158] For telecommunications, see Ch.4.

> "... a state of unbalanced or asymmetric information benefits the regulated by comparison with not only the regulator, but also actual and potential competitors and customers."[159]

Regulated bodies have a number of tactics to reduce the effectiveness of the regulatory machinery. They may produce too little information; they may give too much in a form that is unclear or opaque; or they may offer the desired information too slowly.[160] An effective regulatory scheme requires the production of relevant information on a periodic basis, set against the background of clear objectives as to why the information is needed.[161] The information should be geared to detection of the offences the regulatory regime hopes to control.[162]

A second aspect of effective regulatory control concerns the *objectives* of the regulatory regime. The powers of the regulatory authorities are set out in broad terms, coupled with the more specific proscription of certain types of activity, such as discriminatory pricing. It is clear that a significant part of the remit of the regulatory bodies is economic in nature, whether in the form of protecting consumers from excessive prices or potential competitors from predation. It may be less apparent how far non-economic considerations should feature as part of the regulator's objectives, such as regulating pricing in a way which is geared towards those with low incomes. There are difficulties with this type of regulation. Thus, Foster has argued that it may be more difficult to monitor the data in relation to social offences; there may be a conflict between the pursuit of economic and non-economic goals; non-economic goals can themselves conflict; and the greater the number of divergent aims which are being pursued the more difficult might it be to develop a coherent overall strategy.[163] However, as Prosser has shown, it is clear that the regulators do engage in social regulation, and that this is so even where an element of competition has been introduced into the provision of the relevant service.[164] The social facet of the regulator's task is expressly provided for in the Utilities Act 2000, in relation to gas and electricity. The social dimension of regulation has more generally been developed as a result of initiatives from EU law, concerned with universal service obligations and the like.[165]

11–042 A third aspect of the institutional design of a regulatory system is that it should minimise the possibility of *regulatory failure*. This term can cover a number of differing scenarios. It may mean that the regulated industry is no longer capable of sustaining profitable trading because the regulatory controls do not, for example, allow it to adapt to new market circumstances such as inflation. It may mean that the regulator is no longer capable of properly fulfilling his remit

---

159 Foster, *Privatization, Public Ownership and the Regulation of Natural Monopoly* (1992), p.226.

160 Foster, *Privatization, Public Ownership and the Regulation of Natural Monopoly* (1992), pp.235–236.

161 Foster, *Privatization, Public Ownership and the Regulation of Natural Monopoly* (1992), pp.236–238.

162 Foster, *Privatization, Public Ownership and the Regulation of Natural Monopoly* (1992), pp.250–254.

163 Foster, *Privatization, Public Ownership and the Regulation of Natural Monopoly* (1992), pp.316–323.

164 Prosser, *Law and the Regulators* (1997), Chs 3–7.

165 Prosser, *Law and the Regulators* (1997).

because of governmental interference with the regime, or because there are inadequate powers in the original legislation.

A more general cause of regulatory failure is *regulatory capture*, in the sense that the regulator is captured by the very industries being regulated. We have touched on this issue in the preceding discussion.[166] The Chicago School developed a well-known version of regulatory capture.[167] The essence of the argument is that the monopolist in an industry to be regulated has an economic incentive to influence the content of the legislation, since the regulatory regime will constrain what the monopolist can do with its monopoly profits. This same incentive will also lie behind attempts by the monopolist to influence the regulator once the regulatory regime has been established. The monopolist will predictably be willing to expend a great amount of its monopoly profits on influencing the regulator in order to retain at least some of these profits.

The Public Choice School provides a somewhat different account of regulatory capture or bias.[168] The theory draws analogies between markets for ordinary goods and the making of legislation, which is conceived of as a political market. The content of the legislation will reflect the contesting pressures of the differing interest groups who are concerned with the topic. On this view "trade continues until the marginal value to the politicians and regulator of the obligation assumed by the regulated industry equals its marginal financial cost to the industry".[169]

The theoretical and empirical assumptions underlying these models have been contested. We should nonetheless structure the regulatory regime so as to minimise the likelihood of this occurring. Foster has provided helpful pointers in this regard.[170] There should be an independent regulator who retains discretion to interpret regulatory offences. Formal court procedures should be avoided since these are likely to favour the regulated industry, but there should be appropriate procedural rights, which safeguard the interests of affected parties. Appeals on the merits should be provided in some instances, but preferably to another regulatory agency which has appropriate expertise. The more firms there are within an industry, the less likely will it be that the regulator will be captured by any one firm. There should be the possibility of input from other interested parties, including consumers, since they will act as some counterweight to the power of the regulated industry itself. The scope of any ministerial power should be defined as clearly as possible, in order that the regulated industry is not tempted to by-pass the regulator and seek to capture the minister instead.

---

[166] See paras 11–018 to 11–019.

[167] Stigler, "The Theory of Economic Regulation" (1971) 2 Bell Jnl. Econ. 3; Posner, "Theories of Economic Regulation" (1974) 5 Bell Jnl. Econ. 335; Peltzman, "Towards a More General Theory of Regulation" (1976) 19 Jnl. Law & Econ. 211.

[168] Buchanan and Tullock, *The Calculus of Consent* (1962); Buchanan, *The Limits of Liberty: Between Anarchy and Leviathan* (1975); Buchanan, *Freedom in Constitutional Contract* (1978); Buchanan, *Liberty, Market and State: Political Economy in the 1980s* (1986); Brennan and Buchanan, *The Reason of Rules* (1985); McLean, *Public Choice: An Introduction* (1987); Mueller, *Public Choice* (1979); G. Becker, "A Theory of Competition among Pressure Groups for Political Influence" (1983) 98 Quarterly Jnl. of Econ. 371.

[169] Foster, *Privatization, Public Ownership and the Regulation of Natural Monopoly* (1992), p.387.

[170] Foster, *Privatization, Public Ownership and the Regulation of Natural Monopoly* (1992), p.413.

11–043 The final aspect of a coherent regulatory strategy is to ensure that the regulatory authority observes the requisite *procedural and substantive norms* expected of other public agencies.[171]

In procedural terms, this means that the basic principles of fair procedure apply to decisions made by such bodies, whether in the setting of prices, the grant of licences or the adjudication of offences under the 1992 legislation to be discussed below. This does not mean that such agencies should necessarily have to operate in accordance with the full rigours of the ordinary adversarial/adjudicative conception of fair procedure, modelled as it is upon ordinary court processes.[172] Procedural justice is a more flexible concept, which can be tailored to the needs of the particular area. It is clear that some agencies have adopted ideas of informal adjudication and rule-making used by US agencies, as mandated by the Administrative Procedure Act 1946.[173] This is particularly true in the context of telecommunications where the DGT employed sophisticated regulatory procedures designed to elicit the views of a wide range of people when making regulations relating to price controls and conditions of fair trading. There was a double consultation exercise with a timetable for the receipt of views from interested parties.[174] It is equally clear that not all other regulatory agencies have been as forthcoming in this respect. There is much to be said for Prosser's suggestion that the procedural obligations imposed by the APA in the United States should be required here.[175] This links in more generally with concerns for participation in the administrative process.[176]

In substantive terms, the agencies that oversee the regulated industries are subject to the ordinary principles of judicial review.[177] There is in addition a form of internal appeal on a number of issues, such as when a licence condition is to be changed. The application of the principles of judicial review will be dependent on the structure and content of the enabling legislation. This will provide the background for determining which considerations are deemed to be relevant, and whether agency action is reasonable. We have already seen that the UK agencies undertake social regulation to varying degrees. There may well be lessons to be learned in this respect from experience in France and Italy. Prosser has provided a valuable analysis of the more structured way in which social goals of equality, impartiality, consumer choice and consumer participation have been written into the enabling legislation in, for example, Italy.[178] There has been

> "... a fuller recognition of the plurality of regulatory goals through the establishment of a relatively sophisticated case law dealing with the social requirements of public service, and suggestions that there is something different about basic services linked to citizenship".[179]

---

171 Graham and Prosser, *Privatizing Public Enterprises, Constitutions, the State and Regulation in Comparative Perspective* (1991), Ch.7.

172 See Ch.12.

173 Foster, *Privatization, Public Ownership and the Regulation of Natural Monopoly* (1992), pp.274–275.

174 Prosser, *Law and the Regulators* (1997), pp.84–86.

175 Prosser, *Law and the Regulators* (1997), pp.277–286.

176 See Ch.15.

177 See Chs 12–23.

178 Prosser, *Law and the Regulators* (1997), pp.287–292.

179 Prosser, *Law and the Regulators* (1997), p.292.

It is, moreover, important to place this issue into its broader context. The substantive norms applied by regulatory agencies necessarily raises wider issues as to the way in which we conceptualise public-sector service delivery.[180] This issue has been considered above and reference should be made to that discussion.

E. The Regulatory Regime: The Limits of Public Law

It is clear, as noted above, that the principles of administrative law can apply to the activities of the regulatory agencies themselves.[181] It also seems clear that the exercise of monopoly powers by a local authority in administering an ancient market is susceptible to judicial review concerning the rents which can lawfully be charged.[182] **11–044**

More interesting and controversial is the issue as to whether these procedures and principles could be used directly against the privatised bodies themselves. This raises the vexed topic as to the scope of "public law" for the purposes of remedies.[183] It requires us to judge how far those procedures are appropriate to a corporation which is nominally private, with some degree of monopoly power, which is buttressed directly and indirectly by a statute.

It is readily apparent from the earlier discussion that the courts have in the past found little difficulty in subjecting such institutions to rules that differ from those of the ordinary "private" corporation.[184] It might well be argued that any complainant would have to exhaust the "internal" remedial options before seeking judicial review. The force of this argument would depend upon whether the complaint fell within the relevant internal procedures, and also upon the general law governing the relationship between the pursuit of judicial review and the availability of alternative remedies. The possibility of using judicial review was mooted by Sir Gordon Borrie, who had a wealth of experience as Director General of Fair Trading[185]:

> "Is it satisfactory … that neither private individuals or bodies nor (in many instances) public officials can bring to bear on private centres of power the kind of legal challenge in the courts that has been so effective as the challenges to the exercise of local government power by way of application for judicial review in recent decades? The lack of any possibility for the industrial customers of British Gas or even for a public official such as the Director General of Fair Trading to take British Gas to court to challenge their exercise of monopoly power meant that a reference to the Monopolies and Mergers Commission, which the customers had no right to initiate themselves and which could result only in recommendations for government action, was the only possible way of pursuing the matter."

---

[180] M. Freedland and S. Sciarra (eds), *Public Services and Citizenship in European Law, Public and Labour Law Perspectives* (Oxford University Press, 1998).

[181] For problems which can arise from the government's continued share-holdings in some privatised corporations, C. Graham and T. Prosser, "Privatising Nationalized Industries: Constitutional Issues and New Legal Techniques" (1987) 50 M.L.R. 16.

[182] *R. v Birmingham City Council, Ex p. Dredger and Paget* [1993] C.O.D. 340.

[183] See Ch.27.

[184] See paras 11–026 to 11–027.

[185] Sir G. Borrie "The Regulation of Public and Private Power' [1989] P.L. 552, 560–561.

F. The Regulatory Regime: The Citizen's Charter and Subsequent Legislation

11–045 Some of the force of Sir Gordon's complaint was addressed by legislation, which applied principles contained in the Citizen's Charter: the Competition and Service (Utilities) Act 1992.[186]

Part I of this legislation amended the existing statutes through which utilities were privatised[187] and imposed standards of performance and service to customers. The details of the legislation varied with respect to telecommunications, gas, water and electricity. The description below focuses principally upon gas by way of example.[188]

The Gas and Electricity Markets Authority (the Authority), is empowered to make regulations prescribing standards of performance that ought to be achieved by designated operators in *individual* cases.[189] The regulations require the consent of the secretary of state, and can only be made after consulting the operators and parties likely to be affected by the regulations. Compensation is payable to any person who is affected by failure to meet the specified standard. The Authority will adjudicate on a dispute as to whether the standards have been met, and any order takes effect as if it were a judgment of a county court. The Authority is also empowered to determine *overall* standards[190] of performance for the industry.[191]

The Director is instructed to collect *information* with respect to compensation paid by designated operators in individual cases, and with respect to overall levels of performance.[192] Failure to provide the information is punishable by a fine. The Authority is to publish the information provided at least once a year. There are provisions dealing with more particular issues such as discriminatory pricing, billing disputes and deposits.

11–046 *Penalties* can be imposed for breach of the relevant conditions, and compliance may be made part of the licence conditions under which the firm operates. Where this is so breach of these conditions can lead to an order for compliance by the Authority and a subsequent action brought either by the Authority, or by another for breach of statutory duty. The Regulatory Enforcement and Sanctions Act 2008 further enhanced the range of sanctions that could be imposed by regulators.

The Competition Act 1998 added important powers to the armoury of the regulatory agencies. Section 54 of the Act in effect provides that the authorities responsible for oversight of telecommunications, gas, electricity, water, rail and civil aviation have concurrent powers, within their assigned area, to enforce the provisions relating to agreements and abuse of a dominant position.[193] This

---

186 This Act has been amended by the Utilities Act 2000 ss.90–96 in relation to gas and electricity.

187 Telecommunications Act 1984; Gas Act 1986; Electricity Act 1989; Water Industry Act 1991.

188 The Competition and Service (Utilities) Act 1992 has been amended in significant respects. Thus, the provisions relating to telecommunications were repealed and replaced by provisions in the Communications Act 2003.

189 Gas Act 1986 s.33A.

190 Gas Act 1986 s.33B.

191 See further Utilities Act 2000 ss.90–91.

192 Gas Act 1986 ss.33C–33D; Utilities Act 2000 s.94.

193 Competition Act Sch.10.

means that the Authority that best knows the area can apply the legislation on competition. This serves to reinforce the agencies' powers in regulating for competition.

8. CONCLUSION

No attempt will be made to summarise the entirety of the preceding arguments. **11–047**
What this discussion demonstrates is that administrative law principles must be seen as but part of a larger picture concerned with the institutional design of administrative systems. The "whether", "who" and "how" questions that have formed the framework of this chapter could be applied to any substantive area that is of concern to administrative law.

CHAPTER 12

NATURAL JUSTICE: HEARINGS

1. CENTRAL ISSUES

i. The initial chapters on judicial review deal with process rights: whether an individual has a right to be heard before certain action is taken and if so the content of that right. There are three principal ways in which individuals can be affected by governmental action: through primary legislation, rulemaking and adjudication. Individuals are not accorded any formal rights to be consulted before primary legislation is enacted, although the government will often consult on proposed legislation. Rulemaking connotes a generalised measure, which can take the form of delegated legislation or administrative rules. The common law rules concerning process rights do not apply to rulemaking. The reasons for this, and the extent to which process rights are protected through other means, are considered in Ch.15. Adjudication connotes some form of individualised act addressed to a particular person, or persons. The process rights that attach to adjudication are considered in this chapter and the two which follow. 12–001

ii. Process rights in relation to individualised decisions have traditionally been based on natural justice, which encapsulates two ideas: that the individual be given adequate notice of the charge and an adequate hearing (*audi alteram partem*), and that the adjudicator be unbiased (*nemo judex in causa sua*).[1] The former will be dealt with in this chapter and the next, and the latter in that which follows.

iii. The *audi alteram partem* principle has a long lineage and developed from various types of case. An early group of cases was concerned with deprivation of offices,[2] requiring notice and a hearing prior to the deprivation. Another somewhat later group involved the clergy: penalties or disciplinary measures to which the clergy were subjected had to be preceded by notice and a hearing.[3] In the 19th century the *audi alteram partem* principle was applied to a wide variety of bodies, private as well as public. Clubs,[4] associations[5] and trade unions[6] were included within its

---

[1] J. Mashaw, *Due Process in the Administrative State* (New Haven: Yale University Press, 1985); D. Galligan, *Due Process and Fair Procedures* (Oxford: Oxford University Press, 1996).

[2] *Bagg's Case* (1615) 11 Co. Rep. 93b; *R. v Chancellor of the University of Cambridge* (1723) 1 Str. 557; *Osgood v Nelson* (1872) L.R. 5 HL 636; *Fisher v Jackson* (1891) 2 Ch. 824.

[3] *Capel v Child* (1832) 2 Cr. & J. 588; *Bonaker v Evans* (1850) 16 Q.B. 163; *R v North, Ex p. Oakey* [1927] 1 K.B. 491, CA.

[4] *Dawkins v Antrobus* (1881) 17 Ch. D. 615; *Fisher v Keane* (1878) 11 Ch. D. 353.

ambit. The increase in the regulatory role of public authorities provided a further opportunity for the generalised application of the maxim.

iv. The generality of the requirement of a hearing was evident in *Cooper v Wandsworth Board of Works*,[7] where it was held that demolition powers vested in the defendant Board were to be subject to notice and hearing requirements. The court made clear that the omission of positive words in the statute requiring a hearing was not conclusive, since the justice of the common law would supply the omission of the legislature.[8] The generality and flexibility of the *audi alteram partem* maxim, were brought out once again by Lord Loreburn.[9] He stated that the maxim applied to "everyone who decides anything", while recognising that the manner in which a person's case was heard did not necessarily have to be the same as an ordinary trial. The breadth of the *audi alteram partem* principle was, however, limited in the first half of this century for reasons that will be explored below.

v. There are two rationales for natural justice. The instrumental rationale emphasises the connection between the provision of hearing rights and the correctness of the outcome on the substance of the case. The non-instrumental rationale focuses on the ways in which process rights protect human dignity.

vi. It is necessary in any legal system for there to be some criteria through which to decide on whether natural justice is applicable. In the United Kingdom these criteria have been fashioned largely by the courts and require the existence of a right, interest or legitimate expectation before natural justice is applicable. The common law criteria have, however, been complemented by those drawn from art.6 of the European Convention of Human Rights.

vii. It is also necessary for a legal system to decide on the content of natural justice, assuming that it is applicable to a particular case. This can vary significantly, from a very full set of process rights that approximates to an ordinary trial, to something more modest. This decision is made by the courts and is influenced by three factors: the importance of the interest infringed; the value to the claimant of the additional process right; and the cost of providing the additional procedural safeguard.

viii. The applicability and content of natural justice has proven especially problematic in relation to legislation dealing with terrorism post 9/11. These problems will be considered in the next chapter.

ix. Natural justice is predicated on a model of process rights that reflects that used in an ordinary court. The process rights are modified in their application to administrative bodies, but this does not alter the force of this

---

[5] *Wood v Woad* (1874) L.R. 9 Ex. 190; *Lapointe v L'Association de Bienfaisance et de Retraite de la Police de Montreal* [1906] A.C. 435.

[6] *Wood* (1874) L.R. 9 Ex. 190; *Lapointe v L'Association de Bienfaisance et de Retraite de la Police de Montreal* [1906] A.C. 435.

[7] *Cooper v Wandsworth Board of Works* (1863) 14 C.B. (NS) 180.

[8] *Cooper* (1863) 14 C.B. (NS) 180 at 194; *Hopkins v Smethwick Local Board of Health* (1890) 24 Q.B.D. 713; *Bank Mellat v HM Treasury* [2013] UKSC 39.

[9] *Board of Education v Rice* [1911] A.C. 179, HL at 182.

point. Process rights fashioned in this way are termed adjudicatory, which captures the background model of court procedures that frames natural justice. It is however important to recognise that this is not the only type of process right. Non-adjudicatory process rights may be more suitable for certain types of administrative decision-making, and better attain the instrumental and non-instrumental values that process rights are designed to serve. The circumstances where this is so will be explored at the end of this chapter.

2. THE RATIONALE FOR PROCEDURAL RIGHTS

Justifications for process rights in adjudication vary.[10] One rationale emphasises the connection between procedural due process and the substantive justice of the final outcome. All rules are designed to achieve a particular goal, for example that liquor licences should only be granted to those of good character. Giving a person a hearing before deciding to refuse a licence can help to ensure that this goal is correctly applied. Procedural rights perform an *instrumental* role, in the sense of helping to attain an accurate decision on the substance of the case.[11] Other rationales focus upon *non-instrumental* justifications for procedural rights. Formal justice and the rule of law are enhanced, in the sense that the principles of natural justice help to guarantee objectivity and impartiality.[12] Procedural rights are also seen as protecting human dignity by ensuring that the individual is told why she is being treated unfavourably, and by enabling her to take part in that decision.[13] 12–002

These twin rationales for procedural rights have been recognised by the judiciary. *Doody*[14] was concerned with whether prisoners given a life sentence for murder should be told the reasons relating to the length of their imprisonment. Lord Mustill stated that a prisoner would wish to know why the particular term was selected,

> "... partly from an obvious human desire to be told the reason for a decision so gravely affecting his future, and partly because he hopes that once the information is obtained he may be able to point out errors of fact or reasoning and thereby persuade the secretary of state to change his mind, or if he fails in this to challenge the decision in the courts".

The non-instrumental and instrumental justifications for procedural protection are readily apparent in this quotation. It is perfectly possible to support natural justice for both instrumental and non-instrumental reasons, but it should be recognised

---

[10] Galligan, *Due Process and Fair Procedures* (1996), pp.75–82.

[11] J. Resnick, "Due Process and Procedural Justice", in J. Pennock and J. Chapman (eds), *Due Process* (Nomos, 1977), p.217.

[12] H.L.A. Hart, *Concept of Law* (Oxford: Clarendon Press, 1961), pp.156 and 202; J. Rawls, *A Theory of Justice* (Oxford University Press, 1973), p.235.

[13] F. Michelman, "Formal and Associational Aims in Procedural Due Process", in Pennock and Chapman (eds), *Due Process* (1977), Ch.4; Mashaw, *Due Process in the Administrative State* (1985), Chs 4–7.

[14] *R. v Secretary of State for the Home Department, Ex p. Doody* [1994] 1 A.C. 531, HL at 551.

that the content of natural justice in a particular area may vary depending upon whether one accords primacy to instrumental or non-instrumental considerations.[15]

3. LIMITATION OF THE PRINCIPLE

12–003 The breadth of the *audi alteram partem* principle was limited in the first half of this century. This occurred in a number of ways.

A. Administrative v Judicial

12–004 In the 19th century the right to a hearing was applied in a number of areas that were administrative. In so far as the term judicial was used it was automatically implied whenever a decision was made which affected a person's rights in a broad sense.[16] Despite this the courts began to draw a dichotomy between administrative and judicial decisions, to take a narrow view of what constituted a judicial or quasi-judicial decision and to require this as a condition precedent for a right to a hearing.

For example, in *Errington*[17] it was argued that the minister was in breach of natural justice by conferring with the local authority and receiving further evidence after the close of a public inquiry. The Court of Appeal found that there had been a breach, but the phrasing of the judgment was nonetheless restrictive. Maugham LJ stated that if the minister acted administratively natural justice would not apply, that the minister was in fact acting quasi-judicially, but only because the situation was "triangular" in that the minister was deciding a legal action between the local authority and objectors.[18] In cases where the legal action had not yet been joined the applicant was less successful.[19]

B. Rights and Remedies

12–005 The detailed study waits to be written on the way in which developments in the law of certiorari affected the law on natural justice. The problem can be briefly stated as follows. It was thought that for certiorari to be available there would have to be not just a determination affecting the rights of individuals, but also a superadded duty to act judicially.[20] This view has now been overturned.[21]

---

[15] See paras 12–029 to 12–30.

[16] *Hopkins v Smethwick Local Board of Health* (1890) 24 Q.B.D. 713.

[17] *Errington v Minister of Health* [1935] 1 K.B. 249, CA.

[18] *Errington v Minister of Health* [1935] 1 K.B. 249, CA at 270–273; *Local Government Board v Arlidge* [1915] A.C. 120, HL.

[19] *Offer v Minister of Health* [1936] 1 K.B. 40, CA; *Frost v Minister of Health* [1935] 1 K.B. 286 KBD; *R. v Metropolitan Police Commissioner, Ex p. Parker* [1953] 1 W.L.R. 1150 QBD at 1153–1154; *Nakkuda Ali v Jayaratne* [1951] A.C. 66; *R. v Leman Street Police Station Inspector, Ex p. Venicoff* [1920] 3 K.B. 72 KBD.

[20] *R. v Legislative Committee of the Church Assembly, Ex p. Haynes-Smith* [1928] 1 K.B. 411 KBD at 415 interpreting *R. v Electricity Commissioners, Ex p. London Electricity Joint Committees Co (1920) Ltd* [1924] 1 K.B. 171, CA at 205.

However, while it held sway it was interpreted on occasion to mean not just that there had been a breach of natural justice with no remedy available. The courts went further and said that natural justice itself was not applicable.[22] Thus one reason given in *Ridge v Baldwin* by Lord Reid for the demise of natural justice was misunderstanding over the scope of certiorari.[23]

C. Rights v Privileges

Closely allied to the previous reasons for the limitation of natural justice was the distinction drawn between rights and privileges. In *Nakkuda Ali* one reason the Privy Council denied the application of natural justice was because the cancellation of a licence was characterised as the withdrawal of a privilege and not the determination of a right[24] and in *Parker*[25] the cab licence which was withdrawn was just a "permission". **12–006**

D. Statutory Hearings and Inquiries

The application of natural justice in the context of inquiries has already been touched upon in discussing the administrative-judicial dichotomy. A further example of the limited application of natural justice in this area may be given. In *Arlidge*,[26] the House of Lords considered whether an individual should have an oral hearing before the Local Government Board, and whether the person should be entitled to see the report of the hearing inspector in the context of a statutory scheme to determine whether a closing order on a house should be rescinded. **12–007**

Lord Haldane LC upheld the general principles in the *Rice* case, but refused access to the housing inspector's report or to the Board itself: when a matter was entrusted to a department of state or similar body, Parliament should be taken, subject to contrary intent, to have meant that it could follow its own procedure, which would enable it to work with efficiency. When, therefore, the Board was entrusted with appeals this did not mean that any particular official should undertake the task, nor was the Board bound to disclose the report any more than minutes made on the paper before a decision was arrived at.[27] Some of this reasoning can be accepted, but the failure to disclose the report was a severe set-back in the evolution of inquiry procedures which has taken long to heal.[28]

---

[21] *Ridge v Baldwin* [1964] A.C. 40, HL at 72–76.

[22] *Nakkuda Ali v Jayaratne* [1951] A.C. 66 at 75–77; *Parker* [1953] 1 W.L.R. 1150 at 1153; *R. v St. Lawrence's Hospital Statutory Visitors, Ex p. Pritchard* [1953] 1 W.L.R. 1158 DC.

[23] *Ridge* [1964] A.C. 40 at 72–76.

[24] *Nakkuda Ali* [1951] A.C. 66 at 77–78.

[25] *Parker* [1953] 1 W.L.R. 1150 at 1153; *R. v Leman Street Police Inspector, Ex p. Venicoff* [1920] 3 K.B. 72.

[26] *Local Government Board v Arlidge* [1915] A.C. 120.

[27] *Arlidge* [1915] A.C. 120 at 132–134.

[28] For the position now, see Ch.9.

4. THE PRINCIPLE REVIVED

A. *Ridge v Baldwin*

12–008 While some cases limited the *audi alteram partem* principle,[29] there were nonetheless indications in England,[30] Australia,[31] Canada[32] and New Zealand[33] of a less rigid application of the principle. However, natural justice was at a low ebb prior to the decision of the House of Lords in *Ridge v Baldwin*.[34] Their Lordships held that a chief constable who was dismissable only for cause was entitled to notice of the charge and an opportunity to be heard before being dismissed. The importance of the case lies in the general discussion of the principles of natural justice, especially by Lord Reid.

His Lordship reviewed the 19th-century case law that showed the broad application of natural justice and then gave three reasons why the law had become confused. The first was that natural justice could have only a limited application in the context of the wider duties or discretion imposed upon a minister, but the courts had, unfortunately, applied these limits to other areas where the constraints were unnecessary.[35] The second reason was that the principle had received only limited application during the war. Special considerations that might be pertinent during wartime should not affect the ambit of natural justice now. The third was the confusion between rights and remedies evident in the requirement of a superadded duty to act judicially for certiorari, and the way that this had stilted the development of natural justice.[36]

For Lord Reid, the judicial element in natural justice should be inferred from the nature of the power and its effect on the individual. Lord Morris of Borth-y-Gest also based his judgment on the 19th-century jurisprudence.[37] For Lord Hodson[38] the absence of a legal action between the parties was not decisive, nor was the characterisation of the act as judicial, administrative or executive.[39]

---

[29] A further reason for the non-applicability of the rules of natural justice was said to be if the decision-maker was acting in a disciplinary manner *Ex p. Fry* [1954] 1 W.L.R. 730 at 733. See now *Buckoke v Greater London Council* [1971] 1 Ch. 655 at 669; *R. v Board of Visitors of Hull Prison, Ex p. St. Germain* [1979] Q.B. 425 at 445, 455.

[30] *Hoggard v Worsborough Urban DC* [1962] 2 Q.B. 93.

[31] *Delta Properties Pty Ltd v Brisbane City Council* (1956) 95 C.L.R. 11 at 18–19.

[32] *Alliance des Professeurs Catholiques de Montreal v Labour Relations Board of Quebec* [1953] 2 S.C.R. 140.

[33] *New Zealand Licensed Victuallers' Association of Employers v Price Tribunal* [1957] N.Z.L.R. 167 at 203–205.

[34] *Ridge* [1964] A.C. 40 at 72–76.

[35] *Ridge* [1964] A.C. 40 at 71–72.

[36] *Ridge* [1964] A.C. 40 at 72–78. His Lordship expressly disapproved Lord Hewart CJ's requirement of a superadded duty to act judicially which had been developed in *Church Assembly* [1928] 1 K.B. 411 and disapproved also of *Nakkuda Ali* [1951] A.C. 66 in so far as that case supported the requirement.

[37] *Ridge* [1964] A.C. 40 at 120–121.

[38] *Ridge* [1964] A.C. 40 at 127–132.

[39] Lord Devlin based his judgment primarily upon the application of the police regulations, *Ridge* [1964] A.C. 40 at 137–141. Lord Evershed dissented, at 82–100, and his judgment is considered in Ch.24.

Their Lordships therefore revived the principles of natural justice in two connected ways. They rediscovered the older jurisprudence, which had applied the principle to a broad spectrum of interests and a wide variety of decision-makers. They disapproved 20th-century impediments: the requirements of a a formal action between parties and a superadded duty to act judicially were said to be false constraints. However, little positive guidance is to be found in the case as to when natural justice should apply. The closest to any general formulation is that the applicability of natural justice was dependent on the nature of the power exercised and its effect upon the individual concerned. It is therefore unsurprising that in the years following *Ridge* the courts were faced with many cases concerned not just with the content of natural justice, but with the criterion for its applicability.

B. Natural Justice and Fairness

The years since *Ridge* saw the development of new terminology. The case law is replete with mention of "fairness" or a "duty to act fairly". The terms were initially used by Lord Parker CJ in *HK*.[40] Some courts treat these terms in an omnibus fashion, in the sense that natural justice is said to be but a manifestation of fairness.[41] In other cases courts apply natural justice to judicial decisions, and reserve a duty to act fairly for administrative or executive determinations.[42] It is not uncommon for different members of the same court to be in agreement as to the content of the procedural duty, but to differ as to whether to describe this as resulting from natural justice or fairness.[43] There are differing views as to the significance of the development of fairness. 12–009

There is one view that sees development of fairness as a corollary of the expansion of procedural rights post-*Ridge*. Thus, Megarry VC in *McInnes*[44] stated that natural justice was a flexible term, which imposed distinct requirements in different cases. It was capable of applying to the whole range of situations encapsulated by the terms "judicial", "quasi-judicial", "administrative", or "executive". However, the further that one moved away from anything resembling a "judicial" or "quasi-judicial" situation, the more appropriate it became to use the term fairness rather than natural justice. On this view the distinction between the terms natural justice and fairness is linguistic rather than substantive. The former can cover all cases, but it is felt to be more appropriate to use the term fairness in the context of, for example, company inspectors or immigration officers.

---

40 *HK, Re* [1967] 2 Q.B. 617 at 630.

41 *Wiseman v Borneman* [1971] A.C. 297, HL at 308–309; *McInnes v Onslow-Fane* [1978] 1 W.L.R. 1520 Ch D at 1530; *O'Reilly v Mackman* [1983] 2 A.C. 237, HL at 276.

42 *HK (an infant), Re* [1967] 2 Q.B. 617 QBD at 630; *Pearlberg v Varty* [1972] 1 W.L.R. 534, HL at 550; *Bates v Lord Hailsham* [1972] 1 W.L.R. 1373 Ch D at 1378.

43 *Pergamon Press Ltd, Re* [1971] Ch. 388, CA (Civ Div), 399–400 (Lord Denning MR, "fairly") at 402–403 (Sachs LJ, "natural justice") at 407 (Buckley LJ, "not a judicial function").

44 *McInnes* [1978] 1 W.L.R. 1520 at 1530.

Some commentators take a different view, seeing a broader significance in the shift from natural justice to fairness.[45] It is argued that the basis of natural justice was the desire of the ordinary courts to maintain control over adjudication, and to impose their own procedures on those subject to judicial control. The necessity for the function to be characterised as "judicial" before procedural constraints were imposed was said to be integral to this approach, because only bodies exercising such functions were suited to adjudicative procedures. A corollary of this view was that the content of the rules of natural justice could be relatively fixed and certain. The shift to a broader notion of fairness is said to alter fundamentally the basis of procedural intervention, since it can no longer be restricted to adjudicative settings, and there cannot be fixed standards for determining whether there has been a breach of procedural fairness. The courts are forced to engage in a difficult balancing operation, taking into account the nature of the individuals' interest and the effect of increased procedural protection upon the administration.

12–010 There are however difficulties with this argument. The premise is that natural justice stemmed from a judicial desire to maintain control over adjudication. While this may have formed part of the rationale for natural justice, the major reason for the development of the doctrine was the protection of property rights and interests akin thereto.[46] Moreover, the argument that the term "judicial" was used to ensure that only those bodies suited to adjudicative procedures should be subject to natural justice is not sound. That term was automatically held to be satisfied when the effects on the interests of the individual were felt to be serious enough to warrant procedural protection.[47] Indeed, in cases where the remedy sought was not certiorari, there was often no mention of the "judicial" requirement at all. The rationale for the 20th-century cases that limited natural justice through the judicial–administrative dichotomy was not primarily because it was felt that those categorised as administrative would be unsuited to adjudicative procedures. While this may have been a factor, the case law dealing with aliens, licensing and discipline[48] reflects more a judicial conclusion that those substantive interests were not worthy of judicial protection.[49] A further difficulty with the preceding argument is that the application of natural justice, prior to the introduction of fairness, was never uniform. Courts often explicitly or

---

[45] M. Loughlin, "Procedural Fairness: A Study in Crisis in Administrative Law Theory" (1978) 28 U. Tor. L.J. 215; R. Macdonald, "Judicial Review and Procedural Fairness in Administrative Law" (1979–1980) 25 McGill L.J. 520; (1980–1981) 26 McGill L.J. 1.

[46] See the cases on officers and the clergy, *Bagg's Case* (1615) 11 Co. Rep. 93b; *Chancellor of the University of Cambridge* (1723) 1 Str. 557; *Osgood* (1872) L.R. 5, HL 636; *Fisher* (1891) 2 Ch. 824; *Capel* (1832) 2 Cr. & J. 588; *Bonaker* (1850) 16 Q.B. 163; *Oakey* [1927] 1 K.B. 491 which were particularly influenced by this consideration.

[47] See cases, *Bagg's Case* (1615) 11 Co. Rep. 93b; *Chancellor of the University of Cambridge* (1723) 1 Str. 557; *Osgood* (1872) L.R. 5, HL 636; *Fisher* (1891) 2 Ch. 824; *Capel* (1832) 2 Cr. & J. 588; *Bonaker* (1850) 16 Q.B. 163; *Oakey* [1927] 1 K.B. 491; *Dawkins* (1881) 17 Ch. D. 615; *Fisher* (1878) 11 Ch. D. 353; *Wood* (1874) L.R. 9 Ex. 190; *Lapointe* [1906] A.C. 435; *Cooper* (1863) 14 C.B. (NS) 180 at 194; *Hopkins* (1890) 24 Q.B.D. 713.

[48] See Ch.13.

[49] The thesis holds up best in the context of statutory inquiries, where the nature of the subject matter did influence the courts in reaching the conclusion that it was not suitable for fully adjudicative procedures, and in the unwillingness to accord procedural rights in "legislative" contexts.

implicitly balanced the interests of the individual with the effects on the administration in deciding where the line should be drawn on many issues concerning the content of natural justice.[50]

C. Natural Justice, Fairness and Types of Process Right

What is undoubtedly true is that natural justice has resulted in adjudicative procedural constraints. Process rights are modelled on those of the ordinary courts, and any balancing is undertaken in this context.[51] Whether the introduction of the term fairness causes any modification in this respect depends upon the meaning accorded to that term.[52] **12–011**

It is possible on one view to see fairness as simply fitting into an adjudicative framework, and not necessitating the development of non-adjudicative procedures. The courts determine what adjudicative procedures are required in particular areas. In some, it may approximate to the full panoply of procedural safeguards, including notice, oral hearing, representation, discovery, cross-examination, and reasoned decisions. In others it may connote less. There will be a broad spectrum in between. This is how the system generally works at present. The term fairness can be used to cover all such instances, or the term natural justice can be used for that part of the spectrum that requires a relatively wide range of procedural checks. In so far as fairness is used within the traditional adjudicative framework the balancing involved therein may be different in degree, but not in kind from that which has always been undertaken within natural justice itself. Lord Loreburn LC might well question whether there is really a difference in degree.[53]

It is also possible to take a different view and see the emergence of fairness as having a broader implication. Adjudication is only one form of decision-making with its own distinctive procedure. Mediation, arbitration, contract and managerial direction are other forms of decision-making, and each possesses its own procedural norms. A general concept of procedural fairness could, therefore, lead the courts into developing procedural forms other than classical adjudication. If this transpires then fairness will have a substantial effect on procedural due process.

The discussion now turns to the way in which fairness is presently used in an adjudicative context. This will be followed at the end of the chapter by a look at some of the broader possible implications of fairness, and the way in which that term might aid in the development of procedural forms other than classical adjudication.

---

[50] *Rice* [1911] A.C. 179 at 182, where Lord Loreburn LC openly acknowledged the necessity for flexibility in the operation of the procedural safeguards; *Russell v Duke of Norfolk* [1949] 1 All E.R. 109, CA at 118. See also the cases on notice, hearing and representation, below 12–031, 12–034, 12–037.

[51] See paras 12–001, and 12–023 to 12–030, for further consideration of this point.

[52] The shift in terminology from natural justice to fairness does not, of itself, demand any particular one of these meanings.

[53] *Rice* [1911] A.C. 179 at 182.

5. APPLICABILITY OF PROCEDURAL PROTECTION[54]

12–012 Any legal system will have criteria for determining the applicability of procedural protection, whether this is cast in the language of "natural justice" or a "duty to act fairly". There are a range of options in this regard.[55]

A. Categorisation: Administrative v Judicial v Legislative

12–013 A legal system might decide to render the applicability of procedural protection dependent on categorisation of the nature of the function performed by the body subject to judicial review. This is apparent in the administrative–judicial dichotomy to determine the applicability of natural justice in some cases prior to *Ridge*. Categorisation of this type has however been disapproved of explicitly in the post-*Ridge* case law.[56] The nature of the decision may well be taken into account in determining the content of natural justice, but it has little if any utility over and beyond this for the following reason.

The rationale for rendering the applicability of natural justice dependent on such classification would be certainty and predictability, such that if a case fell within one category certain results would follow. It is however notoriously difficult to decide whether a case should be categorised as judicial, administrative, executive, etc. Moreover, the presumption is that once the characterisation has been made the content of natural justice is fixed and certain: all administrative matters will be subject to the same rules, as will all judicial or quasi-judicial. Yet the variety of matters comprehended within the terms "administrative", "quasi-judicial" or "executive" is vast, however sensitively they are defined, and therefore the same procedural rules may not be appropriate for all cases within the category.[57]

The discussion thus far has concentrated on the distinction drawn between administrative and judicial decisions. The courts have, however, held that rules of a legislative nature are not generally subject to natural justice.[58] The exceptions to this proposition will be considered below.[59] Whether such protection should apply raises broader questions concerning the way in which delegated legislation and rules of a legislative nature are made, and also the type of remedy available.

[54] The phrase procedural protection is used instead of natural justice because this section will be examining types of procedural checks in addition to those of traditional natural justice.

[55] P. Craig, "Perspectives on Process: Common Law, Statutory and Political" [2010] P.L. 275.

[56] *R. v Gaming Board for Great Britain, Ex p. Benaim and Khaida* [1970] 2 Q.B. 417 CA (Civ Div) at 430; *O'Reilly v Mackman* [1983] 2 A.C. 237, HL at 279.

[57] *Wiseman v Borneman* [1971] A.C. 297 at 317.

[58] *Bates v Lord Hailsham* [1972] 1 W.L.R. 1373 Ch D; *R. v Devon CC, Ex p. Baker* [1993] C.O.D. 138 QBD; *R. (BAPIO Action Ltd) v Secretary of State for the Home Department* [2007] EWCA Civ 1139 at 43–46, affirmed on different grounds [2008] 1 A.C. 1003. Compare *R. v Liverpool Corporation, Ex p. Liverpool Taxi Fleet Operators' Association* [1972] 2 Q.B. 299 CA (Civ Div).

[59] See Ch.15.

B. Rights, Interests and Legitimate Expectations

A legal system must necessarily have some criterion for deciding whether procedural protection is applicable. It is common for legal systems to focus on the nature of the applicant's interest. The general approach used by our courts is to consider whether there is some right, interest or legitimate expectation such as to warrant the applicability of procedural protection.[60] The common law meaning of these terms will be explained, followed by examination of the jurisprudence under art.6 ECHR. **12–014**

i. Rights

The term right in this context clearly covers instances in which the challenged action affects a recognised proprietary or personal right of the applicant. Thus, if, for example, the public body's action impinges upon a person's real property, process rights will be required for the action to be legal.[61] This has been equally the case in respect of personal property, and process rights will be applicable where a job is regarded as an office and a species of personal property.[62] Some form of hearing right will also be demanded if the action affects the personal liberty of the individual, more particularly if that action entails some actual loss of liberty.[63] Thus, in the post-*Ridge* era the courts have insisted that procedural fairness applies to disciplinary actions that impact on liberty interests, or adversely affect the individual.[64] **12–015**

ii. Interests

The term interest is looser than that of right, and has been used as the basis for some type of hearing even where the individual would not be regarded in law as having any substantive entitlement or right.[65] Many cases concerning natural justice in the context of clubs, unions and trade associations provide examples of the courts demanding that process rights be accorded where the applicant has an **12–016**

---

[60] *Schmidt v Secretary of State for Home Affairs* [1969] 2 Ch. 149, CA (Civ Div).

[61] *Cooper* (1863) 14 C.B. (NS) 180.

[62] See *Bagg's Case* (1615) 11 Co. Rep. 93b; *Chancellor of the University of Cambridge* (1723) 1 Str. 557; *Osgood* (1872) L.R. 5, HL 636; *Fisher* (1891) 2 Ch. 824.

[63] *R. v Parole Board, Ex p. Wilson* [1992] 1 Q.B. 740.

[64] *Taylor v National Union of Seamen* [1967] 1 W.L.R. 532 Ch D; *R. v Aston University Senate, Ex p. Roffey* [1969] 2 Q.B. 538 DC; *Glynn v Keele University* [1971] 1 W.L.R. 487 Ch D; *St Germain* [1979] Q.B. 425; *R. v Board of Visitors of Hull Prison, Ex p. St Germain (No.2)* [1979] 1 W.L.R. 1401 QBD; *Leech v Parkhurst Prison Deputy Governor* [1988] A.C. 533, HL; G. Richardson, *Law, Process and Custody: Prisoners and Patients* (London: Weidenfeld and Nicolson, 1993); M. Loughlin and P. Quinn, "Prisons, Rules and Courts: A Study in Administrative Law" (1993) 56 M.L.R. 497. In the case of students this is subject to the jurisdiction of the Visitor, *Thomas v University of Bradford* [1987] A.C. 795; *Oakes v Sidney Sussex College, Cambridge* [1988] 1 W.L.R. 431 Ch D, although the courts will exercise limited supervisory review over the visitor, *Page v Hull University Visitor* [1993] A.C. 682; Smith, "The Exclusive Jurisdiction of the University Visitor" (1981) 97 L.Q.R. 610.

[65] The dividing line between rights and interests can be problematic because the definition of what constitutes a right is itself contentious.

interest as such, rather than any substantive right.[66] The application of natural justice or fairness in the context of, for example, licensing and aliens is also based on the individual possessing an interest as opposed to a right stricto sensu.[67]

The willingness to accept that interests that fall short of rights stricto sensu can trigger the applicability of procedural protection is correct in principle. The technical distinction between rights and privileges should not be determinative of the applicability of procedural protection. Many interests may be extremely important to an individual even though they would not warrant the label "right" or "Hohfeldian right".[68] The absence of a substantive right to a particular benefit should not lead to the conclusion that procedural rights are inapplicable, although it might impact on the content of the procedural rights. The absence of substantive protection may well render procedural rights even more important, a point made cogently by Lord Wilberforce in *Malloch*.[69] Thus the mere fact that, for example, an office is held at pleasure should not lead to the denial of procedural protection, more especially because the dividing line between officers who can be dismissed for cause[70] and those who can be dismissed at pleasure can be hard to draw,[71] as can the line between an office and a pure master–servant relationship.[72]

iii. Legitimate expectation

12–017 The concept of legitimate expectations adds to those of right and interest in three different ways.[73]

First, the court may decide that the interest, although not presently held, is important enough that an applicant should not be refused it without having some

[66] See *Dawkins* (1881) 17 Ch. D. 615; *Fisher* (1878) 11 Ch. D. 353; *Wood* (1874) L.R. 9 Ex. 190; *Lapointe* [1906] A.C. 435.

[67] *Gaming Board* [1970] 2 Q.B. 417 at 430; *R. (Quark Fishing Ltd) v Secretary of State for Foreign and Commonwealth Office* [2002] EWCA Civ 1409.

[68] C. Reich, "The New Property" (1964) 73 Yale L.J. 733.

[69] *Malloch v Aberdeen Corporation* [1971] 1 W.L.R. 1578, 1595–1598; *Stevenson v United Road Transport Union* [1977] I.C.R. 893.

[70] Traditionally, the availability of natural justice in the employment context depended upon the nature of the employment relationship. If there is what is regarded by the law as an office then public law remedies are available to protect its holder who is entitled to natural justice. The individual can thus regain the office if dismissed without a hearing, *Bagg's Case* (1615) 11 Co. Rep. 93b ; *Chancellor of the University of Cambridge* (1723) 1 Str. 557 ; *Fisher* (1891) 2 Ch. 824; *Ridge* [1964] A.C. 40 at 66; *R. v East Berkshire Health Authority, Ex p. Walsh* [1985] Q.B. 152; *R. v Secretary of State for the Home Department, Ex p. Benwell* [1985] Q.B. 554. Where the office was held at pleasure then the presumption was that no procedural protection was applicable. *Capel v Child* (1832) 2 Cr. & J. 588; *Bonaker v Evans* (1850) 16 Q.B. 163; *R. v North, Ex p. Oakey* [1927] 1 K.B. 491, CA.

[71] *R. v Darlington School Governors* (1844) 6 Q.B. 682, though the courts often evaded the rule, *Willis v Childe* (1851) 13 Beav. 117.

[72] Contrast *Cooper v Wilson* [1937] 2 K.B. 309, CA and *Ridge* [1964] A.C. 40 (police are office-holders) with *Barber v Manchester Regional Hospital Board* [1958] 1 W.L.R. 181 (consultant surgeon) and *Vidyodaya University Council v Silva* [1965] 1 W.L.R. 77 (university teacher) not office holders. Compare further *Walsh* [1985] Q.B. 152 and *Benwell* [1985] Q.B. 554.

[73] C. Forsyth, "The Provenance and Protection of Legitimate Expectations" (1988) 47 C.L.J. 238; P. Elias, "Legitimate Expectation and Judicial Review", in J. Jowell and D. Oliver (eds), *New Directions in Judicial Review* (London: Sweet & Maxwell, 1988), pp.37–50; P. Craig, "Legitimate Expectations: A Conceptual Analysis" (1992) 108 L.Q.R. 79.

procedural rights. In this sense the courts are protecting future interests. The courts make a normative judgment that a consequence of applying for a substantive interest is that some procedural protection is warranted. Thus, in *McInnes*[74] Megarry VC held that there was a class of case in which the applicant could be said to have a legitimate expectation that an interest would be granted. This was where the applicant was a licence holder who was seeking the renewal of a licence, or where a person was already elected to a position and was seeking confirmation of the appointment from a different body. Precisely which future interests should be deserving of this procedural protection may be contestable.[75]

A second way in which the concept of legitimate expectation adds to the ideas of right and interest is where there is a clear and unequivocal representation.[76] Where this condition is satisfied a representation generating a legitimate expectation can be important in two types of case.

On the one hand, there may be cases in which the representation provides the foundation for the procedural rights, even though in the absence of the representation it is unlikely that the substantive interest would entitle the applicant to natural justice or fairness. In this type of case the interest of the applicant, by itself, would not warrant procedural protection. It is the conduct of the public body, through its representation, which provides the foundation for the procedural protection. In *AG of Hong Kong v Ng Yuen Shiu*[77] it was held that although the rules of natural justice or fairness might not generally be applicable to an alien who had entered the territory illegally, a person could claim some elements of a fair hearing if there was a legitimate expectation of being accorded such a hearing. Such an expectation could arise if, as was the case, the government had announced that illegal immigrants would be interviewed with each case being treated on its merits, albeit there being no guarantee that such immigrants would be allowed to remain in the territory. The point is well captured by Elias, who states that[78]:

> "[I]t was only the legitimate expectation arising from the assurance given by the Government that enabled the court to intervene on behalf of the illegal immigrant: his status as an illegal immigrant would not of itself have created any entitlement to a hearing."

On the other hand, the representation that gives rise to the legitimate expectation may augment the applicant's procedural rights, as exemplified by the *Liverpool Taxi* case.[79] In that case the council had pursued a policy of limiting the number of licensed taxis to 300. The applicants were repeatedly assured that the figure **12–018**

---

[74] *McInnes* [1978] 1 W.L.R. 1520.

[75] Megarry VC in *McInnes* [1978] 1 W.L.R. 1520 held that even a pure applicant would be entitled to a measure of procedural protection, in that the deciding authority should reach its decision without bias and without pursuing a capricious policy.

[76] *R. v Falmouth and Truro Port Health Authority, Ex p. South West Water Ltd* [2001] Q.B. 445, CA (Civ Div); *R. (Galligan) v Chancellor, Masters and Scholars of the University of Oxford* [2002] A.C.D. 33 QBD.

[77] *Attorney General of Hong Kong v Ng Yuen Shiu* [1983] 2 A.C. 629.

[78] Elias, "Legitimate Expectation and Judicial Review", in Jowell and Oliver (eds), *New Directions in Judicial Review* (1988), p.41.

[79] *R. v Liverpool Corporation, Ex p. Liverpool Taxi Fleet Operators' Association* [1972] 2 Q.B. 299, CA (Civ Div).

would not be increased without their being consulted, but the council did so nonetheless. It is unclear whether the court believed that the applicants would have had any procedural rights in the absence of the initial council assurances.[80] It is, however, clear that the content of the applicants' procedural rights were enhanced by the representations. Thus, Lord Denning MR stated that the council ought not to depart from the undertaking,

> "... except after the most serious consideration and hearing what the other party has to say and then only if they are satisfied that the overriding public interest requires it".[81]

Roskill LJ held that the council could not resile from their undertaking, "without notice to and representations from the applicants", and only after "due and proper consideration of the representations of all those interested".[82]

The third way in which legitimate expectations can arise is closely related to, but distinct from, the second. This is where the defendant institution has established criteria for the application of policy in a certain area, an applicant has relied on these criteria, and the defendant then seeks to apply different criteria. In *Khan*[83] the applicant sought to adopt his brother's child from Pakistan. The Home Office, while stating that there was no formal provision for this in the immigration rules, provided a circular stating the criteria used by the Home Secretary. The applicant sought entry clearance for the child on the basis of these criteria, but was refused, and the Home Office indicated that different tests had been used. The court found for the applicant. Parker LJ held that while there was no specific undertaking in this case, the principle from *Liverpool Taxi* was nonetheless applicable. Thus, if the Home Secretary stipulated certain general entry conditions he should not be allowed to depart from them "without affording interested persons a hearing and then only if the overriding public interest demands it".[84] A new policy could be implemented, but the recipient of the letter which set out the previous policy must be given the opportunity to argue that the "old" policy be applied to the particular case.

iv. *Article 6(1) ECHR: "Civil Rights and Obligations"*

12–019 The discussion thus far has focused upon the applicability of procedural protection in accordance with domestic criteria from common law or statute. This

---

[80] Lord Denning MR believed that they would have some such rights, *Liverpool Taxi Fleet* [1972] 2 Q.B. 299 at 307–308, Roskill LJ left the matter open, at 311.

[81] *Liverpool Taxi Fleet* [1972] 2 Q.B. 299 at 308.

[82] *Liverpool Taxi Fleet* [1972] 2 Q.B. 299 at 311. See also, *R. v Secretary of State for Health, Ex p. United States Tobacco International Ltd* [1992] Q.B. 353 DC at 370; *R. (Gates Hydraulics Ltd) v Secretary of State for Communities and Local Government* [2009] EWHC 2187 (Admin); *R. (Niazi) v Secretary of State for the Home Department* [2008] EWCA Civ 755 at [29]–[31]; *R. (Kelly) v Hounslow LBC* [2010] EWHC 1256 (Admin). Compare *R. v Devon County Council, Ex p. Baker* [1993] C.O.D. 138 QBD.

[83] *R. v Secretary of State for the Home Department, Ex p. Asif Mahmood Khan* [1984] 1 W.L.R. 1337 CA (Civ Div).

[84] *Asif Mahmood Khan* [1984] 1 W.L.R. 1337 at 1344. See also, *R. v Rochdale Metropolitan Borough Council, Ex p. Schemet* [1993] C.O.D. 113 QBD. Reliance is required to sustain an action of this nature, *R. v Lloyds of London, Ex p. Briggs* [1993] C.O.D. 66 QBD.

must, however, now be seen in the light of art.6 of the European Convention of Human Rights (ECHR). The Human Rights Act 1998 (HRA) incorporated Convention rights into domestic law, including art.6. The courts have an obligation to interpret legislation to be in accord with these rights,[85] and acts of public authorities that are incompatible with the rights are unlawful.[86] Section 2 of the HRA provides that the national courts must take into account the jurisprudence of the Strasbourg institutions, although they are not bound by it. The Human Rights Act will be considered below,[87] but it is appropriate to consider the implications of art.6 at this juncture. Article 6(1) applies to both civil and criminal cases alike.

> "In the determination of his civil rights and obligations or of any criminal charge against him, everyone is entitled to a fair and public hearing within a reasonable time by an independent and impartial tribunal established by law. Judgment shall be pronounced publicly but the press and the public may be excluded from all or part of the trial in the interests of morals, public order or national security in a democratic society, where the interests of juveniles or the protection of the private life of the parties so require, or the extent strictly necessary in the opinion of the court in special circumstances where the publicity would prejudice the interests of justice."

The first sentence of art.6(1) imposes a duty to provide a hearing where the conditions mentioned are present. The initial trigger for art.6(1) is the existence of "civil rights and obligations". It is important to be clear about the meaning of this phrase.

The *intent of the framers of the ECHR in using this phrase is by no means clear*. On one view, the phrase "civil rights and obligations" was originally intended to cover those rights and obligations that would, in Continental legal systems, be adjudicated on by the civil courts. These were in essence rights and obligations in private law.[88] On another view, it has been argued that studies of the drafting history of art.14 of the International Covenant on Civil and Political Rights, which was used as the model for art.6 ECHR, offer a strong indication that it was not the intent to restrict the scope of art.6 to determinations of rights and obligations of a private law character.[89]

The existence of a civil right is for the autonomous determination of the European Court of Human Rights (ECtHR). It is not resolved solely by the classification adopted by the national legal order. Both the Commission and the ECtHR have stressed that the interpretation of this phrase cannot be answered exclusively by reference to domestic law categorisations. These will be taken into account, but will not be determinative, and the ECtHR will make its own autonomous judgment as to whether a dispute involves civil rights and obligations.[90]

---

[85] Human Rights Act 1998 (HRA) s.3.

[86] HRA s.6.

[87] Ch.20.

[88] *Feldbrugge v Netherlands* (1986) 8 E.H.R.R. 425 at 444, [19]–[21]; *Runa Begum v Tower Hamlets LBC* [2003] 2 A.C. 430 at [28].

[89] P. van Dijk and G. van Hoof, *Theory and Practice of the European Convention on Human Rights*, 3rd edn (Deventer, Netherlands: Kluwer Law International, 1998), p.393.

[90] *Golder v UK* (1975) 1 E.H.R.R. 524 at 536.

The phrase *civil rights and obligations has been interpreted broadly* by the Strasbourg organs so as to include[91]: disputes concerning land use[92]; monetary claims against public authorities[93]; applications for, and revocations of, licences[94]; claims for certain types of social security benefit[95]; and disciplinary proceedings leading to suspension or expulsion from a profession.[96] The rationale for this jurisprudence is in part that administrative decision-making can determine or affect rights and obligations in private law. It is in part that public law rights may closely resemble rights in private law. Article 6(1) is moreover required in initial proceedings if they have a significant influence on later proceedings, or if they are dispositive of the result in later proceedings, where the later proceedings are subject to art.6, even where the initial proceedings, viewed in isolation, would not engage art.6(1).[97]

12–020 There is nonetheless *considerable uncertainty about the outer limits of "civil rights", with distinctions drawn by the ECtHR that are difficult to justify in normative terms*. Van Dijk and van Hoof attest to the lack of clarity and certainty in the Strasbourg case law.[98] They point also to distinctions drawn that have little normative justification. This is especially so insofar as the ECtHR has reasoned from the existence of discretion by public authorities, to the absence of a civil right for the purposes of art.6.[99] The line between a substantive entitlement and a discretionary benefit is notoriously difficult to draw. It is not moreover a valid normative criterion on which to base the existence of procedural protection.[100] The distinction drawn by the ECtHR between rights that the individual has as a private person, and those possessed as a citizen, the latter not being regarded as civil rights for the purposes of art.6, is also deeply problematic.[101] Lord Hoffmann, echoing the sentiments of Laws L.J., stated that

> "... an English lawyer tends to see all claims against the state which are not wholly discretionary as civil rights and to look with indifference upon the casuistry that finds the need to detect analogies with private law".[102]

---

[91] P. Van Dijk, "The Interpretation of 'Civil Rights and Obligations' by the European Court of Human Rights—One More Step to Take", in F. Matscher and H. Petzold (eds), *Protecting Human Rights: The European Dimension: Studies in Honour of Gerard J. Wiarda*, 2nd edn (Carl Heymans Verlag, 1990), pp.131–143.

[92] *Ringeisen v Austria* (1979–80) 1 E.H.R.R. 455; *Sporrong and Lonnroth v Sweden* (1983) 5 E.H.R.R. 35; *Zander v Sweden* (1994) 18 E.H.R.R. 175; *Skarby v Sweden* (1990) 13 E.H.R.R. 90.

[93] *Editions Periscope v France* (1992) 14 E.H.R.R. 597.

[94] *Benthem v Netherlands* (1986) 8 E.H.R.R. 1; *Pudas v Sweden* (1988) 10 E.H.R.R. 380.

[95] *Feldbrugge* (1986) 8 E.H.R.R. 425; *Deumeland v Germany* (1986) 8 E.H.R.R. 448; *Salesi v Italy* (1998) 26 E.H.R.R. 187; *Mennitto v Italy* (2002) 34 E.H.R.R. 1122.

[96] *Le Compte, van Leuven and de Meyere v Belgium* (1982) 4 E.H.R.R. 1; *H v Belgium* (1988) 10 E.H.R.R. 339; *Madan v General Medical Council* [2001] EWHC Admin 577.

[97] *R. (G) v Governor's of X School* [2011] UKSC 30.

[98] Van Dijk and van Hoof, *Theory and Practice of the European Convention on Human Rights* (1998), p.404.

[99] Van Dijk and van Hoof, *Theory and Practice of the European Convention on Human Rights* (1998), p.405.

[100] P. Craig, "The HRA, art.6 and Procedural Rights" [2003] P.L. 753.

[101] Van Dijk and van Hoof, *Theory and Practice of the European Convention on Human Rights* (1998), p.405; *Ferrazzini v Italy* (2002) 34 E.H.R.R. 45.

[102] *Runa Begum* [2003] 2 A.C. 430 at [69].

The *difficulties as to the meaning of civil rights and obligations are apparent in the UK jurisprudence on art.6*. Space precludes a detailed examination of the case law,[103] but three examples will convey the difficulty faced by the courts.[104] 12–021

In *Husain*,[105] the applicant sought judicial review for the withdrawal of financial asylum support. It was accepted that some social security payments were to be classified as civil rights,[106] but that this was not so in relation to discretionary social welfare benefits. The court was consequently required to decide on which side of the line the applicant's claim fell, a task that was not easy.

In *Begum*, the claimant was offered housing as a homeless person, but refused it on the ground that the area in which it was situated suffered from drugs and racism. In the Court of Appeal,[107] Laws LJ held that a right was by definition something to which the individual had an entitlement, and that a discretionary benefit that a public authority could give or refuse as it wished could not be the subject of a right. He acknowledged however that the definition of right was broader than the common law conception of cause of action. He acknowledged also that the administration of the regime under the Housing Act 1996 Pt VII required the authority to resolve a series of matters on a spectrum between the wholly objective and the wholly subjective. In such circumstances the issue of whether there was a civil right could not be answered by a sharp criterion. Laws LJ found that although there was discretion, the applicant possessed a civil right under the housing legislation for the purposes of art.6. The House of Lords in *Begum*[108] left open the issue as to whether the applicant had a civil right for the purposes of art.6. Their Lordships recognised that the Strasbourg jurisprudence had extended the meaning of civil right beyond private rights stricto sensu. They acknowledged that the local authority had some discretion under the relevant statutory provisions, but this did not necessarily preclude the existence of a civil right for the purposes of art.6. When the statutory criteria for providing accommodation were met, the local authority were under a duty to provide it, even though they had some discretion as to the manner in which this would be done. In this sense, the applicant's interest was, in terms of the Strasbourg case law, personal, economic and flowed from specific statutory rules.

In *Ali*[109] the House of Lords decided the issue left open in *Begum* and held that the legislation concerning housing for homeless persons did not give rise to civil rights for the purposes of art.6. Cases where the award of services or benefits in kind was not an individual right of which the applicant could consider himself the

---

103 Craig, "The HRA, art.6 and Procedural Rights" [2003] P.L. 753.

104 See also, *R. (Primary Health Investment Properties Ltd) v Secretary of State for Health* [2009] EWHC 519 (Admin); *R. (Wright) v Secretary of State for Health* [2009] 1 A.C. 739; *R. (Khaled) v Secretary of State for Foreign and Commonwealth Affairs* [2011] EWCA Civ 350; *R. (G) v X School Governors* [2011] UKSC 30; *R. (Puri) v Bradford Teaching Hospitals NHS Foundation Trust* [2011] EWHC 970 (Admin); *Mattu v University Hospitals of Coventry and Warwickshire NHS Trust* [2012] EWCA Civ 641.

105 *R. (Hamid Ali Husain) v Asylum Support Adjudicator* [2001] EWHC 852 (Admin).

106 *Feldbrugge* (1986) 8 E.H.R.R. 425; *Deumeland* (1986) 8 E.H.R.R. 448.

107 *Runa Begum v Tower Hamlets LBC* [2002] 2 All E.R. 668 at [23]–[24].

108 *Runa Begum* [2003] 2 A.C. 430.

109 *Ali v Birmingham City Council* [2010] 2 A.C. 39 SC.

holder, but was dependent on a series of evaluative judgments by the provider as to whether the statutory criteria were satisfied and how the need ought to be met, did not engage art.6(1).

Applicants seek to use art.6 in domestic courts primarily in order to argue that the decision-maker was not independent and impartial as required by that article. The courts are fully aware of this connection. The case law on this will be considered within a later chapter, since it is connected to the issue of bias. Suffice it to say for the present, that the wording of art.6 threatens to embroil the courts in complex disputes as to the meaning of civil right, with the consequence that the obligation to provide an independent and impartial tribunal will often be unpredictable and turn on distinctions that have little or no normative foundation.[110]

6. CONTENT OF PROCEDURAL PROTECTION: BALANCING

12–022 Any legal system must decide how to determine the content of procedural protection, assuming that some natural justice has been held to be applicable. There are a number of options.[111] At one end of the spectrum is the all-embracing procedural code, which addresses such matters in detail. At the other end of the spectrum are ad hoc judicial decisions, with the courts deciding on a case by case basis. There are various options in between. The courts may develop a general formula through which to determine the content of process rights.[112] Legislation may stipulate the content of process rights for hearings of a certain type, for example those that are more formal in nature.[113] The content of hearing rights can alternatively be determined by a mixture of ad hoc case law, combined with sector-specific legislation that applies the courts' precepts and fleshes them out.

The United Kingdom has no general procedural code to determine the detailed content of procedural rights, although sector-specific legislation operates in particular areas, and such codes have been increasingly developed by tribunals.[114] The courts therefore generally undertake a balancing test to determine the content of procedural rights required in a particular case.

A. Balancing: Factors

12–023 The courts take account of a wide variety of factors within this balancing test. These include the nature of the individual's interest; the type of decision challenged; whether it was final or preliminary; the type of subject-matter; how far it was necessary to supplement statutory procedures; and the cost of imposing

[110] See cases, *Primary Health Investment Properties Ltd* [2009] EWHC 519 (Admin); *Wright* [2009] 1 A.C. 739; *Khaled* [2011] EWCA Civ 350; *G* [2011] UKSC 30; *Puri* [2011] EWHC 970 (Admin); Craig, "The HRA, art.6 and Procedural Rights" [2003] P.L. 753.

[111] Craig, "Perspectives on Process: Common Law, Statutory and Political" [2010] P.L. 275.

[112] See, e.g. the approach adopted in relation to the content of constitutional due process in the US, *Mathews v Eldridge* 424 US 319 (1976).

[113] This is the methodology for formal adjudication and formal rulemaking under the Administrative Procedure Act 1946 in the US.

[114] Craig, "Perspectives on Process: Common Law, Statutory and Political" [2010] P.L. 275.

further procedural requirements. In more general terms, the result is arrived at after balancing three types of factor: the individual's interest; the benefits to be derived from added procedural safeguards; and the costs to the administration, both direct and indirect, of complying with these procedural safeguards.

The more important the individual interest, the greater the procedural protection. Thus, in *Wilson*[115] the court was concerned with whether the applicant who was given a discretionary life sentence should be told of the reasons why the Parole Board had refused to recommend his release on licence. In deciding that the applicant should be entitled to this information the court was strongly influenced by the fact that the liberty of the subject was involved.[116] This justified departure from previous authorities, which had held that this information did not have to be disclosed.

The balancing process is exemplified by *Pergamon Press.*[117] Inspectors had been appointed to investigate two companies under the control of Robert Maxwell. The directors were unwilling to respond to questions unless given assurances, and on condition that a judicial type inquiry was conducted. When the inspectors refused to give all the detailed assurances the directors claimed a breach of natural justice. The Court of Appeal found for the inspectors. Although they were under a duty to act fairly, they had not broken this duty. While the potentially serious effect of the report required some procedural protection, this was weighed against the interest of the administration in ensuring confidentiality, added to which were the factors of speed and the preliminary nature of the proceedings.

The *GCHQ*[118] case exemplifies judicial "balancing" in a very different context. **12–024**
Their Lordships decided that past practice in the operation of GCHQ generated a legitimate expectation that those who worked there would be consulted before important changes were made in the terms of their employment. The government decision that workers at GCHQ could no longer belong to national trade unions, which was reached without prior consultation, was prima facie in breach of natural justice. Considerations of national security were, however, held to outweigh those of procedural fairness. The court accepted the view of the executive that to give prior notice of their intentions would run the risk of actions that would disrupt the intelligence services. Whether this approach to considerations of national security was too deferential will be considered below.

The way in which the nature of the affected interest can impact on the procedural rights accorded is evident in licensing cases. Thus in *McInnes*,[119] Megarry VC held that in the case of forfeiture the individual was entitled to an unbiased tribunal, notice and a hearing, whereas in the case of an application less

[115] *Wilson* [1992] 1 Q.B. 740.

[116] See also, *R. v Life Assurance and Unit Trust Regulatory Organisation Ltd, Ex p. Ross* [1993] 1 Q.B. 17; *United States Tobacco International Ltd* [1992] Q.B. 353 DC at 370.

[117] *Pergamon Press Ltd, Re* [1971] Ch. 388 CA (Civ Div); *Wiseman* [1971] A.C. 297; *Maxwell v Department of Trade* [1974] Q.B. 523 CA (Civ Div).

[118] *Council of Civil Service Unions v Minister for the Civil Service* [1985] A.C. 74. GCHQ is the Governmental Communications Headquarters responsible for the security of military and official communications and the provision of signals intelligence to the government.

[119] *McInnes* [1978] 1 W.L.R. 1520. See also, *R. v Calgary, Ex p. Sanderson* (1966) 53 D.L.R. (2d) 477; *R. v Secretary of State for the Environment, Ex p. Brent LBC* [1982] Q.B. 593 DC at 642–643.

was required. Since nothing had been taken away the duty in such a case was to reach an honest conclusion without bias and not in pursuance of a capricious policy. Renewal of a licence fell into an intermediate category. Here, the individual might have a legitimate expectation that the licence would be renewed. These cases were, said Megarry VC, to be treated as closer to forfeiture than to those of initial application.

These distinctions should not however be allowed to become over-rigid. There may well be areas where the interest at stake in an application for a licence is considerably more important than that involved in a forfeiture or failure to renew in a different context. Moreover, the duty owed to the applicant may well be higher in certain areas than that indicated by Megarry VC This was recognised in *Quark Fishing*,[120] where it was accepted that elements of procedural fairness could be required even in application cases, especially where the licence constituted a valuable commodity. The public body could be required to afford the applicant the opportunity to make representations, and to provide information on which the decision was founded.

B. Balancing: Limits

12–025 While the courts generally undertake balancing to determine the content of procedural rights in a particular case, the reality is that where natural justice is applicable there have been core process rights, such as notice and some form of hearing, for all cases. The balancing therefore normally operates outside this core, relating to matters such as whether the claimant has an oral or written hearing, whether legal representation is always available, and whether there can be cross-examination, etc.

Thus, as Lord Denning stated, if "the right to be heard is to be a real right which is worth anything, it must carry with it a right in the accused man to know the case which is made against him".[121] This was forcefully reaffirmed in *Anufrijeva*.[122] Lord Steyn held that notice of a decision was essential to enable the person affected to be able to challenge it. It was an "application of the right of access to justice", which was a "fundamental and constitutional principle of our legal system".[123] The rule of law required that a constitutional state should accord individuals the right to know of a decision before their rights could be affected.

The heightened security concerns of the post 9/11 world posed serious challenges for liberal governments. The implications for process rights were thrown into sharp relief by legislation to combat terrorism that severely curtailed process rights. This will be examined in more detail below.[124] Suffice it to say for

---

[120] *Quark Fishing* [2002] EWCA Civ 1409.

[121] *Kanda v Government of Malaya* [1962] A.C. 322 at 337; *Attorney General v Ryan* [1980] A.C. 718; *Hadmor Productions Ltd v Hamilton* [1982] 2 W.L.R. 322, HL; *Al Rawi v Security Service (Justice and others intervening)* [2011] UKSC 34.

[122] *R. (Anufrijeva) v Secretary of State for the Home Department* [2004] 1 A.C. 604 HL.

[123] *Anufrijeva* [2004] 1 A.C. 604 at [26].

[124] See Ch.13.

the present that the existence of a core minimum of process rights was confirmed by the House of Lords in *AF*, at least for cases involving deprivation of liberty.[125]

The appellants were subject to non-derogating control orders, which were made pursuant to the Prevention of Terrorism Act 2005 s.2 (PTA), on the ground that the secretary of state had reasonable grounds for suspecting that the appellant was, or had been, involved in terrorism-related activity, and that he considered it was necessary to make such an order to protect the public from a risk of terrorism. The issue before the House of Lords was whether the procedure for the making of a control order complied with art.6 ECHR. The appellants argued that art.6 was violated because the judge who made the order relied on material in closed hearing that was not disclosed. **12–026**

Lord Phillips gave the leading judgment. The House of Lords held that there was a core minimum of procedural justice and that this could not be overridden by arguments that the procedural rights would not have made any difference. Their Lordships reached this conclusion through reasoning from case law and from principle, with the consequence that the relevant provisions of the PTA 2005 were read down so as to be compatible with Convention rights. The person subject to the control order must be given sufficient information about the allegations against him to enable him to give effective instructions in relation to those allegations. Provided that this requirement was satisfied there could be a fair trial notwithstanding that the person subject to the control order was not provided with the detail or sources of the evidence forming the basis of the allegations. Where, however, the open material consisted purely of general assertions and the case against the person was based solely or to a decisive degree on closed materials the requirements of a fair trial would not be satisfied, however cogent the case based on the closed materials might be.[126]

The precise boundaries of the ruling in *AF* are, however, not entirely certain. It is clear from *Tariq*,[127] discussed in the next chapter, that providing the claimant with the gist of the case against him, what has become known as gisting, is not required in a case of security vetting. It seems clear also from *Tariq* that gisting will not be mandatory except where the liberty of the subject is at stake, provided that the closed material procedure contains appropriate procedural safeguards. It nonetheless remains unclear precisely what constitutes the liberty of the subject for these purposes. It is moreover also not entirely clear whether the gisting requirement is only applicable in cases where art.6 ECHR applies.

C. Balancing: Causation

An important issue is whether the applicability of procedural protection can be affected by the likelihood that the hearing would make a difference to the result in the case. There are a number of authorities holding that this should be **12–027**

[125] *Secretary of State for the Home Department v AF* [2010] 2 A.C. 269 HL; *AT v Secretary of State for the Home Division* [2012] EWCA Civ 42; Craig, "Perspectives on Process: Common Law, Statutory and Political" [2010] P.L. 275; A. Kavanagh, "Special Advocates, Control Orders and the Right to a Fair Trial" (2010) 73 M.L.R. 836.

[126] *AF* [2010] 2 A.C. 269 at [59].

[127] *Tariq v Home Office* [2011] UKSC 35.

irrelevant.[128] This is surely correct. The path of the law is, as Megarry J stated,[129] strewn with examples of unanswerable charges that were completely answered. A reviewing court is, moreover, not in a good position to calculate whether a hearing would have made a difference.[130] In *Evans*[131] the House of Lords explicitly disapproved of statements made in the Court of Appeal that a court could exercise a general power to consider whether the decision reached was fair and reasonable. It stated that where review was based upon breach of natural justice, the court should only be concerned with the manner in which the decision was reached, and not with the correctness of the decision itself.[132] Some courts have, however, looked to the causal link between the existence of a hearing and the final outcome.

First, a court may regard the likelihood of the hearing making a difference as a reason for denying the existence of natural justice or fairness. In *Cinnamond*[133] a number of minicab drivers had been repeatedly prosecuted by the BAA for touting for passengers at the airport. The BAA prohibited the drivers from entering the airport except as bona fide passengers. The drivers sought a declaration that the ban was invalid arguing that it was in breach of natural justice, since they had not been given an opportunity to make representations before it was imposed. Lord Denning MR stated that where there was no legitimate expectation of being heard there was no requirement for a hearing. Because the drivers had a long record of bad behaviour and convictions no such expectations were held to exist.

Secondly, the likelihood of the hearing making a difference may influence the discretionary power to grant a remedy. In *Glynn*[134] the court found that there had been a breach of natural justice by the failure to give a hearing to a student who had been disciplined. A remedy was refused, the court holding that nothing the student could have said could have affected the decision reached.

12–028 Where review is based on procedural grounds the applicability of such protection should not be placed in jeopardy by the court second-guessing whether a hearing would have made a difference. The weight of authority is firmly against such an

---

128 *General Medical Council v Spackman* [1943] A.C. 627 HL at 644; *Annamunthodo v Oilfield Workers' Trade Union* [1961] A.C. 945 at 956; *Ridge* [1964] A.C. 40; *R. v Thames Magistrates' Court, Ex p Polemis* [1974] 1 W.L.R. 1371 QBD at 1375; *St Germain (No.2)* [1979] 1 W.L.R. 1401 at 1411–1412; *Secretary of State for the Environment, Ex p. Brent LBC* [1982] Q.B. 593 DC at 645–646; *R. v Chief Constable of the Thames Valley Police Forces, Ex p. Cotton* [1990] I.R.L.R. 344 CA (Civ Div); *Waite v United Kingdom* (2003) 36 E.H.R.R. 54 at [58]–[59]; *Smith v North Eastern Derbyshire Primary Care Trust* [2006] 1 W.L.R. 3315 CA (Civ Div); *Secretary of State for the Home Department v AF (No.3)* [2010] 2 A.C. 269, HL; *R. (L) v West London Mental Health NHS Trust* [2014] 1 W.L.R. 3103 CA; Sir Thomas Bingham, "Should Public Law Remedies be Discretionary?" [1991] P.L. 64, 72–73.

129 *John v Rees* [1970] Ch. 345 at 402.

130 *Ridge* [1964] A.C. 40 at 127.

131 *Chief Constable of North Wales Police v Evans* [1982] 1 W.L.R. 1155 HL; *Brent LBC* [1982] Q.B. 593.

132 *Evans* [1982] 1 W.L.R. 1155 at 1160–1161, 1174–1175. Compare *Cheall v APEX* [1983] 2 A.C. 180, HL at 190.

133 *Cinnamond v British Airports Authority* [1980] 1 W.L.R. 582 CA (Civ Div); *Malloch* [1971] 1 W.L.R. 1578 at 1595, 1600.

134 *Glynn* [1971] 1 W.L.R. 487.

approach, and arguments of principle firmly support the predominant approach of the case law. The powerful dictum of Sedley LJ captures this sentiment[135]:

> "[I]t is in my respectful view seductively easy to conclude that there can be no answer to a case of which you have only heard one side. There can be few practising lawyers who have not had the experience of resuming their seat in a state of hubristic satisfaction, having called a respectable witness to give apparently cast-iron evidence, only to see it reduced to wreckage by ten minutes of well-informed cross-examination or convincingly explained away by the other side's testimony. Some have appeared in cases in which everybody was sure of the defendant's guilt, only for fresh evidence to emerge which makes it clear that they were wrong. As Mark Twain said, the difference between reality and fiction is that fiction has to be credible. In a system which recruits its judges from practitioners, judges need to carry this kind of sobering experience to the bench. It reminds them that you cannot be sure of anything until all the evidence has been heard, and that even then you may be wrong. It may be, for these reasons, that the answer to Baroness Hale's question—what difference might disclosure have made?—is that you can never know."

The legal position has regrettably been altered by the Criminal Justice and Courts Act 2015 Pt 4, hereafter the CJCA, which imposes substantive constraints on courts and the Upper Tribunal when exercising judicial review. The CJCA s.84 amends the Senior Courts Act s.31, the latter statute containing the principal framework for judicial review in primary legislation. It does so by limiting the circumstances in which permission to proceed and the award of relief at the substantive hearing can be given.

In deciding whether to grant leave/permission the High Court is now empowered to consider of its own motion whether the outcome for the applicant would have been substantially different if the conduct complained of had not occurred, and it must consider that question if the defendant asks it to do so.[136] If it appears to the High Court to be highly likely that the outcome would not have been substantially different, the court must refuse to grant leave,[137] subject to the caveat that the court can disregard the preceding requirement if it considers that it is appropriate to do so for reasons of exceptional public interest, but must certify that it is making use of this proviso.[138] There are analogous conditions limiting the award of relief if the case proceeds to the substantive hearing, the court being instructed to refuse relief and/or a monetary award if it appears to be highly likely that the outcome for the applicant would not have been substantially different if the conduct complained of had not occurred, subject to the proviso concerning exceptional public interest.[139] The same provisions are rendered applicable to the Upper Tribunal when it exercises its judicial review powers.[140] It remains to be seen how these provisions are interpreted, but they are regrettable for the reasons given above.

---

[135] *Secretary of State for the Home Department v AF (No.3)* [2009] 2 W.L.R. 423, CA (Civ Div) at [113].

[136] Senior Courts Act 1981 s.31(3)(C).

[137] Senior Courts Act 1981 s.31(3)(D).

[138] Senior Courts Act 1981 s.31(3)(E), (F).

[139] Senior Courts Act 1981 s.31(2)(A)–(C).

[140] Tribunals, Courts and Enforcement Act 2007 ss.15(5)(A)–(B), 16(3)(C)–(G).

D. Balancing: Execution

12–029 Balancing necessitates not only identification of the individual's interest, but also some judgment about how much we value it, or the weight which we accord to it. Thus to take some position, as Megarry VC did in *McInnes*,[141] as to whether the renewal of a licence is a "higher" interest than an initial application, is not to engage in rigid conceptualism, but is rather a necessary step in reaching any decision. Provided that we do not assume that all renewal cases warrant more protection than all initial application cases, irrespective of the nature of the subject matter, then such ranking is necessary and helpful. It should also be acknowledged that valuation of the nature of the interest and the other elements in the balancing process, the social benefits and costs of the procedural safeguards, may be problematic. This is not simply a "mathematical" calculus.[142]

We should not moreover conclude that all judicial balancing is necessarily premised on the same assumptions. The premises which underpin an essentially law and economics approach to natural justice or fairness, may be far removed from those which underlie a more rights-based approach to process considerations.[143] A law and economics approach to judicial balancing is apparent in the following extract from Posner[144]:

> "[W]hile most lawyers consider that the question whether there is a right to a trial-type hearing in various administrative contexts, such as the exclusion of aliens … turns on some irreducible concept of 'fairness', the economic approach enables the question to be broken down into objectively analysable, although not simple, inquiries. We begin by asking, what is the cost of withholding a trial-type hearing in a particular type of case? This inquiry has two branches: first, how is the probability of an error likely to be affected by a trial-type hearing? … Second, what is the cost of an error if one occurs? … Having established the costs of error, we then inquire into the costs of the measures—a trial-type hearing or whatever—that would reduce the error costs. If those direct costs are low … then adoption can be expected to reduce the sum of error and direct costs and thus increase efficiency."

This particular species of balancing focuses principally on an instrumental connection between process rights and the correct determination on the substance of the case. The process rights are accorded insofar as they constitute an efficient mechanism for ensuring the correctness of the substantive outcome. There are connections between this mode of thought and utilitarianism.[145]

This approach to judicial balancing has, however, been criticised. There are problems of implementing a calculus of this kind. Thus, Mashaw has pointed out that balancing of this kind "has an enormous appetite for data that is disputable, unknown, and, sometimes, unknowable",[146] and that "the accounting task that a thorough analysis of social costs and benefits would impose on the Court is

[141] *McInnes* [1978] 1 W.L.R. 1520; Judge Friendly, "Some Kind of Hearing" (1975) 123 U. Pa. L.R. 1267.

[142] J. Mashaw, "The Supreme Court's Due Process Calculus for Administrative Adjudication in *Mathews v Eldridge*: Three Factors in Search of a Theory of Value" (1976) 44 U. Chi. L.R. 28, 47–48.

[143] Compare R. Posner, "An Economic Approach to Legal Procedure and Judicial Administration" (1973) 2 J. Legal Studies 399 and Mashaw, *Due Process in the Administrative State* (1985).

[144] *Economic Analysis of Law*, 2nd edn (Boston: Little Brown, 1972), p.430.

[145] Mashaw, *Due Process in the Administrative State* (1985), pp.104–108.

[146] Mashaw, *Due Process in the Administrative State* (1985), p.115.

simply too formidable".[147] Moreover, the "dynamic effects of procedural change are unpredictable".[148] The approach moreover risks undervaluing concerns relating to process rights that are not directly related to the accuracy of the decision-making.[149] It is also inconsistent to test procedural rules by some pure utilitarian calculus in circumstances where one believes that a person has a substantive entitlement of some kind.[150]

Some balancing must, nonetheless, be undertaken. To denominate certain interests as rights for the purposes of procedural protection, and to take no account of other factors in determining the nature of this protection, is implausible given that the costs of such protection have to be borne by society. This has been recognised by Dworkin, who notes that in both the criminal and civil process the individual is provided with less than the optimum guarantee of accuracy, and that "the savings so achieved are justified by considerations of the general public welfare."[151] As Mashaw states[152]: **12–030**

> "[W]e cannot sustain a vision of the world in which rights ring out true and clear, unencumbered by the consideration of conflicting claims of others to scarce resources. It is the fundamentally compromised nature of social life that interest balancing recognizes and confronts."

It is important, therefore, to consider the judicial balancing that would be countenanced by those who disapprove of "pure" cost-benefit analysis, and yet at the same time recognise that society cannot provide an absolute level of procedural protection, which pays no heed to cost considerations. Dworkin advances one such approach.[153] He draws a distinction between the bare harm suffered by an individual who is punished, and the further injury suffered when the punishment is unjust, simply by virtue of that injustice. This injustice factor is termed moral harm.[154] The importance of this element is brought out in the following extract[155]:

> "People are entitled that the injustice factor in any decision that deprives them of what they are entitled to have be taken into account, and properly weighted, in any procedures designed to test their substantive rights. But it does not automatically follow either that they do or do not have a right to a hearing of any particular scope or structure. That depends on a variety of factors, conspicuously including those the court mentioned in *Mathews*.[156] The court was wrong, not in thinking those factors relevant, but in supposing that the claimant's side of the

[147] Mashaw, *Due Process in the Administrative State* (1985), p.127.

[148] Mashaw, *Due Process in the Administrative State* (1985), p.127.

[149] Mashaw, *Due Process in the Administrative State* (1985), p.113. See also, Hart, *Concept of Law* (1961); Rawls, *A Theory of Justice* (1973); Michelman, "Formal and Associational Aims in Procedural Due Process", in Pennock and Chapman (eds), *Due Process* (1977); Mashaw, *Due Process in the Administrative State* (1985).

[150] R. Dworkin, *A Matter of Principle* (1985), pp.79–84.

[151] R. Dworkin, *A Matter of Principle* (1985), p.74.

[152] Mashaw, *Due Process in the Administrative State* (1985), pp.154–155.

[153] R. Dworkin, *A Matter of Principle* (1985), Ch.3.

[154] R. Dworkin, *A Matter of Principle* (1985), p.80.

[155] R. Dworkin, *A Matter of Principle* (1985), pp.100–101.

[156] The case is *Mathews v Eldridge* 424 US 319 (1976), in which the Supreme Court of the United States held that the availability of procedural rights would depend on the following factors: the interest of the individual; the risk of any erroneous deprivation of that interest through the procedures

scales contained only the bare harm he would suffer if payments were cut off. The claimant's side must reflect the proper weighting of the risk of moral harm, though it may well be that the balance will nevertheless tip in the direction of denying a full adjudicative hearing anyway."

It may be contentious whether a court has weighted the injustice factor appropriately. This does not undermine the importance of the point. It is very difficult to reconcile a view of the law as comprising, in part at least, substantive rights or entitlements, while at the same time being content with a view of procedure based on some pure utilitarian cost-benefit calculus. The recognition that there is an injustice factor helps to ensure that the balancing, necessary though it may be, does not undervalue the nature of the individual's interest.[157] It can in fact be argued that the Dworkinian approach does not go far enough, because Dworkin restricts its use to those cases where the individual possesses a substantive right, and as Galligan has persuasively argued this restriction is unwarranted.[158]

7. CONTENT OF PROCEDURAL PROTECTION: SPECIFIC PROCEDURAL NORMS

A. Notice

12–031 Notice is central to natural justice. This was recognised by Lord Denning who said that if,

> "… the right to be heard is to be a real right which is worth anything, it must carry with it a right in the accused man to know the case which is made against him".[159]

Thus, it is contrary to natural justice to inform an individual of only one complaint if there are two,[160] or to find the person guilty of a different offence from the one that she was charged with.[161] Similarly, it was held to be contrary to natural justice to confirm an order on facts that the individual had no opportunity

actually used, and the probable value of additional procedural safeguards; and the governmental interest, including the costs imposed by the additional procedural requirement.

[157] See also, Mashaw, *Due Process in the Administrative State* (1985), Chs 4–7.

[158] D. Galligan "Rights, Discretion and Procedures", in C. Sampford and D. Galligan (eds), *Law, Rights and the Welfare State* (London: Croom Helm, 1986), pp.139–141; Galligan, *Due Process and Fair Procedures* (1996), pp.104–107.

[159] *Kanda* [1962] A.C. 322 at 337; *Ryan* [1980] A.C. 718; *Hamilton* [1982] 2 W.L.R. 322.

[160] *Board of Trustees of the Maradana Mosque v Mahmud* [1967] 1 A.C. 13 at 24–25.

[161] *Lau Luit Meng v Disciplinary Committee* [1968] A.C. 391.

to show to be erroneous.[162] The right to notice extends also to giving the individual a reasonable amount of time in which to prepare the case.[163]

The importance of the right to notice was reaffirmed in *Anufrijeva*.[164] The claimant was an asylum seeker, whose income support was terminated after the Home Secretary rejected her asylum application. This determination was not however communicated to the claimant. Lord Steyn held that notice of a decision was essential in order to enable the person affected to be able to challenge it. It was an "application of the right of access to justice", which was a "fundamental and constitutional principle of our legal system".[165] The rule of law required that a constitutional state should accord to individuals the right to know of a decision before their rights could be affected.

> "The antithesis of such a state was described by Kafka: a state where the rights of individuals are overridden by hole in the corner decisions or knocks on doors in the early hours".[166]

Lord Steyn acknowledged that there could be exceptional cases where notice was not possible, such as with arrests and search warrants, but held that the present case fell within the ambit of the general rule requiring notice. The right to notice was a fundamental right and could therefore only be excluded by Parliament expressly or by necessary implication. He concluded that Parliament had not done so in the relevant legislation.

While the courts have jealously protected an individual's right to notice,[167] they have on occasion interpreted it in a limited manner.[168] In the *Gaming Board*[169] case the Court of Appeal held that applicants for a gaming licence should have the opportunity to respond to the negative views formed by the Gaming Board. The Board did not, however, have to quote "chapter and verse", nor did it have to disclose the source of its information if it would be contrary to

[162] *Fairmount Investments Ltd v Secretary of State for the Environment* [1976] 1 W.L.R. 1255, HL at 1260, 1265–1266. See also, *R. v Deputy Industrial Injuries Commissioner, Ex p. Jones* [1962] 2 Q.B. 677 DC at 685; *Sabey & Co Ltd v Secretary of State for the Environment* [1978] 1 All E.R. 586 QBD; *R. v Secretary of State for the Environment, Ex p. Norwich City Council* [1982] Q.B. 808, CA (Civ Div); *Mahon v Air New Zealand Ltd* [1984] A.C. 808; *R. (X) v Chief Constable of the West Midlands Police* [2004] 2 All E.R. 1 QBD; *R. (London Reading College Ltd) v Secretary of State for the Home Department* [2010] EWHC 2561 (Admin).

[163] *Polemis* [1974] 1 W.L.R. 1371 at 1375; *R. v Grays Justices, Ex p. Graham* [1982] Q.B. 1239 QBD.

[164] *Anufrijeva* [2004] 1 A.C. 604; *R. (S) v Secretary of State for the Home Department* [2011] EWHC 2120 (Admin); *R. (WL (Congo)) v Secretary of State for the Home Department* [2011] 2 W.L.R. 671 SC at [34]–[36]; *Bank Mellat v HM Treasury* [2013] UKSC 39; *R. v (H) v Secretary of State for the Home Department* [2015] EWHC 377 (Admin).

[165] *Anufrijeva* [2004] 1 A.C. 604 at [26].

[166] *Anufrijeva* [2004] 1 A.C. 604 at [28].

[167] *In Hamilton, Re* [1981] A.C. 1038, HL; *R. v Chichester Justices, Ex p. Collins* [1982] 1 W.L.R. 334 DC; *R. v Diggines, Ex p. Rahmani* [1985] Q.B. 1109, CA (Civ Div); *R. v Secretary of State for the Home Department, Ex p. Al-Mehdawi* [1990] 1 A.C. 876, HL; *R. v Bolton Justices, Ex p. Scally* [1990] 1 Q.B. 537.

[168] *R. (M) v Secretary of State for Constitutional Affairs and the Lord Chancellor* [2004] 2 All E.R. 531, CA (Civ Div).

[169] *Gaming Board* [1970] 2 Q.B. 417 at 430–432.

the public interest, nor did the reasons for the refusal have to be given.[170] In *Breen*[171] a majority of the Court of Appeal held that a disciplinary committee of a trade union did not have to tell a shop steward why they had refused to endorse his election. In *McInnes*[172] it was held that the council of the Boxing Board of Control did not have to give an applicant for a manager's licence an outline of its objections to him. The test adopted in both cases was that the decision-maker should not capriciously withhold approval.[173] It is clear moreover from the *Children's Rights Alliance* case[174] that there is no obligation on the public body to provide notice as to the legal effect of executive action.

There is a tension underlying some decisions between the right to notice and the absence of any general duty to give reasons. In the context of, for example, an application for a licence, there is no "charge". Where the applicant has made repeated unsuccessful requests the person may wish to know why a licence has not been granted. This is, however, tantamount to requiring the giving of reasons, a point noted by Megarry VC in *McInnes*.[175] Whether reasons should be given will be considered below.

B. Consultation

12–032 There is no general duty to consult imposed either by common law or statute. When consultation is specified by statute this may be a mandatory requirement or it may only be directory. Where the statute states that consultation "shall" take place the former construction is more common.[176] The legislation will determine who must be consulted. In some areas there will be a general discretion to consult such interests as appear to be appropriate. In other areas the statute may be more explicit as to which interests should be consulted.[177]

Where a statutory duty to consult exists it requires the authority to supply sufficient information to those being consulted to enable them to tender advice, and a sufficient opportunity to tender that advice before the mind of the authority becomes unduly fixed.[178] Where the obligation to consult is mandatory, failure to

---

[170] Compare, *R. v Kent Police Authority, Ex p. Godden* [1971] 2 Q.B. 662, CA (Civ Div); *Denton v Auckland City* [1969] N.Z.L.R. 256.

[171] *Breen v Amalgamated Engineering Union* [1971] 2 Q.B. 175 CA (Civ Div) at [195], [200].

[172] *McInnes* [1978] 1 W.L.R. 1520.

[173] There is some indication that more would have to be disclosed to the applicant if a charge was made against the person, or if the refusal constituted a slur against the applicant or deprived the individual of a statutory right, *McInnes* [1978] 1 W.L.R. 1520 at 1535.

[174] *R. (Children's Rights Alliance for England) v Secretary of State for Justice* [2013] 1 W.L.R. 3667 CA (Civ Div).

[175] *McInnes* [1978] 1 W.L.R. 1520 at 1532.

[176] *May v Beattie* [1927] 3 K.B. 353; *Rollo v Minister of Town and Country Planning* [1948] 1 All E.R. 13 KBD; *Union of Benefices of Whippingham and East Cowes, St James's, Re* [1954] A.C. 245; *Port Louis Corp v Attorney General of Mauritius* [1965] A.C. 1111; *Sinfield v London Transport Executive* [1970] Ch. 550, CA (Civ Div) at 558; *Agricultural, Horticultural and Forestry Industry Training Board v Aylesbury Mushrooms Ltd* [1972] 1 W.L.R. 190 QBD; *Powley v ACAS* [1978] I.C.R. 123 Ch D.

[177] Compare *Post Office v Gallagher* [1970] 3 All E.R. 712 CA (Civ Div) and *Rollo* [1948] 1 All E.R. 13.

[178] See *Rollo* [1948] 1 All E.R. 13; *Port Louis* [1965] A.C. 1111 and *Sinfield* [1970] Ch. 550.

comply with the duty will result in the order subsequently made being held void. The courts' approach is evident in *Gunning*[179]:

> "First, that consultation must be at a time when proposals are still at a formative stage. Secondly, that the proposer must give sufficient reasons for any proposal to permit intelligent consideration and response. Thirdly, that adequate time must be given for consideration and response and finally, fourthly, that the product of the consultation must be conscientiously taken into account in finalising statutory proposals."

Consultation may also take place on a more informal, non-statutory basis. Advisory committees abound and will commonly be brought into discussions concerning proposed rules,[180] as will other interest groups. It is clear that even where consultation is not a legal requirement, if a public body chooses to consult this has to be done properly and fairly.[181]

There may alternatively be a duty to consult from the common law. This will normally flow from the doctrine of legitimate expectation considered above.[182] Thus, if a public body has made a representation to a specific individual or group of individuals that a particular policy will be followed, or that they will be informed before any such change in policy takes place, then the individuals will be entitled to comment before any such change occurs, or before there is a departure from that policy. Similarly if an individual has in the past enjoyed a benefit or advantage which could legitimately be expected to continue, that person may be entitled to a statement of reasons for the change of position, and an opportunity to be consulted thereon.[183]

The existence and content of any legitimate expectation, whether arising from a representation or past practice, will be a matter of construction.[184] The courts have in general denied a common law duty to consult where there is no legitimate

---

[179] *R. v Brent London Borough Council, Ex p. Gunning* (1985) 84 L.G.R. 168. See also, *R. v Secretary of State for Social Services, Ex p. Association of Metropolitan Authorities* [1993] C.O.D. 54 QBD; *R. (Wainwright) v Richmond upon Thames LBC* [2001] EWCA Civ 2062; *R. (Partingdale Lane Residents Association) v Barnet LBC* [2003] EWHC 947 (Admin); *R. (Eisai Limited) v National Institute for Health and Clinical Excellence* [2008] EWCA Civ 438; *R. (East Devon DC) v Electoral Commission Boundary Committee for England* [2009] EWCA Civ 239; *R. (Peat) v Hyndburn BC* [2011] EWHC 1739 (Admin); *R. (Brynmawr Foundation School Governors) v Welsh Ministers* [2011] EWHC 519 (Admin).

[180] Garner, "Consultation in Subordinate Legislation" [1964] P.L. 105.

[181] *R. (easyJet Airline Co Ltd) v Civil Aviation Authority* [2008] EWCA Civ 755; *R. (Save our Surgery Ltd) v Joint Committee of Primary Care Trusts* [2013] EWHC 439 (Admin).

[182] See para.12–017.

[183] *Council of Civil Service Unions v Minister for the Civil Service* [1985] A.C. 374 HL at 408–409; *Khan* [1985] 1 All E.R. 40; *R. v Secretary of State for the Home Department, Ex p. Ruddock* [1987] 1 W.L.R. 1482 QBD; *R. v Birmingham City Council, Ex p. Dredger* [1993] C.O.D. 340.

[184] Compare *Khan* [1985] 1 All E.R. 40; *Dredger* [1993] C.O.D. 340; *R. v Alnwick DC, Ex p. Robson* [1998] C.O.D. 241; *R. (Greenpeace Ltd) v Secretary of State for Trade and Industry* [2007] EWHC 311 (Admin); *Findlay* [1985] A.C. 318.

expectation.[185] There is no general duty to consult imposed by the common law where the order is of a legislative nature.[186]

12–033 The preceding principles are evident in the following cases. In *Guardians ad Litem*[187] the court held that self-employed guardians had a legitimate expectation, based on the defendant's conduct and statements, that they would be consulted before changes in their terms of engagement. In *LH*[188] the court held that a local authority had a common law duty to consult users of a day care centre that was to be closed. In the *Greenpeace* case[189] a government White Paper on energy policy indicated that the government was not minded to support "new nuclear build" and stated that there would be full public consultation before the government reached any decision to change its policy. A consultation exercise was held and the government decided that it would support some element of "new nuclear build". The court held that there was a legitimate expectation that consultation would occur and that the consultation process that took place was seriously flawed for a number of reasons.[190]

The interplay between statute and common law in relation to the duty to consult is evident in *Moseley*.[191] The Supreme Court held that there had been inadequate consultation concerning local authority budget cuts. Lords Wilson and Kerr acknowledged that the duty to consult could arise pursuant to statute or the common law, but held that "irrespective of how the duty to consult has been generated, that same common law duty of procedural fairness will inform the manner in which the consultation should be conducted".[192] Their Lordships endorsed the criteria for lawful consultation laid down in *Gunning*,[193] holding that they were applicable when the consultation was founded on the common law. They held, moreover, that the degree of specificity with which, in fairness, the public authority should conduct its consultation exercise may be influenced by the identity of those whom it is consulting, and that the demands of fairness

---

[185] *Dredger* [1993] C.O.D. 340; *R. v BBC, Ex p. Kelly* [1998] C.O.D. 58; *R. v Secretary of State for Education, Ex p. Southwark LBC* [1994] C.O.D. 298; *R. (BAPIO Action Ltd) v Secretary of State for the Home Department* [2007] EWCA Civ 1139, affirmed on different grounds [2008] 1 A.C. 1003; *R.. (Moseley) v Haringey LBC* [2014] UKSC 56 at [35].

[186] *Bates v Lord Hailsham* [1972] 1 W.L.R. 1373 at 1378; *R. (BAPIO Action Ltd) v Secretary of State for the Home Department* [2007] EWCA Civ 1139 at [43]–[46], affirmed on different grounds [2008] 1 A.C. 1003; *R. (Hillingdon LBC) v Lord Chancellor* [2008] EWHC 2683 (Admin); *Niazi* [2008] EWCA Civ 755.

[187] *R. (National Association of Guardians Ad Litem and Reporting Officers) v Children and Family Court Advisory and Support Service* [2001] EWHC 693 (Admin).

[188] *R. (LH) v Shropshire Council* [2014] EWCA Civ 404.

[189] *R. (Greenpeace Ltd) v Secretary of State for Trade and Industry* [2007] EWHC 311 (Admin); *Niazi* [2008] EWCA Civ 755; *easyJet* [2009] EWCA Civ 1361; J. Thornton, "Greenpeace and the Law of Consultations" [2007] J.P.L. 975.

[190] The potential implications of this case are far-reaching. If a government department or agency formally announces that it will engage in consultation on a particular policy matter then it is arguable that this will in itself create a legitimate expectation that such consultation will occur, and allow the courts to adjudicate on the adequacy of the consultation exercise. This could open the door to judicial review of the adequacy of consultation exercises that are undertaken pursuant to the government's Code of Practice on Consultation, see Ch.15 for discussion of the Code.

[191] *Moseley* [2014] UKSC 56.

[192] *Moseley* [2014] UKSC 56 at [24].

[193] *Gunning* (1985) 84 L.G.R. 168.

would be higher when an authority deprived someone of an existing benefit, than when the claimant was a bare applicant for a future benefit.[194] Lord Reed concurred with the result, but preferred to base the decision on the specific statutory duty to consult in the instant case, rather than drawing on the common law duty to act fairly and legitimate expectations, which were not, in his view, pertinent to the instant case.[195]

C. The Hearing

i. The type of hearing

While hearings will normally be oral, there is no fixed rule that this must be so.[196] **12–034**
An oral hearing will, however, be required where this is necessary for the applicant to be able to present his case effectively to the tribunal or body making the decision, more especially when a liberty interest is at stake.[197] Thus in *Osborn* the Supreme Court held that the parole board had to hold an oral hearing whenever fairness to the prisoner required in order to comply with common law standards of procedural fairness and to act compatibly with art.5(4) when determining an application for release or transfer to open conditions.[198]

The courts will, moreover, avoid construing a statute so as to dispense with a hearing completely. A statute empowering a public body to dispense with a hearing will, for example, be interpreted to allow oral hearings to be omitted, and courts do not look kindly on interference with the right to a hearing through retrospective legislation.[199] There are some cases that appear to hold that natural justice may not require a hearing.[200] These statements must be treated with great reserve. While the type of hearing may differ within different areas, and while it might vary depending upon, for example, the stage the proceedings have reached or the nature of the interest being asserted, to go further than this would be contrary to principle. To assert that, quite apart from the above factors, natural justice could be satisfied even though there was nothing in the nature of a hearing at all would be to denude the concept of all content.[201]

It is axiomatic that the hearing should accord the affected party the opportunity to **12–035**
respond to allegations made against him,[202] the corollary being that the evidence

194 *Moseley* [2014] UKSC 56 at [25]-[26].

195 *Moseley* [2014] UKSC 56 at [34]-[38].

196 *R. v Amphlett (Judge)* [1915] 2 K.B. 223 KBD; *Kavanagh v Chief Constable of Devon and Cornwall* [1974] Q.B. 24 CA (Civ Div); *Attorney General v Ryan* [1980] A.C. 718; *R. (Heather Moor & Edgecomb) v Financial Ombudsman Service* [2009] EWHC 2701 (Admin); *R.(Lynch) v Secretary of State for the Home Department* [2012] EWHC 1597 (Admin); *Clayton v Army Board of the Defence Council* [2014] EWHC 1651 (Admin).

197 *R. (Smith) v Parole Board* [2005] 1 All E.R. 755, HL.

198 *R. (Osborn) v Parole Board* [2014] A.C. 1115 SC.

199 *R. (Reilly) v Secretary of State for Work and Pensions* [2014] EWHC 2182 (Admin).

200 *Roffey* [1969] 2 Q.B. 538 at 552, 556; *Breen v Amalgamated Engineering Union* [1971] 2 Q.B. 175 CA (Civ Div).

201 *AF* [2010] 2 A.C. 269.

202 *R. (Shoesmith) v Ofsted* [2011] EWCA Civ 642.

against him should be made known to the affected party.[203] Courts will therefore lean strongly against allowing a tribunal to decide a matter without giving the individual a chance to see the opposing case and have his own considered,[204] although the difficulties created in this respect by the procedures in the anti-terror legislation will be considered below.[205] There may also be a breach of natural justice where the tribunal referred in its decision to an authority that the parties did not have the opportunity to address, provided that the authority was central to the decision and that a material injustice resulted.[206] The application of these basic precepts can however be contentious, as is evident from *Roberts*.[207] The claimant challenged the decision of the Parole Board that certain sensitive material placed before it by the Home Office should be withheld from the claimant and his solicitor, and that it should only be disclosed to a specially appointed advocate, who would represent the claimant at a closed hearing of the Parole Board. The case provoked sharp division of opinion in the House of Lords. The majority held that this procedure was prima facie compatible with natural justice, and within the powers of the Parole Board. Lord Bingham and Lord Steyn dissented. They held that the procedure was incompatible with the principle that the affected party should have the opportunity to respond to allegations made against him, the corollary being that the evidence should be made known to the affected party.[208] They held moreover that the Parole Board had no power to adopt such a procedure, and that the principle of legality meant that statutes should be interpreted as not interfering with fundamental rights, in this context the right to a fair hearing.[209]

An individual can waive the right to a hearing,[210] but this option will not always be open. Thus, in *Hanson*[211] it was held that where the matter was one in which there was a wider public interest it might not be possible for one party to withdraw without the assent of the other once the proceedings had begun. Even if both parties agreed the issue might not be withdrawn if the tribunal objected. However, where an individual has lost the opportunity to present the case through the fault of her own advisers this could not constitute a breach of natural justice.[212]

---

203 *Official Solicitor v K* [1965] A.C. 201 HL; *D (Minors) (Adoption Reports: Confidentiality), Re* [1996] A.C. 593 HL at 603–604, 615; *Wilson* [1992] 1 Q.B. 740 at 751–752; *Doody* [1994] 1 A.C. 531 at 562.

204 *R. v Housing Appeal Tribunal* [1920] 3 KB 334 KBD; *Wilson, Re* [1985] A.C. 750 HL; *R v Birmingham JJ, ex p Lamb* [1983] 1 WLR 339 DC; *R. v Central Criminal Court, ex p Boulding* [1984] QB 813 QBD; *Wright* [2009] 1 A.C. 739.

205 See Ch.13.

206 *Sheridan v Stanley Cole (Wainfleet) Ltd* [2003] 4 All E.R. 1181, CA (Civ Div).

207 *Roberts v Parole Board* [2005] 2 A.C. 738, HL.

208 *Roberts* [2005] 2 A.C. 738 at [16]–[18], [88]–[97].

209 *Roberts* [2005] 2 A.C. 738 at [25], [93].

210 *R. v Deputy Industrial Injuries Commissioner, Ex p. Moore* [1965] 1 Q.B. 456, CA at 489–490. The onus placed on the individual to request a hearing may well be inappropriate.

211 *Hanson v Church Commissioners* [1978] Q.B. 823, CA (Civ Div).

212 *R. v Secretary of State for the Home Department, Ex p. Al-Mehdawi* [1990] 1 A.C. 876, HL.

ii. *Rules of evidence*

The strict rules of evidence do not have to be followed.[213] Diplock LJ set out the following general principles: the tribunal is not restricted to evidence acceptable in a court of law; provided that it has some probative value the court will not reassess its weight. Where there is an oral hearing, written evidence submitted by the applicant must be considered, but the tribunal may take account of any evidence[214] of probative value from another source provided that the applicant is informed and allowed to comment on it. An applicant must also be allowed to address argument on the whole of the case,[215] but there is no right to cross examine in all cases.[216] **12–036**

These general principles are, however, subject to the following reservation. The overriding obligation is to provide the applicant with a fair hearing and a fair opportunity to controvert the charge.[217] This may in certain cases require not only that the applicant be informed of the evidence, but that the individual should be given a sufficient opportunity to deal with it,[218] more especially when a public consultation has taken place.[219] This may involve the cross-examination of the witnesses whose evidence is before the hearing authority in the form of hearsay.[220] Where there are insuperable difficulties in arranging for that evidence to be questioned it should not be admitted in evidence, or the hearing authority should exclude it from their consideration.

D. Representation

The legal position as to whether an individual can choose a representative, including a lawyer, can be summarised as follows.[221] **12–037**

---

[213] *Moore* [1965] 1 Q.B. 456 at 476–477, 486–490; *Mahon* [1984] A.C. 808 at 820–821.

[214] For the extent to which personal knowledge and impression can be used, *R. v City of Westminster Assessment Committee, Ex p. Grosvenor House (Park Lane) Ltd* [1941] 1 K.B. 53 CA; *Crofton Investment Trust Ltd v Greater London Rent Assessment Committee* [1967] Q.B. 955 at 967; *Wetherall v Harrison* [1976] Q.B. 773 QBD.

[215] *Mahon* [1984] A.C. 808 at 820–821; *R (Afzal) v Election Court* [2005] EWCA Civ 647.

[216] *Kavanagh v Chief Constable of Devon and Cornwall* [1974] Q.B. 624, CA (Civ Div); *Bushell v Secretary of State for the Environment* [1981] A.C. 75, HL; *R. v Commission for Racial Equality, Ex p. Cottrell and Rothon* [1980] 1 W.L.R. 1580 DC; *Chilton v Saga Holidays Plc* [1986] 1 All E.R. 841, CA (Civ Div); *R. v Secretary of State for the Home Department, Ex p. Tarrant* [1985] Q.B. 251 DC, 288–289; *Public Disclosure Commission v Isaacs* [1989] 1 All E.R. 137; *R. (N) v M* [2006] EWCA Civ 1789 at [39]; *R. (JB) v Haddock (Responsible Medical Officer)* [2006] EWCA Civ 961 at [64]; *R. (Bonhoeffer) v General Medical Council* [2011] EWHC 1585 (Admin); *R. (St Matthews (West) Ltd) v HM Treasury* [2014] EWHC 2426 (Admin).

[217] *St Germain (No.2)* [1979] 1 W.L.R. 1401at 1408–1412.

[218] *Smith* [2005] 1 All E.R. 755.

[219] *Edwards* [2005] 1 All E.R. 755; *Smith* [2002] EWHC 2640 (Admin).

[220] *Bonhoeffer* [2011] EWHC 1585 (Admin); *R. (Evans) v Chief Constable of Sussex* [2011] EWHC 2329.

[221] J. Alder, "Representation Before Tribunals" [1972] P.L. 278; Galligan, *Due Process and Fair Procedures* (1996), pp.361–369.

First, there appears to be no absolute right to such representation.[222] Legal representation may be counterproductive, unnecessary or overly cumbersome in cases where a matter must be speedily resolved, and hence the courts have resisted claims that there should be a right to such representation. This must, however, now be seen in the light of the decision in *Ezeh*,[223] where the ECtHR held that a person charged with a criminal offence who does not wish to defend himself in person must be able to have recourse to legal assistance of his own choosing, and that the denial of legal representation constituted a breach of the second limb of art.6(3)(c) of the Convention.

Second, the courts have, however, emphasised that tribunals possess discretion as to whether to allow such representation, and are willing to review the manner in which the discretion is exercised. A tribunal controls its own procedure, and this provides the foundation from which it can permit such representation.[224] Consideration of the statutory scheme within a particular area may convince the court that representation by a lawyer should on construction be excluded.[225] However, the courts are in general reluctant to exclude the possibility of such legal representation in a particular area, and if a tribunal did this it might be regarded as a fetter on discretion.[226] In exercising their discretion whether to permit such representation, tribunals should take the following factors into account[227]: the seriousness of the charge or penalty; whether any points of law are likely to arise; the capacity of a person to present their own case; procedural difficulties; the need for speed in reaching a decision; and the need for fairness as between the individual and the officers concerned.

Third, there does not appear to be any general right to attend a hearing as the friend or adviser of the individual directly concerned. Whether such a right exists depends on the nature of the tribunal in question. Any such tribunal does, however, have discretion to allow the individual to be assisted by such an adviser.[228]

222 *Enderby Town Football Club Ltd v Football Association Ltd* [1971] Ch. 591 at 605; *Fraser v Mudge* [1975] 1 W.L.R. 1132 at 1133, 1134; *R. v Secretary of State for the Home Department, Ex p. Tarrant* [1985] Q.B. 251, 270–272, 295–296; *R. v Board of Visitors of HM Prison, The Maze, Ex p. Hone* [1988] 1 A.C. 379.

223 *Ezeh and Connors v United Kingdom* (2002) 35 E.H.R.R 28; *Bell v United Kingdom* (2007) 45 E.H.R.R. 24; *Kulkarni v Milton Keynes Hospital NHS Trust* [2009] EWCA Civ 789.

224 *Tarrant* [1985] Q.B. 251 at 273.

225 *Maynard v Osmond* [1977] Q.B. 240 CA (Civ Div) at 253, 255.

226 *Enderby Town* [1971] Ch. 591.

227 *Tarrant* [1985] Q.B. 251 at 284–286; *R. v Secretary of State for the Home Department, Ex p. Anderson* [1984] Q.B. 778 QBD; *Hone* [1988] 1 A.C. 379.

228 *Tarrant* [1985] Q.B. 251 at 282–283, 298.

E. Reasons

i. The importance of reasons

There are a number of advantages in the provision of reasons for decisions.[229] First, reasons can assist the courts in performing their supervisory function. Substantive review based on relevancy, propriety of purpose or proportionality is easier to apply if the agency's reasons are evident. Second, an obligation to provide reasons will often help to ensure that the decision has been thought through by the agency. Third, the provision of reasons can help to ensure that other objectives of administrative law are not frustrated. If, for example, we grant consultation rights in certain areas, then a duty to furnish reasons will make it more difficult for the decision-maker merely to go through the motions of hearing interested parties without actually taking their views into account. Finally, it is arbitrary to have one's status redefined without an adequate explanation of the reasons for the action. The provision of reasons can, by way of contrast, increase public confidence in the administrative process and enhance its legitimacy. A duty to provide reasons can, therefore, help to attain both the instrumental and non-instrumental objectives that underlie process rights. **12–038**

The disadvantages of a duty to provide reasons are said to be that it can stifle the exercise of discretion and overburden the administration. It is doubtful whether these objections are convincing. EU law has a general duty to provide reasons embodied in art.296 TFEU, which applies to the making of regulations as well as decisions.[230] This has been a requirement since the EEC was first created and there is no indication that it has overburdened the administration or stifled the exercise of discretion.

There is no general duty to give reasons in English law, although the common law is moving in that direction. While statutory and common law rules impose a duty to provide reasons in certain circumstances, the absence of any general duty is still a gap in our procedural protection.[231] The historical origins of the rule that there is no general duty to provide reasons are obscure.[232] In so far as they are based upon analogy with the position of courts of law, this reasoning is being undermined, as the judiciary increasingly require some statement of reasons

---

[229] M. Akehurst, "Statements of Reasons for Judicial and Administrative Decisions" (1970) 33 M.L.R. 154; G. Flick, "Administrative Adjudications and the Duty to Give Reasons—A Search for Criteria" [1978] P.L. 16; D. Galligan, "Judicial Review and the Textbook Writers" (1982) 2 O.JL.S. 257; G. Richardson, "The Duty to Give Reasons: Potential and Practice" [1986] P.L. 437; P. Craig, "The Common Law, Reasons and Administrative Justice" [1994] C.L.J. 282; Sir Patrick Neil, "The Duty to Give Reasons: The Openness of Decision-Making", in C. Forsyth and I. Hare (eds), *The Golden Metwand and the Crooked Cord* (Oxford: Oxford University Press, 1998), pp.161–184; M. Elliott, "Has the Common Law Duty to Give Reasons Come of Age Yet?" [2011] P.L. 56.

[230] P. Craig, *EU Administrative Law*, 2nd edn (Oxford: Oxford University Press, 2012), Ch.12.

[231] *Administrative Justice, Some Necessary Reforms* (Oxford: Oxford University Press, 1988), pp.46–68; *R v Secretary of State for the Home Dept, Ex p. Harrison* [1988] 3 All E.R. 86; *R. v Civil Service Appeal Board, Ex p. Bruce* [1989] I.C.R. 171, CA (Civ Div).

[232] *Administrative Justice, Some Necessary Reforms* (1988), pp.29–32.

within judgments.[233] An obligation to furnish reasons in a particular case may be imposed by statute, the common law or EU law. These will be considered in turn.

ii. Reasons and statute: general

12–039 Statutory intervention owes much to the Franks Committee, which recommended the giving of reasons.[234] This was enacted in the Tribunals and Inquiries Act 1958,[235] which requires the tribunals listed in the Act to give a statement, written or oral, of the reasons for a decision, if requested by the individual. The statute also applies to ministerial decisions subsequent to statutory inquiries. In addition, primary and secondary legislation has imposed a duty to give reasons in specific situations.[236]

The stringency of the duty to provide reasons will depend on the statutory language and the context. The reasons given must be adequate, intelligible and deal with the substantial points that have been raised. They must enable the individual to assess whether the decision can be challenged.[237] Yet the courts have also held that an alleged deficiency in the provision of reasons will only lead to the decision being quashed if the applicant has been substantially prejudiced.[238] Moreover, the preponderant view appears to be that a mere failure to comply with the duty to provide reasons does not, of itself, provide grounds for appeal on a point of law. The decision will only be quashed if the reasons as stated actually furnish evidence of such an error.[239] Sedley J has however signalled that this issue should be reconsidered, so that the law could be brought

---

[233] *Eagil Trust Co Ltd v Piggott-Brown* [1985] 3 All E.R. 119, CA (Civ Div); *R. v Harrow Crown Court, Ex p. Dave* [1994] C.O.D. 99; *R. v Winchester Crown Court, Ex p. Morris* [1996] C.O.D. 104; *Flannery v Halifax Estate Agencies (t/a Colleys Professional Services)* [2000] 1 W.L.R. 377, CA (Civ Div); *R. v Denton* [2001] 1 Cr. App. R. 16, CA (Crim Div); *English v Emery Reimbold & Strick Ltd* [2002] 1 W.L.R. 2409, CA (Civ Div); *Butler v Thompson* [2005] EWCA Civ 864; *Cunliffe v Fielden* [2006] Ch. 361.

[234] The Franks Report (1957), Cmnd.218, paras 98 and 351.

[235] Tribunals and Inquiries Act 1958 s.12(1), replaced by the Tribunals and Inquiries Act 1992 s.10(1).

[236] *R. v Minister of Housing and Local Government, Ex p. Chichester RDC* [1960] 1 W.L.R. 587 DC; *Givaudan & Co Ltd v Minister of Housing and Local Government* [1967] 1 W.L.R. 250 QBD; *Brayhead (Ascot) Ltd v Berkshire CC* [1964] 2 Q.B. 303 QBD; *French Kier Developments Ltd v Secretary of State for Environment* [1977] 1 All E.R. 296 QBD; *R. v Secretary of State for the Home Department, Ex p. Dannenberg* [1984] Q.B. 766, CA (Civ Div); *Bone v Mental Health Review Tribunal* [1985] 3 All E.R. 330 QBD; *R. v Mental Health Review Tribunal, Ex p. Pickering* [1986] 1 All E.R. 99 QBD; *Westminster City Council v Great Portland Estates Plc* [1985] A.C. 661, HL.

[237] *Poyser and Mills's Arbitration,* [1964] 2 Q.B. 467 QBD at 478; *Westminster City Council v Great Portland Estates Plc* [1985] A.C. 661, HL at 673; *R. v City of Westminster, Ex p. Ermakov* [1996] C.O.D. 391, CA (Civ Div); *R. (Mevagissey Parish Council) v Cornwall Council* [2013] EWHC 3684 (Admin).

[238] *Save Britain's Heritage v Secretary of State for the Environment* [1991] 1 W.L.R. 153, HL; *South Bucks District Council v Porter (No.2)* [2004] 1 W.L.R. 1953, HL.

[239] *Mountview Court Properties Ltd v Devlin* (1970) 21 P. & C.R. 689 QBD; *Crake v Supplementary Benefits Commission* [1982] 1 All E.R. 498 QBD; *R. v Legal Aid Area No.8 (Northern) Appeal Committee, Ex p. Angel* [1990] C.O.D. 355 QBD; *S (A Minor) v Special Educational Needs Tribunal* [1996] 1 All E.R. 171 QBD; Richardson, "The Duty to Give Reasons: Potential and Practice" [1986] P.L. 437, 450–457.

into line with that on judicial review.[240] It is open to the court to refer an inadequately reasoned decision back to the original decision-maker.[241]

iii. *Reasons and statute: HRA and the ECHR*

The general relevance of the ECHR for the content of procedural norms will be considered below. Article 6 ECHR has implications for the provision of reasons where there are civil rights and obligations. While there is no express requirement to give reasons the ECtHR regards this as implicit in the obligation to provide a fair hearing. Reasons do not have to be given on every single point, but they must be sufficient to enable a party to understand the essence of the decision in order to be able to exercise any appeal rights.[242] The Privy Council recognised in *Stefan*[243] that the advent of the HRA, which brought art.6 into domestic law, would therefore require the courts to pay close attention to the giving of reasons in cases involving civil rights and obligations. **12–040**

iv. *Reasons and the common law: indirect techniques for securing reasons*

There is no general common law duty to give reasons,[244] but there are none the less a number of ways in which the common law has imposed such a duty in particular instances. **12–041**

First, it can be argued that the absence of reasons renders any right of appeal or review nugatory, or that it makes the exercise of that right more difficult. This reasoning was originally developed in the context of appeal as illustrated by *Wrights' Canadian Ropes.*[245] Wrights' Canadian Ropes Ltd complained that the minister should have allowed claims for expenses to be set off against tax. The Privy Council held that although the minister was not bound to disclose his reasons, he could not thereby render the company's right of appeal nugatory. The court could look at the facts before the minister, and if those were insufficient in law to support his determination then the court would deem that it must have been arbitrary. The same approach has been adopted in later cases.[246]

If this line of argument were applied to the courts' powers of review it would lead to a general right to a reasoned decision.[247] There are some indications of

240 *R. v Northamptonshire CC, Ex p. Marshall* [1998] C.O.D. 457 QBD at 458.

241 *Emery Reimbold* [2002] 1 W.L.R. 2409; *Adami v Ethical Standards Officer of the Standards Board for England* [2005] EWCA Civ 1754.

242 *Helle v Finland* (1998) 26 E.H.R.R. 159; *Van de Hurk v The Netherlands* (1994) 18 E.H.R.R. 481.

243 *Stefan v General Medical Council* [2000] H.R.L.R. 1.

244 *Minister of National Revenue v Wrights' Canadian Ropes Ltd* [1947] A.C. 109 at 123; *Gaming Board* [1970] 2 Q.B. 417 at 431; *McInnes* [1978] 1 W.L.R. 1520 at 1532; *R. v Civil Service Appeal Board, Ex p. Cunningham* [1991] 4 All E.R. 310, CA (Civ Div).

245 *Wrights' Canadian Ropes* [1947] A.C. 109.

246 *Norton Tool Co Ltd v Tewson* [1973] 1 W.L.R. 45 at 49; *Alexander Machinery (Dudley) Ltd v Crabtree* [1974] I.C.R. 120 at 122; *Bone* [1985] 3 All E.R. 330; *Dannenberg* [1984] Q.B. 766 at 775–776; *Flannery* [2000] 1 W.L.R. 377.

247 *R. v Knightsbridge Crown Court, Ex p. International Sporting Club (London) Ltd* [1982] 2 Q.B. 304 at 314–315; *R. v Immigration Appeal Tribunal, Ex p. Khan* [1983] Q.B. 790.

such a development. *Doody*[248] was concerned with life sentences for murder, and whether the secretary of state should tell the prisoner the reasons why he was deciding on a certain period of time for imprisonment. Lord Mustill reiterated the orthodoxy that there was no general duty to provide reasons. However, he also found that there was a duty to give reasons in this instance, because the reasons would facilitate any judicial review challenge by the prisoner, who might wish to argue that the secretary of state had erred in departing from the sentence originally recommended by the judges.

Second, the courts can indirectly impose a requirement to give reasons by labelling the result reached in their absence as arbitrary. This approach was adopted in *Padfield*,[249] but the scope of this exception to the general rule was limited by *Lonrho*.[250] It was claimed that the secretary of state should have referred a merger between AIT, (Lonrho's rivals), and the House of Fraser to the Monopolies and Mergers Commission. It was argued that in the absence of convincing reasons for not having done so, the decision not to refer should be regarded as irrational. Their Lordships disagreed. They held that if there was no duty to provide reasons in a particular instance, then their absence could not, of itself, provide support for the suggested irrationality of the decision. The only significance of the absence of reasons was that if all known facts appeared to point overwhelmingly in favour of a decision other than that reached, then the decision-maker could not complain if the court drew the inference that there was no rational reason for the decision actually taken.

Third, courts can indirectly inquire into the reasoning process by examining the evidence the decision-maker used to arrive at the jurisdictional findings. The court can then assess whether that evidence justified the findings made.[251]

Fourth, if a public body has created a legitimate expectation that it will act in a certain manner then this may lead to the imposition of a duty to provide reasons as to why it has departed from the course of action which was expected of it.[252]

v. *Reasons and the common law: direct link with procedural fairness*

12–042 The courts have also imposed a duty to provide reasons more directly, by linking the provision of reasons to fairness itself. The court will consider the nature of the decision-maker, the context in which it operates and whether the provision of reasons is required on grounds of fairness.

This was the approach in *Cunningham*.[253] Lord Donaldson MR reaffirmed previous orthodoxy that there was no general duty to provide reasons. However, he imposed such a duty on the Civil Service Appeal Board, which had given the applicant far less compensation for unfair dismissal than he would have received

---

[248] *Doody* [1994] 1 A.C. 531 at 564; *R. v Commissioners of Customs and Excise, Ex p. Tsahl* [1990] C.O.D. 230 QBD at 231.

[249] *Padfield v Minister of Agriculture, Fisheries and Food* [1968] A.C. 997, HL.

[250] *Lonrho Plc v Secretary of State for Trade and Industry* [1989] 2 All E.R. 609, HL.

[251] *Secretary of State for Education and Science v Tameside Metropolitan Borough Council* [1977] A.C. 1014, HL; *Mahon* [1984] A.C. 808 at 832–833; *R. v Sykes* (1875) 1 Q.B. 52; *R. v Thomas* [1892] 1 Q.B. 426.

[252] See para.12–017.

[253] *Cunningham* [1991] 4 All E.R. 310.

under the normal employment protection legislation. The duty was imposed because the CSAB was held to be a judicial body performing functions analogous to those of an industrial tribunal. The latter would have to provide reasons, and fairness demanded that so too should the CSAB. The same approach is evident in later cases.

Thus, in *Wilson*,[254] Taylor LJ based his decision that the applicant should be entitled to know the reasons why the Parole Board was not recommending him for release, on the general ground of natural justice. This method is also apparent in *Doody*.[255] Lord Mustill noted the recent tendency to greater transparency and openness in the making of administrative decisions, and gave an alternative rationale for his judgment to that considered above. His Lordship stated that the statutory scheme should be operated as fairly as possible in the circumstances, and that one should ask whether the refusal to give reasons was fair. On the facts of the case he thought not, since the prisoner had a real interest in understanding how long might be the term of imprisonment and why this particular period was imposed.

The general trend of the case law has been for the courts, while accepting that there is no general duty to provide reasons, none the less to demand them on the facts of the particular case,[256] and to justify this in the light of the reasoning in *Cunningham*, *Wilson*, *Doody*, and the *Dental Surgery* case.[257]

Thus, in *Matson*[258] the applicant complained that he had not been told the reasons **12–043**
why the Court of Aldermen had not confirmed his election. The Court of Appeal held that it must do so. It was influenced by the fact that the applicant had been duly elected, that the Court of Aldermen's verdict was a matter of public record, and that it had made suggestions during an interview with the applicant which indicated that it felt that he was unsuited for the post, but without saying why. In *Hickey*[259] the Home Secretary had ordered substantial police inquiries to decide whether to refer a case of a person who had been convicted to the Court of Appeal. The court held that he must allow the affected individuals to make effective representations concerning the material revealed by his inquiries before deciding whether or not to make the referral. In *Stefan*[260] the Privy Council

---

[254] *Wilson* [1992] Q.B. 740.

[255] *Doody* [1994] 1 A.C. 531; *R. v Dairy Produce Quota Tribunal and Minister for Agriculture, Fisheries and Food, Ex p. Cooper* [1993] C.O.D. 277.

[256] *R. v Criminal Injuries Compensation Board, Ex p. Cobb* [1995] C.O.D. 126 QBD; *R. v Secretary of State for the Home Department, Ex p. Pegg* [1995] C.O.D. 84 DC; *R. v Secretary of State for the Home Department, Ex p. Hickey (No.2)* [1995] C.O.D. 164; *R. v City of London Corporation, Ex p. Matson* [1997] 1 W.L.R. 765, CA (Civ Div); *R. v Secretary of State for the Home Department, Ex p. Follen* [1996] C.O.D. 169; *R. v Secretary of State for the Home Department, Ex p. Murphy* [1997] C.O.D. 478; *R. v Secretary of State for the Home Department, Ex p. McAvoy* [1998] C.O.D. 148; *R. (Wooder) v Fegetter* [2002] 3 W.L.R. 591; *R. (Savva) v Kensington and Chelsea RLBC* [2010] EWCA Civ 1209; *R. (T) v Legal Aid Agency* [2013] EWHC 960 (Admin).

[257] *R. v Higher Education Funding Council, Ex p. The Institute of Dental Surgery* [1994] 1 W.L.R. 242; *R. v Bristol City Council, Ex p. Bailey* [1995] C.O.D. 347; *R. v Royal Borough of Kensington and Chelsea, Ex p. Grillo* (1995) 28 H.L.R. 94; *R. (Asha Foundation) v Millennium Commission* [2003] EWCA Civ 88.

[258] *Matson* [1997] 1 W.L.R. 765.

[259] *R. v Secretary of State for the Home Department, Ex p. Hickey (No.2)* [1995] C.O.D. 164.

[260] *Stefan* [2000] H.R.L.R. 1; *Madan* [2001] EWHC Admin 577.

decided that the General Medical Council was under a common law duty to provide reasons when suspending a practitioner indefinitely, even though there was no express or implied statutory duty to do so.

In *Fayed*[261] the applicants were seeking naturalisation as British citizens. Their application was refused without reasons, and s.44 of the British Nationality Act 1981 expressly provided that reasons did not have to be given. Lord Woolf MR held, however, that while reasons as such did not have to be given, s.44 did not exclude the right to notice, which was a separate aspect of natural justice. This right to notice was then used as the conceptual foundation for an obligation to provide the applicants with sufficient information in order for them to understand the essence of what troubled the Home Secretary.

In some cases the court has however denied a duty to give reasons. In the *Institute of Dental Surgery* case[262] the applicants sought judicial review of the decision by the Higher Education Funding Council, which rated the Institute for research purposes at a lower level than the Institute believed was correct. The Institute challenged the rating on the grounds that reasons for the assessment were not provided and that this was unfair. Sedley J rejected the application, on the grounds that where what was sought to be impugned was no more than an exercise of informed academic judgment, fairness alone would not require reasons to be given.

12–044 Notwithstanding this decision on the facts, the judgment indicates the progress the common law has made in this area. The judgment accepts that reasons should be given either when the interest at stake is so important that fairness demands the provision of reasoned explanation, or where the decision appears to be aberrant. Sedley J also held that where reasons ought to have been given, but were not forthcoming, this in itself constituted a breach of an independent legal obligation with the consequence that the impugned decision was a nullity. It was not necessary to establish that the failure to provide the reasons established some other head of review, such as irrationality or irrelevancy.

Lord Bingham CJ in *Murray*[263] distilled certain principles concerning the duty to give reasons from earlier decisions. His Lordship stated that there was at present no general duty to give reasons, and that the public interest might outweigh the advantages of giving reasons in a particular case. He held that certain factors militated against the giving of reasons: it could place an undue burden on the decision-maker; demand the articulation of inexpressible value judgments; and offer an invitation to the captious to comb the reasons for grounds of challenge. Lord Bingham recognised, however, that there was a perceptible trend towards greater transparency in decision-making. He acknowledged that there were significant factors in favour of giving reasons: it could concentrate the mind of the decision-maker; demonstrate to the recipient that this was so; show that the issues had been properly addressed; and alert the individual to possible justiciable flaws in the process. Where a body had power to affect individuals a

---

[261] *R. v Secretary of State for the Home Department, Ex p. Fayed* [1997] 1 All E.R. 228.

[262] *Dental Surgery* [1994] 1 W.L.R. 242. In *Fegetter* [2002] 3 W.L.R. 591 it was held that the *Dental Surgery* case might now be decided differently on its facts, but see *Millenium Commission* [2003] EWCA Civ 88.

[263] *R. v Ministry of Defence, Ex p. Murray* [1998] C.O.D. 134 DC.

court would therefore readily imply procedural safeguards in addition to any stipulated in the relevant statute if they were necessary to ensure fairness. If a just decision could not be given without the provision of reasons then they should be provided, and so too where the decision appeared to be aberrant. In deciding whether reasons should have been given, the court would take into account the absence of any right of appeal, and the role reasons can play in detecting the kind of error which would entitle the court to intervene by way of review. The fact that a tribunal was carrying out a judicial function was a consideration in favour of the giving of reasons, particularly where personal liberty was concerned.

The courts have made great strides in this area. There is, moreover, little doubt that the criteria laid down in *Murray* will afford later courts with ample opportunity to justify the imposition of a duty to give reasons should they so wish. It would none the less be desirable to shift the focus still further. The general rule should be that reasons should be given, subject to exceptions where warranted. The courts are coming close to this proposition, as evident from the dictum of Lord Clyde in *Stefan*. He stated that while there was no general duty to give reasons there was a strong argument for the view that "what were once seen as exceptions to a rule may now be becoming examples of the norm, and the cases where reasons are not required may be taking on the appearance of exceptions".[264] It would do much to simplify and clarify matters if the legal rule could be expressed in this way.

vi. Reasons, statute and common law: "late evidence of reasons"

A number of cases have considered whether a body that is under a duty to provide reasons should be able to adduce evidence as to the reasons that were given, where the original statement of reasons was inadequate.[265] **12–045**

The position appears to be as follows. Where there is a statutory duty to provide reasons as part of the notification of the decision, the adequacy of the reasons is a condition of the legality of the decision. In such cases it will be very exceptional for a court to accept subsequent evidence of the reasons.

The court will also be cautious about accepting late reasons in other cases, because of attempts by the public body to rationalise its decision after the event. It will take account of a number of factors in this regard. The court will consider whether the new reasons are consistent with the original reasons, merely seeking to elucidate them. It will decide whether the later reasons have been advanced to support the original decision, or whether they are in reality an attempt to support that decision on different grounds. The court will consider whether the decision-maker would have been expected to state in the original decision the reason that he or she was seeking to adduce later.

---

264 *Stefan* [2000] H.R.L.R. 1 at 10.

265 *Angel* [1990] C.O.D. 355; *R. v Westminster City Council, Ex p. Ermakov* [1996] 2 All E.R. 302, CA (Civ Div); *R. v Northamptonshire CC, Ex p. D* [1998] E.L.R. 291 QBD; *R. (Nash) v Chelsea College of Art and Design* [2001] EWHC 538 (Admin); *Leung v Imperial College of Science, Technology and Medicine* [2002] A.C.D. 100 QBD; *R. (Hereford Waste Watchers Ltd) v Herefordshire CC* [2005] EWHC 191 (Admin); *Keane v Law Society* [2009] EWHC 783 (Admin); *R. (Lanner Parish Council) v Cornwall Council* [2013] EWCA Civ 1290.

vii. *Reasons and EU law*

12–046 In EU law there is a duty to give reasons based on art.296 TFEU. The extent of the duty will depend upon the nature of the relevant act and the context in which it was made.[266] The duty is principally imposed upon the EU organs, but it can apply to national authorities where they are acting as agents of the European Union for the application of EU law.[267]

There is also authority for the proposition that where a fundamental EU right is in issue, such as the right to free movement of workers, this can generate a duty to give reasons by the relevant national authorities.[268] Thus, where a Member State seeks to deny a particular worker free movement by claiming, for example, that his qualification for the job is not accepted by that state, the competent national authority must inform the person of the reasons for the refusal, in order that the applicant can decide with full knowledge of the relevant facts whether there is any point in attempting to seek legal redress.

F. Appeals and Rehearing

12–047 An important issue is the extent to which a defect of natural justice can be cured by an appeal within the administrative hierarchy or by a rehearing by the original body. The authorities were reviewed by the Privy Council in *Calvin*.[269] It was argued that a breach of natural justice at the original hearing conducted by racing stewards could not be cured by an appeal to a committee of the Australian Jockey Club since there would be nothing to appeal against, the first decision being a nullity. Lord Wilberforce reviewed the authorities and adopted a tripartite distinction.

First, where the rehearing was by the same body or some more complete form of it, the general rule was that defects at the original hearing could be cured.[270] Second, there were cases where after considering the whole hearing structure in its particular context a fair hearing might be required at the original stage and on appeal, since otherwise the claimant could be deprived of "two cracks of the whip".[271] This second proposition was not, however, an absolute one. His Lordship posited a third situation where, looking again at the whole context, it could be seen whether the end result was fair despite some initial defect. This would depend on the type of appeal process. If, for example, the appeal body was only entitled to a transcript from the original decision then the later hearing

---

[266] Craig, *EU Administrative Law* (2012); *Beus* (5/67) [1968] E.C.R. 83; *Germany v* Commission (24/62) [1963] E.C.R. 63; *Meroni v High Authority* (9/56) [1958] E.C.R. 133.

[267] *Wachauf v Germany* (5/88) [1989] E.C.R. 2609.

[268] *Unectef v Heylens* (222/86) [1987] E.C.R. 4097 at [15].

[269] *Calvin v Carr* [1980] A.C. 574.

[270] *Calvin* [1980] A.C. 574 at 592; *De Verteuil v Knaggs* [1918] A.C. 557; *Ridge* [1964] A.C. 40 at 79; *R. (New London College Ltd) v Secretary of State for the Home Department* [2011] EWHC 856. This must be subject to a caveat for cases where failure to give an initially fair hearing prejudiced the individual in a way that could not be cured by the later rehearing.

[271] *Calvin* [1980] A.C. 574 at 592–593; *Leary v National Union of Vehicle Builders* [1971] Ch. 34 Ch D at 48–58; *Roffey* [1969] 2 Q.B. 538; *Wright* [2009] 1 A.C. 739.

would probably be inadequate.[272] The facts of *Calvin* itself were said to fall into category three. The stewards' inquiry had to make a quick decision. Any defect in natural justice at that stage would be cured by the hearing before the full committee of the Jockey Club.

G. Deciding Without Hearing

A related but distinct issue is how far the decision-maker is allowed to determine a matter without a hearing. This depends on the enabling legislation, the type of function being performed, and the nature of the decision-maker. Thus, it is accepted that if a minister is the decision-maker the decision will often have to be made through officers, who will collect the material, and the officer may even make the decision in the minister's name.[273] **12–048**

In other areas the general principle is that the greater the judicial element involved, the more likely it is that the decision-maker must also hear.[274] Investigation may well be undertaken by a sub-committee, but the deciding authority must then be appraised of that material. Whether the material thus collected can be summarised, and whether all those on the deciding authority must possess all the papers[275] will depend on the nature of the function being performed and the language of the enabling statute.

Evans[276] provides an example of what may be required. A probationer constable sought certiorari to quash the decision of the Chief Constable that he should resign or be discharged. The Chief Constable had decided to dispense with his services because of a report on the probationer constable, which led the Chief Constable to believe that he was not fitted to be a member of the police force. The investigation had been conducted by the deputy Chief Constable. Delegation of the inquiry was allowed provided that a number of conditions were met. The ultimate decision must be made by the Chief Constable. The delegate must tell the constable the nature of the complaint against him and allow him an opportunity to comment on it before the final decision was taken by the Chief Constable. It seems that the Chief Constable must also show the report to the constable and invite his comments before reaching his final decision. On the facts the rules of natural justice had been broken because the constable had had no opportunity to comment upon the allegations made against him.

---

272 *Calvin* [1980] A.C. 574 at 593.

273 *Local Government Board v Arlidge* [1915] A.C. 120, HL.

274 *Barnard v National Dock Labour Board* [1953] 2 Q.B. 18, CA; *Vine v National Dock Labour Board* [1957] A.C. 488, HL; *Jeffs v New Zealand Dairy Board* [1967] 1 A.C. 551 at 568, 569; *R. v Race Relations Board, Ex p. Selvarajan* [1975] 1 W.L.R. 1686, CA (Civ Div).

275 *Selvarajan* [1975] 1 W.L.R. 1686 at 1695–1696, 1698; *R. v Commission for Racial Equality, Ex p. Cottrell and Rothon* [1980] 1 W.L.R. 1580 DC at 1589.

276 *Evans* [1982] 1 W.L.R. 1155 at 1161, 1165.

H. The ECHR and the Content of Procedural Rights

12–049 We have already considered art.6(1) ECHR in relation to determining the applicability of procedural rights, and must now consider its relevance to the content of such rights. The ECtHR has stressed a number of elements as integral to the requirement of a fair hearing pursuant to art.6.

There must be access to a court.[277] There must be procedural equality or what is often termed "equality of arms". This implies that each party must be afforded a reasonable opportunity to present his case, including evidence, under conditions that do not place him at a substantial disadvantage in relation to his opponent.[278] There is a right to a hearing within a reasonable time.[279] There must be some proper form of judicial process, which will often take the form of an adversarial trial where the parties have the opportunity to have knowledge of, and comment on, the observations and evidence adduced by the other side.[280] The requirement that there be a fair hearing will not always mean that the applicant must be present in person, but this should be so where personal character, or manner of life, are relevant to the subject matter of the case. While there is no express requirement to give reasons, the ECtHR regards this as implicit in the obligation to provide a fair hearing. Reasons do not have to be given on every single point, but they must be sufficient to enable a party to understand the essence of the decision in order to be able to exercise any appeal rights.[281]

The Supreme Court has however emphasised that the common law should be regarded as the first source in assessing how the demands of ECHR membership should be met in a particular case. This was evident in *Osborn*,[282] where the Supreme Court considered whether the Parole Board had breached the ECHR by not providing an oral hearing to three prisoners whose sentences it reviewed. Lord Reed gave judgment for the Supreme Court. He held that protection of human rights was not a distinct area of the law, based solely on the jurisprudence of the ECtHR, but permeated the domestic legal system. Compliance with the ECHR should initially be determined through relevant rules of domestic law. This was more especially so given that the ECHR rights were set out at a high level of generality. It followed that "the values underlying both the Convention and our own constitution require that Convention rights should be protected primarily by a detailed body of domestic law".[283] The courts could, pursuant to the Human Rights Act 1998, take account of ECHR obligations in the development of the common law and in the interpretation of legislation. While the importance of the HRA was unquestionable, it did not "however supersede the protection of human rights under the common law or statute, or create a discrete body of law based on the judgments of the European court", with the consequence that "human rights

---

277 *Golder v UK* (1979–80) 1 E.H.R.R. 524.

278 *Dombo Beheer BV v The Netherlands* (1994) 18 E.H.R.R. 213.

279 *Attorney General's Reference (No.2 of 2001), HL* [2004] 2 A.C. 72; *Eastaway v. Secretary of State for Trade & Industry* [2007] EWCA Civ 425.

280 *Ruiz-Mateos v Spain* (1993) 16 E.H.R.R. 505.

281 *Helle v Finland* (1998) 26 E.H.R.R. 159.

282 *Osborn v Parole Board* [2013] UKSC 61; *A v. BBC* [2014] UKSC 25.

283 *Osborn* [2013] UKSC 61 at [56].

continue to be protected by our domestic law, interpreted and developed in accordance with the Act when appropriate".[284]

8. FAIRNESS: NON-ADJUDICATIVE PROCEDURES

A. The Relationship between Decision-making and Procedure

The discussion thus far has been concerned with the applicability and content of procedural fairness, where the norms applied have been developed against the background of adversarial adjudication. It is time now to consider non-adjudicative procedures. **12–050**

> "This whole analysis will derive from one simple proposition, namely that the distinguishing characteristic of adjudication lies in the fact that it confers on the affected party a peculiar form of participation in the decision, that of presenting proofs and reasoned arguments for a decision in his favour. Whatever heightens the significance of this participation lifts adjudication towards its optimum expression. Whatever destroys the meaning of that participation destroys the integrity of adjudication itself."

Thus, wrote Fuller[285] in a paper published after his death, on which he had worked for over 20 years. Fuller laid down what he conceived to be the forms and limits of adjudication. The precise nature of these need not be rehearsed here, although they will be touched on below. What is important is the realisation that adjudication is but one form of decision-making. Our procedural rules are sown in an adjudicative framework.[286] The rules of natural justice are related to the presentation of proofs and reasoned argument. Thus, to give an obvious example drawn from Fuller,[287] participation through reasoned argument loses its meaning if the arbiter of the dispute is insane or hopelessly prejudiced. Similar connections clearly exist in relation to matters such as notice. The development of fairness in the case law has not caused us to depart from this adjudicative framework.

While attention has been paid to modification of adjudicative procedures to meet the requirements of a particular area, there has been little thought directed to the broader question of whether adjudication is the correct decision-making process on which to be fashioning procedures. The important point revealed by Fuller is that just as adjudication is distinguished by the form of participation that it confers, so too are other types of decision-making, and just as the nature of adjudication shapes the procedures relevant to its decisional form, so do other species of decision-making. Nine modes of decision-making are listed by Fuller:

---

[284] *Osborn* [2013] UKSC 61 at [57], citing *R. (Daly) v. Secretary of State for the Home Department* [2001] 2 A.C. 532 and *R (West) v Parole Board* [2005] 1 W.L.R. 350 as examples of this juridical technique.

[285] "The Forms and Limits of Adjudication" (1978) 92 Harv. L.R. 353, 364; J, Allison, "The Procedural Reason for Judicial Restraint" [1994] P.L. 452; Galligan, *Due Process and Fair Procedures* (1996), Chs 8 and 9.

[286] This does not mean that the principal aim of natural justice was to impose uniform adjudicative procedures.

[287] "The Forms and Limits of Adjudication" (1978) 92 Harv. L.R. 353, 364.

mediation; property; voting; custom; law officially declared; adjudication; contract; managerial direction; and resort to chance.

The relationship between each type of decision-making, and its procedural rules, is as follows. The procedural rules will be *generated* by, and will *protect* the integrity of, the type of decision-making in issue. For example, adjudication is one species of decision-making, and the rule against bias is generated by it. It would be inconsistent with our idea of what judging means to allow the decision to be made by one who was biased. In this sense, the procedural rule is there to protect the integrity of what we mean by adjudication. If we demand that an agency uses adjudicatory process rights then we are indirectly forcing it to make its decisions by adjudication rather than some other means.

The relevance of this is that there may well be situations when the procedures modelled on adjudication are not the most appropriate, and where safeguards developed against the backdrop of a different type of decision-making may be more efficacious. The emergence of fairness may help us towards a realisation of this. The point is well put by Macdonald[288]:

> "Rather than ask what aspects of adjudicative procedures can be grafted onto this decisional process reviewing tribunals must ask: what is the nature of the process here undertaken, what mode of participation by affected parties is envisioned by such a decisional process, and what specific procedural guidelines are necessary to ensure the efficacy of that participation and the integrity of the process under review?"

It may well be the case that the very concept of adjudication as applied to disputes between private individuals has to be modified in its application to litigation involving public bodies. This does not negate the point being made by Fuller and MacDonald: it may still be the case that a different decisional form is more appropriate in a particular area.[289] Two brief examples of this idea may be given.

B. Example 1: Statutory Inquiries

12–051 Statutory inquiries have always presented a problem for the application of natural justice.[290] The courts have been troubled by the very nature of the decision-making process, divided between the inspector and the minister. Such inquiries do not fit one of the requisites of classical adjudication, which has been termed strong responsiveness.[291] This expresses the notion that the decision should proceed from the proofs and arguments advanced by the parties. The position of the minister, and the broad range of policy considerations that must be taken into account, precludes this. This also prevents the minister from being an impartial

---

[288] "Judicial Review and Procedural Fairness in Administrative Law: II" (1980–1981) 26 McGill L.J. 1, 19.

[289] A. Chayes, "The Role of the Judge in Public Law Litigation" (1976) 89 Harv. L.R. 1281; M. Eisenberg, "Participation, Responsiveness and the Consultative Process" (1978) 92 Harv. L.R. 400, 426–431; L. Fuller, "Mediation: Its Forms and Functions" (1971) 44 S. Cal. L.R. 305.

[290] *Errington* [1935] 1 K.B. 249; *Offer* [1936] 1 K.B. 40; *Franklin v Minister of Town and Country Planning* [1948] A.C. 87.

[291] Eisenberg, "Participation, Responsiveness and the Consultative Process" (1978) 92 Harv. L.R. 400, 411–412.

adjudicator in the ordinary sense of that term. Despite this lack of harmony between the facts and the ideal, the courts have traditionally seen the procedures for such inquiries against an adjudicative backdrop. It is true that they have recognised that the minister cannot be impartial in the way that a judge would be.[292] It is true also that the courts afford considerable latitude to the public authority in devising its own procedures.[293] Nevertheless, these are seen as modifications within the traditional adjudicatory framework.

What these modifications indicate, however, is that this decisional paradigm may not be the most appropriate. As Fuller makes clear, whatever undermines the meaning of participation that characterises adjudication, undermines the integrity of adjudication itself. Moreover, it is arguable that classical adjudication is in general unsuited to the resolution of what are termed polycentric problems,[294] which may form the subject-matter of statutory inquiries. Judicial realisation that the full implications of the adjudicative model cannot be applied in this area is beneficial. A broad notion of procedural fairness may, however, demand more. It may require us to rethink the type of decision-making process from which we are deriving our procedures. Statutory inquiries may be better seen as a form of mediation or consultation. Some of the legislation in the planning sphere reflects such an approach. If some inquiries were to be viewed in this light then the courts could help to devise procedural rules to fit this type of decision-making. What those rules are would be derived from the type of participation demanded by that decisional process. Some of these may overlap with characteristics found in adjudication, others may not.[295]

C. Example 2: Social Welfare

Social welfare provides a second example of the theme under discussion. **12–052**
Claimants for social welfare provisions have not always been in a good position so far as procedural protection is concerned. There has been a tendency to regard such provisions as government largesse to be dispensed at the unfettered will of the public body. This view has been more manifest in the United States[296] than in this country, although we have not entirely escaped the same phenomenon. The response has been to bolster the procedural checks attendant on the disbursement

---

[292] *R. (Alconbury Developments Ltd) v Secretary of State for the Environment, Transport and the Regions* [2001] 2 W.L.R. 1389, HL.

[293] *Bushell v Secretary of State for Environment* [1981] A.C. 75, HL; *R. v Secretary of State for Transport, Ex p Gwent CC* [1987] 2 W.L.R. 961, CA (Civ Div).

[294] Put simply, this is a problem in which one part interacts with a number of others so that a change in any one will produce ramifications in the whole: the decision of the team captain to move X from centre-back to half-back may necessitate alteration in the whole team; Fuller (1978) 92 Harv. L.R. 353, 384–405; Chayes (1976) 89 Harv. L.R. 1281; Eisenberg (1978) 92 Harv. L.R. 400, 426–431; J King, "The Pervasiveness of Polycentricity' [2008] PL 101.

[295] Fuller, "Mediation: Its Forms and Functions" (1971) 44 S. Cal. L.R. 305; M. Eisenberg, "Private Ordering Through Negotiation, Dispute Settlement and Rule-Making" (1976) 89 Harv. L.R. 637.

[296] C. Reich, "The New Property" (1964) 73 Yale L.J. 773; "Midnight Welfare Searches and the Social Security Act" (1963) 72 Yale L.J. 1347; "Individual Rights and Social Welfare: The Emerging Issues" (1965)74 Yale L.J. 1245; "The Law of the Planned Society" (1966) 75 Yale L.J. 1227. The Supreme Court strengthened the procedural rights of such claimants in *Goldberg v Kelly* 397 US 254 (1970).

of such benefits. These safeguards are framed in an adjudicative fashion, albeit one which is modified to take account of the circumstances. It may however be that this type of procedural check is not the most effective in this area for a number of reasons.

First, giving claimants appeal rights with a hearing before a higher tribunal ignores the factual background from which such cases spring. There will often be a continuing relationship between the claimant and the original officer, which the former is unlikely to want to sully by taking appellate action. To this must be added the nature of the claimants themselves, who may not fully comprehend the mechanics of such an appeal process.[297]

Second, the adversary nature of the adjudicative process may not be well suited to this area. The idea of "opponents" and the "winner take-all" attitude is not necessarily the best form of decision-making for social welfare cases.[298] What this suggests is that a different type of decision-making with correspondingly different procedures may be more relevant. A mixture of consultation and internal management control might well prove a better starting point.[299]

It should be noted that other commentators have expressed reservations about the extent to which informal procedures can be successful, and have pointed to the benefits of a broadly adjudicative appeal regime.[300] We should nonetheless be prepared to think more broadly about what procedural protection connotes. Procedures developed against a backdrop of adjudication may well be the most appropriate in certain areas. They may not, however, be equally suited to all the institutions that comprise administrative law. What is equally important is that other types of procedural norms may in certain circumstances better effectuate the twin rationales for process rights. Procedures developed in the context of consultation may, for example, better attain the instrumental and non-instrumental aims that underlie process rights.[301]

9. CONCLUSION

12–053 The courts have not been idle since the landmark decision in *Ridge v Baldwin*.[302] While many of the subsequent developments are to be welcomed, continuing analysis is required to determine whether the content of the rules in general, and their application to particular areas, is being pitched at the "right" level. There is, for example, a cogent argument for the recognition of a general duty to provide reasons, while improvements in the context of employment relationships and aliens could be made. More thought should also be given to understanding the general nature of the balancing process that operates within fairness. The extent, to which this should be viewed as a utilitarian calculus of some kind, or whether a more dignitarian approach should be pursued, is of considerable importance.

[297] J. Handler, "Controlling Official Behaviour in Welfare Administration" (1966) 54 Cal. L.R. 479; M. Adler and A. Bradley, *Justice, Discretion and Poverty* (Professional Books, 1975).

[298] G. Ganz, *Administrative Procedures* (London: Sweet & Maxwell, 1974), p.35.

[299] J. Mashaw, *Bureaucratic Justice* (Yale University Press, 1983).

[300] N. Wikeley and R. Young, "The Administration of Benefits in Britain: Adjudication Officers and the Influence of Social Security Appeal Tribunals" [1992] P.L. 238.

[301] See para.12–002.

[302] *Ridge* [1964] A.C. 40.

The concluding comments thus far have been directed towards the application and content of natural justice and fairness, seeing both of these terms against an adjudicative framework. This is how they operate at present. Procedures derived from a backdrop of adjudication may not, however, be the most appropriate or effective in particular areas. Other decisional forms, whether they be mediation or managerial direction, may be better in certain contexts. The recognition and development of other types of decision-making, with the procedures necessarily consequent upon them, is one of the important tasks for the administrative lawyer, just as important as the workings of fairness within the traditional adjudicative context.

CHAPTER 13

NATURAL JUSTICE: HEARINGS, PUBLIC INTEREST IMMUNITY AND CLOSED MATERIAL PROCEDURE

1. CENTRAL ISSUES

i. The previous chapter considered the general principles of natural justice as they pertain to hearings. The reality is, however, that the type of hearing available to the individual has always been affected by rules designed to safeguard the national interest. This has been increasingly the case post 9/11. These developments raise important issues of principle. The broad outlines of the story are as follows. **13–001**

ii. The type of hearing available to the claimant has always been subject to the rules on public interest immunity. These rules are of common law origin. The courts transformed this area of the law in the 1960s. Prior to then this area was conceptualised as Crown privilege, this name carrying the implication that it was for the government to decide whether evidence should be withheld. The new language of public interest immunity carried the connotation that the court would decide that certain evidence should be excluded from the case on the grounds that the public interest in withholding the evidence outweighed the public interest in its disclosure.

iii. The normal rules concerning hearings and natural justice have more recently been qualified by the introduction of what are known as closed material procedures, which are statutory creations. A danger is that such proceedings squeeze out the balancing that takes place within public interest immunity. Closed material procedures were introduced by statute in specific areas, such as national security, where it was felt that the public interest so demands. These proceedings have both "open" and "closed" elements. All the material, open and closed, which the government relies on, is placed before the court and a lawyer known as the special advocate. The individual concerned and his legal representatives can be present at the open hearings, and see all the open material used in those hearings. They cannot be present at the closed parts of the proceedings, or see the closed material. The special advocate attends all parts of the proceedings, and sees all the material, including the closed material not disclosed to the individual. He can take instructions from the individual before he reads the closed material, and written instructions after he has seen the closed material. A special advocate can also communicate with the individual after he has seen the material, provided it is with the permission of the court, but this is relatively rare. There are however, difficulties in ensuring that the special advocate can adequately represent the individual's interests within this system.

iv. The compatibility of the closed material procedure with the rules of natural justice was tested before the courts. The Supreme Court made it clear in *AF*[1] that natural justice placed limits on the range of material that could be excluded from the individual, at least in cases concerning liberty where art.6 ECHR was applicable. It subsequently held in *Tariq*[2] that the limits devised in *AF* did not apply to all cases that fell within art.6 ECHR. The Supreme Court further decided in *Al Rawi*[3] that there had to be statutory foundation for the closed material procedure, and that it could not be invoked in the absence of such foundation.

v. The government introduced legislation to clarify certain of these issues and provide the general foundation for closed material proceedings.[4] This has now been done in the Justice and Security Act 2013, which is analysed at the end of the chapter.

2. PUBLIC INTEREST IMMUNITY

A. "Crown Privilege"

13–002 The overall story concerning hearings and restricted material begins with what is now known as public interest immunity. Prior to 1968 it was known as Crown privilege. When an action takes place discovery of documents will often be necessary. A party will ask the other side to produce documents that may be material to the question. Where a party resisted disclosure the court would not order the production of the documents unless it believed that it was necessary either for disposing fairly of the cause or matter, or for saving costs.[5]

Until 1968 the Crown possessed what was known as Crown privilege.[6] It could refuse to reveal documents because it would be contrary to the public interest. This principle was widely drawn as exemplified by *Duncan*.[7] A submarine built by the defendants for the Admiralty sank while on trial. The plaintiff, the widow of one of those drowned, brought an action for negligence. She sought discovery of plans of the submarine. The Admiralty withheld them and claimed Crown privilege. The House of Lords found for the Crown and propounded a broad rule allowing the Crown to withhold documents of two types. They could be withheld either if the disclosure of the "contents" of a particular document would injure the public interest, or where the document was one of a "class" of documents that must be withheld to ensure the proper

1 *Secretary of State for the Home Department v AF* [2010] 2 A.C. 269, HL.

2 *Tariq v Home Office* [2011] UKSC 35.

3 *Al Rawi v Security Service (Justice and others intervening)* [2011] UKSC 34.

4 Green Paper, *Justice and Security* (2011) Cm.8194, see *http://consultation.cabinetoffice.gov.uk/justiceandsecurity/* [Accessed 17 April 2012]; Justice and Security Bill 2012.

5 RSC Ord.24 r.13.

6 J. Jacob, "From Privileged Crown to Interested Public" [1993] P.L. 121.

7 *Duncan v Cammell, Laird & Co Ltd* [1942] A.C. 624, HL.

functioning of the public service. A ministerial statement in the proper form that a document fell into one of these categories would it seems not be challenged by the courts.

The *Duncan* case sanctioned the withholding of documents to a greater extent than had been allowed previously.[8] The potential breadth of the "class category" enabled the government to protect documents that might not have required blanket protection.[9] Dissatisfaction led the Lord Chancellor in 1956 to announce that the government would henceforth not claim privilege in certain areas.[10] This welcome self-denying ordinance proved to be a double-edged sword. The areas where privilege would not be claimed had little if any analytic coherence. Pressure for judicial reconsideration of *Duncan* came from Scotland[11] and the Court of Appeal.[12] The common link was the refusal to accept that the court was bound by every class claim put forward by the government. Despite these promising omens, the Court of Appeal[13] then returned once more to the rigidity of the *Duncan* approach. It was fortunate that the case went to the House of Lords, which took the opportunity for legal reform.

B. From Crown Privilege to Public Interest Immunity

In *Conway v Rimmer*[14] the plaintiff was a former probationary police constable who began an action for malicious prosecution against his former superintendent. The secretary of state objected to the production of five documents, certifying that they fell within classes of document whose disclosure would be injurious to the public interest. The defendant made four of the reports about the plaintiff during his probationary period. The fifth was a report made by him to his chief constable in connection with the prosecution of the plaintiff on a criminal charge on which he was acquitted. It was this criminal charge that was the foundation of the action for malicious prosecution. **13–003**

The *Duncan* case was overturned. The House of Lords asserted the courts' power to hold a balance between the public interest as expressed by the minister who wished to withhold certain documents, and the public interest in ensuring the proper administration of justice. The formulations as to how the balancing was to operate differed. These should not cloud the main principle that was unequivocally asserted: the courts would balance the competing public interests to determine whether disclosure should be ordered. If the court was in doubt as to

[8] *Robinson v South Australia (No.2)* [1931] A.C. 704; *Spiegelman v Hocker* (1933) 50 T.L.R. 87.

[9] *Ellis v Home Office* [1953] 2 Q.B. 135, CA; *Broome v Broome* [1955] P. 190 Probate, Divorce and Admiralty Division.

[10] Reports of witnesses of accidents on the road, on government premises or involving government employees; medical reports concerning civilian employees; medical reports where the Crown was sued for negligence; materials required for the defence against a criminal charge and witnesses' statements to the police; and certain reports on factual matters relating to liability in contract, HL Deb., Vol.197, col.741 (6 June 1956).

[11] *Glasgow Corporation v Central Land Board* 1956 S.C. 1.

[12] *Grosvenor Hotel (London) Ltd (No.2), Re* [1965] Ch. 1210, CA; *Merricks v Nott-Bower* [1965] 1 Q.B. 57, CA; *Wednesbury Corp v Ministry of Housing and Local Government* [1965] 1 W.L.R. 261, CA (Civ Div).

[13] *Conway v Rimmer* [1967] 1 W.L.R. 1031, CA (Civ Div).

[14] *Conway v Rimmer* [1968] A.C. 910, HL.

the outcome of this balancing it could inspect the documents before ordering production. This was done and the court concluded that the documents should be produced. Class claims and contents claims for public interest immunity persisted after *Conway*. What the judgment made clear was that all such claims would be subject to the balancing test.

Given the nature of the balancing operation the *Conway* case required, the name "Crown privilege" was obviously inappropriate. The Crown could not simply decide to withdraw documents from the court. This was recognised in *Rogers*.[15] An application for a gaming certificate had been refused and Rogers wished to know the contents of a letter written by the chief constable to the Gaming Board about him. The Home Secretary sought to prevent discovery of the document and pleaded Crown privilege. While the House of Lords agreed that the letter should not be produced, they disapproved of the term Crown privilege. Lord Reid[16] stated that the term privilege was misleading, and that the real issue was whether the public interest in not disclosing the document outweighed the interest of the litigant in having all the evidence before the court.

C. Public Interest Immunity: The Type of Body that Can Claim Immunity

13–004 This question arose in *D v National Society for the Prevention of Cruelty to Children*.[17] The Court of Appeal decided that public interest immunity was only available where the public interest related to the effective functioning of departments or other organs of central government. This view was rejected by the House of Lords. The NSPCC was an authorised person for the purpose of bringing care proceedings under the Children and Young Persons Act 1969. Although it was not under a statutory duty to bring such actions, this was not decisive. Ensuring the confidentiality of the information was as important here as it had been in *Rogers*.[18]

It is questionable how far beyond the organs of central government one may go and still have the defence available. Their Lordships rejected the view that it only operated where the effective functioning of departments or other organs of central government were involved. They also rejected the very broad approach posited by the NSPCC that whenever a party to legal proceedings claims that there is a public interest to be served by withholding documents it is the duty of the court to weigh that interest against the countervailing public interest in the administration of justice, and to refuse disclosure if the balance tilts that way. Which bodies are entitled to raise the issue must therefore be decided on a case by case approach.[19]

---

[15] *Rogers v Secretary of State for Home Department* [1973] A.C. 388, HL.

[16] *Rogers* [1973] A.C. 388 at 400. See also, 406, 408 and 412.

[17] *D v National Society for the Prevention of Cruelty to Children* [1978] A.C. 171, HL.

[18] *Rogers* [1973] A.C. 388

[19] *BL Cars Ltd (Formerly Leyland Cars) v Vyas* [1980] A.C. 1028, HL; *Buckley v Law Society (No.2)* [1984] 1 W.L.R. 1101 Ch D; *British Steel Corp v Granada Television Ltd* [1981] A.C. 1096, HL; *Shah v HSBC Private Bank (UK) Ltd* [2011] EWHC 1713.

It should also be noted that the Civil Procedure Rules allow a person to apply for an order permitting him to withhold documents on the ground that disclosure would damage the public interest.[20] This provision is held not to affect any rule of law that permits or requires a document to be withheld from disclosure on the ground that its disclosure or inspection would damage the public interest.[21]

D. Public Interest Immunity and Confidentiality

A number of cases have been concerned with the protection of information given in confidence.[22] Confidentiality is not by itself a separate ground for withholding evidence. This was established by *Alfred Crompton*.[23] The company claimed that the assessment of purchase tax based upon the wholesale value of amusement machines was too high. The customs and excise commissioners, as part of their investigation, obtained from Crompton's customers and other sources information concerning the value of the machines. No agreement was reached as to the appropriate tax rate. When the matter went to arbitration the commissioners claimed that the information received from these customers and other sources should be immune from disclosure since it would reveal the commissioners' methods and contained information supplied confidentially. The House of Lords upheld this claim. Disclosure of the information could hinder the commissioners in the discharge of their functions. However, the fact that the information was supplied in confidence was not in itself a reason for non-disclosure. It was not a separate head of privilege, but could be a material consideration when privilege was claimed on the ground of public interest. **13–005**

Confidentiality also played a part in *D v National Society for the Prevention of Cruelty to Children*.[24] The NSPCC relied heavily upon members of the public to give information about possible child abuse. In the instant case, the NSPCC acted on information that subsequently proved to be untrue. The mother claimed damages against the NSPCC, alleging a failure to take reasonable care before investigating an allegation of maltreatment. She demanded discovery of all the documents the society had relating to the case. The House of Lords upheld the public interest defence. They reiterated that confidentiality is not itself a defence but, reasoning by analogy from the case of police informants, it was decided that the documents did not have to be disclosed. Sources of information would dry up

[20] CPR r.31.19(1); *Frankson v Secretary of State for the Home Department* [2003] 1 W.L.R. 1952, CA (Civ Div) at [9].

[21] CPR r.31.19(8).

[22] *Rogers* [1973] A.C. 388; *Lonrho Ltd v Shell Petroleum Co Ltd (No.2)* [1982] A.C. 173, HL; Y. Cripps, "Judicial Proceedings and Refusal to Disclose the Identity of Sources of Information" [1984] C.L.J. 266.

[23] *Alfred Crompton Amusement Machines Ltd v Customs and Excise Commissioners (No.2)* [1974] A.C. 405, HL; *R. (Mohamed) v Secretary of State for Foreign and Commonwealth Affairs (No.2)* [2011] Q.B. 218 CA (Civ Div).

[24] *D v National Society for the Prevention of Cruelty to Children* [1978] A.C. 171, HL; *D (Infants), Re* [1970] 1 W.L.R. 599, CA (Civ Div); *Gaskin v Liverpool City Council* [1980] 1 W.L.R. 1549, CA (Civ Div); *Buckley v Law Society (No.2)* [1984] 1 W.L.R. 1101 Ch D.

if the names of the informants were to be made public, hampering the society in the discharge of its duties. This outweighed the interest of the individual in knowing the name of the informant.[25]

E. Public Interest Immunity: Duty or Discretion

13–006 It was held in *Makanjuola*[26] that public interest immunity could not be waived. The court reasoned that the litigant who asserted public interest immunity was not claiming a right, but observing a duty. Immunity was accorded in certain circumstances where this was warranted by the public interest. It was for this reason that the immunity could not be waived. The judgment led government departments to believe that they should withhold documentation, with the consequence that plaintiffs would have to overcome the hurdles considered below, which are necessary to obtain documents. Thus, in the Matrix Churchill saga, concerning the sale of arms to Iraq, government ministers were advised by the Attorney General that they had no discretion and had to sign certificates claiming public interest immunity.[27]

This must now be seen in the light of *Wiley*,[28] which overruled *Makanjuola*. Lord Woolf, speaking for the House, accepted that public interest immunity could not be waived after the court had determined that the public interest against disclosure outweighed that of disclosure. Matters were, however, different in relation to the situation before that final determination had been made. His Lordship held that ministers possessed discretion as to whether to claim public interest immunity. Thus, it was open to the secretary of state, or the Attorney General, to decide that the public interest in documents being withheld from production was outweighed by the public interest in disclosure. While the court was the ultimate arbiter on this balance Lord Woolf made it clear that it would be extremely rare for the court to reach a different conclusion where the minister was of the view that the documents could be disclosed. This was equally true of class claims and contents claims.

Where however parties other than government departments were in possession of documents in respect of which immunity could be claimed on a class basis matters were rather different. It would not, said Lord Woolf, be right for the individual to decide that the documents should be disclosed, since this could undermine the claim for immunity of documents within that general category. It might, on the facts, be possible for the individual to consult other relevant parties, and the Attorney General, and then to decide that disclosure was not problematic. This view as to the balance of the public interest would in all likelihood be accepted by the court. Where this was not possible then public interest immunity should be claimed and the balancing would be undertaken by the court.

---

[25] See also *Norwich Pharmacal Co v Customs and Excise Commissioners* [1974] A.C. 133, HL.

[26] *Makanjuola v Commissioner of Police of the Metropolis* [1992] 3 All E.R. 617, CA (Civ Div); *Halford v Sharples* [1992] 1 W.L.R. 736, CA (Civ Div).

[27] A. Bradley, "Justice, Good Government and Public Interest Immunity" [1992] P.L. 514; A. Tomkins, "Public Interest Immunity after Matrix Churchill" [1993] P.L. 650, 662–665.

[28] *R. v Chief Constable of the West Midlands Police, Ex p. Wiley* [1995] 1 A.C. 274, HL; *Tchenguiz v Director of the Serious Fraud Office* [2015] 1 W.L.R. 797, CA.

F. Public Interest Immunity: Duty, Discretion and the ECHR

The discussion in *Wiley* focused primarily on the extent to which a minister had discretion to decide that public interest immunity was, on balance, not required in a particular case. The ECHR has an impact in the converse case, concerning the discretion to withhold information on public interest immunity grounds. Applicants have argued that withholding documents on the ground of public interest immunity infringes the right to a fair trial in art.6 ECHR. The European Court of Human Rights (ECtHR) enunciated the following principles.[29] **13–007**

It held that a fundamental aspect of art.6 is equality of arms, which meant that the prosecution should normally disclose all evidence for or against the accused. The ECtHR accepted that this did not constitute an absolute right, and that there might be circumstances where the public interest justified the withholding of information on public interest immunity grounds. It was for the national court, not the ECtHR, to decide whether the non-disclosure was strictly necessary. It was, however, not open to the prosecution to withhold evidence without notifying the trial judge, thereby preventing the latter from making the assessment of whether the claim for public interest immunity was really warranted on the facts, unless the defect had been remedied by a full inter partes hearing by the Appeal Court.[30]

Moreover, where evidence was withheld any difficulties caused for the defence must be counterbalanced by the procedures adopted by the judicial authorities. Thus, the defence should be kept informed and permitted to make submissions in the decision-making process about public interest immunity, so far as this was possible without revealing the material that the prosecution sought to keep secret.

These principles have been acknowledged by the House of Lords. Thus in *R. v H*[31] the House of Lords held that having regard to the overriding principle that the trial process, viewed as a whole, should be fair and to the rule obliging the prosecution to make full disclosure of unused material tending to undermine its case or assist that of the defence, the trial judge on a public interest immunity application was required to give detailed consideration to the material sought to be withheld in the context of the prosecution and defence cases. The trial judge should identify the public interest in question and assess the prejudice claimed, and ensure that any derogation from the full disclosure rule was the minimum necessary to secure the required protection. An application made ex parte without notice to the defence was permitted only in exceptional circumstances. Appointment of special counsel to represent a defendant as an advocate on such an application might in an exceptional case be necessary in the interests of justice, but such an appointment should not be ordered unless the trial judge was satisfied that no other course would adequately meet the overriding requirement

---

[29] *Edwards v United Kingdom* (1993) 15 E.H.R.R. 417; *Rowe and Davis v United Kingdom* (2000) 30 E.H.R.R. 1; *Jasper v United Kingdom* (2000) 30 E.H.R.R. 441; *Atlan v United Kingdom* (2002) 34 E.H.R.R. 33; *Edwards and Lewis v United Kingdom* [2005] 40 E.H.R.R. 24.

[30] The application of these principles was considered in *R. v Botmeh* [2002] 1 W.L.R. 531, CA (Crim Div); *R. v H* [2003] 1 W.L.R. 3006, CA (Crim Div).

[31] *R. v H* [2004] 2 A.C. 134, HL; *R. v May* [2005] 1 W.L.R. 2902, CA (Crim Div); *R. v Lewis* [2005] EWCA Crim 859.

of fairness to the defendant. Material that was damaging to the defendant was not in any event disclosable and should not be brought to the court's attention. Provided the existing procedures were operated in accordance with these principles there would be no violation of art.6.

G. Public Interest Immunity: Disclosure and Public Interest Immunity

13–008 In the past the person claiming discovery had to show that the documents were necessary for fairly disposing of the cause or matter or for saving costs.[32] If this could not be shown then the documents did not have to be disclosed and there was no need to raise a claim of public interest immunity. It might, however, be unclear whether the documents were necessary until they were looked at. The person who was seeking discovery was in danger of being caught in a "Catch 22" dilemma: it might only be possible to show that they were necessary for disposing of the case by seeing the documents themselves. Yet the courts did not wish to sanction fishing expeditions by people who were seeking to establish a cause of action. The resolution of this conundrum was for the applicant to prove that the documents might well be of use to the case. The precise standard demanded by their Lordships differed. In *Burmah Oil*,[33] Lord Wilberforce stated that the court should not inspect the documents unless the party could show a strong positive case that they might help him. Lord Keith[34] used a test of reasonable probability, while Lord Edmund-Davies[35] adopted a test of likelihood. Only if the person seeking access to the documents surmounted this hurdle would the court undertake the balancing operation.

The position under the Civil Procedure Rules (CPR) is as follows.[36] CPR Pt 31 is framed in terms of orders for "standard disclosure" and for "specific disclosure". A party discloses a document by stating that the document exists or has existed.[37] A party to whom a document has been disclosed has, subject to certain exceptions, a right to inspect it.[38] An order to give disclosure is, unless the court otherwise directs, an order to give standard disclosure.[39] It is open to the court to dispense with or limit standard disclosure.[40] Where a court makes such an order then it requires a party to disclose the documents on which it relies, and the documents which adversely affect its own or another party's case, or support another party's case, and such documents which it is required to disclose by a relevant practice direction.[41] The court is also empowered to make an order for specific disclosure or specific inspection, requiring the party to disclose those

[32] RSC Ord.24 r.13; *Air Canada v Secretary of State for Trade (No.2)* [1983] 2 A.C. 394, HL.

[33] *Burmah Oil Co Ltd v Bank of England* [1980] A.C. 1090, HL at 1117.

[34] *Burmah Oil* [1980] A.C. 1090 at 1135–1136.

[35] *Burmah Oil* [1980] A.C. 1090 at 1126.

[36] *R. (A Child) (Care: Disclosure: Nature of Proceedings), Re* [2002] 1 F.L.R. 755 Fam Div.

[37] CPR r.31.2.

[38] CPR r.31.3.

[39] CPR r.31.5(1).

[40] CPR r.31.5(2).

[41] CPR r.31.6.

documents specified in the order.[42] The extent to which the courts will order disclosure in judicial review proceedings will be considered in a later chapter.[43]

A person may apply for an order permitting him to withhold disclosure of a document on the ground that disclosure would damage the public interest.[44] This is a method by which public interest immunity claims are raised and the person seeking to withhold disclosure has the burden or showing that he is entitled to do so.[45] CPR 31.19 is as follows:

> "(1) A person may apply, without notice, for an order permitting him to withhold disclosure of a document on the ground that disclosure would damage the public interest.
> (2) Unless the court orders otherwise, an order of the court under paragraph (1)—(a) must not be served on any other person; and (b) must not be open to inspection by any person.
> (3) A person who wishes to claim that he has a right or a duty to withhold inspection of a document, or part of a document must state in writing—(a) that he has such a right or duty; and (b) the grounds on which he claims that right or duty.
> (4) The statement referred to in paragraph (3) must be made—(a) in the list in which the document is disclosed; or (b) if there is no list, to the person wishing to inspect the document.
> (5) A party may apply to the court to decide whether a claim made under paragraph (3) should be upheld.
> (6) For the purpose of deciding an application under paragraph (1) (application to withhold disclosure) or paragraph (3) (claim to withhold inspection) the court may—(a) require the person seeking to withhold disclosure or inspection of a document to produce that document to the court; and (b) invite any person, whether or not a party, to make representations.
> (7) An application under paragraph (1) or paragraph (5) must be supported by evidence.
> (8) This Part does not affect any rule of law which permits or requires a document to be withheld from disclosure or inspection on the ground that its disclosure or inspection would damage the public interest."

It may be necessary for the court to inspect the documents to determine whether their disclosure should be ordered. This is evident from CPR 31.19(6), and from the general common law on public interest immunity. *Burmah Oil*[46] is authority that inspection can be ordered at this level. This must be correct on principle. The degree of likelihood that the claimant must show for the court to inspect the documents continues to divide the judiciary. Thus, in *Air Canada*[47] their Lordships refused to inspect, but their formulations differed.[48] If the standard is set too high then claimants could find themselves in a position not very different from that prior to *Conway*, since the case will never reach the balancing stage. **13–009**

---

[42] CPR r.31.12.

[43] See Ch.27.

[44] CPR r.31.19.

[45] *Shah* [2011] EWHC 1713.

[46] *Burmah Oil* [1980] A.C. 1090.

[47] *Air Canada* [1983] 2 A.C. 394.

[48] Three of their Lordships held that in order to warrant inspection the plaintiff must show that there was a reasonable probability that the material was necessary for fairly disposing of the case, and that the documents would help his or her case or damage that of the other side, *Air Canada* [1983] 2 A.C. 394 at 435, 439, 442–443. Two of their Lordships held that the plaintiff must show that the documents were likely to be necessary for fairly disposing of the case, and that the court could inspect the documents when it considered that their disclosure might materially assist either of the parties or the court in the determination of the issues, 445–446, 447–449.

It is clear moreover from *Al-Sweady*, that the court will take a very dim view of inaccurate claims to public interest immunity.[49] The secretary of state relied on what was a partly false PII certificate, which asserted that it was not in the public interest, on national security grounds, to disclose certain redacted documents otherwise disclosed to the claimants. However, a significant proportion of the redacted material, which related to the permissible limits of the techniques for tactical questioning of captured individuals, had previously been disclosed in Court Martial proceedings, and was thus in the public domain. The court was sharply critical of the Ministry of Defence and made it clear that until risk of error was removed the court would approach such PII certificates with considerable caution.

H. Public Interest Immunity: The Balancing Process

13–010 The person arguing against disclosure raises the public interest in favour of immunity. How strong a case must be made out is not entirely clear,[50] although the government's practice is not to claim immunity unless it believes that disclosure would cause real damage or harm to the public interest.

If there is doubt about whether a document should be included within a particular class claim the court may inspect it.[51] This must be right in terms of principle. If there is doubt as to whether immunity should be claimed for a particular document, not to inspect would make it possible for the party against disclosure to protect material that did not warrant immunity.

If a class claim is advanced by a public body the court will decide whether it is sustainable. This was the ground for the decision in *Wiley*,[52] where it was held that a class claim did not attach to all documents coming into existence in consequence of an investigation against the police under Pt IX of the Police and Criminal Evidence Act 1984. There were, however, differences of view as to whether class claims in respect of some reports could be sustained. Lord Woolf expressed reservations as to whether this could be so. Lord Slynn did not share these reservations, and felt that much turned on the breadth of the relevant class, as did Lord Lloyd.

Inspection may be required at the balancing stage in order to determine whether the public interest is for or against disclosure. *Conway*[53] endorsed inspection where necessary, in order to decide where the balance lay, as did *Burmah Oil*.[54] Notwithstanding these authorities, some courts have been more

[49] *R. (Al-Sweady) v Secretary of State for Defence* [2009] EWHC 1687 DC (Admin).

[50] In *Burmah Oil* [1980] A.C. 1090 Lord Wilberforce spoke of a claim for public interest immunity having been made on a strong and well-fortified basis, at 1112, while Lord Edmund-Davies spoke of the Chief Secretary establishing a good prima facie case for withholding the documents, at 1125; in *Wiley* [1995] 1 A.C. 274 Lord Templeman spoke of the need for disclosure unless this would cause substantial harm to the public interest, at 281.

[51] *Conway* [1968] A.C. 910 at 995; *Burmah Oil* [1980] A.C. 1090; CPR r.31.19(6).

[52] *Wiley* [1995] 1 A.C. 274.

[53] *Conway* [1968] A.C. 910 at 953, 972, 980, 989, 995–996.

[54] *Burmah Oil* [1980] A.C. 1090 at 1121–1122, 1129, 1134–1135, 1145; *Goodridge v Chief Constable of Hampshire Constabulary* [1999] 1 All E.R. 896 QBD; *Amaryllis Ltd v HM Treasury* [2009] EWHC 1666 at [52].

circumspect about the desirability of such inspection.[55] Varying reasons have been given for this more wary approach. A recurring theme is that to inspect infringes the principle that documents should be available to both sides. This point was well answered by Lord Upjohn[56]: when the judge demands to see the documents for which privilege is claimed he is not considering the main cause of action between the parties, but a distinct issue, viz whether the public interest in withholding the document outweighs the public interest that all relevant documents not otherwise privileged should be displayed in litigation. If on balance the court considers that the document should be produced, it may inspect it before ordering production, particularly if it had not been seen by the court before that stage.[57]

The balancing stage is then reached, the issue being whether the public interest that the evidence be withheld outweighs the public interest in the administration of justice.[58] An important point is whether there are any categories in relation to which balancing does not apply. Their Lordships in *Conway* differed as to whether certain types of documents should automatically be regarded as beyond the reach of the courts and not subject to the balancing approach.[59] The question of whether such a category existed arose in *Burmah Oil*.[60] Burmah Oil was in financial difficulty and a rescue package was put together under which Burmah sold their British Petroleum stock to the Bank. The original intent was that because BP stock was low at the time of the sale, any profit from resale of the stock would be divided between the Bank and Burmah Oil. The government did not, however, accept this part of the scheme. BP stock rose in value, and Burmah Oil alleged that the sale of the stock was unconscionable. It sought to discover documents, including those from ministerial meetings, and those relating to meetings of government officials. The object was to find evidence that the government's rejection of the profit sharing scheme was unfair. Their Lordships held that, while the importance of the documents would be a factor in the balancing process, no classes of document were entirely excluded from that process. Even high level governmental policy could be subjected to this process.[61] **13–011**

This is further exemplified by *Mohammed*.[62] The court held that the confidentiality of working arrangements between allied intelligence services was not absolute. Thus after balancing the public interest in national security against the public interest in open justice as safeguarding the rule of law, free speech and

[55] *Gaskin v Liverpool City Council* [1980] 1 W.L.R. 1549, CA (Civ Div).

[56] *Conway* [1968] A.C. 910 at 995–996.

[57] *Conway* [1968] A.C. 910.

[58] See, e.g. *R. (Mohammed) v Secretary of State for Defence* [2012] EWHC 3454 (Admin); *Worcestershire CC v HM Coroner for Worcestershire* [2013] EWHC 1711 (QB); *R. (Evans) v Secretary of State for Defence* [2013] EWHC 3068 DC (Admin); *R.(A) v Chief Constable of C Constabulary* [2013] EWHC 4120 (Admin); *Commissioner of Police of the Metropolis v Bangs* [2014] EWHC 546 DC (Admin); *R.(X) v Chief Constable of Y* [2015] EWHC 484 (Admin).

[59] *Conway* [1968] A.C. 910 at 952–953, 986–987, 971, 993.

[60] *Burmah Oil* [1980] A.C. 1090.

[61] *Burmah Oil* [1980] A.C. 1090 at 1113, 1129, 1134–1135, 1143–1144.

[62] *R. (Mohamed) v Secretary of State for Foreign and Commonwealth Affairs (No.2)* [2011] Q.B. 218, CA (Civ Div). Compare *Secretary of State for Foreign and Commonwealth Affairs v Assistant Deputy Coroner for Inner North London* [2013] EWHC 3724 DC (Admin).

democratic accountability, certain paragraphs that contained a summary of reports made by the US government to the UK government relating to the detention and treatment of a suspected terrorist ought to be included in a judgment, since they did not contain information which could pose a risk to national security, but did contain information that it was in the public interest to disclose.

The Human Rights Act 1998 has had an impact on the balancing process. Thus, in *McNally*[63] the fact that rights protected by the ECHR were in play inclined the court to accept that there should be a more case-specific balancing to decide whether it should be revealed that a person was a police informer. The courts are more demanding that those who advance a public interest immunity claim should set out with greater particularity than hitherto the harm that will be caused to the public interest by the production of the relevant material.[64]

Various arguments have been used to justify non-disclosure, particularly of high policy documents. The most common are that disclosure would place candour within the public service at risk, and that it would fan ill-formed or captious criticism by those without understanding of how government worked. The candour argument is no longer regarded as such an important factor. There are nonetheless differences of judicial opinion as to its relevance. For example, Lord Reid in *Conway* did not believe that the possibility of disclosure would inhibit candour.[65] This sentiment was echoed even more strongly by Lord Keith in *Burmah Oil*,[66] who regarded the notion that candour would be diminished by the off-chance of disclosure as grotesque. Similarly dismissive statements are to be found in other cases.[67] In *Burmah Oil* Lord Wilberforce, by way of contrast, felt that the candour argument had received an excessive dose of cold water,[68] while Lord Scarman[69] took the view that both the candour argument and the captious public criticism argument were important.[70]

I. Public Interest Immunity: The Change in Governmental Approach

13–012 The use of public interest immunity certificates was criticised in the Scott Report into the Arms to Iraq affair.[71] The inquiry that led to this report considered the use of such certificates in the abortive attempt to prosecute the directors of Matrix Churchill. It was this report, combined with the decision in *Wiley*, which caused

[63] *Chief Constable of the Greater Manchester Police v McNally* [2002] 2 Cr. App. R. 37, CA (Civ Div).

[64] *R. (A Child) (Care: Disclosure: Nature of Proceedings), Re* [2002] 1 F.L.R. 755 Fam Div.

[65] *Conway* [1968] A.C. 910 at 952.

[66] *Burmah Oil* [1980] A.C. 1090 at 1133.

[67] *Science Research Council v Nasse* [1980] A.C. 1028, HL at 1070, 1081; *Campbell v Tameside MBC* [1982] 3 W.L.R. 75, CA (Civ Div); *Williams v Home Office* [1981] 1 All E.R. 1151 QBD.

[68] *Burmah Oil* [1980] A.C. 1090 at 1112.

[69] *Burmah Oil* [1980] A.C. 1090 at 1145. Even where the balance is against disclosure there may be a temporal limit upon the secrecy, *R. v Inland Revenue Commissioners, Ex p. Rossminster Ltd* [1980] A.C. 952, HL.

[70] See also the opinion of Lord Fraser in *Air Canada* [1983] 2 A.C. 394.

[71] *The Report of the Inquiry into the Export of Defence and Dual Use Goods to Iraq and Related Prosecutions*, HC Paper No.115 (Session 1995–96).

the government to rethink its approach to this issue. There was a consultation exercise, followed by statements from the Lord Chancellor and the Attorney General.[72] The new approach only applies when it is the government that is claiming immunity.

i. *The new approach*

Ministers will only claim public interest immunity when it is believed that disclosure of a document will cause real damage or harm to the public interest. The harm might be direct or indirect. Ministers will therefore perform the balancing exercise specified in *Wiley*. The damage might relate to the safety of an individual, to the regulatory process, to international relations, the nation's economic interests or national security. The nature of the harm will be explained by the minister when immunity is claimed. **13–013**

The former division into class claims and contents claims will no longer be applied. Ministers will not therefore claim immunity to protect, for example, internal advice or national security merely by pointing to the general nature of the document. The factors which will be taken into account in a properly reasoned certificate relating to, for example, internal advice, will include: the public importance of the topic; the level of the discussion; the degree of controversy; the expectation of the parties that the exchanges would be confidential; and the likelihood that the disclosure will have damaging consequences of a specific and important nature.

ii. *Evaluation*

The new approach to public interest immunity by the government is to be welcomed. There are, however, features of the policy which are still a cause for concern.[73] The criterion of real damage or harm used by the government should not be read as a lower standard than that of substantial harm set out by Lord Templeman in *Wiley*.[74] It is encouraging that the government does not wish to persist with class claims, which have long been criticised.[75] The dividing line between a class claim and a contents claim can nonetheless be a fine one. Thus, while the government has stated that it will not use class claims, it is also clear that it will use "sampling": ministers may assert immunity "for a number of documents after examining a sample of the documents, rather than each one".[76] The government accepts that it will be for the court to decide whether the sampling that has been done is sufficient, but the very idea of sampling blurs the line between class and contents claims. **13–014**

The government view was that the same approach should be applied to civil and criminal cases,[77] albeit recognising that the balancing might operate

[72] *Hansard*, HL, cols 1507–1508, HC cols 949–950 HC (18 December 1996).

[73] M. Supperstone and J. Goudie, "A New Approach to Public Interest Immunity" [1997] P.L. 211.

[74] *Wiley* [1995] 1 A.C. 274 at 281.

[75] Sir Richard Scott, "The Acceptable and Unacceptable Use of Public Interest Immunity" [1996] P.L. 427, 436–443.

[76] *Report on Public Interest Immunity*, December 18, 1996, para.6.3.

[77] *Report on Public Interest Immunity*, para.1.9.

differently within the criminal context. It is, however, questionable whether the balancing approach is really suited to criminal cases. Sir Richard Scott argued cogently that it cannot readily be transferred to such cases. Thus, referring to the balancing process that applies in civil cases, he questioned whether that has anything to do with the public interest that a defendant should have fair trial and that an innocent man should not be convicted.[78] It should in any event be borne in mind that the principles applied by the courts in criminal cases discussed in the previous section will be controlling, and that criminal procedural rules now deal with this issue.[79]

3. CLOSED MATERIAL PROCEDURES

A. Closed Material Procedures: Nature

13–015 A closed material procedure (CMP) involving special advocates is a procedure whereby relevant material the disclosure of which would harm the public interest ("closed material"), can still be considered in the proceedings rather than being excluded as with public interest immunity. The aim is therefore to provide individuals with "a substantial measure of procedural justice in the difficult circumstances where, in the public interest, material cannot be disclosed to them".[80]

The proceedings have both "open" and "closed" elements. All the material, both open and closed, relied on by the government is laid before the court and the special advocate.[81] The individual and his legal representative are present at the open hearings, and have access to the open material. They cannot be present at the closed parts of the proceedings, or see the closed material. A special advocate is appointed who attends all parts of the proceedings, and sees all the material, including the closed material not disclosed to the individual. He is able to take instructions from the individual before he reads the closed material, and written instructions after he has seen the closed material. A special advocate can also communicate with the individual after he has seen the material, subject to permission from the court, but this is relatively rare. The special advocate is a security cleared barrister/advocate, who is given special training for this role.

The special advocate acts for the individual's interests in relation to closed material and closed hearings, but the individual is not their client. The special advocates ensure that the closed material is subject to independent scrutiny and adversarial challenge, and they can make submissions in closed session as to whether or not the closed material should be disclosed to the individual. It is for the court, not the secretary of state, to decide whether material should be withheld.

The closed material procedure was initially introduced in the context of immigration deportation decisions, with the stimulus coming from the European

---

78 Scott, "The Acceptable and Unacceptable Use of Public Interest Immunity" [1996] P.L. 427, 434.
79 Criminal Procedure Rules 2011 (SI 1709/2011).
80 Green Paper, *Justice and Security*, p.52.
81 J. Ip, "The Rise and Spread of the Special Advocate" [2008] P.L. 717.

Court of Human Rights.[82] The CMP has subsequently been used by the Special Immigration Appeals Commission, the Proscribed Organisations Appeal Commission, Employment Tribunal cases concerning national security, control order cases under the Prevention of Terrorism Act 2005, financial restrictions proceedings under the Counter-Terrorism Act 2008, and the Sentence Review Commission and Parole Commission in Northern Ireland.

B. Closed Material Procedures: Compatibility with Natural Justice

The compatibility of the CMP with natural justice has been tested before the courts. The heightened security concerns of the post 9/11 world posed serious challenges for liberal governments, which led to difficult cases where the courts considered the compatibility of legislation to combat terrorism with human rights.[83] The control order regime in the Prevention of Terrorism Act 2005 was enacted after the decision in *A v Secretary of State for the Home Department*,[84] where the House of Lords held that s.23 of the Anti-terrorism, Crime and Security Act 2001, which gave the secretary of state power to detain a suspected international terrorist with a view to his intended deportation, was incompatible with arts 5 and 14 ECHR. **13–016**

The compatibility of the control order regime with natural justice was considered in *Secretary of State for the Home Department v AF*[85] where the House of Lords affirmed the existence of a core minimum of natural justice. The appellant was subject to a non-derogating control order made pursuant to the Prevention of Terrorism Act 2005 s.2 (PTA), on the ground that the secretary of state had reasonable grounds for suspecting that the appellant was, or had been, involved in terrorism-related activity, and that he considered it was necessary to make such an order to protect the public from a risk of terrorism. If this criterion was met it was not necessary to prove that the person subject to the control order had actually committed any further offence. The PTA and Civil Procedure Rules[86] made provision for a CMP and special advocates. The issue before the House of Lords was whether the procedure for the making of a control order complied with art.6 ECHR and hence, with the Human Rights Act 1998.

The making of such orders could be supervised by the court pursuant to PTA 2005 s.3, which included provision of a hearing to determine whether the conditions in PTA 2005 s.2(1), were met. The compatibility of the control order

---

[82] *Chahal v United Kingdom* (1996) 23 E.H.R.R. 413.

[83] K. Ewing, "The Futility of the Human Rights Act" [2004] P.L. 829; A. Lester, "The Utility of the HRA: A Reply to Keith Ewing" [2005] P.L. 249; K. Ewing and J. Tham, "The Continuing Futility of the Human Rights Act" [2008] P.L. 829; A. Sandell, "Liberty, Fairness and the UK Control Order Cases: Two Steps Forward, Two Steps Back" [2008] E.H.R.L.R. 120; A. Kavanagh, "Judging the Judges under the Human Rights Act: Deference, Disillusionment and the 'War on Terror'" [2009] P.L. 287.

[84] *A v Secretary of State for the Home Department* [2005] 2 A.C. 68 HL.

[85] *AF* [2010] 2 A.C. 269; P. Craig, "Perspectives on Process: Common Law, Statutory and Political" [2010] P.L. 275; A. Kavanagh, "Special Advocates, Control Orders and the Right to a Fair Trial" (2010) 73 M.L.R. 836.

[86] CPR 76.

regime in the PTA 2005 with the ECHR had been raised in *MB*,[87] but the ratio was unclear and this caused difficulties in subsequent cases, in which lower courts took rather different messages from the speeches in *MB*.[88]

13–017 The difficulties generated by *MB* led the House of Lords to revisit the issue in the *AF* case.[89] It held that there was a core minimum of procedural justice and that this could not be overridden by arguments that the procedural rights would not have made any difference. The consequence was that the relevant provisions of the PTA 2005 were read down so as to be compatible with Convention rights. Their Lordships were influenced by the decision of the ECtHR in *A v United Kingdom*,[90] which held that non-disclosure could not deny a party knowledge of the essence of the case against him, in cases where the consequences were of the kind that flowed from a control order.[91] The regime of Special Advocates could alleviate the problems caused by non-disclosure of closed material to the affected party, by testing the evidence and putting arguments on behalf of the detainee during the closed hearings. However, the very fact that special advocates could not make contact with the affected party once the closed material had been seen meant that there were real limits to the representation that they could provide, since unless the detainee had sufficient information as to the allegations against him, he could not give meaningful instructions to the special advocate. This was especially problematic where the open material consisted of mere general assertions, and the entirety of the case against the detainee was contained in closed material.[92]

The House of Lords accepted the decision of the ECtHR, stating that it established that the person subject to the control order must be given sufficient information about the allegations against him to enable him to give effective instructions in relation to those allegations. Provided that this requirement was satisfied there could be a fair trial notwithstanding that the person was not provided with the detail or the sources of the evidence forming the basis of the allegations. Where, however, the open material consisted purely of general assertions and the case against that person was based solely or to a decisive degree on closed materials the requirements of a fair trial would not be satisfied, however cogent the case based on the closed materials might be.[93]

The argument from case law was reinforced by that from principle. Lord Phillips adduced instrumental and non-instrumental reasons that underlie natural justice to support the preceding conclusion.[94] Thus, in instrumental terms Lord

---

87 *Secretary of State for the Home Department v MB* [2008] 1 A.C. 440, HL.

88 *Secretary of State for the Home Department v AE* [2008] EWHC 132; *Secretary of State for the Home Department v E* [2008] EWHC 585; *R. (Secretary of State for the Home Department) v H* [2008] EWHC 1045 (Admin); *Secretary of State for the Home Department v R* [2008] EWHC 3164 (Admin); *Secretary of State for the Home Department v Rideh* [2008] EWHC 1993 (Admin).

89 *AF* [2010] 2 A.C. 269; *AT v Secretary of State for the Home Division* [2012] EWCA Civ 42; *Bank Mellat v HM Treasury* [2014] EWHC 3631 (Admin); *Secretary of State for the Home Department v CC* [2014] 1 W.L.R. 4240, CA; *ZZ (France) v Secretary of State for the Home Department* [2014] Q.B. 820, CA.

90 *A v United Kingdom* Application No.3455/05, 19 February 2009.

91 *A v United Kingdom* Application No.3455/05, 19 February 2009 at [216]–[220].

92 *A v United Kingdom* Application No.3455/05, February 19, 2009 at [220].

93 *AF* [2010] 2 A.C. 269 at [59], [81], [85], [96], [101], [108], [114].

94 *AF* [2010] 2 A.C. 269 at [56], [58], [60]–[66].

Phillips noted that there were strong policy considerations to support a rule that a trial procedure could never be considered fair if a party was kept in ignorance of the case against him, since there would be many cases where it would be impossible for the court to be confident that disclosure would make no difference. This was more especially so where the criteria for the control order, viz reasonable suspicion of involvement in terrorism related activity, might be founded "on misinterpretation of facts in respect of which the controlee is in a position to put forward an innocent explanation".[95] This conclusion was reinforced by non-instrumental or dignitarian considerations, since resentment would undoubtedly be felt by the controlee and the family where there was no proper explanation for the control order: they and the wider public "need to be able to see that justice is done rather than being asked to take it on trust".[96]

The courts subsequently confirmed the idea of a core minimum of process rights,[97] and made clear that failure to comply with the requirements in *AF* lead to the decision being struck down as void.[98] The control order regime nonetheless remains inherently problematic from the perspective of the individual and the government. **13–018**

From the individual's perspective, the underlying principle of the PTA 2005 was that a control order would only be made where there was no realistic prospect of successfully prosecuting the subject of the order for a terrorism-related offence.[99] The consequence was that the person was subject to significant constraints based on reasonable suspicion in circumstances where he might not be able to see the full evidence against him. The decision in *AF* is to be welcomed in affirming the existence of a core minimum of process rights, but later courts must still adjudicate on the difficult line as to whether the claimant has received enough information about the essence of the allegations against him to enable him to defend himself,[100] and on whether the closed material procedure can be used to submit evidence on behalf of the claimant, subject to strict duties of non-disclosure of the evidence where it might endanger the witness.[101]

From the government's perspective, the decision in *AF* is seen as problematic because it has to "balance the importance of protecting the public from the risk of terrorism posed by the individual against the risk of disclosing sensitive material".[102] The consequence is that where the disclosure required by the court cannot be made because the potential damage to the public interest is too high, the government must withdraw the information from the case, and the control order will then be quashed if it cannot be sustained on the remaining material.

---

[95] *AF* [2010] 2 A.C. 269 at [63].

[96] *AF* [2010] 2 A.C. 269 at [63], [83].

[97] *Bank Mellat v HM Treasury* [2010] 3 W.L.R. 1090.

[98] *Secretary of State for the Home Department v AF* [2010] EWHC 42 (Admin); *N v Secretary of State for the Home Department* [2010] EWCA Civ 869; *R. (BB (Algeria)) v Special Immigration Appeals Commission* [2011] EWHC 336 (Admin); *AT* [2012] EWCA Civ 42.

[99] *Secretary of State for the Home Department v E* [2008] 1 A.C. 499, HL.

[100] *AH v Secretary of State for the Home Department* [2011] EWCA Civ 787; *Secretary of State for the Home Department v CD* [2011] EWHC 2087; *Bank Mellat v HM Treasury* [2014] EWHC 3631 (Admin).

[101] *W (Algeria) (FC) v Secretary of State for the Home Department* [2012] UKSC 8.

[102] Green Paper, *Justice and Security*, p.54.

C. Closed Material Procedures: Limits of *AF*

13–019 The decision in *AF* required, as we have seen, that the essence of the case should be conveyed to the individual in open proceedings. This has come to be known as providing the individual with the gist of the case against him, or gisting. The precise circumstances in which this will be required is, however, not entirely clear, as is apparent from *Tariq*.[103]

T was employed by the Home Office as an immigration officer. His security clearance was withdrawn after the arrest of his brother and cousin during an investigation into a suspected terrorist plot. T's brother was released without charge, but the cousin was convicted of various offences. There was, however, no information that T was involved with the plot. The secretary of state argued that the decision was made to safeguard national security. The employment tribunal used a CMP to determine the case, as provided for under the relevant legislation. T argued that there was an absolute requirement flowing from art.6 that he could see the allegations in sufficient detail to give instructions to his legal representatives so that the allegations could be challenged effectively.

The Supreme Court found against T and held that the CMP was compatible with art.6 ECHR. It held that national security could justify use of a closed material procedure, in which a party was unable to know material by reference to which his complaint was determined, provided that there were sufficient safeguards. The Supreme Court took account of the following factors in this regard: the decision as to use of the CMP was made by the employment tribunal after hearing argument; the employment tribunal kept the closed procedure under review throughout the proceedings; the special advocate procedure was part of the CMP; the case concerned employment rather than deprivation of fundamental rights; and the Home Office would have to concede the case if it could not prevent disclosure of the vetting process. The Supreme Court concluded that balancing the disadvantage to the claimant, as mitigated by the CMP, against the need to protect the integrity of the security vetting process, the balance was in favour of the Home Office. The majority of the Supreme Court therefore found that gisting was not required in every context in which art.6 was engaged and that it was not necessary in a context such as national security vetting in *Tariq*. There was therefore no absolute requirement flowing from art.6 that T could see the allegations in sufficient detail to give instructions to his legal representatives so that the allegations could be challenged effectively.[104]

It is clear from *Tariq* that gisting is not required in a case of security vetting. It seems clear also from *Tariq* that gisting will not be mandatory except where the liberty of the subject is at stake, provided that the CMP contains appropriate procedural safeguards. It nonetheless remains unclear precisely what constitutes the liberty of the subject for these purposes. It is, moreover, also not entirely clear whether the gisting requirement is only applicable in cases where art.6 ECHR

---

[103] *Tariq* [2011] UKSC 35; *CF v Security Service* [2014] EWHC 3171 (QB).

[104] *Tariq* [2011] UKSC 35 at [67]–[69], [81]–[83], [86]–[92], [138], [143]–[147], [158].

applies. The uncertainties in this regard led the government to legislate to clarify the circumstances in which the gisting requirement derived from *AF* is not applicable.[105]

D. Closed Material Procedures: The Need for Statutory Foundation

The Supreme Court placed limits on the use of closed material procedure in *Al Rawi*.[106] The judgment is complex, but the majority of the Supreme Court held in essence that a closed material procedure could only be introduced by statute, and that it was not open to the courts to do so pursuant to the courts' power to regulate its own procedure. **13–020**

The claimants had been detained by foreign authorities at foreign locations and allegedly suffered ill-treatment. They sought damages in tort against the defendants for causing or contributing to their detention and suffering. The defendant security services denied liability for such detention or ill-treatment and wished to rely on material that could not be disclosed without real risk of harm to the public interest. They argued therefore that they should be able to set out this material in closed pleadings which would be withheld from the claimants and their legal advisers, but which would be considered by special advocates representing their interests.

The majority of the Supreme Court held that Parliament alone could introduce such a closed material procedure as a replacement for the existing common law process for dealing with claims for public interest immunity in ordinary civil claims for damages, and it was not open to the courts to do so in reliance on power to regulate its own procedures. They held that the principles of open and natural justice whereby proceedings generally take place and judgments are delivered in public and parties know and can respond to the cases against them, calling witnesses and cross-examining opposing witnesses, were fundamental features of a common law trial. While the court had inherent power to regulate its own procedures, it could not, in doing so, deny parties' rights to participate in litigation in accordance with those principles.

The majority distinguished closed material procedures from claims for public interest immunity. In relation to public interest immunity as developed by the common law, the principles of fairness and equality of arms applied, with the consequence that documents were either disclosed to or withheld from all the parties and no party was excluded from participation in the litigation. However, a closed material procedure, which excluded a party from part or the whole of a closed hearing and prevented him from seeing and challenging the evidence, except to the limited extent possible through assistance of a special advocate, was a departure from those principles and could not be regarded as a development of the common law. **13–021**

105 Green Paper, *Justice and Security*, paras 2.39–2.46.

106 *Al Rawi* [2011] UKSC 34; *R. (B) v Westminster Magistrates' Court* [2014] 3 W.L.R. 1336 SC; A Zuckerman, "Closed Material Procedure—Denial of Natural Justice: Al Rawi v Security Service" (2011) 30 C.J.Q. 345.

Lord Mance and Baroness Hale took a different view. They concluded that a closed material procedure was not outside the court's jurisdiction. However, they also held that in the absence of statutory authority such a procedure should only be used where, after a conventional public interest immunity exercise, the judge concluded that there should be no disclosure of the documents held by the defence and that as a result the case was untriable. The court might then adopt some form of closed material procedure, if the claimant consented.

The decision in *Al-Rawi* was qualified by *Bank Mellat*[107] where it was held that the Supreme Court could use a CMP, even though there was no express statutory provision for it to do so. The majority was willing to construe the Constitutional Reform Act 2005 to legitimate use of a CMP by the Supreme Court, more especially because such a procedure had been used in the High Court in the instant case, and it would therefore be difficult for the appeal to be conducted by the Supreme Court if it could not use such a procedure. The Supreme Court now has express power to use a closed material procedure pursuant to the Justice and Security Act 2013.[108]

4. JUSTICE AND SECURITY ACT 2013

A. Key Features

13–022 The government published a wide-ranging Green Paper in which it addressed issues concerning natural justice, public interest immunity and the closed material procedure in the light of the case law considered above.

The government's approach to reform was predicated on seeking to maximise "the amount of relevant material that is considered by the court while at the same time ensuring that, where the material is sensitive, it is protected from potentially harmful disclosure".[109] The assumption was that it is "fairer in terms of outcome to seek to include relevant material rather than to exclude it from consideration altogether".[110] It proposed legislation to make CMPs available wherever necessary in civil proceedings, thereby overcoming the obstacles of *Al Rawi*.[111]

Most worrying was the proposal to vest the decision whether to use a CMP in the Secretary of State on the ground that he is "best placed to assess the harm that may be caused by disclosing sensitive information".[112] It was accepted that this decision could be judicially reviewed, but it would have been difficult for the claimant to succeed, since in most instances the court would be asked to review the exercise of ministerial discretion and this would be subject to limited rationality review. This proposal was strongly criticised in the consultation process.

---

[107] *Bank Mellat v HM Treasury* [2014] A.C. 700 SC at [38]-[42].
[108] Justice and Security Act 2013 s.6(11).
[109] Green Paper, *Justice and Security*, para.2.2.
[110] Green Paper, *Justice and Security*, para.2.2.
[111] *Al Rawi* [2011] UKSC 34; Green Paper, *Justice and Security*, para. 2.5.
[112] Green Paper, *Justice and Security*, para. 2.6.

The Justice and Security Act 2013 did not retain this feature. It is for the court to make a declaration allowing a CMP procedure in relevant civil proceedings.[113] The application may be made by the Secretary of State, or any party to the proceedings, or it may be made of the court's own motion.[114] Two conditions must be satisfied before the court issues such a declaration. The first condition is that a party to the proceedings would be required to disclose sensitive material in the course of the proceedings to another person, or that a party to the proceedings would be required to make such a disclosure were it not for one or more circumstances specified in the Act.[115] The second condition is that it is in the interests of the fair and effective administration of justice in the proceedings to make a declaration.[116] Sensitive material is defined to be material the disclosure of which would be damaging to national security.[117] The court has a duty to keep the CMP under review, and may revoke it at any time if it considers that it is no longer in the interests of the fair and effective administration of justice in the proceedings.[118] Special advocates are part of the CMP regime.[119] The secretary of state has an obligation to report on the use of the CMP procedure each year,[120] and must appoint a person to review the operation of the CMP schema in the 2013 Act.[121]

B. Evaluation

Tomkins is assuredly right that the Justice and Security Act 2013 benefited from close scrutiny by the House of Lords, which secured a number of valuable amendments during the legislative process.[122] There is also little doubt that there are tensions integral to the closed material procedure, and that its generalised availability through the 2013 legislation exacerbates those tensions. **13–023**

i. *The legislative premise*

The premise to the reforms was that extension of CMPs was the most just way to ensure that sensitive cases were litigated with the maximum available material before the court. This would, in the government's view, be preferable to the public interest immunity system, since it would allow the court to consider all the relevant material, regardless of security classification; render it less likely that cases would have to be dropped or settled; "enable the courts to deal effectively **13–024**

---

[113] Relevant civil proceedings are defined in the Justice and Security Act 2013 s.6(11), as any proceedings (other than proceedings in a criminal cause or matter) before the High Court, the Court of Appeal, the Court of Session, or the Supreme Court; *Al Fawwaz v Secretary of State for the Home Department* [2015] EWHC 468 (Admin).

[114] Justice and Security Act 2013 s.6(1)–(2).

[115] Justice and Security Act 2013 s.6(4).

[116] Justice and Security Act 2013 s.6(5).

[117] Justice and Security Act 2013 s.6(11).

[118] Justice and Security Act 2013 s.7(2).

[119] Justice and Security Act 2013 s.9.

[120] Justice and Security Act 2013 s.12.

[121] Justice and Security Act 2013 s.13.

[122] A. Tomkins, "Justice and Security in the United Kingdom" (2014) 47 Israel L. Rev. 305.

with the challenges in all the contexts in which they arise"[123]; and reduce the risk of damaging disclosure of sensitive material. This premise seems uncontroversial, but on further reflection is not for the reason given by Lord Kerr in *Al Rawi*.[124]

> "The defendants' second argument proceeds on the premise that placing before a judge all relevant material is, in every instance, preferable to having to withhold potentially pivotal evidence. This proposition is deceptively attractive—for what, the defendants imply, could be fairer than an independent arbiter having access to all the evidence germane to the dispute between the parties? The central fallacy of the argument, however, lies in the unspoken assumption that, because the judge sees everything, he is bound to be in a better position to reach a fair result. That assumption is misplaced. To be truly valuable, evidence must be capable of withstanding challenge. I go further. Evidence which has been insulated from challenge may positively mislead. It is precisely because of this that the right to know the case that one's opponent makes and to have the opportunity to challenge it occupies such a central place in the concept of a fair trial. However astute and assiduous the judge, the proposed procedure hands over to one party considerable control over the production of relevant material and the manner in which it is to be presented. The peril that such a procedure presents to the fair trial of contentious litigation is both obvious and undeniable."

ii. CMP and PII

13–025 There is nothing logically inconsistent in having both traditional PII and a CMP. Thus it would be perfectly possible to proceed initially by way of public interest immunity to determine whether, after conducting the balancing exercise, the information could be disclosed. Insofar as the answer was negative, it would then be possible to use a CMP. The political reality is that the government envisaged that its proposals for a general statutory power to use CMPs will lead to a "much reduced role for PII",[125] the aim being for CMPs to replace PII in most instances.

This is significant for the reasons adverted to in *Al Rawi*.[126] PII is predicated on fairness and equality of arms, such that documents are disclosed or withheld from all parties and no party is excluded from participation in the litigation. CMP is predicated on the exclusion of a party from the closed hearing, who is unable to challenge the evidence, except for the efforts of a special advocate. The serious implications of doing away with PII balancing have been noted by the Supreme Court.[127] The government has moreover different incentives under PII and CMP, as noted by Lord Kerr.[128]

> "At the moment with PII, the state faces what might be described as a healthy dilemma. It will want to produce as much material as it can in order to defend the claim and therefore will not be too quick to have resort to PII. Under the closed material procedure, all the material goes before the judge and a claim that all of it involves national security or some other vital public interest will be very tempting to make."

The preceding concerns are borne out by the Justice and Security Act 2013, which reflects the government preference for CMPs over PII. This is apparent

[123] Green Paper, *Justice and Security*, para.2.3.
[124] *Al Rawi* [2011] UKSC 34 at [93].
[125] Green Paper, *Justice and Security*, para.2.82.
[126] *Al Rawi* [2011] UKSC 34.
[127] *Al Rawi* [2011] UKSC 34 at [92], [130], [152].
[128] *Al Rawi* [2011] UKSC 34 at [96].

from the combination of s.6(7) and s.6(4).[129] Section 6(7) merely requires the secretary of state to have "considered" whether to make an application for PII before seeking to invoke the CMP. Section 6(4) sets out the first condition for seeking a CMP,[130] which is that a party would be required to disclose sensitive material to another person, or that a party would be required to make such a disclosure were it not for the possibility of a claim for public interest immunity in relation to the material.[131] The tensions between PII and CMP were explored by Irwin J in *CF*.[132] He took the view that the two procedures were antithetical, and that particular difficulties could exist where a case involved issues of national security, which could justify a CMP, and other issues, such as harm to international relations, which might be the ground for PII.

iii. CMPs and special advocates

The special advocate system is crucial to the CMP and the Green Paper considered ways in which its effectiveness could be enhanced, by providing for better arrangements for communication with the party whose interests they are representing after service of closed material. Concerns in this respect have been central to the critique of the special advocate system. The limit of what they can achieve has been noted by those with first-hand experience of the role. Thus, Chamberlain pointed to assumptions that underpinned judicial treatment of special advocates.[133] **13–026**

It was assumed that the special advocates' ability to adduce evidence to rebut the closed material contributed to their ability to ensure procedural justice. The reality was that special advocates lacked access to independent expertise and advice, such that it was difficult to proffer evidence to challenge expert assessments of the Security Service. A second assumption was that special advocates could challenge effectively the government's objections to disclosure of the closed case. However, without access to independent expert evidence, the special advocate could not contest the government's argument that disclosure could cause harm to the public interest. The result was that unless the special advocate could point to an open source for the information in question, governmental assessment about what could be disclosed could not effectively be challenged. A third assumption was that the fact that the special advocate could communicate with the claimant after seeing the closed material, albeit with the court's permission, was significant in achieving procedural justice. This was however, not very effective since the government would often object to such communication and the special advocate would not wish to disclose litigation strategy.[134]

---

[129] *R. (Sarkandi) v Secretary of State for Foriegn and Commonwealth Affairs* [2014] EWHC 2359 (Admin); *CF v Security Service* [2014] 1 W.L.R. 1699 (QB).

[130] Justice and Security Act 2013 s.6(4)(a).

[131] Justice and Security Act 2013 s.6(4)(b)(i).

[132] *CF* [2014] 1 W.L.R. 1699 at [56]-[62].

[133] M. Chamberlain, "Special Advocates and Procedural Fairness in Closed Proceedings" (2009) 28 C.J.Q. 314

[134] Green Paper, *Justice and Security*, paras 2.29–2.30.

Some of these limitations have been appreciated by the courts. The difficulties were captured by Lord Dyson[135]:

> "[I]t is obviously true that party A who is in possession of the closed material will know whether there is material on which it may wish to rely and will therefore be in a position to decide whether to ask the court to order a closed procedure in relation to that material. But it is difficult to see how opposing party B will know whether his case will be assisted by, or even depend to a significant extent on, the closed material held by A without knowing what the material is and what it contains. If a special advocate is appointed, he might be able to assess the importance of some of the documents, but the scope for doing so without being able to take instructions from B is bound to be limited. It follows that, if the power to order a closed material procedure turns on such considerations, it is likely to operate in favour of A and to the disadvantage of B. In my view, this is an approach which is inherently unfair. It is certainly not necessary in the interests of justice."

Parliamentary committees have also noted the limits of what can be achieved by special advocates within the CMP regime. The Joint Committee on Human Rights expressed strong sentiments in this regard[136]:

> "After listening to the evidence of the special advocates, we found it hard not to reach for well-worn descriptions of it as 'Kafkaesque' or like the Star Chamber. The special advocates agreed when it was put to them that, in the light of the concerns they had raised, 'the public should be left in absolutely no doubt that what is happening … has absolutely nothing to do with the traditions of adversarial justice as we have come to understand them in the British legal system.' Indeed, we were left with the very strong feeling that this is a process which is not just offensive to the basic principles of adversarial justice in which lawyers are steeped, but it is very much against the basic notions of fair play as the lay public would understand them."

The government's Green Paper noted some of these difficulties, and the difficulties in resolving them.[137] The Civil Procedure Rules made pursuant to the Justice and Security Act 2013 that relate to special advocates largely track analogous provisions under earlier legislation.[138]

5. CONCLUSION

13–027 Reconciliation of the demands for procedural justice and the need to safeguard national security is an endemic problem for all liberal states. The case law reveals the difficult judgments that have to be made in this respect. There is little doubt that enactment of a general statute legitimating recourse to closed material procedure has a significant impact on pre-existing hearing rights. These concerns are heightened by the fact that the Justice and Security Act 2013 severely constrains proceedings whereby the claimant seeks disclosure of material from a

135 *Al Rawi* [2011] UKSC 34 at [42].

136 Counter-Terrorism Policy and Human Rights: 28 days, intercept and post-charge questioning, *19th Report of Session 2006–07*, HL Paper No.157/HC Paper No.394 (Session 2006–07), para.210; Counter-Terrorism Policy and Human Rights (16th Report), *Annual Renewal of Control Orders Legislation 2010, 9th Report of Session 2009–2010*, HL Paper No.64/HC Paper No.395 (Session 2009–10).

137 Green Paper, *Justice and Security*, paras 2.33–2.34.

138 CPR r. 82.10-11.

person to prove wrongdoing by another.[139] It remains to be seen how the courts interpret the legislation. Lord Neuberger's guidelines in *Bank Mellat* prior to the 2013 Act about use of the CMP nonetheless remain relevant.[140]

[139] Justice and Security Act 2013 s.17.

[140] *Bank Mellat* [2014] A.C. 700 SC at [68]–[74]. They can be summarised as follows. First, where a judge gives both open and closed judgments, it is highly desirable in the open judgment, that the judge identifies every conclusion reached using closed material, and says that this is what has been done. Second, a judge who has relied on closed material in a closed judgment should say in the open judgment as much as possible about the closed material relied upon. Third, on appeal against an open and closed judgment, an appellate court should only be asked to conduct a closed hearing if it was strictly necessary for fairly determining the appeal. Fourth, if the appellate court decided to look at closed material, careful consideration should be given by the advocates, and by the court, to whether it would nonetheless be possible to avoid a closed substantive hearing. Fifth, if the court decided that a CMP was necessary, the parties should try and agree a way of avoiding, or minimising the extent of, a closed hearing. Sixth, if there is a closed hearing, the lawyers representing the party relying on the closed material, as well as that party itself, should ensure in advance of the appeal that the excluded party is provided with as much information as possible about closed documents relied on, and the special advocates are given as full information as possible regarding the nature of the passages relied on in closed documents and the arguments that will be advanced in relation thereto. Lastly, appellate courts should be robust about acceding to applications to go into closed session or even to look at closed material.

CHAPTER 14

NATURAL JUSTICE: BIAS AND INDEPENDENCE

1. CENTRAL ISSUES

i. The second limb of natural justice is that decisions should be made free from bias or impartiality.[1] The issue can arise in two main contexts. First, the decision-maker might have some pecuniary or personal interest in the proceedings. Second, there can be problems where the decision-maker is interested in the result of an inquiry or investigation, not in any personal sense, but because the institution that is represented wishes to attain a certain objective. 14–001

ii. There has been considerable discussion on the appropriate test for establishing bias. The legal test has now become more settled. The chapter will examine the controversies surrounding the nature of the test for bias and consider how the current test has been interpreted by the courts.

iii. The Human Rights Act 1998 added a further dimension to this inquiry. Article 6 of the European Convention on Human Rights (ECHR) establishes a right to a fair trial. The relevance of art.6 for the applicability and content of procedural rights was considered in an earlier chapter.[2] The present discussion will focus on another important aspect of art.6 ECHR. This is the requirement that the hearing should be by "an independent and impartial tribunal established by law".

iv. The application of art.6 can be problematic. This is because it may require significant modification of the pre-existing methods for the making of administrative decisions. The extent to which the previous administrative landscape should be altered in the light of the demands of art.6 will be considered in this chapter.

2. BIAS: PERSONAL INTEREST

A. Pecuniary Interest

The courts have long insisted that any pecuniary interest disqualified the decision-maker be he high or low. Thus, in *Dimes*[3] the House of Lords reversed a decision made by the Lord Chancellor, Lord Cottenham, when the latter had 14–002

[1] D. Galligan, *Due Process and Fair Procedures* (Oxford: Oxford University Press, 1996), pp.437–450.
[2] See Ch.12.
[3] *Dimes v Grand Junction Canal Co Proprietors* (1852) 3 H.L.C. 759, HL.

affirmed decrees by the Vice-Chancellor in relation to a company in which the Lord Chancellor held some shares. There was no imputation of any actual bias against Lord Cottenham, but it was held that the principle that no man can be a judge in his own cause must be sacred.[4] The courts have consistently held that if there was a pecuniary interest it was not necessary to consider reasonable suspicion or real likelihood of bias.[5] It is therefore important to establish what will constitute a pecuniary interest.

Blackburn J held that any pecuniary interest, however small, will be sufficient.[6] Some qualification is, however, required to this statement. If the pecuniary interest is not personal to the decision-maker then the matter will fall to be considered as a challenge on the grounds of favour.[7] Moreover, if the alleged pecuniary interest is extremely remote,[8] or based on contingencies that are unlikely to materialise,[9] then the matter will similarly be treated as a challenge on the grounds of favour. Subject to these qualifications, the prohibition of pecuniary interest seems to be absolute and is not further qualified by any requirement that the interest be substantial.[10]

B. Other Personal Interests

14–003 Other personal interests may disqualify the decision-maker if the courts find that the interest gave rise to a reasonable suspicion or real danger of bias. Much will depend on the factual nexus between the decision-maker and another party involved in the dispute. Family relationship,[11] business connections, and commercial ties[12] are examples of the interests that can disqualify the decision-maker, as is membership of an organisation interested in the dispute.[13] It may, on occasion, be someone other than the actual adjudicator who has been involved. Nevertheless, provided that he has, or may appear to have, an influence on the decision given, then that will be sufficient to render the determination invalid.[14]

---

[4] *Dimes* (1852) 3 H.L.C. 759 at 793–794.

[5] *R. v Rand* (1866) L.R. 1 Q.B. 230; *Leeson v General Council of Medical Education and Registration* [1889] 43 Ch. D. 366.

[6] *R. v Hammond* (1863) 9 L.T. (N.S.) 423; *Rand* (1866) L.R. 1 Q.B. 230 at 232.

[7] In the *Rand* case those challenged were two justices who were trustees for a hospital and friendly society respectively, which bodies had funds invested in a corporation which had applied to the justices.

[8] *R. v McKenzie* [1892] 2 Q.B. 519.

[9] *R. v Burton, Ex p. Young* [1897] 2 Q.B. 468 QBD.

[10] *R. v Gaisford* [1892] 1 Q.B. 381 QBD, the interest of a ratepayer was held to be a pecuniary interest.

[11] *Metropolitan Properties (FGC) Ltd v Lannon* [1969] 1 Q.B. 577, CA (Civ Div).

[12] *R v Barnsley Licensing JJ, Ex p. Barnsley and District Licensed Victuallers Association* [1960] 2 Q.B. 167, CA; *R. v Hendon Rural DC, Ex p. Chorley* [1933] 2 K.B. 696 KBD; *R. v Chesterfield BC, Ex p. Darker Enterprises Ltd* [1992] C.O.D. 466.

[13] *Leeson* [1889] 43 Ch. D. 366; *Allinson v General Council of Medical Education and Registration* [1894] 1 Q.B. 750, CA.

[14] *R. v Sussex Justices, Ex p. McCarthy* [1924] 1 K.B. 256 KBD (clerk to the justices was member of a solicitor's firm acting for one of the parties in a collision out of which the prosecution of the other party arose); *Cooper v Wilson* [1937] 2 K.B. 309, CA (chief constable who had purported to dismiss a policeman sat with the Watch Committee when they heard the policeman's case); *R. v Kent Police*

3. BIAS: INSTITUTIONAL

A. Prosecutor and Judge

A different way in which bias can manifest itself is when the prosecutor of an offence is also the judge. This may happen directly as in *Shaw*,[15] where the sanitary committee of a town council instructed the town clerk to prosecute a person and one of the justices before whom he was prosecuted was a member of that committee. The court held that the decision could not stand.[16] The matter can also arise indirectly where the decision-maker belongs to an organisation that initiated the proceeding, but where he himself has taken no part in the decision to prosecute. In *Leeson*,[17] the General Medical Council had disqualified a doctor for infamous misconduct in a prosecution brought by the Medical Defence Union, an organisation designed to uphold the character of doctors and to suppress unauthorised practitioners. Two of the 29 who held the inquiry were members of the Medical Defence Union, but not of its managing body. The court found that, looked at in substance and fact, the two Medical Defence Union members on the General Council were not accusers as well as judges and that they could not reasonably be suspected of bias.[18] The court may also overturn a decision if it is felt that, for example, a justice has pre-judged the matter before hearing the full case.[19] More recently in *ILEX*[20] it was held that the vice-president of the Institute of Legal Executives was disqualified by her leading role in ILEX, and so her inevitable interest in ILEX's policy of disciplinary regulation, from sitting on a disciplinary or appeal tribunal. 14–004

This can be contrasted to the ruling in *Pinochet Ugarte (No.2)*.[21] The applicant was the former head of state of Chile. He challenged a decision of the House of Lords that he could be extradited in respect of acts committed while he was still head of state. The foundation for the challenge was that one of the Law Lords who had heard the matter, Lord Hoffmann, was the director and chairperson of Amnesty International Charity Ltd (AICL), a body which had been incorporated to carry out the charitable work of Amnesty International (AI). AI had been given leave to intervene in the contested proceedings and had argued that Pinochet should be extradited. The House of Lords made it clear that there was no

Authority, Ex p. Godden [1971] 2 Q.B. 662, CA (Civ Div) (in deciding whether a policeman should be compulsorily retired a report should not be sought from a psychiatrist who had already formed an adverse view of the person); *R. v Barnsley MBC, Ex p. Hook* [1976] 1 W.L.R. 1052, CA (Civ Div) (market manager in the position of a prosecutor should not give evidence to a committee in the absence of the accused).

15 *R. v Lee, Ex p. Shaw* [1882] 9 Q.B.D. 394.

16 See also *R. v Gaisford* [1892] 1 Q.B. 381 QBD; *R. v Pwllheli JJ, Ex p. Soane* [1948] 2 All E.R. 815 DC; *Frome United Breweries Co Ltd v Bath Justices* [1926] A.C. 586, HL; *Roebuck v National Union of Mineworkers (Yorkshire Area) (No.2)* [1978] I.C.R. 676 Ch D.

17 *Leeson* [1889] 43 Ch. D. 366; *S (A Barrister), Re* [1981] Q.B. 683 Visitors to the Inns Court.

18 See also, *Allinson* [1894] 1 Q.B. 750; *Burton* [1897] 2 Q.B. 468. Compare *Law v Chartered Institute of Patent Agents* [1919] 2 Ch. 276 Ch D.

19 *R. v Romsey JJ, Ex p. Gale* [1992] C.O.D. 323 DC.

20 *R. (Kaur) v Institute of Legal Executives Appeal Tribunal* [2011] EWCA Civ 1168.

21 *R. v Bow Street Metropolitan Stipendiary Magistrate, Ex p. Pinochet Ugarte (No.2)* [2000] 1 A.C. 119, HL; T. Jones, "Judicial Bias and Disqualification in the *Pinochet* case" [1999] P.L. 391; Sir D. Williams, "Bias, the Judges and the Separation of Powers" [2000] P.L. 45.

allegation of any actual bias against Lord Hoffmann, but held that the earlier decision could nonetheless not stand. The principle that a judge was automatically disqualified from hearing a matter in his own cause was, said their Lordships, not restricted to cases where the judge had a pecuniary interest in the outcome, but applied also to cases where the judge's decision would lead to the promotion of a cause in which the judge was involved with one of the parties. This did not preclude judges from sitting on cases concerning charities which they were involved with, and they would normally only have to recuse themselves, or disclose the position to the parties, where they had an active role as trustee or director of a charity which was closely allied to, and acting with, a party to the litigation.[22] In the instant case, Lord Hoffmann was a director of a charity closely related to AI, in a case where AI had argued directly for a particular result, and therefore the original decision could not be allowed to stand.

In *ILEX*[23] the Court of Appeal held that it was possible to see the doctrine of automatic disqualification of judges and the doctrine of apparent bias as two strands of a single over-arching requirement that judges should not sit, or should face recusal or disqualification, where there was a real possibility on the objective appearance of things, assessed by the fair-minded and informed observer, that the tribunal could be biased. The two doctrines could be analytically reconciled by regarding the automatic disqualification test as dealing with cases where the personal interest of the judge concerned, if judged sufficient on the basis of appearances to raise the real possibility of preventing him bringing an objective judgment to bear, was deemed to raise a case of apparent bias.

The difficulty discussed in this section is more acute in the context of governmental agencies that have responsibility both for adjudication and prosecution, a combination more normal in the USA than in this country. In response to this problem the 1946 Federal Administrative Procedure Act s.5(c) established an internal separation of function between decider and prosecutor.[24]

B. Institutional Opinion

14–005 Overlapping with, but nevertheless separate from the mixture of function between prosecutor and judge, is the fact that administrators of a particular scheme may well have "strong views" or "preconceived ideas" concerning the issue before them.[25] This may be of a discretionary or regulatory nature and while these elements should not exclude proscriptions against bias they are likely to modify their application. Administrators may have guidelines to help them to interpret a broadly worded statute, the application of which should not in itself constitute bias. Clear pre-judgment of a case is to be disapproved of, but the success of

---

[22] *Leeson* [1889] 43 Ch. D. 366; *Allinson* [1894] 1 Q.B. 750; *Meerabux v Attorney General of Belize* [2005] 2 A.C. 513.

[23] *ILEX* [2011] EWCA Civ 1168.

[24] S. Breyer, R. Stewart, C. Sunstein and M. Spitzer, *Administrative Law and Regulatory Policy, Problems, Text and Cases*, 5th edn (Aspen Publishers, 2002), Ch.7.

[25] G. Flick, *Natural Justice* (Sydney: Butterworths, 1979), pp.122–129.

legislation may well depend on the administrator enforcing the institution's policies with rigour. Indifference to the end in view, even if it were possible, might well be undesirable.[26]

Seen against this background the decision in *Franklin*,[27] although influenced by the judicial conservatism of the time, would probably not be different today.[28] The House of Lords stated that the Minister had a duty to give genuine consideration to a report of an inspector concerning the siting of a new town at Stevenage and to consider objections to that position. It was held that reference to bias was out of place in this context. However, while the result might well be the same, the reasoning of the Court of Appeal is to be preferred: complete impartiality could not be expected and the term impartiality when used in the context of a minister making a decision such as the siting of a new town, would not necessarily be the same as when applied to a magistrate deciding a case of nuisance.

While complete impartiality cannot always be expected in such a case, natural justice may still require that a minister hear representations. In the *Brent LBC* case,[29] the applicant local authorities claimed that they should be entitled to make representations to the minister as to how he should exercise his powers concerning local authority grants. Representations had been made prior to the passage of the legislation, but the court held that the minister was still under a duty to act fairly in the way in which he exercised his discretion under the legislation. He should, therefore, have listened to representations made after the Act received the Royal Assent, but before he actually exercised his discretion. The court accepted that the minister would not be expected to hear such representations as if he were a judge. The minister would not be expected to approach the matter with an empty mind, but his mind should, in the words of the court, at least be ajar.

The problem adverted to above can also manifest itself at local as well as at central level. Thus, it has been held that licensing justices are not precluded from hearing an appeal for a licence, even though some of them had been concerned with an earlier application: the nature of the licensing function required those with local knowledge to form a policy for their area which they could have regard to when hearing individual applications, and the limited number of licensing justices meant that they might, on occasion, hear an appeal when they had been concerned with an earlier application.[30]

---

[26] Committee on Ministers' Powers Report (1932), Cmd.4060, p.78.

[27] *Franklin v Minister of Town and Country Planning* [1948] A.C. 87, HL; *Turner v Allison* [1971] N.Z.L.R. 833. An expression of opinion by the adjudicator will not constitute bias, *R. v London County Council, Re The Empire Theatre* (1894) 71 L.T. 638; *R. v Nailsworth Licensing Justices, Ex p. Bird* [1953] 1 W.L.R. 1046 DC.

[28] *R. (Lewis) v Redcar and Cleveland BC* [2009] 1 W.L.R. 83.

[29] *R. v Secretary of State for the Environment, Ex p. Brent LBC* [1982] Q.B. 593 DC.

[30] *R. v Crown Court at Bristol, Ex p. Cooper* [1990] 2 All E.R. 193 CA (Civ Div); *Darker Enterprises Ltd v Dacorum BC* [1992] C.O.D. 465.

4. BIAS: THE TEST FOR BIAS

A. Past Confusion

14–006 There has been considerable confusion concerning the test for determining bias in cases other than those concerning pecuniary interest. Two tests were espoused by the courts, that of "real likelihood of bias", and that of "reasonable suspicion of bias".[31] In the 19th-century cases the former test held sway: if there was no pecuniary interest the court inquired whether there was a real likelihood of bias.[32] However, in *McCarthy*,[33] Lord Hewart CJ said that a reasonable suspicion of bias was sufficient to quash the determination. The tide appeared to be shifting back to the higher test for in two prominent cases the courts expressly adopted that criteria and disapproved of Lord Hewart CJ's formulation.[34] Certainty was not however to last for in *Lannon* Lord Denning MR "rescued" Lord Hewart's reasonable suspicion test.[35] The root of the confusion for later cases was that Lord Denning MR began by approving the Hewart test and ended by talking of real likelihood. Not surprisingly, later cases found *Lannon* difficult to interpret.[36]

B. From *Gough* to *Porter*

i. The Porter test

14–007 The House of Lords attempted to clarify the law in *Gough*.[37] It held that the same test should be applied in all cases of apparent bias, whether concerned with justices, tribunals, jurors, arbitrators and coroners. In terms of the *degree of bias* the test should be whether there was a real danger of bias on the part of the relevant member of the tribunal, etc. in the sense that he might unfairly regard with favour or disfavour the case of the party under consideration by him. In terms of the *perspective from which bias should be viewed*, it was not necessary, said Lord Goff, to formulate the test in terms of the reasonable man, because the court personified the reasonable man, and because the court had to ascertain the relevant circumstances from the evidence that might not be available to the ordinary observer.

This test was, however, criticised by courts in other common law jurisdictions, because it emphasised the court's view of the facts and gave inadequate attention to the public perception of the incident being challenged.[38] The House of Lords

[31] R. Cranston, "Disqualification of Judges for Interest, Association or Opinion" [1979] P.L. 237; H. Rawlings, "The Test for the Nemo Judex Rule" [1980] P.L. 122.
[32] *Rand* (1866) L.R. 1 Q.B. 230; *R. v Sunderland JJ* [1901] 2 K.B. 357, CA.
[33] *R. v Sussex Justices, Ex p. McCarthy* [1924] 1 K.B. 256 KBD at 259.
[34] *R. v Camborne JJ., Ex p. Pearce* [1955] 1 Q.B. 41 QBD; *Barnsley Licensing* [1960] 2 Q.B. 167, CA.
[35] *Metropolitan Properties (F.G.C.) Ltd v Lannon* [1969] 1 Q.B. 577, CA (Civ Div) at 598–600, 606.
[36] *Hannam v Bradford Corp* [1970] 1 W.L.R. 937, CA (Civ Div); *R. v Altrincham JJ, Ex p. Pennington* [1975] Q.B. 549 DC.
[37] *R. v Gough* [1993] A.C. 646, HL; *R. v HM Coroner for Inner West London, Ex p. Dallaglio and Lockwood Croft* [1994] 4 All E.R. 139, CA (Civ Div).
[38] *Webb v R* (1994) 181 C.L.R. 41.

indicated that it might review the test in *Gough*.[39] The Court of Appeal undertook such a review[40] and its approach, with some modification, was confirmed in *Porter*.[41] This review was precipitated by continuing uncertainty over the correctness of the test, and its compatibility with the criterion used by the Strasbourg Court, which considered whether there was an objective risk of bias in the light of the circumstances identified by the court.[42]

The test adopted in *Porter* was whether, having regard to the relevant circumstances as ascertained by the court, the fair-minded and informed observer, having considered the facts, would conclude that there was a real possibility that the tribunal was biased.[43] Courts have applied this test in subsequent cases.[44] Thus, in *Davidson* it was held that a risk of apparent bias arose where a judge was called upon to rule judicially on the effect of legislation that he had drafted or promoted during the Parliamentary process.[45]

The courts have, on occasion, found that there was no bias according to this test by attributing detailed knowledge of the workings of the judicial system,[46] and the substantive law,[47] to the "fair-minded and informed observer". This renders it more difficult for the claimant to succeed. It was, moreover, held in *Condron*[48] that how the person to whom words were addressed had interpreted them was not determinative. The question was whether the fears expressed by the complainant were objectively justified. There was, said the court, a clear distinction between a legitimate predisposition towards a particular outcome and an illegitimate predetermination of the outcome. The court therefore rejected a claim of bias in relation to a casual statement by a member of the Welsh Assembly, prior to the hearing on the matter, that he was minded to agree with the report of a planning inspector concerning a mining operation to which the claimant objected.

---

39 *Pinochet Ugarte (No.2)* [2000] 1 A.C. 119, HL at 136.

40 *Medicaments and Related Classes of Goods (No.2), Re* [2001] 1 W.L.R. 700, CA (Civ Div).

41 *Porter v Magill* [2002] 2 A.C. 357 HL.

42 *Piersack v Belgium* (1982) 5 E.H.R.R. 169 at 179–180; *Pullar v UK* (1996) 22 E.H.R.R. 391 at 402–403.

43 *Porter* [2002] 2 A.C. 357 at [102]–[103].

44 *Taylor v Lawrence* [2002] 3 W.L.R. 640, CA (Civ Div); *Lawal v Northern Spirit Ltd* [2002] I.C.R. 486 EAT; *Taylor v Williamsons (A Firm)* [2002] EWCA Civ 1380; *Hart v Relentless Records Ltd* [2002] EWHC 1984; *Jones v DAS Legal Expenses Insurance Co Ltd* [2003] EWCA Civ 1071; *Lawal v Northern Spirit Ltd* [2004] 1 All E.R. 187, HL; *R. (Carroll) v Secretary of State for the Home Department* [2005] 1 W.L.R. 688, HL; *Gillies v Secretary of State for Work and Pensions* [2006] 1 W.L.R. 781, HL; *El Farargy v El Farargy* [2007] EWCA Civ 1149; *R. v Abdroikov* [2007] 1 W.L.R. 2679, HL; *R. (Compton) v Wiltshire Primary Care Trust* [2009] EWHC 1824 (Admin); *Virdi v Law Society* [2010] EWCA Civ 100; *De-Winter Heald v Brent LBC* [2010] 1 W.L.R. 990, CA (Civ Div); *Belize Bank Ltd v Attorney General of Belize* [2011] UKPC 36; *O'Neill (Charles Bernard) v HM Advocate* [2013] UKSC 36; *Mitchell v Georges* [2014] UKSC 43 (PC); *Rasool v General Pharmaceutical Council* [2015] EWHC 217 (Admin).

45 *Davidson v Scottish Ministers (No.2)* [2004] H.R.L.R. 34, HL.

46 *Taylor v Williamsons* [2002] EWCA Civ 1380.

47 *Hart* [2002] EWHC 1984.

48 *R. (Condron) v National Assembly for Wales* [2006] EWCA Civ 1573.

ii. *The bodies subject to the Porter test*

14–008 The test as formulated in *Gough* applied to the bodies specified in that judgment: justices, tribunals, jurors, arbitrators and coroners. The test as re-formulated in *Porter* was framed in terms of tribunals. It is clear, however, that the House of Lords in *Porter* regarded itself as modifying the test as laid down in *Gough*, and therefore the *Porter* test covers at least the same range of bodies as in *Gough*.

This still leaves open the issue as to whether a different test might apply when bias is alleged against a body other than one in the above list. This issue has been considered in a number of cases involving allegations of bias against bodies such as local authorities, and other administrative bodies that might have an interest in the policy outcome.[49] The precise test used in such cases has not always been clear, and this is in part because the relationship between predetermination and apparent bias has not been fully clarified.

The judgment of Beatson J in *Persimmon Homes* is helpful in this respect.[50] He correctly noted that they were distinct concepts. Predetermination was the surrender by a decision-maker of its judgment by having a closed mind and failing to apply it to the task. By way of contrast in a case of apparent bias, the decision-maker may in fact have applied its mind quite properly to the matter, but a reasonable observer would consider that there was a real danger of bias on its part. Thus bias "is concerned with appearances whereas predetermination is concerned with what has in fact happened".[51]

Predetermination and apparent bias can nonetheless become intertwined in judgments and the reason is not hard to divine: it can be difficult to decide as a matter of fact whether there has been predetermination by, for example, a local authority and thus claimants may allege that there has been apparent bias. It is, however, difficult to establish predetermination or apparent bias in relation to bodies such as elected councillors, who are entitled to take into account policy considerations when making their decisions. Thus in *Lewis*[52] the Court of Appeal held that councillors determining a planning application were not in a judicial or quasi-judicial position, but were democratically accountable decision-makers, who had been elected to pursue policies, and were therefore entitled to be predisposed to determine the application in accordance with their political views and policies, provided that they had regard to all material considerations and gave fair consideration to relevant points raised with them. Thus, where predetermination was alleged, the test was whether the committee members had made their

---

49 *R. v St Edmundsbury Borough Council, Ex p. Investors in Industry Commercial Properties Ltd* [1985] 1 W.L.R. 1168 DC; *R. v Sevenoaks DC, Ex p. Terry* [1985] 3 All E.R. 226 QBD; *Darker Enterprises Ltd v Dacorum BC* [1992] C.O.D. 465; *R. v Chesterfield BC, Ex p. Darker Enterprises* [1992] C.O.D. 466; *R. v Secretary of State for the Environment and William Morrison Supermarkets Plc, Ex p. Kirkstall Valley Campaign Ltd* [1996] 3 All E.R. 304 QBD; *R. (Georgiou) v Enfield LBC* [2004] EWHC 779 (Admin); *Condron* [2006] EWCA Civ 1573; *R. (Ware) v Neath Port Talbot CBC* [2007] EWHC 913 (Admin); *Lewis* [2009] 1 W.L.R. 83; *R (Siraj) v Kirklees MC* [2010] EWHC 444 (Admin).

50 *R. (Persimmon Homes Ltd) v Vale of Glamorgan Council* [2010] EWHC 535 (Admin).

51 *Vale of Glamorgan Council* [2010] EWHC 535 (Admin) at [116].

52 *Lewis* [2009] 1 W.L.R. 83; *R. (Berky) v Newport City Council* [2012] EWCA Civ 378 at [25]–[30]; *R. (Nestwood Homes Developments Ltd) v South Holland DC* [2014] EWHC 863 (Admin).

decision with closed minds, or the circumstances gave rise to such a real risk of closed minds that the decision ought not in the public interest to be upheld.

5. BIAS: EXCEPTIONS

A. Necessity

The normal rules against bias will be displaced where the individual whose impartiality is called in question is the only person empowered to act. Thus, in the *Dimes*[53] case it was held that the Lord Chancellor's signature on an enrolment order which was necessary in order for the case to proceed to the House of Lords, was unaffected by his shareholding in the company because no other person was empowered to sign. Similarly, in *Phillips*[54] it was held that the Governor of a colony could validly assent to an Act of Indemnity which protected his own actions because the relevant Act had to receive this signature. **14–009**

B. Statute

Parliament has made statutory exceptions to the rule against bias, allowing justices to sit who have some interest in the subject-matter of the action.[55] The courts have construed such statutory provisions strictly.[56] Thus, in *Shaw*[57] s.258 of the Public Health Act 1872, which enabled a justice of the peace to sit even though a member of a local authority, was held not to protect him where he acted in a prosecutorial and adjudicatory capacity. In other areas statute may, for example, create an offence to take part in a decision on a matter in relation to which a person has a pecuniary interest, and yet will allow acts thus made to remain valid.[58] **14–010**

C. Waiver

It is permissible for an individual to waive the interests of an adjudicator,[59] and the courts were quick to infer such a waiver.[60] Later courts have been more reluctant to so infer, particularly where the applicant did not know of the right to object at that stage. In order for a waiver to be valid the party waiving the right **14–011**

---

[53] *Dimes* (1852) 3 H.L.C. 759 at 787.

[54] *Phillips v Eyre* (1870) L.R. 6 Q.B. 1. See also *Re Manchester (Ringway Airport) Compulsory Purchase Order* (1935) 153 L.T. 219; *Jeffs v New Zealand Dairy Production and Marketing Board* [1967] 1 A.C. 551.

[55] Justices Jurisdiction Act 1742.

[56] *Frome United Breweries Co Ltd v Bath Justices* [1926] A.C. 586, HL.

[57] *Shaw* [1882] 9 Q.B.D. 394. Compare *Soane* [1948] 2 All E.R. 815.

[58] Local Government Act 1972 ss.82, 94 and 97. Similar provisions in licensing legislation have been strictly construed, *Barnsley Licensing Justices* [1960] 2 Q.B. 167. It is unclear whether actual bias would have to be shown in order to circumvent the statutory provisions, see Rawlings, "The Test for the Nemo Judex Rule" [1980] P.L. 122, 125–126.

[59] *Nailsworth Licensing Justices* [1953] 1 W.L.R. 1046.

[60] *R. v Williams, Ex p. Phillips* [1914] 1 K.B. 608 KBD.

had to be aware of all the material facts and the consequences of the choice open to him and should be given a fair opportunity to reach an unpressured decision.[61] This restriction on waiver is to be welcomed. Such a surrender of rights should not be inferred lightly. It is in fact open to question whether it should be allowed at all, at least in certain types of cases. The premise behind the ability to waive is that it is only the individual who is concerned, and thus if that person "chooses" to ignore the fact that the adjudicator is an interested party then so much the worse for the applicant. However, there may well be a wider interest at issue, in that it may be contrary to the public interest for decisions to be made where there may be a likelihood of favour to another influencing the determination.

6. THE HRA AND THE ECHR

A. Article 6(1): The ECHR Legal Requirements

14–012 The Human Rights Act 1998 brought many Convention rights into domestic law. This includes art.6 ECHR, which provides the guarantees of a fair trial. An earlier chapter considered the impact of art.6 on the applicability and content of process rights.[62] The present discussion is concerned with the requirement that there should be an "independent and impartial tribunal established by law". Article 6(1) provides that:

> "In the determination of his civil rights and obligations or of any criminal charge against him, everyone is entitled to a fair and public hearing within a reasonable time by an independent and impartial tribunal established by law. Judgment shall be pronounced publicly but the press and the public may be excluded from all or part of the trial in the interests of morals, public order or national security in a democratic society, where the interests of juveniles or the protection of the private life of the parties so require, or the extent strictly necessary in the opinion of the court in special circumstances where the publicity would prejudice the interests of justice."

It is clear from the Strasbourg jurisprudence that in deciding whether a body is independent, regard will be given to the manner of its appointment, its term of office, the existence of guarantees against outside pressure, and whether the body presents an appearance of independence.[63] A decision of a court or tribunal will not satisfy this requirement if, for example, some other authority is able to decide whether or not the judgment of the court or tribunal should be implemented,[64] nor where the court or tribunal is biased. The requirement of "independence" also means that the decision-maker should be independent from the parties and the

---

[61] *R. v Essex Justices, Ex p. Perkins* [1917] 2 K.B. 475; *Pinochet Ugarte (No.2)* [2000] 1 A.C. 119; *Smith v Kvaerner Cementation Foundations Ltd (General Council of the Bar intervening)* [2007] 1 W.L.R. 370, CA (Civ Div).

[62] See Ch.12.

[63] *Bryan v UK* (1996) 21 E.H.R.R. 342; *Kingsley v UK* (2001) 33 E.H.R.R. 288; (2002) 35 E.H.R.R. 177; *Stefan v UK* (1998) 25 E.H.R.R. CD 130.

[64] *Van de Hark v The Netherlands* (1994) 18 E.H.R.R. 481.

Executive.[65] This has important consequences for decisions made by, for example, local authorities and government departments, since these will normally not satisfy this requirement.[66]

It is also clear from the Strasbourg jurisprudence that this requirement of independence does not have to be satisfied at every stage of the decision-making process. Where an administrative body does not comply with the duty imposed by art.6 it must be subject to the control of a judicial body that does so comply.[67] It has been recognised by both the Commission and the European Court of Human Rights (ECtHR) that many initial decisions are made by local authorities or government departments. The compatibility of such decision-making with art.6 then depends on whether there are adequate appeal rights, or judicial review, to a judicial body that has "full jurisdiction" and provides the guarantees of art.6(1). The article does not require that the appellate or review body has the power to substitute judgment on issues of expediency or the merits.[68] The ECtHR will, when assessing the sufficiency of review or appeal, consider the subject-matter in issue within its entire statutory context. In *Crompton* the ECtHR held that in order to determine whether a tribunal had "full jurisdiction", or provided "sufficiency of review" to remedy a lack of independence at first instance, it was necessary to have regard to factors such as the subject matter of the decision appealed against, the manner in which that decision was arrived at and the content of the dispute, including the desired and actual grounds of appeal.[69]

Thus, in *Bryan* in the context of an appeal from an inspector's decision in the planning sphere,[70] the ECtHR found that a planning inspector was not independent for the purposes of art.6, because of the minister's power over his determinations. It held that the sufficiency of review would be judged taking account of factors such as the subject-matter of the decision, the manner in which that decision was arrived at, and the content of the dispute. The Strasbourg Court stressed in *Bryan* the "safeguards" attendant on the procedure before the inspector. These were the quasi-judicial nature of the decision-making process, the duty to exercise independent judgment, the fact that the inspector made decisions in accord with principles of openness, fairness and impartiality and the requirement that the inspector must not be subject to any improper influence.[71] It was sufficient that the High Court had power to overturn findings of fact if they were irrational. This was the limit of what could be expected given the specialised nature of the subject-matter, and the nature of the preceding inquiry. **14–013**

The preceding decision can be contrasted with *Tsfayo*.[72] The applicant for housing and council tax benefit failed to submit her benefit renewal form in time. Her claim was rejected by the council because she had failed to show "good

[65] *Ringeisen v Austria* (1979–80) 1 E.H.R.R 455.

[66] *Tre Traktorer AB v Sweden* (1991) 13 E.H.R.R. 309; *Benthem v Netherlands* (1986) 8 E.H.R.R. 1; *Bryan* (1996) 21 E.H.R.R. 342.

[67] *Albert and Le Compte v Belgium* (1983) 5 E.H.R.R. 533.

[68] *Kaplan v UK* (1994) 76A D.R. 90; *ISKON v UK* (1994) 76A D.R. 90. See, however, *W v UK* (1987) 10 E.H.R.R. 29.

[69] *Crompton v UK* (2010) 50 E.H.R.R. 36 at [71].

[70] *Bryan* (1996) 21 E.H.R.R. 342.

[71] *Bryan* (1996) 21 E.H.R.R. 342 at [46].

[72] *Tsfayo v UK* [2007] L.G.R. 1; J. Howell QC, "*Alconbury* Crumbles" [2007] J.R. 9.

cause" as to why she had not claimed benefits earlier. Her appeal to the Housing Benefit Review Board was dismissed. She sought judicial review on the grounds that the HBRB was not an independent and impartial tribunal. The ECtHR concluded that there had been a violation of art.6(1), notwithstanding the availability of judicial review.[73] It held that the decision-making process was significantly different from that in earlier cases such as *Kingsley*, *Bryan* and *Runa Begum*. In those cases, the issues to be determined required a measure of professional knowledge or experience and the exercise of administrative discretion pursuant to wider policy aims. In *Tsfayo*, by way of contrast, the HBRB was deciding a simple question of fact, whether there was "good cause" for the applicant's delay in making a claim. This was moreover not merely incidental to the reaching of broader judgments of policy or expediency, which it was for the democratically accountable authority to take. Moreover, the HBRB was not merely lacking in independence from the Executive, but was directly connected to one party to the dispute, since it included five councillors from the local authority, which would be required to pay the benefit if it was awarded. The ECtHR concluded that the HBRB's procedures were not adequate to overcome this fundamental lack of objective impartiality.

B. Article 6(1) in Domestic Courts: Fairness and Waiver

14–014 The centrality of the requirement that the tribunal should be independent and impartial was vividly emphasised in *Millar*.[74] The defendants were convicted by temporary sheriffs in Scotland. In another case it was held that temporary sheriffs were not independent and impartial for the purposes of art.6(1). The convicted parties contended, in reliance on that case, that their prosecutions had been unlawful, since the Lord Advocate had no power to do an act incompatible with a Convention right. It was argued by way of defence that the accused had in fact received fair trials, since the critical issue under art.6(1) was the fairness of the proceedings as a whole.

The Privy Council held that the right of the accused in criminal proceedings to be tried by an independent and impartial tribunal could not be compromised, unless validly waived by the accused. The appearance of independence and impartiality was just as important as whether those qualities existed in fact. A claim that art.6(1) had been breached could not, therefore, be met by asking whether the proceedings overall had been fair. An accused could moreover only be held to have waived art.6(1) by a voluntary, informed and unequivocal election by a party not to claim a right, or raise an objection.

[73] *Tsfayo* [2007] L.G.R. 1 at [46]–[47].

[74] *Millar v Dickson (Procurator Fiscal, Elgin)* [2002] 1 W.L.R. 1615.

C. Article 6(1) in Domestic Courts: Planning and the Distinction between Policy and Fact-Finding

The impact of art.6(1) on the freedom of the legislature to choose who should make decisions in the planning sphere was a central issue in *Alconbury*.[75] It was alleged that the role of the Secretary of State for the Environment, Transport and the Regions (SSETR) in making decisions relating to different pieces of legislation was inconsistent with art.6(1) ECHR. One case[76] involved decisions by the minister to call in applications for planning permission.[77] The local council normally decides planning applications, but the minister has the power to call in such applications and to make the decision himself. Another case[78] involved what is known as a recovered appeal against a refusal of planning permission.[79] The SSETR decided that he should hear and determine the appeal against the refusal of planning permission, instead of the inspector. The third case[80] was concerned with proposed highway orders, and related compulsory purchase orders, in connection with a scheme to improve the A34/M4 junction. 14–015

The minister accepted that he was not an independent tribunal for the purposes of art.6. He argued, however, that the decision-making process as a whole, including judicial review, complied with art.6. He relied on the *Bryan* case,[81] where the Strasbourg Court held that an inspector did not constitute an independent tribunal because the minister could revoke the inspector's power. It found nonetheless that the courts' powers of appeal and review were sufficient to ensure that the decision-making process as a whole complied with art.6. The minister argued in the alternative that if the whole process did not comply with art.6 then the court should expand its powers of judicial review pursuant to ss.3 and 6 HRA, so as to make it do so.

The Divisional Court found for the claimants.[82] The House of Lords overturned this decision.[83] Their Lordships accepted that the minister was not an impartial tribunal as required by the Convention. They held, however, that the decision-making process taken as a whole was compatible with the Convention, since there was sufficient review of legality through judicial review. Two issues were central to the case: the role of the minister, and the sufficiency of control by way of review.

---

[75] *R. (Alconbury Developments Ltd) v Secretary of State for the Environment, Transport and the Regions HL; R. (Holding & Barnes Plc) v Secretary of State for the Environment, Transport and the Regions HL; Secretary of State for the Environment, Transport and the Regions v Legal and General Assurance Society Ltd* [2003] 2 A.C. 295, HL.

[76] *Holding and Barnes Plc* [2003] 2 A.C. 295

[77] Town and Country Planning Act 1990 s.77.

[78] *Alconbury Developments Ltd* [2003] 2 A.C. 295.

[79] Town and Country Planning Act 1990 ss.78 and 79.

[80] *Legal and General* [2003] 2 A.C. 295.

[81] *Bryan* (1996) 21 E.H.R.R. 342.

[82] *R. (Holding and Barnes Plc) v Secretary of State for the Environment, Transport and the Regions* (2001) 3 L.G.L.R. 21 DC.

[83] *Alconbury* [2003] 2 A.C. 295.

i. *The role and position of the minister*

14–016 There was a marked difference of view between the Divisional Court and the House of Lords on the role of the minister. Both courts regarded the legality of the ministerial power to make policy, and adjudicate thereon, as the nub of the issue.

The premise of the Divisional Court's judgment was that this duality of function was wrong. It felt that the minister made important policy decisions in these areas, and also adjudicated on individual matters, without there being sufficient safeguards to prevent him acting in his own self-interest when making such decisions.[84]

The premise of the House of Lords' judgment was precisely the opposite. Their Lordships felt that the ministerial role was quite proper. Lord Slynn refused to accept that a policy maker could not be a decision-maker, or that the final decision could not be that of a democratically elected person or body.[85] Lord Nolan held that a degree of central control was essential to orderly planning. Parliament had entrusted this task to the minister, who was accountable to it. To substitute for the minister an "independent and impartial body with no electoral accountability would not only be a recipe for chaos: it would be profoundly undemocratic".[86] Lord Clyde stated that once

> "... it is recognised that there should be a national planning policy under a central supervision, it is consistent with democratic principle that the responsibility for that work should lie on the shoulders of a minister answerable to Parliament".[87]

Lord Hutton noted that the minister would be answerable to Parliament for the exercise of his power.[88] Lord Hoffmann was most forceful in this respect. He accepted, with the Divisional Court, that the minister was not an independent and impartial tribunal. Lord Hoffmann, however, strongly disagreed with the lower court that it was objectionable in terms of art.6 that the minister should be judge in his own cause where his policy was in play. For Lord Hoffmann, the question was not whether he should be a judge in his own cause, but whether he should be regarded as a judge at all.[89] Lord Hoffmann did not think of the minister in this way: the minister's constitutional role was to formulate and apply government policy.[90]

ii. *The sufficiency of the controls via judicial review*

14–017 The differing views on the propriety of the minister's role had a marked effect on the second issue, which was the sufficiency of the controls provided by judicial review. We have seen that the Strasbourg jurisprudence stipulated that the

84 *Alconbury* [2003] 2 A.C. 295 at [56].
85 *Alconbury* [2003] 2 A.C. 295 at [48].
86 *Alconbury* [2003] 2 A.C. 295 at [60].
87 *Alconbury* [2003] 2 A.C. 295 at [141]. See also, [142]–[144], [159].
88 *Alconbury* [2003] 2 A.C. 295 at [176].
89 *Alconbury* [2003] 2 A.C. 295 at [124].
90 *Alconbury* [2003] 2 A.C. 295 at [127].

requirements of art.6 could be met either if the initial decision-maker was independent and impartial, or if there was control by a judicial body with full jurisdiction, which provided the guarantees of art.6.[91] In *Alconbury* the Divisional Court found that the "safeguards" mentioned in *Bryan* were insufficient where the minister, rather than the inspector, made the decision. This was because he was free to make his own decision after taking account of internal legal and policy elucidation.[92]

The House of Lords reached the opposite conclusion. Lord Slynn emphasised the detailed procedural rules applicable when the minister made a decision on a called in planning application, or recovered appeal. These rules were pertinent when the minister differed from the inspector on a matter of fact, or took into account new evidence, and was disposed to disagree with the inspector. He was required to notify persons entitled to appear at the inquiry, to give reasons for his differences with the inspector and to allow written representations.[93] It was this, combined with judicial review, which Lord Slynn felt to be determinative in concluding that the procedure as a whole was compatible with art.6.[94]

Lord Clyde examined the factors mentioned in *Bryan* relevant to the sufficiency of control by way of review. He considered the subject matter of the dispute, the manner in which the decisions were taken, and the content of the dispute. His conclusion was that, judged by these criteria, judicial review was sufficient to ensure that the decision-making process as a whole complied with art.6.[95] Lord Hutton was of the opinion that the principles in *Bryan* could be applied to the instant case, notwithstanding that the minister rather than the inspector made the decision.[96]

Lord Hoffmann held that the lower court had misunderstood the relevance of the "safeguards" mentioned in *Bryan*, by finding that they were necessary before appeal or review could satisfy art.6 whatever the issues actually were.[97] This was, he said, the opposite of what had been intended in *Bryan* itself. Where the question was one of policy or expediency these "safeguards" were irrelevant. The reason why judicial review was sufficient in such cases had nothing to do with the "safeguards", but depended on respect for the ministerial decision on matters of expediency. The fact that the parties were not privy to departmental processes of decision-making was "no more than one would expect",[98] given that the constitutional role of the minister in formulating and applying government policy required the advice and assistance of civil servants. It was only where findings of fact, and evaluation of fact, were in issue that the safeguards were essential for the acceptance of limited review of fact by the appellate tribunal.[99] In this respect

---

91 *Albert* (1983) 5 E.H.R.R. 533; *R (Kehoe) v Secretary of State for Work and Pensions* [2004] Q.B. 1378, CA (Civ Div).
92 *Alconbury* [2003] 2 A.C. 295 at [94]–[95].
93 Town and Country Planning (Inquiries Procedure) (England) Rules 2000 r.17(5).
94 *Alconbury* [2003] 2 A.C. 295 at [16]–[19] and [49]–[56].
95 *Alconbury* [2003] 2 A.C. 295 at [155]–[160].
96 *Alconbury* [2003] 2 A.C. 295 at [188]–[189].
97 *Alconbury* [2003] 2 A.C. 295 at [116].
98 *Alconbury* [2003] 2 A.C. 295 at [127].
99 *Alconbury* [2003] 2 A.C. 295 at [117].

the procedural rules on planning, combined with controls on fact-finding through judicial review, were sufficient to satisfy art.6.[100]

iii. *Policy and fact finding after Alconbury*

14–018 The application of art.6 in the context of planning continued to be problematic. The discussion in cases after *Alconbury* focused on whether the requirements of art.6 are satisfied where the initial decision is not made by a planning inspector, as was the case in *Alconbury* itself, but by a local planning authority. This issue arose in *Kathro*,[101] where the applicants argued that the grant of planning permission by the local authority did not comply with art.6, notwithstanding that the authority's decisions were subject to judicial review. It was accepted that a planning authority was not independent for the purposes of art.6. The issue before the court was whether the procedure taken as a whole, including judicial review, was nonetheless compliant with art.6. Richards J concluded that the finding in *Alconbury* that the decision-making process was compatible with art.6 was based to a significant extent on the fact-finding role of the inspector, with its attendant procedural safeguards. There was, said Richards J, no equivalent to these safeguards in the decision-making process of the local planning authority. There was a right to make representations, and submit evidence, and persons could be heard orally by the relevant committee. There was, however, "nothing like a public inquiry, no opportunity for cross-examination and no formal procedure for evaluating the evidence and making findings of fact".[102] This considerably reduced the scope for effective scrutiny of the planning decision by way of judicial review.

The issue came before the court again in *Friends Provident*,[103] in the context of a challenge to the grant of planning permission by the local council for a large retail complex in Norwich. It was accepted that the local council was not independent for the purposes of art.6. It was argued that the only way for the procedure to be compatible with art.6 was for the secretary of state to call in the planning application, and establish a public inquiry presided over by an inspector. Forbes J disagreed. He recognised that a decision made by a local authority, combined with judicial review, might not comply with art.6 where there were contested issues of primary fact.[104] He felt however that the principal issue in the present case was the retail impact assessment that was made as part of the planning decision. This did not, said Forbes J,

[100] *Alconbury* [2003] 2 A.C. 295 at [128]; *R. (Aggregate Industries UK Ltd) v English Nature* [2002] A.C.D. 67 QBD at [12].

[101] *R. (Kathro, Evans, Evans, Grant, Llantwit Fadre Community Council) v Rhondda Cynon Taff County BC* [2002] Env. L.R. 15 QBD.

[102] *Kathro* [2002] Env. L.R. 15 at [28].

[103] *Friends Provident Life & Pensions Ltd v Secretary of State for Transport, Local Government and Regions* [2002] 1 W.L.R. 1450 QBD.

[104] *Friends Provident* [2002] 1 W.L.R. 1450 at [93].

> "… give rise to the type of investigation of fact which requires the safeguards attaching to a public inquiry before an independent inspector in order to be in compliance with art.6, since that assessment was principally a matter of 'local planning judgment, policy and expediency'."[105]

D. Article 6(1) in Domestic Courts: Housing and the Re-evaluation of the Policy/Fact-Finding Distinction

The impact of art.6 has not been confined to the planning sphere. The courts have had to grapple with it in other areas, such as housing. The courts' general approach was to apply the distinction between policy and fact-finding, developed in the planning cases, to this area.[106] **14–019**

This approach must be reappraised in the light of the House of Lords' decision in *Begum*.[107] The claimant was offered housing as a homeless person, but refused it on the ground that the area in which it was situated suffered from drugs and racism. Her decision to decline the offer was reviewed by an officer of the local authority, who found that the offer was suitable. She appealed to the county court, which found that the failure of the local authority to refer the matter to an independent tribunal constituted a breach of art.6. The House of Lords held to the contrary. It assumed for the purposes of the case that art.6 was engaged because the claimant had a civil right.

Lord Hoffmann gave the leading judgment. He agreed that the reviewing officer did not constitute an independent and impartial tribunal for the purposes of art.6, since she was an employee of the local authority, and hence could not be independent when deciding whether it had discharged its duty to the applicant. The live issue was, therefore, whether this was cured by the right of appeal to the county court, so as to satisfy art.6. The county court's jurisdiction was in substance the same as that of the High Court in judicial review. It was, however, acknowledged that the county court could not make fresh findings of fact. The applicant argued that this meant that it could not satisfy art.6: when a case turned on contested facts it was necessary either that the appellate body should have full jurisdiction to review the facts, or that the primary decision-making process should have sufficient safeguards to make it virtually judicial.[108] Reliance was placed[109] on a dictum of Lord Hoffmann in *Alconbury*,[110] that the safeguards mentioned in *Bryan* would be required in relation to the evaluation of facts. Lord Hoffmann in *Begum* stated that this was an incautious remark,[111] and adopted a rather different approach to the policy/fact distinction than he had articulated in *Alconbury*.

Lord Hoffmann held that the rule of law required that decisions made about private rights, and breaches of the criminal law, must be entrusted to the judicial **14–020**

[105] *Friends Provident* [2002] 1 W.L.R. 1450 at [94].

[106] *Runa Begum v Tower Hamlets LBC* [2002] 2 All E.R. 668, CA (Civ Div); *R. (Personal Representatives of Beeson) v Dorset CC* [2002] EWCA Civ 448.

[107] *Runa Begum v Tower Hamlets LBC* [2003] 2 A.C. 430, HL.

[108] *Begum* [2003] 2 A.C. 430 at [37].

[109] *Begum* [2003] 2 A.C. 430 at [39].

[110] *Alconbury* [2003] 2 A.C. 295 at [117].

[111] *Begum* [2003] 2 A.C. 430 at [40].

branch of government. This basic principle did not yield to utilitarian considerations that it would be cheaper to have such matters decided by administrators. The possibility of an appeal could not compensate for the lack of independence and impartiality on the part of the primary decision-maker.[112] Matters were, however, different in relation to social welfare or regulatory functions, such as licensing or the grant of planning permission. In these areas regard could be had to considerations, such as efficient administration, democratic accountability and the sovereignty of Parliament. It was, in particular, legitimate for Parliament not to over-judicialise dispute procedures. It would therefore not be appropriate to require that findings of fact should be made by a body other than the primary decision-maker, and there did not need to be a mechanism for independent findings of fact or full appeal.[113]

This left open the issue as to precisely how the shortcomings of the reviewing officer, who did not satisfy art.6, were cured by having regard to the entire procedure, including the role of the county court. Lord Hoffmann's response was that even though there did not need to be a mechanism for independent findings of fact, or full appeal, the overall procedure had to be lawful and fair.[114] This was to be determined in part by the procedure attendant on the initial decision. Thus, even though the reviewing officer might not be independent for the purposes of art.6, the rules regulating the way in which such reviews were conducted would be relevant for the purpose of deciding whether the overall process was lawful and fair. The other safeguard to be taken into account was the supervisory power of the county court judge, which was, as stated above, akin to judicial review. Lord Hoffmann acknowledged that it was open to such a court to adopt a more intensive scrutiny of the rationality of the reviewing officer's decision, by considering whether it had been made on a misunderstanding or ignorance of an established and relevant fact, or where rights were at stake by using proportionality.[115] Lord Hoffmann nonetheless declined to say that this was necessary. He held that where no human rights other than art.6 were engaged then conventional judicial review would suffice.[116]

Space precludes a detailed examination of the implications, positive and normative, of the above jurisprudence.[117] Suffice it to say for the present that while the desire not to over-judicialise the administrative process may be laudable, the approach adopted in *Begum* may nonetheless be problematic. It requires, in terms of positive law, the drawing of difficult lines between cases involving private rights and social/regulatory schemes. This may be especially difficult in circumstances where some aspects of a single area, such as enforcement of planning notices, are held to be akin to cases of private rights, while others, such as planning permissions, are not.[118] It raises, moreover, important normative issues as to the type of procedural protection that should apply in cases involving private rights, and social/regulatory policy.

---

[112] *Begum* [2003] 2 A.C. 430 at [42].
[113] *Begum* [2003] 2 A.C. 430 at [43]–[47].
[114] *Begum* [2003] 2 A.C. 430 at [47].
[115] *Begum* [2003] 2 A.C. 430 at [49].
[116] *Begum* [2003] 2 A.C. 430 at [50].
[117] P. Craig, "The HRA, art.6 and Procedural Rights" [2003] P.L. 753.
[118] *Begum* [2003] 2 A.C. 430 at [41]–[42].

E. Article 6(1) in Domestic Courts: Developments since Begum

UK courts have continued to grapple with the requirements of art.6 in subsequent cases. The issue in *Wright*[119] concerned the Care Standards Act 2000, which introduced a listing system for the protection of vulnerable adults. Care workers who were included on the lists were prevented from working as carers of vulnerable adults. Under s.82(4) if the secretary of state felt that it might be appropriate for the worker to be included on the list from information submitted with the reference, he had to include the worker provisionally on the list pending a determination of the reference. The secretary of state took several months between receiving a reference and making the decision required in s.82(4). An aggrieved worker could try to convince the secretary of state that the listing was unjustified. The issue was whether the provisional listing procedure was compatible with art.6 ECHR. **14–021**

The House of Lords held that it was not. Baroness Hale, giving judgment, acknowledged that under art.6 decisions that were determinative of civil rights and obligations could be made by administrative authorities, provided that there was access to an independent and impartial tribunal which exercised "full jurisdiction".[120] What amounted to "full jurisdiction" varied according to the decision that was made. It did not, said Baroness Hale, always require access to a court or tribunal even for the determination of disputed issues of fact, and much depended on the subject matter of the decision and the quality of the initial decision-making process. If there was a classic exercise of administrative discretion, even though determinative of civil rights and obligations, and there were safeguards to ensure that the procedure was fair and impartial, then judicial review might be adequate to supply the necessary access to a court, even if there was no jurisdiction to examine the factual merits of the case. In the instant case, art.6 was engaged and had been breached because the process did not begin fairly, by offering the care worker an opportunity to answer the allegations made against her, before a decision that could lead to irreparable damage to her employment or prospects of employment.

In *Ali*[121] the House of Lords decided the issue left open in *Begum* and held that the legislation concerning housing for homeless persons did not give rise to civil rights for the purposes of art.6. Cases where the award of services or benefits in kind was not an individual right of which the applicant could consider himself the holder, but was dependent on a series of evaluative judgments by the provider as to whether the statutory criteria were satisfied and how the need ought to be met, did not engage art.6(1). The House of Lords, however, also considered whether the procedures in the instant case satisfied the requirements of art.6, and held that they did comply. The claimant had argued that a letter from the local authority had not been received and that the procedures to resolve this issue did not comply with art.6. The claimant sought, not surprisingly, to rely on *Tsfayo*.[122] Lord Hope, however, distinguished that case. He held that an answer to the question whether

---

[119] *R. (Wright) v Secretary of State for Health* [2009] 1 A.C. 739, HL.

[120] *Wright* [2009] 1 A.C. 739 at [23].

[121] *Ali v Birmingham City Council* [2010] 2 A.C. 39 SC.

[122] *Tsfayo* [2007] L.G.R. 1.

or not the local housing authority's letters were received was incidental to a more searching and judgmental inquiry into the accommodation's suitability. It was a staging post on the way to the much broader judgment that had to be made. These cases were therefore different from *Tsfayo*, where no broad questions requiring professional knowledge or experience had to be addressed once the question whether there was good cause had been answered. Given that this was so, Lord Hope was content to apply *Begum* and conclude that the absence of a full fact-finding jurisdiction in the court to which an appeal lay under the legislation did not prevent it from complying with art.6.[123]

7. A COMMON LAW REQUIREMENT OF "AN INDEPENDENT AND IMPARTIAL TRIBUNAL"

14–022 The discussion thus far has focused on the traditional concept of bias developed at common law, and the requirement for an independent and impartial tribunal that flows from art.6 of the ECHR. There is, however, authority for the proposition that the latter is also a requirement of the common law. The Court of Appeal held this to be so in the *Medicaments* case,[124] although the claim in that case related to bias rather than structural independence.

The issue of independence came more squarely before the court in *Bewry*.[125] The case was concerned with housing benefit, and whether the Housing Benefit Review Board, which included members of the council that had rejected the initial application, was independent. Moses J considered the existence of a common law right to an independent and impartial tribunal because the facts occurred before the HRA came into force. He held that the

> "... right of review of a determination of statutory entitlement is akin to the right of access to a court and carries with it a right to an independent and impartial review".[126]

The common law therefore provided no lesser protection than the ECHR.[127] This reasoning fits with the general stance of the courts prior to the HRA, where they made it clear that the common law protected the rights contained in the ECHR.[128]

It might be thought that the common law recognition of this right was no longer of importance, now that the HRA has come into force. This conclusion would be premature. The protection afforded by art.6 only applies where there is a civil right. Moses J's formulation of the common law requirement of an independent and impartial tribunal is that it applies in cases of statutory entitlement. There is, however, no reason in principle why the common law

---

[123] See also, *Walsall MBC v Secretary of State for Communities and Local Government* [2013] EWCA Civ 370; *R. (King) v Secretary of State for Justice* [2012] EWCA Civ 376.

[124] *Medicaments* [2001] 1 W.L.R. 700 at [35].

[125] *R. (Bewry) v Norwich City Council* [2002] H.R.L.R. 2 QBD.

[126] *Bewry* [2002] H.R.L.R. 2 at [29], relying on *Medicaments* [2001] 1 W.L.R. 700 at [35], and *R. v Secretary of State for the Home Department, Ex p. Saleem* [2001] 1 W.L.R. 443 at 457–458.

[127] The reasoning in *Bewry* was questioned in *R. (McLellan) v Bracknell Forest BC* [2002] Q.B. 1129 CA (Civ Div) at [75]–[78], but these doubts appear to relate to the application of the common law principle, rather than its existence.

[128] See Ch.19.

requirement should necessarily be limited to cases where the applicant has a right. It may be fortuitous whether the legislation is framed in terms of a right, or the grant of discretion. It may be debatable whether the statutory language should be read as conferring a right or discretion. The normative arguments in favour of an independent and impartial tribunal are, moreover, strong even where the public body has been accorded discretion. The absence of a substantive right should not lead to the conclusion that this important procedural guarantee is inapplicable.

CHAPTER 15

RULE-MAKING

1. CENTRAL ISSUES

i. We saw in an earlier chapter that people may be affected not only through individualised adjudication, but also through the application of pre-determined rules. These rules will have to be applied to the case at hand, but they will often be determinative of the result, or will strongly influence the outcome. This chapter considers the procedural and substantive constraints on rule-making. 15–001

ii. The term rule-making is used here, instead of delegated legislation, because the latter is but one species of the former. The test of whether a rule is subject to legislative checks is one of form. A primary statute that empowers a minister to make rules will specify whether they are to be regarded as statutory instruments for the purposes of the Statutory Instruments Act 1946. This Act contains the provisions for publication and legislative scrutiny. There are two areas not touched by the legislative controls: there are rules that are not expressed to be statutory instruments and are therefore outside the 1946 legislation; and there are areas in which administrative institutions develop rules, even if they are not expressly empowered to do so.

iii. The making of detailed rules pursuant to a primary statute is a common feature of all polities. There are a number of reasons why this is so. First, the area may be technically complex, making it difficult to set out all the permutations in the original statute. Second, the subject-matter may be novel. Time may be needed to experiment and to determine how the legislation is operating, making delegated legislation the most appropriate tool. Third, the Executive may wish to implement the legislation at a later stage, or to alter its detail.

iv. We are concerned about rule-making, whatever form it takes, because our ideas of representative government tell us that legislative norms achieve validation and legitimacy through consent by the legislature. The existence of rules of a legislative character, other than primary statutes, poses the problem of how this is to be accomplished. That is the central concern of this chapter.

v. There are four broad mechanisms for the control of rule-making: consultation, publication, legislative scrutiny and judicial review. Consultation is designed to secure consideration of the rule by interested parties prior to its passage. Publication ensures knowledge of the rule. Legislative supervision takes the form of parliamentary scrutiny. Consultation and legislative scrutiny are general methods of control, and the focus is on the merits of the rule as well as its technical legality. Judicial supervision by way of contrast is ex post facto, particular and focuses on the legality of the measure and not its merits. It takes place when the rule has been made.[1] It is dependent on an individual invoking the court's assistance and is in this sense particular, and because of the constitutional position of our courts they cannot, overtly at least, attack the merits of the rule. Judicial decisions may nonetheless have an effect on the making of future rules by prescribing procedural standards, or by decisions on aspects of legality. The judicial process is nonetheless unsuited to any generalised control over the content of rules. For this, checks in the form of consultation, legislative supervision and publication must remain the chief weapons.

vi. We will examine first the existing constraints on delegated legislation and then take a closer look at the problem of administrative rule-making. The final section of the chapter will consider the importance of EU law.

2. DELEGATED LEGISLATION: HISTORY, RATIONALE AND FORM

A. History

15–002 Delegated legislation is not a new phenomenon.[2] While the Statute of Proclamations 1539 giving Henry VIII extensive powers to legislate by proclamation proved to be a relatively short-lived measure, the Statute of Sewers 1531 was the harbinger of a more general trend. The latter vested the Commissioners of Sewers with full powers to make laws and decrees concerning drainage schemes and the levying of rates to pay for them.[3]

It was, however, the social and economic reforms of the 19th century that was the origin of delegated legislation on the scale to which we have now become accustomed. The Poor Law Amendment Act 1834 vested the Poor Law Commissioners with power to make rules for the management of the poor,[4] and many other 19th-century statutes contained power to make rules. After 1890 statutory rules and orders were published annually. Between 1901–1914 the average number of orders made was 1,349, which increased in the war years to 1,459.[5]

---

[1] Subject to the judicial role in enforcing compliance with the requirements of consultation. As to whether the courts would intervene by injunction to prevent the passage of delegated legislation, see Ch.26.

[2] C. Allen, *Law and Orders: An Inquiry into the Nature and Scope of Delegated Legislation and Executive Powers in English Law*, 3rd edn (London: Stevens, 1965), Ch.2; C. Carr, *Delegated Legislation: Three Lectures* (Cambridge: Cambridge University Press, 1921); J. Griffith and H. Street, *Principles of Administrative Law*, 5th edn (London: Pitman, 1973), Chs 2 and 3; R. Baldwin, *Rules and Government* (Oxford: Oxford University Press, 1995).

[3] The Commissioners of Sewers are also a good example of a body vested with administrative, judicial and executive powers, P. Craig, *UK, EU and Global Administrative Law: Foundations and Challenges* (Cambridge: Cambridge University Press, 2015), Ch. 1.

[4] See Ch.2.

[5] Allen, *Law and Orders: An Inquiry into the Nature and Scope of Delegated Legislation and Executive Powers in English Law* (1965), p.32.

The advent of war increased not only the amount, but also the complexity and generality of delegated legislation. The Defence of the Realm Act 1914 gave the government power to make regulations for securing public safety and the defence of the realm, a power liberally used. Regulations were made on dog shows and the supply of cocaine to actresses, neither of which was of prime concern to the war effort. While the generality of the empowering provisions diminished immediately after the First World War, it did not entirely wane. Thus, the Emergency Powers Act 1920 gave the government extensive powers to deal with peace-time emergencies.[6] The advent of the Second World War found the draftsmen ready with the Emergency Powers (Defence) Acts 1939 and 1940. This legislation empowered the Crown to make regulations for public safety, the defence of the realm, the maintenance of order, the maintenance of supply and the detention of persons whose detention appeared to the secretary of state to be expedient in the interests of public safety, or the defence of the realm.

While wide delegated powers could be accepted during war or civil emergency, there was growing disquiet about their scope in peacetime. Some, like Lord Hewart,[7] felt that delegated legislation was out of control. While controls over delegated legislation were desirable Lord Hewart's general attack upon such delegation was overplayed, as was made apparent by the Committee on Ministers' Powers. The Committee was appointed to consider delegated legislation and the making of judicial or quasi-judicial decisions by ministers.[8] Its conclusions were that delegated legislation was inevitable, but could be improved by a clearer use of terminology; by defining the delegated powers as clearly as possible; and by adequate facilities for publication and legislative scrutiny.

B. Rationale and Constitutional Concerns

Few have doubted the continuing need for delegated legislation: 3,292 statutory instruments were made in 2013 and 3,492 such instruments were made in 2014.[9] **15–003**
The exigencies of the modern state have increasingly led to statutes containing delegated power. This is so for a number of reasons.

First, the area may be technically complex, making it difficult to set out all the permutations in the original statute. Second, the subject-matter may be novel. Time may be needed to determine how the legislation is operating. Only then can all the details be filled in, making delegated legislation the most appropriate tool. Third, even where the area is well known, the executive may wish to implement the legislation at a later stage, or to alter its detail. Delegated legislation is a useful mechanism for achieving these ends. A fourth reason is the advantage that such legislation gives to the Executive. For a government with an onerous legislative timetable, or only a small majority, there is the temptation to pass

[6] The Act was used in the general strike 1926, the 1948 and 1949 dock strikes, the 1955 rail strike, the 1966 seamen's strike, the 1970 dock strike and the coal strike of 1973.

[7] Lord Hewart, *The New Despotism* (London: Ernest Benn, 1929).

[8] Donoughmore Committee, *Report of the Committee on Ministers' Powers* (1932), Cmd 4060.

[9] See *http://www.legislation.gov.uk/uksi* [accessed 13 July 2015].

skeleton legislation, with the details being etched in by the minister. These details may contain important aspects of the legislation, and legislative scrutiny may not always be effective.

While all accept the need for delegated legislation there are certain types which give rise to particular constitutional concern. The Scott Report[10] was, for example, critical of the broad delegated powers given to the executive by statutes such as the Import, Export and Customs Powers (Defence) Act 1939, which was used to control exports until 1990, and its successor statute the Import and Export Control Act 1990.[11] More generally, the use of skeleton legislation is a cause for concern. The passage of such legislation is now common, with power being given to the executive not merely to fill in technical details, but also to decide broad issues of policy, thereby leading to a consequential shift in the balance of power between Parliament and the Executive.[12]

The type of delegated legislation that is most constitutionally problematic is that which contains a "Henry VIII" clause. This is the nickname for clauses that allow a minister to amend the primary statute, or some other statute, through delegated legislation. The use of such clauses has increased,[13] as exemplified by the Deregulation and Contracting Out Act 1994, and the Regulatory Reform Act 2001.[14] It should also be remembered that the Human Rights Act 1998 contains what is in effect a Henry VIII clause to enable a minister expeditiously to alter legislation which a court has held to be inconsistent with the Convention rights recognised by the Act.[15]

C. Form

15–004 There are a bewildering variety of names for delegated legislation. Orders in Council, rules, regulations, byelaws and directions all jostle one another upon the statute book. The key to sanity is the realisation that nothing turns upon the precise nomenclature.[16] A word about the differing devices is nonetheless necessary. Orders in Council tend to be the more important pieces of subordinate legislation. The Executive will draft the legislation, but it will be enacted as an Order of the Privy Council. The authority to make such Orders will be derived

---

[10] *Report of the Inquiry into the Export of Defence Equipment and Dual-Use of Goods to Iraq and Related Prosecutions*, HC Paper No.115 (Session 1995–96) (the Scott Report).

[11] G. Ganz, "Delegated Legislation: A Necessary Evil or a Constitutional Outrage?", in P. Leyland and T. Woods (eds), *Administrative Law Facing the Future: Old Constraints and New Horizons* (Oxford: Blackwell, 1997), Ch.3.

[12] Ganz, "Delegated Legislation: A Necessary Evil or a Constitutional Outrage?", in Leyland and Woods (eds), *Administrative Law Facing the Future: Old Constraints and New Horizons* (1997), pp.63–64.

[13] Lord Rippon, "Henry VIII Clauses" (1989) 10 Stat. L. Rev. 205 and "Constitutional Anarchy" (1990) 11 Stat. L. Rev. 184.

[14] Ganz, "Delegated Legislation: A Necessary Evil or a Constitutional Outrage?", in Leyland and Woods (eds), *Administrative Law Facing the Future: Old Constraints and New Horizons* (1997), pp.65–66; M. Freedland, "Privatising *Carltona*: Part II of the Deregulation and Contracting Out Act" [1995] P.L. 21, 22.

[15] Human Rights Act 1998 s.10.

[16] The Donoughmore Committee recommended that each of these terms should be used for a specific purpose, but their ideas were not implemented, Cmd.4060, p.64.

from statute.[17] Regulations and rules are used widely to denote subordinate law-making power. The power will normally be conferred upon a minister of the Crown. Agencies and local authorities may also pass regulations, rules or orders. Byelaws are commonly promulgated by local authorities, but can also be made by agencies.[18]

3. DELEGATED LEGISLATION: PASSAGE AND PUBLICATION

A. The Statutory Instruments Act 1946

Section 1(1) of the 1946 Act states[19]: **15–005**

> "1(1) Where by this Act or any Act passed after the commencement[20] of this Act power to make, confirm, or approve orders, rules, regulations or other subordinate legislation is conferred on His Majesty in Council or on any Minister of the Crown then, if the power is expressed—
> (a) in the case of a power conferred on His Majesty, to be exercised by Order in Council;
> (b) in the case of a power conferred on a Minister of the Crown, to be exercisable by statutory instrument,
>
> any document by which that power is exercised shall be known as a 'statutory instrument' and the provisions of this Act shall apply thereto accordingly."

The Act therefore provides for two different types of cases. All Orders in Council made pursuant to a statutory power must be exercised by statutory instrument.[21] Other rules, regulations or orders must be exercised by statutory instrument only when the particular statute states that the power must be so exercised. The test is one of form. Moreover, s.1(1)(b) only applies when the power is conferred on a minister of the Crown. This is defined flexibly: if there is any question whether any board, commissioner or other body on whom any such power is conferred is a government department, or which minister of the Crown is in charge of them, the question is to be referred to the minister for the Civil Service.[22] As s.1 makes clear, it is sufficient if the minister of the Crown has power to make, confirm or approve the subordinate legislation.[23]

---

[17] The Privy Council can, however, pass legislation which is not subordinate legislation on matters within the Royal Prerogative, provided that the power to do so has not been restricted by statute, *Attorney General v De Keyser's Royal Hotel* [1920] A.C. 508, HL.

[18] For special problems concerning byelaws see J. Garner, *Administrative Law* in B. Jones and K. Thompson, 8th edn (London: Butterworths, 1996), pp.99–106. There are also devices known as Provisional Orders and Special Procedure Orders (for the latter see the Statutory Orders (Special Procedure) Act 1945) which are intended to expedite the passage of private Acts, see Allen, *Law and Orders: An Inquiry into the Nature and Scope of Delegated Legislation and Executive Powers in English Law* (1965), pp.76–82.

[19] Statutory Instruments Act 1946 (1946 Act) s.1(1A) makes provision for Wales.

[20] 1 January 1948.

[21] Orders in Council made in pursuance of the Royal Prerogative are not covered.

[22] 1946 Act s.11(2).

[23] A third type of case is dealt with in the Statutory Instruments Act 1946 s.1(2), which covers statutes passed before 1946, and provides the criterion as to when rules passed pursuant to such statutes after 1946 should count as statutory instruments. See further Statutory Instruments Regulations 1947 (SI 1948/1).

B. Publication and Making

15–006 A principal purpose of the 1946 Act is to provide for the publication of statutory instruments. This is dealt with in s.2(1): immediately after the making of any statutory instrument it shall be sent to the King's printer of Acts of Parliament and numbered in accordance with regulations made under the 1946 Act. Copies shall be printed[24] and sold as soon as possible, subject to any exception in Acts passed after the 1946 Act, or in any regulations made under the 1946 Act. Statutory instruments must contain a statement of the date on which they become operative.[25]

The main exceptions from the requirement for publication are as follows: local instruments, which connote local and personal or private Acts[26]; and general instruments[27] certified by the responsible authority to be a class of documents which would otherwise be regularly printed.[28] The Reference Committee[29] may direct that such an instrument should be published. Exemptions from publication also exist for temporary instruments,[30] the publication of bulky schedules,[31] and for confidential instruments.[32]

It might be thought that a failure to publish would affect the validity of the statutory instrument, since the public would not otherwise have the opportunity to know the law being applied to them. This is not however the case. Primary statutes take effect as soon as they have received the Royal Assent. It was at one time thought that subordinate legislation required publication in order to be valid. There is some authority for this proposition,[33] but the weight of authority is against this view.

15–007 In *R. v Sheer Metalcraft Ltd*,[34] a company was prosecuted for infringing an Iron and Steel Prices Order. The Order had been printed but certain schedules had not, and no certificate of exemption had been obtained. Streatfeild J held that the existence of s.3(2) of the 1946 Act indicated that the Order was valid despite failure to publish. That section provides a defence to an action for contravention of a statutory instrument where the instrument has not been issued at the date of the contravention, unless it can be shown that reasonable steps were taken to bring it to the public's knowledge. If an Order was ineffective before publication then s.3(2) would be redundant, as there would be no law contravened. Streatfeild

---

24 The Statutory Instruments (Production and Sale) Act 1996 was passed in order to facilitate the contracting-out of the printing of statutory instruments.

25 1946 Act s.4(2).

26 Statutory Instruments Regulations 1947 (SI 1948/1) reg.4(2).

27 General instruments are those in the nature of a public general Act, SI 1948/1 reg.4.

28 SI 1948/1 reg.5.

29 Two or more persons nominated by the Lord Chancellor and Speaker of the House of Commons, SI 1948/1 reg.11(1).

30 SI 1948/1 reg.6.

31 SI 1948/1 reg.7.

32 SI 1948/1 reg.8. This exception only applies so as to restrict publication before the instrument comes into operation

33 *Johnson v Sargent* [1918] 1 K.B. 101 KBD.

34 *R. v Sheer Metalcraft Ltd* [1954] 1 Q.B. 586 QBD. See also, *Jones v Robson* [1901] 1 Q.B. 673 QBD.

J stressed that the making of the instrument was one thing and the issue of it another. An instrument was valid once it was made by the minister and laid before Parliament.[35]

This still leaves the issue as to when the instrument is "made" by the minister. The enabling legislation may state that an instrument shall not be made until it has been laid before Parliament. There may also be a provision stipulating when the instrument should come into operation. In the absence of such provisions the statutory instrument would appear to be made when either enacted by the Queen in Council, or signed by the competent authority, who will normally be a minister or a civil servant with authority to sign for the minister.[36]

C. Publication and Making: Exceptions

Whatever the deficiencies of the 1946 Act, it does ensure publication of statutory instruments. There are, however, five categories of case where there is no guarantee of publication. **15–008**

First, some statutory instruments may, as noted above, be exempted from publication under regulations made pursuant to the 1946 Act.

Second, there is no requirement for publication where Orders in Council are made in exercise of the Prerogative.

Third, publication is not required where delegated legislation is passed in furtherance of a statute that does not deem that legislation to be a statutory instrument.

Fourth, it is doubtful whether sub-delegated legislation is covered by the 1946 Act. This is legislation made under a power conferred by a regulation or other legislative instrument not being itself an Act of Parliament. The 1946 Act requires that the delegated legislation be made under powers conferred by an Act of Parliament. Whether this excludes all sub-delegated legislation is questionable. The answer depends in part on the meaning of "confer". If this word is interpreted so as to include "derive" then some, at least, sub-delegated legislation will be included. Such legislation can be traced back to the primary statute, which originally conferred the power to make the rules from which the sub-delegated legislation originated. The answer also depends on the breadth given to the term "minister of the Crown", which is left open-ended by s.11 of the 1946 Act, and on how much sub-delegated legislation is actually legislation, as opposed to administrative direction or executive order. While circulars and the like may be published by departments, if they are not the citizen will be faced with a mass of

[35] There is some doubt whether validity requires the instrument even to be laid before Parliament, *Starey v Graham* [1899] 1 Q.B. 406 at 412, and in any event not all instruments are required to be laid. However, when a statute provides that a statutory instrument is to be laid before Parliament after being made the general rule is that it must be laid before coming into operation, Statutory Instruments Act 1946 s.4.

[36] Allen, *Law and Orders: An Inquiry into the Nature and Scope of Delegated Legislation and Executive Powers in English Law* (1965), p.114.

literature which may well be dispositive of the case, but the contents of which cannot be ascertained. As Streatfeild J has said, such power is four times cursed[37]:

> "First, it has seen neither House of Parliament; secondly, it is unpublished and is inaccessible even to those whose valuable rights of property may be affected; thirdly it is a jumble of provisions, legislative, administrative, or directive in character and sometimes difficult to disentangle one from the other; and, fourthly, it is expressed not in the precise language of an Act of Parliament or an Order in Council but in the more colloquial language of correspondence, which is not always susceptible of the ordinary canons of construction."

The final category where there is no guarantee of publication is rules made by the administration. What distinguishes these from sub-delegated legislation is that there may be no express power to make rules, whether derived from an Act of Parliament or other legislative instrument. This does not mean that administrative rule-making is either unlawful or to be regretted. It is neither as we shall see below. Such rules may however be unpublished and hence unknown. This problem will be considered below.[38]

4. DELEGATED LEGISLATION: CONTROL BY PARLIAMENT

A. Scrutiny by the House

15–009 There are instances where there is no requirement that the subordinate legislation be laid before Parliament.[39] Where delegated legislation must come before the House there are numerous ways in which this can occur.[40] Three principal methods can, however, be identified.

First, the empowering legislation may simply require the subordinate legislation to be laid before the House after it has been made. In such cases the laying is simply a mechanism to inform Parliament of its content before it becomes operative. Questions may be asked, but no direct attack upon the delegated legislation is possible. If a document has been presented to the House it has been laid,[41] and the laying should take place before the instrument comes into force. Where it is vital that it should become operational before being laid this can occur, provided that notification is sent to the Speaker of the House of Lords and the Speaker of the House of Commons.[42]

The second mechanism offers some measure of parliamentary control: this is the affirmative resolution procedure. This requires the subordinate legislation to be subject to an affirmative resolution of each House, or the House of Commons

[37] *Patchett v Leathem* (1949) 65 T.L.R. 69 at 70. See also, *Blackpool Corp v Lockyer* [1948] 1 K.B. 349, CA at 369. Allen, *Law and Orders: An Inquiry into the Nature and Scope of Delegated Legislation and Executive Powers in English Law* (1965), pp.194–195, reaches no definite conclusion on the publication of sub-delegated legislation.

[38] See paras 15–043 to 15–051.

[39] J. Kersell, *Parliamentary Scrutiny of Delegated Legislation* (London: Stevens, 1960), p.19.

[40] Allen, *Law and Orders: An Inquiry into the Nature and Scope of Delegated Legislation and Executive Powers in English Law* (1965), pp.122–125.

[41] *R. v Immigration Appeal Tribunal, Ex p. Joyles* [1972] 1 W.L.R. 1390 DC. The effect of the Laying of Documents before Parliament (Interpretation) Act 1948 is that each House is a master of the meaning of laying.

[42] 1946 Act s 4.

alone. The procedure can vary as between areas. A statute may state that instruments made there under do not have any effect until parliamentary approval has been secured. If there is no such provision the instrument will have effect as soon as it is made, with a rider that if it is not approved within the requisite period it should not be invalidated retrospectively.[43] The debate on the measure will automatically take place within a delegated legislation standing committee, unless the government agrees to a debate on the floor of the House. The standing committee can, however, only vote on an unamendable motion that it has considered the measure. The substantive vote on whether the measure should be approved takes place on the floor of the House without further debate. Instruments taken on the floor of the House are debated for up to an hour and a half, also on an unamendable motion. Relatively few instruments are subject to the affirmative procedure for the very reason that the government then has to find time to secure their passage.[44]

The third principal way in which statutory instruments are processed through Parliament is by the negative resolution procedure. It is the private member who must secure time to attack the delegated legislation. The instrument is open to a prayer for annulment within 40 days of being laid. Such instruments are as a general rule to be laid before becoming operative.[45] The prayer for annulment may be moved in either House, but it is not easily secured. A member must ensure a quorum to retain the House in session. There is no provision for amendment, only outright rejection. Debates on annulment resolutions are subject to time limits and there is insufficient time for such debates.[46] Even if a prayer for annulment succeeds this does not of itself administer the death-blow to the subordinate legislation. A successful prayer precludes further action from being taken under the instrument and empowers Her Majesty to pass an Order in Council revoking it. It does not invalidate anything done prior to the prayer, nor does it bar the making of a new statutory instrument.[47]

Many instruments are subject to the negative resolution procedure,[48] but no real principle guides the choice between the available options. It is clear that the most important types of instrument should be subject to the affirmative resolution procedure and only purely technical matters should be exempt from the need to be laid. While the affirmative procedure has been used for important matters such as those affecting statutes and the grant of very broad delegated powers, this practice is by no means uniform. It is common to find the affirmative and negative procedures used indiscriminately to implement the same statute. Moreover, while instruments not subject to the requirement of laying should be **15–010**

---

43 Allen, *Law and Orders: An Inquiry into the Nature and Scope of Delegated Legislation and Executive Powers in English Law* (1965), p.123.

44 A. Adonis, *Parliament Today*, 2nd edn (Manchester: Manchester University Press, 1993), p.113; Select Committee on Procedure, *First Report: Delegated Legislation*, HC Paper No.48 (Session 1999–2000), paras 24–25.

45 This is the effect of s.5 of the 1946 Act which applies s.4 to the negative resolution procedure.

46 *Making the Law*, The Report of the Hansard Society Commission on the Legislative Process (1993) p.93.

47 1946 Act s.5.

48 A further mechanism is for laying the instrument in draft, see the 1946 Act s.6.

reserved for minor matters, subordinate legislation of such "peripheral importance" as the alteration of county council electoral boundaries and the constitution of Regional Hospital Boards have passed in this manner.[49]

Some oversight is exercised by the House of Lords' Delegated Powers Scrutiny Committee, which was established in 1992 and is now called the Delegated Powers and Regulatory Reform Committee. It has the power to report whether the provisions of a Bill inappropriately delegate legislative power, or whether they subject the exercise of legislative power to an inappropriate degree of Parliamentary scrutiny.[50]

The effectiveness of control on the floor of the House is constrained by the shortage of time for debate and the difficulty of securing sufficient support to move a prayer for annulment. Some such prayers are moved after the period in which the instruments can be annulled, in which case they can only be discursive, while others are attended by relatively few members. Nor is there any requirement that there be consultation with MPs prior to the promulgation of the rules.[51] Sir Carleton Kemp Allen concluded that it was a constitutional fiction to say that Parliament exercised any real safeguards over delegated legislation.[52]

B. Scrutiny in Committee: Delegated Legislation Committees

15–011 Statutory instruments may be referred to Delegated Legislation Committees, which are according to the standing orders of the House of Commons regarded as General Committees.[53] There shall be one or more Delegated Legislation Committees at any point in time and the Speaker of the House of Commons distributes such instruments as are referred between them.[54] The remit of these committees is however limited. The Delegated Legislation Committee cannot make any amendments to the measure and merely "considers" the instrument. The meetings are limited to one and half hours, but normally last no longer than 30 minutes.

C. Scrutiny in Committee: The Joint Committee on Statutory Instruments

15–012 Control on the floor of Parliament is supplemented by scrutiny in committee. In 1944 a Scrutiny Committee was appointed and in 1973 a Joint Committee on Statutory Instruments was formed from the committees of the Commons and

[49] Allen, *Law and Orders: An Inquiry into the Nature and Scope of Delegated Legislation and Executive Powers in English Law* (1965), pp.128–133. Joint Committee, *Second Report: Delegated Legislation*, HL Paper No.204, HC Paper No.408 (Session 1972–73) recommended that the affirmative procedure should be used for rules which substantially affect the provisions of primary legislation, impose or increase taxation, or otherwise involve special considerations.

[50] C. Himsworth, "The Delegated Powers Scrutiny Committee" [1995] P.L. 34.

[51] J. Beatson, "Legislative Control of Administrative Rulemaking: Lessons from the British Experience" (1979) 12 Corn. I.L.J. 199, 213–215.

[52] Allen, *Law and Orders: An Inquiry into the Nature and Scope of Delegated Legislation and Executive Powers in English Law* (1965), p.136.

[53] Standing Orders of the House of Commons (HMSO, 2015), Order 84(h).

[54] Standing Orders of the House of Commons (HMSO, 2015), Order 118.

Lords. Its terms of reference require that it should examine every statutory instrument, rule, order or scheme laid or laid in draft before Parliament in order to determine whether the attention of the House should be drawn to an instrument for any of the following reasons[55]: that it imposes a tax or charge; that it is made under a statute which prevents challenge in the courts; that it appears to make an unusual or unexpected use of powers conferred by the statute; that it purports to have retrospective effect without statutory authorisation; that there seemed to be unwarranted delay in the publication or laying of the instrument; that the statutory instrument has not been laid and that notification to the Speaker has not been prompt; that it is unclear whether the instrument is intra vires; that for any special reason its form or purport requires elucidation; and that the drafting appears to be defective.

Scrutiny of technical legality has been of value.[56] In 2008 the Joint Committee scrutinised 1,486 statutory instruments and found cause to draw the special attention of each House to 59 instruments, 4 per cent of the total scrutinised.[57] The attentions of the Joint Committee have improved drafting and increased the number of explanatory notes provided by departments. The very presence of the Committee sounds a warning to departments. The Joint Committee monitors departments in order to determine the action taken on instruments in relation to which the Committee has drawn special attention.[58]

There are nonetheless limitations to the existing controls. Only about one half of statutory instruments are reviewed by the Joint Committee in any one year. The departmental response to Joint Committee reports drawing special attention to a particular instrument is mixed and there is variance in the extent to which different departments address the concerns raised by the Joint Committee.[59] The Committee's power is moreover limited. It can refer an instrument to the House, but it has no means of ensuring that a prayer for annulment or debate will occur following its report. Nor can it be sure that its report will reach the House before the period for annulment is over, and debate may well ensue on the merits of an instrument before technical scrutiny has occurred.[60] Beatson concluded that[61]:

> "The British system of legislative veto has proved less than satisfactory in rendering administrators accountable to their political superiors and protecting those affected by administrative rules. This limited success stems from many factors. These include de facto executive control of the legislature, the unavailability of information about the substance of a

---

[55] Standing Orders of the House of Commons (HMSO, 2010), Order 151.

[56] Joint Committee on Statutory Instruments, *Thirty-ninth Report*, HL Paper No.178, HC Paper No.135 xxxix, (2002).

[57] Joint Committee on Statutory Instruments, *Scrutinising Statutory Instruments: Departmental Returns, 2008*, HL Paper No.136, HC Paper No.884 (Session 2008–09), para.1.

[58] Committee on Statutory Instruments, *Scrutinising Statutory Instruments: Departmental Returns, 2008*, paras 9–14.

[59] Committee on Statutory Instruments, *Scrutinising Statutory Instruments: Departmental Returns, 2008*, paras 15–20.

[60] Beatson, "Legislative Control of Administrative Rulemaking: Lessons from the British Experience" (1979) 12 Corn. I.L.J. 199, 215, 218. See also, J. Hayhurst and P. Wallington, "The Parliamentary Scrutiny of Delegated Legislation" [1988] P.L. 547.

[61] Beatson, "Legislative Control of Administrative Rulemaking: Lessons from the British Experience" (1979) 12 Corn. I.L.J. 199, 222.

rule in the time available for control, the limited time available for debate, and the apparent unwillingness of Members of Parliament to take an interest in scrutiny, especially of technical infirmities."

These sentiments were echoed by Alan Beith MP,[62] who emphasised the control wielded by government business managers over the scrutiny of delegated legislation, whether on the floor of the House or in committee. This is all the more important given the fact that delegated legislation will often be concerned not just with issues of detail, but also with major issues of social policy.[63]

D. Scrutiny in Committee: The House of Lords Secondary Legislation Scrutiny Committee

15–013 In 2003 the House of Lords established the Merits of Statutory Instruments Committee, the initial catalyst for which came from recommendations of the Royal Commission on the Reform of the House of Lords in 2000, the Wakeham Commission. It was renamed the Secondary Legislation Scrutiny Committee in 2012. It considers the policy merits of any statutory instrument laid before each House and upon which proceedings may be, or might have been, taken in either House of Parliament under an Act of Parliament. It can also consider proposals for such instruments.[64]

It draws the attention of the House to an instrument, draft or proposal on the grounds that: it is politically or legally important or gives rise to issues of public policy likely to be of interest to the House; it may be inappropriate in view of changed circumstances since the enactment of the parent Act; it may inappropriately implement EU legislation; it may imperfectly achieve its policy objectives; it is insufficiently clear as to its policy objectives; or there were inadequacies in consultation concerning the instrument. The criteria for referring a matter to the House therefore allow the Committee to consider the merits of a statutory instrument in the way that is not normally undertaken by the Joint Committee. The Secondary Legislation Scrutiny Committee has however no power to block the passage of a statutory instrument.

The Committee has performed a valuable function since its inception. It has made perceptive comments on particular statutory instruments. It has also undertaken more general studies, concluding that defective management processes used by government departments when making statutory instruments were responsible for some of the defects found in particular instruments.[65] The

[62] Alan Beith MP, "Prayers Unanswered: A Jaundiced View of the Parliamentary Scrutiny of Statutory Instruments" (1981) 34 *Parliamentary Affairs* 165, 170.

[63] Hayhurst and Wallington, "The Parliamentary Scrutiny of Delegated Legislation" [1988] P.L. 547, 573–574.

[64] See, *http://www.parliament.uk/business/committees/committees-a-z/lords-select/secondary-legislation-scrutiny-committee/role/* [accessed 13 July 2015].

[65] House of Lords Merits of Statutory Instruments Committee, *Twenty-ninth Report: The Management of Secondary Legislation*, HL Paper No.149 (Session 2006–07).

Committee made a number of recommendations for improvement in departmental management of statutory instruments,[66] which will be considered below when discussing possible reforms in relation to delegated legislation. More recently, the Committee undertook valuable studies of post-implementation review of statutory instruments designed to test their efficacy,[67] and of the operation of the Public Bodies Act 2011.[68]

E. Scrutiny of Regulatory Reform: A Special Regime

A separate procedure operates for statutory instruments dealing with regulatory reform. The Regulatory Reform Act 2001 modified the earlier scheme enshrined in the Deregulation and Contracting Out Act 1994. The Regulatory Reform Act 2001 has now largely been repealed and replaced by the Legislative and Regulatory Reform Act 2006. The 2006 Act enables a minister of the Crown to make an order for the purpose of reforming legislation that has the effect of imposing burdens on persons carrying on any activity. The substantive details of the legislation were considered in the discussion of regulation.[69] It is the procedure for the making of such orders that is relevant here. 15–014

The Legislative and Regulatory Reform Act 2006, stipulates that an order made under the legislation must be made by statutory instrument.[70] The minister has an obligation to consult about the content of any proposed order.[71] A draft of the order and an explanatory document setting out the reasons for the order and the way in which it fulfils the conditions of the Act is then laid before Parliament.[72] The minister provides a reasoned recommendation in the explanatory document as to whether the order should be subject to the negative resolution procedure, the affirmative resolution procedure or the super-affirmative resolution procedure. The minister's recommendation applies unless, within 30 days of the draft being laid before the House, either House of Parliament specifies that a more onerous procedure should apply.[73] It is also open to the Regulatory Reform Committee of the House of Commons or the Delegated Powers and Regulatory Reform Committee of the House of Lords that report on draft orders under the Act to recommend that a particular draft order is subject to a higher level of procedure than recommended by the minister, and if it does so this will prevail unless it is rejected by resolution of the House.[74]

---

66 House of Lords Merits of Statutory Instruments Committee, *Twenty-ninth Report: The Management of Secondary Legislation*, para.126.

67 House of Lords Merits of Statutory Instruments Committee, *Thirtieth Report: What Happened Next? A Study of Post-Implementation Reviews of Secondary Legislation*, HL Paper No.180 (Session 2009–10) and Government Response, HL Paper No.43 (Session 2010–12).

68 House of Lords Secondary Legislation Scrutiny Committee, *Twenty-second Report: Special Report Public Bodies Act 2011: Two Years On,* HL Paper No. 98 (Session 2013-14).

69 See Ch.11.

70 Legislative and Regulatory Reform Act 2006 s.12.

71 Legislative and Regulatory Reform Act 2006 s.13.

72 Legislative and Regulatory Reform Act 2006 s.14.

73 Legislative and Regulatory Reform Act 2006 s.15.

74 Legislative and Regulatory Reform Act 2006 s.15(6).

15–015 If the negative procedure is used then within 40 days of the draft being laid either House of Parliament must resolve that the draft order should not be adopted.[75] The 2006 Act, however, also in effect gives the committee of each House charged with reporting on the draft order a veto power, in the sense that it may, after 30 days and before the expiry of the 40 day period, recommend that the draft order should not be made. The minister may not then make the order, unless the committee recommendation is rejected by resolution of that House.[76]

If the affirmative procedure is adopted the draft must be approved by resolution of each House of Parliament within 40 days of its being laid. The relevant committees once again have a form of veto power: if either committee recommends after 30 days and before the expiry of the 40 day period that the draft order should not be made, then no proceedings can be taken in relation to that draft order unless the recommendation is rejected by resolution of that House in the same Session.[77]

The super-affirmative procedure operates as follows.[78] The minister must have regard to any representations, any resolution of either House of Parliament, and any recommendations of a committee of either House of Parliament charged with reporting on the draft order, made during the 60-day period with regard to the draft order. If, after the expiry of the 60-day period, the minister wishes to make an order in the terms of the draft, he must lay before Parliament a statement indicating whether any representations were made and if so he must give details of them. The minister can then make an order in the terms of the draft if it is approved by a resolution of each House of Parliament. The relevant committees once again have a form of veto power: the committee of either House charged with reporting on the draft order may, at any time after the laying of the ministerial statement and before the draft order is approved by that House, recommend that no further proceedings be taken in relation to the draft order. If it does so then no proceedings may be taken in relation to the draft order in that House unless the recommendation is, in the same Session, rejected by resolution of that House. There is provision for the minister to make a revised version of the order with material changes after the 60-day period. This too must be approved by each House and the relevant committees have the same power in relation to the revised order as they do in relation to the original draft order.

The "super affirmative" procedure that applied under the Regulatory Reform Act 2001 generally worked well and enabled detailed scrutiny of draft deregulation and regulatory reform orders.[79] This was, however, the only procedure for the making of orders under the 2001 Act. The 2006 Act, as we have seen, provides for the possible use of the negative and affirmative procedures as

75 Legislative and Regulatory Reform Act 2006 s.16.

76 Legislative and Regulatory Reform Act 2006 s.16(4)–(5).

77 Legislative and Regulatory Reform Act 2006 s.17(3)–(4).

78 Legislative and Regulatory Reform Act 2006 s.18.

79 D. Miers, "The Deregulation Procedure: An Expanding Role" [1999] P.L. 477; Deregulation and Regulatory Reform Committee, *Third Special Report: The Handling of Regulatory Orders (III)*, HC Paper No.1272 (2001–02); Deregulation and Regulatory Reform Committee, *First Special Report: The Handling of Regulatory Reform Orders*, HC Paper No.389 (Session 2001–02); Deregulation and Regulatory Reform Committee, *Second Special Report: The Operation of the Regulatory Reform Act: Government's Response to the Committee's First Special Report of Session 2001–02*, HC Paper No.1029 (Session 2002–03).

well as the super-affirmative procedure. It is true that the committees' powers are enhanced, in the sense that they can play a role in the choice of procedure to govern the making of a particular order, and also have the qualified veto power set out above as to whether a particular order is approved. The degree of scrutiny will therefore depend on how far ministers seek to use the lower level procedures and how far the committees exercise their power to press for higher level procedures and how far they recommend against the making of particular orders.[80]

F. Scrutiny of European Legislation

The United Kingdom's accession to the European Union produced novel problems of supervision and control. European legislation can be directly applicable within the Member States.[81] This means that once enacted by the European Union it is automatically incorporated into municipal law without the normal requirements of adoption or transformation. 15–016

In terms of machinery,[82] Committees of the House of Commons have been established to consider whether delegated legislation is necessary in order to implement,[83] for example, an EU directive, and also to scrutinise proposals that emerge from the European Union, in order to provide Parliament with information about impending European legislation. Concern that legislation from Europe was not receiving proper attention led the House of Commons' Procedure Committee to propose the establishment of five standing committees, although only three were established.

The system works in the following way. The European Scrutiny Committee examines EU documents, such as draft proposals for legislation, and reports on the "legal and political importance" of each document. The scrutiny is conducted in the light of the Explanatory Memorandum produced by the relevant government department on the EU documents. The Committee considers approximately 1,100 documents each year, half of which are deemed to be of legal or political importance, such that the Scrutiny Committee reports substantively on them. It recommends approximately 40 such documents per year for further consideration by one of the European Standing Committees, and

---

[80] The Regulatory Reform Committee, in considering the changes required to its standing orders as the result of the 2006 Act, pressed hard for the power to refer a draft order for debate in a Delegated Legislation Committee, in order to provide MPs with the opportunity to consider such draft orders that warranted such scrutiny because of their political or legal significance, Regulatory Reform Committee, *Second Special Report 2006–07, Revised Standing Orders*, HC Paper No.385 (Session 2006–07); Regulatory Reform Committee, *Government's Response*, HC Paper No.610 (Session 2007–08).

[81] See Ch.10.

[82] T. St J.N. Bates, "European Community Legislation before the House of Commons" (1991) 12 Stat. L.R. 109; E. Denza, "Parliamentary Scrutiny of Community Legislation" (1993) 14 Stat. L.R. 56; The European Union Scrutiny System in the House of Commons (2015), *http://www.parliament.uk/documents/commons-committees/european-scrutiny/European-Scrutiny-Committee-Guide-May15.pdf* [accessed 13 July 2015].

[83] The Legislative and Regulatory Reform Act 2006 s.27 amended the European Communities Act 1972 s.2(2) by providing that Community provisions could be implemented in the UK not only by regulations, but also by orders, rules or schemes.

approximately six per year for debate on the floor of the House. The latter only occurs if the House decides that they should be considered in this way.

15–017 There are three European Standing Committees[84] and the relevant committee will consider the merits of the issues. The reports of the European Scrutiny Committee are clearly and succinctly presented.[85] They show an awareness of the legal and political importance of complex issues. The committee's evaluation may support the relevant government minister, but may take a differing line. The very fact that there is a body within the UK looking at such issues, other than the relevant department of state, is undoubtedly beneficial. The European Scrutiny committee will also liaise where necessary with departmental select committees. The regime has undoubtedly had a positive impact.[86]

It has in the past been hampered by the brevity of time left for discussion before the EU legislation is considered by the Council. The Lisbon Treaty was designed to alleviate this problem. Documents such as Green and White Papers are sent to national parliaments as soon as they are published, and draft legislative acts are transmitted to them at the same time as they are sent to the Council and European Parliament.[87] The general rule is that an eight-week period must elapse between transmission of a draft legislative act to national parliaments, and it being placed on a provisional agenda for the Council for its adoption or for adoption of a position under a legislative procedure.[88] The national parliaments also receive the agendas and outcomes of Council meetings at the same time as national governments.[89]

There is in addition a House of Lords' Select Committee on the European Union. It is chaired by a salaried officer of the House and considers any EU proposal that it believes should be drawn to the attention of the House. The Committee functions through a number of subcommittees which are subject-matter based.[90] These subcommittees will co-opt other members of the House of Lords for the investigation of particular issues. The House of Lords' Select Committee is therefore different from that in the House of Commons. The latter

[84] A. Energy and Climate Change; Environment, Food and Rural Affairs; Transport; Communities and Local Government; Forestry Commission. B. HM Treasury; Work and Pensions; Foreign and Commonwealth Office; International Development; Home Office; Justice; and matters not otherwise allocated. C. Business, Innovation and Skills; Children, Schools and Families; Culture, Media and Sport; and Health.

[85] See, e.g. Select Committee on European Scrutiny, *Twenty Seventh Report*, HC Paper No.34-xxvii (1999); European Union Scrutiny Committee, *Third Report: The European Union's Annual Policy Strategy 2006*, HC Paper No.34-iii (2005); European Union Scrutiny Committee, *Fourteenth Report, Aspects of the EU's Constitutional Treaty*, HC Paper No.38-xiv-1 (2005); European Union Scrutiny Committee, *Fourteenth Report: 2008–09, Free Movement of Workers in the EU*, HC Paper No.324 (2009); European Scrutiny Committee, *Eleventh Report, Ukraine and Russia: EU Restrictive Measures*, HC No. 219-xi (2014).

[86] The European Union Scrutiny System in the House of Commons (2015).

[87] TEU art.12; Protocol (No.1) On the Role of National Parliaments in the European Union art.1.

[88] Protocol (No.1) art.4.

[89] Protocol (No.1) art.5.

[90] There are six such subcommittees which deal with: economic and financial affairs; internal market, infrastructure and employment; external affairs; agriculture, fisheries, environment and energy; justice, institutions and consumer protection; home affairs, health and education.

will sift through EU legislation and refer matters on to the standing committee where this is warranted. The House of Lords' committee will produce its own valuable reports on particular issues.[91]

5. DELEGATED LEGISLATION: CONSULTATION

A. General Principles

There is no general duty to consult, imposed either by common law or statute. **15–018** Consultation may be required by the terms of a particular statute, or there may, in certain instances, be a duty to consult imposed by the common law. There is no common law duty to consult where the order is of a legislative nature[92]; the right to a reasoned decision does not apply where the order is of a legislative character[93]; and question marks hang over the application of the prerogative orders to legislative instruments. The absence of any common law duty to consult is matched by the lack of any such general statutory duty. The relevant statutes and case law have been considered in an earlier chapter.[94]

It is, however, clear from *Bank Mellat*[95] that the fact that a statute makes some provision for the procedure to be followed before or after the exercise of a statutory power does not of itself impliedly exclude the duty of fairness, or the duty of prior consultation, where they would otherwise arise. In the instant case a direction to a specific bank was required to be made in subordinate legislation, subject to Parliamentary approval. While a court might conclude in the case of some statutory powers that Parliamentary review was enough to satisfy the requirement of fairness, such as where the measure impugned was of a general legislative nature, matters were different where the relevant Treasury direction was in effect a command targeted at a specific individual.

There is no necessary connection between the existence of an obligation to consult about the making of an order or regulation and its characterisation as a statutory instrument. It all depends on the enabling legislation. It is perfectly possible for there to be, for example, a statutory duty to consult, and for the resulting measure to be a statutory instrument. It is equally possible for there to be such an obligation where the resultant order or regulation is not a statutory instrument.

---

[91] See, e.g. Select Committee on the European Communities, *Third Report*, HL Paper No.23 (1999), dealing with reforms to Comitology procedures; Select Committee on the European Communities, *Nineteenth Report*, HL Paper No.101 (1999), dealing with the then forthcoming European Council meeting which was the first such meeting to deal with justice and home affairs; European Union Committee, *Tenth Report: The Future Regulation of Derivatives Markets: Is the EU on the Right Track?* HL Paper No.93 (2010); European Union Committee, *Second Report: EU Data Protection Law: "A Right to be Forgotten?"* HL Paper No.40 (2014).

[92] *Bates v Lord Hailsham* [1972] 1 W.L.R. 1373 Ch D at 1378; *R. (BAPIO Action Ltd) v Secretary of State for the Home Department* [2007] EWCA Civ 1139 at [43]–[46], affirmed on different [2008] 1 A.C. 1003; *R. (Hillingdon LBC) v Lord Chancellor* [2008] EWHC 2683 (Admin); *R. (Niazi) v Secretary of State for the Home Department* [2008] EWCA Civ 755. The Rules Publication Act 1893 was the nearest which we have ever come to providing any general duty to consult.

[93] Tribunals and Inquiries Act 1992 s.10(5)(b).

[94] See paras 12–032 to 12–033.

[95] *Bank Mellat v HM Treasury* [2013] UKSC 39 at [35], [46].

B. Consultation Rights: Benefits

15–019 There are a number of advantages of prior consultation. The Rippon Commission rightly regarded developments with respect to consultation as an important way to improve the quality of secondary legislation. Moreover, the Cabinet Office has, as will be seen below, issued a Code of Practice on Consultation.

The principal arguments for participation rights are as follows[96]: it enables views to be taken into account before an administrative policy has hardened into a draft rule; it can assist Parliament with technical scrutiny; it can improve the quality of rules by input from interested parties with knowledge of the area being regulated; and allows those outside government to play some role in shaping of policy.

It is moreover not immediately self-evident why a hearing should be thought natural when there is some form of individualised adjudication, but not where rules are being made. The unspoken presumption is that a "hearing" will be given to a rule indirectly in Parliament, via representative democracy. We have already seen how far reality falls short of this ideal. Moreover, many of the rules are not statutory instruments and have, therefore, never seen the Parliamentary light of day at all.

C. Consultation Rights: Contentious Issues

15–020 Commentators who favour increased participation rights look approvingly at the USA where such rights are fostered to a greater extent than here, although that regime is not without difficulties.[97] Three principal issues can be identified if we wish to develop such rights.

First, there is the type of consultative process that might be established. There are a range of options. Thus, the US Administrative Procedure Act 1946 provides that notice of any proposed rule-making is to be published in the Federal Register, including a statement of the time and place of the rule-making proceedings and the terms or substance of the proposed rule.[98] There are three modes of participation, with varying degrees of formality. Most administrative rules are subject to what is termed *notice and comment*: the proposed rule is published and interested parties can proffer written comments. A small number of rules are subject to a *full trial type hearing*, which can include the provision of oral testimony and cross-examination.[99] Yet other rules are governed by an

---

[96] D. Galligan, *Due Process and Fair Procedures* (Oxford: Oxford University Press, 1996), Ch.4.

[97] R. Stewart, "The Reformation of American Administrative Law" (1975) 88 Harv. L.R. 1667; Baldwin, *Rules and Government* (1995), pp.74–80.

[98] Except where notice or hearing is required by statute, this does not apply to interpretative rules, general statements of policy, rules of agency organisation, procedure or practice, or in any situation in which the agency for good cause finds that notice and public procedures are impracticable, unnecessary, or contrary to the public interest.

[99] This more formal procedure operates when rules are required by statute to be made on the record after opportunity for an agency hearing, s.553(c). This criterion is narrowly construed, *United States v Florida East Coast Railway* 410 US 224 (1973).

intermediate or *hybrid process*, which entails more formality than notice and comment, but less than the trial type hearing.[100]

Second, there is the possibility that *dominant groups may exert excessive pressure* on the rulemaking authority. Pluralist writers in the United Kingdom recognised the existence of groups that influenced the political process.[101] They did not, however, regard groups as equal in power. Corporatist arguments, which postulate the existence of a dominant group with a "monopoly" of representational status, serve to underline this point. Some theorists go further and argue that agencies can be "captured" by the group they regulate. The agency comes to protect the client group and its interests rather than advancing the public interest.[102]

While the problem of inequality of group power is a real one it must, however, be kept within perspective. Given that such inequality exists, it is difficult to believe that the less advantaged groups will do better where there are no participatory rights. The more powerful groups will exert influence upon a public body even where there are no formal rights, through the very fact of their power. The introduction of a more structured system of participatory rights gives the less advantaged groups a chance to air their views. **15–021**

The problem can in any event be tackled in a number of differing ways. The courts should insist that the agency give adequate consideration to the range of groups who proffered evidence. This is valuable, but such intervention may come "too late". Certain less powerful groups may simply not be in a good position to advance their views before the agency. We may therefore need to devise strategies to help such disadvantaged groups put their case. This may entail direct financial aid, relief from costs and the provision of assistance in formulating and advancing their views.

Third, it might be argued that greater participatory rights can cause problems of *time, cost, and delay*. There are, however, responses to such concerns. It can be contended that such costs are worth bearing. If an autocrat made all decisions, they would doubtless be made more speedily. A cost of democracy is precisely the cost of involving more people. The argument for increased participatory rights is, moreover, based on the idea that the people consulted may improve the draft rule. If a less good rule emerges where there is no consultation then the total costs may be greater if the rule fails to achieve its objective. It is in any event recognised that there are certain areas where participatory rights are not suitable, for example, where time is of the essence, such as when it is necessary to combat an outbreak of foot and mouth disease.

---

[100] *International Harvester Co v Ruckelshaus* 478 F 2d 615 (DC Cir 1973); *Portland Cement Assn v Ruckelshaus* 486 F 2d 375 (DC Cir 1973); *Vermont Yankee Nuclear Power Corp v Natural Resources Defence Council, Inc* 435 US 519 (1978); A. Aman and W. Mayton, *Administrative Law*, 3rd edn (St Paul, MN: West, 2014), Chs 2–4.

[101] See paras 1–030 to 1–034.

[102] M. Bernstein, *Regulating Business by Independent Commission* (Princeton: Princeton University Press, 1955), p.270. Compare R. Posner, "Theories of Economic Regulation" (1974) 5 Bell Jnl. of Econ. & Mgmt. Sci. 335, 342.

D. Consultation and the Code of Practice

15–022 While there is no general legal right to be consulted in the United Kingdom, there is nonetheless a political code. The Cabinet Office was initially in the driving seat and issued a Code of Practice on Written Consultations, which applied from 1 January 2001,[103] replaced by a version in 2008, which was administered by the Department for Business, Innovation and Skills.[104] The 2008 Code was replaced by a set of Consultation Principles in 2013.[105]

15–023 The object of the Consultation Principles is to make written consultations more effective, to improve decision-making and to open up decision-making to a wider group of people. It does not have legal force. The governing principle is proportionality of the type and scale of consultation to the potential impact of the proposal or decision being taken. The subject matter which should be subject to consultation is less clear in the 2013 Principles than in the previous Codes, this being left largely to individual departments. This is also true in relation to the criteria for consultation.

The 2008 Code set out seven criteria for consultation: it should occur early enough to affect the policy outcome; there should be a minimum of 12 weeks for written consultation; there should be clarity about the proposals, the questions asked and the timescale for responses; the consultation should be clearly targeted and accessible; the burden on those consulted should be minimised so that consultations can be effective; consultation responses should be analysed carefully, feedback should be given regarding the responses received and how the consultation process influenced the policy; and officials running consultation exercises should seek guidance as to the best manner of doing so and share best practice.

The 2013 Principles are less clear in this respect. Some of the preceding criteria can be found in the 2013 Principles, such as the need for early consultation, clarity about the object of the consultation, taking it seriously, giving feedback on the consultation, and there is increased emphasis on digital consultation. However the 2013 Principles have changed the length of the consultation period, which is now specified as between 2–12 weeks, it being clear that the longer period is only contemplated for new and contentious policies.

The House of Lords' Secondary Legislation Scrutiny Committee was critical of some of the changes introduced by the 2013 Principles: it regarded six weeks as the minimum consultation period, save for exceptional cases; it was concerned that the governmental instruction to avoid disproportionate cost could be used to avoid the need for consultation, or unduly curtail it; the Committee stressed the need for active monitoring of the consultation process and for a redress mechanism where consultation did not comply with the principles; and it argued

---

[103] Cabinet Office, *Better Regulation Executive, Code of Practice on Consultation* (2005).

[104] See *http://www.berr.gov.uk/files/file47158.pdf* [accessed 20 July 2015].

[105] Cabinet Office, *Consultation Principles, https://www.gov.uk/government/uploads/system/uploads/attachment_data/file/255180/Consultation-Principles-Oct-2013.pdf* [accessed 20 July 2015].

that if secondary legislation was laid within the 12 weeks allowed for governmental response to consultation then the views of those consulted should be made available to Parliament.[106]

E. Conclusion

The political dimension to consultation is to be welcomed. The very fact that there is a centralised initiative that is regarded as binding on government departments and agencies, even if it is not enshrined in law, is a step forward. It can moreover be argued that this approach to consultation avoids the excessive legalism that can be attendant upon affording legally binding consultation rights. There is some force in this argument. **15–024**

The limits of the non-legal approach should, however, also be borne in mind. Thus, there is evidence of room for improvement in the way that consultation exercises are conducted in relation to, for example, delegated legislation.[107] Departments had considerable discretion as to whether to undertake consultation pursuant to the 2008 Code, and even more so under the 2013 Principles. There is moreover considerable variance in the use of consultation across government departments.

We should moreover not forget that where the relevant statute does not mandate consultation, claimants who are not consulted have no legal redress, unless they can show a legitimate expectation. This will be so even though they are affected significantly by the change in policy.

The *Greenpeace* case[108] demonstrates, however, the potential implications of the legitimate expectations doctrine. If a government department or agency formally announces that it will engage in consultation on a particular policy matter then it is arguable that this creates a legitimate expectation that such consultation will occur, and allows the courts to adjudicate on the adequacy of the consultation exercise. This could therefore open the door to judicial review of the adequacy of consultation exercises that are undertaken pursuant to the Consultation Principles.[109] *Niazi*[110] provides some support for this view. It held that while the Code did not commit the government to hold a consultation, the Code nonetheless applied when the government chose to consult. Moreover, in *EasyJet*[111] it was held that that even where consultation was not a legal requirement, if it was embarked on it had to be conducted properly and fairly.

---

[106] House of Lords Secondary Legislation Scrutiny Committee, *Seventeenth Report: The Government's Review of Consultation Principles,* HL Paper No.75 (Session 2013–14).

[107] House of Lords Merits of Statutory Instruments Committee, *Twenty-ninth Report: The Management of Secondary Legislation*, paras 91–93.

[108] *Greenpeace* [2007] EWHC 311 (Admin).

[109] The court was influenced in *Greenpeace* by the fact that the UK was a signatory to the Aarhus Convention, which required the government to provide opportunities for public participation in relation to the environment. This consideration however, affected the issue of whether it was open to the government to grant or withhold consultation in this area. It does not affect the point being made in the text that if the government does promise consultation then this can trigger a legitimate expectation allowing the court to adjudicate on the adequacy of the consultation.

[110] *Niazi* [2008] EWCA Civ 755.

[111] *easyJet* [2008] EWCA Civ 755.

This principle was endorsed in *Rusal*, where the Court of Appeal held that the principles from *Gunning* as to the adequacy of the consultation would be applied.[112] It is nonetheless clear from *Rusal* that the public body has discretion as to which options require consultation, and that the adequacy of the consultation depended on the sufficiency of the information in the context of the particular case.

6. DELEGATED LEGISLATION: JUDICIAL REVIEW

A. Procedural Ultra Vires and Formal Invalidity

15–025 We have already seen that delegated legislation may be enacted by a variety of procedures. If the requisite procedure is not followed, and that procedure is held to be mandatory rather than directory, it will lead to the invalidation of the legislation. This is exemplified by the mandatory statutory requirement to consult.

The secondary legislation will also be invalidated if it is formally outside the parent Act.[113] In one case a notice requisitioning certain property was held to be void because the notice did not exclude furniture and the power to requisition did not extend to furniture.[114] In another, a byelaw restricting access to a military site was impugned because the enabling legislation only allowed such byelaws to be made on condition that they did not infringe upon any rights of common.[115] On some occasions it may be necessary to pass legislation to correct an earlier mistake, such as when it was realised that certain regulations concerning fire services had never been laid as required by the parent Act. An Act of Indemnity was passed to correct the error.[116]

B. Substantive Ultra Vires

15–026 Delegated legislation may also be struck down because its substance infringes the parent Act, another primary statute, or constitutional principle. The courts have on occasion, especially during wartime, liberally construed statutory instruments,[117] but they generally undertake more searching review.

i. *Infringement of the primary Act*

15–027 A court may decide that the challenged regulation was illegal because it was outside the powers of the enabling legislation, or conflicted with rights granted by other legislation. The process of statutory interpretation will be affected by the importance of the rights at stake.

[112] *R. (United Company Rusal Plc) v London Metal Exchange* [2015] 1 W.L.R. 1375 at [25], CA (Civ Div); *R. v Brent London Borough Council, Ex p Gunning* (1985) 84 LGR 168.
[113] *R. (C) v Secretary of State for Justice* [2009] Q.B. 657, CA (Civ Div).
[114] *Patchett v Leathem* (1949) 65 T.L.R. 69.
[115] *DPP v Hutchinson* [1990] 2 A.C. 783, HL.
[116] National Fire Service Regulations (Indemnity) Act 1944.
[117] *R. v Halliday* [1917] A.C. 260, HL; *Liversidge v Anderson* [1942] A.C. 206, HL.

In the *Joint Council for the Welfare of Immigrants*[118] the secretary of state had made certain regulations acting under powers conferred by the Social Security Contributions and Benefits Act 1992 in order to discourage asylum claims by economic migrants. The effect of the regulations was to remove benefits from many of those seeking asylum. Simon Brown LJ held the regulations ultra vires, primarily because they rendered nugatory the rights of asylum seekers under the Asylum and Immigration Appeals Act 1993. Parliament could not, he said, have intended a significant number of genuine asylum seekers to be impaled on the horns of an intolerable dilemma[119]: "the need either to abandon their claims to refugee status or alternatively to maintain them as best they can but in a state of utter destitution". This could only be done by primary legislation.

In *Javed*[120] the Court of Appeal held that it was entitled to review subordinate legislation on grounds of illegality, impropriety or irrationality, notwithstanding that it had been approved by affirmative resolution, but that when reviewing for irrationality account would be taken of the nature and purpose of the enabling legislation. In the instant case the applicant challenged the legality of the subordinate legislation on the ground that it wrongly designated Pakistan as a country in respect of which there was no serious risk of persecution. The court accepted that the minister had a margin of appreciation in deciding whether there was such a risk in Pakistan, but decided nonetheless on a review of the evidence that there was such a risk for women, especially those who belonged to the applicant's minority sect.

ii. Breach of constitutional principle

Although we have no written constitution the courts use constitutional principles when construing delegated legislation. An instrument that contravenes such principles will be declared void, unless there is express statutory authority to justify the action. **15–028**

In *Wilts United Dairies*,[121] the Food Controller was empowered to regulate the sale, purchase, etc. of food and to regulate price. A dairy company was granted a licence to trade in milk, but it had to pay a charge of 2d per gallon. This condition was initially accepted by the company, but it later resisted and refused to pay. Despite its express consent to the condition, the court held that its refusal to pay was justified. The charge infringed the provision in the Bill of Rights 1689 that no money should be levied to the use of the Crown without the consent of Parliament. A power to charge would not be implied from the general power to control that trade.

---

118 *R. v Secretary of State for Social Security, Ex p. Joint Council for the Welfare of Immigrants* [1997] 1 W.L.R. 275, CA (Civ Div); *R. (BC) v North Yorkshire CC* [2014] EWHC 3335 (Admin).

119 *Council for the Welfare of Immigrants* [1997] 1 W.L.R. 275, CA (Civ Div) at 293.

120 *R. (Asif Javed) v Secretary of State for the Home Department* [2002] Q.B. 129, CA (Civ Div); *R. (MD (Gambia)) v Secretary of State for the Home Department* [2011] EWCA Civ 121.

121 *Attorney General v Wilts United Dairies Ltd* (1921) 39 T.L.R. 781.

The use of constitutional presumptions is also apparent in *Leech*.[122] The court struck down a rule that authorised a prison governor to read every letter from a prisoner and stop any that were objectionable or of inordinate length. The court held that the more fundamental the right interfered with, and the more drastic the interference, the more difficult was it to imply a rule-making power of this kind. The fundamental right in question was the right of access to court and it was held that the rule could not be upheld because of the extent to which it impeded the exercise of that right.

15–029 A different constitutional principle was evident in *Pankina*.[123] The Immigration Rules had to be laid before Parliament. The issue before the court was whether those rules could lawfully incorporate provisions from another document which had not itself been laid before Parliament. Sedley LJ held that this was not possible. The law could not, he said, abandon a constitutional principle which had stood for four centuries as a pillar of the separation of powers in what was a democracy under the rule of law. Parliament expected the Home Secretary to lay before it any rules that were proposed to manage immigration. The courts would expect such rules, like any other source of law, to be only those that had Parliament's approval.

The importance of constitutional principle was apparent once again in *A v HM Treasury*.[124] The House of Lords struck down orders made pursuant to the United Nations Act 1946, which were to implement in the UK resolutions from the UN concerning the freezing of assets of suspected terrorists. The 1946 Act was framed so as to give the executive broad power to make such Orders in Council as were deemed necessary or expedient to effectuate the UN resolutions. Notwithstanding this broad wording the House of Lords held that the contested orders were ultra vires. It reasoned that the rule of law demanded that decisions as to what was "necessary" or "expedient" could not be left to the uncontrolled judgment of the Executive. This would be unacceptable and conflict with the basic rules that lay at the heart of our democracy. Clear parliamentary authority would have to be shown if the Executive wished to be able restrict the basic rights of citizens in the manner contemplated by the contested orders and the 1946 Act would not be read so as to authorise what had occurred.

iii. Purpose, relevancy and reasonableness

15–030 Subordinate legislation will also be subject to the substantive controls that apply to administrative action in general. The courts will apply notions of purpose, relevancy and reasonableness to constrain discretionary power.[125]

Powers are granted for certain purposes. If it can be shown that subordinate legislation is being used for an improper purpose, other than that intended by the

[122] *R. v Secretary of State for the Home Department, Ex p. Leech (No.2)* [1994] Q.B. 198, CA (Civ Div); *Joint Council for the Welfare of Immigrants* [1997] 1 W.L.R. 275, CA (Civ Div) at 293; *R. v Lord Chancellor, Ex p. Witham* [1998] Q.B. 575 QBD; *Chester v Bateson* [1920] 1 K.B. 829.

[123] *Secretary of State for the Home Department v Pankina* [2011] Q.B. 376, CA (Civ Div).

[124] *A v HM Treasury* [2010] 2 A.C. 534 SC, relying on *R. v Secretary of State for the Home Department, Ex p. Simms & O'Brien* [2000] 2 A.C. 115, HL.

[125] See Chs 19 and 21.

parent Act, it will be declared void.[126] The courts will also intervene if the exercise of the delegated power is held to be unreasonable. An instrument will not be held to be unreasonable merely because the particular judge disagrees with its content, or believes that it goes further than is prudent, necessary, or convenient. The instrument must be manifestly unjust, involve the oppressive or gratuitous interference with the rights of those subject to it such as could find no justification in the minds of reasonable men, disclose bad faith, or be partial and unequal in its operation as between different classes.[127] An instrument may also be unreasonable if it is too vague, but the courts have in some instances construed statutory instruments generously.

In *McEldowney*,[128] a regulation was challenged that created a criminal offence of belonging to an organisation describing itself as a "republican club" or "any like organisation howsoever described". The person convicted belonged to such a club, and a majority upheld the conviction. This was despite the fact that no threat to public order was apparent, and notwithstanding that the wording of the regulation was vague to say the least. By way of contrast in *Bugg*,[129] the court struck down a byelaw restricting access to a military base on the ground that the area covered by the byelaw was not delineated clearly enough. This ruling must, however, now be seen in the light of *Percy*.[130] The court held that a byelaw should be regarded as valid unless it was so uncertain in its language as to have no ascertainable meaning, or so unclear in its effect as to be incapable of certain application in any case.

The substantive controls can be applied with varying degrees of intensity. This will be discussed in more detail below,[131] and is apparent in the *McEldowney* case. The courts have, moreover, made this explicit. In the *Nottinghamshire County Council* case,[132] the local authority challenged expenditure limits imposed by the secretary of state. Failure to comply with those limits led to a reduction in the rate support grant available to the local authority. The limits required the approval by resolution of the House of Commons before they could take effect. The local authority argued that these limits were unreasonable. Lord Scarman held that the courts should be reluctant to intervene on this ground. This was in part because the subject matter, public financial administration, inevitably involved political judgment by the minister. It was also because approval of the House of Commons had been given. The court would intervene if there had been a misconstruction of the statute. It would, however, be constitutionally inappropriate for the court to interfere on the ground of unreasonableness unless **15–031**

---

126 *Attorney General for Canada v Hallett & Carey Ltd* [1952] A.C. 427 ; *R. v HM Treasury, Ex p. Smedley* [1985] Q.B. 657, CA (Civ Div).

127 *Kruse v Johnson* [1898] 2 Q.B. 91 QBD. See also, *Monro v Watson* (1887) 57 L.T. 366; *Repton School Governors v Repton Rural DC* [1918] 2 K.B. 133, CA; *Sparks v Edward Ash Ltd* [1943] 2 K.B. 223.

128 *McEldowney v Forde* [1971] A.C. 632, HL.

129 *Bugg v DPP* [1993] Q.B. 473 DC.

130 *Percy v Hall* [1997] Q.B. 924, CA (Civ Div). The Court of Appeal preferred the formulation by Lord Denning in *Fawcett Properties Ltd v Buckingham CC* [1961] A.C. 636, HL at 677–678, to that of Mathew J in *Kruse v Johnson* [1898] 2 Q.B. 91 QBD at 108.

131 See Ch.19.

132 *R. v Secretary of State for the Environment, Ex p. Nottinghamshire CC* [1986] A.C. 240, HL.

the minister had abused his power, in the sense of deceiving the House or producing expenditure limits so absurd that he must have taken leave of his senses.[133] The House of Lords has endorsed this approach.[134]

While the subject-matter in such cases, economic regulation, may warrant less intensive review, the relevance of a resolution by the Commons may be questioned. We have already seen that the passage of such a resolution does not indicate any meaningful legislative scrutiny, and hence the effect of this approval is largely symbolic. This was acknowledged in *Orange Personal Communications*.[135] The court held that, when making regulations pursuant to s.2(2) of the European Communities Act 1972, the Executive must tell Parliament in clear terms what primary legislation was being repealed or amended for the purposes of applying the Community law in question. This was especially so, given that parliamentary scrutiny under s.2(2) was so limited.

C. Delegation

15–032 The normal principles concerning delegation apply. These will be dealt with below,[136] and can be briefly summarised here. The general rule is that a power must be exercised by the person on whom it is conferred. A necessary qualification exists in the case of ministers, where officials will exercise powers in the name of the minister. How far delegation will be allowed will depend upon the nature of the power in question and the general circumstances of the case. In principle, legislative power should be exercised by those in whom it is vested.[137]

D. Remedies

15–033 The presumption is that invalidity may be raised collaterally or directly.[138] This is particularly so when a criminal sanction may be imposed pursuant to, for example, a byelaw which the individual claims to be invalid. This can be challenged by way of defence to the criminal action. Collateral challenge may also take the form of a defence to a contract or tort action. There may, however, be instances where the statute is held to indicate that a direct challenge by way of an application for judicial review is the only way to raise certain kinds of error.[139]

A statutory instrument may be attacked directly through the declaration. Subject to the doubts voiced below,[140] the direct action should be brought as an

---

[133] *Ex p. Nottinghamshire CC* [1986] A.C. 240 at 247, 250–251.

[134] *R. v Secretary of State for the Environment, Ex p. Hammersmith and Fulham LBC* [1990] 1 A.C. 521; *Bank Mellat* [2013] UKSC 39 at 44.

[135] *R. (Orange Personal Communications Ltd) v Secretary of State for Trade and Industry* [2001] 3 C.M.L.R. 36 QBD; *R. (C)* [2009] Q.B. 657, CA (Civ Div).

[136] See Ch.18.

[137] See *Hawke's Bay Raw Milk Products Co-operative Ltd v New Zealand Milk Board* [1961] N.Z.L.R. 218. In the First World War sub-delegation of legislative power was not expressly authorised, but the Emergency Powers (Defence) Act 1939 allowed further delegation. This could produce as many as five tiers of authority; a veritable wedding cake of regulations.

[138] *Boddington v British Transport Police* [1999] 2 A.C. 143, HL.

[139] *R. v Wicks* [1998] A.C. 92, HL.

[140] See Ch.26.

application for judicial review for a declaration or injunction. The prerogative orders of certiorari and prohibition were traditionally regarded as applying only to judicial functions and hence as being inapplicable to delegated legislation. The inroads that have been made on this principle are considered below.[141] The scope of locus standi to challenge secondary legislation is not entirely clear. It has traditionally been assumed to be quite wide. However, in *Bugg* it was held that individuals have no right to complain of procedural defects in delegated legislation unless they have been prejudiced by the default.[142] It is unclear whether this aspect of the ruling survives the overruling of the case on other grounds. The possibilities of an injunction to prevent a minister from proceeding with making an instrument[143] and the possible immunisation of delegated legislation from judicial control[144] are considered later.

7. DELEGATED LEGISLATION: POSSIBLE REFORMS

There is no ready-made solution to solve, at the stroke of a pen, the problems with delegated legislation. Improvements are, however, possible. A Hansard Society Report, produced under the chairmanship of Lord Rippon, highlighted the problems.[145] Its recommendations for change in the primary legislative process have already been discussed. The Commission recognised that much delegated legislation was of real importance.[146] It stated that "we consider the whole approach of Parliament to delegated legislation to be highly unsatisfactory".[147] The Commission made a number of suggestions for improvement. **15–034**

A. Hansard Society 1993

i. Publication and access to the law

The Commission made its views on the present arrangements for publication and access to the law very clear.[148] **15–035**

> "At present the accessibility of statute law to users and the wider public is slow, inconvenient, complicated and subject to several impediments. To put it bluntly, it is often very difficult to find out what the text of the law is—let alone what it means. Something must be done."

It recommended that as far as possible new laws should not come into effect before they are published, and that the government should press ahead as fast as possible with a Statute Law Database, which would facilitate the publication and

---

141 See Ch.26. Mandamus seems to be subject to no such limitations and has been used in relation to byelaws, *R. v Manchester Corporation* [1911] 1 K.B. 560.

142 *Bugg* [1993] Q.B. 473.

143 See paras 26–031 to 26–032.

144 See Ch.28.

145 Hansard Society Commission on the Legislative Process, *Making the Law*, (1993).

146 Hansard Society Commission on the Legislative Process, *Making the Law*, p.89.

147 Hansard Society Commission on the Legislative Process, *Making the Law*, pp.89–90.

148 Hansard Society Commission on the Legislative Process, *Making the Law*, p.108.

updating of statute law.[149] There should, moreover, be financial assistance provided to bodies such as Citizens Advice Bureaus to help them to explain the law to the public.[150]

The Commission also addressed the problems that exist where a primary statute is to be implemented by delegated legislation. It suggested that the government should indicate the general nature of the regulations it intended to introduce, and that this could be done by a White Paper, or through an explanatory statement published with the Bill.[151]

ii. The subject-matter scrutinised by Parliament

15–036 We have already seen that the definition of a statutory instrument is purely formal, with the consequence that many rules of a legislative nature are not open to scrutiny by Parliament. The Commission did not consider this matter in any depth, but it did touch on the issue. The Commission noted that much sub-delegated legislation was not, and could not be, debated in Parliament. This was not, said the Commission, acceptable. It recommended that all Acts and delegated legislation should be drafted so that all important regulations and delegated legislation can be debated in Parliament.[152] The realisation of this particular recommendation is, as will be seen below, problematic.

iii. Debates on statutory instruments

15–037 The ineffectiveness of the regime for debating statutory instruments on the floor of the House has been noted above. The Rippon Commission proposed a number of significant alterations, which centred on greater use of standing committees.

For those statutory instruments subject to affirmative resolution the Commission suggested the following new procedure.[153] Unless the House otherwise ordered, all statutory instruments which require affirmative resolution should be automatically referred to standing committee for debate. This now represents current practice, since such instruments are referred to delegated legislation committees.[154] The Commission recommended that longer or more complex instruments could be referred to a special standing committee. Such standing committees should have the power to question ministers on the meaning, purpose and effect of the instrument.

For those statutory instruments subject to negative resolution then, unless the House otherwise ordered, all prayers for the annulment of such instruments should be referred to a standing committee. The procedure within the committee would be the same as for affirmative instruments, except that the MP who tabled the prayer would either move a motion for annulment of the instrument, or a

---

149 Hansard Society Commission on the Legislative Process, *Making the* Law, p.109.

150 Hansard Society Commission on the Legislative Process, *Making the* Law, p.113.

151 Hansard Society Commission on the Legislative Process, *Making the* Law, p.112.

152 Hansard Society Commission on the Legislative Process, *Making the* Law, p.93.

153 Hansard Society Commission on the Legislative Process, *Making the* Law, pp.91–93, 149.

154 House of Commons Information Office, Statutory Instruments (2008), pp.7–8, available at *http://www.parliament.uk/documents/commons-information-office/l07.pdf* [Accessed 20 July 2015]; Standing Orders of the House of Commons (HMSO, 2015), Order 118(3).

motion recommending its amendment. The current reality is that the Delegated Legislation Committees can consider the "prayer" against a statutory instrument subject to the negative procedure.[155]

These suggestions are to be welcomed. The centrality accorded to the standing committee as an initial vehicle for scrutiny is designed to alleviate the real difficulty of finding time to conduct the whole procedure on the floor of the House.

iv. *Committee scrutiny*

The function of the committees described above is to render the debate by Parliament more workable and thorough. There is still room for reform of the pre-existing committee regime. The Commission suggested a number of such reforms. **15–038**

Some relate to the work of the Joint Committee on Statutory Instruments. It proposed that, except in cases of emergency, no statutory instrument should be debated until the Joint Committee reported. Furthermore, if that committee reported that an instrument is ultra vires or otherwise defective, there should be no motion approving the instrument without a resolution to set aside the committee's findings.[156]

A further suggestion is for scrutiny of delegated legislation to be assigned to the departmental select committee responsible for that area, which would then report on those instruments that raise matters of public importance.[157] There is much to be said for this idea, which would help to alleviate the present malaise.[158]

The current committee system is beset by difficulties. These include the workload placed on the Joint Committee; its lack of expertise in many subject matter areas; lack of interest among MPs in the committee's work; and the hazy division between technical scrutiny and the merits. If departmental select committees reviewed statutory instruments then this would meet some of these problems. The workload would be spread among these committees, which are staffed by those with knowledge of the area.

v. *Consultation*

The Rippon Commission prefaced its recommendations about consultation and delegated legislation with this observation[159]: **15–039**

> "The importance of proper consultation on delegated legislation should not be underestimated. For many bodies its importance is equal to—or greater than—the importance of consultation on bills. And from the point of view of those directly affected, it is equally important to get

[155] Standing Orders of the House of Commons (HMSO, 2015), Order 118(4).

[156] Hansard Society Commission on the Legislative Process, *Making the Law*, p.91.

[157] Hansard Society Commission on the Legislative Process, *Making the Law*, p.90.

[158] The Procedure Committee also recommended the use of a departmental select committee for very important orders, coupled with the two-stage procedure which applies in the case of deregulation orders, Procedure Committee Delegated Legislation para.9.

[159] Hansard Society Commission on the Legislative Process, *Making the Law*, p.42.

> delegated legislation right. Delegated legislation may be of secondary importance to Ministers and those in Parliament … but to those to whom the law applies or to the practitioners … who have to apply it, the method by which the law is made is of little significance. Primary and delegated legislation are equally the law of the land."

This observation is to be welcomed, as are the suggestions which flow from it. The Commission recommended that there should be consultation where appropriate at the formative stage of delegated legislation, and that wherever possible departments should consult outside experts and affected bodies on the drafts of instruments they propose to submit to Parliament. Moreover, the guidelines for consultation on primary bills should be applied with suitable modification to delegated legislation.

The problem with this proposal relates not to its substance, but to its application. The force of law may well be required to ensure that departments really do consult in the desired manner, rather than by "marking" certain groups which are regarded as acceptable, with the consequence that others are unable to play any real part in this consultative process.

B. Hansard Society 2014

15–040 The Hansard Society returned to delegated legislation in its 2014 Report, aptly titled *The Devil is in the Detail*.[160] The Report makes for depressing reading, insofar as it highlights the continuing problems that beset this area, including: the lack of effective scrutiny on the floor of the House or in committee; the fact that many statutory instruments are simply made by the minister and not subject to any scrutiny at all; the fact that many such instruments come into force before consideration by the relevant committee; and the fact that only 16 statutory instruments out of over 169,000, 0.01%, in 65 years have been rejected.

C. The Select Committee on Procedure

15–041 The Select Committee on Procedure also made valuable suggestions for reform of delegated legislation. It issued a major report in 1996,[161] and returned to the topic in a report in 2000,[162] in which it endorsed the conclusions reached in the earlier study. Both reports stressed the failings of the existing system, describing it as palpably unsatisfactory.

First, statutory instruments do not receive scrutiny in proportion to their importance or merits. This was because certain trivial matters were subject to the affirmative procedure, while some important matters were dealt with by the negative resolution procedure. The Committee recommended the establishment of a Sifting Committee, which would examine all statutory instruments subject to

---

160 Hansard Society, *The Devil is in the Detail: Parliament and Delegated Legislation* (2014).

161 Select Committee on Procedure, *Delegated Legislation*, HC Paper No.152 (Session 1995–96). See also, Select Committee on Modernisation of the House of Commons, *First Report*, HC Paper No.190 (Session 1997–98), para.83.

162 Select Committee on Procedure, *First Report: Delegated Legislation*, HC Paper No.48 (Session 1999–2000).

annulment.[163] The Committee would recommend those instruments that were of sufficient political importance for debate in standing committee and put down a motion to this effect. The debate would then take place before the time limit for prayers had expired. This committee would also liaise with departmental select committees, a proposal welcomed by the Liaison Committee.[164]

Second, the debates on such instruments in standing committee were criticised as being meaningless, because they did not take place on a substantive amendable motion. The Committee recommended that the motions in delegated legislation standing committees should be substantive and amendable, and that where the government was defeated there should be up to an hour's further debate in the House.

Third, the Committee felt that there was need for a "super-affirmative" procedure, to allow more thorough scrutiny of a small number of complex statutory instruments by departmental select committees. This would be modelled on the procedure used for deregulation and regulatory reform orders. The later report of the Committee also left open the possibility of greater use of departmental select committees more generally in relation to delegated legislation.[165]

C. The House of Lords' Merits of Statutory Instruments Committee

The House of Lords' Merits of Statutory Instruments Committee also made recommendations for improvement, and focused on departmental management of statutory instruments.[166] It recommended that in each department there should be one member of top management accountable to the relevant minister for the efficiency and effectiveness in preparing statutory instruments, as well as for ensuring that the finished products met the requirements of good regulation. Departments should prepare annual management plans for their statutory instruments, and they should be given guidance on best practice regarding the planning and management of secondary legislation programmes. Statutory instruments and their explanatory memoranda should be subject to review in the course of preparation by a senior official who was sufficiently detached from the subject matter to be able to assess its intelligibility to the layman reader. Departmental plans for secondary legislation should also include a target date for post-implementation review of each statutory instrument.[167] **15–042**

The Merits Committee also had reservations about the existing consultation regime. Thus, it recommended that: government should take action to ensure that the 12-week consultation requirement from the Consultation Code of Practice was met other than in exceptional cases; consultation should be mandatory for all

[163] Select Committee on Procedure, *Delegated Legislation*, paras 33–36; Select Committee on Procedure, *First Report: Delegated Legislation*, paras 14–15.

[164] Liaison Committee, *First Report*, HC Paper No.323-I (1996–97), para.33.

[165] Select Committee on Procedure, *First Report: Delegated Legislation*, para.54.

[166] House of Lords Merits of Statutory Instruments Committee, *Twenty-ninth Report: The Management of Secondary Legislation*, para.126.

[167] House of Lords Merits of Statutory Instruments Committee, *Thirtieth Report: What Happened Next? A Study of Post-Implementation Reviews of Secondary Legislation*.

instruments that transpose EU obligations into UK law; there should be an opportunity for ordinary citizens, as well as representative groups, to make their views known; and departments should report the outcome of the consultation in the explanatory memorandum.

The Merits Committee in addition directed certain recommendations towards government rather than individual departments. The government should take action to ensure that no instrument is laid before Parliament less than 21 days before it is due to come into force unless there are clear and compelling reasons for doing so. The government should moreover put more impetus behind the process of consolidation and should aim to publish consolidated electronic versions of each instrument following amendment. Once a public database of statute law is available, it should be extended as quickly as possible to cover secondary as well as primary legislation.

8. RULES MADE BY THE ADMINISTRATION

A. Type and Rationale

15–043 There is a duality latent in the term legislative instrument. When we speak of delegated legislation we mean the grant of power by the parent legislature to a minister or other body to make rules or regulations. While the test of what is to count as a statutory instrument in the 1946 Act is primarily one of form,[168] the idea of publication and legislative scrutiny is premised on the hypothesis that the rules thus made are themselves legislative in nature. Legislative in this sense signifies that the rule has a generality of application that distinguishes it from a mere executive order. Sub-delegated legislation poses problems at both levels. It may be unclear whether Parliament delegated power to a particular person, and it may be questionable whether the rule thus made really was legislative in character or not.

There is, however, an important category of rules outside that of sub-delegated legislation. There may be no express legislative mandate to make rules, the administration nonetheless makes rules that are legislative in character, using that term in the second sense. They are of a generality of application such that if they were juxtaposed to real statutory instruments they would be indistinguishable in terms of their nature or content. Thus, although such rules may be made by the administration, they are not necessarily administrative rules. Some of them may be, but many are not. Such rule-making can enhance justice in that it allows interference with private interests only on the condition that the individual knows of the rule in advance and can plan his or her actions accordingly.

There are various *types* of such rules. Codes of practice, circulars, directions, rules and regulations are all to be found within the administrative landscape. These labels are not terms of art. A suggested classification categorises administrative rules in the following manner[169]: procedural rules; interpretive

[168] Except for rules made after the 1946 Act came into force under statutes existing prior to that date.
[169] R. Baldwin and J. Houghton, "Circular Arguments: The Status and Legitimacy of Administrative Rules" [1986] P.L. 239, 240–244.

guides; instructions to officials; prescriptive/evidential rules; commendatory codes; voluntary codes; rules of practice; management and operation; and administrative pronouncements.

There are differing *rationales* for such rules, and for preferring them to more formal delegated legislation. Four such reasons can be distinguished.[170] First, even where no explicit power to make regulations is granted to a department or agency, it will often make rules to indicate how it will exercise its discretion. This is a natural tendency for bureaucracies when faced with a recurring problem. The debate about rules versus discretion will be addressed below.[171] Second, non-legal rules facilitate the use of non-technical language, as exemplified by the Highway Code, and the Health and Safety Codes. Third, such rules may be preferred because they are more flexible than statutory instruments, and hence can be changed more easily. Finally, these rules may be preferred to delegated legislation precisely because they are not legally binding. They enable policies to be developed voluntarily in the sense that "persuasion may be preferable to compulsion".[172] **15–044**

We should not therefore deprecate the use of such rules. The cogency of particular arguments used in favour of informal rules must nonetheless be carefully analysed. For example, the argument that informal rules are preferred because they reflect a voluntary approach whereby reliance is placed on co-operation and consent rather than the force of law, could mean three very different things.

It could indicate that a policy approved by the legislature is then implemented by a code, rather than formal legislation, because it is felt that this will be more efficacious. It could alternatively exemplify a "corporatist strategy", whereby the Executive and a major interest group bargain independently of the legislature to attain a goal, which may be opposed by other less powerful interest groups, and/or the legislature. It could finally mean that a powerful executive implements a code or rule which the relevant interest groups oppose, but which they are powerless to fight. Legislative scrutiny can be avoided, and the minimum of legal formalism troubles the Executive in pursuit of its aim. Not all informal rules are therefore necessarily more truly consensual in nature than those norms which emerge as legislation.

B. Legal Status

The precise legal status of these rules may differ depending on the type of rule in question. Three points of general importance can, however, be made. **15–045**

First, the fact that a department or agency does not have express power to make rules does not render them invalid. The capacity to make such rules flows from the way in which they are allowed to exercise their discretion. The courts

[170] G. Ganz, *Quasi-Legislation: Recent Developments in Secondary Legislation* (London: Sweet & Maxwell, 1987), Ch.6; Baldwin, *Rules and Government* (1995), Ch.4.

[171] See Ch.18.

[172] Ganz, *Quasi-Legislation: Recent Developments in Secondary Legislation* (1987), pp.97–98.

have held that rules or policy guidelines are valid provided that they are not too rigidly applied, and provided that certain other conditions are met.[173]

Second, the precise legal status of any particular rule can only be discerned by examining the relevant statutory provisions. Thus legislation may, for example, stipulate that a code, such as the Highway Code, should have a certain degree of legal force in legal proceedings, by identifying the weight to be given to a breach of the code in any such action.[174] Codes may also possess "indirect" legal effect.[175] Non-compliance with the provisions may provide a reason why, for example, a television programme contractor should not have its franchise renewed.[176] Non-compliance with a code may also furnish the rationale for the passage of a statutory instrument, the object of which is to provide "full" legal force for the attainment of the code's objectives.[177] It is not therefore surprising that the judiciary can be divided as to the status of a rule, even within a particular area.[178]

Third, even if a particular rule is not "related to" primary legislation in any of the ways considered earlier, it may still have legal consequences in a double sense: provided that the rule is not too rigidly applied, it can be dispositive of a person's case[179]; and the existence of such a rule may, as we have seen, generate consultation rights if the public body seeks to resile from the application of its rule.[180]

C. Rules made by the Administration: Problems

15–046 The first problem presented by such rules is that their promulgation by the Executive, together with the relevant interest group, may bypass the legislature and foreclose the possibility of parliamentary scrutiny. As Stewart states,[181] "the ultimate problem is to control and validate the exercise of essentially legislative powers that do not enjoy the formal legitimation of one-person one-vote election". A second problem flows from the first, in that particular pressure groups may exercise excessive influence over the rules that emerge. It may be difficult for the general public to have input into the proposed rule. A third cause for concern centres upon the rule of law. Many of the rules are unpublished, or not readily accessible, and their legal status may be unclear. Yet other rules fit poorly with the relevant parent legislation, and appear to countenance action inconsistent with the enabling statute. Finally, such rules have been used on

[173] See Ch.18.

[174] See, e.g. Road Traffic Act 1988 s.38(7).

[175] Ganz, *Quasi-Legislation: Recent Developments in Secondary Legislation* (1987), pp.16–18.

[176] Communications Act 2003 ss.319 and 325.

[177] Local Government, Planning and Land Act 1980 ss.2–3.

[178] Compare *R. v Heathrow Airport Immigration Officer, Ex p. Bibi* [1976] 1 W.L.R. 979 CA (Civ Div), *R. v Home Secretary, Ex p. Hosenball* [1977] 1 W.L.R. 766, CA (Civ Div), *R. v Immigration Appeal Tribunal, Ex p. Bakhtaur Singh* [1986] 1 W.L.R. 910, HL, *Pankina v Secretary of State for the Home Department* [2011] Q.B. 376, CA (Civ Div) on the status of immigration rules.

[179] See Ch.18.

[180] See para.15–022.

[181] Stewart, "The Reformation of American Administrative Law" (1975) 88 Harv. L.R. 1667, 1668.

issues of considerable political contention, thereby rendering the law "most vague at the points where it should be most clear".[182]

D. Rules made by the Administration: Possible Solutions

i. Direct control by Parliament

Direct control would require any rule of a legislative character to be subject to parliamentary scrutiny. This would reverse the formalistic premise of the Statutory Instruments Act 1946: delegated legislation is subject to parliamentary scrutiny and publication only where the instrument is described as a statutory instrument.[183] If we desire direct validation by Parliament the basic premise of the 1946 Act would, therefore, have to be modified so that any legislative rule formulated by a public body, whether under express delegation or not, would be subject to legislative oversight, subject to limited exceptions for rules of internal organisation and the like.[184] There are two difficulties with this approach. **15–047**

The first problem is that it may be difficult to decide what constitutes a "legislative rule". This point must, however, be kept within perspective. Criticism of the distinction between legislative and executive, or legislative and administrative, has force because it is thought to be irrelevant as a criterion for the application of, for example, certiorari. The position is different here. The distinction is important in this context. It is rules of a legislative character that we believe ought to be controlled by the legislature. The 1946 Act with its formalistic approach simply ducks the whole matter. More precisely, it allows the decision to reside with the government. The Executive will frame the legislation, and will therefore decide whether the delegated powers should be termed statutory instruments.

The second problem is the effectiveness of any such control. We have already seen the constraints on effective legislative scrutiny. Adding extra tasks to an already overburdened system of legislative control, both on the floor of the House and in committee, will give cause for hope only to the most sanguine.[185] These problems should, therefore, be borne in mind when assessing proposals, such as that of the Rippon Commission, that Acts and delegated legislation should be drafted to ensure that all important regulations can be debated in Parliament.[186]

ii. Legislative specification of standards

Parliament in its initial grant of authority could specify the standards it wishes the public body to apply. It could, alternatively, empower the relevant minister to **15–048**

[182] Baldwin and Houghton, "Circular Arguments: The Status and Legitimacy of Administrative Rules" [1986] P.L. 239, 268.

[183] Although all Orders in Council made under statutory as opposed to prerogative power are automatically so regarded.

[184] Administrative Procedure Act 1946 s.553(b) (US).

[185] Certain pieces of quasi-legislation are subject to legislative oversight and scrutiny by select committee, Ganz, *Quasi-Legislation: Recent Developments in Secondary Legislation* (1987), pp.26–32.

[186] Hansard Society Commission on the Legislative Process, *Making the Law*, para.382.

supply guidelines or directions to the body in the course of its operations. This is a device that has been used in relation to nationalised industries and other agencies. There is no doubt that it could be used to a greater extent than at present. Legislative specification of standards may, however, be of limited utility for novel problems, where the precise interests to be weighed are unclear at the outset. This problem can be partially circumvented by granting power to the minister to give directions after consultation with the public body. This is in itself constrained by the type of public institution in question. If it is one that warrants a high degree of autonomy from party political pressures then ministerial directives will be inappropriate.

iii. Consultation

15–049 Consultation in the rule-making process is another option. The extent to which statute and the common law presently provide consultation rights has been considered earlier. Consultation is even more central here than in the context of delegated legislation. The latter will at least see the light of day through publication and will be subject to some legislative scrutiny. If we decide that other forms of rule-making are not suited to legislative scrutiny, then validation and control by a different method becomes more important. Consultation through the representation of interested parties can go some way to achieving this. The previous discussion is relevant here, as is the Cabinet Office's Consultation Principles.

iv. Judicial control

15–050 There is clearly an overlap between judicial control and consultation rights, since it is the judiciary that interprets such rights. However, the judiciary have a role to play in this area independent of the issue of consultation. The courts' role is as follows.[187]

First, the court will decide whether the code or circular is susceptible to judicial review. For example, in *Gillick*[188] Lord Bridge stated that the general rule was that the reasonableness of advice contained in non-statutory guidance could not be subject to judicial review, but that there was an exception to this general rule. If a government department promulgated advice in a public document that was erroneous in law the court could correct this.

Second, in so far as codes, circulars, etc. are given certain evidentiary or substantive force within legal proceedings, it is the judiciary who will interpret the meaning they should bear.[189] They will also review the interpretation of a

[187] Ganz, *Quasi-Legislation: Recent Developments in Secondary Legislation* (1987), pp.41–46; Baldwin, *Rules and Government* (1995), pp.85–119.

[188] *Gillick v West Norfolk and Wisbech Area Health Authority* [1986] A.C. 112, HL; *R. v Secretary of State for the Home Department, Ex p. Westminster Press Ltd* [1992] C.O.D. 303 DC; *R. (Axon) v Secretary of State for Health* [2006] Q.B. 539 QBD; *R. (Association of British Travel Agents Ltd (ABTA)) v Civil Aviation Authority* [2006] EWHC 13 (Admin); *R. (Letts) v Lord Chancellor* [2015] EWHC 402 (Admin).

[189] *R. v Secretary of State for the Home Department, Ex p. Lancashire Police Authority* [1992] C.O.D. 161 QBD.

code where it has been applied by an administrative agency.[190] The intensity of any such review may vary from area to area,[191] and courts may disagree upon the appropriate intensity of review in a particular area.[192]

Third, the existence of an agency rule or code will generate an obligation of consistency in relation to its application, such that it should not be departed from without cogent reasons,[193] and it might lead to enforceable legitimate expectations.[194]

Finally, the courts can apply the tests of purpose, relevancy, reasonableness and fettering of discretion to determine whether a rule is within the ambit of the relevant empowering legislation, or whether undue weight has been given to one circular and another has been ignored.[195] These tests are normally applied to the individual exercise of discretion. Departmental or agency choices should not however, be immune from such oversight merely because they assume the form of a rule.[196] The courts' willingness to invalidate a rule on the grounds of, for example, unreasonableness may differ from area to area. It appears that the courts are more willing to consider this where the rule is made in the context of a relatively clear statutory framework, against which its vires and reasonableness can be judged.[197] The court will then pronounce upon the legality of the rule, even if it is non-statutory.

v. *Conclusion*

Quasi-legislation has been present for a considerable time. The term was already current in the 19th century,[198] and concern was expressed 70 years ago.[199] Renewed interest is timely,[200] given the importance of the issue addressed. No single, simple solution is likely to be forthcoming. There is a range of options, none of which is free from difficulty. At the very least quasi-legislation should be published, and rendered accessible to those affected by it. **15–051**

---

190 *HTV v Price Commission* [1976] I.C.R. 170, CA (Civ Div).

191 *R. v Secretary of State for the Home Department, Ex p. Gangadeen* [1998] C.O.D. 216, CA (Civ Div).

192 See, e.g. *R. v Criminal Injuries Compensation Board, Ex p. Schofield* [1971] 1 W.L.R. 926 DC; *R. v Criminal Injuries Compensation Board, Ex p. Thompstone* [1984] 1 W.L.R. 1234, CA (Civ Div).

193 *R. (Munjaz) v Mersey Care NHS Trust* [2006] 2 A.C. 148, HL.

194 See Ch.22.

195 *JA Pye (Oxford) Estates Ltd v West Oxfordshire DC and the Secretary of State for the Environment* [1982] J.P.E.L. 557.

196 See Ch.18.

197 *Gillick* [1986] A.C. 112; *Royal College of Nursing of the UK v Department of Health and Social Security* [1981] A.C. 800, HL.

198 A. Todd, *On Parliamentary Government in England* (1867–1869), Vol.I, p.288; H. Parris, *Constitutional Bureaucracy* (1969), pp.193–194.

199 R. Megarry, "Administrative Quasi-Legislation" (1944) 60 L.Q.R. 125.

200 Baldwin and Houghton "Circular Arguments: The Status and Legitimacy of Administrative Rules" [1986] P.L. 239, 240–244; Ganz, *Quasi-Legislation: Recent Developments in Secondary Legislation* (1987); Baldwin, *Rules and Government* (1995).

9. THE IMPACT OF EU LAW

15–052 We have already considered the mechanisms for the scrutiny of EU law by parliamentary committees. The discussion would, however, be incomplete if it did not also advert to the broader significance of EU law for rule-making. This is not the place for detailed exegesis on the European Union's legislative process, which can be found elsewhere.[201] The present object is to make clear the impact of EU law on the subject at hand.

First, it should be recognised that regulatory competence in many areas has shifted to the European Union and away from the nation state. In many areas the main body of rules will emanate from the European Union.

Second, it would, however, be mistaken to conclude that all regulatory competence within these areas now resides with the European Union. The precise allocation of power as between national and Union authorities varies from area to area. It is not uncommon to find regulatory competence shared between the nation state and the European Union. This has led commentators to depict the regulatory process as multi-level governance, in which sub-national, national and EU actors take part.

Third, the process by which the European Union makes rules which would, in all probability, otherwise have been made by national delegated legislation or rule-making, is problematic. Space precludes detailed exegesis of the complex procedures that operate within the European Union.[202] Suffice it to say that the problems of ensuring legitimacy, accountability and control are just as difficult when rules are made by the European Union as when they are made by a nation state.

[201] P. Craig and G. de Búrca, *EU Law, Text, Cases and Materials*, 6th edn (Oxford: Oxford University Press, 2015), Ch.5; P. Craig, "Institutions, Power and Institutional Balance", in P. Craig and G. de Búrca (eds), *The Evolution of EU Law*, 2nd edn (Oxford: Oxford University Press, 2011), Ch.3.
[202] P. Craig, *EU Administrative Law*, 2nd edn (Oxford University Press, 2012), Ch.5.

CHAPTER 16

ERROR OF LAW

1. CENTRAL ISSUES

i. A public body is given authority to decide on a particular issue. If a furnished tenancy exists the public body may adjudicate on the rent. If an employee is unfairly dismissed she may be awarded compensation. All such grants of authority may be expressed in the following manner: if X exists the public body may or shall do Y. X may consist of a number of different elements, factual, legal and discretionary. An individual contends that the public authority has made an error of law in the meaning of the term employee, which is part of the X question. **16–001**

ii. Judicial review traditionally dealt not with the correctness of the findings, but with their legality. For a full rehearing of the merits, appeal, a creature of statute, is required. The inherent power of the courts to review the findings of a public body has, by way of contrast, been concerned with ensuring that the decision-maker remains within its jurisdiction. Whether the distinction between review and appeal is sustainable will be considered in due course

iii. If judicial review is drawn too narrowly then the spectre is raised of the public body becoming a power unto itself. The Albert Hall is deemed to be a furnished tenancy and a rent set for it. However, if review is drawn too broadly it will approximate to appeal on law. The findings made by the public body will be binding only if judged right by the reviewing court.

iv. The conceptual basis for judicial review over the conditions of jurisdiction was examined above.[1] In essence the courts' control over jurisdiction was premised on the assumption that they ensured that the public body remained within the boundaries of what Parliament intended it to examine by ensuring that those conditions were present. However, this gave little guidance as to the extent of control.

v. The courts from the 16th to the 20th century used either the collateral fact doctrine or the theory of limited review to determine the extent of control. Both theories were premised on a distinction between jurisdictional and non-jurisdictional issues, although they drew the divide differently. The assumption was that a jurisdictional error of law was reviewable, but a non-jurisdictional error of law was not, unless the error of law was on the

---

[1] See Ch.1.

face of the record. The divide between jurisdictional and non-jurisdictional error was, however, always fraught with difficulty for reasons that will be explained below.

vi. The modern approach, which dates from the latter part of the 20th century, rejected the jurisdictional/non-jurisdictional divide. The starting assumption is that all errors of law are subject to judicial review and that the reviewing court will substitute judgment for that of the primary decision-maker on such issues.

vii. This approach avoids the difficulties of the jurisdictional/non-jurisdictional divide. There are, however, difficulties with the modern approach. It is based on the twin assumptions that reviewing courts should substitute judgment on all such legal issues and that this is the only way to maintain control over the organs of the administrative state. The courts have more recently signalled variation in the test for review primarily in the context of decisions made by tribunals.

viii. The final part of the chapter will consider the broader policy arguments concerning the scope of review, and will examine experience in some other common law jurisdictions, notably the USA and Canada.

2. THEORIES OF JURISDICTION

A. Introduction

16–002 A general word concerning the theories will be helpful in understanding what follows. The first two theories attempted to draw the following distinction. Errors which related to the *type* or *kind* or *scope* of case into which a public body could inquire were regarded as jurisdictional. Errors which related to the *truth* or *detail* of the findings that it made were categorised as non-jurisdictional. The line between the two was said to provide the justification for judicial review. The court only intervened when the public body was outside the "scope" assigned to it by the legislature. The judiciary would not intervene if the public body made an error within its assigned area, since this would eradicate the distinction between review of legality and appeal. The first two theories drew this distinction in different ways, and there were very real difficulties with this dichotomy.

The following analysis is not predicated on the assumption that the jurisdictional/non-jurisdictional distinction was always used in a purely logical manner. Some courts used the ambiguity inherent in that dichotomy in an instrumental fashion: the decision whether to label an X factor as jurisdictional or non-jurisdictional was influenced by a judicial desire to intervene or not as the case may be. It would nonetheless be wrong to assume that most judges viewed the distinction in an instrumental fashion. It is clear from reading the case law that many believed that a real division could be drawn in analytical terms.

The more recent approaches, by way of contrast, largely ignore any distinction between scope and truth/detail. Judicial intervention is based on error of law as the organising principle. While this approach avoids the difficulties of the earlier theories it is not unproblematic. Thus, there are issues of classification to be resolved, such as the division between law and fact. There are also important policy issues which require discussion, such as whether the courts are always better suited to resolve issues of law than are the public bodies they are reviewing.

B. Collateral Fact Doctrine

Until the 1960s the most widely accepted theoretical explanation of which issues should be held to go to jurisdiction was the collateral or preliminary or jurisdictional fact doctrine. It has a long historical lineage, but the most sophisticated explanation was that given by Diplock LJ,[2] as he then was. **16–003**

i. The core thesis: preliminary questions and merits

A public body is given power on the existence of certain conditions. There are certain preliminary questions that it must decide before it can proceed to the merits. These include matters such as whether the public body was properly constituted and whether the case was of a kind referred to in the statute. The public body must make an initial determination on such matters, but its decision is not conclusive. If the court on review believes that the requisite situation spoken of in the statute did not exist then the conclusion reached by the public body will be a nullity. Such preliminary questions can involve fact, law or discretion. **16–004**

ii. Difficulties: ambit of the preliminary question

The crucial issue is therefore the ambit of the preliminary or collateral question. The nature of this dilemma can be described as follows. Let us revert to the example used before of a public body with power to decide whether a furnished tenancy exists. The existence of a furnished tenancy may be expressed as follows: **16–005**

$$f\,(a,\, b,\, c,\, d\, \ldots\, n) = \text{furnished tenancy}$$

This equation is merely convenient shorthand. The elements within the bracket constitute the furnished tenancy or, conversely, the term furnished tenancy is a shorthand description of the presence of those elements. Thus, here "*a*" would represent the need for time certain in a lease, "*b*" the intent of the parties, "*c*" the fixtures and fittings required to render the tenancy furnished. These factors can be law, fact, mixed fact and law or discretion. The letter "*f*" is simply shorthand for indicating that a furnished tenancy will be determined by the elements within the bracket. This picture is a simplified one. The position will often be more complex. It is very common for a statute to say if X1, X2, X3 exist the public body may or shall do Y. X2 and X3 would, like X1, be shorthand descriptions presuming the existence of elements within the bracket

[2] *Anisminic Ltd v Foreign Compensation Commission* [1968] 2 Q.B. 862, CA (Civ Div) at 887–905. Compare Lord Diplock's view in *Racal Communications Ltd, Re* [1981] A.C. 374, HL.

he collateral fact doctrine was predicated on the assumption that certain X ors could be said to be jurisdictional, while other such factors would be rded as non-jurisdictional. The fundamental problem was that in an everyday se all the elements relating to X, or, to X1, X2, X3, could be said to condition jurisdiction. The enabling statute always states if X1, X2, X3 exist, you may or shall do Y. Yet, if X1, X2, and X3, and all the elements constituting them, were always held to be jurisdictional, the dividing line between review and appeal would disappear and the public body would only have power to give the right answer, this being that which accorded with the opinion of the reviewing court.

Diplock LJ attempted to solve this conundrum by drawing the following distinction: a misconstruction of the enabling statute describing the *kind* of case into which the public body was meant to inquire would go to jurisdiction, but misconstruing a statutory description of the *situation* that the public body had to determine would, at most, be an error within jurisdiction.

It is however impossible to draw this line with certainty, because the definition of "kind" or "type" is *inevitably* comprised of descriptions in the statute of the "situation" which the public body has to determine. The former represents the sum, the latter the parts. This is simply demonstrated. If one were asked to produce a summary of the *kind* of case into which the public body was intended to inquire one would do so by looking at the *situations* which the public body had to determine as mentioned in the statute. These situations consist of the statutory terms in the enabling legislation. Thus, in a case such as *Anisminic* one would say that if there was property in Egypt, which belonged to a British national or successor in title at the relevant dates, which had been seized, the FCC should award compensation. The *kind* of case is comprised of the *situations described in the statute* which the public body has to determine. The distinction between *kind* and *type* on the one hand, and *truth* or *detail* or *situation* on the other, proved illusory. There was no predictability as to how a case would be categorised before the court pronounced on the matter. There was also no ex post facto rationality that could be achieved by juxtaposing cases and asking why one case went one way and another was decided differently.[3]

C. Limited Review

i. The core thesis: relative rather than absolute facts

16–006 This theory was strongly advocated by Gordon.[4] If a public body is given jurisdiction over a certain topic the question is whether the facts relating to that

[3] In *Anisminic* [1968] 2 Q.B. 862 at 904–905, Diplock LJ found that the error was, at most, one within jurisdiction. It did not relate to the "kind" of case into which the FCC could inquire. No indication is given as to why the error was categorised in this way. See, further, the examples given in D. Gordon, "The Relation of Facts to Jurisdiction" (1929) 45 L.Q.R. 458.

[4] Gordon, "The Relation of Facts to Jurisdiction" (1929) 45 L.Q.R. 458; "Observance of Law as a Condition of Jurisdiction" (1931) 47 L.Q.R. 386, 557; "Conditional or Contingent Jurisdiction of Tribunals" (1959–1963) 1 U.B.C.L. Rev. 185; "Jurisdictional Fact: An Answer" (1966) 82 L.Q.R. 515; "What did the *Anisminic* Case Decide?" (1971) 34 M.L.R. 1. See also P. Hogg, "The Jurisdictional Fact Doctrine in the Supreme Court of Canada; *Bell v Ontario Human Rights Commission*" (1971) 9 Osgoode Hall L.J. 203.

topic exist in the opinion of the public body. Thus, if a public body is given jurisdiction over assault the question is whether an assault exists in the opinion of that public body. Any public body might err in a finding that it makes: no public body is infallible. But so long as the public body decides the question assigned to it by the law, its relative opinion will bind, subject to appeal. Jurisdiction must involve the power to make a wrong as well as a correct decision. The public body's jurisdiction was limited, but that limit was determined not by the truth or falsehood of its findings, but by their scope or nature. It was sufficient that the charge was laid in the correct form. Thus, jurisdiction was determined at the commencement not at the conclusion of the inquiry.

ii. Difficulties: distinction between scope and truth

There are real difficulties with the Gordon theory. It may, for example, be hard to decide when an inquiry commences. It may also be that this limited review is unacceptable on policy grounds. The policy issues will be discussed in detail later. For the present, attention will be focused on the most crucial part of the theory, the distinction between scope and truth. **16–007**

For Gordon it was fallacious to say that if a public body made a mistake as to the factors involved in a subject-matter properly before it, and thereby misconceived the questions that it should consider, that it thereby exceeded its jurisdiction. Any error was only an error within jurisdiction. This can best be understood by reverting to our previous example concerning a furnished tenancy, which could be expressed as:

$$f(a, b, c, d \ldots n) = \text{furnished tenancy}$$

The elements in the bracket represent the need for time certain, intent of the parties, amount of fixture and fittings, etc. The premise underlying Gordon's argument was that scope or subject-matter meant simply the assertion of the existence of a furnished tenancy by the public body. Any error concerning *a, b, c,* etc. would, at most, be an error within jurisdiction. What Gordon sought to do, therefore, was to avoid the pitfalls of the collateral fact doctrine by erecting a wall between the words furnished tenancy and the bracket. The court was not allowed to consider the meanings assigned to those elements, except to find a non-jurisdictional error. Gordon's argument was therefore premised on a formal separation between the term furnished tenancy, which went to scope, and the elements within the bracket which constituted it. An error relating to scope would be jurisdictional and thus, if the wrong term was used instead of furnished tenancy, a court should intervene. Mistakes concerning elements within the bracket were, however, non-jurisdictional at most.

The words furnished tenancy are however only a shorthand description of the presence of the elements, factual and legal, within the bracket, and therefore to regard an error relating to them as jurisdictional, but mistakes concerning *a, b, c* or *d* as not, makes little sense. People may disagree as to whether, for example, an assault has in fact occurred. But to argue from this that we can divorce the term furnished tenancy or assault from the elements within the bracket does not follow.

It would mean that an assault could exist without any of the elements which comprise that term. No one would, for example, have to be placed in fear for their bodily safety. This would have fundamental consequences for the way we use legal language. The words furnished tenancy or assault would be empty vessels into which anything could be poured. The formal incantation of such words would suffice for the public body to remain within the scope of its authority.

It might be argued that the content of the bracket constituting the term furnished tenancy or employee or assault should be for the relative opinion of the public body. This might happen in a particular area. There is nothing to prevent the legislature preferring a public body's interpretation of the term, for example, employee, to that of the reviewing court. Gordon's argument is however dependent upon showing not just that this might happen, but that it must happen. There is no reason why this should be so.

D. Extensive Review: The Academic Argument

16–008 A theory of extensive review was advanced by Gould.[5] A similar approach represents the current law. Gould's argument will be considered within this section, while the case law will be analysed in the following section.

i. The core thesis: preliminary questions and substance

16–009 Gould's argument was as follows. A public body had to answer a preliminary question, which was whether it was empowered to answer the issue placed before it. This could not be decided finally by the public body itself. A decision that jurisdiction existed was a necessary precondition to the exercise of jurisdiction, and it was not therefore a question on which the public body could go right or wrong.

The factors which came within this category were those which must exist independently of the substance to be decided. These factors were given. Their meaning could not be altered by the public body itself. It was not that they were facts in the absolute. Gould, like Gordon, agreed that they were relative. However, they were for the relative opinion of the reviewing courts, not the public body. These factors were all legal rules and concepts, because such rules must have a given meaning established by the courts. Thus, all legal terms within the bracket would go to jurisdiction and worrisome problems of jurisdictional versus non-jurisdictional errors of law are left behind.

ii. Difficulties: the rationale for the underlying assumption

16–010 The key to the theory is the argument that all issues of law are "given", to be determined by the courts. Three reasons can be extracted from the argument as to why this should be so.

[5] B. Gould, "*Anisminic* and Jurisdictional Review" [1970] P.L. 358; H. Rawlings, "Jurisdictional Review after Pearlman" [1979] P.L. 404.

1. Parliamentary intent

Legal issues are "given" Gould argued because Parliament intended them to be decided by the ordinary courts. This argument could be regarded as a *rebuttable* presumption, but then the inexorable logic of the theory would break down. It could not be said that legal rules were always to be determined by the ordinary courts. Insofar as there is a rebuttable presumption that all questions of law should be for the ordinary courts this is not to be derived from an allegedly logical a priori argument that all legal questions are "given". The argument must therefore be based upon an *irrebuttable* presumption as to parliamentary intent. This might be derived from constitutional theory or judicial practice. **16–011**

There are difficulties with the argument based on *constitutional theory*. Parliament is sovereign and in theory it can give the task of determining the legal meaning of a term to, for example, a tribunal or inferior court. It manifests an explicit intent to do so when it places a privative clause in a statute empowering a public body. The courts, it is true, have construed such clauses to mean that jurisdictional errors are not protected.[6] It is equally true that Lord Diplock stated[7] that the normal presumption is that Parliament intends questions of law to be decided by the courts, but his Lordship did not state that this was an irrebuttable presumption. This presumption has been repeated in *Page*, but their Lordships were clear that this was not, in all cases, to be viewed as an irrebuttable presumption. The fact that it is not an irrebuttable presumption was reinforced more recently in *Cart*[8] and *Jones*.[9] It should moreover be emphasised that allowing a public body to give the meaning to a statutory term does not entail the absence of judicial control, since the courts could still review the rationality of the public body's interpretation.

We can now turn to *judicial practice*. It could be argued that Gould's irrebuttable presumption finds support in the fact that the judiciary makes the ultimate decision on questions of law. However, the courts have not for the last 300 years recognised, nor have they acted upon, a logic which renders all questions of law jurisdictional. To the contrary, review differed over time, but it is indisputable that the judiciary accepted that non-jurisdictional errors of law could exist. A number of courts gave substantial latitude to the decision-maker. The judicial approach has altered in recent years, as the courts have taken authority over most legal questions. It is however difficult to build an *irrebuttable* presumption on 40 years' judicial practice, given the contrary position that prevailed for 300 years hitherto.[10]

---

6 See Ch.28.

7 *Racal Communications Ltd, Re* [1981] A.C. 374, HL; *O'Reilly v Mackman* [1983] 2 A.C. 237, HL.

8 *R. (Cart) v Upper Tribunal* [2011] UKSC 28.

9 *R. (Jones) v First-tier Tribunal* [2013] UKSC 19.

10 The argument presented within this section assumes a variety of guises. It should not, however, be confused with the principle that the courts always have jurisdiction to declare the law unless that jurisdiction is specifically excluded by Parliament. This principle finds its application in the construction of privative clauses and alternative remedies, and is designed to preserve the *possibility* of judicial review. It says nothing as to the *scope* of review.

2. The impossibility argument

16–012 It would not, said Gould, be possible to talk of error of law at all unless such elements had a "given" meaning, because such language implied a departure from a criterion laid down by the courts. This is to confuse cause and effect. When the legal meaning of a term is determined by the courts, then the phrase "error of law" implies a deviation from that standard. It cannot provide the *reason why* all matters of law should have an interpretation provided by the ordinary courts. It is perfectly possible for the legal meaning to be provided by the public body, subject to control through rationality review.

The possibility of the latter occurring is not contrary to the rule of law. Many legal terms have a number of possible meanings, each of which is reasonable. Words or phrases such as "furnished tenancy", "successor in title", "course of employment", "trade dispute", "boat" and "resources", are open to a spectrum of reasonable meanings. The statement that the public body made an "error of law" means that the construction placed on the term by the court is preferred to that of the public body. Parliament might, however, prefer the particular construction adopted by the specialist public body to that given by the generalist court. The courts can maintain control through review of the rationality of the public body's interpretation, rather than simply substituting their own preferred meaning.

3. The uniformity argument

16–013 A third argument is that it is only by giving the legal meaning of a term to the courts that uniformity can be achieved, as opposed to diverse interpretations of the same term being given by different public bodies. The limits of this argument should be noted. It will not apply to public bodies with an internal hierarchy, the top of which can impose a uniform meaning, nor will it necessarily apply where there is only one tribunal in an area. The need for uniformity is greatest where there are a number of parallel tribunals deciding the same point. Uniformity should be achieved by providing an appeal rather than by distorting review to become appeal, or by insisting that the particular meaning adopted by one of the set of tribunals should be applied consistently by those in a similar position.

E. Extensive Review: The Judicial Argument

i. The core thesis: review for error of law

16–014 Judicial indications that the courts would no longer follow the collateral fact doctrine were apparent for some time.[11] These were confirmed by the House of Lords in the *Page* case.[12] A detailed analysis of the case will be provided below. The present discussion is confined to the general assumptions that underlie the decision.

[11] *Anisminic* [1969] 2 A.C. 147, *Racal Communications Ltd, Re* [1981] A.C. 374, HL, and *O'Reilly v Mackman* [1983] 2 A.C. 237, HL.

[12] *R. v Hull University Visitor, Ex p. Page* [1993] A.C. 682, HL.

Lord Browne-Wilkinson gave the leading judgment.[13] He held that the effect of the *Anisminic* case was to render obsolete the distinction between errors of law on the face of the record, and other errors of law, by extending the doctrine of ultra vires. Thenceforward, it was to be taken that Parliament had only conferred a decision-making power on the basis that it was to be exercised on the correct legal basis, such that misdirection in law when making the decision rendered it ultra vires. The general rule was that any (relevant) error of law could be quashed. The constitutional basis of the courts' power was that the tribunal's unlawful decision was ultra vires. In general, the law applicable to an administrative institution was the ordinary law of the land. Therefore, "a tribunal or inferior court acts *ultra vires* if it reaches its conclusion on a basis erroneous under the general law".[14] It is clear from the judgment that the presumption that any error of law is reviewable can be rebutted, and the strength of this presumption can vary depending on the institution being reviewed.[15]

ii. *Difficulties: assumptions and consequences*

It is necessary to distinguish between four different aspects of the reasoning used in the *Page* decision. First, there is disapproval of the collateral fact doctrine. This is to be welcomed. The difficulties with that doctrine have been discussed, and it is high time that it was discarded. **16–015**

Second, there is the replacement of that doctrine with the test that all errors of law are open to scrutiny. The similarity between this approach and Gould's is readily apparent. Some of the concerns expressed about the Gould theory are therefore equally relevant here. If *Page* were taken to mean that the court would substitute its view for that of the public body in relation to *any* X factor that involves *any* element of law then it would be problematic. The courts would become embroiled in the minutiae of disputed interpretations as to what many, or all, of the X conditions meant. The approach is based on the presumption that the courts' interpretation of phrases such as "employee" or "course of employment" is necessarily to be preferred to that of the agency, and that substitution of judgment is the only way to exercise control over such agency interpretations. Neither of these assumptions is well founded. The courts' particular interpretation of such terms may not necessarily be better than that of the agency, and adequate control may be maintained through a different standard of review.[16]

Third, although Lord Browne-Wilkinson based judicial intervention on the ultra vires principle, it was given a different meaning than hitherto. When that principle was the basis for intervention under the collateral fact doctrine, there was a distinction between jurisdictional and non-jurisdictional errors. The former would result in the decision being ultra vires and void, because the tribunal acted outside its jurisdiction. The latter were errors within jurisdiction and could only be challenged if the error of law was on the face of the record. However, the ultra

[13] Lord Slynn and Lord Mustill dissented on other grounds, but agreed with the majority on this general issue, *Page* [1993] A.C. 682 at 705–706.
[14] *Page* [1993] A.C. 682 at 702.
[15] *Page* [1993] A.C. 682 at 702–704.
[16] See para.16–040.

vires principle as used in *Page* bears a different meaning. Any error of law may lead to the decision being ultra vires, because the tribunal reached its conclusion on a basis that was erroneous under the general law. Sir John Laws argued that once the distinction between jurisdictional and non-jurisdictional errors was discarded, there was no longer any need for the ultra vires principle as such, since the courts were in reality intervening to correct errors of law.[17] The rationale for the judicial persistence with the principle is that it provides a legitimating device for the exercise of the courts' power. Sir John Laws captures this idea[18]:

> "'Ultra vires' is, in truth, a fig-leaf; it has enabled the courts to intervene in decisions without an assertion of judicial power which too nakedly confronts the established authority of the Executive or other public bodies … The fig-leaf was very important in *Anisminic*; but fig-leaf it was. And it has produced the historical irony that *Anisminic*, with all its emphasis on nullity, nevertheless erected the legal milestone which pointed towards a public law jurisprudence in which the concept of voidness and the ultra vires doctrine have become redundant."[19]

Fourth, there is a duality latent in the meaning given to the ultra vires principle by Lord Browne-Wilkinson.[20] One reading sees it as being based on legislative intent, in the sense that Parliament intended that all errors of law should be open to challenge. Thus his Lordship stated that Parliament "had only conferred the decision-making power on the basis that it was to be exercised on the correct legal basis",[21] with the consequence that misdirection in law when making the decision rendered it ultra vires. A different reading of the ultra vires principle is found later in the judgment. Ultra vires is equated with the general law of the land, which includes the common law. On this view the ultra vires principle is no longer based exclusively on legislative intent. It simply becomes the vehicle through which the common law courts develop their controls over the administration[22]:

> "[T]he constitutional basis of the courts' power to quash is that the decision of the inferior tribunal is unlawful on the grounds that it is *ultra vires*. In the ordinary case, the law applicable to a decision made by such a body is the general law of the land. Therefore, a tribunal or inferior court acts *ultra vires* if it reaches its conclusion on a basis erroneous under the general law."

F. Conclusion

16–016 Two conclusions can be drawn from the preceding analysis. The first is that the line between scope and truth/detail cannot furnish a satisfactory guide as to what should, and what should not, be regarded as jurisdictional. The second point is equally important. The scope of jurisdictional review is not self-defining. It is not

[17] Sir John Laws "Illegality: The Problem of Jurisdiction", in M. Supperstone and J. Goudie (eds), *Judicial Review* (London: Butterworths, 1992), Ch.4.

[18] Laws "Illegality: The Problem of Jurisdiction", in Supperstone and Goudie (eds), *Judicial Review* (1992), p.67.

[19] By laying the foundation for the idea that all errors of law can be reviewed.

[20] P. Craig, "Ultra Vires and the Foundations of Judicial Review" [1998] C.L.J. 63, 79–80; Laws "Illegality: The Problem of Jurisdiction", in Supperstone and Goudie (eds), *Judicial Review*.

[21] *Page* [1993] A.C. 682 at 701.

[22] *Page* [1993] A.C. 682 at 702.

capable of being answered by linguistic or textual analysis of the statute alone, however assiduously that is performed. The critical question, the answer to which underlies any statement concerning jurisdictional limits, is whose relative opinion on the relevant issue should be held to be authoritative. All theories encapsulate a view about this, although it is often not openly expressed. The answer resides not in a logic which compels, for example, that all questions of law must always be for the courts or the tribunal. Such logic is flawed. A response must ultimately be based on a value judgment, the precise content of which will not necessarily always be the same. We shall consider this in more detail after examining the case law.

3. CASE LAW HISTORY

The present attitude of the courts towards judicial review cannot be adequately understood without some idea of 18th- and 19th-century case law. This history reveals the differing judicial views as to how far they should be reviewing tribunals and other inferior bodies. **16–017**

A. Limited Intervention

A number of leading authorities supported only limited review. To revert to our example of the equation, they were saying that if the subject-matter lies within the tribunal's jurisdiction, the factors within the bracket constituting that subject-matter would not be reassessed. In *Bolton*[23] magistrates found that the plaintiff had occupied a parish house as a pauper and that a formal notice to quit had been served on him. They directed constables to enforce the notice. The applicant sought certiorari. He wished to show by affidavit evidence that he had not occupied the house as a pauper, but had paid rates and carried out repairs, and that he had not therefore been chargeable on the parish during the period of his occupation. **16–018**

Lord Denman CJ drew the following distinction. Where the charge laid before the magistrate did not constitute the offence over which the statute gave him jurisdiction, affidavit evidence could be introduced. So too could it where the charge was insufficient, but had been misstated. In both cases, extrinsic evidence could be introduced to show a want of jurisdiction. However, where the charge had been well laid before the magistrate, on its face bringing itself within his jurisdiction, any error would be only an error within jurisdiction.

The question of jurisdiction depended not on the truth or falsehood of the charge, but upon its nature and was determinable at the commencement not at the conclusion of the inquiry. The limit of the inquiry must be whether the magistrates had jurisdiction, supposing the facts alleged in the information to be true. The magistrates' return contained all that was needed to give them

---

[23] *R. v Bolton* (1841) 1 Q.B. 66 KBD at 72–74. See also, *Brittain v Kinnaird* (1819) 1 B. & B. 432 at 442; *Ackerley v Parkinson* (1815) 3 M. & S. 411; *Wilson v Weller* (1819) 1 B. & B. 57; *Fawcett v Fowlis* (1827) 7 B. & C. 396; *R. v Justices of Cheshire* (1838) 8 Ad & E 398; *Re Baines* (1840) Cr. & Ph. 31; *Cave v Mountain* (1840) 1 M. & G. 257.

jurisdiction over the subject-matter: occupation of a parish house belonging to the hamlet and service of a notice to quit. The application for certiorari was therefore rejected. There were many examples of the same approach.[24]

B. Collateral or Preliminary Fact Cases

16–019 There were also numerous cases that applied the collateral fact doctrine. Certain facts were required to be proven to the satisfaction of the reviewing court before the magistrate or tribunal could go right or wrong. An early example can be seen in *Nichols.*[25] The plaintiff lived in Totteridge and was evaluated for the poor rates by the assessors for Hatfield. In a trespass action the plaintiff's case was upheld. Hatfield and Totteridge were separate places and the one could not levy rates for the other. A number of similar cases concerned with the Poor Laws followed.[26]

What had been implicit in the above cases was made explicit in *Bunbury.*[27] The plaintiff brought an action in debt against the defendant owner of the land, claiming the amount due as being for tithes. The defendant argued that part of the land was exempt from tithes, but an assistant tithe commissioner denied this. The defendant claimed that the determination was an excess of jurisdiction. Coleridge J found for the defendant. The existence of land subject to a tithe was a point collateral to the decision of the assistant tithe commissioner.[28]

> "Now it is a general rule, that no court of limited jurisdiction can give itself jurisdiction by a wrong decision on a point collateral to the merits of the case upon which the limit to its jurisdiction depends; and however its decision may be final on all particulars, making up together that subject-matter which, if true, is within its jurisdiction, and, however necessary in many cases it may be for it to make a preliminary inquiry, whether some collateral matter be or be not within the limits, yet, upon this preliminary question, its decision must always be open to inquiry in the superior court."

[24] See *Bolton* (1841) 1 Q.B. 66; *Brittain* (1819) 1 B. & B. 432; *Ackerley* (1815) 3 M. & S. 411; *Wilson* (1819) 1 B. & B. 57; *Fawcett* (1827) 7 B. & C. 396; *Justices of Cheshire* (1838) 8 Ad & E 398; *Re Baines* (1840) Cr. & Ph. 31; *Cave* (1840) 1 M. & G. 257; *Mould v Williams* (1844) 5 Q.B. 469; *Allen v Sharp* (1848) 2 Ex 352; *R. v Buckinghamshire JJ* (1843) 3 Q.B. 800; *R. v Wilson* (1844) 6 Q.B. 620; *R. v Wood* (1855) 5 El. & Bl. 49; *Revell v Blake* (1872) 7 C.P. 300; *Usill v Hales* (1878) 3 C.P.D. 319; *R. v Whitfield* (1885) 15 Q.B.D 122; *R. v Justices of the Central Criminal Court* (1886) 17 Q.B.D 598.

[25] *Nichols v Walker* (1632–1633) Cro. Car. 394.

[26] *Milward v Caffin* (1778) 2 Black. W. 1330; *Lord Amherst v Lord Somers* (1788) 2 T.R. 372; *Weaver v Price* (1832) 3 B. & Ad. 409; *Governors of Bristol Poor v Wait* (1834) 1 A. & E. 264; *Fernley v Worthington* (1840) 1 Man. & G. 491. See also, cases on title, *Thompson v Ingham* (1850) 14 Q.B. 710 at 718; *Dale v Pollard* (1847) 10 Q.B. 505; *Chew v Holroyd* (1852) 8 Ex. 249.

[27] *Bunbury v Fuller* (1853) 9 Ex. 111.

[28] *Bunbury* (1853) 9 Ex. 111 at 140; *R. v Badger* (1856) 6 El. & Bl. 138; *R. v Stimpson* (1863) 4 B. & S. 301; *Ex p. Vaughan* (1866) L.R. 2 Q.B. 114; *Elston v Rose* (1868) L.R. 4 Q.B. 4; *Ex p. Bradlaugh* (1878) 3 Q.B.D 509.

C. Attempts at Reconciliation

There cannot be any reconciliation on the basis that some judges preferred more limited, while others opted for more extensive review.[29] The most common strategy was to say that both groups of cases were equally valid and that differences turned on the legislative instrument.[30] 16–020

Thus in *R. v Commissioners for Special Purposes of Income Tax*[31] Lord Esher MR distinguished between two types of tribunal. There were tribunals which had jurisdiction if a certain state of facts existed but not otherwise; it was not for the inferior tribunal to determine conclusively on the existence of such facts. There could, however, be a tribunal which had jurisdiction to determine whether the preliminary state of facts existed; here it would be for the inferior tribunal to decide on all the facts.

This reconciliation does not with respect withstand examination. It is impossible by juxtaposing the legislative instruments in these cases to determine why one case should fall in one category rather than the other. All statutes say if X exists, you may or shall do Y. The answer as to who is to determine X (and the factors constituting X) is dependent on which theory of jurisdiction is accepted. The two groups of cases discussed above reflect different answers to that question, and Lord Esher's analysis simply reiterates ex post facto that divergence. The analysis does not provide an ex ante tool to determine which group a case should fall into. This is not to say that a statute might not assign the relative meaning of "if X", as between courts and tribunals, differently in diverse areas. It is to say that whether it has done so cannot be determined by asking whether the statute requires a certain state of facts to exist before a decision is reached: all statutes always do this.

4. Current Case Law

A. Impact of *Anisminic*

The passing of the Victorian age, significant in so many spheres, brought no great change in this area. There is no magic in the divide between the 19th and 20th centuries so far as the scope of judicial review is concerned. There were still cases advocating only limited review.[32] These were the heirs of *Brittain* and *Bolton*. There were also decisions which adopted a more interventionist 16–021

---

[29] Lord Denman CJ decided *R. v Bolton* (1841) 1 Q.B. 66 and *Governors of Bristol Poor v Wait* (1834) 1 A. & E. 264; Coleridge J decided *R. v Buckinghamshire JJ* (1843) 3 Q.B. 800 and *Bunbury v Fuller* (1853) 9 Ex. 111: and see Coleridge J *arguendo* in *Thompson v Ingham* (1850) 14 Q.B. 710 at 713.

[30] For a different, and unsuccessful, attempt at reconciliation, see *Thompson* (1850) 14 Q.B. 710 at 718.

[31] *R. v Commissioners for Special Purposes of Income Tax* (1888) 21 Q.B.D 313. See also, *Colonial Bank of Australasia v Willan* (1874) L.R. 5 P.C. 417.

[32] *R. v Mahony* [1910] 2 I.R. 695; *R. v Bloomsbury Income Tax Commissioners* [1915] 3 K.B. 768 KBD; *R. v Nat Bell Liquors Ltd* [1922] 2 A.C. 128; *R. v Swansea Income Tax Commissioners* [1925] 2 K.B. 250 KBD; *R. v Minister of Health* [1939] 1 K.B. 232, CA; *Tithe Redemption Commission v Wynne* [1943] K.B. 756, CA.

attitude,[33] using the collateral or preliminary fact doctrine. These were the descendants of *Bunbury*. It was still difficult to determine which matters should be characterised as collateral or preliminary, and it was admitted that there could be errors of law within jurisdiction which, if they appeared on the face of the record, would be quashed.[34]

The scope of review was markedly affected by *Anisminic*.[35] The plaintiff was an English company that owned property in Egypt prior to 1956. In November 1956 the property was sequestrated by the Egyptian authorities, and in April 1957 the sequestrator sold the property to TEDO, an Egyptian organisation. Anisminic put pressure on their customers not to buy ore from TEDO, as a result of which an agreement was reached in November 1957 whereby the plaintiff sold the mining business to TEDO for £500,000. In February 1959 a Treaty was made between the United Kingdom and the United Arab Republic, which provided for the return of sequestrated property, except property sold between October 1956 and August 1958. A sum of £27,500,000 was paid by the United Arab Republic in final settlement of claims to property which was not being returned. Orders in Council were passed setting out the conditions for participation in the fund.

The Foreign Compensation Commission (FCC) found that Anisminic did not qualify. The Foreign Compensation (Egypt) (Determination and Registration of Claims) Order 1962[36] stated in art.4(1)(b)(ii) that the applicant and the successor in title should be British nationals on October 31, 1956 and February 28, 1959. The FCC interpreted this to mean that they had to inquire whether there was a successor in title and, if so, whether the person qualified under art.4(1)(b)(ii). TEDO was a successor in title according to the FCC and was not a British national at the relevant dates, therefore the plaintiff failed. The plaintiff claimed that the nationality of the successor in title was irrelevant where the claimant was the original owner and sought a declaration that the determination was a nullity.

The House of Lords[37] found for the plaintiffs. Lord Reid stated that jurisdiction in a narrow sense meant only that the tribunal should be entitled to enter on the inquiry. There were, however, a number of ways in which, having correctly begun the inquiry, the tribunal could do something which rendered its decision a nullity. Misconstruction of the enabling statute so that the tribunal failed to deal with the question remitted to it, failure to take account of relevant considerations, and asking the wrong question were, said Lord Reid, examples of this.[38] The plaintiff's construction of successor in title was correct and the decision by the FCC was a nullity. Lord Reid's judgment significantly broadened the scope of review. A court, if it wished to interfere, could always characterise an alleged error as having resulted from asking the wrong question, or having taken account of irrelevant considerations.

---

[33] *R. v Fulham, Hammersmith and Kensington Rent Tribunal, Ex p. Zerek* [1951] 2 K.B. 1 KBD; *R. v Fulham, Hammersmith and Kensington Rent Tribunal, Ex p. Hierowski* [1953] 2 K.B. 147.

[34] *R. v Paddington North and St. Marylebone Rent Tribunal, Ex p. Perry* [1956] 1 Q.B. 229 DC.

[35] *Anisminic Ltd v Foreign Compensation Commission.* [1969] 2 A.C. 147, HL.

[36] SI 1962/2187.

[37] *Anisminic* [1969] 2 A.C. 147. The case was also concerned with privative clauses, Ch 28.

[38] *Anisminic* [1969] 2 A.C. 147 at 171.

Lord Pearce and Lord Wilberforce reached their conclusions in similar way.[39] The tribunal had a limited authority, and it was for the reviewing court to keep it within its assigned area. It was for the court to determine the true construction of a statute delineating that area. Lack of jurisdiction could arise in various ways, such as absence of a condition precedent to the tribunal's jurisdiction, irrelevancy, and asking the wrong question. Lord Pearson agreed that if there had been an error it would have been jurisdictional, but found no such mistake.[40] Lord Morris dissented. He realised the implications of the majority judgments and pointed out that the Order "bristled" with words requiring statutory construction. It could not, said his Lordship, be the case that any misconstruction of any of these terms would involve a jurisdictional error.[41] Three points can be made about the case. 16–022

First, "asking the wrong question" or "irrelevancy" tell one that an error has been made, not whether the error was jurisdictional.[42] The step from "asking the wrong question", to the error being regarded as jurisdictional, presupposes that any "condition" to the exercise of jurisdiction becomes jurisdictional. The assumption is that questions of law are for the ordinary courts. The tribunal must give what the reviewing court regards as the correct meaning to the statutory terms, before the tribunal can be properly within the sphere of its jurisdiction. Concepts such as "asking the wrong question" simply function as the vehicle through which the court substitutes its views on the meaning of the statutory term for that of the tribunal. This reasoning reduces the division between jurisdictional and non-jurisdictional error to vanishing point.

Second, the language of judicial intervention should not conceal the issue in cases such as *Anisminic*, which is the meaning of an X condition. The language of "asking the wrong question" and the like is simply an indirect way for the court to express the conclusion that it believes that a different construction of the term should be substituted for that adopted by the agency.

Third, notwithstanding the broad potential for jurisdictional error, Lord Reid reaffirmed the continued existence of errors of law within jurisdiction.[43] This is difficult to reconcile with the general tenor of his judgment. Later case law has drawn out the implications of *Anisminic* more fully, and held that the case eradicated the distinction between jurisdictional and non-jurisdictional error.

B. From *Anisminic* to *Racal*

It was over a decade before the House of Lords considered the issue again in the *Racal* case. In the meantime *Anisminic* provided a broad armoury for later courts. If a court wished to categorise an error as jurisdictional it could do so by using the "wrong question" or "irrelevant consideration" formula. However, the courts could choose whether to use this armoury. If the court did not wish to intervene it 16–023

[39] *Anisminic* [1969] 2 A.C. 147 at 194–195, 207–210.
[40] *Anisminic* [1969] 2 A.C. 147 at 220–222.
[41] *Anisminic* [1969] 2 A.C. 147 at 182–190.
[42] A point made by Diplock LJ in the Court of Appeal [1968] 2 Q.B. 862 at 904–905. See also *R. v Furnished Houses Rent Tribunal for Paddington and St. Marylebone, Ex p. Kendal Hotels Ltd* [1947] 1 All E.R. 448 at 449; *R. v Paddington North and St. Marylebone Rent Tribunal, Ex p. Perry* [1956] 1 Q.B. 229 at 237–238.
[43] *Anisminic* [1969] 2 A.C. 147 at 174.

could achieve this result by saying that there was no error at all, by characterising the error as one within jurisdiction, or by defining jurisdiction more narrowly than in *Anisminic*. Two cases may be contrasted by way of example.

In *Moore*,[44] the claimant sought certiorari on the basis that the Supplementary Benefits Commission had misinterpreted the meaning of the term "resources" for the purposes of calculating supplementary benefits. Lord Denning MR found that the interpretation of the Commission was correct, but made it clear that he did not wish the legislation to become a hunting ground for lawyers whereby the court, on review, would have to interpret every minute point of law.

This may be contrasted with Lord Denning MR's decision in *Pearlman*.[45] The question was whether the installation of central heating was "an improvement made by the execution of works amounting to a structural alteration" within the Housing Act 1974. Lord Denning held that the line between errors of law which went to jurisdiction and those within jurisdiction was a fine one, and that the characterisation would often be dependent upon whether the court wished to intervene. Distinctions between errors within and errors going to jurisdiction should be discarded. Any error of law should be jurisdictional if the case depended upon it.[46]

C. The Uncertainty of *Racal*

16–024 Despite Lord Denning's observations, it was too early to build a pyre on which to consign conventional doctrine to its timely end. The courts continued to equivocate as to whether the traditional approach should be maintained. Put more accurately, individual judges may have been clear as to their preferences, but those preferences did not always coincide. This is clear from *Racal Communications Ltd, Re*.[47] Lord Diplock, with whom Lord Keith agreed, drew a tripartite distinction as to the scope of review.[48]

First, administrative tribunals or authorities were subject to the full rigours of the *Anisminic* judgment: the parliamentary intent was presumed, subject to a clear contrary indication, to be that questions of law were to be decided by the courts. The distinction between errors within jurisdiction and errors going to jurisdiction was, for practical purposes, abolished, and any error of law would automatically result in the tribunal having asked itself the wrong question. The resultant decision would be a nullity. Second, inferior courts were subject to a different test. It would depend on the construction of the statute whether Parliament intended questions of law to be left to an inferior court. There was no presumption that it did not so intend. The third category was the High Court. These courts were not subject to judicial review, which only applied to

[44] *R. v Preston Supplementary Benefits Appeal Tribunal, Ex p. Moore* [1975] 1 W.L.R. 624, CA (Civ Div); *R. v Industrial Injuries Commissioner, Ex p. Amalgamated Engineering Union (No.2)* [1966] 2 Q.B. 31; *Allen and Mathews Arbitration, Re* [1971] 2 Q.B. 518 QBD.

[45] *Pearlman v Keepers and Governors of Harrow School* [1979] Q.B. 56, CA (Civ Div); *ACT Construction Ltd v Customs and Excise Commissioners* [1981] 1 W.L.R. 49, CA (Civ Div), the point was not touched on in the House of Lords [1982] 1 All E.R. 84.

[46] *Pearlman* [1979] Q.B. 56 at 69–70.

[47] *Racal Communications Ltd, Re* [1981] A.C. 374, HL.

[48] *Racal Communications Ltd, Re* [1981] A.C. 374 at 381–382.

administrative authorities and inferior courts. Appeal was the only corrective for a mistake by a High Court judge. There was, however, little support in the other judgments either for Lord Diplock's tripartite standard of review, or for the extensive review which his Lordship advocated for administrative institutions.[49]

D. The Impact of *Page*

It was to be over a decade before the House of Lords (though not the Privy Council) had another detailed look at the issue. Decisions between *Racal* and *Page* did little to establish a uniform approach to the scope of review. Some decisions, such as *South East Asia Fire*,[50] persisted with the traditional collateral fact doctrine, rejecting arguments that the distinction between jurisdictional and non-jurisdictional error had been discarded. Others, such as *O'Reilly*,[51] stated that *Anisminic* rendered unnecessary the distinction between jurisdictional and non-jurisdictional errors of law. Yet other cases accepted in principle that review for error of law flowed from *Anisminic* and *O'Reilly,* but qualified it by emphasising that such review was only a presumption, which could be rebutted by the statutory language.[52] **16–025**

The decision in *Page*[53] became the leading authority. Page, a lecturer at Hull University, was made redundant. He argued that his appointment did not allow termination of his employment on this ground. The university visitor dismissed the argument, and Page then sought judicial review of the visitor's decision. Much of the case turned on reviewability of the visitor. However, there were also more general observations concerning the scope of jurisdictional review, which can be summarised as follows.

First, Lord Browne-Wilkinson, who gave the leading judgment, held that *Anisminic,* combined with Lord Diplock's dictum in *O'Reilly,* had rendered obsolete the distinction between errors of law on the face of the record and other errors of law, and had done so by extending the ultra vires doctrine. Thenceforward, it was to be taken: **16–026**

> "... that Parliament had only conferred the decision making power on the basis that it was to be exercised on the correct legal basis: a misdirection in law in making the decision therefore rendered the decision *ultra vires*."[54]

[49] *Racal Communications Ltd, Re* [1981] A.C. 374 at 386, 389–390.

[50] *South East Asia Fire Bricks Sdn Bhd v Non-Metallic Mineral Products Manufacturing Employees Union* [1981] A.C. 363.

[51] *O'Reilly v Mackman* [1983] 2 A.C. 237, HL. See also *Council of Civil Service Unions v Minister for the Civil Service* [1985] A.C. 374, HL at 410–411.

[52] *R. v Registrar of Companies, Ex p. Central Bank of India* [1986] Q.B. 1114, CA (Civ Div) at 1175–1176.

[53] *R. v Hull University Visitor, Ex p. Page* [1993] A.C. 682, HL.

[54] *Page* [1993] A.C. 682 at 701. Lord Slynn and Lord Mustill dissented in relation to certain aspects of the case concerning the Visitor. However, on the general point concerning the scope of review for error of law they were of the same view as the majority, at 705–706.

In general therefore, "any error of law made by an administrative tribunal or inferior court in reaching its decision can be quashed for error of law."[55]

Second, the constitutional foundation for the court's power was the ultra vires doctrine. In an ordinary case,[56] the law applicable to a decision made by such a body was the general law of the land. A tribunal or inferior court would, therefore, act ultra vires if it reached a decision that was erroneous under the general law.[57]

Third, it was, however, only "relevant" errors of law that would lead to the decision being quashed. The error had to be one which affected the actual making of the decision and the decision itself. The mere existence of an error of law at some earlier stage of the proceedings would not vitiate the decision.[58]

Finally, the case was unclear as to whether varying presumptions existed for administrative bodies on the one hand, and for inferior courts on the other. A distinction still appeared to exist. Lord Browne-Wilkinson cited the dicta from Lord Diplock in *Racal*, and reasoned on the assumption that differing presumptions existed in the two situations.[59] Lord Griffiths' reasoning was also based on the continued vitality of the distinction.[60]

E. The Impact of *South Yorkshire Transport*

16–027 In *South Yorkshire Transport Ltd*[61] the secretary of state had power under the Fair Trading Act 1973 s.64(1)(a), to refer a merger to the Monopolies and Mergers Commission (MMC) where it appeared to him that the two or more enterprises ceased to be distinct and that as a result the supply of over 25 per cent of the services of any description "in a substantial part of the United Kingdom" would be carried on by one person. The MMC investigated a merger between two companies that operated bus services in an area which was 1.65 per cent of the total United Kingdom, and which contained only 3.2 per cent of the total population. The companies claimed that the investigation should be set aside because the jurisdictional condition relating to a "substantial part of the UK" had not been fulfilled. Lord Mustill gave judgment for the MMC. He reasoned as follows.

---

55 *Page* [1993] A.C. 682 at 702. See also, *R. v Bedwelty Justices, Ex p. Williams* [1997] A.C. 225, HL.

56 The visitor was regarded as being in a special position in this respect, since he was not applying the general law, but a special domestic legal regime.

57 *Page* [1993] A.C. 682 at 702.

58 *Page* [1993] A.C. 682 at 702, explaining *R. v Independent Television Commission, Ex p. TSW Broadcasting Ltd Independent* 27 March 1992. See also, *R. (Warren) v Mental Health Review Tribunal London & North East Region* [2002] A.C.D. 84.

59 *Page* [1993] A.C. 682 at 703–704.

60 *Page* [1993] A.C. 682 at 693–694.

61 *R. v Monopolies and Mergers Commission, Ex p. South Yorkshire Transport Ltd* [1993] 1 W.L.R. 23, HL; *R. (Goodman) v Lewisham LBC* [2003] EWCA Civ 140; *R. (BBC) v Information Tribunal* [2007] 1 W.L.R. 2583; *R. (Wye Valley Action Association Ltd) v Herefordshire Council* [2011] EWCA Civ 20.

First, the term "substantial" was open to a range of possible meanings, from "not trifling" to "nearly complete". In between these two senses of the term there were many others which drew colour from the statutory context in which they were found.[62]

Second, it was for the court to decide where along the "spectrum of possible meanings"[63] the term was to be placed. When the court had pronounced on this matter the fact that the chosen meaning was formerly part of a range of possible meanings on which opinions might legitimately differ became simply a matter of history.[64]

Third, the criterion which was chosen might, however, itself be so imprecise that different decision-makers could rationally reach different conclusions when applying it to the facts of a given case:

> "In such a case the court is entitled to substitute its opinion for that of the person to whom the decision has been entrusted only if the decision is so aberrant that it cannot be classed as rational: *Edwards v. Bairstow* ... The present is such a case. Even after eliminating inappropriate senses of 'substantial' one is still left with a meaning broad enough to call for the exercise of judgment rather than an exact quantitative measurement."[65]

F. The Impact of *Cart*

Judicial review of tribunals under the Tribunals, Courts and Enforcement Act 2007 is more limited than the general test established by *Page*. *Cart* is the leading decision.[66] C and R failed in appeals to the social security and child support, and the immigration and asylum, chambers of the First-tier Tribunal respectively. They were refused permission to appeal to the Upper Tribunal by both the First-tier Tribunal and Upper Tribunal. They could not appeal this refusal to the Court of Appeal, because the refusal of permission to appeal by the Upper Tribunal was an "excluded decision" for the purposes of the TCE Act, which signified that it was not amenable to further onward appeal.[67] They therefore sought judicial review by the Divisional Court of the refusal of permission by the Upper Tribunal. **16–028**

The government initially argued that the Upper Tribunal was immune from judicial review, because it was a "superior court of record".[68] This argument was rejected by Laws LJ in the Divisional Court on the ground that designation of a body as a superior court of record did not suffice to exclude judicial review. The Supreme Court endorsed this reasoning. It held moreover that the TCE Act 2007 did not contain the clear words necessary to oust or exclude judicial review of unappealable decisions of the Upper Tribunal. Judicial review was, said the Supreme Court, an artefact of the common law, the object being to ensure that insofar as possible decisions were taken in accordance with the law, and in particular the governing statute in the particular area.

[62] *South Yorkshire Transport* [1993] 1 W.L.R. 23 at 29.
[63] *South Yorkshire Transport* [1993] 1 W.L.R. 23 at 30.
[64] *South Yorkshire Transport* [1993] 1 W.L.R. 23 at 32.
[65] *South Yorkshire Transport* [1993] 1 W.L.R. 23 at 32.
[66] *Cart* [2011] UKSC 28; *Eba v Advocate General for Scotland* [2011] UKSC 29.
[67] Tribunals, Courts and Enforcement Act 2007 s.13(1) and (8)(c).
[68] Tribunals, Courts and Enforcement Act 2007 s.3(5).

The Supreme Court acknowledged that neither tribunals nor courts were infallible and a judge at any level might be wrong in law. It concluded that there should be the possibility that a second judge, who should always be someone with more experience or expertise than the judge who first heard the case, could check for errors in the case. If the decision of the Upper Tribunal to refuse permission to appeal to itself was never amenable to judicial review, there was, said the Supreme Court, a real risk of the Upper Tribunal becoming the final arbiter of the law, even when it was wrong in law, so that errors of law of real significance could be perpetuated. There had therefore to be some possibility of judicial review.

The Supreme Court was nonetheless mindful of the status of the new tribunal regime. This was reflected in the "restrained" test adopted as to when the ordinary courts would review the Upper Tribunal. The Supreme Court reasoned by analogy from s.13(6) of the 2007 Act, which limits the circumstances in which there can be a second-tier appeal: it is for the claimant to show that the proposed appeal raises some important point of principle or practice, or there was some other compelling reason for the appellate court to hear the appeal. This was adopted as the criterion for judicial review. Thus, judicial review of the Upper Tribunal is available, but only when the claimant comes within the preceding test.[69]

G. The Impact of *Jones*

16–029 Judicial review for error of law, and the distinction between law and fact, must now be seen in the light of the Supreme Court's decision in *Jones*.[70] Some back ground concerning the law/fact distinction is necessary to appreciate the significance of this decision.

i. *The law/fact distinction*

16–030 The traditional case law on judicial review prior to *Anisminic* provided little guidance as to the divide between law and fact. This was because the test for judicial review was the collateral fact doctrine or the theory of limited review. Both theories applied equally to law and fact: provided for example that the court categorised the issue as collateral it would substitute judgment, whether the issue was one of fact or law.[71]

The shift in *Page* to the idea that all errors of law are jurisdictional meant that the distinction between law and fact became more significant. Much of the literature on the law/fact distinction arose from cases concerned with appeal,

[69] *R. (Khalil) v Truro CC* [2011] EWHC 3335 (Admin); *PR (Sri Lanka) v Secretary of State for the Home Department* [2011] EWCA Civ 988; *R. (Amir) v Secretary of State for the Home Department* [2012] EWHC 4229 (Admin); *JD (Congo) v Secretary of State for the Home Department* [2012] EWCA Civ 327; *A v Secretary of State for the Home Department* [2013] EWHC 1272 (Admin).

[70] *R. (Jones) v First-tier Tribunal* [2013] UKSC 19.

[71] The courts might have felt less inclined to intervene in relation to matters which were purely factual, but the juridical basis of intervention was never premised on the need to distinguish between law and fact. The only real occasion for the distinction was when the court intervened to quash an error of law on the face of the record.

which is commonly only available on questions of law. The case law has been discussed above.[72] There are three themes in the literature.

First, there can be analytical disagreement as to whether a question should be deemed to be one of law or fact.[73] Thus the case law and the academic commentary display diversity of opinion on whether the meaning given to a statutory term such as employee, trade, boat or successor in title should always be regarded as a question of law. The answer on analytical grounds is probably in the affirmative.[74] **16–031**

Second, there can be disagreement as to the conclusions that follow from attachment of the labels law and fact. Thus, some courts have reasoned that if an issue is deemed to be one of law then this must inevitably lead to substitution of judgment by the court; conversely where a statutory term is open to a spectrum of reasonable interpretations some courts have held that it must be a question of fact.[75] Both propositions are contestable: judicial review over issues of law may take the form of rationality review, it does not have to lead to substitution of judgment; and a legal issue does not cease to be such simply because the term in question is open to a range of possible meanings.

Third, the courts have not always adopted an analytic approach. The labels law and fact have been attached depending on whether the courts wished to intervene or not. This is exemplified by Lord Hoffmann's dictum that "there are questions of fact; and there are questions of law as to which lawyers have decided that it would be inexpedient for an appellate tribunal to have to form an independent judgment."[76] This approach informed the ruling in *Jones*.

ii. Jones

In *Jones* the claimant was injured when his car was hit by a lorry that swerved to avoid a person who stepped into the road. His claim for compensation was rejected by the Criminal Injuries Compensation Authority because there had been no crime of violence, which was the trigger for payment under the scheme. The claimant contended that the crime of grievous bodily harm had been committed, but this was rejected by the First-tier Tribunal (FTT) because the deceased's aim **16–032**

---

[72] See paras 9–022 to 9–024; W. Wilson, "A Note on Fact and Law" (1963) 26 M.L.R. 609 and "Questions of Degree" (1969) 32 M.L.R. 361; E. Mureinik, "The Application of Rules; Law or Fact?" (1982) 98 L.Q.R. 587; J. Beatson, "The Scope of Judicial Review for Error of Law" (1984) 4 O.J.L.S. 22; T. Endicott, "Questions of Law" (1998) 114 L.Q.R. 292; R. Williams, "When is an Error not an Error? Reform of Jurisdictional Review of Error of Law and Fact" [2007] P.L. 793; L. Jaffe, "Judicial Review: Question of Law" (1955) 69 Harv. L.R. 239; L. Jaffe, "Judicial Review: Question of Fact" (1955) 69 Harv. L.R. 1020.

[73] *Moyna v Secretary of State for Work and Pensions* [2003] 1 W.L.R. 1929, HL.

[74] See paras 9–022 to 9–024, and the articles, Wilson, "A Note on Fact and Law" (1963) 26 M.L.R. 609 and "Questions of Degree" (1969) 32 M.L.R. 361; Mureinik, "The Application of Rules; Law or Fact?" (1982) 98 L.Q.R. 587; *R. v Barnet London Borough Council, Ex p. Shah (Nilish)* [1983] 2 A.C. 309, HL; *ACT Construction Ltd v Customs and Excise Commissioners* [1981] 1 W.L.R. 49, aff'd [1981] 1 W.L.R. 1542. For a different view, see Endicott, "Questions of Law" (1998) 114 L.Q.R. 292 who argues that there can be an analytical approach which does not lead to this conclusion. This argument, however, explicitly builds pragmatic considerations into the analytical approach.

[75] *Edwards v Bairstow* [1956] A.C. 14 at 33–36.

[76] *Moyna* [2003] 1 W.L.R. 1929 at [44]; *Lawson v Serco* [2006] ICR 250 at [34].

was to commit suicide and therefore there was no mens rea for the criminal offence. This decision was challenged by way of judicial review before the Upper Tribunal (UT),[77] which upheld the FTT's decision. The UT's decision was then challenged by way of appeal, which is available on a point of law, to the Court of Appeal and then to the Supreme Court.[78] The Supreme Court rejected the claim. It is important to disaggregate two linked issues that arose in the case, both of which concerned the law/fact distinction albeit in different ways.

First, there was the issue as to whether the tribunal should be accorded some interpretive leeway in the legal meaning of "crime of violence". The Supreme Court held that where the interpretation and application of a specialised statutory scheme had been entrusted by Parliament to the new tribunal system, it was for the Upper Tribunal to develop structured guidance on the use of expressions that were central to the scheme, so as to reduce the risk of inconsistent results by different panels at the First-tier level. The development of a consistent approach to the expression "crime of violence" within the statutory scheme was primarily for the tribunals, not the appellate courts. The extent of the leeway accorded to the tribunal is not entirely clear from the judgments. Thus Lord Hope gave interpretive leeway in part because of the tribunal's relative expertise and in part because he believed that issues concerning "crimes of violence" would often be factual, while recognising that the legal meaning/application of other offences might admit of only one legal answer.[79] Lord Carnwath framed the issue more broadly. He emphasised that the distinction between law and fact could be affected by policy and expediency, and that relevant factors in this regard included the relative competence of the tribunal and court. He was moreover willing to give interpretive weight to a tribunal's conclusion on an issue of law.[80] How much interpretive weight the courts are willing to give, and what test of review is brought to bear in such instances, remains to be seen.[81]

Second, the law/fact distinction was also relevant in relation to the determination of when an appeal could lie to the ordinary courts from the tribunal, and also from one the FTT to the UT. The Supreme Court held that a pragmatic approach should be taken to the dividing line between law and fact, so that the expertise of tribunals at the First-tier and that of the Upper Tribunal could be used to best effect. An appeal court should not venture too readily into this area by classifying as law issues that were best left for determination by the specialist appellate tribunals.

---

77 Tribunals, Courts and Enforcement Act 2007 s.15.

78 Tribunals, Courts and Enforcement Act 2007 s.13.

79 *Jones* [2013] UKSC 19 at [17]–[18].

80 *Jones* [2013] UKSC 19 at [65]; Lord Carnwath, "Tribunal Justice—A New Start" [2009] PL 48, 63-64; *Obrey v Secretary of State for Work and Pensions* [2013] EWCA Civ 1584 at [14]; *N v Advocate General for Scotland* [2014] UKSC 30 at [26]–[28]; *Pendragon Plc v Revenue and Customs Commissioners* [2015] UKSC 37 at [49]–[51]; *AM v Secretary of State for Work and Pensions* [2015] UKSC 47 at [45].

81 *Revenue and Customs Commissioners v Atlantic Electronics Ltd* [2013] EWCA Civ 651; *Criminal Injuries Compensation Authority v First-tier Tribunal (Social Entitlement Chamber)* [2014] EWCA Civ 1554; *ZP (South Africa) v Secretary of State for the Home Department*, 2 July 2015.

H. Summary

i. The courts have the power to review any error of law, and will in general no longer use distinctions between jurisdictional and non-jurisdictional error. When an error has been made the court will normally substitute its view for that of the body subject to review. There are six qualifications to this basic proposition. **16–033**

ii. The error of law must be relevant or material in the sense discussed above.

iii. The court will not necessarily substitute its judgment for that of the agency where having defined the meaning of the statutory term, the particular interpretation is still inherently imprecise. In such instances the court will only intervene if the application of the term is so aberrant as to be irrational.[82]

iv. If the institution subject to review is an inferior court there is no presumption that Parliament did not intend questions of law to be left to that court.[83]

v. If the institution subject to review is the Upper Tribunal and there have been two unsuccessful appeals within the tribunal regime then judicial review to the ordinary courts will only be available where the claimant can show that the claim raises an important point of principle or practice, or where there is some other compelling reason for the reviewing court to give permission for judicial review.[84]

vi. If the institution subject to review is a tribunal within the Tribunals, Courts and Enforcement Act 2007 then it will be accorded interpretive leeway when making decisions on issues of law, and the reviewing court will take pragmatic considerations into account, including relative expertise, when deciding on the division between law and fact.[85] The standard of review that is applicable in such cases is unclear. The interpretive leeway accorded to tribunals must be bounded by something akin to a rational basis test of the kind that is used in the USA and Canada. It is moreover unclear how far this interpretive leeway will apply to other decision-makers.

vii. The courts continue to regard the grant of a remedy as discretionary, and will not necessarily grant the remedy merely because an error of law has been committed during, for example, an inquest.[86]

---

[82] *South Yorkshire Transport* [1993] 1 W.L.R. 23.

[83] However, even in this latter instance it appears to be the case that, for example, a legislative finality clause, which purports to render a decision of an inferior court final and conclusive, will only protect that body from errors of law within jurisdiction, *Page* [1993] A.C. 682 at 703.

[84] *Cart* [2011] UKSC 28.

[85] *Jones* [2013] UKSC 19.

[86] *R. v Inner South London Coroner, Ex p. Douglas-Williams* [1999] 1 All E.R. 344, CA (Civ Div) at 347, citing *R. v Greater Manchester Coroner, Ex p. Tal* [1985] Q.B. 67 QBD at 83. The court was however influenced by the legislation relating to coroners which specifies that a new inquest should not be held unless it is necessary or desirable in the interests of justice.

I. Error of Law within Jurisdiction

16–034 In addition to review for jurisdictional error, the courts have, in the past, maintained control over errors of law within jurisdiction if they appeared on the face of the record. Certiorari developed to control this very type of error.[87] Control over such errors declined during the latter half of the 19th century,[88] and was only "rediscovered" 100 years later.[89] This control was exercised if the defect appeared on the face of the record. The courts construed this broadly to include the documents which initiated the proceedings, the pleadings and the adjudication.[90] The reasons for the decision might also be held to be part of the record.[91] The Tribunals and Inquiries Act 1958 s.12 initiated a right to reasoned decisions which were to be treated as part of the record, but only in the sphere covered by the Act.

The revival of this head of review was greeted enthusiastically. Whether it continued to survive depended on whether the collateral fact doctrine continued to be used by the courts. Although *Anisminic*[92] affirmed the continued existence of non-jurisdictional errors of law, *Page*[93] discarded the distinction between jurisdictional and non-jurisdictional error. A separate category of error of law within jurisdiction is, therefore, largely redundant.

The only instances where error of law within jurisdiction might still be relevant[94] are where there is a finality clause and the court believes that Parliament might have intended that the decision-maker should be the final arbiter on questions of law. In such circumstances the finality clause might immunise the decision from attack if there is an error of law within jurisdiction. This is equally true if the common law has recognised that decisions of, for example, university visitors are final and conclusive. Provided that the University Visitor has jurisdiction in the narrow sense to consider the relevant matter, the courts will not interfere further and will not review errors of law committed within jurisdiction.[95]

---

[87] A. Rubinstein, *Jurisdiction and Illegality* (Oxford: Oxford University Press, 1965), Ch.4.

[88] The primary reason was the passage of the Summary Jurisdiction Act 1848 which authorised a truncated form of record in which the charge, evidence and reasoning to support it were no longer required to be set out in criminal convictions, *R. v Nat Bell Liquors Ltd* [1922] 2 A.C. 128 at 159.

[89] *R. v Northumberland Compensation Appeal Tribunal, Ex p. Shaw* [1951] 1 K.B. 711 KBD; [1952] 1 K.B. 338 CA.

[90] *Shaw* [1952] 1 K.B. 338 at 352.

[91] *R. v Medical Appeal Tribunal, Ex p. Gilmore* [1957] 1 Q.B. 574, CA; *Baldwin and Francis Ltd v Patents Appeal Tribunal* [1959] A.C. 663, HL; *R. v Knightsbridge Crown Court, Ex p. International Sporting Club (London) Ltd* [1982] Q.B. 304 QBD; *R. v Chertsey JJ, Ex p. Franks* [1961] 2 Q.B. 152 DC.

[92] *Anisminic* [1969] 2 A.C. 147.

[93] *Page* [1993] A.C. 682 at 701.

[94] *Page* [1993] A.C. 682 at 703.

[95] *Page* [1993] A.C. 682 at 702–703; *R. (Ferguson) v Visitor of the University of Leicester* [2003] EWCA Civ 1082; *R. (Varma) v Duke of Kent* [2004] E.L.R. 616 QBD.

J. Statutory Review

16–035 A number of statutes contain provisions allowing review only within a limited period, commonly being six weeks. The effect of the six-week time limit will be considered in the context of exclusion of remedies.[96] What is considered here is the effect of a specific statutory formula which allows challenge within the six-week period on certain grounds. The statute will normally establish two grounds of review. These are that the order impugned is not within the powers of the Act, or that any requirement of the Act has not been complied with. If the latter is the ground of attack, there is often the additional requirement that the interests of the applicant have been substantially prejudiced.

There has been considerable difference of judicial opinion as to the construction of these clauses. If such statutory clauses were ever intended to reflect the common law, and this is not clear, the distinction between the two heads of review now makes little sense given the expansion of non-statutory review. Moreover, the very existence of the two heads of control has exacerbated the problem as judges sought to find a meaning for each of the terms.

This can be seen in *Smith*[97] where there were differing views as to the meaning of "not within the powers of this Act". Lord Reid[98] held that bad faith and unreasonableness were outside the statute completely and therefore could be impugned even after six weeks. A similar result was reached by Lord Somervell.[99] The majority, however, decided that challenge for fraud was precluded after six weeks. Lord Morton construed the statutory terms extremely narrowly as permitting challenge only if express statutory requirements were violated.[100]

16–036 The sensible interpretation would be to read the phrase, "not within the powers of this Act" so as to include any traditional head of ultra vires, and there is authority for this position.[101] Later courts have given the formula a broad interpretation. It has been held to encompass not only traditional forms of jurisdictional error, but also no evidence, and any error of law.[102] The puzzles of *East Elloe* will therefore probably be quietly forgotten.

Despite this broad formulation, the courts continued to use the second limb of the formula: "a requirement of the Act has not been complied with".[103] It may well be best that this should be confined to the challenge of directory provisions,

---

[96] See Ch.28.

[97] *Smith v East Elloe Rural District Council* [1956] A.C. 736, HL.

[98] *Smith* [1956] A.C. 736 at 763.

[99] *Smith* [1956] A.C. 736 at 772.

[100] *Smith* [1956] A.C. 736 at 755.

[101] *Webb v Minister of Housing and Local Government* [1965] 1 W.L.R. 755, HL at 770 (Lord Denning MR). See cases, *Ashbridge Investments Ltd v Minister of Housing and Local Government* [1965] 1 W.L.R. 1320, CA; *Coleen Properties Ltd v Minister of Housing and Local Government* [1971] 1 W.L.R. 433, CA (Civ Div); *Gordondale Investments Ltd v Secretary of State for the Environment* (1971) 70 L.G.R. 158, CA (Civ Div); *Peak Park Planning Board v Secretary of State for the Environment* (1980) 39 P. & C.R. 361 QBD.

[102] *Ashbridge* [1965] 1 W.L.R. 1320; *Coleen Properties* [1971] 1 W.L.R. 433; *Gordondale* (1971) 70 L.G.R. 158; *Peak Park* (1980) 39 P. & C.R. 361.

[103] *Gordondale* (1971) 70 L.G.R. 158; *Miller v Weymouth Corporation* (1974) 27 P. & C.R. 468 QBD.

allowing a court to quash an order if non-compliance with such provisions has caused substantial prejudice to the applicant.

5. THE TEST FOR REVIEW: POLICY CONSIDERATIONS

A. Clearing the Deck: The Demise of the Collateral Fact Doctrine and Limited Review

16–037 The demise of the collateral fact doctrine is to be welcomed. It was always arbitrary and uncertain in its application. The difficulty of distinguishing between the *kind* of case which a tribunal had to determine, and the statutory description of the *situation* which the tribunal had to decide, was the root cause of the problem. It was not possible to predict in advance the way in which a case would be categorised, nor was there any ex post facto rationality to explain why cases were categorised in different ways.

The Gordon thesis of limited review was also unsatisfactory. It was analytically flawed and unacceptable on policy grounds. While the spectre of the Albert Hall being deemed a furnished tenancy haunts the annals of legal literature rather than the real world, we nonetheless require more control than allowed by Gordon's commencement theory.

B. Judicial Control and Agency Autonomy: Remembering the Past when Constructing the Future

16–038 It is important to pause and consider an important issue, which is why the courts persisted with the collateral fact doctrine and limited review for so long. No answer is found in the modern case law. The judges in cases such as *Racal* and *Page* simply regard the distinctions between jurisdictional and non-jurisdictional error as esoteric and unnecessary. The implicit message is that the earlier decisions failed to realise that such distinctions were not needed, and that the judiciary could now impose more far-reaching controls. This is, with respect, to do a disservice to the older jurisprudence.

It is clear from a reading of this case law that the courts did not feel that they were bound by some *a priori* logic to employ either of the discredited theories. They acknowledged the possibilities open to them when devising the tests for jurisdictional control. The truth is that they adopted the collateral fact doctrine or the theory of limited review because they believed that these best captured the appropriate balance between judicial control and agency autonomy.[104] The courts did not believe that they should be substituting judgment on every issue of law which comprised the "if X" question, since this would emasculate autonomy over issues that had been assigned to the agency by Parliament. They realised also that

[104] P. Craig, "Jurisdiction, Judicial Control and Agency Autonomy", in I. Loveland (ed.), *A Special Relationship, American Influences on Public Law in the UK* (Oxford: Oxford University Press, 1995), Ch.7.

some judicial control was required. The collateral fact doctrine and limited review were the tools used to preserve control, while giving some leeway to agency autonomy.

These tests were defective, but we are, nonetheless, in danger of forgetting the rationale for them. We do not have to accept the balance between judicial control and agency autonomy adopted by earlier courts, but we should not forget that there is an issue here at all. Courts in other common law jurisdictions are fully cognisant of this underlying policy issue. This should be borne in mind when considering the modern law.

C. The Modern Law: Review for Errors of Law

The effect of *Anisminic*, as interpreted in *Racal*, *O'Reilly* and *Page*, is that all errors of law became susceptible to review. Three comments are warranted. **16–039**

First, this scope of review is not logically demanded. There is no *a priori* reasoning which dictates that the courts' view on the meaning of an "if X" issue should necessarily and always be preferred to that of the agency, tribunal or inferior court. The answer resides not in some logically compelled statement as to whose opinion should count, but in a normative judgment as to whose relative opinion on a particular matter we wish to adopt.

Second, the typical case concerns a contested interpretation of a statutory term. The courts regard misconstruction of many such terms as errors of law, and substitute their view for that of the tribunal. However, terms such as "resources", "employee", or "structural alteration" can have a spectrum of possible meanings depending on the policy of the legislation. The ordinary courts' interpretation of all such terms will not necessarily be better than that of the primary decision-maker. The latter is established partly because of its expertise, and this is not confined solely to fact finding. The meaning of "course of employment" in a particular statute may be better decided by a tribunal staffed with a lawyer chairman and "wing" members representing the interests of trade unionists and employers rather than the ordinary courts.[105] Control can be maintained through a rationality test.

Third, it is, as we have seen, possible to interpret the law/fact distinction in a more pragmatic, functional or policy-oriented way, which takes into account the desirability of interfering with the agency decision, and the relative abilities of the court and the agency for deciding the question in issue. As Beatson stated,[106] "a system that uses the pragmatic approach is not using the concept of error of law as an organizing principle" as such, but rather as a facade behind which to weigh the relative competence of court and agency. There is increased evidence of this approach within the case law. *South Yorkshire Transport* went some way in this direction, but only to a limited extent.[107] Some later cases, such as

[105] J. Beatson, "The Scope of Judicial Review for Error of Law" (1984) 4 O.J.L.S. 22, 40–42; , J. Black, "Reviewing Regulatory Rules: Responsibility to Hybridisation", in J. Black, P. Muchlinski and P. Walker (eds), *Commercial Regulation and Judicial Review* (Oxford: Hart Publishing, 1998), Ch.6.

[106] Beatson, "The Scope of Judicial Review for Error of Law" (1984) 4 O.J.L.S. 22, 43.

[107] *South Yorkshire Transport* [1993] 1 W.L.R. 23 at 29. Their Lordships decided on the meaning of the open-textured statutory term, even though the primary decision-maker had very considerable

CENTRO,[108] explicitly acknowledged issues of relative institutional expertise, while in other cases, such as *Wiles*,[109] the court was respectful of tribunal findings because of their expertise. The most significant decisions in this respect are those concerning the new tribunal regime, in *Cart*,[110] *Eba*[111] and *Jones*.[112] It remains to be seen whether the reasoning in *Jones* is extended beyond the tribunal regime.

D. A Middle Way: Rightness and Reasonable Basis

i. The USA

16–040 It is important to consider the possibility that control can be achieved without the court automatically substituting judgment for that of the tribunal, and without allowing the tribunal to have unlimited power.

The leading decision on this issue in the United States is *Chevron*.[113] The Supreme Court drew the following distinction. If a court reviewing an agency's construction of a statute decided that Congress had a specific intention on the precise question in issue then that intention should be given effect to. The court substituted judgment for that of the agency and imposed the meaning Congress intended. If, however, the reviewing court decided that Congress had not directly addressed the point of statutory construction, the court considered whether the agency's answer was based on a permissible construction of the statute. The agency finding might be upheld even though it was not the interpretation which the court itself would have adopted, and even though it was only one of a range of permissible such findings that could be made.[114] Thus, the court could not substitute its own construction of a statutory provision for a reasonable interpretation made by the administrator of an agency.[115] *Chevron* therefore established a two-part test. Cases which fall under part one lead to substitution of judgment by the reviewing court; cases which fall under part two result in a less intensive standard of review, that of reasonableness or rational basis.

A good example of a case pre-dating *Chevron* which applied a rationality test is *Hearst Publications*.[116] Hearst published newspapers and refused to bargain

expertise. The latitude afforded the primary decision-maker was at a second-order level: where the meaning given by the court was itself inherently open-textured then it would only intervene if the agency's decision was irrational.

108 *R. (CENTRO) v Secretary of State for Transport* [2007] EWHC 2729 (Admin).

109 *Eba* [2011] UKSC 29; *R. (Wiles) v Social Security Commissioners* [2010] EWCA Civ 258.

110 *Cart* [2011] UKSC 28.

111 *Eba* [2011] UKSC 29.

112 *Jones* [2013] UKSC 19.

113 *Chevron USA Inc v NRDC* 467 US 837 (1984). There is a vast literature on *Chevron*, some of the leading works are considered in P. Craig, "Judicial Review of Questions of Law: A Comparative Perspective", in S. Rose-Ackerman and P. Lindseth (eds), *Comparative Administrative Law* (Cheltenham: Edward Elgar, 2011), Ch.26. See also, P. Daly, "Deference on Questions of Law" (2011) 74 M.L.R. 694; M. Aronson, "Should We Have a Variable Error of Law Standard?", in M. Elliott and H. Wilberg (eds), *The Scope and Intensity of Substantive Review, Traversing Taggart's Rainbow* (Oxford: Hart, 2015), Ch. 10.

114 *Chevron* 467 US 837 (1984) at 842–843.

115 *Chevron* 467 US 837 (1984) at 844.

116 *National Labour Relations Board v Hearst Publications, Inc* 322 US 111 (1944).

collectively with a union representing newsboys, who distributed the papers. Hearst argued that the newsboys were not "employees" within the relevant legislation. The aim of the legislation was to enhance good labour relations, and Rutledge J decided that this encompassed people outside the traditional common law classification of an employee. There could nonetheless be differences of opinion as to which workers should be termed "employees" for the purposes of the statute, since there were "myriad forms of service relationship" within the economy.[117] The Board's determination would, said the court, be accepted if it had warrant in the record and a reasonable basis in law, as judged in the light of the overall statutory objective. The court did not simply substitute its own view: Congress had assigned the task primarily to the agency which, because of its greater experience, placed it in a better position to resolve the matter than the court.

There have, however, been difficulties with application of the *Chevron* test.[118] There has been disagreement as to the meaning of the two-part test, especially part one. In *Cardozo-Fonseca*[119] the Supreme Court decided that a particular statutory term was clear within the first limb of the test, because the court could divine its meaning through the normal tools of statutory construction. This provoked a powerful separate opinion from Justice Scalia. He felt that the majority approach would radically undermine the *Chevron* formula, given that a court could always conclude that the meaning of a statutory term was clear through the use of "normal tools of statutory construction". By way of contrast in *Rust*[120] Rehnquist CJ interpreted the first limb of *Chevron* to apply only where the congressional meaning of the term really was evident on the face of the statute. If this was not so then the matter would fall to be determined under the rationality part of the formula. The tendency in recent case law has been towards less deference, with greater reliance on the "plain" meaning of statutory terms.[121] This has led to more cases being characterised as falling within part one of the *Chevron* test, even if there is sharp disagreement within the Supreme Court as to what the relevant statutory term actually means.[122] The law has moreover been complicated by the difficult ruling in the *Mead* case,[123] which limits the circumstances in which the *Chevron* approach is deemed applicable.

ii. Canada

The Canadian courts also engaged in extensive analysis of the proper standard of **16–041**
judicial review. There were remnants of reasoning in terms of jurisdictional error, but the general approach was to use varying intensities of review: correctness,

[117] *National Labour Relations Board* 322 US 111 (1944) at 126.

[118] Craig, "Judicial Review of Questions of Law: A Comparative Perspective", in S. Rose-Ackerman and P. Lindseth (eds), *Comparative Administrative Law* (2011), Ch.26.

[119] *Immigration and Naturalization Service v Cardozo-Fonseca* 480 US 421 (1986).

[120] *Rust v Sullivan* 111 S Ct 1759 (1991).

[121] *MCI Telecommunications Corp v American Telephone & Telegraph Co* 512 US 218 (1994); *Brown v Gardner* 513 US 115 (1994); *Food and Drug Administration v Brown & Williamson Tobacco Corp* 529 US 120 (2000).

[122] *Brown & Williamson Tobacco* 529 US 120 (2000)

[123] *US v Mead Corporation* 533 US 218 (2001); *Alaska Department of Environmental Conservation v Environmental Protection Agency* 540 US 461 (2004).

reasonableness *simpliciter*, and patent unreasonableness.[124] The Supreme Court in *Pushpanathan*[125] identified factors that would be taken into account when deciding on their applicability, including: the existence or not of a privative clause and its nature; the relative expertise of the decision-maker; the purpose of the legislation and of the particular contested provision; and the nature of the problem, more especially, whether it was law, fact or involved elements of both. The Canadian approach was, therefore, "functional and pragmatic". Insofar as the term jurisdictional was used it was as a label for a provision that a court determined must be answered correctly, in accord with the preceding approach.

However, in *Dunsmuir*[126] the Supreme Court reduced the tests for review to correctness and reasonableness, abolished the distinction between reasonableness *simpliciter* and patent unreasonableness, and renamed the test the "standard of review analysis" rather than the "pragmatic and functional analysis". The correctness test connoted judicial substitution of judgment with no deference accorded to the tribunal. Rationality review embraced process, how the decision was reached, its transparency and intelligibility. It also embraced substance, that is, whether it was within the range of reasonable outcomes. Deference, construed as respect for the primary decision-maker, informed the rationality test on fact and law.

The following criteria were held relevant to the choice between correctness and rationality. The correctness test was applicable to "true" jurisdictional issues, whether the tribunal had authority to make the inquiry, and questions of law that were of central importance for the legal system and outside the agency's area of expertise, such as issues of constitutional interpretation or the jurisdictional divide between two agencies. Rationality review would normally be appropriate where there was a privative clause; there was a discrete administrative regime and the tribunal had expertise; the review was of fact or discretion; or there was an issue of law that did not warrant correctness review, more especially where the factual and legal issues were closely intertwined, and/or where the agency was interpreting its own statute. The court thereby affirmed that while some legal issues were subject to correctness review, there was nothing unprincipled about

---

124 Madame L'Heureux-Dube J, "The "Ebb" and "Flow" of Administrative Law on the "General Question of Law", in M. Taggart (ed.), *The Province of Administrative Law* (Oxford: Hart Publishing, 1997), Ch.14; D. Mullan, "Establishing the Standard of Review: The Struggle for Complexity?" (2003) 17 Can. J. Admin. Law & Prac. 59; G. Huscroft, "Judicial Review from *CUPE* to *CUPE*: Less is not Always More", in G. Huscroft and M. Taggart (eds), *Inside and Outside Canadian Administrative Law, Essays in Honour of David Mullan* (University of Toronto Press, 2006), pp.296–326; D. Mullan, "*Dunsmuir v. New Brunswick*, Standard of Review and Procedural Fairness for Public Servants: Let's Try Again!" (2008) 21 *Canadian Journal of Administrative Law and Practice* 117; M. Walters, "Jurisdiction, Functionalism and Constitutionalism in Canadian Administrative Law", in C. Forsyth, M. Elliott, S. Jhaveri, A. Scully-Hill, M. Ramsden (eds), *Effective Judicial Review: A Cornerstone of Good Governance* (Oxford: Oxford University Press, 2010), p.300; Daly, "Deference on Questions of Law" (2011) 74 M.L.R. 694; Chief Justice Beverly McLachlin, "Administrative Tribunals and the Courts: An Evolutionary Relationship", May 27, 2013, *http://www.scc-csc.gc.ca/court-cour/judges-juges/spe-dis/bm-2013-05-27-eng.aspx* [accessed 13 November 2015].

125 *Pushpanathan v Canada (Minister of Citizenship and Immigration)* [1998] 1 S.C.R. 982.

126 *Dunsmuir v New Brunswick* [2008] 1 S.C.R. 190.

the application of rationality review to other legal issues. The decision is to be broadly welcomed, but there are nonetheless issues that are unresolved or uncertain.[127]

E. The Middle Way: Challenges

i. Constitutional principle

It is clear in the light of the decisions in *Cart*[128] and *Jones*[129] that the Supreme Court believes that variable intensity of review for error of law, combined with flexibility in relation to the law/fact distinction, is compatible with constitutional principle in the UK. This is assuredly so. The conceptual basis of judicial review, that the courts are thereby enforcing the legislative will by ensuring that the authority remains within its assigned area, has never provided any sure guide as to the scope of review. Almost any answer can be formally accommodated within the language of jurisdiction. It is high time that we assessed the desirability of judicial intervention in its own terms. **16–042**

ii. Certainty

It might be felt that the approaches considered above would produce uncertainty. It is important in this respect to distinguish between two different senses of uncertainty. **16–043**

First, uncertainty might relate to the difficulty of predicting which test for review, rational basis or rightness would be adopted in any particular case. This objection can be conceded. If the courts rigorously applied the idea that all errors of law are jurisdictional, defined the word law in a purely analytical way so that it embraced any application of a statutory term and substituted judgment on the meaning of that term, then a claimant would be clear that the courts would intervene using that standard. This certainty would mean reducing the competence of the initial decision-maker to a mere fact-finder, denying any weight to its opinion on the interpretation of the constituent parts of the X question, and embroiling the courts in the minutiae of all the elements which comprise the conditions of jurisdiction.

A second meaning of certainty relates to the probability that the court would uphold the initial decision-maker's findings, which is a practical concern for the claimant. It may be difficult for an experienced adviser to predict whether the reviewing court will accept that the interpretation of a term adopted by the initial decision-maker was right. There would, by way of contrast, be greater certainty in those areas covered by the rational basis part of the test, since this is a narrower

[127] Mullan, "*Dunsmuir v. New Brunswick*, Standard of Review and Procedural Fairness for Public Servants: Let's Try Again!" (2008) 21 *Canadian Journal of Administrative Law and Practice* 117; J. Evans, "Standards of Review in Administrative Law" (2012) 26 *Canadian Journal of Administrative Law and Practice* 67; P. Daly, "The Struggle for Deference in Canada", in Elliott and Wilberg (eds), *The Scope and Intensity of Substantive Review* (Oxford: Hart, 2015), Ch.12.

[128] *Cart* [2011] UKSC 28.

[129] *Jones* [2013] UKSC 19.

standard of review. There is a greater chance that the original decision will be upheld as having a rational basis, even if the interpretation is not the precise one which the court itself would have chosen.

iii. Criteria

16–044 There are two key issues involved in the application of variable intensity of review.

The first is the type of criterion used to distinguish between the standards of review. The US criterion focuses predominantly on whether Congress has spoken to the meaning of the contested issue. If it has the court substitutes its judgment for that of the agency; if it has not then rationality review is used instead. Many of the difficulties in the US case law stem from different judicial interpretations as to whether Congress has spoken to the meaning of the contested term. While this should be a relevant factor, it should not be the only consideration that conditions the test for review. It is indeed somewhat paradoxical that in the pre-Chevron case law the courts used a wider range of factors in determining the applicable standard of review. The richer set of factors used in the Canadian jurisprudence is to be preferred. This coheres with the approach in *Cart*,[130] *Eba*[131] and *Jones*[132] where the Supreme Court justified the interpretive leeway given to tribunals by looking at a range of factors, including relative expertise, and the nature of the contested issue considered by the tribunal.

The second issue is the type of body that is subject to the variable test for review. Thus, for example, the *Chevron* approach in the USA applies across the spectrum of administrative institutions broadly conceived. In the UK the reasoning in *Cart* and *Jones* has been crafted for tribunals, and it is clear that the court-like nature of such bodies, combined with their expertise, was central to the judgments. It remains to be seen whether the court is willing to apply such reasoning to other parts of the administrative state, and if so which.

---

130 *Cart* [2011] UKSC 28.
131 *Eba* [2011] UKSC 29.
132 *Jones* [2013] UKSC 19.

CHAPTER 17

ERROR OF FACT

1. CENTRAL ISSUES

i. The previous chapter considered the scope of review for errors of law. We saw that the divide between issues of law and fact could be contentious, and reference should be made to that discussion.[1] This chapter considers the test for judicial review of questions of fact and the related issue of how far the courts will review evidentiary material. **17–001**

ii. It was surprising that until recently the courts had not addressed the criteria for judicial review and appeal of fact in a principled manner. Text writers advocated expansion and consolidation of this head of review.[2] The Court of Appeal in *E v Secretary of State for the Home Department*[3] attempted to bring some order into this area, and the issue was also addressed by the House of Lords in *Croydon*.[4]

iii. The discussion begins by considering the variety of situations covered by the general category of mistake of fact. The meaning of fact for the purposes of judicial review is under-explored, and the discussion will therefore shed light on the different meanings that the term mistake of fact can bear.

iv. This is followed by an overview of the earlier case law. The rationale for the confusion in the case law will be explained, and was evident in the existence of broad and narrow views concerning the scope of review for error of fact.

v. The discussion then shifts to analysis of the reasoning in the *E* case, and the four-part test for review of fact established by the Court of Appeal. This decision was not however, referred to by the House of Lords in the *Croydon* case, and the four-part test was not used. The best "legal fit" between the two authorities will be analysed.

vi. The *E* case has nonetheless been much cited and applied in subsequent case law dealing with a variety of subject matter. The four parts of the test are

---

[1] See paras 9–022 to 9–24, 16–029 to 16–032, 16–039, 16–043, 16–044.

[2] P. Craig, *Administrative Law*, 5th edn (London: Sweet and Maxwell, 2003), pp.502–510; S. de Smith, Lord Woolf and J. Jowell, *Judicial Review of Administrative Action*, 5th edn (London: Sweet and Maxwell, 1995), paras 5–091 to 5–096; H.W.R. Wade and C. Forsyth, *Administrative Law* 8th edn (Oxford: Oxford University Press, 2000), pp.266–268, 278–285.

[3] *E v Secretary of State for the Home Department* [2004] Q.B. 1044, CA (Civ Div).

[4] *R. (A) v Croydon LBC* [2009] 1 W.L.R. 2557 SC.

therefore examined in the light of this subsequent case law, as is the judicial approach to the admission of fresh evidence to prove the existence of a factual error.

vii. The chapter concludes by considering the limits of judicial intervention in relation to factual claims, with particular emphasis on the respective roles of the court and initial decision-maker in relation to factual findings.

2. MISTAKE OF FACT: MEANING

17–002 It is important to consider the meaning of mistake of fact. There has been considerable academic discussion of the divide between law and fact for the purposes of appeal and judicial review.[5] This is readily explicable given the expansion in review for error of law. There has, however, been less attention paid to the meaning of mistake of fact. It has for the most part been treated as a "residual unitary category" embracing cases where there is no error of law. It is however clear that the category of mistake of fact includes a variety of different situations.

We can begin with the paradigm where a *simple factual finding made by the decision-maker is challenged as being incorrect*. This covers the type of case where the initial decision was premised on the existence of certain relatively simple or straightforward primary facts, such as whether a person was in a certain place at a certain time, or whether two towns were separate with the consequence that one could not levy rates for poor relief on inhabitants of the other.[6]

This leads to cases involving *more complex factual findings, which require a greater degree of evaluative judgment*. Thus, in *Kibiti* the applicant sought asylum, and the Immigration Appeals Tribunal made a finding that there was a civil war in the Congo.[7] This was important because it had an impact on the test for persecution used when deciding on asylum applications.[8] Kibiti argued that the IAT had erred factually, because there was no civil war in the Congo, but the court found against him, holding that the evidence available to the IAT amply justified its factual finding. *Turgut*[9] provides another good example. The applicant claimed that he faced a real risk of persecution and ill-treatment if returned to Turkey, since he was a Turkish Kurd who had evaded the draft. The decision on this factual issue required a considerable degree of evaluative judgment, prompting the court to discuss the respective roles of the court and the secretary of state in relation to the assessment of the factual evidence.[10]

17–003 There is then a category of case where *the primary decision-maker factually misinterpreted or misunderstood evidence presented at the hearing*. The *Haile*

[5] See paras 9–022 to 9–024, 16–029 to 16–032, 16–039, 16–043, 16–044.

[6] *Nichols v Walker* (1632–1633) Cro. Car. 394; *Milward v Caffin* (1778) 2 Black W. 1330; *Lord Amherst v Lord Somers* (1788) 2 T.R. 372; *Weaver v Price* (1832) 3 B. & Ad. 409; *Governors of Bristol Poor v Wait* (1834) 1 A. & E. 264; *Fernley v Worthington* (1840) 1 Man. & G. 491.

[7] *Romain Kibiti v Secretary of State for the Home Department* [2000] Imm. A.R. 594, CA (Civ Div).

[8] *Adan v Secretary of State for the Home Department* [1999] 1 A.C. 293, HL.

[9] *R. v Secretary of State for the Home Department, Ex p. Turgut* [2001] 1 All E.R. 719, CA (Civ Div).

[10] See also *K v Secretary of State for the Home Department* [2006] EWCA Civ 1037.

case[11] exemplifies this type of case. The essence of the complaint, upheld by the court, was that the special adjudicator in an asylum case had found against the applicant because he, the adjudicator, had mixed up the names of two organisations in Ethiopia. The special adjudicator had thought that the applicant was referring to membership of a body called the EPRF, when in fact the applicant was referring to the EPRP. The adjudicator felt that certain of the applicant's evidence was not credible, on the assumption that it referred to the EPRF, whereas it actually referred to the EPRP and when read in that way it made sense.

We can move on to a fourth type of case where the *decision-maker makes a mistake of fact by failing to take account of crucial evidence when it made its initial decision*. The prime modern example is the *CICB* case.[12] The Criminal Injuries Compensation Board denied the applicant's claim for compensation in ignorance of the report by a police doctor that lent weight to her allegations that she had been sexually assaulted, and in reliance on a statement from a member of the police force that ran counter to the findings of the police doctor.

There is a fifth type of case where the *decision is made on certain factual assumptions and the applicant seeks to show, sometimes through the admission of fresh evidence, that these factual assumptions were mistaken*. This was in essence the claim in *Tameside*.[13] The secretary of state had intervened in the local authority's education plans because he did not believe that the school selection procedures could be applied within the required time, and therefore the local authority was acting unreasonably so as to justify his intervention. The House of Lords held that this assumption was not made out on the facts of the case. This was also the nature of the claim in the *E* case.[14] The decision of the adjudicator and the IAT was based on the factual assumption that membership of the Muslim Brotherhood would not render E liable to persecution, more especially since his involvement had been at a low level. E sought to rely on subsequent evidence in the form of two reports revealing that membership of the Muslim Brotherhood would lead to a serious risk of detention and torture. The same was true in the related case of *R* who claimed asylum on the ground that he was a convert from Islam to Christianity and would therefore face persecution if he was returned home. His claim was rejected because the adjudicator and the IAT felt that he did not have a well-grounded fear of persecution since the Taliban were no longer in power. He argued that the IAT should have taken into account a report from April 2003, which indicated that apostates were still at risk of persecution or death.[15]

There is a sixth category, which is closely related to, but distinct from, the fifth. **17–004**
This is where *the initial decision was made on certain general factual assumptions about, for example the degree of risk faced by a certain category of persons, but these general assumptions are then modified in the light of later*

[11] *R. (Haile) v Immigration Appeal Tribunal* [2002] I.N.L.R. 283, CA (Civ Div).

[12] *R. v Criminal Injuries Compensation Board, Ex p. A* [1999] 2 A.C. 330, HL.

[13] *Secretary of State for Education and Science v Tameside MBC* [1977] A.C. 1014, HL.

[14] *E* [2004] Q.B. 1044; See also, *A v Secretary of State for the Home Department* [2003] I.N.L.R. 249, CA (Civ Div); *R. (Bagdanavicius) v Secretary of State for the Home Department* [2003] EWCA Civ 1605.

[15] *E* [2004] Q.B. 1044.

evidence. Thus, in *Polat*[16] the claimant was a Turkish Kurd who sought asylum. The IAT rejected the claim and based its decision on the assumption that such a person could not succeed unless he could show something more than that the Turkish authorities would have a record of his involvement in a separatist organisation. Later information came to light which caused the IAT in a subsequent case to modify its view about the risks faced by this category of person, such that suspected membership of, or support for, a separatist organisation would result in the person being handed over to the Turkish anti-terror branch, with the attendant risk of torture.

It is important moreover to appreciate that the category of *jurisdictional facts may cut across the preceding categories* and it should also be recognised that *factual issues can occur in the context of rulemaking*. The discussion thus far, has been concerned with the various meanings of factual error in the context of individual determinations. It is perfectly possible for an applicant to contest the factual basis behind a rule promulgated by an agency, or the factual assumptions that underlie an agency policy determination. The relationship between courts and agency in such instances will be considered more fully below.

3. SCOPE OF REVIEW: THE PRIOR LAW

A. Rationale for Uncertainty

17–005 The extent to which facts were susceptible to review or appeal was, until recently, unclear, notwithstanding the importance of the issue.[17] There were numerous cases dealing with review and appeal for fact, but there was little principled judicial guidance as to when facts ought to be susceptible to judicial scrutiny. This was in part because of the malleability of the categories of judicial review, with the consequence that courts could choose to catch factual error through a doctrinal category such as relevancy if they were so inclined. It was in part because courts intervened in relation to factual error where they felt that this was warranted, without too close an inquiry as to whether such intervention was justified under existing case law. It was in part also because judicial indications that the scope of review for fact might be broader than hitherto perceived were often dicta in cases where this was not the main issue before the court. The net effect was uncertainty as to the scope of review for fact. There was authority for a narrow and a broader view.

[16] *Bulent Polat v Secretary of State for the Home Department* [2003] EWCA Civ 1059.

[17] T. Jones, "Mistake of Fact in Administrative Law" [1990] P.L. 507; M. Kent, "Widening the Scope of Review for Error of Fact" [1999] J.R. 239; P. Craig, "Judicial Review, Appeal and Factual Error", [2004] P.L. 788; C. Forsyth and E. Dring, "The Final Frontier: The Emergence of Material Error of Fact as a Ground for Judicial Review", in C. Forsyth, M. Elliott, S. Jhaveri, A. Scully-Hill and M. Ramsden (eds), *Effective Judicial Review: A Cornerstone of Good Governance* (Oxford: Oxford University Press, 2010), Ch.15.

B. Narrow View

The narrower view was that judicial review for error of fact only existed in limited circumstances. It was accepted that review could lie for jurisdictional fact.[18] These were facts that related to the existence of the public body's power over the relevant area. Thus, as seen in the previous chapter, a statute will always stipulate certain preconditions for the exercise of the agency's power. In a simple paradigm it will state that if an employee is injured at work then compensation can or should be granted. The statutory conditions may be factual, legal or discretionary in nature. A classic factual precondition is that a person should be of a particular age to qualify for a benefit; a simple legal stipulation is provided by the meaning of the term employee; a discretionary precondition is where the statute provides that if a minister has reasonable grounds to believe that a person is a terrorist then he may be detained. Claims of factual error can arise in all three types of case. It might be argued that the agency was mistaken about the applicant's age, because it confused the applicant with a different person. It might be claimed that the agency misapplied the legal meaning of the term employee to the applicant's case because of a factual error. It might be contended that the minister did not have sufficient factual material to sustain a reasonable ground for believing that the applicant was a terrorist. **17–006**

In addition to review for jurisdictional fact, it was accepted that review was also available where the fact was the only evidential basis for the decision,[19] or where the fact related to a matter that had, expressly or impliedly, to be taken into account. However, leaving aside special considerations in relation to planning and asylum, there was no general right to challenge the decision of a public body on fact alone.[20]

C. Broad View

There was also authority for a broader view of review for error of fact. Thus, Scarman LJ in *Tameside* held that misunderstanding or ignorance of an established and relevant fact could be a ground for review.[21] Lord Wilberforce in *Tameside* stated that if a judgment required, before it could be made, the existence of certain facts, then while the evaluation of those facts was for the minister, the court could inquire whether the facts existed and had been taken into account, whether the judgment was made on a proper self-direction as to those **17–007**

[18] *Nichols* (1632–1633) Cro. Car. 394; *Milward* (1778) 2 Black W. 1330; *Lord Amherst* (1788) 2 T.R. 372; *Weaver* (1832) 3 B. & Ad. 409; *Wait* (1834) 1 A. & E. 264; *Fernley* (1840) 1 Man. & G. 491; *Eleko* [1931] A.C. 662.

[19] *R. v Secretary of State for Education, Ex p. Skitt* [1996] C.O.D. 270; *R. v Bedwelty Magistrates, Ex p. Williams* [1997] A.C. 225, HL.

[20] *R. v London Residuary Body* July 24, 1987; *Wandsworth LBC v A* [2000] 1 W.L.R. 1246, CA (Civ Div).

[21] *Tameside* [1977] A.C. 1014 at 1031–1032.

facts, and whether irrelevant facts had been taken into account.[22] There were also planning cases in which the courts intervened where there was factual error.[23]

More recent support for the broader view was evident in other cases. In the *CICB* case[24] Lord Slynn was willing to characterise a failure to take account of certain factual evidence as justifying judicial review on the grounds of unfairness. It was Lord Slynn once again who alluded to the courts' powers over fact finding in *Alconbury*,[25] stating that they could quash for misunderstanding or ignorance of an established and relevant fact.[26] Lord Clyde noted that fact could be subject to review where the decision-maker was mistaken or where account had been taken of irrelevant facts,[27] while Lord Nolan was willing to countenance review of fact at least where the factual finding had no justifiable basis.[28]

4. SCOPE OF REVIEW: *E V SECRETARY OF STATE FOR THE HOME DEPARTMENT*

17–008 It was this uncertainty that prompted the Court of Appeal in the *E* case[29] to take stock and attempt to bring some order to this area.

A. The Facts

17–009 The decision of the Court of Appeal arose out of two joined cases concerned with immigration and asylum.

In one of the cases E, an Egyptian national, who had lived outside Egypt all his life, came to the United Kingdom in 2001 from Bangladesh and claimed asylum. He argued that if he returned to Egypt he would be at risk of detention and torture, because he was a sympathiser with the Muslim Brotherhood and his family were involved in its activities. His application for asylum was refused by the Home Secretary, and this was confirmed by the adjudicator and by the IAT. The decision was based in part on the factual assumption that membership of the Muslim Brotherhood would not render him liable to persecution, more especially since his involvement had been at a low level. E sought to rely on subsequent evidence in the form of two reports revealing that membership of the Muslim Brotherhood would lead to a serious risk of detention and torture. The IAT refused permission to appeal to the Court of Appeal, stating that the IAT could

[22] *Tameside* [1977] A.C. 1014 at 1047. See also *Ashbridge Investments v Minister of Housing and Local Government* [1965] 1 W.L.R. 1320, CA at 1326; *Coleen Properties Ltd v Minister of Housing and Local Government* [1971] 1 W.L.R. 433, CA (Civ Div); *General Electric Co Ltd v Price Commission* [1975] I.C.R. 1.

[23] *Hollis v Secretary of State for the Environment* (1984) 47 P. & C.R. 351; *Jagendorf v Secretary of State and Krasucki* [1985] J.P.L. 771; *Simplex GE (Holdings) Ltd v Secretary of State for the Environment* (1989) 57 P. & C.R. 306.

[24] *A* [1999] 2 A.C. 330 at 343–346.

[25] *R. v Secretary of State for the Environment, Ex p. Alconbury* [2003] 2 A.C. 295, HL at [53].

[26] This was relevant in deciding whether the courts' powers were sufficient for the purposes of art.6 of the European Convention on Human Rights.

[27] *Alconbury* [2003] 2 A.C. 295 at [169].

[28] *Alconbury* [2003] 2 A.C. 295 at [62].

[29] *E* [2004] Q.B. 1044.

only decide a case on the evidence before it at the time of hearing, and the reports relied on by E were not before the tribunal when it made its decision.

In the other case R was an Afghan national who came to the United Kingdom in 2001 and claimed asylum on the ground that he was a convert from Islam to Christianity and would face persecution if he was returned home. His claim was refused because the adjudicator and the IAT felt that he did not have a well-grounded fear of persecution, since the Taliban were no longer in power. The IAT hearing was held in April 2003, but the decision was not promulgated until August 2003. R sought permission to appeal to the Court of Appeal. He claimed that the IAT should have taken into account a report from April 2003, which indicated that apostates were still at risk of persecution or death. The IAT refused permission to appeal, holding that the relevant report was not available until May 2003, and that it decided the case on the material available at the time.

B. Judicial Review, Appeal and Fact

The essence of E and R's claim was that the IAT had erred by not admitting the relevant evidence, and that this could be appealed even where, as under this statutory regime, the right of appeal was limited to questions of law. Carnwath LJ gave the judgment of the Court of Appeal. **17–010**

The judgment proceeded on the assumption that there should be no material difference as to whether the case arose as an application for judicial review or an appeal on a point of law. There had been a general assimilation of the various forms of review, statutory and common law, such that "it has become a generally safe working rule that the substantive grounds for intervention are identical".[30] The main practical dividing line was between instances where appeal or review was accorded on fact and law, and those where it was confined to law. The key issue was whether a decision reached on an incorrect basis of fact could be challenged on an appeal that was limited to points of law.

C. The Test for Review of Error of Fact

The Court of Appeal analysed the existing jurisprudence concerning judicial review for factual error. It noted the differences between the narrow and broad view in the pre-existing case law,[31] and concluded that clarification was required. **17–011**

The Court of Appeal held that cases concerned with factual error could be dealt with under a separate ground of review based on fairness.[32] In categorising matters in this way it followed Lord Slynn's approach in the *CICB* case.[33] Carnwath LJ, giving judgment, held that this was a convincing explanation of the cases where decisions had been set aside for mistake of fact[34] and stated that if this was felt to take fairness beyond the traditional confines of procedural

---

30 *E* [2004] Q.B. 1044 at [42], [50].

31 *E* [2004] Q.B. 1044 at [44]–[60].

32 *E* [2004] Q.B. 1044 at [63].

33 *CICB* [1999] 2 A.C. 330.

34 *E* [2004] Q.B. 1044 at [64].

irregularity it was going no further than the use of fairness in previous cases.[35] The court concluded that mistake of fact giving rise to unfairness was a separate head of challenge in an appeal on a point of law "at least in those statutory contexts where the parties share an interest in co-operating to achieve the correct result",[36] asylum being regarded as one such area. There were four requirements to show the requisite unfairness and hence justify setting aside a decision for mistake of fact[37]:

> "First, there must have been a mistake as to an existing fact, including a mistake as to the availability of evidence on a particular matter. Secondly, the fact or evidence must have been 'established', in the sense that it was uncontentious and objectively verifiable. Thirdly, the appellant (or his advisers) must not have been responsible for the mistake. Fourthly, the mistake must have played a material (not necessarily decisive) part in the Tribunal's reasoning."

D. The Test for Admission of Evidence to Prove a Mistake of Fact

17–012 The judgment then considered the circumstances in which evidence could be admitted to prove the mistake of fact. The court has discretion under the CPR to admit new evidence.[38] This is, however, generally subject to the principles in *Ladd v Marshall*,[39] which established that for fresh evidence to be admitted it must be shown that it could not with reasonable diligence have been obtained for use at the trial, that if the evidence had been given it would probably have had an important influence on the result of the case, and that it was credible, albeit it did not have to be incontrovertible. Carnwath LJ analysed the extent to which these principles should be relevant in public law cases. He distinguished between two different types of case.

There were, on the one hand, cases where the courts had admitted fresh evidence without reference to the principles in *Ladd*. This was explicable, said Carnwath LJ, because the cases turned on the legality of a ministerial decision, where the evidence was not available when the minister made the initial determination, but the minister had continuing responsibility over the matter.[40] *Launder*[41] and *Simms*[42] were seen as examples of such cases. Carnwath LJ did not regard them as controlling for a body with finite jurisdiction, such as the IAT.[43]

There were, on the other hand, cases dealing with challenges to decisions made by tribunals such as the IAT, where the applicant sought to introduce fresh evidence in order to prove the factual error. Some courts had been willing to

35 *E* [2004] Q.B. 1044 at [65], citing *HTV Ltd v Price Commission* [1976] I.C.R. 170 CA (Civ Div) and *R. v IRC, Ex p. Preston* [1985] A.C. 835 HL.

36 *E* [2004] Q.B. 1044 at [66].

37 *E* [2004] Q.B. 1044 at [66].

38 CPR 52.11(2).

39 *Ladd v Marshall* [1954] 1 W.L.R. 1489, CA.

40 *E* [2004] Q.B. 1044 at [73]–[75].

41 *R. v Secretary of State for the Home Department, Ex p. Launder (No.2)* [1997]1 W.L.R. 839 at 860–861.

42 *R. v Secretary of State for the Home Department, Ex p. Simms* [2000] 2 A.C. 115, HL at 127.

43 *E* [2004] Q.B. 1044 at [74]–[75], [77].

admit such evidence, notwithstanding the fact that the error could have been detected by the applicant's advisers when the IAT made its decision, such as in *Haile*.[44] Carnwath LJ held that the principles in *Ladd* should be treated as the starting point, albeit with discretion to depart from them in exceptional circumstances, and the *Haile* case should be seen as an instance where this was warranted.[45] He was mindful of the dangers of statutory appeals on law or judicial review being used too readily as a mechanism for the re-evaluation of factual matters, and this was the rationale for the emphasis accorded to the principles in *Ladd* in public law.

The Court of Appeal decided that it was within the powers of the IAT to re-open its decision to take account of evidence that existed before its decision, where the evidence was only drawn to its attention when an application to appeal was made. The IAT should, however, be satisfied that there was a risk of serious injustice because of evidence that had been overlooked at the hearing.[46] The case was therefore remitted to the IAT to reconsider in the light of the principles laid down by the Court of Appeal in this case.

5. SCOPE OF REVIEW: *CROYDON* CASE

The scope of review for factual error must also be assessed in the light of the *Croydon* case, a decision of the House of Lords.[47] The claimants were asylum seekers who sought judicial review of the local authority's decision, which had denied that they were children and hence not entitled to accommodation by the local authority. The House of Lords held that the Children Act 1989 drew a clear distinction between whether a person was a child and whether that child was in need within the meaning of the Act. The former question was one of fact, which admitted only one answer, and was to be decided by the ultimate determination of the court, even though it might be difficult to decide the issue in any particular case. The House of Lords gave two reasons for this conclusion. **17–013**

Baroness Hale held firstly that the court would make the ultimate determination because the issue admitted of a right or wrong answer and this was so notwithstanding the difficulties of making this determination.[48] This was also the primary rationale for Lord Hope.[49] Baroness Hale made clear that this rationale was based on the wording of the Children Act 1989 and was independent[50] of a second argument adduced by the claimants, which was that the court should make the determination as to whether the person was a child because

---

44 *Haile* [2002] I.N.L.R. 283.

45 *E* [2004] Q.B. 1044 at [81]–[82], [91]; *JG (Jamaica) v Secretary of State for the Home Department* [2015] EWCA Civ. 215.

46 *E* [2004] Q.B. 1044 at [35], [97]–[98].

47 *R. (A) v Croydon LBC* [2009] 1 W.L.R. 2557.

48 *R. (A) v Croydon LBC* [2009] 1 W.L.R. 2557 at [26]–[27].

49 *R. (A) v Croydon LBC* [2009] 1 W.L.R. 2557 at [51].

50 *R. (A) v Croydon LBC* [2009] 1 W.L.R. 2557 at [29].

it was a jurisdictional fact[51] in the traditional sense of that phrase. Baroness Hale was willing to conclude that the existence of a "child" was a jurisdictional fact for the purposes of this legislation.[52]

The House of Lords made no mention of the *E* case,[53] which prompts inquiry as to the fit between *Croydon* and the *E* case. There is nothing in *Croydon* that casts doubt on the authority of the ruling in the *E* case, and the latter has, as will be seen below, been applied on numerous occasions since the decision in *Croydon*.[54] This still leaves open the "fit" between the two decisions. The "literal" answer subject to any later judicial guidance would be as follows.

17–014 A court can review fact on three grounds: where there is an objective fact that is susceptible to only one answer and it is decided that Parliament intended the courts to provide that answer; where there is a jurisdictional fact; and where there are facts that fulfil the criteria in the *E* case. On this view, if a claimant can bring the case within the first or second grounds it will not be necessary to satisfy the four conditions in the *E* case, and the doctrine of jurisdictional fact still provides an independent ground on which a claimant can seek judicial review of fact. This formally reconciles *Croydon* and *E*, but this "solution" is problematic for two reasons.

First, it is difficult to find authority for the proposition that courts can review facts simply because they are susceptible to only one answer to be provided by the reviewing court. If this had been established doctrine the history of judicial review of fact would have been very different, and the divide between this ground for intervention and traditional conceptions of jurisdictional fact would be difficult to say the least. The reality is that later cases raising the same point have treated *Croydon* as a case about jurisdictional fact.[55] The reality is also that cases dealing with different subject matter have resisted the argument that the court should provide the answer on the ground that the fact is objective, holding that this aspect of *Croydon* was dependent on the particular statute.[56]

Second, if the first ground of review in *Croydon* is accepted then it would transform judicial review and consume the other grounds. This is not an objection in and of itself. It does mean that we should be mindful of the significance of accepting such reasoning.

---

51 See para.16–019; *Bunbury v Fuller* (1853) 9 Ex. 111; *R. v Fulham, Hammersmith and Kensington Rent Tribunal, Ex p. Zerek* [1951] 2 K.B. 1 KBD; *R. v Secretary of State for the Home Department, Ex p. Khawaja* [1984] A.C. 74, HL.

52 *Croydon* [2009] 1 W.L.R. 2557 at [31]–[32].

53 *E* [2004] Q.B. 1044.

54 See para.17–020.

55 *R. (CJ) v Cardiff CC* [2011] EWCA Civ 1590; *R. (S) v Croydon LBC* [2011] EWHC 2091 (Admin); *R. (AS) v Ealing LBC* [2012] EWHC 356 (QB); *R. (AA (Afghanistan)) v Secretary of State for the Home Department* [2013] UKSC 49; *R. (Bluefin Insurance Ltd) v Financial Ombudsman Service Ltd* [2014] EWHC 3413 (Admin); *R. (GE (Eritrea)) v Secretary of State for the Home Department* [2014] EWCA Civ 1490.

56 *Bubb v Wandsworth BC* [2011] EWCA Civ 1285.

6. THE TEST FOR MISTAKE OF FACT: FOUNDATIONS

The approach to mistake of fact in the *E* case represents a compromise between two pairs of rival considerations. There is the obvious tension between the primary role of the initial decision-maker in relation to findings of fact, and the judicial desire to provide relief through review or appeal where a factual error occurred. There is also the tension resulting from the limitation of appeals in certain areas to questions of law. This rendered it necessary to produce a ground of intervention for mistake of fact that could be couched in terms of error of law. It is difficult to reconcile these competing considerations, and there will be differences of opinion as to whether the *E* case achieved this. **17–015**

It will be argued that the Court of Appeal was on the right lines. The test in the *E* case brings a degree of order to an area that was lacking hitherto. It was regrettable that the pre-existing law on appeal and review for mistake of fact was so unclear. This was especially so given the practical importance of the topic for courts and litigants alike. Thus, as the court noted, there were widely differing views as to the scope of review for mistake of fact, but in practice administrative court judges tended to set aside decisions on this ground when justice so required.[57] A judgment to instil some order and principle was therefore timely.

A. Looking Back: Difficulties with the Pre-Existing Narrow View

The pre-existing narrow view of intervention for mistake of fact was difficult to apply. Mistake of fact could vitiate the decision only where the fact was a condition precedent to an exercise of jurisdiction, where the fact was the only evidential basis for the decision, or where the fact related to a matter that had, expressly or impliedly, to be taken into account. The difficulty was as to whether these categories were really separable from other instances of factual error. **17–016**

Thus, the category of jurisdictional fact assumes that there is a clear divide in the powers accorded to a public body between those factual matters that can be regarded as jurisdictional and other factual matters that condition the exercise of power that are not to be so regarded. The reality is that this divide is very difficult to draw. Insofar as the jurisdiction of a public body is defined by a series of statutory conditions, some of which relate to facts, it is not possible to decide in a principled manner that some of these factual conditions should be treated as jurisdictional, while others should not. The reality is that all such factual jurisdictional terms condition the ability of the primary decision-maker to proceed to the substance of the case.[58] The real issue is the degree of judicial control over such factual findings, whether they choose to substitute judgment or accord some degree of autonomy to the factual findings made by the initial decision-maker.

There were similar problems with the category of intervention where the fact was the only evidential basis for the decision. It could be difficult to decide whether the contested fact really was the only evidential basis for the decision.

---

[57] *Bubb* [2011] EWCA Civ 1285 at [52].

[58] See para.16–005.

Even if it was this still left open the issue of principle, as to why the courts should not be able to intervene where the fact was not the only evidential basis for the decision, but nonetheless had a marked causal impact thereon.

The final category for review of fact allowed by the narrow view was that the fact related to a matter that had expressly or impliedly to be taken into account. This provided the courts with a flexible tool to allow intervention or not as they chose, but it did little to enhance certainty, and merely concealed the judicial value judgments in any particular case.

B. Looking Forward: The Conceptual Foundation for Judicial Intervention

17–017 The conceptual foundation for judicial intervention in relation to mistake of fact is explicable. It would have been perfectly possible, if there had not been the need to accommodate appeals on questions of law, to justify judicial review squarely on mistake of fact, without the necessity of conceptualising this as an error of law. There has long been intervention in relation to factual matters within judicial review. The issue has always been the scope of this head of judicial review, rather than its existence.

The court in the *E* case decided that the substantive grounds of intervention should be the same in relation to statutory appeals limited to law and judicial review.[59] The choice of fairness as the ground for intervention was motivated in part by the need to ensure that intervention for mistake of fact could be accommodated within the remit of appeals limited to questions of law and within the general framework of judicial review.[60] It was necessary to construct a rationale that could be couched in terms of error of law, and it was the unfairness resulting from the mistake of fact that provided the requisite link.

It might be argued that where the legislature limited appeals to questions of law this revealed an intention not to allow appeal in relation to fact. It is however the very meaning of law that is in issue. It cannot simply be assumed that factual error can never lead to an error of law, since that would be to presume the answer to the question at issue.

17–018 The reality is that the conception of "legality" within judicial review is used as a label to cover a variety of more specific grounds of challenge relating to the rule of law. The courts have on a number of previous occasions forged the link between factual mistake and error of law in order to facilitate judicial intervention.[61] In that sense, the reasoning in the *E* case was following a well-trodden path. Judicial review for "illegality" embraces a wide range of situations. Thus, there are classic errors of law in the sense that the public body has, in the opinion of the reviewing court, misconstrued a legal term in the

---

[59] *E* [2004] Q.B. 1044 at [42], [50].

[60] *E* [2004] Q.B. 1044 at [63], [66].

[61] *R. v Deputy Industrial Injuries Commissioner, Ex p. Moore* [1965] 1 Q.B. 456 CA, 488; *Ashbridge Investments* [1965] 1 W.L.R. 1320, CA at 1326; *Coleen Properties* [1971] 1 W.L.R. 433; *General Electric* [1975] I.C.R. 1; *R. v Secretary of State for the Environment, Ex p. Ostler* [1977] Q.B. 122, CA (Civ Div) at 123; *Mahon v Air New Zealand* [1984] A.C. 808 at 821; *Williams* [1997] A.C. 225; *Reid v Secretary of State for Scotland* [1999] 2 W.L.R. 28 at 54 HL.

empowering legislation. Illegality also covers matters such as action for improper purposes, and the taking account of irrelevant considerations, or the failure to take account of relevant considerations. These are treated as species of illegality because they involve statutory construction to delimit the ambit of the public body's power. The line between failing to take account of relevant considerations and factual error may however be a fine one, which explains why relevancy has in the past been used as a surrogate doctrinal device through which to deal with factual mistake. The denomination of factual error leading to unfairness as giving rise to an appeal on a point of law is not therefore so odd when the category of legal error is viewed in this manner.

The Court of Appeal recognised that unfairness when used in this context went beyond its traditional role as an aspect of procedural irregularity,[62] but held that its application in this context went no further than in previous cases such as *HTV*[63] and *Preston*.[64] The Court of Appeal did not say that the cases on mistake of fact and unfairness were the same as *HTV* and *Preston*.[65] The argument was that the use of fairness as the ground for intervention in relation to mistake of fact was warranted because it went no further than its use in these cases, and that in both types of case the unfairness could occur even though there was no fault on the part of the public body.

This can be accepted. It should nonetheless be recognised that fairness plays only a limited role in relation to mistake of fact. It is not a matter to be proven independently of the four requirements laid down by the Court of Appeal. It is rather the necessary consequence of finding that those requirements are met. If they are then the requisite unfairness will exist.

7. THE TEST FOR MISTAKE OF FACT: CURRENT LAW

A. Jurisdictional Error

Whether there should be different tests for review of jurisdictional fact and other factual error will be considered later.[66] The existing law, as exemplified by the *Croydon* case,[67] is, however, predicated on the continued existence of the distinction in the following sense: if the claimant can show that the error concerns a jurisdictional fact then the court will review the determination and will not require the claimant to prove the four criteria in the *E* case. In other instances the claimant must show that the four criteria in the *E* case have been met. It is to these that we now turn. 17–019

62 *E* [2004] Q.B. 1044 at [65].
63 *HTV* [1976] I.C.R. 170.
64 *Preston* [1985] A.C. 835.
65 Those cases were concerned with the unfairness that could result from the public body's attempt to resile from representations on which the representee had detrimentally relied.
66 See paras 17–030, 17–033.
67 *R. (A) v Croydon LBC* [2009] 1 W.L.R. 2557.

B. The *E* Case: Mistake as to Existing Fact including Mistake as to Availability of Evidence

17–020 The *E* case has been applied in many subsequent decisions. The subject matter has varied from asylum to planning, from disability discrimination to parole and from health care to human rights.[68] Some of the cases arise via appeal, others by way of judicial review. Yet other cases reach the court pursuant to statutory provisions allowing applicants to challenge decisions made that were not within the powers of the statute, or on the ground that the relevant requirements in making the decision had not been complied with.[69]

The first limb of the guidance in the *E* case makes it clear that intervention is possible in principle for all species of mistake of existing fact, including mistake as to availability of evidence, subject to the other criteria that make up the test. This is important given the different types of case that come within the umbrella of mistake of fact. The demarcation of types of factual error that are susceptible to review/appeal, and those that are not, would involve protracted litigation concerning the boundaries of the respective categories leading to uncertainty of the kind that bedevilled the jurisprudence prior to the *E* case.

Such demarcation would, moreover, only serve a valid purpose if the distinctions between different types of factual error made sense in normative terms. It is however not self-evident that, for example, a factual error materially affecting the exercise of discretion is less deserving of judicial attention than other types of factual error, more especially where the error relating to the exercise of discretion can impact on the applicant's human rights.

17–021 The test does, however, require a mistake as to an "existing" fact. This is exemplified by *Kaydanyuk*.[70] The applicant sought asylum, but his application was denied. The IAT took note of a report from a psychiatrist to the effect that the applicant was suffering from depression and that deportation would increase the risk that he would commit suicide. His state of mind declined sharply when he learned that his application for asylum had been rejected. He argued that the IAT's determination was based on a mistake of fact, because his real state of mind only became apparent after the IAT's determination. The Court of Appeal disagreed and held that the applicant did not meet the first part of the test: the IAT

---

[68] *R. (Iran) v Secretary of State for the Home Department* [2005] EWCA Civ 982, asylum; *R. (Ross) v West Sussex Primary Care Trust* [2008] EWHC 2252 (Admin), primary care; *MS (Democratic Republic of Congo) v Secretary of State for the Home Department* [2009] EWCA Civ, asylum; *R. (Lunt) v Liverpool City Council* [2009] EWHC 2356 (Admin), disability discrimination; *Historic Buildings and Monuments Commission for England (English Heritage) v Secretary of State for Communities and Local Government* [2009] EWHC 2287 (Admin), planning; *R. (Connolly) v Havering LBC* [2009] EWCA Civ 1059, planning; *R. (Nukajam) v Secretary of State for the Home Department* [2010] EWHC 20 (Admin), human rights; *Jobson v Secretary of State for Communities and Local Government* [2010] EWHC 1602 (Admin), planning; *Cox v Secretary of State for Communities and Local Government* [2010] EWHC 104 (Admin), planning; *H v Parole Board* [2011] EWHC 2081 (Admin), parole; *Hiam v Secretary of State for Communities and Local Government* [2014] EWHC 4112 (Admin), planning; *R. (SO (Eritrea)) v Barking & Dagenham LBCR* [2014] EWCA Civ 1486 (social welfare); *R. (Gopikrishna) v Office of the Independent Adjudicator for Higher Education* [2015] EWHC 207 (Admin), higher education.

[69] Town and Country Planning Act 1990 s.288.

[70] *Kaydanyuk v Secretary of State for the Home Department* [2006] EWCA Civ 368 at [20]–[21].

had taken full account of the medical report, which included the risk of suicide, and the increase in this risk after its decision did not mean that the decision was based on a mistake of existing fact.

This can be contrasted with the *L* case.[71] The Special Educational Needs and Disability Tribunal decided that a child with autism should be educated at school A rather than school B. The decision was based in part on the assumption that school B was to be closed, whereas the reality was that there was a proposal that it should be closed. Jack J held that this constituted a mistake as to existing fact and therefore allowed the appeal by the local authority.

C. The *E* Case: The Fact or Evidence must be Uncontentious and Objectively Verifiable

The second limb of the guidance is that the fact or evidence must have been established, in the sense that it was uncontentious and objectively verifiable. The paradigm is a case such as *CICB*,[72] where the error was failure to mention the police doctor's report. The requirement that the fact or evidence must be uncontentious has been the ground for rejecting a number of claimants in later cases.[73] **17–022**

The requirement that the fact or evidence should be objectively verifiable is not problematic in principle. The difficulty resides rather with the requirement that the fact or evidence should be uncontentious. It is unproblematic insofar as it requires the claimant to adduce evidence to show that the alleged factual error occurred.[74] There are, however, other possible interpretations of this requirement. Thus, for example, it might be contended that a fact is contentious because it requires "evaluation", as opposed to mere "observation", and hence there could be disagreement about the resulting evaluation. It might alternatively be contended that a fact is contentious because it is not crucial or reliable to the initial determination. These constructions will be examined in turn.

i. Contentious and complex

It would be regrettable if the term uncontentious were interpreted so as to exclude judicial consideration of more complex factual findings that require evaluation as opposed to mere observation. This narrow construction would mean that only simple errors of primary fact, falling into the first of the categories articulated above,[75] would suffice to raise this head of review/appeal. This would exclude more complex cases where the factual determination requires evaluative judgment, on the ground that such evaluative judgment might well be "contentious". This would be regrettable, since there are many cases that fall within this and the other categories articulated above. **17–023**

[71] *R. (L) v London Borough of Wandsworth* [2006] EWHC 694 (Admin).

[72] *CICB* [1999] 2 A.C. 330.

[73] *W v Staffordshire CC* [2006] EWCA Civ 1676 at [25]–[26]; *Phelps v First Secretary of State* [2009] EWHC 1676.

[74] *Richmond Upon Thames LBC v Kubicek* [2012] EWHC 3292 (QB).

[75] See para.17–002.

It is moreover questionable how far this narrow construction of the term "uncontentious" is compatible with earlier case law. It is clear from case law prior to the *E* case that the courts engaged in review or appeal of fact in cases where the facts could not, in reality, be regarded as uncontentious in the narrow sense of the term. This is exemplified by cases such as *Kibiti*,[76] *Turgut*,[77] and *Polat*.[78]

This is also clear from the earlier case law dealing with review of subjectively worded statutory conditions. If the statute states that the "Minister may intervene if he thinks it necessary or desirable", there may be no term, such as successor in title, or resources, which the courts can insist should bear a certain meaning. The courts therefore sought to ensure that the decision-maker had some reasonable grounds for the action, and reviewed the facts and evidence on which the minister acted. They initially exercised this control where there was no evidence to support the finding that was made.[79] This control was extended to cover cases where, for example, a minister reached a decision to which on the evidence he could not reasonably have come.[80] The control was further reinforced in *Tameside*,[81] in particular the judgment of Lord Wilberforce considered above.[82] The factual and evidentiary issues raised in many of these cases could not readily be regarded as "uncontentious" in the narrow sense of that term considered above. The courts nonetheless exercised control over these determinations. It would therefore be regrettable if the term "uncontentious" were to be construed too narrowly in the jurisprudence post the *E* case.

ii. Contentious and reliable

17–024 The requirement that the fact should be uncontentious may, however, relate to the extent to which it is crucial and reliable to the initial determination, rather than complexity. This appears to be the meaning accorded to it by Brooke LJ in *Shaheen*.[83] He expressed concern about a prior case, *Cabo Verde*,[84] where the court held that there was a mistake of fact because the IAT had made its asylum determination on the basis that the applicant was badly treated in Angola, whereas subsequent evidence indicated that he was in Portugal at the relevant time. In *Shaheen* Brooke LJ expressed his concern in the following terms.[85]

---

76 *Kibiti* [2000] Imm. A.R. 594.

77 *Turgut* [2001] 1 All E.R. 719. See also more recently, *K* [2006] EWCA Civ 1037.

78 *Polat* [2003] EWCA Civ 1059.

79 See *Skitt* [1996] C.O.D. 270; *Williams* [1997] A.C. 225; *London Residuary Body* July 24, 1987; *A* [2000] 1 W.L.R. 1246. Compare *R v Nat Bell Liquors Ltd* [1922] 2 A.C. 128 at 151–154.

80 See cases *Moore* [1965] 1 Q.B. 456, 488; *Ashbridge Investments* [1965] 1 W.L.R. 1320; *Coleen Properties* [1971] 1 W.L.R. 433; *General Electric* [1975] I.C.R. 1; *Ostler* [1977] Q.B. 122; *Mahon* [1984] A.C. 808; *Williams* [1997] A.C. 225; *Reid* [1999] 2 W.L.R. 28; *Allinson* [1894] 1 Q.B. 750; *Lee* [1952] 2 Q.B. 329.

81 *Tameside MBC* [1977] A.C. 1014 at 1047; *Mahon* [1984] A.C. 808 at 821, 832–833; *Alconbury* [2003] 2 A.C. 295 at [53]; *CICB* [1999] 2 A.C. 330.

82 See para.17–007.

83 *Shaheen v Secretary of State for the Home Department* [2005] EWCA Civ 1294. See also *R. (Iran)* [2005] EWCA Civ 982 at [50].

84 *Cabo Verde v Secretary of State for the Home Department* [2004] EWCA Civ 1726.

85 *Shaheen* [2005] EWCA Civ 1294 at [28].

> "We seem to be in danger, in this area, of slipping from the identification of an uncontentious and objectively verifiable fact such as the prior existence of crucial and reliable documentary evidence into a willingness to re-open appeals for error of law merely because a witness has been subsequently found who could have made a witness statement challenging the factual conclusions that were reached by the original decision-maker in ignorance of such evidence."

Controls over fact and evidence should not lead to decisions being challenged on questionable or spurious grounds. It is nonetheless necessary to disaggregate two related, albeit distinct, issues.

The first is whether the fact or evidence is uncontentious and objectively verifiable, which clearly entails that it is reliable, and perhaps also that it is crucial to the initial determination, although this captured by the fourth limb of the test. The second issue is whether fresh evidence should be admitted. If the fresh evidence could with reasonable diligence have been obtained when the initial determination was made, or it is not credible, it should be rejected on these grounds. If however this is not so then it should be admitted to prove the initial mistake and the matter remitted to the primary decision-maker.

D. The *E* Case: Responsibility for the Mistake

The third limb of the guidance is that the applicant or his advisers should not have been responsible for the mistake.[86] This clearly makes good sense. It prevents the applicant from taking advantage of his or her own wrongdoing and provides a potent incentive for the applicant to disclose the full and accurate facts when the initial determination was made. 17–025

E. The *E* Case: The Mistake should have Played a Material Part in the Tribunal's Reasoning

The final requirement is that the mistake should have played a material, albeit not necessarily decisive, part in the tribunal's reasoning.[87] Thus, to amount to an error of law, a mistake by which a decision-maker was deprived of evidence had to be material, in the sense that if it had been available to the decision-maker it would or could have played a material part in her thinking.[88] 17–026

F. The Admissibility of Fresh Evidence

The full impact of the *E* case can only be understood when the four part guidance is read in tandem with the approach to the admissibility of fresh evidence. The Court of Appeal wished to keep a tighter rein on admissibility of fresh evidence in public law than had been so in some previous cases. The rationale for this was 17–027

---

86 *Richmond Upon Thames LBC v Kubicek* [2012] EWHC 3292 (QB).

87 *Montes v Secretary of State for the Home Department* [2004] EWCA Civ 404; *R. (Morton) v Parole Board* [2009] EWHC 188 (Admin); *Hiam* [2014] EWHC 4112 (Admin).

88 *Speers v Secretary of State for Communities and Local Government* [2014] EWHC 4121 (Admin); *Ecotricity Next Generation Ltd v Secretary of State for Communities and Local Government* [2015] EWHC 189 (Admin).

readily apparent, given that it had expanded appeal/review for mistake of fact. It was mindful of the dangers of statutory appeals on law or judicial review being used too readily as a mechanism for the re-evaluation of factual matters.[89] Thus the court held that the principles in *Ladd*[90] should be treated as the starting point, albeit with discretion to depart from them in exceptional circumstances.[91]

In cases dealing with a body with finite jurisdiction, such as the IAT, the principles in *Ladd* were to be treated as the starting point. Thus, in *Montes*[92] an application for fresh evidence to be considered was rejected on the ground that it could have been obtained with reasonable diligence for use at the IAT hearing, and that in any event the evidence was unlikely to have led to any different conclusion. By way of contrast in *Gungor*[93] Collins J held that it would be dangerous to rely merely on the fact that the evidence would have been available at the time of the initial hearing as entitling it to be disregarded, and it should have been considered whether such evidence might have affected the result.

The Court of Appeal distinguished the preceding type of case from that concerned with the legality of a ministerial decision, where the evidence was not available when the minister made the initial determination and where the minister had continuing responsibility over the matter.[94] It is the continuing responsibility of the minister that explains the greater willingness to admit evidence that was not available when the initial decision was made.

8. THE TEST FOR MISTAKE OF FACT: ROLE OF THE REVIEWING COURT

17–028 The preceding summation of the existing law raises a number of issues concerning the role of the reviewing court in assessing whether the factual error has occurred.

A. The Standard of Proof Required in Relation to Facts

17–029 It is axiomatic that the existence or not of a factual error may well depend on the standard of proof demanded in relation to the relevant facts. It is for the reviewing court to determine the standard of proof required for the establishment of facts by the primary decision-maker.

The *Khawaja* case[95] provides a clear example. The House of Lords held that an illegal entrant under the Immigration Act 1971 could cover a person who had obtained leave to enter by deception or fraud, as well as a person who had entered by clandestine means. Their Lordships then considered the standard of proof required of the immigration officer if his decision on the facts that a person had

---

[89] *E* [2004] Q.B. 1044 at [85]; *Bagdanavicius* [2003] EWCA Civ 1605 at [72]; *JG (Jamaica) v Secretary of State for the Home Department* [2015] EWCA Civ. 215.

[90] *Ladd* [1954] 1 W.L.R. 1489.

[91] *E* [2004] Q.B. 1044 at [81]–[82], [91].

[92] *Montes* [2004] EWCA Civ 404; *AM (Iran) v Secretary of State for the Home Department* [2006] EWCA Civ 1813.

[93] *R. (Gungor) v Secretary of State for the Home Department* [2004] EWHC 2117 (Admin).

[94] *E* [2004] Q.B. 1044 at [73]–[75], [77].

[95] *R. v Secretary of State for the Home Department, Ex p. Khawaja* [1984] A.C. 74.

entered by deception was to be upheld. The House of Lords held that it was insufficient for the immigration officer to show that he had some reasonable grounds for his action. The standard should be higher when a power to affect liberty was in issue. An immigration officer would have to satisfy a civil standard of proof to a high degree of probability that the entrant had practised such deception. The court would determine whether that standard of proof had been met.

Rehman[96] provides a more controversial example of the interrelationship between the meaning of the statutory term, and the standard of proof required to satisfy its existence on the facts of the case. R was a Pakistani national with temporary leave to stay the UK, who had applied for indefinite leave to remain. The Home Secretary, acting on the advice of the security service, decided that R's activities were intended to further the cause of a terrorist organisation abroad. The Home Secretary therefore refused his application to remain in the UK, and decided that R's departure would be in the interests of national security. The House of Lords held that the term national security could, as a matter of law, cover not only direct threat to the UK, but also action against a foreign state that might indirectly affect the security of the UK. It held that preventative or precautionary action could be taken in these circumstances.

The House of Lords then considered the standard of proof to determine whether R's actions constituted a threat to national security. The Special Immigration Appeals Commission had applied a test of a "high civil balance of probabilities". The House of Lords disagreed. It held that in determining whether there was a real possibility of activity harmful to national security, the Home Secretary did not have to prove this according to a high civil degree of probability in the manner akin to a trial. While there had to be past proven action relied on as grounds for deportation, the Home Secretary was also entitled to have regard to R's potential action, in accord with the preventative principle. The court should, moreover, give considerable weight to the Home Secretary's assessment in this regard, since he was in the best position to determine what national security required.

B. The Reviewing Court's Options: De Novo Review of Fact

It is important to clarify the issue discussed in this and the next section. There will be cases of relatively simple factual error where there is no meaningful issue concerning the respective role of the court and the initial decision-maker in relation to the determination of the factual error. The existence of the factual error will be uncontentious. Thus, in the *CICB* case there was no doubt that the relevant doctor's report had not been placed before the Board.[97] Similarly in the *Haile* case[98] it was clear that the special adjudicator had confused the names of the relevant organisations in Ethiopia. 17–030

There will, however, be other cases concerned with assessment of more complex factual issues, requiring evaluative judgment, where the "correct"

[96] *Secretary of State for the Home Department v Rehman* [2002] 1 All E.R. 122.
[97] *CICB* [1999] 2 A.C. 330.
[98] *Haile* [2002] I.N.L.R. 283.

factual answer will often not follow inexorably from the data. The court will have to decide, explicitly or implicitly, the extent to which it should be making its own de novo judgment about the relevant factual matter, and the extent to which it should be acting in a more supervisory capacity.

In such instances the court should not generally be making its own de novo decision about the existence of those facts. The court should not regard itself as the primary fact-finder, nor as a general rule should it substitute its judgment about the relevant factual matter for that of the initial fact-finder.[99] The court is not well-equipped or well-placed to undertake de novo review. The finding and evaluation of facts is quintessentially a matter accorded to the initial decision-maker, who will normally have dealt with many such cases. It will have developed an understanding and expertise in the relevant area that a generalist court cannot match.

17–031 It would, moreover, be inappropriate for the courts to exercise de novo judgment in circumstances where the initial decision-maker has conducted an oral hearing, and evaluated the cogency of witnesses. The reviewing court will rarely wish or be able to replicate this process. If it did so with any degree of frequency and proceeded to make a de novo judgment in cases where the factual issues were complex then this would seriously overburden the courts.

If the reviewing court is to engage in de novo review this must be justified by the special circumstances of the particular case, for example where it is felt that the fact finding procedures used by the primary decision-maker are inadequate,[100] or where the facts relate to matters over which the courts have expertise greater than that of the body being reviewed.

The courts should not, however, engage in de novo review merely because the allegation relates to a jurisdictional fact that conditions the existence of the public body's power. The rationale for caution can best be expressed through an example. It may well be that the power of an agency is conditioned on the existence of a "trade dispute". The court stipulates the legal meaning that this term should bear, and it is then for the agency to decide on the facts whether such a dispute exists. This finding is contested before the courts. It is important to distinguish two related issues that arise in such cases.

It is generally accepted that the courts can receive evidence to affirm or controvert the finding of fact made by the agency.[101] If the evidence was not before the agency that made the initial decision, but the court admits it and finds it compelling then to that extent the court will be making its own judgment on the relevant factual matter.

The applicant may, however, simply argue before the reviewing court that the facts which were before the agency did not warrant the finding of a trade dispute. There is in such instances no reason why the reviewing court should substitute its own independent assessment of the facts for that of the agency. It can properly recognise the agency's expertise in relation to the factual matter, while maintaining judicial control, through a test which is less intrusive than

[99] *Bubb* [2011] EWCA Civ 1285 at [27]–[43].

[100] *Citizens to Preserve Overton Park v Volpe* 401 US 402, 415 (1971).

[101] *Eshugbayi Eleko v Government of Nigeria* [1931] A.C. 662 at 670–672.

substitution of judgment. It can, for example, deploy a substantial evidence test and decide whether the factual finding made by the agency is sustainable according to this standard of review.[102]

This has been recognised by the courts. Thus, in *Rolls*[103] it was held that Parliament must have intended that if the local authority applied the correct legal test to determine the meaning of the word "gypsy", the question of whether particular persons were as a matter of fact gypsies within this test was pre-eminently a matter for the local authority, subject to review on *Wednesbury* grounds of unreasonableness. A similar conclusion was reached in *Begum*[104] concerning the duties of a local authority in the housing context. It was held that a decision by a local authority that a person lacked the capacity to make an application for housing, because he could not understand or act on the offer of accommodation could only be challenged if it could be shown to be *Wednesbury* unreasonable. 17–032

We see the same reasoning in *Moyna*,[105] where the claimant sought a disability allowance because she was so severely disabled that she could not prepare a main cooked meal for herself. The House of Lords set out the legal meaning of the statutory term and then held that whether facts fell within the legal category thus defined was a question of fact for the tribunal. It could therefore only be overturned by an appellate body limited to questions of law if the tribunal's conclusions fell outside the bounds of reasonable judgment. This is evident once again in the *Croydon* case,[106] where Baroness Hale made clear that a court would take account of the initial factual determination and that the "better the quality of the initial decision-making, the less likely it is that the court will come to any different decision upon the evidence".

C. The Reviewing Court's Options: Sufficiency of Evidence or Rationality

If a court chooses to act in a more supervisory capacity then it can deploy a substantial evidence test, rationality scrutiny or intervene for manifest error. The substantial evidence test is used extensively in the USA in relation to the assessment of more formal factual findings resulting in a record of the proceedings. The courts will uphold the agency finding if there is substantial evidence in the record as a whole, even if the court might not have made those findings if it had been the initial decision-maker.[107] There must be such relevant evidence as a reasonable mind might accept as adequate to support a conclusion.[108] The test of manifest error for review of fact in EU law is also 17–033

[102] *Universal Camera Corp v NLRB* 340 US 474 (1951).

[103] *Rolls v Dorset County Council* [1994] C.O.D. 448.

[104] *R. v Tower Hamlets LBC, Ex p. Begum* [1993] A.C. 509.

[105] *Moyna v Secretary of State for Work and Pensions* [2003] 1 W.L.R. 1929; *Bubb* [2011] EWCA Civ 1285.

[106] *Croydon* [2009] 1 W.L.R. 2557 at [33].

[107] A. Aman and W. Mayton, *Administrative Law*, 2nd edn (St Paul, MN: West Publishing, 2001), pp.453–460.

[108] *Consolidated Edison Co v NLRB* 305 U.S. 197, 229 (1938).

predicated on the assumption that the courts act in a supervisory capacity when reviewing fact, and do not generally substitute judgment.[109]

The courts might, alternatively, use a test for review couched in terms of rationality or arbitrariness. Such tests have been deployed in the USA in relation to factual findings resulting from less formal adjudicatory proceedings, and in relation to informal rule-making, the argument being that criteria framed in terms of rationality or arbitrariness are better suited to situations where there is no formal record. These tests tend to converge with the substantial evidence test, in the sense that a finding unsupported by substantial evidence is regarded as arbitrary.[110] There will be differences of view as to the application of the substantial evidence test and the rationality/arbitrariness test in particular instances. These differences reflect different views about the degree of deference that should be accorded to the initial fact finder in the specific case.[111]

Factual review in relation to rule-making involves particular difficulties. This is in part because the consequences of invalidation may be more dramatic, in the sense that it might involve overturning an agency rule that has been many years in the making. This is in part because there is a danger in the courts being overzealous in their deployment of this head of review, requiring a degree of factual certainty or probability for a rule that might not be attainable in the light of the existing scientific or technical data. Caution in this respect is therefore warranted. There is no magical way of avoiding this problem, but awareness of the danger will go some way towards preventing its occurrence.

17–034 The role of the court in relation to the initial decision-maker was at the forefront of the decision in *Turgut*.[112] The applicant was a Turkish Kurd, who had evaded the draft in Turkey, and sought asylum in the UK. The special adjudicator found him to be lacking in credibility and rejected the claim. The applicant argued nonetheless that he should be given exceptional leave to remain in the UK, because any young Turkish Kurd who evaded the draft would be subject to a real risk of ill-treatment or torture if returned home. The forced return would therefore be a violation of art.3 ECHR.

The Court of Appeal considered whether it should have the role of primary fact-finder, and decide for itself on all the available material whether the applicant was subject to the risk in question, or whether the court was still exercising an essentially supervisory jurisdiction, albeit heightened because of the human rights context. Simon Brown LJ concluded that the court was not the primary fact-finder: it was not for the court to form its own independent view of the facts, which would prevail over that of the secretary of state.[113] The courts' role was to subject the secretary of state's decision to rigorous examination by considering the underlying factual material to see whether or not it compelled a different conclusion. While the court was not therefore the primary fact-finder, it would not accord any special deference to the secretary of state's conclusion on

---

[109] P. Craig, *EU Administrative Law*, 2nd edn (Oxford: Oxford University Press, 2012), Ch.15.

[110] *Associated Industries v US Dept of Labor* 487 F 2d 342, 350 (2d Cir 1973); *Association of Data Processing Service Organizations, Inc v Board of Governors of the Federal Reserve System* 745 F 2d 677, 683 (DC Cir 1984).

[111] *Allentown Mack Sales and Service v National Labor Relations Board* 522 US 359 (1998).

[112] *Turgut* [2001] 1 All E.R. 719.

[113] *Turgut* [2001] 1 All E.R. 719 at 728–729.

the facts. This was because of the human rights' context; because the court was hardly less well-placed than the minister to make the assessment once it had the material before it; and because of the possibility that the minister might, albeit unconsciously, have underplayed the risk.

The same tension is apparent in other cases, even if it features less explicitly in the court's judgment. Thus, in *Kibiti* the court decided that there was ample evidence on which the IAT could have concluded that there was civil war in the Congo, rather than making its own primary judgment on the point.[114]

The courts' role in these types of case should be supervisory for the reasons discussed above, while accepting that the supervisory review may be more or less intensive depending on the nature of the factual inquiry before the court. The judicial role will also be influenced by the relevant statutory language. Thus, in *Tameside*[115] the minister could only intervene and give directions if the local authority was acting unreasonably. The factual allegations concerning the viability of conducting the selection procedures within the specified time were assessed within this statutory frame. The minister had to show in the light of the factual issues concerning the selection procedures that the local authority was acting so unreasonably that no local authority would have attempted to organise their schooling in such a manner. The House of Lords held that he had failed to demonstrate that this was so.

D. The Reviewing Court's Role: Factual Error only Apparent in the Light of Fresh Evidence

The role of the court viz-á-viz the initial decision-maker in relation to fact finding raises particular considerations where the factual error is only apparent in the light of fresh evidence. The reviewing court may choose to remit the case to the initial decision-maker to consider it again. This was the approach adopted in the *E* case.[116] It remitted the matter to the IAT to consider, in the light of the principles enunciated by the Court of Appeal concerning the admissibility of fresh evidence, whether the new material warranted a re-hearing.[117] However, before remitting the case to the IAT the Court of Appeal took a look at the fresh evidence in order to decide whether there was something that might have affected the IAT's original findings. **17–035**

There are, however, other cases where, having decided to admit the fresh evidence, the reviewing court will make the determination itself, rather than remit the case to the initial decision-maker, more especially when it feels that the fresh evidence admits only one possible conclusion. Thus, in the *A* case[118] the applicant claimed asylum and also that return to Jamaica would be in violation of arts 2 and 3 ECHR. She had informed on a gang member who had killed her daughter, was threatened by other gang members and moved to a different part of Jamaica. She was not however safe in those areas, because the structure of the social order was

[114] *Kibiti* [2000] Imm. A.R. 594.
[115] *Tameside* [1977] A.C. 1014.
[116] *E* [2004] Q.B. 1044.
[117] *E* [2004] Q.B. 1044 at [95]–[98].
[118] *A* [2003] I.N.L.R. 249 at [21]–[34].

such that inhabitants of one part of Jamaica were not welcome in another area. She was harassed, sexually and non-sexually. The IAT concluded that she could settle in a different area of Jamaica. The applicant presented fresh evidence that this was not feasible, and that she would continue to be at serious risk of harm from the original gang. The Court of Appeal admitted the fresh evidence, decided that it admitted of only "one sensible interpretation",[119] which was supportive of the applicant, found in her favour and declined to remit the matter to the IAT.

The approach in the *E* case should be the "default position". The court should remit the case to the original decision-maker to decide whether the new material should be admitted in the light of the principles developed by the courts for the admission of such evidence. It is the original decision-maker who will often be best placed to decide whether the new material warrants a re-hearing, given its greater familiarity with the details of the contested decision, as well as decisions in related cases. The court should therefore be cautious about departing from this default position and should only do so where the fresh evidence that has been admitted really does only allow of one sensible interpretation.

9. CONCLUSION

17–036 The doctrine concerning review for error of fact has been clarified by recent case law, but issues still require resolution. It is important to be mindful of the respective roles of courts and initial decision-makers in deciding whether a factual error has occurred. There are, as seen above, well-developed tests for maintaining judicial control over facts without the courts thereby assuming the role of primary fact-finder. The divide between issues of law and fact is also important, and reference should be made to the previous discussion of this issue.[120]

[119] *A* [2003] I.N.L.R. 249 at [33].

[120] See paras 9–022 to 9–024, 16–029, 16–032, 16–039, 16–043, 16–044.

CHAPTER 18

FAILURE TO EXERCISE DISCRETION

1. CENTRAL ISSUES

i. We saw in the previous chapter that all grants of power to public bodies could be broken into two parts: if X exists, you may or shall do Y. This chapter is principally concerned with judicial constraints on the Y level. Discretion may also exist on the X level, in the conditions which determine the scope of the tribunal's jurisdiction. **18–001**

ii. This is not the place for a jurisprudential analysis on the nature of discretion.[1] Discretion for the purposes of this and related chapters will be defined as existing where there is power to make choices between courses of action or where, even though the end is specified, a choice exists as to how that end should be reached. There are three principal ways in which such discretion can be controlled. This and the following chapters deal with these topics.

iii. First, the courts can impose controls on the *way in which* the discretion has been exercised, with the objective of ensuring that there has been no *failure* to exercise the discretion. Limitations on delegation, and on the extent to which an authority can proceed through policies or rules, are the two principal controls of this type.

iv. Second, constraints can be placed to ensure that there has been no *misuse of power*. The judiciary can impose substantive limits on the power of an administrative body on the ground that it is thereby ensuring that the body does not act *illegally*, outside the remit of its power.

v. Third, the courts can develop principles to make sure that the administrative authority does not misuse its power by acting *irrationally*, thereby placing substantive limits on the power of that authority.

vi. The traditional rationale for judicial intervention has been examined earlier.[2] When the courts intervene to control the X factor they do so in purported fulfilment of the legislative will, by delineating the boundaries of one institution's powers from that of another. A public body adjudicating on furnished tenancies cannot trespass on the territory of a different body dealing with unfurnished tenancies. The rationale for judicial intervention on the Y level has always been more indirect. The authority is within its assigned area, in the sense that it is, for example, properly adjudicating on

---

[1] D. Galligan, *Discretionary Powers, A Legal Study of Official Discretion* (Oxford: Oxford University Press, 1986).

[2] See Ch.1.

furnished tenancies. The issue now is as to the rationale for judicial control over, for example, the fair rent that should be charged for such premises. Traditional theory posited the link with sovereignty and the ultra vires doctrine in the following manner: Parliament only intended that such discretion should be exercised on relevant and not irrelevant considerations, or to achieve proper and not improper purposes. Any exercise of discretion which contravened these limits was ultra vires. The ease with which the judicial approach can be reconciled with sovereignty demonstrates the limits of the ultra vires concept as an organising principle for administrative law. Almost any such controls can be formally squared with legislative intent.

vii. It is in part because of this that the more modern conceptual rationale bases judicial intervention on rather different grounds. Legislative intent and the will of Parliament are still regarded as relevant, but the judicial controls are seen as being as much concerned with supplementing legislative intent as with implementing it. On this view the judicial role is to fashion and enforce principles of fair administration.[3] The implications of this will become apparent in the discussion which follows.

2. DELEGATION

A. General Principles

18–002 The general starting point is that if discretion is vested in a certain person it must be exercised by that person. This principle finds its expression in the maxim *delegatus non potest delegare*. The maxim is however expressive of a principle and not a rigid rule. Whether a person other than that named in the empowering statute is allowed to act will depend on the statutory context. The nature of the subject-matter, the degree of control retained by the person delegating, and the type of person or body to whom the power is delegated, will be taken into account.[4]

Thus in *Allingham*[5] the court held that it was unlawful for a wartime agricultural committee, to which powers concerning cultivation of land had been delegated by the Minister of Agriculture, to delegate to an executive officer the choice of which particular fields should be subject to a certain type of cultivation. In *Ellis*[6] a condition imposed by the licensing committee of a county council that it would not allow films to be shown unless certified for public exhibition by the

[3] See Ch.1; Sir Harry Woolf, *Protection of the Public-A New Challenge* (London: Sweet & Maxwell, 1990), pp.122–124.

[4] J. Willis, "Delegatus non Potest Delegare" (1943) 21 Can. B.R. 257.

[5] *Allingham v Minister of Agriculture* [1948] 1 All E.R. 780, DC.

[6] *Ellis v Dubowski* [1921] 3 K.B. 621 KBD.

Board of Film Censors, was held invalid as involving a transfer of power to the latter.[7] There are numerous other instances where the courts found that an unlawful delegation occurred.[8]

The type of power that is delegated will be important, though not conclusive. Thus, the courts are reluctant to allow further delegation of delegated legislative power.[9] Similarly, the courts are reluctant to sanction the delegation of judicial power. In *Barnard*,[10] the National Dock Labour Board had lawfully delegated powers, including those over discipline, to the local Boards. The latter purported to delegate these to the port manager who suspended the plaintiff from work. This was held to be unlawful, the court stressing that a judicial function could rarely be delegated. The House of Lords in *Vine* reached the same conclusion, though emphasising that there was no absolute rule that judicial or quasi-judicial functions could never be delegated. The golden rule was always to consider the entire statutory context.[11]

B. Agency and Delegation

The relationship between agency and delegation is difficult and the case law is often contradictory. It is best therefore to approach the matter by considering first principles. **18–003**

i. *The creation of agency and delegation*

Both delegation and agency involve an authorisation that someone may act on behalf of another. The things which may be delegated are, as we have seen, limited. There are also limits on the capacity of an agent. An agent can perform any act on behalf of a principal which the principal could execute, except for the purpose of executing a right, or power, or performing a duty imposed on the principal personally, the exercise of which requires discretion or skill, or where the principal is required by statute to do the act personally.[12] Although the ability to delegate and to appoint an agent is limited, there is a difference as to presumption. Where public bodies possess powers the presumption is that the power should be exercised by the person named in the statute, though this is rebuttable. Where private parties are concerned the norm is that a principal should be able to appoint an agent, subject to the limits mentioned above. **18–004**

---

[7] *Mills v London CC* [1925] 1 K.B.; *R. v Greater London Council, Ex p. Blackburn* [1976] 1 W.L.R. 550, CA (Civ Div); *R. v Police Complaints Board, Ex p. Madden* [1983] 1 W.L.R. 447 QBD.

[8] *Jackson, Stansfield & Sons v Butterworth* [1948] 2 All E.R. 558, CA; *H Lavender & Son Ltd v Minister of Housing and Local Government* [1970] 1 W.L.R. 1231 QBD; *Ratnagopal v Attorney General* [1970] A.C. 974, HL. Compare *R. (Ealing LBC) v Audit Commission* [2005] EWCA Civ 556; *Thames Water Utilities Ltd v Transport for London* [2013] EWHC 187 (Admin).

[9] *King-Emperor v Benoari Lal Sarma* [1945] A.C. 14; *Noon v Matthews* [2014] EWHC 4330 (Admin); P. Thorp, "The Key to the Application of the Maxim 'Delegatus non Potest Delegare'" (1972–1975) 2 Auck. U.L.J. 85.

[10] *Barnard v National Dock Labour Board* [1953] 2 Q.B. 18, CA.

[11] *Vine v National Dock Labour Board* [1957] A.C. 488, HL; *Phonepayplus Ltd v Ashraf* [2014] EWHC 4303 (Ch).

[12] *Bowstead and Reynolds on Agency*, 19th edn (London: Sweet & Maxwell, 2010), para.2.017.

This difference in presumption is important and failure to comprehend it has led the courts into error. The error is the belief that principles of agency can "cure" an unlawful delegation. In *Lever Finance*[13] a planning officer represented to a developer that minor changes in a building plan were not material. The developer built the houses, the residents complained, the developer applied for planning permission for the modifications and his application was rejected by the planning committee, the body duly authorised to make the decision. Lord Denning MR held that the public body was estopped from contesting the representation made by its planning officer who had acted within the scope of his ostensible authority. It was clear from the statutory context that delegation to the planning officer would have been ultra vires.[14] This could not be circumscribed by calling the officer an agent who acted within his ostensible authority. If the initial delegation to the officer would have been unlawful that was an end to the matter. It could not be cured by saying that the officer possessed apparent authority, since a necessary condition to make the parent responsible for the acts of its agent is that the parent was not deprived of the capacity to delegate authority of that kind to the agent.[15]

Denning LJ stated the correct position in the *Barnard* case. It was argued that the unlawful delegation to the port manager could be cured by ratification of the Labour Board. Denning LJ rejected this, stating that the effect of ratification was to make the action equal to a prior command. However, since a prior command in the form of delegation would have been unlawful, so also would ratification.[16]

A second example can be taken from cases concerning local authorities. A number of cases have raised the problem of a delegate who takes certain action, for example, to institute legal proceedings, without prior approval. The authority whose approval is required then purports to ratify the action already undertaken.[17] One issue is whether ratification could occur at the stage the proceedings had reached. The other is whether the officer instituting the proceedings was capable of doing so and thus, whether that task could have been validly delegated to that person.

ii. Delegation and retention of authority by the delegator

18–005 There has been uncertainty as to whether the person delegating retains power concurrently with the delegate, in the way that a principal retains power with an agent. There is authority supporting this view.[18]

However, Scott LJ in *Locker*[19] reached the opposite conclusion. The Minister of Health had delegated power to the corporation or their town clerk to

---

13 *Lever Finance Ltd v Westminster (City) LBC* [1971] 1 Q.B. 222, CA (Civ Div).

14 P. Craig, "Representations by Public Bodies" (1977) 93 L.Q.R. 398, 404–408.

15 *Freeman & Lockyer v Buckhurst Park Properties (Mangal) Ltd* [1964] 2 Q.B. 480, CA, at 506.

16 *Barnard* [1953] 2 Q.B. 18 at 39–40. See also *Western Fish Products Ltd v Penwith DC* [1981] 2 All E.R. 204, CA (Civ Div).

17 *Firth v Staines* [1897] 2 Q.B. 70; *R. v Chapman, Ex p. Arlidge* [1918] 2 K.B. 298 KBD; *Bowyer, Philpott & Payne Ltd v Mather* [1919] 1 K.B. 419 KBD; *Warwick Rural District Council v Miller-Mead* [1962] Ch. 441, CA.

18 *Huth v Clark* (1890) 25 Q.B.D. 391; *Gordon Dadds & Co v Morris* [1945] 2 All E.R. 616 at 621. Compare *Battelley v Finsbury LBC* (1958) 56 L.G.R. 165.

19 *Blackpool Corp v Locker* [1948] 1 K.B. 349, CA, Asquith LJ agreed with Scott LJ.

requisition property subject to certain conditions, which were not complied with on the facts of the case, thereby rendering the requisition by the corporation inoperative. Scott LJ stated that the relationship between the minister and corporation or town clerk was not one of principal/agent, that there had been a sub-delegation of legislative power and that this divested the minister of any concurrent power unless he had expressly reserved such power to himself.[20] In the absence of any such reservation a later attempt by the minister to requisition the property was inoperative.

The case has been criticised by writers[21] and doubted in the courts. In *Roberts*,[22] Denning LJ, on similar facts, stated that the town clerk was an agent of the Ministry, that the delegation, whether general or specific, was not a legislative act, and that it did not divest the government of its powers. The *Locker* case was said to turn on the inability of the minister to ratify the acts of an agent who had exceeded the assigned authority.

The relevant authorities were more recently reviewed in *Robertson*.[23] Burton J held that he was bound by *Locker*. He held, moreover, that he preferred the proposition that the ordinary consequence of delegation was divestment of the delegator of the powers delegated, unless there was an express or implied retention of some or all of the powers, whether with or without a provision for notice to the delegate, rather than the proposition that the delegator retained power unless something was stated to the contrary. This was so irrespective of whether the power delegated was administrative or legislative in nature. The principal rationale for Burton J's position was that the possession of concurrent authority by delegator and delegate could lead to uncertainty and that it would not normally be appropriate for the delegator to do for himself what had just been delegated.

C. Government Departments

i. General principles

It is accepted that where powers are granted to a minister they can be exercised by the department. This is known as the *Carltona* principle.[24] It is clearly sensible since it would be impossible for the minister personally to give consideration to each case. The minister need not personally confer the authority for the official to act. It may be granted in accordance with departmental practice,[25] but it is unclear **18–006**

---

[20] *Blackpool Corp* [1948] 1 K.B. 349 at 365, 367–368, 377.

[21] R. Jackson, "County Agricultural Executive Committees" (1952) 68 L.Q.R. 363, 375–376.

[22] *Lewisham LBC v Roberts* [1949] 2 K.B. 608, CA at 621–622.

[23] *Robertson v Department for the Environment, Food and Rural Affairs* [2004] I.C.R. 1289 EAT. The matter was not considered in depth by the Court of Appeal, *Robertson v Department for the Environment, Food and Rural Affairs* [2005] EWCA Civ 138 at [41].

[24] *Carltona Ltd v Commissioners of Works* [1943] 2 All E.R. 560.

[25] *Carltona* [1943] 2 All E.R. 560; *Roberts* [1949] 2 K.B. 608; *R. v Skinner* [1968] 2 Q.B. 700, CA (Crim Div); *Golden Chemical Products Ltd, Re* [1976] Ch. 300 Ch D; *Bushell v Secretary of State for the Environment* [1981] A.C. 75, HL; *R. v Secretary of State for the Home Department, Ex p. Oladehinde* [1991] 1 A.C. 254, HL; *Castle v Crown Prosecution Service* [2014] EWHC 587 (Admin); D. Lanham, "Delegation and the Alter Ego Principle" (1984) 100 L.Q.R. 587.

whether it is necessary for the officer to act explicitly on behalf of the minister.[26] There are judicial indications that the delegation of power should be subject to a requirement that the seniority of the official exercising a power should be of an appropriate level, having regard to the nature of the power in question.[27] The ability to delegate may be limited where the empowering statute explicitly states that the minister in person must perform certain functions.[28] Where civil servants are acting on behalf of ministers the better view is that there is no delegation as such at all. The responsible officer is the *alter ego* of the minister who maintains responsibility before parliament.[29]

It is uncertain whether there is a class of case in which the minister must personally direct his or her mind to the issue. It has been stated that such a distinction would be impossible to apply and that it is not established by the case law.[30] Some other cases dealing with personal liberty such as deportation[31] and fugitive offenders[32] left the matter more open. However, it was held by the House of Lords in *Oladehinde*[33] that the power to deport can be delegated to immigration inspectors who were of a suitable grade and experience, provided that this did not conflict with the officers' own statutory duties.

An important qualification to *Carltona* is apparent in the *Health Stores* case.[34] It was held that *Carltona* only established that the act of a duly authorised civil servant was in law the act of the minister. It did not decide that what the civil servant knew was in law the minister's knowledge, regardless of whether the latter actually knew it. It followed that a minister who reserved a decision to himself, and a civil servant who was authorised by the minister to take a decision, must know or be told enough to ensure that nothing that it was necessary, because legally relevant, for him to know was left out of account. The minister or civil servant must know enough to enable him to make an informed judgment.

ii. The application of Carltona to other public bodies

18–007 It has been held that the *Carltona* principle is not limited to government departments. In *Birmingham Justices*,[35] Sedley LJ held, contrary to earlier indications,[36] that the *Carltona* principle was not dependent on the particular status of civil servants as the alter ego of the minister. The principle could also

---

26 *Woollett v Minister of Agriculture and Fisheries* [1955] 1 Q.B. 103, CA at 120–121.

27 *DPP v Haw* [2007] EWHC 1931 at [29].

28 *R. v Secretary of State for the Home Department, Ex p. Oladehinde* [1991] 1 A.C. 254, HL at 303; *Haw* [2007] EWHC 1931 at [33].

29 See, e.g. *R. v Skinner* [1968] 2 Q.B. 700, CA (Crim Div) at 707; *Nelms v Roe* [1970] 1 W.L.R. 4 DC at 8; *Castle* [2014] EWHC 587 (Admin).

30 *Golden Chemical Products Ltd, Re* [1976] Ch. 300 Ch D at 309–310.

31 *R. v Superintendent of Chiswick Police Station, Ex p. Sacksteder* [1918] 1 K.B. 578, CA at 585–586, 591–592.

32 *R. v Governor of Brixton Prison, Ex p. Enahoro* [1963] 2 Q.B. 455 QBD at 466.

33 *Oladehinde* [1991] 1 A.C. 254.

34 *R. (National Association of Health Stores) v Secretary of State for Health* [2005] EWCA Civ 154; *Secretary of State for the Home Department v AT* [2009] EWHC 512; *R. (Seabrook Warehousing Ltd) v Revenue and Customs Commissioners* [2010] EWCA Civ 140.

35 *R. (Chief Constable of the West Midlands Police) v Birmingham Justices* [2002] EWHC 1087 (Admin).

36 *Nelms* [1970] 1 W.L.R. 4.

allow a Chief Constable to discharge functions through an officer for whom he was answerable. This was so provided that the function could, consistently with the statute, be delegated, and provided also that a suitable person was entrusted with the task. In *Austin*,[37] by way of contrast, it was held that the Police Regulations precluded the Chief Constable from delegating power to dismiss a probationary constable.

This approach was affirmed in *Haw*.[38] Lord Phillips CJ stated that the *Carltona* principle could apply to the exercise of prerogative powers that were not conferred by statute. Where powers were conferred on a minister by statute, the *Carltona* principle would apply to those powers unless the statute, expressly or by implication, provided to the contrary. Where a statutory power was conferred on an officer who was a creature of statute, whether that officer had the power to delegate depended upon the interpretation of the relevant statute or statutes. Where the responsibilities of the office created by statute were such that delegation was inevitable, there would be an implied power to delegate. In such circumstances there would be a presumption, where additional statutory powers and duties were conferred, that there was a power to delegate unless the statute conferring them, expressly or by implication, provided to the contrary.

iii. Government departments and executive agencies

The decision in *Sherwin*[39] provides guidance as to how the preceding principles will apply where the relevant power has been de facto exercised by an executive agency, as opposed to a civil servant within the parent department. **18–008**

Regulation 37 of the Social Security (Claims and Payments) Regulations 1987 gave the secretary of state power to suspend the payment of a benefit where there was an appeal pending on a point which affected payment of that benefit. Regulation 37A gave the secretary of state the same suspensory power where another case was being used as a test case on the same point. A decision to suspend payment had to be made within one month. The applicant's benefit was suspended by a district manager of the Benefit Agency in Birmingham, and this was an executive agency operating within the Department of Social Security. It was argued on behalf of the applicant that notice was not given within the requisite period of one month, because the district manager of the agency could not be said to speak for the minister via the *Carltona* principle.[40] The Divisional Court disagreed, holding that the *Carltona* principle could apply notwithstanding that the officer who made the decision operated within an executive agency.

This decision clearly has much to recommend it. These agencies do not have separate legal status, and powers are still formally vested in the name of the minister. Given that this is so the policy underlying the *Carltona* principle can be seen to have continuing force in this context: the minister cannot literally be expected to address his or her mind to each such decision and must, of necessity,

---

[37] *Austin v Chief Constable of Surrey* [2010] EWHC 266 (Admin).

[38] *Haw* [2007] EWHC 1931 at [33]; *R. (Hamill) v Chelmsford Justices* [2014] EWHC 2799 (Admin).

[39] *R. v Secretary of State for Social Services, Ex p. Sherwin* (1996) 32 B.M.L.R. 1 QBD; *Castle* [2014] EWHC 587 (Admin).

[40] *Carltona* [1943] 2 All E.R. 560.

act through officials. Moreover, the result serves to ensure that it will be the minister who will continue to have ultimate legal responsibility for the decision which has been taken.

The creation of executive agencies has, however, created a tension in this area. These agencies are, as we have seen, designed to have authority over operational matters.[41] They are meant to function de facto more independently from the minister, as compared to the situation when all matters are undertaken by a unitary government department. The idea of the framework agreement, the appointment of a Chief Executive and the growing autonomy these agencies have over pay and conditions, are all factors that serve to reinforce this sense of separation. The particular framework agreement which governed this area expressly emphasised the idea that there was a delegation of operational autonomy to this agency.[42] There is therefore a tension between this institutional scheme and the idea that a decision taken by an official in such a case can really be regarded as one taken on behalf of the secretary of state.

iv. Government departments and contracting-out

18–009 The application of the *Carltona* principle to situations where power has been contracted-out to a private undertaking is legally clearer and also significant. The Deregulation and Contracting Out Act 1994 Pt II makes provision for the contracting-out of certain functions by government to bodies that will normally be private. Government departments have frequently contracted-out functions independently of this Act.[43] The statute was passed in order to enable the body to which the power has been contracted-out to operate in the name of the minister, by analogy with the *Carltona* principle.

Section 69 enables functions which, by virtue of any enactment or rule of law, can be performed by an officer of a minister, to be contracted-out to an authorised party.[44] Section 69(5)(c) makes it clear that the minister may still exercise the function to which the authorisation relates.

Section 71(1) imposes certain limits upon the functions that can be contracted-out. Thus, a function is excluded from ss.69 and 70 where: it would constitute the exercise of jurisdiction of any court or of any tribunal which exercises the judicial power of the state; or its exercise, or a failure to exercise it, would necessarily interfere with or otherwise affect the liberty of any individual; or it is a power or right of entry, search or seizure into or of any property[45]; or it is a power or duty to make subordinate legislation.

18–010 Section 72(2) is designed to render the minister ultimately responsible for action taken by the body to whom the power has been contracted-out, although its meaning is not free from doubt. It is clear from s.72(3)(b) that s.72(2) does not apply in respect of any criminal proceedings brought against the person to whom the power has been contracted out. The precise import of s.72(3)(a) is far less

[41] See Ch.4.

[42] See, e.g. para.4 of the Framework Agreement.

[43] *Quaquah v Group 4 Securities Ltd (No.2)* [2001] Prison L.R. 318 QBD.

[44] Deregulation and Contracting Out Act 1994 s.70 contains provisions concerning local authorities.

[45] This is subject to exceptions listed in Deregulation and Contracting Out Act 1994 s.71(3).

clear. This states that s.72(2) does not apply "for the purposes of so much of the contract made between the authorised person and the Minister, office-holder or local authority as relates to the exercise of the function". It is as, Freedland states,[46] difficult to know what is meant by a rule which says that where a contract brings about the treatment of the acts or omissions of one party as those of the other, that treatment nevertheless does not occur "for the purposes of" so much of the contract as relates to the exercise of the function. An interpretation of this section would enable the minister to plead the terms of the contract against third parties to show that the act or omission of the contractor should not be seen as that of the minister, although this would emasculate s.72(2).

It is readily apparent from discussion of the legislation in the House of Commons that the government regarded these sections as merely technical amendments involving no issue of principle. They were depicted as minor changes to facilitate contracting-out by sweeping away unnecessarily restrictive distinctions as to what had to be done by civil servants as opposed to outside contractors.[47] It is nonetheless difficult to regard these changes with such equanimity. Thus, although Pt II of the legislation is entitled "Contracting-Out" s.69 is actually framed so as to empower an outside body to exercise the functions of the minister. The donee of the power is not simply the alter ego of the minister, but the actual repository of the statutory power.[48] Moreover, the very idea that one can transfer the *Carltona* principle to private bodies to which power has been contracted-out is itself contentious. The point is captured well by Freedland[49]:

> "One cannot read the unanimous judgment of the Court of Appeal in the *Carltona* case without concluding that it would have been unthinkable to that court that their doctrine could be extended so that the functions of a Minister could be exercised by a private sector employee linked to the minister only by a chain of contracts and not by any public service relationship. They would have been amazed that the Minister could be expected on the one hand to seek and maintain a commercial relationship with an outside contractor, while on the other hand treating that contractor as the very embodiment of himself. It requires some ingenuity thus to treat somebody as standing in one's shoes, yet at the same time to keep that person at arm's length."

[46] M. Freedland, "Privatising *Carltona*: Part II of the Deregulation and Contracting-Out Act 1994" [1995] P.L. 21, 25.
[47] Freedland, "Privatising *Carltona*: Part II of the Deregulation and Contracting-Out Act 1994" [1995] P.L. 21, 22.
[48] Freedland, "Privatising *Carltona*: Part II of the Deregulation and Contracting-Out Act 1994" [1995] P.L. 21, 24–25.
[49] Freedland, "Privatising *Carltona*: Part II of the Deregulation and Contracting-Out Act 1994" [1995] P.L. 21, 25.

D. Statutory Power

18–011 Power to delegate will often be granted by statute, a prominent example of this being the Local Government Act 1972 authorising local authorities to discharge any of their functions by committees, officers, or acting jointly with other local authorities.[50] Similar powers exist in other areas such as planning.

3. FETTERING OF DISCRETION: RULES, POLICIES AND DISCRETION

18–012 Unlawful delegation is one way in which a public body may be held to have failed to exercise its discretion. A second is where the public body adopts a policy which precludes it from considering the merits of a particular case. This involves two related issues. First, assuming the public body has a policy or rule, there is the test applied to determine whether it should be allowed to stand. Second, there is the issue of whether the court should encourage public bodies to make rules if they do not currently exist. The words policy and rule will be used interchangeably for the present.

A. An Existing Rule or Policy: The Present Law

i. *General principles*

18–013 A public body endowed with statutory discretionary powers is not entitled to adopt a policy or rule which allows it to dispose of a case without any consideration of the merits of the individual applicant. In *Corrie*[51] the court quashed a decision refusing the applicant permission to sell pamphlets at certain meetings. The decision had been taken in reliance upon a council bylaw that nothing was to be sold in parks. Darling J stated that each application must be heard on its merits. There could not be a general resolution to refuse permission to all.[52] This does not preclude the public body from having any general policy/rule. This is allowed provided that due consideration of the merits of an individual case takes place, and provided that the content of the policy is intra vires.[53]

---

50 Local Government Act 1972 ss.101 and 102; *R. v Secretary of State for the Environment, Ex p. Hillingdon LBC* [1986] 1 W.L.R. 192 QBD, affirmed [1986] 1 W.L.R. 807; *R. (Friends of Hethel Ltd) v South Norfolk DC* [2011] 1 W.L.R. 1216, CA (Civ Div); *R. (Couves) v Gravesham BC* [2015] EWHC 504 (Admin).

51 *R. v London County Council, Ex p. Corrie* [1918] 1 K.B. 68 KBD.

52 *Corrie* [1918] 1 K.B. 68 at 73; *R. v Flintshire County Council Licensing (Stage Plays) Committee, Ex p. Barrett* [1957] 1 Q.B. 350, CA; *Attorney General, ex rel. Tilley v Wandsworth LBC* [1981] 1 W.L.R. 854, CA (Civ Div); *R. (Hardy) v Sandwell MBC* [2015] EWHC 890 (Admin).

53 See, e.g. *Boyle v Wilson* [1907] A.C. 45, HL; *R. v Torquay Licensing Justices, Ex p. Brockman* [1951] 2 K.B. 784 KBD; *Merchandise Transport Ltd v British Transport Commission* [1962] 2 Q.B. 173, CA at 186, 193; *R. v Commissioner of Police of the Metropolis, Ex p. Blackburn* [1968] 2 Q.B. 118, CA (Civ Div) at 136, 139; *R. v Commissioner of Police of the Metropolis, Ex p. Blackburn (No.3)* [1973] Q.B. 241, CA (Civ Div); *R. v Tower Hamlets LBC, Ex p. Kayne/Levenson* [1975] 1 Q.B. 431 at 440, 453.

Most discretionary power is accorded by statute. The position in relation to common law discretionary power has been treated differently by the courts. In *Elias*[54] the claimant who had been interned by the Japanese was denied access to the UK government's ex gratia compensation scheme, because only civilian internees who had been born in the United Kingdom, or one of whose parents or grandparents had been born in the United Kingdom, were eligible to receive payment. She argued, by analogy with the case law on statutory discretion, that the secretary of state had unlawfully fettered his common law power by refusing to consider whether to make an exception to the criteria for compensation.

The Court of Appeal rejected the analogy.[55] It held that it was lawful to formulate a policy for the exercise of statutory discretionary power, but the person who fell within the statute could not be completely debarred, and continued to have a statutory right to be considered by the person entrusted with the discretion. These considerations did not, said the court, apply in the case of an ordinary common law power, since it was within the power of the decision-maker to decide on the extent to which the power was to be exercised when, for example, setting up a scheme. It might be decided that there should be no exceptions to the criteria in the scheme, and that "bright line" criteria should determine eligibility for payments from public funds. Such criteria should not be regarded as a fetter on an existing common law discretionary power to decide each application according to the circumstances of each individual case.

The decision was endorsed by the Supreme Court in *Sandiford*,[56] where the claimant challenged the blanket rule that financial assistance would not be given to fund legal representation in death penalty cases. The secretary of state's power to provide assistance, including legal funding, to British citizens abroad was derived from the prerogative, not statute. There was, said the Supreme Court, no necessary implication, from the mere existence of prerogative powers, that the State as their holder must keep open the possibility of their exercise in more than one sense. There was no necessary implication that a blanket policy was inappropriate, or that there must always be room for exceptions, when a policy was formulated for the exercise of a prerogative power. The policy would, however, be subject to review for irrationality.

ii. The weight to be given to the policy/rule

The courts have not always been uniform in deciding on the weight which the public body is to be allowed to accord to its policy or rule in the context of statutory discretionary power.[57] The dominant line of authority allows the body to apply its rule provided only that the individual is granted the opportunity to contest its application to the particular case. **18–014**

---

[54] *R. (Elias) v Secretary of State for Defence* [2006] 1 W.L.R. 3213, CA (Civ Div).

[55] *R. (Elias) v Secretary of State for Defence* [2006] 1 W.L.R. 3213, CA (Civ Div) at [191]–[192].

[56] *R. (Sandiford) v Secretary of State for Foreign and Commonwealth Affairs* [2014] UKSC 44, [2014] 1 W.L.R. 2697 SC.

[57] D. Galligan, "The Nature and Function of Policy within Discretionary Power" [1976] P.L. 332, 346–355.

Thus, in *Kynoch* Bankes LJ[58] contrasted two situations, the former being permissible, the latter not. It was lawful for an authority to adopt a policy, to intimate to the applicant what that policy was, and to tell that person that it would apply the policy after a hearing, unless there was something exceptional in the case. It was, however, not permissible for the authority to make a determination not to hear any application of a particular character. A similar approach was adopted in *British Oxygen*.[59] The Board of Trade exercised its discretion under the Industrial Development Act 1966 not to give grants towards expenditure of less than £25. BOC had spent a large sum on gas cylinders, the individual cost of which was only £20 and it sought a declaration that the Board of Trade's practice was unlawful. Lord Reid disagreed. His Lordship stated that while anyone possessing discretion could not shut his ears to an application, and while there might be cases where it should listen to arguments that its "rules" should be changed, an authority was entitled to have a policy. This policy would have evolved over many similar cases and might well have become so precise that it could be called a rule. That was acceptable provided that the authority was willing to listen to anyone who had something new to say.[60]

There are, however, some cases which allow only a more minor role to be played by the policy. It can be but one relevant factor used by the public body in arriving at its determinations. Thus, in *Stringer*[61] Cooke J reviewed the legality of a policy that restricted planning permission for developments which could interfere with the Jodrell Bank telescope. He held that the general policy could stand provided that it did not inhibit the taking account of all issues relevant to each individual case which came up for determination.[62]

The preponderance of authority favours the less restrictive approach,[63] and the reasons for preferring this will be examined below. The difference between the two approaches is brought out well by Galligan[64]:

> "The implications of this more restrictive approach are that not only must an authority: (a) direct itself to whether in the light of the particular situation a predetermined policy ought to be altered; but also (b) must refrain from regarding a policy as anything more than one factor

---

[58] *R. v Port of London Authority, Ex p. Kynoch Ltd* [1919] 1 K.B. 176, CA at 184; *Boyle* [1907] A.C. 45 at 57.

[59] *British Oxygen Co Ltd v Board of Trade* [1971] A.C. 610, HL.

[60] *British Oxygen* [1971] A.C. 610 at 625; *Cumings v Birkenhead Corp* [1972] 1 Ch. 12; *R. v Tower Hamlets LBC, Ex p. Kayne-Levenson* [1975] 1 Q.B. 431; *Kilmarnock Magistrates v Secretary of State for Scotland* (1961) S.C. 350; *R. v Secretary of State for the Environment, Ex p. Brent LBC* [1982] Q.B. 593 DC at 640–642; *R. v Chief Constable for the North Wales Police Area Authority, Ex p. AB and DC* [1997] C.O.D. 395 DC; *R. (S) v Chief Constable of South Yorkshire* [2002] 1 W.L.R. 3223, CA (Civ Div).

[61] *Stringer v Minister of Housing and Local Government* [1970] 1 W.L.R. 1281 QBD at 1297–1298.

[62] *H Lavender & Son Ltd v Minister of Housing and Local Government* [1970] 1 W.L.R. 1231 QBD at 1240–1241; *Sagnata Investments Ltd v Norwich Corp* [1971] 2 Q.B. 614, CA (Civ Div).

[63] *R. v Rochdale Metropolitan Borough Council, Ex p. Cromer Ring Mill Ltd* [1982] 3 All E.R. 761 QBD; *R. v Eastleigh Borough Council, Ex p. Betts* [1983] 2 A.C. 613, HL at 627–628; *Re Findlay* [1985] A.C. 318, 334–336. Compare *R. v Windsor Licensing Justices, Ex p. Hodes* [1983] 1 W.L.R. 685, CA (Civ Div); *R. v Secretary of State for the Environment, Ex p. Brent LBC* [1982] Q.B. 593 DC at 640–642; *P. v Hackney LBC* [2007] EWHC 1365.

[64] D.J. Galligan, "The nature and functions of policies within discretionary power" [1976] P.L. 332, 349.

amongst others to take into account. In other words a policy may not become a norm which, subject only to (a) determines the outcome of particular decisions."

iii. Control over the substance of the policy

It is clear that the policy must be legitimate given the statutory framework within which the discretion is exercised.[65] It must be based on relevant considerations and must not pursue improper purposes.[66] These controls are necessary since otherwise a public authority could escape the normal constraints on the exercise of discretion by framing general policies. Thus, in *Venables*[67] it was held that the governing statute required the Home Secretary to have regard to the interests of a child offender when sentencing, and therefore that it was unlawful for him to adopt a policy that failed to take this into account. 18–015

However, the extent of control that the courts should exercise is more questionable, in particular when the courts demand evidence and facts for hypotheses that are not susceptible to clear-cut analysis. Thus, while one could test factually whether the Jodrell Bank telescope would function less efficiently if planning permission were granted for houses, it is less easy to test assumptions such as whether amusement arcades have a socially deleterious effect on young people. The courts have, however, struck down decisions in pursuance of policies of the latter type for this reason.[68] To insist on the type of factual "back-up" which the majority demanded in the *Sagnata* case is excessive.[69]

iv. Rules and process rights: claimant seeks non-application of the policy

The existence of a rule or policy that is upheld by the courts raises issues concerning process rights. There is no general right to participate in rule-making.[70] The individual may, however, wish to argue that the policy *should not be* applied to the particular case. There is authority for the view that such an applicant should be informed of what the policy entails, since this was necessary for any effective right to challenge it.[71] The extent of this right is unclear. There may, depending on the circumstances, be a right to a hearing. It is, however, unclear whether the individual will be entitled to an oral hearing,[72] although this will be so if the applicant would normally be so entitled. Equally it is not certain whether the individual can only challenge the application of the policy in the 18–016

[65] *British Oxygen* [1971] A.C. 610 at 623–624; *Cumings* [1972] 1 Ch. 12 at 37–38; *R. v London Lambeth LBC, Ex p. Ghous* [1993] C.O.D. 302.

[66] See Ch.19.

[67] *R. v Secretary of State for the Home Department, Ex p. Venables* [1998] A.C. 407, HL.

[68] *Sagnata Investments Ltd v Norwich Corp* [1971] 2 Q.B. 616.

[69] The test should not be not what evidence a social scientist with full research grant and expertise, etc. could produce, but what evidence would be available to the corporation, apart from the general feeling that such places were a bad influence on the young.

[70] See Ch.15.

[71] See, e.g. *Kynoch* [1919] 1 K.B. 176 at 184; *Brockman* [1951] 2 K.B. 784 at 788; *R. v Criminal Injuries Compensation Board, Ex p. Ince* [1973] 1 W.L.R. 1334, CA (Civ Div) at 1344–1345.

[72] In the *British Oxygen* [1971] A.C. 610 case Lord Reid stated that the hearing did not have to be oral at 625.

instant case, or whether the substance of the policy can be questioned. The latter issue can clearly be raised on judicial review, the question being whether the individual can raise the matter before the authority itself.[73]

v. *Rules and process rights: claimant seeks application of the policy*

18–017 The individual may conversely wish to argue that an established policy *should be* applied to the particular case, while the public body may wish to change its policy or depart from it. This involves consideration of legitimate expectations, which is discussed later.[74] Suffice it to say the following for the present.

First, if a public body has made a representation to a specific individual or group of individuals that a particular policy will be followed, or that they will be informed before any such change in policy takes place, then the individuals will be entitled to comment before any such change occurs, or before there is a departure from that policy.[75] The change in policy may, moreover, only be countenanced in the instant case if the public interest so demands. Similarly, if an individual has in the past enjoyed a benefit or advantage which could legitimately be expected to continue, that person may be entitled to a statement of reasons for the change of position, and an opportunity to be consulted thereon.[76] A duty to consult will not be derived from the duty to act fairly, independently of a legitimate expectation based on a prior representation or a prior practice of consultation.[77]

Second, the principle of consistency creates a presumption that a public body will follow its own policy. If it seeks to depart from that policy then there must be good reasons for the departure and these must be given to the applicant.[78]

---

[73] Contrast *Boyle* [1907] A.C. 45 at 57, where the court doubted whether the applicant could challenge the policy itself, with *British Oxygen* [1971] A.C. 610, where Lord Reid thought that there were instances where this was possible, at 625. The latter view is supported by *Ince* [1973] 1 W.L.R. 1334 at 1344.

[74] See Ch.22.

[75] *Attorney General of Hong Kong v Ng Yuen Shiu* [1983] 2 A.C. 629; *R. v Liverpool Corporation, Ex p. Liverpool Taxi Fleet Operators' Association* [1972] 2 Q.B. 299, CA (Civ Div); *R. v Secretary of State for the Home Department, Ex p. Khan* [1985] 1 All E.R. 40, CA (Civ Div); *Council of Civil Service Unions v Minister for the Civil Service* [1985] A.C. 374, HL at 408–409; *R. v Secretary of State for the Home Department, Ex p. Ruddock* [1987] 1 W.L.R. 1482 QBD; *R. v Secretary of State for the Home Department, Ex p. Gangadeen* [1998] C.O.D. 216, CA (Civ Div); *R. (Niazi) v Secretary of State for the Home Department* [2008] EWCA Civ 755; *R. (Luton BC) v Secretary of State for Education* [2011] EWHC 217 (Admin).

[76] *CCSU* [1985] A.C. 374 at 408–409; *Khan* [1985] 1 All E.R. 40; *Ruddock* [1987] 1 W.L.R. 1482; *R. v Birmingham City Council, Ex p. Dredger* [1993] C.O.D. 340.

[77] *R. v Birmingham City Council, Ex p. Dredger* [1993] C.O.D. 340 QBD; *R. v BBC, Ex p. Kelly* [1998] C.O.D. 58; *R. v Secretary of State for Education, Ex p. Southwark LBC* [1994] C.O.D. 298 QBD; *R. (BAPIO Action Ltd) v Secretary of State for the Home Department* [2007] EWCA Civ 1139, affirmed on related grounds [2008] 1 A.C. 1003.

[78] *R. v Secretary of State for the Home Department, Ex p. Urmaza* [1996] C.O.D. 479 QBD; *R. v Secretary of State for the Home Department, Ex p. Gangadeen* [1998] C.O.D. 216 CA (Civ Div); *R. (Lowe) v Governor of Liverpool Prison* [2008] EWHC 2167 (Admin).

B. No Existing Rule or "Insufficient" Rules

i. *The debate over rules v discretion*

The discussion thus far has focused on the appropriate judicial response to a situation where an agency has made rules. There is, however, an important literature concerning the extent to which an agency should be encouraged to make rules rather than proceed by way of individual discretionary decisions. Davis did much of the early work in this area.[79] He made clear the importance of discretionary action. It was vital for the individualisation of justice, and no society existed in which discretion was absent. Writers[80] who yearned for rule-based government from which discretion was expunged, what Davis termed the extravagant version of the rule of law, were postulating an ideal that could never be attained. Davis nonetheless argued that while discretion was indispensable, there was "too much of it".[81] He suggested three principal ways in which it could be curtailed. **18–018**

The first was to eliminate unnecessary discretionary power or "confine" it within necessary bounds.[82] This could be achieved by encouraging administrators to make standards and rules that clarified vague legislative criteria. Courts should require an administrative agency to achieve this within a reasonable time. The agency should not feel hesitant about making rules for fear that they would involve too broad a generalisation, for Davis argued that such rules could be limited to a narrow spectrum of cases. Development of agency policy through rule-making was felt to be preferable to this occurring through adjudication, because it allowed more participation by interested parties.

The second method of controlling discretion was to ensure that it was "structured".[83] Whereas confining discretion sought to keep it within certain boundaries, structuring discretion was aimed at controlling how discretionary power was exercised within those boundaries. Davis suggested a number of ways in which this could be achieved: open plans, open policy statements and rules, open findings, open reasons, open precedents and fair procedure. The overall aim was not to eliminate discretion. It was to find the optimum degree of structuring in respect of each discretionary power.

The third limb of Davis' argument was that discretion should be "checked" by, for example, supervision by superiors, administrative appeals and judicial review.

A number of writers have pursued similar themes. Jowell[84] tabulated the merits and demerits of rules. The former included the clarification of organisational aims, thereby rendering it less likely that an official would take a decision based **18–019**

---

[79] K.C. Davis, *Discretionary Justice, A Preliminary Inquiry* (Baton Rouge: Louisiana State University Press, 1969), and *Discretionary Justice in Europe and America* (Urbana: University of Illinois Press, 1976).

[80] F. Hayek, *The Road to Serfdom* (Chicago: University of Chicago Press, 1944) and *The Constitution of Liberty* (Chicago: University of Chicago Press, 1960).

[81] Davis, *Discretionary Justice, A Preliminary Inquiry* (1969), Chs 1–2.

[82] Davis, *Discretionary Justice, A Preliminary Inquiry* (1969), Ch.3.

[83] Davis, *Discretionary Justice, A Preliminary Inquiry* (1969), Ch.4.

[84] J. Jowell, *Law and Bureaucracy, Administrative Discretion and the limits of Legal Action* (New York: Dunellen, 1975), Ch.1.

upon improper criteria, and that rules would be more exposed to public scrutiny, thereby rendering the administration more accountable. There were, moreover, the benefits of like cases being treated alike and the possibility of greater public participation in the formulation of goals. The defects of rules are familiar, including the legalism and rigidity that can be attendant upon them.[85] Despite such disadvantages other writers joined the call for more structuring of discretion.[86]

Reservations have also been expressed. It has been argued that where the issue is inherently subjective, such as that of "need" within social welfare, rules are unsuitable. Rules are also said to be of limited value where the problem is polycentric, with a number of interacting points of influence, such that alteration of one variable produces an effect on all others.[87] A related point is made by those who argue that agencies may not make rules because the issues are complex or controversial, with the consequence that the agency does not yet feel able to commit itself, or wishes to gain more experience before doing so.[88]

ii. Organisations, the decision-making process, rules and discretion

18–020 An assessment of the relative merits of rules and discretion will often be based on assumptions as to how bureaucracies are structured and operate. The relevant literature can assist in the debate about rules and discretion.

Interest in organisational structure emerged earlier last century with the work of the "classical" school of scientific management, the object being to discover the most efficient method of performing an assigned task, and the type of command structure most likely to achieve the organisational purpose.[89] The work of the scientific school was directed initially at private industry, but was viewed with increasing interest by governments who sought to apply such ideas to public functions.[90]

Weber focused more directly on the public sector when constructing his "ideal-type" bureaucracy.[91] The main attributes of a Weberian bureaucracy were

---

[85] Jowell, *Law and Bureaucracy, Administrative Discretion and the limits of Legal Action* (1975), p.22; "For example, a parking meter will not show understanding or mercy to the person who was one minute over the limit because he was helping a blind man across the street". See also J. Jowell, "Legal Control of Administrative Discretion" [1973] P.L. 178.

[86] C. Reich, "The New Property" (1964) 73 Yale L.J. 733.

[87] Jowell, *Law and Bureaucracy, Administrative Discretion and the limits of Legal Action* (1975), Ch.5.

[88] D. Shapiro, "The Choice of Rulemaking or Adjudication in the Development of Administrative Policy" (1965) 78 Harv. L.R. 921; G. Robinson, "The Making of Administrative Policy: Another Look at Rule-Making and Adjudication and Administrative Procedures Reform" 118 U Pa LR (1970); R. Baldwin and K. Hawkins, "Discretionary Justice: Davis Reconsidered" [1984] P.L. 570.

[89] H. Fayol, *General and Industrial Management* (London: Pitman, 1949); F. Taylor, *Scientific Management* (New York: Harper, 1947).

[90] R. Brown and D. Steel, *The Administrative Process in Britain*, 2nd edn (London: Methuen, 1979), pp.156–157.

[91] M. Weber, *The Theory of Social and Economic Organisation*, translated by Henderson and Talcott Parsons (New York: Free Press, 1947), pp.302–313; M. Weber, *Essays in Sociology* (Oxford: Oxford University Press, 1946), pp.196–245.

that[92]: duties should be distributed in a fixed way as official duties; officers should be hierarchically ordered, being responsible to the person above, and responsible for those below; the institution should apply abstract rules to particular cases; the official should operate "without hatred or passion", neutrally applying the given rules; and advancement and dismissal should be objectively assessed. The Weberian scheme was designed to ensure the objective, efficient pursuit of the agency's task, but whether it did so was debatable. For example, reserved detachment could hinder development of esprit de corps, while the insistence on conformity could engender rigidity and inhibit the rational exercise of judgment.[93]

Later theory reacted against the "mechanistic" aspects of earlier analysis. It emphasised the role of more complex motivational considerations that operated on the individual.[94] Systems theory drew analogies from the biological sciences, such that organisations were perceived as systems which have inputs, process those inputs and produce outputs.[95] The processing of inputs will have technical, social and structural aspects, which combine to determine the shape of the organisation. Structural influences would be whether work was organised in terms of specific client groups, or on geographical criteria. Social influences would include the organisation's perception of its primary goals. The outputs would encompass the rules produced by the organisation. These had to satisfy the demands placed upon the organisation by government, client groups, and affected parties. **18–021**

This has implications for the rules/discretion debate. Lawyers tend to view decisions as relatively simple and discrete.[96] A more realistic picture would view them as "complex, subtle and woven into a broader process",[97] resulting from a variety of intersecting inputs. This has three consequences for the debate on rules and discretion.

First, if we decide that a certain administrative area should be more "rule based", then we must be aware that this can lead to problems of displacement. Limiting discretion in one part of the system can lead to its re-emergence elsewhere: "squeeze in one place, and, like toothpaste, discretion will emerge at another".[98] Rendering sentencing more rule-based may, for example, increase the pre-trial **18–022**

[92] P. Blau and M. Meyer, *Bureaucracy in Modern Society*, 2nd edn (New York: Random House, 1971), pp.18–23.

[93] Blau and Meyer, *Bureaucracy in Modern Society* (1971), pp.23–24; M. Crozier, *The Bureaucratic Phenomenon* (Chicago: University of Chicago Press, 1964); T. Burns and G. Stalker, *The Management of Innovation*, 2nd edn (London: Tavistock, 1966); M. Meyer, *Change in Public Bureaucracies* (Cambridge: Cambridge University Press, 1979).

[94] J. March and H. Simon, *Organisations* (New York: Wiley, 1958), Ch.3; C. Argyris, *Personality and Organisation* (New York: Harper, 1957).

[95] J. Bourn, *Management in Central and Local Government* (London: Pitman, 1979); Brown and Steel, *The Administrative Process in Britain* (1979), pp.167–169; P. Self, *Administrative Theories and Politics: An Inquiry into the Structure and Processes of Modern Government* (London: Allen & Unwin, 1973), pp.48–50; W. Evan, *Organisation Theory: Structures, Systems and Environments* (New York: Wiley, 1976).

[96] Baldwin and Hawkins, "Discretionary Justice: Davis Reconsidered" [1984] P.L. 570, 580–586.

[97] Baldwin and Hawkins, "Discretionary Justice: Davis Reconsidered" [1984] P.L. 570, 580.

[98] Baldwin and Hawkins, "Discretionary Justice: Davis Reconsidered" [1984] P.L. 570, 582.

discretion exercised by prosecutors since a person knows that if there is a guilty plea on a certain charge, there will be a particular sentence.[99]

Second, the Davis thesis emphasises the "external aspect" of discretion, this being the potential for arbitrary action if agencies possess broad, unstructured discretionary power. However, organisational theory also emphasises the internal aspect of discretion: systems theory stresses that execution of a programme may be materially affected by the "managerial structures which are built and sustained in connection with it".[100] To enshrine the external aspect of discretion, through its formulation in rules, without any regard for the internal aspect could simply reinforce existing imbalances. Thus, if the internal organisational structure of an agency has been so constructed that the inputs and outputs favour particular interests, a requirement that the agency should make rules to confine the external aspect of its discretion could simply reinforce these existing imbalances.[101]

Third, the balance between rules and discretion will be affected by the purpose that the organisation is seeking to achieve. Thus, the structure of an organisation distributing benefits for disability will depend on the objective behind such a scheme. One such objective has been termed "professional treatment", the idea being that decisions should provide support or therapy viewed from the perspective of a particular professional culture.[102] Given this model, "the incompleteness of facts, the singularity of individual context, and the ultimately intuitive nature of judgment are recognised, if not exalted".[103] In such a system considerations of hierarchy and rules would have little role to play. To insist upon the structuring of discretion could undermine the very purpose of regulation.

iii. Conclusion

18–023 The optimum balance between rules and discretion will vary from area to area. Only careful analysis of particular regulatory contexts can reveal that balance. Given that this is so, suggestions that the courts should force or persuade agencies to develop rules should be treated with considerable reserve. The judiciary are not in a good position to assess whether the complex arguments for and against rule-making should lead to an increase in the prevalence of such rules in a particular area.

---

[99] Baldwin and Hawkins, "Discretionary Justice: Davis Reconsidered" [1984] P.L. 570, 582–583.

[100] P. Selznick, *TVA and the Grass Roots* (Berkeley: University of California Press, 1949), p.67; Brown and Steel, *The Administrative Process in Britain* (1979), pp.193–194.

[101] Such rules might make existing biases more overt and hence more open to attack. It is more likely that they would be built into the system and become the accepted way of administering it, but not be apparent on the face of the rules. Such rules need not appear absurd or even openly biased, see, e.g. the subtle but real prejudices at work within the TVA in favour of wealthier farming interests, Selznick, *TVA and the Grass Roots* (1949), Chs 3–5.

[102] J. Mashaw, *Bureaucratic Justice* (New Haven: Yale University Press, 1983), pp.25–27.

[103] Mashaw, *Bureaucratic Justice* (Yale University Press, 1983), pp.27–28; P. Craig, "Discretionary Power in Modern Administration", in M. Bullinger (ed.), *Verwaltungsermessen im modernen Staat* (1986), pp.79–111.

4. FETTERING OF DISCRETION: CONTRACTS AND THE EXERCISE OF DISCRETION

A. The Problem

The preceding discussion concerned the situation where a public body has discretion and the extent to which it can nonetheless use rules to determine the application of the relevant policy. We have seen that the courts are willing to allow such rules provided that they do not unduly fetter the exercise of the public body's discretion. 18–024

A similar problem can arise where there is a clash between a discretionary power and a contractual obligation which the public body has undertaken. More general issues concerning contracts and public bodies were considered in an earlier chapter.[104] The present discussion focuses on contract and the fettering of discretion. A public body, whether a statutory corporation, governmental department or local authority, has a variety of statutory powers and duties to perform. The issue is the effect of a clash between such a power or duty and an existing contractual obligation that the public body has with a private individual.[105] The courts have to decide when the contractual obligation will be declared ineffective as a fetter on the statutory power or duty, and whether the private individual should have compensation. A public body cannot however escape from a contract merely because it has made a bad bargain.[106]

B. The Incompatibility Test

i. *The origins of the incompatibility test*

The problem was posed clearly in the 19th century case of *Leake*.[107] The court had to decide whether land vested in commissioners responsible for drainage could be dedicated to the public as a highway, it having been thus used for 25 years. Parke J expounded a test based upon compatibility. If the objects prescribed by the statute were incompatible with the land being dedicated as a highway then the commissioners could not in law do such a thing. However, if such use by the public was not incompatible with the statutory purposes then the dedication could take place. On the facts no incompatibility was found to exist. 18–025

This test has much to commend it. If the rule were that no contract could stand if it were hypothetically to be a fetter on another of the body's powers then very few contracts could subsist. This would be disadvantageous to the public body as

---

104 See Ch.5.

105 H. Street, *Governmental Liability* (Cambridge: Cambridge University Press, 1953), Ch.3; J.D.B. Mitchell, *Contracts of Public Authorities* (London: University of London, 1954); S. Arrowsmith, *Civil Liability and Public Authorities* (Winteringham: Earlsgate Press, 1992), pp.72–79; A. Davies, "Ultra Vires Problems in Government Contracts" (2006) 122 L.Q.R. 98.

106 *Attorney General v Lindegren* (1819) 6 Price 287; *Municipal Mutual Insurance Co Ltd v Pontefract Corp* (1917) 33 T.L.R. 234; *Commissioners of Crown Lands v Page* [1960] 2 Q.B. 274, CA.

107 *R. v Inhabitants of Leake* (1833) 5 B. & Ad. 469.

well as the contractor, since the former needs to make contracts where it might be acting as an ordinary commercial undertaking. A balance is required between the necessity for the public body to make contracts, fairness to the contractor, and the need to ensure that the contracts do not stifle other statutory powers. Parke J's incompatibility test achieved this by allowing the contract to stand unless it was incompatible with another statutory power or duty.

ii. Development of the test

18–026 Cases after *Leake* can be divided into two groups. The first group concerns decisions that may have been correct on the facts, in the sense that the contract may have been incompatible with the statutory power. However, the language in these cases was suggestive of a stricter test, to the effect that whenever a statutory power and a contract touched on the same subject-matter the latter would be void. For example, in *Ayr Harbour*[108] trustees were concerned with the management of a harbour and were empowered by statute to take certain lands to carry out specified works. They acquired part of Oswald's land and took a restrictive covenant that they would allow access from his remaining land to the harbour, thereby reducing the amount of compensation they would have to pay. The House of Lords held that the covenant could not stand. Where the legislature had conferred powers to take land compulsorily, a contract purporting to bind them not to use those powers was void. It may well have been that the covenant could be seen as a sterilisation of the "statutory birthright" given to the trustees and hence incompatible with the statute. The court did not, however, speak in terms of incompatibility, the cases cited used a stricter test[109] and *Ayr Harbour* became the cornerstone of arguments that a public body should be freed from a private law obligation. Other cases gave the same impression of a test stricter than that in *Leake*, or at least of the application of that test with undue strictness.[110]

The second group of cases reaffirmed the incompatibility test and applied it less strictly. The Court of Appeal confirmed that a public body or statutory undertaking could grant an easement,[111] or take a restrictive covenant,[112] provided that these were not incompatible with the statutory powers. It emphasised that it could be disadvantageous for a public body not to be able to do so since a potential vendor would be less likely to agree to a sale. Decisions of the House of Lords followed. In *Birkdale District Electricity Supply*[113] Lord Sumner refused to hold ultra vires a contract by Birkdale Electricity Supply that it would not increase the price for electricity higher than that charged by Southport Corporation. His Lordship held that the contract was not incompatible with a statutory power to charge what it wished up to a certain maximum. The *Ayr Harbour* case was distinguished as being concerned with proprietary rights and *Leetham*[114] was disapproved.

[108] *Ayr Harbour Trustees v Oswald* (1883) 8 App. Cas. 623.
[109] *Mulliner v Midland Railway* (1879) 11 Ch. D. 611.
[110] *York Corp v H Leetham & Sons Ltd* [1924] 1 Ch. 557 Ch D; *Amphitrite* [1921] 3 K.B. 500.
[111] *South Eastern Ry Co v Cooper* [1924] 1 Ch. 211, CA.
[112] *Stourcliffe Estates Co Ltd v Bournemouth Corp* [1910] 2 Ch. 12, CA.
[113] *Birkdale District Electricity Supply Co Ltd v Southport Corp* [1926] A.C. 355, HL.
[114] *Leetham* [1924] 1 Ch. 557.

This more lenient approach was endorsed in the *British Transport Commission* case.[115] The question was whether a footpath across an accommodation bridge could be dedicated to the public. This was opposed by the railway authority, which argued that statutory powers enabled it to discontinue the bridge and therefore the footpath across it could not be dedicated to the public. Viscount Simonds endorsed the incompatibility test of *Leake*, and found that there was no incompatibility on the facts of the *British Transport Commission* case. He said of *Ayr Harbour* that "it was in fact an example of incompatibility not a decision to the effect that incompatibility does not supply a test".[116]

iii. *The determination of incompatibility: reasonable foresight*

18–027 The incompatibility test was firmly established in the *British Transport Commission* case.[117] Compatibility is to be judged by reasonable foresight. The issue is whether it is reasonably foreseeable that a conflict will arise between the contract and the statute. The existence of a mere possibility that this might occur is insufficient.[118] Whether incompatibility exists is therefore in part a factual question and in part dependent on construction of the legislation.[119] In *Kilby*[120] the legislation was decisive, the court holding that where a statute specifically stated that the local authority's contractual tenancies could be varied by unilateral notice, a system which circumscribed that power by giving to tenants' representatives an absolute veto was incompatible with the statute. Two factors that have been held relevant in the determination of incompatibility require further mention.

iv. *The determination of incompatibility: contract and property rights*

18–028 In the *Birkdale* case[121] Lord Sumner made statements which could be interpreted to mean that only where the contract created something akin to a property right would it be deemed to be incompatible with the statutory power. Thus, when distinguishing the *Ayr Harbour* case his Lordship said that in that case the trustees were, by the covenant, forbearing to acquire all that the statute intended them to acquire and hence sterilising part of their birth right. This was distinguished from a mere contract, even if in perpetuity. Thus, Lord Sumner believed that if the trustees had covenanted with Oswald to allow him to moor his barges in perpetuity at any wharf the decision could have been different. It was on this ground also that the *Leetham* case was criticised, since the contract was only

---

[115] *British Transport Commission v Westmoreland CC* [1958] A.C. 126, HL; *R. (Newhaven Port and Properties Ltd) v East Sussex CC* [2015] UKSC 7, [2015] 2 W.L.R. 601 SC.

[116] *British Transport Commission* [1958] A.C. 126 at 143; Lord Radcliffe at 152–153.

[117] See also *Ransom and Luck Ltd v Surbiton BC* [1949] Ch. 180, CA; *Marten v Flight Refuelling Ltd* [1962] Ch. 115 Ch D; *Triggs v Staines Urban DC* [1969] 1 Ch. 10 Ch D; *Board of Trade v Temperly Steam Shipping Co Ltd* (1927) 27 Ll. L. Rep. 230; *William Cory and Son Ltd v London Corp* [1951] 2 K.B. 476, CA; *Commissioners of Crown Lands v Page* [1960] 2 Q.B. 274, CA; *Smith v Muller* [2008] EWCA Civ 1425.

[118] *British Transport Commission* [1958] A.C. 126 at 144.

[119] *Newhaven Port and Properties Ltd* [2015] UKSC 7, [2015] 2 W.L.R. 601 SC at [91]–102].

[120] *R. (Kilby) v Basildon DC* [2007] EWCA Civ 479.

[121] *Birkdale* [1926] A.C. 355.

concerned with trading profit, not the land itself.[122] While the possibility of incompatibility is increased if the right is proprietary rather than contractual, it is doubtful whether the distinction should be taken any further than that. There may well be cases where even though there is no proprietary right there is a clear incompatibility between the contract and the statutory power.

v. *The determination of incompatibility: "valid exercises of statutory power"*

18–029 In *Dowty Boulton Paul*[123] the defendant corporation had conveyed to an aircraft company a plot of land for the erection of a factory in 1936, together with the right of the company to use the municipal airport for business purposes for 99 years, or so long as the corporation should maintain the airport as a municipal airport, whichever should be the longer. The conveyance also stated that, without prejudice to the corporation's powers to deal with the airport, they should not, in exercise of their powers, unreasonably affect the plaintiff's rights. The corporation changed its mind in 1970, wishing to use the area for housing, and therefore refused to renew the licence for the airfield. The plaintiff relied on its lease and the corporation argued that this was ultra vires as fettering its statutory powers to provide housing.

Pennycuick VC found for the plaintiff, and reasoned as follows. The cases on incompatibility were concerned with attempts to fetter in advance the future exercise of statutory powers otherwise than by the valid exercise of a statutory power. They were not concerned with the position where a statutory power had been validly exercised creating a right extending over a term of years. The existence of that right excluded other statutory powers in relation to the same subject-matter, but it could not be held to be a fetter on the future exercise of powers.[124]

If this means that whenever a contract or lease is created pursuant to one statutory power it can never be incompatible with a second statutory power then it must be wrong. It is quite possible for one statute to give a public body a general power of leasing land, the lease so granted becoming incompatible with a later statutory power.

18–030 The point is well illustrated by *Blake*.[125] The corporation had acquired land for a park under a statute of 1875 and claimed that the beneficial ownership was, for rating purposes, in the public. This was contested by the valuation officer who argued that such a dedication would be incompatible with the Local Government Act 1933, which allowed a local authority to grant leases. The corporation could not do this in relation to the park if the beneficial ownership was in the public. Where two statutory powers might conflict they had, said Devlin LJ, to be

---

122 *Birkdale* [1926] A.C. 355 at 371.

123 *Dowty Boulton Paul Ltd v Wolverhampton Corp* [1971] 1 W.L.R. 204 Ch D.

124 The case was decided differently, on other grounds, in *Dowty Boulton Paul Ltd v Wolverhampton Corp (No.2)* [1976] Ch. 13, CA (Civ Div).

125 *Blake (Valuation Officer) v Hendon Corp (No.1)* [1962] 1 Q.B. 283, CA; *R. v Hammersmith and Fulham LBC, Ex p. Beddowes* [1987] Q.B. 1050, CA (Civ Div). Compare *Kilby* [2007] EWCA Civ 479.

construed. Here the power to lease in the 1933 Act was subordinate to that in the 1875 Act. However, Devlin LJ could envisage a situation in which the 1933 Act would predominate, for example if the Act contained a specific provision allowing the leasing of parkland, on which hypothesis the beneficial ownership could not be in the public.

Devlin LJ's approach must be correct. The two statutory powers must be construed, and a decision made as to whether the later in time really does render incompatible what was done under the earlier power. It cannot be presumed that the grant of a lease under the first statutory power is immune from the effect of a later statute. The latter may, as in Devlin LJ's example, contain provisions that mandate an outcome inconsistent with the exercise of the earlier statutory power.

There may, however, be cases where the later statute simply contains a broad discretion and the public body seeks to exercise this in a manner that is inconsistent with the contract or property right created pursuant to the earlier statutory power. In such instances Davies has argued persuasively that the court should be able to evaluate whether it is really necessary to disrupt the contract in order to exercise the later statutory discretion. The courts could use a proportionality test, require the public body to identify the public interest goal promoted by the exercise of the later statutory power, and decide whether this constituted an overriding public interest sufficient to justify the disruption to the contractor.[126]

C. Compensation

The issue is whether the contractor should be entitled to some form of compensation if a contract is found to be incompatible with a statutory power or duty. **18–031**

i. Damages for breach of contract

It might be argued that the incompatibility test only tells us that a contract incompatible with a statutory power should not be specifically enforced. It does not mean that the contractor should not obtain damages for breach of the contract. This argument is, however, flawed. A condition precedent to the grant of damages for breach of a contract is that there has been a breach. A party is failing to do something which it has expressly or impliedly promised to do. It is however, difficult to identify any breach of a promise by the public body in these cases. The loss caused to the private contractor flows from the exercise by the public body of its other powers or duties. This is simply a manifestation of the fact that such bodies act both commercially and as public authorities. An allegation of breach of contract would therefore have to be framed such that the public body was promising expressly or impliedly that it would do nothing in its public role that was incompatible with such a contract. Such a promise is clearly unrealistic **18–032**

---

[126] Davies, "Ultra Vires Problems in Government Contracts" (2006) 122 L.Q.R. 98, 110.

and would never be made by a public authority. An express promise would certainly be ultra vires and thus no such promise could be implied.[127]

ii. *Frustration*

18–033 A second possible way of granting compensation would be to say that the contract had been frustrated. There are, however, a number of difficulties.

First, it is not clear whether on normal principles the contract would be held to be frustrated. For example, in the *Cory* case, although the corporation had conceded frustration the point was not argued, and it is unclear whether the contract would have been frustrated since the essence of the claim was simply that it was now less profitable to do the work. Moreover, the compensation available under the Law Reform (Frustrated Contracts) Act 1943 might not be adequate or appropriate.

Second, the suggestion that the public body's action in this type of case should be deemed self-induced frustration is misconceived.[128] The premise behind this concept is that a party cannot rely on frustration brought about by its own conduct, act or election. The party is still liable to perform the contract or pay damages for breach, because it has deliberately or perhaps negligently, without legal constraint, brought about the event in question. A public body has no freedom in this sense. It has either exercised a statutory duty with which the contract is incompatible, or it has decided intra vires to exercise its statutory powers in a particular way with the same result. The action, unlike that of the private individual, is done under these legal constraints and thus, cannot be deemed self-induced frustration.[129]

The third difficulty is perhaps the most important. The frustration solution is predicated on the idea that the contract should be at an end, and that neither the public body nor the private party have any interest in its continuity. This was felt to be the case by Lord Sumner in *Birkdale*.[130] This assumption is not sound, in many cases at least.

18–034 The *Cory* case[131] provides a good example. The plaintiffs in 1936 made a contract with the defendant corporation to dispose of its refuse. In 1948 the defendant, acting as Port of London Health Authority, made bylaws which caused refuse disposal to be more expensive. Cory claimed that this was a breach of contract, arguing that the 1936 contract contained an implied term that the defendant would not do anything which made the contract more onerous. This argument was rejected. The essence of the plaintiff's argument was that it had offered a price presuming that certain costs would be involved and that these costs had risen due to the bylaws. If Cory could not make any profit it would be forced into liquidation. This was of no concern to Lord Sumner since a different

---

[127] *William Cory and Son Ltd v London Corp* [1951] 2 K.B. 476, CA; *Commissioners of Crown Lands v Page* [1960] 2 Q.B. 274, CA at 291.

[128] C. Harlow, "'Public" and "Private" Law: Definition without Distinction" (1980) 43 M.L.R. 241, 248–249.

[129] The argument from self-induced frustration is simply a damages action by the backdoor.

[130] *Birkdale* [1926] A.C. 355 at 374–375.

[131] *Cory* [1951] 2 K.B. 476.

company would undertake refuse collection. Yet, presuming that Cory was a reasonably efficient firm, any other firm which tendered for the contract would set its price taking account of the more expensive nature of the job resulting from the 1948 bylaws. The defendant corporation, therefore, had an interest in the continuity of performance of the task. The simplest solution would be to allow Cory to revise their price upwards to take account of the greater costs incurred. On the facts it appeared that Cory had made a bad bargain from which it was seeking to escape. The general point being made, that a public body may well have an interest in the continuity of the relationship, is nonetheless still important. If the firm undertaking the refuse collection had made a reasonable bargain, which was only rendered unreasonable by regulations that applied *solely* to that firm, then a remedy allowing revision of the price would be beneficial.

iii. A specialised remedy

The particular problems created by public authority contracts, where the public body may be acting in a "public" and a "private" role, is the key to understanding the remedy which should be given. Normal contract principles have as their premise the necessity for one party to show that the other has committed a wrong in order to found a claim for breach of contract. This does not work here. A public body cannot promise not to exercise its statutory or common law powers so as not to interfere with one of its contracts. However, this may be hard on the private contracting party who may have suffered considerable loss. What is required is a remedy that recognises the legality of the public body's action, but which nevertheless accepts that compensation should be payable provided that certain conditions are met. **18–035**

Such remedies exist in other countries[132] such as France, which recognises administrative contracts as a separate entity.[133] The central idea is the predominance of the public interest. It is acknowledged that in certain circumstances the public body may in its public role be required to take action that is detrimental to the other contracting party, and can to this end suspend or vary the contract. Three remedies are of a particular interest.

Imprévision is similar to frustration subject to two important differences. It is based on the continuity of the relationship and not necessarily its termination. It does not require that the contract should have become legally or physically incapable of being performed, and applies when circumstances upset the economic substance of the contract, rendering it more difficult than contemplated, over and beyond the normal risk. The contractor, when this occurs, may, for example, continue to perform the contract, but at a revised rate. **18–036**

The second and perhaps most interesting of the three is a remedy called *fait du prince*. An unforeseeable loss may be shared by the two parties, and the contractor can obtain an indemnity for increased costs. This applies where the contract is affected by something done by the public body in its public role which

---

[132] P. Craig, "Specific Powers of Public Contractors", in R. Noguellou and U. Stelkens (eds), *Comparative Law on Public Contracts* (Brussels: Bruylant, 2010), pp.173–198.

[133] Mitchell, *Contracts of Public Authorities* (University of London, 1954), Ch.4; N. Brown and J. Bell, *French Administrative Law*, 5th edn (Oxford: Clarendon Press, 1998), pp.202–210.

renders the bargain less profitable. The remedy may constitute an indemnity for the private party, or an authorisation to increase the charge. *Fait du prince* will not apply where the loss is caused by legislation affecting all people equally.

A third doctrine, *supervision*, allows the administration to modify the contractual terms in the public interest, but it has to pay an indemnity to the other party if, on the facts, that is the fair balance.

iv. A specialised remedy: standard form contracts

18–037 The flexibility provided by the French remedies is to be envied. Recognising the specialised nature of the problem, specialised solutions have been found. English law, by way of contrast, is inadequate in this respect. While the rules developed as to when a contract should fall are now satisfactory, the consequences are not. Care must be taken to ensure that the person contracting with the public body is not placed in a better position than the party to a purely private contract. However, where action taken by a public authority does not affect people generally then a remedy akin to *fait du prince* would be welcome.[134]

The reality is, however, that much the same solution is reached in UK law through the provisions built into government model terms of contract.[135] The contracting authorities of particular departments are strongly encouraged to adopt these terms and conditions, with any tailoring necessary to reflect individual circumstances.[136] Thus, the Model Terms and Conditions of Contracts for Goods include unilateral powers for the public body. Clause F3 deals with variation of the contract. It provides in essence that the public body may request a variation of the contract, and that the contractor should be given time to consider this and also whether a change in the price is required as a consequence of the variation. If the contractor is unable to accept the variation proposed by the public body, the latter has two options. It can allow the contractor to proceed in accord with the original terms of the contract. The public body can alternatively terminate the contract, except where the contractor has already delivered all or part of the goods, or where the contractor can show evidence of substantial work carried out to fulfil the requirements of the specification.[137] The Model Terms also contain provisions about termination that accord some unilateral power to the public body. Thus, cl.H3 provides that the public body "shall have the right to terminate the Contract at any time by giving [3] Months' written notice to the Contractor", thereby giving the public body a unilateral right to terminate provided that some relatively small notice period is complied with.

The Model Terms and Conditions also deal with compensation. The contractor is required to have adequate insurance cover. Subject to this, cl.H4.2 states that where the public body terminates the contract under cl.H3, the break clause, the

---

[134] In a case such as *Cory* [1951] 2 K.B. 476 the plaintiffs should not be granted compensation, since it is difficult to see how the company was in any worse position than anyone else who would be affected by the new byelaws.

[135] P. Craig and M. Trybus, "England and Wales", in R. Noguellou and U. Stelkens (eds), *Comparative Law on Public Contracts* (Brussels: Bruylant, 2010), pp.338–366.

[136] See, e.g. *http://www.hse.gov.uk/sellingtohse/tandcgoods.pdf; http://dwp.gov.uk/supplying-dwp/doing-business-with-dwp/terms-and-conditions/* [Accessed 22 August 2015].

[137] Model Terms and Conditions for Goods cl.F3.3b

public body shall indemnify the contractor against any commitments, liabilities or expenditure which represent an unavoidable direct loss to the contractor by reason of the termination of the contract, provided that the contractor takes all reasonable steps to mitigate such loss. Where the contractor holds insurance, the public body shall only indemnify the contractor for those unavoidable direct costs that are not covered by the insurance available.

5. THE POSITION OF THE CROWN

The problems when a public body acts in a dual capacity, as a contracting party and as the holder of statutory powers, is not altered by the public body being the Crown. The same principles outlined above should be applied, as to when any contract should fall, and as to whether compensation should be granted. Rowlatt J's decision in the *Amphitrite*[138] does, however, suggest a stricter test. **18–038**

Neutral ship owners, aware of the danger of their ships being detained in British ports, obtained undertakings from the British government that if the ship carried a particular type of cargo it would not be detained. The ship was nevertheless detained and the ship owners sought damages. Rowlatt J denied the claim. It was, he said, competent for the Crown to bind itself by an ordinary commercial contract, but the present agreement was not a contract. It was an arrangement whereby the government purported to say what its future executive action would be, and was an expression of intent and not a contract. Rowlatt J characterised matters in this way because he felt that the government could not fetter its future executive action, which had to be determined by the needs of the community. Reliance was placed upon the cases concerning Crown service.

The case has been criticised in later authorities,[139] and ignored in at least one case to which it might have been applied.[140] On principle the judgment of Rowlatt J is too extreme. It can be accepted that the Crown, like any other public body, cannot enter into a contract that would be incompatible with its executive powers. However, the judgment implies that any contract that in any way fetters the discharge of any executive power must fall, or be deemed not to be a contract at all. This, like the judgment in the *Ayr Harbour* case, is unnecessarily draconian. The position of the Crown should be brought into line with that of other public bodies and the incompatibility test should be applied.

---

138 *Amphitrite* [1921] 3 K.B. 500.

139 *Robertson v Minister of Pensions* [1949] 1 K.B. 227 KBD; *Howell v Falmouth Boat Co* [1951] A.C. 837, HL.

140 *Steaua Romana* [1944] P. 43.

CHAPTER 19

ABUSE OF DISCRETION

1. CENTRAL ISSUES

i. The courts have since the origins of judicial review exercised control to prevent abuse of discretionary power. There are essentially two differing levels at which the judicial controls can operate. The courts can intervene because the tribunal has used its discretionary power for a purpose not allowed by the legislation at all. They can, in addition, intervene because the tribunal, while able in principle to use its power to reach a certain end, has done so in a manner felt to be unreasonable, irrational, or disproportionate. Lord Diplock's distinction in GCHQ[1] between review for illegality and for irrationality captures this idea. **19–001**

ii. This chapter will be concerned with controls that relate to illegality, while those pertaining to irrationality will be considered in later chapters. It may not however always be easy to distinguish between the two levels. Courts and commentators may differ as to which category a particular case should be placed in.

iii. The reason is that statutes conferring broad discretionary powers do not have neat corners, nor is the process of statutory construction self-executing. The determination of legitimate purpose and relevant considerations may therefore entail judicial value judgment and use of substantive principles, not merely discernment of something that is evident from the very face of the enabling legislation.

iv. The discussion of illegality within this chapter will be structured in the following manner. The next three sections will address the basic structure of the Wednesbury test, the types of power that can be judicially controlled and the intensity of judicial review. There will then be a discussion of the constraints that relate directly to illegality. Until recently these were principally of common law origin, and focused on the purpose for which the power was exercised and the relevancy of the considerations that were taken into account. The Human Rights Act 1998 (HRA) added an important head of statutory illegality, which will be analysed in the following chapter.

[1] *GCHQ* [1985] A.C. 374 at 410–411.

2. REASONABLENESS: THE TWO MEANINGS

19–002 The distinction drawn above concerning the levels of review is apparent in the two senses of unreasonableness found in the oft-cited judgment of Lord Greene MR in the *Wednesbury* case.[2] The corporation was empowered to grant licences for Sunday entertainment subject to such conditions as it thought fit. A picture house was licensed subject to the condition that no children under 15 should be admitted. This condition was challenged as unreasonable and ultra vires. Lord Greene MR stressed that the court should not substitute its view for that of the corporation, and then analysed the meaning of the term unreasonable. Two such meanings emerged from his judgment.

The first can be called the "umbrella sense". Unreasonable was used as a synonym for a host of more specific grounds of attack, such as taking account of irrelevant considerations, acting for improper purposes and acting mala fide, which, as Lord Greene MR said, tend to run into one another. The second meaning may be termed the "substantive sense" of unreasonableness: a decision may be attacked if it is so unreasonable that no reasonable public body could have made it. To prove this required something extreme, Lord Greene MR giving the example of a teacher being dismissed because of red hair.

Unreasonableness in its substantive sense was conceived of as a safety net to be used after tests such as relevancy or purpose.[3] The court looked firstly to see whether, for example, the body had acted for improper purposes. If it had not the decision might still be struck down if it was unreasonable in the substantive sense. The two senses of the term unreasonable reflected the two levels of judicial control set out above.

19–003 It is evident that neither of Lord Greene MR's interpretations of the term reasonable accord with the dictionary meaning of that word. The special interpretation of the term reasonableness was said to be warranted by the constitutional position of the courts.[4] They should not intervene simply because they believed that a different way of exercising discretionary power would be more reasonable than that chosen by the public body. This would be to substitute a judicial view as to, for example, the most appropriate way in which to allocate aid, or to disburse licences, for that of the public body. Hence, the controls over the ends that can be pursued by an administrative authority are expressed in terms of relevancy, purpose or unreasonableness in its substantive sense. By phrasing control in these terms, the courts preserve the impression that they are thereby only fulfilling the legislative will. They will not dictate which result should be reached, but they will impose limits on which ends cannot be pursued.

However, what are relevant considerations or proper purposes will often not be self-evident; decisions about these factors will involve social and political

---

[2] *Associated Picture Houses Ltd v Wednesbury Corp* [1948] 1 K.B. 223, CA at 228–230.

[3] *Wednesbury Corp* [1948] 1 K.B. 223 at 233–234.

[4] *Pickwell v Camden LBC* [1983] Q.B. 962 QBD; *Council of Civil Service Unions v Minister for the Civil Service* [1985] A.C. 374, HL at 410–411.

value judgments. Moreover, the boundary line between this form of intervention and more direct substitution of opinion by the judiciary may well become blurred.[5]

3. JUDICIAL REVIEW: TYPES OF POWER CONTROLLED

A. Statutory Power

The UK courts have not traditionally held it to be within their power to invalidate primary legislation, this being regarded as inconsistent with parliamentary sovereignty, although there are dicta countenancing the possibility that primary statute might be judicially challenged in certain exceptional cases.[6] The courts will, however, exercise control over primary legislation in certain instances. 19–004

Thus, it is open to the courts to interpret primary legislation in the manner that best fits with the precepts of judicial review. Primary statutes can moreover be challenged for compatibility with EU law. They are subject to the Human Rights Act 1998, in that the courts have a duty to interpret legislation to be compatible with the Convention rights mentioned in the Act. The courts have in addition heard a claim that primary legislation was not properly made in accordance with the Parliament Acts, and that the Parliament Act 1949 was invalid.[7] Delegated or secondary legislation is subject to judicial review.[8] So too is discretionary power exercised pursuant to a statute and the majority of cases are of this nature.

B. Prerogative Power

It is now clear that prerogative powers are subject to judicial review. The previous orthodoxy was that courts would control the existence and extent of prerogative power, but not the manner of exercise,[9] although there were dicta supporting a wider review power.[10] 19–005

This position was modified by the *GCHQ*[11] case. Their Lordships emphasised that the reviewability of discretionary power should be dependent on the subject-matter, and not whether its source was statute or the prerogative. Certain exercises of prerogative power would, because of their subject-matter, be less justiciable, and Lord Roskill compiled the broadest list of such forbidden

[5] P. Craig, "Political Constitutionalism and the Judicial Role: A Response" (2011) 9 I-CON 112.

[6] *R. (Jackson) v Attorney General* [2006] 1 A.C. 262, HL at [101]–[102].

[7] *Jackson* [2006] 1 A.C. 262.

[8] See Ch.15.

[9] *Case of Monopolies* (1602) 11 Co. Rep. 84b; *Prohibitions del Roy* (1607) 12 Co. Rep. 63; *Burmah Oil Co Ltd v Lord Advocate* [1965] A.C. 75, HL; *Attorney General v De Keyser's Royal Hotel Ltd* [1920] A.C. 508, HL; *Chandler v DPP* [1964] A.C. 763, HL; P. Craig, "Prerogative, Precedent and Power", in C. Forsyth and I. Hare (eds), *The Golden Metwand and the Crooked Cord, Essays in Honour of Sir William Wade* (Oxford: Oxford University Press, 1998), pp.65–91.

[10] *Chandler* [1964] A.C. 763 at 809–810 (Lord Devlin); *Laker Airways Ltd v Department of Trade* [1977] Q.B. 643, CA (Civ Div) (Lord Denning MR).

[11] *Council of Civil Service Unions* [1985] A.C. 374 at 417–418.

territory.[12] Thus, their Lordships held that although the minister had to adduce evidence that the decision to ban national unions at GCHQ was based on considerations of national security, the question of whether such considerations outweighed the prima facie duty of fairness was for the minister himself to decide.[13] Subject to this important caveat, their Lordships were willing, albeit in varying degrees, to consider the manner of exercise of prerogative power, as well as adjudicating on its existence and extent. The success of such a challenge might be affected by the ground of attack,[14] as well as the nature of the subject-matter.

Later courts have been prepared to reassess the extent to which any particular prerogative subject-matter is immune from review, and the general trend has been to reduce such islands of immunity. Thus in *Bentley*[15] it was held that the prerogative of mercy was subject to judicial review, and the court could stipulate the types of consideration which could be taken into account when exercising this power. In *Abbasi*[16] the court held that it was no answer to a claim for judicial review to say that the source of the power of the Foreign Office was the prerogative, since it was the subject-matter that was determinative. In *Bancoult*[17] Sedley LJ opined that a number of the examples given by Lord Roskill might be regarded as questionable in the modern day and that the grant of honours for reward, the waging of a war of manifest aggression or a refusal to dissolve Parliament could well call in question immunity based purely on subject-matter. The House of Lords in *Bancoult* held that there was no reason in principle why prerogative legislation should not, like other prerogative acts, be reviewable by the courts on ordinary principles of legality, rationality and procedural impropriety.[18] There can nonetheless be sharp differences of view about the application of the principles of review in a particular case, as evident from *Bancoult* discussed below.[19] While the courts are more willing to review prerogative power than hitherto, the nature of the particular prerogative may still affect the incidence of review.[20]

---

[12] *Council of Civil Service Unions* [1985] A.C. 374 at 418. The making of treaties, the defence of the realm, the dissolution of parliament, the appointment of Ministers, as well as other areas where the subject-matter was not justiciable.

[13] *Council of Civil Service Unions* [1985] A.C. 374 at 402–403, 406–407, 412–413, 420–421, unless it seems the minister's decision was one which no reasonable minister could make, 406. See also, *R. v Secretary of State for the Home Department, Ex p. Ruddock* [1987] 1 W.L.R. 1482, where the court emphasised that the evidence concerning national security must be cogent and that the court could, if necessary, hear such evidence in camera; *R. v Secretary of State for Foreign and Commonwealth Affairs, Ex p. Everett* [1989] 2 W.L.R. 224.

[14] Lord Diplock stated that an applicant would be more likely to succeed if alleging illegality or procedural impropriety, as opposed to irrationality, *Council of Civil Service Unions* [1985] A.C. 374 at 411; C. Walker, "Review of the Prerogative: The Remaining Issues" [1987] P.L. 62.

[15] *R. v Secretary of State for the Home Department, Ex p. Bentley* [1994] Q.B. 349 DC.

[16] *R. (Abbasi) v Secretary of State for Foreign and Commonwealth Affairs* [2002] EWCA Civ 1598 at [106].

[17] *R. (Bancoult) v Secretary of State for Foreign and Commonwealth Affairs* [2007] EWCA Civ 498 at [46]. The Court of Appeal's judgment was overturned by the House of Lords, but this did not affect the point made in the text.

[18] *R. (Bancoult) v Secretary of State for Foreign and Commonwealth Affairs* [2008] UKHL 61; *R. (Misick) v Secretary of State for Foreign and Commonwealth Affairs* [2009] EWHC 1039 (Admin).

[19] See para.19–011.

[20] *R. (Harrow Community Support Ltd) v Secretary of State for Defence* [2012] EWHC 1921 (Admin).

Certain prerogative powers, notably those relating to the civil service and ratification of Treaties, have been placed on statutory footing, thereby increasing parliamentary scrutiny and control over what had hitherto been prerogative discretionary power.[21]

C. Common Law Discretionary Power

There is debate as to whether there is a category of power that is neither statutory nor prerogative in nature, but which is more properly to be classified as common law discretionary power.[22] Whether this category is required depends in part on the definition of prerogative power. **19–006**

Dicey described the prerogative as the lawful basis of all executive action which could be done without the authority of Parliament.[23] On this view there would be no need for a third source of power, since all executive action that could be done without statute would be treated as within the prerogative. Blackstone however took a narrower view. The prerogative referred to those rights and capacities which the King enjoyed alone, in contradistinction to others, and not to those which he enjoyed in common with his subjects, since "if once any prerogative of the Crown could be held in common with the subject, it would cease to be prerogative any longer".[24] For Blackstone it was only those non-statutory powers that really were unique to the executive, and were not possessed by ordinary persons, that should be termed prerogative powers. The power to make contracts, ex gratia payments and the like did not, on this view, come within the prerogative. They were simply common law powers held by the Crown, which had the same capacity in this respect as an ordinary person. The courts themselves may be uncertain as to how to classify certain powers. Thus in *Elias* the court appeared to conceptualise a ministerial ex gratia compensation scheme as a common law discretionary power separate from the prerogative, although there were also statements that appeared to regard the ministerial power as part of the prerogative.[25]

The courts have tended towards the Blackstonian rather than the Diceyan view. They have held that the powers of the Crown were not confined to those conferred by statute or prerogative, but extended, subject to any relevant statutory or public law constraints and to the competing rights of other parties, to anything that could be done by a natural person.[26] The Court of Appeal in the *Shrewsbury* case concluded that this residual category of ministerial power was exceptional.

---

[21] *Governance of Britain* (2007), Cm.7170, paras 14–51; Constitutional Reform and Governance Act 2010.

[22] B.V. Harris, "The 'Third Source' of Authority for Government Action" (1992) 109 L.Q.R. 626; M. Freedland, "Public Law and Private Finance—Placing the Private Finance Initiative in a Public Law Frame" [1998] P.L. 288; B.V. Harris, "The 'Third Source' of Authority for Government Action Revisited" (2007) 123 L.Q.R. 225.

[23] Dicey, *Law of the Constitution*, 10th edn (Liberty Fund, 1967), p.425.

[24] Sir W. Blackstone, *Commentaries on the Law of England*, 16th edn (1825), Vol.I, p.239.

[25] *R. (Elias) v Secretary of State for Defence* [2006] 1 W.L.R. 3213, CA (Civ Div) at [185], [193].

[26] *R. v Somerset CC, Ex p. Fewings* [1995] 1 W.L.R. 1037, CA (Civ Div); *R. v Secretary of State, Ex p. C* [2000] 1 F.L.R. 627, CA (Civ Div); *R. (Shrewsbury and Atcham BC) v Secretary of State for Communities and Local Government* [2008] EWCA Civ 148.

Thus, although the Crown was not a creature of statute and had power to do whatever a private person could do, as an organ of government it could only exercise that power for the public benefit, and for identifiably "governmental" purposes within limits set by the law.[27] Richards LJ dissented in part. He contended that it was necessary to explain the basis on which the ordinary business of government was conducted and that the simplest and most satisfactory explanation was that it depended heavily on the third source of powers, namely the normal powers, capacities and freedoms of a corporation with legal personality. It was, in Richards LJ's view, unnecessary and unwise to introduce qualifications to the effect that the powers could only be exercised for the public benefit or for identifiably "governmental" purposes.

The existence of the third source of government authority was endorsed by Lord Sumption, who gave the majority judgment in *New London College*.[28] He held that it had long been recognised that the Crown possessed some general administrative powers to carry on the ordinary business of government, which were not exercises of the royal prerogative and did not require statutory authority, although he also acknowledged that the extent of such powers and their exact juridical basis were controversial. He accepted that in previous case law[29] the juridical base of such power was said to be the Crown's status as a common law corporation sole, with all the capacities of a natural person, subject to any particular limits imposed by law. Lord Sumption, however, questioned whether the analogy with a natural person was really apt for public or governmental action, as opposed to purely managerial acts of a kind that any natural person could do, such as making contracts, acquiring or disposing of property, hiring and firing staff and the like. The issue was not resolved on the facts of the case, because the Supreme Court held that the Secretary of State's statutory power to administer immigration control necessarily extended to a range of ancillary and incidental administrative powers not expressly spelt out in the Act.

19–007 Insofar as there is this further type of power the trend of the case law is, as seen in the context of the prerogative, to base reviewability on the subject-matter of the power and not its source. Thus, in *Elias* the court duly considered the claim that there had been a fettering of ministerial power in relation to the ex gratia compensation scheme, and was willing to do so irrespective of whether this was conceptualised as a common law discretionary power or a prerogative power.[30]

This is surely correct as a matter of principle. The courts quite rightly broke down previous barriers between review of statutory and prerogative discretionary power, and held that review should be dependent on the subject matter rather than the source of the power. Insofar as a separate category of common law discretionary power is recognised then it too should be subject to the same precepts. This view has been reinforced by the House of Lords' Constitution Committee, which criticised the "Ram doctrine" named after its creator, Sir

---

[27] *Shrewsbury and Atcham* [2008] EWCA Civ 148; *R. (W) v Secretary of State for Health* [2014] EWHC 1532 (Admin).

[28] *R. (New London College Ltd) v Secretary of State for the Home Department* [2013] UKSC 51, [2013] 1 W.L.R. 2358 SC at [28].

[29] *Ex p. C* [2000] 1 F.L.R. 627, CA (Civ Div); *Shrewsbury and Atcham* [2008] EWCA Civ 148.

[30] [2006] 1 W.L.R. 3213 at [193].

Granville Ram.[31] The Committee was critical of the proposition that a minister could do anything a natural person could do, unless prohibited by legislation, and emphasised that ministerial power, unlike that of a private person, was subject to constraints derived from public law precepts, including the Human Rights Act 1998.

There has been greater uncertainty as to the extent to which the courts will review contracting power, and the relevant case law has been affected by the extent to which the courts have been willing to conclude that a public body exercising such power is exercising a public function.[32]

D. Non-statutory Bodies

The courts have also imposed controls on the way in which power is exercised by bodies that are not the creature of statute. The law in this area has been driven principally by developments relating to remedies, and its precise metes and bounds are still being worked out. There will be detailed consideration of this in the chapter on remedies.[33] **19–008**

4. JUDICIAL REVIEW: INTENSITY

Judicial review can vary in intensity, which alters depending on the subject-matter of the action. The intensity of review can affect the application of irrationality or proportionality, as exemplified by the courts' willingness to protect individual rights even prior to the Human Rights Act 1998,[34] and by the variable intensity of review that prevails even under the Human Rights Act 1998, flowing from the fact that not all rights are equally important.[35] This can be briefly demonstrated by contrasting two decisions. **19–009**

In *Brind*,[36] to be considered fully later, their Lordships made it clear that if the exercise of discretionary power impinged upon a fundamental right then the courts would require an important competing public interest to be shown in order to justify this intrusion. By way of contrast, in the *Hammersmith* case,[37] the House of Lords reviewed charge capping by the secretary of state, which the applicant local authorities claimed was in breach of the relevant statute. Lord Bridge held that while the court could intervene if the secretary of state had acted illegally, that is for improper purposes, or on irrelevant considerations, it should in the sphere of economic policy, be wary of irrationality review unless there was some manifest absurdity or bad faith.

---

[31] See also Constitution Committee, *Thirteenth Report: The pre-emption of Parliament*, HL Paper 165 (Session 2012-13), paras 49–65.
[32] See paras 27–022 to 27–024.
[33] See Ch.27.
[34] See paras 19–021 to 19–024.
[35] See paras 20–051 to 20–064.
[36] *R. v Secretary of State for the Home Department, Ex p. Brind* [1991] 1 A.C. 696, HL.
[37] *R. v Secretary of State for the Environment, Ex p. Hammersmith and Fulham LBC* [1991] 1 A.C. 521, HL.

It is nonetheless important to note that while intensity of review can vary when the courts consider irrationality or proportionality, the judicial approach taken to challenges cast in terms of improper purposes and relevancy is different. The general judicial approach is that courts substitute judgment for that of the primary decision-maker as to whether a purpose is proper, or whether a consideration is relevant. The rationale is, as noted above, that the courts conceive of themselves as delimiting the ambit of what the statute allows through a normal process of statutory interpretation. This conceptualisation is reinforced by thinking of improper purposes and relevancy as heads of illegality.

The reality is that whether a case concerning discretion is classified as falling within purpose/relevancy, or whether it is held to come within irrationality/proportionality, can be contestable and dependent on the relative breadth with which the court defines the relevant considerations.[38] The reality is also that statutory construction can often involve difficult value choices, and complex issues of interpretation. It is therefore arguable that the courts should be willing to accord some measure of deference or weight to the views of the administration when determining whether a purpose is proper, or whether a consideration is relevant. This does not mean that the administration's view should be determinative in this regard, but it does mean taking seriously the considered judgment of the administration as to why, for example, a consideration should or should not be felt relevant to the exercise of discretion under a particular statute.[39]

5. ILLEGALITY: COMMON LAW CONSTRAINTS

19–010 The courts have, ever since the origins of judicial review, exerted control over discretion to prevent power from being misused or abused. Thus, in *Rooke's Case*,[40] Commissioners of Sewers had repaired a river bank and taxed Rooke for the whole amount, despite the fact that other landowners benefited from the work. The Commissioners had discretion as to the levying of the money, but the court struck the decision down: the discretion was to be exercised according to reason and law and it was unreasonable for Rooke to bear the whole burden.

---

[38] See para.21–007. Take the classic example of the unreasonable decision, dismissal of a teacher because of the colour of her hair. If the considerations relevant to dismissal of a teacher are broadly defined as "any physical characteristic" then dismissal on the above ground is relevant. However, the question could and should be posed more specifically, distinguishing between the types of physical characteristics relevant to teaching and those, such as hair colour, which were not.

[39] H. Wilberg, "Deference on Relevance or Purpose? Wrestling with the Law/Discretion Divide", in H. Wilberg and M. Elliott (eds.), *The Scope and Intensity of Substantive Review, Traversing Taggart's Rainbow* (Oxford: Hart Publishing, 2015), Ch.11.

[40] *Rooke's Case* (1598) 5 Co. Rep. 99b; *Hetley v Boyer* (1614) Cro. Jac. 336; *R. v Askew* (1768) 4 Burr. 2186; *Leader v Moxon* (1773) 2 W. Bl 924.

A. Improper Purposes

The law reports abound with examples of courts striking down discretionary decisions where the discretion has been used for an improper purpose. A public body with power to construct lavatories could not use that power in order to build a subway under a street[41]; deportation could not be used to achieve extradition[42]; the Home Secretary could not use his powers to revoke television licences where people had bought a new licence early in order to avoid a price rise[43]; a local authority had no power to enter into speculative financial swap transactions[44]; a local authority could not refuse to renew a lease for a solicitor's firm in retaliation for the firm bringing actions against it[45]; a local authority could not use its conservation powers improperly to prevent demolition of a particular building[46]; and a local authority could not use its power to dispose of land to promote the electoral advantage of the dominant party on the council.[47] The courts determine the purpose of a particular statute as a matter of construction. While they maintain that they are only keeping the authority within the boundaries of its power and not substituting their view, the dividing line can be a fine one. **19–011**

For example, planning authorities may grant planning permission unconditionally, or subject to such conditions as they think fit. A number of cases have turned on the legality of such conditions. The general position adopted has been that the conditions must fairly and reasonably relate to the permitted development.[48] In applying this test the courts have upheld fairly broad conditions,[49] but they have also struck down others by using concepts that are open to debate. Thus, the court held invalid conditions attached to the grant of a caravan site licence which required site rents to be agreed with the council and security of tenure to be provided for caravan owners.[50] The House of Lords found that the legislation only allowed terms to be attached that related to the use of the site, and not to the types of contract the site owner could make with the caravan owners. In reaching this conclusion the court argued that freedom of contract was a fundamental right, and that if Parliament intended to empower a third party to make conditions that affected the provisions of a contract between others then this should be expressed

---

41 *Westminster Corp v L & NW Ry* [1905] A.C. 426, HL; *Galloway v London Corporation* (1866) L.R. 1 H.L. 34, HL.

42 *R. v Governor of Brixton Prison, Ex p. Soblen* [1963] 2 Q.B. 243, CA.

43 *Congreve v Home Office* [1976] Q.B. 629, CA (Civ Div).

44 *Hazell v Hammersmith and Fulham LBC* [1992] 2 A.C. 1, HL.

45 *R. (Trafford) v Blackpool BC* [2014] EWHC 85 (Admin).

46 *R. (Silus Investments SA) v Hounslow LBC* [2015] EWHC 358 (Admin).

47 *Porter v Magill* [2002] 2 A.C. 357, HL.

48 *Pyx Granite Co Ltd v Ministry of Housing and Local Government* [1958] 1 Q.B. 544 at 572, affirmed [1960] A.C. 260, HL; *Newbury District Council v Secretary of State for the Environment* [1981] A.C. 578, HL.

49 *Fawcett Properties Ltd v Buckingham CC* [1961] A.C. 636, HL.

50 *Chertsey Urban DC v Mixnam Properties Ltd* [1965] A.C. 735, HL.

in clear terms.[51] In other cases the courts relied on the principle that private rights of property should not be taken without compensation unless there exists clear authority in the statute.[52]

This is not to say that either of the decisions was wrong. The balance between presumptions as to freedom of contract and the protection of private property rights unless due compensation is paid, and the overall direction of the planning system, is a complex one on which opinions may differ. There is, however, no doubt that the denomination of a purpose as proper or improper raises issues of political and social choice, which do not cease to be so by being expressed in the language of vires. Later authority has held that planning law is of a "public character", and that the courts should not introduce private law principles unless these are expressly authorised by parliament or are necessary to give effect to the legislative purpose.[53]

19–012 Cases raising such issues are not restricted to the planning field. In *Roberts*,[54] Poplar Council had decided to pay their low grade workers £4 per week. The relevant statute empowered the council to pay such wages as it thought fit.[55] Despite this the House of Lords found that the payment was excessive: the statute was to be read subject to an implied condition that the wages should be reasonable, which was to be judged by current rates payable in the industry. Anything above this was a gratuity. The advancement of a social purpose, such as payment of a minimum wage, was unlawful.[56]

The decision in *Bromley* further exemplifies the difficulties of determining the purposes for which a statutory power can be used.[57] The Transport (London) Act 1969 s.1 imposed on the GLC a duty to develop policies that promoted the provision of integrated, efficient and economic transport facilities for Greater London. The policies were implemented by the London Transport Executive (LTE), which was required, so far as was practicable, to make up any deficit incurred in one accounting period within the next.[58] The legislation empowered the GLC to take such action as was necessary and appropriate in order to enable the LTE to comply with this obligation.[59] The GLC also had power to make grants to the LTE for any purpose.[60]

The GLC decided to implement a resolution, which had been included by the majority group in their manifesto, to reduce fares by 25 per cent. To this end, the GLC issued a supplementary precept for rates to all London boroughs. The

---

51 *Mixnam Properties Ltd* [1965] A.C. 735 at 763–764.

52 *Minister of Housing and Local Government v Hartnell* [1965] A.C. 1134, HL. Compare *Kingston LBC v Secretary of State for the Environment* [1973] 1 W.L.R. 1549 DC.

53 *Pioneer Aggregates (UK) Ltd v Secretary of State for the Environment* [1985] A.C. 132, HL at 140–141; *R. v St Edmunsbury Borough Council, Ex p. Investors in Industry Commercial Properties Ltd* [1985] 1 W.L.R. 1157 DC.

54 *Roberts v Hopwood* [1925] A.C. 578. Compare *Pickwell* [1983] Q.B. 962.

55 Metropolis Management Act 1855 s.62.

56 See also, *Prescott v Birmingham Corp* [1955] Ch. 210, CA; *Taylor v Munrow* [1960] 1 W.L.R. 151 DC; *Bromley LBC v Greater London Council* [1983] 1 A.C. 768, HL.

57 *Bromley LBC* [1983] 1 A.C. 768. See *R. v London Transport Executive, Ex p. Greater London Council* [1983] Q.B. 484 DC, in which a revised fares reduction scheme was held to be lawful.

58 Transport (London) Act 1969 s.7(3)(b).

59 Transport (London) Act 1969 s.7(6).

60 Transport (London) Act 1969 s.3(1).

money would be paid by the GLC to the LTE as a grant, to enable the latter to balance its accounts. An indirect result of the fare reduction was that the GLC would lose approximately £50 million of the rate support grant. Bromley LBC sought to quash the supplementary rate, arguing that it was either beyond the powers of the GLC under the 1969 Act, or that it was an invalid exercise of discretion under that legislation.

The House of Lords upheld the claim. Their Lordships recognised that the power to make grants contained within s.3 conferred a wide discretion, and that such grants could be made to supplement the revenue received by the LTE from fares. This discretion was, however, limited. The LTE's basic obligation was to run its operations on ordinary business principles, which the fare reduction contravened. The GLC could not use its grant making powers to achieve a social policy that was inconsistent with these obligations. Reduction of the fares was also invalid because it involved a breach of fiduciary duty owed by the GLC to the ratepayers. The effect of the 25 per cent reduction in fares would be to place an inordinate burden on the ratepayers, since it would lead to a loss of rate support grant. Nor could the GLC defend its policy on the basis that it possessed a mandate to lower fares. Those who were elected were representatives and not delegates. They could not regard themselves as irrevocably bound by their manifesto. **19–013**

The case is interesting in many respects.[61] The statutory language was, Lord Diplock admitted,[62] sometimes opaque and elliptical, and this is reflected in the fact that although the House of Lords reached a unanimous conclusion, their Lordships differed in their interpretation of the legislation.

The idea that a local authority owes a fiduciary duty to its ratepayers is not new,[63] but it was not subject to thorough judicial investigation. The idea seems self-evident: a local authority occupies a position of trust, or a fiduciary duty, in relation to the ratepayers whose money it is using, and who are the beneficiaries of its services. Closer analysis reveals a shakier foundation.[64] Ratepayers do not provide even the majority of local authority revenue, which comes from central government. The fiduciary duty operates, moreover, in an asymmetrical fashion. It serves to quash expenditure deemed to be in breach of this duty, but does not impose any obligation to spend money that is unreasonably withheld.[65] Given that ratepayers were, as their Lordships admitted, only one part of those to whom the local authority owed duties, it was then necessary to determine the balance between their interests and those of others in local society. This was a difficult determination and it is arguable that the determination made by the elected representatives should have been allowed to stand.

The response of the House of Lords to the argument based upon the election manifesto is, in many ways, incontrovertible. A person who is elected is not a **19–014**

---

[61] J. Dignan, "Policy-Making, Local Authorities and the Courts: the 'GLC Fares' Case" (1983) L.Q.R. 605; M. Loughlin, *Local Government in the Modern State* (Oxford: Oxford University Press, 1986), Ch.3.

[62] *Bromley LBC* [1983] 1 A.C. 768 at 822–823.

[63] *Roberts* [1925] A.C. 579; *Prescott* [1955] Ch. 210.

[64] Note, Griffiths (1982) 41 C.L.J. 216.

[65] D. Williams, "The Control of Local Authorities", in J. Andrews (ed.), *Welsh Studies in Public Law* (Cardiff: University of Wales Press, 1970), pp.132–133.

delegate for the voters, but a representative who must act in the best interests of all constituents. The representative cannot be irrevocably bound to fulfil election promises. This is unexceptionable, but it does not sit easily with the views of the House of Lords in the *Tameside*[66] case, where their Lordships placed much emphasis on the fact that the local authority had a virtual mandate to retain certain grammar schools in the area. It was a significant factor to be taken into account when assessing the reasonableness of the local authority's conduct in attempting to allocate children to the correct school.

The difficulties concerning interpretation of the scope of a power and the divide between proper and improper purposes are not confined to cases where the power is derived from statute. The issue is equally apparent in cases where it is founded on the prerogative, as exemplified by *Bancoult*.[67] The case concerned the legality of Orders in Council made pursuant to the prerogative that removed any right of abode and disentitled the Chagos islanders from entry or presence on the islands without permission from the United Kingdom. The claimants challenged the legality and rationality of the Orders in Council. The majority held that the Orders in Council should be regarded as lawful, in the sense that they could exclude the islanders from returning to their island. The right of abode was regarded as a "creature of the law", which the law gave and could take away.[68] The minority, by way of contrast, concluded that the Order in Council was invalid, because there was no warrant for saying that it could be used to exclude an indigenous population from its homeland. There was, said Lords Bingham and Mance, no historical authority for such a power and it was contrary to principle.[69] There were similar differences of view in relation to irrationality. For the majority, the exercise of the prerogative power was consonant with ordinary principles of judicial review. It should not be struck down because it was not unreasonable to refuse resettlement, more especially because of the security considerations relating to a US military base. For the minority, the Order in Council forbidding resettlement was irrational, in part because there was no good reason for making it[70] and in part because an order removing the islanders' right of abode abrogated a fundamental right and hence called for heightened scrutiny.[71]

It would be a simple world in which an authority always acted for one purpose only. Complex problems can arise where one of the purposes is lawful and one is regarded as unlawful. The courts have used various tests to resolve this problem. One test considers the true purpose for which the power was exercised. Provided that the legitimate statutory purpose was achieved it is irrelevant that a subsidiary object was also attained.[72] A second approach analyses the dominant purpose for

66 *Secretary of State for Education and Science v Tameside MBC* [1977] A.C. 1014, HL.

67 *Bancoult* [2008] UKHL 61.

68 *Bancoult* [2008] UKHL 61 at [45].

69 *Bancoult* [2008] UKHL 61 at [69]–[70], [155]–[157].

70 *Bancoult* [2008] UKHL 61 at [72].

71 *Bancoult* [2008] UKHL 61 at [172].

72 *Westminster Corp* [1905] A.C. 426; *R. v Brixton Prison Governor, Ex p. Soblen* [1963] 2 Q.B. 243, CA.

which the power was exercised.[73] A third test considers whether any of the purposes were authorised, although this has less support in the case law than the previous two tests. A fourth approach is to examine whether any of the purposes was unauthorised and had an effect on the decision. If this was so the decision was overturned as being based on irrelevant considerations.[74]

B. Relevancy

The second principal method of controlling the exercise of discretion is relevancy: a decision will be declared ultra vires if it is based upon irrelevant considerations, or if relevant considerations are not taken into account. Relevancy overlaps with control maintained through improper purposes and a number of the cases could be classified under one section or the other. **19–015**

In exercising control based upon relevancy, the courts have, for example, defined the types of considerations which licensing justices can take into account. These included the character and needs of an area,[75] but not the terms on which an applicant conducted the business, if those terms did not affect the applicant's fitness to hold the licence.[76] Similar control is maintained over other areas such as education,[77] housing,[78] the police,[79] the mentally disordered,[80] asylum,[81] disabled people,[82] sentencing[83] and nationalised industry,[84] although the courts have been more reluctant to specify the considerations deemed to be relevant in conduct of foreign relations.[85]

The stringency with which the courts have applied the criterion of relevancy has varied in different areas,[86] and there has been an unwillingness to declare invalid administrative decisions simply because the applicant could point to one

[73] *R. v Immigration Appeals Adjudicator, Ex p. Khan* [1972] 1 W.L.R. 1058 DC; *R. v Greenwich LBC, Ex p. Lovelace* [1991] 1 W.L.R. 506 DC.

[74] *Hanks v Minister of Housing and Local Government* [1963] 1 Q.B. 999 QBD at 1016, 1020, 1037; *R. v Inner London Education Authority, Ex p. Westminster City Council* [1986] 1 W.L.R. 28 QBD; *R. v Broadcasting Complaints Commission, Ex p. Owen* [1985] Q.B. 1153 DC.

[75] *Sharp v Wakefield* [1891] A.C. 173.

[76] *R. v Hyde* [1912] 1 K.B. 645 KBD; *R. v Bowman* [1898] 1 Q.B. 663 QBD; *R. v Wandsworth Licensing JJ, Ex p. Whitbread and Co Ltd* [1921] 3 K.B. 487 KBD; *R. v Birmingham Licensing Planning Committee, Ex p. Kennedy* [1972] 2 Q.B. 140, CA (Civ Div).

[77] *Sadler v Sheffield Corp* [1924] 1 Ch. 483 Ch D; *Short v Poole Corporation* [1926] Ch. 66, CA.

[78] *Bristol District Council v Clark* [1975] 1 W.L.R. 1443, CA (Civ Div); *Cannock Chase District Council v Kelly* [1978] 1 W.L.R. 1, CA (Civ Div); *Victoria Square Property Co Ltd v Southwark LBC* [1978] 1 W.L.R. 463, CA (Civ Div).

[79] *R. v Commissioner of Police of the Metropolis, Ex p. Blackburn* [1968] 2 Q.B. 118, CA (Civ Div); *R. v Commissioner of Police of the Metropolis, Ex p. Blackburn (No.3)* [1973] Q.B. 241, CA (Civ Div).

[80] *Retarded Children's Aid Society Ltd v Barnet LBC* [1969] 2 Q.B. 22 DC.

[81] *R. (Refugee Action) v Secretary of State for the Home Department* [2014] EWHC 1033 (Admin).

[82] *R. (South Tyneside Care Home Owners Association) v South Tyneside Council* [2013] EWHC 1827 (Admin).

[83] *R. v Secretary of State for the Home Department, Ex p. Venables* [1998] A.C. 407, HL.

[84] *South of Scotland Electricity Board v British Oxygen Co Ltd* [1956] 1 W.L.R. 106; [1959] 1 W.L.R. 587, HL.

[85] *R. (Al Rawi) v Secretary of State for Foreign and Commonwealth Affairs* [2007] 2 W.L.R. 1219, CA (Civ Div).

[86] *Fletcher's Application, Re* [1970] 2 All E.R. 527, CA (Civ Div).

"relevant" factor which the authority did not take into account. This is particularly so where it is felt that the consideration did not have a causal effect upon the authority's determination and where the decision being impugned was not determinative of rights, such as a decision by a local authority to refer a landlord to a rent tribunal.[87]

19–016 While the courts will intervene if a relevant consideration has not been taken into account, they will not generally have regard to the weight it has been accorded, this being seen as the function of the primary decision-maker.[88] The courts can, however, have regard to such matters where the weighing was *Wednesbury* unreasonable, or where there was evidence that the decision-maker had fettered its discretion.

An important issue that has arisen in a number of cases is whether a local authority is allowed to take account of shortage of resources when deciding how to fulfil its statutory duties.[89] In *Barry*[90] the House of Lords considered whether the availability of resources could be taken into account under the Chronically Sick and Disabled Persons Act 1970 s.2(1). This provided that if a local authority was satisfied that it was necessary to make arrangements in order to meet the needs of a chronically sick or disabled person then it was the duty of that authority to make those arrangements. The applicant had been provided with cleaning and laundry services pursuant to this provision, but the local authority withdrew these services due to cuts in funding from central government. A majority of the House of Lords held that, as a matter of construction, the needs of such a person for services could not sensibly be assessed without having some regard for the costs of providing them.

The same issue arose in *Tandy*.[91] The House of Lords decided as a matter of construction that the question of "suitable education" for the purposes of the Education Act 1993 s.298, was to be determined solely by reference to educational considerations, in the sense that the education had to be efficient and suitable for the child's age and ability. Resources were not relevant to this determination, although they were relevant when choosing between different ways of making such provision. Lord Browne-Wilkinson distinguished the *Barry* case. He held that the statutory provision in *Barry* was somewhat strange in that it imposed a duty to meet the "needs" of disabled persons, even though the lack of

---

[87] *R. v Barnet and Camden Rent Tribunal, Ex p. Frey Investments Ltd* [1972] 2 Q.B. 342, CA (Civ Div); *R. v Secretary of State for Social Services, Ex p. Wellcome Foundation Ltd* [1987] 1 W.L.R. 1166, CA (Civ Div).

[88] *Tesco Stores Ltd v Secretary of State for the Environment* [1995] 1 W.L.R. 759, HL.

[89] Fredman, "Social, Economic and Cultural Rights", in D. Feldman (ed.), *English Public Law* (2004), Ch.10; Syrett, "Opening Eyes to the Reality of Scarce Health Care Resources?" [2006] P.L. 664; King, "The Justiciability of Resource Allocation" (2007) 70 M.L.R. 197; Pillay "Courts, Variable Standards of Review and Resource Allocation: Developing a Model for the Enforcement of Social and Economic Rights" [2007] E.H.R.L.R. 616; Newdick, "Judicial Review: Low-Priority Treatment and Exceptional Case Review" [2007] Med. L.R. 236; Palmer, *Judicial Review, Socio-Economic Rights and the Human Rights Act* (2007); King, *Judging Social Rights* (2012).

[90] *R. v Gloucestershire CC, Ex p. Barry* [1997] A.C. 584; *R. (Savva) v Kensington and Chelsea RLBC* [2010] EWCA Civ 1209; *R. (KM) v Cambridgeshire CC* [2010] EWHC 3065 (Admin); *R. (Nestwood Homes Developments Ltd) v South Holland DC* [2014] EWHC 863 (Admin).

[91] *R. v East Sussex CC, Ex p. Tandy* [1998] A.C. 714; *R. (JL (A Child)) v Islington LBC* [2009] EWHC 458 (Admin); *R. (Kebede) v Newcastle City Council* [2013] EWCA Civ 960.

the benefits enumerated in the section could not possibly give rise to "need" in any stringent sense of the word. The 1970 Act had, moreover, not provided any guidance as to how such needs were to be assessed. Given that this was so it was not, he said, surprising that the House of Lords had held that resources could be taken into account. In *Tandy*, by way of contrast, the statute imposed an immediate obligation to make arrangements for "suitable education", which was defined by objective criteria.

The courts have had to decide whether the availability of resources is a relevant consideration under other social welfare legislation, or how statutory provisions with resource implications should be exercised, and have generally made their decisions by way of statutory interpretation.[92] Where the statute is construed as imposing a specific duty for the benefit of particular individuals the court will be considerably less willing to listen to arguments concerning limited resources, but there can be significant differences of view by judges in the same case as to whether the statute can be regarded as imposing duties and the precise content of such obligations.[93] The issue concerning resources can also arise in the context of a challenge to the rationality of administrative action.[94] **19–017**

The difficulties with statutory interpretation and identification of relevant/irrelevant considerations are exemplified by the *Corner House* decision.[95] In 2004 the Director of the Serious Fraud Office (SFO), acting under the Criminal Justice Act 1987, began an investigation into allegations of corruption against a UK company. This included a valuable arms contract between the UK and Saudi Arabia, for which the company was the main contractor. During the investigation the company represented to the SFO that disclosure of information required by a statutory notice served on it would adversely affect relations between the UK and Saudi Arabia and jeopardise the arms contract. Following communications and meetings, the director took the view that he had a duty to investigate crime and that the investigation should continue, which it did. In the autumn of 2006 the SFO intended to investigate bank accounts in Switzerland to ascertain whether payments had been made to an agent or public official of Saudi Arabia. This provoked an explicit threat by the Saudi authorities that if the investigation continued Saudi Arabia would withdraw from the existing bilateral counter-terrorism co-operation arrangements with the UK, withdraw co-operation from the UK in relation to its strategic objectives in the Middle East and end the negotiations for the procurement of Typhoon aircraft. Following further discussion, the director in December 2006 decided that the investigation should be discontinued.

The claimants sought judicial review of his decision, contending that it had been unlawful to permit a threat to influence it. The Divisional Court quashed the decision. It decided that in yielding to the threat the director had ceased to exercise his powers under the 1987 Act independently, without surrendering them

---

[92] *R. v Sefton BC, Ex p. Help the Aged Ltd* [1997] 4 All ER 532, CA (Civ Div); *R. v Norfolk CC, Ex p. Thorpe* [1998] C.O.D. 208 QBD; *R. v Bristol City Council, Ex p. Penfold* [1998] C.O.D. 210 QBD; *R. (G) v Barnet LBC* [2004] 2 A.C. 208, HL; *R. (Spink) v Wandsworth LBC* [2005] 1 W.L.R. 2884, CA (Civ Div); *R. (Conville) v Richmond upon Thames LBC* [2006] 1 W.L.R. 2808, CA (Civ Div).

[93] *Barnet LBC* [2004] 2 A.C. 208.

[94] *R. (Rogers) v Swindon NHS Primary Care Trust* [2006] 1 W.L.R. 2649, CA (Civ Div).

[95] *R. (Corner House Research) v Director of the Serious Fraud Office* [2009] 1 A.C. 756, HL.

to a third party; that there had been no sufficient appreciation of the damage to the rule of law caused by submission to a threat directed at the administration of justice; and that submission to a threat was lawful only when it was demonstrated to a court that there was no alternative course open to the decision-maker.

19–018 The House of Lords reversed the decision. The director of the SFO had legal authority in the narrow sense to make the decision whether a prosecution could continue, since this was demanded of him by the empowering legislation. It was how he exercised this discretionary power that was in issue. The House of Lords considered whether it was legitimate for the SFO to take account of the threat by the Saudis at all, and if so whether the SFO gave undue weight to that threat and thereby abdicated responsibility. The answer on the first issue was affirmative. There was no basis in the empowering statute, or in normative principle, to say that the SFO should never be able to take any account of such threats. So the issue was the weight to be accorded to that threat in the light of the other values to be served by prosecution of fraud cases. The House of Lords held that: it was legitimate to take account of such a threat in deciding whether to pursue a prosecution; the SFO was in a good position to assess its weight; the SFO did not abdicate its discretionary power; and made its own considered judgment in the light of the evidence before it.

The House of Lords' decision has been criticised for being insufficiently searching in this respect and for undervaluing the rule of law. This critique is contestable. It is certainly true that the courts should insist that challenged decisions should have sufficient evidential base. Having said this, it is not clear why the views of the reviewing court on the issue of the weight of the relevant consideration and the balancing involved therein should be substituted for that of the SFO. What the *Corner House* decision does undoubtedly show is that statutory interpretation to identify relevant considerations, and the weight to be accorded to them, is not a self-executing exercise.

C. Bad Faith

19–019 The concept of bad faith has remained either largely in the region of hypothetical cases,[96] or has been treated as synonymous with improper purposes or relevancy.[97] Bad faith would automatically render applicable control mechanisms in terms of purpose or relevancy. This is not to say that spite, malice or dishonesty may not exist. It clearly can.[98] It is to question the necessity of its being a separate method of control.[99]

---

[96] *Smith v East Elloe Rural DC* [1956] A.C. 736, HL at 770.

[97] *Westminster Corp* [1905] A.C. 426; *Webb v Minister of Housing and Local Government* [1965] 1 W.L.R. 755, CA, 784.

[98] *Roncarelli v Duplessis* (1959) 16 D.L.R. (2d) 689.

[99] It may be easier to evade a clause excluding judicial review if the allegation is of bad faith, *Lazarus Estates Ltd v Beasley* [1956] 1 Q.B. 702, CA at 712–713, 722. Compare *R. v Secretary of State for the Environment, Ex p. Ostler* [1977] Q.B. 122, CA (Civ Div) at 138–139.

6. HUMAN RIGHTS: THE COMMON LAW BACKGROUND

The Human Rights Act 1998 has, as will be seen in the next chapter, created a new statutory head of illegality and requires public authorities to comply with the rights laid down in the European Convention of Human Rights. Before examining this important innovation it is necessary to understand how far the common law protected fundamental rights, since there may be situations in which it is still relevant.[100] On the traditional theory of sovereignty Parliament is omnipotent. This constitutional orthodoxy has, moreover, been taken to mean that talk of fundamental rights within our system is simply a misnomer: what we have are residual liberties. This may represent the traditional position. It ceased, however, accurately to reflect the reality of the common law jurisprudence. **19–020**

A. Common Law Jurisprudence

It is clear that our courts had, even prior to the Human Rights Act 1998, begun to give a special status to fundamental rights and to engage in more searching scrutiny in such instances. **19–021**

i. Heightened rationality review and alignment of common law and ECHR

In *Brind*,[101] the Home Secretary had issued directives under the Broadcasting Act 1981 requiring the BBC and the IBA to refrain from broadcasting certain matters by persons who represented organisations that were proscribed under legislation concerning prevention of terrorism. The ambit of this proscription was limited to direct statements made by the members of the organisations. It did not, for example, prevent the broadcasting of such persons on film, provided that there was a voice-over account paraphrasing what had been said. The applicant's claim based directly on the European Convention of Human Rights failed for reasons considered in the next chapter. The decision none the less contained interesting dicta on rights at common law. Lord Bridge, having noted the absence of any code of rights in domestic law, then had this to say[102]: **19–022**

> "But … this surely does not mean that in deciding whether the secretary of state, in the exercise of his discretion, could reasonably impose the restriction he has imposed on the broadcasting organisations, we are not perfectly entitled to start from the premise that any restriction of the right to freedom of expression requires to be justified and nothing less than an important competing public interest will be sufficient to justify it."

While the primary judgment as to whether the public interest warranted the restriction rested with the minister, the court could exercise a secondary judgment by asking whether a reasonable minister could reasonably make that judgment on the material before him.[103] Lord Templeman reasoned in a similar manner. He

---

[100] M. Hunt, *Using Human Rights Law in English Courts* (Oxford: Hart Publishing, 1997).

[101] *Brind* [1991] 1 A.C. 696.

[102] *Brind* [1991] 1 A.C. 696 at 748–749.

[103] *Brind* [1991] 1 A.C. 696 at 749.

held that freedom of expression was a principle of every democratic constitution; that the court must inquire whether a reasonable minister could reasonably have concluded that the interference with this freedom was justifiable; and that "in terms of the Convention" any such interference must be both necessary and proportionate.[104]

The courts went further in other cases. They took the important step of aligning the position at common law with that under the ECHR. In the *Spycatcher* case[105] Lord Goff, in delineating the ambit of the duty of confidentiality, stated that he saw no inconsistency between the position under the Convention and that at common law. The dictum of Lord Goff was used in the *Derbyshire* case.[106] Their Lordships held that, as a matter of principle, a local authority should not be able to maintain an action in its own name for defamation, since this would place an unwarranted limitation on freedom of speech. Lord Keith, giving judgment for the House, reached this conclusion on the basis of the common law and echoed Lord Goff's statement that there was no difference in principle between the common law and the Convention.

19–023 The "green light" given by the House of Lords was not lost on lower courts. It became normal for there to be searching scrutiny in rights-based cases.[107] In *Leech*[108] the court considered the validity of a rule that allowed a prison governor to read letters from prisoners and stop those that were inordinately long or objectionable. The court held that the more fundamental the right interfered with, the more difficult was it to imply any such rule-making power in the primary legislation.

The same approach was evident in *Smith*,[109] where there was a challenge to the policy of prohibiting gay men and women from serving in the armed forces. Sir Thomas Bingham MR held that the more substantial the interference with human rights, the more the court would require by way of justification before it would accept that the decision was reasonable.[110]

In *McQuillan*[111] the applicant challenged the legality of an exclusion order prohibiting him from entering Great Britain on the ground that he had been involved in terrorism. He maintained that he was no longer a member of a terrorist organisation and that his life was in danger if he stayed in Northern Ireland. The Home Secretary refused to revoke the exclusion order. Sedley J recognised that freedom of movement, subject only to the general law, was a fundamental value of the common law.[112] The power given to the Home

---

104 *Brind* [1991] 1 A.C. 696 at 750–751.

105 *Attorney General v Guardian Newspapers (No.2)* [1990] 1 A.C. 109, HL at 283–284.

106 *Derbyshire CC v Times Newspapers Ltd* [1993] A.C. 534, HL.

107 *R. v Broadcasting Complaints Commission, Ex p. Granada Television Ltd* [1995] C.O.D. 207, CA (Civ Div); *R. v Secretary of State for the Home Department, Ex p. Norney* (1995) 7 Admin. L.R. 861 QBD; *R. v Secretary of State for the Home Department, Ex p. Moon* [1996] Imm. A.R. 477; *R. v Secretary of State for Social Security, Ex p. Joint Council for the Welfare of Immigrants* [1997] 1 W.L.R. 275, CA (Civ Div); *R. v Chief Constable for the North Wales Police Area Authority, Ex p. AB and DC* [1997] 3 W.L.R. 724 DC.

108 *R. v Secretary of State for the Home Department, Ex p. Leech* [1994] Q.B. 198, CA (Civ Div).

109 *R. v Ministry of Defence, Ex p. Smith* [1996] Q.B. 517, CA (Civ Div).

110 *Smith* [1996] Q.B. 517 at 554.

111 *R. v Secretary of State for the Home Department, Ex p. McQuillan* [1995] 4 All E.R. 400 QBD.

112 *McQuillan* [1995] 4 All E.R. 400 at 421–422.

Secretary to restrict this freedom, not by modifying the general law, but by depriving certain persons of the full extent of this right, was a draconian measure, which could be justified only by a grave emergency. It was for this reason that the courts would scrutinise the minister's reasoning closely and "draw the boundaries of rationality tightly around his judgment".[113] This was equally true in relation to the right to life. This too was recognised and protected by the common law and "attracted the most anxious scrutiny by the courts of administrative decision-making".[114]

ii. The principle of legality and the interpretation of legislation

The courts also created a priority rule, to the effect that legislation would not be held to allow an interference with a common law constitutional right unless this was sanctioned by Parliament. **19–024**

Thus, in *Witham*[115] Laws J held that access to the court was a constitutional right and that the Executive could only abrogate that right if it was specifically permitted to do so by Parliament. Laws J accepted that Parliament might expressly limit this right, but stated that he could not conceive of anything short of this which would convince the court that the right had been limited by implication. The class of case where the right might be limited by necessary implication was a class with no members.[116]

A similar approach is apparent in *Simms*.[117] Legislation was to be read subject to a principle of legality, which meant that fundamental rights could not be overridden by general or ambiguous words. This was, said Lord Hoffmann, because there was too great a risk that the full implications of their unqualified meaning might have passed unnoticed in the democratic process. In the absence of express language, or necessary implication to the contrary, the courts would therefore presume that even the most general words were intended to be subject to the basic rights of the individual. Parliament had, therefore, to squarely confront what it was doing and accept the political cost. Lord Hoffmann left open the possibility that a fundamental right could be overridden by necessary implication, as well as by express words. It seems clear that he would only accept that this was so in extreme cases, and this is the import of the phrase "necessary implication". Viewed in this way his approach was very similar to that of Laws J.

---

113 *McQuillan* [1995] 4 All E.R. 400 at 422.

114 *McQuillan* [1995] 4 All E.R. 400 at 422.

115 *R. v Lord Chancellor, Ex p. Witham* [1998] Q.B. 575 QBD at 585–586.

116 Compare *R. v Lord Chancellor, Ex p. Lightfoot* [1999] 2 W.L.R. 1126 QBD.

117 *R. v Secretary of State for the Home Department, Ex p. Simms & O'Brien* [2000] 2 A.C. 115, HL; *R. (Morgan Grenfell & Co Ltd) v Special Commissioner of Income Tax* [2003] 1 A.C. 563, HL; *R. (Anufrijeva) v Secretary of State for the Home Department* [2004] 1 A.C. 604, HL; *A v HM Treasury* [2010] 2 A.C. 534 SC.

B. Secondary Literature

19–025 The preceding case law was complemented by a rich secondary literature, in which many of the contributions were from judges. Different strands of reasoning are apparent in this literature.

A prominent strand was that the courts should recognise and employ a general presumption against interference with human rights, which was grounded in the common law. Thus, Lord Browne-Wilkinson[118] argued that the presumption should apply not only when there was ambiguity in the domestic provisions, but also where there was general statutory language.[119] Sir John Laws[120] drew a distinction between reliance upon the European Convention as a legal instrument stricto sensu, and reliance upon the content of the Convention as a series of propositions that were either already inherent in our law, or could be integrated into it by the judiciary through the normal process of common law adjudication. It was not for the courts themselves to incorporate the Convention, since that would be to trespass on the legislature's sphere. The courts could, however, legitimately pursue the latter approach and consider the Convention jurisprudence as one source for charting development of the common law. The standard of review would, moreover, be more intensive in rights-based cases[121]:

> "[T]he greater the intrusion proposed by a body possessing public power over the citizen in an area where his fundamental rights are at stake, the greater must be the justification which the public authority must demonstrate … It means that the principles [of review] are neither unitary nor static; it means that the standard by which the court reviews administrative action is a variable one. It means, for example, that while the secretary of state will largely be left to his own devices in promulgating national economic policy … the court will scrutinise the merits of his decisions much more closely when they concern refugees or free speech."

The argument in a second strand of this literature went further. There were suggestions that the courts would not always feel constrained to obey the will of Parliament in areas concerned with fundamental rights, or with the basic structures of a democratic society. Lord Woolf[122] argued that if Parliament were to do the unthinkable and seek to abolish or radically curtail the courts' power of review, then the courts too "would also be required to act in a manner which would be without precedent".[123] There were, in his Lordship's view, limits to the supremacy of Parliament, which it was the courts' duty to identify and uphold. The existence of rights-based limits to the sovereignty of Parliament also featured in the work of Sir John Laws.[124] The survival of democracy in which rights are respected and enshrined "requires that those who exercise democratic, political power must have limits set to what they may do: limits which they are not allowed to overstep".[125] Democratic power cannot therefore be absolute. The

---

118 Lord Browne-Wilkinson, "The Infiltration of a Bill of Rights" [1992] P.L. 397, 404.

119 "The Infiltration of a Bill of Rights" [1992] P.L. 397, 406.

120 Sir John Laws, "Is the High Court the Guardian of Fundamental Constitutional Rights?" [1993] P.L. 59.

121 Laws, "Is the High Court the Guardian of Fundamental Constitutional Rights?" [1993] P.L. 59, 69.

122 Lord Woolf, "Droit Public—English Style" [1995] P.L. 57.

123 Woolf, "Droit Public—English Style" [1995] P.L. 57, 69.

124 Sir John Laws, "Law and Democracy" [1995] P.L. 72.

125 Laws, "Law and Democracy" [1995] P.L. 72, 81.

effective protection of basic rights, and also the essential structural workings of a democracy, such as free and regular elections, necessitates a higher order law, which cannot be abrogated by Parliament.[126] Lord Steyn voiced similar sentiments in the *Jackson* case,[127] stating that the Diceyan idea of absolute supremacy of Parliament was out of place in the modern UK. The supremacy of Parliament might, said Lord Steyn, still be regarded as the general principle of our constitution. It was, however, a construct of the common law, which had been created by the courts. It was not therefore unthinkable that circumstances might arise where the courts would have to qualify that principle, such as where the legislature attempted to abolish judicial review or the ordinary role of the courts.

A third strand in this rich vein of literature is to be found in the writings of Sir Stephen Sedley.[128] He did not subscribe to the idea of a higher order law against which the legality of governmental action was to be tested.[129] He believed, however, that the reinvigoration of judicial review was motivated, in part at least, by the desire of the judiciary to repair dysfunction in the democratic process, and to fill "lacunae of legitimacy in the functioning of democratic polities".[130] This led to a refashioning of our constitutional order, away from the traditional Diceyan paradigm of parliamentary sovereignty, and towards a

> "… bi-polar sovereignty of the Crown in Parliament and the Crown in its courts, to each of which the Crown's ministers are answerable—politically to Parliament, legally to the courts".[131]

For Sir Stephen Sedley, it was equally important to realise that the government of the day had no separate sovereignty: the sharpest of all lessons from Eastern Europe was that "it is when state is collapsed into party that democracy founders".[132]

---

[126] Laws, "Law and Democracy" [1995] P.L. 72, 84–85. See also, Laws, "The Constitution, Morals and Rights" [1996] P.L. 622 and "The Limitations of Human Rights" [1998] P.L. 254.

[127] *Jackson* [2006] 1 A.C. 262 at [102].

[128] Sir Stephen Sedley, "Human Rights: A Twenty-First Century Agenda" [1995] P.L. 386.

[129] Sedley, "Human Rights: A Twenty-First Century Agenda" [1995] P.L. 386, 389–390.

[130] Sedley, "Human Rights: A Twenty-First Century Agenda" [1995] P.L. 386, 388.

[131] Sedley, "Human Rights: A Twenty-First Century Agenda" [1995] P.L. 386, 389.

[132] Sedley, "Human Rights: A Twenty-First Century Agenda" [1995] P.L. 386, 389.

CHAPTER 20

HUMAN RIGHTS ACT

1. CENTRAL ISSUES

i. This chapter considers the impact of the Human Rights Act 1998 (HRA), on judicial review. The HRA brought certain rights from the European Convention on Human Rights (ECHR) into UK law.[1] Prior to the HRA, the UK was bound by the ECHR as an international Treaty, but the rights could not be directly relied on in domestic law, although they were indirectly used in litigation in a various ways. The Labour government in 1998 decided that the Convention rights should be "brought home", so that claimants could use them in national courts. It has had a significant impact on judicial review by the emphasis thereby given to what has been termed the culture of justification.[2] This requires the primary decision-maker not merely to explain the challenged decision, but to proffer a reasoned argument, which the courts will scrutinise within the framework of proportionality to determine whether the limitation of the right was normatively justified. **20–001**

ii. The discussion begins with the structure of the HRA. This includes analysis of the status of the ECHR prior to the HRA, and the principal provisions of the HRA. It also includes discussion of the status of case law from the European Court of Human Rights in Strasbourg, (ECtHR), when national courts adjudicate under the HRA, which is controversial.

iii. The focus then shifts to the HRA ss.3 and 4, which are concerned with claims that primary legislation is contrary to Convention rights. The framers of the HRA were influenced by UK precepts of parliamentary sovereignty. The HRA does not therefore embody what can be termed classic constitutional review, whereby courts can invalidate a statute if it violates constitutional rights. The HRA embodies a softer form of judicial review, whereby the courts are obliged insofar as possible to interpret

---

[1] C. Gearty (ed.), *European Civil Liberties and the European Convention on Human Rights* (Kluwer, 1997); P. Van Dijk and Y. Arai, *Theory and Practice of the European Convention of Human Rights*, 4th edn (Antwerp: Intersentia, 2006); A. Mowbray, *Cases and Materials on the European Convention on Human Rights*, 2nd edn (Oxford: Oxford University Press, 2007); M. Janis, R. Kay and A. Bradley, *European Human Rights Law: Text and Materials* 3rd edn (Oxford: Oxford University Press, 2008); Jacobs, White and Ovey, *European Convention on Human Rights*, 6th edn (Oxford: Oxford University Press, 2014); D. Harris, M. O'Boyle, E. Bates, C. Buckley, *Law of the European Convention of Human Rights*, 3rd edn (Oxford: Oxford University Press, 2014); E. Bjorge, *Domestic Application of the ECHR: Courts as Faithful Trustees* (Oxford: Oxford University Press, 2015).

[2] D. Dyzenhaus, "The Politics of Deference: Judicial Review and Democracy", in M. Taggart (ed.), *The Province of Administrative Law* (Oxford: Hart, 1997), Ch.13; M. Taggart, "The Tub of Public Law", in D. Dyzenhaus (ed.), *The Unity of Public Law* (Oxford: Hart, 2004), Ch.17.

national law to be in accord with Convention rights. If this is not possible, the courts then issue a declaration of incompatibility, with the consequence that the legislation is sent back to Parliament, which can decide whether to amend it so that it is consistent with Convention rights. The declaration of incompatibility does not, however, affect the validity of the law prior to any change by Parliament. The extent to which this is really softer than classic constitutional review has been debated in the literature.[3]

iv. The other principal provision is s.6 HRA, which renders it illegal for a public authority to act incompatibly with Convention rights. This enables claimants to argue that measures other than primary legislation, (or secondary legislation that is strictly dependent on primary legislation), should be declared illegal for breach of Convention rights.

v. This is followed by discussion of the standard of review under the HRA. A claimant will only succeed if able to show breach of a Convention right. Whether this is possible will depend on the standard of judicial review under the HRA. There will be analysis of the circumstances in which the courts substitute judgment under the HRA, and the extent to which they apply proportionality when reviewing legislation or governmental action. There has been considerable judicial and academic debate as to the extent to which the courts should show some measure of deference/discretionary area of judgment/respect/weight to the view of the legislature or executive when adjudicating under the HRA. This debate will be examined in the course of the subsequent analysis.

vi. The chapter concludes by consideration of the relevant principles of EU law concerning rights. This is a topic of considerable importance, more especially since the EU Charter of Rights was made binding by the Lisbon Treaty.

vii. There are two significant shadows that affect the material discussed in this chapter. First, the Conservative Party is committed to introducing a British Bill of Rights to replace the HRA. The detailed content of such a measure, and how far it would differ from the HRA, is however unclear at the time of writing. Second, in relation to Brexit, the UK remains bound by EU law, including the material discussed in this chapter, while withdrawal discussions are ongoing under art.50 TEU. This material may continue to have relevance post-exit depending on the nature of the withdrawal agreement.

[3] S. Gardbaum, "The New Commonwealth Model of Constitutionalism" (2001) 49 A.J.C.L. 707; J. Hiebert, "Parliamentary Bills of Rights: An Alternative Model?" (2006) 69 M.L.R. 7; M. Tushnet, "New Forms of Judicial Review and the Persistence of Rights and Democracy-based Worries" (2003) 38 Wake Forest L. Rev. 813; R. Bellamy, "Political Constitutionalism and the Human Rights Act" (2011) 9 I-CON 86.

2. HUMAN RIGHTS ACT 1998

A. Status of the ECHR prior to the HRA

Prior to enactment of the HRA the ECHR could be relied on in UK courts in limited circumstances.[4] *Brind* established that there was no presumption that statutory discretion should be exercised in conformity with the Convention.[5] There were, however, instances where the courts regarded it as acceptable to have regard to the ECHR[6]: it could be used as an aid in the construction of primary legislation where there was an ambiguity;[7] as an aid in the interpretation of legislation enacted as a result of an adverse judgment from the European Court of Human Rights[8]; it could be of assistance in determining the ambit of common law rights[9]; it could be a factor that shaped the exercise of judicial discretion[10]; courts began to take increasing notice of the ECHR when determining irrationality claims in cases concerned with rights[11]; some case law suggested that it could be regarded as a relevant consideration[12]; and the ECHR jurisprudence could also be applied in and by our courts through EU law.[13] **20–002**

B. "Bringing Rights Home"

It was nonetheless felt to be wrong that applicants should be forced to have recourse to the Convention institutions in Strasbourg. The government's objective in enacting the HRA was to "bring rights home", thereby allowing our courts to adjudicate directly on ECHR rights.[14] To this end s.1 HRA lists the "Convention **20–003**

---

[4] M. Hunt, *Using Human Rights Law in English Courts* (Oxford: Hart, 1997); M. Beloff and H. Mountfield, "Unconventional Behaviour? Judicial Uses of the European Convention of Human Rights in England and Wales" [1996] E.H.R.L.R. 467.

[5] *R. v Secretary of State for the Home Department, Ex p. Brind* [1991] 1 A.C. 696, HL.

[6] Lord Bingham, HC Deb., col.146 (3 July 1996).

[7] *Garland v British Rail Engineering Ltd* [1983] 2 A.C. 751, HL at 771; *R. v Chief Immigration Officer, Heathrow Airport, Ex p. Bibi* [1976] 1 W.L.R. 979, CA (Civ Div), at 984, 988.

[8] *R. v Secretary of State for the Home Department, Ex p. Norney* (1995) 7 Admin. L.R. 861 QBD.

[9] *Derbyshire CC v Times Newspapers Ltd* [1993] A.C. 534, HL.

[10] *Attorney General v Guardian Newspapers (No.2)* [1990] 1 A.C. 109, HL at 283–284.

[11] *R. v Ministry of Defence, Ex p. Smith* [1996] Q.B. 517, CA (Civ Div).

[12] *R. v Secretary of State for the Home Department, Ex p. Chahal* [1993] Imm. A.R. 362 QBD.

[13] See paras 20–066 to 20–071.

[14] T. Campbell, K. Ewing, and A. Tomkins (eds), *Sceptical Essays on Human Rights* (Oxford: Oxford University Press, 2001); F. Klug, *Values for a Godless Age: The Story of the UK's New Bill of Rights* (London: Penguin, 2000); J. Jowell and J. Cooper (eds), *Understanding Human Rights Principles* (Oxford: Hart, 2001); D. Feldman, *Civil Liberties and Human Rights in England and Wales*, 2nd edn (Oxford: Oxford University Press, 2002); C. Gearty, *Principles of Human Rights Adjudication* (Oxford: Oxford University Press, 2004); H. Fenwick, G. Phillipson, R. Masterman (eds), *Judicial Reasoning under the UK Human Rights Act* (Cambridge: Cambridge University Press, 2007); J. Beatson, S. Grosz, T. Hickman, R. Singh with S. Palmer, *Human Rights: Judicial Protection in the UK* (London: Sweet & Maxwell, 2008); A. Kavanagh, *Constitutional Review under the UK Human Rights Act* (Cambridge: Cambridge University Press, 2009); A. Young, *Parliamentary Sovereignty and the Human Rights Act* (Oxford: Hart, 2009); R. Clayton and H. Tomlinson, *The Law of Human Rights*, 2nd edn (Oxford: Oxford University Press, 2009); Lord Lester and Lord Pannick (eds), *Human Rights Law and Practice*, 3rd edn (London: LexisNexis, 2009); T. Hickman, *Public Law after the Human Rights Act* (Oxford: Hart, 2010); H. Fenwick and G. Phillipson, *Text, Cases and Materials*

rights" that can be used in domestic litigation pursuant to the Act. They are arts 2–12 and 14 of the ECHR, arts 1–3 of the First Protocol, and arts 1–2 of the Sixth Protocol as read with arts 16–18 of the Convention. The articles are set out in Sch.1 of the HRA. The HRA came into force on 2 October 2000.[15]

C. ECHR Case Law

20–004 The HRA s.2 provides that a court or tribunal determining a question which has arisen under the HRA in connection with a Convention right must take into account any judgment, decision, declaration or advisory opinion of the ECtHR; opinion of the Commission given in a report adopted under art.31 of the ECHR; decision of the Commission in connection with art.26 or 27(2) of the ECHR; or decision of the Committee of Ministers taken under art.46 of the ECHR. The courts are therefore not bound by the Strasbourg jurisprudence but have an obligation to take it into account. The courts continue to apply domestic rules of precedent, with the consequence that if a judge feels that a decision is inconsistent with Strasbourg authority he has to follow the binding precedent, but can give leave to appeal as appropriate.[16]

The more precise interpretation of s.2 has been contentious.[17] The general approach has been termed the "mirror principle" as enunciated by Lord Bingham in *Ullah*. On this view it was the duty of the national courts "to keep pace with the Strasbourg jurisprudence as it evolves over time: no more, but certainly no less".[18] The mirror principle embodies a view as to the floor and ceiling of human rights protection.

---

on Public Law and Human Rights, 3rd edn (London: Routledge, 2011); J. Wadham, H. Mountfield, E. Prochaska and R. Desia, *Blackstone's Guide to the Human Rights Act 1998*, 7th edn (Oxford: Oxford University Press, 2015).

[15] The extent to which the HRA can have an impact on matters prior to this date has proven to be controversial, *R. v Benjafield* [2001] 3 W.L.R. 75, CA (Crim Div); *R. v Lambert* [2002] 2 A.C. 545, HL; *R. v Kansal (No.2)* [2002] 2 A.C. 69, HL; *R. (Hurst) v HM Coroner for Northern District London* [2007] 2 A.C. 189, HL.

[16] *Kay v Lambeth LBC* [2006] 2 A.C. 465, HL; *Leeds City Council v Price* [2005] 1 W.L.R. 1825, CA (Civ Div).

[17] R. Masterman, "Section 2(1) of the Human Rights Act 1998: Binding Domestic Courts to Strasbourg?" [2004] P.L. 725; R. Masterman, "Taking the Strasbourg Jurisprudence into Account: Developing a 'Municipal Law of Human Rights' under the Human Rights Act" (2005) 54 I.C.L.Q. 907; F. Klug and H. Wildbore, "Follow or Lead? The Human Rights Act and the European Court of Human Rights" [2010] E.H.R.L.R. 621; J. Wright, "Interpreting Section 2 of the Human Rights Act: Towards an Indigenous Jurisprudence of Human Rights" [2009] P.L. 595; N. Bratza, "The Relationship between the UK Courts and Strasbourg" [2011] E.H.R.L.R. 505; R. Clayton, "Smoke and Mirrors: The Human Rights Act and the Impact of the Strasbourg Case Law" [2012] P.L. 639; E. Bjorge, "The Courts and the ECHR: A Principled Approach to the Strasbourg Jurisprudence" [2013] C.L.J. 289.

[18] *R. (Ullah) v Special Adjudicator* [2004] 2 A.C. 323, HL at [20]; *R.(S) v Chief Constable of South Yorkshire Police* [2004] UKHL 39 at [27]; *R.(Quark Fishing) v Secretary of State for Foreign and Commonwealth Affairs* [2006] 1 A.C. 529, HL at [34]; *R. (Al-Skeini) v Secretary of State for Defence* [2008] 1 A.C. 153 at [90], [106]; *R. (Smith) v Oxfordshire Assistant Deputy Coroner* [2011] 1 A.C. 1 SC at [60], [93], [147]; *McGowan (Procurator Fiscal, Edinburgh) v B (Scotland)* [2011] UKSC 54; *Ambrose v Harris (Procurator Fiscal, Oban)* [2011] UKSC 43 at [20].

The idea that Strasbourg case law provides a floor, a minimum below which the national courts should not fall, has been supported both on grounds of principle and practicality, since if the national courts fall below this minimum a claimant will have a strong incentive to pursue a claim before the ECtHR.[19] This is so notwithstanding that there are instances where national courts resist Strasbourg case law because they feel that the ECtHR has misunderstood UK legal rules when finding a breach of the ECHR.[20] **20–005**

The idea that Strasbourg case law should operate as a ceiling to human rights protection has been more controversial. It has been argued that UK courts should be able to accord more extensive protection than that given by Strasbourg where it is felt appropriate, and should be able to apply Convention rights in the way suited to national traditions and values.[21] Thus, in *Re P* [22] the claimants, an unmarried heterosexual couple, were prevented from adopting a child by statutory regulations in Northern Ireland. The Strasbourg court had not yet pronounced on the issue. The House of Lords nonetheless found that the fixed rule precluding adoption was disproportionate. The majority held that, given the developing state of its jurisprudence, it was likely that the ECtHR would hold that the challenged provision was discriminatory and that the House should not be inhibited from going further than the ECtHR, since the margin of appreciation available to member states in delicate areas of social policy was not automatically appropriated by the legislature. It held moreover that Convention rights under the HRA were domestic rights, not international rights and that the House was therefore free to give what it considered to be a principled interpretation to the concept of discrimination on grounds of marital status.

Lord Kerr has, moreover, been notable for willingness to question this dimension of the mirror principle. He held that it was not open to our courts "to adopt an attitude of agnosticism and refrain from recognising such a right simply because Strasbourg has not spoken" [23] The Strasbourg court would not, said Lord Kerr, resolve all issues concerning the meaning of Convention rights, many of which would be determined by national courts without formal guidance from the ECtHR. It remained the duty of the Supreme Court to consider those issues when they arose, even if the existing Strasbourg case law was unclear, and this duty was reinforced by s.6 HRA.[24] Bjorge has argued convincingly that this principled approach to the ECHR is preferable to strict adherence to *Ullah*, and that it coheres well with common law tradition.[25]

---

[19] *R. (Alconbury Developments Ltd) v Secretary of State for the Environment, Transport and the Regions* [2003] 2 A.C. 295, HL at [26]; *R. (Anderson) v Secretary of State for the Home Department* [2003] 1 A.C. 837, HL at [18]; *R. (Amin) v Secretary of State for the Home Department* [2004] 1 A.C. 653, HL at [44].

[20] *R. v Horncastle* [2010] 2 A.C. 373 SC; E. Bjorge, "Exceptionalism and Intentionalism in the Supreme Court: Horncastle and Cadder" [2011] P.L. 475.

[21] *Begum v Tower Hamlets LBC* [2002] H.R.L.R. 24, CA (Civ Div) at [17]; *R. (ProLife Alliance) v British Broadcasting Corp* [2002] 3 W.L.R. 1080, CA (Civ Div) at [33]–[34].

[22] *In P (Adoption: Unmarried Couples), Re* [2008] 3 W.L.R. 76, HL; *Rabone v Pennine NHS Care Foundation Trust* [2012] UKSC 2 at [112]; *Sugar v BBC* [2012] UKSC 4 at [59].

[23] *Ambrose* [2011] UKSC 43 at [128].

[24] *Ambrose* [2011] UKSC 43 at [129].

[25] Bjorge, "The Courts and the ECHR: A Principled Approach to the Strasbourg Jurisprudence" [2013] C.L.J. 289.

3. LEGISLATION: THE INTERPRETATIVE OBLIGATION AND THE DECLARATION OF INCOMPATIBILITY

A. The Statutory Provisions

20–006 The framers of the HRA were not in favour of what might be termed "hard constitutional review" such as exists in countries where the courts can strike down legislation that is incompatible with fundamental rights. This was felt to be unsuitable for the UK with its traditions of parliamentary sovereignty. The HRA therefore encapsulates a "softer" form of constitutional review in relation to the scrutiny of legislation.[26]

Before any legislation is passed the relevant Minister must comply with s.19 HRA.[27] This stipulates that a minister of the Crown in charge of a Bill in either House of Parliament must, before the second reading of the Bill, make a statement that in his view the provisions of the Bill are compatible with Convention rights.[28] This is known as a "statement of compatibility".[29] The minister can, alternatively, make a statement to the effect that although he is unable to make a statement of compatibility the government wishes the House to proceed with the Bill.[30]

If legislation is challenged s.3 HRA provides that "so far as it is possible to do so, primary legislation and subordinate legislation must be read and given effect in a way which is compatible with the Convention rights". This interpretative obligation applies to any legislation whenever enacted.[31] Section 3 does not, however, affect the validity, continuing operation or enforcement of any incompatible primary legislation,[32] or of any incompatible secondary legislation if, leaving aside any possibility of revocation, primary legislation prevents the removal of the incompatibility.[33]

20–007 Where a court is satisfied that primary legislation is incompatible with a Convention right then it can, pursuant to s.4 HRA, make a declaration of that incompatibility.[34] It can also do in relation to secondary legislation where, leaving aside any possibility of revocation, the primary legislation prevents removal of the incompatibility.[35] The courts that can make such a declaration are

---

[26] P. Craig, "Constitutional and Non-Constitutional Review" [2001] C.L.P. 147.

[27] N. Bamforth, "Parliamentary Sovereignty and the Human Rights Act 1998" [1998] P.L. 572, 575–582.

[28] D. Feldman, "Parliamentary Scrutiny of Legislation and Human Rights" [2002] P.L. 323.

[29] HRA s.19(1)(a).

[30] HRA s.19(1)(b).

[31] HRA s.3(2)(a).

[32] HRA s.3(2)(b).

[33] HRA s.3(2)(c).

[34] HRA s.4(1)–(2).

[35] HRA s.4(3)–(4); A. Bradley, "The Impact of the Human Rights Act 1998 upon Subordinate Legislation Promulgated before October 2, 2000" [2000] P.L. 358; R. Allen and P. Sales, "Joint Note for the Court of Appeal in *R. v Lord Chancellor, Ex p. Lightfoot*" [2000] P.L. 361.

limited by the HRA, with the lowest court being the High Court.[36] This may well be problematic, particularly because challenges to legislation may originate in lower courts or tribunals.[37]

The declaration of incompatibility does not affect the validity, continuing operation or enforcement of the provision in respect of which it has been given, and is not binding on the parties to the proceedings in which it is made.[38] The Crown is accorded the right to notice where a court is considering whether to make a declaration of incompatibility and a minister of the Crown is entitled to be joined as a party to the proceedings.[39]

While a declaration of incompatibility does not affect the validity of the challenged legislation, it does trigger s.10 HRA, which applies where a declaration of incompatibility has been made and any appeal rights have either been exhausted, attempted or are not intended to be used. Section 10 can also apply where it appears to a minister that primary legislation is incompatible with the ECHR as a result of a ruling by the ECtHR in a case concerning the United Kingdom. In either of these circumstances s.10(2) states that if **20–008**

> "... a Minister of the Crown considers that there are compelling reasons for proceeding under this section, he may by order make such amendments to the legislation as he considers necessary to remove the incompatibility".

The HRA therefore gives a power to amend the offending legislation through secondary legislation. It is, in this sense, an example of a Henry VIII clause, which was considered when discussing delegated legislation.[40] The justification for such a power here is to remove speedily legislative provisions that offend HRA rights.

The remedial orders made under s.10 can amend or repeal primary or secondary legislation, including legislation other than that which contains the incompatible provisions.[41] The orders can also be retrospective.[42] The orders are statutory instruments,[43] and are therefore subject to the Statutory Instruments Act 1946.[44] A remedial order is subject to the affirmative resolution procedure and must be approved by resolution of each House of Parliament made after 60 days beginning with the day on which the draft was laid.[45] The order cannot be made until the end of the 60-day period, and this is intended to provide an opportunity for representations to be made to the minister about the measure. This process is facilitated by the existence of an obligation on the minister to provide information[46] about the nature of the incompatibility, and a statement of the

---

[36] The courts which can make such a declaration are listed in HRA s.4(5).

[37] I. Leigh and L. Lustgarten, "Making Rights Real: The Courts, Remedies and the Human Rights Act" [1999] C.L.J. 509.

[38] HRA ss.3(2) and 4(6).

[39] HRA s.5.

[40] See Ch.15.

[41] HRA Sch.2 para.1(2).

[42] HRA Sch.2 para.1(1)(b).

[43] HRA s.20.

[44] See Ch.15.

[45] HRA Sch.2 para.2(a).

[46] HRA Sch.2 para.5.

reasons for proceeding under s.10. Where representations have been made during this period, they must be summarised, and details given of any changes made to the draft order as a result of the representations.[47] There are exceptions to the need to secure parliamentary approval in cases of urgency.[48]

B. Legislative History

20–009 The courts are instructed by s.3 that "so far as it is possible to do so" legislation must be read and given effect in a way which is compatible with the Convention rights.[49] The more the courts are willing to construe legislation to be in conformity with Convention rights, the less they will need to issue declarations of incompatibility. A strident approach to the interpretation of s.3 means that the courts retain the matter in their own hands. Parliamentary choice as to whether to comply with a declaration of incompatibility will not arise where no such declaration is issued.

The legislative history of s.3 provided little by way of firm guidance as to the meaning of s.3.[50] The Lord Chancellor thought that it gave the courts broad power to interpret legislation whenever possible so as to be compatible with the Convention.[51] It was not necessary to find an ambiguity.[52] In relation to statutes passed after the HRA, Parliament should be presumed to legislate compatibly with the Convention, and the courts should only find the contrary where it was impossible to construe a statute in that way.[53] The Home Secretary, however, noted that the courts should not distort the meaning of statutory language so as to produce implausible meanings.[54]

C. Judicial Interpretation of Section 3: Early Case Law

20–010 In the early case law judges adopted somewhat differing interpretations of s.3. This is evident from *R. v A.*[55] It was argued that s.41 of the Youth Justice and Criminal Evidence Act 1999 violated art.6 of the Convention. Section 41 severely restricted the cross-examination of a rape victim about her sexual conduct, which might otherwise be relevant to a defence based on consent. The House of Lords held that s.41 must be read subject to s.3 HRA, and that the test for the admissibility of such evidence should be whether it was so relevant to the issue of consent that to exclude it would endanger the fairness of the trial and thus violate art.6 ECHR. Lord Steyn held that s.3 required the courts to "subordinate the

---

47 HRA Sch.2 para.3.

48 HRA Sch.2 paras 2(b) and 4.

49 See Ch.10 for consideration of the interpretative obligation flowing from EU law, *Von Colson and Kamann v Land Nordrhein-Westfalen* (14/83) [1984] E.C.R. 1891; *Marleasing SA v La Commercial International De Alimentation SA* (C-106/89) [1990] E.C.R. I-4135.

50 F. Klug, "The Human Rights Act 1998, *Pepper v Hart* and All That" [1999] P.L. 246, 252–255.

51 *Hansard*, HL Deb., col.795 (24 November 1997).

52 Lord Irvine, "The Development of Human Rights in Britain under an Incorporated Convention on Human Rights" [1998] P.L. 221, 228.

53 *Hansard*, HL Deb., cols 535, 547 (18 November 1997).

54 *Hansard*, HC Deb., cols 421–422 (3 June 1998).

55 *R. v A* [2002] 1 A.C. 45.

niceties of the language in s.41(3) to broader considerations of relevance".[56] He reached that conclusion on certain assumptions about the meaning of s.3[57]:

> "[T]he interpretative obligation under s.3 … is a strong one. It applies even if there is no ambiguity in the language in the sense of the language being capable of two different meanings … Under ordinary methods of interpretation a court may depart from the language of the statute to avoid absurd consequences: s.3 goes much further. Undoubtedly, a court must always look for a contextual and purposive interpretation: s.3 is more radical in its effect … In accordance with the will of Parliament as reflected in s.3 it will sometimes be necessary to adopt an interpretation which linguistically may appear strained. The techniques to be used will not only involve the reading down of express language in a statute but also the implication of provisions. A declaration of incompatibility is a measure of last resort. It must be avoided unless it is plainly impossible to do so. If a *clear* limitation of convention rights is stated in *terms*, such an impossibility will arise … There is, however, no limitation of such a nature in the present case."

Lord Hope gave a more cautious reading of s.3.[58] He acknowledged that there was no need to identify an ambiguity or absurdity, but emphasised that s.3 was only a rule of interpretation, which did not entitle the judges to act as legislators. A Convention-compliant interpretation would not therefore be possible if the UK legislation contained provisions that expressly contradicted the meaning which the enactment would have to be given to make it compatible, or where the inconsistency followed by necessary implication from the UK legislation.

There were instances in the early case law where *the courts saved legislation from incompatibility through s.3*. They "read in" provisions, normally by implying words in a statute, or "read down" legislation, by according it a narrower interpretation to ensure that it remained valid.[59] The line between these two techniques may be a fine one. In *R. v A*, the House of Lords modified the test for the admissibility of evidence contained in the primary legislation, by reading words into the statute.[60] In *Lambert* the House of Lords read down s.28 of the Misuse of Drugs Act 1971 that imposed a reverse burden of proof.[61] The ordinary meaning of s.28 was that it imposed the legal burden of proof on the accused, but the House of Lords decided that it should be construed, pursuant to s.3 HRA, as imposing only an evidential burden, so as to render it compatible with art.6(2) ECHR. **20–011**

There *were other decisions where the courts were unable to "save the legislation" through s.3 and issued declarations of incompatibility.*[62] This is exemplified by *Matthews*.[63] The court held that the Crown Proceedings Act 1947

---

[56] *A* [2002] 1 A.C. 45 at [45].

[57] *A* [2002] 1 A.C. 45 at [44]. Italics in the original.

[58] *A* [2002] 1 A.C. 45 at [108]; *R. v Lambert* [2002] 2 A.C. 545, HL at [79]–[81]; *S (children: care plan), Re* [2002] 2 A.C. 291, HL at [40].

[59] R. Clayton, "The Limits of What's 'Possible': Statutory Construction under the Human Rights Act" [2002] E.H.R.L.R. 559, 562–563.

[60] *A* [2002] 1 A.C. 45.

[61] *R. v Lambert* [2002] 2 A.C. 545.

[62] *Wilkinson v Inland Revenue Commissioners* [2002] S.T.C. 347 QBD; *R. (D) v Secretary of State for the Home Department* [2002] EWHC 2805 (Admin); *Poplar Housing & Regeneration Association Ltd v Donoghue* [2002] Q.B. 48, CA (Civ Div); *R.(H) v Mental Health Review Tribunal for the North and East London Region* [2002] Q.B. 1, CA (Civ Div).

[63] *Matthews v Ministry of Defence* [2002] 3 All E.R. 513, CA (Civ Div).

s.10, which prevented in certain circumstances an action in tort against the Crown by a serviceman, did not infringe art.6 ECHR, because a serviceman had no civil right that engaged this article. Counsel for the claimant argued, drawing on *R. v A*,[64] that the court should read down s.10, by adding a sentence to the effect that the section would not be used unless the secretary of state was satisfied that the injury occurred in warlike conditions. The court rejected this argument, in part because Convention rights were not engaged. Lord Phillips MR held moreover that it would be beyond the courts' power under s.3 HRA to imply such a clause, since the fundamental alteration of the scope of s.10 would amount to legislation by the court, which was not permissible.[65] The reluctance to rewrite legislation was evident once again in *Roth*.[66] The Immigration and Asylum Act 1999 provided for fixed penalties on hauliers who intentionally or negligently allowed a person to gain illicit entry to the United Kingdom, and imposed a reverse burden of proof. The court found the scheme to be inconsistent with Convention rights. It could not be saved by s.3 HRA, since a radically different approach would be required to comply with the Convention.[67] This would entail a fundamental re-orientation of the roles of the minister and the court under the scheme, such that the "rewritten scheme would not be recognisable as the scheme which Parliament intended".[68]

D. Judicial Interpretation of Section 3: *Ghaidan v Godin-Mendoza*

20–012 The leading decision on s.3(1) HRA is now *Ghaidan*.[69] The case concerned differential treatment of homosexual couples by way of comparison with heterosexual couples in relation to legal succession to a tenancy when one partner died. The House of Lords found that the legislation was discriminatory, but held that it could be read compatibly with Convention rights. Their Lordships gave more general guidance on the interpretation of s.3(1). The following principles emerged from the case.

First, the application of s.3 is not dependent on ambiguity in the legislation being interpreted. Thus, even if construed according to the ordinary principles of interpretation the meaning of the legislation is not in doubt, s.3 may none the less require the legislation to be given a different meaning.[70]

Second, it followed that s.3 could require the court to depart from the unambiguous meaning the legislation would otherwise bear.[71] It followed also that while the natural starting point was the wording used by Parliament, this was not determinative. In the words of Lord Nicholls[72]:

---

64 *A* [2002] 1 A.C. 45.

65 *Matthews* [2002] 3 All E.R. 513 at [76]. The point was not considered in the House of Lords, *Matthews v Ministry of Defence* [2003] 1 A.C. 1163, HL.

66 *R. (International Transport Roth GmbH) v Secretary of State for the Home Department* [2003] Q.B. 728, CA (Civ Div).

67 *International Transport Roth GmbH* [2003] Q.B. 728 at [66].

68 *International Transport Roth GmbH* [2003] Q.B. 728 at [156].

69 *Ghaidan v Godin-Mendoza* [2004] 2 A.C. 557, HL.

70 *Ghaidan* [2004] 2 A.C. 557 at [29], [44], [67].

71 *Ghaidan* [2004] 2 A.C. 557 at [30].

72 *Ghaidan* [2004] 2 A.C. 557 at [31]. See also [49], Lord Steyn.

> "[O]nce it is accepted that s.3 may require legislation to bear a meaning which departs from the unambiguous meaning the legislation would otherwise bear, it becomes impossible to suppose Parliament intended that the operation of s.3 should depend critically upon the particular form of words adopted by the parliamentary draftsman in the statutory provision under consideration. That would make the application of s.3 something of a semantic lottery. If the draftsman chose to express the concept being enacted in one form of words, s.3 would be available to achieve Convention-compliance. If he chose a different form of words, s.3 would be impotent."

Third, it was therefore open to the court to read in words which changed the meaning of the enacted legislation, so as to make it Convention-compliant, and could modify the meaning of primary and secondary legislation, subject to the constraint that this constituted a "possible" interpretation of the legislation.[73]

Fourth, there were however limits to the use of s.3(1). Thus, the courts should not adopt a "meaning inconsistent with a fundamental feature of legislation"[74]; the meaning imported "must be compatible with the underlying thrust of the legislation being construed"[75]; any word implied must "go with the grain of the legislation"; and the courts should moreover not use s.3 to adopt an interpretation of legislation for which they were ill-equipped, such as where the interpretation would bring about far-reaching change of a kind that was best dealt with by Parliament.

These features were said in *Ghaidan*[76] to explain previous decisions, *Re S* and *Bellinger*, in which the courts had concluded that the legislation could not be made Convention compliant through s.3. **20–013**

S, Re[77] was concerned with the Children Act 1989 s.38. The Court of Appeal had, pursuant to s.3 HRA, read into s.38 of the 1989 Act a wider discretion to make an interim care order, and introduced a new procedure by which certain essential elements of a care plan would be identified and elevated to a starred status. It would then be for a court to check whether the starred elements were met. Lord Nicholls held that the starring system could not be justified under s.3 HRA. Parliament had entrusted local authorities under the 1989 Act, not the courts, with the responsibility for looking after children who were subject to care orders. The starring system departed substantially from that system, and constituted an amendment of the 1989 Act, not its interpretation: a "meaning which departs substantially from a fundamental feature of an Act of Parliament is likely to have crossed the boundary between interpretation and legislation".[78]

In *Bellinger*[79] the applicant contended that legislation was contrary to Convention rights because it precluded a post-operative transsexual from being regarded as a woman for the purposes of marriage. The House of Lords held that the legislation could not be interpreted to be in accord with Convention rights by using s.3 HRA, because such recognition of the validity of the marriage would

---

[73] *Ghaidan* [2004] 2 A.C. 557 at [32].

[74] *Ghaidan* [2004] 2 A.C. 557 at [33]; *R. (Anderson) v Secretary of State for the Home Department* [2003] 1 A.C. 837, HL.

[75] *Ghaidan* [2004] 2 A.C. 557 at [33].

[76] *Ghaidan* [2004] 2 A.C. 557 at [34], [49], [114].

[77] *S (children: care plan), Re* [2002] 2 A.C. 291.

[78] *S, Re* [2002] 2 A.C. 291 at [40].

[79] *Bellinger v Bellinger* [2003] 2 A.C. 467, HL. See also, *R. (Chester) v Secretary of State for Justice* [2010] EWCA Civ 1439.

represent a major change in the law relating to gender reassignment that would have far reaching ramifications, necessitating extensive enquiry and the widest possible consultation. The issues were ill-suited for judicial determination and were pre-eminently a matter for Parliament, more especially since the government had said that it would introduce primary legislation on the subject.

E. Judicial Interpretation of Section 3: The Post-*Ghaidan* Case Law

20–014 The reasoning in *Ghaidan* has been the touchstone for courts in later cases. Thus, in *Sheldrake*[80] the House of Lords concluded that s.11(2) of the Terrorism Act 2000, which placed on the defendant the burden of proving that the relevant organisation was not proscribed, was intended by Parliament to place the legal burden of proof on the defendant. Their Lordships held, however, that there was a real risk that a person who was innocent, but who was unable to establish a defence under s.11(2), might fall within s.11(1), thereby resulting in a clear breach of the presumption of innocence and an unfair conviction. They therefore, pursuant to s.3 HRA, read down s.11(2) so as to impose on the defendant an evidential burden only, even though that was not Parliament's intention when enacting the subsection.

The judicial willingness to interpret legislation to be compatible with Convention rights is also apparent in other cases.[81] In *Hammond*[82] the legislation allowed the judge to decide the minimum term to be served by a prisoner serving a mandatory life sentence without an oral hearing. The House of Lords held that this was incompatible with the right to a fair trial in art.6 ECHR, but it was willing, following a concession made by the government, to accept that the legislation should be read subject to an implied condition whereby the judge could allow an oral hearing where this was necessary to ensure fairness and compliance with art.6. In *GC*[83] the Supreme Court read s.64(1)A of the Police and Criminal Evidence Act 1984 so as not to mandate indefinite retention of biometric samples taken from those questioned by the police, and did so in order to comply with a ruling from the Strasbourg Court.

It would nonetheless be mistaken to conclude that the statutory language can always be interpreted consistently with Convention rights. Where the court believes that this is not possible, it will issue a declaration of incompatibility under s.4 HRA.[84] This is exemplified by *A v Secretary of State for the Home*

---

[80] *Sheldrake v DPP* [2005] 1 A.C. 264, HL; *R. v Webster* [2010] EWCA Crim 2819.

[81] See, e.g. *R. (O) v Crown Court at Harrow* [2007] 1 A.C. 249, HL; *Secretary of State for the Home Department v MB* [2007] 3 W.L.R. 681, HL; *Thomas v Bridgend CBC* [2011] EWCA Civ 862; *Pomiechowski v Poland* [2012] UKSC 20; *Adesina v Nursery and Midwifery Council* [2013] EWCA Civ. 818; *Warren v Care Fertility (Northampton) Ltd* [2014] EWHC 602 (Fam).

[82] *R. (Hammond) v Secretary of State for the Home Department* [2006] 1 A.C. 603, HL.

[83] *R. (GC) v Commissioner of Police of the Metropolis* [2011] UKSC 21.

[84] *AS (Somalia) v Entry Clearance Officer (Addis Ababa)* [2009] UKHL 32; *R. (Wright) v Secretary of State for Health* [2009] 1 A.C. 739, HL; *R. (F) v Secretary of State for the Home Department* [2011] 1 A.C. 331 SC; *Benkharbouche v Embassy of Sudan* [2015] EWCA Civ. 33.

Department.[85] The UK government, as part of the response to the situation post 9/11, enacted the Anti-terrorism, Crime and Security Act 2001, s.23 of which provided for the detention of non-nationals if the Home Secretary believed their presence in the UK was a risk to national security and he suspected that they were terrorists who, for the time being, could not be deported because of fears for their safety or other practical considerations. The House of Lords held that s.23 was discriminatory and disproportionate, since it did not apply to UK nationals who might pose the same threat, and issued a declaration of incompatibility.

F. Reflections on the Courts' Jurisprudence

There have unsurprisingly been differences in the academic literature on the construction of s.3 HRA,[86] and how far the courts should go in reading legislation so as to make it compatible with Convention rights.[87] The following points should be borne in mind in this respect. **20–015**

First, there are two senses of legislative intention at play in the case law. There is the legislative intent expressed in the legislation that is said to be incompatible with Convention rights. There is also the legislative intent expressed in s.3 HRA, that such legislation, whether enacted before or after the HRA, should insofar as possible be read so as to be compatible with Convention rights. The most natural reading of s.3 HRA is to accord the courts more latitude to interpret legislation to be in accord with Convention rights than would flow from the ordinary principles of statutory interpretation.

---

[85] *A v Secretary of State for the Home Department* [2005] 2 A.C. 68, HL; *R. (Wilkinson) v Inland Revenue Commissioners* [2005] 1 W.L.R. 1718, HL; *R. (Clift) v Secretary of State for the Home Department* [2007] 1 A.C. 484, HL.

[86] G. Marshall, "Interpreting Interpretation in the Human Rights Bill" [1998] P.L. 167; D. Pannick, "Principles of Interpretation of Convention Rights under the Human Rights Act and the Discretionary Area of Judgment" [1998] P.L. 545; G. Marshall, "Two Kinds of Compatibility: More about Section 3 of the Human Rights Act 1998" [1999] P.L. 377; Lord Lester of Herne Hill, "The Art of the Possible: Interpreting Statutes under the Human Rights Act" in University of Cambridge Centre for Public Law, *The Human Rights Act and the Criminal Justice and Regulatory Process* (1999); F. Bennion, "What Interpretation is 'Possible' under Section 3(1) of the Human Rights Act 1998?" [2000] P.L. 77; C. Gearty, "Reconciling Parliamentary Democracy and Human Rights" (2002) 118 L.Q.R. 248; R. Clayton, "The Limits of What's 'Possible': Statutory Construction under the Human Rights Act" [2002] E.H.R.L.R. 559; G. Phillipson, "(Mis)-reading Section 3 of the Human Rights Act" (2003) 119 L.Q.R. 183; C. Gearty, "Revisiting Section 3(1) of the Human Rights Act" (2003) 119 L.Q.R. 551; R. Ekins, "A Critique of Radical Approaches to Rights Consistent Statutory Interpretation" [2003] E.H.R.L.R. 641; D. Nicol, "Statutory Interpretation and Human Rights after *Anderson*" [2004] P.L. 274; A. Kavanagh, "Statutory Interpretation and Human Rights after *Anderson*: A More Contextual Approach" [2004] P.L. 537; A. Kavanagh, "The Elusive Divide between Interpretation and Legislation under the Human Rights Act 1998" (2004) 24 O.J.L.S. 259; A. Kavanagh, "Unlocking the Human Rights Act: The 'Radical' Approach to Section 3(1) Revisited" [2005] E.H.R.L.R. 259; A. Young, "*Ghaidan v Godin-Mendoza*: Avoiding the Deference Trap" [2005] P.L. 23; A. Kavanagh, "The Role of Parliamentary Intention in Adjudication under the Human Rights Act 1998" (2006) 26 O.J.L.S. 179; P. Sales, "A Comparison of the Principle of Legality and Section 3 HRA" (2009) 125 L.Q.R. 598; R. Buxton, "The Future of Declarations of Incompatibility" [2010] P.L. 213.

[87] See, e.g. the critique by Buxton, "The Future of Declarations of Incompatibility" [2010] P.L. 213 of *R. (H) v Secretary of State for Health* [2006] 1 A.C. 441 and *R.(Nasseri) v Secretary of State for the Home Department* [2010] 1 A.C. 1.

Second, the House of Lords' decision in *Ghaidan*[88] is now the leading authority on what can and cannot be achieved via s.3 HRA. The House of Lords adopted a position midway between the radical view of Lord Steyn, which seemed to indicate that s.3 could resolve all cases by reading down the primary legislation or reading in provisions, save where it contained a clear limitation on Convention rights, and the more cautious view of Lord Hope set out above. Thus, their Lordships made clear in *Ghaidan* that s.3 could be used in the absence of legislative ambiguity, the corollary of which is that the legislation may be interpreted differently from the unambiguous meaning of the wording used. The wording of the statute is not therefore conclusive, and the court inclined against a purely linguistic or semantic approach, expressing its willingness to read down and read in provisions to render the legislation compatible with Convention rights. This aspect of the reasoning in *Ghaidan* was, however, tempered by the limits imposed by their Lordships: the courts should not adopt a meaning that was inconsistent with the fundamentals of the legislation being reviewed, nor should they use s.3 to adopt an interpretation of legislation for which they were ill-equipped, such as where the interpretation would bring about far-reaching change of a kind that was best dealt with by Parliament. There will doubtless be differences of view in particular cases as to whether s.3 HRA as interpreted in *Ghaidan* can render legislation compatible with Convention rights. That is inevitable. *Ghaidan* nonetheless provides welcome guidance, more especially because the midway approach is more nuanced than that in previous cases.

20–016 Third, the interpretation of s.3 HRA has a marked impact on the relationship between the courts and the legislature. The more cases that are resolved through s.3, the fewer that will be returned to the legislature, since there will be no need to make a declaration of incompatibility. The desire to accord primacy to s.3 in the remedial scheme of the HRA, with the consequence that the declaration of incompatibility becomes a matter of last resort,[89] should not, however, be pressed too far. We should, for example, be wary of allowing s.3 as interpreted in *Ghaidan* to be used where it would involve a significant revision of the statutory scheme, since the impact of such revisions on the workability of the scheme as a whole may be profound and Parliament may be best placed to revise the legislation to comply with the court's judgment, should it be minded to do so, which it normally will. We should also be mindful of the cautionary words of Sir Jack Beatson[90]:

> "Words that are read in, added, or read down are not made part of the statute by s.3, but they have a stronger force than the product of ordinary statutory interpretation because it is accepted that those words can change the meaning of the statute. It must be recognised that, quite apart from any complexity and difficulty of understanding caused by the nature of the subject matter or the drafting technique used, we are going to have statutes that simply do not mean what the words say. That is, it is submitted, not good for the law because it increases its opacity. What is the solution? One possibility … is that where s.3 has been used to read and give effect to a statute in a way that is Convention compliant but changes the meaning of the enacted words, textual amendments should be made to the statute. But this would only be a

---

88 *Ghaidan* [2004] 2 A.C. 557.

89 *Ghaidan* [2004] 2 A.C. 557 at [46], Lord Steyn.

90 Sir Jack Beatson, "Common Law, Statute and Constitutional Law" [2006] Stat. L. Rev. 1, 13–14.

solution if the state provides an updated version of our statutes. Without that, we must recognise that the quest for transparency and clarity faces a considerable obstacle, an obstacle that has nothing to do with drafting styles."

4. ACTS OF PUBLIC AUTHORITIES: A NEW HEAD OF ILLEGALITY

A. Section 6(1) HRA

The other main legal innovation of the HRA is s.6(1), which provides that it is "unlawful for a public authority to act in a way which is incompatible with a Convention right".[91] **20–017**

Section 6(1) creates a new statutory head of illegality for breach of a Convention right. It is a free-standing statutory ground of challenge. We have already seen that the common law had increased the protection of rights. It was not, however, possible at common law to argue that administrative action was unlawful simply because there had been a breach of a right. The breach of a right might, by way of contrast, signal more intensive review under the *Wednesbury* test, or it might convince the court that a relevant consideration had not been taken into account. It is now possible to argue that an act of a public authority is unlawful because it is incompatible with a Convention right. However, s.6(1) only renders the act of the public authority unlawful if there has been a breach of a Convention right. Much therefore depends on the standard of review used to decide whether a Convention right has been broken.

Sections 3 and 4 HRA received most attention when the HRA was debated, because the subject matter of the action concerned primary legislation, with all the attendant concerns about sovereignty. Applicants will, however, often be most concerned about a concrete remedy and will use s.6 if this is possible. The importance of s.6(1) is further enhanced because s.6(6) states that an "act" for these purposes includes also a failure to act, albeit not a failure to legislate. This means that the courts have the power to compel public authorities to take positive action.[92] This is all the more significant when read in conjunction with the fact that the state may, under the jurisprudence of the ECtHR, be responsible for the violation of a Convention right by another private party.[93]

B. Section 6(2) HRA

Section 6(1) HRA is qualified by s.6(2) HRA, which is designed to prevent legislation from being indirectly attacked under s.6(1), since the proper method of challenging such legislation is through ss.3 and 4. Section 6(2) provides that: **20–018**

"(2) Subs.(1) does not apply to an act if—

---

[91] For consideration of the territorial scope of s.6 HRA, *Quark Fishing* [2006] 1 A.C. 529 at [34]; *Al-Skeini* [2008] 1 A.C. 153; *R. (Al-Saadoon) v Secretary of State for Defence* [2010] Q.B. 486, CA (Civ Div); *Smith* [2011] 1 A.C. 1.

[92] *Rose v Secretary of State for Health, Human Fertilisation and Embryology Authority* [2002] UKHRR 1329 QBD at [45], [49]–[51].

[93] A. Clapham, *Human Rights in the Private Sphere* (Oxford: Oxford University Press, 1993), Ch.7.

(a) as the result of one or more provisions of primary legislation, the authority could not have acted differently; or

(b) in the case of one or more provisions of, or made under, primary legislation which cannot be read or given effect in a way which is compatible with the Convention rights, the authority was acting so as to give effect to or enforce those provisions."

i. *An example: Wilkinson*

20–019 The interpretation of s.6(2) HRA can be exemplified by *Wilkinson*.[94] The claimant was a widower who, if he had been a widow, would have received a widow's bereavement allowance by way of deduction from liability for income tax under s.262 of the Income and Corporation Taxes Act 1988. He argued that the failure to pay such an allowance constituted discrimination under the ECHR. Lord Hoffmann held that s.262 of the 1988 Act only authorised the payment of the allowance to widows and not widowers, and that it could not be read so as to include the latter,[95] and that this was so even in the light of the approach to s.3 HRA taken in *Ghaidan*. It followed that the IRC were protected by s.6(2)(a) of the HRA, since they were required by the 1988 Act to pay the benefit to women and had no power to pay the equivalent benefit to men.

The courts will nonetheless construe the protection afforded by s.6(2) narrowly. Thus, it was held in *Bono*[96] that it protects the public authority only where the primary legislation cannot be read or given effect in a way that is compatible with Convention rights. It does not give protection in relation to subordinate legislation where there is some incompatibility, but it is not the necessary consequence of the primary legislation.[97]

ii. *The relationship between section 6(2)(a) and (b): Hooper*

20–020 The relationship between s.6(2)(a) and (b) was considered in *Hooper*.[98] The claimants argued that the provision of certain benefits to widows and not widowers was in breach of arts 14 and 8 ECHR. The claim was brought not under s.3 HRA, but under s.6, since they wished to secure the benefits, which a declaration of incompatibility made under s.4 could not have given them. The House of Lords held that there was objective justification for the differential treatment so far as it concerned widows' pensions. In relation to the payment of other benefits, the widow's payment and the widowed mother's allowance, the secretary of state argued by way of defence that the claim under s.6(1) could not succeed because of s.6(2)(b).

Their Lordships agreed that the general purpose of s.6(2) was to prevent the principles in the HRA from being undermined. The logic of s.3 is that if primary legislation cannot be interpreted to be compatible with Convention rights, then Parliament is given the option of revising the legislation to render it compatible with the Convention. The purpose of s.6(2) is to prevent this from being

---

94 *Wilkinson* [2005] 1 W.L.R. 1718.

95 *Wilkinson* [2005] 1 W.L.R. 1718 at [17]–[18].

96 *R. (Bono) v Harlow DC* [2002] 1 W.L.R. 2475 QBD at [34].

97 See also *R. (H) v Secretary of State for Health* [2006] 1 A.C. 441, HL.

98 *R. (Hooper) v Secretary of State for Work and Pensions* [2005] 1 W.L.R. 1681, HL.

undermined by applicants who challenge as unlawful an act of the relevant minister made pursuant to the primary legislation said to be inconsistent with the HRA.[99] There was nonetheless disagreement between Lord Hope and Lord Brown about the interrelationship between s.6(2)(a) and (b).

For *Lord Hope*, the key to the two limbs of s.6(2) was the distinction between duty and discretion. Section 6(2)(a) captured the situation where the legislation imposed a duty to act. Thus, if an authority could not have acted differently because of one or more provisions of primary legislation the disputed act could not be regarded as unlawful under s.6(1), and the claimant would have to challenge the primary legislation directly under s.3. It thus covered the situation where the "authority is obliged to act in the manner which the legislation lays down even if the legislation requires it to act in a way which is incompatible with a Convention right".[100] **20–021**

Lord Hope held that s.6(2)(b) by way of contrast captured the situation where the authority has discretion derived from primary legislation, which cannot be read or given effect in a way that is compatible with Convention rights.[101] In such cases, the discretion could not be read to be compatible with Convention rights, and the exercise of that discretion in an instant case could not therefore be challenged under s.6(1). The proper mode of attack would be to challenge the primary legislation itself under s.3.[102]

Lord Brown agreed with Lord Hope as to the general purpose of s.6(2) HRA, this being to safeguard the sovereignty of Parliament by preventing an act or failure to act under legislation that could not be read compatibly with Convention rights under s.3 from being declared unlawful under s.6(1).[103] He regarded the case as falling squarely within s.6(2)(a): Parliament intended the benefits to be payable only to widows, the legislation could not be read so as to include widowers,[104] and the secretary of state could not have acted differently.[105]

Lord Brown, however, disagreed about the interpretation of s.6(2)(b). He accepted that it would provide a defence where the discretion could never be exercised in a manner that was Convention compliant and therefore the primary legislation would be set at naught. He held, however, that this was different from cases where the argument was that the power must always be exercised in order to be Convention compliant. It was, said Lord Brown, generally accepted in many cases that discretion must be exercised in a particular way in order to be compliant with Convention rights and there was no suggestion that s.6(2)(b) would be applicable in such circumstances. It should not then make a difference if the statutory discretion was one that had to be exercised in every case in order to ensure Convention compliance.[106] The fact that this converted a power into a

---

[99] *Hooper* [2005] 1 W.L.R. 1681 at [51], [70], [92], [105].

[100] *Hooper* [2005] 1 W.L.R. 1681 at [71].

[101] *Hooper* [2005] 1 W.L.R. 1681 at [72]–[73], Lord Hope gave the following cases as examples: *Alconbury* [2003] 2 A.C. 295 and *R. v Kansal (No.2)* [2002] A.C. 69 at [86]–[88].

[102] *Hooper* [2005] 1 W.L.R. 1681 at [73].

[103] *Hooper* [2005] 1 W.L.R. 1681 at [105].

[104] *Hooper* [2005] 1 W.L.R. 1681 at [122].

[105] *Hooper* [2005] 1 W.L.R. 1681 at [124].

[106] *Hooper* [2005] 1 W.L.R. 1681 at [118].

duty was said Lord Brown no bar in this respect since this was often required to ensure Convention-compliant decision-making.

iii. The relationship between section 6(2)(a) and (b): conclusions

20–022 The difference of opinion as to the reach of s.6(2)(b) made no difference in the instant case since Lord Brown decided that s.6(2)(a) was applicable. The difference of view between Lord Hope and Lord Brown does, however, have significant repercussions for the ambit of s.6(2)(b).

Lord Hope's view was premised on a symmetrical reading of s.6(2)(b). He held that it was applicable either where it would not be possible to exercise the discretion in a manner compliant with Convention rights, or where the discretion had to be exercised in order to be compliant with such rights. In either eventuality s.6(2)(b) would provide a defence to an action under s.6(1), and the applicant would have to proceed via ss.3 and 4 HRA.

Lord Brown's view was premised on a denial of this symmetry. He accepted that s.6(2)(b) provided a defence where the power could not be exercised without breaching Convention rights, since otherwise the primary legislation would be set at naught. He held, however, that matters were different in cases where the discretion had to be exercised. The effect of this reading of s.6(2)(b) is that it would rarely apply so as to provide a defence to exercise of discretionary power, which would have to be compliant with Convention rights. If it was not the defendant could not take the benefit of s.6(2)(b). Similarly, if compliance with Convention rights could only be secured by always exercising the discretion, then this should be done and it would not be open to the defendant to rely on s.6(2)(b) by way of defence.

The reasoning in *Hooper* should also be seen in the light of the subsequent decision in *Morris*.[107] Sedley LJ, having considered the judgment in *Hooper*, held that where a statutory provision could not be read to be compatible with Convention rights then it fell prima facie within s.6(2) HRA. This did not, however, prevent a public authority from using other statutory powers that it possessed, although it was not under a duty to do so, provided that it did not use such alternate powers solely as the means to circumvent the provisions of the statute that were not compatible with the HRA.

C. Acts of Public Authorities: The Scope of Section 6

i. Two types of public authority

20–023 The scope of s.6 HRA is clearly important.[108] Section 6(1) provides that it is unlawful for a public authority to act in a way which is incompatible with a Convention right. Section 6(3) provides that a public authority includes: "a court or tribunal" (s.6(3)(a)), and "any person certain of whose functions are functions

[107] *R. (Morris) v Westminster City Council* [2005] 1 W.L.R. 505.

[108] D. Oliver, "The Frontiers of the State: Public Authorities and Public Functions under the Human Rights Act" [2000] PL. 476; G. Morris, "Public Employment and the Human Rights Act 1998" [2001] P.L. 442.

of a public nature" (s.6(3)(b)). It does not include either House of Parliament, or a person exercising functions in connection with proceedings in Parliament. The guidance is augmented by s.6(5), which states that in relation to a particular act, a person is not a public authority by virtue only of s.6(3)(b) if the nature of the act is private. Private action by a private body is not therefore within the remit of the HRA, subject to what will be said below concerning the horizontal effect of the HRA.

These sections draw a distinction between core public bodies stricto sensu, such as government departments, which are always within the ambit of s.6 whatever the nature of the act complained of, and other hybrid bodies which are only caught because certain of their functions are of a public nature within s.6(3)(b). This is important because bodies caught by virtue of s.6(3)(b) can argue, based on s.6(5), that they are not within the HRA if the nature of the act was private.

The distinction between core public authorities, which are bound by the HRA in respect of everything they do, and hybrid public authorities, which are bound by the HRA in respect of their public but not their private functions, is apparent in the debates on the Bill in Parliament, and in subsequent case law.

Thus in the debates in Parliament, the Home Secretary stated that it would not be possible to list all the bodies to which the HRA would be applicable, and that a non-exhaustive definition of a public authority was adopted in s.6. He then added that "obvious public authorities, such as central Government and the police are caught in respect of everything they do", and that "public—but not private—acts of bodies that have a mix of public and private functions are also covered".[109]

This distinction has been recognised in the case law. Thus, in *Aston Cantlow*[110] their Lordships accepted the distinction between core and hybrid public authorities. Lord Nicholls stated that a core public authority was bound by the HRA in respect of "everything it does",[111] as did Lord Rodger[112]; Lord Hope stated that core public bodies were public authorities "through and through"[113] with the consequence that s.6(5) did not apply to them, the assumption being that everything done by such an authority constituted a public function for the purposes of the HRA[114]; and Lord Hobhouse held that core public authorities were those bodies all of whose functions were of a public nature, so that s.6 applied to all of their actions.[115] Hybrid public authorities, by way of contrast, were only bound by the HRA in relation to functions of a public nature. Similarly in *YL*[116] Lord Neuberger held that a core public authority was bound by s.6 in relation to "every one of its acts whatever the nature of the act concerned",[117] **20–024**

[109] HC Deb., col.775 (16 February 1998).

[110] *Aston Cantlow and Wilmcote with Billesley Parochial Church Council v Wallbank* [2004] 1 A.C. 546, HL.

[111] *Aston Cantlow* [2004] 1 A.C. 546 at [7].

[112] *Aston Cantlow* [2004] 1 A.C. 546 at [144].

[113] *Aston Cantlow* [2004] 1 A.C. 546 at [35].

[114] *Aston Cantlow* [2004] 1 A.C. 546 at [41].

[115] *Aston Cantlow* [2004] 1 A.C. 546 at [85].

[116] *YL v Birmingham City Council* [2008] 1 A.C. 95, HL.

[117] *YL* [2008] 1 A.C. 95 at [131], [129].

with the consequence that there was no need to distinguish between private and public acts or functions of a core public authority. A hybrid public authority was, however, only bound by s.6 in relation to an act which was not private in nature, and which was pursuant to, or in connection with, a public function.

This twin-track approach fits with that adopted by the ECtHR. It has applied the Convention to state institutions stricto sensu even where it has been argued that the challenged action concerned the exercise of power by the state qua employer rather than qua legislator or Executive, and it rejected the contention that the Convention could not impose obligations on the state which were not incumbent on private employers.[118]

It is interesting to reflect on the rationale for subjecting all actions of core public authorities to the HRA. It might be felt that such bodies never do anything that could be regarded as private. This empirical claim is debatable. It might, alternatively, be argued that bodies which are "so public" should set an example and that acts which might be felt to be private if performed by others should none the less be subject to the HRA when undertaken by a core public authority. This is a normative claim that might well be warranted, but which should be openly acknowledged. A third possible rationale might be a mix of the previous two. It might be felt that "not many" acts of such bodies would be classified as private, and that it would not be good if these bodies were to seek to evade the HRA in such instances, since this would send the wrong message about the government's overall commitment to the legislation.

ii. The test for core public authorities

20–025 It follows from the above that there must be some criterion for dividing between core and hybrid public authorities. The case law provides guidance in this respect, both as to the criteria that should be used and as to the criteria that are not determinative.

The principal criterion used by the courts to determine the meaning of core public authority is whether the relevant body is, in the words of Lord Nicholls, "governmental in a broad sense of that expression",[119] such that the government is answerable for the relevant body under the ECHR. Lord Nicholls gave by way of example government departments, local authorities, the police and the armed forces. Underlying this classification were factors such as the "possession of special powers, democratic accountability, public funding in whole or in part, an obligation to act only in the public interest, and a statutory constitution".[120] The judicial interpretation of core public authority has been influenced by the consequences of inclusion within this category: the core public authority is bound by the HRA in respect of all its actions, and cannot enjoy Convention rights.[121] The latter consideration has inclined the courts to be cautious about defining core

---

[118] *Swedish Engine Drivers' Union v Sweden* (1979) 1 E.H.R.R. 617; *Schmidt and Dahlstrom v Sweden* (1979) 1 E.H.R.R. 632.

[119] *Aston Cantlow* [2004] 1 A.C. 546 at [7].

[120] *Aston Cantlow* [2004] 1 A.C. 546 at [7].

[121] *Aston Cantlow* [2004] 1 A.C. 546 at [8].

public authority too broadly. They have concluded that, for example, non-governmental organisations should not generally be regarded as falling within the category of core public authorities, since this would thereby deny them the benefit of Convention rights, more especially because such organisations are included within the list of those who are allowed to bring actions before the ECtHR under art.34 ECHR.[122]

The courts have also provided guidance as to the criteria that should not be determinative of the category of core public authority. Thus, the case law on the amenability of a body to judicial review is properly regarded as not being conclusive, since it was developed for different purposes.[123] The courts have in addition made it clear that case law concerning the meaning of the "state" developed by other courts is of limited utility in answering the salient issues under the HRA. The ECJ's jurisprudence concerning the meaning of the "state" for the purposes of deciding whether a directive can be enforced against a particular body, has therefore been rightly said to provide limited assistance for the purposes of the definitional issues that arise under the HRA.[124]

iii. *The test for hybrid public authorities*

The courts have also furnished guidance concerning hybrid public authorities, indicating the relevant criteria and those that are not determinative. The dominant approach is to consider a range of factors to decide whether the function performed by the body can be regarded as public and hence render it subject to the HRA as regards that function. This is apparent from the judgment of Lord Nicholls in *Aston*[125]: **20–026**

> "What, then, is the touchstone to be used in deciding whether a function is public for this purpose? Clearly there is no single test of universal application. There cannot be, given the diverse nature of governmental functions and the variety of means by which these functions are discharged today. Factors to be taken into account include the extent to which in carrying out the relevant function the body is publicly funded, or is exercising statutory powers, or is taking the place of central government or local authorities, or is providing a public service."

A similar approach is evident in later cases. Thus, in *YL* Lord Bingham echoed Lord Nicholls' reasoning, and listed factors that should be taken into account in construing "public function" in s.6(3)(b) HRA.[126] These included: the role and responsibility of the state in relation to the subject matter in question; the nature and extent of the public interest in the function in question; the nature and extent

---

[122] *Aston Cantlow* [2004] 1 A.C. 546 at [8], [47], [87].

[123] *Aston Cantlow* [2004] 1 A.C. 546 at [52], [87].

[124] *Aston Cantlow* [2004] 1 A.C. 546 at [55], [87]. The ECJ's case law is concerned with whether such bodies are sufficiently public to be regarded as part of the state for the purposes of vertical direct effect, with the consequence that a directive can be pleaded against them, P. Craig and G. de Búrca, *EU Law, Text, Cases and Materials*, 6th edn (Oxford: Oxford University Press, 2015), Ch.7. The issue under the HRA is as to which bodies should be regarded as "obviously public", with the consequence that they should bound in all their activities, public or private, by the HRA.

[125] *Aston Cantlow* [2004] 1 A.C. 546 at [12].

[126] *YL* [2008] 1 A.C. 95 at [5]–[11]. Lord Bingham dissented on the facts, but that does not undermine the force of his observations as to the approach to be adopted to deciding on the meaning of a hybrid public authority.

of any statutory power or duty in relation to that function; the extent to which the state, directly or indirectly, regulates, supervises and inspects the performance of that function, taking into account the extent to which it imposes penalties on those who fail to meet the requisite standards; the extent to which, whether directly or indirectly, the state was willing to pay for the function that is at issue; and the extent of the risk that improper performance of the function might violate an individual's Convention rights. A factor-based approach was also endorsed by Baroness Hale,[127] Lord Mance,[128] Lord Scott,[129] and Lord Neuberger.[130]

The courts have also indicated factors that should not be regarded as determinative or particularly helpful in deciding whether a body should be regarded as a hybrid public authority, such as the amenability of bodies to judicial review and the EU case law on the definition of the "state" for the purposes of direct effect of directives.[131]

iv. The application of the test for hybrid public authorities

20–027 The very fact that a range of factors are taken into account in deciding whether a body falls within s.6(3)(b) HRA inevitably means that there will be differences of view as to the application of those factors in a particular case.

This is exemplified by *Aston Cantlow*. The parochial church council served a notice on the defendants to repair the chancel of the parish church. The defendants resisted payment, alleging that the notice infringed its rights under art.1 of the First Protocol. The Court of Appeal concluded that the parochial church council could be regarded as within the HRA, either because it was a core public authority, or that it fell within the category of hybrid public authority.[132]

The House of Lords, however, held that the parochial church council could not be regarded as falling in either category.[133] It concluded that although the Church of England had special links with central government and performed certain public functions, it was essentially a religious organisation and not a governmental organisation. The functions of parochial church councils were primarily concerned with pastoral and administrative matters. They were not wholly of a public nature, and therefore were not core public authorities under s.6(1). The fact that the public had certain rights in relation to their parish church was not sufficient to characterise the actions of a parochial church council in maintaining the fabric of the parish church as being of a public nature, so that when the plaintiff took steps to enforce the defendants' liability for the repair of the chancel, it was not performing a function of a public nature, which rendered it a hybrid public authority under s.6(3)(b).

---

127 *YL* [2008] 1 A.C. 95 at [64]–[72].
128 *YL* [2008] 1 A.C. 95 at [91].
129 *YL* [2008] 1 A.C. 95 at [64].
130 *YL* [2008] 1 A.C. 95 at [154]–[160].
131 *Aston Cantlow* [2004] 1 A.C. 546 at [52], [55], [87]; *YL* [2008] 1 A.C. 95 at [12].
132 *Aston Cantlow PCC v Wallbank* [2002] Ch. 51, CA (Civ Div).
133 *Aston Cantlow* [2004] 1 A.C. 546.

v. The application of the test for hybrid public authorities: contracting out

The meaning accorded to s.6(3)(b) has been especially problematic in cases where a public body has contracted out the provision of certain services. **20–028**

This is exemplified by the *Donoghue* case.[134] A housing association had been created by a local authority, and transferred to it a substantial proportion of the local authority's housing stock. The relevant issue was whether the housing association was a public authority for the purposes of s.6 HRA. Lord Woolf CJ gave the judgment of the Court of Appeal and reasoned as follows[135]:

> "The fact that a body performs an activity which otherwise a public body would be under a duty to perform cannot mean that such a performance is necessarily a public function. A public body in order to perform its public duties can use the services of a private body. Section 6 should not be applied so that if a private body provides such services, the nature of the functions are inevitably public. If this were to be the position, then when a small hotel provides bed and breakfast accommodation as a temporary measure, at the request of a housing authority that is under a duty to provide that accommodation, the small hotel would be performing public functions and required to comply with the Human Rights Act 1998. That is not what the Human Rights Act 1998 intended … Section 6(3) means that hybrid bodies, who have functions of a public and private nature are public authorities, but *not* in relation to acts which are of a private nature. The fact that through the act of renting by a private body a public authority may be fulfilling its public duty, does not automatically change into a public act what would otherwise be a private act … ".

Lord Woolf set out a list of factors to determine whether a body such as the housing association should be regarded as a public authority for the purposes of the HRA[136]: the existence of statutory authority could mark out the act as being public; so too could the extent of control over the function exercised by a body that was a public authority; and the more closely enmeshed were the prima facie private acts with the activities of a public body, the more likely they were to be treated as public. However, the mere fact that a public regulatory authority supervised the acts would not suffice in this respect. The housing association was, judged by these criteria, deemed to be performing a public function and subject to the HRA: the housing association had been created by the local authority, members of the local authority sat on its board, and it was subject to guidance by the local authority. The housing association was therefore subject to the HRA and Convention rights. The court, however, held that there was no breach of art.8 ECHR.

The Court of Appeal considered the issue again in the *Leonard Cheshire* case.[137] **20–029**
The appellants were long-term patients in a home run by the Leonard Cheshire Foundation (LCF), and sought judicial review of LCF's decision to close the home. They argued that they had been promised a "home for life" in their current accommodation, that the decision to close the home was in breach of art.8 ECHR, and that this was so even though alternative accommodation in community based

---

134 *Poplar Housing and Regeneration Community Association Ltd v Donoghue* [2002] Q.B. 48, CA (Civ Div).

135 *Donoghue* [2002] Q.B. 48 at 67. Italics in original.

136 *Donoghue* [2002] Q.B. 48 at 69.

137 *R. v Leonard Cheshire Foundation (A Charity)* [2002] 2 All E.R. 936, CA (Civ Div).

units would be provided. The majority of the residents had been placed there by the social services departments of their local authority or by their health authority. The placements were paid for by the authorities and were made pursuant to statutory powers.[138] The legislation made it clear that the accommodation could be provided either "in house", by the local authority itself,[139] or it could be contracted out to third parties.[140]

Lord Woolf CJ adhered to the approach in *Donoghue*. If the local authority itself provided accommodation, it would be performing a public function. This would also be so where it made arrangements for the accommodation to be provided by LCF. This did not however mean that LCF should be regarded as performing a public function so as to come within the HRA.[141] Lord Woolf then considered the factors in *Donoghue* to determine whether the LCF should be regarded as a public authority for the purposes of the HRA.[142] He concluded that it should not. The mere fact of public funding by the local authority for the accommodation was not determinative of whether the functions were public or private.[143] There was, said Lord Woolf, no other evidence of there being a public flavour to the functions of LCF or LCF itself, which did not exercise statutory powers in caring for the appellants.[144]

20–030 The reasoning and result in *Leonard Cheshire* were challenged before the House of Lords in *YL*.[145] The claimant, who was 84, suffered from Alzheimer's disease. The defendant council had a statutory duty under the National Assistance Act 1948 to make arrangements for providing her with residential accommodation,[146] and it chose to fulfil that duty, as it was allowed to,[147] by contracting with the second defendant company, an independent provider of health and social care services, for the claimant to be placed in one of its care homes, which accommodated both privately funded residents and those whose fees were paid by the council in full or in part. The claimant's fees were paid by the council, save for a small top-up fee paid by her relatives. The company subsequently sought to terminate the contract for her care and remove her from the home. The claimant argued that the company fell within s.6(3)(b) HRA and that its actions were in breach of arts 2, 3 and 8 ECHR.

The majority of the House of Lords rejected the claim. The reasoning was complex, but in essence was as follows. The majority distinguished between the function of a local authority in making arrangements pursuant to the 1948 Act for those in need of care and accommodation who were unable to make such arrangements for themselves, and that of a private company in providing such

[138] The National Assistance Act 1948 s.21(1), required the local authority to provide accommodation for the claimants, being people who by reason of age, illness or disability were in need of care and attention that was not otherwise available to them.

[139] National Assistance Act 1948 s.21(4)–(5).

[140] National Assistance Act 1948 s.26.

[141] *Leonard Cheshire* [2002] 2 All E.R. 936 at [15].

[142] *Leonard Cheshire* [2002] 2 All E.R. 936 at [16]–[28].

[143] *Leonard Cheshire* [2002] 2 All E.R. 936 at [35(i)].

[144] *Leonard Cheshire* [2002] 2 All E.R. 936 at [35(ii)].

[145] *YL* [2008] 1 A.C. 95.

[146] National Assistance Act 1948 s.21.

[147] National Assistance Act 1948 s.26.

care and accommodation under contract with the authority, on a commercial basis rather than by subsidy from public funds. They held that the actual provision of such care and accommodation by the private company, as opposed to its regulation and supervision pursuant to statutory rules, was not an inherently public function and thus fell outside s.6(3)(b). Thus, while the claimant retained public law rights as against the local authority that had arranged the accommodation, she did not have Convention rights as against the care home.

There was a powerful dissent by Lord Bingham and Baroness Hale, who reasoned as follows. The duty imposed on the local authority by the 1948 legislation could be discharged either by arranging for residential care itself, or through another local authority or a voluntary organisation, such as the second defendant. These were "alternative means by which the responsibility of the state may be discharged".[148] They rejected the distinction, which was crucial to the majority's reasoning, between arranging for and providing such accommodation. Parliament intended that residential care should be provided. This duty had to be performed, and the means by which it was done were not important.[149] The factors listed by Lord Bingham as indicative of a "public function" undertaken by a hybrid public authority all inclined to the conclusion that the second defendant fell within this category.[150] Lord Bingham concluded,[151]

> "When the 1998 Act was passed, it was very well known that a number of functions formerly carried out by public authorities were now carried out by private bodies. Section 6(3)(b) of the 1998 Act was clearly drafted with this well-known fact in mind. The performance by private body A by arrangement with public body B, and perhaps at the expense of B, of what would undoubtedly be a public function if carried out by B is, in my opinion, precisely the case which s.6(3)(b) was intended to embrace. It is, in my opinion, this case."

vi. The application of the test for hybrid public authorities and contracting out: an assessment

The application of s.6(3)(b) HRA to cases where a public body contracts out the performance of its duties remains highly problematic in the light of *YL* and the dissent is to be preferred. The reasons are as follows.[152] **20–031**

---

[148] *YL* [2008] 1 A.C. 95 at [16].

[149] *YL* [2008] 1 A.C. 95 at [16].

[150] *YL* [2008] 1 A.C. 95 at [65]–[72], as applied by Baroness Hale.

[151] *YL* [2008] 1 A.C. 95 at [20].

[152] P. Craig, "Contracting Out, the Human Rights Act and the Scope of Judicial Review" (2002) 118 L.Q.R. 551; M. Sunkin, "Pushing Forward the Frontiers of Human Rights Protection: The Meaning of Public Authority under the Human Rights Act" [2004] P.L. 643; C. Donnelly, "*Leonard Cheshire* Again and Beyond: Private Contractors, Contract and Section 6(3)(b) of the Human Rights Act" [2005] P.L. 785; H. Quane, "The Strasbourg Jurisprudence and the Meaning of a 'Public Authority' under the Human Rights Act" [2006] P.L. 106; Joint Committee on Human Rights, *Ninth Report: The Meaning of Public Authority under the Human Rights Act*, HL Paper No.77, HC Paper No.410 (Session 2006–07); C. Donnelly, *Delegation of Governmental Power to Private Parties, A Comparative Perspective* (Oxford: Oxford University Press, 2007), Ch.6; S. Palmer, "Public, Private and the Human Rights Act 1998: An Ideological Divide" (2007) 66 C.L.J. 559; A. Williams, "*YL v Birmingham City Council*: Contracting out and 'Functions of a Public Nature'" [2008] E.H.R.L.R. 524; Lord Pannick, "Functions of a Public Nature" [2009] J.R. 109; C. Campbell, "The Nature of the Power as Public in English Judicial Review" (2009) 68 C.L.J. 90; C. Donnelly, "Positive Obligations and Privatisation" (2010) 61 N.I.L.Q. 209; A. Williams, "A Fresh Perspective on Hybrid Public

First, s.6(3)(b) may be applicable either in cases where there is no contracting out, such as *Aston Cantlow*, or where there is, such as *YL*. This has implications for the test to determine "public function" under s.6(3)(b). It may well be right to apply the "list of factors" approach developed in *Aston Cantlow* to the former situation, precisely because there is no single criterion that can be used to determine whether a nominally private body should be subject to the HRA. It is, however, questionable whether this approach should be relevant to the latter cases, where there is contracting out. If it is decided that a core public authority is performing a public function pursuant to a statutory duty or power cast upon it, then that should be decisive. The nature of the function does not change if the task is contracted out to a body that is nominally private. That is the essence of the quotation from Lord Bingham set out above, and it is surely correct. The same point can be put in a different way. The fact that a core public authority is bound under the HRA in respect of all its actions, does not preclude us from deciding that, as will commonly be the case, its action in a particular instance is properly regarded as fulfilment of a public function cast upon it in the public interest by legislation. Where this is so the fact that it contracts out the performance of the task to a private body does not alter its nature: if it was properly regarded as a public function when performed by the public authority itself, then it should be so regarded when the same task is performed by the body to whom the power has been contracted out.

Second, it cannot be correct as a matter of principle for the availability of Convention rights to be dependent upon the fortuitous incidence as to how the core public authority chooses to discharge its functions. It is increasingly the case that public authorities contract out some of the duties cast upon them. There may be good reasons for this. The choice whether to do so should not however place in jeopardy the applicability of Convention rights, since this would make the protections secured by the HRA a lottery.

20–032 Third, the preceding arguments can be tested against the facts of *YL* itself. The statutory duty cast on local authorities by the National Assistance Act 1948 to make arrangements for providing accommodation for those who could not do so for themselves for reasons of age, infirmity, disability, etc. was, as recognised by Baroness Hale, part of the post-war Beveridge social welfare reforms.[153] It was quite clearly a public function, imposed in the public interest. It did not change its nature by the fact that it could be fulfilled through a voluntary organisation. The distinction that lies at the heart of the majority judgment between making arrangements for such accommodation, and the provision of such accommodation, is, with respect, not supported by the words of the statute,[154] or by the

Authorities under the Human Rights Act 1998: Private Contractors, Rights-stripping and 'Chameleonic' Horizontal Effect" [2011] P.L. 139; S. Choudry, "Children in 'Care' after *YL*—The Ineffectiveness of Contract as a means of Protecting the Vulnerable" [2015] P.L. 519; K. Gledhill, "The Public Function Test: Have we Been Asking the Right Question?" [2015] J.R. 73.

153 *YL* [2008] 1 A.C. 95 at [49].

154 The actual wording of the National Assistance Act 1948 s.21(1) is that the local authority shall "make arrangements for providing". This is simply reflective of the fact that the local authority has choice under the legislation as to how the duty should be fulfilled. It does not mean that there is no duty in relation to the provision of the accommodation. This reading would make no sense of the legislative scheme and is inconsistent with, for example s.21(4).

legislative intent underlying the statutory scheme. The legislative intent was, as Lord Bingham noted, that residential care should be provided, while leaving choice as to the means by which this was done.[155] The dissent is to be preferred. This is so whether one applies the "list of factors" approach to conclude that the second defendant was performing a public function,[156] or whether, as argued above, one reaches the same conclusion by saying that the local authority was performing a public function in the public interest, such that when the task was contracted out the second defendant was also performing a public function and hence bound by the HRA.

Fourth, the majority in *YL* were concerned that if the HRA was applicable to the instant case then there would be inequality between those who were resident in care homes as a result of the local authority fulfilling its statutory duties, and others who resided in a purely private capacity. There is some force in this argument. The counter argument is, however, that the schema of the HRA as applied to this type of case means that there will always be an equality issue. The decision in *YL* means that there will be differential treatment in terms of the HRA between the infirm, ill, etc. who are housed in local authority accommodation, who would take the benefit of Convention rights, and those who are housed in accommodation pursuant to a contracting out scheme, who would be denied such rights.

Finally, the actual decision in *YL* was reversed by the Health and Social Care Act 2008, s.145 of which made provision of care home accommodation an exercise of a public function for the purposes of s.6(3)(b) HRA.[157] It has now been replaced by the Care Act 2014 s.73. The 2008 and 2014 legislation did not, however, alter the general reasoning in *YL*, which is still applicable to other instances where functions are contracted out. A Private Members' Bill, the Human Rights Act (Meaning of Public Authority) Bill 2009–2010, would have made this change if it had been enacted. It followed the lead of the Joint Committee on Human Rights[158] and defined "function of a public nature" to include a function which is required or enabled to be performed wholly or partly at public expense, irrespective of the legal status of the person who performed the function, and irrespective of whether the person who performed the function did so pursuant to a contract. The Bill was not, however, taken up by the government and did not become law.

---

[155] *YL* [2008] 1 A.C. 95 at [16].

[156] *R. (Weaver) v London and Quadrant Housing Trust* [2010] 1 W.L.R. 363, CA (Civ Div).

[157] This did not however render all relations between the care home and local authority to be of a public nature for the purposes of judicial review, *R. (Broadway Care Centre Ltd) v Caerphilly CBC* [2012] EWHC 37 (Admin).

[158] Joint Committee on Human Rights, *Ninth Report: The Meaning of Public Authority under the Human Rights Act*, para.150.

D. Acts of Public Authorities: The Horizontal Effect of the Human Rights Act

i. *Vertical and horizontal impact: general theory*

20–033 Any legal system that protects fundamental rights must decide how far those protections are to apply.[159] The traditional sphere of application for such protections is "vertical", operating between state and individual. An important issue is how far they can apply "horizontally" as between private individuals, or between the public body acting in a private capacity and an individual. The vertical view is premised, as Hunt has argued, on a

> "... rigid distinction between the public and private sphere and presupposes that the purpose of fundamental rights protection is to preserve the integrity of the private sphere against coercive intrusion by the state".[160]

Legal relations between individuals are, by way of contrast, seen as part of private autonomy, with the consequence that the choices individuals make about how to live their lives and deal with each other should not be dictated by the state.

The alternative view that rights-based protections should apply even as between private parties is premised ultimately on the hypothesis that all legal relations are constituted by the state, in the sense that the law itself is constructed and supported by the state.[161] Viewed from this perspective, choices are constantly made and expressed through legal rules as to the limits on private freedom of action. Legal rules, both statutory and common law, frequently impose limits on private choice whether in the sphere of contract, tort, property or restitution.

When the matter is viewed in this light the formal divide between the public and private sphere is much less secure. The issue becomes which types of restraint on private action are felt to be normatively warranted. It becomes more difficult to argue that rights-based protections should have no application in the

---

[159] M. Hunt, "The 'Horizontal Effect' of the Human Rights Act" [1998] P.L. 423; B. Markesinis, "Privacy, Freedom of Expression and the Horizontal Effect of the Human Rights Bill: Lessons from Germany" (1998) 114 L.Q.R. 47; Sir W. Wade, "The United Kingdom's Bill of Rights", in *Constitutional Reform in the United Kingdom: Practice and Principles* (University of Cambridge Centre for Public Law, 1998), Ch.6; G. Phillipson, "The Human Rights Act, 'Horizontal Effect' and the Common Law: A Bang or a Whimper" (1999) 62 M.L.R. 824; I. Leigh, "Horizontal Rights, the Human Rights Act and Privacy: Lessons from the Commonwealth" (1999) 48 I.C.L.Q. 57; N. Bamforth, "The Application of the Human Rights Act 1998 to Public Authorities and Private Bodies" [1999] C.L.J. 159; Sir R. Buxton, "The Human Rights Act and Private Law" (2000) 116 L.Q.R. 48; Sir W. Wade, "Horizons of Horizontality" (2000) 116 L.Q.R. 217; A. Young, "Remedial and Substantive Horizontality: The Common Law and *Douglas v Hello! Ltd*" [2002] P.L. 232; J. Morgan, "Questioning the 'True Effect' of the Human Rights Act" (2002) 22 L.S. 259; S. Pattinson and D. Beyleveld, "Horizontal Applicability and Horizontal Effect" (2002) 118 L.Q.R. 623; A. Young, "Horizontality and the Human Rights Act 1998", in K. Ziegler (ed.), *Human Rights and Private Law: Privacy as Autonomy* (Oxford: Hart, 2007), p.35; G. Phillipson and A. Williams, "Horizontal Effect and the Constitutional Constraint" (2011) 74 M.L.R. 878; G. Phillipson, "Privacy and Breach of Confidence: The Clearest Case of Horizontal Effect?", in D. Hoffman (ed.), *The Impact of the UK Human Rights Act on Private Law* (Cambridge: Cambridge University Press, 2011).

[160] Hunt, "The 'Horizontal Effect' of the Human Rights Act" [1998] P.L. 423, 424.

[161] Clapham, *Human Rights in the Private Sphere* (1993).

private sphere, more especially since power which is nominally private may be just as potent as power which is formally public. If constitutional rights are applied horizontally this does not preclude differences in their interpretation in public and private contexts.

ii. *Vertical and horizontal impact: the HRA*

20–034 It might be thought that the preceding discussion has no immediate application here, since s.6 HRA only applies to public authorities and therefore embodies a legislative choice to limit the HRA to vertical relations between citizen and state. The matter is not, however, so straightforward.

It should be noted at the outset that ss.3 and 4 HRA can be relied on in actions between private parties. The obligation in s.3 to read and give effect to legislation in a manner that is consistent with Convention rights is general in scope and can be applied to the interpretation of legislation in actions between private parties.[162]

Subject to this, the general view is that the HRA does not have "direct horizontal effect". It is not open to a private party to contend that action by the private defendant is unlawful for violation of Convention rights. The wording of s.6 HRA, limited as it is to public authorities, precludes such an independent cause of action between private parties.[163]

20–035 It is also generally accepted that the HRA does not thereby preclude all horizontal effect. To the contrary, the text and the legislative history reveal that some element of "indirect horizontal effect" is intended by the legislation. The textual indication is to be found in the inclusion of courts and tribunals as public authorities in s.6(3). Such bodies are bound by the obligation in s.6(1) to act compatibly with Convention rights.[164] The text takes us only so far. It does not in itself indicate that courts and tribunals are under this obligation when deciding purely private disputes between private parties. That this was the framers' intention is, however, clear from consideration of the legislative history. Hunt[165] has shown that the government rejected an amendment to the Bill designed to prevent it from having any horizontal effect. The amendment would have altered s.6(1) so as to prevent it from applying where "the public authority is a court or a tribunal and the parties to the proceedings before it do not include any public authority". The Lord Chancellor rejected the amendment. He stated that it was right as a matter of principle for the courts to have the duty to act compatibly with the Convention not only in cases involving other public authorities, but also in developing the common law in deciding cases between individuals.[166]

It is therefore important to consider what is meant by "indirect horizontal effect" in cases between private individuals. Canadian and German jurisprudence

---

[162] See, e.g. *Ashdown v Telegraph Group Ltd* [2002] Ch. 149; *Ghaidan* [2004] 2 A.C. 557; *CGU International Insurance Plc v Astrazeneca Insurance Co Ltd* [2006] EWCA Civ 1340; *Mykoliw v Botterill* [2010] CSOH 84.

[163] The argument for direct horizontality is put by Wade, "Horizons of Horizontality" (2000) 116 L.Q.R. 217 and Pattinson and Beyleveld, "Horizontal Applicability and Horizontal Effect" (2002) 118 L.Q.R. 623.

[164] *Hammerton v Hammerton* [2007] EWCA Civ 248.

[165] Hunt, "The 'Horizontal Effect' of the Human Rights Act" [1998] P.L. 423, 440.

[166] HL Deb., col 783 (24 November 1997).

indicate that the values and principles enshrined in the protection of rights may influence the rules applicable as between private parties.[167] These values can therefore be used to help shape the development of, for example, the common law rules in a particular area of private law.[168] This still leaves open the more precise way in which Convention rights can shape the development of the common law. This issue has generated a sophisticated literature,[169] which cannot be fully explored here.

Suffice it to say that strong and weak versions of indirect horizontality have been identified.[170] Under a model of strong horizontality, the courts are under a duty to develop the common law so as to be compatible with Convention rights, and should link the common law very closely with the rights as interpreted by the Strasbourg institutions. Under a model of weak indirect horizontality, the courts have a power to develop the common law so as to be compatible with Convention rights, and have greater latitude in allowing the common law to develop differently from the precise jurisprudence of the Strasbourg institutions.[171]

20–036 Hunt has articulated a view about the possible impact of the HRA on private relations that is more extensive than encapsulated by "indirect horizontal effect".[172] Drawing on case law from South Africa,[173] he posits a view about the effect of such rights on private parties, which is different from both direct and indirect horizontal effect. On this view fundamental rights are applicable to "all law", irrespective of the parties to the action. This does not thereby destroy private autonomy, since it is still open to individuals to conduct their affairs as they choose however unpleasant the criteria may be. What it does mean is that the law will not protect these bigoted choices where they conflict with protected rights.

Phillipson and Alexander have more recently argued convincingly for a constitutional constraint model. This requires courts to develop the common law compatibly with the Convention, but only where this can be achieved by incremental development, by developing the law in a judicial rather than legislative manner, "that is on a piecemeal and principled basis that takes due account of pre-existing legal frameworks established by Parliament and previous

---

[167] Hunt, "The 'Horizontal Effect' of the Human Rights Act" [1998] P.L. 423; Markesinis, "Privacy, Freedom of Expression and the Horizontal Effect of the Human Rights Bill: Lessons from Germany" (1998) 114 L.Q.R. 47

[168] It follows that even if a public authority successfully brings itself within s.6(5), and claims that it is not bound by s.6(1) because the nature of the act was private, it will still be open to the court to consider the values underlying the Convention rights in any private litigation between it and another party.

[169] Hunt, "The 'Horizontal Effect' of the Human Rights Act" [1998] P.L. 423.

[170] Young, "Remedial and Substantive Horizontality: The Common Law and *Douglas v Hello! Ltd*" [2002] P.L. 232; Phillipson, "The Human Rights Act, 'Horizontal Effect' and the Common Law: A Bang or a Whimper" (1999) 62 M.L.R. 824.

[171] Young, "Remedial and Substantive Horizontality: The Common Law and *Douglas v Hello! Ltd*" [2002] P.L. 232, 236.

[172] Hunt, "The 'Horizontal Effect' of the Human Rights Act" [1998] P.L. 423, 434–435, 441–442.

[173] *Du Plessis v Du Klerk* 1996 3 S.A. 850 at 914–915, Kriegler J.

judicial decisions".[174] Subject to the constraint of incrementalism, this model allows courts to create new causes of action.

There are some case law indications of indirect horizontality. Thus, in the *Douglas* case,[175] the claimants sought an injunction against *Hello!* magazine, because it had published pictures of their wedding, which they had promised exclusively to another magazine. The court, while refusing to grant the injunction, accepted that s.6 HRA required the court to have regard to art.8 ECHR when considering a common law claim to privacy as between private parties. There are, however, also decisions that evince a more cautious approach.[176]

E. Proceedings and Standing under Section 6

The forum in which claims under the HRA can be brought is dealt with in ss.7 and 9 HRA. Section 7(1) provides that: **20–037**

> "A person who claims that a public authority has acted (or proposes to act) in a way which is made unlawful by s.6(1) may—
> (a) bring proceedings against the authority[177] under this Act in the appropriate court or tribunal, or,
> (b) rely on the Convention right or rights concerned in any legal proceedings, but only if he is (or would be) a victim of the unlawful act."

Section 7(3) makes it clear that the need for the claimant to be a victim operates when the proceedings are brought by way of judicial review. The phrase "appropriate court or tribunal" within s.7(1)(a) means such court or tribunal as may be determined in accordance with rules[178] to be made by the secretary of state or the Lord Chancellor.[179] The phrase "legal proceedings" within s.7(1)(b) includes proceedings brought by or at the instigation of a public authority, and an appeal against the decision of a court or tribunal.[180] Proceedings brought under s.7(1)(a) in respect of a judicial act[181] may be brought only by exercising a right of appeal, or by way of judicial review, or in such other forum as may be prescribed by rules.[182] This does not, however, affect any rule of law, which prevents a court from being the subject of judicial review.[183]

---

[174] Phillipson and Williams, "Horizontal Effect and the Constitutional Constraint" (2011) 74 M.L.R. 878, 887.

[175] *Douglas v Hello! Ltd* [2001] Q.B. 967, CA (Civ Div) at [111], [167]; *Douglas v Hello! Ltd (No.6)* [2006] Q.B. 125, CA (Civ Div); *Campbell v MGN* [2004] 2 A.C. 457 at [132]; *Berezovsky v Forbes (No.2)* [2001] E.M.L.R. 45, CA (Civ Div) at [10]; *In A Local Authority (Inquiry: Restraint on Publication), Re* [2004] 2 W.L.R. 926 Fam Div.

[176] *Wainwright v Home Office* [2004] 2 A.C. 406, HL; *Money Markets International Stockbrokers Ltd (in liquidation) v London Stock Exchange Ltd* [2002] 1 W.L.R. 1150 at [137]–[140]; *McDonald v McDonald* [2014] EWCA Civ. 1049 CA (Ch).

[177] This covers a counterclaim or similar proceeding, HRA s.7(2).

[178] HRA s.7(2); *A v B (Investigatory Powers Tribunal: Jurisdiction)* [2010] 2 A.C. 1 SC.

[179] HRA s.7(9).

[180] HRA s.7(6).

[181] Defined as a judicial act of a court, including an act done on the instructions, or on behalf, of a judge, HRA s.9(5).

[182] HRA s.9(1).

[183] HRA s.9(2).

The time limits are specified in s.7(5).[184] Where proceedings are brought under s.7(1)(a) they must be commenced before the end of one year from the date when the act complained of took place, or such longer period as the court or tribunal considers equitable having regard to all the circumstances.[185] This is, however, expressly subject to any rule imposing a stricter time limit in relation to the procedure in question. The effect of this proviso is that if, for example, the procedure chosen is the application for judicial review then the shorter time limit applicable to such proceedings will operate.

Convention rights can be used offensively as covered by s.7(1)(a), whereby the individual instigates the action based on the infringement of s.6(1). Convention rights can also be used defensively as covered by s.7(1)(b), where the action is brought against an individual by a public authority and the former relies on a breach of s.6(1) by the authority as a defence. The limitation period in s.7(5) only applies to offensive actions. Where the individual relies on a breach of Convention rights by way of defence pursuant to s.7(1)(b) he will often have no control over the timing of the action, and might be unaware of the possible s.6(1) illegality until the public authority seeks to enforce an order against him, which he believes to violate Convention rights.[186]

20–038 Many s.6(1) actions will be brought by way of application for judicial review and will be linked with other possible heads of illegality. The implications which this has for the operation of the ordinary judicial review procedure will be considered later.[187]

The test for standing in relation to s.6(1) is that the person must be a victim of the unlawful act.[188] A person will only be deemed to be a "victim" if he would be a victim for the purposes of art.34 ECHR as interpreted by the ECtHR.[189] This criterion is different from that in ordinary judicial review applications, where the test is one of sufficiency of interest. This caused some disquiet during the passage of the Bill. The meaning of the term victim in the jurisprudence of the ECtHR will be discussed within the general context of standing.[190]

If it should transpire that a s.6(1) action is not allowed to proceed, because the applicant is not deemed to be a victim, then the courts can always use the common law jurisprudence. This was considered earlier,[191] and there is nothing in the HRA that overrules this body of doctrine. If, therefore, a public interest group which complained of a violation of a Convention right was held not to be a victim for the purposes of the HRA, it could argue that the challenged action was ultra vires in accord with the common law protections for fundamental rights.

---

[184] *Dunn v Parole Board* [2009] 1 W.L.R. 728 CA (Civ Div); *M (A Child) v Ministry of Justice* [2009] EWCA Civ 419.

[185] *Cameron v Network Rail Infrastructure Ltd (formerly Railtrack Plc)* [2007] 1 W.L.R. 163 QBD; *XYZ v Chief Constable of Gwent* [2014] EWHC 1448 (QB).

[186] Similar considerations affect judicial review actions, see Ch.27.

[187] See Ch.27.

[188] *Savage v South Essex Partnership NHS Foundation Trust* [2009] 1 A.C. 681, HL.

[189] HRA s.7(7).

[190] See paras 25–029 to 25–30.

[191] See paras 19–021 to 19–025.

F. Remedies for Breach of Section 6

Section 8(1) HRA provides that "in relation to any act (or proposed act) of a public authority which the court finds is (or would be) unlawful, it may grant such relief or remedy, or make such order, within its powers as it considers just an appropriate". The courts are therefore given a wide discretion concerning remedies. A declaration that the act of the public authority was unlawful, or an order to quash the act, will be the normal remedy. The appropriate relief may be prohibition or an injunction to prevent an unlawful act from being committed, since s.8(1) expressly contemplates a remedy being granted where a proposed act would be unlawful. The fact that s.6(6) defines an act to include a failure to act means that mandatory orders may also be ordered where the court believes that this is just and appropriate. **20–039**

Section 8(1) contains the proviso that the remedy must be within the powers of the court that makes it, and s.8(6) defines court to include a tribunal. We have seen that actions for breach of s.6(1) may be brought before an appropriate court or tribunal.[192] It may well be that a particular tribunal lacks the power to award certain types of remedy. This issue is addressed by s.7(11). It states that the minister who has power to make rules in relation to a particular tribunal may by order add to the relief or remedies which the tribunal may grant, or the grounds on which it may grant them, to the extent to which he considers this necessary to ensure that the tribunal can provide an appropriate remedy for the purposes of a s.6(1) action.

The application of s.8(1) to cases where the defendant public authority is a court or tribunal poses interesting problems. The acts of superior courts are not amenable to judicial review and therefore there would be no power to issue certiorari to such a body. The decision of the offending court could be set aside on appeal, on the ground of error of law.

The HRA also provides for the possibility of a remedy in damages. This will be considered in detail when discussing damages.[193] The bare outline of the relevant provisions will be given here. Section 8(1) is framed broadly enough to include such a remedy, and this is clearly contemplated by the legislation since s.8(2) stipulates that "damages may be awarded only by a court which has power to award damages, or to order the payment of compensation in civil proceedings". While damages can be given for breach of s.6(1), the intention is that they should be awarded only where other relief cannot afford just satisfaction to the claimant. This is the import of s.8(3): **20–040**

> "No award of damages is to be made unless, taking account of all the circumstances of the case, including—
> (a) any other relief or remedy granted, or order made, in relation to the act in question (by that or any other court), and
> (b) the consequences of any decision (of that or any other court) in respect of that act, the court is satisfied that the award is necessary to afford just satisfaction to the person in whose favour it is made."

---

192 HRA s.7(1)(a).

193 Ch.30.

5. STANDARD OF REVIEW: JUDICIAL PERSPECTIVE

20–041 The discussion thus far has been concerned with ss.3–4 and 6 HRA. We now consider the standard of judicial review under the HRA, which has generated significant case law and academic comment.

A. Standard of Review under the ECHR: Proportionality and Margin of Appreciation

20–042 The paradigm circumstance in which this issue arises is where the court decides that there has been a prima facie interference with a Convention right, and the defendant argues that this was warranted on the facts of the case. The national court will decide whether the interference was "in accordance with the law", or "prescribed by law" as demanded by the Convention. Compliance with these precepts requires not only that there must be some proper source of law authorising the interference, but also that it has the quality of "law". It must be adequately accessible to the citizen, it must be sufficiently clear so that the individual can foresee the consequences of his action and it must not leave excessive discretion to the public authorities.[194]

The national court may then have to decide whether the limitation on a Convention right serves a legitimate aim. Many ECHR articles allow for restrictions of the rights protected therein, but only on specified grounds. Thus, for example, art.10 concerning freedom of speech, and art.11 concerning freedom of assembly and association require that the restriction falls within the specified list of recognised exceptions.

It will then be for the national court to determine whether the interference with the right was proportionate. Even if it can be argued that a restriction on speech can be linked to, for example, the protection of health or morals, the ECHR specifies that it must be "necessary in a democratic society" for the protection of the relevant interest. In the *Sunday Times* case[195] the ECtHR made it clear that while the word "necessary" was not synonymous with indispensable, nor did it have the flexibility of expressions such as "admissible", "useful", "reasonable" or "desirable". The word necessary implied a "pressing social need". The interference had to be proportionate to the legitimate aim pursued, having regard to the facts prevailing in the instant case, and application of this test is affected by the nature of the right.

20–043 The Strasbourg institutions apply a "margin of appreciation" when reviewing the compatibility of state action with Convention rights. The doctrine is associated with cases such as *Handyside*.[196] The ECtHR held that in determining whether interference with a protected right was "necessary in a democratic society" some deference would be given to the state authority, which would be in a better

---

[194] *Sunday Times v UK* (1979) 2 E.H.R.R. 245; *Winterwerp v The Netherlands* (1979) 2 E.H.R.R. 387; *Kruslin v France* (1990) 12 E.H.R.R. 547; *Groppera Radio v Switzerland* (1990) 12 E.H.R.R. 321; *R. (Wardle) v Crown Court at Leeds* [2002] 1 A.C. 754, HL.

[195] *Sunday Times* (1979) 2 E.H.R.R. 245 at [59], [62], [65]; *Silver v UK* (1983) 5 E.H.R.R. 347 at [97]; *Olsson v Sweden* (1988) 11 E.H.R.R. 259.

[196] *Handyside v UK* (1979) 1 E.H.R.R. 737 at [48].

position than the international judge to determine the needs within its own country. The margin of appreciation doctrine is a settled feature of the ECHR jurisprudence. The justification for the doctrine is integrally connected with the supranational nature of the ECHR. The doctrine helps to define the relationship between a supranational court and national authorities, including national courts. The rationale for the doctrine is premised on the assumption that what might be necessary to attain the stated interests might vary from state to state even within democratic societies, and that the distance of the ECtHR from local circumstance as compared to the national executive means that some deference should be accorded to the latter. Viewed in this way the margin of appreciation is recognition of subsidiarity inherent in the ECHR system.[197]

The standard of review under the HRA will now be considered, beginning with proportionality and then moving to discussion of the deference, respect or weight that should be accorded to the initial decision-maker.

B. Standard of Review under the HRA: Proportionality

i. Proportionality: Daly

The courts have adopted proportionality as the appropriate standard of review under the HRA, subject to considerations of deference/discretionary area of judgment/respect/weight, which will normally be considered within the proportionality analysis.[198] *Daly*[199] is the leading authority. The applicant challenged the policy, made pursuant to s.47(1) of the Prison Act 1952, whereby a prisoner could not be present during a search of his cell, when prison officers examined legally privileged correspondence. He argued that this infringed his common law right to communicate confidentially with his legal adviser, and art.8 ECHR. **20–044**

Lord Steyn clarified the test for review under the HRA. He referred to the judgment in *Mahmood*,[200] which was cast in terms of heightened scrutiny under the *Wednesbury* test, in the manner laid down in cases such as *Smith*.[201] This heightened level of scrutiny had been held to be insufficient by the Strasbourg

[197] R. Ryssdal, "The Coming of Age of the European Convention on Human Rights" [1996] E.H.R.L.R. 18 at 24–25, 27.

[198] See cases *P and Q and QB* [2001] 1 W.L.R. 2002; *Samaroo v Secretary of State for the Home Department* [2001] UKHRR 1150; *R. (Farrakhan) v Secretary of State for the Home Department* [2002] Q.B. 139, CA (Civ Div). See also *R. (Ponting) v Governor of HMP Whitemoor, and Secretary of State for the Home Department* [2002] EWCA Civ 224; *R. (E) v Ashworth Hospital Authority* [2001] EWHC 1089 (Admin); *R. (L) v Manchester City Council* [2001] EWHC 707 (Admin); *R. (Hirst) v Secretary of State for the Home Department* [2002] 1 W.L.R. 2929 QBD; *R. (X) v Headteachers and Governors of Y School* [2007] H.R.L.R. 20 QBD; *Animal Defenders International* [2008] 1 A.C. 1312, HL.

[199] *R. (Daly) v Secretary of State for the Home Department* [2001] 2 A.C. 532, HL; *R. v Shayler* [2003] 1 A.C. 247, HL at [33]; *E (A Child) v Chief Constable of Ulster* [2009] 1 A.C. 536; *R. (B) v Chief Constable of Derbyshire* [2011] EWHC 2362; *Bank Mellat v HM Treasury* [2011] EWCA Civ 1.

[200] *R. (Mahmood) v Secretary of State for the Home Department* [2001] 1 W.L.R. 840, CA (Civ Div) at 857. See also, *R. v Secretary of State for the Home Department, Ex p. Isiko* [2001] H.R.L.R. 15, CA (Civ Div) at [30]–[31].

[201] *R. v Ministry of Defence, Ex p. Smith* [1996] Q.B. 517, CA (Civ Div).

Court in *Smith and Grady*.[202] This was because it effectively excluded any consideration by the national court of whether the interference with the applicant's rights answered a pressing social need, or was proportionate to national security or public order.

Lord Steyn held[203] that there was a material difference between the heightened scrutiny test, and one framed in terms of proportionality. While Lord Steyn accepted that many cases would be decided the same way under either test, he held that the intensity of review would be greater under proportionality for two reasons. Proportionality could, said Lord Steyn, require the reviewing court to assess the balance struck by the decision-maker, not merely whether it was within the range of reasonable decisions. The proportionality test could, second, oblige the court to pay attention to the relative weight accorded to relevant interests, in a manner not generally done under the traditional approach to review. The proper intensity of review was, said Lord Steyn, guaranteed by the twin requirements that the limitation of the right was necessary in a democratic society, in the sense of meeting a pressing social need, and really was proportionate to the legitimate aim being pursued.[204] Three points should be made by way of clarification concerning the standard of review articulated in *Daly*.

20–045 First, it is clear that the courts substitute judgment on certain issues under the HRA. This is so in relation to the meaning of many of the Convention terms that arise before the courts pursuant to the HRA. Thus, the courts decide for themselves what constitutes speech, an assembly and other interpretative issues that arise under the legislation.[205] However, the *Daly* proportionality test applies as the standard of review in the paradigm case where the public authority argues that the restriction of a right was necessary in the interests of a democratic society on one of the grounds specified in the relevant article.

Second, there is no inconsistency in principle in having proportionality as a test for review, and recognising that deference/respect/discretionary area of judgment/weight will impact on how proportionality is applied in a particular case. Deference/respect/weight, insofar as the courts choose to accord it, is taken into account in the three stages of the proportionality inquiry. The classic formulation is whether the measure was necessary to achieve the desired objective, whether it was suited to doing so, and whether it nonetheless imposed excessive burdens on the individual.[206]

Third, later courts have recognised that considerations of weight and balance can also be relevant in reasonableness review. Thus in *Kennedy*[207] Lord Mance

[202] *Smith and Grady v United Kingdom* (1999) 29 E.H.R.R. 493 at [138].

[203] *Daly* [2001] 2 A.C. 532 at [26].

[204] *Daly* [2001] 2 A.C. 532 at [27].

[205] *Secretary of State for the Home Department v JJ* [2008] 1 All E.R. 613, HL; *Secretary of State for the Home Department v E* [2008] 1 All E.R. 699, HL.

[206] In *Daly* [2001] 2 A.C. 532 at [27], Lord Steyn relied on the formulation of Lord Clyde in *de Freitas v Permanent Secretary of Ministry of Agriculture, Fisheries and Housing* [1999] 1 A.C. 69 PC at 80. Lord Clyde formulated the three-part test in terms of whether the objective was sufficiently important to justify limiting a fundamental right, whether the measures designed to achieve the objective were rationally connected to it, and whether the means used to impair the right were no more than necessary to accomplish the objective.

[207] *Kennedy v Charity Commission* [2014] UKSC 20 at [54].

held that reasonableness review and proportionality involved considerations of weight and balance, with the intensity of the scrutiny and the weight to be given to any primary decision maker's view depending on the context. This was reiterated by Lord Mance, Lord Carnwath and Lord Sumption in *Pham*.[208]

Daly established proportionality as the test for review. The role of the courts in the proportionality analysis has been discussed in subsequent House of Lords' and Supreme Court cases, notably in *Denbigh*,[209] *Huang*,[210] *Miss Behavin' Ltd*,[211] *Bank Mellat*[212] and *Carlile*.[213] It is important to disaggregate a number of related issues that affect this inquiry.

ii. Proportionality: judicial ultimate determination, not substitution of judgment

It is for the reviewing court to make the ultimate decision as to whether the impugned action violates the proportionality principle. Thus, as Lord Bingham stated in *Denbigh* proportionality must be judged objectively by the court.[214] This was echoed by Lord Hoffmann, Lord Mance and Lord Neuberger in *Miss Behavin'*, who made it clear that it was for the court to decide whether the challenged action infringed a Convention right, including in this respect the proportionality analysis.[215] **20–046**

It is, however, equally important to note that proportionality does not entail substitution of judgment on the merits by the courts for that of the primary decision-maker. This was made clear by Lord Sumption and Lord Reed in *Bank Mellat*.[216] The point was reiterated in *Carlile*,[217] where the Supreme Court emphasised that no review, however intense, could entitle the court to substitute its judgment for that of the constitutional decision-maker. Thus while the court makes the ultimate determination concerning proportionality it will commonly accord some respect or weight to the views of the primary decision-maker.[218]

iii. Proportionality: the weight accorded to the view of the initial decision-maker

The fact that the ultimate decision as to compliance with proportionality resides with the court does not tell us how much weight will be accorded to the view of **20–047**

208 *Pham v Secretary of State for the Home Department* [2015] UKSC 19 at [60], [95], [109]-[110]. Lord Neuberger, Lord Wilson and Lady Hale agreed with Lord Carnwath, Lord Mance and Lord Sumption.

209 *R. (Begum) v Denbigh High School Governors* [2007] 1 A.C. 100, HL.

210 *Huang* [2007] 2 A.C. 167; *Machado v Secretary of State for the Home Department* [2005] EWCA Civ 597.

211 *Belfast City Council v Miss Behavin' Ltd* [2007] 1 W.L.R. 1420.

212 *Bank Mellat v HM Treasury* [2013] UKSC 39.

213 *R. (Lord Carlile of Berriew QC) v Secretary of State for the Home Department* [2014] UKSC 60.

214 *Denbigh* [2007] 1 A.C. 100 at [30].

215 *Miss Behavin'* [2007] 1 W.L.R. 1420 at [13], [44], [88]; *DL v Newham BC* [2011] EWHC 1127.

216 *Bank Mellat* [2013] UKSC 39 at [21], [71]; *First City Trading* [1997] 1 C.M.L.R. 250 at 278–279.

217 *Carlile* [2014] UKSC 60 at [20], [31], [57]-[58], [67]-[68], [86]-[89], [105], [111].

218 The relevant legislation may, however, be interpreted so as to give the court broader power to decide the issue de novo, as in *Huang* [2007] 2 A.C. 167.

the initial decision-maker. The courts may distinguish types of case, to which different standards of proportionality review are applicable. These differential standards will have implications for the weight attached to the views of the primary decision-maker.

It is traditional in rights-based cases for the courts to adopt a strict form of judicial review. The court inquires whether the limitation placed on the right is really necessary, often, but not always, demanding that it be the least restrictive in all the circumstances, and if it is not then it is deemed to be disproportionate. While review according to this standard is searching and intensive it does not preclude the court from taking account of the views of the initial decision-maker when deciding whether this version of the proportionality test is met or not.

In other types of case the courts may adopt a test of lower intensity, whereby the claimant must show that the decision was manifestly disproportionate or something akin thereto. This test is common in cases where the initial decision is concerned with discretionary, social and economic choices, as exemplified by the ECJ's jurisprudence considered in the following chapter. It will still be for the reviewing court to decide whether the initial decision meets proportionality interpreted in this manner, but the views of the initial decision-maker will be of considerable importance in making this determination, since the test demands that the claimant shows that the initial decision was manifestly disproportionate.

20–048 It is, nonetheless, important to recognise that even where the courts adopt a strict form of proportionality review for rights-based cases there can be variation in the intensity of such review, which leads the courts to accord different degrees of weight to the views of the initial decision-maker in different types of case. This is so for two reasons.

First, not all rights are of the same importance, and the differences can impact on the application of proportionality review. This was recognised by Baroness Hale in *Countryside Alliance*, who held that what might be necessary in a democratic society had to take into account the comparative importance of the right infringed in the scale of rights protected, with the consequence that a proportionate interference with a less important right might be a disproportionate interference with a more important right. [219] The point was reiterated by Lord Sumption in *Carlile*, who noted that not all rights protected by the Convention were of equal weight, and that not all subjects called for the same degree of respect for the judgment of the executive.[220]

Second, there can be significant differences concerning the importance of the same right in different cases. Thus most people would accept that freedom of speech is an important right. It can however be deployed in very different types of case, ranging from protection of free speech during elections, as in *Prolife*,[221] to the use of free speech to justify a shop selling pornography, as in *Miss Behavin'*.[222] Courts will engage in more intensive proportionality review in the former type of case than the latter.

---

219 *Countryside Alliance* [2008] 1 A.C. 719 at [124].

220 *Carlile* [2014] UKSC 60 at [20].

221 *R. (ProLife Alliance) v BBC* [2004] 1 A.C. 185, HL.

222 *Miss Behavin'* [2007] 1 W.L.R. 1420.

The courts will, therefore, take account of a range of factors in deciding on the respect/weight accorded to the primary decision-maker when applying the proportionality test. They include the nature of the Convention right, the extent to which the issues require consideration of social, political and economic factors, the extent to which the court has expertise, whether the rights claimed are of especial importance, the democratic status of the primary decision-maker, and the nature of the subject matter area in which the decision has been taken.[223] **20–049**

In *Roth*, Laws LJ articulated four principles that would guide the courts.[224] The first was that greater deference would be paid to an Act of Parliament than to a decision of the Executive or subordinate measure. The second principle was that there was more scope for deference where the Convention required a balance to be struck, much less so where the right was stated in unqualified terms, although even in the latter instance there could be room for differences of view as to how the requirements of a Convention right could be met. Third, greater deference was due to the democratic powers where the subject-matter was peculiarly within their constitutional responsibility, such as defence of the realm, and less when it was more within the constitutional responsibility of the courts, which were concerned with maintenance of the rule of law. The final principle was that greater or lesser deference would be due according to whether the subject matter was more readily within the actual or potential expertise of the democratic powers or the courts. It was for this reason that government decisions in the area of macro-economic policy were relatively remote from judicial control.

The judicial approach is further exemplified by *Denbigh*. A school banned the wearing of Muslim dress in the form of the jilbab, while allowing a different form of Muslim dress, the shalwar kameeze. It was argued that this constituted an infringement of art.9 ECHR safeguarding freedom of religion. The House of Lords held that the school ban on the jilbab was proportionate. Their Lordships made the ultimate decision on proportionality, but took account of the school's views on the dress code that was most appropriate for their pupils. Thus Lord Bingham noted that different schools had different uniform policies, influenced by the composition of their student population and each school had to decide what uniform would best serve its wider educational purposes.[225] Lord Hoffmann applied the proportionality analysis in accord with the discretionary area of judgment applicable to the circumstances of the case: Parliament had left the decision about uniforms to individual schools and it was the school that was best placed to weigh and consider the factors that should influence its particular choice of uniform.[226] For Baroness Hale the school's choice of dress code was devised to meet the social conditions prevailing in that area at that time and was a proportionate response to the need to balance social cohesion and religious diversity.[227]

---

[223] *Samaroo* [2001] UKHRR 1150; *Farrakhan* [2002] Q.B. 139; *Ponting* [2002] EWCA Civ 224; *Langley v Liverpool City Council* [2005] EWCA Civ 1173; *Miss Behavin'* [2008] 1 A.C. 1420; *Denbigh* [2007] 1 A.C. 100; *Countryside Alliance* [2008] 1 A.C. 719.

[224] *Roth* [2003] Q.B. 728 at [83]–[87]; *R.(Wilson) v Wychavon DC* [2007] EWCA Civ 52.

[225] *Denbigh* [2007] 1 A.C. 100 at [33].

[226] *Denbigh* [2007] 1 A.C. 100 at [63]–[65].

[227] *Denbigh* [2007] 1 A.C. 100 at [97]–[98].

Thus, while the House of Lords in *Denbigh* disapproved of the process approach articulated by Brooke LJ in the Court of Appeal,[228] it is nonetheless clear that there will be a greater likelihood of the public body's decision being regarded as proportionate if it consciously addressed the Convention issues when making its decision. In that sense, while the House of Lords rejected Brooke LJ's formulaic process-based approach, a public body would still be advised that the chances of its decision being treated as proportionate will be greater if it has addressed a number of the issues articulated by Brooke LJ.[229]

20–050 The same point is evident in relation to *Miss Behavin'*. A local authority decided pursuant to statutory licensing powers that the appropriate number of licensed sex shops in a particular locality should be nil. The claimant argued that this decision infringed the right of free speech protected by art.10 ECHR. The House of Lords disagreed. Lord Hoffmann emphasised that the key issue was whether the local authority's action infringed the Convention right, not the reasoning process that it adopted. He nonetheless held that the licensing of sex shops was an area of social control in which the Strasbourg Court accorded Member States a wide margin of appreciation and that this translated at domestic level to a broad power of judgment entrusted to local authorities. It would therefore require unusual facts for it to amount to a disproportionate restriction on Convention rights.[230] Baroness Hale held that when the court was deciding whether there was a breach of Convention rights, it was bound to acknowledge that the local authority was much better placed than the court to decide whether the right of sex shop owners to sell pornography should be restricted for the protection of the rights of others or the protection of health and morals. It would therefore be difficult for the court to overturn that balance when it had been made expressly by the local authority. Where there was no indication that the local authority had undertaken that balance, the court had no alternative but to strike the balance itself, but even then it would give due weight to the "judgments made by those who are in much closer touch with the people and the places involved than the court could ever be".[231] Lord Mance took a similar view. He held that it was for the court itself to assess the proportionality of the challenged decision,[232] and then considered the interrelationship between this precept and judicial recognition of a discretionary area of judgment afforded to the initial decision-maker. The existence of this area of judgment necessarily meant, said Lord Mance, that there could be decisions "which a court would regard as proportionate, whichever way they went".[233] Where, however, the decision-maker had not addressed its mind to Convention values then the court would be deprived of its considered opinion on Convention issues, with the consequence that he, like Baroness Hale, concluded that the court

---

[228] *R. (Begum) v Denbigh High School Governors* [2005] 1 W.L.R. 3372, CA (Civ Div) at [81].

[229] See also R. Gordon, "Structures or Mantras? Some New Puzzles in HRA Decision-Making" [2006] J.R. 136; D. Mead, "Outcomes Aren't All: Defending Process-Based Review of Public Authority Decisions under the Human Rights Act" [2012] P.L. 61; A. Kavanagh, "Reasoning about Proportionality under the Human Rights Act 1998: Outcomes, Substance and Process" (2014) 130 L.Q.R. 235.

[230] *Miss Behavin'* [2008] 1 A.C. 719 at [16].

[231] *Miss Behavin'* [2008] 1 A.C. 719 at [37].

[232] *Miss Behavin'* [2008] 1 A.C. 719 at [44].

[233] *Miss Behavin'* [2008] 1 A.C. 719 at [46].

would have to strike the balance for itself, but nonetheless "giving due weight to such judgments as were made by the primary decision-maker on matters he or it did consider".[234] Lord Neuberger reasoned in a similar manner.[235]

C. Standard of Review under the HRA: Deference/Discretionary Area of Judgment/Respect/Weight

We have touched on concepts of deference/respect/weight in the preceding discussion. It is however necessary to consider this issue more closely. **20–051**

i. The ECHR margin of appreciation has not been adopted

UK courts have not adopted the margin of appreciation doctrine developed by the ECtHR. The twin rationales for the Strasbourg doctrine set out above are not appropriate where Convention rights are applied by domestic courts. It would, as Sir John Laws stated, be inapt to the administration of the Convention in the domestic courts for the very reason that they are domestic. They will not be subject to an "objective inhibition generated by any cultural distance between themselves and the state organs impleaded before them".[236] **20–052**

ii. A domestic concept of deference/discretionary area of judgment/respect

The courts nonetheless recognised early in their jurisprudence a domestic concept of deference within the HRA.[237] Lord Hope in *Kebilene*[238] held that the margin of appreciation doctrine was not available to national courts under the HRA for the reasons considered above. He held that national courts should however recognise that difficult choices might have to be made between the rights of the individual and the needs of society. It followed that in some circumstances the courts should acknowledge an area of judgment "within which the judiciary will defer, on democratic grounds, to the considered opinion of the elected body or person whose actual decision is said to be incompatible with the Convention".[239] Such an area of judgment would more readily be found where the Convention required a balance to be struck, or where the case raised issues of social and economic policy. It would be less likely to be found where the right was unqualified, or where the rights were of high constitutional importance which the courts were well placed to assess.[240] **20–053**

---

234 *Miss Behavin'* [2008] 1 A.C. 719 at [47].

235 *Miss Behavin'* [2008] 1 A.C. 719 at [91].

236 Sir John Laws, "The Limitations of Human Rights" [1998] P.L. 254 at 258; D. Pannick, "Principles of Interpretation of Community Rights under the Human Rights Act and the Discretionary Area of Judgment" [1998] P.L. 545 at 548–549.

237 *Brown v Stott (Procurator Fiscal, Dunfermline)* [2003] 1 A.C. 681; *R. (Marper) v Chief Constable of South Yorkshire* [2002] EWCA Civ 1275; *Lambert* [2002] 2 A.C. 545; *Holder v Law Society* [2003] 1 W.L.R. 1059, CA (Civ Div).

238 *R. v DPP, Ex p. Kebilene* [2000] 2 A.C. 326, HL.

239 *Kebilene* [2000] 2 A.C. 326 at 380.

240 *Kebilene* [2000] 2 A.C. 326 at 380.

The importance of deference, and its limits, was brought out forcefully by Lord Hoffmann in *Alconbury*.[241] He stated that "in a democratic country, decisions as to what the general interest requires are made by democratically elected bodies, or persons accountable to them".[242] Parliament might lay down general policy through legislation. It might, however, not be possible to formulate general rules in advance, and what the general interest required would be decided on a case by case basis, as with planning. Parliament delegated such decision-making to ministers, or local authorities, thereby preserving the democratic principle. In such instances the "only fair method of decision is by some person or body accountable to the electorate".[243] The HRA "was no doubt intended to strengthen the rule of law but not inaugurate the rule of lawyers".[244] There were, however, limits to deference. Certain basic individual rights "should not be capable in any circumstances of being overridden by the majority, even if they think that the public interest so requires".[245] These were rights which belonged to individuals "simply by virtue of their humanity, independently of any utilitarian calculation".[246] The protection of these rights from majority decision required an independent and impartial tribunal.

The significance of deference/respect is apparent once again in the *Countryside Alliance* case,[247] in which it was alleged that the Hunting Act 2004, which prohibited the hunting of wild mammals with dogs, infringed Convention rights. The House of Lords concluded that art.1 of the First Protocol was engaged, since the 2004 Act limited the use that an owner could make of his land. It nonetheless held that the restriction was proportionate and in reaching this conclusion accorded the legislature a wide margin of discretionary judgment on a controversial matter of social policy. Lord Bingham was duly mindful of the dangers of subverting the democratic process if "on a question of moral and political judgment, opponents of the Act achieve through the courts what they could not achieve in Parliament".[248]

iii. Terminology

20–054 There have nonetheless been differences of judicial view as to the label that best captures the courts' approach to review under the HRA. The label "deference" has been used by a number of courts. So too has the phrase "discretionary area of judgment".[249]

Lord Hoffmann in *Prolife* was however unhappy about the language of deference, since he believed that it had overtones of servility.[250] It was, said Lord Hoffmann, necessary in a society based on the rule of law and the separation of

---

241 *Alconbury* [2003] 2 A.C. 295.
242 *Alconbury* [2003] 2 A.C. 295 at [69].
243 *Alconbury* [2003] 2 A.C. 295 at [70].
244 *Alconbury* [2003] 2 A.C. 295 at [129].
245 *Alconbury* [2003] 2 A.C. 295 at [70].
246 *Alconbury* [2003] 2 A.C. 295 at [70].
247 *R. (Countryside Alliance) v Attorney General* [2008] 1 A.C. 719, HL.
248 *Countryside Alliance* [2008] 1 A.C. 719 at [45].
249 *R. (P and Q and QB) v Secretary of State for the Home Department* [2001] 1 W.L.R. 2002, CA (Civ Div); *Samaroo* [2001] UKHRR 1150; *Farrakhan* [2002] Q.B. 139.
250 *R. (ProLife Alliance) v BBC* [2004] 1 A.C. 185, HL at [75]–[76].

powers, to decide which branch of government had decision-making power and what the legal limits of that power were. That was a question of law to be decided by the courts. The inevitable consequence was that the courts themselves would often have to decide the limits of their own decision-making power.[251]

> "But it does not mean that their allocation of decision-making power to the other branches of government is a matter of courtesy or deference. The principles upon which decision-making powers are allocated are principles of law. The courts are the independent branch of government and the legislature and executive are, directly and indirectly respectively, the elected branches of government. Independence makes the courts more suited to deciding some kinds of questions and being elected makes the legislature or executive more suited to deciding others. The allocation of these decision-making responsibilities is based upon recognised principles. The principle that the independence of the courts is necessary for a proper decision of disputed legal rights or claims of violation of human rights is a legal principle. It is reflected in art.6 of the Convention. On the other hand, the principle that majority approval is necessary for a proper decision on policy or allocation of resources is also a legal principle. Likewise, when a court decides that a decision is within the proper competence of the legislature or executive, it is not showing deference. It is deciding the law."

In *Huang* Lord Bingham expressed some impatience with prolonged discussion about due deference, discretionary area of judgment, democratic accountability, relative institutional capacity and the like.[252] He stated that giving weight to factors legitimately taken into consideration by the initial decision-maker was not properly described as deference. It was rather "performance of the ordinary judicial task of weighing up the competing considerations on each side and according appropriate weight to the judgment of a person with responsibility for a given subject matter and access to special sources of knowledge and advice", which was "how any rational judicial decision-maker is likely to proceed".[253]

Different judges and commentators may well have preferences as to the language that should be used when the courts undertake review under the HRA. It is, however, doubtful whether anything necessarily follows from the choice of this terminology, at least insofar as judicial practice is concerned. Thus the mere fact that a court uses the language of deference does not in itself indicate that it is likely to leave more leeway to Parliament or the executive than if it had adopted the approach of Lord Hoffmann or Lord Bingham, since much depends on how it weighs the factors that incline in favour of, or against, deference on the facts of the case. **20–055**

The same point can be put from the opposite perspective, by taking Lord Bingham's approach by way of example. The considerations central to debates about due deference, respect, discretionary area of judgment and the like, are not foreclosed or excluded by framing the inquiry in terms of what constitutes giving "appropriate weight" to the initial decision-maker. The same factors will be taken into account, as exemplified by Lord Bingham's judgment in *Animal Defenders*,[254] delivered after *Huang*. In deciding that a blanket ban on political

[251] *ProLife Alliance* [2004] 1 A.C. 185 at [76].

[252] *Huang v Secretary of State for the Home Department* [2007] 2 A.C. 167, HL at [14].

[253] *Huang* [2007] 2 A.C. 167 at [16].

[254] *R. (Animal Defenders International) v Secretary of State for Culture, Media and Sport* [2008] 1 A.C. 1312, HL at [33].

advertising was compatible with Convention rights, Lord Bingham held that the weight to be accorded to Parliament's judgment depended on the circumstances and the subject-matter.

He gave it significant weight in the instant case because: it was reasonable to expect that democratically-elected politicians would be sensitive to measures necessary to safeguard the integrity of our democracy; Parliament had resolved that the prohibition of political advertising on television might infringe art.10 ECHR, but nonetheless decided to proceed with the legislation and Parliament's judgment on this issue should not be lightly overridden; and legislation had to lay down general rules, which meant that a line must be drawn, and it was for Parliament to decide where. Thus, irrespective of whether one necessarily agrees with Lord Bingham's reasoning in this respect, it is clear that framing the inquiry in terms of appropriate weight, rather than respect or deference, does not alter the nature of the inquiry.

6. THE STANDARD OF REVIEW: ACADEMIC PERSPECTIVE

20–056 There has been considerable academic commentary on proportionality and the HRA,[255] and more generally on the concept of deference.[256] It is not possible within the confines of this chapter to do justice to all of the varied positions

[255] D. Feldman, "Proportionality and the Human Rights Act 1998", in E. Ellis (ed.), *The Principle of Proportionality in the Laws of Europe* (Oxford: Hart, 1999), pp.117–144; J. Jowell, "Beyond the Rule of Law: Towards Constitutional Judicial Review" [2000] P.L. 671; M. Elliott, "The Human Rights Act 1998 and the Standard of Substantive Review" [2001] C.L.J. 301; R. Clayton, "Regaining a Sense of Proportion: The Human Rights Act and the Proportionality Principle" [2001] E.H.R.L.R. 504; I. Leigh, "Taking Rights Proportionately: Judicial Review, the Human Rights Act and Strasbourg" [2002] P.L. 265; M. Fordham and T. de la Mare, "Identifying the Principles of Proportionality", in Jowell and Cooper, *Understanding Human Rights Principles* (2001), pp.27–89; S. Attrill, "Keeping the Executive in the Picture: A Reply to Professor Leigh" [2003] P.L. 41; Lord Woolf, "On the Occasion of the Opening of the Judicial Year at the European Court of Human Rights", 23 January 2003, pp.3–4; Lord Irvine, "The Human Rights Act Two Years On: An Analysis", 1 November 2002, pp.6–9; C. Knight, "Proportionality, the Decision-maker and the House of Lords" [2007] J.R. 221; C. Chan, "Proportionality and Invariable Baseline Intensity of Review" (2013) 33 L.S. 1; Kavanagh, "Reasoning about Proportionality under the Human Rights Act 1998: Outcomes, Substance and Process" (2014) 130 L.Q.R. 23; A. Barak, *Proportionality: Constitutional Rights and their Limitations* (Cambridge: Cambridge University Press, 2012); G. Huscroft, B. Miller, G. Webber (eds.), *Proportionality and the Rule of Law: Rights, Justification, Reasoning* (Cambridge: Cambridge University Press, 2014); J. Rivers, "The Presumption of Proportionality" (2014) 77 M.L.R. 409; M. Elliott and H. Wilberg (eds.), *The Scope and Intensity of Substantive Review, Traversing Taggart's Rainbow* (Oxford: Hart, 2015), Chs 3, 4, 5.

[256] Dyzenhaus, "The Politics of Deference: Judicial Review and Democracy", in M. Taggart (ed.), *The Province of Administrative Law* (1997), Ch.13; Taggart, "The Tub of Public Law", in Dyzenhaus (ed.), *The Unity of Public Law* (2004), Ch.17; P. Craig, "The Courts, the Human Rights Act and Judicial Review" (2001) 117 L.Q.R. 589; R. Edwards, "Judicial Deference and the Human Rights Act" (2002) 65 M.L.R. 859; Lord Hoffmann, "Separation of Powers" [2002] J.R. 137; J. Jowell, "Judicial Deference and Human Rights: A Question of Competence", in P. Craig and R. Rawlings (eds), *Law and Administration in Europe, Essays in Honour of Carol Harlow* (Oxford: Oxford University Press, 2003), Ch.4; J. Jowell, "Judicial Deference: Servility, Civility or Institutional Capacity" [2003] P.L. 592; F. Klug, "Judicial Deference under the Human Rights Act 1998" [2003] E.H.R.L.R. 125; M. Hunt, "Sovereignty's Blight: Why Contemporary Public Law Needs the Concept of 'Due Deference'", in N. Bamforth and P. Leyland (eds), *Public Law in a Multi-Layered Constitution* (Oxford: Oxford University Press, 2003), Ch.13; T. Allan, "Common Law Reason and

staked out in this rich literature.[257] The discussion will therefore focus on some of the principal contending lines of argument.

A. Deference/Respect/Weight: Special Doctrine or Part of Ordinary Judicial Review

There has been considerable academic dispute as to how one should conceptualise what the courts are and should be doing, whether it should be regarded as a special doctrine, or part of the existing fabric of judicial review. 20–057

There are some writers, notably Allan and Hickman, who object to the articulation of any distinct doctrine of deference as such. They do not object to the idea that the courts should show some restraint when reviewing the exercise of discretionary power in a rights-based or non-rights-based context. They nonetheless believe that there is no need for any special doctrine of deference, since the factors that the courts take into account when showing judicial restraint are properly taken into account through application of the normal processes of judicial review. For Allan, any doctrine of deference is thus either empty in merely repeating what is currently done within standard judicial review doctrine, or it is pernicious if it accords any latitude over and beyond this, since this is unwarranted and leads to the vice of double counting, whereby weight is given to considerations such as administrative expertise twice over.[258] Hickman expresses analogous concerns, contending that there should be no special doctrine of deference because it would "require the reasons for affording weight to the assessments made by the primary decision-makers to be crystallized into rules or

---

the Limits of Judicial Deference", in D. Dyzenhaus (ed.), *The Unity of Public Law* (Oxford: Hart, 2004), Ch.11; L. Tremblay, "The Legitimacy of Judicial Review: The Limits of Dialogue Between Courts and Legislatures" (2005) 3 I-CON 617; R. Clayton, "Judicial Deference and 'Democratic Dialogue': The Legitimacy of Judicial Intervention under the Human Rights Act" [2004] P.L. 33; Lord Steyn, "Deference: A Tangled Story" [2005] P.L. 346; T. Hickman, "Constitutional Dialogue, Constitutional Theories and the Human Rights Act" [2005] P.L. 306; D. Nicol, "Law and Politics after the Human Rights Act" [2006] P.L. 722; T. Allan, "Human Rights and Judicial Review: A Critique of 'Due Deference'" [2006] C.L.J. 671; Lord Justice Dyson, "Some Thoughts on Judicial Deference" [2006] J.R. 103; R. Clayton, "Principles for Judicial Deference" [2006] J.R. 109; M. Beloff, "The Concept of 'Deference' in Public Law" [2006] J.R. 213; T. Poole, "The Reformation of English Administrative Law", LSE Working Papers 12/2007; T. Hickman, "The Courts and Politics after the Human Rights Act: A Comment" [2008] P.L. 84; J. King, "Institutional Approaches to Judicial Restraint" (2008) 28 O.J.L.S. 409; A. Young, "In Defence of Due Deference" (2009) 72 M.L.R. 554; A. Kavanagh, "Defending Deference in Public Law and Constitutional Theory" (2010) 126 L.Q.R. 222; A. Brady, *Proportionality and Deference under the Human Rights Act 1998: An Institutionally Sensitive Approach* (Cambridge: Cambridge University Press, 2012); P. Daly, *A Theory of Deference in Administrative Law: Basis, Application and Scope* (Cambridge: Cambridge University Press, 2012); M. Elliott, "Proportionality and Deference: The Importance of a Structured Approach", University of Cambridge, Legal Studies Research Paper Series, 32/2013; P. Craig, *UK, EU and Global Administrative Law: Foundations and Challenges* (Cambridge: Cambridge University Press, 2015), pp.236–255.

[257] My views are set out in greater detail in Craig, *UK, EU and Global Administrative Law: Foundations and Challenges* (Cambridge: Cambridge University Press, 2015), pp.236–255.

[258] Allan, "Human Rights and Judicial Review: A Critique of 'Due Deference'" [2006] C.L.J. 671, 675–676.

principles which would then prescribe a certain test or judicial approach", which would be of limited utility because the reasons could only be given at a high-level of abstraction.[259]

There are other writers, such as Kavanagh, Young and King, who contend that there is more to be said in favour of articulating the factors that do and should that play into judicial restraint. For Kavanagh the phrase "doctrine of deference" simply captures her view as to the more particular considerations that should be taken cognizance of when deciding on the appropriate degree of restraint that a court should give to the primary decision-maker, while making clear that this does not amount to a call for judicial abstention or non-justiciability. Young's view concerning the precise role to be played by deference is not the same as Kavanagh's, but she shares the assumption that it will refine the way in which judicial review operates, and denies that it will lead to double counting or some independent doctrine unrelated to the existing confines of judicial review.[260] King does not advance a separate doctrine of deference, but seeks to flesh out the types of factors that should inform our view as to when it is fitting for courts to show restraint.[261]

20–058 It is clear that deference/respect/weight must be located within the standard fabric of judicial review. It is not and cannot be a free-standing concept in its own right. Deference/respect/weight are not in and of themselves tests for review at all, and this is so whatever their content. They are considerations that inform the way in which a test for review, such reasonableness or proportionality, should be applied. It would therefore be meaningless to conclude that considerable weight should be accorded to the primary decision-maker without posing the inquiry in the context of a test for review, since no answer could logically be forthcoming. Deference and respect modulate application of, for example, proportionality. They are not in themselves tests for review.

While Allan is assuredly correct in this respect, the issue is a red herring given that no one argues to the contrary. Kavanagh, Young and King do not contend deference/respect/weight should be perceived as independent of the existing fabric of judicial review. They are therefore not guilty of the charge of being "pernicious" by fostering some latitude to be accorded to the legislature or executive over and beyond what would result from application of the ordinary principles of review. They are by way of contrast determining what that ought to be, more particularly in a post-HRA world.

The contention that the existing tools of judicial review give us all that we need to determine the meaning of a right, or to shape the application of reasonableness/proportionality, is far from self-evident. There are to be sure strictures that courts should not substitute judgment on the merits for that of the primary decision-maker, reflecting thereby an important precept of the separation of powers. There are also well-established principles concerning the variability of reasonableness review in cases dealing with rights, or where socio-economic choices are made by the legislature. The idea that this is the best that we can do does not readily withstand examination. Properly understood the literature on

[259] Hickman, *Public Law after the Human Rights Act*, pp.137–138.
[260] Young, "In Defence of Due Deference" (2009) 72 M.L.R. 554.
[261] King, "Institutional Approaches to Judicial Restraint" (2008) 28 O.J.L.S. 409, 410.

deference seeks to refine and flesh out the factors that should affect this, whether they arise in the definition of the initial right, or in the context of proportionality review.

B. Deference/Respect/Weight: The Relevant Factors

There has also been considerable academic debate concerning the more particular types of factor that should be relevant when according deference/respect/weight to the initial decision-maker. We might do so for three reasons: epistemic, institutional or constitutional. The primary decision-maker might have knowledge of the relevant matter that is greater than could be matched by any reviewing court; it might, independent of epistemic considerations, have a deeper understanding of the contested issue by reason of its institutional place within the fabric of government; the legislature might express a considered view as to the meaning of a right in legislation in circumstances where it has no particular epistemic or institutional advantage over courts. **20–059**

Commentators generally agree that it is legitimate for epistemic and institutional considerations to be taken into account by courts when applying the precepts of judicial review. The courts give respect to the primary decision-maker in accord with such considerations. They do not abjure judgment on the matter, which remains in the hands of the court.[262]

Commentators disagree to a greater extent as to whether deference, respect or weight should be given on constitutional grounds. The paradigm instance of this dispute is as to whether such weight or respect ought to be given to the legislature, by reason of its democratic pedigree.

Jowell argued that while it was legitimate for courts in certain instances to defer to the legislature or executive on grounds of institutional competence, they should not do so on the mistaken belief that they lacked constitutional competence, in the sense of judicial authority to decide the relevant issue.[263] He is correct that the courts should not be regarded as constitutionally disabled from making difficult decisions in relation to Convention rights, nor should they be constitutionally required to defer to Parliament or the Executive on such matters.[264] There should not be any "islands of immunity" that are off-limits on the ground that the courts are not constitutionally competent to undertake judicial review at all.

This should not, however, preclude deference/respect/weight being accorded to the legislature on constitutional grounds by reason of its democratic pedigree. We can for the sake of argument presuppose that there are no independent epistemic or institutional reasons to give weight to the legislature's determination. If any such weight is to be given it must then be on constitutional grounds by virtue of its democratic pedigree. The rationale for affording weight to the legislative **20–060**

---

[262] See para.20–047.

[263] Jowell, "Judicial Deference and Human Rights: A Question of Competence", in Craig and Rawlings (eds), *Law and Administration in Europe, Essays in Honour of Carol Harlow* (2003), p.73.

[264] Jowell, "Judicial Deference and Human Rights: A Question of Competence", in Craig and Rawlings (eds), *Law and Administration in Europe, Essays in Honour of Carol Harlow* (2003), pp.74–75, 80.

choice resides ultimately in the fact that there is room for legitimate disagreement as to the meaning and application of constitutional rights.[265] The courts do not have a monopoly of wisdom in this respect, and judges not infrequently disagree among themselves as to what is demanded by a particular right in particular circumstances. A considered legislative choice is therefore deserving of respect as embodying its reflective view as to what the right means in a particular legislative context. It deserves this respect on constitutional grounds as the elected legislature charged with making such choices. To afford such respect is not inconsistent with the HRA, its wording or the principles underlying it. The argument is not for the courts to abstain or capitulate, but to take cognizance of the legislative choice when making its own final determination.

This is in reality what Lord Bingham did in *Animal Defenders*.[266] We see the same theme in Lord Sumption's judgment in *Carlile* where he stated that "even in the context of Convention rights, there remain areas which although not immune from scrutiny require a qualified respect for the constitutional functions of decision-makers who are democratically accountable",[267] examples being decisions involving important policy choices, broad questions of economic and social policy, or issues involving the allocation of finite resources. The same approach is evident in other cases, such as *Carson*,[268] where the House of Lords adopted the US distinction between strict scrutiny for discrimination on grounds of race, gender, sexual orientation and the like, with rationality review being applicable to other forms of differential treatment.

The court did not abstain from adjudication, or merely accept without more the legislative choice as conclusive, but nor did it simply substitute its view for that of the legislature. The courts considered the choice concerning rights against the backdrop of the problem that the legislation sought to resolve, giving due weight to the reasons for that choice. This was surely the correct approach, and its application will perforce depend on the extent to which there is evidence that the legislature has addressed the salient issue. There will, by way of contrast, be rights-based claims made in relation to legislation where the legislature was not aware in advance that a particular legislative provision was problematic, since the issue only became apparent when the legislation became live.

20–061 The procedural dimension to such claims is important, as emphasised by Hunt[269] and Clayton.[270] The defendant should be required to give a properly reasoned explanation as to why it adopted the challenged act. This facilitates judicial review. It enables the courts to apply the proportionality analysis more fully aware of the factors that played into the contested decision, and evaluate the

---

265 J. Waldron, *Law and Disagreement* (Oxford: Oxford University Press, 1999).

266 *Animal Defenders* [2008] 1 AC 1312.

267 *Carlile* [2014] UKSC 60 at [28].

268 *R. (Carson) v Secretary of State for Work and Pensions* [2006] 1 AC 173; *R (Nicklinson) v Ministry of Justice* [2014] UKSC 38; *R (Hooper) v Secretary of State for Work and Pensions* [2005] 1 WLR 1681.

269 Hunt, "Sovereignty's Blight: Why Contemporary Public Law Needs the Concept of 'Due Deference'", in Bamforth and Leyland (eds), *Public Law in a Multi-Layered Constitution* (2003).

270 Clayton, "Principles for Judicial Deference" [2006] J.R. 109.

evidentiary basis of those reasons.[271] This is exemplified by *Quila*,[272] in which the claimant challenged a government policy that a visa would not be granted to a foreign national where either party to the marriage was under 21. The Supreme Court held that this was in breach of art.8 ECHR. It accepted in principle that the policy could be defended as pursuing a legitimate aim, which was to prevent forced marriages. The Supreme Court nonetheless concluded that the policy was disproportionate because the Home Secretary had failed to produce robust evidence that the policy would have a deterrent effect on forced marriages, more especially given that it would prevent bona fide marriages.

C. Deference/Respect/Weight: Democratic Dialogue

There is a strand of the academic literature that focuses on the notion of democratic dialogue between courts, legislature and Executive within the HRA.[273] It is helpful to disaggregate the following points. **20–062**

First, the concept of democratic dialogue can bear different meanings,[274] and commentators differ sharply on which version, if any, should be used under the HRA. Thus, for some it connotes the idea that because the meaning of rights entails contestable value judgments, so judicial decisions should be regarded simply as one way in which they should be interpreted, with Parliament free to choose an alternative interpretation.[275] Others reject this view and regard dialogue as something far more limited, connoting the ability of courts, if they so wish, to avoid issues of principle.[276] Yet others adopt an intermediate position.[277] Suffice it to say for the present that unless an approach allows divergence of view concerning the meaning of rights to be taken into account it is questionable whether it should be regarded as a species of democratic dialogue.

Second, an element of democratic dialogue is built into the HRA through ss.3 and 4. If the court feels unable to interpret the contested legislation so as to be compatible with Convention rights then it issues a declaration of incompatibility. This does not affect the validity of the legislation and it is for Parliament to decide whether to amend it so as to render it compatible with Convention rights. This can be regarded in dialogic terms: the courts proffer an interpretation of the

---

[271] A reading of the leading cases on arts 8–11 reveals the close attention paid by the ECtHR to the reasons given by the national authorities to determine whether they could be said to meet the criterion of pressing social need. Many cases are decided at this point, with the ECtHR deciding that the reasons advanced by the state do not suffice to show a pressing social need

[272] *R. (Aguilar Quila) v Secretary of State for the Home Department* [2011] UKSC 45.

[273] Clayton, "Judicial Deference and 'Democratic Dialogue': The Legitimacy of Judicial Intervention under the Human Rights Act" [2004] P.L. 33; Clayton, "Principles for Judicial Deference" [2006] J.R. 109; Hickman, "Constitutional Dialogue, Constitutional Theories and the Human Rights Act" [2005] P.L. 306; D. Nicol, "Law and Politics after the Human Rights Act" [2006] P.L. 722; T. Hickman, "The Courts and Politics after the Human Rights Act: A Comment" [2008] P.L. 84; A. Young, "Is Dialogue Working under the Human Rights Act 1998?" [2011] P.L. 773; P. Sales and R. Ekins, "Rights-Consistent Interpretation and the Human Rights Act 1998" (2011) 127 L.Q.R. 217.

[274] Hickman, "Constitutional Dialogue, Constitutional Theories and the Human Rights Act" [2005] P.L. 306

[275] Nicol, "Law and Politics after the Human Rights Act" [2006] P.L. 722.

[276] Hickman, "The Courts and Politics after the Human Rights Act: A Comment" [2008] P.L. 84.

[277] Young, "Is Dialogue Working under the Human Rights Act 1998?" [2011] P.L. 773.

challenged legislation that is found to be incompatible with Convention rights, which is the catalyst for Parliament to rethink its view in the original legislation and modify it in the light of the court's judgment.[278]

Third, the opportunities for democratic dialogue under the HRA are limited. In relation to primary legislation, Parliament will only be accorded a second bite of the cherry if the court makes a declaration of incompatibility under s.4 HRA. If the court decides the case under s.3 HRA then Parliament has no opportunity to respond, subject to the fact that Parliament can enact new legislation, which is expressive of a different view from the court's original judgment. Moreover, national courts generally decide cases in accord with Strasbourg case law, and Parliament must accept the result or risk confrontation with Strasbourg.[279] There may nonetheless be room for national choice either when this is part of the relevant Strasbourg jurisprudence, or when that case law has not yet dealt with the issue that has come before the national court,[280] or when the court interprets the relevant Convention right so as to give latitude to the views of the legislature or Executive. There are also limits on democratic dialogue under s.6 HRA, since there is nothing equivalent to s.4 HRA.

20–063 Finally, it is important to be mindful about the nature of the dialogue that occurs, as is apparent from the debates in Canada. The idea of democratic dialogue was developed in the Canadian jurisprudence and used to measure legislative responses to judicial decisions under the Canadian Charter.[281] There has, however, been debate about what constitutes democratic dialogue, with some contending that legislative repeal of the offending enactment should not count as dialogue for these purposes,[282] while others argue that dialogue theory does not assess matters qualitatively, but simply identifies legislative responses, whatsoever they may be.[283] The theory has also been challenged concerning the very nature of the envisioned dialogue.[284] Thus, it has been argued that the proponents of dialogue theory conceive of it as one in which the court is free to interpret the Charter, with the legislature required to act within such parameters as the Court

[278] Clayton, "Principles for Judicial Deference" [2006] J.R. 109, 125.

[279] Sales and Ekins, "Rights-Consistent Interpretation and the Human Rights Act 1998" (2011) 127 L.Q.R. 217.

[280] Subject to the discussion concerning HRA s.2 at para.20–004.

[281] P. Hogg and A. Bushell, "The *Charter* Dialogue between Courts and Legislatures (or perhaps the Charter isn't such a bad thing after all)" (1997) 35 Osgoode Hall L.J. 75; P. Hogg, A. Bushell-Thornton and W. Wright, "*Charter* Dialogue Revisited—Or 'Much Ado About Metaphors'" (2007) 45 Osgoode Hall L.J. 51.

[282] C. Manfredi and J. Kelly, "Six Degrees of Dialogue: A Response to Hogg and Bushell" (1999) 37 Osgoode Hall L.J. 513; P. Hogg and A. Thornton, "Reply to Six Dialogues" (1999) 37 Osgoode Hall L.J. 529.

[283] G. Huscroft, "Rationalizing Judicial Power: The Mischief of Dialogue Theory", in C. Manfredi and J. Kelly (eds), *Contested Constitutionalism: Reflections on the Canadian Charter of Rights and Freedoms* (Vancouver: University of British Columbia Press, 2009), Ch.3.

[284] G. Huscroft, "Constitutionalism from the Top Down" (2007) 45 Osgoode Hall L.J. 91; A. Petter, "Taking Dialogue Theory Much Too Seriously (Or Perhaps *Charter* Dialogue Isn't Such a Good Thing After All)" (2007) 45 Osgoode Hall L.J. 147.

allows. It has been argued that this is not dialogue, but "top-down constitutionalism",[285] to be contrasted with a vision of democratic dialogue in which the court would respect and be influenced by the legislature's interpretation of the Canadian Charter.

D. Deference/Respect/Weight: The Critique Revisited

It may be helpful by way of conclusion to this section to revisit Allan's critique of deference in the light of the preceding discussion.[286] He rejects the idea that the courts should be swayed by factors that might be regarded as "external" to the intrinsic quality of the decision under review. He accepts however that the courts should cede to Parliament and government an appropriate sphere of decision-making protected from judicial interference, to be determined by the circumstances of the particular case. The judge should therefore only defer to the extent that the reasons proffered are persuasive, and any deference should be regarded as "internal" to the ordinary principles of review applied by the courts with due regard for the particularities and circumstances of the case. A number of comments can be made about this thesis. **20–064**

First, there is a sense in which he is attacking a straw man. He is undoubtedly correct that deference should not be regarded as some trump, such that the mere mention of "democratic credential" leads the court to refrain from judicial review, or accept without more the view taken by the legislature or executive. No one, however, maintains such a position. This is not the view taken by Hunt or Kavanagh, who make it manifestly clear that any deference has to be earned by the reasons advanced by the primary decision-maker. Nor is it the view taken by the courts.

Second, the reality is that Allan's disagreement with others is more about form than substance. He is willing to accord deference to the primary decision-maker.[287] He is content for factors such as expertise to be taken into account, provided that they are warranted on the facts and conceptualised as internal to the "intrinsic quality" of the decision when applying the ordinary precepts of judicial review, rather than as "external factors". The crucial issue is the factors regarded as relevant in deciding on the degree of latitude afforded to the primary decision-maker, not whether one regards those as "internal" or "external" to the remainder of the legal determination. There is moreover much to be gained in terms of transparency by making such factors explicit.

Third, Allan's distinction between matters that are "internal" to the determination of the right and those that are "external" is an imperfect guide, in relation to epistemic, institutional or constitutional rationales for restraint. It presupposes a neat two-step inquiry in which the meaning of the right is elaborated, the internal inquiry, and there is then a further determination as to whether that might be **20–65**

[285] Huscroft, "Constitutionalism from the Top Down" (2007) 45 Osgoode Hall L.J. 91.

[286] Allan, "Human Rights and Judicial Review: A Critique of 'Due Deference'" [2006] C.L.J. 671 and "Judicial Deference and Judicial Review: Legal Doctrine and Legal Theory" (2011) 127 L.Q.R. 96.

[287] Allan, "Common Law Reason and the Limits of Judicial Deference", in D. Dyzenhaus (ed.), *The Unity of Public Law* (2004), p.97.

modified through taking cognizance of epistemic, institutional or constitutional considerations, the external inquiry. Thus in cases such as *Animal Defenders* the House of Lords did not make an abstract determination of whether freedom of speech was violated by the legislative constraint, and then consider any possible legislative excuse. To the contrary, the legislative rationale for placing this constraint was crucial to the judicial inquiry as to whether the right had been violated and whether there were justifications for the limitation. The same is true for the mode of judicial inquiry in most cases where epistemic or institutional considerations are taken into account in deciding whether a limitation of a right was proportionate or not, such factors being part of the initial legal determination on this issue, not something undertaken as an external inquiry after an internal assessment has been made.[288] The fact that it is the democratically elected legislature that made the initial choice is not determinative of its legality, but nor is it something external to the intrinsic quality of the decision. To accord respect to the legislative determination does not mean submission,[289] nor does it entail judicial abdication of responsibility. It is reflective of the contested nature of rights determinations, and a judicial willingness to consider seriously the interpretation given to a right by the democratic branch of government.

7. RIGHTS: THE EU DIMENSION

20–066 An individual may derive rights from EU law, which can be used to challenge primary legislation, or executive action. In relation to the result of the Brexit referendum, the UK remains bound by EU law while the withdrawal negotiations under art.50 TEU are ongoing.

A. Legislative Competence and Human Rights

20–067 The European Union has some legislative competence in the field of human rights. Article 2 TEU provides that the "Union is founded on the principles of liberty, democracy, respect for human rights and fundamental freedoms and the rule of law, principles which are common to the laws of the Member States". Specific legislative competence is found in art.19 TFEU, which provides that the Union legislature may, within the limits of the EU's powers, take "appropriate action to combat discrimination based on sex, racial or ethnic origin, religion or belief, disability, age or sexual orientation". This article does not in and of itself ban such discrimination, but empowers the European Union to adopt measures to combat such discrimination within the scope of the powers otherwise granted in

---

[288] See, e.g. *Samaroo* [2001] UKHRR 1150; *R. (Bloggs 61) v Secretary of State for the Home Department* [2003] 1 W.L.R. 2724; *Denbigh* [2007] 1 A.C. 100.

[289] Dyzenhaus, "The Politics of Deference: Judicial Review and Democracy", in Taggart (ed.), *The Province of Administrative Law* (1997); Taggart, "The Tub of Public Law", in Dyzenhaus (ed.), *The Unity of Public Law* (2004).

the Treaty. When such measures are enacted they can be relied on by individuals in their national courts, assuming that the measures are sufficiently certain and precise.[290]

B. Rights and Direct Effect

Individuals can gain rights from Treaty provisions or norms made thereunder via the concept of direct effect. This concept has been described above,[291] and has been applied to an increasing number of EU norms. Certain directly effective Treaty provisions deal with subject matter that would merit inclusion in any list of constitutional or fundamental rights. **20–068**

An obvious example is art.157 TFEU, which is concerned with equal pay and gender discrimination. This was held to be directly effective in the seminal case of *Defrenne*.[292] Defrenne was employed as an air hostess with Sabena. She argued that her conditions of service were discriminatory, as compared with those of male cabin stewards who performed the same tasks. The ECJ held that art.119 EEC as it then was had direct effect, in some cases at least, that Defrenne therefore derived rights from the Treaty and that these were enforceable against the airline. There have been many similar cases.

C. Fundamental Rights

An individual may also make use of the EU concept of fundamental rights.[293] The original Treaty contained no list of traditional fundamental rights, in part because its original rationale was principally economic. The initial catalyst for the creation of such rights was the threat of revolt by some national courts. Individuals who were dissatisfied with the provisions of, for example, a regulation would contend before their national court that it was inconsistent with rights in their own national constitutions and argue that these rights could not have been given away by the state when acceding to the European Union. **20–069**

This argument was made before the German courts in *Internationale Handelsgesellschaft*.[294] The threat this posed to the supremacy of EU law was not lost on the ECJ, and it stated that Union norms could not be challenged in this manner. However, in order to stem any national rebellion the ECJ declared that fundamental rights were part of the general principles of EU law, and that the compatibility of an EU norm with such rights would be tested by the ECJ itself.[295]

---

[290] Council Directive 2000/78 of 27 November 2000, Establishing a General Framework for Equal Treatment in Employment and Occupation [2000] OJ L303/16; Council Directive 2000/43 of 29 June 2000, Implementing the Principle of Equal Treatment between Persons Irrespective of Racial or Ethnic Origin [2000] OJ L180/22.

[291] See Ch.10.

[292] *Defrenne v Sabena* (43/75) [1976] E.C.R. 455.

[293] Craig and de Búrca, *EU Law, Text, Cases and Materials* (2015), Ch.11.

[294] *Internationale Handelsgesellschaft* (11/70) [1970] E.C.R. 1125.

[295] *Internationale Handelsgesellschaft* (11/70) [1970] E.C.R. 1125 at 1134.

The fundamental rights doctrine has been used primarily as a way of attacking EU norms, such as regulations or decisions, but national norms can also be challenged for compliance with fundamental rights in a number of different situations.[296] This will be so where Member States are applying provisions of EU law which are based on the protection for human rights[297]; where they are enforcing EU rules on behalf of the Union or interpreting EU rules[298]; or where Member States are seeking to derogate from a requirement of EU law.[299] The supremacy doctrine will operate in such instances and national norms, including primary legislation, which are inconsistent with EU law, will have to be altered.

D. The EU Charter of Rights

20–070 A claimant might also seek to use the EU Charter of Fundamental Rights.[300] The immediate catalyst for the Charter came from the European Council. In June 1999 the Cologne European Council[301] decided that there should be a European Union Charter of Fundamental Rights to consolidate the fundamental rights applicable at Union Level. It was made clear that the document should include economic and social rights, as well as traditional civil and political rights. A body called the Convention was established, with representatives of the Member States, a member of the Commission, members of the European Parliament, and representatives from national Parliaments. The Charter was accepted by the Member States in 2000.[302] It includes a broad array of rights, including civil, political, social and economic rights. Chapter VII of the Charter contains important general provisions. Article 51(1) defines the scope of application of the Charter. It is addressed to the institutions and bodies of the Union with due regard to the principle of subsidiarity, and to Member States when they are implementing Union law, which means for these purposes when they act in the scope of EU law.[303] The Charter was drafted so as to be capable of being legally binding. Its precise legal status was left undecided in 2000, but art.6 TEU of the Lisbon Treaty made the Charter legally binding and gave it the same legal status as the Treaties. There is a Protocol that affects the application of the Charter to the UK and Poland, but this does not constitute an opt-out from the rights contained in the Charter.[304]

---

[296] Craig and de Búrca, *EU Law, Text, Cases and Materials* (2015)

[297] *Johnston v Chief Constable of the Royal Ulster Constabulary* (222/84) [1986] E.C.R. 1651.

[298] *Wachauf v Germany* (5/88) [1989] E.C.R. 2609; *R. v Kent Kirk* (63/83) [1984] E.C.R. 2689.

[299] *Elliniki Radiophonia Tileorassi AE v Dimotki Etairia Pliroforissis and Sotirios Kouvelas* (C-260/89) [1991] E.C.R. I-2925; *Society for the Protection of Unborn Children Ireland Ltd v Grogan* (C-159/90) [1991] E.C.R. I-4685.

[300] Charter of Fundamental Rights of the European Union [2000] OJ C364/1, [2010] OJ C83/389.

[301] 3–4 June 1999.

[302] Charter 4955/00, Convent 51, 17 October 2000.

[303] *Åklagaren v Hans Åkerberg Fransson* (Case C-617/10), EU:2013:C:105; *Benkharbouche v Sudan Embassy* [2015] EWCA Civ. 33; *R. (Davies) v Secretary of State for the Home Department* [2015] EWHC 2092 (Admin).

[304] Protocol (No.30); *NS v Secretary of State for the Home Department* (C-411 and 493/10), EU:C:2011:865.

E. The ECHR, HRA and European Union

20–071 It is important by way of conclusion to consider in outline the interrelationship between protection of Convention rights via the HRA, and protection of rights via the European Union. The ECJ's approach to the ECHR has in the past provided the Convention with a peremptory force in national courts it lacked prior to the passage of the HRA.[305] EU law would take account of the ECHR in fashioning its own fundamental rights doctrine, and this would then bind Member States in the types of case mentioned above. Convention rights mediated through EU law may still provide a more potent weapon than the HRA, particularly where the incompatibility with Convention rights flows from primary legislation. In such instances the courts are limited to making a declaration of incompatibility under s.4 HRA. However, the supremacy of EU law applies in relation primary legislation. The national courts could then declare the primary legislation to be inapplicable to the instant case, rather than simply making a declaration of incompatibility under s.4 HRA.

It is important also to consider the national court's obligation if there is a difference between the CJEU and the ECtHR on the meaning of Convention rights, where the case before the national court has an EU law component. National courts are bound by EU law, and the supremacy doctrine applies to all species of national law. If there is a divergence in the meaning of the relevant Convention right as between the CJEU and the ECtHR then the national court must adopt the CJEU's interpretation. Under the HRA national courts have an obligation to take account of the Strasbourg case law. They are not bound to follow it. The national courts are bound to apply EU law, irrespective of the way in which the issue arises, or the forum in which it arises. The binding nature of EU law is applicable just as much to adjudication under the HRA as any other, provided that the case has an EU law dimension. The issue posed in this paragraph is however unlikely to arise. This is because the Charter of Rights obliges the European Union to accord the same meaning and scope to Charter rights that correspond to those in the ECHR.[306] The European Union does, moreover, have an obligation to join the ECHR,[307] although the draft agreement for accession was found to be unacceptable in certain respects by the CJEU.[308]

---

[305] N. Grief, "The Domestic Impact of the European Convention on Human Rights as Mediated through Community law" [1991] P.L. 555.

[306] Charter art.52(3), although the European Union can provide more extensive protection.

[307] TEU art.6(2).

[308] *Accession of the European Union to the European Convention for the Protection of Human Rights* (Opinion 2/13), EU:C:2014:2454.

CHAPTER 21

RATIONALITY AND PROPORTIONALITY

1. CENTRAL ISSUES

i. This chapter is concerned with rationality and proportionality, and their respective roles in judicial review of administrative action. 21–001

ii. The traditional position in UK law has been to test administrative action for rationality. This control is exercised after the court is satisfied that the challenged action withstands scrutiny under the tests of propriety of purpose and relevancy considered in an earlier chapter.[1] The traditional form of rationality review has been limited: the court has to be satisfied that the challenged decision was so unreasonable that it would not have been made by any reasonable public authority. This narrow test was fashioned on the assumption that the public body had passed the hurdles of purpose and relevancy and was therefore within the "four corners" of its allowed power. It was felt therefore that judicial intervention on grounds of rationality should be very limited. Whether this assumption is warranted will be considered later.

iii. The judiciary modified this very narrow form of rationality review in cases concerned with fundamental rights. Courts have also used more searching rationality review even in some cases where there are no fundamental rights, because the traditional version of rationality review, literally interpreted, would almost never give a claimant any protection.

iv. Review for proportionality is at present required in a limited number of areas, principally in cases decided under the Human Rights Act 1998, and in cases dealing with EU law. It is also used in some cases dealing with legitimate expectations. Proportionality is not at present a general head of review in UK law. Whether it should be will be examined later.

v. This chapter begins by considering two foundational points that are central to this area: the limits of substantive intervention, and the interrelationship between procedural and substantive review. The focus then shifts to the *Wednesbury* test of rationality review, and considers the assumptions underlying the test, the way in which it is used at present and its likely future. This leads to discussion of proportionality. It begins with analysis of the meaning of proportionality, followed by examination of its place in UK law. This is followed by an overview of the way in which proportionality is used in EU law, where it is a general head of judicial review. The chapter

[1] See Ch.19.

concludes by considering the future roles of rationality and proportionality and whether the latter should be a general head of judicial review.

2. TWO CENTRAL FOUNDATIONS

A. Limits of Substantive Intervention

21–002 It is important at the outset to be clear about the limits of judicial intervention over discretion: it is not for the courts to substitute their choice as to how the discretion ought to have been exercised for that of the administrative authority. They should not substitute judgment for that of the administration. They should not intervene, reassess the matter afresh and decide, for example, that funds ought to be allocated in one way rather than another. Decisions as to political and social choice are made by the legislature, or by a person assigned the task by the legislature.[2] To sanction general judicial intervention simply because the court would prefer a different choice to that of the administrator runs counter to this fundamental assumption, and would entail a re-allocation of power from the legislature and bureaucracy to the courts.

The courts accept that it is not their task to substitute judgment. This is exemplified by the *Cambridge Health Authority* case.[3] The applicant, B, was a 10-year-old girl who was extremely ill. She had received a bone marrow transplant, which had not proven effective. The hospital, acting on the advice of specialists, decided that B had only a short time to live and that further major therapy should not be given. B's father sought the opinion of two further specialists, who thought that a second bone marrow transplant might have some chance of success. Such treatment could, however, only be administered privately because there were no beds in the National Health Service within a hospital which could carry out such therapy. The proposed treatment would take place in two stages, the first of which would cost £15,000 and have a 10–20 per cent chance of success; the second stage would cost £60,000 with a similar 10–20 per cent chance of success. B's father requested the health authority to allocate the funds necessary for this therapy. It refused to do so, given the limited nature of the funds at its disposal and the small likelihood that the treatment would be effective. B's father sought judicial review, but failed before the Court of Appeal. Sir Thomas Bingham MR recognised the tragic nature of B's situation, but stressed that the courts were not the arbiters of the merits in such cases. It was not for the courts to express any opinion as to the likely success or not of the relevant medical treatment.[4] The courts should, said the Master of the Rolls, confine themselves to the lawfulness of the decision under scrutiny. The basic rationale for the health authority's refusal to press further with treatment for B was scarcity of resources. The court's role in this respect was perforce limited[5]:

---

[2] *R. v Ministry of Agriculture, Fisheries and Food, Ex p. First City Trading* [1997] 1 C.M.L.R. 250 QBD at 278.

[3] *R. v Cambridge Health Authority, Ex p. B* [1995] 2 All E.R. 129, CA (Civ Div); *R. (Wells) v Parole Board* [2007] EWHC 1835 (Admin) at [39], overruled on other grounds [2008] EWCA Civ 30.

[4] *Cambridge Health Authority* [1995] 2 All E.R. 129 at 135–136.

[5] *Cambridge Health Authority* [1995] 2 All E.R. 129 at 137.

> "I have no doubt that in a perfect world any treatment which a patient … sought would be provided if doctors were willing to give it, no matter how much it cost, particularly when a life was potentially at stake. It would however, in my view, be shutting one's eyes to the real world if the court were to proceed on the basis that we do live in such a world. It is common knowledge that health authorities of all kinds are constantly pressed to make ends meet. They cannot pay their nurses as much as they would like; they cannot provide all the treatments they would like; they cannot purchase all the extremely expensive medical equipment they would like; they cannot carry out all the research they would like; they cannot build all the hospitals and specialist units they would like. Difficult and agonising judgments have to be made as to how a limited budget is best allocated to the maximum advantage of the maximum number of patients. That is not a judgment which the court can make. In my judgment, it is not something that a health authority such as this authority can be fairly criticised for not advancing before the court."

While all accept that it is not for the courts to substitute judgment, it is also recognised that there should be some control over the rationality of the decisions made by the administration. This is exemplified by *Rogers*.[6] The defendant had funds available to provide treatment with a breast cancer drug for all patients who fulfilled the clinical requirements for such treatment and whose clinician had prescribed it. However, its policy was to refuse funding for such treatment, save where exceptional personal or clinical circumstances could be shown. The Court of Appeal held that the defendant's policy was irrational, since there were no relevant exceptional circumstances that could justify giving the drug to one patient rather than another. **21–003**

The theme that runs throughout this area is therefore the desire to fashion a criterion that will allow judicial control, without thereby leading to substitution of judgment or too great an intrusion on the merits. The distinction found in some case law and literature between merits review and non-merits review is, nonetheless, not especially helpful. All tests of substantive judicial review entail the judiciary in taking some view of the merits of the contested action. This is so even in relation to the classic *Wednesbury* test.[7] What distinguishes different tests for review is not whether they consider the merits or not, but the stringency of the judicial scrutiny. It is possible in this regard to range different tests for review along a spectrum. Classic, limited *Wednesbury* review is at one end of the spectrum, judicial substitution of judgment, whereby the court imposes what it believes to be the correct result lies at the opposite end of the spectrum. Heightened *Wednesbury* review and proportionality occupy intermediate positions,[8] with the latter being more intensive than the former.

B. Interrelation between Procedure and Substance

It is equally important to understand the intimate connection between procedural and substantive principles in any scheme of judicial review. This is especially so in relation to procedural notions of reasoned justification. The proper application of rationality or proportionality requires reasoned justification by the agency in order that the court can properly assess whether the test has been met or not. This **21–004**

[6] *R. (Rogers) v Swindon NHS Primary Care Trust* [2006] 1 W.L.R. 2649, CA (Civ Div). See also, *R. (Walker) v Secretary of State for the Home Department* [2008] EWCA Civ 30.

[7] *Associated Picture Houses Ltd v Wednesbury Corp* [1948] 1 K.B. 223, CA at 233–234.

[8] *First City Trading* [1997] 1 C.M.L.R. 250 at 278–279.

is equally true in relation to, for example, governmental justifications for departing from an established policy with respect to a particular individual. It may be difficult to decide how much to demand by way of reasoned justification. There must be enough in order that the principles of substantive review can operate meaningfully. Bland statements set at a high level of generality, or justifications rationalised ex post facto, do not ensure proper accountability.[9]

This is exemplified by the decision in *Quila*,[10] in which the claimant challenged a government policy that a visa would not be granted to a foreign national where either party to the marriage was under 21. The Supreme Court held that this was in breach of art.8 ECHR. It accepted in principle that the policy could be defended as pursuing a legitimate aim, which was to prevent forced marriages. The Supreme Court nonetheless concluded that the policy was disproportionate, because the Home Secretary had not produced robust evidence that the policy would deter forced marriages, more especially given that it would prevent bona fide marriages.

The need for evidence and reasoned decision-making is particularly important given that much decision-making will take place within "bounded rationality".[11] It will normally be incremental. Officials rarely have the full range of choices before them. Since officials will often not be viewing the whole picture comprehensively, it is all the more important that the reasons for a particular course of conduct should be articulated. Moreover, while we should be aware that no official can ever literally take "all" relevant considerations into account, the courts have a role[12] in redressing a bureaucratic tendency to adopt a very narrow bounded rationality, which thereby forecloses policy choices.

21–005 The courts should, at the same time, be wary of requiring too much by way of reasoned justification. This is because decisions may have to be made in, for example, areas of scientific uncertainty.[13] Public bodies will make decisions about the level of acceptable risk where there is imperfect information about the consequences of a certain substance on the environment or on human physiology. There may well be many instances where "we do not even know what we do not know", but where regulation is nonetheless warranted. To wait until we have more perfect information may mean that the problem cannot be tackled, or that there will already have been consequences that cannot be remedied. To demand "perfect" reasoned justification would stultify important regulatory initiatives. It could also lead to "paralysis by analysis", whereby those opposed to the regulation seek to use the courts to overturn such initiatives on the grounds that not every piece of data relied on by the agency could be perfectly proven. This

[9] *First City Trading* [1997] 1 C.M.L.R. 250 at 279; *R. (L) v Manchester City Council* [2002] A.C.D. 45 QBD at [15]–[16].

[10] *R. (Aguilar Quila) v Secretary of State for the Home Department* [2011] UKSC 45.

[11] C. Lindblom, "The Science of Muddling Through" (1959) 19 Pub. Adm. Rev. 79; D. Braybrooke and C. Lindblom, *A Strategy of Decision, Policy Evaluation as a Social Process* (New York: Free Press, 1963).

[12] I. Harden and N. Lewis, *The Noble Lie, The British Constitution and the Rule of Law* (London: Hutchinson, 1986).

[13] I have benefited from discussions on this issue with Elizabeth Fisher, and see E. Fisher, *Risk Regulation and Administrative Constitutionalism* (Oxford: Hart, 2007).

can lead to public bodies becoming excessively cautious, or unwilling to suggest a regulation unless they have a veritable mountain of data.

It follows from the above that two legal systems can have similar substantive grounds for review, but these may have differing degrees of force because of the way in which procedural principles, such as reason giving and the like, are applied.

Thus, in the USA agency findings could be set aside if they were found to be "arbitrary, capricious or an abuse of discretion".[14] This criterion was narrowly interpreted, it being sufficient for the agency to show some minimal connection between the statutory goal and the choice actually made. The standard of review was akin to having Lord Greene MR's narrow sense of unreasonableness as the only basis for attack. The label "hard look" developed because the US courts began to desire more control than allowed by this limited test.

In the *State Farm*[15] case the Supreme Court founded its intervention on the arbitrary and capricious test, but then gave a broader reading to that phrase than in earlier cases. The court accepted that it should not substitute its judgment for that of the agency. It could, however, intervene if any of the following defects were present: if the agency relied on factors which Congress had not intended it to consider; failed to consider an important aspect of the problem; offered an explanation which ran counter to the evidence before the agency; was so implausible that it could not be sustained; or failed to provide a record which substantiated its findings. **21–006**

The hard look doctrine therefore represented a shift from a previously more minimal standard of review, where judicial intervention would occur only if there was serious irrationality, to one where the courts would interfere where the broader list of defects set out above are present. That list bears analogy to the totality of Lord Greene MR's list, purpose, relevancy and reasonableness.

The hard look test was however a more powerful tool than the *Wednesbury* formula, because of the greater concern for the provision of reasons, and the demand for a more developed record. It also provided a foundation for interested parties to express their views, particularly in the context of rule-making.[16] This is not to say that the system of review in the USA has been unproblematic. There have been problems resulting from an excessive demand for information and justification by the courts, which has led to the very phrase "paralysis by analysis".

---

[14] Administrative Procedure Act 1946 s.706(2)(a).

[15] *Motor Vehicle Manufacturers Assn v State Farm Mutual Automobile Insurance Co* 463 US 29, 42–43 (1983).

[16] R. Stewart, "The Reformation of American Administrative Law" 88 Harv. L. Rev. 1667 (1975).

3. *WEDNESBURY* UNREASONABLENESS: PAST, PRESENT, AND FUTURE

A. *Wednesbury* Unreasonableness: "The Touchstone of Legitimate Judicial Intervention"

21–007 In this section we will consider the "past" of *Wednesbury* unreasonableness, and examine the conceptual rationale for the meaning given to unreasonableness in that case. We saw in an earlier chapter[17] that Lord Greene MR used the word unreasonableness in two different senses. It was used to describe the various grounds of challenge which went to the legality of the public body's actions. This "umbrella sense" of unreasonableness was used to describe actions based on illegality, irrelevancy and the like. He also gave unreasonableness a "substantive" meaning in its own right. If an exercise of discretion successfully negotiated the hurdles of propriety of purpose and relevancy it could still be invalidated if it was so unreasonable that no reasonable body could reach such a decision. The two senses of unreasonableness were designed to legitimate judicial intervention over discretionary decisions, and to establish the limits to any such intervention.

The first meaning of the term allowed the courts to intervene where the decision was of a type that could not be made at all, and was therefore illegal. It was outside the four corners of the power that Parliament had given to the decision-maker, and the courts should therefore step in. Where, however, the primary decision-maker was within the four corners of its power then the courts should be reluctant to interfere. The courts should not substitute their view for that of the public body, nor should they overturn a decision merely because they felt that there might have been some other reasonable way for the agency to have done its task. Some control over decisions within the four corners of the public body's power was, however, felt to be warranted.

This was the rationale for the substantive meaning of unreasonableness. If the challenged decision really was so unreasonable that no reasonable body could have made it, then the court was justified in quashing it. The very fact that something extreme would have to be proven legitimated the judicial oversight, and served to defend the courts from the charge that they were intervening too greatly on the merits. It is clear from Lord Greene MR's judgment that he conceived of it being used only in the extreme and hypothetical instance of "dismissal for red hair type of case". Lord Diplock in *GCHQ* was equally clear that this species of irrationality would only apply to a "decision which is so outrageous in its defiance of logic or of accepted moral standards that no sensible person who had applied his mind to the question could have arrived at it".[18] We shall consider in due course whether the test needs to be this limited in order that the court should not be regarded as overstepping its proper bounds.

It should be recognised that the courts have always had an inherent discretion as to whether to classify a case as relating to illegality or unreasonableness in its substantive sense. Let us take the classic example of the unreasonable decision, dismissal of a teacher because of the colour of her hair.[19] If the considerations

---

[17] See Ch.19.

[18] *Council of Civil Service Unions v Minister for the Civil Service* [1985] A.C. 374, HL at 410.

[19] *Short v Poole Corp* [1926] Ch. 66.

relevant to dismissal of a teacher are broadly defined as "any physical characteristic" then of course dismissal on the above ground is relevant. However, common sense dictates that this is not the way that we would approach the matter. The question would be posed more specifically, distinguishing between the types of physical characteristics that were felt to be relevant to teaching and those, such as hair colour, which were not. Other decisions could equally be resolved through traditional conceptions of purpose and relevancy.[20]

B. *Wednesbury* Unreasonableness: The Present Law

The *Wednesbury* test has been the principal tool to control discretionary decisions, which have passed the legality hurdles of propriety of purpose and relevancy. The wording of the test, combined with the overlay provided by Lord Greene and Lord Diplock as to when it would apply, might lead one to think that few cases would be condemned. The reality is, however, that the courts have developed the substantive meaning of unreasonableness in two ways, and they have also articulated a test for review independent of *Wednesbury*, based on abuse of power. These will be considered in turn. 21–008

i. *The application of Wednesbury in cases not concerned with rights*

The courts have "loosened" the *Wednesbury* test in some cases that have nothing to do with fundamental rights. They have, for example, applied the test to discretionary decisions that could not, whether right or wrong, be classified as of the "red hair type". The test has been used in the planning sphere to invalidate conditions attached to planning permission. An obligation on the developer to construct an ancillary road over the frontage of the site, to which rights of passage should be given to others,[21] was struck down, so too was an obligation that a property developer should allow those on a council housing list to occupy the houses with security of tenure for 10 years.[22] The test has also been adopted in the context of industrial relations.[23] These cases may have been correctly decided. It is, however, difficult to regard the subject-matter under attack as determinations which were so unreasonable that no reasonable authority could have made them, at least not when viewed as Lord Greene MR visualised the notion. The test was applied in a way that made it closer to asking whether the court believed that the exercise of discretion was reasonable.[24] 21–009

[20] *Williams v Giddy* [1911] A.C. 381; *UKAPE v ACAS* [1981] A.C. 424, HL.

[21] *Hall & Co Ltd v Shoreham-by-Sea Urban DC* [1964] 1 W.L.R. 240, CA.

[22] *R. v Hillingdon LBC, Ex p. Royco Homes Ltd* [1974] Q.B. 720 QBD.

[23] *UKAPE* [1981] A.C. 424; See also, *R. v Boundary Commission for England, Ex p. Foot* [1983] Q.B. 600, CA (Civ Div); *R. v Crown Court of St Albans, Ex p. Cinnamond* [1981] Q.B. 480 QBD.

[24] This is just a sample: *Niarchos v Secretary of State (No.2)* [1981] J.P.L. 118, CA (Civ Div); *West Glamorgan County Council v Rafferty* [1987] 1 W.L.R. 457, CA (Civ Div); *R. v Bridgnorth DC, Ex p. Prime Time Promotions Ltd* [1999] C.O.D. 265 QBD; *R. v Secretary of State for the Home Department, Ex p. Tawfick* [2001] A.C.D. 28 DC; *R. v Secretary of State for Health, Ex p. Wagstaff* [2001] 1 W.L.R. 292 DC; *R. (Howard) v Secretary of State for Health* [2002] EWHC 396 (Admin); *R. (Von Brandenburg) v East London and the City Mental Health Trust* [2002] Q.B. 235, CA (Civ Div); *R. (Paul-Coker) v Southwark LBC* [2006] EWHC 497 (Admin); *Walker* [2008] EWCA Civ 30; *R.*

This has become more explicit in later cases. In *Saville*,[25] Lord Woolf MR held that to label a decision as irrational would often not do justice to the decision-maker, who could be the most rational of persons. In many such cases the true explanation for the decision being flawed was that although such perversity could not be established, the decision-maker had misdirected itself in law. In *Balchin*,[26] Sedley J held that a decision would be *Wednesbury* unreasonable if it disclosed an error of reasoning, which robbed the decision of its logical integrity. If such an error could be shown then it was not necessary for the applicant to demonstrate that the decision-maker was "temporarily unhinged". In *Coughlan*,[27] the court held that rationality covered not only decisions that defied comprehension, but also those made by "flawed logic".[28] In *Kennedy*[29] Lord Mance held that the common law no longer insisted on the uniform application of the rigid test of irrationality once thought applicable under the so-called *Wednesbury* principle and that the nature of judicial review in each case depended upon the context. This was reiterated in *Pham*.[30] It is nonetheless still the case that the traditional *Wednesbury* test can be a significant hurdle in many cases.[31]

The loosening of Lord Greene's test received explicit support from Lord Cooke in the *ITF* case.[32] He regarded the formulation used by Lord Greene as tautologous and exaggerated. It was not, said Lord Cooke, necessary to have such an extreme formulation in order to ensure that the courts remained within their proper bounds as required by the separation of powers. He advocated a simpler and less extreme test: was the decision one that a reasonable authority could have reached. Lord Cooke returned to the topic in more forthright terms in *Daly*[33]:

> "[I] think that the day will come when it will be more widely recognised that … *Wednesbury* … was an unfortunately retrogressive decision in English administrative law, insofar as it suggested that there are degrees of unreasonableness and that only a very extreme degree can bring an administrative decision within the legitimate scope of judicial invalidation. The depth

(LH) v Lambeth LBC [2006] EWHC 1190 (Admin); *Rogers* [2006] 1 W.L.R. 2649; *R. (Bradley) v Secretary of State for Work and Pensions* [2008] EWCA Civ 36; *R. (Boyejo) v Barnet LBC* [2009] EWHC 3261 (Admin); *Barnett v DPP* [2009] EWHC 2004 (Admin); *Icon Display Ltd v Paine* 2009 WL 4248563 EAT at [13]; *Stagecoach Group Plc v Competition Commission* [2010] C.A.T. 14; *Budd v Office of the Independent Adjudicator for Higher Education* [2010] EWHC 1056 (Admin); *R. (Technoprint Plc) v Leeds City Council* [2010] EWHC 581 (Admin); *R. (Pampisford Estate Farms Ltd) v Secretary of State for Communities and Local Government* [2010] EWHC 131 (Admin); *R. (O) v Hammersmith and Fulham LBC* [2011] EWCA Civ 925; A. Le Sueur, "The Rise and Ruin of Unreasonableness?" [2005] J.R. 32.

25 *R. v Lord Saville of Newdigate, Ex p. A* [1999] 4 All E.R. 860, CA (Civ Div) at [33].

26 *R. v Parliamentary Commissioner for Administration, Ex p. Balchin* [1997] C.O.D. 146 QBD.

27 *R. v North and East Devon Health Authority, Ex p. Coughlan* [2001] Q.B. 213, CA (Civ Div).

28 *Coughlan* [2001] Q.B. 213 at [65].

29 *Kennedy v Charity Commission* [2014] UKSC 20 at [51]. Lord Neuberger and Lord Clarke agreed.

30 *Pham v Secretary of State for the Home Department* [2015] UKSC 19 at [94], [109]–[110]. Lord Neuberger, Lady Hale and Lord Wilson agreed.

31 See, e.g. *R. (J) v Special Educational Needs and Disability Tribunal (SENDIST)* [2005] EWHC 3315 (Admin); *R. (AA (Afghanistan)) v Secretary of State for the Home Department* [2006] EWCA Civ 1550.

32 *R. v Chief Constable of Sussex, Ex p. International Trader's Ferry Ltd* [1999] 2 A.C. 418, HL at 452.

33 *R. v Secretary of State for the Home Department, Ex p. Daly* [2001] 2 A.C. 532, HL at 549; *R. (Farrakhan) v Secretary of State for the Home Department* [2002] 3 W.L.R. 481, CA (Civ Div) at [66].

> of judicial review and the deference due to administrative discretion vary with the subject matter. It may well be, however, that the law can never be satisfied in any administrative field by a finding that the decision under review is not capricious or absurd."

ii. *The application of Wednesbury in cases concerned with rights*

The courts have varied the intensity with which they apply the *Wednesbury* test in cases concerned with rights. We have already considered the approach of the common law courts prior to the Human Rights Act 1998.[34] The growing recognition of the importance of rights was accommodated by modification of the substantive meaning of unreasonableness. It is now common to acknowledge that the courts apply the principles of judicial review, including the *Wednesbury* test, with varying degrees of intensity depending on the nature of the subject-matter.[35] **21–010**

Lord Bridge in *Brind*[36] said that in cases concerned with rights, the court must inquire whether a reasonable secretary of state could reasonably have made the primary decision being challenged. The court should begin its inquiry from the premise that only a compelling public interest would justify the invasion of the right. Sir Thomas Bingham MR's formulation was very similar.[37] The court was to consider whether the decision was beyond the range of responses open to a reasonable decision-maker, and the greater the interference with human rights the more the court would require by way of justification.

It is possible to argue that this is merely the *Wednesbury* test, which is being applied with due regard to the nature of the subject matter.[38] Much, however, depends upon what one means by the word "same". The idea that heightened scrutiny in cases concerning rights can be seen *simply* as a variant of the original *Wednesbury* test is problematic in both linguistic and conceptual terms.[39]

In linguistic terms, it is difficult to regard the tests as the same, which is readily apparent when they are juxtaposed. Lord Greene's formulation required the decision to be so unreasonable that no reasonable public body could have made it. The formula applied in cases concerned with rights directs the court to consider whether the decision was beyond the range of responses open to a reasonable decision-maker, and the greater the interference with human rights the more the court would require by way of justification. The court does not rest content with inquiring whether the decision of the minister interfering with rights was so unreasonable that no reasonable minister could have made it. It is true that the degree of linguistic difference between the two fades if one adopts the formulation proposed by Lord Cooke. This is of course because this latter formulation is itself a modification of Lord Greene's test. **21–011**

---

[34] See Ch.19.

[35] Sir John Laws, "*Wednesbury*", in C. Forsyth and I. Hare (eds), *The Golden Metwand and the Crooked Cord, Essays in Honour of Sir William Wade* (Oxford: Oxford University Press, 1998), pp.185–202.

[36] *R. v Secretary of State for the Home Department, Ex p. Brind* [1991] 1 A.C. 696, HL at 748–749.

[37] *R. v Ministry of Defence, Ex p. Smith* [1996] Q.B. 517, CA (Civ Div).

[38] Laws, "*Wednesbury*", in C. Forsyth and I. Hare (eds), *The Golden Metwand and the Crooked Cord, Essays in Honour of Sir William Wade* (Oxford: Oxford University Press, 1998).

[39] P. Craig, "Unreasonableness and Proportionality in UK Law", in E. Ellis (ed.), *The Principle of Proportionality in the Laws of Europe* (Oxford: Hart, 1999), pp.85–106.

In conceptual terms, it is equally difficult to regard judicial review in rights cases merely as a variant of traditional *Wednesbury*, since the premises that underlie review in the two contexts differ. The premise that underpins the classic *Wednesbury* approach, as overlaid by Lord Diplock, is that the courts should be aware of their limited role. Social and political choices have been assigned by Parliament to a minister or agency and it was not for the courts to overstep their legitimate bounds when engaged in judicial review. It was this premise which shaped the *Wednesbury* test. The court would intervene to ensure that the agency remained within the four corners of its powers, through concepts such as propriety of purpose and relevancy, but would only exercise very limited control over the rationality of the decision through *Wednesbury* unreasonableness. The premise differs in cases concerned with rights. The courts continue to accept that they should not substitute judgment. It is also generally accepted that traditional notions of sovereignty mean that the courts cannot invalidate primary legislation on the ground that it infringes rights.[40] The courts do not, however, operate on the assumption that decisions about rights made by the political arm of government, or another public body, must necessarily be accorded the same respect or judicial deference as, for example, allocative decisions of an economic nature. The majoritarian will is quite properly accorded less force in rights-based cases than in others. This serves to explain, and is reflected in, the different meaning given to "reasonableness review". The level of unreasonableness which the applicant must prove is less extreme than in the traditional *Wednesbury* formula,[41] and the court requires more compelling justification before it is willing to accept that an invasion of rights was warranted.

iii. The non-application of Wednesbury in legitimate expectation cases: rationality and abuse of power

21–012 The case law on legitimate expectations will be examined in the following chapter. This case law is, however, of more general relevance for the standard of review. In *Coughlan*,[42] the court held that judicial intervention could be premised on bare rationality, as reflected in the *Wednesbury* test. This test was rejected as being insufficiently searching in cases where a public body sought to resile from a substantive legitimate expectation.[43] The court held that intervention could, alternatively, be premised on abuse of power, citing *Preston*[44] as the principal authority. The court's task was to ensure that the power to alter policy was not abused by unfairly frustrating an individual's legitimate expectations. This standard of review was more far-reaching than bare rationality.[45] While it was for the public body to decide when to change policy, the applicant's substantive legitimate expectation could not be frustrated unless there was an overriding

[40] See, however, Sir John Laws, "Law and Democracy" [1995] P.L. 72 and "The Constitution: Morals and Rights" [1996] P.L. 622; Lord Woolf, "Droit Public—English Style" [1995] P.L. 57.

[41] This is so even taking account of the discussion in the previous section

[42] *Coughlan* [2001] Q.B. 213.

[43] *Coughlan* [2001] Q.B. 213 at [66].

[44] *R. v Inland Revenue Commissioners, Ex p. Preston* [1985] A.C. 835, HL.

[45] *Coughlan* [2001] Q.B. 213 at [74], [77].

public interest, and whether this existed or not was a matter for the court.[46] The appropriate standard of review in legitimate expectation cases will be considered in detail below.[47] Two points should be emphasised in the present context.

On the one hand, abuse of power may properly be regarded as the *conceptual rationale* for judicial intervention to protect substantive legitimate expectations. It encapsulates the conclusion that the applicant had some normatively justified expectation, since there would otherwise have been no foundation for finding such an abuse. The term abuse of power can also capture the conclusion that the court has found the public body's argument for going back on the expectation to be unconvincing.

On the other hand, it must also be recognised that abuse of power does not, in itself, furnish a *standard of review* for deciding whether a public body can resile from a proven substantive expectation.[48] Abuse of power can express the conclusion reached under any such standard, but does not constitute a standard of review itself. The standard should, as recognised in *Coughlan*, be more searching than bare rationality. There are two possible standards of review that could be employed: a modified *Wednesbury* test, and proportionality. The choice between these tests in legitimate expectation cases will be considered below.[49] The following discussion in this chapter is also of relevance.

C. *Wednesbury* Unreasonableness: The Future of the Test

The *Wednesbury* test has long occupied centre stage in the control of discretion. **21–013**
Its very malleability has helped it to survive. Whether it continues to do so is dependent upon three factors.

First, there is the empirical issue as to how many cases which have, up until now, been adjudicated pursuant to this test, will be recast as rights-based claims under the Human Rights Act 1998 (HRA). Some challenges will be recast in this manner, and the indications post the HRA is that many cases include a rights-based claim. This is important because, as we have seen,[50] the test for review under the HRA is more demanding than the *Wednesbury* test as originally conceived. It would, for example, be a "nice" question as to how *Wednesbury* itself would be argued under the HRA.[51] The applicants might well contend that the restriction imposed in that case, to the effect that a cinema could open on a Sunday, but could not admit children under 15, was contrary to the right to family life, or perhaps even free speech. This might be thought to be fanciful, but the general point holds true none the less: many cases litigated under the *Wednesbury* test could be pleaded under the HRA. This is obviously true in relation to cases such as *Brind*, *Smith* or *McQuillan*, which clearly involve rights-based claims. It

---

[46] *Coughlan* [2001] Q.B. 213 at [76].

[47] See paras 22–017 to 22–022.

[48] See also, *R. (S) v Secretary of State for the Home Department* [2007] EWCA Civ 546 at [39]–[45].

[49] See Ch.22.

[50] See para.20–044.

[51] Sir Robert Carnwath, "The Reasonable Limits of Local Authority Powers" [1996] P.L. 244 at 247–248.

is, however, also true of other cases, such as those concerning the imposition of conditions on a planning permission. There is little doubt that some of these cases would now be brought under the HRA.

21–014 The second factor that will affect the status of the *Wednesbury* test is more normative in nature. This is the impact of the standard of review under EU law and the HRA. It is clear that EU law uses proportionality as a criterion for review. It is clear also that proportionality is the test applied under the HRA. We shall consider proportionality immediately hereafter. For the present we are concerned with the affect this might have on the *Wednesbury* test.

It may be that *Wednesbury* will survive and continue to be used in cases where there is no link with EU law, and where there is no claim under the HRA. Indeed, some courts might feel that precisely because there are no connections with EU law or the HRA, therefore the traditional *Wednesbury* test remains the most appropriate standard for review.

It may, however, transpire that *Wednesbury* ceases to operate as an independent test in its own right. It might be caught in the "pincers" of the tests used in EU law and the HRA. This is in part because a proportionality test can be applied with varying degrees of intensity. The constitutional concerns about the limits of the judicial role that underpinned *Wednesbury* could, therefore, be accommodated within a proportionality inquiry. It is in part because it will be increasingly difficult for courts to apply different tests to different allegations made in an application for judicial review. It will be common for cases to feature claims under the HRA, and independent assertions of ultra vires conduct. It is possible for courts to use different tests for review in relation to each claim. The attractions of applying a single test, albeit one which can be applied with varying degrees of intensity may, however, prove difficult to resist over time. This is particularly so given that the courts will become more accustomed to a proportionality inquiry via the HRA. We shall see that Lord Slynn in *Alconbury* called for proportionality to be recognised as an independent head of review.[52]

The third factor is related to, but distinct, from the second. This is the precise meaning given to the *Wednesbury* test. If the courts adopt the modified version of the test suggested by Lord Cooke it raises the issue of how different this is from a proportionality test. His contributions are to be welcomed. Lord Cooke recognised the separation of powers principle which underlies this area, but believed that this could be properly respected by framing a reasonableness test in less extreme terms than articulated by Lord Greene. This will be considered when proportionality has been analysed.

---

[52] *R. (Alconbury Developments Ltd) v Secretary of State for the Environment, Transport and the Regions* [2003] 2 A.C. 295, HL at [51].

4. PROPORTIONALITY IN UK LAW: STATUS, MEANING AND APPLICATION

The discussion will begin with the present status of this concept within our law, to be followed by more general consideration of the meaning of proportionality and the desirability of developing this head of review.[53] **21–015**

A. Legal Status of Proportionality

i. Proportionality in domestic law: Brind

Brind[54] is a leading authority on the status of proportionality. The Home Secretary issued directives under the Broadcasting Act 1981 requiring the BBC and the IBA to refrain from broadcasting certain matters by persons who represented organisations that were proscribed under legislation concerning the prevention of terrorism. The proscription was limited to direct statements made by the members of the organisations. It did not prevent the broadcasting of such persons on film, provided that there was a voice-over account paraphrasing what had been said. The objective was both to deny such organisations any appearance of political legitimacy, and also to prevent intimidation. The applicants argued that the directives were disproportionate. **21–016**

Their Lordships rejected the argument. Lord Bridge held that the restrictions on freedom of speech were not unreasonable in scope, and he did not believe that the applicants' case could be improved by invoking proportionality.[55] Lord Bridge, however, agreed with Lord Roskill that proportionality might at some time be incorporated within UK law. Lord Roskill acknowledged that Lord Diplock had, in the *GCHQ* case,[56] held this open as a possible future development. Lord Roskill did not, however, think that this was an appropriate case for such a development, believing that it would lead the courts into substituting their view for that of the Home Secretary.[57] Similar concerns are apparent in the judgments of Lord Ackner and Lord Lowry. Thus, Lord Ackner reasoned that if proportionality were to add something to existing law, then it would be a more intensive standard of review than traditional *Wednesbury* unreasonableness. This would mean that an "inquiry into and a decision upon the merits cannot be avoided", in the sense that the court would have to balance the

---

53 J. Jowell and A. Lester, "Beyond Wednesbury: Substantive Principles of Administrative Law" [1987] P.L. 368; Craig, "Unreasonableness and Proportionality in UK Law", in E. Ellis (ed.), *The Principle of Proportionality in the Laws of Europe* (1999); G. de Búrca, "Proportionality and Wednesbury Unreasonableness: The Influence of European Legal Concepts on UK Law", in M. Andenas (ed.), *English Public Law and the Common Law of Europe* (London: Key Haven, 1998), Ch.4; G. Gerapetritis, *Proportionality in Administrative Law* (Athens: Sakkoulas, 1997); M. Elliott, "The Human Rights Act and the Standard of Substantive Review" [2001] C.L.J. 301; T. Hickman, "Proportionality: Comparative Law Lessons" [2007] J.R. 31; R. Clayton and K. Ghaly, "Shifting Standards of Review" [2007] J.R. 210; J. Rivers, "Proportionality and the Variable Intensity of Review" [2006] C.L.J. 174.

54 *R. v Secretary of State for the Home Department, Ex p. Brind* [1991] 1 A.C. 696, HL.

55 *Brind* [1991] 1 A.C. 696 at 748–749.

56 *GCHQ* [1985] A.C. 374 at 410.

57 *Brind* [1991] 1 A.C. 696 at 696, 749–750.

pros and cons of the decision being challenged.[58] Lord Lowry felt that the judges were not well equipped by training or experience to "decide the answer to an administrative problem where the scales are evenly balanced".[59] He also feared that recognition of proportionality would lead to an increase in the number of applications for judicial review, with a consequential increase in costs for litigants and court time.[60]

It is not surprising, in the light of *Brind*, to find cases where the courts declined to apply proportionality as an independent standard of review.[61] It is clear that any change will require a decision from the Supreme Court. Thus in the *ABCIFER* case,[62] Dyson LJ held proportionality was only applicable in cases concerned with EU law and the HRA, and that it was not for the Court of Appeal to perform the burial rites to the *Wednesbury* test, this being something that would have to be done by the House of Lords. Dyson LJ nonetheless added that he had difficulty in seeing what purpose was served by retention of the *Wednesbury* test. More recently in *Keyu* a Supreme Court panel composed of five declined to decide whether proportionality should be regarded as a general independent head of review in UK law, stating that this matter should only be decided by a larger panel.[63]

ii. Proportionality in domestic law: direct or indirect recognition

21–017 The historical reality is that a concept of "proportionability" was part of UK judicial review from the 17th century.[64] There are, moreover, more modern domestic cases where the courts have either explicitly applied proportionality, or reasoned in a manner analogous thereto. This current in the jurisprudence is especially noteworthy in cases dealing with penalties or fundamental rights.

There are a number of decisions where the courts have applied proportionality expressly or impliedly. This is exemplified by *Hook*,[65] where a stallholder had his licence revoked for urinating in the street and using offensive language. Lord Denning MR struck down the decision in part because the penalty was excessive and out of proportion to the offence.[66] In *Nadarajah*[67] Laws LJ held that a public body could resile from a prima facie legitimate expectation only where it had a

58 *Brind* [1991] 1 A.C. 696 at 762.

59 *Brind* [1991] 1 A.C. 696 at 767.

60 *Brind* [1991] 1 A.C. 696 at 767.

61 See, e.g. *R. v International Stock Exchange, Ex p. Else* [1992] B.C.C. 11 Ch D; *R. v Chief Constable of Kent, Ex p. Absalom* 5 May 1993; *R. v Secretary of State for the Home Department, Ex p. Hargreaves* [1997] 1 All E.R. 397.

62 *R. (Association of British Civilian Internees: Far East Region) v Secretary of State for Defence* [2003] Q.B. 1397, CA (Civ Div) at [34]–[35].

63 *Keyu v Secretary of State for Foreign and Commonwealth Affairs* [2015] UKSC 69.

64 P. Craig, "Proportionality and Judicial Review: A UK Historical Perspective", in S. Vogenauer and S. Weatherill (eds), *General Principles of Law: European and Comparative Perspectives* (Oxford: Oxford University Press, 2016).

65 *R. v Barnsley MBC, Ex p. Hook* [1976] 1 W.L.R. 1052, CA (Civ Div) at 1057.

66 See also, *R. v Warwick Crown Court, Ex p. Smalley* [1987] 1 W.L.R. 237 QBD; *R. v Highbury Magistrates' Court, Ex p. Uchendu* (1994) 158 J.P. 409; *R. v Secretary of State for the Environment, Ex p. NALGO* [1993] Admin L.R. 785; *R. v Manchester Metropolitan University, Ex p. Nolan, The Independent*, 14 July 1993 DC; *Bolton v Law Society* [1994] C.O.D. 295 CA (Civ Div); *R. v Admiralty Board of the Defence Council, Ex p. Coupland* [1996] C.O.D. 147 QBD; *B v Secretary of State for the*

legal duty to do so, or where it was otherwise a proportionate response having regard to a legitimate aim pursued by the public body in the public interest.

A similar trend is apparent in cases where the affected interest is a fundamental right. While the House of Lords in *Brind* denied that proportionality was an independent ground of review, a number of their Lordships reasoned in an analogous manner. Lord Templeman[68] held that the court was not restricted in such cases to asking whether the governmental action was perverse or irrational. The judge must rather inquire whether a reasonable minister could reasonably conclude that the interference with the right in question was justifiable. Any such interference must be necessary and proportionate to the damage that the restriction was designed to prevent. Lord Bridge's reasoning was similar. The same approach is evident in other cases involving rights.[69]

More recently the Supreme Court in *Youssef*[70] confirmed that proportionality was the test for review in cases concerning fundamental rights. The Supreme Court however emphasised that the decision would not necessarily differ from that reached by more intensive rationality review, and that the court conducting proportionality review should accord the requisite respect to the determination made by the executive. **21–018**

The jurisprudence considered thus far, has applied proportionality or a test akin thereto in specific types of case. The range of such cases is, however, expanding beyond the strict confines of cases concerned with EU law and the HRA. Thus, as we have seen proportionality has been applied in cases concerned with legitimate expectations. In *Walker*, Laws LJ opined that *Wednesbury* unreasonableness now seemed an "old-fashioned legal construct".[71] The courts were, said Laws LJ, increasingly accustomed to the framing of substantive challenges to public decisions in terms of proportionality, and not only in the context of EU law and human rights. Lord Slynn in *Alconbury* expressed the view that proportionality should be recognised as a general head of review within domestic law, irrespective of whether the case was concerned with the HRA or EU law.[72]

It remains to be seen whether the courts will take this step, and the policy arguments in this respect will be considered below.[73] The Supreme Court has not yet decided whether proportionality can be a general head of review,[74] but has nonetheless made a number of statements that are relevant in this respect. Thus in

Home Department [2000] H.R.L.R. 439, CA (Civ Div); *South Buckinghamshire DC v Porter* [2003] 2 A.C. 558; *Chaudhury v General Medical Council* [2002] UKPC 41; *R. (Livermore) v Nursing and Midwifery Council* [2005] EWHC 2339 (Admin).

67 *R. (Nadarajah) v Secretary of State for the Home Department* [2005] EWCA Civ 1363.

68 *Brind* [1991] 1 A.C. 696 at 751.

69 *Smith* [1996] Q.B. 517; *Bugdaycay v Secretary of State for the Home Department* [1987] A.C. 514, HL at 531; *R. v Secretary of State for the Home Department, Ex p. Leech* [1994] Q.B. 198, CA (Civ Div); *R. v Secretary of State for the Home Department, Ex p. McQuillan* [1995] 4 All E.R. 400 QBD; *Saville* [1999] 4 All E.R. 860 at [34]–[37]; See para.19–022.

70 *R. (on the application of Youssef) v Secretary of State for Foreign and Commonwealth Affairs* [2016] UKSC 3 at [55]–[59].

71 *Walker* [2008] EWCA Civ 30 at [38].

72 *Alconbury* [2003] 2 A.C. 295 at [51].

73 See paras 21–031 to 21–047.

74 *Keyu* [2015] UKSC 69.

Kennedy[75] Lord Mance held that reasonableness review and proportionality involved considerations of weight and balance, with the intensity of the scrutiny and the weight to be given to any primary decision maker's view depending on the context. This was reiterated by Lord Mance, Lord Carnwath and Lord Sumption in *Pham*.[76] Lord Sumption in *Pham* held, moreover, that although UK law had not adopted a general principle of proportionality review, it had "for many years stumbled towards a concept which is in significant respects similar, and over the last three decades has been influenced by European jurisprudence even in areas of law lying beyond the domains of EU and international human rights law."[77] Lord Reed held that although proportionality and more intensive rationality review were not identical, the application of reasonableness review and proportionality could yield the same outcome, more especially so given that the intensity of proportionality review could itself vary.[78]

iii. Proportionality in domestic law: the Human Rights Act 1998

21–019 We have already considered in detail the role of proportionality in HRA cases, and reference should be made to that discussion.[79] In *Daly*[80] Lord Steyn held that there was a material difference between a rationality test cast in terms of heightened scrutiny, and a proportionality test. He accepted that many cases would be decided the same way under either test, but acknowledged that the intensity of review would be greater under proportionality. Proportionality could require the reviewing court to assess the balance struck by the decision-maker, not merely whether it was within the range of reasonable decisions. A proportionality test could also oblige the court to pay attention to the relative weight accorded to relevant interests, in a manner not generally done under the traditional approach to review. It had to be shown that the limitation of the right was necessary in a democratic society, to meet a pressing social need, and was proportionate to the legitimate aim being pursued.

The Supreme Court in *Kennedy* and *Pham* has, however, as seen above, held that considerations of weight and balance are relevant in rationality cases as well as in proportionality cases.[81]

---

[75] *Kennedy* [2014] UKSC 20 at [54].

[76] *Pham* [2015] UKSC 19 at [60], [95], [109]–[110]. Lord Neuberger, Lord Wilson and Lady Hale agreed with Lord Carnwath, Lord Mance and Lord Sumption.

[77] *Pham* [2015] UKSC 19 at [105], [107].

[78] *Pham* [2015] UKSC 19 at [115]–[117].

[79] See paras 20–041 to 20–055.

[80] *Daly* [2001] 2 A.C. 532 at 547. See also, *Sudesh Madan v General Medical Council* [2001] A.C.D. 3 QBD; *Samaroo v Secretary of State for the Home Department* [2001] EWCA Civ 1139 at [29]–[35]; *Manchester City Council* [2002] A.C.D. 45 QBD at [21]; *Southampton Port Health Authority v Seahawk Marine Foods Ltd* [2002] EWCA Civ 54 at [34]; *Farrakhan* [2002] 3 W.L.R. 481, CA (Civ Div) at [65]; *Chaudhury* [2002] UKPC 41.

[81] *Kennedy* [2014] UKSC 20 at [54]; *Pham* [2015] UKSC 19 at [60], [95], [107]–[110]; P. Craig, "The Nature of Reasonableness Review" [2013] C.L.P. 1.

iv. *Proportionality: cases with an EU law component*

It is clear that national courts are bound to apply EU law principles, and they have applied proportionality in cases which have an EU law element.[82] **21–020**

This is exemplified by the *ITF* case.[83] The applicants were exporters of live animals across the Channel. There were serious protests against such exports at the docks. The Chief Constable of Sussex deployed significant manpower to control the protests, but then decided that because of his limited resources he could only provide the requisite police cover for the exporters two days per week. ITF argued that this decision was irrational under domestic law and contrary to EU law. The domestic law argument failed: it was for the Chief Constable to decide how to use his limited resources, and that decision was not *Wednesbury* unreasonable. The EU law claim was that the Chief Constable's decision constituted an export ban, which was prohibited by art.35 TFEU. The House of Lords accepted that if there had been a breach of art.35, proportionality would be relevant in deciding on the application of art.36 TFEU, which allows a defence for limitations on the free movement of goods for reasons of, inter alia, public security or public health, provided that the limitation is not disproportionate. The Chief Constable's decision was held to be a proportionate response.

B. Proportionality: Place and Meaning

It is important to be clear as to the *place* of proportionality within the general scheme of review, and its relationship with other methods of control. It is clear, as a matter of principle, that to talk of proportionality assumes that the public body was entitled to pursue its desired objective. The presumption is, therefore, that the general objective was a legitimate one, and that the public body was not seeking to achieve an improper purpose. If the purpose was improper then the exercise of discretion should be struck down on this ground, without any investigation as to whether it was disproportionate. Proportionality should only be considered when the controls of purpose and relevancy have been satisfied. If we bypass this level of control then the danger is that the courts will assume that the public body was able to use its discretion for the purpose in question, the only live issue being whether it did so proportionately. **21–021**

Let us turn now to the *meaning* of the concept itself. Proportionality involves some balance between interests or objectives, and an appropriate relationship between means and ends. We must therefore identify the relevant interests, and ascribe some weight to them. A decision must then be made as to whether the

---

[82] See, e.g. *R. v Minister of Agriculture, Fisheries and Food, Ex p. Bell Line* [1984] 2 C.M.L.R. 502 QBD; *R. v Ministry of Agriculture, Fisheries and Food, Ex p. Roberts* [1990] 1 C.M.L.R. 555; *International Stock Exchange* [1992] B.C.C. 11; *R. v Secretary of State for the Home Department, Ex p. Adams* [1995] All E.R. (EC) 177; *First City Trading* [1997] 1 C.M.L.R. 250; *R. v Ministry of Agriculture, Fisheries and Food, Ex p. Astonquest Ltd* [2000] Eu. L.R. 371; *B* [2000] H.R.L.R. 439; *R. (Hoverspeed Ltd) v Customs and Excise Commissioners* [2002] EWHC 1630 (Admin); *R. (Castille Ltd) v Secretary of State for Trade and Industry* [2002] EWHC 16 (Admin); *Gough v Chief Constable of Derbyshire* [2002] 3 W.L.R. 289, CA (Civ Div); *R. (Lumsdon) v Legal Services Board* [2015] UKSC 41.

[83] *International Trader's Ferry* [1999] 2 A.C. 418, HL.

public body's decision was proportionate or not, in the light of the preceding considerations. The most common formulation[84] is a three-part analysis. The court considers:

i. whether the measure was suitable to achieve the desired objective;
ii. whether the measure was necessary for achieving the desired objective; and
iii. whether it none the less imposed excessive burdens on the individual. The last part of this inquiry is often termed proportionality stricto sensu.

The court will decide how *intensively* to apply these criteria, which may require the court to consider *alternative strategies* for attaining the desired end. This follows from the fact that the court will, in fundamental rights cases, consider whether there was a less restrictive method for attaining the desired objective. The need to consider alternative strategies may well also arise in other cases. Where the decision is of a technical or professional nature it may require specialist evidence as to the practicability of alternative strategies.[85]

C. Proportionality: Application

21–022 The proportionality test might well produce differing results depending upon the circumstances of the case. That much is obvious. We can, however, go further in providing some guidance as to how proportionality will be applied in differing types of case. Three types of case can be differentiated. It will be seen that proportionality is easier to apply in the first two situations than it is in the third.

i. Proportionality and rights

21–023 The first type of situation is where the exercise of discretion impinges upon, or clashes with, a recognised fundamental right. We have already seen that proportionality is part of the test for review under the HRA, and there is authority that proportionality also applies in relation to fundamental rights recognised at common law.[86] Our courts must take the jurisprudence of the European Court of Human Rights on proportionality into account, even though it is not binding on them.

It is clear as a matter of principle that some such test should apply in this area, quite apart from the persuasive force of the Strasbourg case law. The reason is as follows. If we recognise certain interests as being of particular importance, and categorise them as fundamental rights, then this renders the application of proportionality the natural standard of review.

[84] *Hickman* [2007] J.R. 31 provides a valuable analysis of different versions of the proportionality test.
[85] *Seahawk Marine Foods* [2002] EWCA Civ 54 at [34]–[35].
[86] *Quila v Secretary of State for the Home Department* [2010] EWCA Civ 1482. The point was not addressed by the Supreme Court *Quila* [2011] UKSC 45. See more generally A. Barak, *Proportionality, Constitutional Rights and their Limitations* (Cambridge: Cambridge University Press, 2012).

This is because the very denomination of an interest as a fundamental right means that any invasion should be kept to a minimum. It can be accepted that many rights are not absolute, and that therefore some limitations may be warranted. Nonetheless there is a presumption that any inroad should interfere with the right as little as possible, and no more than is merited by the occasion. It is natural therefore to ask whether the interference with the fundamental right was the least restrictive possible in the circumstances. Proportionality review is facilitated because the fundamental nature of the interest, such as freedom of speech, has been acknowledged, although the court will still have to decide whether the invasion of the right was proportionate, and this may well be controversial.

ii. *Proportionality and penalties*

The second type of case is where the penalty is deemed to be disproportionate to the offence committed. People may disagree as to the precise penalty which is appropriate for a particular offence. Nonetheless we know the penalty that has been imposed; we know the offence; and we know also the interest affected by the penalty. This interest may be personal liberty in the case of imprisonment, or it may be loss of livelihood as in *Hook*. It is a recognised principle of justice that penalties should not be excessive, as acknowledged in the Bill of Rights 1689. A court is unlikely to intervene unless the disproportionality is reasonably evident,[87] and judicial review of this kind is to be welcomed. The application of proportionality in this type of case is also made easier because the applicant will not normally be challenging the administrative rule itself, but simply the penalty imposed for the breach. **21–024**

iii. *Proportionality and administrative discretion*

The third type of case covers those situations not dealt with by the previous two. There are no fundamental rights at stake, and no excessive penalties. The paradigm of this third category is where the public body decides to exercise its discretion in a particular manner, this necessitates the balancing of various interests, and a person affected argues that the balancing was disproportionate. The application of a proportionality test may be more difficult in this type of case. **21–025**

This is in part because it requires us to weight, for example, the respective values of ratepayers and transport users in a *Fares Fair*[88] type of case. It is in part because many administrative decisions involve balancing, which is the essence of political determinations and administrative choices. It cannot therefore be right for the judiciary to overturn a decision merely because the court would have balanced the conflicting interests differently. This would amount to substitution of judgment by any other name.

This does not mean that proportionality has no role to play in this type of case. This is especially so given that administrative policy choices should be

---

[87] *Customs and Excise Commissioners v P & O Steam Navigation Co* [1993] C.O.D. 164 DC.

[88] *Bromley LBC v Greater London Council* [1983] 1 A.C. 768.

susceptible to judicial scrutiny.[89] What it does mean is that the intensity of proportionality review is crucial in this type of case. A less intensive form of proportionality review can, however, be utilised for cases in this area, as exemplified by the EU jurisprudence on proportionality.

D. Proportionality, the Role of the Court and the Standard of Review

21–026 The discussion thus far has considered the legal status of proportionality within UK law. The precise role of the courts in the proportionality analysis has been the subject of discussion in prominent cases, notably in *Denbigh*,[90] *Huang*,[91] and *Miss Behavin' Ltd*.[92] This issue was addressed in the previous chapter,[93] and reference should be made to that discussion. A further point concerning the nature and standard of judicial review should nonetheless be considered here.

The cases mentioned above contain a number of statements contrasting the judicial role in HRA cases, with its role in ordinary judicial review. Thus, Lord Hoffmann in *Denbigh* stated that in domestic judicial review the court was usually concerned with whether the decision-maker reached its decision in the right way, rather than with whether he reached what the court might think is the right answer, whereas under the HRA the court was concerned with substance and not procedure,[94] and this view was echoed in later cases.[95] This contrast should not be pressed too far.[96] The reality is that the court is concerned with substance and procedure in HRA cases and ordinary judicial review.

In relation to HRA cases, it is true that the court will be concerned with ensuring that the result reached by the public body complied with Convention rights. Thus, the mere fact that the public body used immaculate procedure will not prevent a decision from being struck down, if it is felt not to be a correct interpretation of the Convention right. In that respect the focus is indubitably on substance. However, as we have seen,[97] the court is still willing to give some respect to the judgment of the public body when deciding whether the Convention right has been broken, and insofar as it does so it is acknowledging that, within the confines of that area, there may be more than one substantive result that is consistent with the Convention right. Moreover, the extent to which the public body's decision-making process consciously addressed Convention issues will influence the extent to which the court is willing to accept the decision.[98]

---

[89] Harden and Lewis, *The Noble Lie, The British Constitution and the Rule of Law* (1986).

[90] *R. (Begum) v Denbigh High School Governors* [2007] 1 A.C. 100 HL.

[91] *Huang v Secretary of State for the Home Department* [2007] 2 W.L.R. 581 HL.

[92] *Belfast City Council v Miss Behavin' Ltd* [2007] 1 W.L.R. 1420 HL.

[93] See paras 20–041 to 20–055.

[94] *Denbigh* [2007] 1 A.C. 100 at [68].

[95] See, e.g. *Miss Behavin'* [2007] 1 W.L.R. 1420 at [31], Baroness Hale; at [45], Lord Mance.

[96] A. Kavanagh, "Reasoning about Proportionality under the Human Rights Act 1998: Outcomes, Substance and Process" (2014) 130 L.Q.R. 235.

[97] See paras 20–046 to 20–055.

[98] See also D. Mead, "Outcomes Aren't All: Defending Process-Based Review of Public Authority Decisions under the Human Rights Act" [2012] P.L. 61.

In relation to ordinary judicial review, it is true that some aspects of the standard doctrinal armoury address the decision-making process, rather than stipulating a particular substantive conclusion that must be reached. It would nonetheless be mistaken to conceptualise these doctrines as solely, or even primarily, about the decision-making process. Thus, judicial intervention on grounds of relevancy or propriety of purpose will not directly stipulate a particular substantive result that should be reached, although it may do so indirectly, but the very denomination of what constitutes a relevant consideration or a proper purpose will be a substantive determination, which constrains the range of results that the public body can arrive at. The same is true for proportionality in cases that are not concerned with human rights. Judicial application of the necessity and suitability tests will involve consideration of the administrative decision-making process, but it will also indubitably place substantive limits on outcome or result.

5. PROPORTIONALITY: THE EU DIMENSION

Proportionality is a general principle of EU law, and our courts must therefore apply it in cases with an EU law dimension.[99] These general principles have been developed by the ECJ and draw their inspiration from the laws of the Member States. They can be relied on in actions to contest the legality of EU measures, or national measures designed to implement EU law. Proportionality has been applied in all three types of case described above. **21–027**

A. Proportionality and Rights

There have been a number of cases concerned with proportionality in the context of rights granted by the EU Treaties. A common scenario is where the Member State seeks to take advantage of a public policy exception to, for example, the free movement of workers. This right is guaranteed by art.45 TFEU, and the public policy exception finds expression in art.45(3). The ECJ has insisted that derogation from the fundamental principle of art.45 can only be sanctioned where there is a genuine and serious threat to public policy, and then only if the measure is the least restrictive possible in the circumstances.[100] The same principle is evident in cases on freedom to provide services, which is protected by art.56 TFEU. In *Van Binsbergen*[101] the court held that residence requirements limiting this freedom may be justified, but only where they were strictly necessary to **21–028**

---

99 P. Craig, *EU Administrative Law*, 2nd edn (Oxford: Oxford University Press, 2012), Chs 19–20; T. Tridimas, *The General Principles of EU Law*, 2nd edn (Oxford: Oxford University Press, 2006), Chs 3–5; G. de Búrca, "The Principle of Proportionality and its Application in EC Law" (1993) 13 Y.B.E.L. 105.

100 *Rutili v Minister of the Interior* (36/75) [1975] E.C.R. 1219; *R. v Bouchereau* (30/77) [1977] E.C.R. 1999.

101 *Van Binsbergen v Bestuur van de Bedrijfsvereniging Metaalnijverheid* (33/74) [1974] E.C.R. 1299; *Coenen v Sociaal Economische Raad* (39/75) [1975] E.C.R. 1547; *Corsten* (C-58/98) [2000] E.C.R. I-7919; *Canal Satelite Digital SL v Aministacion General del Estado and Distribuidora de Television Gigital SA (DTS)* (C-390/99) [2002] E.C.R. I-607.

prevent the evasion by those residing outside the territory of professional rules applicable to the activity in question. A similar approach is evident in cases concerning the right to free movement of goods. Thus, in the famous *Cassis de Dijon* case[102] the ECJ decided that a German rule which prescribed minimum alcohol content for an alcoholic beverage impeded the free movement of goods under art.34 TFEU, and assessed whether the rule was necessary to protect consumers from being misled. The court rejected the defence, because the interests of the consumers could be safeguarded in other less restrictive ways, by displaying the alcohol content upon the packaging of the drinks.

Application of proportionality can also be seen in cases where individuals claim that EU regulations infringe their fundamental rights. Thus, in *Hauer*[103] the ECJ held that a regulation that restricted the areas in which wine could be grown, and thus limited the applicant's property rights, must not constitute a disproportionate and excessive interference with the rights of the owner.[104]

B. Proportionality and Penalties

21–029 The principle has been often applied where the applicant claims that the penalty is disproportionate to the offence committed.[105] This is exemplified by *Man (Sugar)*.[106] The applicant was required to give a security deposit to the Board when seeking a licence to export sugar outside the Community. The applicant was four hours late in completing the relevant paperwork. The board, acting pursuant to a Community regulation, declared the entire deposit of £1,670,370 to be forfeit. The ECJ held that the automatic forfeiture of the entire deposit in the event of any failure to fulfil the time requirement was too drastic.[107]

In addition to cases dealing with penalties stricto sensu the ECJ applied proportionality in the field of economic regulation, scrutinising the level of charges imposed by the European Union. Thus, in *Bela-Muhle*[108] the court held that a scheme whereby producers of animal feed were forced to use skimmed milk in their product, in order to reduce a surplus, rather than soya, was unlawful because skimmed milk was three times more expensive than soya. The obligation to purchase the milk, therefore, imposed a disproportionate burden on the animal feed producers.

---

102 *Rewe-Zentrale AG v Bundesmonopolverwaltung für Branntwein* (120/78) [1979] E.C.R. 649; *Commission v Germany* (178/84) [1987] E.C.R. 1227; *Commission v United Kingdom* (40/82) [1984] E.C.R. 2793; *Commission v Belgium* (C-217/99) [2000] E.C.R. I-10251; *Kemikalieinspektionen v Toolex Alpha AB* (C-473/98) [2000] E.C.R. I-5681; *Criminal Proceedings against Burmanjer, Van der Linden and de Jong* (C-20/03) [2005] E.C.R. I-4133.

103 *Hauer v Land Rheinland-Pfalz* (44/79) [1979] E.C.R. 3727.

104 See also, *Council v Hautala* (C-353/99) [2001] E.C.R. I-9565.

105 Craig, *EU Administrative Law* (2012), Ch.19.

106 *R. v Intervention Board, Ex p. Man (Sugar) Ltd* (181/84) [1985] E.C.R. 2889.

107 *Sugar* [1985] E.C.R. 2889 at [29]; *Atlanta Amsterdam BV v Produktschap voor Vee en Vlees* (240/78) [1979] E.C.R. 2137; *Buitoni SA v Fonds d'Orientation et de Regularisation des Marches Agricoles* (122/78) [1979] E.C.R. 677; *Portugal v Commission* (C-365/99) [2001] E.C.R. I-5645.

108 *Bela-Muhle Josef Bergman v Grows-Farm* (114/76) [1977] E.C.R. 1211.

C. Proportionality and Discretion

Proportionality has also been applied in cases of the third type described in the previous section. The meaning given to proportionality is of particular interest. *Fedesa*[109] provides a good example. The applicants challenged the legality of a Council directive prohibiting the use of certain substances that had a hormonal action in livestock farming. The ECJ stressed that the Community institutions must pursue their policy by the least onerous means, and that the disadvantages must not be disproportionate to the aims of the measure. It then continued as follows[110]: **21–030**

> "However, with regard to judicial review of compliance with those conditions it must be stated that in matters concerning the common agricultural policy the Community legislature has a discretionary power which corresponds to the political responsibilities given to it by arts 40 and 43[111] of the Treaty. Consequently, the legality of a measure adopted in that sphere can be affected only if the measure is manifestly inappropriate having regard to the objective which the competent institution is seeking to pursue."

The guiding principle was stated in *British American Tobacco*[112]: this measure of review will be deemed appropriate whenever the EU legislature exercises a broad discretion involving political, economic or social choices requiring it to make complex assessments. A decision will only be overturned if it is "manifestly disproportionate" to the objective being pursued.

It would nonetheless be mistaken to conclude that there is no difference between proportionality as interpreted in this manner and *Wednesbury* unreasonableness. The test may be cast in terms of manifest disproportionality, but the reality is that the EU courts will normally examine the claimant's allegations in considerably more detail than is commonly to be found within *Wednesbury* review.[113]

The case law furnishes interesting insights into why the ECJ adopted this more limited form of review. An important consideration is that the ECJ did not wish to be continually faced with challenges to EC norms in areas where the Community institutions had discretionary power and had to balance variables, which could often conflict. If the ECJ countenanced more intensive review for proportionality in, for example, the agricultural sphere then it would be continually faced with arguments that the variables should have been balanced in some other way.

---

[109] *R. v The Minister of Agriculture, Fisheries and Food and the Secretary of State for Health, Ex p. Fedesa* (C-331/88) [1990] E.C.R. I-4023.

[110] *Fedesa* [1990] E.C.R. I-4023 at 4063; *Schrader v Hauptzollamt Gronau* (265/87) [1989] E.C.R. 2237.

[111] Now arts 40–43 TFEU.

[112] *R. v Secretary of State for Health, Ex p. British American Tobacco (Investments) Ltd and Imperial Tobacco Ltd* (C-491/01) [2002] E.C.R. I-11453 at [123]; *The Queen (Swedish Match AB and Swedish Match UK Ltd) v Secretary of State for Health* (C-210/03) [2004] E.C.R. I-11893 at [48]; *The Queen (S.P.C.M. SA) v Secretary of State for the Environment, Food and Rural Affairs* (C-558/07) [2009] E.C.R. I-5783 at [41]–[42]; *The Queen (Vodafone Ltd) v Secretary of State for Business, Enterprise and Regulatory Reform* (C-58/08) [2010] E.C.R. I-4999 at [51]–[53].

[113] Craig, *EU Administrative Law* (2012), Ch.19.

Evidence of reluctance to overturn the Community's choices in relation to agriculture is evident in other cases,[114] and in the secondary literature.[115]

The relative intensity with which proportionality is applied in the agricultural sphere is not necessarily indicative of how the concept is used in other cases that come within this third category. There are other areas where the ECJ is willing to intervene with a more searching form of inquiry, particularly where the discretionary power is more narrowly circumscribed. This third category of cases may, therefore, have to be broken down into more discrete categories to reflect this fact.

6. REASONABLENESS, PROPORTIONALITY AND REVIEW

21–031 It is now appropriate to consider how the general shape of substantive review might develop. There is a vibrant debate as to whether proportionality should be regarded as a general head of review, or whether the terrain of substantive review should continue to be divided between rationality and proportionality, with the latter confined to rights-based cases and those concerning EU law.[116]

---

[114] *Balkan Import-Export GmbH v Hauptzollamt Berlin Packhof* (5/73) [1973] E.C.R. 1091; *Stolting v Hauptzollamt Hamburg-Jonas* (138/78) [1979] E.C.R. 713; *Racke v Hauptzollamt Mainz* (98/78) [1979] E.C.R. 69; *Ludwigshafener Walzmuhle Erling KG v Council* (197–200, 243, 245, 247/80) [1981] E.C.R. 3211; (C-8/89) *Zardi v Consorzio Agrario Provinciale di Ferrara* (C-8/89) [1990] E.C.R. I-2515 at 2532–2533; *R. (Omega Air Ltd) v Secretary of State for the Environment, Transport and the Regions* (C-27/00) [2002] E.C.R. I-2569; *Maatschap Toeters and MC Verberk v Productschap Vee en Vlees* (C-171/03) [2004] E.C.R. I-10945; *Denka International BV v Commission* (334/07) [2009] E.C.R. II-4205 at [139]; *Gowan Comércio Internacional e Serviços Lda v Ministero della Salute* (C-77/09) [2010] E.C.R. I 3533 at [82].

[115] C. Vajda, "Some Aspects of Judicial Review within the Common Agricultural Policy—Part II" (1979) E.L. Rev. 341, 347–348.

[116] M. Elliott, "The Human Rights Act 1998 and the Standard of Substantive Review" (2001) 60 C.L.J. 301; M. Taggart, "Reinventing Administrative Law", in N. Bamforth and P. Leyland (eds), *Public Law in a Multi-layered Constitution* (Oxford: Hart, 2003), Ch.12; M. Taggart, "Proportionality, Deference, Wednesbury" [2008] N.Z.L.R. 423; M. Hunt, "Against Bifurcation", in D. Dyzenhaus, M. Hunt and G. Huscroft (eds), *A Simple Common Lawyer—Essays in Honour of Michael Taggart* (Oxford: Hart, 2009), Ch.6; T. Hickman, *Public Law after the Human Rights Act* (Oxford: Hart, 2010), Ch.9; P. Craig, "Proportionality, Rationality and Review" [2010] N.Z.L.R. 265; T. Hickman, "Problems for Proportionality" [2010] N.Z.L.R. 303; J. King, "Proportionality: a Halfway House" [2010] N.Z.L.R. 327; D. Knight, "Calibrating the Rainbow of Judicial Review: Recognizing Variable Intensity" [2010] N.Z.L.R. 393; D. Mullan, "Proportionality—A Proportionate Response to an Emerging Crisis in Canadian Judicial Review Law?" [2010] N.Z.L.R. 233; J. Goodwin, "The Last Defence of Wednesbury" [2012] P.L. 445; T. Endicott, "Proportionality and Incommensurability" Oxford University Legal Research Paper Series, No 40/2012; C. Chan, "Proportionality and Invariable Baseline Intensity of Review" (2013) 33 L.S. 1; Sir P. Sales, "Rationality, Proportionality and the Development of the Law" (2013) 129 L.Q.R. 223; P. Craig, "The Nature of Reasonableness Review" [2013] C.L.P. 1; Lord Carnwath, "From Rationality to Proportionality in the Modern Law" (2014) 44 H.K.L.J. 1; Lady M. Arden, *Human Rights and European Law, Building New Legal Orders* (Oxford: Oxford University Press, 2015), Ch.4; J. Jowell, "Proportionality and Reasonableness: Neither Merger nor Takeover", in M. Elliott and H. Wilberg (eds.), *The Scope and Intensity of Substantive Review, Traversing Taggart's Rainbow* (Oxford: Hart, 2015), Ch.3; J. Varuhas, "Against Unification", ibid. Ch.5; P. Craig, *UK, EU and Global Administrative Law: Foundations and Challenges* (Cambridge: Cambridge University Press, 2015), pp.256–260, 268–271; P. Craig,

A. Retention of Traditional *Wednesbury* alongside Proportionality

The courts could persist with *Wednesbury* review outside those areas where they have to apply proportionality. Different grounds of challenge would be dealt with under different heads of review, and *Wednesbury* would be interpreted in the traditional sense articulated by Lord Greene as overlaid by Lord Diplock. Those who favour this approach argue that it prevents the courts from intruding too far into the merits and obviates the need for any complex balancing, both of which are said to be undesirable features of proportionality. It is argued that the traditional approach preserves the proper boundaries of judicial intervention. This was Taggart's preferred approach. Proportionality should be the test in rights-based cases, with narrow rationality review remaining the test for what he described as "public wrongs". Taggart explicitly limited rationality review to the narrow form of *Wednesbury* unreasonableness.[117] He thereby rejected proportionality as a general head of review, and the broader form of rationality review articulated by some courts that will be considered below. The "rainbow of judicial review" was therefore starkly divided, with rights-based cases subject to proportionality, while "public wrongs" would only be overturned if Lord Greene M.R.'s extreme form of irrationality could be established. This is a possible approach, but there are however two problems with it, the first being practical, the second being normative. **21–032**

i. Practical objection

The practical objection is that rationality review *cast in these terms*[118] would almost never avail claimants. It is difficult to think of any cases in which the real facts match up to the standard of irrationality required by Lord Greene and Lord Diplock. We live in the real world, and the consequences of any test must be evaluated with respect to real world situations, not hypothetical examples, however famous they might be. The classic example of the decision that is so unreasonable that no reasonable public authority would have made it is the dismissal of the teacher because of the colour of her hair. Lord Diplock spoke in similarly extreme terms. **21–033**

Taggart's solution is therefore dependent on the claimant in a case concerning "public wrongs" being able to prove irrationality of this magnitude. It will rarely if ever be possible. This test, if taken seriously, constitutes an almost insurmountable hurdle for claimants. Decisions of such extremity might in principle occur. This should not mask the reality, which is that it is very difficult, if not impossible, to come up with real world cases in which such extreme irrationality has been present. It is for this very reason that the reality in terms of

"Proportionality and Judicial Review: A UK Historical Perspective", in S. Vogenauer and S. Weatherill (eds.), *General Principles of Law: European and Comparative Perspectives* (Oxford: Oxford University Press, 2016).

[117] Taggart, "Proportionality, Deference, Wednesbury" [2008] N.Z.L.R. 423 at 471–472, 477–479.

[118] It is of course possible to find cases that come within broader tests of rationality review, the discussion in the text is as to whether it is possible to satisfy a test framed in the terms Lord Greene and Lord Diplock, cf. Baroness Hale *Keyu* [2015] UKSC 69.

positive law[119] is that the courts have stretched the concept of rationality, often without admitting that they are doing so, and used it to catch administrative action that could not be regarded as coming within the very narrow sense of rationality advanced by Lord Greene and Lord Diplock. We shall return to this point.

ii. Normative objection

21–034 Taggart's view is also problematic from a normative perspective. There is little in the way of detailed normative justification given for rationality review cast in the form used by Lord Greene and Lord Diplock. The explanations proffered tend to rest content with generalities couched in terms of the courts not substituting judgment on the merits of discretionary determinations, because of separation of powers concerns. These claims must however be substantiated, not merely asserted.

It can be accepted that the courts should not substitute judgment on the merits of discretionary determinations. There are good reasons for this grounded in the separation of powers. It does not, however, provide the normative justification for the narrowness of traditional rationality review. All tests for substantive review place constraints on the decision that can be reached by the administrator, and that is true also for narrow rationality review. It is the extent and nature of the constraint that is in issue. There are various other judicial options in terms of tests for review, which do not entail judicial substitution of judgment on the merits, but which nonetheless entail more searching scrutiny of the challenged decision. It is therefore insufficient to invoke some mantra as to separation of powers and the avoidance of merits review as if this provided a complete argument in favour of very narrow rationality review.

This was recognised most explicitly in the judicial arena by Lord Cooke.[120] He accepted the separation of powers rationale for the courts not substituting judgment on the merits, but denied that this should lead to a very narrow form of rationality review of the kind espoused by Lord Greene and Lord Diplock. It was not necessary to have such an extreme formulation in order to ensure that the courts remained within their proper bounds as required by the separation of powers, and advocated a simpler and less extreme test: was the decision one that a reasonable authority could have reached.

Taggart presented his argument of narrow rationality review as part of the "rainbow of review", but the difference for claimants who fall within the respective parts of the rainbow is stark indeed. The limit of rationality review for

---

[119] See *Niarchos* [1981] J.P.L. 118; *Rafferty* [1987] 1 W.L.R. 457; *Prime Time Promotions* [1999] C.O.D. 265; *Tawfick* [2001] A.C.D. 28; *Wagstaff* [2001] 1 W.L.R. 292; *Howard* [2002] EWHC 396 (Admin); *Von Brandenburg* [2002] Q.B. 235; *Paul-Coker* [2006] EWHC 497 (Admin); *Walker* [2008] EWCA Civ 30; *LH* [2006] EWHC 1190 (Admin); *Rogers* [2006] 1 W.L.R. 2649; *Bradley* [2008] EWCA Civ 36; *Boyejo* [2009] EWHC 3261 (Admin); *Barnett* [2009] EWHC 2004 (Admin); *Paine* 2009 WL 4248563; *Stagecoach Group* [2010] C.A.T. 14; *Budd* [2010] EWHC 1056 (Admin); *Technoprint Plc* [2010] EWHC 581 (Admin); *Pampisford Estate Farms* [2010] EWHC 131 (Admin); *O* [2011] EWCA Civ 925; A. Le Sueur, "The Rise and Ruin of Unreasonableness?" [2005] J.R. 32; *A* [1999] 4 All E.R. 860; *Balchin* [1997] C.O.D. 146.

[120] *ITF* [1999] 2 A.C. 418 at 452; *Daly* [2001] 2 A.C. 532 at 549.

those who fall within the "public wrongs" part of this spectrum means that it will be rare if ever for such claimants to satisfy the test for review advanced by Taggart. We should not live in a world where "public wrongs" are subject to no meaningful judicial scrutiny. It does not fit the reality of the positive law, nor is it desirable in normative terms. This is more especially so given that there are many interests that do not qualify as rights, but are nonetheless of real significance for the individuals concerned.

B. Retention of Modified *Wednesbury* alongside Proportionality

We have already noted that many decisions in effect embody a broader sense of rationality review than that used by Lord Greene and Lord Diplock.[121] The courts could then retain the *Wednesbury* test for those areas not covered by the European Union or the HRA, but give it the tougher meaning ascribed by Lord Cooke: a decision would be overturned if it was one which a reasonable authority could or should not have made. This standard of review could also vary in intensity, depending on the subject matter. This option is, somewhat paradoxically, more unstable than that just considered, and the reasons why this is so are revealing. **21–035**

The premise of Lord Cooke's thesis is undoubtedly correct. His Lordship argued that the proper boundaries between courts and administration could be secured by a test that was less exaggerated than the traditional *Wednesbury* formulation. To be sure the courts should not substitute their judgment on the merits for that of the administration, but this could be avoided even where the reasonableness test was formulated in the manner articulated by Lord Cooke.

The instability of this option becomes apparent when we probe further. We should recall that the "virtue" of the traditional Lord Greene reading of the test was that there was no need to press further. The really outrageous decision would be all too evident and indefensible. If we shift to Lord Cooke's reading of the test this no longer holds true. It would be incumbent on the judiciary to articulate in some ordered manner the rationale for finding that an administrative choice was one which could not reasonably have been made, where that choice fell short of manifest absurdity. If the courts are not obliged to explain their own findings in this manner then the new test will create unwarranted judicial discretion.

It is, however, difficult to see that the factors that would be taken into account in this regard would be very different from those used in the proportionality calculus. The courts would in some manner want to know how necessary the measure was, and how suitable it was, for attaining the desired end. These are the first two parts of the proportionality calculus. It is also possible that under Lord **21–036**

[121] See *Niarchos* [1981] J.P.L. 118; *Rafferty* [1987] 1 W.L.R. 457; *Prime Time Promotions* [1999] C.O.D. 265; *Tawfick* [2001] A.C.D. 28; *Wagstaff* [2001] 1 W.L.R. 292; *Howard* [2002] EWHC 396 (Admin); *Von Brandenburg* [2002] Q.B. 235; *Paul-Coker* [2006] EWHC 497 (Admin); *Walker* [2008] EWCA Civ 30; *LH* [2006] EWHC 1190 (Admin); *Rogers* [2006] 1 W.L.R. 2649; *Bradley* [2008] EWCA Civ 36; *Boyejo* [2009] EWHC 3261 (Admin); *Barnett* [2009] EWHC 2004 (Admin); *Paine* 2009 WL 4248563; *Stagecoach Group* [2010] C.A.T. 14; *Budd* [2010] EWHC 1056 (Admin); *Technoprint Plc* [2010] EWHC 581 (Admin); *Pampisford Estate Farms* [2010] EWHC 131 (Admin); *O* [2011] EWCA Civ 925; A. Le Sueur, "The Rise and Ruin of Unreasonableness?" [2005] J.R. 32; *A* [1999] 4 All E.R. 860; *Balchin* [1997] C.O.D. 146.

Cooke's formulation a court might well, expressly or impliedly, look to see whether the challenged measure imposed excessive burdens on the applicant, the third part of the proportionality formula. If these factors are taken into account, and some such factors will have to be, then it will be difficult to persist with the idea that this is really separate from a proportionality test. There will then be an impetus to extend proportionality from the areas where it currently already applies, the European Union and the HRA, to general domestic law challenges.

It might be argued that rationality review of the kind advocated by Lord Cooke, or something akin thereto, is correct in normative terms and consonant with the separation of powers, but that it does not collapse into proportionality review. This argument must however be sustained, not just asserted, and it would have to be shown to be preferable in terms of substantive legitimacy. It would therefore have to be shown that the kinds of inquiry explicitly undertaken via proportionality analysis, necessity, suitability, etc. would not implicitly occur when resolving the rationality of the challenged action. It would have to be shown why, insofar as this inquiry entails some assessment of the relative weight of the respective interests and the balance between them, that this is not substantively legitimate outside the sphere of rights, more especially because the inquiry would be undertaken via varying intensity of review. It would also have to be shown that more intensive rationality review could be undertaken without explicitly or implicitly assessing the relative weight of the respective interests and the balance between them.

C. Proportionality as the General Criterion of Review: Arguments in Favour

21–037 "Proportionability" was part of judicial review from the 17th century and is thus not alien to the common law. The current debate is as to whether proportionality should be a head of review applicable to all administrative action. It does not mean, as argued by Hickman, that proportionality should be the only substantive ground of review, or that the whole doctrinal ensemble of judicial review would be controlled by proportionality.[122] The other grounds of substantive judicial review such as review for error of law, error of fact, propriety of purpose, relevancy, legitimate expectations, and equality would continue to exist. Proportionality is a general head of review in EU law and subsists alongside other well-recognised heads of judicial review. Insofar as proportionality is part of UK doctrinal inquiry in cases concerned with, for example, equality and legitimate expectations, this is because the courts have decided for good reason that it should play a role when adjudicating on these concepts. This is, however, already so under the existing law. It is not dependent on whether proportionality is a general head of review.

---

[122] Hickman, *Public Law after the Human Rights Act* (2010), pp.272–273; Hickman, "Problems for Proportionality" [2010] N.Z.L.R. 303; P. Craig, "Proportionality and Judicial Review: A UK Historical Perspective", in S. Vogenauer and S. Weatherill (eds.), *General Principles of Law: European and Comparative Perspectives* (Oxford: Oxford University Press, 2016).

i. *Simplicity*

21–038 It would, other things being equal, be advantageous for the same test to be used to deal with claims arising under EU law, the HRA, and other non-HRA domestic law challenges. This is particularly so because it will be common to find at least two such claims in an application for judicial review, and it is not uncommon to find cases where all three may be relevant. There will moreover be difficult borderline cases concerning application of the HRA. The nature of the test to be applied should not differ radically depending on which side of the borderline a case is said to fall.

ii. *Structured inquiry*

21–039 The proportionality test provides a structured form of inquiry. The three-part proportionality inquiry focuses the attention of the agency being reviewed, and the court undertaking the review. The agency has to justify its behaviour in the terms demanded by this inquiry. It has to explain why it thought that the challenged action really was necessary and suitable to reach the desired end, and why it felt that the action did not impose an excessive burden on the applicant. If the reviewing court is minded to overturn the agency choice it too will have to do so in a manner consonant with the proportionality inquiry. It will be for the court to explain why it felt that the action was not necessary, etc. in the circumstances. It is precisely this more structured analysis which has often been lacking when the "monolithic" *Wednesbury* test has been applied. This was recognised by Lord Mance in *Kennedy*, where he stated that[123]:

> "The advantage of the terminology of proportionality is that it introduces an element of structure into the exercise, by directing attention to factors such as suitability or appropriateness, necessity and the balance or imbalance of benefits and disadvantages. There seems no reason why such factors should not be relevant in judicial review even outside the scope of Convention and EU law. Whatever the context, the court deploying them must be aware that they overlap potentially and that the intensity with which they are applied is heavily dependent on the context. In the context of fundamental rights, it is a truism that the scrutiny is likely to be more intense than where other interests are involved."

iii. *Reasoned inquiry*

21–040 A corollary is that proportionality facilitates a reasoned inquiry of a kind that is often lacking under the traditional *Wednesbury* approach. This is brought out forcefully by Laws J who stated that under proportionality:

> "… it is not enough merely to set out the problem, and assert that within his jurisdiction the Minister chose this or that solution, constrained only by the requirement that his decision must have been one which a reasonable Minister might make".

It was rather for the court to

---

[123] *Kennedy* [2014] UKSC 20 at [54]; *Pham* [2015] UKSC 19 at [95].

> "… test the solution arrived at, and pass it only if substantial factual considerations are put forward in its justification: considerations which are relevant, reasonable and proportionate to the aim in view".[124]

It will often only be possible to test the soundness of an argument by requiring reasoned justification of this kind.

iv. *Intensity of review*

21–041 EU law shows that proportionality can be applied with varying degrees of intensity so as to accommodate different types of decision subject to judicial review.[125] If proportionality were to become a general head of review this does not therefore mean that it would apply in the same way to rights and non-rights cases. This has not been advocated by any commentator, it is not demanded by the concept of proportionality, nor is it required by judicial doctrine. There is an emerging sophisticated body of work elaborating the types of factor that should be taken into account in deciding on the appropriate intensity of review in cases concerned with resource allocation and social and economic rights.[126]

EU law reveals the benefits of proportionality review, even where it is applied with low intensity. It is often assumed that low intensity proportionality review is much the same as the *Wednesbury* test. The conclusion reached on the respective tests may be the same, but this nonetheless masks important differences in the way they are applied. Thus, the structured form of the proportionality inquiry will normally lead the ECJ to examine the arguments of the parties in a degree of detail that is rarely found in cases employing the *Wednesbury* test.[127]

D. Proportionality as the General Criterion of Review: Arguments Against

i. *Intrusive*

21–042 It is argued that proportionality allows too great an intrusion into the merits. Proportionality does not, however, entail substitution of judgment on the merits by the courts for that of the agency.[128] Proportionality does entail some view about the merits, since otherwise the three-part inquiry could not be undertaken. The test is also applied with varying intensity of review. However, the way in which Lord Greene's test has been applied in practice to strike down agency action falling far short of the absurd also demands some view of the merits. The

[124] *First City Trading* [1997] 1 C.M.L.R. 250 at 279.

[125] Craig, *EU Administrative Law* (2012), Chs 19–20.

[126] K. Syrett, "Opening Eyes to the Reality of Scarce Health Care Resources?" [2006] P.L. 664; J. King, "The Justiciability of Resource Allocation" (2007) 70 M.L.R. 197; A. Pillay, "Courts, Variable Standards of Review and Resource Allocation: Developing a Model for the Enforcement of Social and Economic Rights" [2007] E.H.R.L.R. 616; C. Newdick, "Judicial Review: Low-Priority Treatment and Exceptional Case Review" [2007] Med. L.R. 236.

[127] Craig, *EU Administrative Law*, Ch.19.

[128] *Bank Mellat v HM Treasury* [2013] UKSC 39 at [21], [71]; *First City Trading* [1997] 1 C.M.L.R. 250 at 278–279.

same can be said a fortiori about the revised meaning of the reasonableness test proposed by Lord Cooke. Arguments to the effect that proportionality is too intrusive are therefore predicated on some assumption as to what the appropriate intensity of review should be, which brings us back to the earlier inquiry.

I do not believe that adherence to very low intensity rationality review cast in terms of the Lord Greene/Diplock test is desirable, nor do I believe that it is demanded by the separation of powers. In practical terms, litigants would never get beyond the court door if the strictures of this version of the rationality test were taken seriously. In normative terms, it has never been apparent precisely why the separation of powers is thought to demand this exiguous form of judicial oversight. Nor is it self-evident why the divide between rights and non-rights based cases is felt to warrant this chasm in the test for judicial review. This is more especially so, given that the far more demanding test used in relation to rights is premised on the assertion that a right might have been infringed, not that it necessarily has been. There are many interests falling short of rights that are of real importance for individuals, which warrant meaningful judicial oversight, even if this is not as intense as that which pertains in rights-based cases.[129]

There is, moreover, no reason to believe that the level of proportionality protection would be pitched at too high a level, simply because the test is cast in terms of necessity. This is a concern voiced by King.[130] He argues that rationality admits of more than one solution, and hence is capable of embracing the disagreement that characterises plural societies. He maintains that necessity is an absolute and precludes the taking account of such differences of view. This does not cohere with the application of the necessity test by courts in the UK, EU or ECHR. Thus to take one example, Lord Sumption in *Bank Mellat* rejected counsel's suggestion that a measure would be disproportionate if any more limited measure was capable of achieving the objective. The "effectiveness of the measure and the degree of interference are not absolute values but questions of degree, inversely related to each other", and thus the question was whether "a less intrusive measure could have been used without unacceptably compromising the objective".[131] The very fact that some measure of deference/respect/weight is accorded to the primary decision-maker even in rights-based cases serves, moreover, to moderate the application of necessity, thereby enabling the views of the executive or legislature to be taken into account when deciding whether the action was indeed necessary. This is reflective of the fact that people can disagree as to whether action is indeed necessary, and that the views of the legislature or executive may be deserving of some respect/weight in that regard. This is of course a fortiori so in relation to the application of proportionality in non-rights based cases.

[129] See also to similar effect, Mullan, "Proportionality—A Proportionate Response to an Emerging Crisis in Canadian Judicial Review Law?" [2010] N.Z.L.R. 233; Hunt, "Against Bifurcation" in Dyzenhaus, Hunt and Huscroft (eds), *A Simple Common Lawyer—Essays in Honour of Michael Taggart* (2009).

[130] King, "Proportionality: a Halfway House" [2010] N.Z.L.R. 327.

[131] *Bank Mellat* [2013] UKSC 39 at [20].

ii. Inappropriate

21–043 It is contended that proportionality cannot readily be applied in cases that do not concern rights, because it is difficult or impossible to decide on the interests to be balanced and the weight to be ascribed to such interests. Thus, Taggart maintains that "without the anchor of 'rights' as a starting point the proportionality methodology loses many of its touted advantages as a transparent and visible tool for ensuring reasonable or proportionate decision-making", with the result that "it has a 'determinate-looking' structure without the reality of determinacy".[132] Taggart therefore concludes that review must remain bifurcated between rights and non-rights cases. This objection to proportionality review is misplaced for four reasons.

First, the argument is premised on certain assumptions as to the application of proportionality review in rights-based cases. The assumption is that the constitution or the legislature has stated that certain rights are deserving of judicial protection, and that this "anchors" proportionality in a way that is not possible in non-rights cases. This premise conceals as much as it reveals. The constitution or the legislature may well indicate that certain interests are worthy of special protection by denominating them as rights and enshrining them in a constitution, or a statute such as the Human Rights Act 1998. This does not, however, render the balancing process in such cases straightforward, or less problematic than if proportionality were to be applied in non-rights cases. The reason is not hard to divine. Constitutional or statutory recognition of certain interests as rights still leaves open all the difficult issues that are routinely addressed in the case law, both in the UK and elsewhere. These include the relative importance of the rights included within the constitution or governing statute, the range of justificatory responses open to the government or legislature, and the fact that the same right, even if prima facie high on the list of protected rights, can be deployed in very different circumstances. These issues are played out in the case law on proportionality in rights-based cases, and in the related jurisprudence on the extent to which the courts should accord the initial decision-maker some deference/respect/weight when making the proportionality calculus. The reality is that identification of a right affected by the challenged governmental action constitutes merely the starting point for the proportionality analysis, and does not in itself resolve the issues identified above.

Second, the identification of the respective interests that are considered within the proportionality calculus in non-rights based cases is readily apparent from systems, such as the European Union. The proportionality analysis is framed by the parties' arguments. The claimant will contend that, for example, a certain regulatory measure is disproportionate in relation to its trade interests. The defendant will then adduce arguments as to why the measure was necessary and suitable. Its argument will be grounded on the legislation. It will contend that the contested measure was necessary or suitable in the light of the statutory objectives, and if the case reaches this point it will also contend that the challenged measure does not violate the third limb of the proportionality test. The court will evaluate the contending arguments. The purposes underlying the

[132] Taggart, "Proportionality, Deference, Wednesbury" [2008] N.Z.L.R. 423, 477.

legislation thus form the natural focus for the proportionality analysis, coupled with the impact of the regulatory power on the claimant. This is exactly what one would expect and the EU courts undertake the requisite inquiry day in day out.

It can be readily accepted that the judicial inquiry is evaluative in terms of its identification of the statutory objectives, the application of the different limbs of the proportionality test and the weight accorded to the claimant's interest. No one has contended to the contrary. There is, however, no warrant for saying that the proportionality inquiry requires greater normative evaluation in cases where rights are not present than in those where they are, more especially because the former category of case will normally entail low intensity proportionality review. Nor is there any warrant for the view expressed by Taggart that proportionality loses many of its touted advantages when applied in non- rights cases. To the contrary, it continues to provide a structured framework for inquiry through which to decide whether the contested action should survive judicial scrutiny.[133]

Third, it is no answer to the preceding point to contend that the courts should not be making such evaluative judgments in non-rights cases concerning the importance of the claimant's interest, and the purposes that the legislative scheme is designed to serve, since rationality review of the kind articulated by Lord Cooke or anything akin thereto cannot be undertaken without recourse to such normative evaluation. It could indeed be said with justification that to attempt such rationality scrutiny without addressing such issues would itself be irrational. We have already seen that the original conception of rationality articulated by Lord Greene and Lord Diplock is not reflected in the courts' jurisprudence. Some courts have applied a test more akin to that espoused by Lord Cooke, even if they have not been willing to admit this. Rationality review of this nature cannot be applied without implicitly or explicitly according some weight to the claimant's interest. It cannot be undertaken without assessment of the objectives underlying the statutory scheme. The decision as to whether the decision is rational requires the courts to undertake much the same inquiry as that done explicitly via proportionality, albeit not so overtly or clearly. **21–044**

Fourth, there may be certain types of case that are unsuited to a proportionality analysis.[134] This argument was made by Lord Hoffmann in relation to the Sunday trading cases, which required national courts to decide whether national bans on Sunday trading were proportionate in terms of their restriction on cross-border trade for the purposes of EU law. The ECJ became mindful of these difficulties and resolved the proportionality itself, rather than leaving it to national courts.[135] Whatever view one takes about this particular example, it is not an argument for rejecting proportionality as a general head of review, but for ensuring that its application is subject to the same threshold principles which apply generally within administrative law. The reach of proportionality must be limited by

---

[133] Craig, *EU Administrative Law*, Ch 19.

[134] Lord Hoffmann, "The Influence of the European Principle of Proportionality upon English Law", in Ellis (ed.), *The Principle of Proportionality in the Laws of Europe* (1999), pp.107–115.

[135] *Stoke on Trent City Council v B & Q* [1991] 1 A.C. 49.

justiciability.[136] The same is also true for any form of rationality scrutiny that ventures over and beyond the bare minimum countenanced by the literal reading of Lord Greene's and Lord Diplock's tests.

iii. Legal certainty

21–045 It is argued that proportionality would lead to legal uncertainty,[137] because invocation of proportionality tells one little as to the standard of review, or the intensity with which it is applied. It can be acknowledged that judges may on occasion differ as to which test of proportionality review should be applicable in a particular case.[138]

This criticism of proportionality is nonetheless striking to say the very least, given the uncertainty that besets the meaning of irrationality. It is over 60 years post-*Wednesbury*, and over 300 years since the advent of some form of rationality review in the United Kingdom. The bottom line remains that we cannot produce a modern definition of rationality review, which is legally authoritative *and* where the mode of application coheres with the legal test. What we have is a legal test, *Wednesbury*, which cannot explain the current case law. This is coupled with various ad hoc modifications of the legal test by dicta in individual cases.

A sample of 200 recent rationality cases that did not involve rights revealed the following. Some courts continued to cite Lord Greene and/or Lord Diplock, while at the same time adjudicating on cases which would have been stopped at the outset if those criteria of rationality review had been taken seriously, since the alleged error came nowhere close to the kind of irrationality demanded by them.[139] Some cases simply concluded that the *Wednesbury* test had not been met on the facts, without any further indication as to how demanding the court perceived the test to be. In other cases the precise language of rationality review was modified so as to countenance more searching scrutiny, although there was no consistency in the actual wording used.[140] In yet other cases, the courts deployed the term "anxious scrutiny", the precise import of which varied within this sub-part of the jurisprudence.[141]

---

[136] W. Van Gerven, "The Effect of Proportionality on the Actions of Member States of the EC: National Viewpoints from Continental Europe", in Ellis (ed.), *The Principle of Proportionality in the Laws of Europe* (1999), pp.37–63.

[137] Hickman, "Problems for Proportionality" [2010] N.Z.L.R. 303.

[138] *R. (Sinclair Collis) v Secretary of State for Health* [2011] EWCA Civ 437.

[139] See for example *Niarchos* [1981] J.P.L. 118; *Rafferty* [1987] 1 W.L.R. 457; *Prime Time Promotions* [1999] C.O.D. 265; *Tawfick* [2001] A.C.D. 28; *Wagstaff* [2001] 1 W.L.R. 292; *Howard* [2002] EWHC 396 (Admin); *Von Brandenburg* [2002] Q.B. 235; *Paul-Coker* [2006] EWHC 497 (Admin); *Walker* [2008] EWCA Civ 30; *LH* [2006] EWHC 1190 (Admin); *Rogers* [2006] 1 W.L.R. 2649; *Bradley* [2008] EWCA Civ 36; *Boyejo* [2009] EWHC 3261 (Admin); *Barnett* [2009] EWHC 2004 (Admin); *Paine* 2009 WL 4248563; *Stagecoach Group* [2010] C.A.T. 14; *Budd* [2010] EWHC 1056 (Admin); *Technoprint Plc* [2010] EWHC 581 (Admin); *Pampisford Estate Farms* [2010] EWHC 131 (Admin); *O* [2011] EWCA Civ 925; A. Le Sueur, "The Rise and Ruin of Unreasonableness?" [2005] J.R. 32; *A* [1999] 4 All E.R. 860; *Balchin* [1997] C.O.D. 146.

[140] See for example *Niarchos* [1981] J.P.L. 118; *Rafferty* [1987] 1 W.L.R. 457; *Prime Time Promotions* [1999] C.O.D. 265; *Tawfick* [2001] A.C.D. 28; *Wagstaff* [2001] 1 W.L.R. 292; *Howard* [2002] EWHC 396 (Admin); *Von Brandenburg* [2002] Q.B. 235; *Paul-Coker* [2006] EWHC 497 (Admin); *Walker* [2008] EWCA Civ 30; *LH* [2006] EWHC 1190 (Admin); *Rogers* [2006] 1 W.L.R. 2649; *Bradley* [2008] EWCA Civ 36; *Boyejo* [2009] EWHC 3261 (Admin); *Barnett* [2009] EWHC

The reality is therefore that in many cases the courts have been applying rationality review that was broader, albeit still not easy to satisfy, than that articulated by Lord Greene and Lord Diplock. The problem is that we were never told definitively what that is, and indeed it is still not clear. Lord Cooke was exceptional and notable for his willingness to question openly the traditional orthodoxy, and to suggest a reformulated rationality test that better reflected the practice of what at least some courts had been doing, as well as being preferable in normative terms. **21–046**

The idea that there would be some net detriment in terms of legal certainty if proportionality were to be available as a general head of review is therefore predicated on a picture of the status quo that does not cohere with legal or practical reality. Working out the varying intensity of proportionality review would, moreover, not begin with a clean slate. To the contrary it would build on what was already in the UK case law, and draw on experience from elsewhere. Hickman's concern that legal certainty would be jeopardised by the "adoption of a single, entirely flexible, meta-principle of substantive review",[142] which would obscure the differentiated range of protection under the present law,[143] is misplaced. The reality is that the current law operates with varying intensities of review, and in that sense embodies a sliding scale.[144] This would not change if proportionality were to become a principle of review applicable to all kinds of administrative action.

iv. Cost

A final objection to proportionality review advanced by King is that it would lead to cost increases and greater ossification of administrative action.[145] These are important concerns. I do not, however, believe that the argument has been made out in relation to either concern. Space precludes detailed consideration of why this is so, which can be found elsewhere.[146] **21–047**

Suffice it to say for the present that there is no empirical evidence to sustain the conclusion that insofar as proportionality entails more searching review it would increase overall costs for the administration. The calculus of the likely overall cost implications of a change in the standard of review is complex, taking into account factors such as how many cases would be fought, how many would be settled and the length of the litigation. There is no reason to believe that viewed in the light of such factors proportionality would lead to an increase in costs, and it might well lead to a decrease. Nor is there empirical evidence that proportionality will ossify the capacity for administrative action. There is no

2004 (Admin); *Paine* 2009 WL 4248563; *Stagecoach Group* [2010] C.A.T. 14; *Budd* [2010] EWHC 1056 (Admin); *Technoprint Plc* [2010] EWHC 581 (Admin); *Pampisford Estate Farms* [2010] EWHC 131 (Admin); *O* [2011] EWCA Civ 925; A. Le Sueur, "The Rise and Ruin of Unreasonableness?" [2005] J.R. 32; *A* [1999] 4 All E.R. 860; *Balchin* [1997] C.O.D. 146.

141 P. Craig, "Judicial Review and Anxious Scrutiny: Foundations, Evolution and Application" [2015] P.L. 60.

142 Hickman *Public Law after the Human Rights Act* (2010), p.275.

143 Hickman *Public Law after the Human Rights Act* (2010), pp.275–277.

144 *Kennedy* [2014] UKSC 20; *Pham* [2015] UKSC 19.

145 King, "Proportionality: a Halfway House" [2010] N.Z.L.R. 327.

146 Craig, "Proportionality, Rationality and Review" [2010] N.Z.L.R. 265, 281–284.

evidence of this in the EU where proportionality is a general head of review, and the causes of any ossification-type problems in the USA, which does not use proportionality review, are different.

CHAPTER 22

LEGITIMATE EXPECTATIONS

1. CENTRAL ISSUES

i. The discussion in the previous chapter focused on reasonableness and proportionality and the way in which these concepts controlled abuse of discretion. The present chapter considers the way in which legal certainty and legitimate expectations influence the exercise of discretion.[1] 22–001

ii. The phrase "procedural legitimate expectation" denotes the existence of some process right the applicant claims to possess as the result of a promise or behaviour by the public body that generates the expectation. The procedural role of legitimate expectations has been discussed earlier.[2]

iii. The phrase "substantive legitimate expectation" captures the situation in which the applicant seeks a particular benefit or commodity, such as a welfare benefit or a licence, as the result of some promise, behaviour or representation made by the public body. The claim to such a benefit is founded on governmental action that is said to justify the existence of the relevant expectation.

iv. The issue concerning substantive legitimate expectation can arise where the representation, behaviour or promise made by the public body was prima facie lawful, in the sense that it was within the powers accorded to that

---

[1] C. Forsyth, "The Provenance and Protection of Legitimate Expectations" [1988] C.L.J. 238; P. Elias, "Legitimate Expectation and Judicial Review", in J. Jowell and D. Oliver (eds), *New Directions in Judicial Review* (London: Sweet & Maxwell, 1988), pp.37–50; P. Craig, "Legitimate Expectations: A Conceptual Analysis" (1992) 108 L.Q.R. 79; R. Singh, "Making Legitimate Use of Legitimate Expectations" (1994) 144 N.L.J. 1215; P. Craig, "Substantive Legitimate Expectations in Domestic and Community Law" [1996] C.L.J. 289; P. Craig, "Substantive Legitimate Expectations and the Principles of Judicial Review", in M. Andenas (ed.), *English Public Law and the Common Law of Europe* (London: Key Haven, 1998), Ch.3; Y. Dotan, "Why Administrators should be Bound by their Policies" (1997) 17 O.J.L.S. 23; P. Craig and S. Schonberg, "Substantive Legitimate Expectations after *Coughlan*" [2000] P.L. 684; S. Schonberg, *Legitimate Expectations in Administrative Law* (Oxford: Oxford University Press, 2000); R. Clayton, "Legitimate Expectations, Policy, and the Principle of Consistency" [2003] C.L.J. 93; P. Sales and K. Steyn, "Legitimate Expectations in English Public Law: An Analysis" [2004] P.L. 564; I. Steele, "Substantive Legitimate Expectations: Striking the Right Balance?" (2005) 121 L.Q.R. 300; R. Moules, *Actions Against Public Officials: Legitimate Expectations, Misstatements and Misconduct* (London: Sweet and Maxwell, 2009); C. Knight, "Expectations in Transition: Recent Developments in Legitimate Expectations" [2009] P.L. 15; J. Watson, "Clarity and Ambiguity: A New Approach to the Test of Legitimacy in the Law of Legitimate Expectations" (2010) 30 L.S. 633; C. Forsyth, "Legitimate Expectations Revisited" [2011] J.R. 429; P. Reynolds, "Legitimate Expectations and the Protection of Trust in Public Officials" [2011] P.L. 330.

[2] Ch.12.

body and the officer who made the representation. This is dealt with in the first half of the chapter. Important doctrinal issues that arise in this area include the rationale for according protection to such expectations, the conditions that must be satisfied before a prima facie expectation can be said to arise and the test for judicial review that should be applied when a public body seeks to resile from an unambiguous and specific representation.

v. The issue concerning substantive legitimate expectation can also arise where the representation was ultra vires the power of the public body, or officer who made the representation. This is considered in the second half of the chapter. The case law establishes that there can be no actionable legitimate expectation flowing from an ultra vires representation. The rationale for this will be examined below, as will the limited exceptions to this basic proposition. The current law can cause hardship to an individual who may have bona fide relied on a representation and had no reason to suspect that it was ultra vires. Possible reforms will be considered in the course of the analysis.

2. NATURE OF THE PROBLEM

A. Actual and Apparent Retroactivity

22–002 The connected concepts of legal certainty and legitimate expectations are found in many legal systems[3] although their precise content may vary.[4] The most obvious application of legal certainty is in the context of rules or decisions with an *actual retroactive effect*. Following Schwarze,[5] actual retroactivity covers the situation where a rule is introduced and applied to events that have already been concluded. This may occur either where the date of entry into force precedes the date of publication; or where the regulation applies to circumstances concluded before the entry into force of the measure.[6] The arguments against allowing such measures to have legal effect are compelling.[7] A basic tenet of the rule of law is that people ought to be able to plan their lives, with knowledge of the legal consequences of their actions.[8] This precept is violated by application of measures not in force at the time that the events took place.

There are also problems presented by cases of *apparent retroactivity*.[9] A person may have planned her actions on the basis of a policy choice made by the administration, and seeks redress when the chosen policy alters, even though this

---

[3] P. Craig, *EU Administrative Law*, 2nd edn (Oxford: Oxford University Press, 2012), Ch.18.

[4] J. Schwarze, *European Administrative Law* (London: Sweet & Maxwell, 1992), Ch.6.

[5] Schwarze, *European Administrative Law* (1992), p.1120.

[6] There can be complex issues concerning retroactivity, as exemplified by *AXA General Insurance Ltd v HM Advocate* [2012] UKSC 46.

[7] See, e.g. *Test Claimants in the FII Group Litigation v Revenue and Customs Comrs (formerly Inland Revenue Comrs)* [2012] UKSC 19 at [238]–[244].

[8] J. Raz, *The Authority of Law* (Oxford: Clarendon Press, 1979), Ch.11.

[9] The distinction between actual and apparent retroactivity is sometimes expressed alternatively in terms of a division between primary and secondary retroactivity, *Bowen v Georgetown University Hospital* 488 US 204 (1988).

alteration is only prospective and not retrospective. The problem of apparent retroactivity arises when rules change for the future, but have an impact on plans made in the past. The moral arguments against allowing laws to have actual retroactive effect are powerful. The category of apparent retroactivity is more problematic because the administration must have power to alter its policy for the future, even though this may have implications for the conduct of private parties planned on the basis of the pre-existing legal regime.

B. Legal Certainty, Legitimate Expectations and Legality

A public body may have made a representation that it would exercise its discretion in a particular manner, which has been reasonably relied on by the individual. This representation may be said to generate a legitimate expectation that the power would be exercised in this way. The *principle of legal certainty* would indicate that the individual ought to be able to plan her action on that basis.[10] There can, however, be a clash between this principle and the *principle of legality*, which has two meanings in this context. **22–003**

First, a public body may have made a representation within its power, but then seeks to depart from it. Or it may have published policy criteria for dealing with a particular issue, which criteria were intra vires, but it might now wish to adopt new tests for dealing with the same topic, these new criteria also being lawful. The individual may seek to rely on the initial representation or original statement of policy. A traditional objection to the individual being able to do so is that this would be a fetter on the discretion of the public body, which should be able to develop policy in the manner it believes to be in the public interest. The principle of legality is apparent in the doctrine that such a fetter on discretion would itself be ultra vires.

Second, the representation may have been outside the power of the public body or the officer who made it. The principle of legality manifests itself here in the simple form that the representation was ultra vires and therefore should not bind the public body.

The discussion within the first half of this chapter will be concerned with cases where the representation itself was intra vires, the first type of situation. This will be followed in the second half of the chapter by analysis of cases where the representation was ultra vires, the second type of situation.

3. INTRA VIRES REPRESENTATIONS: TYPES OF CASE

Problems of legal certainty and legitimate expectations can arise in a variety of circumstances. The second type of case also raises issues of equality. **22–004**

i. A general norm or policy choice, which an individual has relied on, has been replaced by a different policy choice.
ii. A general norm or policy choice has been departed from in the circumstances of a particular case.

[10] Schwarze, *European Administrative Law* (1992), pp.874–1173.

iii. There has been an individual representation relied on by a person, which the administration seeks to resile from in the light of a shift in general policy.
iv. There has been an individualised representation that has been relied on. The administrative body then changes its mind and makes an individualised decision that is inconsistent with the original representation.

The European Union and many continental systems recognise that these cases raise problems concerning legal certainty and legitimate expectations,[11] although distinctions may be drawn between types of case when devising the appropriate rules. Cases falling into the fourth category are normally treated as the strongest. This is because an unequivocal representation carries a particular moral force, and because holding the public body to that representation is less likely to have serious consequences for the administration. Cases falling into the first category are, by way of contrast, generally regarded as more problematic for reasons to be discussed later. Different principles of judicial review may, therefore, be appropriate in this type of case.

4. INTRA VIRES REPRESENTATIONS AND SUBSTANTIVE LEGITIMATE EXPECTATIONS: THE CONTENDING ARGUMENTS

A. Arguments in Favour[12]

i. Fairness in Public Administration

22–005 In *Hamble Fisheries* Sedley J put the case for recognition of substantive legitimate expectations in terms of fairness in public administration[13]:

> "[T]he real question is one of fairness in public administration. It is difficult to see why it is any less unfair to frustrate a legitimate expectation that something will or will not be done by the decision-maker than it is to frustrate a legitimate expectation that the applicant will be listened to before the decision-maker decides whether to take a particular step. Such a doctrine does not risk fettering a public body in the discharge of public duties because no individual can legitimately expect the discharge of public duties to stand still or be distorted because of that individual's peculiar position."

It is important to recognise that there are different values that should properly be taken into account in this regard; thus it would be wrong to allow changes of policy to be unduly fettered. There is, however, also the value of legal certainty, which encapsulates the fundamental idea that those who have relied on a particular policy choice made by an agency may have a valid claim for some protection when that policy alters. This is so notwithstanding that there may be room for debate as to the more detailed conditions that should be satisfied before such a claim can proceed.

---

[11] Schwarze, *European Administrative Law* (1992), Ch.6.
[12] Schonberg, *Legitimate Expectations in Administrative Law* (2000), Ch.1.
[13] *R. v Ministry of Agriculture, Fisheries and Food, Ex p. Hamble (Offshore) Fisheries Ltd* [1995] 2 All E.R. 714 QBD, at 724.

ii. *Reliance and trust in government*

The normative argument for according protection to substantive legitimate expectations is especially strong where the individual has detrimentally relied on a specific representation made by a public body. The meaning of detrimental reliance will be explored later. Suffice it to say for the present that where the individual has suffered such detriment as a result of justified reliance on a specific representation made by a public body, this generates a normative argument that some legal protection should be accorded. This is so notwithstanding the fact that the public body may need to resile from the expectation where the public interest so demands, since this can be part of the doctrinal legal rule. The very fact that a legal system does accord protection to substantive legitimate expectations can moreover enhance trust in government,[14] which is not only a good in itself, but may well render discharge of government business more efficient. 22–006

iii. *Equality*

Equality provides a further normative argument in favour of protecting substantive legitimate expectations. It is especially relevant in those instances where a public body seeks to depart from an existing policy in relation to a particular individual, while preserving the policy intact. The basic precept that like cases should be treated alike is clearly infringed in such instances. 22–007

iv. *Rule of law*

The argument thus far can be reinforced by rule of law considerations. The concept of legal certainty, which underlies much continental and EU thinking,[15] has close connections with the formal conception of the rule of law, with its concern for autonomy and the ability to plan one's life. 22–008

There is one aspect of the rule of law that is of particular relevance. It is concerned with the importance of considering matters across time. This idea is to be found in Raz's work.[16] Space precludes any detailed examination of his thesis. Suffice it to say for the present that Raz stresses the "principled faithful application of the law",[17] in which the courts, while faithful to legislation, act in a principled manner so as to "facilitate the integration of particular pieces of legislation with the underlying doctrines of the legal system".[18] This is justified in part to mix "the fruits of long-established traditions with the urgencies of short-term exigencies".[19]

It is precisely because the legislature or the executive can be susceptible to short-term influences, whether generated by elections or the need to respond

---

[14] Reynolds, "Legitimate Expectations and the Protection of Trust in Public Officials" [2011] P.L. 330; Forsyth, "Legitimate Expectations Revisited" [2011] J.R. 429.

[15] Schwarze, *European Administrative Law* (1992), Ch.6.

[16] J. Raz, *Ethics in the Public Domain* (Oxford: Oxford University Press, 1994), Ch.17.

[17] Raz, *Ethics in the Public Domain* (1994), p.373.

[18] Raz, *Ethics in the Public Domain* (1994), p.375.

[19] Raz, *Ethics in the Public Domain* (1994), p.376.

quickly to public pressure, that the courts should have a role as the guardians of longer-term tradition. This argument is important where the applicant has an expectation that is normatively justified. Raz's thesis can best be met by ensuring that the new policy choice should be interpreted by the courts in a manner which takes account of that expectation.

B. Arguments Against

22–009 The central argument against a doctrine of substantive legitimate expectations is that the government must be free to make policy changes,[20] and therefore existing policy should not be ossified or unduly fettered. The following points are relevant in this context.

First, the relevant aspect of the no fettering of discretion principle is derived from case law concerning the extent to which public bodies can be bound by contracts, which was considered earlier.[21] The limits of the argument must be borne firmly in mind. In a literal sense any form of contractual arrangement, more especially a long-term contract, circumscribes the ability of the public body to make choices concerning the relevant subject matter. If the no fettering argument was taken absolutely then such contracts would be illegal. Public bodies need, however, to make contracts in many areas. It is precisely for this reason that the case law makes clear that a public body is only precluded from making contracts where they are incompatible with the exercise of the statutory power or duty. The incompatibility must be reasonably foreseeable, and a possibility that this might occur is not sufficient in this respect. The doctrine of legitimate expectations should be subject to the same limit, but this does not preclude recognition of substantive legitimate expectations. It merely places a limit thereon.

Second, we should moreover be mindful of the reality of public contracting and the limited application of the no fettering principle. This principle has, for example not precluded the creation of PFI contracts worth billions of pounds.[22] This is so notwithstanding the fact that such contracts place constraints on the exercise of discretion in the relevant area, and are often scheduled for terms of 10, 15 or 25 years. While we should therefore be mindful of the need to ensure that the doctrine of legitimate expectations does not unduly fetter discretionary choices, we should also keep this in perspective. The constraints placed by PFI contracts far exceed any such constraining effect flowing from the doctrine of legitimate expectations. This is more especially so given that many such cases are concerned with the timing of the new policy, rather than precluding the policy choice.[23]

---

[20] *Hughes v Department of Health and Social Security* [1985] 1 A.C. 776 at 778; *R. (Niazi) v Secretary of State for the Home Department* [2008] EWCA Civ 755 at [41]; Forsyth, "Revisited" [2011] J.R. 429.

[21] See Ch.18. The fettering of discretion argument is also deployed to prevent a public body from adopting a policy that precludes it from disposing of a case without consideration of the merits of the individual applicant. This is not relevant here.

[22] See Ch.5.

[23] *R. v Secretary of State for the Home Department, Ex p. Hargreaves* [1997] 1 W.L.R. 906, CA (Civ Div).

Third, a doctrine of substantive legitimate expectations still requires an applicant to prove the requisite expectation on the facts of the case. The mere fact that there has been some change of policy does not mean that those who operated under the old policy would be able to prove the existence of such an expectation. EU law and German law, both of which protect substantive legitimate expectations, contain helpful jurisprudence on this issue. **22–010**

Fourth, the proof of the expectation is but the first step in the analysis. There is a second legal step, in which the courts inquire whether the public body had sufficient reasons to depart from the expectation. The test that should apply at this level will be examined below.

Finally, the preceding points help to explain why there is no evidence that recognition of substantive legitimate expectations in other legal systems has had any undue impact on the administration's freedom to develop policy.

5. INTRA VIRES REPRESENTATIONS AND LEGITIMATE EXPECTATIONS: *COUGHLAN*

The analysis begins with the case law prior to *Coughlan*,[24] when there was uncertainty as to whether the doctrine of substantive legitimate expectations was part of UK law. *Coughlan* will then be analysed. This will be followed by consideration of the factors taken into account in deciding whether an expectation is legitimate or not. The focus then shifts to the standard of review that applies in deciding whether a public body can resile from a substantive expectation that has been found to exist. We shall then discuss the application of the doctrine to the different types of case set out above. **22–011**

A. Prior to *Coughlan*

There was, prior to *Coughlan*, uncertainty as to whether substantive legitimate expectations were recognised within UK law, especially in the *first type of case* dealing with change of policy. In *Hamble Fisheries*[25] Sedley J argued strongly in favour of substantive legitimate expectations. Hamble Fisheries had purchased two small fishing vessels with the purpose of transferring fishing licences from those vessels to a larger vessel operated by the company. At the time of purchase, the policy of the Ministry was to allow such transfers. When that policy was subsequently changed, Hamble Fisheries claimed a breach of legitimate expectations. It accepted that policy could be altered for the future, but argued that the introduction of severe measures such as a moratorium with immediate effect constituted a breach of its legitimate expectations. Sedley J held, for the reasons given above, that a policy or practice could create legitimate expectations protected by administrative law. Moreover, in *Unilever*,[26] the Court of Appeal held that the Inland Revenue could not without prior warning discontinue a **22–012**

[24] *R. v North and East Devon Health Authority, Ex p. Coughlan* [2001] Q.B. 213, CA (Civ Div).

[25] *Hamble Fisheries* [1995] 2 All E.R. 714; *R. v Gaming Board of Great Britain, Ex p. Kingsley* [1996] C.O.D. 241 QBD.

[26] *R. v Inland Revenue Commissioners, Ex p. Unilever Plc* [1996] S.T.C. 681, CA (Civ Div).

practice, applied for 25 years, of accepting annual tax refund claims after the expiry of a statutory time limit. Its sudden change of conduct was an unfair breach of the applicant's legitimate expectations and therefore an abuse of power.

There was, however, another line of authority, which cast doubt on the existence of substantive legitimate expectations. In *Hargreaves*,[27] the Home Secretary had changed policy on prisoners' home leave with immediate effect in the light of concerns over crimes committed by prisoners on leave. This change had a traumatising effect on some prisoners. However, the Court of Appeal held that the Home Office had acted lawfully. Relying primarily on *Findlay*,[28] it rejected the approach taken in *Hamble Fisheries* as "heresy" and "wrong in principle".[29] There were aspects of the judgment that could be read as being opposed to any doctrine of substantive legitimate expectations. An alternative reading of the judgment was that no such expectation existed on the facts, and if it did exist the court would review the change of policy which disappointed that expectation only on the *Wednesbury* test.

22–013 There was, however, authority for substantive legitimate expectations in the *second type of case*, where a general policy or practice had been departed from in a particular case. In *Khan*[30] the applicant alleged that the Home Office had departed from a policy, communicated to him in writing, concerning approval of adoption of family members from abroad. Parker LJ held, drawing on Lord Denning's dicta in *HTV*[31] and *Laker Airways*,[32] that a public authority could only go back on a legitimate expectation after granting a hearing and then only if the overriding public interest demanded it.[33] In *Ruddock*[34] the applicant sought judicial review of a decision to intercept her telephone calls. Taylor J accepted her argument that fairness might require more than procedural protection, and that she could legitimately expect that the police would comply with published criteria for when telephone interception would take place, unless a departure was required for reasons of national security. In *Gangadeen*,[35] the Court of Appeal reaffirmed that "the Home Secretary is in ordinary circumstances obliged to act in accordance with his declared policy"[36] concerning deportation of foreigners with children lawfully residing in Britain.

There was also authority for a concept of substantive legitimate expectations in the *fourth type of case*, where a public body made an individual representation, which was relied on and the body subsequently sought to go back on the representation. In *Preston*[37] the applicant was assured by the Revenue in 1978

[27] *R. v Home Secretary, Ex p. Hargreaves* [1997] 1 W.L.R. 906, CA (Civ Div); *R. v Secretary of State for Transport, Ex p. Richmond upon Thames London LBC* [1994] 1 W.L.R. 74, CA (Civ Div); *R. v Secretary of State for Health, Ex p. US Tobacco International Inc* [1992] Q.B. 353 DC at 368–369.

[28] *Findlay, Re* [1985] A.C. 318.

[29] *Hargreaves* [1997] 1 W.L.R. 906 at 921.

[30] *R. v Home Secretary, Ex p. Khan* [1984] 1 W.L.R. 1337, CA (Civ Div).

[31] *HTV v Price Commission* [1976] I.C.R. 170, CA (Civ Div) at 185.

[32] *Laker Airways v Department of Trade* [1977] Q.B. 64,3 CA (Civ Div) at 707.

[33] *Khan* [1984] 1 W.L.R. 1337 at 1344.

[34] *R. v Home Secretary, Ex p. Ruddock* [1987] 1 W.L.R. 1482 QBD at 1487.

[35] *R. v Home Secretary, Ex p. Gangadeen* [1998] 1 F.L.R. 762, CA (Civ Div).

[36] *Gangadeen* [1998] 1 F.L.R. 762 at 766; *R. v Home Secretary, Ex p. Urmaza* [1996] C.O.D. 479 QBD.

[37] *R. v Inland Revenue Commissioners, Ex p. Preston* [1985] A.C. 835, HL.

that it would not raise further inquiries on certain tax affairs if he agreed to forgo interest relief he had claimed and to pay certain capital gains tax. The House of Lords held that the Revenue could not bind itself not to perform its statutory duties. It could therefore in principle go back on its assurance when it received new information about the applicant's dealings. A court could however hold the Revenue to its assurance where the unfairness to the applicant caused by exercising the statutory duty would amount to an abuse of power. The principles laid down in *Preston* were developed further in *MFK*.[38] These judgments were couched in terms of abuse of power and substantive fairness, rather than explicitly in terms of legitimate expectations. However, the reason why the administration's actions could be deemed abusive was that the representations had created normatively justified expectations and reliance in the affected individuals.

B. *Coughlan*

The law must now be seen in the light of *Coughlan*.[39] Coughlan had been very seriously injured in a traffic accident in 1971, and was cared for in Newcourt Hospital. The hospital was considered unsuited for modern care, and therefore Coughlan and other patients were moved to Mardon House in 1993. The patients were persuaded to move by representations made on behalf of the Health Authority that Mardon House would be more appropriate for their needs. The patients relied on an express assurance that they could live there for as long as they chose. In October 1998 the Health Authority decided to close Mardon House, and to move the patients to other facilities. A consultation paper issued in August 1998 preceded this decision, and recognised the force of the promise made to the residents in 1993. The consultation paper was placed before the Health Authority when it made its decision in October 1998. The Health Authority recognised that it had a number of options. It could continue to support Mardon House; it could, in breach of the original promise, assist residents to move elsewhere; or it could move other NHS services into Mardon House. In October 1998 the Health Authority decided to close the facility and move the residents elsewhere. The applicant challenged this as being in breach of the promise that she would have a home for life. The Court of Appeal distinguished between three situations. **22–014**

In the first, the court might decide that the public authority was only required to bear in mind its previous policy or other representation, giving it the weight it thought fit before deciding to change course. In such cases the court was confined

[38] *R. v Inland Revenue Commissioners, Ex p. MFK Underwriting Agencies Ltd* [1990] 1 W.L.R. 1545 QBD. See also *Matrix Securities Ltd v Inland Revenue Commissioners* [1994] 1 W.L.R. 334, HL.

[39] *Coughlan* [2001] Q.B. 213; *R. v Merton, Sutton and Wandsworth Health Authority, Ex p. P* [2001] A.C.D. 9 QBD; *R. (Theophilus) v London Borough of Lewisham* [2002] 3 All E.R. 851 QBD; *R. (B) v London Borough of Camden* [2001] EWHC 271 (Admin); *Niazi* [2008] EWCA Civ 755.

to reviewing the decision on *Wednesbury* grounds. *Findlay*[40] and *Hargreaves*[41] were treated as examples of this type of case.[42]

The second situation was where the court decided that there was a legitimate expectation of being consulted before a decision was taken. In such cases the court would require there to be an opportunity for consultation, unless there was an overriding reason to resile from the undertaking. The court would judge for itself the adequacy of the reason for the change of policy.[43] This situation was regarded as one where the court exercised "full review", deciding for itself whether what happened was fair.[44] The decision in *Ng Yuen Shiu*[45] was cited as an example of this type of case.

The third situation was where the court considered that a lawful promise had induced a substantive legitimate expectation. The court relied on previous authority for review in this type of case.[46] The court would decide whether the frustration of the expectation was so unfair that to take a new and different course of action would amount to an abuse of power. When the legitimacy of the expectation had been established, the court would weigh "the requirements of fairness against any overriding interest relied upon for the change of policy".[47] Most cases within this category were likely to be those where the expectation was confined to one person, or a few people. The present case was held to come within the third category.

22–015 The recognition of substantive legitimate expectations as part of UK law is to be welcomed. The House of Lords acknowledged the concept in subsequent cases.[48] The divide between the three types of case in *Coughlan* should, nonetheless, be treated with caution. The first category was created in order to deal with cases, primarily *Hargreaves*, which might have hindered recognition of substantive legitimate expectations within UK law. This category is now confined to cases where the original promise was merely to consider taking action.[49] The second category is concerned primarily with procedural legitimate expectations. The dividing line between the first and third categories cannot however be regarded as "hermetically sealed".[50]

---

40 *Findlay* [1985] A.C. 318.

41 *Hargreaves* [1997] 1 W.L.R. 906.

42 *Coughlan* [2001] Q.B. 213 at [57].

43 *Coughlan* [2001] Q.B. 213 at [57].

44 *Coughlan* [2001] Q.B. 213 at [62].

45 *Attorney General For Hong Kong v Ng Yuen Shiu* [1983] 2 A.C. 629; *British Dental Association v General Dental Council* [2014] EWHC 4311 (Admin); *R. (LH) v Shropshire Council* [2014] EWCA Civ 404.

46 *Coughlan* [2001] Q.B. 213 at [61], [67]–[69], relying on *Preston* [1985] A.C. 835; *Laker Airways* [1977] Q.B. 643; *HTV* [1976] I.C.R. 170; *MFK* [1990] 1 W.L.R. 1545; *Unilever* [1996] S.T.C. 681. *Khan* [1984] 1 W.L.R. 1337; *Ruddock* [1987] 1 W.L.R. 1482; and *Council of Civil Service Unions v Minister for the Civil Service* [1985] A.C. 374, HL at 410–411 were also seen as recognising substantive legitimate expectations, *Coughlan* [2001] Q.B. 213 at [77].

47 *Coughlan* [2001] Q.B. 213 at [57].

48 *R. v Ministry of Defence, Ex p. Walker* [2000] 1 W.L.R. 806, HL; *R. v Secretary of State for the Home Department, Ex p. Zeqiri* [2002] UKHL 3, Lord Hoffmann at [44].

49 *R. (Abbasi) v Secretary of State for Foreign and Commonwealth Affairs* [2002] EWCA Civ 1598 at [99].

50 *R. v Secretary of State for Education and Employment, Ex p. Begbie* [2000] 1 W.L.R. 1115 at 1130, 1133–1134.

6. INTRA VIRES REPRESENTATIONS: THE DETERMINATION OF WHETHER THE EXPECTATION IS REASONABLE AND LEGITIMATE

22–016 The court will consider a number of factors when determining whether an expectation was reasonable and legitimate.

i. The most important factor concerns the nature of the representation. A clear and unambiguous promise, undertaking or representation provides the strongest foundation for a claim.[51] Thus, where a public authority had issued a promise or adopted a practice that represented how it was supposed to act in a given area, the law would require the promise or practice to be honoured unless there was a good reason not to do so.[52] The representation may arise from words or conduct or from a combination of the two.[53] There is, however, authority that consistent conduct over a long period of time may give rise to an expectation, even if it was not a clear and unambiguous representation.[54] Some decisions as to whether a representation was sufficiently specific and unambiguous to create a legitimate expectation can be controversial and divide the members of the court.[55]
ii. A representation may be based on a variety of sources, including an individual statement, a circular, a report or an agreement. It will be easier to establish a reasonable expectation the more specific is the representation.[56]
iii. An expectation will not be regarded as reasonable or legitimate if the applicant could have foreseen that the subject matter of the representation was likely to alter, or that it would not be respected by the relevant agency. Similarly if the person claiming the benefit knew that the representor did

---

[51] *MFK* [1990] 1 W.L.R. 1545; *R. v Independent Television Commission, Ex p. Flextech Plc* [1999] E.M.L.R. 880 QBD. For cases where the court decided that there was no such representation, or that it was not deemed to be clear or sufficiently precise, see e.g. *R. (Association of British Civilian Internees (Far East Region)) v Secretary of State for Defence* [2002] EWCA Civ 473; *R. (Fivepounds.co.uk Ltd) v Transport for London* [2005] EWHC 3002 (Admin); *R. (Wheeler) v Office of the Prime Minister* [2008] EWHC 1409 (Admin); *R. (Hillingdon LBC) v Lord Chancellor* [2008] EWHC 2683 (Admin); *Niazi* [2008] EWCA Civ 755; *R. (Stamford Chamber of Trade and Commerce) v Secretary of State for Communities and Local Government* [2009] EWHC 719 (Admin); *R. (Baird) v Tribunals Service* [2010] EWHC 1257 (Admin); *R. (Luton BC) v Secretary of State for Education* [2011] EWHC 217 (Admin); *R. (Davies) v Revenue and Customs Commissioners* [2011] UKSC 47; *R. (Badger Trust) v Secretary of State for the Environment, Food and Rural Affairs* [2014] EWCA Civ 1405; *R. (Karia) v Leicester City Council* [2014] EWHC 3105 (Admin); *R. (Project Management Institute) v Minister for the Cabinet Office* [2014] EWHC 2438 (Admin); *Hossain v Secretary of State for the Home Department* [2015] EWCA Civ 207.

[52] *R. (Nadarajah) v Secretary of State for the Home Department* [2005] EWCA Civ 1363; *R. (Montpeliers and Trevors Association) v City of Westminster* [2005] EWHC 16 (Admin); *R. (Greenpeace Ltd) v Secretary of State for Trade and Industry* [2007] EWHC 311 (Admin); *Paponette v Attorney General of Trinidad and Tobago* [2011] 3 W.L.R. 219; *R. (GSTS Pathology LLP) v Revenue and Customs Commissioners* [2013] EWHC 1801 (Admin); *R (Patel) v General Medical Council* [2013] EWCA Civ 327; *R. (Simpson) v Chief Constable of Greater Manchester* [2013] EWHC 1858 (Admin); *R. (C) v Westminster CC*, 23 October 2015.

[53] *MFK* [1990] 1 W.L.R. 1545; *R. v Gaming Board of Great Britain, Ex p. Kingsley* [1996] C.O.D. 241 QBD.

[54] *Unilever* [1996] S.T.C. 681.

[55] *R. (Bancoult) v Secretary of State for Foreign and Commonwealth Affairs* [2009] 1 A.C. 453, HL.

[56] *Hamble* [1995] 2 All E.R. 714; *United States Tobacco* [1992] Q.B. 353.

not intend his statements to create an expectation then this will tell against the expectation being reasonable or legitimate.[57]

iv. If an individual knew or ought to have known that an assurance could only be obtained in a particular way, and a purported assurance was obtained in a different way, it will not be an abuse of power to go back on the assurance.[58]

v. Detrimental reliance will normally be required in order for the claimant to show that it would be unlawful to go back on a representation,[59] since if the individual has suffered no hardship there is no reason based on legal certainty to hold the agency to its representation. It should not, however, be necessary to show monetary loss or anything equivalent thereto. There may be moral detriment flowing from disappointment when an expectation is not honoured,[60] although disappointment will not suffice in this respect.[61] While in a strong case there will be both reliance and detriment, there may also be cases where there is reliance, without measurable detriment. It may still be unfair to thwart a legitimate expectation in such circumstances.[62]

vi. Where an agency seeks to depart from an established policy in relation to a particular person detrimental reliance should not be required. Consistency of treatment and equality are at stake in such cases, and these values should be protected irrespective of whether there has been any reliance as such.[63]

vii. An expectation will not be regarded as reasonable or legitimate if the potential beneficiary has not placed "all cards face up on the table".[64] All relevant issues must therefore be disclosed.

viii. The courts will not readily infer a legitimate expectation where it would confer an unmerited or improper benefit, which offended against fairness and justice.[65]

ix. The subject-matter can render application of legitimate expectations more problematic. Thus, planning is regulated by a comprehensive statutory code, and the courts have held that a legitimate expectation arising from the conduct of a local planning authority could only occur in exceptional circumstances, for example where there was no third party or public interest.[66]

---

[57] *Kingsley* [1996] C.O.D. 241.

[58] *Matrix Securities* [1994] 1 W.L.R. 334.

[59] *R. v Secretary of State for the Environment, Ex p. NALGO* [1992] C.O.D. 282; *R. v Jockey Club, Ex p. RAM Racecourses* [1993] 2 All E.R. 223; *Matrix Securities* [1994] 1 W.L.R. 334; *Walker* [2000] 1 W.L.R. 806; *Begbie* [2000] 1 W.L.R. 1115 at 1123, 1131, 1133; *R. v London Borough of Newham and Manik Bibi and Ataya Al-Nashed* [2002] 1 W.L.R. 237, CA (Civ Div) at [29]; *R. (Association of British Civilian Internees (Far East Region)) v Secretary of State for Defence* [2002] EWHC 2119 (Admin) at [34]–[35]; *R. (Lindley) v Tameside MBC* [2006] EWHC 2296 (Admin).

[60] *Bibi* [2002] 1 W.L.R. 237 at [54]–[55].

[61] *The Association of British Civilian Internees* [2002] EWCA Civ 473 at [36].

[62] *Bibi* [2002] 1 W.L.R. 237 at [31].

[63] *Bibi* [2002] 1 W.L.R. 237 at [29]–[30]; *R. (Rashid) v Secretary of State for the Home Department* [2005] EWCA Civ 744; *R. (K. and A.C. Jackson & Son) v Department for the Environment, Food and Rural Affairs* [2011] EWHC 956 (Admin).

[64] *MFK* [1990] 1 W.L.R. 1545 at 1569; *Matrix Securities* [1994] 1 W.L.R. 334.

[65] *Kingsley* [1996] COD 241, 243; *Matrix Securities* [1994] 1 W.L.R. 334.

[66] *Henry Boot Homes Ltd v Bassetlaw DC* [2002] EWCA Civ 983; *R. (Wandsworth LBC) v Secretary of State for Transport, Local Government and the Regions* [2003] EWHC 622 (Admin).

x. Even if the expectation is reasonable and legitimate there may be good reasons why the public body needs to act so as to defeat it. The standard of review which should apply in such circumstances is crucial, and it is to this issue that we should now turn.

7. INTRA VIRES REPRESENTATIONS: THE STANDARD OF REVIEW APPLIED WHEN THE ADMINISTRATION SEEKS TO DEFEAT A LEGITIMATE EXPECTATION

A. *Coughlan*

i. The court's reasoning

The distinction between the types of case was regarded as important in *Coughlan* for the standard of review. In the first type of case the normal *Wednesbury* test would apply. In the second, the court would engage in "full review", deciding for itself whether the departure from a procedural legitimate expectation was fair. It is the standard of review in the third type of case that is of particular interest. This will be a live issue where, as in *Coughlan*, the public body seeks to resile from the legitimate expectation on the ground that the public interest demands that this should be so. 22–017

The court in *Coughlan* accepted that public bodies must be able to change policy, and that undertakings were therefore open to modification or abandonment.[67] It followed that the court's task was

> "… not to impede executive activity but to reconcile its continuing need to initiate or respond to change with the legitimate interests or expectations of citizens or strangers who have relied, and have been justified in relying, on a current policy or an extant promise".[68]

This was especially so given that there were two lawful exercises of power in this type of case: the promise and the policy change.[69] This consideration led the court to distinguish between two standards of judicial review of discretion.

There was, on the one hand, bare or intrinsic irrationality, through which a court could quash a decision that defied comprehension in the sense articulated by Lord Greene[70] and Lord Diplock.[71] Such cases were rare. Rationality also embraced decisions made on the basis of flawed logic. The court in *Coughlan* rejected this criterion. Where there were, as here, two lawful exercises of power,

> "… a bare rationality test would constitute the public authority judge in its own cause, for a decision to prioritise a policy change over legitimate expectations will almost always be rational from where the authority stands, even if objectively it is arbitrary or unfair".[72]

---

67 *Coughlan* [2001] Q.B. 213 at [64].
68 *Coughlan* [2001] Q.B. 213 at [65].
69 *Coughlan* [2001] Q.B. 213 at [66].
70 *Associated Picture Houses Ltd v Wednesbury Corp* [1948] 1 K.B. 223, CA at 228–230.
71 *Council of Civil Service Unions* [1985] A.C. 374 at 410–411.
72 *Coughlan* [2001] Q.B. 213 at [66].

There was, on the other hand, intervention on the grounds of abuse of power. A power which had been abused had not been lawfully exercised.[73] The court's task was to ensure that the power to alter policy was not abused by unfairly frustrating individual legitimate expectations. *Preston*[74] was treated as the principal authority for judicial review for abuse of power, although a number of other cases[75] were cited in support.[76] Abuse of power could take many forms. To renege on a lawful promise made to a limited number of individuals without adequate justification was one such type of case. There was, said the Court of Appeal, no suggestion in *Preston*, or other relevant cases,[77] that the final arbiter of a decision which frustrated a substantive legitimate expectation was, rationality apart, the decision-maker rather than the court.[78] Nor was there any suggestion that judicial review in such instances was confined to the bare rationality of the decision.[79] The court would intervene where there had been an abuse of power, and this was a matter for the court to determine.[80] Policy was for the public authority. The court's task was "limited to asking whether the application of the policy to an individual who has been led to expect something different is a just exercise of power".[81] The applicant's substantive legitimate expectation could not be frustrated unless there was an overriding public interest, and whether this existed was a matter for the court.[82] The court found in favour of the applicant on the facts of the case.

ii. *Assessment*

22–018 The reasons given in *Coughlan* for rejecting the *Wednesbury* test[83] in the original manner conceived of by Lord Greene MR are convincing. It would require the individual to show that the agency's decision to act inconsistently with the legitimate expectation was so unreasonable that no reasonable agency would have done it. It would, as recognised in *Coughlan*, be almost impossible for the individual to succeed on this criterion.[84]

The court in *Coughlan* preferred to use abuse of power as the criterion for testing whether a public body could resile from a prima facie legitimate expectation. This is, however, problematic for the following reason. Abuse of power may well be regarded as the *conceptual rationale* for judicial intervention to protect substantive legitimate expectations.[85] It encapsulates the conclusion that the applicant had some normatively justified expectation, since there would

73 *Coughlan* [2001] Q.B. 213 at [70].
74 *Preston* [1985] A.C. 835.
75 *Unilever* [1996] S.T.C. 681; *HTV* [1976] I.C.R. 170; *Laker* [1977] Q.B. 643; *MFK* [1990] 1 W.L.R. 1545.
76 *Coughlan* [2001] Q.B. 213 at [67]–[69].
77 *R. v Devon County Council, Ex p. Baker* [1995] 1 All E.R. 73.
78 *Coughlan* [2001] Q.B. 213 at [69], [74].
79 *Coughlan* [2001] Q.B. 213 at [74], [77].
80 *Coughlan* [2001] Q.B. 213 at [81].
81 *Coughlan* [2001] Q.B. 213 at [82].
82 *Coughlan* [2001] Q.B. 213 at [76].
83 *Wednesbury* [1948] 1 K.B. 223.
84 *Coughlan* [2001] Q.B. 213 at [66].
85 *Coughlan* [2001] Q.B. 213 at; *Unilever* [1996] S.T.C. 681; *Zeqiri* [2002] UKHL 3.

otherwise have been no foundation for finding such an abuse. The term abuse of power can also capture the conclusion that the court has found the public body's argument for going back on the expectation to be unconvincing. Abuse of power does not, however, furnish a *standard of review* for deciding whether a public body can resile from a proven substantive expectation. It can be used to express the conclusion reached under any such standard, but does not itself constitute a standard of review.[86]

B. *Nadarajah*

i. *The court's reasoning*

22–019 The decision in *Nadarajah* is to be welcomed for clarifying this issue.[87] The normal position under the 1999 Asylum Act was that an asylum seeker who sought asylum in another country and then sought asylum in the UK would be returned to the other country, provided it was regarded as safe. This was qualified by the Family Links Policy (FLP), which provided that potential third country cases would nonetheless be considered in the UK where the applicant's spouse was in the UK. This included presence of the spouse in the UK as an asylum seeker. N's spouse came to the UK, was refused asylum, but appealed that decision. N did not know of the FLP. The secretary of state said that the FLP was not applicable, because N's spouse had been denied entry as an asylum seeker, even though she was appealing that decision. The High Court decided to the contrary and held that she was still an asylum seeker while her appeal was pending. N claimed that he had a legitimate expectation that the FLP should be applied to him and that there was in effect a departure from that policy in the instant case. The secretary of state argued that there had been no abuse of power, since N had not known of the FLP, and hence there was no reliance.

The judgment of the Court of Appeal was given by Laws LJ. He held that the concept of abuse of power might well underlie the law in this area, in the sense that it captured the idea that an act of a public authority that was not legally justified would be an abuse of power, but he recognised that the concept of abuse of power would not in itself tell one in a particular case whether public action was lawful or not. It could therefore be a conclusory label but little more.

Laws LJ then addressed the legal test that should apply when a public body sought to depart from a legitimate expectation. He held that where a public authority issued a promise or adopted a practice which represented how it

---

[86] See further, *R. (S) v Secretary of State for the Home Department* [2007] EWCA Civ 546 at [39]–[42].

[87] *Nadarajah* [2005] EWCA Civ 1363; *R. (Bamber) v Revenue and Customs Commissioners* [2005] EWHC 3221 (Admin); *R. (Fingle Glen Junction Business and Community Action Group) v Highways Agency* [2007] EWHC 2446 (Admin); P. Sales, "Legitimate Expectations" [2006] J.R. 186; C. Hilson, "Policies, the Non-Fetter Principle and the Principle of Substantive Legitimate Expectations: Between a Rock and a Hard Place?" [2006] J.R. 289; M. Elliott, "Legitimate Expectations and the Search for Principle: Reflections on *Abdi & Nadarajah*" [2006] J.R. 281; C. Knight, "The Test that Dare not Speak its Name: Proportionality Comes out of the Closet?" [2007] J.R. 117.

proposed to act in a particular area the law required the practice or promise to be honoured unless there was a good reason not to do so.[88] The underlying rationale was good administration.

A public body's promise or practice could, said Laws LJ, only be denied or departed from where to do so was the public body's legal duty, or was otherwise a proportionate response of which the court was the last judge having regard to a legitimate aim pursued by the public body in the public interest. The

> "... principle that good administration requires public authorities to be held to their promises would be undermined if the law did not insist that any failure or refusal to comply is objectively justified as a proportionate measure in the circumstances".[89]

The existence of detrimental reliance was no more than a factor to be weighed in deciding whether denial of the expectation was proportionate.[90] This approach was held to apply to both procedural and substantive legitimate expectations.

ii. Assessment

22–020 The proportionality test articulated by Laws LJ for deciding whether a public body can go back on or depart from a legitimate expectation has beneficially clarified this area of the law,[91] although the application of the test to the facts was more questionable. Abuse of power does not encapsulate a standard of review, although it might well be a fitting conclusory label to append to the application of any other test. The traditional *Wednesbury* test would be too narrow. The applicant would almost never win on such a test and it was ruled out by *Coughlan*. The *Wednesbury* test could be applied more intensively in cases of this kind,[92] or the courts could adopt the interpretation of the reasonableness test by Lord Cooke.[93] We have, however, seen that the factors taken into account when reasonableness is interpreted in this manner would be very like those considered in proportionality.[94]

Proportionality review is therefore the best option, and it will only be relevant if the applicant establishes a substantive legitimate expectation. If the applicant surmounts this hurdle then it is fitting in normative terms that a proportionality test should be used to determine the legality of action that purports to resile from the substantive legitimate expectation. The proportionality test provides a structured analysis which facilitates review, and forces the agency to give a reasoned justification for its course of action. The reasoning used in *Coughlan* to decide whether the public body could resile from the applicant's expectation was very close to a proportionality inquiry. The way in which the standard of review

---

88 *Nadarajah* [2005] EWCA Civ 1363 at [68].

89 *Nadarajah* [2005] EWCA Civ 1363 at [68].

90 *Nadarajah* [2005] EWCA Civ 1363 at [70].

91 *Bancoult* [2009] 1 A.C. 453 at [182], Lord Mance reserved the issue as to whether proportionality should be the test for deciding if a public body could resile from a prima facie expectation, but he nonetheless made it clear that the test should involve weighing the interests of the public body seeking to resile from the expectation with those of the claimant.

92 C. Forsyth, "*Wednesbury* Protection of Substantive Legitimate Expectations" [1997] P.L. 375.

93 *R. v Chief Constable of Sussex, Ex p. International Trader's Ferry Ltd* [1999] 1 All E.R. 129.

94 See para.21–035.

is applied will depend on the nature of the case. The courts will be more reluctant to interfere with general changes of policy, than with cases where a representation is made to a discrete group.[95] This variability can, however, be accommodated within a proportionality inquiry. It is moreover incumbent on the public body to adduce evidence as to why it believes that the public interest requires it to resile from the legitimate expectation,[96] and the reviewing court will be influenced by the importance of the public interest that is said to justify departure from the legitimate expectation.[97]

The precise meaning of the condition that a public authority could depart from a prima facie expectation where it had the legal duty to do so is not entirely clear. It could be intended to capture the situation where the initial representation was intra vires, but where there was then some supervening legal duty embodied in a subsequent statute that required the public authority to depart from the representation. It could, in addition, be intended to cover the case where the initial representation was ultra vires.

C. *Bibi*

i. *The court's reasoning*

The court might decide to remit the case back to the original decision-maker where a legitimate expectation has been found to exist. The *Bibi* case provides a good example.[98] The applicants had been provided with accommodation for the homeless. The local authority promised that it would provide them with security of tenure. It had made this promise because it thought, wrongly, that it was under a duty to provide permanent accommodation. The local authority sought to renege on the promise, having become aware that it did not have a duty to give permanent accommodation. Schiemann LJ held that the promise had created a substantive legitimate expectation.[99] He held further that when an authority, without even considering that it is in breach of a promise giving rise to a legitimate expectation, acts at variance with the promise, then the authority is abusing its power.[100] **22–021**

The court did not, however, order the local authority to provide the secure accommodation. It remitted the case to the local authority and imposed a duty on it to consider the applicants' housing on the basis that they had a legitimate expectation that they would be given secure accommodation. The reason for this strategy was that while the applicants had a legitimate expectation, so too did other people on the council's accommodation list, and the overall stock of

[95] *Begbie* [2000] 1 W.L.R. 1115 at 1130–1131.

[96] *Paponette* [2011] 3 W.L.R. 219.

[97] *R. (Alansi) v Newham LBC* [2013] EWHC 3722 (Admin); *Solar Century Holdings Ltd v Secretary of State for Energy and Climate Change* [2014] EWHC 3677 (Admin); *R. (Birks) v Commissioner of Police of the Metropolis* [2014] EWHC 3041 (Admin).

[98] *Bibi* [2002] 1 W.L.R. 237; *Theophilus* [2002] 3 All E.R. 851 at [27]–[29]; *B* [2001] EWHC 271 (Admin) at [32]; *R. (HSMP Forum Ltd) v Secretary of State for the Home Department* [2008] EWHC 664 (Admin).

[99] *Bibi* [2002] 1 W.L.R. 237 at [46].

[100] *Bibi* [2002] 1 W.L.R. 237 at [39], [49]–[51].

housing was limited. The local authority might be able to help the applicants in some other way, if it felt unable to give them secure housing.[101] The court nonetheless made it clear that the assumption was that effect should be given to the legitimate expectation. If the local authority decided not to do so, it had to provide reasons, which the applicants could test in court.[102]

ii. Assessment

22–022 The option of remitting the case back to the public body is useful. This is especially so, in cases such as *Bibi*, where there are others who can be directly affected by enforcement of the legitimate expectation. The assumption is that the public body will give effect to the expectation, and if this transpires it side steps difficult issues about the standard of review. If this assumption is not borne out, the applicant can challenge the resultant decision.

8. INTRA VIRES REPRESENTATIONS AND LEGITIMATE EXPECTATIONS: TYPES OF CASE

22–023 We have examined the criteria used to determine whether a legally enforceable expectation exists, and the test for deciding whether a public body can resile from such an expectation. We should now consider the application of these precepts to different types of legitimate expectation case.

A. Changes of Policy

22–024 The cases in this category are the most problematic. Public bodies must be able to change their policy.[103] The fact that a policy will normally continue until the time for its cessation, or until there is a shift in thinking about the area, will not therefore suffice to ground a substantive legitimate expectation.[104] This does not mean that the doctrine could never apply to this type of case. This would create difficult boundary problems between this category and the others, since the line between a general policy and an individual representation may be difficult to draw. It does mean as Laws LJ stated[105] that a claimant will have to show a "specific undertaking, directed at a particular individual or group, by which the relevant policy's continuance is assured".

The fact situations in cases such as *Hamble Fisheries*,[106] *Hargreaves*,[107] and *Godfrey*[108] provide examples of situations in which a change of policy might give rise to a substantive legitimate expectation claim. This is so notwithstanding the fact that the claims failed in these cases. The individual may nonetheless properly

[101] *Bibi* [2002] 1 W.L.R. 237 at [58].
[102] *Bibi* [2002] 1 W.L.R. 237 at [59].
[103] *Niazi* [2008] EWCA Civ 755 at [41].
[104] *Niazi* [2008] EWCA Civ 755 at [34]–[36].
[105] *Niazi* [2008] EWCA Civ 755 at [43].
[106] *Hamble Fisheries* [1995] 2 All E.R. 714.
[107] *Hargreaves* [1997] 1 All E.R. 397.
[108] *R. (Godfrey) v Conwy CBC* [2001] EWHC 640 (Admin).

argue that there was a legitimate expectation based on the old policy, which was ignored in the transition to the new policy. This argument would be even stronger where there were no transitional provisions between the two policies. Whether the individual can show the legitimate expectation will depend on the facts and the public body can argue that there was an overriding public interest to defeat any such expectation.

Whether such an expectation exists can be controversial, as exemplified by *Bancoult*.[109] The inhabitants of the Chagos Islands were compulsorily removed from their land by an Immigration Ordinance in 1971, which was quashed on the ground that the exclusion of an entire population from its land was ultra vires the relevant order. The government stated that it accepted the court's ruling and would allow the Chagossians to return home. However, the government later decided that resettlement was not feasible and that the territory was still wanted for defence purposes. It therefore enacted Orders in Council, which prevented the Chagossians from returning home.

The Court of Appeal held that the secretary of state had impermissibly frustrated the claimants' legitimate expectation that they would be allowed to return home.[110] The public promise made by the secretary of state to right the wrong exposed by the earlier judgment had been implemented by the enactment in 2000 of a right of return for Chagossians, and the Orders in Council of 2004 had gone back on that undertaking. The majority of the House of Lords held, however, that the ministerial statement in 2000 was not sufficiently unambiguous to create a legitimate expectation that the islanders would be allowed to return home. The dissenting view of Lords Bingham and Mance, who held that there was an unequivocal assurance given in 2000, better coheres with the facts and is to be preferred.

B. Departure from an Existing Policy

The status of policy, and the legal rules which should apply when an agency seeks to depart from an established policy, have been considered in a number of cases.[111] There are cases where the public authority seeks to depart from an existing policy in relation to a particular applicant. These are less difficult than those where there is a general change of policy for the future. **22–025**

In *Ruddock*[112] the applicant, who had been a prominent member of the Campaign for Nuclear Disarmament, sought judicial review of a decision to

109 *Bancoult* [2009] 1 A.C. 453

110 *R. (Bancoult) v Secretary of State for Foreign and Commonwealth Affairs* [2008] Q.B. 365 CA (Civ Div) at [72]–[76], [100].

111 A prominent example of departure from an existing policy was *Rashid* [2005] EWCA Civ 744; M. Elliott, "Legitimate Expectation, Consistency and Abuse of Power: The *Rashid* Case" [2005] J.R. 281. The decision was however overruled by the Supreme Court in *R. (TN (Afghanistan)) v Secretary of State for the Home Department* [2015] UKSC 40. The rationale for the SC's decision was that asylum appeals should be determined by reference to the position at the time of the appellate decision, rather than by reference to the factual situation at the time of the original decision against which the appeal was brought, and solely on the basis as to whether the evidence showed that the appellant was presently exposed to a risk entitling him to refugee protection.

112 *Ruddock* [1987] 1 W.L.R. 1482.

intercept her telephone calls. She argued that she had a legitimate expectation that the published criteria as to when this would be done would be followed. Taylor J recognised that where there would be no right to be heard before making the interception order, it was particularly important that the ministerial undertaking should be followed. The publication of a policy did not preclude any future change, nor did it prevent its non-application in a particular case for reasons of national security. The minister had not, however, argued that the policy should be dispensed with on these grounds, and therefore the applicant had a legitimate expectation that the published criteria would be applied.[113]

There has been debate as to whether these cases should be regarded as coming within legitimate expectations, since considerations of equality and consistency should suffice for the claim, unless the agency can show convincing reasons for departure from the policy,[114] and because there may be instances where the claimant did not know of the policy departed from and hence it is difficult to regard him as having a legitimate expectation in relation to that policy.[115]

22–026 This was recognized in *Mandalia*.[116] Lord Wilson, giving judgment for the Supreme Court, held that the ascription of the legal effect of policy to the doctrine of legitimate expectations was strained in circumstances where those who invoke it were unaware of the policy until after the determination adverse to them was made, and was also strained where reliance was placed on guidance issued by one public body to another. The applicant's right to the determination of his application in accordance with policy should therefore be taken to flow from a free-standing principle, albeit one that was related to the doctrine of legitimate expectation. The principle, which Lord Wilson took from *Nadarajah*,[117] was that where a public authority issued a promise or adopted a practice that represented how it proposed to act in a given area, the law would require the promise or practice to be honoured unless there was good reason not to do so, this being based on a requirement of good administration, by which public bodies ought to deal straightforwardly and consistently with the public. The following principles capture the current case law.[118]

---

[113] The applicant failed on the facts because the court held that the minister could have concluded that the criteria were applicable.

[114] *Bibi* [2002] 1 W.L.R. 237 at [29]–[30]; Dotan, "Why Administrators should be Bound by their Policies" (1997) 17 O.J.L.S. 23.

[115] Forsyth, "Legitimate Expectations Revisited" [2011] J.R. 429.

[116] *Mandalia v Secretary of State for the Home Department* [2015] UKSC 59 at [29]–[31].

[117] *Nadarajah* [2005] EWCA Civ 1363 at [68]; *R (WL (Congo)) v Secretary of State for the Home Department* [2012] 1 A.C. 245 at [35].

[118] *Urmaza* [1996] C.O.D. 479; *Gangadeen* [1998] 1 F.L.R. 762; *R. v Secretary of State for the Environment, Ex p. West Oxfordshire DC* [1994] C.O.D. 134 QBD; *R. (Coghlan) v Chief Constable of Greater Manchester* [2005] 2 All E.R. 890 QBD; *R. (Gill) v Lord Chancellor's Department* [2003] EWHC 156 (Admin); *R. (Munjaz) v Mersey Care NHS Trust* [2006] 2 A.C. 148, HL; *R. (S) v Secretary of State for the Home Department* [2011] EWHC 2120 (Admin); *Eastlands Homes Partnership Ltd v Whyte* [2010] EWHC 695 (Q.B.); *R. (Kambadzi) v Secretary of State for the Home Department* [2011] 1 W.L.R. 1299 SC; *R. (Lumba) v Secretary of State for the Home Department* [2011] UKSC 12; *R. (Manchester Ship Canal Co Ltd) v Environment Agency* [2011] EWHC 1643 (QB); *Mandalia* [2015] UKSC 59.

i. The legal principle of consistency in the exercise of public law powers creates a presumption that the agency or minister will follow a declared policy. This presumption flows from the very purpose of such a policy, which is to secure consistency.

ii. There is a duty to publish current policy and to follow that published policy so that a person affected by it can make informed and meaningful representations before a decision is made. A decision-maker cannot rely on an unpublished policy to render lawful something that is inconsistent with a published policy.

iii. It is for the court to decide the legal meaning of the policy.[119] Thus where the policy is framed in ordinary English, the court will ensure that it is not given an interpretation which is inconsistent with its plain and ordinary meaning. Similarly, where the decision is predicated on the existence of certain legal categories the court will hold the agency to these. Thus, "consistency, in the eye of the law, does not extend to being consistently wrong".[120] Where the policy contains specialist terms, or jargon, the court respects evidence as to its meaning, but not so as to subvert the object of the policy.

iv. If there is a departure from the policy then reasons must be given to justify this. The decision-maker should, when considering a departure from an established policy, weigh the interests of those affected by the existing policy with the need to depart from it in the instant case. There has been some difference of opinion as the standard of review to determine the legality of a departure from an established policy. In *Urmaza* Sedley J held that the courts were not restricted to a bare rationality test in this regard.[121] In *Gangadeen* Hirst LJ held that review should be limited to traditional grounds,[122] and disapproved of Sedley J's suggestions that it should be more intensive. This ruling was, however, given prior to *Coughlan*[123] and *Gangadeen* was disapproved in *Mandalia*.[124] The argument in *Coughlan* and *Nadarajah* for more intensive review than bare rationality is especially apposite here, given that it is a departure from an existing policy which is in issue.

C. Individualised Representations

A number of the cases in this area are concerned with representations made to specific individuals. Thus, in *Preston*,[125] P made an agreement with the Revenue in 1978 to forgo interest relief which he had claimed and he also paid some capital gains tax. In return, the inspector said that he would not raise any further inquiries on certain tax affairs. The Revenue, however, decided to apply 22–027

[119] *Mandalia* [2015] UKSC 59 at [31].
[120] *Urmaza* [1996] C.O.D. 479 at 484.
[121] *Urmaza* [1996] C.O.D. 479 at 483–485.
[122] *Gangadeen* [1998] C.O.D. 216 at 218.
[123] *Coughlan* [2001] Q.B. 213.
[124] *Mandalia* [2015] UKSC 59 at [31].
[125] *Preston* [1985] A.C. 835.

provisions of the tax legislation in 1982, following receipt of new information concerning the same transaction. P sought judicial review of this decision. Lord Templeman stated that P would have no remedy for breach of the representation as such, because the Revenue could not bind itself in 1978 not to perform its statutory duty in 1982.[126] Judicial review was, however, available[127]: a court could direct the Revenue to abstain from performing its statutory duties or exercising its powers where the unfairness to the applicant of doing so rendered such insistence an abuse of power.[128] Conduct by the Revenue that was equivalent to a breach of representation could constitute such abuse of power.[129] The Revenue's action could only have been thus regarded if its prior representation gave rise to some normative expectation that was worthy of protection.

Further authority is provided by the *MFK* case.[130] The applicants approached the Inland Revenue as to whether investments would be taxed as capital or income. The initial response convinced the applicants that the investments would be taxed as capital, but the Revenue later taxed the assets as income. Bingham LJ held that the applicants must fail if the representation was in breach of the Revenue's statutory duty. This was not so, since the Revenue was exercising its proper managerial discretion. The Revenue could not therefore withdraw from its representation if this would cause substantial unfairness to the applicant, and if the conditions for relying on the representation were present: the applicant should give full details of the transaction on which the Revenue's ruling was sought; the applicant should make it apparent that it was seeking a considered ruling on which it intended to rely; and the ruling would have to be clear and unambiguous.[131] It is clear from *Matrix Securities*[132] that the courts will insist strictly on full disclosure of the relevant material, more particularly where the purported assurance has been given in relation to, for example, a tax avoidance scheme which should never have been authorised in this manner.

If the public body argues that there is some public interest justifying departure from its initial representation it must give the person who has a substantive legitimate expectation the opportunity to present arguments as to why the expectation should not be defeated by the public body's subsequent change of view,[133] and the *Nadarajah* test of proportionality[134] will be applicable to this type of case. The argument for more intensive review is especially forceful here, since where a public body seeks to resile from an individual representation it is less likely for there to be wider repercussions of the kind that can arise where there is a shift from one policy to another.

---

126 *Preston* [1985] A.C. 835 at 862.

127 *Preston* [1985] A.C. 835 at 862–863.

128 *Preston* [1985] A.C. 835 at 864. Lord Templeman drew on Lord Denning MR in *HTV* [1976] I.C.R. 170 at 185–186.

129 *Preston* [1985] A.C. 835 at 866–867. The applicant failed on the facts, at 867–871.

130 *MFK* [1990] 1 W.L.R. 1545; *Davies* [2011] UKSC 47.

131 *MFK* [1990] 1 W.L.R. 1545 at 1568–1569.

132 *Matrix Securities* [1994] 1 W.L.R. 334; *Corkteck Ltd v Revenue and Customs Commissioners* [2009] EWHC 785 (Admin); *R. (Medical Protection Society) v Revenue and Customs Commissioners* [2009] EWHC 2780 (Admin).

133 *R. (Machi) v Legal Services Commission* [2002] A.C.D 8 QBD.

134 *Nadarajah* [2005] EWCA Civ 1363.

The assumption in the preceding cases was that the representation was intra vires.[135] However, if a court believes that no balancing should be undertaken if the representation is ultra vires, but it wishes to consider the effects of the representation on the individual, this may cause the court to categorise the representation as intra rather than ultra vires.[136] This is because if a public authority has made an ultra vires representation the courts are reluctant to accord the representation any binding force.

D. Decisions, Final Determinations and Estoppel by Record

i. *Final determinations*

The discussion in the previous section was concerned with cases where there has been a representation, which the individual seeks to rely on. This should be distinguished from the case where there has been a final determination, which cannot be altered because it is a dispositive decision in that case. **22–028**

This is exemplified by the *Denton Road* case.[137] The plaintiff's house was damaged during the war and later demolished by the local authority. The preliminary determination by the War Damage Commission was that the property was a total loss. This was later altered, the Commission saying that the loss was non-total. A third turn of the wheel caused them to revert to the categorisation of total loss. Greater compensation would be paid where the loss was non-total. It was held that the second determination was final and that where Parliament had imposed a duty of deciding any question that affected the rights of subjects, such a decision, when made and communicated in terms which were not preliminary, was final and conclusive. It could not, in the absence of express statutory power or the consent of the person affected, be withdrawn.[138] The intra vires decision was binding as a valid decision.[139]

The scope of the holding in this case is not, however, clear. In *Rootkin*[140] the plaintiff's daughter was given a place at a school, which the local authority believed to be over three miles from her home. They thereby were obliged to provide transport or to reimburse travelling expenses, and decided upon the latter. They later measured the distance once again and, having decided that it was less than three miles, withdrew the funding. The plaintiff relied on the *Denton Road* case. The argument was rejected, the court saying that it had no application where

---

135 *MFK* [1990] 1 W.L.R. 1545.

136 *MFK* [1990] 1 W.L.R. 1545; *Bibi* [2002] 1 W.L.R. 237.

137 *56 Denton Road, Twickenham, Middlesex, Re* [1953] Ch. 51 Ch D. See also, *Livingstone v Westminster Corp* [1904] 2 K.B. 109 KBD, at 120; *R. v Ministry of Agriculture, Fisheries and Food, Ex p. Cox* [1993] 2 C.M.L.R. 917 QBD; *R. (Gleeson Developments Ltd) v Secretary of State for Communities and Local Government* [2014] EWCA Civ 1118.

138 *56 Denton Road, Re* [1953] Ch. 51 at 56–57.

139 *56 Denton Road, Re* [1953] Ch. 51 at 57. No reliance on the original decision will be possible where that decision was based upon facts which have been falsified by the applicant, *R. v Dacorum Borough Council, Ex p. Walsh* [1992] C.O.D. 125 QBD.

140 *Rootkin v Kent CC* [1981] 1 W.L.R. 1186, CA (Civ Div).

the citizen was receiving only a discretionary benefit as opposed to a statutory right, since this would fetter the discretion of the public body.[141]

22–029 The principle in *Denton Road* is surely correct. When a public body makes a lawful final decision this should be binding on it, even in the absence of detrimental reliance. A citizen should be entitled to assume that it will not be overturned by a second decision, even if the latter is equally lawful. The principle of legal certainty has a particularly strong application in these circumstances. Where the initial decision is changed because of a mistake or misinterpretation of the facts then, if there has been detrimental reliance, compensation should be granted. Provided that the applicant has not misled the public body then the onus of ensuring that the facts are correctly applied should be on the public body.

It should make no difference whether the initial decision was the determination of a statutory right or the exercise of discretion. The line between the two may well be a fine one. Moreover, once discretion is exercised the argument that the person should be able to rely upon it is equally strong as in the case of a decision about rights. This is supported by *MFK*.[142] The applicant failed on the facts, but the case clearly demonstrates that a discretionary determination will not necessarily be defeated by the argument that to sanction such a result would be a fetter on the general discretion of that body.[143] Any lawful decision will perforce limit the way in which discretion can be used by ruling out other options.

ii. *Estoppel by record*

22–030 A decision may also be final because of the doctrine of estoppel by record or, as it is often known, estoppel per res judicatem.[144] There are two species of this estoppel. One is known as cause of action estoppel. If the same cause of action has been litigated to a final judgment between the same parties, or their privies, litigating in the same capacity, no further action is possible, the principle being that there must be an end to litigation. The other form of estoppel by record is issue estoppel. A single cause of action may contain several distinct issues. Where there is a final judgment between the same parties, or their privies, litigating in the same capacity on the same issue, then that issue cannot be reopened in subsequent proceedings.[145]

The application of the res judicata doctrine in the public law context was reaffirmed in *Thrasyvoulou*.[146] It was held that in relation to adjudication that was subject to a comprehensive self-contained statutory code, the presumption was that where the statute had created a specific jurisdiction for the determination of any issue which established the existence of a legal right, the principle of res

[141] *Rootkin* [1981] 1 W.L.R. 1186 at 1195–1197, 1200.

[142] *MFK* [1990] 1 W.L.R. 1545.

[143] See also, *Preston* [1985] A.C. 835; *Gillingham Borough Council v Medway (Chatham) Dock Co Ltd* [1992] 3 W.L.R. 449.

[144] *Cross and Tapper on Evidence*, 11th edn (Oxford: Oxford University Press, 2007), pp.94–105.

[145] *R. (Shamsun Nahar) v Social Security Commissioners* [2002] A.C.D 28 QBD, for an unsuccessful attempt to plead issue estoppel against a public body.

[146] *Thrasyvoulou v Secretary of State for the Environment* [1990] 2 A.C. 273, HL at 289.

judicata applied to give finality to that determination, unless an intention to exclude that principle could be inferred as a matter of construction from the statutory provisions.[147]

Res judicata expresses the binding nature of a matter litigated to final judgment. In administrative law jurisdictional matters decided by a public body are not final in this sense. They will be determined by the reviewing court.[148] This is exemplified by *Hutchings*.[149] A local Board of Health applied to the justices under the Public Health Act 1875 to recover the expenses of repairing a street from a person whose property was on that street. The claimant contended that it was a public highway repairable by the inhabitants at large. This contention was upheld by the justices. Some years later the Board of Health made an application against the same person, and on this occasion the justices did order payment of expenses. The plea that the matter was res judicata because of the earlier decision was rejected. It was held that, on construction, the justices had no power to decide whether the street was or was not a public highway. Their only jurisdiction was to determine whether a sum of money should be paid or not.[150] Even where the subject-matter is clearly within the jurisdiction of the tribunal, there may be a temporal limit to the conclusiveness of its findings which limits the application of res judicata. This is illustrated by cases concerning rating and taxes.[151]

Provided that the issue is within the subject-matter and temporal jurisdiction of the public body, res judicata will prevent the same matter being litigated before the original tribunal over again. Whether the public body is performing administrative rather than judicial tasks is not relevant for the application of res judicata, nor is the existence of a lis inter partes.[152] **22–031**

The label res judicata is, however, only required where an applicant attempts to litigate the matter over again before the original decision-maker. In circumstances where the individual has received one decision from the public body, and then attempts to have this reversed on appeal or review, the label is not required. If the original decision is intra vires then it is binding as a lawful decision given by the appropriate body. The term res judicata is of use to prevent frequent attempts to determine the same point. Thus, if an applicant attempts to obtain a decision from one tribunal, fails, tries later on the same point, still fails, and then seeks appeal or review, res judicata is an appropriate label to apply provided that the original decision was intra vires.

---

[147] See, e.g. *Special Effects Ltd v L'Oreal SA* [2007] EWCA Civ 1; there can be exceptional circumstances justifying non-application of the cause of action estoppel rule, *R. (East Hertfordshire DC) v First Secretary of State* [2007] EWHC 834 (Admin).

[148] See Ch.16.

[149] *R. v Hutchings* [1881] 6 Q.B.D 300 at 304–305; *R. v Secretary of State for the Environment, Ex p. Hackney LBC* [1984] 1 W.L.R. 592, CA (Civ Div).

[150] Compare *Wakefield Corp v Cooke* [1904] A.C. 31, HL.

[151] *Society of Medical Officers of Health v Hope* [1960] A.C. 551, HL; *Caffoor v Income Tax Commissioner (Colombo)* [1961] A.C. 584.

[152] *Caffoor* [1961] A.C. 584 at 597–599.

9. ULTRA VIRES REPRESENTATIONS AND LEGITIMATE EXPECTATIONS: THE CURRENT LAW

22–032 The discussion thus far has been concerned with intra vires representations. We now consider ultra vires representations. The law is based on the jurisdictional principle, which means that representations made by an agent who lacks authority, or representations leading to decisions which are ultra vires the public body itself, cannot be binding.[153] It is for this reason that it is said that estoppel can have no role in this area. It will be argued that there are circumstances in which it is possible to allow even an ultra vires assurance to bind without the dire results predicted by traditional theory.

A. Jurisdictional Principle: The Relationship of Ultra Vires, Agency and Delegation

22–033 Two questions can arise when a public body makes a representation. The first is whether the agent acting for the public body had authority, actual or apparent, to make the representation. This is dependent on the law of agency. The second is whether the decision resulting from the representation made by the public body or agent is intra vires or ultra vires. This is dependent on the extent of the powers given to that body.

For the jurisdictional principle to be effective a limit must be imposed on the apparent authority of the agent, which cannot extend to a matter that is ultra vires. The decision resulting from the representation may be outside the powers of the public body, or within its power but incapable of being made by that public officer. Thus, in theory at least, it can be said that whenever a public official has apparent authority the decision must be intra vires, since otherwise the agent would not have had authority.

This is not an exceptional position. Company law had to deal with the relationship of ultra vires and agency arising from limitations on the corporation imposed by its memorandum and articles of association. The similarity between the formulation laid down above and that of Diplock LJ in *Freeman*[154] is due to the conceptual identity of the problem in public law and company law.

22–034 The *Silva* case[155] exemplifies application of these principles in a public law context. The Collector of Customs in Ceylon advertised property for sale by auction in March 1947. He was mistaken in treating this as saleable, for in

[153] G. Treitel, "Crown Proceedings: Some Recent Developments" [1957] P.L. 321 at 335–339; G. Ganz, "Estoppel and Res Judicata in Administrative Law" [1965] P.L. 237; M. Fazal, "Reliability of Official Acts and Advice" [1972] P.L. 43; P. Craig, "Representations By Public Bodies" (1977) 93 L.Q.R. 398; A. Bradley, "Administrative Justice and the Binding Effect of Official Acts" (1981) C.L.P. 1; M. Elliott, "Unlawful Representations, Legitimate Expectations and Estoppel" [2003] J.R. 71; M. Elliott, "Legitimate Expectations and Unlawful Representations" [2004] C.L.J. 261; D. Blundell, "*Ultra Vires* Legitimate Expectations" [2005] J.R. 147.

[154] *Freeman and Lockyer v Buckhurst Park Properties (Mangal) Ltd* [1964] 2 Q.B. 480, CA at 506; *Bowstead and Reynolds on Agency*, 20th edn (London: Sweet & Maxwell, 2014), arts 5, 22, 72, 73.

[155] *Attorney General for Ceylon v AD Silva* [1953] A.C. 461; *R. (Bloggs 61) v Secretary of State for the Home Department* [2003] 1 W.L.R. 2724, CA (Civ Div).

November 1946 an officer of the Ministry of Supply had taken over the goods and had contracted to sell them to a Ceylon firm in January 1947. The plaintiff was the buyer at the sale organised by the Collector of Customs. The Collector became aware of the earlier sale, and refused to deliver the goods to the plaintiff, who brought an action for breach of contract. The case turned on whether the Collector had any authority to make the sale.

The Privy Council considered whether the Collector had actual authority to make the sale. Such authority could be derived from the Customs Ordinance or, arguably, independently of it. The court rejected the argument. As to the former, the argument was dismissed because the court found that the Customs Ordinance did not bind the Crown.[156] As to the latter, it was said that the mere fact that the Collector was a public officer did not give him the right to act on behalf of the Crown in all matters concerning the Crown. This must be established by reference to statute or otherwise.[157] This is an application of the theory stated above: even if the act of selling was intra vires, the contract could not be upheld if the agent had no authority to make it.

The Privy Council denied that the Collector had apparent authority to sell the goods.[158] Such authority involved a representation by the principal as to the extent of the agent's authority. No representation by the agent could amount to a holding out by the principal.

The court went on to consider whether the defendant was bound because the Collector had authority, simply from his position as Collector, to represent that the goods delivered were saleable even though they were not. This argument was also rejected.[159] The Collector might have authority to do acts of a particular class, namely to enter on behalf of the Crown into sales of certain goods. Such authority was, however, limited to those areas covered by the Ordinance. Thus, although the Collector had authority derived from his position as Collector this would not extend beyond the limits of the Ordinance: he could not have authority to commit an ultra vires act.

B. Jurisdictional Principle: Application

While the principles are clear, they have not always been applied. Confusion has been compounded by vague use of the terms delegation and agency. The strain placed on legal language stems partly from the hardship that can be produced if the representation cannot bind the public body.[160] The conclusions of the traditional logic could be avoided by assuming that the decision was intra vires, even though it might be dubious whether it could be so regarded. 22–035

Lever Finance[161] is one such case. Developers had obtained planning permission in March 1969. They later made a slight alteration in their plans. The

[156] *Silva* [1953] A.C. 461 at 473–478.
[157] *Silva* [1953] A.C. 461 at 479.
[158] *Silva* [1953] A.C. 461 at 479–480.
[159] *Silva* [1953] A.C. 461 at 480–481.
[160] B. Schwartz, *Administrative Law* (Boston: Little Brown, 1976), p.134. This hardship was acknowledged in *Silva* [1953] A.C. 461 at 480–481.
[161] *Lever Finance Ltd v Westminster (City) London Borough Council* [1971] 1 Q.B. 222, CA (Civ Div).

local authority planning officer said no further consent was required. The developers went ahead with their altered plans and the local residents objected. The planning authority then told the developers that they would require planning permission for the variation. It was the practice of planning authorities to allow their planning officers to decide whether any proposed minor changes were material or not and, if not, for the developer to continue without any further planning permission. Lord Denning MR, with whom Megaw LJ agreed, referred to the many statements[162] that public authorities cannot be estopped from performing their public duty, but said that these statements must be taken with reserve. He propounded the following principle[163]:

> "There are many matters which public authorities can now delegate to officers. If an officer acting within the scope of his ostensible authority makes a representation on which another acts, then the public authority may be bound by it, just as much as a private concern would be."

We have seen that a decision may be ultra vires in one of two senses: the decision resulting from the representation may be outside the powers of the public body, or within its power but incapable of being made by that public officer. The decision in *Lever* was clearly not ultra vires in the former sense, but it almost certainly was in the latter sense, because the statutory powers gave no power to delegate to the officer.[164] If delegation is forbidden by a statute expressly or impliedly then it will be ultra vires. It cannot be converted into an intra vires act by saying that what the officer does with ostensible authority will bind the principal. There cannot be ostensible or apparent authority to bind the principal where the act committed is ultra vires in either sense identified above.[165] Even if the delegation had been permissible in the *Lever* case, Lord Denning MR's words were broad enough to allow estoppel to validate ultra vires decisions, which is inconsistent with higher authority.[166]

22–036 The decision in *Western Fish*[167] reaffirmed orthodoxy. The plaintiff company purchased an industrial site that had previously been used for production of fertiliser from fish and fishmeal. The company intended to make animal fertiliser from fishmeal and also to pack fish for human consumption. It alleged that it had an established user right, which would entitle it to carry on business without the need for planning permission. The planning officer wrote a letter which, the

[162] *Minister of Agriculture and Fisheries v Hulkin*, unreported but cited in *Minister of Agriculture and Fisheries v Mathews* [1950] 1 K.B. 148. For similar reasoning in the USA, *Utah Power and Light Co v United States* 243 US 389 (1917); *Federal Crop Insurance Corporation v Merrill* 332 US 380 (1947); *Schweiker v Hansen* 450 US 785 (1981); *Office of Personnel Management v Richmond* 496 US 414 (1990).

[163] *Lever Finance* [1971] 1 Q.B. 222 at 230; *Robertson v Minister of Pensions* [1949] 1 K.B. 227 KBD, which was criticised in *Howell* [1951] A.C. 837.

[164] Craig, "Representations by Public Bodies" (1977) 93 L.Q.R. 398, 405–406.

[165] *Southend-on-Sea Corporation v Hodgson (Wickford) Ltd* [1962] 1 Q.B. 416 DC; *R. v Leicester City Council, Ex p. Powergen UK Ltd* [2000] J.P.L. 629 QBD; Craig, "Representations By Public Bodies" (1977) 93 L.Q.R. 398, 406.

[166] See paras 22–043 to 22–044.

[167] *Western Fish Products Ltd v Penwith District Council* [1981] 2 All E.R. 204; *Brooks and Burton Ltd v Secretary of State for the Environment* (1976) 75 L.G.R. 285 at 296; *Rootkin* [1981] 1 W.L.R. 1186; *South Bucks DC v Flanagan* [2002] 1 W.L.R. 2601 at [18].

plaintiff claimed, represented that the officer had accepted the established user right. Work on renovating the factories was begun even though planning permission had not yet been obtained. This permission was subsequently refused by the full council and enforcement notices were served on the plaintiff. The latter claimed that the statements of the planning officer estopped the council from refusing planning permission. This was rejected by the Court of Appeal.

Megaw LJ stated that the planning officer, even acting within his apparent authority, could not do what the Town and Country Planning Act 1971 required the council itself to do. The Act required that the decision concerning planning permission be made by the council, not the officer. No representation by the planning officer could inhibit the discharge of these statutory duties. While specific functions could be delegated to the officer, the determination of planning permission had not been thus delegated.[168]

C. Jurisdictional Principle: The Conceptual Language, Estoppel or Legitimate Expectations

The discussion thus far has used the language of estoppel, since it was used in the case law. This must now be revised in the light of the *Reprotech* case.[169] Lord Hoffmann, giving judgment, held that private law concepts of estoppel should not be introduced into planning law.[170] He acknowledged that there was an analogy between estoppel and legitimate expectations, but held that it was no more than an analogy because "remedies against public authorities also have to take into account the interests of the general public which the authority exists to promote".[171] Lord Hoffmann recognised that earlier cases had used the language of estoppel, but said that was explicable because public law concepts of legitimate expectations and abuse of power were underdeveloped at that time. Public law had now absorbed whatever was useful from the moral values underlying estoppel, and "the time has come for it to stand upon its own two feet".[172] Three comments are relevant here. 22–037

First, the shift from the language of estoppel to that of legitimate expectations does not touch the jurisdictional principle as explicated above. Representations made by an agent who lacks authority, or representations leading to decisions which are ultra vires the public body, will not bind that body. The consequence, prior to *Reprotech*, was to say that estoppel cannot apply in such circumstances. This result would now be expressed by saying that there was no legitimate

[168] *Western Fish* [1981] 2 All E.R. 204 at 219. Compare the more liberal approach to delegation in *R. v Southwark London Borough Council, Ex p. Bannerman* [1990] C.O.D. 115.

[169] *R. v East Sussex CC, Ex p. Reprotech (Pebsham) Ltd* [2003] 1 W.L.R. 348, HL. See also, *Powergen* [2000] J.P.L. 629; *Flanagan* [2002] 1 W.L.R. 2601; *Powergen UK Plc v Leicester City Council* [2000] J.P.L. 1037, CA (Civ Div); *Coghurst Wood Leisure Park Ltd v Secretary of State for Transport, Local Government and the Regions, Rother District Council* [2002] EWHC 1091 (Admin); *R. (Clear Channel UK Ltd) v Southwark LBC* [2006] EWHC 3325 (Admin); *Flattery v Secretary of State for Communities and Local Government* [2010] EWHC 2868 (Admin).

[170] *Reprotech* [2003] 1 W.L.R. 348 at [33].

[171] *Reprotech* [2003] 1 W.L.R. 348 at [34].

[172] *Reprotech* [2003] 1 W.L.R. 348 at [35].

expectation.[173] The result in, for example, *Western Fish* would not have been any different had the language of legitimate expectation been used, rather than estoppel.[174]

Second, there is a close analogy between estoppel and legitimate expectations. The foundation of both concepts is a representation, which provides the rationale for holding the representor to what has been represented, where the reliance was reasonable and legitimate in the circumstances. The fact that the remedy against a public body would take account of the broader public interest was moreover recognised by judges who used the language of estoppel.[175]

Third, cases that would, under the previous terminology, have been pleaded in terms of estoppel, are now considered under the heading of legitimate expectations.[176]

D. Jurisdictional Principle: Qualifications

22–038 *Western Fish* reaffirmed, as we have seen, the traditional view. If the representation is ultra vires either because it is outside the powers of the public body, or because it cannot be delegated to the particular officer, then the claimant will not succeed. It remains to consider whether there are exceptions to this principle and to consider their legal status in the light of *Reprotech*.

i. Procedural irregularity

22–039 There is authority that a procedural irregularity *may* be subject to estoppel. Whether it in fact is depends on construction of the statutory provision setting out the procedure.[177] This exception may survive *Reprotech*, subject to the caveat that it has to be expressed in the language of legitimate expectation rather than estoppel.

ii. Delegation and finality of decision

22–040 There was also authority that where a power had been delegated to an officer to determine specific questions, any decision made could not be revoked, this being regarded as akin to res judicata.[178] This suggests that the conceptual rationale for the exception was more akin to the finality of completed decisions,[179] than estoppel by representation. Sullivan J doubted whether this exception survived *Reprotech*.[180]

The exception, even if it does survive, is limited. The statute must allow the power to be delegated to this type of officer, since otherwise the force of the

173 *Flanagan* [2002] 1 W.L.R. 2601 at [18].

174 *Powergen* [2000] J.P.L. 629.

175 *Laker Airways* [1977] Q.B. 643 at 707.

176 *Flanagan* [2002] 1 W.L.R. 2601 at [16]–[17].

177 *Western Fish* [1981] 2 All E.R. 204 at 221; *Wells* [1967] 1 W.L.R. 1000; *Re L.(A.C.) (an infant)* [1971] 3 All E.R. 743 at 752.

178 *Western Fish* [1981] 2 All E.R. 204 at 221–222.

179 See para. 22–028.

180 *Wandsworth* [2003] EWHC 622 (Admin) at [20]–[21].

proposition that a representation cannot validate an ultra vires act would be negated. If the delegation is lawful there is a further issue as to how far an individual can assume that it has occurred. The answer from *Western Fish* was that it depends on the circumstances.[181] The individual could not assume that any resolution necessary to delegate authority had been passed, nor was the seniority of the officer conclusive. If, however, there was some further evidence that the officer regularly dealt with cases of a type which the individual might expect that official to be able to determine, this could be sufficient to entitle the individual to presume that delegation had occurred even if it had not.

iii. European Convention on Human Rights

The jurisdictional principle is qualified to a certain extent by the ECHR, as exemplified by *Stretch*.[182] The claimant complained that the refusal to exercise a renewal option on the ground that it was ultra vires the local authority landlord's powers violated his property rights under art.1 of the First Protocol ECHR. The claimant was granted a 22-year lease on industrial land by the local authority in 1969, with an option to renew for an additional 21 years. When the initial lease expired, S entered into negotiations for a renewal, but was then informed that the option had been granted in excess of the authority's powers. **22–041**

The Strasbourg Court found that there had been a breach of art.1 of the First Protocol, because the refusal on ultra vires grounds was a disproportionate interference with the claimant's peaceful enjoyment of his possessions. He had entered into the lease on the basis of the option and in reliance on it he had built on the land, paid ground rent to the authority and granted subleases. The ultra vires nature of the grant was only raised late in the renewal negotiations, with the result that S had a legitimate expectation that the lease would be renewed. The court acknowledged that the ultra vires doctrine was important in preventing abuse of power, but concluded that application of the doctrine did not respect proportionality in the instant case. It took into account the fact that there was no third party interest affected, nor would any other statutory function be prejudiced by giving effect to the renewal option.

In *Rowland*[183] the court acknowledged the force of the ECHR jurisprudence. It held that a legitimate expectation relating to property could be a "possession" protected by art.1 of the First Protocol ECHR, even if the representation giving rise to the expectation was ultra vires. It would then be for the public body to show that interference with that possession was justified and proportionate, which was held to be so on the facts of the case.

[181] *Western Fish* [1981] 2 All E.R. 204 at 220–222.

[182] *Stretch v United Kingdom* [2004] 38 E.H.R.R. 12; *Europlus Trading Ltd v Revenue and Customs Commissioners* [2011] UKFTT 635.

[183] *Rowland v Environment Agency* [2005] Ch. 1 at [88], [152].

10. ULTRA VIRES REPRESENTATIONS: REASSESSING THE JURISDICTIONAL PRINCIPLE

22–042 The preceding conclusions have a pristine symmetry. The logic of the jurisdictional principle is followed through to its inexorable end. A moment's reflection will, however, reveal the hardship to the individual. The person who reasonably relies on a representation made by a public body will be left without a remedy. It may be possible in theory for the individual to ascertain the limits of the public body's power, and that of its officers, but theory does not always accord with practical reality. This hardship may well incline courts to construe the empowering legislation so as to, for example, confer validity on a mistaken certificate unless and until it has been revoked,[184] or otherwise interpret the legislation so as to render the public body's action intra rather than ultra vires.[185] This will however not always be plausible and the cogency of the traditional theory must now be examined.[186]

A. The Policy behind the Jurisdictional Principle: The First Rationale

22–043 The first rationale was stated by Lord Greene MR in *Hulkin*[187]: if estoppel were to be allowed to run against the government the donee of a statutory power could make an ultra vires representation and then be bound through the medium of estoppel, or legitimate expectations. This would lead to the collapse of the ultra vires doctrine with public officers being enabled to extend their powers at will. The jurisdictional principle is said to protect the public, or that section of it to which the duty relates.[188] The soundness of this reasoning can be tested against the two ways in which a public body might extend its powers: intentionally or inadvertently.

The cases on representations by public officers do not contain any example of *intentional* extension of power, but let us presume that this has occurred. The jurisdictional principle deals with this by preventing the representee from relying on the representation against the public body. To prevent intentional extension of power the "burden" is imposed on the innocent representee. It would, however, be better to deal with rare cases of intentional excess of power by penalising the public officer involved.[189] The typical situation is, however, *inadvertent* extension of power. A public officer construes a statute, and this is then

---

[184] *Ejaz v Secretary of State for the Home Department* [1995] C.O.D. 72, CA (Civ Div).

[185] *MFK* [1990] 1 W.L.R. 1545; *Bibi* [2002] 1 W.L.R. 237.

[186] It has been shown that sovereign immunity did not prevent estoppel applying against the Crown, F. Farrer, "A Prerogative Fallacy—'That the King is not Bound by Estoppel'" (1933) 49 L.Q.R. 511; H. Street, *Governmental Liability, A Comparative Study* (Cambridge: Cambridge University Press, 1953), p.157.

[187] *Hulkin*, unreported but cited in *Mathews* [1950] 1 K.B. 148. For similar reasoning in the US, *Utah Power* 243 US 389 (1917); *Merrill* 332 US 380 (1947); *Hansen* 450 US 785 (1981); *Richmond* 496 US 414 (1990).

[188] *Silva* [1953] A.C. 461 at 481; *Merrill* 332 US 380 (1947).

[189] Local Government Act 1972 s.161, and *Dickson v Hurle-Hobbs* [1947] K.B. 879 DC.

overturned by a higher officer[190]; or a practice develops that a parti individual can undertake a certain task when the statute places the duty different body.[191] Lord Greene's reasoning will have little if any deterrent e It may be possible to deter negligent conduct by making the actor more careful. However, in the present context the official will normally be acting in the bona fide belief that the construction of the statute is correct, or that the representation is within that officer's authority. Moreover, even where there has been carelessness there is little in the present system to deter the officer. The sole effect of a careless representation, which turns out to be ultra vires, is that the representee cannot rely.

B. Policy behind the Jurisdictional Principle: The Second and Third Rationales

The second argument underlying the jurisdictional principle is that estoppel or legitimate expectations cannot be applied to a public body so as to prevent it from exercising its statutory powers or duties,[192] and the third is that to allow an ultra vires representation to bind a public body could prejudice third parties who might be affected. There is force in these arguments. There will nonetheless be circumstances where the detriment to the public, who are the beneficiaries of the ultra vires doctrine, does not outweigh the harsh effect upon the individual. **22–044**

This can be exemplified by *Robertson*.[193] The plaintiff had relied on a representation given by the wrong body that his injury was attributable to military service, as a result of which he had not obtained an independent medical opinion to confirm this. It can be presumed that the representation was ultra vires.[194] The immediate effect of allowing the ultra vires assurance to bind would be a loss to the department concerned. The loss would be in the form of having to pay a pension that could have been withheld.

In any system there is bound to be a certain percentage of such mistakes. The issue is whether to leave the loss with the representee, or to pass it to the department. The latter will mean that the loss is spread through those who benefit from performance of the public duty. The inadvertent misrepresentation could have happened to any person. It was fortuitous that it befell this individual. The effect of allowing the representation to bind would be to impose the loss on those who take the benefit. The detriment to the public interest would not outweigh the harm to the individual.

---

190 *Clairborne Sales Co v Collector of Revenue* 99 So 2d 345 (1957).

191 *Lever Finance* [1971] 1 Q.B. 222.

192 *Maritime Electric Co Ltd v General Dairies Ltd* [1937] A.C. 610 at 620; *Inland Revenue Commissioners v Brooks* [1915] A.C. 478, HL, at 491; *Thrasyvoulou v Secretary of State for the Environment* [1990] 2 A.C. 273, HL at 289; *R. v Inland Revenue Commissioners, Ex p. MFK Underwriting Agents Ltd* [1990] 1 W.L.R. 1545 QBD at 1568; *R. v Criminal Injuries Compensation Board, Ex p. Keane and Marsden* [1998] C.O.D. 128 QBD; *Rowland* [2005] Ch. 1 at [67], [81]; *R. (Albert Court Residents' Association) v Westminster City Council* [2011] EWCA Civ 430; *R. (Jackley) v Secretary of State for Justice* [2015] EWHC 342 (Admin).

193 *Robertson* [1949] 1 K.B. 227.

194 G. Ganz, "Estoppel and *Res Judicata* in Administrative Law" [1965] P.L. 237, 244–245.

There are of course many situations where the loss to the public will outweigh that of the individual. This will be dependent on the context, planning, social security or tax, in which the representation occurs. Planning is a prime example where the public interest in the strict enforcement of the statutory norms is especially strong. This is reinforced by the detriment to third party interests that would occur if invalid representations could be relied on.[195]

11. ULTRA VIRES REPRESENTATIONS: THREE POSSIBLE STRATEGIES

A. Limited Qualifications to the Jurisdictional Principle

i. Government-proprietary distinction

22–045 The distinction between governmental and proprietary functions is not a test separate from the jurisdictional principle.[196] It was developed in some US jurisdictions as an exception to the general rule that estoppel should not bind a public body.[197] It permits the application of the doctrine when the body is acting in a proprietary rather than governmental capacity, and where the agent making the representation had authority to do so.[198] This approach does, however, have limitations. The distinction between what is a governmental and what is a proprietary function is difficult to draw. More importantly, it is based on the premise that it should not apply to governmental matters which the law does not sanction or permit, which takes us back to the jurisdictional principle.

ii. Internal dealing

22–046 A representation could be allowed to bind so far as the internal management of the public body is concerned, but not for those matters that are substantively ultra vires. The idea has analogies with company law.[199] In the public law context it would operate to validate certain types of representation. It would apply to situations where the subject-matter of the representation was within the power of the public body, and the officer who gave the assurance was not prohibited, expressly or impliedly, from doing so. For example, if a public body has power to delegate certain functions to an officer, the representee could assume that the appropriate procedure had been followed and that the delegation had taken place,

[195] *Henry Boot* [2002] EWCA Civ 983; *Wandsworth* [2003] EWHC 622 (Admin); *Reprotech* [2003] 1 W.L.R. 348; *Powergen* [2000] J.P.L. 629; *Flanagan* [2002] 1 W.L.R. 2601; *Powergen* [2000] J.P.L. 1037; *Coghurst* [2002] EWHC 1091 (Admin); *Clear Channel* [2006] EWHC 3325 (Admin); *Flattery* [2010] EWHC 2868 (Admin).

[196] J.F. Conway, "Equitable Estoppel of the Federal Government and Application of the Proprietary Function Exception to the Traditional Rule" (1987) 55 Fordham L.R. 707.

[197] A. Aman and W. Mayton, *Administrative Law*, 2nd edn (St Paul, MN: West Publishing, 2001), pp.334–336.

[198] *Branch Banking and Trust Company v United States* 98 F Supp 757 (1951) (US Court of Claims); *United States v Georgia-Pacific Company* 421 F 2d 92 (1970) (US Court of Appeals, Ninth Circuit); *FDIC v Harrison* 735 F 2d 408 (1984) (11th Cir.); *Mobil Oil Exploration & Producing Southeast Inc v US* 530 US 604 (2000).

[199] *Lever Finance* [1971] 1 Q.B. 222 at 230–231.

provided that there was nothing to put the individual on inquiry. A limited exception of this nature was allowed by *Western Fish*.[200]

B. Balancing the Public and Individual Interest

i. *Balancing legality and legal certainty: nature of the argument*

It is possible to modify the ultra vires principle beyond the options considered above. The ultra vires principle is the embodiment of the *principle of legality*. This principle can, however, clash with the *principle of legal certainty*, and does so when an individual has detrimentally relied on an ultra vires representation. Where the harm to the public would be minimal compared to that to the individual, there is good reason to consider allowing the representation to bind. This would be to recognise that the principle of legality might, on occasion, be outweighed by that of legal certainty. There will nonetheless be many situations where the public interest must take precedence over that of the individual. The existence of a legitimate expectation would be a necessary, but not sufficient, condition for the representation to bind the public body. **22–047**

It might be objected that a representee could never have a "legitimate" expectation if the representation was ultra vires. This is, however, merely a restatement of the general rule that ultra vires representations cannot bind, which is the very question in issue. It adds nothing to that statement. It is in any event inconsistent with Convention jurisprudence, which is premised on the assumption that an expectation can be legitimate even if it is based on an ultra vires representation. It is also misleading in that it conveys the impression that the individual harboured an illegitimate or unwarranted expectation that the representation would be fulfilled. The reality is that the representee may have had no reason to expect that the representation was outside the complex powers of the public body.

The existence of a legitimate expectation is not, however, a sufficient condition for binding the public body, precisely because the representation is ultra vires. The existence of a legitimate expectation serves, nonetheless, as a signal that issues of legal certainty are involved in a case. The existence of such an expectation should, therefore, operate as a trigger to alert a court that a balance between the principles of legality and legal certainty may be required.

ii. *Balancing legality and legal certainty: case law and statute*

The application of a balancing approach through the *courts* is apparent in some American jurisdictions. Many cases have followed the Supreme Court in *Federal Crop*,[201] denying estoppel where it would validate an ultra vires decision, but there have been some exceptions. In *Mansell*,[202] the Supreme Court of California acknowledged the existence of two competing lines of authority, one of which **22–048**

200 *Western Fish* [1981] 2 All E.R. 204.

201 *Federal Crop* 332 US 380 (1947).

202 *City of Long Beach v Mansell* 476 P 2d 423 (1970).

applied estoppel where justice and right required it, the other which denied estoppel where the representation was beyond the power of the public body and where it would defeat a policy adopted to protect the public. The court propounded the following principle.[203]

> "The government may be bound by an equitable estoppel in the same manner as a private party where the elements requisite for such an estoppel against a private party are present, and in the considered view of a court of equity the injustice which would result from a failure to uphold an estoppel is of sufficient dimension to justify any effect upon public interests or policy which would result from the raising of an estoppel."

There is some authority for the balancing approach within UK law. Not surprisingly it came from Lord Denning MR. His Lordship stated[204]:

> "The underlying principle is that the Crown cannot be estopped from exercising its powers, whether given in a statute or by common law, when it is doing so in the proper exercise of its duty to act for the public good, even though this may work some injustice or unfairness to the private individual ... It can, however, be estopped when it is not properly exercising its powers, but is misusing them; and it does misuse them if it exercises them in circumstances which work injustice or unfairness to the individual without any countervailing benefit to the public."[205]

Lord Denning MR provides support for the balancing approach, and conceptualises it in an interesting manner. The formulation makes the binding nature of the representation flow from fulfilment of, not derogation from, the ultra vires principle: where the public body exercises its powers such as to work injustice to the individual without any countervailing benefit to the public this is itself a misuse of powers. If the jurisdictional principle is the trump card, his Lordship trumps this by making this notion of fairness part of the constraints on the use of discretion.

The balancing approach in later cases appears confined to cases where the representation was intra vires, and this view has been reinforced by recent case law.[206] However, if a court believes that no balancing should be undertaken if the representation is ultra vires, but it wishes to consider the effects of the representation, this may incline it to categorise the representation as intra rather than ultra vires.[207] It should also be recognised that there will be often be balancing within the ultra vires principle itself. This can take the form of a value judgment as to whether to categorise an error as one of law, fact, discretion or no error at all.

---

[203] *Mansell* 476 P 2d 423 (1970) at 448. The court did, however, reserve the question of what would happen where the body totally lacked the power to achieve that which estoppel would accomplish against it, at 450.

[204] *Laker Airways* [1977] Q.B. 643 at 707.

[205] Citing *Robertson* [1949] 1 K.B. 227; *R. v Liverpool Corporation, Ex p. Liverpool Taxi Fleet Operators' Association* [1972] 2 Q.B. 299 and *HTV* [1976] I.C.R. 170.

[206] *Reprotech* [2003] 1 W.L.R. 348; *Powergen* [2000] J.P.L. 629; *Flanagan* [2002] 1 W.L.R. 2601; *Powergen* [2000] J.P.L. 1037; *Coghurst* [2002] EWHC 1091 (Admin); *Clear Channel* [2006] EWHC 3325 (Admin); *Flattery* [2010] EWHC 2868 (Admin).

[207] *MFK* [1990] 1 W.L.R. 1545; *Bibi* [2002] 1 W.L.R. 237; *Ejaz* [1995] C.O.D. 72.

A balancing approach is undertaken by the Strasbourg Court and by the ECJ,[208] and in *Rowland* May LJ considered favourably the general idea of a balancing approach.[209] The court in *Rowland* recognised that some balancing might be required as a result of the Convention jurisprudence. It held, as we have seen, that a legitimate expectation relating to property could be a "possession" protected by art.1 of the First Protocol ECHR, even if the representation giving rise to the expectation was ultra vires. The expectation would not necessarily entitle the party to its realisation, but could entitle him to some other form of relief that was within the powers of the public body. This might take the form of the benevolent exercise of discretion to alleviate the injustice, or the payment of compensation. **22–049**

The balancing approach has the advantage of allowing the court the very flexibility that the jurisdictional principle treats as a foregone conclusion. It manifests a willingness to inquire whether the disadvantages to the public interest really do outweigh the injustice to the individual. In many areas where the representation relates to a purely financial matter, such as a claim by the government for tax or a citizen seeking social security benefits, the hardship to the individual who has detrimentally relied will outweigh any public disadvantage. There are other areas where the balance would be different.[210] Thus, third party interests and the public interest are of particular importance in the planning context. This explains the reluctance to consider modification of the general statutory scheme through giving effect to representations.[211]

It is also possible for balancing to be sanctioned or mandated by *legislation*. This could take one of two forms. A clause dealing with the problem might be inserted in particular statutes.[212] There could, alternatively, be a general statute. This could provide a defence for bona fide reliance on a rule or opinion, where the rule or opinion was made by the body responsible for administering that law, and the rule was promulgated to guide the class of persons to which the representee belonged. The particular statutes to which this defence would apply could be stipulated and additions could be made.[213] These statutes provide a defence to money claims against the representee. This is a valuable first stage in the protection of the representee, but it will often not be sufficient. The individual may need not just relief from a penalty, but the ability to pursue the course of conduct which he was induced to follow by the representation.

---

[208] Craig, *EU Administrative Law*, 2nd edn (2012).

[209] *Rowland* [2005] Ch.1 at [115]–[120].

[210] This is one reason why the example given by Y. Vanderman, "Ultra Vires Legitimate Expectations: An Argument for Compensation" [2012] P.L. 85, 92, is wrong, the other being that the claimant would not satisfy the conditions for an actionable expectation.

[211] *Powergen* [2000] J.P.L. 629; *Flanagan* [2002] 1 W.L.R. 2601; *Powergen UK Plc v Leicester City Council* [2000] J.P.L. 1037 CA (Civ Div); *Reprotech* [2003] 1 W.L.R. 348; *Coghurst* [2002] EWHC 1091 (Admin); *Henry Boot Homes Ltd v Bassetlaw DC* [2002] EWCA Civ 983.

[212] See in the USA Portal-to-Portal Act 1947, 29 USCA ss.258 and 259; Trust Indenture Act 1939, 15 USCA s.77(c); Public Utility Holding Act 1939, 15 USCA s.79 I(d); Defence Production Act 1950, 50 USCA s.2157.

[213] F. Newman, "Should Official Advice be Reliable?—Proposals as to Estoppel and Related Doctrines in Administrative Law" (1953) 53 Col. L. Rev. 374.

iii. Balancing legality and legal certainty: objections

22–050 The central objection to the judicial balancing test is that it would offend against constitutional principle. If Parliament has laid down limits to the powers of a body it might be felt that the courts should not balance the public versus individual interest in the manner suggested above.[214] There is force in this objection.

The strength of the argument is, however, diminished because there are at least four areas in which the jurisdictional principle is compromised, and balancing is accepted as legitimate or inevitable: in the law relating to invalidity, de facto officers, waiver and delay. It is therefore incumbent on those who object to judicial balancing in relation to representations to suggest why it is acceptable in other areas, to distinguish them, or to conclude that the law in such areas is wrong and explain how it should be dealt with in the alternative. This normative exercise is not undertaken by critics, thereby considerably weakening their argument.[215] If the constitutional objection is determinative then it assumes the following principle: it is forbidden for courts to use any public law doctrine whereby the ultra vires nature of a public body's act is mitigated or qualified. This proposition is, however, untenable as a matter of positive law.

In the law relating to invalidity there are situations where the courts have qualified the concept of retrospective nullity, because the effect on the administration or an individual are regarded as unacceptable.[216] This also underlies the doctrine of de facto officers. We allow waiver to operate with the effect that there will be no remedy for an ultra vires decision.[217] This is so also in relation to remedies and delay. The detailed rules on delay will be considered later.[218] Suffice it to say for the present that s.31(6) of the Senior Courts Act 1981 allows the court to refuse a remedy where there has been undue delay in making the application, if it considers that the granting of relief would cause substantial hardship to, or substantially prejudice the rights of, any person or would be detrimental to good administration. The effect of the law in these areas is to countenance balancing, usually against the individual, where an ultra vires act has occurred, even though we deny any such balancing in favour of the innocent individual who has been misled by an ultra vires representation made by a public body. A number of objections might be made to this analysis.

22–051 First, it might be argued that balancing is justified in the context of, for example, delay because there is legislative sanction. This will not withstand examination. The argument misconstrues the position at common law prior to the Senior Courts Act 1981.[219] The courts, prior to this Act, took a wide variety of factors into account in determining whether to withhold a remedy or not, including: administrative convenience, effectiveness, hardship to third parties, and broad

---

214 Aman and Mayton, *Administrative Law* (2001), pp.328–329.

215 The arguments in this section are not addressed in Vanderman, "Ultra Vires Legitimate Expectations: An Argument for Compensation" [2012] P.L. 85.

216 See Ch.24.

217 See para.26–010.

218 See Ch.27.

219 Moreover, if legislative sanction was held to be required then Ord.53 r.4 would have been ultra vires prior to the passage of the Senior Courts Act 1981.

notions of justice.[220] The courts were, in such instances, balancing the ultra vires nature of the conduct against the consequences of granting a remedy. Viewed in this way s.31(6) was little more than a declaration of the previous common law position.

A second objection to the analogies drawn from invalidity, de facto officers, waiver and delay might be cast as follows. In these instances the ultra vires nature of the act is not touched. It is simply the remedy that is refused or modified. This will not do. There may well be reasons why we would wish the courts to exercise their balancing discretion at the remedial level, rather than by manipulating vires itself.[221] Let us not, however, allow form to blind us to substance: in whichever way the balancing is expressed it is still balancing. The full effects of the ultra vires principle are still being compromised. There is in any event no reason to suggest that the balancing which would take place in the context of representations could not be expressed in the same way. If such balancing were to be allowed we would not be saying that the public body could now lawfully do something outside its powers. We would accept that the public body had made an ultra vires representation, but conclude that because of the minimal effect on the public interest, as compared to the harm to the representee, that the representation should bind in this instance.

A third possible objection is that there might be third party interests affected, who would have no opportunity to put their views when determining whether the representation should bind. This will be taken into account in the balancing process. The problem of third party interests is, however, every bit as real when the balancing takes place in relation to invalidity, waiver or delay, yet it has not been regarded as a reason for rejecting balancing in these areas.

A final objection would be to argue that the balancing within invalidity, waiver and delay is justified because it is in favour of the public body, and that such balancing is warranted because the public body represents a wider public interest. A process of weighing is not, it might be argued, legitimate "the other way round", where the only interest affected by the misleading representation is that of the individual. This objection is unconvincing. Granted that the public body represents a wider public interest, this does not explain why an ultra vires representation should never be allowed to bind if the detriment to the individual outweighs the harm to the public interest. The argument is, in any event, mistaken in its own terms. When the courts balance within invalidity, waiver, and delay they do not only take account of administrative convenience. They have considered a much broader range of factors, such as effectiveness, third party interests, the detriment to the applicant, and more amorphous considerations of justice.

---

220 See paras 26–010, 26–016, 26–024 to 26–026, 26–035 and 27–046 to 27–051.

221 See Ch.24.

C. Compensation

22–052 It might be argued that it would be much simpler to give compensation to the aggrieved representee than to allow an ultra vires representation to bind. A monetary remedy would be helpful in this context and should be developed.[222] There are however two points that should be made in relation to this suggestion.

The first is that in some circumstances it would be tantamount to doing the same thing. Giving compensation in cases like *Robertson*[223] would have the same effect as holding the agency to the representation.

The second point is more important. Let us assume that X has been given an assurance that alterations to property do not require further planning permission. X builds the property with the alterations. The assurance given was ultra vires the representor. The cost of compensating X will be £20,000.[224] Let us assume that Y received an assurance that he could operate a new transport service, and invested £25 million. The assurance was ultra vires the body that made it.[225]

Any system of compensation will derive its funds from society, directly or indirectly, whether through taxation or local rates. It is a trite, though important, proposition that funds for compensation are scarce. If by balancing the public and private interest it can be shown that the detriment to the former is outweighed by that of the latter, it is not clear why we should give compensation rather than allow the representation to bind. The ultra vires principle operates to keep bodies within the ambit of their powers, and does so to protect society or a certain section of it.

If it can be shown that society is not going to suffer in comparison to the individual, then to insist that, for example, Y's investment should lay idle, and that Y should be compensated, would be a waste of these resources. Society is compensating X and Y for the destruction of things the presence of which did not really harm it. It is doubtful whether this is the most pressing object on which to spend scarce societal resources. Compensation for wrongful administrative action may well be needed.[226] It should not, however, be an alternative to allowing the representation to bind when there has been an ultra vires assurance. It should be a complement.

---

222 *Rowland* [2005] Ch. 1 at [80]; A. Brown, "Justifying Compensation for Frustrated Legitimate Expectations" [2011] *Law and Philosophy* 699.

223 *Robertson* [1949] 1 K.B. 227.

224 *Lever Finance* [1971] 1 Q.B. 222.

225 *Laker Airways* [1977] Q.B. 643 at 707.

226 Ch.30. There may, for example, be good reason to compensate Z who has suffered loss of amenity due to the ultra vires assurance given to X.

CHAPTER 23

EQUALITY

1. CENTRAL ISSUES

i. The relevance of equality for judicial review has been touched on in previous discussion. It is nonetheless important to treat this topic separately.[1] This chapter does not purport to cover all equality law, since this would require book-length treatment. The focus is on equality as a precept of judicial review. Equality features in judicial actions in four principal ways. 23–001

ii. First, although slow to develop, there is now case law concerning equality as a common law precept of judicial review, such that differential treatment of like groups can lead to invalidation of the contested decision.

iii. Second, statute has made the major contribution to equality law, with specific statutes dealing with different aspects of equality, such as race, sex and disability. This legislation has been brought together in the Equality Act 2010. The details of this legislation are outside the scope of this book, but there is discussion of the public sector equality duty that imposes important procedural obligations on public bodies.

iv. Third, the Human Rights Act 1998 brought Convention rights into UK law, including art.14 ECHR, which enshrines the principle of equality. It has been relied on in numerous important cases under the HRA.

v. Fourth, EU law is a further source of equality rights that can be enforced through national courts, for cases that come within the scope of EU law. EU conceptions of equality have been further enhanced by the EU Charter of Rights, which became legally binding by the Lisbon Treaty. EU law remains binding on the UK while withdrawal negotiations are ongoing.

---

[1] J. Jowell, "Is Equality a Constitutional Principle?" (1994) 7 C.L.P. 1; Lord Lester, "Equality and United Kingdom Law: Past, Present and Future" [2001] P.L. 77; C. McCrudden, "Equality and Discrimination", in D. Feldman (ed.), *English Public Law*, 2nd edn (Oxford: Oxford University Press, 2009), Ch.11; R. Singh QC, "Equality: The Neglected Virtue" [2004] E.H.R.L.R. 141; S. Fredman, "From Deference to Democracy: The Role of Equality under the Human Rights Act 1998" (2006) 122 L.Q.R. 53; K. Monaghan, *Monaghan on Equality Law* (Oxford: Oxford University Press, 2013); B. Hepple, *Equality the New Legal Framework* 2nd edn (Oxford: Hart Publishing, 2014); A. McColgan, *Discrimination, Equality and the Law* (Oxford: Hart, 2014).

2. COMMON LAW

A. The Principle of Treating Like Groups Alike

i. The basic precept

23–002 Historically, the common law was not at the forefront in the protection of equality. The common law was, as McCrudden states, often a source of discrimination,[2] especially for women, although there were, as he points out, several islands of non-discrimination norms in the common law, as exemplified by those dealing with the obligations of common carriers.[3]

The idea that like groups should be treated in a like manner, and that different groups should be treated differently, is a central precept of equality. The decision as to whether a certain group should be regarded as the same or different from another inevitably requires the making of value judgments. It should also be recognised that the basic precept of treating like cases alike conceals choices as to whether to think of equality in terms of consistency, results or opportunity.[4] The choice can have a marked impact on the legitimacy of distinctions drawn by government, including the legitimacy of affirmative action.[5]

23–003 Thus, formal equality or equality as consistency dictates that like should be treated alike and that different cases should be treated differently. This important precept is integral to equality law in most legal systems. It does not, however, dictate any particular substantive result, and can be met whether people are treated equally badly or equally well.[6]

Equality of results, by way of contrast, "goes beyond a demand for consistent treatment of likes, and requires instead that the result be equal", thereby recognising that "apparently identical treatment can in practice reinforce inequality because of past or on-going discrimination".[7] There are, however, as Fredman notes, ambiguities in the meaning accorded to results for these purposes. The focus might be on the particular individual, it might be on the group to which the individual belongs, or it might be on equality of outcome designed to overcome under-representation of a particular group within certain types of employment.[8]

Equality of opportunity constitutes a third conception of equality, and is a *via media* between formal equality and equality of result. Using the metaphor of a race, equality of opportunity is premised on the assumption that real equality cannot be achieved if individuals begin this race from different starting points. There are difficulties with the more precise meaning of this conception of equality, with some emphasising its procedural dimension, and others placing

[2] *Nairn v University of St Andrews* [1909] A.C. 147.

[3] McCrudden, "Equality and Discrimination" in D. Feldman (ed.), *English Public Law* (2009), Ch.11.

[4] S. Fredman, *Discrimination Law*, 2nd edn (Clarendon Press, 2011), Ch.1.

[5] Fredman, *Discrimination Law* (2011), Ch.5.

[6] Fredman, *Discrimination Law* (2011), pp.7–11.

[7] Fredman, *Discrimination Law* (2011), p.11.

[8] Fredman, *Discrimination Law* (2011), pp.11–14.

greater emphasis on substance so as to ensure that "persons from all sections of society have a genuinely equal chance of satisfying the criteria for access to a particular social good".[9]

ii. The case law

The dictate that like cases should be treated alike, and that different groups should be treated differently, has been taken into account by our courts. This has sometimes been under existing heads of review, such as improper purpose or relevancy. The more recent tendency is to ground intervention openly on the basis of equality. **23–004**

In *Kruse*[10] the court held that a bylaw could not be partial or unequal in its operation as between different classes. Lord Denning in *Edwards*[11] held that the courts would not allow a power to be exercised arbitrarily or with unfair discrimination. In *Ali*[12] the court held that the devolution of power by a local authority to neighbourhoods to decide on the allocation of power to the homeless was unfair and irrational, since variable criteria were applied. In *Urmaza*, *Gangadeen*, *WL Congo*, *Mandalia* and other cases[13] it was held that the legal principle of consistency in the exercise of public law powers created a presumption that the agency or minister would follow a declared policy. This presumption flowed from the very purpose of such a policy, which was to secure consistency. A departure from such a policy would require the giving of reasons, and would have to be justified in substantive terms.

The centrality of non-discrimination as a common law concept has been increasingly emphasised by the courts. Thus Lord Woolf CJ in *A v Secretary of State* stated that the right not to be discriminated against was one of the most significant requirements of the rule of law, and that the common law recognised the importance of not discriminating long before the HRA came into force.[14] In *Hall*[15] Lord Hoffmann adverted to the fundamental principle of justice that people should be treated equally and that like cases treated alike. In *Gurung*,[16] the applicants were Gurkhas. They claimed that the decision of the Ministry of

---

9 Fredman, *Discrimination Law* (2011), p.15.

10 *Kruse v Johnson* [1898] 2 Q.B. 91.

11 *Edwards v SOGAT* [1971] Ch. 354.

12 *R. v Tower Hamlets LBC, Ex p. Ali* (1992) 25 H.L.R. 158.

13 *R. v Home Secretary, Ex p. Urmaza* [1996] C.O.D. 479 QBD; *R. v Home Secretary, Ex p. Gangadeen* [1998] 1 F.L.R. 762, CA (Civ Div); *R. v Secretary of State for the Environment, Ex p. West Oxfordshire DC* [1994] C.O.D. 134 QBD; *R. (Coghlan) v Chief Constable of Greater Manchester* [2005] 2 All E.R. 890 QBD; *R. (Gill) v Lord Chancellor's Department* [2003] EWHC 156 (Admin); *R. (Munjaz) v Mersey Care NHS Trust* [2006] 2 A.C. 148, HL; *R. (S) v Secretary of State for the Home Department* [2011] EWHC 2120 (Admin); *Eastlands Homes Partnership Ltd v Whyte* [2010] EWHC 695 (QB); *R. (Kambadzi) v Secretary of State for the Home Department* [2011] 1 W.L.R. 1299 SC; *R. (WL (Congo)) v Secretary of State for the Home Department* [2011] 2 W.L.R. 671 SC; *Mandalia v Secretary of State for the Home Department* [2015] UKSC 59 SC.

14 *A v Secretary of State for the Home Department* [2004] Q.B. 335, CA (Civ Div) at [7]. The decision on the facts was reversed by the House of Lords, but this did not affect the substance of the point made in the text, *A v Secretary of State for the Home Department* [2005] 2 A.C. 68.

15 *Arthur JS Hall v Simons* [2002] 1 A.C. 615, HL at 688.

16 *R. (Gurung) v Ministry of Defence* [2002] EWHC 2463 (Admin); *Rodriguez v Minister of Housing of Gibraltar* [2009] UKPC 52.

Defence to exclude them from an ex gratia scheme of compensation for prisoners of war held by the Japanese was contrary to common law principles of equality. McCombe J held that their exclusion was irrational and inconsistent with the principle of equality that formed a cornerstone of UK law.[17] Lord Hoffmann in *Matadeen*[18] reinforced the basic precept concerning equality, while adverting to the difficulties that could attend adjudication thereon. Referring to the precept that persons should be treated uniformly, unless there was some valid reason for differential treatment, Lord Hoffmann stated that:

> "Their Lordships do not doubt that such a principle is one of the building blocks of democracy and necessarily permeates any democratic constitution. Indeed, their Lordships would go further and say that treating like cases alike and unlike cases differently is a general axiom of rational behaviour. It is, for example, frequently invoked by the courts in proceedings for judicial review as a ground for holding some administrative act to have been irrational ... But the very banality of the principle must suggest a doubt as to whether merely to state it can provide an answer to the kind of problem which arises in this case. Of course persons should be uniformly treated, unless there is some valid reason to treat them differently. But what counts as a valid reason for treating them differently? And, perhaps more important, who is to decide whether the reason is valid or not? Must it always be the courts? The reasons for not treating people uniformly often involve, as they do in this case, questions of social policy on which views may differ. These are questions which the elected representatives of the people have some claim to decide for themselves. The fact that equality of treatment is a general principle of rational behaviour does not entail that it should necessarily be a justiciable principle—that it should always be the judges who have the last word on whether the principle has been observed. In this, as in other areas of constitutional law, sonorous judicial statements of uncontroversial principle often conceal the real problem, which is to mark out the boundary between the powers of the judiciary, the legislature and the executive in deciding how that principle is to be applied."

3. STATUTORY INTERVENTION AND STATUTORY INTERPRETATION

A. General

23–005 This is not the place for detailed analysis of the complex body of statute law concerning various aspects of equality.[19] Suffice it to say for the present that Parliament intervened and dealt with discrimination on a variety of grounds. These include race,[20] gender discrimination and equality[21] and disability.[22] This legislation has now been consolidated by the Equality Act 2010.[23] The very existence of these prohibitions on discrimination means that groups cannot be validly distinguished merely because of, for example, their respective ethnic

---

[17] Compare *The Association of British Civilian Internees Far East Region v Secretary of State for Defence* [2002] EWHC 2119 (Admin) at [53]–[54].

[18] *Matadeen v Pointu* [1999] 1 A.C. 98 at 109.

[19] Fredman, *Discrimination Law* (2011); McCrudden, "Equality and Discrimination", in D. Feldman (ed.), *English Public Law* (2009); Hepple, *Equality the New Legal Framework* (2011).

[20] Race Relations Act 1976; Race Relations (Amendment) Act 2000; *R. (European Roma Rights Centre) v Immigration Officer, Prague Airport* [2005] 2 A.C. 1; *R. (Elias) v Secretary of State for Defence* [2006] EWCA Civ 1293.

[21] Equal Pay Act 1970; Sex Discrimination Act 1975.

[22] Disability Discrimination Act 1995; Disability Rights Commission Act 1999.

[23] Hepple, *Equality the New Legal Framework* (2011).

backgrounds. These foundational statutes have been amended, in part because of the need to comply with initiatives from EU law.

The centrality of non-discrimination can also be seen in the way in which the courts use this principle as an interpretative device when considering statutes. Thus, in *Fitzpatrick*[24] the House of Lords was willing to construe the word "family" within legislation to include a same sex partner. The word could legitimately bear a different meaning in 1999, as compared to the meaning when it was initially enacted in 1920.[25]

B. Public Sector Equality Duties

While the complex body of statute law concerning equality is beyond the remit of this book, it is important to focus on certain public sector equality obligations that are especially important for public bodies.[26] The classic approach of anti-discrimination legislation has been on specific actions brought by an individual against another individual or institution that violated the statutory prohibition on race, sex or disability discrimination. It was nonetheless felt that this approach was too limited, because studies showed the persistence of status inequalities, notwithstanding the legislative proscription of such discriminatory treatment. **23–006**

The response was the enactment of public sector equality duties that imposed obligations on public bodies to pay due regard to the need to eliminate a certain type of discrimination. Such duties, which differed somewhat in detail, were incorporated as amendments to legislation on race, sex and disability discrimination.[27] The public sector equality duty is now contained in the Equality Act 2010 s.149.[28] The protected characteristics referred to in s.149 are age, disability, gender reassignment, pregnancy and maternity, race, religion or belief, sex and sexual orientation[29]:

> "(1) A public authority must, in the exercise of its functions, have due regard to the need to—
> (a) eliminate discrimination, harassment, victimisation and any other conduct that is prohibited by or under this Act;
> (b) advance equality of opportunity between persons who share a relevant protected characteristic and persons who do not share it;
> (c) foster good relations between persons who share a relevant protected characteristic and persons who do not share it.
>
> (2) A person who is not a public authority but who exercises public functions must, in the exercise of those functions, have due regard to the matters mentioned in subsection (1).

---

[24] *Fitzpatrick v Sterling Housing Association Ltd* [2001] 1 A.C. 27, HL.

[25] See also *R. v R* [1992] 1 A.C. 599; *Ghaidan v Godin-Mendoza* [2002] 2 A.C. 557.

[26] M. Bell, "Judicial Enforcement of the Duties on Public Bodies to Promote Equality" [2010] P.L. 672; Sir P. Sales, "The Public Sector Equality Duty" [2011] J.R. 1; S. Fredman, "The Public Sector Equality Duty" (2011) 40 I.L.J. 405; T. Hickman, "Too Hot, too Cold or Just Right? The Development of the Public Sector Equality Duties in Administrative Law" [2013] P.L. 325.

[27] Race Relations Act 1976 s.71(1); Sex Discrimination Act 1975 s.76A(1); Disability Discrimination Act 1995 s.49A.

[28] There is in addition a different public sector duty in relation to socio-economic inequality in s.1 of the Equality Act 2010, but this section has not yet been brought into force, S. Fredman, "Positive Duties and Socio-Economic Disadvantage: Bringing Disadvantage onto the Equality Agenda" [2010] E.H.R.L.R. 290.

[29] Equality Act 2010 s.149(7).

(3) Having due regard to the need to advance equality of opportunity between persons who share a relevant protected characteristic and persons who do not share it involves having due regard, in particular, to the need to—
(a) remove or minimise disadvantages suffered by persons who share a relevant protected characteristic that are connected to that characteristic;
(b) take steps to meet the needs of persons who share a relevant protected characteristic that are different from the needs of persons who do not share it;
(c) encourage persons who share a relevant protected characteristic to participate in public life or in any other activity in which participation by such persons is disproportionately low."

23–007 The duty applies to public authorities as listed in Sch.19 of the 2010 Act and to bodies exercising a public function, which is defined as a function of a public nature for the purposes of the Human Rights Act 1998.[30] It is, moreover, open to a minister of the Crown to impose specific duties on public authorities for the better performance of the duties contained in s.149(1).[31] Failure in respect of these duties does not give rise to a cause of action in private law,[32] but it can be the subject of judicial review. The nature of the duty in s.149 can be best understood through the case law interpreting the analogous duties under the earlier legislation on race, sex and disability discrimination.

The initial case law was not especially promising,[33] but the potential of the new duties was revealed in *Elias*.[34] The applicant was born in Hong Kong, her mother was from Iraq and her father from Iraq or India. They were all British subjects, and were interned by the Japanese for four years in 1941. The applicant had lived in the UK since 1976. The government in 2000 introduced an ex gratia payment of £10,000 for British civilians interned by the Japanese during the war, but imposed a birth link such that a person did not qualify unless the claimant, or a parent/grandparent was born in the UK. The applicant argued that the government was in breach of its equality duty under the Race Relations Act 1976. Elias J held that the criteria for compensation had an obvious discriminatory effect, and that even if this was not so obvious consideration of the race equality duty was still required. There was no evidence that the defendant had assessed the extent of any adverse impact, nor other ways in which it might have been eliminated or minimised. This omission could not be corrected after the policy had been adopted. While this aspect of the case was not contested on appeal, Arden LJ nonetheless stated that[35]:

> "It is the clear purpose of s.71 to require public bodies to whom that provision applies to give advance consideration to issues of race discrimination before making any policy decision that may be affected by them … this provision must be seen as an integral and important part of the mechanisms for ensuring the fulfilment of the aims of anti-discrimination legislation."

---

30 Equality Act 2010 s.150(5).
31 Equality Act 2010 ss.153 and 155.
32 Equality Act 2010 s.156.
33 *R. (Elliott) v The Electoral Commission* [2003] EWHC 395 (Admin).
34 *R. (Elias) v Secretary of State for Defence* [2005] EWHC 1435 (Admin).
35 *Elias* [2006] EWCA Civ 1293 at [274].

Subsequent cases further emphasised the importance of considering the relevant equality duty prior to the contested decision.[36] The duty is to have "due regard" to the matters listed in s.149(1). This is not an obligation to achieve a particular result, but is, as Sales suggests,[37] best conceptualised as a mandatory relevant consideration that has to be taken into account when demanded by the criteria in s.149. This still leaves open what precisely a public authority must do in order to comply with s.149. It requires, as seen above, consideration of the equality duty prior to the making of the contested decision, but does not necessarily demand express reference to the equality duty.[38] In more general terms, the duty has been held to be the regard that is appropriate in all the circumstances,[39] and the courts implicitly if not explicitly apply proportionality when making this determination.[40] The reality is that the public authority will have to produce some evidentiary consideration to show that it has complied with the equality duty, and this may require something akin to an impact assessment.

In *Brown* the court put forward the following principles in deciding whether due regard had been given or not[41]: the relevant officials within the authority should be made aware of their public-sector equality duties; the duty to have due regard must be addressed before the decision is taken; the duty must be undertaken with vigour, it was not an exercise in just ticking boxes; the duty was non-delegable, such that if the assessment is undertaken by a third party the public authority must ensure that it is subject to proper supervision; the duty was a continuing one; and it was good practice for a public authority to keep a record of how it had complied with the equality duty. **23–008**

It is readily apparent that although the public-sector equality duty is couched in terms of procedure and not substance it can nonetheless impose significant demands on public authorities who seek to ensure that they comply with it when making their decisions. This is exemplified by the complex impact assessment undertaken by Brent before deciding to close some local libraries because of the need to make budget cuts. The subsequent legal challenge, although not upheld, nonetheless demonstrated that even explicit, detailed, and careful assessment does not necessarily safeguard the authority against the possibility of such a challenge.[42] The courts will have to tread a careful line[43] between vigorous interpretation of the important duty in s.149[44] and the burdens thereby placed on

---

[36] *R. (Kaur and Shah) v Ealing LBC* [2008] EWHC 2062 (Admin); *R. (C) v Secretary of State for Justice* [2009] Q.B. 657.

[37] Sales, "The Public Sector Equality Duty" [2011] J.R. 1, 6–9.

[38] *R. (Baker) v Secretary of State for Communities and Local Government* [2008] EWCA Civ 141; *R. (Macdonald) v Royal Borough of Kensington and Chelsea* [2011] UKSC 33 at [24]. See however, *R. (Harris) v Haringey LBC* [2010] EWCA Civ 703.

[39] *Baker* [2008] EWCA Civ 141; *Macdonald* [2011] UKSC 33 at [23].

[40] Sales, "The Public Sector Equality Duty" [2011] J.R. 1, 30.

[41] *R. (Brown) v Secretary of State for Work and Pensions* [2008] EWHC 3158 (Admin); *R. (Domb) v London Borough of Hammersmith and Fulham* [2009] EWCA Civ 941; *R. (Bapio Action Ltd) v Royal College of General Practitioners* [2014] EWHC 1416 (Admin); *R. (MA) v Secretary of State for Work and Pensions* [2014] EWCA Civ 13.

[42] *R. (Bailey) v Brent LBC* [2011] EWCA Civ 1586.

[43] Hickman, "Too Hot, Too Cold or Just Right?" [2013] P.L. 325.

[44] *Pieretti v Enfield BC* [2010] EWCA Civ 1104; *R. (Bracking) v Secretary of State for Work and Pensions* [2013] EWCA Civ 1345.

the authorities that have to make the determinations.[45] This is more especially so because, as exemplified by *Bailey* dealing with library closure,[46] there may be tensions concerning the solution that gives best due regard to the different characteristics protected under s.149(1). A decision that accords best due regard to, for example, race will not necessarily be the same as that which shows the best due regard to, for example, age.

4. THE HRA

A. Article 14 and Protocol 12 ECHR

23–009 Many cases raising issues of equality and discrimination now rely on the Human Rights Act 1998,[47] which brought Convention rights into domestic law, including art.14 ECHR. This article does not enshrine equality as a free-standing principle. It does, however, provide that the enjoyment of the rights and freedoms set out in the Convention shall be secured without discrimination on any ground such as sex, race, colour, language, religion, political or other opinion, national or social origin, association with a national minority, property, birth or other status.[48] It is clear that while there cannot be a violation of art.14 in isolation,[49] there may be a breach of this article when considered together with other Convention articles, even if there would have been no breach of those other articles.[50]

This important proposition was established in the *Belgian Linguistic* case.[51] An example cited by the court will make this clear. Article 6 ECHR does not compel states to establish appeal courts. If, however, such courts are set up then access must not be discriminatory since this would violate art.14. The ECtHR in the same case also gave important guidance on the meaning of discrimination: art.14 did not prohibit every difference in treatment, but only those which had no objective and reasonable justification. This was to be assessed in relation to the aims and effects of the measure in question. The differential treatment must not only pursue a legitimate aim. It had to be proportionate: there had to be a reasonable relationship of proportionality between the means employed and the aim sought to be realised.[52]

Mention should also be made of Protocol 12 ECHR. It is important because it provides for a general prohibition of discrimination, by way of contrast to art.14

[45] *R. (Aspinall) v Secretary of State for Work and Pensions* [2014] EWHC 4134 (Admin); *R. (A) v Secretary of State for Work and Pensions* [2015] EWHC 159 (Admin); *IS v Director of Legal Aid Casework* [2015] EWHC 1965 (Admin).

[46] *Bailey* [2011] EWCA Civ 1586.

[47] Fredman, "From Deference to Democracy: The Role of Equality under the Human Rights Act 1998" (2006) 122 L.Q.R. 53.

[48] The UK courts have acknowledged that the list in art.14 is not exhaustive, while holding that the phrase "other status" means that the list is not unlimited, *R. (Clift) v Secretary of State for the Home Department* [2007] 1 A.C. 484, HL; *R. (M) v Secretary of State for Work and Pensions* [2009] 1 A.C. 311, HL.

[49] *Abdulaziz, Cabales and Balkandali v UK* (1985) 7 E.H.R.R. 471 at [71].

[50] Jacobs, White and Ovey, *The European Convention on Human Rights*, 5th edn (Oxford: Oxford University Press, 2010), pp.554–556.

[51] *Belgian Linguistic* judgment of July 23, 1968, Series A, No.6.

[52] See also *Lithgow v UK* (1986) 8 E.H.R.R. 329.

ECHR, which only prohibits discrimination in the enjoyment of one or the other rights guaranteed by the Convention. Protocol 12 removes this limitation and guarantees that no-one shall be discriminated against on any ground by any public authority. Thus, art.1 of the Protocol states that:

> "1. The enjoyment of any right set forth by law shall be secured without discrimination on any ground such as sex, race, colour, language, religion, political or other opinion, national or social origin, association with a national minority, property, birth or other status.
>
> 2. No one shall be discriminated against by any public authority on any ground such as those mentioned in paragraph 1."

The Protocol entered into force in 2005 for those states that had ratified, when the requisite ten ratifications had been secured. The UK has not, however, signed or ratified this Protocol.[53]

B. The Determination of Discrimination

i. Michalak

Article 14 ECHR has been applied by the UK courts pursuant to the HRA. The issues to be considered were initially laid down by Brooke LJ in *Michalak*.[54] The House of Lords expressed reservations about this approach, but it was influential in the early case law and their Lordships' reservations can only be understood in the light of Brooke LJ's approach: **23–010**

> "(i) Do the facts fall within the ambit of one or more of the substantive Convention provisions … (ii) If so, was there different treatment as respects that right between the complainant on the one hand and other persons put forward for comparison ('the chosen comparators') on the other? (iii) Were the chosen comparators in an analogous situation to the complainant's situation? (iv) If so, did the difference in treatment have an objective and reasonable justification: in other words, did it pursue a legitimate aim and did the differential treatment bear a reasonable relationship of proportionality to the aim sought to be achieved? The third test addresses the question whether the chosen comparators were in a sufficiently analogous situation to the complainant's situation for the different treatment to be relevant to the question whether the complainant's enjoyment of his Convention right has been free from article 14 discrimination."

The initial question was therefore whether the facts fell within the ambit of a Convention right. If they did so the court had to consider whether there was different treatment as respects that right as between the complainant and other persons put forward for comparison, the chosen comparators. It was for the court to decide whether the chosen comparators were in an analogous situation to the complainant. It was also for the court to decide whether the difference of treatment was on a ground that fell within art.14 ECHR. This article lists a number of specific discriminatory grounds, but these are prefaced by the words

---

[53] See *http://conventions.coe.int/Treaty/Commun/ChercheSig.asp?NT=177&CM=8&DF=&CL=ENG* [Accessed 10 August 2015].

[54] *Michalak v Wandsworth LBC* [2003] 1 W.L.R. 617 CA (Civ Div) at [20].

"on any grounds such as". It has been held that if the ground relied on is not specifically listed in art.14 then it must be broadly of the same kind.[55]

If there is some prima facie discriminatory treatment judged by the above criteria, the court will then determine whether there is an objective and reasonable justification for the difference in treatment. This requires the court to decide whether the difference in treatment was in pursuit of a legitimate aim, and whether there was a reasonable relationship to the aim sought to be achieved. In general terms, the test for review will be that laid down by Lord Steyn in *Daly*.[56] This test has been considered earlier.[57]

ii. Carson

23–011 The approach in *Michalak* for deciding on art.14 ECHR was called into question in *Carson*,[58] the facts of which will be considered later. Doubts had been raised in earlier case law,[59] and these concerns were reiterated in *Carson* and later cases.[60] The essence of the concern was that the *Michalak* approach could be over rigid, and there could be overlap between the different stages of the analysis, more especially questions two, three and four.[61] There is force in this view and the taxonomy of issues to be decided in discrimination cases should not hinder the resolution of cases by forcing the courts to divide stages of the analysis in an overly rigid manner.

It should, however, also be recognised that the substance of the issues set out in the *Michalak* formula will normally have to be addressed by the court. Thus, it is axiomatic that an applicant will have to satisfy the court that the facts fall within a provision of the ECHR, since if they do not then art.14 cannot be invoked. It is also clear that the applicant will have to show that the alleged discrimination is on a ground covered by art.14. Nor is it possible to avoid discussion of comparators. To be sure this discussion should not obscure resolution of the case before the court, but it is nonetheless central to the very idea of discrimination. It is important moreover to recognise that objective justification is a separate issue that becomes pertinent once a prima facie case of discrimination has been found to exist.[62]

Given that this is so, it is interesting to reflect on why the *Michalak* test was problematic. The difficulty with the *Michalak* formula resides in the division between questions two and three and in that between questions three and four.

---

[55] *Waite v London Borough of Hammersmith and Fulham* [2002] EWCA Civ 482.

[56] *R. (Daly) v Secretary of State for the Home Department* [2001] 2 A.C. 532, HL at [26].

[57] See paras 20–044 to 20–049.

[58] *R. (Carson) v Secretary of State for Work and Pensions* [2006] 1 A.C. 173, HL.

[59] *Nasser v United Bank of Kuwait* [2002] 1 W.L.R. 1868, CA (Civ Div) at [56]; *Ghaidan v Godin-Mendoza* [2004] 2 A.C. 557 at [134]; *Shamoon v Chief Constable of the Royal Ulster Constabulary* [2003] 2 All E.R. 26 at [11].

[60] *Esfandiari v Secretary of State for Work and Pensions* [2006] H.R.L.R. 26, CA (Civ Div); *AL (Serbia) v Secretary of State for the Home Department* [2008] UKHL 42; *Langford v Secretary of State for Defence* [2015] EWHC 875 (Ch).

[61] *Carson* [2006] 1 A.C. 173 at [29]–[33], [61]–[70]; *Esfandiari* [2006] H.R.L.R. 26 at [8].

[62] A. Baker, "Comparison Tainted by Justification: Against a "Compendious Question" in Art 14 Discrimination" [2006] P.L. 476.

23–012 The very division between question two and three was premised on the assumption that one could identify in relatively abstract terms a person or group as the appropriate comparator with the applicant, and then make a separate, more concrete determination as to whether the chosen comparators were in an analogous situation to the applicant, this latter inquiry being designed to decide whether the difference in treatment constituted discrimination. This division can be problematic and artificial, especially where on closer examination the applicant and the chosen comparator are not truly in a sufficiently analogous situation for the difference in treatment to constitute prima facie discrimination.[63] The natural inclination is to run together questions two and three from *Michalak* and simply ask whether the applicant and the chosen comparator really are in an analogous situation.

This is in effect the approach taken by the Strasbourg Court, as exemplified by a case such as *Van der Mussele*.[64] The applicant argued that provisions of Belgian law requiring advocates to give legal assistance to those who needed it were contrary to arts 4 and 14 ECHR, given that such obligations were not placed on other professionals such as doctors, dentists, veterinary surgeons and the like. The Strasbourg Court rejected the claim, holding that the applicant and the other professionals were not in an analogous situation, since there were differences concerning their legal status, manner of entry to the profession, the nature of their functions and the manner in which they were performed. Each profession was characterised by a corpus of rights and obligations and it would be artificial to isolate one aspect thereof.[65]

The Strasbourg Court did not in this and other cases consider whether the applicant and another individual or group might in abstract terms be regarded as comparators, and then decide whether in more concrete terms they were in an analogous situation. It proceeded directly to the latter stage of the inquiry to decide whether in relation to the provision of services to those in need, the applicant and members of other professions were in an analogous situation. It did not thereby ignore the comparator issue. This is, as stated above, central to the very idea of discrimination. The Strasbourg approach indicates that it is only by paying attention to the specific allegations of differential treatment that one can decide whether the two individuals really are in an analogous situation and hence whether there has been discrimination.

23–013 The division between stages three and four of the *Michalak* formula can also be problematic. Courts may simply go straight to the issue of objective justification, where they believe that this is the heart of the issue, without bothering unduly with the other stages of the inquiry. The very idea of objective justification can, moreover, be brought into play within stage three as well as within stage four.[66] Thus, it is open to a court to conclude that a relevant difference between two groups means that they are not in an analogous situation and hence that there has been no discrimination. In such instances, the existence of the relevant difference

---

[63] *R. (Cossey) v Secretary of State for Justice* [2013] EWHC 3029 (Admin); *R. (Mahoney) v Secretary of State for Communities and Local Government* [2015] EWHC 589 (Admin).

[64] *Van der Mussele v Belgium* (1984) 6 E.H.R.R. 163.

[65] *Van der Mussele* (1984) 6 E.H.R.R. 163 at [46].

[66] This was recognised by Lord Hoffmann in *Carson* [2006] 1 A.C. 173 at [30]–[32].

is the justification for the difference in treatment. The concept of objective justification is also used in cases where a court has found that the two groups are in an analogous situation, and hence the differential treatment is prima facie discriminatory, but can be saved because there is some objective justification for the difference, such as the need to correct past discrimination. It will normally be for the state or public body to discharge the burden of proof if a case is resolved on objective justification in this second sense.[67]

The difficulties of maintaining the distinction between questions two and three, and between questions three and four are exemplified by *Carson* itself. The applicant had immigrated to South Africa from the UK. She received a pension to which she was entitled at the age of 60, since she had paid all necessary national insurance contributions. Pensioners who were resident in the UK received annual cost of living increases, as did those living in countries that had reciprocal Treaty arrangements with the UK, but the applicant did not receive any such increases. She argued that this constituted discrimination contrary to art.14 ECHR, read in conjunction with art.1 of the First Protocol.

The House of Lords rejected the claim. The relevant comparator for the applicant was the way in which pensioners in the UK were treated in relation to annual increments to the pension. The essence of their Lordships' decision was, however, that while pensioners in the UK and abroad might, in abstract terms, be regarded as the appropriate comparator, closer inquiry revealed that they were not in an analogous situation, because the provision of pensions was regarded as but one part of the overall regime of taxation and social security and the former paid tax in the UK while the latter did not. The distinction between the two groups was therefore justified, in the first of the senses identified above: the relevant difference was the justification for the difference in treatment.

C. Strict Scrutiny and Rationality Review

23–014 The issue as to how far the court should defer to the Executive, or accord it a discretionary area of judgment, has arisen in litigation under art.14, in much the same way as it has in relation to other Convention articles. There was an interesting tension in the courts' jurisprudence. Some courts were willing to accord such a discretionary area of judgment where the justification for the differential treatment raised issues of social and economic policy.[68] Other courts were less willing to do so, even where the subject matter related to social and economic policy. The very fact that the claim concerned discrimination in relation to such policy was seen as raising issues of high constitutional importance, with the consequence that there was searching scrutiny to determine whether there was a proper and rational justification for the difference in treatment.[69] This issue should now be seen in the light of the House of Lords' decision in *Carson*.

---

[67] See, however, the cautionary observations by Lord Walker, *Carson* [2006] 1 A.C. 173 at [69].

[68] *Michalak* [2003] 1 W.L.R. 617 at [41]; *Matadeen* [1999] 1 A.C. 98 at 109.

[69] *Ghaidan* [2002] 2 A.C. 557 at [18], [44].

i. *Strict scrutiny and rationality review: the distinction*

It is common for legal systems to distinguish between different types of equality claims and to apply different degrees of scrutiny accordingly. This approach has been endorsed by the House of Lords in *Carson*,[70] the facts of which were set out above. It was accepted that pension rights constituted possessions within the meaning of art.1 of the First Protocol and that her foreign residence was a "personal characteristic" for the purposes of art.14 ECHR. The key issue before the House of Lords was whether the differential treatment between the applicant and those who received annual increases constituted discrimination for the purposes of art.14. The House of Lords held that it did not. **23–015**

It was acknowledged that the applicant was treated differently from a pensioner who lived in the UK. Discrimination meant, however, the failure to treat like cases alike, or treating cases alike where there were differences between them.[71] Whether cases were sufficiently alike was "partly a matter of values and partly a matter of rationality".[72] A differential standard of review applied depending on the ground of the alleged discrimination.

Thus, Lord Hoffmann stated that characteristics such as race, caste, noble birth, membership of a political party, gender and sexual orientation were seldom if ever acceptable grounds for difference in treatment and the courts would carefully examine the reasons for differential treatment in relation to such characteristics. Discrimination on such grounds could not be justified on utilitarian grounds, since that would offend the "notion that everyone is entitled to be treated as an individual and not a statistical unit".[73] Lord Walker also followed US law and treated such grounds of discrimination as suspect, such that they would be subject to especially severe scrutiny.[74]

The standard of review for other forms of discrimination was less demanding. Where differences of treatment were made on grounds such as ability, occupation, wealth or education the courts would demand some rational justification. These differences in treatment were said Lord Hoffmann normally dependent on considerations of the public interest, which were "very much a matter for the democratically elected branches of government".[75] Lord Walker also endorsed less exacting rationality scrutiny for this second general category of differential treatment.[76] **23–016**

Their Lordships placed the present case firmly in the second category. There was no discrimination on a suspect ground such as sex or race. The case therefore fell to be decided on criteria of rationality, taking due account of the choices made by the democratically elected government. The differential treatment of

[70] *Carson* [2006] 1 A.C. 173. The leading judgments were given by Lord Hoffmann and Lord Walker. Lord Nicholls and Lord Rodger agreed with both judgments. Lord Carswell dissented; Baker, "Comparison Tainted by Justification: Against a 'Compendious Question' in Art 14 Discrimination" [2006] P.L. 476.

[71] *Carson* [2006] 1 A.C. 173 at [14], Lord Hoffmann.

[72] *Carson* [2006] 1 A.C. 173 at [15], Lord Hoffmann.

[73] *Carson* [2006] 1 A.C. 173 at [16].

[74] *Carson* [2006] 1 A.C. 173 at [55].

[75] *Carson* [2006] 1 A.C. 173 at [16].

[76] *Carson* [2006] 1 A.C. 173 at [55].

pensioners at home and abroad was justified in essence because pensions were regarded as part of the overall system of taxation and social security. The fact that the applicant paid national insurance contributions was not a sufficient condition for entitlement to the same retirement pension as paid to pensioners in the UK. Such contributions were not exclusively linked to pensions, but were rather a source of revenue used to fund social security in general as well as the NHS. The interlocking nature of the taxation and social security system viewed as a whole meant that it was impossible to separate a single element, retirement pensions, and treat it in a disaggregated manner.[77] There were therefore valid reasons for differentiating between the applicant resident abroad, and pensioners resident in the UK. Given that this was so, the courts should, moreover, respect the choice made by Parliament as to how much she should receive.[78]

ii. *Strict scrutiny and rationality review: application*

23–017 The idea that strict scrutiny review should be applied to cases of the kind listed in *Carson* fits with other prominent decisions, such as *A v Secretary of State for the Home Department*.[79] The claimants were foreign nationals who had been certified by the secretary of state as suspected international terrorists under s.21 of the Anti-Terrorism, Crime and Security Act 2001, on the ground that they posed a threat to national security under s.23 of the Act. They were detained without trial or charge and argued that s.23 was discriminatory since it did not provide for the detention of suspected international terrorists who were UK nationals. The House of Lords agreed. Their Lordships held that the legislation, which had been introduced to combat threats posed by Al-Qaeda post 9/11, was discriminatory and disproportionate, because of the differential treatment of nationals and non-nationals who might constitute a terrorist threat. In reaching this conclusion their Lordship made it clear that deference was not appropriate in cases of discrimination where the effect of the challenged measure entailed a significant deprivation of liberty.

The *Carson* approach has been followed in subsequent cases. Thus, in *Baiai*[80] Silber J considered the legality of a statutory regime designed to prevent sham marriages. The new regime required that those who were subject to immigration control and who wished to marry, other than according to the rites of the Church of England, had to apply to the secretary of state for a certificate of approval at a cost of £135. The marriage could only take place if approval was given by the secretary of state. The applicants challenged the regime under arts 12 and 14 ECHR. It is the latter claim that is of interest here. The applicants contended that the statutory scheme discriminated on grounds of religion and nationality, since the requirement for a certificate of approval did not apply to those who married in the Church of England. Silber J held, following the approach in *Carson*, that discrimination on grounds of religion and nationality should be subject to strict

[77] *Carson* [2006] 1 A.C. 173 at [21]–[22], [76]–[78].

[78] *Carson* [2006] 1 A.C. 173 at [25]–[27].

[79] *A v Secretary of State for the Home Department* [2005] 2 A.C. 68, HL; *Clift* [2007] 1 A.C. 484; *R. (Morris) v Westminster City Council (No.3)* [2006] 1 W.L.R. 505, CA (Civ Div).

[80] *R. (Baiai) v Secretary of State for the Home Department, Joint Council for the Welfare of Immigrants* [2006] EWHC 853 (Admin).

scrutiny, and that weighty reasons would have to be proffered to justify such discrimination. He concluded that when judged by this criterion the scheme could not be upheld, since there was no reason to believe that sham marriages were more likely when the ceremony occurred in a place other than the Church of England.

The *Esfandiari* case[81] provides a useful contrast. The applicants argued that the refusal to apply certain regulations under which contributions would be made to funeral expenses, in circumstances where Muslims chose to send the deceased back to their home state for burial, constituted discrimination contrary to art.14 ECHR. The Court of Appeal held that even if recent migrants had an identifiable status for the purpose of art.14 the case would not attract the highest scrutiny, but would rather fall within the second category laid down in *Carson*, since the allocation of public funds was an issue of social policy. The rationale given by the secretary of state for not contributing to the cost of such burials, that it would render the system more complex and considerably more expensive, was held to be defensible.

AL (Serbia)[82] provides a further interesting application of the *Carson* decision. 23–018
The appellant was born in 1984 in Kosovo, left the country in 1999 after being threatened by the authorities, became separated from his parents and arrived in the UK in 2000. His claim for asylum was rejected, but he was granted exceptional leave to remain until his 18th birthday in 2002. His application for an extension was refused. He argued that his removal would, however, be contrary to arts 8 and 14 ECHR. This was because in 2003 the Home Secretary announced the family amnesty policy, which involved the grant of indefinite leave to remain in the UK. In order to qualify, a person had to be an adult who had at least one dependant who was under 18, and the appellant did not satisfy this condition because he had arrived in the UK alone.

The House of Lords acknowledged that it was not entirely easy to decide whether the instant case fell within the strict scrutiny category of *Carson*, or whether it was to be judged by rationality review. It decided that the claimant's status for the purposes of art.14 as a single young adult did not require particularly weighty reasons before differential treatment could be justified, and there was no indication that single young adults were targeted for unfavourable treatment. It held therefore that the policy was a proportionate response to the problems it addressed, and the difference in treatment to which the claimants were subject could be justified.

A final example of the need for care in the application of the principles in *Carson* can be found in *Wilson*.[83] The claimant, a Romany gypsy, sited a residential caravan in breach of planning control on land owned by her family. The council issued a "stop notice" under the planning legislation,[84] requiring her to cease using the land for the stationing of caravans. The claimant argued that

---

[81] *Esfandiari* [2006] H.R.L.R. 26 at [11]–[13]. See also, *M* [2009] 1 A.C. 311; *British Gurkha Welfare Society v Ministry of Defence* [2010] EWCA Civ 1098; *Stewart v Secretary of State for Work and Pensions* [2011] EWCA Civ 907.

[82] *AL (Serbia)* [2008] UKHL 42.

[83] *R. (Wilson) v Wychavon DC* [2007] Q.B. 801.

[84] Town and Country Planning Act 1990 s.183.

the legislation was discriminatory, since it exempted dwelling houses, but not residential caravans, from the stop notice regime, and therefore indirectly discriminated against gypsies, in breach of arts 8 and 14 ECHR. The secretary of state accepted that the legislation was indirectly discriminatory, but argued that it was justified by the need to protect the public against the serious environmental harm caused by unauthorised caravan sites.

The Court of Appeal found against the claimant. Richards LJ found that the inclusion of residential caravans within the general stop notice regime was aimed legitimately at protecting the public against serious harm to amenity. The indirect discriminatory impact on gypsies made it appropriate, said Richards LJ, for the court to examine with intense scrutiny the secretary of state's objective justification for the rule. This did not, however, preclude according to the legislature some discretionary area of judgment, albeit narrower than that usually given in matters of planning policy. Thus, there was, said Richards LJ, no objection in art.14 cases to the adoption of a bright line rule with regard to residential caravans. Provided that the rule fell within the discretionary area of judgment allowed to the legislature, it could not be impugned on the ground that a different balance might have been struck or a less restrictive rule devised, although the existence of a less restrictive alternative might be relevant in examining the cogency of the claimed justification, so that the narrower the discretionary area of judgment, or the more intense the degree of scrutiny required, the more significant it might be that a less restrictive alternative could have been adopted. The court concluded that there were cogent reasons for a simple bright line rule exempting dwelling houses, but not residential caravans, from the stop notice regime.

D. Gender and Positive Discrimination

23–019 While *Carson* is important for judicial endorsement of differential standards of review depending on the nature of the discrimination, *Hooper*[85] is significant for judicial acceptance of justification for discrimination cast in terms of remedying past disadvantages.

The claimants were four widowers, whose wives had died in the period 1995–2000. If they had been widows, they would have received one of a number of widows' benefits depending on their particular circumstances: a widow's payment of £1,000, a widowed mother's allowance for those who had children until they ceased to be dependent, and a widow's pension. Legislation dating from 1999 abolished the widows' benefits for widows whose husbands died on or after 9 April 2001.[86] A new scheme of benefits was introduced that were payable to widows and widowers alike, but the rights of existing widows to the widows' pension were preserved. The claimants argued that once the HRA came into force the denial to them of benefits paid to widows constituted discrimination through a combination of arts 14 and 8 ECHR.

The House of Lords held that there was objective justification for the differential treatment in relation to payment of widows' pensions. Lord Hoffmann

[85] *R. (Hooper) v Secretary of State for Work and Pensions* [2005] 1 W.L.R. 1681 HL.

[86] Welfare Reform and Pensions Act 1999.

surveyed the rationale for and history of such pensions. The payment of this pension was not dependent on the resources of the particular widow: it was paid to all widows who satisfied the age criterion, the premise being that "older widows as a class were likely to be needier than older widowers as a class".[87] The rationale for the provision of the widows' pension was that "in the social conditions which prevailed for most of the last century, it was unusual for married women to work and that it was unreasonable to expect them to be equipped to earn their own living if they were widowed in middle age".[88] While the proportion of older women active in the labour market had increased by the turn of the century, a significant proportion of these worked part-time and there was a higher concentration of women than men in relatively low paid occupations: "the comparative disadvantage of women in the labour market had by no means disappeared".[89]

It was against this background that the House of Lords considered whether the continued payment of the widows' pension in the period 1995–2001 and its continuation for women bereaved before 9 April 2001 was objectively justified. The Court of Appeal concluded that there was no such justification, reversing the decision of Moses J. The House of Lords reversed the Court of Appeal. The House of Lords' reasoning in *Hooper* indicates that while the courts should, as stated in *Carson*, review gender based discrimination strictly this does not necessarily translate into substitution of judgment.

Lord Hoffmann, with whom the other Law Lords agreed on this issue, stated that the Strasbourg Court allowed Member States to treat groups unequally in order to correct factual inequalities and that in making decisions about social and economic policy, in particular those concerned with the equitable distribution of public resources, the Strasbourg Court allowed Member States a margin of appreciation. In a domestic system these decisions were "ordinarily recognized by the courts to be matters for the judgment of the elected representatives of the people",[90] and the mere fact that the complaint concerned gender discrimination was not "in itself a reason for a court to impose its own judgment".[91] **23–020**

Once it is accepted that older widows were historically an economically disadvantaged class which merited special treatment but were gradually becoming less disadvantaged, the question of the precise moment at which special treatment is no longer justified becomes a social and political question within the competence of Parliament.[92]

The recognition that the remedying of past disadvantage can constitute objective justification for differential treatment under the HRA is to be welcomed.[93] The nature of the judicial review undertaken was finely tuned. The key issue was the timing of the shift from the old regime according special benefits to widows, to the new regime under which benefits were granted to

[87] *Hooper* [2005] 1 W.L.R. 1681 at [16].
[88] *Hooper* [2005] 1 W.L.R. 1681 at [17].
[89] *Hooper* [2005] 1 W.L.R. 1681 at [31].
[90] *Hooper* [2005] 1 W.L.R. 1681 at [32].
[91] *Hooper* [2005] 1 W.L.R. 1681 at [32].
[92] *Hooper* [2005] 1 W.L.R. 1681 at [32].
[93] S. Fredman, "Affirmative Action and the Court of Justice: A Critical Analysis", in J. Shaw (ed.), *Social Law and Policy in an Evolving European Union* (Oxford: Hart, 2000), Ch.9.

widows and widowers alike. The House of Lords did not impose its own judgment on this matter. Its willingness to afford Parliament some latitude as to the timing of the change should nonetheless be seen against the fact that the House of Lords had satisfied itself that there was valid reason for differential treatment in relation to widows' pensions in the past.

5. EU LAW

23–021 EU law is of relevance for equality in a number of ways.[94] The principle of equality and the prohibition of discrimination are found expressly within a number of Treaty articles,[95] but the ECJ held at an early stage that these were merely specific enunciations of the general principle of equality as one of the fundamental principles of EU law,[96] which must be observed by any court.[97]

A. Discrimination and Nationality

23–022 EU law proscribes any discrimination on the grounds of nationality. This is a central feature of EU law and is enshrined in general terms in art.18 TFEU. The general prohibition on nationality discrimination in art.18 TFEU has been especially significant, in particular when read with the provisions on citizenship contained in arts 20–21 TFEU.[98] The proscription of nationality discrimination finds more specific recognition in, for example, arts 45, 49 and 56 TFEU, which prohibit discriminatory treatment in relation to free movement of workers, freedom of establishment and freedom to provide services in another Member State. These provisions have direct effect, both vertical and horizontal, and thus can be relied upon in national courts against either the state or a private individual. The proscription of discrimination on grounds of nationality has an economic and a social rationale.[99]

The basic economic objective is to ensure the optimal allocation of resources within the EU, by enabling factors of production to move to the area where they are most valued. Thus, labour is one factor of production, which may be valued more highly in some areas than others. This is so if there is an excess of supply over demand for labour in southern Italy, and an excess of demand over supply in certain parts of Germany. In this situation labour is worth more in Germany than in Italy. The value of labour within the EU as a whole is, therefore, maximised if

[94] P. Craig, *EU Administrative Law* 2nd edn (Oxford: Oxford University Press, 2012), Ch.17.

[95] K. Lenaerts, "L'Egalite de Traitement en Droit Communautaire" (1991) 27 C.D.E. 3.

[96] *Ruckdeschel v Hauptzollamt Hamburg-St Annen* (117/76 and 16/77) [1977] E.C.R. 1753 at [7].

[97] *Milac GmbH v Hauptzollamt Freiburg* (8/78) [1978] E.C.R. 1721 at [18].

[98] *Maria Martinez Sala v Freistaat Bayern* (C-85/96) [1998] E.C.R. I-2691; *Rudy Grzelczyk v Centre Public D'Aide Sociale d'Ottignes-Louvain-la-Neuve (CPAS)* (C-184/99) [2001] E.C.R. I-6193; *Trojani v Centre Public D'Aide Sociale de Bruxelles (CPAS)* (C-456/02) [2004] E.C.R. I-7573; *R. (Bidar) v Ealing LBC and Secretary of State for Education* (C-209/03) [2005] E.C.R. I-2119.

[99] *Phil Collins v Imtrat Handelsgesellschaft mbH* (C-92/92) [1993] E.C.R. I–5145 at 5163, Attorney General Jacobs.

workers are free to move within the Union to the area where they are most valued, and such movement is not impeded by discrimination on grounds of nationality.

There has, however, always been a social as well as an economic rationale underlying the proscription of nationality discrimination within the four freedoms. This is at its most fundamental the idea that it should be regarded as natural that, for example, workers should be employed or firms should carry on business in Member States other than their home state, and that when they did so they could not be treated in a disadvantageous manner as compared with nationals of that state. This was integral to the very idea of a "community". There are barriers to the realisation of this ideal, some practical, others cultural in nature, which provisions embodied in a Treaty cannot in themselves dispel. This can be accepted, while at the same time recognising that the four freedoms are designed to facilitate this integration.

B. Discrimination and Gender

The Treaty has, since its inception, prohibited discrimination in relation to pay on gender grounds, and this was extended to cover equal treatment, art.157 TFEU. **23–023** The principles concerning gender discrimination were further elaborated through legislation, in particular Directive 75/117[100] and Directive 76/207.[101] Action by the state or a private party, which infringes art.157, can be challenged via art.267 TFEU in national courts.

This is exemplified by the well-known *Defrenne* case.[102] The applicant, who was an air hostess, brought an action for discrimination against her employer Sabena, because she was paid less than male colleagues who did the same job. The principal issue was whether art.119 EEC, now art.157 TFEU, should have direct effect. The ECJ said that this question should be considered in the light of the "nature of the principle of equal pay, the aim of this provision and its place in the scheme of the Treaty".[103] The ECJ held that there were two aims underlying this article.

The market-integration objective was designed,

> "... to avoid a situation in which undertakings established in States which have actually implemented the principle of equal pay suffer a competitive disadvantage in intra-Community competition as compared with undertakings established in States which have not yet eliminated discrimination against women workers as regards pay".[104]

The second aim was social in nature: art.119,

[100] Directive 75/117 of 10 February 1975 on the approximation of the laws of the Member States relating to the application of the principle of equal pay for men and women [1975] OJ L45/19.

[101] Directive 76/207 of 9 February 1976 on the implementation of the principle of equal treatment for men and women as regards access to employment, vocational training and promotion, and working conditions [1976] OJ L39/40.

[102] *Defrenne v Société Anonyme Belge de Navigation Aérienne* (43/75) [1976] E.C.R. 455.

[103] *Defrenne* [1976] E.C.R. 455 at [7].

[104] *Defrenne* [1976] E.C.R. 455 at [9].

> "… forms part of the social objectives of the Community, which is not merely an economic union, but is at the same time intended, by common action, to ensure social progress and seek the constant improvement of the living and working conditions of their peoples, as is emphasised by the Preamble to the Treaty".[105]

This double aim, economic and social, was indicative of the foundational role played by the principle of equal pay within the EU.[106] This conclusion reinforced the court's resolve that what is now art.157 should have direct effect, notwithstanding the fact that it was couched in general terms and required further elaboration through Community legislation.

23–024 In *Schröder*[107] the ECJ went further, holding that the social objective underlying art.157 took precedence over the economic. The case was concerned with entitlement to membership of an occupational pension scheme by part-time workers, the great majority of whom were women. If the social aim were accorded priority, then it would be permissible for German law to apply the equal pay principle retroactively so as to permit part-time workers access to such a scheme. However, if the economic aim were to take priority the opposite result might be reached, since it was argued that by allowing retroactive membership of the scheme German firms would be placed at a competitive disadvantage as compared with those in other Member States.

The ECJ reiterated the twin objectives of what is now art.157 that had been elaborated in *Defrenne*. It then pointed to subsequent decisions where it had held that the right not to be discriminated against on grounds of sex was a fundamental human right, whose observance the court had a duty to ensure.[108] The ECJ concluded in the light of this case law that the economic aim pursued by art.157, namely the elimination of distortions of competition between undertakings established in different Member States, "is secondary to the social aim pursued by the same provision, which constitutes the expression of a fundamental human right".[109]

23–025 The third way in which EU law relating to equality can impact on domestic law is via art.19 TFEU, which gives the EU legislative competence to take appropriate action to combat discrimination based on sex, racial or ethnic origin, religion or belief, disability, age or sexual orientation.[110] Two directives were adopted in 2000.

There is a Directive prohibiting discrimination on grounds of race and ethnic origin.[111] There is also the so-called framework employment Directive, covering discrimination in the field of employment on the grounds listed in art.19 (other than race, ethnic origin or sex, which are already covered by other legislation):

---

[105] *Defrenne* [1976] E.C.R. 455 at [10].

[106] *Defrenne* [1976] E.C.R. 455 at [12].

[107] *Deutsche Telekom v Schröder* (C-50/96) [2000] E.C.R. I-743.

[108] *Schröder* [2000] E.C.R. I-743 at [56], citing *Defrenne III* (149/77) [1978] E.C.R. 1365 at [26]–[27], *Razzouk and Beydoun v Commission* (75 and 117/82) [1984] E.C.R. 1509 at [16], and *P v S and Cornwall County Council* (C-13/94) [1996] E.C.R. I-2143 at [19].

[109] *Schröder* [2000] E.C.R. I-743 at [57].

[110] M. Bell, *Anti-Discrimination Law and the EU* (Oxford: Oxford University Press, 2002).

[111] Directive 2000/43 of 29 June 2000 implementing the principle of equal treatment between persons irrespective of racial or ethnic origin [2000] OJ L180/22.

religion, belief, disability, age and sexual orientation.[112] While art.19 specifies that the EU can only act within the limits of the Union's powers, art.3 of the anti-racism Directive gives it an apparently wide scope, including a prohibition on discrimination in relation to social protection, healthcare, housing and education.

Individuals can rely on provisions of the directives in national courts where those provisions meet the conditions for direct effect. This means that a person aggrieved by government action may have recourse both to Convention rights concerning discrimination, and EU measures passed pursuant to art.19. It should also be recognised that the latter are more potent in an important respect. National law that is inconsistent with art.19 will be invalid, and even primary legislation can be declared inapplicable where it conflicts with an EU norm.[113]

D. Discrimination and Common Policies

Discrimination is also relevant in relation to the EU's common policies, such as the Common Agricultural Policy (CAP). The principle of non-discrimination performs what More[114] aptly terms a regulatory role in these areas, in that it constrains the regulatory choices that can be made by the administration. **23–026**

Article 39 TFEU is the foundational provision of the CAP. It is of a broad discretionary nature and sets out a range of general objectives to be served by the CAP. They include increase in agricultural productivity, with the object of ensuring a fair standard of living for the agricultural community; the stabilisation of markets; assuring the availability of supplies; and reasonable prices for consumers. These objectives can clash.[115] The Commission and Council therefore have to make difficult discretionary choices. Whether the resultant choices discriminate between producers may be contentious. The ECJ has, not surprisingly, accepted that the Union institutions have a considerable choice as to how to balance these objectives.[116] The principle of non-discrimination must therefore be viewed against this background. Article 40(2) TFEU provides that:

> "The common organisation established in accordance with paragraph 1 may include all measures required to attain the objectives set out in Article 39, in particular regulation of prices, aids for the production and marketing of the various products, storage and carryover arrangements and common machinery for stabilising imports or exports."

[112] Directive 2000/78 of 27 November 2000 establishing a general framework for equal treatment in employment and occupation [2000] OJ L303/16.

[113] See Ch.10.

[114] G. More, "The Principle of Equal Treatment: From Market Unifier to Fundamental Right", in P. Craig and G. de Búrca (eds), *The Evolution of EU Law* (Oxford: Oxford University Press, 1999), pp.530–535.

[115] *Germany v Commission* (34/62) [1963] E.C.R. 131; *Beus v Hauptzollamt München* (5/67) [1968] E.C.R. 83.

[116] *Ludwigshafener Walzmühle Erling KG v Council* (197–200, 243, 245, 247/80) [1981] E.C.R. 3211; *KG in der Firma Hans-Otto Wagner GmbH Agrarhandel v Bundesanstalt für Landwirtschaftliche Marktordnung* (8/82) [1983] E.C.R. 371; *Firma A Racke v Hauptzollamt Mainz* (283/83) [1984] E.C.R. 3791.

The common organisation shall be limited to pursuit of the objectives set out in art.39 and shall exclude any discrimination between producers or consumers within the Union.

A necessary condition for an applicant to be able to rely successfully on non-discrimination in art.40(2) is therefore that it is in a comparable situation to that of another producer or consumer and is being treated differently, or that it is in a different situation and is being treated in the same manner. Comparability is a necessary condition for successful invocation of art.40(2). It is not, however, sufficient. The applicant will also have to rebut arguments concerning objective justification. Thus the defendant, normally the Commission and/or the Council, may argue that the differential treatment was objectively justified to attain one of the objectives in art.39. The interplay between comparability and objective justification is apparent in the leading cases.[117]

E. Discrimination and the Charter of Rights

23–027 EU law is also relevant for equality because of the Charter of Fundamental Rights. The Lisbon Treaty made the Charter of Rights binding, and it is accorded the same legal value as the Treaties.[118] The Lisbon Treaty is premised on the version of the Charter as amended by the Intergovernmental Conference in 2004,[119] and this version was reissued in the Official Journal.[120]

The UK and Poland negotiated a Protocol designed to limit the application of the Charter in certain respects.[121] The Protocol contains a lengthy preamble, which reaffirms that art.6 TEU requires the courts of the UK and Poland to interpret and apply the Charter in accord with the explanations referred to. The preamble moreover "notes" the wish of Poland and the UK to clarify certain aspects of the application of the Charter.

The Protocol has two substantive articles. Article 1(1) states that the Charter does not extend the ability of the EU courts, or any court or tribunal of Poland or of the UK, to find that the laws, regulations or administrative provisions, practices or action of Poland or of the UK are inconsistent with the fundamental rights, freedoms and principles that it reaffirms. Article 1(2) further states that nothing in Title IV of the Charter, which concerns solidarity rights, creates justiciable rights applicable to Poland or the UK except in so far as Poland or the UK has provided for such rights in its national law. Article 2 provides that insofar as a provision of the Charter refers to national laws and practices, it shall only apply to Poland or the UK to the extent that the rights or principles that it contains are recognised in the law or practices of Poland or of the UK.

---

[117] *Ruckdeschel* [1977] E.C.R. 1753; *Royal Scholten-Honig v Intervention Board for Agricultural Produce* (103 and 145/77) [1978] E.C.R. 2037.

[118] TEU art.6(1).

[119] Brussels European Council, 21–22 June 2007, 25, note 21.

[120] Charter of Fundamental Rights of the European Union [2010] OJ C83/389; Explanations Relating to the Charter of Fundamental Rights [2007] OJ C303/17.

[121] Protocol (No.30) on the Application of the Charter of Fundamental Rights of the European Union to Poland and to the United Kingdom.

The ECJ rightly held that the Protocol did not by its wording constitute an opt-out of the Charter for the UK and Poland, but that art.1(1) merely re-affirmed orthodoxy in art.51(2) of the Charter, that the Charter did not extend the ability of EU or national courts to pronounce on fundamental rights.[122] **23–028**

Chapter III of the Charter deals with equality. It contains a basic equality before the law guarantee, as well as a provision similar, though not identical, to that in art.19 TFEU. There is also a reference to positive action provisions in the field of gender equality, protection for children's rights, and some weaker provisions guaranteeing "respect" for cultural diversity, for the rights of the elderly and for persons with disabilities. The Charter is binding on Member States when they implement EU law,[123] which means that Member States are bound by Charter provisions whenever they act within the scope of EU law.[124] The Charter may also have an indirect horizontal impact as between private parties.[125] Applicants will therefore be able to rely not only on the HRA and Convention rights, but also on EU law, at least insofar as the facts of the case fall within the scope of EU law.

122 *NS v Home Secretary* (C-411 and 493/10) EU:C:2011:865.

123 Charter art.51(1).

124 *Åklagaren v Hans Åkerberg Fransson* (C-617/10) EU:2013:C:105.

125 Craig, *EU Administrative Law* (2012), pp.498–505.

CHAPTER 24

INVALIDITY

1. CENTRAL ISSUES

i. This chapter is concerned with the result of finding that a decision is ultra vires and the status of the decision pending such a finding. A person who wishes to challenge a decision may do so directly or collaterally, and the relationship between the two is considered in the next section. 24–001

ii. The basic principle is as follows. If the decision-maker had no power to take the contested action then the decision should have no effect. It will be void ab initio, retrospectively null. Void is, however, a relative not an absolute concept. Thus, if an ultra vires act has occurred, and it is challenged by the right person in the correct proceedings within the specified time limits, it will then be retrospectively null. There are nonetheless two principal difficulties with application of this foundational proposition.

iii. First, if the correct person successfully challenges the administrative act in the correct proceedings, within the time lime limits, and there are no bars to relief then the act is retrospectively void. However, the implications this has for other acts done after the act that was successfully challenged is a separate conceptual issue. The initial invalid act will often appear to be factually valid and people may well have acted on that assumption. The validity of the later acts depends on whether the second actor has legal power to act even though the first act is invalid. This issue is determined by looking at the relationship between the two sets of acts. The empowering statute will normally provide little guidance on this issue, and the reviewing court will decide whether any of the acts done pursuant to the initial unlawful act can be regarded as valid.

iv. Second, the foundational proposition that invalid acts are retrospectively void has on occasion been obscured by judicial use of the term voidable to describe the consequences of invalid action, rather than void. The rationale for doing so has varied, but the general answer is that some courts have sought to escape from the conclusions that will follow if they find that the contested decision was made outside jurisdiction and hence retrospectively invalid. They have used the term voidable in order to express the conclusion that the contested order should only be ineffective from the date when it was found to be invalid by the court, and not from the date when it was first made. The nature of this problem and the appropriate way of dealing with it will be considered later in this chapter.

2. TYPES OF CHALLENGE

A. Direct and Collateral Attack: Classification

24–002 There are two ways in which governmental action can be challenged, directly or collaterally. The distinction may refer to the form of remedy sought. Thus, direct attack would cover the prerogative orders, injunction, declaration and possibly habeas corpus. The individual is seeking a remedy that directly impugns the administrative order. The problem with this classification is that it groups together remedies that go only to the validity of the challenged finding, with those which pertain to the merits. Examples of the latter are certiorari when used to challenge an error within jurisdiction and appeal. On this hypothesis collateral attack would cover the many ways in which a decision can be challenged indirectly, such as by way of defence to enforcement proceedings or in a tort action.

Alternatively, the distinction between direct and collateral attack may be determined by the scope of review given by the remedy and not by its form. Collateral proceedings would be those in which the nullity of the decision is at issue, and direct proceedings would cover challenges to the merits.[1] The difficulty with this classification is that a remedy such as declaration, which was traditionally regarded as available only for jurisdictional defects, would be regarded as a collateral challenge while having little connection with an incidental form of attack by way of a tort action.

It is, however, clear that collateral attack covers many forms of incidental challenge and has been recognised for over 300 years. It constituted the early method of attacking decisions and pre-dated the general development of the prerogative writs.[2] For example, in the *Case of the Marshalsea*[3] the plaintiff brought an action for trespass and false imprisonment, claiming that the Marshalsea Court possessed no jurisdiction over him as he was not of the King's House. The court held that an action would lie where the challenged authority had no jurisdiction over the case, the entire proceedings being coram non judice. No such action would lie where the error was one within jurisdiction. There are many other ways in which collateral attack can occur.[4] An accuser's guilt may be dependent on the validity of a ministerial order. If the order is ultra vires then the accused will be exonerated.[5] A ratepayer can resist a demand for rates or charges by claiming that the demand is invalid.[6]

---

[1] A. Rubinstein, *Jurisdiction and Illegality* (Oxford: Oxford University Press, 1965), pp.37–39.

[2] Rubinstein, *Jurisdiction and Illegality* (1965), Ch.4.

[3] (1612) 10 Co Rep 68b; *Terry v Huntington* (1668) Hard 480; *Fuller v Fotch* (1695) Carth 346; *Doswell v Impey* (1823) 1 B & C 163.

[4] Rubinstein, *Jurisdiction and Illegality* (1965), pp.39–46.

[5] *DPP v Head* [1959] A.C. 83, HL.

[6] *Daymond v Plymouth City Council* [1976] A.C. 609, HL.

B. Relationship between Direct and Collateral Attack: The General Principle

Collateral attack will only be an option where the defect alleged is jurisdictional.[7] 24–003
Errors of law on the face of the record could therefore not be impeached collaterally, but only by way of certiorari. The rationale was that the court in a collateral action could take account of the invalidity of a challenged order. It was acting in a "declaratory" role. If, however, the decision was valid, albeit tainted with some error, it could only be challenged by appeal, or by certiorari where the error was one of law on the face of the record. A court not possessed of appellate jurisdiction could not obliquely assume such.[8] This point is, however, less important now given the expansion of jurisdictional error and the consequential demise of error of law within jurisdiction.

The general principle is that any defect that would be treated as jurisdictional in direct proceedings is equally available in a collateral action. Thus, in *Foster*[9] it was held that Social Security Commissioners hearing appeals under the Social Security Act 1975 had jurisdiction to determine any challenge to the vires of a provision in regulations made by the secretary of state, on the ground that it was beyond the scope of the enabling power, whenever this was necessary to decide whether a decision under appeal was legally erroneous.

This general principle was re-affirmed in *Boddington*.[10] Boddington was convicted by a stipendiary magistrate for smoking in a railway carriage, contrary to a byelaw of the British Railways Board. The House of Lords held that it was open to a defendant in criminal proceedings to challenge subordinate legislation, or an administrative decision made there under, where the prosecution was premised on its validity, unless there was a clear legislative intent to the contrary. It was, said their Lordships, unacceptable in a democracy based on the rule of law for a magistrate to be able to convict a person who would be precluded from relying on a defence that he might otherwise have had. A direct action for judicial review was an inadequate safeguard: the defendant might be out of time before becoming aware of the byelaw; he might not have the resources for such a challenge; leave might be refused; or a remedy might be denied pursuant to the court's discretionary power over such matters. Their Lordships held, moreover, that there was no distinction in this respect between cases of substantive and procedural invalidity and overruled *Bugg*.[11]

---

[7] See further *Groenvelt v Burwell* (1700) 3 Salk 354; *Gahan v Maingay* (1793) Ridg. L. & S. 20.

[8] *Gahan v Maingay* (1793) Ridg. L. & S. 20.

[9] *Chief Adjudication Officer v Foster* [1993] A.C. 754, HL; *Howker v Secretary of State for Work and Pensions* [2003] I.C.R. 405 CA (Civ Div); *Dong v National Crime Agency* [2014] UKFTT 369.

[10] *Boddington v British Transport Police* [1999] 2 A.C. 143; *Howker* [2003] I.C.R. 405; *R. v Searby (Alan Edward)* [2003] 3 C.M.L.R. 15 CA (Crim Div); *EN (Serbia) v Secretary of State for the Home Department* [2010] Q.B. 633, CA (Civ Div) at [86]–[87]; *R. (Draga) v Secretary of State for the Home Department* [2011] EWHC 1825 (Admin); P. Craig, "Collateral Attack, Procedural Exclusivity and Judicial Review" (1998) 114 L.Q.R. 535; C. Forsyth, "Collateral Challenge and the Foundations of Judicial Review: Orthodoxy Vindicated and Procedural Exclusivity Rejected" [1998] P.L. 364.

[11] *Bugg v DPP* [1993] Q.B. 473 DC.

C. Relationship between Direct and Collateral Attack: Qualifications to the General Principle

24–004 The general principle that defects that can be raised in direct actions can also be raised collaterally is, however, subject to certain qualifications.

i. The particular statute

24–005 A court may interpret a particular statute to preclude or limit collateral attack.[12] Moreover, merely because one individual might have a direct action should not necessarily mean that a different individual should be able to use this invalidity in a collateral action.[13] It was accepted in *Boddington* that there could be cases where a collateral challenge to the validity of an order could be defeated by statutory provisions, which indicated that only a direct action was possible.

This is exemplified by *Wicks*.[14] The House of Lords held that whether a defendant charged with failing to comply with an order made under statutory powers was entitled by way of defence in criminal proceedings to challenge the lawfulness of the order depended on the construction of the statute. There could be cases where the statute allowed any public law claim to be raised collaterally by way of defence. There could also be cases where the statute on its true construction merely required that the act which had been done under statutory authority appeared to be formally valid and had not been quashed by judicial review. In this latter type of case, only the formal validity of the act was of relevance before the court in a prosecution.[15]

The premise behind *Boddington* is, however, that the normal position is that a defendant should be able to raise the invalidity of the byelaw, or an administrative decision based on it, by way of defence in a criminal case. It will be for the prosecution to convince the court that the exception based on the reasoning in *Wicks* is applicable in the instant case.

ii. Court orders

24–006 *Boddington* was distinguished in *DPP v T*.[16] It was held that the normal rule in relation to an order of the court was that it must be treated as valid unless and until it was set aside. Thus, even if the order should not have been made, a person could be liable for any breach committed before it was set aside. The court held that the person against whom an ASBO was made could challenge that order on appeal, and there was no obvious reason why he should be allowed to raise that issue as a defence in subsequent breach proceedings rather than by way of appeal.

[12] *R. v Davey* [1899] 2 Q.B. 301 QBD.
[13] See, e.g. Rubinstein, *Jurisdiction and Illegality* (1965), p.47, Rubinstein's cogent critique of *DPP v Head* [1959] A.C. 83, HL.
[14] *R. v Wicks* [1998] A.C. 92, HL. See also, *DPP v Memery* [2003] RTR 18; *DPP v T* [2007] 1 W.L.R. 209 DC; *Lindum Construction Co Ltd v Office of Fair Trading* [2014] EWHC (Ch); *Lalli v Commissioner of Police of the Metropolis* [2015] EWHC 14 (Admin).
[15] Compare *Palacegate Properties Ltd v Camden LBC* [2001] A.C.D 23 DC, with *Dilieto v Ealing LBC* [2000] Q.B. 381 DC.
[16] *DPP v T* [2007] 1 W.L.R. 209 DC.

The policy consideration that influenced the finding in *Boddington* that the magistrates' court had jurisdiction to determine the validity of a byelaw or administrative decision was absent when the issue was the validity of an order of the court.

iii. *The general law on remedies*

The reform of remedies raised important questions as to how far an individual should be able to challenge a decision outside the Order 53 procedure.[17] The House of Lords held in *O'Reilly v Mackman*[18] that the application for judicial review was the only way to secure a remedy against a public body (procedural exclusivity), the rationale being that this procedure contained certain protections for a public body that would be circumvented by bringing an action in another way. This was always subject to exceptions, most notably where the invalidity of the decision arose as a collateral matter in a claim for the infringement of private rights. Later case law made it clear that procedural exclusivity will only be insisted upon where the sole object of the action is to challenge a public law act or decision. It does not apply in a civil case when an individual seeks to establish private law rights that cannot be determined without examining the validity of the public law decision. Nor does it apply where a defendant in a civil or criminal case seeks to defend himself by questioning the validity of the public law decision.[19] **24–007**

iv. *Positive and negative decisions*

Collateral attack will by its nature not normally be available to challenge decisions denying an individual something which the person desires, unless the individual can show some common law or statutory right to it. If a public body refuses a licence or a social welfare benefit then if the applicant does nothing no licence will be granted, or no benefit will be paid. Attack by prerogative order or declaration is the only recourse available to the aggrieved individual. This may be contrasted with a demand by the public body for rates or duties. The individual can wait to be sued and then assert the invalidity of the order. **24–008**

v. *De facto judges and officers*

A long-standing exception to collateral attack applies where the appointment of judges or public officers is defective. The courts have not allowed collateral challenge where the judge or officer was acting de facto as such, even though the appointment was de jure invalid.[20] The rationale for this limitation is essentially practical: annulment of all subsequent acts because the appointment was invalid could have serious consequences.[21] **24–009**

---

[17] See Ch.27.

[18] *O'Reilly v Mackman* [1983] 2 A.C. 237, HL.

[19] Subject to the point about the interpretation of a particular statute made above.

[20] Rubinstein, *Jurisdiction and Illegality* (1965), pp.205–208.

[21] *Crew v Vernon* (1627) Cro. Car. 97.

The protection accorded to de facto officers appears to have its origin in connection with officers or judges whose appointment was valid when made, but where the appointment was subsequently rendered invalid.[22] The doctrine has, however, been extended to encompass appointments invalid at their inception. Thus, a justice who had not taken the requisite oath was still regarded as a de facto justice[23]; the acts of assessors and collectors of taxes who did not fulfil residency requirements were treated as valid[24]; a rate levied by vestrymen, one of whom was not duly elected, was not annulled[25]; and the doctrine also covered a judge who was mistaken as to the status of the court in which he was sitting, rather than as to the nature or the extent of his own jurisdiction.[26]

It has moreover been held in *Coppard*[27] that the doctrine not only validated acts done by a de facto judge, but validated the judge's office itself. Thus a person who was believed and believed himself to have the necessary judicial authority was regarded in law as possessing such authority. A de facto judge was a tribunal whose authority was established by the common law. This complied with art.6 ECHR, provided that the doctrine did not lead to the ratification of acts of those who knew themselves to lack authority, did not operate arbitrarily and was limited to the correction of mistakes of form rather than of substance.

There are nonetheless limits to the doctrine. It appears to operate only where there is some "colour of authority".[28] It is in any event clear from *Coppard*[29] that the de facto doctrine cannot validate the acts nor ratify the authority of a person who, though believed by the world to be a judge of the court in which he sits, knows that he is not. A person who knows he lacks authority includes a person who has shut his eyes to that fact when it is obvious, but not a person who has simply neglected to find it out. Such a person is termed a usurper.

3. VOID AND VOIDABLE: CORRECT AND INCORRECT USES

24–010 If a public body makes a decision that is ultra vires this means that it had no power to make such a decision, and the decision should in principle have "no effect", although, as we shall see, this principle might have to be compromised in certain cases because of the draconian consequences that can ensue.

22 *Aldridge, Re* (1893) 15 N.Z.L.R. 361 at 369–370.

23 *Margate Pier Company v Hannam* (1819) 3 B. & Ald. 266.

24 *Waterloo Bridge Company v Cull* (1858) 1 El. & El. 213, affirmed (1859) 1 El. & El. 245.

25 *Scadding v Lorant* (1851) 3 H.L.C. 418.

26 *Baldock v Webster* [2006] Q.B. 315, CA (Civ Div).

27 *Coppard v Customs and Excise Commissioners* [2003] Q.B. 1428, CA (Civ Div).

28 *Baldock* [2006] Q.B. 315 at [15]. This is in accord with the preponderance of earlier authority. In *Crew* (1627) Cro. Car. 97 the commissioners' acts seemed only to be valid until they received notice of the death of James I. In *R. v Bedford Level Corporation* (1805) 6 East 356 the officer in question was a deputy whose principal had died. It was held that once the principal dies and this becomes known the de facto authority of the deputy ceases. In *Adams v Adams* [1971] P. 188 the court rejected the argument that a Rhodesian judge held office de facto if not de jure, one reason being that the illegality of the Rhodesian regime was widely known. The court in *Aldridge* (1893) 15 N.Z.L.R. 361 was more divided on this question.

29 *Coppard* [2003] Q.B. 1428 at [18]; *Fawdry & Co v Murfitt* [2003] Q.B. 104, CA (Civ Div).

A. Void: A Relative not Absolute Concept

The effect of finding that a decision is ultra vires is best approached from first principles. If the decision-maker had no power then the decision should have no effect. Translated into the lingua franca of our profession, we would say that such a decision was void ab initio, retrospectively null. Void is, however, a relative not an absolute concept, the meaning of which can be explained as follows.[30] **24–011**

In administrative law there are rules of locus standi, time limits and other reasons for refusing a remedy such as acquiescence. It is only if an applicant for relief surmounts these hurdles that a remedy will be given. The sequence is therefore as follows. An administrative decision is taken. An individual feels aggrieved and challenges the decision. *If* the court finds that the individual has standing, is within the time limits, and that there is no reason to deny a remedy *then* the decision will be found to be void ab initio. This is a description of the conclusion that an ultra vires act has occurred, and that it is being challenged by the right person in the correct proceedings. It is, as Lord Diplock said,[31] confusing to speak of the terms void or voidable before the validity of an order has been pronounced on by a court of competent jurisdiction. The Criminal Justice and Courts Act 2015 s.84 added a further condition, requiring the reviewing court to refuse a remedy where it is highly likely that the outcome would not have been substantially different.

If, by way of contrast, void were to be used in an absolute as opposed to a relative sense the word "void" would, in effect, be moved earlier in the sentence. This would now read: if there is an ultra vires act, the finding thus made is void ab initio and therefore any person can take advantage of it. Applied literally there could be no limits of standing and no discretion in granting the remedy. Two examples of the use of void or nullity in this absolute sense may be given.

In *Ridge*, Lord Evershed stated that because the declaration is a discretionary remedy, therefore a breach of natural justice must render the decision voidable and not void. This was because his Lordship felt that if the decision was a complete nullity the court would have to say so.[32] A similar usage is apparent in *Durayappah*.[33] A minister dissolved the Jaffna City Council after a commissioner made a report to him. The commissioner had inquired into the council's activities, **24–012**

[30] H.W.R. Wade, "Unlawful Administrative Action: Void or Voidable?" (1967) 83 L.Q.R. 499; (1968) 84 L.Q.R. 95; M. Akehust, "Void or Voidable? Natural Justice and Unnatural Meanings" (1968) 31 M.L.R. 2, 138; P. Cane, "A Fresh Look at Punton's Case" (1980) 43 M.L.R. 266; D. Oliver, "Void and Voidable in Administrative Law: A Problem of Legal Recognition" [1981] C.L.P. 43; G. Peiris, "Natural Justice and Degrees of Invalidity of Administrative Action" [1983] P.L. 634; M. Taggart, "Rival Theories of Invalidity in Administrative Law: Some Practical and Theoretical Consequences", in M. Taggart (ed.), *Judicial Review of Administrative Action in the 1980s: Problems and Prospects* (Oxford: Oxford University Press, 1986), pp.70–103; C. Forsyth, "'The Metaphysic of Nullity': Invalidity, Conceptual Reasoning and the Rule of Law", in C. Forsyth and I. Hare (eds), *The Golden Metwand and the Crooked Cord* (Oxford: Oxford University Press, 1998), pp.141–160; D. Feldman, "Error of Law and Flawed Administrative Acts" (2014) 73 C.L.J 275.

[31] *Hoffmann-La Roche Co AG v Secretary of State for Trade and Industry* [1975] A.C. 295, HL at 366; *Isaacs v Robertson* [1985] A.C. 97; *Bugg* [1993] Q.B. 473; *R. v Hendon Justices, Ex p. DPP* [1993] C.O.D. 61 QBD.

[32] *Ridge v Baldwin* [1964] A.C. 40 at 87–88, 91–92.

[33] *Durayappah v Fernando* [1967] 2 A.C. 337.

but had not given a hearing to any member. The mayor sought certiorari, claiming that the dissolution was in breach of natural justice. Lord Upjohn found that there had been a breach of natural justice, and then considered whether the mayor could complain of this. His Lordship stated that it depended on whether the decision was a complete nullity, of which any person having a legitimate interest could complain, or whether it was voidable only at the instance of the party affected.[34] Lord Upjohn found that it was the latter. It could not therefore be attacked by the mayor when the council had chosen not to challenge it.[35]

Lord Evershed and Lord Upjohn used void or nullity in the absolute sense described above. An ultra vires act was found, and it was said not to be void because that would leave the court no discretion in granting the remedy and no control over standing. This can be contrasted to the relative meaning of the term void: it is only if, in addition to finding an ultra vires act, the person has standing and there are no other reasons to refuse the remedy that the decision will be held to be void ab initio.

Lord Diplock endorsed this relative concept of void in *Hoffmann-La Roche*,[36] where he stated that *Durayappah* was best explained as a case relating to standing. There is, therefore, nothing odd in a decision that can be rendered void by one person but not another, or in a decision which would be void if challenged within the correct time, being valid if not so challenged.[37] When a successful challenge is made by the right person in the correct proceedings the decision is retrospectively null.[38]

It should not, however, be thought that an aggrieved individual must always challenge an action directly. If the decision requires, for example, a payment by the individual to a public body then the individual could resist the demand, wait to be sued, and then attack the decision collaterally. In this limited sense statements by Lord Denning MR that there is no need for an order to quash a nullity are correct[39]: the individual can impugn the decision collaterally rather than directly. If the finding is not attacked directly or collaterally it will, however, remain valid irrespective of whether, if it had been challenged, it would have been ultra vires. It will not in some Houdini sense disappear.

B. The Decision as to whether an Error Renders the Administrative Act Void

24–013 We have seen thus far, that if a decision is challenged by the right person, in the right proceedings, within the relevant time limits, it will be void. The applicant must however show that the error was of a kind that led to the challenged action

[34] *Durayappah* [1967] 2 A.C. 337 at 353–354.

[35] *Durayappah* [1967] 2 A.C. 337 at 354–355.

[36] *Hoffmann-La Roche* [1975] A.C. 295 at 366. See also Lord Wilberforce at 358.

[37] *Smith v East Elloe Rural DC* [1956] A.C. 736, HL at 769, Lord Radcliffe.

[38] *McLaughlin v Governor of the Cayman Islands* [2007] UKPC 50; *Mossell (Jamaica) Ltd (t/a Digicel) v Office of Utilities Regulations* [2010] UKPC 1 at [44]; *R. (Ellerton) v Secretary of Justice* [2010] EWCA Civ 906.

[39] *Head* [1959] A.C. 83 at 111–112; *R. v Paddington Valuation Officer, Ex p. Peachey Property Corp Ltd* [1966] 1 Q.B. 380, CA at 402. Reference should, however, be made to the discussion of the presumptive exclusivity of s.31 of the Senior Courts Act 1981 in Ch.27.

being outside the decision-maker's power. This will normally not be problematic. Where a jurisdictional error, abuse of discretion or failure to comply with natural justice has been proven, the court will regard the decision as being outside the power of the decision-maker.

The courts have been more cautious in relation to statutory procedural irregularities. The traditional approach was to distinguish between procedural requirements that were mandatory and those that were directory.[40] The assumption was that any breach of the former would render the decision void. The courts now pay less regard to the mandatory/directory distinction.

In *London and Clydeside Estates*,[41] Lord Hailsham held that the terms mandatory and directory could often be expressive of over-rigid classification. In *Jeyeanthan*,[42] Lord Woolf MR accepted that if statutory language states that a certain procedural requirement "shall" be done, then the requirement is not optional. It was nonetheless for the court to determine the consequences of non-compliance with such a requirement. A court should, said Lord Woolf, be slow to find that any departure from the procedural requirement rendered the decision retrospectively null. The decision as to whether a procedural requirement was mandatory or directory was only the first step. The court should also take account of other factors in deciding on the consequences of non-compliance. The court should consider whether there had been substantial compliance with the requirement, and whether this could meet the statutory condition. It should consider whether the non-compliance was capable of being waived, and whether it had been waived in the particular case. If the provision was not capable of being waived, or had not been waived, the court should then address the consequences of the non-compliance.

C. The Consequences of Holding that an Act is Void

If the correct person successfully challenges the administrative act in the correct proceedings, within the time lime limits, and there are no common law or statutory bars to relief then the act will be void in the sense of retrospectively null. The implications this has for other acts done after the act which was successfully challenged is a separate conceptual issue, as exemplified by the case law on de facto officers considered above. The initial invalid act will often appear to be factually valid and people may well have acted on that assumption. Forsyth correctly points out that the validity of the later acts depends on the legal powers of the second actor: "the crucial issue to be determined is whether that second actor has legal power to act validly notwithstanding the invalidity of the first act", 24–014

[40] See e.g. *Johnson v Secretary of State for Health* [2001] Lloyd's Rep. Med. 385.

[41] *London and Clydeside Estates Ltd v Aberdeen DC* [1980] 1 W.L.R. 182, HL.

[42] *R. v Secretary of State for the Home Department, Ex p. Jeyeanthan* [2000] 1 W.L.R. 354, CA (Civ Div); *Westminster City Council v Mendoza* [2001] EWCA Civ 216; *Apex Asphalt & Paving Co Ltd v Office of Fair Trading* [2005] C.A.T. 4; *R. (McKay) v First Secretary of State* [2005] EWCA Civ 774; *R. (P) v Haringey LBC* [2008] EWHC 2357 (Admin); *R. (CM (Jamaica)) v Secretary of State for the Home Department* [2010] EWCA Civ 160; *Avon Freeholds Ltd v Regent Court RTM Co Ltd* [2013] UKUT 213 (LC); *Elim Court RTM Co Ltd v Avon Freeholds Ltd* [2014] UKUT 397 (LC). Compare *Wallace v Quinn* [2004] N.I. 164; *Seal v Chief Constable of South Wales* [2005] 1 W.L.R. 3183, CA (Civ Div).

and this is to be decided against the background that "an unlawful act is void".[43] This issue will be determined by looking at the relationship between the two sets of acts. The empowering statute will however normally provide little guidance on this issue, and the reviewing court will decide whether any of the acts done pursuant to the initial unlawful act can be regarded as valid.

In some circumstances, the nullity of the initial act will not render unlawful everything done there under.[44] In *Boddington* Lord Browne-Wilkinson stated that an ultra vires act may be capable of having some legal effect between the doing of the act and the recognition of its invalidity by a court, since people will have regulated their lives on the basis that the act is valid: "the subsequent recognition of its invalidity cannot rewrite history as to all other matters done in the meantime in reliance on its validity".[45] This is exemplified by *Percy*.[46] The plaintiffs had been arrested for breach of byelaws later held to be invalid. They brought an action for damages against the police for false imprisonment and wrongful arrest. The court rejected the claim. It reasoned that at the time when the plaintiffs were arrested the byelaws were apparently valid. While a subsequent finding that the byelaws were invalid entitled the plaintiffs to have the conviction set aside, it did not transform what, judged at the time, was a lawful discharge of the police officer's duty into what might later be regarded as tortious conduct.

In other circumstances, the nullity of the initial act will have more far-reaching consequences for acts done prior to the nullity being found to exist. This is evident from *Evans (No.2)*.[47] The applicant had been sentenced to a term of imprisonment, and was entitled to conditional release after a specified period. The prison governor calculated this period in the light of the prevailing case law. This method of calculation was held to be wrong in a subsequent case, the consequence being that she should have been released earlier. She claimed damages for false imprisonment for this period. The House of Lords held that false imprisonment was a strict liability tort, and that a court decision was declaratory of the law as it had always been, even when overruling prior case law on the point. The assumption was that where previous authorities are overruled, decisions to that effect operate retrospectively.[48] The imprisonment was therefore not lawful and the damages action could lie. Lord Browne-Wilkinson did not, however, think that the ruling in *Evans (No.2)* was necessarily decisive of the issues that arise where a defendant acted in accord with statutory provisions that are later held to be ultra vires and void.[49]

---

[43] Forsyth, "'The Metaphysic of Nullity': Invalidity, Conceptual Reasoning and the Rule of Law", in Forsyth and Hare (eds), *The Golden Metwand and the Crooked Cord* (1998), p.159.

[44] Forsyth, "'The Metaphysic of Nullity': Invalidity, Conceptual Reasoning and the Rule of Law", in Forsyth and Hare (eds), *The Golden Metwand and the Crooked Cord* (1998), pp.146–150.

[45] *Boddington* [1999] 2 A.C. 143 at 164, 165; *R. (Shrewsbury and Atcham BC) v Secretary of State for Communities and Local Government* [2008] EWCA Civ 148.

[46] *Percy v Hall* [1997] Q.B. 924, CA (Civ Div) at 950–952; *R. v Central London County Court, Ex p. London* [1999] Q.B. 1260, CA (Civ Div); *Tchenguiz v Director of the Serious Fraud Office* [2014] EWCA Civ 472; *Secretary of State for the Home Department v Draga* [2012] EWCA Civ 842; *White v Governor HMP Pentonville* [2014] EWHC 1886 (Admin).

[47] *R. v Governor of Brockhill Prison, Ex p. Evans (No.2)* [2001] 2 A.C. 19, HL.

[48] *Evans (No.2)* [2001] 2 A.C. 19 at 36.

[49] *Evans (No.2)* [2001] 2 A.C. 19 at 27.

D. Voidable: Different Uses

The term voidable has not been used uniformly in the case law. At least four distinct meanings have been attributed to the term. 24–015

i. *Indicative of the need to challenge*

Lord Morris of Borth-y-Gest used the term voidable in this sense in *Ridge*.[50] In this context voidable is simply descriptive of the need for the chief constable to challenge his dismissal. Unless he did so the decision of the Watch Committee would prevail. In this sense all decisions are voidable. His Lordship went on to say that if and when the court found for the individual the decision would be null and void. 24–016

ii. *An alternative to locus standi*

This connotation of the term voidable is exemplified by *Durayappah*.[51] The Privy Council did not wish the mayor to be able to challenge the dissolution of the City Council. The Privy Council therefore drew a dichotomy between defects which any person having a legitimate interest could take advantage of, which were nullities, and those defects which only the person affected could raise. The term voidable was used to describe errors of the latter type, and the court held that the case fell within this category. The distinction between acts which are null, and those which are merely voidable, manifested itself in the rules of standing. Why the Privy Council did not wish the mayor to succeed will be considered later. 24–017

iii. *The gravity of the error*

In some cases the term voidable has been used to indicate the relative gravity of the defect. This is exemplified by the *Paddington* case.[52] The basis on which a rating list had been compiled was challenged in the courts. The rating authority argued that if the list were struck down there would be widespread administrative upheaval, particularly if the invalidity meant that the list was retrospectively null. To circumvent this problem Lord Denning MR said that a grave invalidity would render the list a nullity. There would be no need for an order to quash a list tainted by such a defect. Less serious defects would only render the list voidable, with the result that any invalidity would only be prospective, not retrospective. The rating assessments could remain valid until replaced by a new list. 24–018

This reasoning is questionable. The concept of a grave defect leading to a nullity which need not be challenged either directly or collaterally, and yet can still be ignored without ill-effects to the individual, is difficult to comprehend. The offending order will not somehow disappear of its own accord. The formulation of the term voidable is equally questionable. On the law as it existed at the time, a non-jurisdictional error could only be struck down if it was an error

---

[50] *Ridge* [1964] A.C. 40 at 125.

[51] *Durayappah* [1967] 2 A.C. 337.

[52] *Paddington* [1966] 1 Q.B. 380 at 401–402.

of law on the face of the record. There was no patent error in the *Paddington* case. The reasons why Lord Denning MR distorted the meanings of void and voidable in order to avoid the consequences of retrospective nullity will be discussed below.

iv. Errors of law within jurisdiction

24–019 It was legitimate to use the term voidable to describe an error of law within jurisdiction. Such mistakes were valid until quashed, and actions taken in pursuance of an order tainted by a patent non-jurisdictional error remained valid, even when the order had been quashed.

Thus, in *Head*[53] a man was convicted of carnal knowledge with a mental defective. He argued by way of defence that he could not be guilty since the medical certificates did not contain any evidence showing the woman to be a moral defective. The majority of the House of Lords upheld this argument and set the conviction aside. Lord Denning concurred in this result, but his reasoning differed. He stated that the defect in the detention order only rendered it voidable and not void. A voidable order would remain good until set aside. Thus, at the time of the offence the detention order was still good, the woman was legally held, and the accused could be guilty of the crime charged.

The expansion in the scope of jurisdictional error, and the corresponding demise of the category of error of law within jurisdiction means, however, that voidable will no longer have a role to play in this regard.

4. VOID AND VOIDABLE: THEORY, REALITY AND JUDICIAL DISCRETION

24–020 The courts have not always used the term voidable to signify non-jurisdictional errors, and it is necessary to understand why they have done so. The general answer is that some courts have sought to escape from the conclusions that will follow if they find that the contested decision was made outside jurisdiction and hence retrospectively null or invalid. They have used the term voidable in order to express the conclusion that the contested order should only be ineffective from the date when it was found to be invalid by the court, and not from the date when it was first made.

The general argument made below is that the concept of retrospective invalidity, in the relative sense considered above, is the correct starting point in principle. We should not lose sight of this. Cases will arise in which the full effects of retrospective invalidity will be unacceptable, and where the principle will, therefore, have to be modified. The most appropriate manner in which to express these modifications is through discretion exercised at the remedial level, not by manipulating the concepts of void or voidable.

---

[53] *Head* [1959] A.C. 83.

A. Administrative Convenience, Justice and Rigidity

Traditional theory, derived from first principles, is that an ultra vires decision should be void, using that term in its relative sense. The voidness will be retrospective, invalidating action taken in the period between the making of the order and the court decision. Voidable decisions involve only prospective and not retrospective invalidity. The tribunal remains within its jurisdiction, but makes a mistake. Action taken in reliance on the order until the time at which it is struck down will be upheld. The invalidity will be only prospective. The only type of defect that should be termed voidable is an error of law on the face of the record. Other non-patent errors of law within jurisdiction would also be voidable, but could only be subject to appeal and not review. Not all courts have used the terms void and voidable in this way, the common denominator being a dislike of the results produced by retrospective nullity. Three reasons for this can be discerned. **24–021**

The first reason was administrative convenience. This was the prime consideration in the *Paddington* case.[54] Lord Denning MR characterised the error as voidable in order that the challenged rating list could remain in existence until a new list was prepared. If the error made the list retrospectively void then it would never have existed and there would have been a gargantuan unravelling task for the rating authorities.

A second reason for departing from traditional ideas of retrospective nullity has been to facilitate a "just result". In *Head*[55] Lord Denning was reluctant to allow an accused to escape a criminal charge by relying upon a defect in the certificate. Hence his characterisation of the defect as making the certificate only voidable: the woman was therefore lawfully detained at the time of the offence, and the accused could be found guilty. The case proceeded on the assumption that the accused should be able to take advantage of the defect within the certificate. There is, however, as noted by Rubinstein,[56] no necessary reason why conditions for detention, which could have been legitimately raised by the detainee, should have been available for the benefit of the accused. In *Ejaz*[57] the court declined to find that a mistaken certificate of naturalisation was a nullity, primarily because this could lead to great hardship, since a person's status could be affected retrospectively many years after the certificate had been granted. The court therefore construed a mistaken certificate to have validity unless and until it was successfully revoked by the Home Secretary.

A third reason why some courts have expressed dissatisfaction with traditional ideas of nullity is that they are felt to be too rigid. In *London and Clydeside Estates*[58] Lord Hailsham held that terms such as mandatory and directory, void and voidable, and nullity could often be expressive of over-rigid classification. When a public body failed to comply with a statutory requirement there could be different results. At one end of the spectrum, there would be instances of egregious breach of a fundamental obligation: the individual could simply use

---

[54] *Paddington* [1966] 1 Q.B. 380. Similar fears appear to underlie *Durayappah* [1967] 2 A.C. 337.

[55] *Head* [1959] A.C. 83 at 111–112. Lord Denning did not in the end dissent, at 113, 114.

[56] *Evans (No.2)* [2001] 2 A.C. 19 at 47.

[57] *R. v Secretary of State for the Home Department, Ex p. Ejaz (Naheed)* [1994] Q.B. 496, CA (Civ Div).

[58] *London and Clydeside Estates* [1980] 1 W.L.R. 182.

that defect as a defence without having to take positive action. At the other end of the spectrum there could be trivial defects that would probably be ignored by the courts. In the middle, however, there was a large group of cases in which it would be wise for the individual to challenge the public action, and where the effect of the breach would be dependent upon the circumstances. Terms such as void and voidable should not cramp the exercise of judicial discretion in determining the consequences of the breach.[59] We shall consider below whether concepts such as void and voidable entail unwarranted rigidity.

B. Resolving the Problem

i. First principles

24–022 It is not uncommon to see statements that the concepts of void and voidable are unnatural inhabitants of the administrative law world, viewed as alien concepts grafted onto public law from the world of contract and status.[60] This is mistaken. Even if those terms originated within private law, and this is by no means clear, they have been in administrative law ever since we have had such jurisprudence for over 300 years.[61] The traditional meaning of the term void, in the sense of retrospective nullity, captures the natural conclusion that if a decision-maker had no power to act then the act should be of no consequences. As Lord Diplock stated[62]:

> "It would, however, be inconsistent with the doctrine of *ultra vires* as it has been developed in English law as a means of controlling abuse of power by the executive arm of government if the judgment of a court in proceedings properly constituted that a statutory instrument was *ultra vires* were to have any lesser consequence in law than to render the instrument incapable of ever having had any legal effect upon the rights or duties of the parties to the proceedings."

The danger of Lord Hailsham's reasoning in *London and Clydeside Estates*[63] is that this important point of principle will be lost sight of. There might well be some statutory provisions where the consequences of the breach should be taken into account when determining the remedy.[64] This has been affirmed in *Jeyeanthan*.[65] This is however a separate issue from the void/voidable distinction. A condition precedent to a finding of retrospective nullity is that the error is regarded as taking the decision-maker outside its power. Whether this should be the case can, as we have seen,[66] be problematic in relation to procedural irregularities. The courts have decided that the consequences of the breach should

---

[59] *London and Clydeside Estates* [1980] 1 W.L.R. 182 at 190.

[60] See e.g. *Isaacs v Robertson* [1985] A.C. 97 at 102–103.

[61] Rubinstein, *Jurisdiction and Illegality* (1965), Chs 1–4.

[62] *Hoffmann-La Roche* [1975] A.C. 295 at 365; *R. (Wirral HA) v Mental Health Review Tribunal* [2001] EWCA Civ 1901; *Secretary of State for the Home Department v JJ* [2007] UKHL 45 at [26]–[27]; *Mossell* [2010] UKPC 1; *Ellerton* [2010] EWCA Civ 906; *McLaughlin* [2007] UKPC 50.

[63] *London and Clydeside Estates* [1980] 1 W.L.R. 182 at 189.

[64] There are analogies here with the condition-warranty distinction in the law of contract and the development of innominate terms.

[65] *Jeyeanthan* [2000] 1 W.L.R. 354.

[66] See para.24–013.

be considered to determine the result. This does not affect the conclusion that where the consequences are serious enough, the result should be retrospective nullity.

The concept of retrospective invalidity can give rise to problems, but these are the exceptions. Retrospective nullity is and should be the rule. If we need to depart from the principle so be it, but let us be clear that we are departing from the norm, and give cogent explanations for doing so. The exceptions should operate via discretion to refuse or limit the remedy, rather than through a sleight of hand over the meanings of void and voidable. There are three related problems with the manipulation of the terms void and voidable.

First, it conceals what is taking place. It provides a convenient mask of legal form to hide reality. Instead of saying that an applicant cannot, because of the administrative consequences, be granted the desired remedy, the applicant is told that the nature of the defect only renders the decision voidable. Second, such manipulation produces confusion by ascribing numerous meanings to the same terms, which when analysed make little sense. Third, there is a danger that what may have been intended as only an ad hoc exception to the norm of retrospective nullity, will become unintentionally generalised. The terminology takes on a life of its own. Legal form, like Frankenstein's creation, becomes unresponsive to the commands of its creator.

ii. Remedial discretion

While retrospective nullity should remain the foundational principle it is clear from the preceding analysis that it must be qualified. This entails choice and discretion as to when the foundational principle should be qualified. This is so irrespective of the level at which one thinks that the qualifications should operate. To imagine otherwise is simply pretence. **24–023**

Given that this is so, one way to resolve the problem is through discretion to refuse a remedy, or limit its application, so that it only operates prospectively.[67] This does not mean that we should play fast and loose with this discretion. It means that if a departure from the norm of retrospective nullity is warranted we should say that the decision is void, but that for reasons of, for example, practicality the effects must be confined to the future or that the remedy must be monetary, rather than a physical undoing of what has transpired. There are

[67] For examples of cases where the courts have exercised discretion to refuse relief on a variety of grounds, see among many *R. v Herrod, Ex p. Leeds City Council* [1976] Q.B. 540, CA (Civ Div); *R. v Mayor of Peterborough* (1875) 44 L.J. Q.B. 85; *R. v Hampstead Borough Council, Ex p. Woodward* (1917) 116 L.T. 213; *Re Bristol and North Somerset Railway Co* (1877) 3 Q.B.D 10 at 12; *R. v Bristol Corp, Ex p. Hendy* [1974] 1 W.L.R. 498 at 503.

indications that our courts see the utility of prospective rulings,[68] although there are also differences of judicial view.[69] The CJEU has employed the technique on a number of occasions.[70]

It is also possible to vest the courts with a more general power to determine the remedial consequences of invalidity.[71] Thus, art.264 TFEU para.2 provides that the CJEU shall, if it considers this necessary, state which effects of the act it has declared void shall be considered as definitive. This has been used to limit the temporal effect of the court's ruling. Considerations of legal certainty will often be paramount in this respect. The CJEU applies art.264 in order to retain in force the contested measure until a new measure can be adopted in order to avoid the drastic consequences that can be attendant on retroactive nullity.[72]

While there is no such general principle in UK law, particular statutes contain provisions authorising the courts to suspend the consequences of a finding of invalidity.[73] Such statutory provisions can properly be regarded as legislative instructions that prevent the relevant act from being regarded as void ab initio.[74]

iii. *The relevance of compensation*

24–024 It has been argued that manipulation of void and voidable is often a mask to avoid paying damages. Thus if English law developed a more general compensatory remedy for harm caused by ultra vires acts many of the problems concerned with void and voidable would disappear. Lord Wilberforce expressed a powerful argument along these lines.[75] There is no doubt an argument in favour of developing a remedy for loss caused by ultra vires administrative action which will be considered below.[76]

The relevance of this to the general debate on void and voidable must be kept in perspective. It is not a panacea that will solve all complexities attendant upon use of these terms. The common case is where the individual asserts the invalidity of an administrative act, and the public body raises the argument that this could have drastic administrative consequences. A developed system of damages could be useful. If the public body's fears are well founded, a court could say that the action was void, but that the only remedy was compensation, and not an order to quash the act.

---

[68] C. Lewis, "Retrospective and Prospective Rulings in Administrative Law" [1988] P.L. 78; Sir Harry Woolf, *Protection of the Public-A New Challenge* (London: Sweet & Maxwell, 1990), pp.53–56; Lady Arden, "Prospective Overruling" (2004) 115 L.Q.R. 7.

[69] *Evans (No.2)* [2001] 2 A.C. 19 at 26–27, 35–37.

[70] *Defrenne v Sabena* (43/75) [1976] E.C.R. 471; *Blaizot v University of Liege* (24/86) [1988] E.C.R. 379.

[71] P. Craig, *EU Administrative Law*, 2nd edn (Oxford: Oxford University Press, 2012), Ch.22.

[72] *Commission v Council (Generalized Tariff Preferences)* (51/87) [1988] E.C.R. 5459 at [21]–[22]; *European Parliament v Council* (C-392/95) [1997] E.C.R. I-3213 at [25]–[27]; *Portugal v Commission* (C-1159/96) [1998] E.C.R. I-7379 at [52]–[53]; *Austria v Council* (C-445/00) [2003] E.C.R. I-8549 at [103]–[106]; *European Parliament v Council* (C-93/00) [2001] E.C.R. I-10119 at [47]–[48].

[73] See e.g. Scotland Act 1998 s. 102(2)(b); *Salvesen v Riddle* [2013] UKSC 22.

[74] M. Elliott, "Invalid Control Orders: Void or Voidable?" (2011) 70 C.L.J. 22.

[75] *Hoffmann-La Roche* [1975] A.C. 295 at 358–359.

[76] See Ch.30; P. Craig, "Compensation in Public Law" (1980) 96 L.Q.R. 413.

The addition of a damages remedy does not however dispel the need for judicial discretion. If there was a real prospect of administrative upheaval the court could use its discretion to restrict the results of the decision being void instead of juggling with void and voidable. The invalidity would show only in the public body's liability to pay compensation. This may be a preferable way forward. The presence of such a remedy would not, however, show that judicial discretion was unnecessary. It would, rather, provide a more convenient and equitable framework within which to exercise that discretion.

iv. *The relevance of parliamentary redress*

The courts could turn a deaf ear to pleas of injustice or administrative chaos, and contend that it would be for Parliament to redress any resulting confusion. This may be warranted in some cases. There are however difficulties with the idea that Parliament can remedy the problem. In practical terms, it is unlikely that Parliament could pass a series of one-off pieces of legislation to remedy the effects of retrospective nullity. The constitutional problems are more severe, as is apparent from the sequence of events. The court states that administrative action is retrospectively void and this produces problems because it will involve large expenditure, or losses. Parliament is pressed to intervene. The problem with any such intervention is that it would constitute retrospective legislation, which takes away peoples' rights, those having been given by the court's judgment. Such legislation has always been frowned upon, and correctly so.[77] **24–025**

5. VOID AND VOIDABLE: NATURAL JUSTICE

The problem of whether decisions are void or voidable has been particularly prevalent in the context of natural justice. **24–026**

A. Hearings

The majority view in *Ridge*[78] was that failure to comply with the rules as to hearings rendered the decision void. This is in accord with precedent and principle. The rationale for regarding such a failure as leading to a void decision was expressed by Lord Selbourne LC: "there would be no decision within the meaning of the statute if there were anything of that sort done contrary to the essence of justice".[79] There have been many other cases where the courts have stated that a failure to hear renders the decision void or a nullity. Thus, the action of a committee, which purported to expel a person from a club without a hearing, was held to be null and void, as was the refusal of a pension to a policeman who **24–027**

---

[77] *Burmah Oil Co Ltd v Lord Advocate* [1965] A.C. 75, HL, and the subsequent War Damage Act 1965.

[78] *Ridge* [1964] A.C. 40 at 80 Lord Reid; at 125–126 Lord Morris of Borth-y-Gest; at 135–136 Lord Hodson.

[79] *Spackman v Plumstead District Board of Works* (1885) 10 App. Cas. 229 at 240.

had resigned from the force.[80] Cases of collateral attack are also instructive.[81] A number of these cases explicitly held that a failure to hear rendered the decision void.[82] Even where this was not so stated it was implicit in the ability to attack the decision collaterally: if a failure to hear constituted only an error within jurisdiction the decision could not have been attacked collaterally.

Despite this long line of authority Lord Evershed in *Ridge*[83] decided that failure to hear only made the decision voidable. His Lordship did not find the above cases convincing, and relied on *Osgood*[84] as support for the proposition that the court should only interfere if there had been a real and substantial miscarriage of justice. Lord Evershed said that this meant that the decision must be voidable and not void.[85] His Lordship's reasons for distinguishing those cases holding that a failure to hear made the decision void were however unconvincing, and the *Osgood* case did not in reality support Lord Evershed's argument.[86] Moreover, even if the *Osgood* case did provide support for the idea that a finding should only be quashed if there had been a substantial miscarriage of justice, the conclusion that therefore the decision must be voidable rather than void does not follow. It is, like his Lordship's reasoning concerning the declaration, based upon an absolute rather than relative meaning of the term void. Lord Diplock has stated[87] that a breach of the rules of natural justice should render the decision void. This has hopefully laid the argument to rest.

24–028 There are also several authorities for the proposition that bias results in a decision being void: a biased judge ceases to be a judge at all.[88] Further, if bias only made a finding voidable then declaration would not on traditional theory have been available, and the court could not have quashed in the presence of a no certiorari clause, but both occurred.[89] Despite these arguments some maintain that bias only

---

[80] *Fisher v Keane* (1878) 11 Ch. D. 353; *Lapointe v L'Association de Bienfaisance et de Retraite de la Police de Montreal* [1906] A.C. 535. See also, *R. v North, Ex p. Oakey* [1927] 1 K.B. 491, CA; *R. v Huntingdon Confirming Authority, Ex p. George and Stanford Hotels Ltd* [1929] 1 K.B. 698, CA; *Abbott v Sullivan* [1952] 1 K.B. 189, CA; *Disher v Disher* [1965] P. 31; *Hounslow LBC v Twickenham Garden Developments Ltd* [1971] Ch. 233 Ch D; *Firman v Ellis* [1978] Q.B. 886, CA (Civ Div).

[81] *Cooper v Wandsworth Board of Works* (1863) 14 C.B. (N.S.) 182; *Hopkins v Smethwick Local Board of Health* (1890) 24 Q.B.D 712; *Capel v Child* (1832) 2 C. & J. 558; *Innes v Wylie* (1844) 1 Car. & K. 257; *Bonaker v Evans* (1850) 16 Q.B. 162; *Wood v Woad* (1874) L.R. 9 Ex. 190.

[82] As in *Capel* (1832) 2 C. & J. 558; *Innes* (1844) 1 Car. & K. 257; *Bonaker* (1850) 16 Q.B. 162 and *Wood* (1874) L.R. 9 Ex. 190.

[83] *Ridge* [1964] A.C. 40 at 87–92.

[84] *Osgood v Nelson* (1872) L.R. 5 H.L. 636.

[85] *Ridge* [1964] A.C. 40 at 91–92.

[86] There is no reference in the *Osgood* case to void or voidable. The notion of substantial miscarriage of justice appears in the judgment of Martin B (1872) L.R. 5, H.L. 636 at 646. However, there is no indication that Martin B intended to use the notion in the sense used by Lord Evershed.

[87] *O'Reilly v Mackman* [1983] 2 A.C. 237, HL; *McLaughlin* [2007] UKPC 50.

[88] *Serjeant v Dale* (1877) 2 Q.B.D 558 at 566, 568; *Allinson v General Council of Medical Education and Registration* [1894] 1 Q.B. 750 at 757; *R. v Furnished Houses Rent Tribunal for Paddington and St Marylebone, Ex p. Kendal Hotels Ltd* [1947] 1 All E.R. 448 KBD at 449; *R. v Paddington North and St Marylebone Rent Tribunal, Ex p. Perry* [1956] 1 Q.B. 229 DC at 237; *Anisminic Ltd v Foreign Compensation Commission* [1969] 2 A.C. 147, HL at 171.

[89] *Cooper v Wilson* [1937] 2 K.B. 309, CA (declaration); *R. v Cheltenham Commissioners* (1841) 1 Q.B. 467 and *R. v Hertfordshire JJ* (1845) 6 Q.B. 753 (no certiorari clauses).

renders a decision voidable.[90] This view is based on *Dimes*.[91] A decision of the Lord Chancellor in the Court of Chancery was challenged on appeal on the basis that the Lord Chancellor possessed a financial interest in the company that was the subject of the litigation. Parke B, in giving advice to the House of Lords, stated that such bias only resulted in the decision being voidable and not void. There are, however, a number of points to notice about the case.[92] It was concerned with an appeal from one superior court to another and not with review. Appeal is the classic instance of a voidable act,[93] whereas for review to be applicable the act must be void or voidable in the area hitherto covered by patent errors of law within jurisdiction. Moreover, the authorities cited by Parke B do not support his proposition.[94]

C. Waiver

An argument used to support the proposition that a breach of the rules of natural justice only makes a decision voidable and not void is that such rules can be waived.[95] The argument is that jurisdictional defects cannot be waived[96] and, therefore, if the rules of natural justice can be waived this is indicative that the defect is not jurisdictional. There are cases indicating that a plaintiff can be barred from obtaining a remedy by waiver,[97] which will be discussed later.[98] However, this does not lead to the conclusion that a defect of natural justice only renders a determination voidable. **24–029**

In terms of principle, the rationale for saying that jurisdictional defects cannot be waived is that the limits to an administrator's jurisdiction are imposed by statute, and by common law principles. It should not, therefore, be open to the individual to disregard those boundaries, which are not established solely for the individual's benefit but for the general public interest. They cannot therefore be waived at the instance of an individual. This may be correct as a starting point. It is, however, modified in a number of respects.[99] It can be argued that defects of natural justice should be susceptible to waiver, without this involving the

---

[90] Rubinstein, *Jurisdiction and Illegality* (1965), p.203.

[91] *Dimes v Grand Junction Canal Co Proprietors* (1852) 3 H.L.C. 759 at 785–786. See also, *Wildes v Russell* (1866) L.R. 1 C.P. 722 at 741–742; *Phillips v Eyre* (1870) L.R. 6 Q.B. 1 at 22.

[92] H.W.R. Wade, "Unlawful Administrative Action: Void or Voidable?" (1968) 84 L.Q.R. 95 at 106–108.

[93] Rubinstein, *Jurisdiction and Illegality* (1965), pp.5–6.

[94] *Brookes v Earl Rivers* (1668) Hardr. 503; *Company of Mercers and Ironmongers of Chester v Bowker* (1726) 1 Stra. 639.

[95] Rubinstein, *Jurisdiction and Illegality* (1965), p.221.

[96] *Essex Incorporated Congregational Church Union v Essex County Council* [1963] A.C. 808, HL at 820–821.

[97] *R. v Salop JJ* [1859] 2 El. & El. 386 at 391; *Mayor and Alderman of City of London v Cox* (1867) L.R. 2 H.L. 239 at 279–283; *Farquharson v Morgan* [1894] 1 Q.B. 552 at 559; *R. v Williams, Ex p. Phillips* [1914] 1 K.B. 608 KBD at 613–614; *R. v Comptroller-General of Patents and Designs, Ex p. Parke Davis* [1953] 2 W.L.R. 760; *R. v British Broadcasting Corp, Ex p. Lavelle* [1983] 1 W.L.R. 23 QBD at 39.

[98] See Ch.26.

[99] The sanctity of the ultra vires principle is compromised by the balancing process inherent within the time limits for remedies, and in the rules concerning delay, acquiescence and the effect of alternative remedies, see 22–050. See also, the discussion of representations, 22–051.

conclusion that such defects are only voidable and not void. A primary purpose of natural justice is to protect the individual. If the individual is aware that the rules are not being fully complied with, but is content to proceed, he should not be able to raise the defect thereafter.[100] There is nothing inconsistent in admitting a doctrine of waiver and still regarding a procedural defect if not waived as producing a void decision.

In terms of the case law, a number of cases see no inconsistency between waiver and voidness. It would of course be open to society to say that there is a wider public interest underlying the procedural rules over and beyond that of the particular individual. The result would be that procedural defects could never be waived. However, the current case law does not in general adopt this attitude. While it continues to regard the procedural rules as imposed primarily for the benefit of the individual, there is no conceptual inconsistency in admitting that such rules can be waived and yet denominating a breach of those rules as jurisdictional leading to a void decision.[101] It is to be hoped that the remarks of Lord Diplock mentioned above have settled the law in this area.

6. PROBLEMS OF PROOF

A. The Burden of Proof

24–030 The general rule is that the claimant asserting the invalidity of administrative action must produce some evidence that throws doubt upon its apparent validity before the burden shifts to the public body. In this sense the presumption is that the actions of the public body are lawful, and it is for the claimant to lead evidence to the contrary. There is, however, no rule that unlawful acts should be treated as valid. That is an entirely different proposition. The individual will none the less normally have the initial onus of showing some defect in the relevant order. Thus, as Lord Steyn held in *Boddington*, while there is no rule giving validity to invalid acts, the court will assume that subordinate legislation and administrative acts are valid unless persuaded otherwise.[102] This is in accord with the leading authorities.

In *Wrights' Canadian Ropes*,[103] the minister had power to disallow any expense that he felt to be in excess of what was normal or reasonable for the taxpayer's business. The court held that it was for WRC to show that there was some ground for interfering with the minister's determination. A number of other cases support the same proposition.[104] In *Rossminster*,[105] tax legislation empowered revenue officers to seize documents where they had reasonable cause

[100] *Jeyeanthan* [2000] 1 W.L.R. 354

[101] Akehurst [1968] 31 M.L.R. 138 at 149, and *Wade* (1968) 84 L.Q.R. 95 at 109 express a similar idea.

[102] *Boddington* [1999] 2 A.C. 143 at 174.

[103] *Minister of National Revenue v Wrights' Canadian Ropes Ltd* [1947] A.C. 109 at 122.

[104] *Point of Ayr Collieries Ltd v Lloyd-George* [1943] 2 All E.R. 546 at 547; *Potato Marketing Board v Merricks* [1958] 2 Q.B. 316 QBD; *Wilover Nominees Ltd v Inland Revenue Commissioners* [1973] 1 W.L.R. 1393 Ch D at 1396, 1399, affirmed [1974] 1 W.L.R. 1342 at 1347; *Fawcett Properties Ltd v Buckingham CC* [1959] Ch. 543, CA at 575, affirmed [1961] A.C. 636.

[105] *R. v Inland Revenue Commissioners, Ex p. Rossminster Ltd* [1980] A.C. 952, HL.

to believe that they would be required as evidence of tax fraud. Lord Diplock[106] stated that the court should proceed on the presumption that the officers acted intra vires, until the applicant had displaced that presumption.

How much evidence will be required in order to shift the burden of proof will depend on the type of case. If the defect is apparent on the face of the decision, the burden will not be a heavy one. Equally, where the applicant is claiming that the decision-maker has misconstrued a condition of jurisdiction, there is unlikely to be a difficulty. A reasoned assertion that the tribunal misinterpreted, for example, the term employee, would normally suffice to force the tribunal to defend its interpretation. The position will, however, be different where the ground of attack is that of unreasonableness or bad faith. The applicant will also have a heavier task where the statute requires the decision-maker to be satisfied of some matter, or where it is required to form some opinion.[107] The general rule described above is subject to two qualifications.

First, where the applicant alleges what would be a tort in the absence of statutory authority, it seems that the claimant only has to prove the facts which would constitute the wrong. The burden of proof is then on the public body to show justification. This is exemplified by *Rossminster*.[108] Lord Diplock stated that since the handling of a man's property without his permission was prima facie tortious, then in a civil action for trespass to goods based on the seizure of the property, the onus would be on the officer to satisfy the court that there were reasonable grounds for believing that the documents were evidence of a tax fraud.[109] It seems that this qualification will only apply where the allegation is that a statutory condition has not been complied with, and not where the allegation is, for example, one of bad faith.[110] **24–031**

The second possible qualification arises from the law on habeas corpus. The law in this area is, however, unclear. In one case the court held that the public body must show that it had complied with the statutory conditions. It was insufficient for a detaining authority to make a return that was valid on its face. A detainee could be put to proof of an allegation of bad faith, but it was otherwise where the allegation related to compliance with the statutory conditions.[111] This case has been distinguished, the court holding that where the return was good on its face it was for the detainee to show that the detention was illegal.[112] The present position none the less seems to be that the burden of proof rests upon the

---

[106] *Rossminster* [1980] A.C. 952 at 1013.

[107] See cases *Wrights' Canadian Ropes* [1947] A.C. 109; *Point of Ayr Collieries* [1943] 2 All E.R. 546; *Merricks* [1958] 2 Q.B. 316; *Wilover Nominees* [1973] 1 W.L.R. 1393; *Fawcett Properties* [1959] Ch. 543.

[108] *Rossminster* [1980] A.C. 952 at 1011; *R. v Secretary of State for the Home Department, Ex p. Khawaja* [1984] A.C. 74, HL.

[109] See also *St Pancras BC v Frey* [1963] 2 Q.B. 586 DC at 592; *Harpin v St Albans Corp* (1969) 67 L.G.R. 479. But see, *Bristol DC v Clark* [1975] 1 W.L.R. 1443 at 1448 where doubt was cast upon these cases.

[110] *R. v Governor of Brixton Prison, Ex p. Ahsan* [1969] 2 Q.B. 222 DC, explaining *Greene v Secretary of State for Home Affairs* [1942] A.C. 284, HL.

[111] *Ahsan* [1969] 2 Q.B. 222. See also, *Eshugbayi Eleko v Government of Nigeria* [1931] A.C. 662.

[112] *R. v Governor of Risley Remand Centre, Ex p. Hassan* [1976] 1 W.L.R. 971 DC at 976–979.

detaining authority. In *Khawaja*,[113] Lord Scarman stated that the initial burden was on the applicant, but that this was transferred to the detaining authority once the applicant had shown that there was a prima facie case that liberty or property were being interfered with. The burden of proof would then be on the detaining authority to justify the detention. Thus, on the facts of that case, once the applicant had shown that he entered the UK with leave of the immigration officer, the burden of proving that he had obtained leave by deception was on the Executive.

The issue considered here should not be confused with a separate, albeit connected one. We have been considering the status of an order and the question of who has the initial onus of proving a defect. The general answer is that the onus is initially on the person alleging the invalidity. A related but separate issue is what the court will demand of the public body if it is to justify its action. In other words if the individual does shift the burden of proof to the public body, what will that body have to prove and what will be the standard of review. This depends on the statutory context. If the allegation relates to a jurisdictional fact the court will normally substitute its judgment for that of the public body. Where the question is whether the evidence justifies the application of a certain statutory term the standard of proof will differ depending upon the area in question.[114]

B. Validity Pending Determination

24–032 The basic principle set out above means that it will be for the individual to persuade the court that there are grounds for invalidating an administrative decision. This has implications for interim proceedings, as exemplified by *Hoffmann-La Roche*.[115] The secretary of state, acting pursuant to a Monopolies Commission report on the company's profits on certain drugs, laid before Parliament statutory orders directing the company to reduce its price. The company informed the secretary of state that it would not obey the relevant Order. It claimed that the procedures of the Monopolies Commission contravened natural justice and that the order was ultra vires. The secretary of state responded by claiming an interim injunction to restrain the company from charging prices in excess of those specified in the Order. The main argument was whether the interim injunction should be conditional on the Crown giving an undertaking to pay damages, should the company prove successful in the main action. The secretary of state refused to give any such undertaking. Their Lordships found against the company. Their reasoning may be summarised as follows.

The statutory instrument is, unless and until successfully challenged, the law of the land. It has a presumption of validity. If and when it is successfully impugned it will be retrospectively null. The normal judicial practice is to condition the grant of an interim injunction upon an undertaking in damages

[113] *R. v Secretary of State for the Home Department, Ex p. Khawaja* [1984] A.C. 74, HL at 111–112; *R. (Abbasi) v Secretary of State for Foreign and Commonwealth Affairs* [2002] EWCA Civ 1598 at [60]; *Duggal v Secretary of State for the Home Dept* [2011] EWHC 736 (Admin); *R. (Antonio) v Secretary of State for the Home Department* [2014] EWHC 3894 (Admin).

[114] See Ch.17.

[115] *Hoffmann-La Roche* [1975] A.C. 295.

given by the person in whose favour the injunction issues. This is to safeguard the position of the party against whom the injunction issues, should this party prove successful in the main action, and has suffered loss in the period between the interim injunction and the final decision. It was at one time maintained that the Crown would never be required to give such an undertaking, but this rule had been rendered out of date by the Crown Proceedings Act 1947. In principle, therefore, such an undertaking could be extracted from the Crown and would normally be required where the Crown was asserting its purely private law rights of a proprietary or contractual nature.

The position was, however, different where the Crown was enforcing the law of the land. In such cases, although an undertaking in damages could be required as a condition for the grant of an injunction, the private party would have to show a strong case for imposing this condition. The factors which the court would take into account in deciding whether to impose the undertaking in damages included: the strength of the company's prima facie case of invalidity; the financial interest of the Crown, given that the National Health Service was the main buyer of the drugs; the viability of a plan proposed by the company under which it would charge the higher prices, but recompense buyers should the Order be upheld; and the effect upon members of the public who were not parties to the action.[116]

Lord Wilberforce dissented.[117] The Statutory Order could not, said his Lordship, have any presumption of validity since it was now being challenged by the right person in the correct proceedings. The optimum position would be to issue the interim injunction, since the only loss suffered would be pecuniary, but to require the Crown to provide compensation should the final decision be in favour of the company.

The difficulty with the decision is that the issues involved therein, the status of the Order and the undertaking in damages, were linked both in the majority and dissenting judgments, in a way which is apt to mislead. **24–033**

The majority judgment should be accepted in relation to the status of the Order. It should be regarded as presumptively valid. The Order must be presumptively something: it must be either presumptively valid or invalid. A neutral stance is not possible, since it would not be possible to assess the demands for injunctive relief, or decide who had the burden of proof. Lord Wilberforce's argument that no such presumption of validity should exist, because the correct person was challenging the order in the correct proceedings, does not take account of the time scale, and the normal burden of proof. The problems concerning the time scale reflect the fact that the claim was for interim relief. The presumption of validity voiced by the majority is a presumption that applies unless and until the order is challenged in the final action. The burden of proof will, as seen above, rest initially on the person disputing the validity of the order. Lord Hoffmann in *Wicks* stated that the presumption of validity was an evidential matter at the interlocutory stage of proceedings, and the presumption existed pending a final decision by the court.[118]

---

[116] *Hoffmann-La Roche* [1975] A.C. 295 at 341–342, 351–354, 361–370, 370–372.

[117] *Hoffmann-La Roche* [1975] A.C. 295 at 354–360.

[118] *Wicks* [1998] A.C. 92 at 116. This view was supported by Lord Steyn in *Boddington* [1999] 2 A.C. 143 at 174.

There is, however, no logical connection between regarding the order as presumptively valid and the undertaking in damages. It was the latter that Lord Wilberforce was most concerned with. The fact that the statutory order is presumptively valid does not in itself tell us the basis on which it should be enforced in interim proceedings. The majority reasoned that because the Order is presently the law of the land, and because the Crown has a duty to enforce it, therefore the Crown should not always be fettered by the requirement of a damages undertaking,[119] which could be a deterrent to the Crown bringing an action.[120]

This reasoning is however contestable. The equation of a duty to enforce the presumptive law, with the absence of responsibility if that presumption proves unfounded, is open to question. The Crown or a public body is given responsibility for law enforcement because it represents the public interest.[121] The people benefit from such law enforcement. If it transpires that the public body was wrong then the public generally should shoulder the burden, through the losses being placed upon it via taxation. Any distributive windfall gain or loss to a section of society[122] is minimal compared to the burden placed on the private party if no undertaking in damages is required. A public body could be deterred from bringing an action if there was the possibility that it could be liable to pay compensation should it prove to be unsuccessful. But this amounts to no more than saying that doing something with no risk of financial liability is less risky than doing something where there is some such risk. It begs the whole question of where losses from invalid governmental action ought to lie.

24–034 The Supreme Court in *Sinaloa Gold*,[123] however, endorsed the reasoning in *Hoffmann-La Roche*, holding that private litigation and public enforcement were distinct. In the latter a public authority was seeking to enforce the law in the interests of the public generally, often in pursuance of a public duty to do so, and enjoyed only the resources assigned to it for its functions. There was therefore no general rule that a public authority acting pursuant to a public duty should be required to give an undertaking in damages, more especially because there was no general cause of action for damages caused by invalid administrative action.

The House of Lords considered the validity of laws pending their final determination in *Factortame (No.2)*.[124] The plaintiffs sought interim relief against the Crown to prevent it from applying a national law, which they argued was in breach of Community law. It was held that there was no rule that a party challenging the validity of a law must show a strong prima facie case that the law was invalid. The court had discretion in the matter. However, their Lordships also held that the court should not restrain a public authority by interim injunction

[119] *Hoffmann-La Roche* [1975] A.C. 295 at 364, 367, Lord Diplock.

[120] *Hoffmann-La Roche* [1975] A.C. 295 at 371 Lord Cross.

[121] *Gouriet v Union of Post Office Workers* [1978] A.C. 435.

[122] *Hoffmann-La Roche* [1975] A.C. 295 at 367; *Rochdale Borough Council v Anders* [1988] 3 All ER 490.

[123] *Financial Services Authority v Sinaloa Gold* [2013] UKSC 11, [2013] 2 A.C. 28.

[124] *R. v Secretary of State for Transport, Ex p. Factortame Ltd (No.2)* [1991] 1 A.C. 603, HL.

from enforcing an apparently valid law, unless it was satisfied that the challenge was, prima facie so firmly based as to justify this exceptional course of action being taken.[125]

C. Partial Invalidity

A court may under certain conditions hold that the invalid part of an order can be severed, while the remainder is still valid. The court will not, however, "rewrite" the order, and the invalid part must not be inextricably interwoven with the whole order.[126] The leading decision is *Hutchinson*.[127] The appellants were convicted of offences under the Greenham Common Byelaws, in that they entered a protected area as defined by the byelaw. They contended by way of defence that the byelaw was invalid, because it was in breach of the enabling legislation. The statute stated that byelaws could be made provided that they did not interfere with rights of common, and the appellants claimed that the byelaws interfered with such rights. The issue for the House of Lords was, therefore, whether the invalid part of the byelaw could be severed. Their Lordships distinguished between two situations. **24–035**

The first was where textual severance was possible. In this instance a test of substantial severability was to be applied, which would be satisfied when the valid text was unaffected by, and independent of, the invalid. The second situation was where textual severance was not possible. The test was whether the legislative instrument with the parts omitted would be a substantially different law from what it would have been if the omitted parts had been included.

In *National Association of Health Stores*[128] Sedley LJ extended the reasoning in *Hutchinson* to cases of curable omissions in regulations. He stated that

> "... to strike down an entire regulation because of a curable omission which appears to have affected nobody, however cogent the case in legal theory for doing so, would represent a triumph of logic over reason".[129]

If therefore

> "... an omission can be made good without disrupting the existing, presumptively lawful, text, and if so far the omission appears to have done no harm, I see no good reason why, instead of permitting the rule-maker to insert the missing brick, the entire structure should be pulled down."[130]

---

[125] *Factortame Ltd (No.2)* [1991] 1 A.C. 603 at 674.

[126] *Potato Marketing Board v Merricks* [1958] 2 Q.B. 316 QBD; *Kingsway Investments (Kent) Ltd v Kent CC* [1971] A.C. 72, HL; *Dunkley v Evans* [1981] 1 W.L.R. 1522 QBD; *Thames Water Authority v Elmbridge BC* [1983] Q.B. 570, CA Civ Div; *R. v Secretary of State for Transport, Ex p. GLC* [1986] Q.B. 556 QBD; *R. v North Hertfordshire DC, Ex p. Cobbold* [1985] 3 All E.R. 487.

[127] *DPP v Hutchinson* [1990] 2 A.C. 783; A. Bradley, "Judicial Enforcement of *Ultra Vires* Byelaws: The Proper Scope of Severance" [1990] P.L. 293; *R. (Public and Commercial Services Union) v Minister for the Civil Service* [2010] EWHC 1463 (Admin).

[128] *R. (National Association of Health Stores) v Secretary of State for Health* [2005] EWCA Civ 154.

[129] *National Association of Health Stores* [2005] EWCA Civ 154 at [16].

[130] *National Association of Health Stores* [2005] EWCA Civ 154 at [20].

CHAPTER 25

REMEDIES: STANDING

1. CENTRAL ISSUES

i. Locus standi is concerned with whether a particular claimant is entitled to invoke the jurisdiction of the court. This must be distinguished from justiciability, which asks whether the judicial process is suitable for the resolution of this type of dispute, whoever brings it to court. It is also distinct from the issue known in the USA as ripeness,[1] under which premature questions are not adjudicated upon. There is case law on both justiciability and ripeness in the UK,[2] although the concepts are not as developed as in the USA. **25–001**

ii. The law will be examined both prior to and consequent upon the reforms of administrative law remedies.[3] A brief historical perspective is necessary for a proper understanding of the present law. It will be seen that prior to 1978 different tests of standing applied as between the prerogative orders on the one hand and declaration and injunction on the other. There was, moreover, variation in the tests that applied to different prerogative orders and uncertainty as to the precise test that applied to particular remedies.

iii. Reform was therefore required. A test of sufficiency of interest was introduced as part of the remedial reforms in 1978. The reform liberalised the test for standing, but still left questions to be resolved in subsequent cases concerning the meaning of sufficient interest, more especially when the claimant was an interest group rather than an individual.

iv. The discussion of standing would be incomplete if it did not include analysis of the rich literature as to what the standing rules ought to be. This will be examined after the positive law on the meaning of sufficiency of interest has been clarified. The issue of who should be able to invoke the judicial process has been much debated,[4] and the policy arguments will be

---

[1] A. Aman and W. Mayton, *Administrative Law*, 2nd edn (St Pauls, MN: West Publishing, 2001), pp.413–420.

[2] J. Beatson, "Prematurity and Ripeness for Review", in C. Forsyth and I. Hare (eds), *The Golden Metwand and the Crooked Cord, Essays on Public Law in Honour of Sir William Wade* (Oxford: Oxford University Press, 1998), pp.221–252.

[3] SI 1955/1977; SI 2000/1980; Senior Courts Act 1981 s.31.

[4] S. Thio, *Locus Standi and Judicial Review* (Singapore: Singapore University Press, 1971); J. Vining, *Legal Identity, The Coming of Age of Public Law* (New Haven: Yale University Press, 1978); P. Van Dijk, *Judicial Review of Governmental Action and the Requirement of an Interest to Sue* (Alphen aan den Rijn: Sijthoff & Noordhoff, 1980).

considered below.[5] We shall see that assumptions concerning the nature of administrative law, and the role of the courts, are inherent in any response.

2. THE LAW BEFORE 1978[6]

25–002 There is considerable diversity in the older case law on standing, both within each remedy and as between them. The main cause for the confusion was the failure to adopt a clear view as to what the remedies were seeking to achieve, which reflected lack of clarity as to the purpose of administrative law.

A. Certiorari

25–003 There were at least two views as to standing requirements for certiorari. The first was that certiorari had no standing limits as such. Any person could apply for an order, and standing would only be relevant to the granting of the remedy. If the application was made by a person aggrieved, then the court would intervene *ex debito justitiae*, in justice to the applicant. Where the applicant was a stranger, the court considered whether the public interest demanded intervention.[7] A second view was that an applicant must show some interest before being accorded standing.[8] The weight of authority favoured the former view.[9] The degree of practical difference between them should not, however, be overemphasised. If a court did not wish to grant an applicant standing, it could reach that conclusion either by adopting the first view, but refusing in its discretion to admit the applicant, or by adopting the second view and deeming the person not to be an interested party.

B. Prohibition

25–004 The case law on standing to seek prohibition makes that on certiorari seem simple.[10] There was, however, one clear line of authority. The cases held that prohibition must be granted whoever the applicant was, the reason being that an excess of jurisdiction by an inferior court was contempt against the Crown, in the sense of being an infringement of the royal prerogative.[11] The applicant therefore

---

[5] See paras 25–033 to 25–049.

[6] SI 1955/1977 came into effect on January 11, 1978.

[7] *R. v Surrey JJ* (1870) L.R. 5 Q.B. 466 at 473; *R. v Butt, Ex p. Brooke* (1922) 38 T.LR 537; *R. v Stafford JJ, Ex p. Stafford Corp* [1940] 2 K.B. 33, CA; *R. v Brighton Borough JJ, Ex p. Jarvis* [1954] 1 W.L.R. 203 DC; *R. v Thames Magistrates' Court, Ex p. Greenbaum* (1957) 55 L.G.R. 129.

[8] Thio, *Locus Standi and Judicial Review* (1971), Ch.5; D.M. Gordon, "Certiorari and the Problem of Locus Standi" (1955) 71 L.Q.R. 483, 485; *R. v Bradford-on-Avon Urban DC, Ex p. Boulton* [1964] 1 W.L.R. 1136 QBD; *R. v Paddington Valuation Officer, Ex p. Peachey Property Corporation* [1966] 1 Q.B. 380, CA; *R. v Russell, Ex p. Beaverbrook Newspapers Ltd* [1969] 1 Q.B. 342 DC.

[9] Cases cited for the second view appear to be either obiter dictum, *Boulton* [1964] 1 W.L.R. 1136 or ambiguous, *Paddington* [1966] 1 Q.B. 380, where Lord Denning MR purported to apply the *Greenbaum* case (1957) 55 L.G.R. 129, which is supportive of the first view.

[10] J. Shortt, *Informations, Mandamus and Prohibition* (London: W. Clowes and Sons, 1887), p.441.

[11] *De Haber v Queen of Portugal* (1851) 17 Q.B. 171; *Worthington v Jeffries* (1875) L.R. 10 C.P. 379; *R. v Speyer* [1916] 1 K.B. 595 KBD.

approached the court to represent the public interest. This reasoning was indicative of a citizen action[12] approach towards standing. There were, however, also cases that adopted a private rights perspective. Thus, some authorities appeared to require a specific interest in the applicant,[13] while others sought to side-step the reasoning in the first line of authority by arguing that it applied only to patent and not to latent jurisdictional defects.[14]

C. Mandamus

The diversity of approach towards standing is clearly evident in the confused case law on mandamus. One line of cases required the applicant to show infringement of a legal right in the traditional private law sense, such that a cause of action in contract or tort could be maintained against the public body.[15] Other cases used the terminology of private right, but gave the term "right" a broader meaning by granting standing even where no contractual or tortious right had been affected.[16] Another line of authority explicitly regarded a sufficient or special interest as satisfying the requirements for standing.[17] **25–005**

D. Injunction and Declaration

Declarations and injunctions were available through Ord.15 r.16, or by application to the High Court respectively. They may now also be claimed by way of application for judicial review under s.31 of the Senior Courts Act 1981. **25–006**

The circumstances in which an individual could seek an injunction or declaration were narrowly construed. In *Boyce*,[18] Buckley J held that an action for an injunction could only be maintained without joining the Attorney General in two types of case. The plaintiff had to show either that the interference with the public right constituted an infringement of a private right, or there had to be

[12] See para. 25–038.

[13] *Forster v Forster and Berridge* (1863) 4 B. & S. 187; *R. v Twiss* (1869) L.R. 4 Q.B. 407 at 413–414.

[14] *Mayor and Aldermen of City of London v Cox* (1867) L.R. 2 H.L. 239; *Farquharson v Morgan* [1894] 1 Q.B. 552.

[15] *R. v Lewisham Union* [1897] 1 Q.B. 498 at 500; *R. v Industrial Court, Ex p. ASSET* [1965] 1 Q.B. 377 QBD.

[16] *R. v Hereford Corp, Ex p. Harrower* [1970] 1 W.L.R. 1424 DC; *R. v Customs and Excise Commissioners, Ex p. Cook* [1970] 1 W.L.R. 450 DC.

[17] *R. v Paddington Valuation Officer, Ex p. Peachey Property Corporation Ltd* [1966] 1 Q.B. 380, CA at 401; *R. v Commissioners for Special Purposes of Income Tax* (1888) 21 Q.B.D 313; *R. v Manchester Corp* [1911] 1 K.B. 560 KBD; *R. v Commissioner of Police of the Metropolis, Ex p. Blackburn* [1968] 2 Q.B. 118, CA (Civ Div).

[18] *Boyce v Paddington BC* [1903] 1 Ch. 109 Ch D at 114; *Stockport District Waterworks Co v Manchester Corp* (1863) 9 Jur. (NS) 266; *Pudsey Coal Gas Co v Corp of Bradford* (1872) L.R. 15 Eq. 167.

special damage. The House of Lords endorsed this criterion,[19] and later cases on declaration adopted the same reasoning.[20] There are two reasons why the courts adopted these narrow rules for standing.

First, the test in *Boyce* was based upon the criteria for public nuisance, as is clear from the authorities cited.[21] This argument is flawed. In private law there is no separation of standing and the merits. Who can sue is not treated as a distinct issue, but is part of the definition of the cause of action. Thus, for example, a person placed in fear of her bodily safety can claim in assault, or one whose reputation is injured can claim in defamation. The argument from public nuisance therefore tells us who should be able to sue in that action. To infer that the same test should apply in public law is a non-sequitur.[22]

A second argument concerning declarations was based on the wording of Ord.15 r.16.[23] Something akin to a private law right was said to be required because the Order was cast in terms of "declarations of rights". This argument is unconvincing. The declaration fulfils both an original and a supervisory role. In the former sense it is used in cases that have nothing to do with public law, for example to declare the parties' respective rights under a contract. Where, however, the declaration is being used in its supervisory role, to control excess of power by public bodies, there is no reason why the remedy can only be granted where a private law right is present.

25–007 Not all cases required a private law right, in the sense of a cause of action in contract or tort, before the plaintiff could proceed.[24] The prospect of broadening the standing requirement was, however, curtailed by *Gouriet*.[25] The Post Office Act 1953 ss.58 and 68 made it an offence to interfere with the mail. The Union of Post Office Workers (UPW) had called on their members not to handle letters being sent to South Africa. Gouriet sought the consent of the Attorney General to a relator action, but this was not forthcoming. When the case went to the House of Lords the plaintiff no longer asserted that this refusal of consent could be reviewed, rather that the failure to secure the approval was not fatal to the claim.

---

19 *London Passenger Transport Board v Moscrop* [1942] A.C. 332, HL at 342.

20 *Gregory v Camden LBC* [1966] 1 W.L.R. 899 QBD; *Anisminic v Foreign Compensation Commission* [1968] 2 Q.B. 862, CA (Civ Div) at 910–911; *Wilson, Walton International (Offshore Services) Ltd v Tees and Hartlepool Port Authority* [1969] 1 Lloyd's Rep. 120; *Booth and Co (International) Ltd v National Enterprise Board* [1978] 3 All E.R. 624 QBD.

21 *Winterbottom v Lord Derby* (1867) L.R. 2 E.x. 316; *Benjamin v Storr* (1874) L.R. 9 C.P. 400.

22 P. Cane, "The Function of Standing Rules in Administrative Law" [1980] P.L. 303 at 305.

23 The courts have, however, held that public law cases must generally be brought within the new public law procedure save in exceptional cases, see Ch.27.

24 (a) on declaration: *Nicholls v Tavistock Urban District Council* [1923] 2 Ch. 18 Ch D; *Prescott v Birmingham Corp* [1955] Ch. 210, CA; *Brownsea Haven Properties v Poole Corp* [1958] Ch. 574, CA; *Eastham v Newcastle United Football Club* [1964] Ch. 413 Ch D; *Thorne Rural DC v Bunting* [1972] Ch. 470 Ch D; *Tito v Waddell (No.2)* [1977] Ch. 106 Ch D at 260; *R. v Greater London Council, Ex p. Blackburn* [1976] 1 W.L.R. 550, CA (Civ Div); (b) on injunction: *Chamberlaine v Chester and Birkenhead Ry Co* (1848) 1 Ex. 870; *Bradbury v Enfield LBC* [1967] 1 W.L.R. 1311, CA (Civ Div), cf. *RCA Corp v Pollard* [1982] 3 W.L.R. 1007, CA (Civ Div) and *Lonrho Ltd v Shell Petroleum (No.2)* [1982] A.C. 173, HL, restrictively interpreting *Ex p Island Records Ltd* [1978] Ch. 122, CA (Civ Div); and *Barrs v Bethell* [1982] Ch. 294 Ch D not following *Prescott*, or *R. v Greater London Council, Ex p. Blackburn*.

25 *Gouriet v Union of Post Office Workers* [1978] A.C. 435, HL; *Eaton v Natural England* [2012] EWHC 2401 (Admin); *Law Society of England and Wales v Shah* [2015] 1 W.L.R. 2094 (Ch).

Their Lordships rejected this argument. The reasoning is permeated by a conception of the role of the citizen in public law. Put shortly, the citizen has no such role. In the absence of the Attorney General a citizen could enforce his or her private rights, but public rights could be enforced only through the Attorney General as representative of the public interest. It therefore followed that consent to a relator action was not something fictitious or nominal, to be circumvented at will. It was the substantive manifestation of the principle that public rights were to be represented by the Attorney General.[26] The precise ambit of the term private right was not clear,[27] and there was some uncertainty as to whether special damage was still an alternative basis for declaratory or injunctive relief.[28]

The decision illustrates a conception of standing based on the vindication of private rights. The difficulties of this approach will be considered later,[29] but a particular difficulty should be mentioned here. An applicant who sought a prerogative order was not tied to the enforcement of private law rights, and was vindicating the public interest to some degree. The premise underpinning *Gouriet*, that individuals enforce private rights and the Attorney General enforces public rights, cannot therefore be accepted as an accurate description of what the courts had been doing.[30] Gouriet argued that the broader notion of interest for standing within the prerogative orders should apply in injunction/declaration cases. Their Lordships rejected this argument, and the cogency of the reasoning will be examined below.[31]

3. THE ATTORNEY GENERAL, PUBLIC AUTHORITIES AND STATUTORY APPEALS

The rules of standing that operate in certain areas are distinct. These will be examined before considering the general rules on standing that operate in ordinary judicial review actions. 25–008

A. Attorney General

The Attorney General as the legal representative of the Crown represents the interests of the Crown qua Sovereign, and also qua parens patriae. This jurisdiction was initially invoked in relation to public nuisance and the administration of charitable and public trusts. The initial impetus seemed to stem from private law proprietary interests, the Crown possessing a jus publicum for the use of highways and rivers, coupled with the desire to prevent multiplicity of 25–009

[26] *Gouriet* [1978] A.C. 435 at 477–480, 483, 495, 498–499, 508. cf. the view in the Court of Appeal [1977] 1 Q.B. 729 at 768–772, 773–779.

[27] *Gouriet* [1978] A.C. 435 at 483–484, 495, 501–502, 514–515.

[28] Lord Wilberforce was the only one of their Lordships to mention special damage, but this might be because special damage was not pleaded. In *Barrs* [1982] Ch. 294 it was held that an individual could proceed in his own name if he could prove such damage.

[29] See para.25–034.

[30] See also Wade, "Note" (1978) 94 L.Q.R. 4.

[31] See para.25–015.

litigation. The Attorney General may act on his own initiative, as guardian of the public interest, to restrain public nuisances and prevent excess of power by public bodies.[32]

Particular problems arise where the Attorney General seeks to buttress the criminal law. In *Attorney General v Smith*[33] an injunction was granted to prevent S from making repeated applications for planning permission for a caravan site, despite the presence of penalties in the relevant legislation. In *Attorney General v Harris*[34] a flower vendor who contravened police regulations many times was prevented from continuing to do so by an injunction. Their Lordships in *Gouriet*[35] felt that this power should be used sparingly, and should be reserved for cases where there were continued breaches of the law, or serious injury was threatened.

It is not entirely clear whether the Attorney General seeking an injunction is in an especially privileged position. The law appears to be as follows. The Attorney General has discretion to decide whether to bring an action.[36] If an action is brought and the breach proven the court is not bound to issue an injunction in the Attorney General's favour, but exceptional circumstances would have to exist before the claim was refused. It will be regarded as a wrong in itself for the law to be flouted.[37]

The Attorney General may proceed at the relation of an individual complainant where she does not possess the requisite interest to bring a case in her own name. The consent of the Attorney General is necessary, the procedure being known as a relator action. We have already seen that the failure to secure this consent cannot be circumvented. In a relator action the Attorney General is the plaintiff, but in practice the private litigant will instruct counsel, and will remain liable for costs.

B. Public Authorities

25–010 The courts in the past restrictively construed the locus standi of public authorities. The public authority was required to show an interference with proprietary rights, special damage or that it was the beneficiary of a statutory duty, in order that the action could be maintained without the Attorney General. Thus, in *Tozer*[38] the corporation failed to obtain an injunction when complaining that the defendant's building constituted the laying out of a new street in contravention of the byelaws. No proprietary interest of the plaintiff was affected and the courts deprecated the bringing of such actions in the absence of the Attorney General.

---

32 *Attorney General v PYA Quarries Ltd* [1957] 2 Q.B. 169, CA; *Attorney General v Manchester Corp* [1906] 1 Ch. 643 Ch D; *Attorney General v Fulham Corp* [1921] 1 Ch. 440 Ch D.

33 *Attorney General v Smith* [1958] 2 Q.B. 173 at 185.

34 *Attorney General v Harris* [1961] 1 Q.B. 74, CA; *Attorney General v Premier Line Ltd* [1932] 1 Ch. 303 Ch D.

35 *Gouriet* [1978] A.C. 435; *Stoke-on-Trent City Council v B & Q (Retail) Ltd* [1984] A.C. 754, HL; *Attorney General v Able* [1984] Q.B. 975.

36 *London CC v Attorney General* [1902] A.C. 165, HL at 169; *Gouriet* [1978] A.C. 435.

37 *Attorney General v Bastow* [1957] 1 Q.B. 514 QBD; *Attorney General v Harris* [1961] 1 Q.B. 74, CA.

38 *Devonport Corp v Tozer* [1903] 1 Ch. 759, CA; *Attorney General v Pontypridd Waterworks Co* [1909] 1 Ch. 388.

Even where standing seemed to be accorded by a specific statute the courts tended to construe such provisions restrictively,[39] as they have done with more general statutory terms.[40]

The legislature responded to the restrictive judicial approach through the enactment of s.222 of the Local Government Act 1972. This allows a local authority to maintain an action in its own name where the authority considers it expedient for the promotion and protection of the interests of the inhabitants of its area. It enables the local authority to sue without joining the Attorney General, and has been liberally interpreted,[41] although the court will be mindful of the interrelationship between the power given under s.222 and other statutory schemes.[42]

C. Statutory Appeals

The question of standing can also arise where a statute allows a "person aggrieved" to challenge a decision. The case law has similarities with that discussed above. Thus, one line of cases adopted a restrictive meaning of the term person aggrieved, requiring the infringement of a private right or something closely akin thereto. The modern case law has, however, embraced a more liberal philosophy. **25–011**

A leading example of the more restrictive line is *Sidebotham.*[43] S had been declared bankrupt. It was alleged that the trustee in bankruptcy had not been performing his duties properly, an allegation verified by the Comptroller in Bankruptcy, who recommended that the trustee make good certain losses. The latter did not do so and was taken to the county court, which made no order compelling the trustee to make good the deficiency. The Comptroller did not appeal this decision, but S attempted to do so as a person aggrieved. He was unsuccessful, the court interpreting a person aggrieved to require something more than one who was disappointed in a benefit which he might have received. There had to be a legal grievance, a wrongful deprivation of something to which the appellant was entitled. It became the leading decision and was often applied,[44] even though it could have been distinguished.[45]

---

[39] *Wallasey Local Board v Gracey* (1887) 36 Ch. D. 593.

[40] *Prestatyn Urban DC v Prestatyn Raceway Ltd* [1970] 1 W.L.R. 33 Ch D, disapproving a more liberal approach by Lord Denning MR in *Warwickshire County Council v British Railways Board* [1969] 1 W.L.R. 1117, CA (Civ Div) concerning the construction of the Local Government Act 1933 s.276.

[41] *Solihull Metropolitan BC v Maxfern Ltd* [1977] 1 W.L.R. 127 Ch D; *Stafford BD v Elkenford Ltd* [1977] 1 W.L.R. 324, CA (Civ Div); *Thanet DC v Ninedrive Ltd* [1978] 1 All E.R. 703 Ch D; *Kent CC v Batchelor (No.2)* [1979] 1 W.L.R. 213 QBD; *Stoke-on-Trent* [1984] A.C. 754; *Monks v East Northamptonshire DC* [2002] EWHC 473 (Admin); *Guildford BC v Hein* [2005] EWCA Civ 979; *Oldham MBC v Worldwide Marketing Solutions Ltd* [2014] EWHC 1910 (QB).

[42] *Birmingham CC v Shafi* [2009] 1 W.L.R. 1961, CA (Civ Div).

[43] *Ex p Sidebotham* (1880) 14 Ch. D. 458.

[44] *R. v London Quarter Sessions, Ex p. Westminster Corporation* [1951] 2 K.B. 508 KBD; *Ealing Corp v Jones* [1959] 1 Q.B. 384 QBD; *Buxton v Minister of Housing and Local Government* [1961] 1 Q.B. 278 QBD.

[45] The court in *Sidebotham* was influenced by the structure of the relevant legislation and the fact that the debtor had an independent cause of action against the trustee: (1880) 14 Ch. D. 458 at 466.

The restrictive approach was challenged by Lord Denning.[46] The *Sidebotham-Buxton* interpretation was held to be too narrow. While busybodies should, of course, be excluded, any person with a genuine grievance whose interests were affected should be admitted. The House of Lords applied the more liberal philosophy in *Ende*.[47] Their Lordships held that a ratepayer living in the same borough or even in the same precepting area could qualify as a person aggrieved so as to be able to challenge the assessment of another's rates as too low. The applicant did not have to show financial detriment, and the infringement of a legal right was not necessary to maintain a claim.[48]

25–012 The law in this area was clarified by *Cook*.[49] Woolf LJ reviewed the authorities in this area. He recognised that some of the earlier decisions had taken a restrictive view of the term "person aggrieved", but pointed to the liberal approach adopted in later jurisprudence, and held that some of the foundational cases supporting the restrictive view should no longer be treated as good law.[50] Henceforth, the principles set out below should apply when the phrase "person aggrieved" appeared in any statute concerning appeal rights, subject to a clear contrary intent in the particular statute. The principles are as follows.[51]

First, a body corporate, including a local authority, was just as capable as being a person aggrieved as an individual. Second, any person who had a decision made against him, particularly in adversarial proceedings, would be a person aggrieved for the purposes of appealing against that decision, unless the decision amounted to an acquittal of a purely criminal case. Third, the fact that the decision against which the person wished to appeal reversed a decision which was originally taken by that person, and did not otherwise adversely affect him, did not prevent that person being a person aggrieved. To the contrary, it indicated that he was a person aggrieved who could use his appeal rights to have the original decision restored.

The court will nonetheless construe the term "person aggrieved" against the particular statutory context in which it appears. Thus, the term will, for example, be interpreted so as to fit with the needs of the planning system,[52] and the competition regime.[53] This approach was reaffirmed in *Walton*[54] where it was held that the term "person aggrieved" should be interpreted in the light of the relevant legislation; that a broad interpretation was warranted in relation to legislation dealing with the environment, which was of legitimate concern to everyone; and that a person would ordinarily be regarded as aggrieved if they

---

[46] *Attorney General of the Gambia v N'Jie* [1961] A.C. 617 at 634; *Maurice v London CC* [1964] 2 Q.B. 362, CA at 378; *Turner v Secretary of State for the Environment* (1973) 28 P. & C.R. 123 at 134, 139.

[47] *Arsenal Football Club Ltd v Ende* [1979] A.C. 1, HL.

[48] Being a taxpayer was not, however, sufficient.

[49] *Cook v Southend Borough Council* [1990] 2 Q.B. 1, CA (Civ Div).

[50] *Westminster Corp* [1951] 2 K.B. 508 was overruled.

[51] *Cook* [1990] 2 Q.B. 1 at 7.

[52] *Historic Buildings and Monuments Commission for England (English Heritage) v Secretary of State for Communities and Local Government* [2010] EWCA Civ 600.

[53] *Merger Action Group v Secretary of State for Business, Enterprise and Regulatory Reform* [2008] C.A.T. 36.

[54] *Walton v Scottish Ministers* [2012] UKSC 44.

made objections or representations as part of the procedure that preceded the decision challenged, and if their complaint was that the decision was not properly made.

4. STANDING IN JUDICIAL REVIEW ACTIONS

A. Introduction

To describe the common law as unnecessarily confused would be to pay it a compliment. While the general trend was towards liberalisation of standing, particularly in the context of the prerogative orders, the stricter test for injunctions and declarations remained. There were, moreover, differing tests even within the prerogative remedies. **25–013**

The Law Commission disapproved of the restrictive formulations of the legal right test, and of the different requirements that governed each remedy. It recommended that any person adversely affected by a decision should have locus standi.[55] In its subsequent report the Law Commission adopted the general flexible approach favoured by the earlier Working Paper and proposed that a person should have standing when there was a sufficient interest in the matter to which the application relates. This was felt to represent the existing position with regard to the prerogative orders. The law relating to declarations and injunctions was to be liberalised by the application of the sufficiency of interest test.[56]

The test proposed by the Law Commission was adopted in Ord.53 r.3(7). This has now been incorporated in what was previously the Supreme Court Act 1981, now renamed the Senior Courts Act 1981[57] (1981 Act) s.31(3), which states:

> "No application for judicial review shall be made unless the leave of the High Court has been obtained in accordance with rules of court; and the court shall not grant leave to make such an application unless it considers that the applicant has a sufficient interest in the matter to which the application relates."

The procedures for judicial review are now governed by Pt 54 of the Civil Procedure Rules (CPR). This will be discussed later.[58] The test for standing however continues to be governed by the 1981 Act s.31(3).

B. The *IRC* Case

The *IRC* case[59] was the first important decision on the sufficiency of interest test. Casual labour was common on Fleet Street newspapers, the workers often adopting fictitious names and paying no taxes. The Inland Revenue (IRC), made **25–014**

---

[55] Law Commission, *Working Paper No.40* (1970), pp.125–132.

[56] Law Commission, *Report on Remedies in Administrative Law*, Law Com No.73, Cmnd.6407, pp.22–33.

[57] The Supreme Court Act 1981 was renamed the Senior Courts Act 1981, the change has been brought about by the Constitutional Reform Act 2005 Sch.11(1) para.1.

[58] Ch.27.

[59] *R. v Inland Revenue Commissioners, Ex p. National Federation of Self-Employed and Small Businesses Ltd* [1982] A.C. 617, HL; P. Cane, "Standing, Legality and the Limits of Public Law"

a deal with the relevant unions, workers and employers whereby if the casuals would fill in tax returns for the previous two years then the period prior to that would be forgotten. The National Federation argued that this bargain was ultra vires the IRC, and sought a declaration plus mandamus to compel the IRC to collect the back taxes. The IRC argued that the National Federation had no standing. Their Lordships found for the IRC, but it would be misleading to say that they upheld the entirety of its claim.

i. *Distinguishing Gouriet*

25–015 In the lower courts the IRC relied on *Gouriet*, arguing that the National Federation lacked standing to apply for a declaration because no legal right of its own had been affected. The *Gouriet*[60] decision was treated as referring only to locus standi for declaration and injunction in their private law roles, and as having nothing to say about the standing for those remedies in public law. Order 53 r.1(2)[61] was interpreted to allow an applicant to claim a declaration or injunction instead of a prerogative order, but only where a prerogative order would have been available. If an applicant would have had standing to seek a prerogative order then a declaration or injunction could be granted instead, even though the traditional standing requirements for declaration or injunction would not have been met.

To regard *Gouriet* as concerned only with standing in private law is to allow form to blind one to substance. The parties in *Gouriet* might appear "private": a trade union and a private citizen. The real argument in that case was, however, as to whether a private citizen should be able to vindicate the public interest without joining the Attorney General. This was how the case was argued, and this was how their Lordships responded to the argument.

Gouriet and the *IRC* case reflect different philosophies. The former conceived the private citizen as having no role in enforcing the public interest, and thus preserved the dichotomy in the standing criteria for the prerogative orders and declaration and injunction. This ignored the fact that the private citizen was to some extent vindicating the public interest when seeking prerogative relief. The *IRC* case eschewed the historical distinction between the remedies, and took as its touchstone the more liberal rules for prerogative relief, to which standing for declaration and injunction were then assimilated.

ii. *Sufficiency of interest: a uniform test*

25–016 The *IRC* case is complex because two matters were interwoven in the judgments: whether there should be a uniform test for the prerogative orders and whether

---

[1981] P.L. 322. When the IRC case was decided the test for standing was still in Order 53 and had not yet been incorporated in a statute. This was important because the Rules of the Supreme Court can only alter matters of procedure and not substance. If standing were to be regarded as substantive then no change could be effectuated through Order 53, although the change could have been made by the court itself.

60 *Gouriet* [1978] A.C. 435.

61 Order 53 r.1(2) allows a declaration or injunction to be claimed via an application for judicial review in certain circumstances.

there should be a uniform test for all the remedies. Lord Diplock answered both questions affirmatively.[62] The other judgments were less clear. Lord Fraser felt that the differences between the prerogative orders had been eradicated, but that not all the older law had been overthrown.[63] Lord Scarman held that there should be no difference in standing between the prerogative orders, and that the same test should apply when a declaration or injunction was sought in a public law context.[64] Lord Roskill was clear that many of the old technical distinctions between the remedies, particularly the prerogative orders, should be swept away. The inference was that there should be a uniform test for all the remedies, but this was never made absolutely clear.[65] Lord Wilberforce was, by way of contrast, of the opinion that there should be a distinction even between the prerogative orders, with certiorari being subject to a less strict test than mandamus.[66]

The general thrust of the *IRC* case was, nonetheless, that standing should be developed to meet new problems, and that there should not be an endless discussion of previous authority. This furthered the tendency towards a unified conception of standing based upon sufficiency of interest,[67] notwithstanding the ambiguities in the judgments. Arguments that the test for standing should differ between the remedies have been generally absent from subsequent case law. It should, however, be recognised that even when the courts adopt a uniform test this does not mean that individual judges share the same view as to what should count as a sufficient interest. This is evident from the *IRC* case itself.[68]

iii. The determination of sufficiency of interest: fusion of standing and merits

We noted earlier that in private law the merits and standing were not generally regarded as distinct: who could sue was answered by the definition of the cause of action. In public law, by way of contrast, standing was one matter, the merits another. This has to be revised to some extent in the light of the *IRC* case. **25–017**

Their Lordships agreed that standing and the merits could often not be separated in this way. It might be possible to do so in relatively straightforward cases, but for more complex cases it would be necessary to consider the whole legal and factual context to determine whether an applicant possessed a sufficient interest. The term merits here meant that the court would look to the substance of the allegation to determine whether the applicant had standing. This included *the nature of the relevant power or duty, the alleged breach, and the subject-matter of the claim*. The term *fusion* will be used to refer to the process whereby the court considers these factors to determine whether the applicant has standing.

To appreciate how this operates it is necessary to understand that the Senior Courts Act s.31(3) requires the court to consider sufficiency of interest at the

[62] *IRC* [1982] A.C. 617 at 638, 640.
[63] *IRC* [1982] A.C. 617 at 645–646.
[64] *IRC* [1982] A.C. 617 at 649–653.
[65] *IRC* [1982] A.C. 617 at 656–658.
[66] *IRC* [1982] A.C. 617 at 631.
[67] Lord Denning M.R. in *O'Reilly v Mackman* [1982] 3 W.L.R. 604 stated that there was a uniform test.
[68] Compare, *IRC* [1982] A.C. 617 at 644 Lord Diplock, at 661 Lord Roskill.

leave stage. This would, prior to the CPR reforms, often be ex parte, and thus the court might only have evidence from one side. A court might feel at this stage that the applicant demonstrated a sufficient interest. The second stage is the hearing of the application, at which point the court considered evidence from both parties. At this stage the court might take the view that, on consideration of fuller evidence, the applicant did not possess the interest claimed. This conclusion would be reached from appraisal of the nature of the duty on the public body, the nature of the breach, and the position of the applicant. Thus, in the *IRC* case the only evidence at the ex parte stage was from the National Federation. By the time of the hearing the IRC had prepared affidavits giving its view of the case. This caused the House of Lords to dismiss the case.

The reasoning of their Lordships was, however, subtly different. Some[69] relied most heavily on the statutory framework and background to reach the conclusion that the applicant possessed no sufficient interest. A qualification was added that such a person or group might possess sufficient interest if the illegality were to be sufficiently grave. Other Law Lords, while referring to the statutory context, placed more emphasis on the absence of illegality. If at the hearing of the application the applicant had established the allegations made at the leave stage then the case would have proceeded.[70]

iv. Summary

25–018 The general message from the *IRC* case was that there would be a unified test of standing based upon sufficiency of interest, shorn of archaic limitations, which would probably operate in the same way irrespective of the particular remedy sought. In this sense the test for standing is uniform.

The relationship between standing at the leave stage and at the substantive hearing was summarised by Lord Donaldson MR in *Argyll*[71] as follows. At the leave stage an application should be refused only where the applicant has no interest whatsoever, and is a mere meddlesome busybody. Where, however, the application appears to be arguable and there is no other discretionary bar such as dilatoriness, the applicant should be given leave and standing can then be reconsidered as a matter of discretion at the substantive hearing. At this stage the strength of the applicant's interest will be one of the factors to be weighed in the balance. Sedley J in *Dixon*[72] emphasised that the criterion at the leave stage is set merely to prevent an applicant from intervening where there was no legitimate interest. This did not, however, mean that the applicant must show some pecuniary or special personal interest.

The fusion technique means that standing may vary from area to area. It will depend upon the strength of the applicant's interest, the nature of the statutory power or duty in issue, the subject-matter of the claim and the type of illegality asserted.

---

[69] *IRC* [1982] A.C. 617 at 632–633 Lord Wilberforce, at 646 Lord Fraser, at 662–663 Lord Roskill.

[70] *IRC* [1982] A.C. 617 at 637, 644 Lord Diplock, at 654 Lord Scarman.

[71] *R. v Monopolies and Mergers Commission, Ex p. Argyll Group Plc* [1986] 1 W.L.R. 763, CA (Civ Div) at 773; *Greaves v Boston BC* [2014] EWHC 3590 (Admin).

[72] *R. v Somerset County Council and ARC Southern Ltd, Ex p. Dixon* [1998] Env. L.R. 111 QBD.

The application of these criteria may be unclear or uncertain. Where this is so, the determination of standing will depend upon certain more general assumptions of the judge as to the role which individuals should play in public law. This is readily apparent from the *IRC* case. Thus, Lord Diplock approached the process of statutory construction with the explicit assumption that it would be a grave lacuna in our law if an interest group, or a private citizen, could not "vindicate the rule of law and get the unlawful action stopped".[73] This is close to a citizen action view of standing. This assumption was not shared by all of their Lordships, and differences of this kind can affect the interpretive process.

C. Interpretation of the Test

The cases decided after the *IRC* case may be categorised in the following manner. It will become apparent that not all courts have in fact applied the fusion approach. **25–019**

i. Individual challenges: a liberal approach, but no real fusion

There are a number of cases in which the courts have treated the *IRC* decision as a liberalisation of the pre-existing standing rules. Attempts to argue that an applicant must possess something akin to a narrow legal right before being accorded standing have not been successful.[74] This more liberal approach has also been endorsed extra-judicially.[75] **25–020**

The cases discussed in this section do not however show attachment to the fusion technique. In reaching the decision to accord the applicant standing the courts did not undertake any detailed analysis of the nature of the relevant statutory powers, apart from adverting to the seriousness of the alleged illegality.

Thus in *Smedley* a taxpayer who raised a serious question concerning the legality of governmental action in connection with the EC was accorded standing.[76] In *Leigh* a journalist as a "guardian of the public interest" in open justice was held to have a sufficient interest to obtain a declaration that justices could not refuse to reveal their identity.[77] In *Percival* the head of a set of chambers was accorded standing to contest a decision by the Bar Council that another barrister should be charged with a more serious, rather than a less serious,

---

[73] *IRC* [1982] A.C. 617 at 644.

[74] *R. v Secretary of Companies, Ex p. Central Bank of India* [1986] Q.B. 1114, CA (Civ Div) at 1161–1163; *R. v Secretary of State for Social Services, Ex p. Child Poverty Action Group* [1990] 2 Q.B. 540, CA (Civ Div); *R. v International Stock Exchange of the United Kingdom and the Republic of Ireland, Ex p. Else (1982) Ltd* [1993] 1 All E.R. 420, CA (Civ Div) at 432; *R. v Haringey LBC, Ex p. Secretary of State for the Environment* [1991] C.O.D. 135 DC; *R. (Save our Surgery Ltd) v Joint Committee of Primary Care Trusts* [2013] EWHC 439 (Admin); *Gibraltar Betting & Gaming Association Ltd v Secretary of State for Culture, Media and Sport* [2014] EWHC 3236 (Admin); *R. (O) v Secretary of State for International Development* [2014] EWHC 2371 (Admin).

[75] Sir Harry Woolf, "Public Law—Private Law: Why the Divide? A Personal View" [1986] P.L. 220, 231.

[76] *R. v Her Majesty's Treasury, Ex p. Smedley* [1985] Q.B. 657, CA (Civ Div) at 667, 669–670.

[77] *R. v Felixstowe JJ, Ex p. Leigh* [1987] Q.B. 582 QBD, at 595–598; *R.(Garner) v Elmbridge BC* [2010] EWCA Civ 1006.

charge.[78] In *Williams* it was held that a wide range of people could legitimately claim to have an interest in the implementation of a local authority's library policy, and the range extended beyond those who lived, worked or paid taxes in the local authority's area.[79]

In *Dixon*[80] the applicant, who was a local resident, a local councillor and a member of various bodies concerned to protect the environment, challenged the grant of planning permission to extend quarrying in a particular area. Sedley J held that standing at the leave stage should only be refused if it was clear that the applicant was a busybody with no legitimate interest in the matter. The applicant in the instant case was not a busybody, and he was perfectly entitled as a citizen to draw the attention of the court to what he considered to be an illegality in the grant of planning permission which would have an impact on the natural environment.

ii. *Individual challenges: a more restrictive approach, and use of the fusion technique*

25–021 The fusion technique is dependent upon statutory construction and results will therefore differ from area to area. Application of the test can lead to broad or narrow categories of applicant being afforded standing. Some decisions have adopted the fusion approach, but the results have been relatively restrictive.

Thus, in *Bateman*[81] it was held, on construction of the relevant statutory provisions, that a legally-aided client did not have standing to contest an order made as to the taxation of her solicitor's costs, since she was not affected by the result of the taxation. The action could only be brought by the solicitor, and the fact that the applicant was genuinely concerned to see that her solicitor was properly remunerated did not suffice to afford her a sufficient interest for the purposes of judicial review.[82]

In *Johnson*[83] it was held that the applicant did not have standing to question the validity of a notice served on his wife obliging her to answer inquiries into a fraud investigation currently under way against her husband.

25–022 In *Moses*[84] the applicant objected to the grant of planning permission for the extension of an airport runway. She had previously lived close to the end of the runway, but now lived six miles away. She argued that no environmental assessment had been made prior to the grant of planning permission. Scott Baker J considered *Dixon*,[85] but adopted a narrower approach. He held that standing

[78] *R. v General Council of the Bar, Ex p. Percival* [1990] 3 All E.R. 137 DC.

[79] *R. (Williams) v Surrey CC* [2012] EWHC 516 (Admin).

[80] *Dixon* [1998] Env. L.R. 111; *R.(Edwards) v Environment Agency (No.1)* [2004] 3 All E.R. 21.

[81] *R. v Legal Aid Board, Ex p. Bateman* [1992] 3 All E.R. 490 DC.

[82] Nolan LJ accepted that, in cases where it was appropriate, a member of the public could represent the public interest, but regarded the applicant's behaviour here as "at best quixotic", *Bateman* [1992] 3 All E.R. 490 at 496. See also, *R. v Lautro, Ex p. Tee* [1993] C.O.D. 362; *R. v Secretary of State for Defence, Ex p. Sancto* [1993] C.O.D. 144 DC; *R. (Hussein) v Secretary of State for Defence.*[2014] EWCA Civ 1087.

[83] *R. v Director of the Serious Fraud Office, Ex p. Johnson* [1993] C.O.D. 58.

[84] *R v North West Leicestershire District Council, Ex p. Moses* [2000] J.P.L. 733 QBD.

[85] *Dixon* [1998] Env. L.R. 111.

should not be accorded where the applicant has no real or justifiable concern about a public law decision. The court's time should not be expended on cases that were bound to fail. The applicant did not, on this test, possess a sufficient interest.

Moreover, in *Kides*[86] the claimant was refused standing to challenge the grant of planning permission. This was because she sought to challenge the permission on a ground related to the provision of affordable housing, whereas the court held that she had no interest in this matter, and was rather using it to prevent the building of any housing at all. She was, therefore, said to be a mere busybody in relation to affordable housing.

There may well be good policy reasons for limiting standing in certain types of case. Thus, in *Bulger*[87] the father of a murdered child sought to challenge the Lord Chief Justice's decision fixing the tariff term to be served by those who had murdered his son. Rose LJ held that in criminal cases there was no need for a third party to intervene to uphold the rule of law, since the traditional parties to criminal proceedings, the Crown and the defendant, could do so. The Lord Chief Justice when fixing the sentence had taken account of the views of the victim's family. This did not however amount to an invitation to indicate their views on the appropriate tariff, and the claimant could not therefore raise the matter by judicial review.

iii. *Group challenges: associational, surrogate and public interest*

Cane[88] has argued persuasively that there are three kinds of group challenge: associational, surrogate and public interest. The line between these categories can be contestable, but the taxonomy is helpful nonetheless. **25–023**

Associational standing is typified by an organisation suing on behalf of its members. Standing has been accorded in such circumstances where the group consists of persons who are directly affected by the disputed decision.[89] There can equally be cases where one member of a group brings the action on behalf of the group as a whole.[90]

Surrogate standing covers the case where a pressure group represents the interests of others, who may not be well placed to bring the action. The courts allowed challenges by the Child Poverty Action Group to decisions concerning social security that affected claimants. Woolf J reasoned that the CPAG was a body designed to represent the interests of unidentified claimants, who could be deprived of benefits by the secretary of state and that it had a sufficient interest to argue the case.[91] The court also construed the Highgate Projects, a charitable

---

86 *R. (Kides) v South Cambridgeshire DC* [2001] EWHC 839 (Admin) at [109].

87 *R. (Bulger) v Secretary of State for the Home Department, and the Lord Chief Justice of England and Wales* [2001] 3 All E.R. 449 DC.

88 Cane, "Standing up for the Public" [1995] P.L. 276.

89 *Royal College of Nursing of the UK v DHSS*[1981] 1 All E.R. 545 HL at 551; *R. v Chief Adjudication Officer, Ex p. Bland*, February 6, 1985; *R.(National Association of Guardians ad Litem and Reporting Officers) v Children Family Court Advisory Service*[2002] A.C.D. 44 QBD.

90 *R. v Dyfed County Council, Ex p. Manson*[1994] C.O.D. 366 QBD.

91 *Child Poverty Action Group* [1990] 2 Q.B. 540 detailed argument on the standing issue was not heard by the court, at 556.

body providing hostel accommodation to young offenders, as being a "person affected" within the meaning of regulations concerning housing benefit. The young people could have acted for themselves, and were therefore competent to authorise the Project to act as their agent in review proceedings.[92]

Public interest standing is asserted by those claiming to represent the wider public interest, rather than merely that of a group with an identifiable membership. In this type of case the decision may affect the public generally, or a section thereof, but no one particular individual has any more immediate interest than any other, and a group seeks to contest the matter before the courts. Some such claims have failed, but a number have succeeded.

iv. *Public interest challenges by a group or an individual*

25–024 A well-known claim that failed was the *Rose Theatre* case.[93] Developers, who had planning permission for an office block, discovered the remains of an important Elizabethan theatre. A number of people formed a company to preserve the remains. They sought to persuade the secretary of state to include the site in the list of monuments under the Ancient Monuments and Archaeological Areas Act 1979. The secretary of state could do so if the site appeared to him to be of national importance. If the site was thus designated no work could be done without his consent. Although the secretary of state agreed that the site was of national importance he declined to include it within the relevant legislation. Schiemann J found that there had been no illegality, but he also held that the applicants had no locus standi. He accepted that a direct financial or legal interest was not necessary in order for an applicant to have standing, and that it was necessary to consider the statute to determine whether it afforded standing to these individuals in this instance. However, he also approached the matter with the express view that not every person will always have sufficient interest to bring a case; that the assertion of an interest by many people did not mean that they actually possessed one; and that there might be certain types of governmental action which no one could challenge. In the instant case he held that no individual could point to anything in the statute which would give him a greater right or interest than any other that the decision would be taken lawfully. Schiemann J concluded that while in a broad sense we could all expect that decisions be made lawfully that was insufficient to give the applicants standing.[94]

In other cases public interest challenges have been successful. In the *Equal Opportunities Commission* case,[95] the EOC sought locus standi to argue that certain rules concerning entitlement to redundancy pay and protection from unfair dismissal were discriminatory and in breach of EC law. The EOC's duties

---

92 *R. v Stoke City Council, Ex p. Highgate Projects* [1994] C.O.D. 414 QBD.

93 *R. v Secretary of State for the Environment, Ex p. Rose Theatre Trust Co* [1990] 1 Q.B. 504 QBD; Sir Konrad Schiemann, "Locus Standi" [1990] P.L. 342; P. Cane, "Statutes, Standing and Representation" [1990] P.L. 307.

94 See also, *R. v Secretary of State for the Home Department, Ex p. Amnesty International*, 31 January 2000; *Rape Crisis Centre v Secretary of State for the Home Department* [2001] S.L.T. 389; Lord Hope, "Mike Tyson comes to Glasgow—A Question of Standing" [2001] P.L. 294.

95 *R. v Secretary of State for Employment, Ex p. Equal Opportunities Commission* [1995] 1 A.C. 1, HL.

included elimination of discrimination, and promotion of gender equality.[96] The House of Lords held that the EOC had standing. Lord Keith, giving the majority judgment, reasoned that if the contested provisions were discriminatory then steps taken by the EOC to change them could reasonably be regarded as working towards the elimination of discrimination. It would, said his Lordship,[97] be a retrograde step to hold that the EOC did not have standing to "agitate in judicial review proceedings questions related to sex discrimination which are of public importance and affect a large section of the population".

In *Greenpeace*[98] the applicant group challenged the regulation of the Sellafield nuclear site. Otton J made it clear that interest groups would not automatically be afforded standing merely because the members were concerned about a particular matter, but found that the group had standing, and declined to follow the *Rose Theatre* decision. He reached his conclusion by taking a number of factors into account, including: the fact that Greenpeace was a respected international organisation; that a number of its members lived in the Cumbria region; that the issues were serious and complex; that Greenpeace was well-placed to argue them; and that if it did not have standing there might not be any effective way to bring the matter before the court.

A liberal attitude towards public interest challenges is also apparent in the *World Development Movement* case.[99] The WDM challenged the minister's decision to grant aid to fund the construction of the Pergau dam in Malaysia, on the ground that it was outside the relevant statutory powers. The court accorded the group standing, taking into account the fact that no other challenger was likely to come forward, and the importance of vindicating the rule of law by ensuring that the minister remained within his statutory powers.[100] **25–025**

The liberal approach was affirmed in *Walton*,[101] which concerned a challenge to a road scheme. Lord Reed, following the reasoning in *Axa General Insurance*,[102] opined that standing was to vindicate the rule of law, as well as individual grievance against the state. In many contexts it would be necessary for a person to demonstrate some particular interest to demonstrate that he was not a mere busybody,[103] and not every member of the public could complain of every potential breach of duty by a public body.

> "But there may also be cases in which any individual, simply as a citizen, will have sufficient interest to bring a public authority's violation of the law to the attention of the court, without

---

96 Sex Discrimination Act 1975 s.53(1).

97 *Equal Opportunities* [1995] 1 A.C. 1 at 26.

98 *R. v Her Majesty's Inspector of Pollution, Ex p. Greenpeace Ltd (No.2)* [1994] 4 All E.R. 329 QBD.

99 *R. v Secretary of State for Foreign Affairs, Ex p. World Development Movement* [1995] 1 W.L.R. 386 DC.

100 See also, *R. v Secretary of State for Foreign and Commonwealth Affairs, Ex p. Rees-Mogg* [1994] Q.B. 552 DC; *Dixon* [1998] Env. L.R. 111; *R. v Leicester County Council, Hepworth Building Products Ltd and Onyx Ltd, Ex p. Blackfordby & Boothcorpe Action Group Ltd* [2000] E.H.L.R. 215 QBD; *R. (UK Uncut Legal Action Ltd) v Revenue and Customs Commissioners* [2012] EWHC 2017 (Admin).

101 *Walton* [2012] UKSC 44.

102 *Axa General Insurance v HM Advocate* [2012] 1 A.C. 868 (SC).

103 See, e.g., *R. (Ramey) v University of Oxford* [2014] EWHC 4847 (Admin).

> having to demonstrate any greater impact upon himself than upon other members of the public. The rule of law would not be maintained if, because everyone was equally affected by an unlawful act, no-one was able to bring proceedings to challenge it."[104]

The nature of the applicant's interest could, however, be relevant when the court exercised its discretion in relation to the remedy that should be granted.[105]

It is clear from *Blackfordby*[106] and *Save our Surgery*[107] that the court will not readily find that the incorporation of an action group is a bar to the bringing of an action for judicial review.

v. Group challenges and unincorporated associations

25–026 The courts are presently divided as to whether an unincorporated association can bring proceedings in its own name. Auld J in the *Darlington* case,[108] relying on the general principle that such bodies could not sue or be sued in their own name, held that they could not seek review in their own name, and that legal capacity was distinct from standing. Turner J in the "*Brake*" case[109] reached the opposite conclusion. He reasoned that in private law a person asserted private rights, and such rights could only be enjoyed by a legal person. In public law it was the legality of the public body's actions that were of prime concern. The applicant who claimed a sufficient interest was invoking the supervisory jurisdiction of the court to control excess of power by a public body. Such actions could therefore be brought by an unincorporated association. In the *Pig Industry* case, Richards J took the sensible view that there was nothing to prevent an unincorporated association seeking judicial review, provided that adequate provision could be made as to costs.[110]

vi. Standing, fusion and the judicial role

25–027 Two more general points are apparent from the courts' jurisprudence, and these should be borne in mind when reading the cases in this area.

First, it is clear that the fusion approach has been used by the courts to varying degrees, and that the process of statutory construction demanded by the *IRC* methodology can lead to differences of opinion from members of the same court. This is exemplified by the *EOC* case in the Court of Appeal, where three differing views emerged from the process of statutory construction as to whether the applicant body should have standing.[111]

---

104 *Walton* [2012] UKSC 44 at [94].

105 *Walton* [2012] UKSC 44 at [95], [104]–[105].

106 *Blackfordby* [2000] E.H.L.R. 215.

107 *R. (Save our Surgery Ltd) v Joint Committee of Primary Care Trusts* [2013] EWHC 439 (Admin).

108 *R. v Darlington BC and Darlington Transport Company Ltd, Ex p. the Association of Darlington Taxi Owners and the Darlington Owner Drivers Association* [1994] C.O.D. 424 QBD.

109 *R. v Traffic Commissioner for the North Western Traffic Area, Ex p."Brake"* [1996] C.O.D. 248 QBD.

110 *R. v Ministry of Agriculture, Fisheries and Food, Ex p. the British Pig Industry* [2001] A.C.D 3 QBD.

111 *R. v Secretary of State for Employment, Ex p. Equal Opportunities Commission* [1993] 1 All E.R. 1022, CA (Civ Div) at 1030–1032, 1039–1041, 1048–1051.

Second, the process of statutory construction demanded by the *IRC* case will often turn on views concerning the purpose of standing. The very process of statutory construction, looking to the nature of the duties and the subject-matter of the claim, is not self-executing, as exemplified by the differences in the *EOC* case.

The judgment in *Rose Theatre*[112] was premised on the assumption that a citizen action view of standing was not to be accepted, in that area at least. The idea underpinning the citizen action, that citizens should be able to vindicate the public interest without showing individual harm over and above that of the general community, particularly where such harm would be difficult to substantiate, was rejected. **25–028**

The *EOC* case provides a good contrast.[113] The differences of view as to the standing of the EOC as between the Court of Appeal and the House of Lords are not explicable solely because of differences as to statutory interpretation. It is clear that Lord Keith disagreed with the majority in the Court of Appeal in part because he took a different view as to the role that the EOC should have in the regime of sex discrimination. His Lordship approached the statutory interpretation with the view that the EOC should be able to raise questions concerning discrimination, which were of public importance and affected large sections of the population.

D. Locus Standi under the Human Rights Act 1998

We have seen that the Human Rights Act 1998 s.6 created a new statutory head of illegality, which can be used in judicial review actions.[114] The criterion for standing is not the normal test of sufficiency of interest. It is narrower than this, and s.7(1) states that only a victim can plead this head of illegality concerned with breach of Convention rights.[115] This is reinforced by s.7(3), which states that if proceedings are brought for judicial review the applicant is to be taken as having a sufficient interest in relation to the unlawful act only if he is, or would be, a victim of that act. Concerns were expressed about the narrowness of this test during the passage of the Bill. Section 7(6) of the Act stipulates that the criterion as to whether a person is a victim is to be found in the jurisprudence under art.34 ECHR.[116] **25–029**

This article provides that the European Court of Human Rights (ECtHR) may receive a petition from any person, non-governmental organisation or group of individuals claiming to be the victim of a violation of a Convention right. It is

112 *Rose Theatre* [1990] 1 Q.B. 504.

113 *EOC* [1995] 1 A.C. 1.

114 See Ch.20.

115 J. Miles, "Standing under the Human Rights Act 1998: Theories of Rights Enforcement and the Nature of Public Law Adjudication" [2000] C.L.J. 133.

116 The jurisprudence was in fact made under art.25 ECHR. This contained the requirement that the applicant be a victim in order to bring a case before the European Commission of Human Rights. The Convention has been modified by Protocol 11, which abolished the Commission and remodelled the court. The requirement that the applicant be a victim in order to bring a case before the court is now to be found in art.34 of the Convention, but the jurisprudence decided under art.25 will doubtless continue to be applied.

clear from the jurisprudence that there is no actio popularis in this area.[117] This is to be expected given the wording of the article in terms of "victim'. Article 34 is nonetheless broader than might appear at first sight. It allows for actions to be brought by organisations such as trade unions, and it seems that such bodies can sue on behalf of their members.[118] It also countenances actions by groups of individuals, provided that each member of the group can show a violation of the relevant right.[119] The term victim has been further expanded by the recognition of potential and indirect victims.[120] The potential victim has been held to cover the situation where a law has been enacted criminalising homosexuality, and a complaint has been admitted even though the law had not been applied to the complainant.[121] The indirect victim has been used to admit cases brought by, for example, close relatives of the direct victim, and those who have had a close relationship with the direct victim.[122]

25–030 A claimant who has been given some remedy by the ECtHR may still be regarded as a victim for the purposes of a subsequent judicial review action.[123] A claimant under the HRA may nonetheless have difficulty in establishing that he or she is a victim. Thus, in the *PAGB* case it was held that a trade association for manufacturers in the pharmaceutical industry was not a victim for the purposes of an action alleging a breach of art.6 ECHR.[124] In *Adams* the claimant sought to challenge Scottish legislation that criminalised foxhunting, on the ground that it was in breach of the HRA. The court held that membership of a club that supported foxhunting was not equivalent to being actively engaged in it, and therefore the claimant was not a victim for the purposes of the HRA.[125] In *Taylor*[126] the court held that the victim test under s.7 HRA meant that it had not been intended that members of the public should use the Act or the Convention to change legislation which they considered was incompatible with the Convention, but which they were not adversely affected by.

If a claimant is unable to satisfy the victim test all is not lost. It may still be possible to bring an application for judicial review without using the HRA, and relying instead on the common law jurisprudence concerning fundamental

[117] Gomien, Harris and Zwaak, *Law and Practice of the European Convention on Human Rights and the European Social Charter* (Council of Europe, 1996), pp.42–47.

[118] Gomien, Harris and Zwaak, *Law and Practice of the European Convention on Human Rights and the European Social Charter* (1996), p.44.

[119] Gomien, Harris and Zwaak, *Law and Practice of the European Convention on Human Rights and the European Social Charter* (1996), p.43.

[120] Gomien, Harris and Zwaak, *Law and Practice of the European Convention on Human Rights and the European Social Charter* (1996), pp.44–46; *Campbell and Cosans v UK* (1982) 4 E.H.R.R. 293; *Open Door Counselling and Dublin Well Woman v Ireland* (1993) 15 E.H.R.R. 244.

[121] *Norris v Ireland* (1991) 13 E.H.R.R. 186.

[122] Gomien, Harris and Zwaak, *Law and Practice of the European Convention on Human Rights and the European Social Charter* (1996), p.46; *Abdulaziz, Cabales and Balkandali v UK* (1985) 7 E.H.R.R. 471.

[123] *McKerr, Re* [2004] UKHL 12.

[124] *Director General of Fair Trading v Proprietary Association of Great Britain* [2002] 1 W.L.R. 269, CA (Civ Div).

[125] *Adams v Lord Advocate* (2003) S.L.T. 366.

[126] *Lancashire CC v Taylor* [2005] 1 W.L.R. 2668, CA (Civ Div).

rights.[127] It should also be remembered that the test for standing under the HRA will not apply where a claimant seeks to vindicate Convention rights via EU law.[128]

E. Locus Standi Outside s.31

The passage of the revised Ord.53 did not abrogate the previous methods of seeking a declaration or injunction. A plaintiff could still seek a declaration outside Ord.53, subject to the case law concerning the presumptive exclusivity of this procedure.[129] We have already seen that the *IRC*[130] case restricted the *Gouriet*[131] test of private rights and special damage to the private law role of declaration and injunction. The difficulty of regarding *Gouriet* as a purely private law case has already been discussed.[132] It appears nonetheless that the test for standing outside s.31 is still private rights and special damage.[133] The legal right test has been effectively rejected within s.31, and it is therefore important to consider why it should continue to furnish the criterion when a declaration or injunction is sought outside that section. Two reasons can be identified, neither of which is convincing. **25–031**

First, there is the argument that removal of the Attorney General would mean unrestricted access for individuals asserting a public right.[134] This does not follow. The issue is who is to decide the limitations on standing, the courts as in the case of s.31, or the Attorney General for cases outside that section. There are reasons for preferring the courts. The Attorney General is a quasi-political figure, which may not be the most appropriate backdrop from which to decide whether a case should proceed. The public interest is not, as counsel for Gouriet observed,[135] one and indivisible. It is often an amalgam of intersecting and conflicting interests. A balancing process is entailed and the Attorney General may not be best placed to make this determination.

The second argument[136] is that the two-stage procedure within s.31 means that frivolous applications will normally be weeded out without troubling the public body, since the application will be ex parte. Since there is no such procedure in an ordinary action the public body will have to appear and argue that the plaintiff has no standing. There are, however, difficulties with this argument. It has not been made before even though it would have been relevant prior to reform of remedies since the prerogative orders had a two-stage procedure. If people who do not have

---

[127] Ch.19.

[128] See paras 20–069 to 20–071.

[129] Ch.27.

[130] *IRC* [1982] A.C. 617.

[131] *Gouriet* [1978] A.C. 435.

[132] See para.25–015.

[133] *Barrs* [1982] Ch. 294; *Steeples v Derbyshire City Council* [1985] 1 W.L.R. 256 QBD at 290–298; *Ashby v Ebdon* [1985] Ch. 394 Ch D; *Stoke-on-Trent* [1984] A.C. 754 at 766–767, 769–771; *Mortimer v Labour Party*, 14 January 2000; *Shah*.[2015] 1 W.L.R. 2094 (Ch).

[134] *Gouriet* [1978] A.C. 435 at 483, 501–502.

[135] *Gouriet* [1978] A.C. 435 at 461.

[136] *Barrs* [1982] Ch. 294.

private rights are not regarded as vexatious in proceedings under s.31, it is difficult to see why they should suddenly become so when the form of relief alters.

5. INTERVENTION IN JUDICIAL REVIEW ACTIONS

25–032 An issue that is closely related to, but distinct from, standing is that of intervention. The rules on intervention by a third party in judicial review proceedings are as follows. The CPR, which came into force on 29 April 1999, govern this area.[137] They apply to all judicial review applications lodged on or after 2 October 2000.[138] CPR 54.1(2)(f) allows an interested party, other than the claimant and defendant, who is directly affected by the claim, to be served. The court will not consider claims by interested parties that are different from those advanced by the claimant.[139] CPR 54.17 provides that any person may apply for permission to file evidence or make representations at the hearing, but the court has discretion whether to admit interveners.[140]

The "amicus brief" is used quite extensively in other countries such as the USA, Canada, and by the European Court of Human Rights. It can perform a valuable informational function by bringing relevant evidence to the court, which it would not otherwise have heard. The recent liberalisation of standing by our courts has made them more receptive to such interventions.[141]

6. THE FUNCTION OF STANDING

25–033 It is time now to look more generally at the role of locus standi. Any definition of sufficient interest presupposes a particular view of the function to be performed by standing.

A. Vindication of Private Rights

25–034 Legal systems can display points in common. Standing is one such instance. There was early insistence on the presence of a legal right, in the sense of a private law cause of action, and gradual movement away from that criterion. There are two principal reasons why the legal right test assumed a central role.

---

[137] Lord Woolf, *Access to Justice: The Final Report to the Lord Chancellor on the Civil Justice System in England and Wales* (1997); SI 1998/ 3132.

[138] SI 2092/2000.

[139] *R. (McVey) v Secretary of State for Health* [2010] EWHC 1225 (Admin).

[140] *R. (Howard League for Penal Reform) v Secretary of State for the Home Department (No.1)* [2002] EWHC 1750 (Admin); *Secretary of State for Foreign and Commonwealth Affairs v HM Assistant Deputy Coroner for Inner North London* [2013] EWHC 1786 (Admin); *R. (British American Tobacco UK Ltd) v Secretary of State for Health.*[2014] EWHC 3515 (Admin).

[141] *R. v Home Secretary, Ex p. Sivakumaran* [1988] A.C. 958, HL; *R. v Coventry City Council, Ex p. Phoenix Aviation* [1995] 3 All E.R. 37 DC; *R. v Secretary of State for the Home Department, Ex p. Venables* [1998] A.C. 407, HL; *R. v Secretary of State for the Home Department, Ex p. Hargreaves* [1997] 1 W.L.R. 906, CA (Civ Div); *R. v Lord Chancellor, Ex p. Witham* [1998] Q.B. 575 QBD; *R.(Northern Ireland Human Rights Commission) v Greater Belfast Coroner* [2002] UKHL 25; C. Harlow, "Public Law and Popular Justice" (2002) 65 M.L.R. 1.

There was, on the one hand, the unthinking adoption of rules from private law causes of action into the realm of challenges against public bodies, as exemplified by cases such as *Boyce*.[142] There was, on the other hand, the more abstract argument found in *Gouriet*.[143] A role for the individual was specifically etched out, which was the vindication of private rights, with the public interest protected by the Attorney General. This function of the individual mirrored that of the courts, which perceived their role as the settling of private disputes. The courts would adjudicate on a matter of public law at the instance of an individual, provided that it was settling the rights of the latter. This perspective on the role of the individual and the court proved inadequate for three reasons.

First, it presented a distorted picture of what the courts had been doing. The approach within the prerogative orders could not be fitted into a conceptual strait-jacket called private dispute settling. Individuals were to a greater or lesser degree vindicating the public interest. This tension between the prerogative orders, and declaration and injunction, was largely ignored and de facto resolved in favour of the latter in the *Gouriet* case, whereas in *IRC* it was faced more openly, inadequately explained, and resolved in favour of the prerogative orders. **25–035**

A second reason why the private right model proved inadequate was that new values were recognised, which could not be accommodated by the traditional restrictive standing criteria. Broader social, economic, religious and non-economic values are justly prized. Traditional legal rights will often not exist in such areas. No established cause of action arises if they are infringed. If standing were limited to situations in which such a cause of action arose no person could invoke the protection of the court. It could be argued that the law should develop new "rights" or new concepts of "property" to protect these emerging values. This has happened to some extent. There are, however, dangers in pressing the concept of property or legal right too far, and thereby diluting their content.[144] The expansion in the concept of right or property, moreover, undermines the argument that the government is settling a private dispute with an individual.[145]

The final reason why the legal right test was inadequate was that the underlying premise was flawed. The premise was that these cases really were primarily about private rights, and that the court would consider matters of public law only incidentally, so far as necessary to decide whether the private right was infringed. Thus, Sarah claims that a public body has trespassed upon her property. The defence is that this is justified by a compulsory purchase order. Sarah will have standing to challenge the legality of the order because her private rights are at stake. However, in deciding on the legality of the order, Sarah's status as an injured property owner is not determinative. The argument will focus on public law matters concerning the legality of the order, and Sarah will be voicing the interests of the public at large. The effect of a finding that a legal right has been

[142] *Boyce* [1903] 1 Ch 109.

[143] *Gouriet* [1978] A.C. 435.

[144] Compare C. Reich, "The New Property" (1964) 73 Yale L.J. 733 and W. Simon, "Rights and Redistribution in the Welfare System" (1986) 38 Stan. L.R. 1431.

[145] Vining, *Legal Identity, The Coming of Age of Public Law* (1978), p.25; Cane, "The Function of Standing Rules in Administrative Law" [1980] P.L. 303.

infringed will tell one that the order was invalid and hence that a trespass action lies, but that conclusion simply follows from the decision that the order was illegal.[146]

B. Fusion of Standing and Merits

25–036 The argument for the fusion approach is that it is only by looking at the type of injury, the aims of the legislation, and the interest affected, that one can decide who should be able to claim. It has been argued that attempts to decide such matters in the abstract lead to unhelpful generalisation.[147] It is argued further that this is not very different from the way in which such factors are used in private law to determine the existence of a cause of action. These sentiments are clearly evident in the *IRC*[148] decision and the insistence that sufficiency of interest should be seen against the subject-matter of the application, including the nature of the duty and the nature of the breach.[149]

The closest analogy is the rules for determining whether an action lies by an individual for breach of statutory duty: who is enabled to sue will be dependent upon construction of the particular statute. This analogy is also indicative of the problems with the fusion approach. Statutory construction is a notoriously difficult operation because the legislature has often given no thought as to who should have standing. This leads the courts to infer intent from such matters as the nature of the duty and subject-matter of the claim. In breach of statutory duty the courts' inference is not drawn from detailed consideration of the statute. Rather, the judicial process abstracts certain matters and regards these as central or strongly presumptive, such as whether a penalty exists, and the class of persons affected by the statute.[150] The very process of abstracting such criteria recreates standing as a preliminary issue. Moreover, because who can sue is meant to be a result of detailed consideration of the individual statute, and because in many cases it is palpably not,[151] there is judicial disenchantment with the process. This manifests itself in a refusal to be led through the competing lines of cases. The conclusion is both the ultimate generalisation and the ultimate in the ad hoc: the court will allow a person to be a beneficiary of the statute if it thinks it right that this should be so.[152]

---

[146] Vining, *Legal Identity, The Coming of Age of Public Law* (1978), p. 20.

[147] L. Albert, "Standing to Challenge Administrative Action: An Inadequate Surrogate for Claims to Relief" (1973–1974) 83 Yale L.J. 425 and "Justiciability and Theories of Judicial Review: A Remote Relationship" (1976–1977) 50 So Calif. L.R. 1139.

[148] *IRC* [1982] A.C. 617.

[149] Their Lordships framed their judgments as if the fusion technique had been an accepted part of the legal vocabulary. With respect, this was not so. It is true that one can point to cases in which the courts have considered the ambit and purposes of a statutory scheme in order to determine standing. However, these are far outweighed by the cases in which the issue of locus standi has been decided by abstracted categories, such as ratepayers or competitors, without any detailed analysis of the scope of the duty or nature of the breach.

[150] *Markesinis and Deakin's Tort Law*, 7th edn (S. Deakin, A. Johnston and B. Markesinis, Oxford: Oxford University Press, 2013), Ch.7.

[151] *Booth & Co (International) Ltd v National Enterprise Board* [1978] 3 All E.R. 624 QBD.

[152] *Ex p Island Records Ltd* [1978] Ch.122 at 134.

This is not to suggest that a court should decide standing independent of the merits. The argument is that it is unlikely that standing will disappear as an independent issue, to be swallowed up by the merits and re-emerge as a number of distinct "causes of action", in which those who can sue will depend entirely on the subject-matter area.[153] Even if this aim could be realised it would have disadvantages. Access to the courts should, in principle, be as clear as possible and this would not be so under the fusion doctrine. **25–037**

It is apparent from the judgments in the *IRC* case that they did not conceive of having to look to the merits on every occasion. A busybody can be excluded, or an applicant with a strong interest can be admitted, without venturing into detailed consideration of the merits. In later cases many courts have not engaged in detailed analysis of the nature of the statutory power, or subject matter of the claim, when determining who has standing. When the fusion technique has been applied in detail it has, on occasion, generated significant differences of opinion between judges of the same court as to whether the applicant was intended to have standing. Moreover, uncertainty as to what the legislature intended means that the court's judgment will be influenced by more general perceptions as to the role that the individual should have in public law.

C. Citizen Action

i. The arguments for such an action

A citizen action or actio popularis is based on the premise that the main aim of public law is to keep public bodies within their powers. The presumption is that citizens generally should be enabled to vindicate the public interest, without showing individual harm over and above that of the general community. The arguments in favour of such an approach are as follows.[154] The first was put succinctly by Lord Diplock in the *IRC* case[155]: **25–038**

> "It would, in my view, be a grave *lacuna* in our system of public law if a pressure group, like the federation, or even a single public-spirited taxpayer, were prevented by outdated technical rules of locus standi from bringing the matter to the attention of the court to vindicate the rule of law and get the unlawful action stopped."

Second, there are instances of unlawful conduct that affect the general public on matters of importance, but which do not affect the interests of one individual more than another. Such illegalities should be capable of being challenged in our society.[156]

Third, even if the interests of more specific individuals are affected by the disputed governmental action, there may be reasons why such individuals have not directly raised the point and could not be expected to do so.[157]

---

[153] *IRC* [1982] A.C. 617.
[154] See also Schiemann, "Locus Standi" [1990] P.L. 342, 346.
[155] *IRC* [1982] A.C. 617 at 644.
[156] *Walton* [2012] UKSC 44 at [94].
[157] *CPAG* [1990] 2 Q.B. 540 at 546–547.

ii. Practical objections

25–039 The most oft-repeated practical objection is that it would open the courthouse doors to vexatious litigants and busybodies. Scott has provided the most succinct response to this criticism: "The idle and whimsical plaintiff, a dilettante who litigates for a lark, is a spectre which haunts the legal literature, not the courtroom".[158]

A second practical objection is that an applicant who has no personal interest will not be the most effective advocate. This is a non sequitur. No one has demonstrated a correlation between the degree of interest that an applicant has and the effectiveness of the advocacy. The public spirited citizen who challenges governmental action, with no personal stake in the outcome, may well be a more effective litigant because the person will normally feel strongly before bringing a claim.

A final practical objection is that the greater number of suits would distract government from its primary task by taking up its time in defending legal actions and, moreover, would take up scarce court resources.[159] This argument is contestable. The primary task of those who govern is to do just that, but they should govern according to the law. The key issue is, therefore, who should be able to bring potential illegality before the court. It is not clear why an action that affects the public at large, in which no individual is necessarily affected more than any other, is a less deserving distraction from the primary task of governing, or a less deserving use of court time, than an action in which the applicant has some more particularised interest. This is particularly so given that the subject-matter in the former case may well be more important than in the latter.

iii. Conceptual objections: the need for a person

25–040 Vining[160] posits a situation in which the courts have discarded the legal rights test and put nothing in its place, and asks whether that would be possible, answering that it would not. He argues that people possess a number of different identities such as father, businessman, sports player, etc. When a person comes to the court he comes not as a "natural person", but in one of the more particularised guises set out above.

The problem with this argument is that the conclusion follows inevitably from the premise, but it is the premise which is in issue. If the courts continue to require some harm personalised to the applicant then the applicant will fail if he does not fall into the category, such as fathers, which the courts regard as harmed by the activity impugned. However, nothing in the argument demonstrates that the courts have to require such harm. It would be possible for a court, faced with the above example, to say that whether the applicant is or is not a father is not conclusive, and that he possesses a citizen's interest in preventing the challenged

---

[158] K. Scott, "Standing in the Supreme Court—A Functional Analysis" (1973) 86 Harv. L.R. 645 (1973); J. Jolowicz, "Protection of Diffuse, Fragmented and Collective Interests in Civil Litigation: English Law" [1983] C.L.J. 222.

[159] Schiemann, "Locus Standi" [1990] P.L. 342, 348.

[160] Vining, *Legal Identity* (1978), Ch.4.

regulations from being promulgated. The only identity that the court would be concerned with would be the applicant's position as a citizen. The possibility of citizen actions cannot be rejected on the basis that they would be inconsistent with the way in which courts "see" people who come before them.

iv. Conceptual objections: inconsistent with the traditional judicial role

A more complex objection to the citizen action is that it would be inconsistent with the traditional judicial role, or at least place it under severe strain. The argument is as follows.[161] **25–041**

The common law case method serves to prevent use of the judicial process for the articulation of abstract principles of law, as opposed to the settlement of concrete disputes. Thus ripeness focuses on the temporal immediacy of the harm, justiciability on the suitability of the subject-matter for judicial resolution, and standing on the nature of the person's interest. Where the connection between the interest asserted and the type of judicial intervention requested becomes more attenuated, so the possibility of broadly framed challenges increases.[162] The judicial focus shifts from the remedying of private wrongs to the making of abstract determinations of legal principle.[163] The more broadly framed the initial challenge, the more likely it will be that the applicant may fail adequately to represent future applicants affected by the dispute. Narrower standing criteria, by way of contrast, implicitly look to the scope of those affected if the applicant wins or loses, and determine whether the harm alleged by the applicant is proximate enough to that suffered by other possible challengers for the former to "represent" the latter.

There is however, an ambiguity in this argument as to the meaning of the words "abstract" or "broadly framed". Three interpretations are possible, none of which sustain the argument advanced.

The first sees "abstract" or "broadly framed" as meaning that the principles propounded by the courts will be vague or unripe, in the sense of premature, this being juxtaposed to the settlement of "concrete" disputes. This does not follow from the existence of a citizen action. Allowing a broad range of persons to challenge administrative action does not mean that the principles thereby propounded will be vague or untimely. Limits of ripeness and justiciability would still exist. In the *IRC* case the illegality asserted by the National Federation was not abstract in the sense of vague or hypothetical. Nor was it unripe in the sense of being premature. Nor was the issue unsuited for legal resolution. The issue was sharply defined and current, albeit in the end unproven. **25–042**

A second meaning of "abstract" and "broadly framed" is that a decision will not be concrete, and thus will be abstract, if no person is individually affected.

---

[161] R. Brilmayer, "Judicial Review, Justiciability and the Limits of the Common Law Method" 57 Boston ULR 807 (1977).

[162] *Gouriet* [1978] A.C. 435 at 501–502.

[163] See also, Schiemann, "Locus Standi" [1990] P.L. 342, 348–349; Harlow "Public Law and Popular Justice" (2002) 65 M.L.R. 1; T.R.S. Allan, *Constitutional Justice, A Liberal Theory of the Rule of Law* (Oxford University Press, 2001), Ch.6.

But this proves too much for it is a tautology. It amounts to saying no more than that abstract determinations are bad and are determinations not affecting a specific person more than others, therefore, a citizen action is bad because abstract. A person may take such a view, but it has nothing to do with the traditional role of the courts. It is simply a value judgment. Moreover, such a meaning of "abstract" would automatically preclude challenges to important areas of governmental activity, which did not affect any person more than another.

A third interpretation of the phrases "abstract" and "broadly framed" is more complex. The premise behind the argument is that the traditional common law model of adjudication can be applied to public law, provided that we observe certain limits of justiciability, ripeness and standing. The traditional model is one in which the contest is between two individuals; it concerns a completed set of past events; the defendant compensates the plaintiff for some breach of duty committed by him; the judge is a neutral umpire; and the court's involvement ends with the conclusion of the case.[164]

25–043 However, whether the traditional model of adjudication can be applied to public law has very little if anything to do with standing, be it broad or narrow, and much to do with the subject-matter of public law. Public law litigation often sits uneasily with the traditional model. There may be a wide range of persons affected by the case, and the judicial focus may be more prospective than retrospective, being concerned with the modification of a public body's conduct in the future. These differences are reflected in the remedy, which will be formed ad hoc, be forward looking, and one that the judge takes an active role in formulating. These distinctions flow from the fact that public law cases will often involve broad issues of social and political choice. The more "abstract" or "general" nature of the issues presented for judicial determination is not a corollary of who has standing, but of the subject-matter itself. Nor is there any necessary connection between broad standing rules and problems of polycentricity. The fact that the action is brought by a public interest group, does not mean that the issue before the court is polycentric.[165] It may well be technical, and hard-edged, albeit one that does not affect any particular person more than another.

An example may help to clarify these points. Let us take the facts of the *Prescott* case, in which the challenge was to the provision of free bus rides for old age pensioners.[166] Imagine first that only those with private rights are accorded standing. The court will have to consider a broad range of issues, as to the way local authorities hold their funds and the uses to which they can be put, in determining the legality of the scheme. The result may be the vindication of private rights, but the substance of the case will turn on the broader public interest as reflected in the vires issue. Alter the hypothesis so that a broader range of persons is accorded standing. The nature of the judicial inquiry will not be altered in any way by having broader standing rules.

---

[164] A. Chayes, "The Role of the Judge in Public Litigation" 89 Harv LR 1281 (1976).

[165] Compare Harlow, "Public Law and Popular Justice" (2002) 65 M.L.R. 1, 10.

[166] *Prescott* [1955] Ch. 210.

It is undeniably true that because public law issues have this broad reach there is a problem of ensuring that those interested in the suit have a chance to make representations, and that the "person" presenting the case adequately represents future interests. This is, however, because of the subject-matter, not the rules of standing. Narrow standing rules do not solve this problem, they brush it under the carpet. In the example drawn from *Prescott*, if society only allowed those with private rights to argue the public interest about the legality of free bus rides for pensioners this would not mean that others were not concerned with the issue, nor would it ensure that the applicant who possessed the private rights would argue the public interest adequately.

v. *The limits to the citizen action: the relativity of ultra vires*

The most important qualification to the citizen action has been voiced by one of its main proponents. Jaffe advocated broad rules of standing to allow the "private attorney-general" or "non-Hohfeldian plaintiff" to vindicate the public interest.[167] However, Jaffe favoured a two-part test for standing in which those with some interest would have standing as of right, whereas the standing of the citizen applicant would be at the discretion of the court. The rationale for this divide is that there may well be cases in which the interests the law chooses to protect are content with the situation. If this is so a stranger should not be allowed to raise a possible invalidity. Any test of standing should therefore include a concept of the zone of interests the legislation is intended to protect, since this places control of the situation in the hands of those most immediately concerned. Where those possessing a defined legal interest do not adequately represent all interests protected by the legislation and if there are no other devices for public control, or if those devices are unresponsive to unrepresented interests, then the court in its discretion can take jurisdiction at the instance of a private attorney general. 25–044

The essence of his argument is that invalidity is relative and that those who come within the "protected ambit" will differ depending upon the nature of the legislation involved. Thus, there are many cases where, if those affected do not complain, others should not be able to do so. The key issue is whether in a case such as *Ridge v Baldwin*[168] if the person affected had decided not to challenge his dismissal anyone else should have been able to do so. The answer will be a value judgment. The most extreme view would be to say that any citizen has an interest in any government wrong-doing and therefore should have standing. Many would, however, believe that this is wrong. If the Chief Constable does not wish to challenge the decision that is his affair and his life should not be upset by someone else doing so.

[167] L. Jaffe, "Standing to Secure Judicial Review: Public Actions" (1960–1961) 74 Harv. L.R. 1265; L. Jaffe, "Standing to Secure Judicial Review: Private Actions" (1961–1962) 75 Harv. L.R. 255; "The Citizen and Litigant in Public Actions: The Non-Hohfeldian or Ideological Plaintiff" (1967–1968) 116 U. of Penn L.R. 1033; L. Jaffe, "Standing Again" (1970–1971) 84 Harv. L.R. 633; R. Stewart, "The Reformation of American Administrative Law" (1975) 88 Harv. L.R. 1667, 1735–1737; R. Cranston, "Reviewing Judicial Review", in H. Genn and G. Richardson (eds), *Administrative Law and Government Action* (Oxford: Clarendon, 1994), pp.59–61.

[168] *Ridge v Baldwin* [1964] A.C. 40, HL.

Jaffe is surely correct in principle. The citizen action is premised upon the sound reasoning that just because a very large number of people are equally affected this does not mean that no one should have standing if the subject-matter of the dispute is otherwise capable of judicial resolution. This does not logically mean that any person must always be accorded standing.[169] There will be "*Ridge* type" cases where none but the person or persons concerned will be granted locus standi. If they choose not to complain, so be it.

D. Injury in Fact

25–045 Davis favoured a test based purely upon injury in fact.[170] He argued against the other part of the test established by the US Supreme Court, the zone of interests test, saying that it was unworkable, conceptually unsound, and historically unnecessary. Davis is undoubtedly correct in pointing out the dangers in attempting to define legislative intent, but his insistence that injury in fact can provide the sole requirement for standing is questionable.

For Davis, such injury is both a necessary and a sufficient test of standing. The effect of regarding such injury as a necessary test for locus standi is the outright rejection of the citizen action in so far as that allows a citizen who can demonstrate no such injury, apart from a citizen's concern for legality, to impugn governmental action. This, however, leads to fortuitous distinctions being made. Thus cases in which there is ephemeral and indirect individual injury are approved, while actions brought by public interest groups are disapproved.

Treating injury in fact as a sufficient requirement for standing is also open to the objection that such injury is not, in many instances, self-defining. What constitutes injury is itself a normative value judgment, not simply an empirical observation. This value judgment cannot be made in a vacuum and must be decided against the relevant legislative background. The essence of the zone of interests test, rejected by the front door, reappears in a veiled form by the side entrance.

7. STANDING AND INTERVENTION: LOOKING TO THE FUTURE

A. Standing

25–046 The optimal solution would be an approach akin to that propounded by Jaffe. This involves acceptance of citizen actions, particularly in those areas where a large number of people are equally affected by governmental irregularity, but where no particular person is singled out. To deny access in such cases seems indefensible. If the subject-matter is otherwise appropriate for judicial resolution, and the application is timely, to deny standing would be to render important areas of governmental activity immune from censure for no better reason than that they

[169] *Walton* [2012] UKSC 44 at [94], [95], [104]–[105].

[170] "Standing: Taxpayers and Others" (1967–1968) 35 U. Chic. L.R. 601; "The Liberalised Law of Standing" (1969–1970) 37 U Chic. L.R. 450; "Judicial Control of Administrative Action: A Review" (1966) 66 Col. L.R. 635, 659–669.

affect a large number of people. Common sense would indicate the opposite conclusion, that the wide range of people affected was a reason to allow challenge by someone.[171] Judicial support for this approach can be found in Sedley J's judgment in the *Dixon* case,[172] and more recently by Lord Reed and Lord Carnwath in *Walton*.[173]

Public law is concerned with abuse of power, even where there were no private rights at stake. A person or organisation with no personal stake in the outcome might wish to call the court's attention to such an abuse of power, and there were a number of areas where any individual, simply as a citizen, had a sufficient interest to bring the matter before the court.[174] This does not, as seen above, mean that any person should be allowed to raise any issue of invalidity. There will be "*Ridge* type cases", where if the person directly affected does not challenge the act then no one should be able to do so. **25–047**

A citizen should therefore be entitled at the discretion of the court to bring an action alleging invalid public activity, except where it can be shown from a consideration of the statutory framework that the range of persons with standing was intended to be narrower than this. In this latter instance standing should be as of right and limited to the protected class. This should be subject to the qualification that there might be cases where those with a protected legal interest do not adequately represent a wider group affected by the legislation. The wider group should be admitted at the discretion of the court. The presumption is therefore that citizens simply qua citizens have a sufficient interest in governmental legality.

This formulation may be compared to that proposed by Lord Woolf. He advocated a two-track test for standing. The applicant will have a sufficient interest in cases where she has been personally adversely affected by the challenged decision. In other cases standing will be at the discretion of the court, which will take into account matters such as the allocation of scarce resources, the relationship between courts and Parliament, and the screening out of busybodies.[175] In a similar vein the Law Commission proposed a two-track system.[176] An applicant who is personally adversely affected will generally be admitted as a matter of course. Public interest challenges will lie at the discretion of the court, the test being whether the court considers that it is in the public interest for the applicant to make the application.

How far these formulations differ from that presented above depends on the construction of the term "personal adverse effect", and how a court exercises its discretion to admit cases within the second category. The broader the construction

[171] *IRC* [1982] A.C. 617 at 644.

[172] *Dixon* [1998] Env. L.R. 111.

[173] *Walton* [2012] UKSC 44 at [94], [95], [104]-[105].

[174] Sedley J expressly placed reliance on older case law which in effect endorsed a citizen action view of standing: *De Haber* (1851) 17 Q.B. 171; *Worthington* (1875) L.R. 10 C.P. 379; *Speyer* [1916] 1 K.B. 595.

[175] Lord Woolf, "Judicial Review: A Possible Programme for Reform" [1992] P.L. 221, 232–233.

[176] Law Commission, *Administrative Law: Judicial Review and Statutory Appeals* (Report No.226, 1994), pp.41–44.

of the term personal adverse effect, and the more liberally the court interprets the discretion to admit a case in the second category, then the closer will this formulation be to that proposed above.

B. Standing: Individuals and Groups

25–048 When we consider the appropriate test for standing, and whether it should be different for individuals as opposed to groups, we should be mindful of the insights from the literature on public choice concerning the logic of collective action.[177] Collective action entails both direct and indirect costs. The direct costs are those of organising the group. The indirect costs arise from the fact that some individual autonomy is foregone. Collective action also has benefits. The group will often be more powerful than any single individual; it will bring together expertise from diverse areas; the workload will be spread among the members; and it will normally have greater resources than any individual. Collective action will be the preferred option when the benefits of organising in this manner outweigh the costs. In modern society this calculus increasingly comes down in favour of collective action. The complexity of many issues between state and citizen, the very power of the state itself, and the demands of everyday life on individuals, often mean that collective action is preferred. It is therefore to be expected that much of the pressure brought to bear on governments will come from groups.[178] This is important when we think about standing and the tests for individuals and groups.[179]

Associational standing is an obvious manifestation of the logic of collective action. If the court is faced with a group that directly represents its members then it should not treat this body less favourably than if the action had been brought by an individual member: if the individual would be admitted to court as a matter of right, then so should the group.[180]

The courts should also be sympathetic to surrogate standing by groups, especially where the applicant represents a section of the public affected by the challenged decision and the case is unlikely to be brought by those immediately affected. In this type of case the logic of collective action combines with the relative weakness of those immediately affected.

Public interest challenges by groups will always be more controversial. It may well be that the test for standing in these instances should be discretionary, along the lines of the two-track approach considered above. When considering how this

---

[177] J. Buchanan and G. Tullock, *The Calculus of Consent: Logical Foundations of Constitutional Democracy* (Ann Arbor: University of Michigan Press, 1962); M. Olson, *The Logic of Collective Action: Public Goods and the Theory of Groups* (Cambridge, Mass: Harvard University Press, 1965).

[178] C. Harlow and R. Rawlings, *Pressure through Law* (London: Routledge, 1992); R. Rawlings, "Courts and Interests", in I. Loveland (ed.), *A Special Relationship? American Influences on Public Law in the UK* (Oxford: Oxford University Press, 1995), pp.104–105.

[179] P. Cane, "Standing up for the Public" [1995] P.L. 276 and "Standing, Representation and the Environment", in Loveland (ed.), *A Special Relationship? American Influences on Public Law in the UK* (1995), Ch.5; M. Sunkin, "The Problematical State of Access to Judicial Review", in B. Hadfield (ed.), *Judicial Review: A Thematic Approach* (Dublin: Gill and MacMillan, 1995).

[180] For suggestions that there should be some mechanism to ensure that the group does represent the views of its members, see, Cane, "Standing up for the Public" [1995] P.L. 276, 278.

discretion should be exercised we should, however, be mindful of the fact that a group challenge to a matter that affects many individuals equally may be the only realistic option. It is in these areas that the arguments for collective action will be especially strong.

C. Intervention

Cases raising matters of public concern would be the most obvious category in which to allow intervention.[181] This is more especially so if we accept that public interest challenges are warranted in some circumstances, and if we acknowledge that public law litigation may well have implications for people other than those who bring the case. **25–049**

A study by *Justice* and the Public Law Project[182] proposed a new rule of court which would have the effect of recognising public interest interveners as a class of litigant in its own right. Leave to intervene would be needed; the court would have to be satisfied that the case raised a matter of public interest and that the intervention would assist the court. There would also be limits or guides to the form and length of any intervention.

This suggestion has, however, not gone unchallenged. Schiemann[183] expressed concern at the breadth of discretion that would be given to judges as to who should address the court and on what issues. He was worried that such interventions would force the court to consider social policy to a greater extent than hitherto, and that the traditional judicial role would be undermined. Harlow voiced similar concerns that intervention could undermine the bipolar, adversarial nature of adjudication, and that intervenors are not necessarily impartial or representative.[184] These concerns should be taken seriously, but intervention can nonetheless be very valuable, and Fordham renewed the call for enhanced intervention rights.[185]

---

181 S. Grosz, "A Matter of Public Interest: A Justice/PLP Report" [1996] J.R. 147.
182 Justice/Public Law Project, *A Matter of Public Interest* (1996).
183 Sir Konrad Schiemann, "Interventions in Public Interest Cases" [1996] P.L. 240.
184 Harlow, "Public Law and Popular Justice" (2002) 65 M.L.R. 1, 10–11.
185 M. Fordham, ""Public Interest" Intervention: A Practitioner's Perspective" [2007] P.L. 410.

CHAPTER 26

JUDICIAL REMEDIES

1. CENTRAL ISSUES

i. A citizen aggrieved by a decision of a public body has a variety of remedies available.[1] The prerogative orders of mandamus, prohibition and certiorari are, after amendment to the Senior Courts Act 1981 in 2004, known as mandatory, prohibiting and quashing orders.[2] 26–001
ii. The High Court has jurisdiction to make mandatory, prohibiting and quashing orders in those classes of case in which, immediately before 1 May 2004, it had jurisdiction to make orders of mandamus, prohibition and certiorari respectively.[3] Thus, the grounds on which mandatory, prohibiting and quashing orders can be made remain largely the same as prior to 2004.
iii. A citizen can also use the declaration and the injunction, which have been applied to public bodies. Reference will also be made to other remedies. The Crown's involvement in judicial review proceedings is nominal, and the action is between the applicant and the public authority.[4]
iv. The law of remedies was hitherto highly complex, with differing procedures applying to the prerogative orders and to declaration and injunction. Some of this disorder was swept away by reform considered in the following chapter. The reform was, however, principally related to procedure. The grounds on which the remedies can be given are not altered. The procedural reforms are considered in the following chapter.

2. CERTIORARI/QUASHING ORDER AND PROHIBITION/PROHIBITING ORDER

A. Introduction

Certiorari and prohibition have long been remedies for the control of administrative action. The former had its origins as a royal demand for information. The history of the writ is complex, but Rubinstein argues convincingly that certiorari was originally developed to fill a gap left by 26–002

[1] C. Lewis, *Judicial Remedies in Public Law*, 4th edn (London: Sweet & Maxwell, 2009).
[2] Senior Courts Act 1981 s.29, as amended by SI 1033/2004 art.3. The Supreme Court Act 1981 was renamed the Senior Courts Act 1981, see Constitutional Reform Act 2005 Sch.11(1) para.1.
[3] Senior Courts Act 1981 s.29(1)(A).
[4] *R. (Ben-Abdelaziz) v Haringey LBC* [2001] 1 W.L.R. 1485, CA (Civ Div).

collateral attack and the writ of error.[5] Collateral attack, in the form of an action for assault, trespass, etc. lay only for jurisdictional defects, while the writ of error was restricted to some courts of record.[6] The area left unfilled was an error within jurisdiction by an institution not amenable to the writ of error. Certiorari was thus initially aimed at errors within, as opposed to errors going to jurisdiction.[7]

Certiorari began to be used more generally for jurisdictional defects in response to finality clauses. The courts restrictively construed such clauses to render them applicable only for non-jurisdictional error. Where the error went to jurisdiction certiorari was held to be still available. The reach of certiorari was augmented further by the acceptance of affidavit evidence to prove that a jurisdictional defect existed.[8]

Whereas certiorari operated retrospectively to quash a decision already made, prohibition was prospective in its impact, preventing the person addressed from continuing with something that would be an excess of jurisdiction. It was a particularly useful weapon wielded by the King's Bench Division in its struggles with more specialised or ecclesiastical courts. The law reports are replete with judges of the King's Bench castigating such assumptions of authority.[9] Prohibition was also used more generally to control a wide spectrum of inferior bodies.[10]

B. The Scope of Certiorari/Quashing Orders and Prohibition/Prohibiting Orders

26–003 In 1924 Atkin LJ produced the most frequently quoted dictum as to the scope of certiorari[11]:

> "Whenever any body of persons having legal authority to determine questions affecting the rights of subjects, and having the duty to act judicially, act in excess of their legal authority, they are subject to the controlling jurisdiction of the King's Bench Division exercised in these writs."

---

[5] A. Rubinstein, *Jurisdiction and Illegality* (Oxford: Oxford University Press, 1965), Ch.4. See also S.A. de Smith, *Judicial Review of Administrative Action*, 4th edn (London: Sweet & Maxwell, 1980), Appendix 1; *de Smith's Judicial Review*, 6th edn (Lord Woolf, J. Jowell, and A. Le Sueur, London: Sweet & Maxwell, 2007), Ch.15; E. Henderson, *Foundations of English Administrative Law* (Cambridge, Mass: Harvard University Press, 1963); L. Jaffe and E. Henderson, "Judicial Review and The Rule of Law: Historical Origins" (1956) 72 L.Q.R. 345; P. Craig, *UK, EU and Global Administrative Law: Foundations and Challenges* (Cambridge: Cambridge University Press, 2015), pp.25–65.

[6] Such courts had power to fine and imprison or had jurisdiction to try civil causes according to common law where the sum involved exceeded 40 shillings, Rubinstein, *Jurisdiction and Illegality* (1965), p.57.

[7] *Groenvelt v Burwell* (1700) 1 Ld Raym 454. See also, the reports in (1700) 1 Comyns 76; (1700) 12 Mod 386; *Commins v Massam* (1643) March NC 196, 197; *R. v Hide* (1647) Style 60; *R. v Plowright* (1686) 3 Mod 94.

[8] Rubinstein, *Jurisdiction and Illegality* (1965), pp.71–80.

[9] *Mayor and Aldermen of City of London v Cox* (1867) L.R. 2 H.L. 239, HL.

[10] *R. v Local Government Board* (1882) 10 Q.B.D. 309.

[11] *R. v Electricity Commissioners, Ex p. London Electricity Joint Committee Co (1920) Ltd* [1924] 1 K.B. 171, CA at 205.

Prohibition is in general subject to the same rules as certiorari. The dictum of Atkin LJ provides a useful starting point when considering the scope of the remedies.

i. Persons and type of authority

26–004 The general starting point is that certiorari and prohibition apply to quash any decision of a public law nature. The scope of "public law" for these purposes will be considered in the following chapter. Certiorari and prohibition cannot be used to challenge the decision of a superior court.[12] The orders will issue to any person or body that exercises statutory authority, including departments of state,[13] local authorities,[14] individual ministers,[15] magistrates[16] and public bodies.[17]

It is assumed that they will not be available against the Crown, the reason being that the orders are punishable by contempt, being commands from the court. This is anachronistic since the existence of a potentially coercive remedy against the Crown as an institution does not imply that such measures would or could be taken against Her Majesty in person. However, other provisions are based upon similar reasoning.[18] The availability of the prerogative orders against the Crown will be considered later.[19]

The remedies are not restricted to those whose authority is based on statute. They are available to protect common law rights of a public nature,[20] and also to prevent institutions or persons acting under prerogative powers from exceeding their authority.[21]

26–005 The traditional assumption has been that certiorari will not be available where a body is exercising powers that may be of a public nature if the derivation of that power is contractual.[22] There are, however, statements to the contrary,[23] but it is

---

12 *Racal Communications Ltd, Re* [1981] A.C. 374, HL. The exception is Crown courts which are superior courts, but are amenable to the prerogative orders by virtue of the Senior Courts Act 1981 ss.28 and 29.

13 *Board of Education v Rice* [1911] A.C. 179, HL.

14 *R. v London County Council, Ex p. The Entertainments Protection Association Ltd* [1931] 2 K.B. 215, CA.

15 *R. v Minister of Health, Ex p. Yaffe* [1930] 2 K.B. 98, CA.

16 *R. v Bedwelty Justices, Ex p. Williams* [1997] A.C. 22,5 HL.

17 *R. v Milk Marketing Board, Ex p. North* (1934) 50 TLR 559. See also *R. v Blundeston Prison Board of Visitors, Ex p. Fox-Taylor* [1982] 1 All E.R. 646; *R. v Leyland Magistrates, Ex p. Hawthorn* [1979] 1 All E.R. 209 DC.

18 Crown Proceedings Act 1947 s 21.

19 See Ch.28.

20 *R. v Barnsley MBC, Ex p. Hook* [1976] 1 W.L.R. 1052, CA (Civ Div), 1057, at 1060.

21 *R. v Criminal Injuries Compensation Board, Ex p. Lain* [1967] 2 Q.B. 864 QBD, at 880–881, 884; *Council of Civil Service Unions v Minister for the Civil Service* [1985] A.C. 374, HL.

22 *R. v National Joint Council for the Craft of Dental Technicians (Disputes Committee), Ex p. Neate* [1953] 1 Q.B. 704 DC; *Vidyodaya University Council v Silva* [1965] 1 W.L.R. 77; *Herring v Templeman* [1973] 3 All E.R. 569, CA (Civ Div) at 585 and *R. v Post Office, Ex p. Byrne* [1975] I.C.R. 221 DC at 226.

23 *O'Reilly v Mackman* [1982] 3 W.L.R. 604 (Lord Denning MR); [1983] 2 A.C. 237, HL at 279 (Lord Diplock).

nonetheless doubtful whether an institution that derives its powers solely from contract is amenable to the prerogative orders.[24] The case law will be discussed in the following chapter.[25]

The argument underlying such cases is not that there is some "analytical" reason precluding the application of the prerogative orders to bodies that derive their power from contract. It is rather that the facts of these cases disclosed no "public" law issue, but simply one of a private or domestic character.[26] The courts are, moreover, willing to look beyond the source of a body's power, and to inquire into its nature, in order to determine whether it is susceptible to judicial review.[27]

ii. *The determination of rights*

26–006 The decision challenged need not be "determinative" in the sense of final. In the *Electricity Commissioners*[28] case, the commissioners had to report their findings to the minister and if he confirmed them he would then lay them before Parliament. The court held that this did not preclude certiorari. This has been subsequently affirmed.[29] There are, however, cases that regard the necessity for approval or confirmation by another as preventing the orders from issuing.[30] The Senior Courts Act 1981 s.31(2) rendered this less important, since if the decision is not sufficiently final for certiorari then declaratory or injunctive relief may be claimed instead.[31]

The word "rights" has been broadly interpreted. It includes personal security,[32] traditional property interests[33] and an interest in continued membership of a profession.[34] It is not, however, thus restricted and includes many interests that would, in Hohfeldian terms, be described as privileges.[35] Two cases illustrate how liberally the courts have interpreted this requirement.

---

[24] *R. v BBC, Ex p. Lavelle* [1983] 1 W.L.R. 23 QBD at 31; *Law v National Greyhound Racing Club Ltd* [1983] 3 All E.R. 300, CA (Civ Div); *R. v Panel on Take-overs and Mergers, Ex p. Datafin Plc* [1987] Q.B. 815, CA (Civ Div) at 847, approving *Ex p. Neate* [1953] 1 Q.B. 704.

[25] See para. 27–027.

[26] *Lavelle* [1983] 1 W.L.R. 23 at 31; *Datafin* [1987] Q.B. 815 at 834–837, 847–849.

[27] See para.27–023.

[28] *Electricity Commissioners* [1924] 1 K.B. 171 at 192, 208; *Church v Inclosure Commissioners* (1862) 11 C.B. (N.S.) 664.

[29] *Estate and Trust Agencies (1927) Ltd v Singapore Investment Trust* [1937] A.C. 898 at 917; *R. v Kent Police Authority, Ex p. Godden* [1971] 2 Q.B. 662, CA (Civ Div); *R. v Board of Visitors of Hull Prison, Ex p. St Germain* [1979] Q.B. 425, CA (Civ Div).

[30] *R. v St Lawrence's Hospital Statutory Visitors, Ex p. Pritchard* [1953] 1 W.L.R. 1158 DC.

[31] *R. (Shrewsbury and Atcham BC) v Secretary of State for Communities and Local Government* [2008] EWCA Civ 148.

[32] *R. v Boycott, Ex p. Keasley* [1939] 2 K.B. 651 KBD.

[33] *R. v Agricultural Land Tribunal for the Wales and Monmouth Area, Ex p. Davies* [1953] 1 W.L.R. 722 DC.

[34] *General Medical Council v Spackman* [1943] A.C. 627; *Vidyodaya University Council v Silva* [1965] 1 W.L.R. 77.

[35] *R. v Woodhouse* [1906] 2 K.B. 501; *R. v Gaming Board for Great Britain, Ex p. Benaim and Khaida* [1970] 2 Q.B. 417, CA (Civ Div); *R. v Liverpool Corporation, Ex p. Liverpool Taxi Fleet Operators' Association* [1972] 2 Q.B. 299, CA (Civ Div).

In *Lain*[36] the applicant sought certiorari to quash a decision made by the Criminal Injuries Compensation Board. It was argued that the board made ex gratia payments and therefore did not determine rights. The court rejected this contention. It was not necessary that the board make decisions creating or affecting rights in a narrow sense. Although the precise formulations given by the court differed, they concurred in holding the board amenable to certiorari. In *St Germain*,[37] there was a challenge to disciplinary proceedings before a prison visitor consequent upon a prison riot. It was argued that the visitor's decision did not interfere with the prisoners' rights, but only affected their expectations of having a privilege conferred on them, the privilege being remission for good behaviour. Counsel's endeavour to convince the court of the need for accurate Hohfeldian categorisation was to no avail. It was, said the court, irrelevant whether a privilege or right was at stake. This is obviously correct. Administrative law has been plagued for long enough by distinctions based upon rights versus privileges.

iii. Duty to act judicially

If the dichotomy between rights and privileges was one plague visited upon administrative law, a second was that between administrative and judicial functions. The history of the rise and fall of this confusion can be traced as follows. **26–007**

In the early years certiorari and prohibition were used partly to control inferior courts, and hence bodies exercising judicial functions. However, even in their early infancy the writs were also used to control many activities of an administrative nature, such as those undertaken by commissioners of sewers or of tithes.[38] Government departments, individual ministers and quasi-governmental undertakings were all within their purview. Defences to the application of certiorari or prohibition based upon the non-judicial nature of the proceedings were treated dismissively by the courts.[39]

Atkin LJ spoke of certiorari applying where the rights of subjects were affected and where the body had the duty to act judicially.[40] He saw the judicial element as inferred from the nature of the power and its effect on individuals. Nonetheless, some later courts held that apart from an effect on the rights of individuals there must be a superadded duty to act judicially.[41] This conceptual confusion led to bad decisions. The courts held, for example, that disciplinary proceedings, not being judicial, were not susceptible to certiorari.[42]

---

36 *R. v Criminal Injuries Compensation Board, Ex p. Lain* [1967] 2 Q.B. 864 QBD.

37 *R. v Board of Visitors of Hull Prison, Ex p. St Germain* [1979] Q.B. 425, CA (Civ Div); *O'Reilly v Mackman* [1983] 2 A.C. 237, HL, where Lord Diplock talked of common law or statutory rights and obligations.

38 *Commins v Massam* (1643) March N.C. 196; *R. v Hide* (1647) Style 60.

39 *R. v Woodhouse* [1906] 2 K.B. 501, CA at 534–535; *Electricity Commissioners* [1924] 1 K.B. 171 at 198.

40 *Electricity Commissioners* [1924] 1 K.B. 171 at 205.

41 *R. v Legislative Committee of the Church Assembly, Ex p. Haynes-Smith* [1928] 1 K.B. 441 KBD.

42 *R. v Metropolitan Police Commissioner, Ex p. Parker* [1953] 1 W.L.R. 1150 QBD.

All was not darkness in these years, but the occasional ray of clarity was the more apparent for being exceptional.[43] In *Ridge v Baldwin*[44] one reason given by Lord Reid for natural justice becoming unduly restricted was the confusion introduced by the requirement of a superadded duty to act judicially as a condition for certiorari, which was adopted in some natural justice cases. The judicial element was, said Lord Reid, simply to be inferred from the nature of the power.[45] Forty years on, the stance adopted by Atkin LJ in the *Electricity Commissioners* case was restored both for remedies and natural justice. Certiorari was subsequently held applicable to discipline by a prison visitor[46] and to decisions by a local planning authority.[47] The argument that the judicial or administrative nature of the proceedings should not be relevant for the purposes of certiorari was confirmed by *O'Reilly v Mackman*.[48] Lord Diplock, giving the unanimous decision of the court, stated that there was no longer a requirement of a superadded duty to act judicially before the prerogative orders could apply. It was, said his Lordship, no longer necessary to distinguish between judicial and administrative acts.

iv. Certiorari and subordinate legislation

26–008 It was assumed in the past that certiorari should not readily apply to legislative functions. In *Ridge* Lord Reid, while disapproving of the superadded duty requirement, agreed with the result in the *Church Assembly*[49] case, because the process involved was legislative. It is by no means self-evident that this should be so. The prerogative orders cannot be used to challenge primary legislation, because of the sovereignty of Parliament. It is not evident why other "legislation" should be immune from the prerogative orders, more particularly given that the declaration will issue against secondary legislation. The prerogative orders have issued to stages in the legislative process, as exemplified by the *Electricity Commissioners*[50] decision and other cases where the courts expressed their willingness to award certiorari where the function was defined as legislative.[51] There is no reason on principle why the prerogative orders should not be available against secondary legislation stricto sensu and to impugn rules of a legislative character made by a public body.[52] There have been cases in which it was assumed that certiorari was available to quash a statutory instrument, even

---

43 *R. v Manchester Legal Aid Committee, Ex p. R. A. Brand and Co Ltd* [1952] 2 Q.B. 413 DC at 425–431.

44 *Ridge v Baldwin* [1964] A.C. 40, HL.

45 *Ridge* [1964] A.C. 40 at 74–78.

46 *R. v Board of Visitors of Hull Prison, Ex p. St Germain* [1979] Q.B. 425, CA (Civ Div).

47 *R. v Hillingdon LBC, Ex p. Royco Homes Ltd* [1974] Q.B. 720 QBD.

48 *O'Reilly v Mackman* [1983] 2 A.C. 237, HL.

49 *Church Assembly* [1928] 1 K.B. 411; *Ridge* [1964] A.C. 40 at 72.

50 *Electricity Commissioners* [1924] 1 K.B. 171; *Church v Inclosure Commissioners* (1862) 11 C.B. (N.S.) 664.

51 *Minister of Health v R, Ex p. Yaffe* [1931] A.C. 494, HL at 532, 533.

52 *Attorney General of Hong Kong v Ng Yuen-Shiu* [1983] 2 A.C. 629; *R. v Secretary of State for the Home Department, Ex p. Khan* [1985] 1 All E.R. 40, CA (Civ Div).

though the courts decided in their discretion not to order the remedy.[53] There have also been cases where they have quashed statutory instruments.[54]

This is surely correct. The line between decisions made individually or ad hoc, and those institutionalised into rules, may be fine and fortuitous. Moreover, there is force in Buxton LJ's observation that

> "… the imperative that public life should be conducted lawfully suggests that it is more important to correct unlawful legislation, that until quashed is universally binding and used by the public as a guide to conduct, than it is to correct a single decision, that affects only a limited range of people".[55]

Insofar as the scope of the prerogative orders is meant to reflect the ambit of "public law", the orders would be defective if they did not cover an important area which is indubitably public.

C. Grounds for the Award of Certiorari and Prohibition

The grounds for the award of certiorari and prohibition are those set out in Pt II: jurisdictional defects including natural justice, and excess, abuse, or failure to exercise a discretionary power. Errors of law on the face of the record were also susceptible to certiorari, but this concept is now largely redundant. **26–009**

D. Limitations on the Grant of the Remedies

An applicant may be denied relief because of undue delay in seeking relief, or because of alternative remedies. The relevant rules will be considered later.[56] An applicant may also fail because of waiver. The general rule is that, unless there is a statutory exception, jurisdiction cannot be conferred on a public body by acquiescence.[57] A decision made without jurisdiction is void. The case law is, however, complex. The most problematic part concerned prohibition. Some 19th-century courts took the view that any person could have standing to seek prohibition, because excess of jurisdiction by an inferior court would infringe the royal prerogative, all courts deriving their authority from the Crown, and because to allow a patent defect to stand could establish a bad precedent.[58] Neither the lateness of the application, nor the triviality of the sum was a bar, since the essence of the action was not the vindication of a personal right, but of the royal prerogative. This reasoning did not readily admit any conception of waiver. **26–010**

---

[53] *R. v Secretary of State for Social Services, Ex p. Association of Metropolitan Authorities* [1986] 1 W.L.R. 1 QBD; *R. (English Speaking Board (International) Ltd) v Secretary of State for the Home Department* [2011] EWHC 1788 (Admin).

[54] *R. v Secretary of State for Health, Ex p. United States Tobacco International Inc* [1992] Q.B. 353 DC; *R. (C) v Secretary of State for Justice* [2009] Q.B. 657, CA (Civ Div); *R. (Evans) v Secretary of State for Justice* [2011] EWHC 1146 (Admin).

[55] *R. (C)* [2009] Q.B. 657 at [41].

[56] See paras 27–046 to 27–051, 27–062 to 27–064.

[57] *Essex Incorporated Congregational Church Union v Essex CC* [1963] A.C. 808, HL; *Rydqvist v Secretary of State for Work and Pensions* [2002] 1 W.L.R. 3343, CA (Civ Div).

[58] *De Haber v Queen of Portugal* (1851) 17 Q.B. 171 KBD; *Worthington v Jeffries* (1875) L.R. 10 C.P. 379.

However, certain other cases accepted the basic premise of the above argument and yet wished to prevent an unworthy applicant from securing prohibition. A line was drawn. If the want of jurisdiction was patent on the face of the proceedings, then acquiescence or waiver was irrelevant: the protection of the royal prerogative and preventing the establishment of a bad precedent were supreme. Where, however, the defect was latent, and where the defect lay within the knowledge of the applicant who neglected to bring it forward earlier, then the court in its discretion could refuse to issue the writ or order. Here the fault or tardiness of the applicant was allowed to outweigh the public interest represented in the royal prerogative.[59] The distinction between patent and latent defects was overlaid by that between total and partial want of jurisdiction. Some cases were explained on the hypothesis that a total want of jurisdiction could not be cured, but that a partial one could.[60]

In terms of principle, the basic proposition should be that a defect is not curable by acquiescence or waiver. The limits on a tribunal are imposed for the public interest. An individual should not be able to extend that tribunal's jurisdiction by waiving limits to its authority. In this sense the ultra vires principle holds supreme and a void act cannot be validated by the individual. The defect itself cannot be cured. However, this general principle could lead to undesirable results, especially where the defect is within the knowledge of the applicant who neglected to bring it forward earlier. In such cases the best solution would be to state that the public body's action was ultra vires, but that the waiver or acquiescence affected the discretion to grant a remedy. This was in effect the solution in the leading 19th-century authorities. Waiver in this sense of precluding a remedy rather than curing the defect should in principle be possible whatever the type of defect. The importance of the ultra vires activity, the knowledge of the defect by the applicant, and the extent to which the defect was personal to the applicant or could have wider ramifications, would be relevant factors to be taken into account.

E. The Effect of an Award of Certiorari/Quashing Order

26–011 When certiorari is issued it will serve to quash the offending decision and render it retrospectively null. The meaning of retrospective nullity has been considered earlier.[61] The reviewing courts now possess a further useful power. In circumstances where there are grounds for quashing the decision the court can remit the case to the original decision-maker with a direction to reconsider the matter and reach a decision in accord with the judgment of the court.[62] Thus, instead of merely quashing the original decision and leaving the applicant to make a fresh application, the court can now, for example, quash the refusal to grant a benefit to the applicant, and remit the matter for reconsideration by the

[59] *Mayor and Alderman of City of London v Cox* (1867) L.R. 2 H.L. 239, HL; *Farquharson v Morgan* [1894] 1 Q.B. 552, CA; *R. v Comptroller-General of Patents and Designs, Ex p. Parke Davis* [1953] 2 W.L.R. 760.

[60] *Jones v Owen* (1845) 5 D. & L. 669; *Moore v Gamgee* (1890) 25 Q.B.D 244.

[61] Ch.24.

[62] Senior Courts Act 1981 s.31(5); SI 2092/2000, CPR 54.19(2).

decision-maker in the light of the court's judgment. The court also has the power, subject to any statutory provision giving power to a specific tribunal, person or body, to take the decision itself where there is no purpose to be served by remitting the matter to the initial decision-maker.[63]

3. MANDAMUS/MANDATORY ORDER

A. Introduction

The early history of the writ of mandamus is by no means clear. Commands from the King were, as de Smith points out, a common feature among the early writs, but it is doubtful whether any real connection existed between these early writs and what we now know as mandamus.[64] The seminal case for the emergence of the writ is *Bagg's Case*[65] and few legal rules can be said to have had so colourful a birth. Bagg was a chief burgess of Plymouth who had been removed from office for unseemly conduct, consisting of calling the mayor "a cozening knave", threatening to make his "neck crack" as well as other offensive gestures. Despite this behaviour a mandamus was issued against Plymouth, because Bagg had been disenfranchised without a hearing. Similar cases of deprivation of office followed.[66] It was, however, Lord Mansfield who fully exploited the potential in mandamus stating that[67]: **26–012**

> "It was introduced, to prevent disorder from a failure of justice, and defect of police. Therefore it ought to be used upon all occasions where the law established no specific remedy, and where in justice and good government there ought to be one."

From these beginnings a large jurisprudence developed, which compelled Tapping[68] to undertake the Herculean task of categorising the case law by subject-matter. A glance through the treatise reveals the diversity of this subject-matter, including Abbots and Yeoman. The reform of local government in the 19th century diminished the need for mandamus, as did the gradual disappearance of the freehold office, and the emergence of alternative remedies such as appeal.

B. The Ambit of Mandamus/Mandatory Order

i. Type of duty

For mandamus to lie there must be a public duty owed to the applicant. This involves two distinct requirements. **26–013**

[63] SI 2092/2000, CPR 54.19(3).

[64] de Smith, *Judicial Review of Administrative Action* (1980), Appendix 1, pp.591–592; Henderson, *Foundations of English Administrative Law* (1963), pp.45–65.

[65] *Bagg's Case* (1615) 11 Co. Rep. 93b.

[66] See, e.g. *R. v Chancellor of the University of Cambridge* (1723) 1 Str. 557.

[67] *R. v Barker* (1762) 3 Burr. 1265 at 1267; *R. v Askew* (1768) 4 Burr. 2186.

[68] T. Tapping, *The Law and Practice of the High Prerogative Writ of Mandamus, as it obtains both in England and Ireland* (London: W. Benning and Co, 1848).

First, the duty must be of a public as opposed to a private character. The remedy was therefore held to be inappropriate when requested against a private arbitral tribunal, and when sought in relation to reinstatement in a trade union.[69] Provided that the duty is public, it may flow from statute, prerogative, common law, charter, custom or even contract.[70]

Second, even if the duty is of a public character it must be owed to an individual. In *R. v Secretary of State for War*[71] an officer sought mandamus to compel the secretary of state to upgrade the compensation he received on his retirement. He failed. The duty incumbent upon the secretary of state was held to be owed to the Crown alone. This need not be so, as admitted in the case. Whether it is or not will be a matter of construction. In the modern day the general rule of construction is that duties imposed on ministers are owed to the public, or a section thereof, rather than to the Crown alone.

The courts might also decline mandamus where, although the duty is of a public character, its terms are so open textured as to indicate that the statute is not enforceable by individuals. The courts might reach this conclusion by saying that the issue is not justiciable. It is more likely that the courts will retain control in principle. They assert that mandamus might issue, but find on the facts that there is no cause. This approach will be considered in more detail later.

ii. Type of defect

26–014 Mandamus will issue where the tribunal has made a jurisdictional error, and has thereby declined to exercise a power or duty that it ought to have exercised. Older cases distinguished between situations where the tribunal reached an erroneous decision on the merits, and those in which it refused to consider the merits at all, because it felt that they were outside its power. Mandamus would issue in the latter, but not in the former situation. This approach is now of questionable validity. The case law was based upon the narrow commencement theory of jurisdiction, under which very few defects would be categorised as jurisdictional. The necessary corollary was that no remedy would be available.

For example in *Dayman*[72] the applicant claimed that expenses he had incurred for paving a new street had not been met. The magistrate decided after hearing the parties that the street was not a new street, and the applicant sought mandamus. His application failed. The magistrate had, said the court, heard and determined the matter. That was all that was required of him. It was irrelevant that the court might believe that the magistrate's view of "new street" was mistaken. The expansion in the concept of jurisdictional error considered earlier[73]

[69] *R. v Industrial Court, Ex p. ASSET* [1965] 1 Q.B. 377 QBD. See however, *Imperial Metal Industries (Kynoch) Ltd v AUEW (Technical, Administrative and Supervisory Section)* [1979] I.C.R. 23 CA (Civ Div) at 33 where the court approved of the principle but disapproved of its application in the *ASSET* case; *Armstrong v Kane* [1964] N.Z.L.R. 369.

[70] *Ex p. Napier* [1852] 18 Q.B. 692 at 695; *R. v Secretary of State for War* [1891] 2 Q.B. 326, CA at 335; *R. v Criminal Injuries Compensation Board, Ex p. Clowes* [1977] 1 W.L.R. 1353 DC.

[71] *R. v Secretary of State for War* [1891] 2 Q.B. 326, CA; *Napier* (1852) 18 Q.B. 692.

[72] *R. v Dayman* (1857) 7 El. & Bl. 672 at 676, 677, 679; *R. v Cheshire JJ, Ex p. Heaver* (1913) 108 L.T. 374.

[73] Ch.16.

would be likely to produce a different result. The reviewing court would reassess for itself the meaning of "new street", the magistrate would be held to have made a jurisdictional error, and mandamus would issue.

Mandamus can also be used to correct a mistaken exercise of discretion. Thus, the remedy is available if a decision is reached on the basis of irrelevant considerations or improper purposes,[74] if a pre-determined policy is applied too rigidly,[75] if the wrong question is answered,[76] if the body has not properly considered whether to exercise its discretion[77] or for other misuses of power.[78] Where, however, the duties are broadly framed and involve competing claims upon limited resources the court is less likely to find any ultra vires behaviour or, even if it does, it may in its discretion refuse the remedy.[79]

iii. Demand and refusal

The traditional approach was that before seeking mandamus the applicant must have made a specific demand to the respondent that the latter perform the relevant duty. In exceptional circumstances this requirement could be dispensed with,[80] and the duty to make a specific demand was never an absolute one.[81] It is doubtful whether this formalistic requirement will be insisted upon in the modern day. It will normally be unrealistic to expect an individual to make a formal demand that the duty should be performed.[82] **26–015**

C. Limits on the Availability of Mandamus/Mandatory Order

The relevance of an alternative remedy for the grant of mandamus will be considered below.[83] It is generally accepted that mandamus is a discretionary remedy.[84] A variety of factors have influenced the court in deciding how the discretion should be exercised. The need for constant supervision has been one factor taken into account in refusing the award of the order,[85] as has been the willingness of the public body to comply voluntarily.[86] Public inconvenience has **26–016**

---

[74] *R. v Birmingham Licensing Planning Committee, Ex p. Kennedy* [1972] 2 Q.B. 140, CA (Civ Div).

[75] *R. v Port of London Authority, Ex p. Kynoch Ltd* [1919] 1 K.B. 176, CA.

[76] *Board of Education v Rice* [1911] A.C. 179, HL.

[77] *R. v Tower Hamlets London Borough Council, Ex p. Chetnik Developments* [1988] A.C. 858, HL.

[78] *Padfield v Minister of Agriculture, Fisheries and Food* [1968] A.C. 997, HL.

[79] *R. v Commissioner of Police of the Metropolis, Ex p. Blackburn* [1968] 2 Q.B. 118, CA (Civ Div) at 136, 148–149; *R. v Commissioner of Police of the Metropolis, Ex p. Blackburn (No.3)* [1973] Q.B. 241, CA (Civ Div) at 254; *R. v Bristol Corporation, Ex p. Hendy* [1974] 1 W.L.R. 498, CA (Civ Div); *R. v Kensington and Chelsea RLBC, Ex p. Birdwood* (1976) 74 L.G.R. 424.

[80] de Smith, *Judicial Review of Administrative Action* (1980), pp.556–557.

[81] *R. v Hanley Revising Barrister* [1912] 3 K.B. 518 KBD.

[82] See, however, *R. v Horsham DC, Ex p. Wenman* [1995] 1 W.L.R. 680 QBD.

[83] See para.27–062 to 27–064.

[84] See, e.g. *R. v Churchwardens of All Saints Wigan* (1876) 1 App. Cas. 611 at 620; *Chief Constable of the North Wales Police v Evans* [1982] 1 W.L.R. 1155, HL.

[85] *R. v Peak Park Joint Planning Board, Ex p. Jackson* (1976) 74 L.G.R. 376 at 380; *Chief Constable of the North Wales Police v Evans* [1982] 1 W.L.R. 1155, HL.

[86] *R. v Northumberland Compensation Appeal Tribunal, Ex p. Shaw* [1952] 1 K.B. 338, CA at 357; *Peak* (1976) 74 L.G.R. 376.

received varying treatment, some courts viewing this as an improper consideration in deciding whether to issue the order,[87] others being willing to take it into account.[88] The court will not normally order a respondent to undertake the impossible,[89] nor will it make orders that cannot be fulfilled for other practical or legal reasons.[90] Moreover, as has already been seen, if a public body has a wide discretion and limited resources this will enter into the court's decision as to whether a remedy should be given.[91] The applicant's motives will normally not be relevant in deciding whether an order should be issued. However, in some instances the courts have stated that a particular statutory provision can only be enforced by one who is advancing the general interests of the community, as opposed to his or her own private concerns.[92]

4. DECLARATION

A. Introduction

26–017 The development of declaration is interesting, largely because the main catalyst was not the courts.[93] Indeed, it might well be said that declaration flowered despite judicial opposition. Declaratory judgments, as opposed to purely declaratory orders, appear to be a relatively novel development. A wealth of dicta can be found in the mid-19th century asserting that the courts should not give a declaration of rights per se.[94] Moreover, as de Smith observes,[95] Lord Brougham's campaign advocating the introduction of the declaration only makes sense against such a background. Certain limited exceptions existed in which the courts could grant some declaratory relief.

There was, however, judicial reluctance to make use of declaratory relief and this was evident in the courts' treatment of the Court of Chancery Procedure Act 1852 s.50. This stated that no suit should be open to objection on the ground that a merely declaratory decree or order was being claimed, and that the courts could make binding declarations of right without granting consequential relief. The legislation was largely nullified by judicial interpretation: declaratory relief was

[87] See, e.g. *R. v Kerrier DC, Ex p. Guppys (Bridport) Ltd* (1976) 32 P. & C.R. 411, CA (Civ Div) at 418.

[88] See, e.g. *R. v Paddington Valuation Officer, Ex p. Peachey Property Corporation Ltd* [1966] 1 Q.B. 380, CA at 402, 416.

[89] *Bristol and North Somerset Railway Co, Re* (1877) 3 Q.B.D 10 at 12.

[90] *R. v Pembrokeshire JJ* (1831) 2 B. & Ad. 391 KBD; *R. v National Dock Labour Board, Ex p. National Amalgamated Stevedores and Dockers* [1964] 2 Lloyds L.R. 420 at 429; *Evans* [1982] 1 W.L.R. 1155.

[91] *R. v Bristol Corporation, Ex p. Hendy* [1974] 1 W.L.R. 498, CA (Civ Div) at 503; *R. v Inner London Education Authority, Ex p. Ali* [1990] C.O.D. 317 QBD; *R. v Lancashire CC, Ex p. Guyer* [1980] 1 W.L.R. 1024, CA (Civ Div).

[92] *R. v Mayor of Peterborough* (1875) 44 L.J. Q.B. 85; *R. v Hampstead Borough Council, Ex p. Woodward* (1917) 116 L.T. 213.

[93] I. Zamir, Lord Woolf, J. Woolf and Lord Clyde, *The Declaratory Judgment*, 3rd edn (London: Sweet & Maxwell, 2002).

[94] *Elliotson v Knowles* (1842) 11 L.J. Ch. 399, at 400; *Clough v Ratcliffe* (1847) 1 De. G. and S. 164 at 178–179; *Barraclough v Brown* [1897] A.C. 615, HL at 623.

[95] *de Smith's Judicial Review* (2007), p.806.

held to be available unaccompanied by any consequential relief, but only where the plaintiff would have been entitled to other relief if it had been sought.[96]

In 1883, consequent upon powers conferred by the Judicature Acts, the Rule Committee passed Order 25 r.5. This repeated the substance of the 1852 legislation with the important alteration that a declaration could be made whether any consequential relief "is or could be claimed, or not". This was intended to circumvent the restrictive interpretation given to the 1852 legislation, but it was to be 30 years before the courts exploited this new potential.

The breakthrough came in *Dyson*.[97] Dyson was served with a notice by the Inland Revenue Commissioners, which required him to supply certain particulars under pain of a penalty. Dyson refused. He sought declarations that the demand was unauthorised and was ultra vires the Finance Act. He relied on Order 25 r.5, and upon Exchequer precedents prior to 1842. The Court of Appeal accepted that his method of proceeding was a proper one, and regarded it as a convenient and beneficial way to test the legality of government action. The *Dyson* case represented a landmark in the development of the declaration.[98] The current rule omits any reference to rights and provides that the court may make binding declarations whether or not any other remedy is claimed.[99]

B. The Scope of Declaration

i. The broad reach of the declaration

26–018 The period following *Dyson* was still characterised by judicial restraint.[100] However, as time progressed the courts became more aware of its potential, especially when contrasted with the limitations surrounding the prerogative orders. Judicial statements countenanced the broad reach of the declaration and its freedom from constraint.[101]

The declaration can operate both as an original and a supervisory remedy. In the former instance a court will declare what rights the parties have, for example, under a contract or over land. In the latter case, the remedy will control decisions made by other bodies, such as declaring the attachment of planning conditions to be invalid. This duality strengthens the declaration. It allows a court to declare invalid action by a public body in pursuance of the supervisory role, and then, if appropriate, to pronounce on the parties' rights, in pursuance of the original role.

---

[96] *Jackson v Turnley* (1853) 1 Dr. 617 at 628.

[97] *Dyson v Attorney General* [1911] 1 K.B. 410, CA. See also, [1912] 1 Ch. 159.

[98] In *Guaranty Trust Co of New York v Hannay and Co* [1915] 2 K.B. 536, CA, the court rejected the argument that Ord 25 r.5 was itself ultra vires.

[99] CPR 40.20.

[100] *Smeeton v Attorney General* [1920] 1 Ch. 85 Ch D at 97; *Russian Commercial and Industrial Bank v British Bank of Foreign Trade Ltd* [1921] 2 A.C. 438 at 445.

[101] *Pyx Granite Co Ltd v Ministry of Housing and Local Government* [1958] 1 Q.B. 554, CA at 571; *Ibeneweka v Egbuna* [1964] 1 W.L.R. 219 at 224.

No finite list of areas to which declaration applies can be provided. The subject-matter includes administrative decisions or orders,[102] subordinate legislation,[103] and, in areas covered by EU law, primary legislation.[104] Rights to pursue a trade[105] and issues of status[106] are also subject to declaration. In addition, the scope of a person's financial obligations is subject to the declaratory procedure,[107] as are questions relating to the scope of obligations imposed upon a public body,[108] or sporting body,[109] and the construction of contracts with public authorities.[110]

ii. Types of defect

26–019 While the subject-matter covered by the declaration is therefore broad, there has been uncertainty as to the type of defects that it will operate against. It is clearly available against jurisdictional defects, but it was doubtful whether it would issue to control an error of law on the face of the record. The rationale for this limitation was that such an error only rendered the tribunal's decision voidable and not void. The original decision would stand and therefore if the plaintiff were to seek a declaration of her rights she would be faced with the problem that the tribunal had already determined what those rights were, and that the court could not assume an appellate jurisdiction for itself to make a second decision different from that still extant made by the tribunal. Such a declaration would be of no effect unless the tribunal had power to rescind its original finding, or unless the declaration prevented the tribunal from acting on the decision.[111] It is doubtful whether this reasoning was correct in its own terms,[112] but in any event the courts have rendered the concept of error of law within jurisdiction largely redundant and this problem is, therefore, no longer a real one. The defect will in future be regarded as jurisdictional.

---

[102] *Hall and Co Ltd v Shoreham-by-Sea Urban DC* [1964] 1 W.L.R. 240, CA; *Congreve v Home Office* [1976] Q.B. 629, CA (Civ Div).

[103] *Nicholls v Tavistock Urban DC* [1923] 2 Ch. 18 Ch D; *Brownsea Haven Properties Ltd v Poole Corporation* [1958] Ch. 574, CA.

[104] *R. v Secretary of State for Employment, Ex p. Equal Opportunities Commission* [1995] 1 A.C. 1, HL.

[105] *Eastham v Newcastle United Football Club Ltd* [1964] Ch. 413 Ch D; *Nagle v Feilden* [1966] 2 Q.B. 633, CA; *Bucknell & Son Ltd v Croydon LBC* [1973] 1 W.L.R. 534 QBD; *Racal Communications Ltd v Pay Board* [1974] 1 W.L.R. 1149 Ch D.

[106] *Sadler v Sheffield Corporation* [1924] 1 Ch. 483 Ch D; *Ridge v Baldwin* [1964] A.C. 40, HL.

[107] *Nyali v Attorney General* [1957] A.C. 253, HL.

[108] *Attorney General v St Ives Rural DC* [1961] 1 Q.B. 366, CA; *Human Fertilisation & Embryology Authority v Amicus Healthcare Ltd* [2005] EWHC 1092 (Admin).

[109] *Mullins v McFarlane* [2006] EWHC 986 (Q.B.).

[110] *Staffordshire Area Health Authority v South Staffordshire Waterworks Co* [1978] 1 W.L.R. 1387, CA (Civ Div).

[111] *Punton v Ministry of Pensions and National Insurance* [1963] 1 W.L.R. 186, CA; *Punton v Ministry of Pensions and National Insurance (No.2)* [1964] 1 W.L.R. 226, CA.

[112] P. Cane, "A Fresh Look at Punton's Case" (1980) 43 M.L.R. 266.

C. Limits on the Availability of Declaration

The effect of alternative remedies on the availability of the declaration will be considered in a later section.[113] **26–020**

i. *Exclusion of original jurisdiction*

The possibility of the original jurisdiction being excluded operates in the following manner. Parliament may assign a certain topic to a particular public authority. When it does so the question arises as to whether an individual can nevertheless have the same matter adjudicated on by the High Court in the exercise of its original jurisdiction to grant a declaration. If the determination made by the tribunal is ultra vires this will be subject to the court's supervisory jurisdiction, subject to any possible limits to this role. The issue here is whether the grant of power will exclude the original jurisdiction of the court. **26–021**

In answering this question two principles have to be reconciled. There is the presumption that when the legislature has created new rights and obligations and has empowered a specific tribunal to adjudicate upon them then recourse must be had to that body. The other principle is the courts' dislike of anything that takes away their jurisdiction. The outcome has depended upon which principle has been accorded greater weight.

There are a number of cases holding that the jurisdiction of the High Court has been excluded, one of the best known of which is *Barraclough*.[114] The plaintiff was empowered to remove boats that had sunk in a river if the owner did not do so. Expenses were recoverable from the owner in a court of summary jurisdiction. The plaintiff sought a declaration in the High Court that he was entitled to these expenses. His action failed despite the permissible words of the statute. The plaintiff could not at one and the same time claim to recover by virtue of the statute and insist on doing so by means other than those prescribed by that statute.[115]

There are, however, cases that deny exclusive jurisdiction to the appointed public body. Thus, in *Pyx Granite*[116] the plaintiffs carried on the business of quarrying and claimed that they should be able to pursue this without recourse to planning permission.[117] This was denied by the defendants, who further argued that under the relevant legislation there was a specified procedure for determining whether **26–022**

---

113 See paras 27–062 to 27–064.

114 *Barraclough v Brown* [1897] A.C. 615, HL.

115 *Barraclough* [1897] A.C. 615 at 619–620. See also, *Baron Reitzes de Marienwert v Administrator of Austrian Property* [1924] 2 Ch. 282, CA; *Wilkinson v Barking Corp* [1948] 1 K.B. 721, CA; *Gillingham Corp v Kent CC* [1953] Ch. 37 Ch D; *Healey v Minister of Health* [1955] 1 Q.B. 221, CA; *Square Meals Frozen Foods Ltd v Dunstable Corp* [1974] 1 W.L.R. 59, CA (Civ Div); *Waltham Forest LBC v Roberts* [2004] EWCA Civ 940; *Autologic Holdings Plc v Inland Revenue Commissioners* [2006] 1 A.C. 118, HL; *R. (A) v Director of Establishments of the Security Service* [2010] 2 A.C. 1 SC.

116 *Pyx Granite Co Ltd v Ministry of Housing and Local Government* [1960] A.C. 260, HL; *Manchester City Council v Pinnock* [2010] 3 W.L.R. 1441 SC.

117 The reason being that they claimed entitlement to do so under a private Act of Parliament, and further argued that such statutes were exempt from the requirement of planning permission.

planning permission was required or not,[118] which procedure was exclusive and prevented an application for a declaration. The House of Lords distinguished *Barraclough*. Whereas in that case the statute had created new rights to be determined by a certain procedure, in the *Pyx* case the plaintiff was simply relying on his common law rights, the only question being how far they had been removed.[119]

The distinction drawn between common law and statutory rights is questionable in its application to the facts of the case[120] and on principle. Whether an original jurisdiction granted to a public body should be taken to be exclusive should be determined by a consideration of the subject-matter, and not whether the rights are derived from common law or statute. The ability to side-step the enacted procedure should be dependent on the type of procedure and its suitability for resolving the kind of question in issue. If there is little dispute as to the facts, and a point of general legal importance is at stake, then a declaration may well be more appropriate,[121] but unless such special considerations exist the particular regime established to determine the issue should be used, and this has been emphasised in more recent judgments.[122]

ii. Exclusion of supervisory jurisdiction

26–023 Whether the supervisory jurisdiction of the High Court has been excluded will be considered as a separate topic.[123] The difference between exclusion of original and supervisory jurisdiction is clear in *Fullbrook*.[124] Section 35 of the Local Government Superannuation Act 1937 provided that any question concerning the rights and liabilities of an employee should be determined initially by the local authority and then, if the employee was dissatisfied, by the minister whose decision would be final. The plaintiff was deprived of his superannuation benefits. He challenged this by a declaration claiming that he had been denied a hearing. The defendants relied on s.35 and on cases mentioned in the previous section. This argument failed. While s.35 might exclude the original jurisdiction to grant a declaration, the essence of the plaintiff's claim was the invocation of the supervisory jurisdiction of the courts, a power to declare void action that was ultra vires. This survived and could not be abrogated by the finality clause within s.35.

---

[118] Town and Country Planning Act 1947 s.17(1).

[119] *Pyx Granite* [1960] A.C. 260 at 286–287, 290, 302, 304.

[120] G. Borrie, "Note" [1960] P.L. 14, 14–17.

[121] These factors influenced the court in the *Pyx Granite* case [1960] A.C. 260. See also, *Ealing LBC v Race Relations Board* [1972] A.C. 342, HL.

[122] *Roberts* [2004] EWCA Civ 940; *Autologic Holdings* [2006] 1 A.C. 118; *Security Service* [2010] 2 A.C. 1.

[123] See Ch.28.

[124] *Fullbrook v Berkshire Magistrates' Courts Committee* (1970) 69 L.G.R. 75.

iii. *Hypothetical questions: ripeness and mootness*

The issues of ripeness and mootness are integral to a rational system of remedies, but are not as fully developed in the UK as they are in the USA.[125] **26–024**

The courts dislike deciding hypothetical questions. Historically, this is because the Stuart monarchs placed pressure on judges to respond to advisory opinions in the manner most favourable to the Crown. More modern rationales for being wary of hypothetical questions include: fear of a flood of litigation;[126] concern that there might be a difference between the abstract question posed and the way in which the issue arose in real terms, thereby casting doubt upon the probative value of the earlier judgment; concern that the parties most interested in the dispute might not be before the court;[127] and wastage of judicial resources because the hypothetical event might never materialise.[128] If advice on difficult points is required then the Judicial Committee Act 1833 s.4 empowers the Crown to seek legal advice from the Privy Council.

There is, however, the important counter-argument that a legal system should enable people to operate their lives with as much certainty as possible, with knowledge of the legal rights and obligations thereby entailed. If the concept of hypothetical question is drawn too broadly it will prevent this function of a legal system from being performed. It has been held that the courts possess an inherent jurisdiction to make advisory declarations as a matter of discretion.[129] Lord Woolf noted that it may be advantageous for a public body to be able to obtain an anticipatory ruling, particularly where there is doubt as to the legality of its proposed course of action.[130] Recommendations that there should be power to make advisory declarations on matters of general public importance were made by Lord Woolf in his report on the civil justice system,[131] and by the Law Commission.[132]

The courts have treated as hypothetical, questions which come too early and are thus unripe, or which come too late and are therefore moot. An example of the former is *Draper*.[133] The defendant optical association informed the plaintiff that it believed him to be in breach of its code of ethics, and that a meeting would be **26–025**

[125] J. Jaconelli, "Hypothetical Disputes, Moot Points of Law and Advisory Opinions" (1985) 101 L.Q.R. 587; J. Beatson, "Prematurity and Ripeness for Review", in C. Forsyth and I. Hare (eds), *The Golden Metwand and the Crooked Cord, Essays on Public Law in Honour of Sir William Wade* (Oxford: Oxford University Press, 1998), pp.221–252.

[126] *Re Clay* [1919] 1 Ch. 66 at 78–79.

[127] *R. v DPP, Ex p. Merton LBC* [1999] C.O.D. 358; *Maerkle v British Continental Fur Co Ltd* [1954] 1 W.L.R. 1242, CA at 1248.

[128] *R. (Rusbridger) v Attorney General* [2004] 1 A.C. 357, HL.

[129] *R. v Secretary of State for the Home Department, Ex p. Mehari* [1994] Q.B. 474 DC at 491; *R. v Ministry of Agriculture, Fisheries and Food, Ex p. Live Sheep Traders Ltd* [1995] C.O.D. 297; Sir John Laws, "Judicial Remedies and the Constitution" (1994) 57 M.L.R. 213.

[130] Sir Harry Woolf, *Protection of the Public-A New Challenge* (London: Sweet & Maxwell, 1990), p.47.

[131] Lord Woolf, *Access to Justice: The Final Report to the Lord Chancellor on the Civil Justice System in England and Wales* (1997), p.251.

[132] Law Commission, *Administrative Law: Judicial Review and Statutory Appeals* (Law Com No.226, 1994), paras 8.9–8.14.

[133] *Draper v British Optical Association* [1938] 1 All E.R. 115; *Carnavon Harbour Acts, Re* [1937] Ch. 72; *Barnato, Re* [1949] Ch. 258, CA; *Lever Brothers & Unilever Ltd v Manchester Ship Canal Co*

held to determine whether his name should be removed from the list of members. In advance of this the plaintiff sought a declaration that the association could not enforce the code against him or remove him from the list of members. Farwell J held the application premature: the association had not yet done anything to the plaintiff and the meeting had not yet been held. The court is more likely to take jurisdiction when it feels that a legal decision will prevent possible disruptive action. In *Lee*[134] the plaintiff local authority asked for a declaration that the defendant's caravans were temporary buildings and thereby liable to be removed. The defendant argued that no dispute existed. In rejecting this argument the court was influenced by the possibility of a fight if the local authority attempted to remove the caravans without having first clarified the legal position.

Disputes may also be held to be hypothetical when they come too late and are in this sense moot,[135] where the point has become of academic interest,[136] or where the dispute has ceased to be of practical importance.[137] Thus, the courts refused to issue a declaration in relation to the legality of a statutory scheme concerning the export of live animals where the scheme had been repealed prior to the application for judicial review.[138] However, where the courts feel that an important point of legal principle is involved they may give judgment even though the matter has ceased to have practical import for the parties.[139] In *Salem*[140] Lord Slynn held that the courts have discretion to hear a case even where there is no longer a live claim that will affect the rights and obligations of the parties. Lord Slynn held that this discretion should, however, be exercised with caution. Appeals that were academic between the parties should not be heard unless there was a good reason in the public interest for doing so. There would be a good reason where there was a discrete point of statutory construction, which did not involve detailed consideration of facts, and where there were likely to be a large number of similar cases so that the point would, in any event, have to be decided in the near future. The decision in *Salem* was overruled by the House of

---

(1945) 78 Ll. L.R. 507; *R. v Personal Investments Authority Ombudsman, Ex p. Burns Anderson Independent Network plc* [1997] C.O.D. 379, CA (Civ Div); *R. (Robinson) v Torridge DC* [2007] 1 W.L.R. 871 QBD.

134 *Ruislip-Northwood Urban DC v Lee* (1931) 145 L.T. 208 at 214, 215.

135 *Everett v Ryder* (1926) 135 L.T. 302; *Whyte, Ridsdale & Co Ltd v Attorney General* [1927] 1 Ch. 548 Ch D; *Harrison v Croydon LBC* [1968] Ch. 479 Ch D; *Howard v Pickford Tool Co* [1951] K.B. 417.

136 *R. v Her Majesty's Inspectorate of Pollution, Ex p. Chapman* [1996] C.O.D. 154 QBD; *MD v Secretary of State for the Home Department* [2011] EWCA Civ 453.

137 *R. v Head Teacher and Governors of Fairfield Primary School and Hampshire CC, Ex p. W* [1998] C.O.D. 106.

138 *Live Sheep Traders Ltd* [1995] C.O.D. 297.

139 *Eastham v Newcastle United Football Club Ltd* [1964] Ch. 413 Ch D; *West Ham Corporation v Sharp* [1907] 1 K.B. 445 KBD; *R. v Secretary of State for the Home Department, Ex p. Abdi* [1996] 1 W.L.R. 298, HL.

140 *R. v Secretary of State for the Home Department, Ex p. Salem* [1999] 1 A.C. 450, HL at 456–457.

Lords in *Anufrijeva*.[141] The reasons for the overruling did not, however, affect the issue of whether the courts have discretion to hear a case even where there is no longer a live claim.[142]

Closely allied to but distinct from the cases discussed in the last paragraph are those in which a declaration is refused because of the practical impossibility of its terms being fulfilled, or because the inconvenience caused by issuing the remedy would be great compared with the benefits to be obtained. *Coney*[143] provides an example of the latter. A school reorganisation scheme was challenged for failure to comply with minor requirements concerning the posting of notices. The court characterised the requirements as directory rather than mandatory, but it made clear that it would in any event have exercised its discretion to refuse relief. Granting the remedy would at most have postponed the whole scheme for a year.

iv. Justiciability

To ask whether a dispute is justiciable is to consider whether the dispute is suitable for resolution by the judicial process, irrespective of who is bringing the action. Justiciability has been most explicitly recognised in tort actions against public authorities.[144] The term is used relatively rarely in other areas, but it has influenced a number of different decisions, some of which concern the declaration. **26–026**

For example, in reaching the conclusion that broadly framed duties under the Education Act 1944 were to be enforced through the minister, the courts were clearly influenced by the difficulties of adjudicating on such subject-matter. While the possibility of judicial intervention was not totally excluded, it was restricted to the more extreme and obvious forms of unlawful behaviour.[145] In some cases the courts have been more willing to tackle such issues, but this must be read against the type of illegality being asserted.[146]

The nature of the subject-matter has influenced the courts in other areas. The effect has been that the courts have declined to intervene, or have done so on narrower grounds. Alleged breaches of duty by university examiners provide an example of the former[147] and the provision of accommodation by a local authority an example of the latter.[148] The decision that no declaration would be

141 *R. (Anufrijeva) v Secretary of State for the Home Department* [2004] 1 A.C. 604, HL.

142 *R. (Zoolife International Ltd) v Secretary of State for the Environment, Food and Rural Affairs* [2007] EWHC 2995 (Admin); *R. (Raw) v Lambeth LBC* [2010] EWHC 507 (Admin); *PO (Nigeria) v Secretary of State for the Home Department* [2011] EWCA Civ 132.

143 *Coney v Choyce* [1975] 1 W.L.R. 422 Ch D at 436–437; *Maerkle v British and Continental Fur Co Ltd* [1954] 1 W.L.R. 1242, CA; *Attorney General v Colchester Corp* [1955] 2 Q.B. 207 QBD.

144 See Ch.30; *Anns v Merton LBC* [1978] A.C. 728, HL; *Rowling v Takaro Properties Ltd* [1988] A.C. 473.

145 *Watt v Kesteven County Council* [1955] 1 Q.B. 408, CA; *Bradbury v Enfield LBC* [1967] 1 W.L.R. 1311, CA (Civ Div); *Cumings v Birkenhead Corporation* [1972] Ch. 12, CA (Civ Div).

146 *Meade v Haringey LBC* [1979] 1 W.L.R. 637, CA (Civ Div); *Thornton v Kirklees MBC* [1979] 3 W.L.R. 1, CA (Civ Div).

147 *Thorne v University of London* [1966] 2 Q.B. 237, CA.

148 *R. v Bristol Corporation, Ex p. Hendy* [1974] 1 W.L.R. 498, CA (Civ Div).

granted to preclude the Crown from undertaking an international obligation was also influenced by considerations of justiciability.[149]

D. The Impact of the Declaration

26–027 The normal impact of a declaration is to render the decision challenged retrospectively invalid or void ab initio. There may, however, be instances in which its impact is prospective rather than retrospective. The court may in effect refuse to grant relief in the instant case, but nonetheless proceed to give a declaration on the general point of law.[150] The reasons for employing this technique are similar to those encountered when discussing invalidity.[151] To render the contested decision retrospectively null may have a profound effect on the administration, or may adversely affect the rights of third parties. The court may decide to refuse relief in the instant case,[152] or it may, while declining relief in the instant case, take the opportunity to clarify the law in the area.[153] The desirability of modifying the concept of retrospective nullity in this fashion has been considered in the earlier discussion of invalidity.[154]

E. Practice and Procedure

26–028 A court can grant a binding declaration irrespective of whether any other remedy is claimed.[155] The judicial review procedure may be used in a claim for judicial review where the claimant is seeking a declaration.[156] This procedure will be analysed in the following chapter. The Senior Courts Act s.31(2) sets out the circumstances in which a court can grant a declaration in a claim for judicial review, and this will be considered in the following chapter. Where the claimant is seeking a declaration or injunction in addition to a mandatory, prohibiting or quashing order, then the judicial review procedure must be used.[157] A "gap" in the courts' jurisdiction was the inability to grant an interim declaration of rights. This

---

149 *Blackburn v Attorney General* [1971] 1 W.L.R. 1037, CA (Civ Div).

150 *R. v Panel on Take-overs and Mergers, Ex p. Datafin* [1987] Q.B. 815, CA (Civ Div); *R. v Secretary of State, Ex p. Association of Metropolitan Authorities* [1986] 1 W.L.R. 1 QBD; C. Lewis, "Retrospective and Prospective Rulings in Administrative Law" [1988] P.L. 78; Woolf, *Protection of the Public-A New Challenge* (1990), pp.53–54.

151 See Ch.24.

152 *R. v Monopolies and Mergers Commission, Ex p. Argyll Group Plc* [1986] 1 W.L.R. 763, CA (Civ Div).

153 *Datafin* [1987] Q.B. 815.

154 See para.24–023.

155 CPR 40.20.

156 SI 2092/2000, CPR 54.3(1).

157 CPR 54.3(1).

was important when claims were brought against the Crown since injunctive relief was not available.[158] The Civil Procedure Rules now provide for an interim declaration.[159]

5. INJUNCTION

A. Introduction

The injunction has had an impact on public law for many years,[160] as exemplified by case law on public nuisance and the administration of charitable or public trusts. The latter was, as de Smith pointed out,[161] of particular importance. The Attorney General's intervention was founded on the Crown as parens patriae. This role existed not only for charities, infants, and those infirm in mind, but also included a visitatorial authority over those charitable and ecclesiastical corporations that lacked visitors of their own. Proceedings by the Attorney General often arose because such bodies defaulted in performance of their functions. The general right of the Attorney General to prevent ultra vires action grew out of a broad conception of the prerogative of protection.[162] **26–029**

Despite the respectability of its historical lineage, the injunction remained largely on the periphery of public law. The principal reason was that the prerogative orders existed, but it was also because the injunction remained shackled by its history. The criteria for individual standing were derived from those of public nuisance.[163] If these were not satisfied the Attorney General had to bring the action. This reasoning was criticised in the discussion of standing.[164] The rules were, however, reaffirmed in *Gouriet*.[165] The fetters binding the injunction have indeed been tightened. Whereas the old rules from public nuisance could have been liberalised, the reasoning in the *Gouriet* case rendered this much less likely. The court's reasoning was predicated on the assumption that the citizen could not protect the public interest unless he was settling a private dispute, or one in which he had a special interest, with a public body. The courts do, however, take a more liberal attitude to standing under the Senior Courts Act 1981 s.31 than at common law.[166]

Injunctions can be negative or positive, prohibiting certain action from being done or commanding the performance of certain action. In addition, an injunction **26–030**

[158] *Underhill v Ministry of Food* [1950] 1 All E.R. 591 Ch D; *International General Electric Co of New York Ltd v Customs and Excise Commissioners* [1962] Ch. 784, CA; *R. v Inland Revenue Commissioners, Ex p. Rossminster Ltd* [1980] A.C. 952; *Clarke v Chadburn* [1985] 1 W.L.R. 78 Ch D.

[159] CPR 25.1(1)(b); *X NHS Trust v T (Adult Patient: Refusal of Medical Treatment)* [2005] 1 All E.R. 387 Fam Div.

[160] Many of the cases brought against local authorities were injunction cases.

[161] *de Smith's Judicial Review* (2007), pp.800–804.

[162] de Smith, *Judicial Review of Administrative Action* (1980), p.433; *de Smith's Judicial Review* (2007), pp.803–804.

[163] *Boyce v Paddington Borough Council* [1903] 1 Ch. 109 Ch D.

[164] See para.25–006.

[165] *Gouriet* [1978] A.C. 435; *Barrs v Bethell* [1982] Ch. 294 Ch D.

[166] Ch.25.

can be perpetual or interim. The former is granted at the end of the action and conclusively determines the respective rights and liabilities of the parties. Interim injunctions are designed to preserve the status quo pending trial of the main action.[167] The plaintiff must show that there is some arguable point of law and that the balance of convenience indicates that relief should be granted pending trial of the main action.[168]

It has, however, been held by Lord Goff that a public authority should not normally be restrained from enforcing an apparently valid law unless the court is satisfied that the challenge to the validity of the law is prima facie so firmly based as to justify so exceptional a course being taken.[169] It may be difficult to assess the balance of convenience in public law cases, because the public body will be representing a wider public interest when making the challenged decision. It is therefore unsurprising that the courts are likely to take into account the strength of the applicant's case in challenging the act when deciding where the balance of convenience lies. The party in whose favour the interim relief is granted will normally have to give an undertaking in damages lest he proves to be unsuccessful and the defendant suffers loss. However, where the challenge is to government policy that is not enshrined in legislation this will affect the weighing process and the balance of convenience.[170]

The award of an interim injunction will be affected where there is a challenge involving EU law.[171] It will also be affected by the Human Rights Act 1998 s.12(3), which provides that where a claim might affect the right to freedom of expression, no such relief is to be granted so as to restrain publication before trial unless the court is satisfied that the applicant is likely to establish that publication should not be allowed.[172]

C. The Scope of Injunctive Relief

i. Injunctions: general

26–031 Injunctions can be issued in a wide range of situations: to prevent a public body from committing what would be a private wrong such as a trespass[173] or a nuisance[174]; to restrain a public body from acting unlawfully[175]; to restrain the

[167] CPR 25.1(1)(a).

[168] *American Cyanamid Co v Ethicon Ltd* [1975] A.C. 396, HL; *R. v Secretary of State for Transport, Ex p. Factortame (No.2)* [1991] 1 A.C. 603, HL; *Douglas v Hello! Ltd (No.1)* [2001] Q.B. 967, CA (Civ Div); J. Martin, "Interlocutory Injunctions: *American Cyanamid* Comes of Age" (1993–94) King's Coll. L.J. 52.

[169] *Factortame (No.2)* [1991] 1 A.C. 603.

[170] *R. (Medical Justice) v Secretary of State for the Home Department* [2010] EWHC 1425 (Admin).

[171] *R. v Ministry of Agriculture, Fisheries and Food, Ex p. Monsanto Plc* [1999] Q.B. 1161 DC; *R. v Secretary of State for Health, Ex p. Scotia Pharmaceuticals International Ltd (No.2)* [1997] Eu. L.R. 650 DC; *R. v Secretary of State for Health, Ex p. Imperial Tobacco Ltd* [2001] 1 W.L.R. 127, HL.

[172] *Cream Holdings Ltd v Banerjee* [2005] 1 A.C. 253, HL; *Greene v Associated Newspapers Ltd* [2005] Q.B. 972, CA (Civ Div); *R. (Newby Foods Ltd) v Food Standards Agency* [2013] EWHC 2132 (Admin).

[173] *Broadbent v Rotherham Corp* [1917] 2 Ch. 31 Ch D.

[174] *Pride of Derby and Derbyshire Angling Association Ltd v British Celanese Ltd* [1953] Ch. 149, CA.

implementation of an unlawful decision[176]; and to enforce public duties, provided that they are not too vague.[177] The remedy can be used by the Attorney General, who can seek an injunction to prevent a public body from acting ultra vires.[178] The Attorney General has also used the injunction to prevent repeated breaches of the criminal law, and in circumstances where injury to the person is threatened.[179]

ii. Injunctions and Parliament

Possible challenge to the legality of public statutes immediately enmeshes one in debates on sovereignty. This is not the place to consider this debate.[180] Even before a measure has received the Royal Assent it is dubious whether it could be successfully challenged in the courts.[181] **26–032**

The courts have, however, asserted that, in principle, they would be willing to issue an injunction to prevent a breach of contract where that breach consists of a promise not to oppose a private Bill. The key word in the above sentence is "principle", since the courts have in fact declined to intervene even in what appears to be a strong case. Thus in *Bilston Corp v Wolverhampton Corporation*[182] the latter had contracted with Bilston Corporation that it would not oppose any application to Parliament by Bilston whereby Bilston sought a local Act of Parliament for securing a water supply. Despite this promise and the fact that it had been enshrined in an earlier local Act, the court declined to issue the injunction, the reasoning being that Parliament should have the opportunity to hear the argument of both parties in order to decide whether Wolverhampton Corporation should be released from its obligations by statute.

Challenge to subordinate legislation is subject to different considerations. When such legislation has been enacted it is open to attack as being ultra vires, and a declaration or injunction can be granted to a plaintiff. If a person wishes to bring an action prior to the final enactment of the order the issue is more problematic. An injunction will not issue against Her Majesty in Council, nor it seems against a minister of the Crown who is making a statutory instrument. A declaration might be possible if an appropriate defendant could be found. Where

---

175 *Bradbury* [1967] 1 W.L.R. 1311.

176 *R. v North Yorkshire CC, Ex p. M* [1989] Q.B. 411 QBD.

177 *R. v Kensington and Chelsea London Borough Council, Ex p. Hammell* [1989] Q.B. 518, CA (Civ Div); *South Buckinghamshire DC v Porter (No.1)* [2003] 2 A.C. 558, HL.

178 *Attorney General v Manchester Corp* [1906] 1 Ch. 643 Ch D; *Attorney General v Fulham Corp* [1921] 1 Ch. 440 Ch D.

179 *Attorney General v Smith* [1958] 2 Q.B. 173 QBD; *Attorney General v Chaudry* [1971] 1 W.L.R. 1614, CA (Civ Div). See Ch.24.

180 P. Craig, "Parliamentary Sovereignty after *Factortame*" (1991) 11 Y.B.E.L. 221.

181 de Smith, *Judicial Review of Administrative Action* (1980), pp.465–466; de Smith, Woolf and Jowell, *Judicial Review of Administrative Action*, 5th edn, (London: Sweet & Maxwell, 1995), pp.725–726.

182 *Bilston Corp v Wolverhampton Corp* [1942] Ch .391 Ch D. However, in *Attorney General v London and Home Counties Joint Electricity Authority* [1929] 1 Ch. 513 Ch D, it was accepted that the Attorney General could have an injunction to prevent unauthorised expenditure of corporate funds to promote a bill.

an order has been laid before Parliament, and has been approved by both Houses of Parliament, the courts will be reluctant to intervene.[183]

26–033 Even where the legislative process is not involved, the courts will not award an injunction where to do so would interfere with the right of the House to regulate its own internal proceedings.[184] There are, however, dicta that it would be possible, albeit unusual, for a court to grant a mandatory injunction ordering a minister to lay a statutory instrument before Parliament.[185]

The position with respect to EU law and the legislative process is different. The courts have accepted that EU law must take supremacy in the event of a clash with domestic law. This was the essence of the holding in *Factortame (No.2)*.[186] The House of Lords held that an interim injunction could be granted under s.37 of the Senior Courts Act 1981 preventing the enforcement of the domestic legislation, pending the final resolution of the disputed matter before the ECJ. It remains to be seen what the courts would do if it were alleged that the domestic legislature was about to enact legislation that was felt to be in breach of EU law. It is clear that, as a matter of EU law, Parliament is under an obligation not to enact legislation contrary to EU obligations. However, it is likely that our courts would require strong evidence before accepting that domestic legislation that was to be enacted was in breach of EU law. If such evidence were forthcoming then it is not inconceivable that an interim injunction could be issued pending the final resolution of the substantive issue by the ECJ. In the event that the ECJ found that the proposed legislation was contrary to EU law then a final order could be addressed to the relevant minister. This could be in the form of a prohibiting order, or in the form of an injunction.

iii. Injunctions and public offices

26–034 An information in the nature of quo warranto was, until 1938, the procedure by which challenges to the usurpation of a public office were made. In 1938 the information in the nature of quo warranto was abolished and replaced by the injunction.[187] The substance of the action remained the same, and only the form of the remedy was altered. Thus, the office must be public in character, and the usurper must have actually acted in pursuance of it; a claim per se was insufficient. The office itself had to be not only public but "substantive", as distinct from mere employment at the will of others. Standing to secure the remedy was broadly construed,[188] but acquiescence or undue delay would operate to defeat the plaintiff. Specific statutory provisions govern challenges to particular types of office.[189]

---

183 *Harper v Home Secretary* [1955] Ch. 238, CA; *Nottinghamshire CC v Secretary of State for the Environment* [1986] A.C. 240, HL. See, however, *Hoffman-La Roche & Co AG v Secretary of State for Trade and Industry* [1975] A.C. 295, HL.

184 *Bradlaugh v Gossett* (1884) 12 Q.B.D 271.

185 *R. v HM Treasury, Ex p. British Telecomunications Plc* [1995] C.O.D. 56, CA (Civ Div).

186 *Factortame (No.2)* [1991] 1 A.C. 603.

187 Administration of Justice (Miscellaneous Provisions) Act 1938 s.9; Senior Courts Act 1981 s.30.

188 *R. v Speyer* [1916] 1 K.B. 595 KBD, (affirmed [1916] 2 K.B. 858).

189 See, e.g. Local Government Act 1972 s.92 applies to challenges to the qualifications of members of a local authority.

D. Limits to Injunctive Relief

The injunction is an equitable remedy and equitable principles will influence the way in which it is applied by the courts. Undue delay or acquiescence will bar the plaintiff. The adequacy of a monetary remedy will also influence the court. Considerations of practicality have been treated differently by the courts. They will not order a defendant to do the impossible[190] and will weigh the inconvenience caused by the public body's defective action with the cost of requiring it to comply with the statutory procedure to the letter.[191] The courts will not, however, refuse the remedy because of general pleas by a public body of its disruptive effects, or difficulty of complying with the court order.[192] Particular problems have surrounded the award of injunctive relief against the Crown, which is dealt with later.[193] The availability of a different remedy, and the effect of this upon the ability to claim injunctive relief, will also be considered.[194] **26–035**

E. Practice and Procedure

Injunctions, like declarations, can be claimed under s.31 of the Senior Courts Act 1981, and independently of this procedure. The judicial review procedure may be used in a claim for judicial review where the claimant is seeking an injunction.[195] The Senior Courts Act s.31(2) sets out the circumstances in which a court can grant an injunction in a claim for judicial review, and this will be considered in the following chapter. Where the claimant is seeking an injunction in addition to one of the prerogative orders, then the judicial review procedure must be used.[196] **26–036**

An injunction may also be sought independently of a judicial review action. In 1875 the power to grant an injunction, which had previously resided solely with courts of equity, was made available to all divisions of the High Court where the award of the remedy appeared to be just and convenient.[197] The effect of the provision was to allow the High Court to grant an injunction where it would previously have granted a common law remedy. Where no remedy would have been available at common law or equity an injunction could not be given.[198]

6. OTHER REMEDIES

A person aggrieved with action taken by a public body may be able to bring a civil claim in tort or contract. The scope of these causes of action will be considered below. **26–037**

---

190 *Attorney General v Colchester Corp* [1955] 2 Q.B. 207 QBD.

191 *Coney v Choyce* [1975] 1 W.L.R. 422 Ch D.

192 *Pride of Derby* [1953] Ch. 149; *Bradbury* [1967] 1 W.L.R. 1311.

193 See paras 29–007 to 29–010.

194 See paras 27–062 to 27–064.

195 SI 2092/2000, CPR 54.3(1).

196 CPR 54.3(1).

197 Supreme Court of Judicature Act 1873 s.25(8); Senior Courts Act 1981 s.37.

198 *North London Ry v Great Northern Ry* (1883) 11 Q.B.D 30.

A. Habeas Corpus

26–038 If an individual is detained the writ of habeas corpus may be sought to challenge the legality of the administrative order on which the detention was based.[199] A brief outline of this remedy will be provided here. Fuller treatment may be found elsewhere.[200]

The immediate progenitor of the present writ was the writ of habeas corpus cum causa, which developed in the 14th century as a mechanism for testing the legality of detention. Reforms expediting the procedure were introduced by the Habeas Corpus Act 1679, which also contained financial penalties for those, whether they were judges or jailers, who refused service of the writ or impeded its effective execution. The detainee will normally make the application, unless the circumstances of the imprisonment preclude this and the writ will be served on the person who has the applicant in custody.

The cases on scope of review in a habeas corpus action are a minefield, evidencing a bewildering variety of terminology. Starting from first principles, it seems clear that the writ cannot be used to challenge the correctness of the detention, but only its validity. Correctness can only be challenged on appeal.[201] This is simply an application of the traditional principles of judicial review, but it remains to be seen how far the expansion of jurisdictional error affects this area so as to render the above distinction redundant. Jurisdictional error provides a clear reason for awarding the writ.[202] It is less clear whether habeas corpus can be awarded for an error on the face of the record, but the answer appears to be in the affirmative,[203] and the courts will also consider whether the evidence justifies the holding of the detainee.[204] In general, while the courts insist that they are looking at validity rather than correctness, they will not normally be prevented from releasing a detainee who they feel ought to be released by inquiry into the jurisprudential niceties of errors going to and errors within jurisdiction.[205] Such distinctions are, in any event, now largely of historical interest given the courts' expansion of the concept of jurisdictional error. A purely technical flaw in the process leading to detention may lead the court to decline to issue the writ.[206]

26–039 Habeas corpus will be available to determine whether the detention itself was valid,[207] and the courts will normally apply the general principles of administrative law when determining this issue.[208] Where, however, an applicant seeks to attack the underlying administrative decision, which was the cause of the

199 For related challenges based on collateral attack, see Ch.24.

200 R. Sharpe, *The Law of Habeas Corpus*, 2nd edn (Oxford: Clarendon, 1989); de Smith, *Judicial Review of Administrative Action* (1980) App 2; *de Smith's Judicial Review* (2007), pp.865–871.

201 *Ex p. Hinds* [1961] 1 W.L.R. 325.

202 *Eshugbayi Eleko v Government of Nigeria* [1931] A.C. 662.

203 *R. v Governor of Brixton Prison, Ex p. Armah* [1968] A.C. 192, HL.

204 *Armah* [1968] A.C. 192; *Knowles v Government of the United States of America* [2007] 1 W.L.R. 47 at [14]; *Gibson v The Government of the United States of America* [2007] UKPC 52 at [18]; *R. v Board of Control, Ex p. Rutty* [1956] 2 Q.B. 109 DC.

205 Rubinstein, *Jurisdiction and Illegality* (1965), p.115.

206 *R. v Governor of Pentonville Prison, Ex p. Osman (No.3)* [1990] 1 W.L.R. 878 DC.

207 *Rahmatullah v Secretary of State for Foreign and Commonwealth Affairs* [2012] UKSC 48.

208 *R. v Governor of Pentonville Prison, Ex p. Osman* [1990] 1 W.L.R. 277 QBD.

detention, judicial review should be used rather than habeas corpus.[209] There is a more general tendency to prefer challenges by way of judicial review, with resort to habeas corpus where no other mode of challenge is available.[210] Where a claimant challenged via judicial review and habeas corpus, the proceedings should be harmonised.

The Lord Chancellor put forward proposals that affect the relationship between judicial review and habeas corpus.[211] The principal recommendation was that habeas corpus should, subject to permission, be available in judicial review proceedings for all civil cases. The Lord Chancellor also sought views on whether habeas corpus should be wholly subsumed into judicial review, and whether the discretionary elements of judicial review in relation to permission, time limits and remedies, should also apply to a claim for habeas corpus within judicial review proceedings.[212]

B. Default Powers

Many statutes contain provisions which enable a more senior body in the administrative hierarchy or the minister to exercise powers where the original grantee has failed to do so. Normally the defaulting authority will be warned and given time to fulfil its duties. Failing this, the duties will be transferred to the minister, to an independent body, or new members may be appointed to replace those in default. **26–040**

The courts on some occasions have treated the existence of such powers as excluding other remedies. Thus in *Pasmore*[213] the existence of default powers in the Public Health Act 1875 was held to prevent a private person from obtaining mandamus to enforce a duty to provide such sewers as might be necessary for draining a district. In other cases the courts have held that other remedies are available despite the presence of default powers in cases involving, for example, education[214] and television.[215]

It is odd to regard default powers as an alternative remedy that is equally beneficial as a declaration or mandamus. In some ways it is not a legal remedy at

[209] *R. v Secretary of State for the Home Department, Ex p. Cheblak* [1991] 1 W.L.R. 890, CA (Civ Div); *R. v Secretary of State for the Home Department, Ex p. Muboyayi* [1992] Q.B. 244, CA (Civ Div); *S-C (Mental Patient, Re)* [1996] Q.B. 599, CA (Civ Div); *R. v Stoke-on-Trent Justices, Ex p. Cawley* [1996] C.O.D. 292 DC; *Rahman, Re* [1996] C.O.D. 465 QBD.

[210] *MB v The Managers of Warley Hospital*, 30 July 1998; *R. v BHB Community Healthcare NHS Trust, Ex p. B* [1999] 1 F.L.R. 106, CA (Civ Div); *R. v Leeds Crown Court, Ex p. Hunt* [1999] 1 W.L.R. 841 DC; *Sheikh v Secretary of State for the Home Department* [2001] A.C.D 33, CA (Civ Div); Sir Simon Brown, "Habeas Corpus—A New Chapter" [2000] P.L. 31.

[211] Lord Chancellor's Department Consultation Paper, *The Administrative Court: Proposed Changes to Primary Legislation following Sir Jeffrey Bowman's Review of the Crown Office List* (2001), paras 3–10.

[212] See however *Rahmatullah* [2012] UKSC 48, where the SC emphasised the non-discretionary nature of habeas corpus.

[213] *Pasmore v Oswaldtwistle Urban District Council* [1898] A.C. 387, HL, applying *Doe d. Bishop of Rochester v Bridges* (1831) 1 B. & Ad. 847; *Bradbury*, [1967] 1 W.L.R. 1311; *Wood v Ealing LBC* [1967] Ch. 364 Ch D; *Southwark LBC v Williams* [1971] Ch. 734, CA (Civ Div).

[214] *Meade v Haringey LBC* [1979] 1 W.L.R. 637, CA (Civ Div).

[215] *Attorney General, ex rel. McWhirter v Independent Broadcasting Authority* [1973] Q.B. 629, CA (Civ Div).

all.[216] The cases which regard default powers as excluding other remedies should therefore be narrowly construed. Those cases where such powers have been regarded as exclusive are perhaps better explained as ones in which the nature of the duty rendered it unsuited to enforcement by individuals. There are indications in the case law that the courts have had this factor in mind when construing the relevant statute.[217]

Although default powers will only be used as a last resort they are a potent threat, particularly when the relationship between central and local government is under strain.[218] The exercise of such powers will be subject to judicial review. If the minister acts on irrelevant considerations or misdirects himself in fact or law, then the intervention will be ultra vires. The court should not interfere simply because they took a different view from that of the minister.[219]

---

216 *R. v Leicester Guardians* [1899] 2 Q.B. 632 QBD at 639.

217 *Southwark LBC* [1971] Ch. 734 at 743.

218 *Asher v Secretary of State for the Environment* [1974] Ch. 208, CA (Civ Div).

219 *R. v Secretary of State for the Environment, Ex p. Norwich CC* [1982] Q.B. 808, CA (Civ Div). Lord Denning MR also suggests that the minister has a procedural duty to hear the local authority's view before exercising his powers.

CHAPTER 27

REMEDIES AND REFORM

1. CENTRAL ISSUES

i. The range of remedies available to a claimant described in the previous chapter was always a mixed blessing. The principal remedies of certiorari and declaration had advantages and disadvantages. **27–001**

ii. Certiorari could apply to all types of error, the standing rules were relatively wide and interim relief was available. Its disadvantages included the impossibility of combining certiorari with a damages action, a relatively short time limit, and the difficulty of adjudicating on fact.

iii. The declaration was meant to be the shining white charger cutting through outmoded limitations encrusted on the prerogative orders,[1] and so it might have been. It was unencumbered by the limitations mentioned above and its dual capacity as supervisory and original remedy gave it added flexibility. It could be combined with other claims for relief, was not subject to a short time limit, and could be attended by full discovery. The promise that declaration might bloom into a general remedy, with the prerogative orders being left to atrophy from lack of use, did not however come to pass. It was thought that no interim declaration could be granted, there were question marks surrounding the availability of declaration for non-jurisdictional error of law, and the standing criteria, as laid down in the *Gouriet* case,[2] were restrictive.

iv. The preceding complexity led to reform of remedies, preceded by Law Commission reports. The core of the new procedure is now termed the claim for judicial review. This is the mechanism by which a range of remedies can be claimed against a public body. The reforms introduced in the 1970s removed some of the complexities from the previous law. It nonetheless brought new difficulties into the law, two of which are especially significant.

v. First, the courts construed the new procedure as prima facie exclusive, in the sense that claims against public bodies would have to be brought via the new procedure. This was because the procedure contained protections for public bodies in terms of the need for the claimant to secure permission before seeking judicial review, and in the form of short time limits. It was felt that it would be an abuse of process for a claimant to avoid these

---

[1] *Barnard v National Dock Labour Board* [1953] 2 Q.B. 18, CA.

[2] *Gouriet* [1978] A.C. 435.

safeguards by proceeding outside the new procedure. The courts nonetheless created exceptions to this prima facie exclusivity, the scope and application of which gave rise to much case law.

vi. Second, the reformed procedure also generated much case law as some claimants sought to bring their case within the new procedure. This was because they felt that the remedy under the public law procedure would either be better than they would otherwise secure, or because there was doubt as to whether they would be able to secure any other remedy. The courts therefore had to decide whether the case was "sufficiently public" to warrant recourse to public law procedures.

2. THE CLAIM FOR JUDICIAL REVIEW

A. The Ordinary Courts: The Legal Foundations of the Existing Procedure

27–002 The reform of remedies was the result of the Law Commission's Report No.73, which was the culmination of earlier studies.[3] By the time that Report No.73 was published the Law Commission felt that it must confine itself to questions of procedure. The earlier Working Paper had undertaken a wider-ranging study encompassing time limits, ouster clauses, and damages. These were felt to be outside the Law Commission's brief.

What emerged was a revised Ord.53,[4] as amended by a later statutory instrument.[5] Some of the key provisions were incorporated into what was the Supreme Court Act 1981[6] s.31, which has now been renamed the Senior Courts Act 1981. The foundations for the public law procedures continued to be revised Ord.53, and the 1981 Act, for 20 years.

These legal foundations have now changed.[7] The catalyst was reform of the civil justice system flowing from the Woolf Report.[8] This led to a radical revision of the rules on civil procedure. The initial impact on judicial review was marginal, since Ord.53, subject to minor change, was appended to the new Civil Procedure Rules. The position altered as a result of the Bowman Report into the Crown Office.[9] Judicial review is now governed by CPR 8, as modified by a new Pt 54. These provisions apply to all judicial review applications lodged on or after

---

[3] Law Commission No.20 (1969), Cmnd 4059; Law Commission Working Paper No.40 (1971); Law Commission No.73 (1976), Cmnd.6407.

[4] SI 1955/1977.

[5] SI 2000/1980.

[6] The change was brought about by the Constitutional Reform Act 2005 Sch.11(1) para.1.

[7] C. Lewis, *Judicial Remedies in Public Law*, 4th edn (London: Sweet & Maxwell, 2009).

[8] Lord Woolf, *Access to Justice: The Final Report to the Lord Chancellor on the Civil Justice System in England and Wales* (1997); SI 3132/1998.

[9] Review of the Crown Office List (LCD, 2000); Lord Chancellor's Department Consultation Paper, *The Administrative Court: Proposed Changes to Primary Legislation following Sir Jeffrey Bowman's Review of the Crown Office List* (2001).

2 October 2000.[10] The legal foundations for judicial review will henceforth be based on the CPR, the Senior Courts Act 1981 s.31 and Practice Directions. The detailed procedure under CPR 54 will be considered below.[11] The Crown Office has been renamed the Administrative Court.[12] It is clear that although the claim for judicial review is brought in the name of the Crown, the Crown's involvement is nominal. The real contest is between the claimant and the defendant.[13]

B. The Upper Tribunal: Legal Foundations for New Judicial Review Power

The power of judicial review has traditionally vested in the ordinary courts. The Tribunals, Courts and Enforcement Act 2007 altered this. The Act was considered in an earlier chapter.[14] Suffice it to say for the present that it enables, subject to certain conditions, the Upper Tribunal to exercise judicial review functions[15] and allows for the transfer of certain judicial review cases to it from the High Court.[16] The procedure for judicial review before the Upper Tribunal is, however, largely the same as that in ordinary judicial review applications to the High Court, in relation to matters such as the need for permission, time limits and the like. **27–003**

C. The Application/Claim for Judicial Review

The 1977 reform was based on the application, or as it is now termed, claim for judicial review. The prerogative orders and declaration and injunction are subject to this mechanism, and the remedies may be sought in the alternative or cumulatively depending upon the type of case.[17] When revised Ord.53 was first passed it was thought that declaration and injunction would still be obtainable under their pre-existing procedures. It would, however, be inappropriate for those remedies to be claimed under the new procedure unless the case was of a public law nature. **27–004**

Section 31(2) of the Senior Courts Act 1981 defines when cases will be of this kind. Declarations and injunctions can be granted pursuant to an application for judicial review if the court considers, having regard to the nature of the matters and the nature of the persons and bodies against whom a remedy may be granted by the prerogative orders, and all the circumstances of the case, that it would be just and convenient for the declaration to be made or for the injunction to be granted. The test is therefore both functional and institutional. It is clear, after

---

[10] SI 2092/2000; M. Fordham, "Judicial Review: The New Rules" [2001] P.L. 4; T. Cornford and M. Sunkin, "The Bowman Report, Access and the Recent Reforms of the Judicial Review Procedure" [2001] P.L. 11.

[11] See below, paras 27–057 to 27–060.

[12] Practice Direction (Administrative Court: Establishment) [2000] 1 W.L.R. 1654.

[13] *R. (Ben-Abdelaziz and Kryva) v London Borough of Hackney and the Secretary of State for the Home Department* [2001] 1 W.L.R. 1485, CA (Civ Div) at [29].

[14] See Ch.9.

[15] Tribunals, Courts and Enforcement Act 2007 s.15.

[16] Tribunals, Courts and Enforcement Act 2007 s.19, inserting s.31A into the Senior Courts Act 1981.

[17] Senior Courts Act 1981 s.31(1).

some earlier doubts,[18] that a declaration or an injunction can be granted even if a prerogative order would not be available,[19] provided that the subject-matter of the application is of a public law nature and hence suited to judicial review.[20]

This general approach has been retained by CPR 54 Pt 1 of which deals with judicial review. A claim for judicial review is defined in CPR 54.1(2)(a) to be a claim to review the lawfulness of an enactment or decision, action or failure to act in the exercise of a public function. CPR 54.2 provides that the judicial review procedure must be used where the claimant is seeking a mandatory, prohibiting or quashing order,[21] or an injunction under the Senior Courts Act 1981 s.30. It must also be used where the claimant seeks a declaration or injunction in addition to a mandatory, prohibiting or quashing order. CPR 54.3(1) provides that the judicial review procedure may be used in a claim for judicial review where the claimant is seeking a declaration or an injunction. The Senior Courts Act 1981 s.31(2) continues to provide the circumstances in which a claimant can seek a declaration or injunction in a claim for judicial review. Damages, restitution or the recovery of a sum due can be claimed in conjunction with the other remedies, but a claim for judicial review may not seek such remedies alone, CPR 54.3(2). This does not, however, create a new remedy where none existed before. The court must be satisfied that if the claim had been made in an ordinary action the applicant would have been awarded the remedy.[22]

The Senior Courts Act 1981 was amended by the Criminal Justice and Courts Act 2015. In deciding whether to grant leave/permission the High Court is now empowered to consider of its own motion whether the outcome for the applicant would have been substantially different if the conduct complained of had not occurred, and it must consider that question if the defendant asks it to do so.[23] If it appears to the High Court to be highly likely that the outcome would not have been substantially different, the court must refuse to grant leave,[24] subject to the caveat that the court can disregard the preceding requirement if it considers that it is appropriate to do so for reasons of exceptional public interest, although it must certify that it is making use of this proviso.[25] There are analogous conditions limiting the award of relief if the case proceeds to the substantive hearing, the court being instructed to refuse relief and/or a monetary award if it appears to be highly likely that the outcome for the applicant would not have been substantially different if the conduct complained of had not occurred, subject to the proviso concerning exceptional public interest.[26] The same provisions are applicable to the Upper Tribunal when it exercises its judicial review powers.[27]

---

[18] *R. v Inland Revenue Commissioners, Ex p. National Federation of Self-Employed and Small Businesses Ltd* [1982] A.C. 617, HL at 647–648.

[19] *R. v Secretary of State for Employment, Ex p. Equal Opportunities Commission* [1995] 1 A.C. 1, HL.

[20] *R. v British Broadcasting Corp, Ex p. Lavelle* [1983] 1 W.L.R. 23 QBD at 30–31.

[21] These are the new names for mandamus, prohibition and certiorari, Senior Courts Act 1981 s.29, as amended by SI 1033/2004 art.3.

[22] Senior Courts Act 1981 s.31(4).

[23] Senior Courts Act 1981 s.31(3)(C).

[24] Senior Courts Act 1981 s.31(3)(D).

[25] Senior Courts Act 1981 s.31(3)(E),(F).

[26] Senior Courts Act 1981 s.31(2)(A)-(C).

[27] Tribunals, Courts and Enforcement Act 2007 ss.15(5)(A)–(B), 16(3)(C)–(G).

D. O'Reilly v Mackman

The application for judicial review must be read in the light of the decision in *O'Reilly v Mackman*.[28] This case limited the circumstances in which a declaration or an injunction in a public law case could be sought outside the Senior Courts Act 1981 s.31. Lord Diplock gave judgment for the House of Lords, and reasoned as follows. The prerogative orders had, prior to the reforms, been subject to limitations. There was no right to discovery, damages could not be claimed in conjunction with the orders and cross-examination upon affidavits occurred very rarely if at all. These limitations justified the use of the declaration under Ord.15 r.16. However, the reformed Ord.53 had removed these defects by providing for discovery, allowing damages to be claimed, and making provision for cross-examination. The reformed procedure also provided important safeguards for the public body, including the requirement of leave to bring the case and a time limit short enough so that the public body would not be kept in suspense as to the validity of its actions. **27–005**

It would therefore normally be an abuse of process to seek a declaration outside of s.31. Two exceptions were mentioned: certain types of collateral attack and cases where none of the parties objected to a remedy being sought outside s.31. The possibility that other exceptions might exist was left open. Lord Diplock also felt that within s.31 the prerogative orders should be the main remedies. The declaration was seen as useful, while the prerogative orders were unduly limited. Now that the latter had been liberated from their constraints, they should assume pride of place within s.31. When the sole aim was to quash a decision, certiorari and not declaration should be used.

The decision in *O'Reilly* raised a number of important questions. First, what are the exceptions to *O'Reilly*: how do you "get out" of the judicial procedure? Second, how public must a case be to be brought within the judicial review procedure: how do you "get into" this procedure? Finally, do we need a separate procedure for judicial review cases?

3. THE EXCEPTIONS: "GETTING OUT" OF THE JUDICIAL REVIEW PROCEDURE

A. The Reasons for Seeking to Proceed outside Section 31

It is important to understand why applicants sought to proceed outside s.31. The principal reason is that if they were forced to bring their cases within s.31 they would be outside the short time limit and hence their claims would fail. This problem could be particularly acute when the person seeking to raise the public law issue was the defendant and therefore not in control of the time within which the action was brought. **27–006**

A secondary reason for seeking to bring the claim outside s.31 is that the applicant may wish to investigate factual issues and to undertake cross-examination. While this can occur within s.31 proceedings it is not normal. Prior

[28] *O'Reilly v Mackman* [1983] 2 A.C. 237, HL.

to 1977 grant of leave to cross-examine under the prerogative orders was very rare. This was a reason why applicants preferred to use the declaration or the injunction, since unless one could cross-examine it might be impossible to prove the alleged error. The new procedure made provision for discovery and cross-examination. Notwithstanding these provisions there were early indications that the ability to cross-examine should be used sparingly, and that the ordinary trial procedure was preferable for complex factual questions.[29] Later judicial[30] and extra-judicial[31] statements appeared to confirm the reluctance to allow discovery and cross-examination within s.31, because of the delays and extra costs generated by such concessions to the individual.

This was somewhat paradoxical. A principal reason for making the new procedure exclusive was that the reforms removed defects in the previous law, including the inability to cross-examine and seek discovery. This was the justification for confining the individual to s.31, with its protections for the public body. If however the applicant is rarely allowed to use these procedural aids, they may be unable to prove the invalidity alleged. The courts have sometimes allowed a case to proceed outside s.31 because of the complex factual issues involved. It will also be seen that the courts have, more recently, indicated that disclosure should be somewhat more readily available in judicial review cases than hitherto.[32]

The interpretation of the private rights exception has altered since *O'Reilly*. The analysis will therefore consider the approach in the period immediately after *O'Reilly*, and then focus on later case law.

B. Collateral Attack and Private Rights: The Initial Approach

27–007 The difficulty of applying this exception can be exemplified by contrasting three of the leading cases decided in the years shortly after *O'Reilly*.

In *Cocks*,[33] the plaintiff claimed a declaration and damages alleging a breach by the defendant council of its duties under the Housing (Homeless Persons) Act 1977. The House of Lords insisted that the action should be brought via judicial review for the following reason. The existence of a duty to inquire whether the applicant might be made homeless and whether the applicant might be entitled to temporary or permanent housing, were public law questions. The determination of these issues in the applicant's favour was a condition precedent to the

[29] *R. v Inland Revenue Commissioners, Ex p. Rossminster Ltd* [1980] A.C. 952, HL at 1027.

[30] *O'Reilly* [1983] 2 A.C. 237; *R. v Secretary of State for the Home Department, Ex p. Khawaja* [1984] A.C. 74, HL; *Air Canada v Secretary of State for Trade (No.2)* [1983] 2 A.C. 394, HL; *Lonrho Plc v Tebbit* [1992] 4 All E.R. 280, CA (Civ Div); *R. v Inland Revenue Commissioners, Ex p. Taylor* [1989] 1 All E.R. 906, CA (Civ Div); *R. v Secretary of State for the Environment, Ex p. Doncaster BC* [1990] C.O.D. 441; *R. v Secretary of State for the Home Department, Ex p. BH* [1990] C.O.D. 445; *R. v Secretary of State for Education, Ex p. J* [1993] C.O.D. 146; *R. v Secretary of State for Transport, Ex p. APH Road Safety Ltd* [1993] C.O.D. 150 QBD; *R. v Secretary of State for Health, Ex p. Hackney LBC* [1994] C.O.D. 432 QBD; *R. v Arts Council of England, Ex p. Women's Playhouse Trust* [1998] C.O.D. 175 QBD.

[31] Sir H. Woolf, "Public Law–Private Law: Why the Divide? A Personal View" [1986] P.L. 220, 229, 231.

[32] *Tweed v Parades Commission for Northern Ireland* [2007] 1 A.C. 650, HL.

[33] *Cocks v Thanet DC* [1983] 2 A.C. 286, HL.

establishment of a private law right. Such issues must therefore be brought within the Senior Courts Act s.31, because at that stage the applicant did not yet have private law rights allowing him to proceed outside s.31 by way of an ordinary action.

The decision in *Cocks* can be contrasted with *Davy*.[34] The plaintiff was the owner of premises making pre-cast concrete. He made an agreement with the council in 1979 that he would not oppose an enforcement notice terminating his right to use the premises, provided that the council did not enforce this notice for three years. In 1982 the plaintiff brought a damages action claiming that he had been negligently advised of his rights under the planning legislation, and that the 1979 agreement was ultra vires and void. The council argued that the action should be brought under s.31, since any defence that Davy had to the enforcement notice was a right to which he was entitled to protection under public law. The House of Lords rejected this argument. Lord Fraser regarded the negligence claim as "simply" an ordinary tort action, which did not raise any matter of public law as a "live issue".[35] The *Cocks* case was distinguished.[36] In that case the plaintiff had to impugn the defendant's decision that he was intentionally homeless, the "public law" issue, as a condition precedent to the establishment of a private law right. In *Davy* the plaintiff's private right did not depend on the enforcement notice. The plaintiff was not challenging the enforcement order but rather claiming damages because he had lost his chance to impugn it. The council would not, therefore, be kept "in suspense" as to the validity of their enforcement notice.[37]

Winder[38] exemplified a further dimension to the private rights exception. The plaintiff local authority had raised the rent of Winder's flat. Winder refused to pay the increase, paying only such an amount as he considered reasonable. The local authority sued for arrears of rent and possession of the flat. Winder argued in defence that the council had acted ultra vires by charging excessive rents. The authority contended that the legality of the rent could only be tested via judicial review under s.31. The House of Lords found for Winder. *O'Reilly* and *Cocks* were distinguished for two reasons. First, the plaintiffs therein did not have private rights, whereas Winder complained of the infringement of a contractual right in private law. Second, the individual had initiated the action in the earlier cases, whereas Winder was the defendant who did not select the procedure to be adopted.

C. Collateral Attack and Private Rights: Broadening the Exception

The preceding cases revealed the difficulty of deciding whether a particular interest should be characterised as a private right. The precise effect of this characterisation was also unclear. It was not certain whether the presence of a private right meant that the principle in *O'Reilly* should no longer be applicable at **27–008**

[34] *Davy v Spelthorne BC* [1984] A.C. 262, HL.
[35] *Davy* [1984] A.C. 262 at 273.
[36] *Davy* [1984] A.C. 262 at 273–274.
[37] *Davy* [1984] A.C. 262 at 274.
[38] *Wandsworth LBC v Winder* [1985] A.C. 461, HL.

all, or whether the existence of such a right was merely an important factor which could lead the court to make a discretionary exception to the *O'Reilly* principle.

This ambiguity was brought to the fore in *Roy*.[39] The applicant was a doctor who was paid certain sums under National Health Service (NHS) regulations for treating patients. The regulations provided that the doctor would only be paid the full basic rate if he devoted a substantial part of his time to treating patients on the NHS, as opposed to private practice. The Kensington Committee decided that the applicant was not complying with this condition and therefore reduced his allowance by 20 per cent. The applicant claimed that this was a breach of contract. The Committee argued that the action should have been brought under s.31 by way of judicial review. The application would then have failed since it would have been outside the time limit. The House of Lords found for the applicant, with judgments given by Lord Bridge and Lord Lowry.

27–009 Lord Bridge[40] acknowledged that *O'Reilly* had been subject to much academic criticism but was not persuaded that it should be overruled, although it should be kept within proper bounds. If the case turned exclusively on a purely public law right, then the only remedy was by way of judicial review under s.31. If, however, the case involved assertion of a private law right, the fact that the existence of the private law right might incidentally involve the examination of a public law issue did not prevent the applicant proceeding by way of an ordinary action outside s.31. The present case came within the latter category.

Lord Lowry gave the other judgment and proffered two possible interpretations of the exception in *O'Reilly*.[41] The "broad approach" was that the "rule in *O'Reilly v Mackman*" did not generally apply against bringing actions to vindicate private rights where the action involved a challenge to a public law act or decision, but that it merely required the aggrieved person to proceed by judicial review only when private rights were not at stake. The "narrow approach" assumed that the rule applied generally to all proceedings in which public law acts or decisions were challenged, subject to some exceptions when private law rights were involved. There was no need in *O'Reilly v Mackman* to choose between these approaches. Lord Lowry preferred the broad approach but did not decide the matter in the instant case since it had not been argued before the court. His Lordship found for the applicant for the following reasons. The applicant had a bundle of rights derived from statute, even if they were not contract rights. When individual rights were claimed there should be no need for leave or a special time limit and the relief should not be discretionary. Although the applicant sought to enforce performance of a public duty under the relevant National Health Service regulations, his private rights dominated the action. The facts were in dispute and were better resolved in an ordinary action.

---

[39] *Roy v Kensington and Chelsea and Westminster Family Practitioner Committee* [1992] 1 A.C. 624, HL.

[40] *Roy* [1992] 1 A.C. 624 at 628–630.

[41] *Roy* [1992] 1 A.C. 624 at 653.

Lord Lowry's preference for the broad view of the exception, the effect of which is to render the rule in *O'Reilly* inapplicable when cases involve private rights, has been generally adopted in later cases.[42]

In *Boddington*[43] the House of Lords held that it was open to a defendant in criminal proceedings to challenge a byelaw, or an administrative decision made there under, where the prosecution was premised on its validity, unless there was a clear parliamentary intent to the contrary. The challenge to the measure did not have to be brought by way of judicial review. The inability to plead the invalidity of a byelaw in the course of a criminal prosecution was, said Lord Steyn, contrary to principle and precedent.[44] **27–010**

His Lordship felt that it was wrong in principle for a magistrate to be able to convict a person who would be precluded from relying on a defence he might have. That was unacceptable in a democracy based on the rule of law. This general argument of principle was reinforced by the case law on procedural exclusivity. Lord Steyn held that later case law[45] had made it clear that procedural exclusivity would only be insisted upon where the sole object of the action was to challenge a public law act or decision. It did not apply in a civil case when an individual sought to establish private law rights, which could not be determined without an examination of the validity of the public law decision. Nor did it apply where a defendant in a civil case sought to defend themselves by questioning the validity of the public law decision. Nor equally did it apply in a criminal case where the liberty of the subject was at stake.[46]

Judicial review was felt by Lord Steyn to be an inadequate safeguard for the individual. The defendant might be out of time before becoming aware of the existence of the byelaw. He might not have the resources for such a challenge. Leave might be refused, or a remedy denied pursuant to the court's discretionary power. The possibility of judicial review could not therefore be said to compensate the individual "for the loss of *the right to* defend himself"[47] in the criminal proceedings.

It was accepted in *Boddington*[48] that there could be cases where a challenge to the validity of an order other than by way of judicial review could be defeated by special statutory provisions, as exemplified by *Wicks*.[49] In *Wicks* the House of Lords adopted a functional approach. Whether a defendant who was charged with failing to comply with an order made under statutory powers was entitled by way of defence in criminal proceedings before the court to challenge the lawfulness of the order depended on the construction of the statute under which the prosecution

---

42 *Lonrho Plc v Tebbit* [1991] 4 All E.R. 973 Ch D; [1992] 4 All E.R 280; *Trustees of the Dennis Rye Pension Fund v Sheffield CC* [1998] 1 W.L.R. 840, CA (Civ Div); *British Steel Plc v Customs and Excise Commissioners* [1997] 2 All E.R. 366, CA (Civ Div); *Bunney v Burns Anderson Plc* [2007] EWHC 1240 (Ch).

43 *Boddington v British Transport Police* [1999] 2 A.C. 143, HL.

44 *Boddington* [1999] 2 A.C. 143 at 172.

45 Lord Steyn referred to *Roy* [1992] 1 A.C. 624, *Winder* [1985] A.C. 461, *Chief Adjudication Officer v Foster* [1993] A.C. 754, HL and *Mercury Communications Ltd v Director General of Telecommunications* [1996] 1 W.L.R. 48, HL.

46 *Boddington* [1999] 2 A.C. 143 at 172.

47 *Boddington* [1999] 2 A.C. 143 at 173. Italics in the original.

48 *Boddington* [1999] 2 A.C. 143 at 173.

49 *R. v Wicks* [1998] A.C. 92, HL.

had been brought, and also upon whether the relevant statute indicated which forum was appropriate for a challenge to the validity of the order.[50] The premise behind *Boddington* is nonetheless that a defendant should normally be able to raise the invalidity of the byelaw, or an administrative decision based on it, by way of defence in a criminal case. It will be for the prosecution to convince the court that the exception based on *Wicks* is applicable in the instant case.

D. Collateral Attack: Beyond Private Rights

27–011 The exceptions to *O'Reilly* may go beyond those in the preceding case law.[51] This seems to be so from a reading of *Mercury*.[52] In 1986 two companies, Mercury (M) and British Telecommunications (BT), made an agreement for the provision of services pursuant to condition 13 of BT's licence. The agreement provided for a reference to the Director General of Telecommunications (DGT) where there was a dispute between M and BT. The parties referred a matter to the DGT concerning pricing for the conveyance of calls. The DGT made his determination and M challenged this, arguing that the DGT had misinterpreted the costs to be taken into account when resolving the pricing issue. M's challenge was by way of originating summons for a declaration. The DGT and BT argued that the case should have been brought by way of Ord.53. Lord Slynn gave the judgment for a unanimous House of Lords in favour of M.

His Lordship acknowledged the rationale for the presumptive exclusivity of judicial review given in *O'Reilly*, but noted also that this exclusivity was only ever presumptive rather than conclusive. The criterion that should be used to decide whether a case could be brought outside Ord.53 was whether "the proceedings constitute an abuse of the process of the court".[53]

The abuse of process test does not on its face require the existence of any private right as a condition precedent for an applicant to be able to proceed outside Ord.53. This is further confirmed by the way in which the test was applied in *Mercury*. In allowing M to bring its case by way of originating summons, Lord Slynn did not mention the rights-based criterion derived from *Roy*. Nor did he frame his judgment that M should be allowed to bring its case by way of originating summons on the ground that its private rights were at stake. It would have been difficult to find private rights that M had as against the DGT. Lord Slynn held that there was no abuse of process, because the essence of the

---

[50] There could, on the one hand, be cases where the statute required the prosecution to prove that the contested act was not open to challenge on any ground available in public law, or where it might be a defence to show that it was open to challenge in that way. In such cases it would be for the court before which the prosecution was brought to rule on the validity of the act. There could, on the other hand, be cases where the statute on its true construction merely required that the act which had been done under statutory authority appeared to be formally valid and had not been quashed by judicial review. In this latter type of case, only the formal validity of the act was of relevance to an issue before the court in a prosecution.

[51] P. Craig, "Proceeding Outside Order 53: A Modified Test?" (1996) 112 L.Q.R. 531.

[52] *Mercury* [1996] 1 W.L.R. 48.

[53] *Mercury* [1996] 1 W.L.R. 48 at 57; *R. (Valentines Homes & Construction Ltd) v Revenue and Customs Commissioners* [2010] EWCA Civ 345.

action was a contractual dispute between M and BT, and because the relevant issues could be better determined by the Commercial Court, rather than via Ord.53.

It would seem that if an applicant has private rights then the case will be allowed to proceed outside Ord.53, even if it does involve a public law matter, and this will be deemed not to be an abuse of process. However, even where there are no such rights it will be open to an applicant to convince the court that recourse to an ordinary action does not constitute an abuse of process. **27–012**

The impact of this reasoning on *O'Reilly* is significant. In *O'Reilly* the assumption was that it would be an abuse of process for an applicant to proceed outside Ord.53, precisely because this would deprive the public body of the protections enshrined in the judicial review procedure. This starting assumption was qualified by the exceptions concerning consent and private rights. In *Mercury* the same concept, abuse of process, has a very different meaning. Here the assumption is that an applicant should be allowed to bring a case outside Ord.53, unless this constitutes an abuse of process. The fact that the public body will be deprived of the protections contained in Ord.53 does not however constitute such an abuse. Provided that the applicant can convince the court that there are good reasons for allowing the claim to be brought by way of ordinary action, no such abuse will be found.

E. The Impact of the Human Rights Act 1998

The Human Rights Act 1998 (HRA) has been considered earlier.[54] The present discussion is concerned with its impact on the cases that may be brought outside s.31 by way of ordinary action. It is clear from s.7 of the HRA that a person who claims that a public authority has acted unlawfully in breach of s.6(1) may bring proceedings against the authority in the appropriate court or tribunal as determined in accordance with rules to be made on the matter. An application for judicial review is one way in which such proceedings may be brought, as is apparent from s.7(3). **27–013**

Claimants may, however, have an incentive to proceed other than by way of judicial review where there is a danger that they will otherwise be out of time. Section 7(5) specifies a basic time limit of one year for violations of s.6 in cases where the illegality is used offensively by the individual, but qualifies this by providing that it is subject to any rule imposing a stricter time limit in relation to the procedure actually used. This means that if an application for judicial review is brought for a breach of s.6 of the HRA, then the time limit for judicial review actions will operate. This limit will be considered in detail later,[55] although suffice it to say for the present that the basic rule is three months. We have already seen that a major reason why claimants sought to proceed outside s.31 is that they would otherwise be time barred, and this is likely to continue to be a significant consideration in cases brought under the HRA.

[54] See Ch.20.

[55] See paras 27–046 to 27–050.

The fact that s.6 actions may be brought other than by way of judicial review is, in formal legal terms, unproblematic. Section 7 expressly contemplates that actions can be brought other than by way of judicial review. Furthermore, the jurisprudence considered earllier concerning the circumstances in which cases can proceed outside s.31 of the Senior Courts Act 1981 has made it clear that this is possible where private rights are at stake. If claims that Convention rights have been violated in breach of s.6 are treated in this way, then proceedings for breach of the HRA will simply be another exception to procedural exclusivity. The scope of this qualification to procedural exclusivity may, however, be greater than might initially be thought.

There will be many public law cases where the claim will be for breach of the HRA. Such claims will not, however, exist in isolation. They may arise as one of a number of allegations of ultra vires conduct. A colourable allegation that there has been a breach of s.6 may serve to take a case outside s.31 of the Senior Courts Act, even if it ultimately proves to be unfounded. The other allegations may normally have been brought within the judicial review procedure because they were pure public law claims. Where the HRA claim fails it is, however, unlikely that the court will insist that the case revert to the judicial review procedure, more particularly if the applicant would be out of time. We may well therefore see more pure public law claims being litigated by way of ordinary action, where the initial rationale for proceeding in this manner was an allegation of a breach of s.6 that proved unfounded.

F. The Impact of the CPR

27–014 The Civil Procedure Rules (CPR), introduced as a result of the Woolf reforms, will have a marked impact on the relationship between the public law procedures and the ordinary procedures for civil action. This is because a central theme of the CPR is to accord the court more control over ordinary civil actions than previously existed.

The implications for procedural exclusivity and the exceptions thereto are apparent from *Clark*.[56] The claimant brought a contract action against a university in relation to the classification of her degree. The university argued that the claim should have been brought by judicial review. It contended that the ordinary contract action was an abuse of process, because it was brought well beyond the three-month time limit for judicial review. Lord Woolf MR held that exclusivity should be seen in the light of the new CPR. This was because the CPR contained safeguards for public bodies even where there was an ordinary civil action. The safeguards related to the stopping of the action and the time in which it could be brought.

If proceedings involving public law issues were begun by ordinary action under CPR Pts 7 or 8, they would be subject to CPR Pt 24. This enabled the court

[56] *Clark v University of Lincolnshire and Humberside* [2000] 1 W.L.R. 1988, CA (Civ Div).

to give summary judgment where it believed that the applicant had no real prospect of success. This restricted the inconvenience to public bodies by the pursuit of hopeless claims.[57]

The normal time limit for a civil action is six years. Lord Woolf acknowledged that it would in the past not have been appropriate to regard delay within the six-year period as a reason for characterising the action as abusive. The position was, said Lord Woolf, different under the CPR. Delay in commencing proceedings under the CPR could be a factor in deciding whether the proceedings were abusive. This was especially so where the action could have been brought by judicial review.[58]

G. Summary

It might be helpful to summarise the law and to state when an individual will be allowed to proceed by an ordinary action outside s.31. **27–015**

i. The courts will only insist on a case being brought via the judicial review procedure if the primary aim is to challenge a public law act or decision.[59]
ii. A civil case can be brought outside s.31 where the individual seeks to establish private rights, even if this requires an examination of the validity of the public law decision.
iii. A defendant in a civil case can challenge a public law decision in the course of defending the private law action. It is not absolutely certain whether it is enough to be the defendant, or whether the defendant must also be able to assert that their rights are being infringed. Some cases have emphasised the first of these factors, without inquiring too closely whether the individual had private rights which were affected, or what the precise nature of these rights were.[60] Other cases suggested that an individual should have some private right in order to be able to raise the invalidity of a public body's action by way of defence in an ordinary action outside s.31.[61] However, the formulation by Lord Steyn in *Boddington* indicated that being a defendant was sufficient in itself, and this approach has been followed in later cases.[62]
iv A defendant in a criminal case will normally be able to raise the invalidity of the subordinate legislation or order on which the prosecution is based by way of defence to the criminal charge, unless there is a clear indication from the relevant statute that such a challenge can only be made via judicial review.

---

57 *Clark* [2000] 1 W.L.R. 1988 at [27]–[28].
58 *Clark* [2000] 1 W.L.R. 1988 at [35]–[36].
59 *Jones v Powys Local Health Board* [2008] EWHC 2562 (Admin); *Trim v North Dorset DC* [2011] 1 W.L.R. 1901, CA (Civ Div); *R. (Townsend) v Secretary of State for Works and Pensions* [2011] EWHC 3434 (Admin) are examples where the courts insisted that the public law procedure should be used.
60 *West Glamorgan CC v Rafferty* [1987] 1 W.L.R. 457, CA (Civ Div); *R. v Crown Court at Reading, Ex p. Hutchinson* [1987] 3 W.L.R. 1062 QBD.
61 *Waverley BC v Hilden* [1988] 1 W.L.R. 246 Ch D.; *Avon CC v Buscott* [1988] 2 W.L.R. 788 Ch D.
62 *Boddington* [1999] 2 A.C. 143 at 172–173; *Bunney v Burns Anderson Plc* [2007] EWHC 1240 (Ch); *R. (WL (Congo)) v Secretary of State for the Home Department* [2011] 2 W.L.R. 671 SC at [70].

v. A person may be able to proceed outside s.31 even where no private rights are present, provided that the court decides that to do so is not an abuse of process.

vi. In cases of doubt the advice of Lord Woolf[63] was that the action should be brought by way of judicial review. If the matter was raised in an ordinary action and there was an application to strike out the case on the ground that it should have been brought by way of judicial review, it was open to the court to consider whether leave would have been granted under the s.31 procedure. If the answer was in the affirmative, then this was a good indication that the ordinary action should not be struck out.

vii. The degree of difference between bringing an ordinary civil action and a claim for judicial review has however diminished under the CPR, as interpreted in *Clark*.[64] The court read the CPR to provide some protection for public bodies even in ordinary civil actions, thereby diminishing to some extent the incentive to proceed outside the judicial review procedure.

H. Assessment

27–016 The approach in *Roy*, *Boddington*, *Mercury* and other cases has limited the force of *O'Reilly*.[65] The principle of presumptive exclusivity in *O'Reilly* was based on the assumption that public bodies warranted the protections of narrow time limits and leave, or permission as it is now known, and that these protections should not be circumvented by allowing applicants to proceed through a different action. The reasoning in later cases indirectly undermined this assumption in two ways, one practical, the other conceptual.

It undermined that principle in practical terms simply because there were fewer cases to which the protections afforded to the public body would apply. Those protections would not apply in cases concerning private rights, or in the other instances set out above. The term "private right" is, moreover, a malleable one. This is exemplified by *Roy*, in which the House of Lords gave a broad construction to "private rights", without too nice an inquiry as to the nature of the rights possessed by the applicant. The very determination of whether a right should be characterised as a private, as opposed to a public right, and whether it can be viewed as distinctive from a "public law" issue which the case raises, is not resolvable by some mechanical formula.[66]

The conceptual foundation of *O'Reilly* was also weakened by later decisions. The premise behind the post-*O'Reilly* jurisprudence was that protections for the public body, in terms of time limits and leave, were overridden when an individual asserted private rights against a public body, and that this was so even if the case involved public law issues. It is clear that even where a case concerns

[63] *Dennis Rye Pension Fund* [1998] 1 W.L.R. 840.

[64] *Clark* [2000] 1 W.L.R. 1988.

[65] See also J. Alder, "Hunting the Chimera—The End of *O'Reilly v Mackman*" [1993] 13 L.S. 183.

[66] See, e.g. (a) the criticism of the *Winder* case by the Rt Hon Sir H. Woolf, "Public Law–Private Law: Why the Divide? A Personal View" [1986] P.L. 220, 233–236. Compare J. Beatson, "'Public' and 'Private' in English Administrative Law" (1987) 103 L.Q.R. 34, 59–61; (b) the reasoning in *Gillick v West Norfolk and Wisbech Area Health Authority* [1986] A.C. 112, HL at 163, 177–178.

private rights it would be mistaken to believe that it is principally about private rights as opposed to public law. This can be easily demonstrated. A public body makes a demolition order on the claimant's property which is said to be ultra vires.[67] The claimant brings an action in trespass. The action involves a private right, but the action is not solely "about" private rights. Whether the claimant wins in the trespass action will be dependent on the validity of the demolition order. This will be the issue in the case, and it is manifestly a public law matter, the resolution of which depends on construction of the legislation. The consequence of this finding will determine whether the claimant can succeed in the tort claim, and in that sense vindicate their private rights, but this does not mean that the case is principally about private rights.[68]

The reality is that the courts were, and still are, ambivalent about the principle in *O'Reilly*. They wished to preserve the protections in s.31, in terms of short time limits and permission. There is also a recurring theme in the case law that the hurdles created by *O'Reilly* were merely technical and legalistic, using those terms in a pejorative sense. Judges referred to the complexity of the law in this area and compared it to the forms of action in the 19th century,[69] or to the difficulties in civil law systems based on the public/private divide.[70] The corollary was that it really did not matter too much whether individuals were allowed to proceed outside s.31. **27–017**

The *Clark* decision[71] is important in this respect. The premise underlying the case was that the differences between ordinary actions and those for judicial review should be minimised. It recognised that an action involving private rights may well involve public law issues. The civil procedure rules on ordinary civil actions were interpreted to allow protection for public bodies, so as to stop hopeless actions and modify the time in which they must be brought. *Clark* therefore accepted that cases involving private rights could proceed by ordinary action, as opposed to judicial review, but sought to diminish the incentives for doing so. These incentives, although diminished, nonetheless still exist. In a judicial review action the claimant must still seek permission to proceed, and the time limit is three months. In an ordinary action, even as interpreted by *Clark*, it will be for the defendant to establish that the case should be stopped because it has no prospect of success. It will also be for the defendant to convince the court that bringing the action within, for example, 18 months, constituted an abuse of process, even though it was well within the limitation period.

---

67 *Cooper v Wandsworth Board of Works* (1863) 14 C.B. (N.S.) 180.

68 This point applies equally to *Roy* [1992] 1 A.C. 624. The case involved private rights, arising from Roy's relationship with the Family Practitioner Committee and the fact that he was seeking a contract-type remedy. However, the case also raised general public law matters. The committee had statutory powers to allocate fees derived from public funds. Whether Roy won on the substance of the case turned on the construction of the statutory norms, in order to determine what it meant to say that a doctor must devote a substantial amount of his time to NHS work.

69 *Doyle v Northumbria Probation Committee* [1991] 4 All E.R. 294 at 300.

70 *Mercury* [1996] 1 W.L.R. 48.

71 *Clark* [2000] 1 W.L.R. 1988.

4. PUBLIC LAW CASES: "GETTING INTO" THE JUDICIAL REVIEW PROCEDURE

A. The Reasons for Wishing to Use the Section 31 Procedure

27–018 The preceding discussion has concentrated upon cases where individuals wish to proceed outside s.31. The traffic has not, however, been purely "one way". There have been many cases where individuals have sought to argue their way into s.31, what one judge[72] has termed the "obverse" of the situation in *O'Reilly*. There are three principal reasons why litigants have sought to do so.

The first is that the applicant may have no other cause of action. In the *Datafin* case, the applicants could not frame a convincing action in contract or tort against the Take-Overs Panel, and this predisposed the court in their favour.[73] Some employment cases are also explicable on this ground. Thus, in *Benwell*, a prison officer was dismissible at pleasure. He could not use the employment protection legislation, and this inclined the court to admit him into s.31.[74]

A second reason why applicants use the public law procedures is because they believe that the remedy will be more effective. This explains some of the employment cases.[75] An employee will be entitled to hearing rights in accord with the law on unfair dismissal. Breach of these rights will give the employee a damages action, compensation for unfair dismissal and a possible order for reinstatement. The public law remedy may nonetheless be preferred because it will afford the applicant more chance of getting the job back. Certiorari will quash the dismissal and leave the applicant in "possession" of the job. This reflects the historical status of employment in a public office: the office was regarded as akin to a property right which the applicant was entitled to have restored if improperly deprived of it. The question of whether employees should have job security rights is a complex one, and the rationale for differential treatment between public and private employment may well be historically outdated. The courts have been wary of expanding indirect job security rights by allowing potentially large categories of employees into s.31. Cases are likely therefore to turn on the court's perception of whether a type of individual should have such security.

The third reason why applicants are keen to use the application for judicial review is because the scope of the obligations imposed on the defendant exceeds those that would be imposed in a private law cause of action. Thus, in the *Aga Khan* case[76] the applicant sought judicial review to determine the legality of the club's actions against the substantive and procedural norms used to test the validity of a public body's behaviour.

---

[72] *R. v East Berkshire Health Authority, Ex p. Walsh* [1985] Q.B. 152, CA (Civ Div).

[73] *R. v Panel on Take-Overs and Mergers, Ex p. Datafin Plc* [1987] Q.B. 815, CA (Civ Div).

[74] *R. v Secretary of State for the Home Department, Ex p. Benwell* [1985] Q.B. 554 QBD at 571, 572; *R. v Bishop of Stafford, Ex p. Owen* [2001] A.C.D. 14, CA (Civ Div).

[75] See, e.g. *Walsh* [1985] Q.B. 152.

[76] *R. v Disciplinary Committee of the Jockey Club, Ex p. Aga Khan* [1993] 1 W.L.R. 909, CA (Civ Div).

B. Public Law: Possible Tests

The meaning of public law for the purposes of s.31 is crucial, since only public law cases are subject to the presumptive exclusivity of the *O'Reilly* decision. Only cases about public law are allowed into s.31. There is however no simple test to determine the meaning of public law for these purposes. Three possibilities can be considered.[77] 27–019

i. Source of the power

The most obvious test is to consider the source of the authority's power: if that power is derived from statute then the body is presumptively public. There are two difficulties with this test. First, if applied literally it would bring within public law the activities of any organisation regulated by statute, even if it generally operated within the private commercial sphere. The second problem is a converse of the first. A body may owe the source of its authority to statute. However, not all of its operations should be regarded as raising public law issues. Local authorities and other public bodies frequently operate in an ordinary commercial capacity. 27–020

ii. Scope of the prerogative remedies

If we are to have a separate set of remedies for public law, then to regard the scope of the prerogative orders as indicative of the scope of public law might be reasonable, particularly given the centrality accorded to such orders within s.31. The problem with this criterion is that there has been a tendency to see the ambit of such orders as fixed. There is little justification for this. Historically the orders were used flexibly to provide a remedy against institutions not covered by existing forms of redress.[78] There are indications that they could be used to cover any duty of a public nature, whether it was derived from statute, custom, prerogative or contract, a view echoed by Lord Diplock.[79] The tendency to regard their boundaries as immutable is a more recent phenomenon. There is no reason why a duty may not be of a public law nature, whatever its derivation. 27–021

To focus on the scope of the prerogative orders as the criterion for the meaning of public law however leads to the following conundrum. If their scope is interpreted flexibly in the above manner, they cease to furnish a criterion that is distinguishable from the third test to below. The nature of a "public" as opposed

---

[77] J. Beatson, "'Public' and 'Private' in English Administrative Law" (1987) 103 L.Q.R. 34; P. Cane, "Public Law and Private Law: A Study of the Analysis of and Use of a Legal Concept", in J. Eekelaar and J. Bell (eds), *Oxford Essays in Jurisprudence*, 3rd Series (Oxford: Oxford University Press, 1987), Ch.3; J. Allison, *A Continental Distinction in the Common Law: A Historical and Comparative Perspective on English Public Law* (Oxford: Oxford University Press, 1996); N. Bamforth, "The Public Law–Private Law Distinction: A Comparative and Philosophical Approach", in P. Leyland and T. Woods (eds), *Administrative Law Facing the Future: Old Constraints and New Horizons* (Oxford: Blackstone, 1997), Ch.6; C. Campbell, "The Nature of Power as Public in English Judicial Review" [2009] C.L.J. 90.

[78] Ch.26; *Groenvelt v Burwell* (1700) 1 Ld. Raym. 454.

[79] *O'Reilly* [1983] 2 A.C. 237 at 279.

to a "private" duty still has to be determined, and if the ambit of the prerogative orders simply covers any "public law" obligation, we are no further forward in deciding whether such an obligation exists in a particular case.[80] If, however, a narrow definition of the prerogative orders is adopted so that they apply only to bodies created by statute or pursuant to the prerogative, then we have a formalistic criterion.[81]

iii. "Nature" of the power

27–022 The difficulties of a formalistic test have inclined the courts towards a more open-textured criterion which requires them to consider the nature of the power. For example, Lloyd LJ in *Datafin*[82] stated that if the source of the power was statutory then the body would be subject to judicial review. However, this would not be the case if the source of power were contractual, but that between these "extremes" it was necessary to consider the nature of the power. Thus, if the body was exercising public law functions, or such functions had public law consequences, then s.31 would be applicable. This formulation appears to beg the question, as do statements that a public duty will be subject to public law. Lord Donaldson MR, by way of contrast, seemed only to be concerned with the source of a body's power in order to exclude institutions whose power was based upon contract or consent.[83] Any other body could be subject to review if there was a sufficiently public element. How far power that is based upon contract is subject to judicial review will be considered more fully below.

The uncertainty of this third test is the price to be paid for moving away from formalistic tests based upon the source of power or on the narrow definition of the prerogative. Statements that a body must have a sufficiently "public element" or must be exercising a public duty, function as conclusory labels. In *Datafin* the court was influenced by a number of such factors including: the undoubted power wielded by the Panel, the statutory cognisance given to its existence, the penalties, direct and indirect, which could follow from non-compliance with its rules, and the absence of any other redress available to the applicants.

C. Boundaries of Public Law

27–023 Traditional public bodies are subject to the application for judicial review. We are concerned here with what other bodies can be subject to the public law procedure.

i. Public bodies and executive agencies

27–024 The applicability of public law principles to executive agencies has been considered earlier.[84] It is clear in principle that such agencies must be subject to

[80] *Walsh* [1985] Q.B. 152 at 162.
[81] H.W.R. Wade, "Procedure and Prerogative in Public Law" (1985) 101 L.Q.R. 180.
[82] *Datafin* [1987] Q.B. 815 at 846–869.
[83] *Datafin* [1987] Q.B. 815 at 838–839.
[84] See Ch.4.

the s.31 procedure, given that they are not formally separate from their sponsoring department, and also because most of these agencies are engaged in public service delivery.

ii. Public authorities and contracting-out

Contracting-out has been used increasingly by government as a method of service delivery.[85] A judicial review action may be maintained against the public body that has contracted-out the power. This may however be of limited utility, since there may be no viable claim against the public body. Whether the private body to which power has been contracted-out can be subject to judicial review is therefore important. **27–025**

This can be exemplified by *Servite Houses*.[86] The applicants were elderly residents at a home run by Servite Houses, a charitable housing association. Wandsworth Council had, pursuant to their statutory duties, assessed them as being in need of residential accommodation.[87] The council was allowed to contract-out the provision of such accommodation.[88] Servite decided to close the home in which the applicants lived. They objected, claiming that they had been promised a home for life.[89] The court therefore had to decide whether the private service provider was amenable to judicial review. This was especially important, given that there was no obvious private law redress.[90] Moses J recognised the significance of the issue, as to how the courts should respond to the increasing contractualisation of government,[91] but held that Servite was not amenable to judicial review.

Moses J considered whether Servite could be amenable to review because there was a *statutory underpinning* to its function. There must, he said, be sufficient statutory penetration, which went beyond the statutory regulation of the manner in which the service was provided. This depended on whether the relevant legislation could be said to enmesh Servite's provision of residential accommodation into a statutory system of community care. Moses J denied that this was so, and held that the effect of the legislation was to create a mixed economy provision for community care services, some being provided in house, and others through contracting-out. It followed that the relationship between Servite and the applicants was to be governed solely by private law.[92] Moses J held moreover that the legislation empowering the contracting-out could not constitute the statutory underpinning to enable Servite's functions to be regarded as public functions. The applicants could not successfully contend that "because

---

[85] See Ch.5.

[86] *R. v Servite Houses and Wandsworth LBC, Ex p. Goldsmith and Chatting* (2000) 2 L.G.L.R. 997 QBD.

[87] National Health Service and Community Care Act 1990 s.47.

[88] National Assistance Act 1948 s.26.

[89] *R. v North and East Devon Health Authority, Ex p. Coughlan* [2001] Q.B. 213, CA (Civ Div).

[90] Servite had lawfully terminated its contract with Wandsworth, the applicants had no contract with Servite, and Wandsworth had discharged its obligation by making the initial arrangements with Servite. Wandsworth could not compel Servite to keep the house open, although the local authority would be under an obligation to find alternative accommodation for the applicants.

[91] *Servite Houses* (2000) 2 L.G.L.R. 997 at 1010, 1025.

[92] *Servite Houses* (2000) 2 L.G.L.R. 997 at 1018.

legislation permits a public authority to enter into arrangements with a private body, the functions of that body are, by dint of that legislation, to be regarded as public functions".[93]

27–026 Moses J considered also *whether the functions performed by Servite could be regarded as public in the absence of any statutory underpinning*. Moses J found "enormous attraction" in this approach[94] but felt unable in the light of existing precedent to adopt it. He held that *Datafin* and *Aga Khan* stood for the proposition that the courts cannot, in the absence of sufficient statutory penetration, impose public standards upon a body the source of whose power is contractual. Servite's powers were said to derive from a purely commercial relationship.

The conclusion that Servite was not amenable to review was cited approvingly by the House of Lords,[95] but it was nonetheless regrettable.[96] There is nothing in the logic of contracting-out that dictates whether the service provider should be subject to private law or public law obligations. The conclusion that the case could not be resolved via statutory underpinning was premised on the irrelevance of the enabling legislation. This conclusion is unwarranted. The concept of statutory underpinning was developed in cases where there was no contracting-out. It served to identify when bodies that were not public in the strict sense of the term, should nonetheless be regarded as susceptible to judicial review. The fact that such a body was recognised directly or indirectly in legislation was relevant in determining the ambit of judicial review. It is central to this reasoning that the legislation is vital in deciding whether the body is amenable to review.

Consider then the application of this idea to situations where there is contracting-out. There is a public function, the provision of care facilities for certain people. The legislation expressly provides that the function can be undertaken in house or contracted-out. This is in reality a stronger instance of statutory underpinning than in a *Datafin*-type case. In the case of contracting-out there is legislation that explicitly and directly, not implicitly and indirectly, tells us that a private party can perform the public function cast on the local authority. However, whereas in the *Datafin*-type of case it is regarded as axiomatic that the legislation is central to deciding whether the body is amenable to review, in the case of contracting-out we are told that it cannot be taken into account.

iii. Public authorities and contracting power: the need for a "public law element"

27–027 If a public body acts pursuant to statutory or prerogative powers then its decisions will be subject to judicial review. We now consider whether a public body that

---

[93] *Servite Houses* (2000) 2 L.G.L.R. 997 at 1019.

[94] *Servite Houses* (2000) 2 L.G.L.R. 997 at 1020; M. Hunt, "Constitutionalism and the Contractualisation of Government", in M. Taggart (ed.), *The Province of Administrative Law* (Oxford: Hart Publishing, 1997), Ch.2; Lord Steyn, "The Constitutionalisation of Public Law" (Constitution Unit, 1999).

[95] *YL v Birmingham CC* [2008] 1 A.C. 95, HL at [120].

[96] P. Craig, "Contracting-out, the Human Rights Act and the Scope of Judicial Review" (2002) 118 L.Q.R. 551.

exercises a contractual power is also subject to judicial review.[97] The traditional tendency was to see contracts, even those made by public bodies, as essentially private matters. The courts have now moved away from this stance, although their attitude towards such contracts is still somewhat ambivalent. The preponderant approach has been to regard contracts made by public authorities as subject to judicial review if there is a sufficiently "public law element" to the case. This phrase can, however, be subject to different interpretations.

In *Hook*[98] the cancellation of a trader's licence was susceptible to review because the council's powers affected a pre-existing common law right to trade in the market. The courts also held that a public body's powers as landlord are subject to review.[99] There is, moreover, authority that procurement decisions are capable of being judicially reviewed. Thus in *Shell* the court reviewed a local authority decision not to deal with Shell, because other companies in the same corporate group had contacts with South Africa.[100] In *Donn*[101] it was held that a legal aid committee was susceptible to judicial review when deciding to award a contract for the conduct of multi-party litigation. Ognall J held that such a case might be regarded as being within public law either because there was a statutory underpinning, or because, irrespective of any connection with a statute or policy, the process might have a sufficient public law element.

There are, however, cases where the court has been unwilling to find the requisite "public law element".[102] Thus, in *Hibbit and Saunders*,[103] the Lord Chancellor's department invited tenders for court reporting services. The unsuccessful applicant sought judicial review on the ground that it had a legitimate expectation that discussions would not be held with some tenderers to enable them to submit lower bids. The court, while sympathetic, held that the decision was not amenable to review, because it lacked a sufficiently public law element. It was not sufficient to create a public law obligation that the respondent was a public body carrying out governmental functions. If such a body entered a contract with a third party then the contract would define the parties' obligations, unless there was some additional element giving rise to a public law obligation. A public law element might be found either where there was some special aim being pursued by the government through the tendering process, which set it apart from ordinary commercial tenders, or where there was some statutory underpinning, such as where there was a statutory obligation to negotiate the contract in a particular way, and with particular terms. In *Pepper* it was held that the mere fact that a public authority was exercising a statutory power when it sold

---

97 S. Arrowsmith, "Judicial Review and the Contractual Powers of Public Authorities" (1990) 106 L.Q.R. 277; S.H. Bailey, "Judicial Review of Contracting Decisions" [2007] P.L. 444.

98 *R. v Barnsley MBC, Ex p. Hook* [1976] 1 W.L.R. 1052, CA (Civ Div); *R. v Birmingham CC, Ex p. Dredger and Paget* [1993] C.O.D. 340 QBD.

99 *Cannock Chase DC v Kelly* [1978] 1 W.L.R. 1, CA (Civ Div); *Sevenoaks CC v Emmett* (1979) 79 L.G.R. 346.

100 *R. v Lewisham LBC, Ex p. Shell UK Ltd* [1988] 1 All E.R. 938 DC; *R. v Enfield LBC, Ex p. Unwin* [1989] C.O.D. 466 DC.

101 *R. v Legal Aid Board, Ex p. Donn & Co* [1996] 3 All E.R. 1 QBD.

102 *R. (Tucker) v Director General of the National Crime Squad* [2003] I.C.R. 599, CA (Civ Div).

103 *R. v Lord Chancellor's Department, Ex p. Hibbit and Saunders* [1993] C.O.D. 326 DC; *R. v Leeds CC, Ex p. Cobleigh* [1997] C.O.D. 69; *R. (Menai Collect Ltd) v Department for Constitutional Affairs* [2006] EWHC 724 (Admin).

land was not enough by itself to render its decision a public law matter. There had to be an additional public law element to the case.[104]

27–028 It is important to consider whether the idea of a "public law element", which serves to distinguish those contracts that are subject to review, is really needed. It is clear in principle that some contracts made by public authorities ought to be susceptible to judicial review. It may be entirely fortuitous whether the government chooses to advance its policy objectives through a regulatory scheme involving statutory discretionary power, or whether it seeks to attain the same regulatory end through a contractual relationship. The choice of method should not affect the application of public law principles.[105] It is however doubtful whether all contracts entered into by public bodies should be subject to judicial review if this is taken to mean that the substantive and procedural principles of public law should be applied. These principles may not be appropriate when a public body makes an ordinary commercial contract for furniture, a lease or the like. It is not self-evident that a private contractor who makes such a contract with a public body should have greater substantive and procedural rights than any other contracting party.

The case law on what constitutes the requisite "public law element" is nonetheless complex and has been justly criticised.[106] The phrase "public law element", while not capable of exact definition, should as a matter of principle focus on two related issues. First, it should denote whether the task being performed by the public body when it makes the contract really partakes in some manner of "governing" or "public regulation", as opposed to private contracting. The phrase "public law element" should, assuming an affirmative answer to the initial inquiry, then capture the ground of the claimant's challenge. If this relates to abuse of power broadly construed then it should be amenable to judicial review.

This can be exemplified by *Molinaro*.[107] The council leased certain land to the claimant for use as a delicatessen. The claimant started to use it as a café. The council served an enforcement notice under the planning legislation. The claimant sought a licence for the new use from the council as landlord, but the council refused, notwithstanding the fact that the claimant received considerable support from local residents for use of the premises as a café. Elias J held that the council's decision was amenable to judicial review.

The judgment can be seen in terms of the analysis in the preceding paragraph. Thus, Elias J acknowledged that contract cases might involve no issue of public law and judicial review would be inappropriate, even where the contract was made pursuant to a statute. Cases where, for example, the public body sued for

---

104 *R. v Bolsover DC, Ex p. Pepper* (2001) 3 L.G.L.R. 20 DC.

105 See also, T. Daintith, "The Techniques of Government", in J. Jowell and D. Oliver (eds), *The Changing Constitution*, 3rd edn (Oxford: Oxford University Press, 1994), Ch.8; S. Fredman and G. Morris, "The Costs of Exclusivity: Public and Private Re-examined" [1994] P.L. 69, 76–78.

106 S. Arrowsmith, "Judicial Review and the Contractual Powers of Public Authorities" (1990) 106 L.Q.R. 277, 291; S.H. Bailey, "Judicial Review of Contracting Decisions" [2007] P.L. 444, 462–463.

107 *R. (Molinaro) v Kensington and Chelsea RLBC* [2001] EWHC 896 (Admin); *R. (A) v B Council* [2007] EWHC 1529 (Admin); *R. (Birmingham and Solihull Taxi Association) v Birmingham International Airport Ltd* [2009] EWHC 1462 (Admin);*R. (A) v Chief Constable of B* [2012] EWHC 2141 (Admin).

arrears of rent raised no special public law principles and there would be no justification for treating the public body differently from private bodies.[108] However, in this case the Council was not acting simply as a private body when it gave effect to its planning policy through contract, but was rather using the contract to effectuate its planning objectives, and this sufficed to inject a public law element into its decision.[109] If the relevant power was abused it should be amenable to review.[110] Public bodies were given powers to be exercised in the public interest and "the public has an interest in ensuring that the powers are not abused",[111] more especially because contracting power enabled "a public body very significantly to affect the lives of individuals, commercial organisations and their employees".[112]

iv. *Regulatory bodies: the "privatisation of the business of government"*

Hoffmann LJ coined this phrase in the *Aga Khan* case,[113] and it provides an apt description of regulatory bodies which are private, but which have been integrated, directly or indirectly, into a system of statutory regulation. **27–029**

Datafin is the seminal decision in this category.[114] The applicants complained that the Panel on Take-Overs and Mergers (the Panel) had incorrectly applied its takeover rules, and had thereby allowed an advantage to be gained by the applicant's rivals who were bidding for the same company. The Panel was a self-regulating body with no direct statutory, prerogative or common law powers, but it was supported by statutory powers that presupposed its existence, and its decisions could lead to penalties. The Panel opposed judicial review, arguing that it was not amenable to the prerogative orders, which had been restricted to bodies exercising powers derived from the prerogative or statute. The court rejected this view. The "source" of a body's powers was not the only criterion for judging whether a body was amenable to public law. The absence of a statutory or prerogative base for such powers did not exclude s.31 if the "nature" of the power rendered the body suitable for judicial review. The nature of the Panel's powers satisfied this alternative criterion for a number of reasons.

First, the Panel, although self-regulating, did not operate consensually or voluntarily, but rather imposed a collective code on those within its ambit.[115] Second, the Panel was performing a public duty as manifested by the government's willingness to limit legislation in this area, and to use the Panel as part of its regulatory machinery.[116] There had been an "implied devolution of power"[117] by the government to the Panel and certain legislation presupposed its

[108] *Molinaro* [2001] EWHC 896 (Admin) at [66].
[109] *Molinaro* [2001] EWHC 896 (Admin) at [63]–[64].
[110] *Molinaro* [2001] EWHC 896 (Admin) at [65].
[111] *Molinaro* [2001] EWHC 896 (Admin) at [67].
[112] *Molinaro* [2001] EWHC 896 (Admin) at [67].
[113] *Aga Khan* [1993] 1 W.L.R. 909.
[114] *Datafin* [1987] Q.B. 815.
[115] *Datafin* [1987] Q.B. 815 at 825–826, 845–846.
[116] *Datafin* [1987] Q.B. 815 at 838–839, 848–849, 850–851.
[117] *Datafin* [1987] Q.B. 815 at 849.

existence. Third, its source of power was only partly moral persuasion, this being reinforced by statutory powers exercisable by the government and the Bank of England.[118] Finally, the applicants did not appear to have any cause of action in contract or tort against the Panel.[119]

Similar reasoning can be found in other cases, such as the *Advertising Standards Authority* case.[120] The applicant complained that an adverse report on it made by the ASA was procedurally irregular. The initial question was whether the ASA was susceptible to judicial review. The court held that it was, following the *Datafin* case. The ASA had no powers granted to it by statute and had no contractual relationship with the advertisers whom it controlled. It was, however, part of a scheme of government regulation of the industry in the following sense. An EC Directive required Member States to control misleading advertising. This was implemented by regulations, which gave the Director General of Fair Trading powers to investigate complaints of misleading advertising. The essence of this regulatory scheme was that the Director General would only take legal proceedings if the matter had not been satisfactorily resolved through the ASA. The court held that in these circumstances the ASA was susceptible to control through judicial review.

v. Regulatory bodies: contract, power and control

27–030 The courts have experienced more difficulty in determining the boundaries of judicial review in a group of cases not far removed from those in the preceding section. These cases also concern regulatory bodies that exercise control over an industry, although there is no governmental involvement in these areas. These regulatory institutions are not part of a schema of statutory regulation. Whether this should make a difference will be considered in due course. The courts have on the whole been unwilling to extend judicial review to cover such cases.

The story begins with the decision in the *Law* case.[121] The plaintiff was a greyhound trainer whose licence was suspended and he sought a declaration outside s.31 that the decision was ultra vires. The NGRC argued that the case should have been brought within s.31. This was rejected by the court. It held that the power exercised by the Greyhound Racing Club was derived from contract

---

[118] *Datafin* [1987] Q.B. 815 at 838–839, 851–852.

[119] *Datafin* [1987] Q.B. 815 838–839. See also, *R. v Panel on Take-Overs and Mergers, Ex p. Guinness Plc* [1990] 1 Q.B. 146; *R. v Civil Service Appeal Board, Ex p. Bruce* [1988] I.C.R. 649; [1989] I.C.R. 171.

[120] *R. v Advertising Standards Authority, Ex p. The Insurance Services Plc* [1990] C.O.D. 42 DC. See also *Bank of Scotland v Investment Management Regulatory Organisation Ltd* (1989) S.L.T. 432; *R. v Financial Intermediaries Managers and Brokers Regulatory Association, Ex p. Cochrane* [1990] C.O.D. 33 DC; *R. v Code of Practice Committee of the Association of the British Pharmaceutical Industry, Ex p. Professional Counselling Aids Ltd* [1991] C.O.D. 228 QBD; *R. v Visitors to the Inns of Court, Ex p. Calder* [1994] Q.B. 1, CA (Civ Div); *R. v Governors of Haberdashers' Aske's Hatcham College Trust, Ex p. Tyrell* [1995] C.O.D. 399 QBD; *R. v BBC and ITC, Ex p. Referendum Party* [1997] C.O.D. 459 QBD; *R. v London Metal Exchange Ltd, Ex p. Albatross Warehousing BV*, 30 March 2000; *R. (Beer (t/a Hammer Trout Farm)) v Hampshire Farmers Markets Ltd* [2004] 1 W.L.R. 233, CA (Civ Div); *R. (Jenkins) v Marsh Farm Community Development Trust* [2011] EWHC 1097 (Admin).

[121] *Law v National Greyhound Racing Club Ltd* [1983] 1 W.L.R. 1302, CA (Civ Div).

and was of concern only to those in this sport. While the exercise of this power could benefit the public by, for example, stamping out malpractice, this was true for many other domestic tribunals, which were not subject to judicial review.

This led to actions concerning the Jockey Club, where the court reluctantly declined to use judicial review because of the holding in the greyhound case.[122] An opportunity to reconsider the point arose in the *Aga Khan* case.[123] The applicant was an owner of racehorses and was therefore bound to register with the Jockey Club and to enter a contractual relationship whereby he adhered to its rules of racing. The applicant's horse was disqualified after winning a major race and he sought judicial review. The Court of Appeal found that in general the Club was not susceptible to judicial review. It rejected the argument that the decision in *Law* had been overtaken by *Datafin*. The court acknowledged that the Club regulated a national activity, and accepted that if it did not regulate the sport then the government would in all probability do so. Notwithstanding this, the court reached its conclusion because the Club was not in its origin, constitution, membership or history a public body, and its powers were not governmental. Moreover, the applicant would have a remedy outside s.31, because he had a contract with the Jockey Club. The court left open the possibility that some cases concerning bodies like the Jockey Club might be brought within public law procedures, particularly where the applicant had no contractual relationship with the Club, or where the Club made rules that were discriminatory.

A similar reluctance to subject the governing authorities' of sporting associations to judicial review is apparent in the *Football Association* case.[124] The FA was the governing authority for football and all clubs had to be affiliated to it. The FA sanctioned various competitions, the most important of which was the Football League (FL). The FL ran the four divisions comprising the league and had a contractual relationship with the FA. The dispute arose from the decision by the FA to establish the Premier League, which would be run by it and not by the FL. In order to facilitate the top clubs breaking away from the FL and forming the Premier League, the FA declared void certain rules of the FL that made it difficult for clubs to terminate their relationship with the FL. The FL sought judicial review of this decision. It argued that the FA had a monopoly over the game, and that although there was a contract between the FA and the FL the rules of the FA were, in reality, a legislative code which regulated an important aspect of national life, in the absence of which a public body would have to perform the same function. Rose J rejected the application and held that the FA was not susceptible to judicial review, notwithstanding its monopolistic powers. It was not underpinned by any state agency, nor was there any real governmental interest in its functions, nor was there any evidence that if the FA did not exist a public body would have to be created in its place. 27–031

---

122 *R. v Disciplinary Committee of the Jockey Club, Ex p. Massingberd-Mundy* [1993] 2 All E.R. 207 DC; *R. v Jockey Club, Ex p. RAM Racecourses Ltd* [1993] 2 All E.R. 225 QBD.

123 *Aga Khan* [1993] 1 W.L.R. 909. See also *R. (Mullins) v Jockey Club Appeal Board (No.1)* [2005] EWHC 2197 (Admin). Compare however *Bradley v The Jockey Club* [2005] EWCA Civ 1056, where the court treated the case as one of private law, but reasoned in a very similar manner to a public law case.

124 *R. v Football Association Ltd, Ex p. Football League Ltd* [1993] 2 All E.R. 833 QBD; *R. v Football Association of Wales, Ex p. Flint Town United Football Club* [1991] C.O.D. 44 DC.

The disinclination to intervene via judicial review with such bodies is not restricted to those in the sporting arena. In the *Lloyd's* case,[125] it was held that Lloyd's of London was not amenable to judicial review in an action brought by "names" who had lost money in insurance syndicates that had covered asbestosis and pollution claims. The court held that Lloyd's was not a public body regulating the insurance market, but rather a body that ran one part of the market pursuant to a private Act of Parliament. The case was concerned solely with the contracts between the names and their managing agents.

27–032 The cases discussed in this section raise in stark form the boundaries of public law. There are three principal strands in the courts' reasoning. The first is that *not all power is public power*. The courts recognise that these regulatory authorities exercise power over their area, although they do not necessarily accept that this should be characterised as public power. Thus in the *Aga Khan* case Hoffmann LJ had this to say about the Jockey Club[126]:

> "But the mere fact of power, even over a substantial area of economic activity, is not enough. In a mixed economy, power may be private as well as public. Private power may affect the public interest and the livelihoods of many individuals. But that does not subject it to the rules of public law. If control is needed it must be found in the law of contract, the doctrine of restraint of trade, the Restrictive Trade Practices Act 1976, arts 85 and 86 of the EEC Treaty and all the other instruments available for curbing the excesses of private power."

A second strand in the courts' reasoning concerns the *suitability of the public law controls* for the types of body under discussion. There are consequences in terms of the procedural and substantive norms held to be applicable to such bodies of attributing the label "public" to them. There is concern as to whether such norms are always well-suited to such bodies. Thus, Rose J in the *Football Association* case stated that[127]:

> "[F]or my part, to apply to the governing body of football, on the basis that it is a public body, principles honed for the control of the abuse of power by government and its creatures would involve what, in today's fashionable parlance, would be called a quantum leap."

A third factor that has influenced the courts is that if these bodies are deemed to fall within public law *it would be difficult to decide where to stop*. Thus, Rose J reflected that if the FA were sufficiently public for judicial review, then so too would the governing authorities of other sports.[128] It was then difficult to see why the exercise of power by private corporate undertakings with a monopolistic position should not be subject to public law.[129] This led to concerns about the

---

[125] *R. v Lloyd's of London, Ex p. Briggs* [1993] 1 Lloyd's Rep. 176. See also *R. v Insurance Ombudsman, Ex p. Aegon Life Insurance Ltd* [1994] C.O.D. 426 DC; *R. v Panel of the Federation of Communication Services Ltd, Ex p. Kubis* [1998] C.O.D. 5 QBD; *R. v Association of British Travel Agents, Ex p. Sunspell Ltd* [2001] A.C.D 16 QBD; *R. v British Standards Institution, Ex p. Dorgard Ltd* [2001] A.C.D 15; *R. (West) v Lloyd's of London* [2004] 3 All E.R. 251, CA (Civ Div).

[126] *Aga Khan* [1993] 1 W.L.R. 909 at 932–933.

[127] *Football Association* [1993] 2 All E.R. 833 at 849.

[128] *Football Association* [1993] 2 All E.R. 833 at 849.

[129] G. Borrie, "The Regulation of Public and Private Power" [1989] P.L. 552.

courts' capacity to deal with this material without becoming "even more swamped with applications than they are already".[130]

Commentators differ as to the cogency of these reasons. Pannick has argued that the exercise of monopolistic power should bring bodies within the ambit of judicial review. To speak of a consensual foundation for a body's power is largely beside the point where those who wish to partake in the activity have no realistic choice but to accept that power.[131] Black has argued that the emphasis given to the contractual foundations for a body's power as the reason for withholding review is misplaced. She contends that the courts are confusing contract as an instrument of economic exchange, with contract as a regulatory instrument.[132] Black argues further that the reliance placed on private law controls, such as restraint of trade and competition law, may be misplaced here. Such controls are designed for the regulation of economic activity in the market place, and they may not be best suited to control potential abuse of regulatory power itself.[133]

vi. Employment relationships: the straining of the public/private divide

There have been numerous cases in which employees have argued that the case was sufficiently public to warrant judicial review. In *Lavelle*,[134] the applicant claimed that she had been dismissed by the BBC in breach of natural justice, and sought judicial review. Woolf J decided that this claim could not proceed under s.31, since it was restricted to matters of a public as opposed to a private nature. The relationship between Lavelle and the BBC was private, and therefore judicial review was inappropriate. The same result was reached in *Walsh*,[135] where a senior nursing officer was dismissed and sought judicial review for breach of natural justice. The court reasoned that judicial review was only available for issues of public law. Ordinary master–servant relationships did not involve any such issue, the only remedy being damages, or relief under the employment legislation. A public law issue could arise if Walsh could be said to hold an office where the employer was operating under a statutory restriction as to the grounds of dismissal.[136] However employment by a public authority did not per se "inject" a public law element; nor did the seniority of the employee or the fact that the employer was required to contract with its employees on special terms. An employee could, however, be a "potential candidate" for administrative law remedies where Parliament "underpinned" the employees' position by directly restricting the freedom of the public authority to dismiss. The preceding cases can **27–033**

130 *Football Association* [1993] 2 All E.R. 833 at 849.

131 D. Pannick, "Who is Subject to Judicial Review and in Respect of What?" [1992] P.L. 1.

132 J. Black, "Constitutionalising Self-Regulation" (1996) 59 M.L.R. 24, 41.

133 J. Black, "Constitutionalising Self-Regulation" (1996) 59 M.L.R. 24, 42.

134 *R. v British Broadcasting Corp, Ex p. Lavelle* [1983] 1 W.L.R. 23 QBD.

135 *Walsh* [1985] Q.B. 152; *R. v Derbyshire CC, Ex p. Noble* [1990] I.C.R. 808, CA (Civ Div); *Krebs v NHS Commissioning Board* [2013] EWHC 3474 (Admin).

136 Following *Ridge v Baldwin* [1964] A.C. 40, HL at 65 and *Malloch v Aberdeen Corporation* [1971] 1 W.L.R. 1578, HL at 1582, 1595.

be contrasted with *Benwell*,[137] where a prison officer was allowed to seek judicial review, the court holding that there was a sufficient statutory underpinning to inject the requisite public law element.

In *McLaren*[138] Woolf LJ distilled some general principles that should apply in employment cases. The starting point, said Woolf LJ, was that employees of public bodies should pursue their cases in the normal way outside s.31, by way of ordinary action. Judicial review could, however, be sought if the public employee was affected by a disciplinary body established under statute or the prerogative to which the employer or employee was required or entitled to refer disputes affecting their relationship. Provided that the tribunal had a sufficiently public law element then s.31 could be used. A public employee could also seek judicial review if attacking a decision of general application and doing so on *Wednesbury* grounds. Even where judicial review was not available because the disciplinary procedures were purely domestic in nature, the employee might seek a declaration outside s.31 to ensure that the proceedings were conducted fairly.[139]

The employment cases have generated a complex case law.[140] The matter has been exacerbated by the fact that public bodies have played the procedural complexities from both sides.[141] Changes in the pattern of governance have rendered it more difficult to distinguish between public and private employment.[142] It is open to question whether *McLaren* achieves the correct balance. The starting assumption is that all employment actions should be brought by ordinary action, on the hypothesis that the employment relationship is intrinsically private, whether the employer operates in the public or private sector. The assumption is then qualified in the manner described above. What unites the exceptions is that something more general is at stake than in the normal employment dispute. However, as Fredman and Morris point out the exceptions could prove to have a wider application than might have been thought[143]:

> "The problem is that this exception could easily engulf the rule. Not only do decisions respecting public employees affect a large number of employees, but they also frequently concern issues which are of public interest and in respect of which the public has the right to expect responsible and accountable behaviour."

---

[137] *Benwell* [1985] Q.B. 554; *R. (Shoesmith) v Ofsted* [2011] EWCA Civ 642.

[138] *McLaren v Home Office* [1990] I.C.R. 824, CA (Civ Div) at 836–837; *Gokool v Permanent Secretary of Health and Quality of Life* [2008] UKPC 54; *R. (Davies) v Pennine Acute Hospitals* [2010] EWHC 2887 (Admin).

[139] *Lavelle* [1983] 1 W.L.R. 23.

[140] S. Fredman and G. Morris, "Public or Private: State Employees and Judicial Review" (1991) 107 L.Q.R. 298 and "A Snake or a Ladder: *O'Reilly v Mackman* Reconsidered" (1992) 108 L.Q.R. 353.

[141] *R. v Civil Service Appeal Board, Ex p. Bruce* [1988] I.C.R. 649 QBD; [1989] I.C.R. 171; *McLaren* [1990] I.C.R. 824.

[142] Ch.5; G. Morris and S. Fredman, "Is There a Public/Private Labour Law Divide?" (1993) 14 *Comparative Labor Law Journal*. 115.

[143] S. Fredman and G. Morris, "The Costs of Exclusivity: the Case of Public Employees", paper delivered to Cambridge Conference on the Law Commission's proposals (1993), pp.5–6; S. Fredman and G. Morris, "Public or Private: State Employees and Judicial Review" (1991) 107 L.Q.R. 298, 307.

vii. Activities within Parliament's proper sphere

27–034 In the *Fayed* case,[144] it was held that the Parliamentary Commissioner for Standards was not amenable to review. His focus was on the activities and workings of those engaged within Parliament. It would therefore be inappropriate for the court to use its supervisory powers in relation to such an investigation, more especially since there was a Committee on Standards and Privileges of the House which performed that role.

viii. Activities which are "inherently private"

27–035 Some activities are regarded as inherently private and hence unsuited to judicial review. *Wachmann*[145] provides an example. The applicant sought judicial review of a disciplinary decision removing him as a Rabbi, because of conduct rendering him morally unfit to continue in the position.

Simon Brown J refused the application, holding that the jurisdiction of the Chief Rabbi was not susceptible to judicial review. He held that the s.31 procedure could only be used when there was not merely a public, but a governmental interest in the decision-making power in question. The Chief Rabbi's functions were said to be essentially intimate, spiritual and religious, and the government could not and would not seek to discharge them if he were to abdicate his regulatory responsibility, nor would Parliament contemplate legislating to regulate the discharge of these functions. Moreover, the reviewing court was not in a position to regulate what was essentially a religious function, whether a person was morally fit to carry out their spiritual responsibilities.

The courts have, however, exercised their review powers on numerous occasions in relation to Church of England clergy. This jurisdiction was reaffirmed in *Owen*,[146] where the court judicially reviewed the decision not to extend a clergyman's term of office. The Supreme Court moreover considered claims concerning discrimination in admissions policy by the Jewish Free School.[147]

ix. The impact of the Human Rights Act 1998

27–036 We have already considered the impact of the Human Rights Act 1998 (HRA) on the types of case which can proceed other than by way of judicial review. The HRA may also have an impact on the converse situation, the claims which can be brought via judicial review.

The relevance of the HRA in this regard stems from the definition of public authority for the purpose of liability under s.6. The HRA contemplates "pure public authorities", all of whose activities are within the ambit of the HRA.

[144] *R. v Parliamentary Commissioner for Standards, Ex p. Fayed* [1998] 1 W.L.R. 669, CA (Civ Div).

[145] *R. v Chief Rabbi of the United Congregations of Great Britain and the Commonwealth, Ex p. Wachmann* [1992] 1 W.L.R. 1036 QBD; *R. v Iman of Bury Park Jame Masjid Luton, Ex p. Sulaiman Ali* [1994] C.O.D. 142, CA (Civ Div).

[146] *Owen* [2001] A.C.D 14.

[147] *R. (E) v JFS Governing Body* [2010] 2 A.C. 728 SC.

However, in relation to "hybrid public authorities", only the public and not private actions are covered. This may affect the type of claim that can be brought by way of judicial review. Employment relationships may serve as an example. We have seen that the basic premise is that such disputes should be brought by way of ordinary action. It might well now be possible for an employee of a pure public authority, which is bound by the HRA in respect of all of its actions, to argue that it can therefore proceed by way of judicial review to vindicate a breach of Convention rights in the employment context.

x. *Future prospects*

27–037 It remains to be seen how far the courts will be willing to take the scope of judicial review. The reservations of some judges have been noted above. Others advocate a broader approach. Thus, Lord Woolf would, it seems, extend review to cover all bodies that exercise authority over another person or body in such a manner as to cause material prejudice to that person or body. These controls could, in principle, apply to bodies exercising power over sport and religion.[148]

If the scope of review is extended thus far, then careful attention must be given to whether the procedural and substantive norms applied against traditional public bodies should also be applied against private bodies. Many of the cases considered within this section were concerned with the application of procedural norms. If we were to follow Lord Woolf's suggestion then we would also have to consider whether substantive public law should be applied to such bodies.

We would then have to decide whether sporting bodies with monopoly power or large companies with similar power, should take account of all relevant considerations before deciding on a course of action, and whether their actions should be subject to proportionality. This would be a significant change to say the very least, and would have ramifications for subjects such as company law, commercial law and contract. It would increase the courts' judicial review case load. It would involve difficult questions as to how such substantive public law principles fit with accepted doctrines of private law. This is not to deny that similar broad principles can operate within the public and private spheres.[149] It is to argue that the broader the reach of "public law", the more nuanced we would have to be about the application of public law principles to those bodies brought within the ambit of judicial review.[150]

---

148 Lord Woolf, "Judicial Review: A Possible Programme for Reform" [1992] P.L. 221, 235.

149 Sir J. Laws, "Public Law and Employment Law: Abuse of Power" [1997] P.L. 467; D. Oliver, "Common Values in Public and Private Law and the Public/Private Divide" [1997] P.L. 630; *Bradley* [2005] EWCA Civ 1056.

150 P. Craig, "Public Law and Control over Private Power", in Taggart (ed.), *The Province of Administrative Law* (1997), pp.196–216.

5. EVALUATION OF THE PRESENT LAW

A. The Unavoidable Issue: Which Bodies are Amenable to Review

The problem of deciding which bodies should be amenable to public law principles would be present even if we had a radically different system of remedies. Let us imagine that we had a unified system of remedies, based broadly on the ordinary civil action. It would still be necessary to decide which bodies were sufficiently "public" for public law principles to be applied to them. The difference between such a regime and the existing one is that at present the resolution of these questions leads to different procedural routes, whereas this would not be so under the new regime being posited. The substantive questions themselves would not, however, disappear. These questions were present long before the 1977 remedial reforms. Put shortly, the substantive issues presented by cases such *Aga Khan* and the like are here to stay. **27–038**

B. The Central Issue: Do Public Bodies Require Special Protection

The central issue concerning procedural reform is whether public bodies require special protection through permission and time limits. If public bodies require such protection then some species of exclusivity or some other form of protection should follow in order to prevent the protections from being by-passed. The idea of presumptive exclusivity, for all its difficulties, was not therefore illogical. The Law Commission did not intend the 1977 procedure to be exclusive,[151] although it failed to reason through the implications of its own proposals. It was the Law Commission that proposed the new procedure, complete with leave requirements and time limits, in order to protect public bodies. **27–039**

Given this initial choice the courts were placed in a dilemma. They could treat the procedure as non-exclusive but the consequences would be odd. The same factual situations would be treated in radically different ways, depending on which remedial route the applicant chose. It could not be rational to allow one applicant to proceed without leave and with no formal time limit, while, on the same facts, another applicant would be subject to leave and a very much shorter time period. As Lord Woolf said,[152] it seems

> "... to be illogical to have a procedure which is designed to protect the public from unnecessary interference with administrative action, and then allow the protection which is provided to be by-passed".

The courts could alternatively insist, as they have done, that s.31 is presumptively exclusive for public law cases, with all the attendant problems this has entailed.

[151] Law Commission No.73 (1976), Cmnd.6407, para.34.

[152] Lord Woolf, "Judicial Review: A Possible Programme for Reform" [1992] P.L. 221, 231.

C. Protecting Public Bodies: Permission

i. Permission: rationale

27–040 The central issue is therefore whether we should retain the protection for public bodies in the form of permission, which has only been required since 1933.[153] Two senses of "protection" should be distinguished.

It could be argued that public bodies must be protected from vexatious litigants and that permission achieves this. This argument is suspect. The vexatious litigant appears to be a hypothetical rather than a real problem. In so far as this spectre assumes a solid form the problem can be solved by adequate provisions as to costs.[154] The case law and literature on the declaration and injunction prior to 1977 contains no evidence that this was a problem even though there was no permission requirement, and evidence about the reformed procedure indicates that the frivolous nature of the application is a very rare ground for refusing permission.[155]

It could alternatively be argued that public bodies must be protected in a broader sense. The argument is that public bodies exist to perform public duties, which are for the benefit of the general public. In deciding whether an action should proceed this wider public interest must be taken into account, as well as that of the applicant, because the public has an interest in seeing that litigation does not unduly hamper the governmental process.[156] A corollary is that the permission requirement exists to protect public bodies from applicants who do not have a chance of winning their case. It is a screening mechanism to prevent the public body from being troubled by cases that are unlikely to succeed.

A crucial issue concerns the test to be applied at the permission stage. There are indications that the test applied by the courts has become stricter over time.[157] Thus the early approach was to refuse leave only in cases that were hopeless or wholly unarguable.[158] Relatively few such cases are likely to exist.[159] However, the test has become stricter, such that the claimant will only be granted permission if the case really was arguable. Thus, judges should refuse permission where they believe that there is no reasonable chance of success, or that the case

---

[153] Administration of Justice (Miscellaneous Provisions) Act 1993 s.5.

[154] The court has, in any event, an inherent jurisdiction to strike out vexatious claims. In addition, there are statutory powers to strike out vexatious claims, Senior Courts Act 1981 s.42, and there are Rules of the Supreme Court which enable provision to be made as to costs; *R. (Ewing) v Office of the Deputy Prime Minister* [2006] 1 W.L.R. 1260, CA (Civ Div).

[155] A. le Sueur and M. Sunkin, "Applications for Judicial Review: the Requirement of Leave" [1992] P.L. 102, 120.

[156] Sir H. Woolf, "Public Law–Private Law: Why the Divide? A Personal View" [1986] P.L. 220, 230; Sir H. Woolf, *Protecting the Public—A New Challenge* (London: Sweet & Maxwell, 1990).

[157] V. Bondy and M. Sunkin, "Accessing Judicial Review" [2008] P.L. 647.

[158] *R. v Secretary of State for the Home Department, Ex p. Doorga* [1990] C.O.D. 109, CA (Civ Div) at 110.

[159] If there are a large number of such cases then there must be something very wrong further back in the system. Public or private money would be wasted by lawyers encouraging the pursuit of such cases. The rational individual is unlikely to wish to press a case if advised by a lawyer that the action was wholly unarguable.

is not reasonably arguable.[160] This formulation will inevitably enable more cases to be disposed of at the permission stage. To refuse permission because the judge believes that the applicant did not have a reasonable chance of success, or some similar test, is nonetheless problematic. The judge will be making a difficult evaluation on fact and law and this evaluation will, after the CPR, be based on written documentation. As Megarry J has stated, albeit in a different context, the law is full of cases which appeared to be open and shut, but which turned out not to be so straightforward.[161]

ii. *Permission: the impact of the CPR and the CJCA 1985*

The reformed Civil Procedure Rules did not unfortunately shed light on this important issue. The permission requirement was retained in CPR 54.4, following the recommendation of the Bowman Report[162] and the earlier recommendation of the Law Commission.[163] The Bowman Report favoured explicit criteria as to when permission should be granted, and a presumption that it should be granted.[164] CPR 54.4 retained the leave requirement, subject to the linguistic alteration from leave to permission, but contained no criteria as to when permission should be granted. **27–041**

It is regrettable that CPR 54.4 contains *no criterion for the grant of permission*, given that there are various possible tests. These include refusal of permission where the case is "wholly unarguable", "if it is not reasonably arguable", "if there is no serious issue to be tried", or "if there is no real prospect of success". The claimant's chances of securing permission may be very different under these different tests.[165] The courts should not employ a test of "serious issue to be tried", since it could be taken to give a court discretion to refuse permission because it felt that the potential illegality was not serious enough to warrant a substantive hearing. The test should be framed in terms of "arguability". A choice then has to be made as to whether to refuse permission

---

160 *R. v Secretary of State for the Home Department, Ex p. Begum* [1990] C.O.D. 107, CA (Civ Div) at 108; *R. v Panel on Takeovers and Mergers, Ex p. Guinness Plc* [1990] 1 Q.B. 146, CA (Civ Div) at 177–178; *R. v Legal Aid Board, Ex p. Hughes* (1992) 24 H.L.R. 698, CA (Civ Div); *Sharma v Brown-Antoine* [2006] UKPC 57; *R. (Fulford Parish Council) v City of York Council* [2013] EWHC 3924 (Admin); *Sky Blue Sports & Leisure Ltd v Coventry CC* [2013] EWHC 3366 (Admin); White Book, *Civil Practice* at [54.4].

161 *John v Rees* [1970] Ch. 345 at 402.

162 Review of the Crown Office List (LCD, 2000); Lord Chancellor's Department Consultation Paper, *The Administrative Court: Proposed Changes to Primary Legislation following Sir Jeffrey Bowman's Review of the Crown Office List*.

163 Law Commission, *Administrative Law: Judicial Review and Statutory Appeals* (Law Commission Report No.226), HC Paper No. 669, (1994), para.5.7; N. Bamforth, "Reform of Public Law: Pragmatism or Principle?" (1995) 58 M.L.R. 722; R. Gordon, "The Law Commission and Judicial Review: Managing the Tension between Case Management and Public Interest Challenges" [1995] P.L. 11.

164 Review of the Crown Office List (LCD, 2000); Lord Chancellor's Department Consultation Paper, *The Administrative Court: Proposed Changes to Primary Legislation following Sir Jeffrey Bowman's Review of the Crown Office List* (2001), para.13.

165 R. Gordon, "The Law Commission and Judicial Review: Managing the Tension between Case Management and Public Interest Challenges" [1995] P.L. 11, 14.

only where a case is unarguable, or whether a more rigorous test is to be applied, which requires the claimant to demonstrate a reasonable chance of success or the like.

CPR 54 modified *the permission stage so that it is now more inter partes than hitherto*. The leave stage was traditionally ex parte, and the respondent might only become involved if leave was given. This has been altered by CPR 54.6–9, which made the permission stage more inter partes than hitherto. The claim form must be served on the defendant and any person the claimant considers an interested party. Any person served with the claim form who wishes to take part in judicial review must file an acknowledgement of service. The acknowledgement must state the grounds on which the party is contesting the claim. The rationale for the change was to get defendants to think about the challenge at the outset, and to ensure that the court was well informed at the permission stage.[166] There are however concerns that the inter partes procedure may disadvantage claimants. The court may regard the defendant's brief response as a knockout blow to the claimant, even where it is not fully supported by evidence.[167] There is also a concern that the permission stage as modified by the CPR will be performing two roles, that of mediating access to judicial review, and managing the substantive dispute, and that it may be difficult to reconcile these roles.[168]

27–042 It is important to realise that *the gap between the judicial review procedure and that for the ordinary action has also narrowed because of changes in the rules governing the latter*. A central theme of the Woolf reforms was to give the courts greater control over the management of civil litigation than hitherto. This is apparent in the general provisions of the CPR.[169] CPR 3.4(2) enables the court to strike out a case if it discloses no cause of action, or if it is an abuse of the court's process. CPR 24 empowers the court to give summary judgment, where it considers that the claimant has no real prospect of success. Increased judicial control over ordinary litigation is also evident in the judicial interpretation of the CPR, as exemplified by *Clark*.[170] The court, as we have seen, made it clear that the CPR relating to ordinary actions would be interpreted to prevent a party gaining unwarranted procedural advantages by proceeding via an ordinary action, as opposed to judicial review. There are nonetheless still differences between the judicial review procedure and that for ordinary actions. Public law applicants are not entitled to pursue a case of their own accord. They must secure permission and argue their way into court, subject to a short time limit. In an ordinary action the claimant is entitled to proceed without any requirement of permission. The onus is on the defendant to argue that the case should be struck out, and the time limit is considerably longer.

---

166 M. Fordham, "Judicial Review: The New Rules" [2001] P.L. 4, 6.

167 T. Cornford and M. Sunkin, "The Bowman Report, Access and the Recent Reforms of the Judicial Review Procedure" [2001] P.L. 11, 19; V. Bondy and M. Sunkin, "Accessing Judicial Review" [2008] P.L. 647.

168 T. Cornford and M. Sunkin, "The Bowman Report, Access and the Recent Reforms of the Judicial Review Procedure" [2001] P.L. 11, 15.

169 CPR Pts 1, 3.

170 *Clark* [2000] 1 W.L.R. 1988.

The criterion for grant of permission has more recently been markedly affected by the Criminal Justice and Courts Act 2015, which as seen,[171] requires courts, subject to limited exceptions, to refuse permission where the outcome would not have been substantially different. This requires the court to make a difficult estimation about causation of a kind that they have largely resisted and with good reason, since it is difficult to determine whether the outcome would have been different.[172] The court will perforce have limited material to hand when it makes this determination and limited time in which to make the assessment.

iii. Permission: empirical evidence

Valuable empirical work has been done on the leave requirement. The principal findings of this work are as follows. **27–043**

First, the most important grounds for applications failing were: delay, the inappropriateness of the public law procedure and the fact that the case was held to be unarguable. The last reason accounted for most unsuccessful applications. Le Sueur and Sunkin concluded that even where a judge expressed himself in forthright language and declared a case to be unarguable, such cases were far from clear: "cases characterised as wholly unarguable at the leave stage have gone on to win on the merits at the full hearing".[173] Many cases were found to be neither wholly unarguable, nor patently arguable, with the consequence that the judge was forced into playing a dangerous guessing game on fact and law.[174] Some cases deemed initially to be wholly unarguable went on to win on the merits at the full hearing, or were granted leave on a renewed application.

Second, the early study by Le Sueur and Sunkin found that success rates at the permission stage varied significantly between judges, thereby rendering this something of a lottery. Some were conservative, granting leave in only 25 per cent of cases; others were more liberal, allowing 82 per cent to proceed; yet others were in the middle of this range, giving leave in 40–60 per cent of cases.[175] A later study by Vardy and Sunkin confirmed the variation in success rates between different judges, with the most generous judge giving permission in 46 per cent of cases, as compared to the success rate before the least generous of 11 per cent.

Third, the overall success rate in gaining permission to seek judicial review has declined markedly over the years. Thus, in 1981, 71 per cent of applications were given leave to proceed, whereas in 2006 the figure was only 22 per cent.[176] This **27–044**

---

[171] See para.27–004.

[172] *John v Rees* [1970] Ch. 345 at 402; *Secretary of State for the Home Department v AF (No.3)* [2009] 2 W.L.R. 423 at [113].

[173] A. Le Sueur and M. Sunkin, "Applications for Judicial Review: the Requirement of Leave" [1992] P.L. 102, 122.

[174] .A. Le Sueur and M. Sunkin, "Applications for Judicial Review: the Requirement of Leave" [1992] P.L. 102, 122.

[175] M. Sunkin, L. Bridges and G. Meszaros, *Judicial Review in Perspective: An Investigation of Trends in the Use and Operation of the Judicial Review Procedure in England and Wales* (Public Law Project, 1993).

[176] V. Bondy and M. Sunkin, "Accessing Judicial Review" [2008] P.L. 647.

decline is in part attributable to the more rigorous test used by the courts when determining whether permission will be given. It is in part a function of changes made by the CPR reforms. Defendants increasingly put in an acknowledgement of service at the permission stage, which contains the core arguments of their defence. This will often convince the judge that the case is not arguable.[177] The lower rate of permission may also be partly explicable because of increased settlement of cases prior to the permission stage being resolved. The cases thus settled appear to be those in which the claimant's case is stronger, thereby leaving the relatively weaker cases to seek permission.[178]

Finally, the studies reveal the dangers of using leave as a method of managing overall case load. There is, as Le Sueur and Sunkin say, "something profoundly ambiguous in giving to the judiciary 'administrative' powers to allocate scarce court resources in a context where the courts are required to supervise the 'administrative' decisions of government", more particularly so where the criteria for decision-making are unclear.[179]

iv. Permission: conclusion

27–045 It was argued prior to the new CPR that suitable techniques for protecting public bodies in ordinary actions could be devised when such protection was warranted. These could take the form of expedited procedures and dismissal of the claim on the ground of undue delay. This choice was favoured by many academics[180] and it has been argued that the changes enshrined in the CPR relating to striking out and summary judgment could be used to protect public bodies, even if separate public law procedures were abolished.[181] Many among the judiciary and government remained convinced that these protections were nonetheless necessary, particularly in the light of the increase in the number of applications for judicial review. It was felt that the ordinary procedures would be too cumbersome for most judicial review applications.[182]

The Tribunals, Courts and Enforcement Act 2007 is relevant here. It was based on the recommendations of the Leggatt Report[183] on tribunals. It is clear that those who favour the retention of the permission requirement are influenced in part by the case-load on judicial review in the ordinary courts. The Tribunals, Courts and Enforcement Act 2007 should alleviate this problem. First-tier Tribunal decisions are subject to a right of appeal on law to the Upper Tribunal,

---

177 V. Bondy and M. Sunkin, "Accessing Judicial Review" [2008] P.L. 647, 656.

178 V. Bondy and M. Sunkin, "Accessing Judicial Review" [2008] P.L. 647, 656–657.

179 A. Le Sueur and M. Sunkin, "Applications for Judicial Review: the Requirement of Leave" [1992] P.L. 102, 126.

180 S. Fredman and G. Morris, "The Costs of Exclusivity" [1994] P.L. 69.

181 T. Cornford and M. Sunkin, "The Bowman Report, Access and the Recent Reforms of the Judicial Review Procedure" [2001] P.L. 11, 15; D. Oliver, "Public Law Procedures and Remedies—Do We Need Them?" [2002] P.L. 91, 93.

182 LCCP, para.5.8; Law Commission, *Administrative Law: Judicial Review and Statutory Appeals* (Report No.226) HC Paper No.669 (1994), para.3.5; Sir J. Laws, "Procedural Exclusivity", paper delivered at Robinson College, Cambridge (15 May 1993).

183 Report of the Review of Tribunals by Sir Andrew Leggatt: *Tribunals for Users—One System, One Service*, (16 August 2001), available at: *http://www.tribunals-review.org.uk* [accessed 23 June 2016].

and then, subject to certain limits, to the Court of Appeal.[184] The Act also makes provision for the Upper Tribunal to exercise judicial review powers, and enables the High Court to transfer a judicial review case to an Upper Tribunal.[185]

D. Protecting Public Bodies: Time Limits

i. *Time limits: current rules*

The rules on time limits and delay are complicated.[186] Before 1977 only certiorari was subject to a six-month time limit, albeit with a discretion to extend beyond this period that was rarely exercised. Declarations and injunctions were not subject to formal limitation periods, but delay could be a factor in the court deciding whether to refuse relief. **27–046**

The rules concerning delay were altered by the 1977 reforms. Order 53 r.4 contained the provision for delay. This was ambiguous[187] and was replaced in 1980.[188] The basic rule was that an application for permission to apply for judicial review should be made promptly and in any event within three months from the date when grounds for the application first arose, unless the court considered that there was good reason for extending time.

Order 53 r.4 was replaced by CPR 54.5(1). This states that the claim form must be filed promptly and in any event not later than three months after the grounds to make the claim first arose. This rule does not apply when any other enactment specifies a shorter time limit for making the claim for judicial review, CPR 54.5(3). The time limit may not be extended by agreement between the parties, CPR 54.5(2). It can however be extended by the court, pursuant to the general power in CPR 3.1(2)(a).[189]

The Senior Courts Act 1981 s.31(6) also contains provisions on delay, although it is framed in different terms. It states that where the High Court considers that there has been undue delay in making an application for judicial review, the court may refuse to grant leave for making the application, or any relief sought on the application, if it considers that the granting of the relief sought would be likely to cause substantial hardship to, or substantially prejudice the rights of, any person, or would be detrimental to good administration. **27–047**

There are three key differences between the formulation in CPR 54.5 and that in the Senior Courts Act s.31(6). First, s.31(6) contains no actual time limit, whereas CPR 54.5 sets a general limit of three months. Second, s.31(6) provides that detriment to good administration and prejudice to a party's rights are to be

[184] Tribunals, Courts and Enforcement Act 2007 ss.11–14.

[185] Tribunals, Courts and Enforcement Act 2007 ss.15–21.

[186] M. Beloff, "Time, Time, Time It's On My Side, Yes It Is", in C. Forsyth and I. Hare (eds), *The Golden Metwand and the Crooked Cord, Essays on Public Law in Honour of Sir William Wade* (Oxford: Oxford University Press, 1998), pp.267–295.

[187] J. Beatson and M. Matthews, "Reform of Administrative Law Remedies: The First Step" (1978) 41 M.L.R. 437, 442–444.

[188] SI 2000/1980 r.3, amending Ord.53 r.4.

[189] *R. v Lichfield DC, Ex p. Lichfield Securities Ltd* [2001] 3 L.G.L.R. 35, CA (Civ Div) at [28]; *R. (M) v School Organisation Committee, Oxford CC* [2001] A.C.D. 77 QBD at [16].

taken into account when there is undue delay. These factors are not found in CPR 54.5. Third, s.31(6) applies both at the permission stage, and at the substantive hearing, whereas CPR 54.5 applies at the permission stage.[190]

The continued existence of two provisions dealing with time limits, cast in different terms, is to be regretted. The complications flowing from this duality have been apparent for over 30 years, and continue to pose problems for the courts.[191] It would be perfectly possible for there to be a single provision dealing with time limits. The fact that this was not done pursuant to the CPR reforms of the judicial review procedure is all the more surprising. The rules on time limits flowing from CPR 54.5 and s.31(6) are as follows.

27–048 The initial issue concerns the point at which time begins to run.[192] This may be clear in some situations,[193] but may be less certain in others, in particular where a challenge is made to a policy determination or rule.[194] The issue is important, given the need to apply promptly and the brevity of the three-month period. It is possible for an applicant to be ruled out of time if the action was brought against a later act when it should have been brought against an earlier one.[195] It was, however, made clear in *Burkett*[196] that it was open to a claimant to challenge grant of planning permission, notwithstanding the fact that there might have been a challenge to an earlier resolution to give the planning permission. Lord Steyn stated that time limits operated to bar review where a public body might have committed an abuse of power. They should be interpreted with this in mind. Courts should not therefore engage in a broad discretionary exercise of determining when the claimant could first reasonably have made the application.[197] The same rules should apply irrespective of the fact that the claimant is a public interest group.[198]

CPR 54.5(1)(a) requires that the decision be made promptly, and in any event within three months after the grounds to make the claim arose. These are separate requirements,[199] and thus applications have been held not to be prompt, even if

[190] *R. v Stratford-on-Avon DC, Ex p. Jackson* [1985] 1 W.L.R. 1319, CA (Civ Div).

[191] See, e.g. *Lichfield* [2001] 3 L.G.L.R. 35.

[192] Ord.53 r.4 stated that where an order of certiorari is sought in respect of any judgment, order, conviction or other proceeding, the date when grounds for the application first arose shall be taken to be the date of that judgment, order, conviction or proceeding. There is no such provision in CPR 54.5.

[193] *Hereward & Foster Ltd v Legal Services Commission* [2010] EWHC 3370 (Admin).

[194] In *R. v Redbridge LBC, Ex p. G* [1991] C.O.D. 398 DC, it was assumed that time ran from when a policy was actually made, but that the fact that the applicant had no knowledge of the policy until it was published later was regarded as a good reason for extending the time limit. However, in *R. v Secretary of State for Trade and Industry, Ex p. Greenpeace (No.2)* [2000] C.O.D. 141 QBD, the court held that time did not begin to run from the date of the contested regulations, since any such claim at that date would have been made in a vacuum;*R. (Nash) v Barnet LBC* [2013] EWCA Civ 1004.

[195] *R. v Avon CC, Ex p. Terry Adams* [1994] Env. L.R. 442, CA (Civ Div); *R. v Commissioners of Customs and Excise, Ex p. Eurotunnel Plc* [1995] C.O.D. 291 DC; *R. v Secretary for Trade and Industry, Ex p. Greenpeace Ltd* [1998] C.O.D. 59 QBD.

[196] *R. v Hammersmith and Fulham LBC, Ex p. Burkett* [2002] 1 W.L.R. 1593, HL.

[197] *Burkett* [2002] 1 W.L.R. 1593 at [44]–[49], disapproving of the first *Greenpeace* case [1998] C.O.D. 59; *R. (De Whalley) v Norfolk CC* [2011] EWHC 3739 (Admin).

[198] The suggestion, in the first *Greenpeace* case [1998] C.O.D. 59 that such groups must be especially prompt was not accepted in the second *Greenpeace* case [2000] C.O.D. 141, or in *Burkett* [2002] 1 W.L.R. 1593.

[199] *Hardy v Pembrokeshire CC (Permission to Appeal)* [2006] EWCA Civ 240.

made within three months.[200] In *Burkett*,[201] doubts were raised as to whether the obligation to act promptly was sufficiently certain to comply with the ECHR. The matter was not decided but a number of their Lordships were concerned that the provision was too uncertain to satisfy Convention jurisprudence. However, in *Hardy*[202] the Court of Appeal concluded that the requirement to act promptly conformed to the ECHR jurisprudence. The concerns expressed in *Burkett* should nonetheless be taken seriously: courts should hesitate before finding that a claim made in less than three months should be struck out because it was not made promptly. It was in any event made clear in *Burkett* that the three-month limit should not be regarded as having been judicially replaced by a period of six weeks.[203]

When an application for leave is not made promptly[204] and in any event within three months, the court can refuse permission on the grounds of delay, unless it considers that there is a good reason for extending the period.[205] The court, in deciding whether to extend time, will consider whether there was a reasonable excuse for late application, the possible impact on third party rights, and the administration, and the importance of the point raised.[206] The issues must be of genuinely public importance, and must be such that they could be best ventilated in the public law context.[207] The courts have held that attempting to reach a negotiated solution with the respondent will not normally be a reason for extension of time,[208] although there are some instances where this has been taken this into account.[209]

It is clear from *Caswell*[210] that where the claim is not made promptly, or within three months, there is undue delay for the purposes of the Senior Courts Act 1981 s.31(6), even if the court extends the time for making the claim. The phrase "undue delay" is the condition precedent for invoking s.31(6). The court may then have regard to hardship to third parties, and detriment to good administration,[211] in deciding whether to refuse permission or refuse relief at the substantive hearing. The court should not, however, refuse to grant permission at the substantive hearing on the basis of hardship to third parties or detriment to **27–049**

---

[200] *Hilditch v Westminster CC* [1990] C.O.D. 434, CA (Civ Div); *R. v ITC, Ex p. T.VNi Ltd and T.VS Ltd*, *The Times*, 30 December 1991; *R. v Minister of Agriculture, Fisheries and Food, Ex p. Dairy Trade Federation* [1995] C.O.D. 3 QBD; *R. v Bath CC, Ex p. Crombie* [1995] C.O.D. 283; *Allman v HM Coroner for West Sussex* 2012] EWHC 534 (Admin).

[201] *Burkett* [2002] 1 W.L.R. 1593 at [6], [53].

[202] *Hardy* [2006] EWCA Civ 240 at [11]–[18].

[203] *Hardy* [2006] EWCA Civ 240 at [53].

[204] *Finn-Kelcey v Milton Keynes BC* [2008] EWCA Civ 1067; *R. (Waste Recycling Group Ltd) v Cumbria CC* [2011] EWHC 288 (Admin).

[205] *R. v Dairy Produce Quota Tribunal, Ex p. Caswell* [1990] 2 A.C. 738 HL.

[206] The second *Greenpeace* case [2000] C.O.D. 141.

[207] *R. v Secretary of State for the Home Department, Ex p. Ruddock* [1987] 1 W.L.R. 1482 QBD; *R. v Collins, Ex p. M.S.* [1998] C.O.D. 52; *School Organisation Committee* [2001] A.C.D 77 QBD at [21]–[31].

[208] *R. v Redbridge LBC, Ex p. G* [1991] C.O.D. 398 DC at 400.

[209] *Owen* [2001] A.C.D 14; A. Lindsay, "Delay in Judicial Review Cases: A Conundrum Solved?" [1995] P.L. 417, 425–426.

[210] *Caswell* [1990] 2 A.C. 738.

[211] *R. (Brown) v Secretary of State for Work and Pensions* [2008] EWHC 3158; *R. (007 Stratford Taxis Ltd) v Stratford on Avon DC* [2011] EWCA Civ 160.

good administration, where permission has already been given, since it is too late to "refuse" permission in such instances. The court should rather refuse relief under s.31(6).[212]

It is clear from *Lichfield*[213] that the same factors will generally be relevant to promptness under CPR 54.5, and undue delay under s.31(6). It is nonetheless in principle open to a court to consider undue delay at the substantive hearing, even where promptness has been considered at the permission stage. The judge at the substantive hearing should however only do so where new material is introduced at the substantive hearing, or if exceptionally the issues as developed at the substantive hearing put a different aspect on promptness, or where the first judge has overlooked a relevant matter.[214]

Where there is undue delay, it will be for the court to decide whether hardship to third parties or detriment to the administration will lead to the denial of relief. Where the impact on third party interests is insufficient in this respect, it will be rarely in the interests of good administration to leave an abuse of power uncorrected.[215]

The rules on time limits will be subject to review by the CJEU where the subject matter falls within the scope of EU law. Thus, the CJEU held that national regulations had failed to implement properly an EU Directive on public procurement. This was because the national regulation required that actions should be brought promptly and in any event within three months and the CJEU held that this was uncertain and hence did not constitute proper implementation of the Directive.[216]

ii. Time limits: justification

27–050 Shorter time limits are said to be required in public law cases because of the greater need for certainty than in private law. There is a wider public interest involved in ensuring that the public service knows whether its actions will be valid or not.[217] There is clearly a need for public bodies to have certainty as to the legal validity of their actions. The following points should nonetheless be borne in mind.

First, there is no evidence that the longer limitation periods in the declaration and injunction cases decided prior to 1977 caused problems. The courts use common law concepts of delay, acquiescence and personal bar to control untimely actions.[218] The Law Commission was, however, against abandoning specific time limits for public law proceedings and against relying on the

---

212 *R. v Criminal Injuries Compensation Board, Ex p. A* [1999] 2 A.C. 330, HL at 340–342.

213 *Lichfield* [2001] 3 L.G.L.R. 35 at [33].

214 *Lichfield* [2001] 3 L.G.L.R. 35 at [34].

215 *Lichfield* [2001] 3 L.G.L.R. 35 at [39].

216 *Uniplex (UK) Ltd v NHS Business Services Authority* (C-406/08), [2010] E.C.R. I-817; C. Knight, "Procuring the End of the Promptness Requirement?" [2010] C.J.Q. 297; *R. (U & Partners (East Anglia) Ltd) v Broads Authority* [2011] EWHC 1824 (Admin);*R. (Berky) v Newport CC* [2012] EWCA Civ 378.

217 *O'Reilly* [1983] 2 A.C. 237 at 249.

218 Lord Clyde and D. Edwards, *Judicial Review* (Edinburgh: W. Green, 2000), para.13.4; *Burkett* [2002] 1 W.L.R. 1593 at [59]–[66].

ordinary limitation periods for civil actions. It believed that the existing three-month period was desirable,[219] subject to discretion to admit cases beyond this period.

Second, in so far as there is a need for short time limits, this is undermined by allowing applicants with private rights to proceed outside s.31.[220] It is true that the court held in *Clark*[221] that it would exercise control over the time in which ordinary actions were brought, where such actions entailed a challenge to the legality of a public body's decision. It nonetheless remains to be seen how often a court will exercise this power where the claimant in an ordinary action is bringing the claim well within the six-year limit, albeit beyond three months.

Third, there are a number of techniques for dealing with this problem. In areas where there is a high premium on certainty, specific statutory provision can be made to ensure that the challenge was brought within a certain defined period. Such provisions are already common in legislation concerning planning. The exercise of discretion in granting types of relief and the development of prospective as opposed to retrospective invalidity could also be employed to resolve problems in particular cases. Moreover, the CPR vests the courts with greater control over actions in general. *Clark*[222] shows the court's willingness to interpret the CPR rules to control the timing of ordinary actions that involve a challenge to the legality of a public body's decision. **27–051**

The final comment on time limits is somewhat different. The increase in the volume of applications for judicial review has been a principal reason for the retention of the permission requirement. The short time limits may, in a paradoxical sense, increase the amount of litigation against the administration. An individual who believes that the public body has acted ultra vires now has the strongest incentive to seek judicial resolution of the matter immediately, as opposed to attempting a negotiated solution, because if the individual forbears from suing they may be deemed not to have applied promptly, or within the three-month time limit.[223] This has been acknowledged by the courts[224]:

> "[A]ny citizen who had a problem with local government, or with any other bureaucracy, was faced with a choice: he could either seek by political means to influence the decision, or could consider whether he had any legal remedy. If he elected to adopt the first course, and achieved nothing, he could not rely on that as a ground for extending time."

It is therefore unsurprising if legal advisers tell their clients that an application for judicial review should be made at once, rather than attempting to negotiate a solution first. Negotiated solutions are possible when litigation has begun. However, the existence of a formal suit can polarise existing positions. There is thus a tension between the rules on time limits and the desire, expressed

[219] Law Commission, *Administrative Law: Judicial Review and Statutory Appeals* (Law Commission Report No.226), para.5.26

[220] J. Beatson, "'Public' and 'Private' in English Administrative Law" (1987) 103 L.Q.R. 34, 44–45.

[221] *Clark* [2000] 1 W.L.R. 1988.

[222] *Clark* [2000] 1 W.L.R. 1988.

[223] This was recognised in *Burkett* [2002] 1 W.L.R. 1593 at [53].

[224] *R. v Redbridge LBC, Ex p. G* [1991] C.O.D. 398 DC at 400.

forcefully by Lord Woolf,[225] that individuals should have resort to any dispute resolution mechanism before seeking judicial review. Lord Woolf CJ returned to this theme in the *Cowl* case.[226] He stated that litigation should be avoided wherever possible, and that maximum use should be made of alternative dispute resolution (ADR) and complaints procedures. It was held that the court could, of its own initiative, hold an inter partes hearing, at which the parties would be asked what use they had made of such procedures. There is obvious good sense behind the drive to use ADR. Legal advisers will, however, only be able to advise their clients to use such mechanisms, if they feel that this will not prejudice a claim for review by it being declared out of time.

E. The Exclusivity Principle

27–052 The "fate" of the exclusivity principle is, as stated above, intimately connected with the decision as to whether special protections for public bodies, in terms of permission and time limits, should be retained. If one believes that special protections are needed then this requires rules to prevent those protections from being side-stepped. It is possible to have a unified procedure if one assumes that the protections are not required, or that any needs of public bodies could be met by the ordinary rules of civil procedure.[227] This is reflected in the three options canvassed by the Law Commission in its discussion of the exclusivity principle.[228]

The principle could be abolished, with the consequence that there would be no special rules for dealing with public law cases. The Law Commission did not favour this option and it has not been adopted: CPR 54 has retained a separate procedure for judicial review, with the distinctive features of permission and short time limits.

The principle could be extended, with the consequence that the current exceptions to the principle would cease to operate. Experience has shown that cases involving public law can arise in a number of ways. To impose requirements of permission and short time limits in all instances could well cause hardship to litigants, and would run counter to the courts' jurisprudence, which had built on the exceptions to *O'Reilly*. This option did not therefore find favour with the Law Commission.

The boundaries of the principle could be delineated more clearly. Cases involving private rights could be brought by ordinary action outside CPR 54. The judicial review procedure would be required only in pure public law cases. The

---

[225] Lord Woolf, *Access to Justice: The Final Report to the Lord Chancellor on the Civil Justice System in England and Wales* (1997), p.251.

[226] *Cowl v Plymouth CC* [2002] 1 W.L.R. 803, CA (Civ Div); *Practice Statement (Administrative Court: Listing and Urgent Cases)* [2002] 1 W.L.R. 810 QBD; *R. (C) v Nottingham CC* [2010] EWCA Civ 790; *R. (Crawford) v Newcastle Upon Tyne University* [2014] EWHC 1197 (Admin).

[227] S. Fredman and G. Morris, "The Costs of Exclusivity: Public and Private Re-examined" [1994] P.L. 69, 83–84.

[228] Law Commission Consultation Paper No.126, *Administrative Law and Statutory Appeals* (1993), pp.18–19, (LCCP).

Law Commission endorsed this position in its Report.[229] This is broadly the view the courts have adopted. There are, as seen, problems with this "result". However, given that exclusivity was unlikely to be abolished or extended to all proceedings, this option was inevitable.

F. Disclosure and Inspection

We have already seen the role played by discovery in the 1977 reforms. The reforms made improved provision for discovery and this was regarded in *O'Reilly* as part of the justification for procedural exclusivity. The reality is that discovery is rarely awarded in judicial review proceedings, because of the cost and time implications.[230] The normal criterion was that discovery would be allowed when it was necessary either for disposing fairly of the cause or for saving costs.[231] **27–053**

The problem for the claimant can be formidable. It can be difficult to sustain certain challenges without discovery and cross-examination. Allegations that an administrator has taken irrelevant considerations into account or has acted for improper purposes are but two such instances. The need for discovery will, moreover, be needed if the courts are to develop emerging doctrines such as proportionality. Openness of decision-making is of real importance, but as Gordon notes,

> "... the restrictive rules that have bedevilled discovery in recent years only permit access to documentation where such is necessary to undermine an apparent lack of candour in the affidavits lodged".[232]

It is clear from the empirical work done by Le Sueur and Sunkin that the most common reason for refusing permission was that the claimant could not, without discovery, establish the factual foundation for the case so as to convince the judge that the claim was arguable.[233]

It remains to be seen how far the CPR make any difference in this respect. CPR 54 is regarded as a modification of CPR 8, which deals with claims where there is no substantial dispute as to fact. CPR 31 deals with disclosure and inspection of documents. A party discloses a document by stating that the document exists or has existed.[234] An order to give disclosure is, unless the court otherwise directs, an order to give standard disclosure.[235] It is open to the court to dispense with or limit standard disclosure.[236] Where a court does make such an order it requires a party to disclose the documents on which it relies, and the documents which adversely affect its own or another party's, case, or support

229 Law Commission, *Administrative Law: Judicial Review and Statutory Appeals* (Law Commission Report No.226), para.3.15.

230 See para.27–006; *Khawaja* [1984] A.C. 74; *Air Canada* [1983] 2 A.C. 394.

231 RSC Ord.24 r.13(1).

232 Law Commission, *Administrative Law: Judicial Review and Statutory Appeals* (Law Commission Report No.226), p.16.

233 A. le Sueur and M. Sunkin, "Applications for Judicial Review: the Requirement of Leave" [1992] P.L. 102.

234 CPR 31.2.

235 CPR 31.5(1).

236 CPR 31.5(2).

another party's case, and such documents which it is required to disclose by a relevant practice direction.[237] A party is under an obligation to make a reasonable search for such documents.[238] The court is also empowered to make an order for specific disclosure or specific inspection, requiring the party to disclose those documents specified in the order.[239] There is little doubt that these rules give the court ample powers through which to require the public body to provide the information needed for the applicant to sustain its case. It is, however, open to the court to dispense with or limit standard disclosure, and the court also has discretion in relation to requests for more specific disclosure. Much will, therefore, depend upon how the courts use the powers at their disposal.[240]

27–054 The House of Lords' decision in *Tweed* is important in this respect.[241] The claimant sought judicial review of a decision placing restrictions on a parade in Northern Ireland, on the ground that it infringed his rights to assembly and free speech protected by the HRA 1998. He sought disclosure of documents referred to in an affidavit sworn by the chairman of the Parades Commission, which made the decision. Their Lordships acknowledged that disclosure had been ordered less readily in judicial review cases than in ordinary actions, in part because judicial review cases often turned on issues of law rather than fact.

They held that disclosure would, however, be more necessary in judicial review cases raising issues of proportionality. This was so here, since the decision of the Parades Commission that imposed restrictions on Convention rights had to be proportionate. The disclosure of documents referred to in affidavits would not however always take place where proportionality was in issue. The proportionality issue formed part of the context in which the court had to consider whether it was necessary for fairly disposing of the case to order the disclosure of such documents. It did not give rise automatically to the need for disclosure of all documents. Whether disclosure should be ordered would depend on a balancing of several factors, of which proportionality was only one, albeit one of some significance. In cases involving issues of proportionality, disclosure should be carefully limited to the issues required in the interests of justice.

Their Lordships also modified the previous practice concerning disclosure and general judicial review actions. The House of Lords held that disclosure would only be necessary in limited cases, but that it was no longer the rule that disclosure would only be ordered where the decision-maker's affidavit could be shown to be materially inaccurate or misleading and the courts should now adopt a more flexible, less prescriptive approach and judge the need for disclosure on the facts of the individual case to see whether it was required to resolve the matter

[237] CPR 31.6.

[238] CPR 31.7(1).

[239] CPR 31.12.

[240] See *Three Rivers DC v Bank of England (Disclosure) (No.1)* [2003] 1 W.L.R. 210 (Civ Div) for analysis of disclosure from a person who is not a party to the case, pursuant to CPR 31.17.

[241] *Tweed v Parades Commission for Northern Ireland* [2007] 1 A.C. 650.

fairly and justly.[242] This liberalisation has been embraced in some later cases, which have ordered disclosure where it was necessary to dispose of the matter fairly and justly.[243]

There are also some decisions showing a greater willingness to order cross-examination in judicial review proceedings. Thus in *Wilkinson*[244] the Court of Appeal held that cross-examination should be ordered where there was a challenge to a decision to administer medical treatment to a patient in judicial review proceedings. The court would have to form its own view as to whether the treatment infringed the applicant's human rights, and cross-examination would be required in order to do this where there were disputed questions of fact. This decision must however be seen in the light of the ruling by the Court of Appeal in *N*.[245] It held that it should not often be necessary to adduce oral evidence with cross-examination where there are disputed issues of fact and opinion in cases where the need for forcible medical treatment of a patient is being challenged on human rights grounds, and that *Wilkinson* should not be regarded as a charter for routine applications to the court for oral evidence in human rights cases generally. Much would depend on the nature of the right that had allegedly been breached and the nature of the alleged breach. A very cautionary approach to the possibility of cross-examination is also evident in *Bubb*.[246] **27–055**

G. Conclusion

There is no doubt that the CPR have narrowed the differences between the judicial review procedure and that in ordinary actions. The former has become more inter partes, and to that extent more like an ordinary action. The latter are now subject to greater judicial control pursuant to the general strategy behind the Woolf reforms. There are nonetheless still real differences between the two forms of procedure. CPR 54 has retained the essential features of Ord.53, the need for permission, plus the short time limits. There continue to be differences of view as to whether these protections are needed, and whether, if they are, they could be provided in the context of ordinary actions, without the need for a separate judicial review procedure. **27–056**

---

242 *Tweed* [2007] 1 A.C. 650 at [3], [32], [56]; *Sky Blue Sports & Leisure Ltd v Coventry CC* [2013] EWHC 3366 (Admin); *R. (Bredenkamp) v Secretary of State for Foreign and Commonwealth Affairs* [2013] EWHC 2480 (Admin); *R. (Perry) v Hackney LBC* [2014] EWHC 1721 (Admin).

243 *R. (Al-Sweady) v Secretary of State for Defence* [2009] EWHC 2387 (Admin); *R. (McVey) v Secretary of State for Health* [2009] EWHC 3084 (Admin); *R. (National Association of Probation Officers) v Secretary of State for Justice* [2013] EWHC 4349 (Admin).

244 *R. (Wilkinson) v Broadmoor Special Health Authority* [2002] 1 W.L.R. 419, CA (Civ Div); *R. (B) v Haddock (Responsible Medical Officer)* [2006] EWCA Civ 961; *Al-Sweady* [2009] EWHC 2387; *T-Mobile (UK) Ltd v Office of Communications* [2009] 1 W.L.R. 1565, CA (Civ Div).

245 *R. (N) v M* [2003] 1 W.L.R. 562, CA (Civ Div) at [36], [39]; *M v South West London & St George's Mental Health NHS Trust* [2008] EWCA Civ 1112.

246 *Bubb v Wandsworth LBC* [2011] EWCA Civ 1285 at [23]–[26].

5. PROCEDURE

A. Permission

27–057 A claimant must seek permission to apply for judicial review, CPR 54.4, and the application must be made promptly and in any event within three months after the grounds for making it first arose, CPR 54. 5. The court has powerful weapons to deter vexatious litigants.[247] The claim for judicial review is made using the CPR 8 claim form, which must in addition to the usual requirements state the following information, CPR 54.6. The claimant must give the name and address of any person considered to be an interested party. The claimant must state that they are requesting permission to seek judicial review, and the remedy being claimed.[248] Where the claimant is raising a point under the HRA, they must specify the Convention right alleged to have been infringed. A Practice Direction issued pursuant to CPR 54 stipulates that the claim form must also state, or be accompanied by a detailed statement of the claimant's grounds for bringing the claim, a statement of the facts relied on, copies of documents relied on by the claimant, relevant statutory material, and a copy of any order that the claimant seeks to have quashed.[249]

The claim form must be served on the defendant and other interested parties within seven days of the date of issue, CPR 54.7. If a person served with the claim form wishes to take part in the judicial review proceedings, they must acknowledge service within 21 days of being served, CPR 54.8(2)(a). This acknowledgement must be served on the claimant and any other person named in the claim form, CPR 54.8(2)(b). The acknowledgement must state whether the person intends to contest the claim, the grounds for doing so, and give the names and addresses of any other person considered to be an interested party, CPR 54.8(4). A person who fails to file an acknowledgement is not allowed to take part in the permission hearing, unless the court allows him to do so, CPR 54.9(1). There is provision for urgent cases.[250]

The criterion that applies to the grant of permission has been considered above.[251] Permission will not be granted unless the applicant has a sufficient interest in the matter to which the application relates.[252] Where permission is given the court may give directions, which may include a stay of the proceedings to which the claim relates, CPR 54.10. Permission decisions will often be made without a hearing. The court must provide reasons for its decision, CPR 54.12(2). A claimant that is refused permission without a hearing may not appeal, but may request, within seven days, for the decision to be reconsidered at a hearing, CPR. 54.12(3). It is not however open to the defendant or any other person served with the claim form to apply to have the permission set aside, CPR 54.13. Where permission has been refused after a hearing, the claimant may apply to the Court of Appeal for permission to appeal, which may, instead of giving permission to

---

247 *Bhamjee v Forsdick* [2004] 1 W.L.R. 88, CA (Civ Div).

248 *R. (Bhatt) v Secretary of State for the Home Department* [2015] EWHC 1724 (Admin).

249 Practice Direction (PD) 54 at [5.6]–[5.7].

250 Practice Statement (Administrative Court: Administration of Justice) [2002] A.C.D. 64.

251 See paras 27–040 to 27–045.

252 Senior Courts Act 1981 s.31(3). See Ch.25.

appeal, give permission for judicial review, CPR 52.15. The case will then be heard in the High Court unless the Court of Appeal indicates to the contrary, CPR 52.15(4).

B. The Substantive Hearing

The defendant and any other person served with the claim form who wishes to contest the claim, or support it on additional grounds, must provide detailed grounds for doing so, together with any written evidence, CPR 54.14. This must be done within 35 days of service of the order giving permission. A claimant must seek the court's permission to rely on grounds other than those for which he has been given permission to proceed, CPR 54.15. Written evidence may not be relied on unless it has been served in accordance with a rule under CPR 54, or direction of the court or the court gives permission, CPR 54.16. Any person may apply for permission to file evidence, or make representations at the judicial review hearing, CPR 54.17.[253] The court may decide the claim for judicial review without a hearing where all the parties agree, CPR 54.18. **27–058**

Where a quashing order is sought, the court may remit the matter to the decision-maker, directing it to reconsider the matter in the light of the court's judgment. Where the court considers that this would serve no useful purpose, it may in addition, subject to any statutory provision, substitute its own decision for the decision in question. However, it can only substitute its own decision if the decision in question was made by a court or tribunal, the decision was quashed for error of law and without the error there was only one lawful decision that the court or tribunal could have reached.[254] If the court does substitute its decision in accord with the previous conditions then, unless the High Court otherwise directs, the substituted decision takes effect as if it were a decision of the relevant court or tribunal.[255]

There are provisions allowing cases to be transferred to and from the Administrative Court, CPR 30. It is open to the court to order a claim to continue as if it had been started under CPR 54, and to give directions about the future management of the claim, CPR 54.20. It is also open to the court, where the relief sought is a declaration or injunction, and the court considers that such relief should not be granted in a claim for judicial review, to order that the case continue as a common law claim under CPR 7. There are provisions concerning the transfer of cases to and from the High Court[256] pursuant to the new power accorded by the Tribunals, Courts and Enforcement Act 2007 to the Upper Tribunal to exercise judicial review functions.[257]

---

[253] *R. (Howard League for Penal Reform) v Secretary of State for the Home Department (No.1)* [2002] EWHC 1750 (Admin); *R. v National Lottery Commission, Ex p. Camelot Group Plc* [2001] EMLR 3 QBD at [3]; M. Fordham, "'Public Interest' Intervention: A Practitioner's Perspective" [2007] P.L. 410.

[254] Senior Courts Act 1981 s.31(5)–(5A).

[255] Senior Courts Act 1981 s.31(5B).

[256] Senior Courts Act 1981 s.31A.

[257] Tribunals, Courts and Enforcement Act 2007 ss.15–19. See Ch.9.

27–059 Where the parties have agreed terms for resolving the case, an order may be obtained from the court to put the agreement into effect, without the need for a hearing. It will be for the judge to decide whether the case can be resolved in this manner.[258] If the judge decides that it would not be appropriate to make such an order, then the case will be heard in the normal manner.

The courts have in the past made a protective costs order, to allow claimants of limited means access to the court without the fear of substantial orders for costs being made against them.[259] The availability of such orders has been limited by the Criminal Justice and Courts Act 2015. They cannot be given prior to leave. An application for such an order requires the applicant to provide information as to resources. The court can then only make such an order if it is satisfied that[260]: the proceedings are public interest proceedings[261]; in the absence of the order, the applicant would withdraw the application for judicial review or cease to participate in the proceedings, and it would be reasonable for the applicant for judicial review to do so. In deciding whether to make such an order, a court must have regard to a range of factors, including[262]: the financial resources of the parties to the proceedings; the extent to which the applicant for the order is likely to benefit if relief is granted to the applicant for judicial review; the extent to which any person who has provided, or may provide, the applicant with financial support is likely to benefit if relief is granted to the applicant for review; whether the applicant's legal representatives are acting free of charge; and whether the applicant for the order is an appropriate person to represent the interests of other persons or the public interest generally.

C. Discretion to Refuse Relief

27–060 The courts exercise discretion in deciding whether to grant a remedy, and take into account a variety of factors. These include waiver, bad faith, the premature nature of the application, the absence of any injustice, the impact on third parties and the administration, and whether the decision would have been the same irrespective of the error.[263] The Court of Appeal recently emphasised that although the court had discretion to withhold relief if there were pressing reasons for not disturbing the status quo, delegated legislation held to be ultra vires had no specially protected position in that respect and there was no principle that it would only be quashed in special circumstances. It was, said the court, more important to correct unlawful legislation, which until quashed was universally binding, than it was to correct a single decision that affected only a limited range of people.[264]

---

258 PD 54 at [17].

259 *R. (Corner House Research) v Secretary of State for Trade and Industry* [2005] 1 W.L.R. 2600, CA (Civ Div); *R. (Buglife: The Invertebrate Conservation Trust) v Thurrock Thames Gateway Development Corp* [2008] EWCA Civ 1209; *R. (Public Interest Lawyers Ltd) v Legal Services Commission* [2010] EWHC 3259 (Admin).

260 Criminal Justice and Courts Act 2015 s.88(6).

261 Criminal Justice and Courts Act 2015 s.88(7)-(8).

262 Criminal Justice and Courts Act 2015 s.89(1).

263 Ch.26.

264 *R. (C) v Secretary of State for Justice* [2009] Q.B. 657, CA (Civ Div).

Whether the courts ought to exercise discretion in refusing relief is a matter on which opinions can differ.[265] Lord Bingham expressed the view that such discretion is acceptable provided that it is strictly limited and the rules for its exercise are clearly understood.[266] There is much to be said for this view. He accepted that differing considerations should apply to the various grounds for refusing relief. Commentators have, for example, been critical of decisions denying a remedy where there has been a failure to comply with natural justice, because the court believed that the outcome would not have been different.[267] It is doubtful whether this should ever be the ground for refusing relief, and Lord Bingham's judgment pointing out the dangers of denying relief on this ground is to be welcomed.[268] This may be contrasted with the situation where the court decides not to award a coercive order because the respondent authority is doing all that it can to comply with its statutory duty,[269] where the error has been substantially cured,[270] where the problem is now moot,[271] or where there would be serious public inconvenience in upsetting the impugned order.[272]

The discretion to refuse relief operates against the individual when the public body has committed an ultra vires act. This is so whether the discretion assumes the form of denying the remedy entirely or rendering the relief only prospectively rather than retrospectively applicable. Either way the ultra vires principle is qualified for good reason. If we are willing to do this then we should also be willing to qualify the ultra vires principle in favour of the individual where, for example, a person has relied upon an ultra vires representation and has suffered loss, provided that there are no dire consequences for the public interest.[273]

6. THE EFFECT OF ALTERNATIVE REMEDIES

A. Choice of Remedies under CPR 54

The traditional view was that the availability of prerogative relief did not operate as a bar to seeking a declaration.[274] The removal of the restrictions on the prerogative orders and the availability of all remedies under a unified procedure have inclined some courts to the view that the prerogative orders should be used whenever the validity of a decision is attacked.[275] Notwithstanding this, it is common for claimants to seek a declaration when challenging the legality of a public body's action. 27–061

[265] C. Forsyth, "The Rock and the Sand: Jurisdiction and Remedial Discretion", University of Cambridge, Legal Studies Research Paper Series, 31/2013.

[266] Lord Bingham, "Should Public Law Remedies be Discretionary?" [1991] P.L. 64.

[267] See Ch.12.

[268] *R. v Chief Constable of the Thames Valley Police Forces, Ex p. Cotton* [1990] I.R.L.R. 344, CA (Civ Div).

[269] *R. v Bristol Corporation, Ex p. Hendy* [1974] 1 W.L.R. 498, CA (Civ Div).

[270] *R. v Secretary of State for Social Services, Ex p. AMA* [1986] 1 W.L.R. 1 QBD.

[271] See Ch.26.

[272] *R. v Secretary of State for Social Services, Ex p. AMA* [1993] C.O.D. 54 QBD.

[273] Ch.22.

[274] *Pyx Granite Co Ltd v Ministry of Housing and Local Government* [1960] A.C. 260, HL at 290.

[275] *Cocks v Thanet DC* [1983] 2 A.C. 286, HL.

B. Alternative Statutory Remedies

27–062 The effect of statutory appeal procedures on the availability of judicial review[276] raises two issues which, although linked, should be distinguished.

First, while it is clear that the existence of such a procedure does not operate as a jurisdictional bar to judicial review, it is less clear how far such a procedure creates a presumption that resort should be had to that procedure rather than judicial review. In *Preston*[277] the House of Lords stated that judicial review should only rarely be available if an appellate procedure existed. This may be contrasted with the more liberal approach of Lord Denning MR in the *Paddington Valuation* case,[278] where his Lordship stated that review would be available where the alternative appellate procedure was "nowhere near so convenient, beneficial and effectual". The dominant view is now that in *Preston*. Lord Woolf, writing extra-judicially,[279] stated that judicial review should normally be a matter of last resort, and returned to this theme in *Cowl*.[280]

Second, the courts have nonetheless been willing to recognise exceptions and allow the judicial review application. The courts will take into account a number of factors in deciding whether to allow an application for judicial review, even though an alternative appellate structure exists.

27–063 Judicial review is unlikely to be ousted where doubt exists as to whether a right of appeal exists,[281] or whether such an appellate right covers the circumstances of the case.[282]

Judicial review will also be available where the statutory appeal mechanism is deemed inadequate as compared to judicial review. Thus, in *Leech*[283] a prisoner

---

[276] C. Lewis, "The Exhaustion of Alternative Remedies" [1992] C.L.J. 138; J. Beatson, "Prematurity and Ripeness for Review", in C. Forsyth and I. Hare (eds), *The Golden Metwand and the Crooked Cord, Essays on Public Law in Honour of Sir William Wade* (1998), pp.229–235.

[277] *R. v Inland Revenue Commissioners, Ex p. Preston* [1985] A.C. 835, HL at 852, 862. See also *R. v Poplar BC (No.1), Ex p. London CC* [1922] 1 K.B. 72, CA at 84–85, 88, 94; *R. v Epping and Harlow General Commissioners, Ex p. Goldstraw* [1983] 3 All E.R. 257, CA (Civ Div) at 262; *R. v Chief Constable of the Merseyside Police, Ex p. Calveley* [1986] Q.B. 424, CA (Civ Div) at 433–434; *Pasmore v Oswaldtwistle Urban DC* [1898] A.C. 387 at 394; *R. v Panel on Take-Overs and Mergers, Ex p. Guinness Plc* [1990] 1 Q.B. 146, CA (Civ Div); *R. v Police Complaints Authority, Ex p. Wells* [1991] C.O.D. 95; *R. v Special Educational Needs Tribunal, Ex p. Fairpo* [1996] C.O.D. 180 QBD; *R. v Secretary of State for the Home Department, Ex p. Capti-Mehmet* [1997] C.O.D. 61; *R. v Secretary of State for the Home Department, Ex p. Watts* [1997] C.O.D. 152; *R. v Falmouth and Truro Port Health Authority, Ex p. South West Water Ltd* [2001] Q.B. 445, CA (Civ Div) at 472–473, 476, 486; *R. (Sivasubramaniam) v Wandsworth County Court* [2002] EWCA Civ 1738; *R. (G) v Immigration Appeal Tribunal* [2005] 1 W.L.R. 1445, CA (Civ Div); *R. (Sinclair Gardens Investments (Kensington) Ltd) v Lands Tribunal* [2005] EWCA Civ 1305; *R. (S) v Hampshire CC* [2009] EWHC 2537 (Admin); *R. (Great Yarmouth Port Co Ltd) v Marine Management Organisation* [2013] EWHC 3052 (Admin); *R. (C) v Financial Services Authority* [2013] EWCA Civ 677.

[278] *R. v Paddington Valuation Officer, Ex p. Peachey Property Corporation* [1966] 1 Q.B. 380, CA at 400. See also, *R. v Leicester Guardians* [1899] 2 Q.B. 632 QBD at 638–639; *R. v North, Ex p. Oakey* [1927] 1 K.B. 491, CA; *Stepney BC v John Walker and Sons Ltd* [1934] A.C. 365.

[279] Lord Woolf, "Judicial Review: A Possible Programme for Reform" [1992] P.L. 221, 235.

[280] *Cowl* [2002] 1 W.L.R. 803.

[281] *R. v Hounslow LBC, Ex p. Pizzey* [1977] 1 W.L.R. 58 DC at 62; *R. v Board of Visitors of Hull Prison, Ex p. St Germain* [1979] Q.B. 425, CA (Civ Div) at 456, 465.

[282] *Preston* [1985] A.C. 835 at 862.

[283] *Leech v Deputy Governor of Parkhurst Prison* [1988] A.C. 533, HL.

was allowed to seek judicial review of a disciplinary decision by a prison governor, notwithstanding the existence of a petition procedure to the secretary of state. Their Lordships were influenced by the fact that the secretary of state did not have the formal power to quash the governor's decision, but merely the power to remit the punishment inflicted on the prisoner.

In deciding whether to allow an applicant to use judicial review the courts will take into account general factors concerning the nature of the appellate procedure, and consider how onerous it is for the individual to be restricted to the statutory mechanism. This is clearly sensible, although the results of this analysis may appear unjust. Thus, in *Calveley*,[284] the court took account of the fact that the alternative procedure was likely to be slow and thus allowed police officers to seek judicial review. However, in *Swati*,[285] an immigrant was restricted to the statutory appeals procedure, save in exceptional circumstances, notwithstanding the fact that this entailed leaving the UK in order to avail himself of that right.

The courts have in the past held that review is more likely to be available where the alleged error is one of law.[286] The judicial approach has, however, changed. The mere existence of an alleged error of law will not in itself serve to displace the presumption that statutory appeal procedures should be used.[287]

An applicant is likely to be restricted to the statutory appeal procedure where the case turns on mixed questions of law and fact,[288] disputed questions of fact, the appellate tribunal possesses expertise,[289] or where issues of criminal law are involved.[290]

The reforms contained in the Tribunals, Courts and Enforcement Act 2007 will reinforce the view that appeal or judicial review within the tribunal system should be used before any possible recourse to judicial review before the High Court.[291]

The long-standing supervisory jurisdiction exercised over magistrates should generally continue to be exercised notwithstanding rights of appeal to the Crown Court.[292]

---

[284] *Calveley* [1986] Q.B. 424 at 434, 440.

[285] *R. v Secretary of State for the Home Department, Ex p. Swati* [1986] 1 W.L.R. 477, CA (Civ Div); *Doorga* [1990] C.O.D. 109 at 111.

[286] *Paddington Valuation* [1966] 1 Q.B. 380; *R. v Hillingdon LBC, Ex p. Royco Homes Ltd* [1974] Q.B. 720 QBD; *Pyx Granite* [1960] A.C. 260; *Wells* [1991] C.O.D. 95; *R. v Devon CC, Ex p. Baker* [1993] 1 All E.R. 73.

[287] *Preston* [1985] A.C. 835; *Poplar BC (No.1)* [1922] 1 K.B. 72; *Goldstraw* [1983] 3 All E.R. 257; *Calveley* [1986] Q.B. 424; *Pasmore* [1898] A.C. 387; *Guinness Plc* [1990] 1 Q.B. 146; *Wells* [1991] C.O.D. 95; *Fairpo* [1996] C.O.D. 180; *Capti-Mehmet* [1997] C.O.D. 61; *Watts* [1997] C.O.D. 152; *South West Water* [2001] Q.B. 445; *Sivasubramaniam* [2002] EWCA Civ 1738; *G* [2005] 1 W.L.R. 1445; *Sinclair Gardens* [2005] EWCA Civ 1305; *S v Hampshire CC* [2009] EWHC 2537 (Admin).

[288] *R. v Epping Forest DC, Ex p. Green* [1993] C.O.D. 81.

[289] *Clark v Epsom Rural DC* [1929] 1 Ch. 287 Ch D.; *Preston* [1985] A.C. 835; *Smeeton v Att Gen* [1920] 1 Ch. 85 Ch D.; *Coney v Choyce* [1975] 1 W.L.R. 422 Ch D. at 434; *Hilditch v Westminster CC* [1990] C.O.D. 434, CA (Civ Div).

[290] *R. v DPP, Ex p. Camelot Group Ltd* [1998] C.O.D. 54 QBD.

[291] *Marine Management Organisation* [2013] EWHC 3052.

[292] *R. v Hereford Magistrates' Court, Ex p. Rowlands* [1998] Q.B. 110 QBD.

C. Conclusion

27–064 The courts have been mindful not to usurp Parliament's choice where it has established a special statutory mechanism to adjudicate on a particular topic. The assumption that litigants must use available statutory machinery has been influenced by the courts' desire to control the case load on judicial review. Specialised statutory appeal mechanisms may, in addition, be better suited to resolving complex issues of fact, and may possess expertise in the relevant area. These are sensible considerations for the courts to take into account. However, as the Law Commission stated,[293] there may well be advantages in determining the effect of alternative remedies at the permission stage.

7. CONCLUSION

27–065 There will be no attempt to summarise the discussion in this and the previous chapter concerning remedies. Cane has rightly pointed out that the way in which we think about remedies in public law should not however, be taken for granted. The claimant is presently required to choose from the range of remedies on offer. The applicant cannot come to court, state the desired object and then ask the court to select a remedy to achieve this end[294]:

> "Just as, under the modern system of pleading, claimants plead facts and ask the court to recognise those facts as giving rise to a cause of action in law, so public law claimants should be free to specify the result they want to achieve by their claim and ask the court to provide an appropriate remedy. A claimant should not be required to specify which remedy is sought; rather it should be for the court to decide if a remedy is available to achieve the claimant's desired end."

[293] LCCP, para.14.14.

[294] "The Constitutional Basis of Judicial Remedies in Public Law", in P. Leyland and T. Woods (eds), *Administrative Law Facing the Future: Old Constraints and New Horizons* (London: Blackstone, 1997), p.245.

CHAPTER 28

REMEDIES: EXCLUSION OF REVIEW

1. CENTRAL ISSUES

i. The legislature has attempted to limit judicial review through various formulae inserted in legislation. These efforts have not in general been successful, since the courts have restrictively construed such legislation. The legislature has attempted to limit judicial review in two types of way. 28–001

ii. First, it has devised a range of clauses, the detailed wording of which differs, designed to exclude judicial review by the ordinary courts. The legislative ingenuity in drafting has been matched by judicial insistence on preservation of the essentials of judicial review. The courts have limited the effect of such clauses through interpretation, which has been influenced by the background legal principle concerning the desirability of ensuring that government is subject to legal control.

iii. Second, the legislature has imposed clauses that limit the time within which judicial review can be claimed. This device has been especially prevalent in areas where certainty of government action is at a high premium, such as planning and land use. The courts have been more tolerant of such clauses than those that seek to oust the jurisdiction of the courts completely.

2. COMPLETE EXCLUSION

A. Finality Clauses

Finality clauses are statutory terms that purport to render the decision of a particular agency unassailable. The courts have given them short shrift, holding that they only protect decisions made on facts and not law.[1] Jurisdictional defects were not immune from judicial scrutiny by such clauses,[2] nor were errors on the face of the record. Thus, in *Gilmore*[3] it was held that the decision of the tribunal was open to attack despite the existence of a finality clause. Denning LJ reviewed the authorities and concluded that the clause only prevented an appeal. Judicial review, whether for jurisdictional error or error on the face of the record, 28–002

---

[1] *R. v Plowright* (1686) 3 Mod. 94.

[2] *R. v Moreley* (1760) 2 Burr. 1040; *R. v Jukes* (1800) 8 TR 542; cf. where certiorari is the creature of statute, *R. v Hunt* (1856) 6 El. & Bl. 409.

[3] *R. v Medical Appeal Tribunal, Ex p. Gilmore* [1957] 1 Q.B. 574, CA.

remained unimpaired.[4] Even this limited effect has been subsequently diminished. Thus, the case law authority for the proposition that a finality clause can prevent an appeal[5] has been characterised as out of date. The Court of Appeal held that, notwithstanding the existence of finality provisions, it was still possible to state a case, at least where declaration or certiorari would themselves have been available.[6]

B. "No Certiorari" Clauses

28–003 Part of the reason for legislative dislike of judicial review was that the courts could overturn decisions for technical errors with an excess of vigour that bordered upon the pedantic. The legislature responded by the insertion of no certiorari clauses within statutes. The judiciary acknowledged that they had been over-technical.[7]

Jurisdictional defects continued, however, to remain unaffected by no certiorari clauses.[8] In *R. v Wood*[9] a byelaw compelling home owners to remove snow from in front of their houses was attacked as ultra vires the parent legislation. The statute concerned the removal of dirt, manure, dung and soil. Lord Campbell CJ held that the no certiorari clause was ineffective. The secretary of state could only give authority to byelaws that were in conformity with the parent legislation, and Lord Campbell rejected any generic identity between these substances and snow.[10]

> "It might possibly have been advisable to extend the power to the case of all snow; but that is not done: the words of the section cannot, by any strain of construction, be extended to untrodden and unsunned snow, which is proverbially pure."

Such clauses, while ineffective to insulate jurisdictional error, could exclude review for error of law on the face of the record, while this concept still had currency. If the clause is contained in a statute enacted prior to August 1958 it will be subject to the Tribunals and Inquiries Act discussed below. Where the preclusive clause is contained in a statute passed after that date, it can be effective, as exemplified by the *South East Asia Fire*[11] case. The Malaysian Industrial Relations Act 1967 s.29(3)(a) contained an "omnibus" exclusion clause. Parliamentary draftsmen had obviously decided that the more types of exclusions the better. Thus, s.29(3)(a) contained a finality clause, a shall not be

---

[4] *Gilmore* [1957] 1 Q.B. 574 at 583–585. See also *R. v Nat Bell Liquors Ltd* [1922] 2 A.C. 128 at 159–160; *R. (Sivasubramaniam) v Wandsworth County Court* [2002] EWCA Civ 1738 at [43]–[45].

[5] *Kydd v Liverpool Watch Committee* [1908] A.C. 327, HL; *Piper v St Marylebone Licensing JJ* [1928] 2 K.B. 221 KBD.

[6] *Tehrani v Rostron* [1972] 1 Q.B. 182, CA (Civ Div) at 187–188, 192. See also *Pearlman v Keepers and Governors of Harrow School* [1979] Q.B. 56, CA (Civ Div) at 68–69, 79.

[7] *R. v Ruyton (Inhabitants)* (1861) 1 B. & S. 534 at 545; *Gilmore* [1957] 1 Q.B. 574 at 586.

[8] *R. v Cheltenham Commissioners* (1841) 1 Q.B. 467 KBD; *R. v Somersetshire JJ* (1826) 5 B. & C. 816 KBD.

[9] *R. v Wood* (1855) 5 El. & Bl. 49 KBD.

[10] *Wood* (1855) 5 El. & Bl. 49 at 55. See also *Ex p. Bradlaugh* [1878] 3 Q.B.D. 509 at 512–513.

[11] *South East Asia Fire Bricks Sdn Bhd v Non-Metallic Mineral Products Manufacturing Employees Union* [1981] A.C. 363.

challenged or questioned section, and a term providing that awards of the industrial court should not be quashed. A dispute between a company and a union was referred to the industrial court, which found in favour of the union. The company sought to have this quashed for error of law on the face of the record.

The Privy Council declined to interfere. Lord Fraser, giving judgment, agreed with the company's argument that the finality provision did not protect the industrial court.[12] The provision within s.29(3)(a) that an award should not be quashed was however sufficient to achieve this end. If it would not suffice by itself, the addition of the words "shall not be called in question in any court of law" were wide enough to cover certiorari. Only errors of law within jurisdiction were immune from attack.[13] A jurisdictional error could still be impugned. The Privy Council rejected the argument that any error of law was now to be regarded as jurisdictional, but, as we have seen, later developments have effectively spelt the end for the concept of error of law within jurisdiction.[14] The expansion of jurisdictional error means that it will be difficult for the legislature to employ this clause to exclude the courts.

C. "Shall not be Questioned" Clauses

Another formula used to exclude the courts has been the "shall not be questioned clause". Any hope that persevering parliamentary draftsmen might have had that this formula would work where all else had failed was to prove unfounded. In *Anisminic*,[15] s.4(4) of the Foreign Compensation Act 1950 stated that a determination of the Commission should not be called in question in any court of law. Their Lordships held that this only protected intra vires determinations. Ultra vires determinations were not determinations at all. They were nullities, which could be of no effect. Section 4(4), or any equivalent provision, could only immunise from attack errors of law within jurisdiction and this concept has itself now largely ceased to exist. **28–004**

The courts however distinguish between the ouster of their jurisdiction in the manner attempted in *Anisminic* and the allocation of adjudicative functions to another tribunal. This is exemplified by the *Security Service* case.[16] The claimant wished to publish a book about the security service in which he had been employed, but the director of the service refused consent. The claimant sought judicial review, arguing that the director's refusal was contrary to freedom of expression as protected by art.10 ECHR. The Supreme Court rejected the claim. It held that s.65(2)(a) of the Regulation of Investigatory Powers Act 2000 gave the Investigatory Powers Tribunal (IPT) the exclusive jurisdiction to hear claims

[12] *South East Asia Fire Bricks* [1981] A.C. 363 at 369–370 following *Gilmore* [1957] 1 Q.B. 574; *Waldron, Re* [1986] Q.B. 824 CA (Civ Div).

[13] *South East Asia Fire Bricks* [1981] A.C. 363 at 370.

[14] See Ch.16.

[15] *Anisminic Ltd v Foreign Compensation Commission* [1969] 2 A.C. 147, HL at 170–171, 181, 200–201, 210; *R. v Secretary of State for the Home Department, Ex p. Mehta* [1992] C.O.D. 484 DC. Cf. *R. v Acting Returning Officer for the Devon and East Plymouth European Constituency, Ex p. Sanders* [1994] C.O.D. 497 QBD.

[16] *R. (A) v Director of Establishments of the Security Service* [2010] 2 A.C. 1 SC. See also *Farley v Secretary of State for Work and Pensions (No.2)* [1986] 1 W.L.R. 1817.

under s.7(1)(a) of the Human Rights Act 1998 against the security services. This did not constitute ouster of the courts' supervisory jurisdiction over the security services, nor did it allow the IPT to determine the scope of its own jurisdiction. Section 65(2)(a) merely allocated scrutiny of HRA claims to the IPT.[17]

D. "As if Enacted" and "Conclusive Evidence"

28–005 A different technique used to insulate subordinate legislation has been to provide that a statutory order shall have effect "as if enacted in this Act", or that confirmation by a designated minister "shall be conclusive evidence that the requirements of this Act have been complied with, and that the order has been duly made and is within the powers of this Act".

Such clauses were condemned by the Committee on Ministers' Powers,[18] which doubted whether they would safeguard an order that was flagrantly ultra vires from judicial censure. Other preclusive clauses have not proven effective even where the invalidity was not extreme.[19] Despite this, both formulations have been successful in excluding review. The authorities upholding the efficacy of the "conclusive evidence" formula date mainly from the earlier part of this century.[20] However, more recent authority has continued to uphold the effectiveness of such clauses.[21]

The current status of the "as if" formula is that there are two decisions of the House of Lords that indicate opposite conclusions and are difficult to reconcile. In the earlier decision their Lordships interpreted the effect of the clause as being to render secondary legislation as immune from censure as if it were part of the parent legislation, the cloak of sovereignty protecting all.[22] If this ruling had been taken literally then the executive could have governed the country de jure as well as de facto. Its scope has, however, been limited. The House of Lords subsequently held that the "as if" formula does not provide protection for secondary legislation which conflicts with the parent Act.[23] This latter statement appears not simply to limit the former but to contradict it, and indeed, there are judgments in the second decision that are difficult to reconcile with the earlier authority. It may be that the clause will be effective if the statutory order in dispute relates generally to the statutory scheme, even though it may be subject to relatively minor errors which would nevertheless, in the absence of the clause, render the decision ultra vires.[24]

---

[17] The Regulation of Investigatory Powers Act 2000 s.67(8) contained an ouster clause, but it was not in issue in the instant case.

[18] Committee on Ministers' Powers (1932) Cmnd.4060, p.41.

[19] *R. v Wood* (1855) 5 El. & Bl. 49 KBD.

[20] *Ex p. Ringer* (1909) 73 J.P. 436; *Reddaway v Lancs CC* (1925) 41 T.L.R. 422; *Minister of Health v R, Ex p. Yaffe* [1931] A.C. 494, HL at 520, 532–533, but see also *Graddage v Haringey LBC* [1975] 1 W.L.R. 241 Ch D.; *County and Nimbus Estates Ltd v Ealing LBC* (1978) 76 L.G.R. 624.

[21] *R. v Registrar of Companies, Ex p. Central Bank of India* [1986] Q.B. 1114, CA (Civ Div), distinguishing such clauses from the type used in the *Anisminic* case.

[22] *Institute of Patent Agents v Lockwood* [1894] A.C. 347, HL.

[23] *R. v Minister of Health, Ex p. Yaffe* [1931] A.C. 494, HL.

[24] This is the view adopted by de Smith, *Judicial Review of Administrative Action*, 4th edn (London: Sweet & Maxwell, 1980), pp.375–376. The formulation in Lord Woolf, J. Jowell and A. Le Sueur, *de*

The difficulty of interpreting the case law is compounded by uncertainty and disagreement as to the purpose of such clauses. One argument is that the formula was intended to have a substantive impact, giving subordinate legislation the same status as a primary Act. The other is that the magic words were a survival from medieval times and now had only a formal function. According to this latter view, the clause was used to indicate that the authority for the creation of secondary legislation was based upon Parliament.[25]

E. Statutory Intervention

In 1958 parliamentary intervention took a different form. There had been much criticism of exclusion clauses. The Franks Committee advocated removal of clauses that purported to oust the prerogative orders.[26] The Tribunals and Inquiries Act 1958 implemented a number of the proposals of the Franks Committee. That Act was replaced by the Tribunals and Inquiries Act 1971, which was replaced by the Tribunals and Inquiries Act 1992 s.12(1) of which provides that as respects England and Wales: **28–006**

> "(a) any provision in an Act passed before 1st August 1958 that any order or determination shall not be called into question in any court, or
> (b) any provision in such an Act which by similar words excludes any of the powers of the High Court, shall not have effect so as to prevent the removal of the proceedings into the High Court by order of certiorari or to prejudice the powers of the High Court to make orders of mandamus."

Three important points about this section should be noted. First, it is subject to two exceptions which are set out in s.12(3), the effect of which is that s.12(1) does not apply to orders or determinations made by courts of law, or to clauses which exclude the courts after a limited period of time. Second, the section only applies to certiorari and mandamus. The declaration is not included. There appears to be no rational reason why this should be so.[27] Third, s.12 has been held not to apply to "conclusive evidence" clauses.[28]

3. TIME LIMITS

In some contexts it may be particularly important to know whether a decision can safely be acted upon. This is particularly so in areas such as planning, compulsory acquisition and the like. Statutes in such areas normally provide a cut-off period of six weeks, after which the decision shall not be called in **28–007**

Smith's Judicial Review, 6th edn (London: Sweet & Maxwell, 2007), pp.187–188, is somewhat different. See also *Foster v Aloni* [1951] V.L.R. 481.

[25] W. Graham-Harrison, *Notes on the Delegation by Parliament of Legislative Powers* (London: Eyre and Spottiswoode, 1931), pp.26–68; J. Willis, *The Parliamentary Powers of English Government Departments* (Cambridge: Harvard University Press, 1933), pp.62–101.

[26] The Franks Committee (1958), Cmnd.218, para.117.

[27] In *Ridge v Baldwin* [1964] A.C. 40, HL at 120–121, Lord Morris of Borth-y-Gest was of the view that the Act did cover the declaration, but in *O'Reilly v Mackman* [1983] 2 A.C. 237, HL it was said that this limit showed a preference for the prerogative orders.

[28] *Central Bank of India* [1986] Q.B. 1114 at 1170, 1178, 1182.

question in any legal proceedings. Within the allowed time there are statutory grounds on which an order can be attacked. The present discussion focuses on the effect of expiry of the six weeks. The scope of review within that period has already been considered in earlier discussion.[29]

The starting point for discussion is the *Smith* case.[30] Smith alleged that a local authority had compulsorily acquired her property in bad faith. Despite the possible presence of fraud their Lordships held that the clause protected the local authority after the expiry of the six weeks.[31] It was unclear how far *Anisminic* affected this decision.[32] The latter also involved a shall not be questioned clause, the difference being that the provision in the Foreign Compensation Act 1950 purported to exclude the courts altogether, whereas in the *Smith* case there was a six-week time limit within which an order could be challenged. In the *Anisminic* case little favour was shown to the *Smith* decision. It was not expressly overruled, although it was distinguished on a variety of grounds. The distinction between complete ouster of jurisdiction and time limitations was not, however, foremost in their Lordships' reasoning.[33]

28–008 *Smith* survived despite this censure. In *Ostler*[34] the applicant sought to quash a road scheme and compulsory purchase order, alleging breach of natural justice and bad faith. The facts of the case were particularly strong. Ostler argued that he was only applying outside the six-week time limit because a covert agreement between a departmental officer and a local merchant had been hidden from him and had changed the whole complexion of the scheme. If the facts had been revealed earlier he would have objected within the time limit.

The six-week time limit was, nonetheless, upheld. *Anisminic* was distinguished for a number of reasons. The distinction between a complete ouster clause and a time limit[35]; the administrative nature of the proceedings in *Smith* as compared with the more judicial nature of the Foreign Compensation Commission[36]; and the allegedly differing degrees of nullity ensuing from the defects in the two cases,[37] were advanced to uphold the clause. The Court of Appeal was also influenced by the fact that a significant part of the scheme had been begun and that nullification would have resulted in considerable disruption and expense.[38]

---

29 See paras 16–035 to 16–036.

30 *Smith v East Elloe Rural DC* [1956] A.C. 736, HL.

31 See also *Woollett v Minister of Agriculture and Fisheries* [1955] 1 Q.B. 103, CA. Compare *Webb v Minister of Housing and Local Government* [1965] 1 W.L.R. 755.

32 *Anisminic* [1969] 2 A.C. 147.

33 *Anisminic* [1969] 2 A.C. 147 at 170–171, 200–201, 210.

34 *R. v Secretary of State for the Environment, Ex p. Ostler* [1977] Q.B. 122, CA (Civ Div).

35 *Ostler* [1977] Q.B. 122 at 135.

36 *Ostler* [1977] Q.B. 122 at 135, 138.

37 *Ostler* [1977] Q.B. 122 at 135, 139, 140.

38 See also *Jeary v Chailey Rural DC* (1973) 26 P. & C.R. 280, CA (Civ Div); *Routh v Reading Corp* (1971) 217 E.G. 1337.

The decisions in *Smith* and *Ostler* have been followed on a number of occasions. Thus, in *Huntington*[39] it was held that an order subject to a six-week time limit clause could only be challenged within that period, and by the method stipulated in the statute. An applicant could not choose to use the ordinary judicial review procedure instead. It made no difference whether the body whose decision was being challenged was quasi-judicial or administrative; and it was irrelevant whether the invalidity was fundamental or not.

However, in *Richards*[40] the Court of Appeal held that time limit clauses should, for constitutional reasons, be narrowly construed. This meant that even if the initial order was immune from review after six weeks because of *Ostler* and *Huntington*, it did not necessarily preclude judicial review of instruments made under that order, since the validity of those instruments depended ultimately on the enabling statute.

The problem considered within this section is now of greater importance given that the time limits for seeking judicial review within proceedings under s.31 of the Senior Courts Act 1981 are short, and given also that the judiciary have insisted that some cases can only be brought by this route. While these provisions on time limits do not contain any explicit "shall not be challenged" clause, the courts have not, on the whole, been willing to allow actions outside this period.[41]

4. THE EFFECT OF THE HUMAN RIGHTS ACT 1998

The HRA is relevant to the viability of ouster clauses. The preclusion of review may offend against the requirement in art.6 ECHR that a decision must be made by an independent tribunal. This will be relevant where there is an ouster clause and the initial decision-maker does not qualify as independent for the purposes of the Strasbourg jurisprudence. The relevant case law has been considered earlier.[42] Thus in *Richards*[43] Neuberger LJ indicated, without deciding the matter, that a time limit clause might not be consistent with art.6 ECHR. A complete ouster would be even more suspect in this regard. 28–009

5. CONCLUSION

A. Complete Ouster Clauses

Whether it would be possible to devise an ouster clause that excluded review is less a matter of semantics than of judicial attitude and legislative response. The courts have always been able to interpret an Act of Parliament and, thus, they can, 28–010

---

39 *R. v Cornwall CC, Ex p. Huntington* [1992] 3 All E.R. 566 QBD, affirmed [1994] 1 All E.R. 694; *R. v Secretary of State for the Environment, Ex p. Kent* [1990] J.P.L. 124, CA (Civ Div); *R. v Secretary of State for the Environment, Ex p. Upton Brickworks Ltd* [1992] C.O.D. 301; *R. v Camden LBC, Ex p. Woolf* [1992] C.O.D. 456.

40 *R. (Richards) v Pembrokeshire CC* [2004] EWCA Civ 1000 at [46]–[47].

41 See paras 27–046 to 27–049.

42 See Ch.14.

43 *Richards* [2004] EWCA Civ 1000 at [37].

if they choose, construe it as only precluding error within jurisdiction or appeal. Short of provoking a constitutional clash by rejecting this judicial interpretation, there is nothing that Parliament can do.

Until recently the courts could, in formal terms, continue to accept Parliamentary authority, even when restrictively construing an ouster clause, by according such clauses some impact, by protecting errors of law within jurisdiction from attack. The expansion of jurisdictional control and the corresponding demise of error within jurisdiction, means that this route is in general no longer open to the judiciary. The options for the future are that the courts either restrictively interpret the clause and deny it any effect, except perhaps in preventing an appeal, or they give the clause some effect by stating that the presumption that all errors of law are open to review has been displaced in a particular area. Even if the courts choose this latter approach some judicial control can still be maintained, as experience in other jurisdictions demonstrates.[44]

The determination of the courts to preserve judicial review in the face of ouster clauses raises important issues. The parliamentary intent was to limit or remove the courts from a particular area.[45] The judicial attitude towards ouster clauses has however hardened over the years. Thus, the government's attempt to include an ouster in legislation relating to asylum provoked a storm of protest from the senior judiciary, which ultimately caused the government to amend the legislation.[46]

28–011 It is not clear what would have happened if the constitutional clash between courts and Parliament had not been averted. The courts might have had recourse to arguments based on the Human Rights Act 1998 concerning the need for a decision to be made by an independent tribunal, although it is not clear that this would have availed them in this particular instance. The courts might, alternatively, have made explicit what has been implicit in their existing jurisprudence on ouster clauses. The case law is ultimately premised on the constitutional principle that access to the courts should not be denied, and that such access is a pre-condition for the protection of other rights guaranteed in our constitutional order.

Given the present judicial attitude to ouster clauses a legislature which is minded to limit judicial intervention might, however, do better by introducing a time limit clause. The courts have accepted that such clauses prevent challenges outside the stipulated period and that any action brought within that time must be by the procedure laid down in the enabling statute, although this case law remains to be tested in the light of the Human Rights Act 1998.

---

[44] The Australian courts have retained power in the face of such terms if there is a clear excess of power, while not interfering if the agency has made a bona fide attempt to exercise its authority in a matter relating to the subject with which the legislation deals, M. Aronson and M. Groves, *Judicial Review of Administrative Action*, 5th edn (Sydney: Lawbook/Thomson Reuters Australia, 2013), Ch.18.

[45] This statement must be qualified in two ways: (a) Parliament enacted the Tribunals and Inquiries Act 1992 s.12; and (b) it has acquiesced, in the sense of continuing to use certain terms even after the legal effect ascribed to them by the courts has become clear.

[46] R. Rawlings, "Review, Revenge and Retreat" (2005) 68 M.L.R. 378; *de Smith's Judicial Review* (2007), Appendix C.

B. Time Limits

Statutes containing time limit clauses raise somewhat different problems. In the modern state there will necessarily be a trade-off between the need for administrative certainty, on the one hand, and justice for the individual and administrative legality on the other. This balancing appears in varying guises throughout administrative law. It arises in the creative decision as to how to categorise an alleged error, as jurisdictional or not, or as law or fact. It rears its head in the way in which we deal with waiver, delay, and representations. It lies behind some of the judicial manipulation of void and voidable. **28–012**

The effect to be given to time limits is another manifestation of this problem. If the *Ostler*[47] decision had gone the other way then some other device, judicial or legislative, would have been required. Where an expensive planning and building project is undertaken then the traditional response of retrospective nullity will be difficult to apply. The method of distinguishing *Anisminic* may or may not have been convincing,[48] but some limit to challenge is required in such areas.

This does not mean that we can be complacent or that there is no room for improvement. Two matters require special attention. The first is to consider whether the length of the time limit is adequate. Six weeks is short and thought needs to be given as to what would be the appropriate balance between the needs of the individual and the requirements of the administration. Second, the provision of a compensatory remedy for those unable to complain needs to be thought through. This is particularly important where the individual's recourse to the statutory machinery is effectively foreclosed by bad faith or fraud. The possibility of such a remedy will be considered later.[49]

---

[47] *Ostler* [1977] QB 122.

[48] J. Alder, "Time Limit Clauses and Judicial Review" (1975) 38 M.L.R. 274; N. Gravells, "Time Limit Clauses and Judicial Review—The Relevance of Context" (1978) 41 M.L.R. 383; N. Gravells, "Time Limit Clauses and Judicial Review—Some Second Thoughts" (1980) 43 M.L.R. 173; J. Alder, "Time Limit Clauses and Conceptualism—A Reply" (1980) 43 M.L.R. 670.

[49] See Ch.30.

8. Time Limits

28-012 [illegible]

[illegible]

[illegible]

[illegible]

CHAPTER 29

CROWN LIABILITY

1. CENTRAL ISSUES

i. The Crown's contractual liability has already been considered.[1] Three matters will be considered in this chapter, which are concerned with the Crown's position in relation to litigation and tort liability. 29–001
ii. First, there are specific legal rules that apply to statutes and the Crown. The law in this respect was more satisfactory 300 hundred years ago, where the simple principle was that the Crown was bound by a statute that was intended to bind it. This principle was however lost sight of in subsequent case law, with the consequence that the current law as to when a statute will bind the Crown is more limited than hitherto.
iii. Second, there have been complications as to the types of remedy that can be awarded against the Crown. The law in this area is now clearer than hitherto, because of statutory changes and more recent case law.
iv. Third, the law prior to 1947 rendered it difficult to claim damages in tort against the Crown. The Crown Proceedings Act 1947 reformed the law in this area, and the applicable rules are, with some modifications, the same as those pertaining to ordinary tort actions.

2. STATUTES AND THE CROWN

A. Statutes Binding the Crown

Whether statutes bind the Crown is problematic, because early decisions have been interpreted in a way they do not warrant, and those subsequent interpretations have become the law. The commonly stated rule is that the Crown is not bound by statute in the absence of express provision or necessary implication. This was not always the case. Street traced the history of this rule and demonstrated the subtle change in the case law.[2] 29–002

In the 16th century the position was that the Crown was bound by a statute intended to bind it.[3] Where the statute touched upon the rights of subjects generally then the Crown would normally also be bound. There was, however, a presumption that a general statute would not affect the prerogative rights of the

[1] See paras 5–053 to 5–057.
[2] H. Street, "The Effect of Statutes upon the Rights and Liabilities of the Crown" (1948) 7 U.T.L.J. 357.
[3] *Willion v Berkley* (1561) 1 Plowden 223.

King, unless he was named therein. The transition from this position to the commonly stated rule set out above occurred largely by accident and misinterpretation.[4] By the 20th century a rule began to be propounded in texts on statute law that the Crown, if not named, would be bound by a statute only if that was the necessary implication. Such an implication would only be necessary if to do otherwise would be to render the statute "unmeaning".[5] This test will only be met if it can be affirmed at the time when the statute was passed that it was apparent from its terms that its purpose would be wholly frustrated if the Crown were not to be bound. The House of Lords endorsed this general rule of construction and made it clear that it applies irrespective of whether the statute in question was passed for the public benefit or not.[6] The courts have, however, been willing to conclude that the Crown is bound by necessary implication, since to do otherwise would frustrate the legislation.[7]

The immunity should in principle be shared by any person who could show that application of the statute to them would prejudice the Crown. On this hypothesis being a Crown servant would be neither a sufficient nor a necessary condition for immunity. It would not be sufficient because it would be possible for a person to be a Crown servant but for the application of the statute not to be prejudicial to the Crown. It would not be necessary, because it would be possible for independent contractors and others to argue that the application of a statute to them would prejudicially affect the Crown.

29–003 A number of problems flow from the existing law. It is unclear when the exception to the present rule will apply. The retention of the present presumption also creates problems with the application to the Crown of statutes concerning tortious liability. The present presumption was left unaltered by the Crown Proceedings Act 1947 s.40(2)(f), except as otherwise expressly provided. Section 2 of the same legislation imposes liability in tort upon the Crown as if it were a private person. A neat question therefore arises as to whether such statutes passed before and after the 1947 Act are rendered automatically applicable to the Crown through the operation of s.2, or whether express provision in the particular statute is required.[8]

The present state of the law is unsatisfactory. The shift from a rule sensibly based on general legislative purpose to the present position was the result of misinterpretation of earlier authority. Little thought has been given to the justification, if any, for this position. It might be argued that the present rule gives rise to no great problems because the Crown can easily be expressly included in the statute. This argument is premised on an ideal, whereby legislators will carefully decide whether to extend an Act to the Crown. The legislative process will often not operate in this way. Whether the Crown should be bound may

[4] *Magdalen College Case* (1615) 11 Co. Rep. 66b.

[5] *Province of Bombay v Municipal Corp of the City of Bombay* [1947] A.C. 58; *Madras Electric Supply Co Ltd v Boarland* [1955] A.C. 667, HL; *Gorton Local Board v Prison Commissioners* [1904] 2 K.B. 165 KBD; *British Broadcasting Corp v Johns* [1965] Ch. 32, CA; cf. *Att Gen v De Keyser's Royal Hotel Ltd* [1920] A.C. 508, HL.

[6] *Lord Advocate v Dumbarton DC* [1990] 2 A.C. 580, HL.

[7] *R. (Revenue and Customs Commissioners) v HM Coroner for Liverpool* [2014] EWHC 1586 (Admin); *R. (Black) v Secretary of State for Justice* [2015] EWHC 528 (Admin).

[8] G. Treitel, "Crown Proceedings: Some Recent Developments" [1957] P.L. 321, 322–326.

receive scant attention or simply be forgotten. A reversal of the present presumption would provide a simple solution: the Crown should be bound unless there is a clear indication to the contrary. This would force the government to take the initiative in practical terms if it wished to secure immunity, and also place upon it the onus of arguing why immunity was required.

B. Statutes Benefiting the Crown

It appears to be the law that the King can take the benefit of statutes even though not named therein.[9] The point has been doubted[10] but appears to be correct. If on true construction of a statute it seems as if the Crown should receive a benefit, then that benefit should indeed be forthcoming even if the Crown is not named expressly therein. This seems to give the Crown a power to claim the benefit but not to take the burden. The problem lies not, however, with the fact that the Crown can take a benefit, even though not named, if the statute was intended to grant the benefit, but with the rule about the Crown not being bound by statutes unless named therein. A related but separate question is whether the Crown could take the benefit of certain statutory rights without the restrictions attendant upon them. The answer, on authority, appears to be negative.[11] **29–004**

The common law position is left unchanged by the Crown Proceedings Act 1947 s.31(1) of which states that the Act shall not prejudice the right of the Crown to take advantage of the provisions of a statute although not named therein and that, in any civil proceedings against the Crown, the Crown, subject to express provision to the contrary, may rely upon the provisions of any Act of Parliament which could, if the proceedings were between subjects, be relied on by the defendant as a defence.

3. PROCEDURE, REMEDIES AND THE CROWN

A. General

In general the rules of civil procedure apply to actions by and against the Crown. This general rule is, however, subject to certain modifications. The Crown is not a party to the proceedings. It is represented, whether as claimant or defendant, by a government department or by the Attorney General. A list of such departments is provided. Where none of these is appropriate, or where there are reasonable doubts as to which is appropriate, the Attorney General should be made the **29–005**

[9] H. Street, *Governmental Liability: A Comparative Study* (Hamden: Archon Books, 1975), pp.154–156; P. Hogg, *Liability of the Crown in Australia, New Zealand and the United Kingdom* (Sydney: Law Book Co, 1971), pp.180–183.

[10] *Cayzer, Irvine & Co Ltd v Board of Trade* [1927] 1 K.B. 269, CA at 274; *Nisbet Shipping Co Ltd v Queen* [1955] 1 W.L.R. 1031 at 1035.

[11] *Crooke's Case* (1691) 1 Show K.B. 208; *Nisbet* [1955] 1 W.L.R. 1031. However, as P. Hogg, *Liability of the Crown in Australia, New Zealand and the United Kingdom* (1971), p.182 points out, this would not be logically impossible as Parliament might intend the Crown not to be subject to certain restrictions.

defendant.[12] The most notable distinction between ordinary actions and those brought against the Crown is in relation to the remedies available. There are two particular points to note in this context.

The first is that it has been argued by Wade and Forsyth that the prerogative remedies cannot lie against the Crown itself since they emanate from the Crown.[13] This is said, however, to be no impediment to the availability of certiorari or prohibition since these remedies lie to control all inferior jurisdictions and therefore apply to ministers of the Crown on whom powers are conferred by Parliament in their own names. It is said to be a problem in relation to mandamus since the Crown itself has public duties. The consequence, in the context of mandamus, is said to be that where the servant of the Crown is merely an instrument selected by the Crown for the discharge of the Crown's duty, any complaint must lie against the Crown itself. Where, however, Parliament has imposed the duty upon a person acting in a particular capacity mandamus will lie even though such a person is acting on the Crown's behalf.[14]

Whether this particular limit upon the availability of mandamus really exists is questionable. In general terms the prerogative orders will issue to ministers of the Crown, and the previous chapters of this book are replete with examples of this. It is clear also that mandamus can issue to a minister who is acting in an official capacity.[15] The objection to the applicability of the prerogative remedies against the Crown itself is also questionable. The authority cited for this proposition[16] gives two reasons for holding that mandamus cannot apply to the sovereign: that it would be incongruous for the sovereign to command herself, and that disobedience results in a writ of attachment.

29–006 These arguments would have force if one were thinking of mandamus applying to the sovereign in a personal capacity. They lose much of this force when applied to the sovereign as personified in and through the government of the day. Viewed in this light it does not appear to be incongruous for the prerogative orders that emanate from the Crown, in the sense that historically the Crown had a judicial capacity, to be applied to the Crown in its governmental capacity. Moreover, as Lord Woolf noted,[17] when a minister is sued in their official capacity, then unless the minister is treated as being distinct from the Crown then the incongruity of the Crown suing the Crown would still be present.

The second point to note is that much of the machinery for enforcing a judgment is excluded. Thus, no execution or attachment or process can issue for enforcing payment by the Crown,[18] and the Crown is not susceptible to an order for specific performance, an injunction or for an order compelling the delivery of

---

[12] Crown Proceedings Act 1947 s.17.

[13] W. Wade and C. Forsyth *Administrative Law*, 11th edn (Oxford: Oxford University Press, 2014), p.530.

[14] W. Wade and C. Forsyth, *Administrative Law* (2014), pp.530–531.

[15] *Padfield v Minister of Agriculture, Fisheries and Food* [1968] A.C. 997, HL; *R. v Customs and Excise Commissioners, Ex p. Cooke and Stevenson* [1970] 1 W.L.R. 450 DC at 455; *M v Home Office* [1994] 1 A.C. 377, HL.

[16] *R. v Powell* (1841) 1 Q.B. 352 QBD at 361.

[17] *M v Home Office* [1994] 1 A.C. 377, HL.

[18] Crown Proceedings Act 1947 s.25(4).

property. The claimant must be content with a declaratory judgment.[19] This will normally create no problem since the Crown will satisfy the judgment. It has, however, given rise to difficulties where the claimant was seeking interim relief as will be seen below. Where the redress required is a money payment, the Act states that the appropriate government department shall pay the amount to the person entitled[20] out of moneys provided by Parliament.[21] The normal rules of indemnity and contribution apply.[22]

B. Injunctions and Interim Relief

The root cause of the problem was that injunctions and interim injunctions were thought not to be available against the Crown or its officers. 29–007

i. *Extending injunctive relief*

The courts took different views as to whether the Crown or its officers were subject to injunctive relief, and hence whether they were also liable for interim injunctive relief. The Crown Proceedings Act 1947 s.21, allows the court in civil proceedings to award any relief against the Crown as it could in proceedings between subjects, provided that it cannot grant injunctions or specific performance, but can instead make a declaratory order. Section 21(2) further provides that the court should not grant an injunction against an officer of the Crown if the effect of doing so would be to give any relief against the Crown, which could not have been obtained in proceedings against the Crown itself. Civil proceedings do not include proceedings for judicial review,[23] but prior to the reform of Ord.53 injunctions could not be sought in judicial review actions. The accepted wisdom was, therefore, that injunctive relief could not be sought against the Crown or its officers. 29–008

The 1977 reforms in the law of remedies allowed injunctions to be claimed when applying for judicial review and this was given statutory force by the Senior Courts Act 1981 s.31. Certain decisions suggested that the absence of injunctive relief had been cured by these reforms, and that injunctions could be sought against officers of the Crown via judicial review.[24] These decisions were overruled in the first *Factortame* case,[25] where Lord Bridge stated that the reforms in the law of remedies could not be taken to have changed the law in this respect: interim injunctive relief against the Crown or officers of the Crown acting as such was not possible.

---

[19] Crown Proceedings Act 1947 s.21; G. Williams, *Crown Proceedings, An Account of Civil Proceedings by and against the Crown as affected by the Crown Proceedings Act, 1947* (London: Stevens, 1948), Ch.7.

[20] Crown Proceedings Act 1947 s.25(3).

[21] Crown Proceedings Act 1947 s.37.

[22] Crown Proceedings Act 1947 s.4.

[23] Crown Proceedings Act 1947 s.38(2).

[24] *R. v Licensing Authority Established under the Medicines Act, Ex p. Smith Kline and French Laboratories Ltd (No.2)* [1990] 2 Q.B. 574; *R. v Secretary of State for the Home Department, Ex p. Herbage* [1987] Q.B. 872 QBD.

[25] *R. v Secretary of State for Transport, Ex p. Factortame Ltd* [1990] 2 A.C. 85, HL.

It was, somewhat paradoxically, the *Factortame* litigation that fuelled the demand for this gap to be filled. The ECJ held that the absence of interim relief against the Crown was itself a breach of Community law, and that any national rule preventing this relief from being claimed must be set aside.[26] In *Factortame (No.2)*[27] the House of Lords accepted the ECJ's ruling and acknowledged that interim relief had to be applicable against the Crown.[28] In formal terms *Factortame (No.2)* only applied to cases with an EU law element. This created an uneasy dualism, since interim injunctive relief could be obtained in cases with an EU law element but not in domestic cases.

The matter rested there until the decision of the House of Lords in *M v Home Office*.[29] The Home Secretary was held in contempt of court for action he had taken in relation to M, who had been refused political asylum. The availability of injunctions against the Crown was relevant because if the courts had no power to make such coercive orders then the judge who made the finding of contempt might have done so without jurisdiction. Lord Woolf, giving the judgment of the court, in effect reversed the holding in the first *Factortame* case, and held that injunctions, including interim injunctions, were available against ministers of the Crown, given the unqualified language of the Senior Courts Act s.31. These remedies could, moreover, be issued even prior to the granting of leave where this was appropriate. The general jurisdiction to issue injunctions should, however, only be exercised in limited circumstances, and his Lordship left open the possibility of the courts being able to grant interim declarations.

ii. *Interim declarations*

29–009 The courts, in the past, set their face against the grant of interim declarations.[30] In *Rossminster*[31] their Lordships differed as to whether interim relief should be available against the Crown. Lord Wilberforce, Viscount Dilhorne and Lord Scarman all expressed doubts about the availability of interim relief against the Crown, and about the advisability of providing this remedy.[32] Lord Diplock was of a different view: the absence of such relief was seen as a serious procedural defect.[33] There have been three main objections to the granting of such relief.

The first was that the very idea of an interim declaration, even between private parties, was simply illogical. A declaration necessarily declared the final rights of the parties and could not simply preserve the status quo. This reasoning is questionable. Thus, it is said that there cannot be an interim declaration because declarations exist to tell people what their rights are and this cannot be achieved

[26] *R. v Secretary of State for Transport, Ex p. Factortame Ltd* (213/89) [1990] 3 C.M.L.R. 867.

[27] *R. v Secretary of State for Transport, Ex p. Factortame Ltd (No.2)* [1991] 1 A.C. 603, HL.

[28] P. Craig, "Administrative Law, Remedies and Europe" (1991) 3 E.R.P.L. 521, 527.

[29] *M v Home Office* [1994] 1 A.C. 377. See also *Davidson v Scottish Ministers (No.1)* [2005] UKHL 74; *Beggs v Scottish Ministers* [2007] 1 W.L.R. 455.

[30] *Underhill v Ministry of Food* [1950] 1 All E.R. 591 Ch D; *International General Electric Co of New York Ltd v Customs and Excise Commissioners* [1962] Ch. 784, CA.

[31] *R. v Inland Revenue Commissioners, Ex p. Rossminster Ltd* [1980] A.C. 952, HL.

[32] *Rossminster* [1980] A.C. 952 at 1001, 1007, 1027.

[33] *Rossminster* [1980] A.C. 952 at 1014–1015.

until the final judgment.[34] However, the claimant is not seeking a final determination of their rights at this stage but is simply asking the court to preserve the status quo. This objection to the grant of interim declaratory relief was rejected by some other high authorities, which saw nothing odd about an interim declaration.[35] It has also been argued that the final declaration might be in different terms from the interim order, and therefore should not be available.[36] Yet it is difficult to see the logic of the argument that because a final order can differ from the interim relief, therefore the interim relief cannot be given. Final injunctions will often differ from an interim injunction granted to preserve the status quo.

The second argument was that to grant an interim declaration would indirectly infringe against the principle that the decisions of the state are presumptively valid unless and until shown to be wrong.[37] This argument is flawed. There is nothing inconsistent in regarding, quite correctly, such decisions as presumptively valid and still leaving open the possibility of granting interim relief. The presumption of validity places the burden of proof upon the party challenging the decision. It does not tell us whether that party should be able to claim interim relief. Provided that the claimant is required to show a sufficiently strong prima facie case of invalidity and provided that the balance of convenience is properly assessed, interim relief is not inconsistent with this principle.[38]

The third argument against the interim declaration was that it would have much the same effect as would the grant of an injunction.[39] This argument is difficult to understand, since the Crown Proceedings Act 1947 s.21, provides for a declaration to be granted instead of an injunction or specific performance. The argument might be that the Crown would feel duty bound to abide by the court's order. This could, however, be said just as much about final declarations. The Crown does comply with them.

The procedure for judicial review is now governed by CPR Pt 54. The judicial review procedure under CPR Pt 54 is a modification of CPR Pt 8.[40] CPR Pt 25 sets out a number of interim orders that a court can grant, including an interim declaration.[41] This is to be welcomed since it provides a valuable additional remedy that can be used against the Crown where it is felt that an injunction is inappropriate. **29–010**

---

[34] *International General Electric* [1962] Ch. 784 at 789; *R. v Collins, Ex p. S (No.2)* [1998] C.O.D. 396, CA (Civ Div) at 399.

[35] *Yotvin v State of Israel* (1979).

[36] *Underhill* [1950] 1 All E.R. 591 at 593; *Rossminster* [1980] A.C. 952 at 1027.

[37] *Rossminster* [1980] A.C. 952 at 1027.

[38] Lord Diplock saw no inconsistency between the presumption of validity and the availability of interim relief, *Rossminster* [1980] A.C. 952 at 1013, 1014–1015, and it was Lord Diplock who gave the exposition of that presumption in *Hoffmann-La Roche & Co AG v Secretary of State for Trade and Industry* [1975] A.C. 295 at 366–367.

[39] *Rossminster* [1980] A.C. 952 at 1001, 1007.

[40] CPR 54.1(2)(e).

[41] CPR 25.1(1)(b); *R. v R* [2000] 1 F.L.R. 451 Fam Div; *X NHS Trust v T* [2005] 1 All E.R. 387 Fam Div.

C. Contempt

29–011 The leading decision is *M v Home Office*.[42] The applicant, M, arrived from Zaire and sought political asylum in the UK. The claim for asylum was rejected by the secretary of state and he made a direction for the removal of M back to Zaire. M then sought leave to apply for judicial review. The judge thought that there was an arguable point and wished M to remain in the UK until the following day when the point could be fully argued. Counsel for the secretary of state then gave what the judge believed to be an undertaking that M would not be removed from the UK pending the hearing. There followed a series of mistakes and mishaps, which culminated in M being returned to Zaire. The judge then issued a mandatory order to the Home Secretary demanding that M be returned to the UK. The Home Secretary challenged this order, after taking legal advice, and the judge, at a hearing on the issue, discharged the order on the basis that he, the judge, had no power to make it. An action was then brought on behalf of M for contempt of court by the Home Secretary on the basis that he had broken the undertaking and the judge's order while it was in force.

The House of Lords held that coercive orders, such as injunctions, could lie against ministers of the Crown, and that if a minister acted in disregard of an injunction made against him in his official capacity the court had jurisdiction to make a finding of contempt against him or his department, albeit not against the Crown itself. The contempt proceedings would, however, differ from normal proceedings of this kind, in that they would not be either personal or punitive: fines and sequestration of assets would not be appropriate in cases involving departments or ministers, although they might be necessary in other instances. There would, said Lord Woolf, still be a point in the finding of contempt since such a finding would vindicate the requirements of justice, and this could be underlined by awarding costs against the government. It would then be for Parliament to decide upon the consequences of the contempt. Any such finding of contempt would be against the authorised department, the minister or the Attorney General, rather than the Crown. It would, moreover, be more normal to make the finding of contempt against the department as opposed to the minister personally. The constitutional precept that the Crown itself can do no wrong was preserved, by presuming that the minister had acted without the authority of the Crown in such circumstances.

The decision was significant for emphasising that the government must obey the law not just as a matter of choice, but ultimately by way of compulsion. Instances of contempt are likely to be rare in practice, although this should not diminish the important point of principle in the House of Lords' ruling, which was brought out by Lord Templeman.[43]

> "My Lords, the argument that there is no power to enforce the law by injunction or contempt proceedings against a minister in his official capacity would, if upheld, establish the

---

[42] *M v Home Office* [1994] 1 A.C. 377; *R. (MA) v Croydon LBC* [2010] 1 W.L.R. 1658 QBD; *R. (Lamari) v Secretary of State for the Home Department* [2012] EWHC 1895 (Admin).

[43] *M v Home Office* [1994] 1 A.C. 377 at 395. See also *Beggs v Scottish Ministers* 2005 S.L.T. 305; *Beggs* [2007] 1 W.L.R. 455.

proposition that the executive obey the law as a matter of grace and favour and not as a matter of necessity, a proposition which would reverse the result of the Civil War."

4. TORT LIABILITY AND THE CROWN

A. The Law Prior to 1947

Until 1947 a citizen's redress against the Crown for tortious conduct committed by its servants was at best indirect. The Petition of Right developed as a means of securing redress against the Crown. In effect the Crown voluntarily referred the content of a Petition by a subject to a court of law, thereby overcoming the objection that the Crown could not be made a defendant in its own courts. By the 19th century it was accepted that the Petition of Right lay for breach of contract or recovery of property, although not for an action which sounded in tort. Such actions were doomed to failure by a combination of the maxim the "king can do no wrong" and a particular conception of vicarious liability. The former embraced the idea that the king has no legal power to do wrong. His powers were derived from the law and the law did not allow him to exceed them. The difficulty of rendering the Crown liable for the torts of its servants was exacerbated by the master's tort theory, which based vicarious liability upon the employer's fault. Neither the illogicality of allowing the Crown to be liable in contract but not in tort, nor the injustice of the immunity in tort impressed the 19th-century judiciary. **29–012**

The servant could still be sued in person and a practice developed whereby the Crown would stand behind actions brought against their servants. Damages would be paid out of public funds and, if it was unclear who should be sued, a defendant would be nominated by the government department. This "solution" was problematic in two ways: some torts only make the employer, not the employee, liable, and the House of Lords came out against the use of nominated defendants.[44] Various reforms were posited before 1947, although these were frustrated by opposition from powerful government departments.[45]

B. Crown Proceedings Act 1947

The old rules were swept away by s.2(1) of the Crown Proceedings Act 1947, which subjects the Crown to the same general principles of tortious liability as if it were a private person of full age and capacity. The Crown is thus rendered liable for torts committed by its servants or agents[46] and has the duties commonly associated with ownership, occupation, possession and control of property. The Crown also owes the normal duties of an employer to its servants. Liability will attach to the Crown even where statute or common law imposes the duty directly upon a minister or other servant; the Crown is held liable as if the minister or servant was acting on instructions from the Crown.[47] Although the Act leaves **29–013**

[44] *Adams v Naylor* [1946] A.C. 543, HL.
[45] J. Jacob, "The Debates behind an Act: Crown Proceedings Reform, 1920–1947" [1992] P.L. 452.
[46] Except where the servant himself would not have been liable. There is no liability outside of the Act, *Trawnik v Lennox* [1985] 1 W.L.R. 532.
[47] Crown Proceedings Act 1947 s.2(3).

unaltered the presumption that the Crown is not bound by statute unless intent to be so bound is expressed or can be implied,[48] the Crown can, subject to the above proviso, be held liable for breach of statutory duty.[49]

The Crown is made responsible for its servants and agents to the same extent as a private person. The term agent includes an independent contractor.[50] For the Crown to be liable for a servant or agent it is not sufficient that the person would have fallen within the common law definitions. The Crown will only be liable if the particular officer[51] was appointed directly or indirectly by the Crown and was at the material time paid wholly out of money provided by Parliament, or out of certain funds certified by the Treasury, or would normally have been so paid.[52] This has the effect of excluding from Crown liability action taken by servants of some statutory corporations and, most importantly, the police who are paid out of local funds. Aside from these specialised provisions, the normal principles will operate to determine whether particular bodies are servants of the Crown.[53] Special rules apply to those discharging responsibilities of a judicial nature[54] and separate rules used to apply to the armed forces.[55]

---

[48] Crown Proceedings Act 1947 s.40(2)(f).

[49] Crown Proceedings Act 1947 s.2(2), the duty must be one which is binding on persons other than the Crown or Crown officers alone, and the normal prerequisites for an action in tort must be present.

[50] Crown Proceedings Act 1947 s.38(2); *GB v Home Office* [2015] EWHC 819 (QB).

[51] Defined in Crown Proceedings Act 1947 s.38(2).

[52] Crown Proceedings Act 1947 s.2(6).

[53] *Tamlin v Hannaford* [1950] 1 K.B. 18, CA; *Morgan v Ministry of Justice* [2010] EWHC 2248 (QB).

[54] Crown Proceedings Act 1947 s.2(5).

[55] Crown Proceedings Act 1947 s.10. *Adams v War Office* [1955] 1 W.L.R. 1116 QBD; *Pearce v Secretary of State for Defence* [1988] A.C. 755, HL; *Mulcahy v Ministry of Defence* [1996] QB 732 (CA); *Matthews v Ministry of Defence* [2003] 1 A.C. 1163, HL; *Roche v United Kingdom* [2006] 42 E.H.R.R. 30; *Smith v Ministry of Defence* [2013] UKSC 41. The Crown Proceedings (Armed Forces) Act 1987 s.1 repealed s.10 of the 1947 Act except in relation to anything done prior to 1987, subject to s.2 of the 1987 Act which allows for the revival of s.10 in certain circumstances.

CHAPTER 30

TORT AND RESTITUTION

1. CENTRAL ISSUES

i. It is important at the outset to consider the foundations of the present law[1] and the options when thinking about damages liability. All legal systems have to decide on the conceptual foundation for damages liability in actions involving public bodies. The principles that underlie the common law regime can be succinctly stated. 30–001

ii. A public body that acts ultra vires is liable in tort if a cause of action is established, just like any private individual would be. There is no general cloak of immunity.[2] However, the basic premise is that an ultra vires act per se will not give rise to damages liability.[3] The claim must therefore be fitted into a recognised private law cause of action.

iii. There are a number of causes of action that might avail a claimant against a public body.[4] These include: negligence; breach of statutory duty; misfeasance in a public office; nuisance; *Rylands v Fletcher*; false imprisonment[5]; and damages under the Human Rights Act 1998. There is no cause of action based simply upon the careless performance of a statutory duty in the absence of any other common law right of action.[6]

iv. We do not therefore have what would be recognised by other legal systems as a general principle of damages liability, nor do we have any wholly separate body of law dealing with damages actions against public bodies.

---

[1] H. Street, *Governmental Liability* (Cambridge: Cambridge University Press, 1953), Ch.2; C. Harlow, *Compensation and Government Torts* (London: Sweet & Maxwell, 1982); S. Arrowsmith, *Civil Liability and Public Authorities* (South Humberside: Earlsgate Press, 1992); B. Markesinis, J.-B. Auby, D. Coester-Waltjen and S. Deakin, *Tortious Liability of Statutory Bodies, A Comparative Analysis of Five English Cases* (Oxford: Hart, 1999); J. Wright, *Tort Law and Human Rights* (Oxford: Hart, 2001); D. Fairgrieve, M. Andenas, and J. Bell (eds), *Tort Liability of Public Authorities in Comparative Perspective* (London: BIICL, 2002); D. Fairgrieve, *State Liability in Tort: A Comparative Law Study* (Oxford: Oxford University Press, 2003); C. Harlow, *State Liability, Tort Law and Beyond* (Oxford: Oxford University Press, 2004); T. Cornford, *Towards a Public Law of Tort* (Aldershot: Ashgate, 2008).

[2] *Entick v Carrington* (1765) 19 St. Tr. 1030; *Leach v Money* (1765) 19 St. Tr. 2002; *Cooper v Wandsworth Board of Works* (1863) 14 C.B. (N.S.) 180; *Pride of Derby and Derbyshire Angling Association Ltd v British Celanese Ltd* [1953] Ch. 149, CA; P. Craig, "Compensation in Public Law" (1980) 96 L.Q.R. 413.

[3] *X (Minors) v Bedfordshire CC* [1995] 2 A.C. 633, HL at 730.

[4] *X* [1995] 2 A.C. 633 at 730–740.

[5] *R. (WL (Congo)) v Secretary of State for the Home Department* [2011] 2 W.L.R. 671 SC; *R. (Kambadzi) v Secretary of State for the Home Department* [2011] 1 W.L.R. 1299 SC.

[6] *X* [1995] 2 A.C. 633.

There are eight basic options available when thinking about monetary liability. Liability can be imposed for: illegality or ultra vires action per se; negligence; a serious breach of duty or discretion; intentional wrongdoing; liability for lawfully caused governmental loss; ex gratia compensation; restitutionary relief; immunity from suit/ The term "fault" may be an imperfect guide for distinguishing between these options, since it is used differently in different legal systems.

vi. First, it may be treated as equivalent to illegality, which is the approach in some civil law systems.[7] Thus, in France, the starting assumption is that illegality connotes fault and hence responsibility in damages. This is also the case in EU law for acts where there is no real discretion. The only circumstance in which the common law approximates to this position is where there has been a finding that a breach of a statute gives rise, in and of itself, to liability in damages.

vii. Second, fault may be seen as distinct from illegality, which is the general approach taken in common law jurisdictions. Proof of illegality, in the sense of an ultra vires act, is not treated as the equivalent of fault for the purposes of damages liability. The claimant has to prove the existence of a duty of care, a breach thereof, and recoverable damage.

viii. A third sense of the term fault is to be found in EU law. Where there is some significant measure of discretion, and/or where the meaning of the EU norm is imprecise, illegality per se will not suffice for liability. The applicant will have to prove that the breach was sufficiently serious. There is, however, no requirement of fault going beyond proof of the serious breach of EU law.

ix. This chapter examines the principal causes of action that are used by individuals when claiming for loss caused by public bodies. The difficulties with sustaining a damages claim against a public body under the existing law will be analysed and the chapter concludes by considering various options for reform that are available.

2. NEGLIGENCE, STATUTORY DUTIES AND STATUTORY POWERS

30–002 We begin with negligence, which is the most common action against a public body. The law concerning negligence and public bodies is complex and still evolving.[8] The tort requires the existence of a duty of care, breach of that duty,

[7] Thus, in France the starting point is that "*toute illegalité constitue par elle-meme une faute*".

[8] H. Street, *Governmental Liability* (1953), pp.40, 56–80; C. Harlow, *Compensation and Government Torts* (1982); S. Arrowsmith, *Civil Liability and Public Authorities* (1992), Ch.6; G. Ganz, "Compensation for Negligent Administrative Action" [1973] P.L. 84; C. Harlow, "Fault Liability in French and English Public Law" (1976) 39 M.L.R. 516; P. Craig, "Negligence in the Exercise of a Statutory Power" (1978) 94 L.Q.R. 428; M. Bowman and S. Bailey, "Negligence in the Realms of Public Law—A Positive Obligation to Rescue" [1984] P.L. 277; T. Weir, "Governmental Liability" [1989] P.L. 40; M. Andenas and D. Fairgrieve, "Sufficiently Serious? Judicial Restraint in Tortious Liability of Public Authorities and the European Influence", in M. Andenas (ed.), *English Public Law and the Common Law of Europe* (London: Key Haven, 1998), Ch.14; S. Bailey and M. Bowman, "Public Authority Negligence Revisited" [2000] C.L.J.; P. Craig and D. Fairgrieve, "*Barrett*, Negligence and Discretionary Powers" [1999] P.L. 626; D. Fairgrieve, "Pushing Back the Frontiers of

causation and damage. This apparently simple formulation conceals a plethora of interpretive issues, which have been problematic in relation to public bodies. It is clear that there can be no cause of action based simply on the careless performance of a statutory duty or power in the absence of any other common law right of action.[9] It is for the claimant to establish that there is a common law duty of care arising from the imposition of a statutory duty or from its performance.[10] The more precise circumstances in which the courts would be willing to impose a duty of care on public bodies have however altered over time. Three approaches can be identified.

A. The "Liberal Approach"

After some initial doubts[11] it was established in *Mersey Docks and Harbour Board Trustees v Gibbs*[12] that a public body could be liable in negligence when exercising a statutory power.[13] The decision was affirmed by the House of Lords,[14] and applied in later cases.[15] The general tendency was to impose liability on public bodies when they failed to take care and caused reasonably foreseeable loss pursuant to a statutory power or duty. 30–003

This was in accord with the general tendency in the law of negligence post-*Donoghue v Stevenson*.[16] The years after this landmark decision saw the courts reassessing areas that were not subject to the normal precepts of negligence liability and they often concluded that such areas should be brought within the framework of the principles laid down by Lord Atkin in *Donoghue*, even if, as for example in the case of liability for negligent misstatement, the principles were modified in their operation in a particular area.

This approach was then embodied in Lord Wilberforce's test in the *Anns* case.[17] If there was sufficient proximity between plaintiff and defendant such that reasonably foreseeable loss would be caused to the plaintiff by the defendant's

Public Authority Liability" [2002] P.L. 288; T. Hickman, "Tort Law, Public Authorities and the Human Rights Act 1998", in D. Fairgrieve, M. Andenas and J. Bell (eds), *Tort Liability of Public Authorities in Comparative Perspective* (2002): T. Hickman, "The Reasonableness Principle: Re-assessing its Place in the Public Sphere" [2004] C.L.J. 166; R. Bagshaw, "Monetary Remedies in Public Law—Misdiagnosis and Misprescription" [2006] L.S. 4; Sir B. Markesinis and J. Fedtke, "Damages for the Negligence of Statutory Bodies: The Empirical and Comparative Dimensions to an Unending Debate" [2007] P.L. 299.

[9] *X* [1995] 2 A.C. 633 at 732–733.

[10] *X* [1995] 2 A.C. 633 at 735–736.

[11] The doubts were raised by a misinterpretation of earlier cases such as *Sutton v Clarke* (1815) 6 Taunt 29, and due to an obiter dictum of Lord Cottenham LC in *Duncan v Findlater* (1839) Macl. & R. 911, HL. See *Mersey Docks and Harbour Board Trustees v Gibbs* (1864–1866) 11 H.L.C. 686 at 719–721.

[12] *Gibbs* (1864–1866) 11 H.L.C. 686.

[13] *Gibbs* (1864–1866) 11 H.L.C. 686 at 719–721.

[14] *Gibbs* (1864–1866) 11 H.L.C. 686 at 725–734.

[15] *Geddis v Proprietors of Bann Reservoir* (1878) 3 App. Cas. 430 at 438, 452, 455–456; *East Fremantle Corp v Annois* [1902] A.C. 213 at 217–219; *Great Central Ry Co v Hewlett* [1916] 2 A.C. 511 HL at 519, 525; *Fisher v Ruislip-Northwood Urban DC and Middlesex CC* [1945] K.B. 584, CA.

[16] *Donoghue v Stevenson* [1932] A.C. 562, HL.

[17] *Anns v Merton LBC* [1978] A.C. 728, HL.

failure to take care then prima facie there was liability, unless the defendant could advance good public policy reasons for this not to be so.

30–004 The application of this reasoning to public bodies was tempered by the policy/operational distinction. The distinction had been alluded to in earlier cases.[18] Thus, in *Dorset Yacht*,[19] borstal boys who had been working on an island under the supervision of officers, escaped and damaged the plaintiff's yacht. The Home Office had instituted a system of open rather than closed borstal institutions, because it felt that it would enhance reform of offenders. This necessarily involved a higher risk of escape, and damage to property. The House of Lords rejected the wide claim for immunity advanced by the Home Office. Their Lordships nonetheless acknowledged that to ask whether the Home Office had been negligent in adopting this policy choice would require the court to balance society's interest in the reform of the offender, the interest of the offender, and the danger to private property, which was something that a court should not do.[20] The decision was one of policy and was non-justiciable. Liability could, however, still exist at the operational level: given that the authorities had chosen a more open prison system, the issue was whether there had been negligence within that framework.[21]

The planning/operational dichotomy was made explicit in *Anns*.[22] The plaintiffs alleged that the council had been negligent in their inspection of foundations, causing cracks in their maisonettes. Assuming that there had been a careless inspection, Lord Wilberforce held that it would be easier to impose a duty of care on the operational rather than the planning level. The latter would encompass the scale of the resources that should be made available to carry out the powers, the number of inspectors, and the type of inspections to be made.[23] Therefore, if the defendants had decided that their inspectors could only carry out limited tests, the costs of more extensive checks being prohibitive, an individual could not claim in negligence merely because a further test would have revealed the defect. Where the inspector was simply careless in performing the prescribed tests, liability would ensue, since this would be purely operational negligence.[24]

Later authority focused directly on justiciability, which underlies the policy/operational dichotomy. In *Rowling*,[25] their Lordships held that this distinction did not itself provide a touchstone of liability. It was rather expressive of the need to exclude altogether those cases in which the contested decision was unsuitable for judicial resolution, as in cases concerning the discretionary allocation of scarce resources or distribution of risks. Classification of a decision

---

[18] *East Suffolk Rivers Catchment Board v Kent* [1940] 1 K.B. 319, CA; [1941] A.C. 74, HL.

[19] *Dorset Yacht Co Ltd v Home Office* [1970] A.C. 1004, HL.

[20] *Dorset Yacht* [1970] A.C. 1004 at 1031–1032, 1036–1037, 1055–1056, 1066–1068.

[21] For an interesting comparison see, *Evangelical United Brethren Church of Adna v State* 407 P 2d 440 (1965).

[22] *Anns* [1978] A.C. 728.

[23] *Anns* [1978] A.C. 728 at 754.

[24] On the alternative hypothesis that the defendant had not exercised the power, Lord Wilberforce held that although the defendant was under no duty to inspect it was under a duty to consider whether it should inspect or not. Negligence liability would ensue if the defendant failed to take reasonable care in its acts or omissions to secure compliance with the bylaws, *Anns* [1978] A.C. 728 at 755.

[25] *Rowling v Takaro Properties Ltd* [1988] A.C. 473. See also *Stovin v Wise* [1996] A.C. 923, HL at 951–952; *Barrett v Enfield LBC* [2001] 2 A.C. 550, HL.

as a policy or planning decision could, therefore, exclude liability. A public authority could not, however, simply assert that it balanced thrift and efficiency in order to evade liability. It would have to show that it reached its decision in this manner and it would then be for the court to decide whether the issue was non-justiciable. There has been considerable discussion of the planning/operational dichotomy. The following points should be borne in mind in this respect.

First, the division was never self-executing. The terms were used in a conclusory role. A court faced with an allegation of negligence would consider the negligence claim and decide whether the allegation was suitable for judicial resolution. When the court felt that it was unsuited for judicial resolution it would apply the label planning decision to express that conclusion. **30–005**

Second, given that justiciability underlies the planning-operational dichotomy, it is preferable to focus directly on this, thereby avoiding any possible confusion caused by misinterpretation of the terms planning and operational.

Third, the mere presence of some discretion does not mean that the matter is non-justiciable. Discretionary judgments made by public bodies, which the courts feel able to assess, should not therefore preclude negligence liability. This does not mean that discretion will be irrelevant to the determination of liability. It will, as seen below, be relevant in deciding whether there has been a breach of the duty of care.

Fourth, the preceding analysis does not necessitate any "separate" tort for public bodies.[26] Where justiciability is relevant it will be one factor which the court considers in determining whether a duty of care should be excluded.[27] This analysis takes place within the reformulated concept of duty, under which the court considers a range of factors to determine whether a duty of care exists.[28]

Finally, notwithstanding the academic and judicial ink devoted to this topic, neither the planning/operational distinction, nor justiciability, has been the principal reason why the courts have denied a duty of care in relation to public authorities. It has been excluded, as will be seen below, because the courts have felt that it would not be fair, just and reasonable to impose a duty of care in particular cases for reasons that have had little if anything to do with justiciability. **30–006**

---

[26] M. Bowman and S. Bailey, "Negligence in the Realms of Public Law—A Positive Obligation to Rescue" [1984] P.L. 277; C. Harlow, "Fault Liability in French and English Public Law" (1976) 39 M.L.R. 516.

[27] *Rowling* [1988] A.C. 473.

[28] *Caparo Industries Plc v Dickman* [1990] 2 A.C. 605, HL; *Governors of the Peabody Donation Fund v Sir Lindsay Parkinson and Co Ltd* [1985] A.C. 210, HL; *Investors in Industry Commercial Properties Ltd v South Bedfordshire DC* [1986] Q.B. 1034 DC; *Murphy v Brentwood DC* [1991] 1 A.C. 398, HL; D. Nolan, "Deconstructing the Duty of Care" (2013) 129 L.Q.R. 559.

B. The "Cautious" or "Restrictive Approach"

30–007 A more cautious or restrictive approach to the existence of the duty of care was apparent in cases such as *X v Bedfordshire*[29] and *Stovin*.[30] This label is warranted for three related reasons.

i. Incrementalism and restriction of the duty of care

30–008 These cases were premised on developments in the general law of negligence that emphasised caution. *Anns* was the subject of judicial criticism and the House of Lords turned away from Lord Wilberforce's two-stage test. It emphasised the cautious and incremental development of the law of negligence. The existence of a duty of care was dependent on three factors: there had to be reasonably foreseeable loss as a result of the failure to take care; there had to be sufficient proximity between plaintiff and defendant; and the imposition of a duty of care had to be fair, just and reasonable.[31]

In deciding whether it was fair just and reasonable to impose a duty of care the courts would construe the relevant statutes to determine the scope of any such duty of care. Thus, in *Peabody*[32] it was held that a local authority was not liable in negligence to building developers because the purpose of the relevant statutory powers was not to safeguard developers against economic loss, but rather to safeguard occupiers of houses and the public generally against dangers to health and safety flowing from defective drainage installations. In *Curran*,[33] a statutory authority which provided funds for accommodation and home improvement was held not liable in negligence to a purchaser to whom they had provided a mortgage when the extension to the house which he had purchased proved to be seriously defective. The statutory authority had furnished funds for the extension to the previous owner. However, it was held that since the relevant provisions gave the authority no power to control the actual building operation, it could not be sued in negligence for the defects to the property.

In deciding whether it was fair, just and reasonable to impose a duty of care, the courts would also take account of a wide range of other policy factors. In practice the most important factor limiting liability was not the policy/operational distinction or justiciability, but rather the judicial determination that it was not fair, just and reasonable to impose such a duty.[34] Justiciability may have been part

---

29 *X* [1995] 2 A.C. 633.

30 *Stovin v Wise* [1996] A.C. 923, HL.

31 *Caparo Industries* [1990] 2 A.C. 605; *Michael v Chief Constable of the South Wales Police* [2015] UKSC 2 at [106]–[116].

32 *Peabody* [1985] A.C. 210 at 241, 245; *Investors in Industry* [1986] Q.B. 1034; *Murphy* [1991] 1 A.C. 398.

33 *Curran v Northern Ireland Co-Ownership Housing Association Ltd* [1987] A.C. 718 at 728.

34 *Peabody* [1985] A.C. 210; *Curran* [1987] A.C. 718; *Yuen Kun-Yeu v Att Gen of Hong Kong* [1988] A.C. 175; *Rowling* [1988] A.C. 473; *Hill v Chief Constable of West Yorkshire* [1989] A.C. 53, HL; *Calveley v Chief Constable of the Merseyside Police* [1989] A.C. 1228, HL; *Clough v Bussan* [1990] 1 All E.R. 431 QBD; *Richardson v West Lindsey DC* [1990] 1 W.L.R. 522, CA (Civ Div); *Kirkham v Chief Constable of the Greater Manchester Police* [1990] 2 Q.B. 283, CA (Civ Div); *Davis v Radcliffe* [1990] 1 W.L.R. 821; *Welsh v Chief Constable of the Merseyside Police* [1993] 1 All E.R. 692 QBD.

of this determination but in many cases there have been other factors leading the courts to conclude that there should be no duty of care.

In *Hill*[35] it was decided that there was no duty of care on the police in relation to the investigation or suppression of crime. Lord Keith was influenced in reaching this conclusion by the fact that the chief police officer had wide discretion as to the manner in which the duty to prevent crime was discharged. It was for him to decide how the available resources should be deployed, whether particular lines of inquiry should be followed and whether certain crimes should be prosecuted. It was not therefore appropriate for there to be any general duty of care to members of the public. It was also felt that such a duty of care would lead to defensive policing and the inefficient diversion of resources.[36] **30–009**

Capital and Counties Plc[37] was concerned with the liability the fire brigade owed when attending a fire. The Court of Appeal decided that there was no common law duty of care to answer the call for help. It also held that there was no sufficiently proximate relationship between the fire brigade and the owner of premises so as to give rise to a duty of care merely because the fire brigade came to fight the fire. Liability in negligence could only arise if the fire brigade had increased the risk of danger to the plaintiff and caused damage that would not otherwise have occurred. The same result was reached in relation to the coastguard services in the *OLL* case.[38]

In *X*[39] there were a number of joined cases, some of which were concerned with allegations of negligence relating to child abuse, others of which concerned claims relating to the provision of special educational needs. The House of Lords held that there was no direct duty of care owed by the local authorities in the child abuse cases. Lord Browne-Wilkinson held that it would not be fair, just and reasonable to impose such a duty. Five reasons can be identified from his judgment.

First, he felt that a duty of care would "cut across the whole statutory system set up for the protection of children at risk".[40] Protection of children from abuse was not the exclusive preserve of the local authority's social services. There was an interdisciplinary system involving the participation of the police, educational bodies, doctors and others. To impose liability for negligence on only one such body would, said Lord Browne-Wilkinson, be manifestly unfair. To impose it on all such bodies would lead to impossible problems of disentangling the respective liability of each of the participants.[41] **30–010**

---

35 *Hill* [1989] A.C. 53.

36 See also *Alexandrou v Oxford* [1993] 4 All E.R. 328, CA (Civ Div); *Vellino v Chief Constable of Greater Manchester* [2002] 1 W.L.R. 218, CA (Civ Div); *Cowan v Chief Constable of Avon and Somerset* [2002] H.L.R. 44, CA (Civ Div). Compare, however, *Swinney v Chief Constable of the Northumbria Police* [1997] Q.B. 464, CA (Civ Div); *Swinney v Chief Constable of the Northumbria Police (No.2)* [1999] Admin. L.R. 811.

37 *Capital and Counties Plc v Hampshire CC* [1997] Q.B. 1004, CA (Civ Div).

38 *OLL Ltd v Secretary of State for Transport* [1997] 3 All E.R. 897 QBD.

39 *X* [1995] 2 A.C. 633.

40 *X* [1995] 2 A.C. 633 at 749.

41 *X* [1995] 2 A.C. 633 at 750.

The second reason was because the local authority's task in dealing with children at risk was "extraordinarily delicate".[42] The relevant legislation required the local authority to have regard to the physical well-being of the child and also to the need not to disrupt the child's family. This duality was reflected in the claims before the court, one of which alleged that the child had been moved precipitately, the other that the child had not been removed soon enough.

The third reason for denying the duty of care was that it could lead the local authorities to a "more cautious and defensive approach to their duties".[43] If the local authority could be made liable for a negligent decision to remove a child then "there would be a substantial temptation to postpone making such a decision until further inquiries have been made in the hope of getting more concrete facts".[44] This would increase the risk of the child being abused.

The availability of alternative remedies laid down in the relevant statute was the fourth reason for denying a duty of care. The final rationale was that in deciding whether to develop novel categories of negligence liability the courts should proceed with caution, particularly where Parliament had charged a body with the task of protecting society from the wrongdoing of others.[45]

ii. Discretion and restriction of the duty of care

30–011 The second reason why the label "cautious" or "restrictive" is warranted is that the House of Lords placed constraints on a negligence action against a public body, which were related to the existence of statutory discretion. Lord Browne-Wilkinson, who gave judgment in *X*, acknowledged that most statutory duties involved discretion as to the extent to which, and the methods by which, the statutory duty was to be performed.[46]

It was held that nothing which the body did within the ambit of its discretion could give rise to an action at common law. In determining whether the challenged action was outside its statutory discretion, the court could not assess factors that were felt to be non-justiciable or within the policy category of the policy/operational dichotomy. In that sense, "a common law duty of care in relation to the taking of decisions involving policy matters cannot exist".[47] Even if a matter was justiciable, the plaintiff, in seeking to show that the authority had acted outside its discretion, would have to prove that it acted manifestly unreasonably so that its action fell entirely outside the ambit of the statutory discretion.[48]

If the challenged decision did fall outside the statutory discretion, it might give rise to a common law duty of care. However, whether it did so would depend on application of the standard tests for determination of such a common law duty. The court would take into account: whether the statute was intended for the

[42] *X* [1995] 2 A.C. 633 at 750.
[43] *X* [1995] 2 A.C. 633 at 750.
[44] *X* [1995] 2 A.C. 633 at 750.
[45] *X* [1995] 2 A.C. 633 at 751.
[46] *X* [1995] 2 A.C. 633 at 736.
[47] *X* [1995] 2 A.C. 633 at 738.
[48] *X* [1995] 2 A.C. 633 at 736–737, 749, 761.

protection of those such as the plaintiff[49]; whether the existence of this common law duty would be inconsistent with or discourage the performance of the statutory duties[50]; and whether the public body was acting pursuant to a statutory duty or statutory power, the courts being more reluctant to impose a common law duty of care in the latter instance than in the former.[51]

iii. Omissions and restriction of the duty of care

The third reason for the appellation "cautious" or "restrictive" is the approach taken to omissions. It was clear from Lord Hoffmann's majority judgment in *Stovin* that the courts would only rarely impose a duty of care on a public body for failure to exercise a statutory power. He reasoned as follows. **30–012**

It was for the court to decide in the light of the statute conferring the power whether the authority was not only under a duty in public law to consider exercising the power, but also under a private law duty to act, which might give rise to a claim in damages.[52] The plaintiff had to show that it was irrational for the authority not to have exercised the power, so that there was in effect a public law duty to act; and there had to be exceptional grounds for holding that the policy of the statute conferred the right to compensation on those who suffered loss if the power was not exercised. The very fact that Parliament had conferred discretion on the public body, rather than a duty, was some indication that the policy of the statute was not to create a right to compensation.[53]

Lord Hoffmann accepted the doctrine of general reliance, developed in the Australian High Court,[54] but only in limited circumstances. The doctrine as propounded by Mason J was based on the idea that the legislature might well have imposed powers on a public body in relation to matters of such complexity or magnitude that individuals could not be expected to take adequate steps for their own protection. Such a situation generated an expectation in the individual that the power would be exercised, and a realisation in the public authority that there would be general reliance on the exercise of that power.

Lord Hoffmann held[55] that it was essential to this doctrine that the benefit or service provided under statutory powers should be of a uniform or routine nature, so that one could describe exactly what the public authority was supposed to do, as in the case of inspection for defects. If a service were provided as routine it would therefore be irrational for a public authority to provide it in one case and arbitrarily to withhold it in another. It was, however, also necessary for the plaintiff to show that there was some policy to provide compensation where the power had not been exercised.

---

49 *Peabody* [1985] A.C. 210; *Curran* [1987] A.C. 718.

50 *X* [1995] 2 A.C. 633 at 739; *Stovin* [1996] A.C. 923 at 952–953.

51 *Stovin* [1996] A.C. 923 at 949, 953. It was also made clear that any such claim would be limited to those instances where the action of the public body had made things worse than if it had not acted at all. There would be no such claim where the plaintiff alleged that there had been a failure to confer a benefit on the plaintiff or a failure to protect him from loss, *Stovin* [1996] A.C. 923 at 949.

52 *Stovin* [1996] A.C. 923 at 949–950.

53 *Stovin* [1996] A.C. 923 at 953.

54 *Sutherland Shire Council v Heyman* (1985) 157 C.L.R. 424 at 464, Mason J. The doctrine now seems to have passed out of favour, *Pyrenees Shire Council v Day* (1998) 192 C.L.R. 330.

55 *Stovin* [1996] A.C. 923 at 953–955.

C. The "Middle Way"

30–013 The law must now be seen in the light of the House of Lords' decisions in *Barrett*[56] and *Phelps*.[57] The hallmarks of this approach are greater unwillingness to allow the duty of care to be excluded in its entirety, with the consequence that problems concerned with the exercise of discretionary power would be considered at the breach level. It is nonetheless important to qualify the extent of the change by recognising that the courts have in certain instances denied the existence of the duty of care and that the judicial approach towards omissions continues to be restrictive.

i. Greater unwillingness to exclude the duty of care in its entirety

30–014 The greater unwillingness to exclude the duty of care in its entirety is evident in two ways in the more recent case law.

First, there is a greater reluctance to decide cases on claims that the action should be struck out. Many important cases had been decided in this way. This involved a preliminary determination of whether the facts as pleaded disclosed a cause of action or not. The dangers of dealing with cases in this way were acknowledged in *Barrett*.[58] Thus, Lord Hutton stated that the court simply could not really know at this stage of the proceedings whether there were non-justiciable matters involved in the claimant's claim, since it was not known what factors the defendant took into account when making decisions about the claimant. It might, said his Lordship, transpire that there were no such issues in the case, so that the trial judge could decide the matter according to normal principles.[59]

Second, we have seen that it was common for claims to fail because the court decided that it was not fair, just or reasonable to impose a duty of care. The decisions in *Barrett* and *Phelps* indicate a greater reluctance to exclude a duty of care on this ground.

30–015 In *Barrett*,[60] the defendant local authority contended that it would not be fair, just and reasonable to impose a duty of care in relation to their responsibilities when undertaking foster care for a child. This argument succeeded in the Court of Appeal.[61] Lord Woolf MR held that the local authority stood in place of the natural parents, and in the same way that a child should not be able to sue the latter for the decisions made as to the child's future, neither should he be able to sue the local authority. The House of Lords disagreed. Lord Hutton stated that the comparison between the local authority and the parent was not entirely apt, since the former would have to take a number of decisions, such as whether a child

---

[56] *Barrett v Enfield LBC* [2001] 2 A.C. 550, HL.

[57] *Phelps v Hillingdon LBC* [2001] 2 A.C. 619, HL.

[58] *Barrett* [2001] 2 A.C. 550 at 557–558.

[59] *Barrett* [2001] 2 A.C. 550 at 586–587; *Phelps* [2001] 2 A.C. 619 at 659–660, 662; *Richards (t/a Colin Richards & Co) v Hughes* [2004] EWCA Civ 266; *Mutua v Foreign and Commonwealth Office* [2011] EWHC 1913.

[60] *Barrett* [2001] 2 A.C. 550.

[61] *Barrett v Enfield LBC* [1998] Q.B. 367, CA (Civ Div).

should be placed with foster parents or sent to a residential home, which would never have to be taken by natural parents.[62] His Lordship also distinguished the policy considerations taken into account in the *X* case, set out above. Lord Hutton felt that these were less persuasive in relation to fostering, than they were in relation to child abuse.[63]

An unwillingness to reject the existence of a duty of care is apparent once again in *Phelps*.[64] There were four separate cases concerning errors allegedly made in the educational system, such as the failure to diagnose dyslexia and the provision of inadequate education to a person with muscular dystrophy. The House of Lords adverted to the considerations that had caused Lord Browne-Wilkinson to exclude the duty of care in the *X* case, but concluded that they were not sufficiently compelling to exclude a duty of care in the instant cases.[65]

ii. Greater willingness to consider issues at the level of breach rather than duty

There are two aspects of the recent case law that are pertinent to the shift in emphasis from duty to breach. They will be considered in turn. **30–016**

First, the House of Lords in *Barrett* and *Phelps* limited the instances in which the courts would deem the matter to be non-justiciable and emphasised that matters concerning discretion could often be dealt with when determining whether there was a breach of the duty of care. Thus, Lord Hutton in *Barrett* accepted that the effect of prior decisions[66] was that the courts would not permit a claim in negligence to be brought where a decision on the existence of negligence would involve the courts in considering matters of policy raising issues which were not justiciable. It was, said Lord Hutton, only where the decision involved the weighing of competing public interests which the courts were not fitted to assess that they would hold that the matter was non-justiciable on the ground that it was made in the exercise of a statutory discretion.[67] It followed said his Lordship that there was nothing to preclude a ruling in the instant case that although the decisions of the defendant were within the ambit of its statutory discretion, nevertheless those decisions did not involve the type of policy considerations which rendered the decisions non-justiciable.[68] It followed also, that provided that no such non-justiciable matters were raised in a particular case, it was preferable for the courts to decide the matter by applying directly the common law concept of negligence. There was no need to advert to any preliminary public law test of *Wednesbury* unreasonableness to determine whether the decision was outside the ambit of the statutory discretion.[69] Lord

[62] *Barrett* [2001] 2 A.C. 550 at 587–588.
[63] *Barrett* [2001] 2 A.C. 550 at 589–590.
[64] *Phelps* [2001] 2 A.C. 619.
[65] *Phelps* [2001] 2 A.C. 619 at 674–675.
[66] *Dorset Yacht* [1970] A.C. 1004; *Anns* [1978] A.C. 728; *Rowling* [1988] A.C. 473.
[67] *Barrett* [2001] 2 A.C. 550 at 583.
[68] *Barrett* [2001] 2 A.C. 550 at 585.
[69] *Barrett* [2001] 2 A.C. 550 at 586.

Slynn in *Barrett* reasoned somewhat differently but reached a similar conclusion.[70] Lord Slynn reaffirmed the *Barrett* approach in *Phelps*.[71]

This approach is clearly sensible. It avoids the necessity for the courts to become embroiled in issues of vires, which are not necessary for the resolution of the case. This conclusion is reinforced by the fact that a finding of ultra vires will not, in itself, be determinative in a subsequent negligence action. Thus, if a policy decision to inspect all buildings of a certain type by tests one and two, rather than half of them by tests one to four, is found to be ultra vires because it was, for example, based upon irrelevant considerations, this merely tells us that the public body in fact took irrelevant considerations into account. It does not in itself show negligence.[72]

30–017 Second, if the courts decide that there is a duty of care, the nature of the statutory discretion and the way in which it was exercised will be relevant in deciding whether there was a breach of that duty.[73] The courts take into account, when assessing breach, the probability that harm will occur, the degree of harm that will occur if that probability comes to pass, and the cost of taking precautions. These factors feature in the determination of whether the defendant has taken reasonable care in all the circumstances.

It will not be easy for the claimant to show that a defendant public authority is in breach of its duty of care, more especially where, as in *Barrett*, there were difficult discretionary decisions to be made as to the appropriate foster home. The claimant raised various claims of negligence as to the way in which he had been frequently moved between foster homes. It is clear that their Lordships did not regard all such matters as non-justiciable. It is equally clear that they accepted that in determining whether any duty of care had been broken, the court would have regard to the difficult nature of the tasks involved. It will be necessary for the claimant to show that the defendant was in breach of the duty of care, as judged by the *Bolam* test.[74] This test requires a professional to exercise the skill of an ordinary competent person exercising that particular art. It was made clear in *Phelps* that this test would apply to determine breach in actions brought against professionals such as teachers, and educational psychologists.[75] It was made equally clear that the courts would not look kindly on those who sought to use negligence actions to pursue ill-founded claims that, for example, a child had underperformed at school.

---

70 *Barrett* [2001] 2 A.C. 550 at 570–572.

71 *Phelps* [2001] 2 A.C. 619 at 653.

72 The claimant might argue that the public body failed to take reasonable care in determining the limits of its powers. However, to reason from a decision of invalidity, to the conclusion that the policy choice when made prior to that decision was made without reasonable care as to the limits of the public body's statutory powers, will only be possible in rare cases where those statutory limits are laid down in clear unambiguous terms. This is not often the case, see, *Dunlop v Woollahra Municipal Council* [1982] A.C. 158; *Rowling* [1988] A.C. 473.

73 *Barrett* [2001] 2 A.C. 550 at 591; *Phelps* [2001] 2 A.C. 619 at 655, 665, 667–668, 672.

74 *Bolam v Friern Hospital Management Committee* [1957] 1 W.L.R. 582 QBD at 586–587.

75 *Phelps* [2001] 2 A.C. 619 at 655, 672; *Bradford-Smart v West Sussex CC* [2002] E.L.R. 139, CA (Civ Div).

iii. *Instances where the courts deny the existence of the duty of care*

The impact of *Barrett* and *Phelps* is apparent in subsequent cases. The general pattern has been for the courts to decide that a duty of care exists and then to determine whether the duty has been breached.[76] **30–018**

There are however instances in the post *Barrett/Phelps* case law where the courts have felt that the policy concerns are sufficiently strong to deny the existence of the duty of care in its entirety. It can be accepted on the *Barrett/Phelps* approach that in some cases it may be correct to decide that it is not fair, just and reasonable to impose a duty of care at all. What *Barrett* and *Phelps* properly emphasise is that this conclusion should only be reached when it is clear that the relevant policy factors really warrant such a conclusion, and there may be disagreement on whether this is so by judges and commentators.

Thus, in *JD*[77] the House of Lords decided that no duty of care was owed by the health care officials to parents accused of child abuse. The majority of the House of Lords felt that the imposition of such a duty would lead to a conflict of interest on the part of the officials in the protection of the child and the protection of the parent. Lord Bingham dissented on the ground that a duty of care could nonetheless be imposed in favour of the parents, albeit making clear that it would be difficult for them to succeed at trial in proving a breach. Whatever one's view about the rightness of the decision reached in this case, it clearly does raise singular problems. The decision that a duty of care should not be imposed in this case should not lead to retreat from the *Barrett/Phelps* approach more generally.

In *Brooks*[78] and *Michael*[79] the House of Lords, while not endorsing all the statements made in *Hill*,[80] nonetheless reaffirmed the general principle that the police owed no duty of care to victims or witnesses in their investigation of crime. Their Lordships rejected the claimant's attempts to fashion certain more specific duties of care that should be imposed on the police in relation to victims and witnesses of crime. They held that this would have detrimental effects on law

---

76 *Reeves v Commissioner of Police of the Metropolis* [2000] 1 A.C. 360, HL; *G (A Child) v Bromley LBC* [2000] 2 L.G.L.R. 237 CA (Civ Div); *Larner v Solihull MBC* [2001] R.T.R. 32, CA (Civ Div); *Watson v British Boxing Board of Control Ltd* [2001] Q.B. 1134, CA (Civ Div); *S v Gloucestershire CC* [2001] 2 W.L.R. 909, CA (Civ Div); *Kane v New Forest DC (No.1)* [2002] 1 W.L.R. 312, CA (Civ Div); *A v Essex CC* [2002] EWHC 2707; *Orange v Chief Constable of West Yorkshire* [2002] Q.B. 347, CA (Civ Div); *Bradford-Smart* [2002] E.L.R. 139; *Devon CC v Clarke* [2005] EWCA Civ 266; *Carty v Croydon LBC* [2005] 1 W.L.R. 2312, CA (Civ Div); *Skipper v Calderdale MBC* [2006] EWCA Civ 238; *Rice v Secretary of State for Trade and Industry* [2007] EWCA Civ 289; *Nuttall v Mayor & Burgesses of Sutton LBC* [2009] EWHC 294 (QB); *Connor v Surrey CC* [2011] Q.B. 429, CA (Civ Div); *Abramova v Oxford Institute of Legal Practice* [2011] EWHC 613 (QB). Compare *Vellino* [2002] 1 W.L.R. 218; *Cowan* [2002] H.L.R. 44.

77 *JD v East Berkshire Community Health NHS Trust* [2005] 2 A.C. 373, HL. See also *B v Att Gen of New Zealand* [2003] UKPC 61; *Lawrence v Pembrokeshire CC* [2007] 1 W.L.R. 2991; *X v Hounslow LBC* [2009] EWCA Civ 286; *Jain v Trent SHA* [2009] 1 A.C. 853; *Mitchell v Glasgow CC* [2009] 1 A.C. 874; *F-D v Children and Family Court Advisory Service* [2014] EWHC 1619 (QB); *ABC v St George's Healthcare NHS Foundation Trust* [2015] EWHC 1394 (QB).

78 *Brooks v Commissioner of Police of the Metropolis* [2005] 1 W.L.R. 1495, HL; *Chief Constable of Hertfordshire v Van Colle* [2008] UKHL 50; *Desmond v Chief Constable of Nottinghamshire* [2011] EWCA Civ 3.

79 *Michael* [2015] UKSC 2.

80 *Hill* [1989] A.C. 53.

enforcement and that the attempt to create more specific duties would create invidious distinctions between those who could sue in negligence and those who could not. The common law did not generally impose negligence liability for the acts of a third party, subject to exceptions where the defendant was in control of the third party, or where the defendant had made a representation and assumed a positive duty to safeguard the claimant.[81]

iv. *Misfeasance and nonfeasance*

30–019 The preceding discussion has been principally concerned with negligence caused by some positive act of the defendant. It is, however, important to consider the applicable legal rules in cases of omissions,[82] more especially because there are indications that the courts have become more restrictive in relation to such cases.

The general rule is that a person is not liable for a negligent omission: a person owes no general duty to assist another. A corollary is that the law will often only award compensation to the person who intervenes carelessly, if the intervention has made the position of the injured party worse than it would otherwise have been.[83] This general proposition is subject to well-recognised exceptions. Thus, it is clear that a case will be regarded as one of misfeasance rather than nonfeasance if the defendant was already under some pre-existing duty, such as the driver who fails to apply the brakes. It is equally well established that there may be duties to act affirmatively to assist others in certain situations because of the relationship between the parties.[84] There are, moreover, circumstances in which the courts will impose a duty on the defendant to take care that a third party does not act to the detriment of the claimant, as exemplified by *Dorset Yacht*,[85] and cases where liability will be imposed because the defendant is taken to have assumed a responsibility to the claimant.[86]

Notwithstanding these exceptions, part of the disquiet caused by *Anns* was because of Lord Wilberforce's willingness to impose liability even on the assumption that the council had not inspected the building at all. His Lordship stated that a public body did not have an unfettered discretion as to whether to exercise its powers, since this discretion could be subject to judicial review. This, said Lord Wilberforce, undermined the argument that if there was no duty to inspect, there was no duty to take care in inspection.[87]

30–020 Later authorities have not endorsed this reasoning and some commentators were critical of this aspect of *Anns*.[88] Thus, the link between a public law duty concerning the control of discretion, and the imposition of a duty of care, has

[81] *Michael* [2015] UKSC 2 at [98]–[100].

[82] D. Nolan, "The Liability of Public Authorities for Failure to Confer a Benefit" (2011) 127 L.Q.R. 260.

[83] *Markesinis and Deakin's Tort Law*, 7th edn (Oxford: Oxford University Press, 2013), pp.178–182; *East Suffolk* [1940] 1 K.B. 319, CA; [1941] A.C. 74, HL.

[84] B. Markesinis, "Negligence, Nuisance and Affirmative Duties of Action" (1989) 105 L.Q.R. 104.

[85] *Dorset Yacht* [1970] A.C. 1004.

[86] *Michael* [2015] UKSC 2 at [98]–[100].

[87] *Anns* [1978] A.C. 728 at 755.

[88] M. Bowman and S. Bailey, "Negligence in the Realms of Public Law–A Positive Obligation to Rescue" [1984] P.L. 277.

been contested.[89] Lord Bridge in *Curran*,[90] was critical of *Anns* for extending the circumstances in which a public body might be under a duty to control the actions of a third party, and for blurring the distinction between misfeasance and nonfeasance.

Lord Hoffmann in *Stovin*[91] was equally reluctant to impose liability for nonfeasance. There were, said his Lordship, two minimum conditions for basing a duty of care on the existence of a statutory power in respect of an omission to exercise the power. It must have been irrational for the authority not to have exercised the power, so that there was in effect a public law duty to act; and there must be exceptional grounds for holding that the policy of the statute conferred the right to compensation on those who suffered loss if the power was not exercised. The very fact that Parliament had conferred discretion on the public body, rather than a duty, was some indication that the policy of the statute was not to create a right to compensation.

This restrictive approach was further emphasised in *Gorringe*.[92] The claimant suffered serious injuries when her car collided with a bus. She had braked sharply just before the crest in the road but her brakes locked and she skidded into the bus. She argued that the local highway authority was liable, since it had not painted the word "SLOW" on the road surface just below the crest. The House of Lords denied liability. Lord Hoffmann stated that the exceptions he had adverted to in *Stovin* may have been ill-advised and that he now found it

> "… difficult to imagine a case in which a common law duty can be founded simply upon the failure (however irrational) to provide some benefit which a public authority has power (or a public law duty) to provide".[93]

This statement applies to both powers and duties and renders it even more difficult for a claimant to succeed than hitherto. Lord Scott was similarly restrictive, stating that:

> "… if a statutory duty does not give rise to a private right to sue for breach, then the duty cannot create a duty of care that would not have been owed at common law if the statute were not there".[94]

The decision is problematic and not easy to reconcile with other relevant case **30–021**
law.[95] While liability for omissions raises difficult issues we should nonetheless be wary of being too restrictive for the following reasons.

First, the position of a public body vested with a discretionary power is not the same as that of a private individual who simply "happens" upon some accident. The reasons for the reluctance to impose liability in cases of pure omission

[89] *Sutherland Shire Council* (1985) 157 C.L.R. 424 at 431.

[90] *Curran* [1987] A.C. 718 at 724, 726.

[91] *Stovin* [1996] A.C. 923.

[92] *Gorringe v Calderdale MBC* [2004] 1 W.L.R. 1057, HL; *St John Poulton's Trustee in Bankruptcy v Ministry of Justice* [2010] EWCA Civ 392; *Desmond v Chief Constable of Nottinghamshire* [2011] EWCA Civ 3; *Furnell v Flaherty* [2013] EWHC 377 (QB).

[93] *Gorringe* [2004] 1 W.L.R. 1057 at [32].

[94] *Gorringe* [2004] 1 W.L.R. 1057 at [70].

[95] D. Nolan, "The Liability of Public Authorities for Failure to Confer a Benefit" (2011) 127 L.Q.R. 260; *Rice* [2007] EWCA Civ 289.

concerning private individuals are questionable,[96] and are not necessarily transferable to public bodies with discretionary powers. As Arrowsmith notes[97]:

> "[O]ne of the main policy reasons for the reluctance to develop duties in private law is that it would impose an unfair burden, and constitute an excessive interference with private autonomy, to require positive action. This argument has no application where there is a public duty to consider whether and how to exercise a particular power."

Second, it is overly formalistic to draw a radical division between those instances in which a public body is granted a statutory discretionary power, with the implication of no liability for omissions, and those areas where it is vested with a statutory duty, with the contrary implication. The very distinction may be difficult to draw as a matter of statutory interpretation. The legislature will often not have given any great thought as to whether the statute is framed in one form rather than the other. Many statutory duties contain discretionary elements. Perhaps most important is the fact that the general assumption underlying the grant of discretionary powers is that they will be exercised in some shape, manner or form. The reason for casting the statute in discretionary rather than mandatory terms is normally reflective of the fact that the problem requires choices to be made by the public body as to how it carries out the statutory remit.

Third, any extension of liability for cases of omission would, in any event, be circumscribed. Thus where a public body makes a legitimate policy decision to exercise its powers in a certain manner, the inevitable consequence will be that it chooses not to act in particular circumstances. However, this species of "omission" is simply the necessary consequence of a policy decision to exercise the powers in one way.

v. The impact of the ECHR

30–022 The considerations that have shaped the law discussed thus far have been domestic in nature. It is, however, also necessary to advert to the impact of the ECHR and the judgment of the ECtHR in *Osman*.[98] The case arose out of a teacher's obsession with a pupil, which culminated in the teacher killing two people and wounding two others. There was a negligence action against the police for a failure to take care in the investigation prior to the fatal shootings. This action failed in the domestic court: the House of Lords in *Hill*[99] held that, for reasons of policy, the police owed no duty of care.

Osman took his case to the ECtHR, which held that the "immunity rule" was in breach of art.6 because it was disproportionate. It did not allow for other public interest considerations to be taken into account, which might favour liability, such as the degree of negligence and the degree of harm in any particular case.[100] The plaintiff had to be able to argue the case on the merits, so that such matters could

[96] P. Cane, *Atiyah's, Accidents, Compensation and the Law*, 7th edn (Cambridge: Cambridge University Press, 2006).
[97] S. Arrowsmith, *Civil Liability and Public Authorities* (1992), pp.183–184.
[98] *Osman v United Kingdom* (1998) 5 BHRC 293.
[99] *Hill* [1989] A.C. 53.
[100] *Hill* [1989] A.C. 53 at [151].

be investigated, rather than having the case struck out on the basis of *Hill*. The ECtHR held that *Hill* infringed art.6 ECHR.

This use of art.6 was problematic, since it is a procedural provision that guarantees a hearing by a tribunal in the determination of a person's civil rights and obligations. The UK argued that the applicant had no "right" in this respect. The very existence of a tortious right was dependent on proof of the constituent elements of a negligence action: proximity, foresight of harm and whether it was fair, just and reasonable to impose a duty of care on the defendant, in this case the police. The House of Lords, which was clearly an independent tribunal, had already determined this issue after full argument. The ECtHR's decision transformed art.6 into a provision that allowed it to pass judgment on the substantive scope of tort liability within a contracting state.

The difficulties with *Osman* were addressed by Lord Browne-Wilkinson in **30–023** *Barrett*[101]: a finding that it was fair, just and reasonable to impose liability was a prerequisite to the existence of a duty of care. Moreover, a decision that it would not be fair, just and reasonable to impose liability was dependent on an aggregate weighing of the detriment to the public interest should negligence liability be held to exist, with the total loss to all would-be claimants if there were held to be no cause of action. When this determination had been made there should not, said his Lordship, be a further weighing of such matters in the context of a particular case. There was also considerable academic criticism of *Osman*.[102]

The ECtHR reconsidered the matter in *Z v UK*,[103] which arose out of the decision in the *X* case.[104] It was argued that the absence of a duty of care in the child abuse cases constituted breach of art.6 ECHR, by parity of reasoning with *Osman*. The ECtHR found that there had been a breach of arts 3 and 13 ECHR, but in effect reversed its ruling in *Osman* concerning the effect of art.6. The absence of a duty of care did not, said the ECtHR, constitute a denial of access to court in violation of art.6. There was simply no substantive right, as judged by UK tort law.[105]

It should nonetheless be recognised that, as in the *Z* case, a claimant may well be able to show a violation of a Convention right other than art.6, and then argue that there must be an effective remedy pursuant to art.13. The latter article was not incorporated into domestic law by the HRA, but Sedley LJ held that art.13 reflected the long-standing principle that where there is a right there should be a remedy.[106]

---

101 *Barrett* [2001] 2 A.C. 550 at 558–560.

102 Lord Hoffmann, "Human Rights and the House of Lords" (1999) 62 M.L.R. 159; T. Weir, "Down Hill—All the Way" [1999] C.L.J. 4; M. Lunney, "A Tort Lawyer's View of *Osman v UK*" [1999] K.C.L.J. 238; P. Craig and D. Fairgrieve, "*Barrett*, Negligence and Discretionary Powers" [1999] P.L. 626; A. Davies, "The European Convention and Negligence Actions: Osman 'Reviewed'" (2001) 117 L.Q.R. 521. Support for *Osman* can be found in J. Wright, "The Retreat from *Osman*: *Z v United Kingdom* in the European Court of Human Rights and Beyond', in D. Fairgrieve, M. Andenas and J. Bell (eds), *Tort Liability of Public Authorities in Comparative Perspective* (2002), Ch.3.

103 *Z v UK* (2002) 34 E.H.R.R. 3.

104 *X* [1995] 2 A.C. 633.

105 *Z* (2002) 34 E.H.R.R. 3 at [96], [101].

106 *R. (K) v Camden and Islington Health Authority* [2002] Q.B. 198, CA (Civ Div) at [54].

Domestic law should be able to satisfy the requirements of art.13 in most instances. This is in part because there is now the damages remedy under the HRA. It is in part because the decisions in *Barrett* and *Phelps* signal that the courts are less likely to deny the existence of a duty of care. It is in part also because the courts may, in the face of a gap, choose to develop the common law so as to provide an appropriate remedy.

3. BREACH OF STATUTORY DUTY

A. Criteria for Liability

30–024 Until the nineteenth century the courts did not inquire closely as to whether the breach of a statute was intended to give a cause of action to individuals, or whether it was only to be enforced by a penalty provided within the statute.[107] A number of 18th- and early 19th-century authorities, some of which dealt with public officers or public bodies, expressed the liability in very general terms: when a public body had a duty imposed upon it an action could be brought by anyone injured by the neglect or refusal to perform it.[108]

However, by the latter part of the 19th century the courts began to restrict the action.[109] Whether an action would lie at the suit of an individual was dependent on a number of factors. The prime consideration was the intent of the legislation.[110] When determining whether the statute was intended to give a cause of action the courts considered whether the existing law of torts provided adequate compensation. If it did, it would usually mean that no action under the statute would lie.[111] Conversely, where a statute simply enacted a pre-existing common law duty this would give rise to an action under the statute.[112] The mere fact that the statute was for the benefit of the public at large would not in itself preclude an action for breach of statutory duty.[113] It might, however, be easier to prove such an action where the statute protected a particular class of which the

[107] K. Stanton, *Breach of Statutory Duty in Tort* (London: Sweet & Maxwell, 1986); R. Buckley, "Liability in Tort for Breach of Statutory Duty" (1984) 100 L.Q.R. 204; K. Stanton et al., *Statutory Torts* (London: Sweet & Maxwell, 2003); K. Stanton, "New Forms of the Tort of Breach of Statutory Duty" (2004) 120 L.Q.R. 324.

[108] Com Dig tit "Action Upon Statute", F; *Sterling v Turner* (1672) 1 Ventris 206; *Rowning v Goodchild* (1772) 2 W. Black 906; *Schinotti v Bumsted* (1796) 6 T.R. 646; *Barry v Arnaud* (1839) 10 Ad. & E. 646; *Ferguson v Kinnoull* (1842) 9 Cl. & F. 251; *Pickering v James* (1873) L.R. 8 C.P. 489.

[109] *Atkinson v Newcastle Waterworks Co* (1877) 2 Ex. D. 441 restricting the broad approach in *Couch v Steel* (1854) 3 E. & B. 402. Despite occasional reference to the broad view as in *Dawson v Bingley Urban DC* [1911] 2 K.B. 149, CA at 159, the courts have applied the criteria which govern breach of statutory duty generally, *Pasmore v Oswaldtwistle Urban DC* [1898] A.C. 387, HL; *Read v Croydon Corporation* [1938] 4 All E.R. 631; *Reffell v Surrey CC* [1964] 1 W.L.R. 358 QBD; *De Falco v Crawley BC* [1980] Q.B. 460, CA (Civ Div); *Booth v NEB* [1978] 3 All E.R. 624 QBD; *Lonrho Ltd v Shell Petroleum (No.2)* [1982] A.C. 173, HL; *R. v Deputy Governor of Parkhurst Prison, Ex p. Hague* [1992] 1 A.C. 58, HL; *X* [1995] 2 A.C. 633 at 731–732; *Peabody* [1985] A.C. 210 at 241; *Curran* [1987] A.C. 718.

[110] *Atkinson* (1877) 2 Ex. D. 441 at 448; *Hague* [1992] 1 A.C. 58; *X* [1995] 2 A.C. 633 at 731–732; *Morrison Sports Ltd v Scottish Power Plc* [2010] UKSC 37.

[111] *Phillips v Britannia Hygienic Laundry Co Ltd* [1923] 2 K.B. 832, CA.

[112] *Ashby v White* (1703) 2 Ld. Raym. 938 at 954.

[113] *Phillips* [1923] 2 K.B. 832; *Lonrho* [1982] A.C. 173.

plaintiff was a member, although the plaintiff will still have to show that the statute was intended to confer private rights.[114] Another factor the court considered was whether the statute provided a penalty for breach. If it did then it might be more difficult to establish a cause of action for an individual, though it was not an impossible hurdle to overcome.[115] In addition, the harm suffered had to be within the risk that the statute was designed to prevent.[116] The courts regarded alternative remedies laid down in the statute, such as default powers, as precluding a civil action.[117] The nature of the duty allegedly broken, and the extent to which the court regarded this as justiciable, influenced its decision as to whether to restrict the plaintiff to the pursuit of a statutory remedy.[118]

B. Application of the Criteria

A claimant who seeks to rely on breach of statutory duty will therefore have to prove this cause of action in accord with the normal criteria. The claimant will have to show that the statute was intended to confer private rights of action and that they came within the protected class. The normal rules of construction will be applied when determining these issues, and the courts have been reluctant to impose strict liability for breach of statutory duty per se. **30–025**

Thus, in *X* Lord Browne-Wilkinson found that general social legislation of the type in question, although passed for the protection of those affected by it, was enacted for the benefit of society as a whole, and therefore no action for breach of statutory duty would lie.[119] A similar reluctance to subject public bodies to liability for breach of statutory duty is apparent in later cases.

Thus, in *Barrett*[120] the claim for breach of statutory duty per se was not pursued before the Court of Appeal or the House of Lords, in the context of an action against a local authority which had taken a child into care, the only live issue being whether there could be a negligence claim.

In *O'Rourke*[121] the House of Lords found that there could be no cause of action for damages for breach of statutory duty arising from s.63 of the Housing Act 1985. Lord Hoffmann, giving judgment, reasoned that the duty to provide accommodation was enforceable in public law via judicial review, but that breach of that duty did not sound in damages. The Act was, said his Lordship, intended for the benefit of society in general, and the existence of the duty to house was **30–026**

[114] *Hague* [1992] 1 A.C. 58.

[115] *Atkinson* (1877) 2 Ex. D. 441; *Groves v Lord Wimborne* [1898] 2 Q.B. 402, CA; *Cutler v Wandsworth Stadium Ltd* [1949] A.C. 398, HL.

[116] *Gorris v Scott* (1875) L.R. 9 Ex. 125; *Peabody* [1985] A.C. 210 at 241; *Curran* [1987] A.C. 718.

[117] *Watt v Kesteven CC* [1955] 1 Q.B. 408, CA; *Wood v Ealing LBC* [1967] Ch. 364 Ch D; *Cumings v Birkenhead Corporation* [1972] Ch. 12, CA (Civ Div); cf. *Meade v Haringey LBC* [1979] 1 W.L.R. 637, CA (Civ Div); *Att Gen ex rel Mcwhirter v Independent Broadcasting Authority* [1973] Q.B. 626 at 649; P. Cane, "*Ultra vires* Breach of Statutory Duty" [1981] P.L. 11.

[118] Compare *Ching v Surrey CC* [1910] 1 K.B. 736, CA and *Reffell v Surrey CC* [1964] 1 W.L.R. 358 QBD, with *Watt* [1955] 1 Q.B. 408 and *Wood* [1967] Ch. 364.

[119] *X* [1995] 2 A.C. 633 at 731–732.

[120] *Barrett* [2001] 2 A.C. 550.

[121] *O'Rourke v Camden LBC* [1998] A.C. 188, HL.

dependent on the local authority's discretion. These factors indicated that the plaintiff's complaint did not give rise to a cause of action in private law for breach of statutory duty.

In *Phelps*,[122] the House of Lords held that the duties cast on local authorities in relation to special educational needs were for the benefit of all children that fell within the relevant area, and were not intended to sound in an action for breach of statutory duty.

In *Michael*[123] the Supreme Court held that the fact that many areas were subject to statutory regulation did not mean that if there was an error in regulatory oversight the state should bear the cost of compensation for wrongs committed by a third party. A similar reluctance to impose liability for breach of statutory duty per se is apparent in other cases.[124]

C. Comment

30–027 Three related comments on this jurisprudence are relevant. The first is that there has been a marked reluctance to find that the conditions for breach of statutory duty have been met in cases concerning public bodies. The statutory construction demanded by the criteria for breach of statutory duty has been explicitly or implicitly underpinned by unwillingness to impose damages liability, more especially where the state is undertaking welfare functions to which the claimant, in the absence of the relevant legislation, would have no "right". The courts' jurisprudence has therefore been premised on certain background assumptions about the correlation, or lack thereof, between statutory duties and consequent monetary claims that are contestable.

The second comment concerns the standard of liability. The impression given in the *X* case is that breach of statutory duty will or must always mean strict liability.[125] This does not have to be so. The standard of liability will depend on construction of the legislation.[126] The duty may be strict, it may simply be one of reasonable care, or it may be an obligation to take action that is reasonably practicable.[127] There is, moreover, no reason why the courts should not be able to apply other standards of liability such as the serious breach test used by the CJEU in assessing state liability in damages. This criterion gives a court room for manoeuvre, which a strict liability standard does not readily provide. The House of Lords decided not to find for the plaintiffs in *X* and *O'Rourke* in part because

---

122 *Phelps* [2001] 2 A.C. 619 at 652.

123 *Michael* [2015] UKSC 2 at [113]–[114].

124 *Clunis v Camden & Islington Health Authority* [1998] Q.B. 978, CA (Civ Div); *Olotu v Home Office* [1997] 1 W.L.R. 328, CA (Civ Div); *Cullen v Chief Constable of the Royal Ulster Constabulary* [2003] 1 W.L.R. 1763; *Gorringe* [2004] 1 W.L.R. 1057, HL; *Neil Martin Ltd v Revenue and Customs Commissioners* [2007] EWCA Civ 1041; *St John Poulton's Trustee in Bankruptcy v Ministry of Justice* [2010] EWCA Civ 392; *Morrison* [2010] UKSC 37.

125 *X* [1995] 2 A.C. 633 at 731–732.

126 *Markesinis and Deakin's Tort Law* (2013), pp.294–299; R.A. Buckley, "Liability in Tort for Breach of Statutory Duty" (1984) 100 L.Q.R. 204, 222–225; K.M. Stanton, "New Forms of the Tort of Breach of Statutory Duty" (2004) 120 L.Q.R. 324, 331–333.

127 *Jayne v National Coal Board* [1963] 2 All E.R. 220; *Edwards v National Coal Board* [1949] 1 K.B. 704, CA.

this would impose strict liability on the defendants. It did not wish to impose an onerous strict duty on the defendants when they had to make complex discretionary determinations. A test akin to that used by the CJEU would have given their Lordships an extra option. They could have held that the statute was intended to give rights to individuals, but that proof of a serious breach was required for a damages action.

Third, it is readily apparent that certain statutory duties contain discretion as to how they should be carried out[128] or they may entail difficult points of statutory construction.[129] The courts have been disinclined to impose strict liability in such circumstances. A test like that used by the CJEU does, however, enable the court to consider such factors in the determination as to whether there has been a serious breach on the facts of a particular case.

4. THE HUMAN RIGHTS ACT

The previous section was concerned with whether the courts would read a statutory duty so as to provide for damages liability. We now consider the Human Rights Act 1998 (HRA), which contains an express provision for damages in certain circumstances.[130] **30–028**

A. Criteria for Liability

Section 8(1) of the HRA provides that the court can grant such relief or remedy within its powers as it considers just and appropriate. This is qualified in s.8(2): damages can only be awarded by a court which has power to do so, or to order the payment of compensation in civil proceedings. Section 8(3) further qualifies this liability by providing that no award of damages is to be made unless taking account of all the circumstances of the case, including any other relief or remedy granted, or order made in relation to the act in question, by that or any other court, and the consequences of any decision, of that or any other court, in respect of that act, the court is satisfied that the award is necessary to afford just satisfaction to the person in whose favour it is made. **30–029**

In determining whether to award damages or the amount, the court must, in accord with s.8(4), take into account the principles of the ECtHR in relation to compensation under art.41 ECHR. It is questionable how far this case law assists the national courts. This is in part because the ECtHR has not developed notably clear principles on compensation.[131] It is in part because the focus of art.41 is

[128] See, e.g. *Haydon v Kent CC* [1978] Q.B. 343, CA (Civ Div).

[129] *Rowling v Takaro Properties Ltd* [1988] A.C. 473.

[130] Law Commission No.266 and Scot Law Commission No.180, *Damages under the Human Rights Act 1998* (2000), Cmnd.4853; D. Fairgrieve, "The Human Rights Act 1998, Damages and Tort Law" [2001] P.L. 695.

[131] Law Commission No.266 and Scot Law Commission No.180, *Damages under the Human Rights Act 1998*, paras 3.4–3.15; Judge Jean-Paul Costa, "The Provision of Compensation under Article 41 of the European Convention on Human Rights", in D. Fairgrieve, M. Andenas and J. Bell (eds), *Tort Liability of Public Authorities in Comparative Perspective* (2002), Ch.1; A. Mowbray, "The European Court of Human Rights Approach to Just Satisfaction" [1997] P.L. 647.

different from the domestic paradigm. Article 41 empowers the ECtHR to award just satisfaction for a violation of the ECHR where the internal law of the defendant state allows only partial reparation to be made. This criterion is of limited relevance for claims within a particular country.

There is, however, nothing to prevent our courts from considering the jurisprudence of other countries concerning damages claims for breach of constitutional rights. Interesting case law on this issue exists in the USA,[132] New Zealand[133] and India[134] to name but three jurisdictions.[135]

Commentators differed as to the nature of the cause of action in s.8,[136] with some analogising it to breach of statutory duty, while others preferred to see it as a free standing tort. It is clear from the case law that there are marked differences between s.8 and traditional torts and hence it may be better to regard s.8 as sui generis.

B. Application of the Criteria

30–030 Section 8 leaves many issues open as to the more particular criteria for assessing damages liability under the HRA. The courts have developed and applied these criteria under the HRA.

i. Damages and the standard of liability

30–031 The standard of liability is of central importance. The general position in domestic law is that some species of fault or intentional wrongdoing is required to establish liability. The HRA provides little direct guidance on this issue, subject to s.9(3) HRA, which stipulates that in proceedings under the HRA in respect of a judicial act done in good faith, damages may not be awarded.[137] This could be interpreted to mean that no such defence is open to other public authorities that act in breach of s.6(1) of the HRA.

The courts might more generally decide that liability should prima facie be strict, in the sense that once a right is violated then damages should follow. They might mitigate this through defences open to the public body that it acted in good faith. They might alternatively decide that the breach has to be especially serious. Lord Woolf argued extra-judicially that the existence of fault should not be a

---

[132] 42 USC section 1983; *Bivens v Six Unknown Named Agents of the Federal Bureau of Narcotics* 403 US 388 (1971).

[133] *Simpson v Attorney General* [1994] 3 N.Z.L.R. 667.

[134] *Nilabati Bahera v State of Orissa* (1993) A.I.R. 1960.

[135] L. Tortell, *Monetary Remedies for Breach of Human Rights: A Comparative Study* (Oxford: Hart, 2006).

[136] Compare D. Fairgrieve, "The Human Rights Act 1998, Damages and Tort Law" [2001] P.L. 695, 696; Law Commission No.266 and Scot Law Commission No.180, *Damages under the Human Rights Act 1998*, para.4.20; A. Lester and D. Pannick, "The Impact of the Human Rights Act on Private Law: The Knight's Move" (2000) 116 L.Q.R. 380, 382; Lord Woolf, "The Human Rights Act 1998 and Remedies", in M. Andenas and D. Fairgrieve (eds), *Judicial Review in International Perspective: Volume II* (Arnhem: Kluwer Law International, 2000), p.432.

[137] Except to compensate a person to the extent required by art.5(5) ECHR.

pre-condition for liability, but that it should not be ignored.[138] It should, moreover, be recognised that breach of certain Convention rights may well entail fault or intentional wrongdoing.[139] The standard of liability must now be seen in the light of the leading cases.

In *Anufrijeva*[140] the claimant argued that the defendant local authority was in breach of art.8 ECHR by failing to discharge its duty to provide accommodation that met the special needs of one member of the family. It is axiomatic that there must be a violation of a Convention right before you can get damages. It is therefore open to courts to limit damages liability by incorporating an element of fault as a requirement for breach of the relevant right. This is what occurred in *Anufrijeva*. The Court of Appeal accepted that art.8 could impose positive obligations on the state to provide the support sought by the claimant. It held, however, that mere breach of a public law obligation to provide the claimant with something to which they were entitled did not automatically breach art.8. Before inaction could lead to breach of art.8 there had to be some culpability, in the sense of knowledge that the claimant's family life was at risk. The impact on family life by not giving the support had to be sufficiently serious and foreseeable,[141] and the culpable delay had to cause substantial prejudice.[142]

The implications of *Anufrijeva* for the standard of liability must be kept in perspective. The case is indicative of the way in which culpability can be taken into account when deciding whether there has been a breach of the Convention right.[143] The nature of such considerations was however affected by the type of case, this being a claim for violation of art.8 ECHR by the state's failure to take positive action to secure for the claimant accommodation sufficient to meet his special needs. **30–032**

These considerations will not necessarily be relevant in relation to breaches of other Convention rights, more especially where there is the paradigm claim that the state infringed the claimant's rights to speech, association, property and the like, or that it violated personal freedom. In such circumstances the courts are more likely to find that breach of the relevant Convention right will at least prima facie allow the claimant to seek damages under s.8 HRA.[144] However, as will be evident from the subsequent discussion, the courts have interpreted s.8 as embodying a broad discretion as to whether damages should be awarded or not. The courts have regarded the seriousness of the violation and the manner in which it occurred as factors to be taken into account in deciding whether to award damages and if so how much. In that sense considerations of culpability have been taken into account, albeit as factors in deciding whether to exercise the discretion to award damages.

---

[138] Lord Woolf, "The Human Rights Act 1998 and Remedies", in M. Andenas and D. Fairgrieve (eds), *Judicial Review in International Perspective: Volume II* (2000), p.433.

[139] D. Fairgrieve, "The Human Rights Act 1998, Damages and Tort Law" [2001] P.L. 695, 700.

[140] *Anufrijeva v Southwark LBC* [2004] Q.B. 1124, CA (Civ Div).

[141] *Anufrijeva* [2004] Q.B. 1124 at [45].

[142] *Anufrijeva* [2004] Q.B. 1124 at [46], [48].

[143] See also *Mitchell* [2009] 1 A.C. 874.

[144] *R. (Infinis Plc) v Gas and Electricity Markets Authority* [2013] EWCA Civ 70.

ii. Damages and discretion

30–033 The standard of liability is therefore of central importance under the HRA. The courts have also maintained control by emphasising that damages under the HRA are discretionary, by way of contrast to common law causes of action where recovery is of right.[145] Thus in *Anufrijeva* Lord Woolf CJ placed emphasis on the wording of s.8 of the HRA, that the court can provide a remedy that it considers just and appropriate, to reinforce the conclusion that the court has a wide discretion as to the award of damages under the HRA. In deciding whether to award damages, and if so how much, the court should balance the interests of the victim and those of the public as a whole.[146] The seriousness of the violation may also be relevant in deciding whether compensation should be awarded, and the manner in which the Convention right was breached may also be a factor in determining whether the violation was serious so as to warrant damages being awarded.[147]

This approach is also evident in *Greenfield*.[148] The claimant was charged with a drugs offence while in prison. His case was heard by the deputy controller, G was found guilty and ordered to serve more days in prison. G argued that this decision was in breach of art.6 ECHR, since it was a determination of a criminal charge and the deputy controller was not an independent tribunal as required by art.6. He sought damages under s.8 of the HRA. Lord Bingham held that the ECHR case law indicated that a finding of a violation was often per se just satisfaction for the violation found, thereby reflecting the ECHR focus, which was the protection of human rights and not the award of compensation.[149] This was especially so because violation of art.6 ECHR did not mean that the outcome would necessarily have been different. It was moreover necessary for the claimant to show that any loss complained of was actually caused by breach of art.6.[150] The House of Lords concluded that damages were not warranted in the instant case.

[145] *Anufrijeva* [2004] Q.B. 1124 at [50], [55].

[146] *Anufrijeva* [2004] Q.B. 1124 at [55]–[56].

[147] *Anufrijeva* [2004] Q.B. 1124 at [64], [66]–[68]; Lord Woolf, "The Human Rights Act 1998 and Remedies", in M. Andenas and D. Fairgrieve (eds), *Judicial Review in International Perspective: Volume II* (2000). See also *R. (Bernard) v Enfield LBC* [2003] L.G.R. 423; *R. (KB) v Mental Health Review Tribunal* [2004] Q.B. 936 QBD; *R. (TH) v Wood Green Crown Court* [2007] 1 W.L.R. 1670 DC; *C (A Child, Re)* [2007] EWCA Civ 2; *R. (Downing) v Parole Board* [2008] EWHC 3198 (Admin); *Dobson v Thames Water Utilities Ltd* [2009] EWCA Civ 28; *R. (Anyasinti) v Secretary of State for the Home Department* [2010] EWHC 1676 (Admin); *R. (Degainis) v Secretary of State for Justice* [2010] EWHC 137 (Admin); *R. (on the application of MG (Iran)) v Secretary of State for the Home Department* [2014] EWHC 3470 (Admin); *DSD v Commissioner of Police of the Metropolis* [2015] EWCA Civ 646.

[148] *R. (Greenfield) v Secretary of State for the Home Department* [2005] 1 W.L.R. 673, HL. See also *R. (Baiai) v Secretary of State for the Home Department* [2006] EWHC 1035 (Admin); *R. (Faulkner) v Secretary of State for Justice* [2010] EWCA Civ 1434; *R. (Faulkner) v Secretary of State for Justice* [2011] EWCA Civ 349.

[149] *Greenfield* [2005] 1 W.L.R. 673 at [9].

[150] *Greenfield* [2005] 1 W.L.R. 673 at [10]–[14].

iii. Damages and quantum

30–034 There has been some judicial disagreement as to how quantum of damages should be calculated under the HRA. In *Anufrijeva* Lord Woolf CJ stated that awards should not be on the low side as compared with tort awards, that domestic courts should be free to depart from the ECHR scale and that English awards by appropriate courts were the fitting comparator.[151]

However, in *Greenfield* Lord Bingham disagreed as to the principles on quantum of recovery.[152] He stated that the HRA was not a tort statute and had different objectives. Thus, even where a finding of a violation of Convention rights did not give the claimant just satisfaction, such a finding would still be an important part of the remedy. The purpose of incorporating the HRA was, said Lord Bingham, not to give victims better remedies at home than in Strasbourg, but to give them the same remedies without the delay and expense of going to Strasbourg. Domestic courts were therefore obliged by s.8(4) of the HRA to take account of ECHR principles not only in deciding whether to award damages, but also in determining the amount of the award. It followed that domestic courts should look to Strasbourg, not to domestic precedent. While they were not bound inflexibly by Strasbourg case law, "they should not aim to be significantly more or less generous than the ECHR might be expected to be in a case where it was willing to make an award".[153] The quantum of damages under the HRA can however reflect the seriousness of the breach of the Convention right.[154]

C. Comment

30–035 It is clear that the courts wish to place limits on the recovery of damages under s.8. This is evident in the repeated emphasis on the discretionary nature of the remedy, coupled with the related idea that a declaration is the primary means of vindicating violations of Convention rights. The factors identified by the courts as relevant to the exercise of their discretion under s.8, such as the balancing of public and private interest, and the limits placed on quantum, serve to reinforce this. There is no doubt that the wording of s.8 of the HRA renders the award of damages discretionary. It can nonetheless be questioned as to whether the courts have interpreted the statutory provisions too restrictively.

Thus, as Clayton has argued in relation to *Anufrijeva*, while the principle of fair balance as between the individual and the public may be inherent in the ECHR as a whole, the ECtHR has not applied "the fair balance principle to questions of just satisfaction", and hence the "idea that the court should expressly balance an individual's rights with the general interest of the community before

---

[151] *Anufrijeva* [2004] Q.B. 1124 at [73]–[74].

[152] *Greenfield* [2005] 1 W.L.R. 673 at [19]; *R. (on the application of Sturnham) v Parole Board for England and Wales* [2013] UKSC 23.

[153] *Greenfield* [2005] 1 W.L.R. 673 at [19].

[154] *Rabone v Pennine Care NHS Trust* [2012] UKSC 2; *D v Commissioner of Police of the Metropolis* [2014] EWHC 2493 (QB).

awarding damages has no basis in ECtHR case law".[155] It is moreover doubtful whether the language of s.8(4) of the HRA, which is cast in terms of taking account of the principles from the ECtHR's case law in deciding whether to award damages, and the amount of any such award, justifies the conclusion in *Greenfield* that HRA damages should generally be at the same level as that in Strasbourg.

In more general terms Varuhas has argued that damages under the HRA should be informed by a tort-based approach, and that this would provide a more coherent foundation for the remedy than the current approach of the courts.[156] In a related vein Steele contends that damages in tort are more regularly given for violation of rights than under the HRA where monetary compensation is somewhat peripheral.[157]

5. MISFEASANCE IN PUBLIC OFFICE

A. Criteria for Liability

30–036 The tort of misfeasance in public office[158] applies specifically to public officers, which has been held to cover those who exercise governmental power.[159] The ambit of this tort was extensively reviewed in *Three Rivers DC v Bank of England (No.3)*,[160] which will be used to analyse the cause of action. The claimants were depositors with a deposit taker (BCCI) licensed by the Bank of England. They lost their money when BCCI went into liquidation. The claimants brought an action in misfeasance in public office, claiming that the Bank had wrongly granted a licence to BCCI and that it had wrongly failed to revoke it.

i. Two limbs of the tort

30–037 In *Bourgoin*[161] it was held that there could be an action where the public body exceeded its powers either maliciously or knowingly. It is accepted that there are

[155] R. Clayton, "Damage Limitation: The Courts and the Human Rights Act Damages" [2005] P.L. 429, 435; M. Andenas, E. Bjorge and D. Fairgrieve "A Fair Price for Violations of Human Rights?" (2014) 130 L.Q.R. 48.

[156] J. Varuhas, "A Tort-Based Approach to Damages under the Human Rights Act 1998" (2009) 72 M.L.R. 750.

[157] J. Steele, "Damages in Tort and under the Human Rights Act: Remedial or Functional Separation?" (2008) 67 C.L.J. 606.

[158] B. Gould, "Damages as a Remedy in Administrative Law" (1972) 5 N.Z.U.L.R.105; C. Harlow, "Fault Liability in French and English Public Law" (1976) 39 M.L.R. 516.

[159] *Society of Lloyd's v Henderson* [2007] EWCA Civ 930, it did not therefore cover the insurers Lloyd's.

[160] *Three Rivers DC v Bank of England (No.3) (Summary Judgment)* [2003] 2 A.C. 1, HL; D. Fairgrieve and M. Andenas, "Misfeasance in Public Office, Governmental Liability, and European Influences" (2002) 51 I.C.L.Q. 757; D. Fairgrieve, "Damages Claims against Public Bodies: The Role for Misfeasance in Public Office" [2007] J.R. 169; J. Murphy, "Misfeasance in a Public Office: A Tort Law Misfit?" (2012) 32 O.J.L.S 51.

[161] *Bourgoin SA v Ministry of Agriculture, Fisheries and Food* [1986] Q.B. 716, CA (Civ Div) at 775–778, 788; *Dunlop* [1982] A.C. 158; *Calveley v Chief Constable of the Merseyside Police* [1989]

two limbs to the tort. A public officer can be liable for misfeasance in public office either: where the public officer performed or omitted to perform an act with the object of injuring the claimant, what is known as targeted malice; or where he performed an act which he knew he had no power to perform, and which he knew would probably injure the claimant.

It was made clear in *Three Rivers* that these were alternative and not cumulative ingredients of the cause of action. Malice in the sense of intent to injure was central to the first limb of the tort, while knowledge on the part of the public officer that he did not have the power to do the act in question was the central element of the second limb of the tort. The litigation in *Three Rivers* was directed towards the more specific requirements necessary to prove the second limb of the cause of action, since there was no allegation that the Bank had been guilty of targeted malice.

ii. The relationship between the two limbs

It is, however, necessary to consider some of the older case law in order to understand the way in which the argument proceeded in the *Three Rivers* case. 30–038
Malicious excess of power had its origin in *Ashby v White*[162] and the dissent by Holt CJ. The plaintiff was wrongfully prevented from voting and he brought an action on the case against the returning officer. He failed in the King's Bench, where the majority gave various reasons for rejecting the claim.[163] But Holt CJ's spirited dissent was upheld by the House of Lords. The plaintiff had a right to vote and he must have a remedy to vindicate that right. It was questionable whether Holt CJ required malice or not.[164] However, later cases held that malice was the essence of the action.[165]

There is, however, a crucial ambiguity in the meaning ascribed to malice in this context. This could be taken to mean that there has to be some intent to injure the claimant. It could alternatively mean something rather broader, akin to a deliberate and wilful abuse of power, albeit without the need to prove any intent to injure as such. In the *Three Rivers* case the Bank argued for the former reading of the older case law, and the claimants for the latter.

This ambiguity as to the meaning of malice persisted in later case law. A number of authorities provide some support for a tort based on malicious excess of power. In *Smith*[166] the plaintiff could not set aside a compulsory purchase order because she was outside the six-week time limit. The House of Lords believed that she could seek damages against the clerk for knowingly, and in bad

---

A.C. 1228, HL. The courts disapproved of the potentially broad application of *Beaudesert Shire Council v Smith* (1966) 120 C.L.R. in *Dunlop* [1982] A.C. 158 at 170–171 and in *Lonhro Ltd v Shell Petroleum (No.2)* [1982] A.C. 173, HL at 188.

162 *Ashby v White* (1703) 2 Ld. Raym. 938; 3 Ld. Raym. 320.

163 The matter was judicial; that it was for Parliament; multiplicity of similar actions, see *Ashby* (1703) 2 Ld. Raym. 938 at 941–942, 943, 947; cf. Holt CJ at 950–954.

164 His dissent in the Kings Bench did not require malice but, cf. *Tozer v Child* (1857) 7 E. & B. 377 at 381, (arguendo Shee Serjt).

165 *Drewe v Coulton* (1787) 1 East 563n; *Harman v Tappenden* (1802) 1 East 555; *Cullen v Morris* (1821) 2 Stark 577; *Tozer v Child* (1857) 7 E. & B. 377.

166 *Smith v East Elloe Rural DC* [1956] A.C. 736, HL at 752, 753.

faith, procuring the confirmation of the order. In *Abdul Cader*[167] the plaintiff alleged that he had been wrongfully and maliciously refused a licence. The court held that if the licence had been maliciously refused a damages action might be brought.[168]

30–039 There is also a group of cases that either deny the need for malice entirely, requiring only a knowing excess of power, or so define malice as to make it equivalent to knowledge. *Farrington*[169] concerned the withdrawal of the plaintiff's liquor licence as a result of which he had to close his hotel. Smith J said that the tort of misfeasance in a public office was constituted by a public officer doing an act which to his knowledge is an abuse of his office and thereby causing damage to another. The defendant had withdrawn the licence knowing that he did not have power to do so. Malice was not needed. In *Roncarelli*[170] the plaintiff claimed that his liquor licence had been withdrawn arbitrarily as punishment for his support of the Jehovah's Witnesses. Rand J in delivering judgment against the defendant, the Prime Minister of Quebec, described the cancellation of the licence on this ground as malicious, but then proceeded to define malice as acting for a reason and purpose knowingly foreign to the administration.[171]

The tensions as to the precise elements of the cause of action for misfeasance in public office were also apparent in Commonwealth cases. In *Mengel*[172] the action was brought by the owners of two cattle stations whose plans to sell their cattle were frustrated by the action of two inspectors who placed the cattle under quarantine without statutory authority to do so. The plurality in the High Court held that misfeasance was not constituted simply by an act of a public officer, which he knew was beyond power and which resulted in damage. It was said that policy and principle required that liability should be more closely confined. The tort should be limited in the same way as other torts that imposed liability for the intentional infliction of harm. Liability required an act that the public officer knew was beyond his power, including reckless disregard of the means of ascertaining the extent of his power, and a foreseeable risk of harm, or reckless indifference to the harm which was caused.[173] In a separate judgment there were dicta by Brennan J, which could be taken to mean that foreseeability of damage was not relevant, provided that the other requisite elements of the cause of action, including causation were present.

---

[167] *David v Abdul Cader* [1963] 1 W.L.R. 835; A. Bradley, "Liability for Malicious Refusal of a Licence" [1964] C.L.J. 4.

[168] *Abdul Cader* [1963] 1 W.L.R. 835 at 839–840; *Jones v Swansea City Council* [1990] 1 W.L.R. 1453, HL.

[169] *Farrington v Thomson* [1959] V.R. 286. See also *Brayser v Maclean* (1875) L.R. 6 P.C. 398 at 405–406; *Whitelegg v Richards* (1823) 2 B. & C. 45.

[170] *Roncarelli v Duplessis* [1959] 16 D.L.R. (2d) 689.

[171] *Roncarelli* [1959] 16 D.L.R. (2d) 689 at 706; *Ferguson v Kinnoull* (1842) 9 Cl. & F. 251 at 303.

[172] *Northern Territory v Mengel* (1995) 69 A.L.J.R. 527.

[173] *Mengel* (1995) 69 A.L.J.R. 527 at 540; *Garrett v Att Gen* [1997] 2 N.Z.L.R. 332; *Rawlinson v Rice* [1997] 2 N.Z.L.R. 651.

B. Application of the Criteria

It was accepted in *Three Rivers* that there were two limbs to the cause of action, the targeted malice limb and the illegality limb. It was the precise elements of the latter that were in issue in the instant case. **30–040**

The claimants argued that malice in the older case law was a relatively loose term akin to a deliberate and wilful abuse of power, without the need to prove any intent to injure as such. They conceived of the targeted malice limb of the tort in just these terms. The corollary was to argue that the illegality limb of the tort should be cast more broadly than found in the ratio of Clarke J and the Court of Appeal. They contended that knowledge of the illegality should be extended to cover objective recklessness, and that the test for recoverable loss should be cast in terms of foreseeability or perhaps directness.

The defendant argued that misfeasance was always an intentional tort and that the early cases that spoke of malice meant that there had to be intent to injure the claimant. The defendant's view of the targeted malice limb had implications for their view of the illegality limb. The defendant argued that knowledge of illegality should be limited to actual knowledge and possibly subjective recklessness, but that it should go no further than that. The test for recoverable loss should therefore be relatively narrow, since this served to ensure that the requisite intent could be found or presumed to exist.

Clarke J's holding in respect of the illegality limb can be summarised as follows.[174] In order to establish that the public officer knew that he had no power to do the act complained of, it was sufficient that the officer had actual knowledge that the act was unlawful, or in circumstances where he believed or suspected that the act was beyond his powers, that he did not ascertain whether or not that was so, or failed to take such steps as an honest and reasonable person would have taken to ascertain the true position. The same test was applied to establish that the officer knew that his act would probably injure the claimant or a person in a class of which the claimant was a member: actual knowledge would suffice, and so too would belief or suspicion that his action would probably cause loss to the claimant, where the public officer did not ascertain whether or not that was so, or where he failed to make the type of inquiries which an honest and reasonable man would have made. **30–041**

The case went to the House of Lords twice, in part because the constituent elements of the cause of action were not entirely clear from the first of these decisions. The summary of the cause of action is therefore taken principally from the second of these cases.[175] **30–042**

The first limb of the tort applied to cases where a public power was exercised for an improper purpose with the specific intention of injuring a person or persons.[176]

The second limb of the tort required an unlawful act or omission made or done in the exercise of power by a public officer. Since the essence of the tort was an

174 *Three Rivers DC v Bank of England (No.3)* [1996] 3 All E.R. 558 QBD.
175 *Three Rivers* [2003] 2 A.C. 1.
176 *Three Rivers DC v Bank of England (No.3)* [2000] 2 W.L.R. 1220, HL.

abuse of power, the act or omission must have been done with the required mental element, and must have been done in bad faith.[177]

The mental element for the second limb was satisfied where the act or omission was done intentionally by the public officer in the knowledge that it was beyond his powers and that it would probably cause injury to the claimant. The fact that the act or omission was done or made without an honest belief that it was lawful was sufficient to satisfy the requirement of bad faith. This could be demonstrated by knowledge of probable loss on the part of the public officer.[178]

The mental element for the second limb of the tort could also be satisfied if the act or omission was done or made recklessly, where the public officer, although he was aware that there was a serious risk that the claimant would suffer loss due to the act or omission that he knew to be unlawful, wilfully chose to disregard that risk. In this version of the second limb, knowledge of the illegality includes subjective recklessness that the act or omission was illegal.[179]

30–043 A public body can be vicariously liable for the acts of its officers.[180] Whether the public body is liable will depend on whether the officers were engaged in a misguided and unauthorised method of performing their authorised duties, or whether the unauthorised acts of the officers were so unconnected with their authorised duties as to be quite independent of and outside those duties.

A claim for exemplary damages can be made in relation to the tort of misfeasance in public office,[181] however, the tort is not actionable per se and hence proof of damage is required.[182]

C. Comment

30–044 The contending arguments in *Three Rivers* threw into sharp relief the nature and reach of the tort of misfeasance in public office. The claimants wished to extend the tort so as to cover damage caused by unlawful governmental action, and hence argued that knowledge of the illegality should embrace objective recklessness. The House of Lords was unwilling to take this step. Subsequent case law has emphasised that the claimant must prove knowledge or subjective recklessness as to the lawfulness of the public officer's acts and the consequences of them, and that mere reckless indifference will not suffice for liability.[183] This renders it difficult for any action to succeed, more especially because it is for the clamant to prove the requisite recklessness. The case law on misfeasance

---

[177] *Three Rivers* [2003] 2 A.C. 1 at [42].

[178] *Three Rivers* [2003] 2 A.C. 1 at [44].

[179] *Three Rivers DC v Bank of England (No.3)* [2000] 2 W.L.R. 1220, HL; *Three Rivers* [2003] 2 A.C. 1 at [42], [45]–[46]; *Southwark LBC v Dennett* [2007] EWCA Civ 1091.

[180] *Racz v Home Office* [1994] 2 A.C. 45.

[181] *Kuddus v Chief Constable of Leicestershire Constabulary* [2002] 2 A.C. 122, HL; *Muuse v Secretary of State for the Home Department* [2010] EWCA Civ 453.

[182] *Watkins v Secretary of State for the Home Department* [2006] 2 A.C. 395, HL; C. Knight, "Constitutionality and Misfeasance in Public Office: Contorting the Tort?" (2011) 16 J.R. 49.

[183] *Dennett* [2007] EWCA Civ 1091; *Henderson* [2007] EWCA Civ 930; *Chagos Islanders v Att Gen* [2004] EWCA Civ 997; *Merelie v General Dentist Council* [2009] EWHC 1165 (QB).

therefore directly raises the issue of whether there should be some redress for those who suffer loss as a result of unlawful governmental action, which will be considered below.[184]

6. NUISANCE

A. Criteria for Liability

The tort of nuisance is commonly defined as covering any substantial and unreasonable interference with the claimant's land or any right over or in connection with its enjoyment.[185] While the gist of liability is unreasonable interference with the claimant's interest, caution is required as to the meaning of the word "reasonable" in this context, so as to avoid confusion with the law of negligence. As Markesinis and Deakin state: 30–045

> "… in nuisance the law does not concentrate so much on the quality of the 'doing' (unreasonableness of the defendant's conduct) as on the quality of the 'deed' (unreasonableness of the result to the claimant)".[186]

While the two sets of considerations are, as the authors accept, not mutually exclusive, the distinction is important: the fact that the creator of the nuisance has taken all reasonable care will not prevent liability if the court decides that the outcome constitutes an unreasonable interference with the claimant's land, or use thereof.[187]

B. Application of the Criteria

The principal hurdle for claimants suing public authorities in nuisance resides not in the constituent elements of the cause of action but rather in the defences, more especially that of statutory authorisation. The courts have held that if the loss is caused pursuant to the lawful exercise of statutory authority, there will be no action. If the loss is the inevitable result of the exercise of the statutory power or duty there will be no action.[188] 30–046

The difficulty is to determine what "inevitable" means. Where the statute prescribes that the public body should act within defined limits and it is obvious that a nuisance must result, no action will lie. Similarly, where the statute confers a power to, for example, build for a particular purpose on a particular site and an

[184] See paras 30–068 to 30–075.

[185] *Markesinis and Deakin's Tort Law* (2013), p.414.

[186] *Markesinis and Deakin's Tort Law* (2013), pp.414–415.

[187] Failure to take care may be relevant where the defendant did not create the initial nuisance, *Sedleigh-Denfield v O'Callaghan* [1940] A.C. 880, HL; *Goldman v Hargrave* [1967] 1 A.C. 645; *Holbeck Hall Hotel Ltd v Scarborough BC* [2000] Q.B. 836, CA (Civ Div).

[188] *R. v Pease* (1832) 4 B. & Ad. 30; *Vaughan v Taff Vale Ry Co* (1860) 5 H. & N. 679; *Hammersmith Ry Co v Brand* (1869) L.R. 4 H.L. 171; *London and Brighton Ry Co v Truman* (1886) 11 App. Cas. 45; *Manchester Corp v Farnworth* [1930] A.C. 171, HL; *Dept of Transport v North West Water Authority* [1984] A.C. 336, HL at 359; A. Linden, "Strict Liability, Nuisance and Legislative Authorization" (1966) Osgoode Hall LJ 196.

individual complains of a nuisance flowing from the normal use of the building for that purpose the action will fail,[189] unless it can be proven that the public body did not use all reasonable diligence to prevent the nuisance from occurring.[190] Thus, actions for nuisance from the running of trains have failed where the preceding criteria have been met,[191] and restrictive covenants have been held to be unenforceable in so far as they clash with the exercise of statutory powers.[192]

Conversely, if the statute is permissive and allows a wide choice of site, area, and method, it has been held that the discretion must be exercised in conformity with private rights. A decision to site a smallpox hospital in Hampstead pursuant to a general power to provide such hospitals was held to be an actionable nuisance unprotected by the statute.[193]

These principles were reaffirmed by the House of Lords in *Allen*[194]: where Parliament, by express direction or by necessary implication, has authorised the construction and use of an undertaking, it has the authority to do what is authorised with immunity from a nuisance action, provided only that there is no negligence.[195] The concept of negligence has a special meaning in this context. It connotes a requirement that the statutory undertaker, in order to enjoy immunity, must carry out the work with all reasonable regard and care for the interests of other persons.[196] On the construction of the statute it was held that, despite the absence of detailed specification as to the building of the refinery, its building and operation were contemplated by the Act, and no nuisance action would lie unless there was negligence.

C. Comment

30–047 There are difficulties with the case law in this area, which relate to the internal coherence of the courts' jurisprudence and its normative foundations.

---

189 *Pease* (1832) 4 B. & Ad. 30; *Vaughan* (1860) 5 H. & N. 679; *Brand* (1869) L.R. 4 H.L. 171; *Truman* (1886) 11 App. Cas. 45; *Farnworth* [1930] A.C. 171; *North West Water Authority* [1984] A.C. 336; *Metropolitan Asylum District v Hill* (1881) 6 App. Cas. 193 at 212.

190 *Farnworth* [1930] A.C. 171; *Tate & Lyle Industries Ltd v Greater London Council* [1983] 2 A.C. 509, HL.

191 *Brand* (1869) L.R. 4 H.L. 171.

192 *Simeon and Isle of Wight Rural DC, Re* [1937] Ch. 525 Ch D; *Marten v Flight Refuelling* [1962] Ch. 115 Ch D.

193 *Hill* (1881) 6 App. Cas. 193; *Vernon v Vestry of St James Westminster* (1880) 16 Ch. D. 449. Where an actionable nuisance has been committed it is no defence that the public authority did what was reasonable in the public interest, *Pride of Derby and Derbyshire Angling Association Ltd v British Celanese Ltd* [1953] Ch. 149, CA. Compare *Smeaton v Ilford Corporation* [1954] Ch. 450 Ch D.

194 *Allen v Gulf Oil Refining Ltd* [1981] A.C. 1001, HL; *Gillingham BC v Medway (Chatham) Dock Co Ltd* [1993] Q.B. 343 QBD.

195 *Allen* [1981] A.C. 1001 at 1014, 1016, 1023–1024. There is an exception to take account of *Hill* (1881) 6 App. Cas. 193. In *Allen* [1981] A.C. 1001this exception is expressed by Lord Wilberforce as applying where the statute is permissive in form, at 1011: in such circumstances a nuisance action will still lie. It would seem that more is required to reconcile *Brand* (1869) L.R. 4 H.L. 171 and *Hill*, or *Hill* and *Allen*: the statute must not only be permissive, but also allow a wide choice of site or area. This view is supported by Lord Diplock, at 1014, and by the fact that there was no real choice of site in the *Allen* case itself. This criterion is critically examined below.

196 *Allen* [1981] A.C. 1001 at 1011; *Dobson v Thames Water Utilities Ltd* [2011] EWHC 3253 (TCC).

There are problems concerning the *internal coherence* of the case law. It is, for example, doubtful whether the test in *Allen* can reconcile all the cases.[197] The test of inevitability set out above may also be inappropriate in the context of statutory powers that require a public body to do a variety of work in a given area as and when the body deems it expedient to do so.[198] More important is the fact that whether the test of inevitability is satisfied can be fortuitous, being dependent on the wording of the enabling statute. Whether the statute is framed in terms of a duty or a power, or within the latter category a power that specifies a site and method, is often dependent upon factors that should not be determinative of whether an action for nuisance survives or not. Many modern statutes are framed in permissive terms for administrative reasons and contain no indication of site or method because the matter is too complex, or best decided by the public body. This tells us nothing about whether a private law action should be sustainable or not.

The *normative foundations* of the courts' jurisprudence are also problematic. It is harsh to make the individual bear the loss arising from socially beneficial activities. There is a strong argument for placing the cost on those who take the benefit of the relevant activity. This was recognised by Lord Blanesburgh in *Farnworth*.[199] It was acknowledged more recently by Lord Phillips MR in the Court of Appeal in *Marcic*.[200] He stated that where a single house was at the risk of flooding by sewerage once every five years, this might not justify the investment to remove the risk. It did not, however, follow that the householder should receive no compensation. The flooding was the consequence of a sewerage system that benefited many. Those who used the sewerage system should therefore be charged a sufficient amount to cover the cost of paying compensation to the minority that suffered damage. The House of Lords reiterated orthodoxy and held that a cause of action in nuisance would be contrary to the statutory scheme,[201] although there were, as will be seen below, dicta recognising the point made by Lord Phillips MR.

It is, in any event, not clear that nuisance is the most appropriate medium whereby compensation should be granted. The criteria for whether private rights of action survive derived from the case law are ill-suited to much modern legislative activity.[202] This is an area where it is necessary to break away from the confines of "normal" legal reasoning, which requires an actionable legal wrong as a pre-condition for the payment of compensation. Justice may require that **30–048**

[197] It is for example difficult to reconcile *London and Brighton Railway Co v Truman* (1886) 11 App. Cas. 45 with *Hill* (1881) 6 App. Cas. 193.

[198] *Marriage v East Norfolk Catchment Board* [1950] 1 K.B. 284, CA at 308, 309; *Hawley v Steele* (1877) 6 Ch. D. 521 at 528, 530.

[199] *Farnworth* [1930] A.C. 171 at 203–204.

[200] *Marcic v Thames Water Utilities Ltd* [2002] Q.B. 929, CA (Civ Div) at [114].

[201] *Marcic v Thames Water Utilities Ltd* [2004] 2 A.C. 42, HL.

[202] The view of the House of Lords in the *Allen* case [1981] A.C. 1001 should be compared in this respect to that of Lord Denning MR in the Court of Appeal, [1980] Q.B. 156 at 168–169. While the Master of the Rolls may have somewhat twisted the authorities, the result he reached may accord better with underlying policy considerations: that the general principle should be that Parliament did not intend to damage innocent people without redress.

compensation should be paid even where the public body's action is lawful.[203] This "just result" has to some extent been achieved by particular statutes and may flow more generally from the HRA. These will be considered in turn.

The Land Compensation Act 1973 provides compensation where the value of an interest in land is depreciated by physical factors caused by the use of public works, whether highways, aerodromes, or other works on land provided or used under statutory powers.[204] Physical factors are defined as noise, smell, smoke, fumes, artificial lighting, and the discharge of any substance onto the land.[205] Interest in land is defined to cover a freeholder or a leaseholder, with three years of the term unexpired. The Act applies to any nuisance which occurred on or after 17 October 1969.[206] The compensation is assessed at prices current on the first day when a claim could be made.[207] Cases where compensation could be obtained through an action in nuisance are in general excluded from the Act.[208]

The HRA is also of relevance for the attainment of the "just result" set out above. Claimants may be able to plead breach of a Convention right in classic nuisance cases. Thus, in *Hatton*,[209] the ECtHR found that the noise flowing from the night-time landing regime at Heathrow airport infringed the applicants' right to family life guaranteed by art.8, and awarded compensation. However, in a subsequent action the ECtHR held in *Hatton* that although a person who was significantly affected by noise or pollution could bring a claim under art.8, states had a margin of appreciation that required them to weigh all the competing interests involved. The extent of the margin of appreciation depended on the facts of each case and the question as to whether the appropriate balance had been struck depended upon the weight given to the different rights and interests involved. When assessing the appropriateness of the balance, the measures available to mitigate the effect of interference with those rights had to be considered and the Strasbourg Court held that the UK had not exceeded the margin of appreciation.[210]

30–049 The possibility of using the HRA and Convention rights was considered in *Marcic*. The claimant's garden and house were periodically flooded by water and sewerage from a system that was adequate when initially constructed, but had become inadequate because of increase in the usage of the system. The Court of Appeal[211] affirmed the claim based on a breach of art.8, protection of the home, and breach of art.1 of the First Protocol, peaceful enjoyment of possessions. The water authority could have prevented the flooding of the claimant's land, but argued that under its system of priorities there was no prospect of the work being

[203] *Burmah Oil Co Ltd v Lord Advocate* [1965] A.C. 75, HL.

[204] Land Compensation Act 1973 s.1; *R. (Plymouth City Airport Ltd) v Secretary of State for the Environment, Transport and the Regions* [2001] EWCA Civ 144; *Chrisostomou v Manchester CC* [2007] R.V.R. 207; *Robertson v Manchester Airport* [2010] UKUT 370; *Thomas v Bridgend CBC* [2011] EWCA Civ 862.

[205] Land Compensation Act 1973 s.1(2).

[206] Land Compensation Act 1973 s.1(8).

[207] Land Compensation Act 1973 s.4; see also ss.5–6.

[208] Land Compensation Act 1973 s.1(6). See also Local Government, Planning and Land Act 1980 ss.112–113.

[209] *Hatton v UK* (2002) 34 E.H.R.R. 1.

[210] *Hatton v UK* (2003) 37 E.H.R.R. 28.

[211] *Marcic* [2002] Q.B. 929.

carried out in the future. The Court of Appeal decided that the company's scheme of priorities did not strike a fair balance between the competing interests of the claimant and other customers.[212] It doubted moreover whether such a scheme could ever be compatible with art.8, if this meant that the claimant would suffer and receive no compensation. There is Strasbourg case law to the effect that while the building of, for example, a power station may be for the public good, the interference with the applicant's right might nonetheless be disproportionate where the individual had to bear an unreasonable burden.[213] Lord Phillips MR said that this case law suggested that:

> "… where an authority carries on an undertaking in the interest of the community as a whole it may have to pay compensation to individuals whose rights are infringed by that undertaking in order to achieve a fair balance between the interests of the individual and the community".[214]

The House of Lords reversed the Court of Appeal, and relying on the approach in the second *Hatton* case,[215] held that there was no breach of Convention rights because the statutory scheme balanced the interests of the defendant's customers whose properties were subject to flooding, with the remainder of its customers whose properties were drained by the sewers, by imposing a general drainage obligation on the defendant and entrusting enforcement to an independent regulator. Lord Nicholls did, however, echo the sentiments of Lord Phillips MR. Thus, Lord Nicholls stated that in principle, if it was not practicable for reasons of expense to carry out remedial works for the time being, those who enjoyed the benefit of effective drainage should bear the cost of paying some compensation to those whose properties endured the sewer flooding, since the flooding was the consequence of the benefit to those making use of the system. Thus, "the minority who suffer damage and disturbance as a consequence of the inadequacy of the sewerage system ought not to be required to bear an unreasonable burden".[216] This did not however give rise to any enforceable legal claim, but was regarded as a matter to be considered by the relevant administrative authorities.

The HRA can nonetheless be of assistance.[217] In *Andrews* there was a claim under art.8 ECHR to recover the cost of noise insulation to combat excessive traffic noise consequent upon a traffic regulation made by the defendants.[218] The court held that a relevant factor in assessing whether the right balance had been struck between the interests of the individual and those of the community was the availability of measures to mitigate the effects of noise. Although the rights of residents were not afforded absolute protection under the 1998 Act, the absence of any possibility of grant, or of any consideration whether such a possibility of compensation should exist, could negate justification for the measure advanced by the defendants. A court subsequently granted compensation.[219] Similarly, in

---

212 *Marcic* [2002] Q.B. 929 at [108]–[110].
213 *S v France* (1990) 65 D.R. 250.
214 *Marcic* [2002] Q.B. 929 at [118].
215 *Hatton* (2003) 37 E.H.R.R. 28.
216 *Marcic* [2004] 2 A.C. 42 at [45]. Lords Steyn, Scott and Hope agreed with Lord Nicholls.
217 *Dobson* [2011] EWHC 3253 (TCC).
218 *Andrews v Reading BC* [2005] Env. L.R. 2 QBD.
219 *Andrews v Reading BC (No.2)* [2005] EWHC 256 (QB).

Dennis[220] Buckley J held that noise flowing from military aircraft engaged in training was justified in the public interest. However, it was not proportionate for specific individuals to bear the cost of the public benefit. The noise was held to constitute a breach of art.8 ECHR and art.1 of the First Protocol and compensation was awarded.

7. RYLANDS V FLETCHER

A. Criteria for Liability

30–050 The principle in *Rylands v Fletcher*[221] imposes liability on a person who for their own purposes brings on to their land something which was not naturally there that is likely to do mischief if it escapes. The central components of the cause of action are therefore accumulation by the defendant, escape and non-natural user of the land. The potential breadth of the cause of action has, however, been significantly reduced by subsequent case law.[222] Thus, the concept of non-natural user was almost certainly intended by Blackburn J in *Rylands* to cover anything that was not naturally on the land. However, in *Rickards*, the term was interpreted far more narrowly to mean some special use bringing increased danger to others and not merely the ordinary user of land, or such use as was proper for the general benefit of the community.[223] The courts also developed a range of defences that further reduced the potential of the cause of action. These restrictive developments reflected the judicial sense that negligence-based liability should be the norm, and hence causes of action that appeared to impose stricter liability should be narrowly confined.

B. Application of the Criteria

30–051 Attempts to apply the principle in *Rylands* against public bodies have not on the whole succeeded. The courts have only applied the doctrine to bodies exercising *statutory powers* where there is a clause imposing liability in nuisance.[224] Where there is a statutory power but there is no section expressly preserving liability for nuisance, no action will lie.[225] If the public body acts under a *statutory duty* rather than a power, there is no liability whether a nuisance section exists or not, if what

220 *Dennis v Ministry of Defence* [2003] EWHC 793 (QB).

221 *Rylands v Fletcher* (1866) L.R. 1 Ex. 265 at 279–280; (1868) L.R. 3 H.L. 330.

222 *Markesinis and Deakin's Tort Law* (2013), pp.518–523; R. Bagshaw, "Rylands Confined" (2004) 120 L.Q.R. 388; D. Nolan, "The Distinctiveness of *Rylands v Fletcher*" (2005) 121 L.Q.R. 421.

223 *Rickards v Lothian* [1913] A.C. 263 at 280; *Cambridge Water Co Ltd v Eastern Counties Leather Plc* [1994] 2 A.C. 264; *Transco Plc v Stockport MBC* [2004] 2 A.C. 1, HL.

224 *Charing Cross Electricity Supply Company v Hydraulic Power Company* [1914] 3 K.B. 772, CA; *Midwood v Manchester Corp* [1905] 2 K.B. 597, CA. A nuisance clause is a specific section in the enabling statute preserving liability in nuisance. Such a clause which *preserves* liability in nuisance has been construed to *exclude* liability unless the public body has been negligent, *Hammond v Vestry of St Pancras* (1874) L.R. 9 C.P. 316 at 322. Not perhaps the most natural construction of such a clause.

225 *Dunne v North Western Gas Board* [1964] 2 Q.B. 806, CA at 837–838 (the liability of Liverpool Corp acting under statutory powers: no nuisance section, no liability).

was done was expressly required by statute or was reasonably incidental to that requirement, and was done without negligence.[226] Even where the statutory duty does not lead inevitably to the loss which occurred, there will be no liability if a nuisance clause is present in the statute.[227]

C. Comment

The justification for this exemption from liability is questionable in terms of principle. Two arguments are interwoven in the judgments, although the courts have not been uniform in their treatment of them.[228] 30–052

There is the "inevitability argument" analogous to that found in the nuisance cases discussed above: if the body is required to act and by implication, or even expressly, cause loss thereby, it should not be liable.[229] The response to this argument is the same as in the case of nuisance and statutory authority. The public body, even if its acts are regarded as lawful rather than tortious, should compensate a person who has suffered loss as a result.

The related argument for denying liability has its roots in the requirements of the *Rylands* doctrine itself. A body which acts not for its own purposes but for the benefit of the community should not be liable. This rationale for excluding the principle reflects mistaken assumptions underlying strict liability. These assumptions have stultified the potential development of this tort into a socially useful instrument by which loss can be spread. Strict liability has no hint of moral censure, nor should it be restricted to socially unusual or abnormal activities. Liability without fault has an important role to play in relation to normal activities that benefit the community, and which involve a relatively high risk of loss or damage. It is because they benefit the community that it is unfair to leave the result of a non-negligent accident to lie fortuitously on a particular individual rather than to spread it among the community generally. Those who take the benefit should bear the burden.[230]

Some piecemeal reform has taken place by statute as, for example, in the Nuclear Installations Act 1965[231] and the Deposit of Poisonous Waste Act 1972.[232] The Land Compensation Act 1973 will cover some cases where recovery is at present denied.[233] It can only be hoped that further such reform will follow. The preceding comments concerning the HRA and nuisance are equally relevant here.

---

[226] *Smeaton v Ilford Corp* [1954] Ch. 450 Ch D at 476–477; *Dunne* [1964] 2 Q.B. 806 at 834–835; *Department of Transport v North West Water Authority* [1984] A.C. 336, HL at 359.

[227] *Smeaton* [1954] Ch. 450 at 477–478.

[228] Compare the view of Sellers LJ in *Dunne* [1964] 2 Q.B. 806 at 832, with Upjohn J in *Smeaton* [1954] Ch. 450 at 468–470, 477–478.

[229] *Smeaton* [1954] Ch. 450; *Dunne* [1964] 2 Q.B. 806.

[230] Law Commission Report No.32 (1970), pp.20–21.

[231] Nuclear Installations Act 1965 s.12.

[232] Deposit of Poisonous Waste Act 1972 s.2.

[233] *Smeaton* [1954] Ch. 450 would be covered, but *Dunne* [1964] 2 Q.B. 806 would not, since the Act is not concerned with physical injury, but with depreciation in the value of land.

8. RESTITUTION

30–053 An individual may wish to claim the return of money that has been paid to a public body rather than damages.[234] A claim for judicial review can include a claim for damages, restitution or the recovery of a sum due, provided that these could have been awarded on a private law claim. However, the claimant may not seek such a remedy alone.[235] Restitutionary claims present a strong case for relief. The law has been shaped by important decisions of the House of Lords in the *Woolwich* case[236] and in *Kleinwort Benson*.[237] In order to appreciate the impact of these decisions it is necessary to understand the previous law. It was generally accepted that to recover money that had been demanded without authority, an individual would have to bring the case within a recognised category in which such recovery was allowed under private law.[238] Duress and mistake were the two principal foundations for a claim to restitution.

A. Duress

30–054 The classic situation is that of money paid to obtain fulfilment of a duty, which the payee is not entitled to charge for at all, or for which a lesser amount should be charged.[239] This is an established category within duress.[240] The utility of the action for money had and received depends upon the meaning given to "compulsion". The broader the idea of compulsion becomes, the more closely will a restitutionary claim approximate to a finding of ultra vires. In *Steele*,[241] the plaintiff applied to the defendant, a parish clerk, for authorisation to search the parish register. The charge was not levied until the search had been completed and there was no right to make the charge at all. Martin B[242] based his decision on a broad ground. The defendant had a duty to receive only what the Act of Parliament allowed him to take and nothing more. It was irrelevant whether the actual payment took place before or after the search had been made. To call such a payment a voluntary payment would be an abuse of language.

There is support for treating demands by a public body differently from those made by an individual in the Commonwealth,[243] and in cases concerning public

---

234 R. Williams, *Unjust Enrichment and Public Law, A Comparative Study of England, France and the EU* (Oxford: Hart, 2010).

235 Senior Courts Act 1981 s.31(4); CPR 54.3(2).

236 *Woolwich Equitable Building Society v Inland Revenue Commissioners (No.2)* [1993] A.C. 70, HL.

237 *Kleinwort Benson Ltd v Lincoln City Council* [1999] 2 A.C. 349, HL.

238 P. Craig, "Compensation in Public Law" (1980) 96 L.Q.R. 413 at 428–435; P. Birks, "Restitution from Public Authorities" (1980) C.L.P. 191; G. Virgo, "Restitution from Public Authorities: Past, Present and Future" [2006] J.R. 370.

239 J. Beatson, "Duress as a Vitiating Factor in Contract" [1974] C.L.J. 97; A. Burrows, "Restitution, Public Authorities and *Ultra Vires*", in A. Burrows (ed.), *Essays on the Law of Restitution* (Oxford: Clarendon, 1991), p.39; J. Alder "Restitution in Public Law: Bearing the Cost of Unlawful State Action" (2002) 22 L.S. 165.

240 *Irving v Wilson* (1791) 4 T.R. 485; *Lovell v Simpson* (1800) 3 Esp. 153.

241 *Steele v Williams* (1853) 8 Ex. 625.

242 *Steele* (1853) 8 Ex. 625 at 632–633. See also *Morgan v Palmer* (1824) 2 B. & C. 729.

243 *Mason v State of New South Wales* (1958–1959) 102 C.L.R. 108.

utilities.[244] In the latter the courts have allowed recovery because of the wrongful demand per se. The compulsion flows from the excess charge, and the claimant does not have to prove any express threat to withhold the service. The statutes are often either technically complex, or contain criteria such as "undue discrimination", which may be difficult for either party to interpret. In this context, to require overt threats by the public body or even protest by the individual is unrealistic. The force implicit in a demand from a public body should suffice. There was a problem that flowed from a wide construction of the term compulsion, in that it came close to granting compensation for pure mistake of law, and such mistakes were, until recently, not thought to ground a restitutionary claim.

B. Mistake

The general principle was that money paid under mistake of fact was recoverable but that money paid under mistake of law was not.[245] The inability to recover for mistake of law was criticised judicially[246] and academically.[247] The problem in the past for those seeking recovery was that the wider recovery for duress became, the finer was the dividing line between cases characterised as involving duress and those classified as involving simple mistake of law.[248] **30–055**

The typical fact situation dealt with until now has been where the claimant has paid money for a service, which the public body should provide for less or for no charge at all. Where, however, the public body simply demanded money that it believed it was entitled to, but the claim was misconceived because of a misconstruction of a statute, the position of the private party was even more difficult. The private party might pay, discover the error and attempt to reclaim the money. This would normally fail because the payment would be made on a mistake of law. Alternatively, the private party might resist the claim. This would be met by an express threat by the public body. The threat would, however, normally be a threat to litigate and such threats were held not to be actionable. This was a development of the principle that a judgment is binding between the parties to it.[249]

The law was transformed by *Kleinwort Benson*.[250] The case was one of many[251] that arose out of the interest rate swaps agreements made by local

[244] *Great Western Railway v Sutton* (1869) L.R. 4 H.L. 226; *South of Scotland Electricity Board v British Oxygen Co Ltd (No.2)* [1959] 1 W.L.R. 587 HL.

[245] *Bilbie v Lumley* (1802) 2 East 469. The reasons given were that: there must be an end to litigation, multiplicity of litigation, and the fact that everyone was presumed to know the law.

[246] *Martindale v Falkner* (1846) 2 C.B. 706 at 718–720; *R. v Mayor of Tewkesbury* (1868) L.R. 3 Q.B. 629 at 635–638; *Kiriri Cotton Co Ltd v Dewani* [1960] A.C. 192 at 203–205; *Nepean Hydro Electric Commission v Ontario Hydro* (1982) 132 D.L.R. (3d) 193, Dickson J.

[247] P. Winfield, "Mistake of Law" (1943) 59 L.Q.R. 327; Law Commission No.227, *Restitution: Mistakes of Law and Ultra vires Public Authority Receipts and Payments* (1994), Cmnd.2731.

[248] Compare *Morgan* (1824) 2 B. & C. 729 and *Steele* (1853) 8 Ex. 625 with *Slater v Mayor of Burnley* (1888) 59 L.T. 636.

[249] J. Beatson, "Duress as a Vitiating Factor in Contract" [1974] C.L.J. 97; *W. Whiteley Ltd v King* (1909) 101 L.T. 741.

[250] *Kleinwort Benson* [1999] 2 A.C. 349.

[251] *Westdeutsche Landesbank Girozentrale v Islington LBC* [1996] A.C. 669, HL.

authorities. These agreements were held to be ultra vires.[252] The agreements were thought to be valid when they were made and had been fully performed. The claim by the bank was struck out in the lower courts, because there was no recovery for mistake of law. The case then went to the House of Lords which held that mistakes, whether of fact or law, could ground a restitutionary claim, subject to general restitutionary defences such as change of position. A blanket rule prohibiting recovery for mistake of law was, said their Lordships, inconsistent with a law of restitution based on unjust enrichment. A claim for mistake of law could also cover the case where payments had been made under a settled understanding of the law, which was subsequently departed from by judicial decision. Payment made under a view of the law which later proved to be erroneous was still money paid over under mistake of law, since the payer believed when he made the payments that he was bound to do so. If it subsequently appeared that on the law held to be applicable at the date of payment that he was not bound to do so then he was entitled to recover the amount paid over.

The House of Lords subsequently held in *Deutsche Morgan Grenfell*[253] that the principle from *Kleinwort Benson* could apply to recovery of taxes paid under a mistake of law. The claimants had paid certain money to the revenue and the statutory regime had been found contrary to EU law by the ECJ. It was held that the claimants could avail themselves of restitutionary relief for mistake of law. This was important on the facts, since the characterisation of the cause of action as mistake of law affected the limitation period that applied and when it would start from.[254]

C. Recovery for Ultra Vires Demands

30–056 The state of the law until recently left many claimants in an unenviable position. If they were unable to prove duress, some form of compulsion or other limited grounds for relief, then it was difficult to sustain an action.[255] This difficulty was compounded by the possibility that the action would be denied because of the then prevailing rule denying recovery for mistake of law. Legislation made provision for recovery in certain circumstances but the scope of any such rights varied from area to area.[256] The decision in *Woolwich*,[257] which was prior to *Kleinwort Benson*, placed litigants in a stronger position.

---

[252] *Hazell v Hammersmith and Fulham LBC* [1992] 2 A.C. 1, HL.

[253] *Deutsche Morgan Grenfell Group Plc v Inland Revenue Commissioners* [2007] 1 A.C. 558, HL; B. Hacker, "Still at the Crossroads" (2007) 123 L.Q.R. 177; G. Virgo, "Restitution from Public Authorities: Past, Present and Future" [2006] J.R. 370; *Sempra Metals Ltd (formerly Metallgesellschaft Ltd) v Inland Revenue Commissioners* [2007] 3 W.L.R. 354, HL.

[254] Limitation Act 1980 s.32(1)(c).

[255] For qualifications to the general rule that recovery was not possible see, Law Commission No.227, *Restitution: Mistakes of Law and Ultra vires Public Authority Receipts and Payments*, pp.53–59.

[256] Law Commission No.120, *Restitution of Payments made under Mistake of Law* (1991), pp.74–84; Law Commission No.227, *Restitution: Mistakes of Law and Ultra vires Public Authority Receipts and Payments*.

The plaintiff building society had paid money to the Inland Revenue on the basis of certain regulations. These were challenged by the Woolwich and held to be ultra vires.[258] The money was repaid to the Woolwich with interest dated from the judgment in the judicial review action. The Woolwich then began a second action, seeking further payment of interest, covering the period from when the money was first paid to the date of the judicial review proceedings. Such an action would only be sustainable if there was a restitutionary right to recover the capital sum. The defendant argued that none of the traditional grounds for restitutionary recovery existed in this case, since there was nothing that could be termed compulsion and no mistake of fact.

It was held by a majority of their Lordships that such a right did indeed exist. Money paid by a subject pursuant to an ultra vires demand was prima facie recoverable as of right at common law together with interest. This was regardless of the circumstances in which the tax was paid, since common justice required that any tax or duty paid by the citizen pursuant to an unlawful demand should be repaid, unless some special circumstances or some policy consideration required otherwise. This result was influenced by the provision in the Bill of Rights that taxes should not be levied without the authority of Parliament: a restitutionary right to claim the return of taxes unlawfully levied was seen as an adjunct of this constitutional principle. The right to repayment vested from the moment when the sums were handed over pursuant to the unauthorised demand and therefore interest could be claimed from the date of the original payment. Moreover, it was made clear that whatever the fate of the rule that money paid under mistake of law was not recoverable should prove to be, that rule was no bar to an action of this kind, based as it was, upon the unlawful nature of the public demand.

The result in the *Woolwich* case was welcome and academic commentators had been pressing for reform along these lines for some time.[259] A number of issues concerning the nature and extent of the *Woolwich* principle remain to be resolved. **30–057**

First, there is the all-important issue concerning the scope of the principle. The strict ratio of the case has been said to be that a citizen who makes a payment in response to an unlawful demand for tax that was unlawful because of the invalidity of the relevant secondary legislation has a prima facie right to restitution of the money, irrespective of whether the payment is mistaken or made under duress.[260] It has, however, been convincingly argued by the Law

[257] *Woolwich* [1993] A.C. 70; *Test Claimants in the FII Group Litigation v Revenue and Customs Commissioners* [2010] EWCA Civ 103; *R. (on the application of Hemming (t/a Simply Pleasure Ltd)) v Westminster CC* [2013] EWCA Civ 591; P. Birks, "'When Money is Paid in Pursuance of a Void Authority …' A Duty to Repay?" [1992] P.L. 580.

[258] *R. v Inland Revenue Commissioners, Ex p. Woolwich Equitable Building Society* [1990] 1 W.L.R. 1400, HL.

[259] P. Birks, "Restitution from the Executive: A Tercentary Footnote to the Bill of Rights", in P. Finn (ed.), *Essays on Restitution* (Sydney: Law Book Co, 1990), p.164; W. Cornish, "'Colour of Office': Restitutionary Redress against Public Authority" [1987] J. Malaysian and Comparative Law 41; S. Arrowsmith, "Ineffective Transactions, Unjust Enrichment and Problems of Policy" [1989] L.S. 307; Virgo, "Restitution from Public Authorities: Past, Present and Future" [2006] J.R. 370.

[260] Law Commission No.227, *Restitution: Mistakes of Law and Ultra vires Public Authority Receipts and Payments*, para.6.33.

Commission that the true scope of the principle is broader.[261] The Law Commission's formulation was that the principle could be applicable to all taxes, levies, assessments, tolls or charges, whether for the provision of services or not, collected by any person or body under a statutory provision that is the sole source of the authority to charge.[262] On this view the *Woolwich* principle was not confined to payments of tax or to governmental or quasi-governmental exactions, or to payments made in accordance with a demand. For the Law Commission, "the crucial element is that the payment is collected by any person or body which is operating outside its statutory authority".[263] The Law Commission also believed that acting ultra vires was not confined to excess of statutory power but also extended to procedural error, abuse of power and error of law by the charging authority.

The decision in *British Steel*[264] confirmed that the *Woolwich* principle could cover a mistaken view of the legal effect of valid regulations, or a mistaken view of the facts of the case, as well as a claim based on regulations that are themselves ultra vires. Moreover, in the *Test Claimants* case[265] the Supreme Court held that the *Woolwich* remedy did not apply only to tax demanded by the Revenue. Where tax was purportedly charged without lawful parliamentary authority, a claim for repayment arose regardless of any official demand. The word "demand" as used in *Woolwich* referred simply to a situation in which payment was required without lawful authority. The *Woolwich* principle covered all sums paid to a public authority in response to, and sufficiently causally connected with, a requirement to pay tax that was without lawful authority.

30–058 The courts will have to decide how to deal with the situation where the invalidity was only technical, or the circumstance where the claimant has not actually suffered any loss because the tax or levy has been passed on to another.[266] In *Stringer*[267] a landlord had been overpaid housing benefits in respect of a tenant who had left his premises. He paid over part of the sum demanded from him by the local authority, but then claimed that the sum should be returned because the request for repayment did not comply with relevant formalities. The court refused to order restitution. It distinguished the case from *Woolwich*, since in *Stringer* the landlord was seeking to resist repayment of money to which he had no entitlement.

Second, there is the relationship between the common law right to restitution and statutory provisions for recovery where they exist. This is a complex issue,

---

[261] Law Commission No.227, *Restitution: Mistakes of Law and Ultra vires Public Authority Receipts and Payments*, paras 6.36–6.41.

[262] Law Commission No.227, *Restitution: Mistakes of Law and Ultra vires Public Authority Receipts and Payments*, para.6.42.

[263] Law Commission No.227, *Restitution: Mistakes of Law and Ultra vires Public Authority Receipts and Payments*, para.6.42.

[264] *British Steel Plc v Customs and Excise Commissioners* [1997] 2 All E.R. 366, CA (Civ Div) at 376.

[265] *Test Claimants in the FII Group Litigation v Revenue and Customs Commissioners* [2012] UKSC 19.

[266] S. Arrowsmith, *Civil Liability and Public Authorities* (1992), pp.273–275.

[267] *Norwich CC v Stringer* (2001) 33 H.L.R. 15, CA (Civ Div).

which cannot be considered in detail here.[268] Suffice it to say for the present that much turns on the construction of the relevant statutory provisions. Thus in *Woolwich*, Lord Goff held that the provisions in the statute did not apply in the instant case, since they presupposed a valid assessment.[269] In *British Steel*,[270] it was held that an unlawful demand for tax was recoverable in a common law restitutionary claim, unless the claim had been removed by the empowering legislation or other legislation. It was clear also that the court would not lightly infer that the common law claim had been excluded by statute.

Third, there is the matter of defences and other grounds for refusing relief. There may well be circumstances in which a restitutionary right of the kind that has been recognised could be problematic if it could be brought within a six-year period by large numbers of claimants. The effect on the finances of public authorities could be significant. This was recognised in *Woolwich*, and there were hints that shorter time limits might have to be set for actions of this kind. It was, moreover, suggested by Lord Goff in *Kleinwort Benson* that in cases concerned with overpaid taxes there is an argument that payments made in accordance with a prevailing practice, or under a settled understanding of the law, should be irrecoverable.[271] In such a situation a large number of taxpayers could be affected and there was an "element of public interest" which militated against repayment of tax in such circumstances.

The Law Commission gave considerable attention to possible defences. It did not **30–059**
feel that there could be completely unrestricted recovery of sums paid in response to ultra vires demands.[272] At the very least the traditional restitutionary defences such as change of position, submission or compromise, estoppel and the limitation period of six years from the date of payment should apply to claims based on the *Woolwich* principle.[273] The courts have, however, held that the change of position defence does not apply to a *Woolwich* claim.[274]

The Law Commission also recommended that overpayments of tax should not be regarded as recoverable merely because the taxpayer paid in accordance with a settled view of the law that payment was due, and later decisions departed from that view.[275] Further defences recommended by the Law Commission included

---

[268] Law Commission No.227, *Restitution: Mistakes of Law and Ultra vires Public Authority Receipts and Payments*, Pt VII; J. Beatson, "Restitution of Taxes, Levies and Other Imposts" (1993) 109 L.Q.R. 401.

[269] *Woolwich* [1993] A.C. 70 at 169–170.

[270] *British Steel* [1997] 2 All E.R. 366. See also *Deutsche Morgan Grenfell* [2007] 1 A.C. 558; *Monro v Revenue and Customs Commissioners* [2008] EWCA Civ 306; *R. (Child Poverty Action Group) v Secretary of State for Work and Pensions* [2011] 2 A.C. 15 SC.

[271] *Kleinwort Benson* [1999] 2 A.C. 349 at 382. See also Law Commission No.227, *Restitution: Mistakes of Law and Ultra vires Public Authority Receipts and Payments*, para.10.20.

[272] Law Commission No.227, *Restitution: Mistakes of Law and Ultra vires Public Authority Receipts and Payments*, paras 10.4–10.7.

[273] Law Commission No.227, *Restitution: Mistakes of Law and Ultra vires Public Authority Receipts and Payments*, para.10.6.

[274] *Littlewoods Retail Ltd v Revenue and Customs Commissioners* [2010] EWHC 1071.

[275] Law Commission No.227, *Restitution: Mistakes of Law and Ultra vires Public Authority Receipts and Payments*, paras 10.20–10.21. The Law Commission would not apply this bar to relief where there was invalidity in the subordinate legislation which created, or was fundamental to, collection of the tax, para.10.30.

submission, contractual compromise,[276] and unjust enrichment by the payer.[277] The Law Commission was, however, against short time limits for bringing actions of this kind.[278] It was also against the introduction of any direct defence of serious disruption to public finance.[279] It did not favour the use of prospective overruling as a technique to prevent financial disruption.[280] It was opposed to the idea that the courts should be empowered to deny recovery to those who had not brought their claims prior to the court's decision, where to allow subsequent claims for recovery would lead to severe disruption to finances.[281]

The decision in *Deutsche Morgan Grenfell*[282] nonetheless shows that the House of Lords is willing to characterise certain actions for recovery of tax as based on mistake of law, even if the consequence is to extend the limitation period, so that it runs from the date when the mistake was, or could with reasonable diligence, have been discovered.

D. Discretionary Payments

30–060 If a claimant cannot sustain a right to repayment of sums paid to a public body, an action may still be brought challenging the discretionary refusal to reimburse such money. Thus, in *Chetnik Developments*[283] the local authority possessed a statutory discretion to refund overpaid rates but refused to reimburse the applicant because the payments had been made under a mistake of law, which would not be recoverable at common law. The House of Lords held that the discretion was not unfettered, and struck down the refusal to reimburse the applicant. It held that such sums paid under a mistake of law or erroneous valuation should not in general be retained unless there were special circumstances warranting the retention. The financial position of the applicant and the general finances of the local authority should not be relevant considerations for the exercise of this discretionary decision. However, there are also indications that the principle in the *Chetnik* case will only apply where there is an express statutory discretion to repay, where the courts will ensure that the discretion is exercised in accordance with the statutory intent.[284]

---

276 Law Commission No.227, *Restitution: Mistakes of Law and Ultra vires Public Authority Receipts and Payments*, para.10.35.

277 Law Commission No.227, *Restitution: Mistakes of Law and Ultra vires Public Authority Receipts and Payments*, para.10.48.

278 Law Commission No.227, *Restitution: Mistakes of Law and Ultra vires Public Authority Receipts and Payments*, para.10.41.

279 Law Commission No.227, *Restitution: Mistakes of Law and Ultra vires Public Authority Receipts and Payments*, paras 11.6 and 11.23.

280 Law Commission No.227, *Restitution: Mistakes of Law and Ultra vires Public Authority Receipts and Payments*, paras 11.7 and 11.23–11.25.

281 Law Commission No.227, *Restitution: Mistakes of Law and Ultra vires Public Authority Receipts and Payments*, para.11.30.

282 *Morgan Grenfell* [2007] 1 A.C. 558.

283 *R. v Tower Hamlets LBC, Ex p. Chetnik Developments Ltd* [1988] A.C. 858, HL.

284 *Woolwich* [1993] A.C. 70 at 171.

E. Restitution from the Individual

The discussion until now has focused upon the ability of the individual to recover money paid to the public body where the demand was unlawful. Restitutionary claims can arise in the converse situation, where the public body seeks to claim back money paid to an individual in circumstances where the payment was ultra vires. Restitutionary relief is available in this situation.[285] The better view is that such a claim applies in the context of any ultra vires payment, and that it should apply irrespective of whether the money is traceable in a technical proprietary sense.[286] The only defence for the individual should be if there has been a change of position in reliance on the payment. The Law Commission recommended that the existing rule should not be altered.[287] A statutory scheme for recovery of sums overpaid to an individual can however exclude a common law restitutionary claim.[288] **30–061**

9. EU LAW: DAMAGES LIABILITY AND RECOVERY OF MONEY

A. Criteria for Liability

The preceding discussion has focused upon domestic law. However, an individual may also be able to claim redress under EU law,[289] more especially by relying on *Francovich*,[290] which introduced the principle of state liability in damages. Italy had failed to pass the laws necessary to implement Directive 80/987, which was concerned with the protection of employees in the event of the insolvency of their employers. The applicants were therefore left with substantial arrears of salary unpaid and sought damages from the Italian government for their losses. The ECJ held that the action was sustainable. It held that the provisions of the Directive did not have direct effect but that the action could be maintained. It reached this result by using arguments of principle and by drawing upon general provisions of the Treaty. **30–062**

[285] *Auckland Harbour Board v R.* [1924] A.C. 318; *R. v Secretary of State for the Environment, Ex p. London Borough of Camden* [1995] C.O.D. 203 QBD.

[286] P. Birks, "'When Money is Paid in Pursuance of a Void Authority …' A Duty to Repay?" [1992] P.L. 580, 588–589.

[287] Law Commission No.227, *Restitution: Mistakes of Law and Ultra vires Public Authority Receipts and Payments*, para.17.21.

[288] *Child Poverty Action Group* [2011] 2 A.C. 15.

[289] P. Craig and G. de Búrca, *EU Law: Text, Cases and Materials*, 6th edn (Oxford: Oxford University Press, 2015), Ch.8; J. Lonbay and A. Biondi (eds), *Remedies for Breach of EC Law* (Chichester: Wiley, 1997); R. Craufurd Smith, "Remedies for Breach of EC Law in National Courts: Legal Variation and Selection", in P. Craig and G. de Búrca (eds), *The Evolution of EU Law* (Oxford: Oxford University Press, 1999), Ch.8; C. Kilpatrick, T. Novitz and P. Skidmore (eds), *The Future of Remedies in Europe* (Oxford: Hart, 2000); M. Dougan, *National Remedies before the Court of Justice, Issues of Harmonisation and Differentiation* (Oxford: Hart, 2004); M. Dougan, "The Vicissitudes of Life at the Coalface: Remedies and Procedures for Enforcing EU Law before the National Courts", in P. Craig and G. de Búrca (eds), *The Evolution of EU Law*, 2nd edn (Oxford: Oxford University Press, 2011), Ch.11.

[290] *Francovich and Bonifaci v Italian Republic* (C-6 and 9/90) [1991] E.C.R. I-5357.

The argument of *principle* was that the full effectiveness of Community law would be called into question, and the protection of the EC rights would be weakened, if individuals could not obtain compensation where their rights were infringed by a breach of Community law by a Member State. This reasoning was reinforced by *textual foundation* drawn from what is now art.4(3) TEU, which provides that states are under an obligation to take all appropriate measures to ensure fulfilment of Treaty obligations. From this the ECJ concluded that states had the duty to make good the unlawful consequences of a breach of Community law.

The precise conditions for liability depended on the nature of the infringement that gave rise to the damage. In cases of non-implementation of a Directive three such conditions had to be satisfied. The Directive must confer rights on individuals; the content of those rights must be apparent from the Directive; and there had to be a causal link between the failure to implement the Directive and the loss suffered by the individual.

Francovich raised many important questions as to the scope of the state's liability in damages for a breach of Community law,[291] which were clarified by the ECJ's later jurisprudence.

B. Application of the Criteria

30–063 In *Brasserie du Pecheur*[292] the claim was brought by a French company against the German government. The company was forced to discontinue selling beer in Germany because the German authorities considered that the beer did not comply with the purity requirements in German law. In a 1987 decision, the ECJ held[293] that this prohibition was contrary to the Treaty provisions on free movement of goods. The French company sought damages for the losses suffered from 1981–1987. In *Factortame* the applicants challenged Pt II of the Merchant Shipping Act 1988 as incompatible with Treaty provisions on freedom of establishment. The ECJ held that the conditions relating to the nationality, residence and domicile of the vessel owners and operators laid down by the 1988 legislation were contrary to Community law.[294] The damages claims related to the losses suffered by those who could not fish in the period before the UK amended its law so as to comply with Community law. The decision in *Brasserie du Pecheur* and *Factortame* may be summarised in the following manner.[295]

---

291 M. Ross, "Beyond *Francovich*" (1993) 56 M.L.R. 55; C. Lewis and S. Moore, "Duties, Directives and Damages in European Community Law" [1993] P.L. 151; D. Curtin, "State Liability under Private Law: a New Remedy for Private Parties" [1992] I.L.J. 74; J. Steiner, "From Direct Effects to *Francovich*" (1993) 18 E.L. Rev. 3; P. Craig, "*Francovich,* Remedies and the Scope of Damages Liability" (1993) 109 L.Q.R. 595.

292 *Brasserie du Pecheur SA v Germany, R. v Secretary of State for Transport, Ex p. Factortame Ltd* (C-46 & 48/93) [1996] E.C.R. I-1029.

293 *Commission v Germany* (178/84) [1987] E.C.R. 1227.

294 *R. v Secretary of State for Transport, Ex p. Factortame Ltd* (C-221/89) [1991] E.C.R. I-3905.

295 P. Craig, "Once More Unto the Breach: The Community, the State and Damages Liability" (1997) 113 L.Q.R. 67; R. Caranta, "Judicial Protection against Member States: A New Jus Commune Takes Shape" (1995) 32 C.M.L.R. 703; C. Deards, "Curioser and Curioser? The Development of Member State Liability in the Court of Justice" (1997) 3 E.P.L. 117; C. Harlow, "*Francovich* and the Problem

First, the principle of state liability in damages exists irrespective of whether the EU norm that was broken was directly effective or not. **30–064**

Second, state liability could exist irrespective of which state entity was responsible for the breach, the legislature, the executive or the judiciary. The rationale was that all state authorities were bound, when performing their tasks, to comply with EU law.[296]

Third, the protection which individuals derived from EU law could not, in the absence of some particular justification, vary depending on whether a national authority or an EU institution was responsible for the breach.[297] Where there was significant discretion an EU institution would not incur damages liability unless it had manifestly and gravely disregarded the limits on its powers. Member States did not always possess such wide discretion when acting under EU law. However, where a Member State had significant discretion, comparable to that of the EU institutions when implementing EU policies, the conditions for liability in damages were the same as those applying to the European Union.[298]

Fourth, the right to damages is dependent on three conditions[299]: the rule of law infringed must have been intended to confer rights on individuals; the breach of the rule of law must have been sufficiently serious; and there must have been a direct causal link between the breach and the damage. The second condition is of particular importance. The decisive test for deciding whether the breach was sufficiently serious is whether the Member State had manifestly and gravely disregarded the limits of its discretion.[300] The following factors can be taken into account when deciding this issue[301]: the clarity and precision of the rule breached; the measure of discretion left to the national authorities; whether the breach and damage were intentional or voluntary; whether any error of law was excusable or inexcusable; whether the position adopted by an EU institution contributed to the act or omission causing loss committed by the national authorities; and whether the national measures had been adopted or retained contrary to EU law.[302] The general or individual nature of the contested measure is not a decisive criterion for identifying the degree of discretion.[303] When it is shown that the state committed a serious breach, the state cannot argue that there should be no monetary liability because there was no subjective fault relating to the conduct that led to the breach. The requirement to prove a sufficiently serious

of the Disobedient State" (1996) 2 E.L.J. 199; W. van Gerven, "Bridging the Unbridgeable: Community and National Tort Laws after *Francovich* and *Brasserie*" (1996) 45 I.C.L.Q. 507.

296 *Factortame* [1996] E.C.R. I-1029 at [34].

297 *Factortame* [1996] E.C.R. I-1029 at [42].

298 *Factortame* [1996] E.C.R. I-1029 at [47].

299 *Factortame* [1996] E.C.R. I-1029 at [51].

300 *Factortame* [1996] E.C.R. I-1029 at [55].

301 *Factortame* [1996] E.C.R. I-1029 at [56].

302 *R. v HM Treasury, Ex p. British Telecommunications Plc* (C-392/93) [1996] E.C.R. I-1631; *Denkavit International v Budesamt fur Finantzen* (C-283, 291 & 292/94) [1996] E.C.R. I-5063; *R. v Ministry of Agriculture, Fisheries and Food, Ex p. Hedley Lomas (Ireland) Ltd* (C-5/94) [1996] E.C.R. I-2553; *Dillenkofer v Germany* (C-178, 179, 188-190/94) [1996] E.C.R. I-4845; *Brinkmann Tabakfabriken GmbH v Skatteministeriet* (C-319/96) [1998] E.C.R. I-5255; *Rechberger v Austria* (C-140/97) [1999] E.C.R. I-3499.

303 *Laboratoires Pharmaceutiques Bergaderm SA and Goupil v Commission* (C-352/98) [2000] E.C.R. I-5291 at [40]–[47].

breach applies to legislative and non-legislative discretionary action.[304] It is for national courts to decide whether there has been a sufficiently serious breach, although the CJEU often gives guidance on this, or even decides the matter if it feels that it has sufficient facts on which to do so.[305]

Finally, the general principle is that the reparation must be commensurate with the damage sustained.[306] In the absence of EU rules, it is for national law to establish the extent of the reparation. This is subject to the qualification that the criteria must not be less favourable than those applied in similar claims based on domestic law, and that they must not make it impossible or excessively difficult to obtain compensation.[307]

C. Implications for Domestic Law

30–065 Three issues must be addressed when considering the impact of the European Union's jurisprudence on domestic law. They are related but distinct.

First, national courts are bound by the CJEU's rulings. A remedy in damages must, therefore, be provided in cases with an EU law component, which fall within the above rules. Thus in *Factortame Ltd (No.5)*[308] the House of Lords decided that the Merchant Shipping Act 1988 constituted a sufficiently serious breach of EU law, so as to lead to damages liability. This was because certain conditions in the legislation, relating to nationality and domicile, were felt to be clearly contrary to EU law, and because the Commission had consistently taken the view that the legislation was contrary to EU law. The fact that the government had sought legal advice as to the compatibility of the 1988 Act with EU law was no defence. By way of contrast Latham J in *Lay and Gage*[309] held that the respondent had made an excusable error in the construction of a complex regulation which was neither clear, nor precise. There was, therefore, no sufficiently serious breach so as to found a claim in damages.

Second, there is the issue as to the nature of the cause of action in cases with an EU law element. They can be treated as giving rise to an autonomous cause of action, without the necessity of fitting into pre-existing domestic categories. There is some older authority to this effect.[310] It is also evident from case law post *Brasserie du Pecheur* and *Factortame* that national courts do not feel the need to fit cases into a pre-existing head of liability, and thus provide support for the idea of an autonomous cause of action. It would, by way of contrast, be possible to modify the cause of action for breach of statutory duty.[311] There are,

---

304 P. Craig and G. de Búrca, *EU Law: Text, Cases and Materials* (2015), Ch.16.

305 *British Telecommunications* [1996] E.C.R. I-1631.

306 *Factortame* [1996] E.C.R. I-1029 at [82].

307 *Factortame* [1996] E.C.R. I-1029 at [83]; P. Craig and G. de Búrca, *EU Law: Text, Cases and Materials* (2015), Ch.8.

308 *R. v Secretary of State for Transport, Ex p. Factortame Ltd (No.5)* [2000] 1 A.C. 524; *Delaney v Secretary of State for Transport* [2014] EWHC 1785 (QB).

309 *R. v Ministry of Agriculture, Fisheries and Food, Ex p. Lay and Gage* [1998] C.O.D. 387.

310 *Application des Gaz v Falks Veritas* [1974] Ch. 381 at 395–396.

311 *Garden Cottage Foods Ltd v Milk Marketing Board* [1984] A.C. 130, HL; *R. v Secretary of State for Transport, Ex p. Factortame (No.6)* [2001] 1 W.L.R. 942 QBD.

however, a number of potential difficulties in conceptualising matters in this way,[312] and it is therefore preferable to regard breach of EU law as an autonomous cause of action.

Third, there is the interesting issue as to whether, and in what way, the CJEU's case law will have an impact on cases where there is no EU law element. Our courts are not bound by EU law in such instances, although they can have regard to such jurisprudence when developing domestic case law. This will be considered below.[313]

D. Recovery of Money

30–066 EU law can also assist individuals who have paid money levied by Member States contrary to EU law and who seek restitutionary relief.[314] The extent to which national remedial rules that limit the vindication of an EU right are lawful under EU law is a complex issue which cannot be fully explored here,[315] but some of the basic principles can be set out.

In *San Giorgio*,[316] the ECJ considered a national rule preventing recovery of taxes wrongfully levied where they had been passed on to third parties. The national rule was based on the rebuttable presumption that the charge had been passed on whenever the goods had been transferred. The ECJ held that the passing on of a charge was a factor that could be properly considered by the national courts. However, it would be contrary to EU law if the burden of proof rendered recovery excessively difficult or virtually impossible. This was so even if the same rule operated in the context of purely domestic cases. It is clear from *Comateb*[317] that whether a charge had been passed on was a question of fact for the national court to decide, and that repayment could only be resisted where the charge was borne in its entirety by someone other than the trader. Even where the whole or part of an unlawful charge had been passed on repayment to the trader would not necessarily constitute unjust enrichment, since the imposition of the unlawful charge might have affected the volume of sales. The court also indicated that a trader might bring a damages action in accord with *Brasserie du Pecheur* and *Factortame* for reparation of loss caused by the levying of unlawful charges, irrespective of whether those charges had been passed on.[318]

[312] P. Craig, "Once More Unto the Breach: The Community, the State and Damages Liability" (1997) 113 L.Q.R. 67, 88–89; M. Hoskins, "Rebirth of the Innominate Tort?", in J. Beatson and T. Tridimas (eds), *New Directions in European Public Law* (Oxford: Hart, 1998), Ch.7; K.M. Stanton, "New Forms of the Tort of Breach of Statutory Duty" (2004) 120 L.Q.R. 324, 328–329.

[313] See paras 30–068 to 30–075.

[314] *Sempra Metals* [2007] 3 W.L.R. 354; *Chalke Ltd v Revenue and Customs Commissioners* [2009] EWHC 952; *Test Claimants in the FII Group Litigation* [2010] EWCA Civ 103.

[315] M. Dougan, "Cutting your Losses in the Enforcement Deficit: A Community Right to the Recovery of Unlawfully Levied Charges" (1998) 1 C.Y.E.L.S. 233; P. Craig and G. de Búrca, *EU Law: Text, Cases and Materials* (2015), Ch.8.

[316] *Amministrazione delle Finanze dello Stato v San Giorgio* (199/82) [1983] E.C.R. 3595; *Amministrazione delle Finanze dello Stato v Denkavit Italiana* (61/79) [1980] E.C.R. 1205.

[317] *Société Comateb v Directeur General des Douanes et Droits Indirects* (C-192–218/95) [1997] E.C.R. I-165.

[318] *Société Comateb* [1997] E.C.R. I-165 at [34].

10. JUDICIAL IMMUNITY

30–067 The law draws a distinction between liability for intra vires and ultra vires acts, and between different types of courts. The precise metes and bounds of liability are not entirely clear, but would appear to be as follows.

No judge, whether of a superior or inferior court, is liable if acting within jurisdiction, even if this is done maliciously.[319] This immunity would appear to apply to justices of the peace.[320]

No judge of a superior court is liable in damages for an act done outside jurisdiction, provided that this was done by the judge in the honest belief that the act was within jurisdiction.[321] Liability will only attach for knowingly acting outside jurisdiction.[322]

An inferior court is one that is subject to the control of the prerogative orders. Justices of the peace can be liable for acts done outside their jurisdiction,[323] and it appears that this liability attaches to other inferior courts.[324] The phrase acting without or in excess of jurisdiction is, however, interpreted more narrowly than in the context of an ordinary action for judicial review which seeks to quash the finding of a public body.[325]

11. REFORM

A. Options for Reform

30–068 It is apparent from the preceding discussion that public bodies can cause loss to individuals in situations where there is at present no redress.[326] This may be because of difficulties of applying tortious principles to public bodies, or because

---

319 *Sirros v Moore* [1975] Q.B. 118 at 132–133; *Re McC (A Minor)* [1985] A.C. 528 at 540–541; *FM (A Child) v Singer* [2004] EWHC 793 (QB).

320 *McC* [1985] A.C. 528 at 533, 541, 559.

321 *Sirros* [1975] Q.B. 118 at 134–135; *McC* [1985] A.C. 528 at 541, 550; *Pius v Fearnley* [2013] EWHC 2216 (Ch).

322 *Sirros* [1975] Q.B. 118 at 136, 149; *McC* [1985] A.C. 528 at 540.

323 *McC* [1985] A.C. 528 at 541, 550, disapproving in this respect *Sirros*. See also *R. v Manchester City Magistrates' Court, Ex p. Davies* [1989] Q.B. 631; *Lloyd v United Kingdom* [2006] RA 329.

324 *McC* [1985] A.C. 528 at 541, 550. Compare *Everett v Griffiths* [1921] 1 A.C. 631.

325 *McC* [1985] A.C. 528 at 542G, 543B, 544E, 546. The precise breadth of this phrase is, however, unclear, at 546–547.

326 P. Craig, "Compensation in Public Law" (1980) 96 L.Q.R. 413 at 435–455; J. McBride, "Damages as a Remedy for Unlawful Administrative Action" [1979] C.L.J. 323; C. Harlow, *Compensation and Government Torts* (London: Sweet & Maxwell, 1982); Sir B. Markesinis, J.-B. Auby, D. Coester-Waltjen and S.Deakin, *Tortious Liability of Statutory Bodies, A Comparative Analysis of Five English Cases* (Oxford: Hart, 1999); R. Caranta, "Public Law Illegality and Governmental Liability", in Fairgrieve, Andenas and Bell (eds), *Tort Liability of Public Authorities in Comparative Perspective* (2002), Ch.10; P. Cane, "Damages in Public Law" (1999) 9 Otago. L.R. 489; B. Markesinis, "Unity or Division: The Search for Similarities in Contemporary European Law", in D. Fairgrieve, M. Andenas and J. Bell, Ch.14; M. Fordham, "Reparation for Maladministration: Public Law's Final Frontier" [2003] J.R. 104; C. Harlow, *State Liability, Tort Law and Beyond* (2004); S. Bailey, "Negligence in the Realms of Public Law—A Positive Obligation to Rescue" [1984] P.L.

public action may cause loss to an individual in circumstances that do not fit recognised heads of liability. If a person is refused a licence, loss may well result, but that loss may not have been occasioned by an established tort. If we wish to develop the law beyond the established heads of civil liability there are various ways in which this could be done. Compensation could be given on the basis of a risk theory, for invalidity, or on an ex gratia basis. Whether the courts or some other agency should administer such a scheme is a separate question.

B. Compensation via a Risk Theory

The risk theory expresses a conclusion, which is that certain interests in society should be protected against *lawful* or *unlawful* interference by government. It does not provide a criterion as to which interests should be thus protected. This is a value judgment for society to make. The conclusion expressed by the risk theory is that the burden of certain public activities should be borne by the community rather than placed on an individual who has been harmed, but cannot prove an established tort. Compensation on the basis of a risk theory or something analogous thereto, is more developed in countries such as France,[327] than the UK. **30–069**

There *is some statutory recognition of the risk theory in the UK*, in the sense that it underlies legislation in certain areas. Which interests are accorded statutory protection on the basis of a risk theory may depend on the strength of the relevant pressure groups,[328] or the degree of public sympathy aroused for the plight of injured individuals,[329] rather than an objective assessment of the importance of that interest when compared to the plight of others who remain unprotected.[330]

There *is however no general common law doctrine based on the risk theory*. The courts have rather made it more difficult to establish tortious liability in nuisance, *Rylands v Fletcher* and breach of statutory duty where the defendant is a public body, as opposed to a private party. A risk theory could be usefully employed in such cases, and in the *Dorset Yacht* type of situation.[331] Society will benefit from the greater reformative effect of open borstals on offenders as compared to closed, high security prisons. The increased risk of individual escape may be an inevitable consequence of such borstals. The cost should be borne by society as a whole and not by the individual who is unable to prove fault. The

277; Sir B. Markesinis and J. Fedtke, "Damages for the Negligence of Statutory Bodies: The Empirical and Comparative Dimensions to an Unending Debate" [2007] P.L. 299; T. Cornford, *Towards a Public Law of Tort* (2008).

327 N. Brown and J. Bell, *French Administrative Law*, 5th edn (Oxford: Oxford University Press, 1998), pp.193–201; R. Caranta, "Public Law Illegality and Governmental Liability", in D. Fairgrieve, M. Andenas and J. Bell (eds), *Tort Liability of Public Authorities in Comparative Perspective* (2002); S. Flogaitis, "State Extra-Contractual Liability in France, England and Greece", in D. Fairgrieve, M. Andenas and J. Bell, Ch.13; Sir B. Markesinis and J. Fedtke, "Damages for the Negligence of Statutory Bodies: The Empirical and Comparative Dimensions to an Unending Debate" [2007] P.L. 299.

328 Land Compensation Act 1973.

329 Vaccine Damage Payment Act 1979.

330 J. Fleming, "Drug Injury Compensation Plans" (1982) 30 Am. J. Comp. Law. 297.

331 *Dorset Yacht* [1970] A.C. 1004.

force of this reasoning was recognised by Lord Phillips MR in *Marcic*, who held that Strasbourg jurisprudence suggested that:

> "… where an authority carries on an undertaking in the interest of the community as a whole it may have to pay compensation to individuals whose rights are infringed by that undertaking in order to achieve a fair balance between the interests of the individual and the community".[332]

However, the House of Lords was, as we have seen, more cautious in this respect.[333]

C. Compensation for Invalidity

30–070 Compensation for invalidity also expresses a conclusion: certain activities in society that cause loss should only give rise to liability when they are invalidly performed. Invalidity becomes a necessary condition of liability. The subject-matter that would commonly come within this area would be losses arising from modern regulatory legislation such as social welfare or licensing. For example, in *Maguire*[334] the applicants had the refusal to grant them cab licences by the local authority quashed, and then sought damages for the losses suffered in the interim. They based their claim on breach of statutory duty, negligence and breach of contract. These arguments failed on the facts, and Schiemann J noted that there was no right to damages for breach of administrative law. There are two reasons, practical and conceptual, why invalidity is a necessary condition of liability.

The *practical reason* is that legislation is constantly enacted to benefit a section of the population, for example through tax changes or selective assistance to industry. If a firm is refused such assistance intra vires there can be no reason to grant compensation, since this would defeat the object of the legislation.[335]

The *conceptual reason* is more contestable. The natural tendency is to assign cases with some private law analogy to the risk theory, whereas losses arising from more modern regulatory legislation are held to require proof of invalidity.[336] We differentiate in this way because of a feeling that the establishment of an open borstal or the building of roads affect "rights" in a way which a statute altering the conditions of manufacturing does not. This achieves plausibility because the loss from the public works has a private law analogy, which "strengthens" the call for sharing the cost among taxpayers when that loss is caused by lawful governmental action. By way of contrast, a statute that detrimentally affects a section of industry, by altering the conditions of business through restrictions on

---

332 *Marcic* [2002] Q.B. 929 at [118].

333 *Marcic* [2004] 2 A.C. 42.

334 *R. v Metropolitan Borough of Knowsley, Ex p. Maguire* [1992] C.O.D. 499 QBD. See also *R. (Quark Fishing Ltd) v Secretary of State for Foreign and Commonwealth Affairs (No.2)* [2003] EWHC 1743; [2006] 1 A.C. 529.

335 There may, however, be cases where the disadvantage to the individual is not the object of the legislation, but only an incident of it. This is a difficult line to draw. In France there is a limited principle allowing recovery for losses caused by legislation, N. Brown and J. Bell, *French Administrative Law* (1998), pp.199–200.

336 Thus, a case in which public works affects property values is regarded as a prime candidate for a risk theory, while one in which public action affects the livelihood of a particular manufacturer is regarded as a candidate for compensation only if there is invalidity.

exports, produces no private law analogy. No private law rights strengthen the call for cost sharing among the public here. The absence of any such common law background does not, however, automatically settle a hierarchy of values or interests. It is, for example, not immediately self-evident that property interests are more precious than livelihood.

There are nonetheless significant problems that would have to be resolved if reform were to proceed.[337] The most serious problem is the breadth of the ultra vires doctrine. A public body may be found to have acted ultra vires for a number of reasons including: breach of natural justice, breach of other mandatory procedural conditions, misconstruction of the enabling statute, or violation of a principle governing the exercise of discretion, such as irrelevancy, propriety of purpose, unreasonableness/proportionality. The consequences of rendering public bodies liable for any species of invalidity per se can be appreciated by focusing upon jurisdictional error and excess of discretion. **30–071**

Cases involving allegations of jurisdictional error, such as *Dunlop*[338] and *Takaro*,[339] demonstrate that statutory provisions will often involve difficult and contestable issues of statutory construction, and as Lord Keith stated, even judges can misconstrue legislation.[340] The "correct" interpretation of enabling legislation is not infrequently a matter on which judges disagree. In *Anisminic*[341] four out of the nine judges involved in the case from the High Court to the House of Lords believed that the FCC's construction of the term successor in title was in fact correct.

These problems are often also present when the challenge is to the manner in which the public body exercised its discretion. There are, to be sure, instances of discretionary behaviour where the public body really abused its power and behaved in an overbearing manner. There are, however, also many instances in which the discretionary decision of the body may be overturned when there is nothing of this sort present on the facts. Whether a particular consideration is deemed to be "relevant" or "irrelevant" will be a matter on which the judiciary can disagree,[342] as will be the result of the balancing process required in the context of proportionality.

It is for such reasons that the ECJ declined to impose liability in damages on the European Union where a regulation made pursuant to a discretionary power caused loss, unless the applicant could show a manifest and flagrant breach of a superior rule of law to protect the individual. Invalidity per se will not suffice for liability in damages. Difficult questions of causation, remoteness and the quantum of recovery would also have to be resolved if any such reform were to be seriously considered.[343] **30–072**

---

337 P. Craig, "Compensation in Public Law" (1980) 96 L.Q.R. 413, 438–443.
338 *Dunlop* [1982] A.C. 158.
339 *Takaro* [1988] A.C. 473.
340 *Takaro* [1988] A.C. 473.
341 *Anisminic* [1969] 2 A.C. 147.
342 See, e.g. *Takaro* [1988] A.C. 473 and many others.
343 P. Craig, "Compensation in Public Law" (1980) 96 L.Q.R. 413, 437–443. The response by the Justice study, *Administrative Justice, Some Necessary Reforms*, Report of the Committee of the Justice—All Souls Review of Administrative Law in the United Kingdom (Oxford: Oxford University

The reform proposed by the Justice study, which advocated damages liability on proof of a wide category of wrongful behaviour, should, therefore, be treated with caution,[344] and the need for such caution was stressed by Lord Woolf.[345] If damages for invalidity were to be granted then the term ultra vires should be more narrowly construed, as it has been in the case law on damages liability of the judiciary. There could alternatively be some qualification as to the manner in which the ultra vires act occurred, requiring the error to be manifest or serious, or there should be proven reliance losses, as in *Maguire*,[346] as a result of a legitimate expectation generated by the defendant's representation.

D. Compensation for Serious Breach

30–073 The idea that compensation be grounded on serious breach was central to the Law Commission's recommendations.[347] It published a Discussion Paper in 2004,[348] followed by a Scoping Report in 2006,[349] a Consultation Paper in 2008[350] and a response to the consultation in 2010.[351] The recommendations were not generally well received and the government was opposed to the suggestions for reform. The Law Commission is therefore not pursuing this aspect of its reform agenda. It is nonetheless important to understand the core of the proposals and the reasons for the opposition.

The Law Commission Consultation Paper 187 was predicated on what was termed modified corrective justice, which connoted the idea that while individuals had a justified claim for redress caused by government wrongdoing, the liability rules should also reflect the special position of public bodies and protect them from unmeritorious claims. The core proposal for public law was that there should be liability for "serious fault" by a public body. The core proposal for private law was that this same basic criterion should be applied to cases that were regarded as "truly public", with ordinary negligence liability being applicable in other cases.

These proposals were criticised, in particular those for private law. The Law Commission reviewed the results of the consultation exercise in its 2010 paper and decided that the general project could not be taken further at present. It

Press, 1988), pp.362–363, to these problems is unsatisfactory. It is true that the law copes with issues of causation in other areas, but the particular way in which the problem arises here is certainly distinctive and problematic, see further, Craig, 438–439.

344 Justice study, *Administrative Justice, Some Necessary Reforms*, pp.362–364. The breadth of the word "wrongful" is conveyed at p.333. In so far as the Report considered these problems they were unmoved by them, p.364.

345 Lord Woolf, *Protection of the Public-A New Challenge* (London: Sweet & Maxwell, 1990), pp.56–62.

346 *Maguire* [1992] C.O.D. 499.

347 The Law Commission papers are available at: *http://www.lawcom.gov.uk/project/administrative-redress-public-bodies-and-the-citizen/* [Accessed 27 January 2016].

348 Law Commission, *Monetary Remedies in Public Law, A Discussion Paper* (2004); R. Bagshaw, "Monetary Remedies in Public Law—Misdiagnosis and Misprescription" [2006] L.S. 4.

349 Law Commission, *Remedies against Public Bodies, A Scoping Report* (2006).

350 Law Commission Consultation Paper No.187, *Administrative Redress: Public Bodies and the Citizen* (2008).

351 Law Commission Paper No.322, *Administrative Redress: Public Bodies and the Citizen* (2010).

nonetheless felt that the core proposal for public law, which attracted considerable support and less criticism than that for private law, had merit and that any problems with it were not insurmountable.

There is force in this view. It is easy when considering the welter of conflicting opinions on this topic to lose sight of the fundamentals. The initial inquiry is whether there are gaps in our law where individuals who are worthy of redress are unable to claim for the reasons adverted to above: either there is no existing cause of action, or there are real difficulties in applying the existing torts to public bodies. It is possible to deny the existence of such gaps, to argue that these are fanciful rather than real, and that the individuals in such circumstances have no "valid" claim against the state for monetary redress. Such arguments must however be substantiated, not just stated. They must be justified in depth, revealing the contestable normative assumptions about what constitutes a legitimate foundation for monetary redress against the state. 30–074

If, having undertaken the above inquiry, one feels that there are indeed gaps in the present law that should be filled, it is then necessary to consider how this should be done. The options are not limitless in this respect. If one believes that liability for invalidity per se would be too harsh a criterion for liability for the reasons given above and those discussed by the Law Commission, then we must use some other test. It would be possible simply to accord a broad discretion to the courts. If however this discretion is unstructured with little if any guidance as to the criteria for the award of compensation then there is a danger that courts will interpret the discretion very differently. A broad, unstructured discretion is also open to the critique that it connotes legislative abdication of responsibility as to what the criterion of liability should be. This leads one back to a test framed in terms of serious breach, or something similar thereto, taking account of the types of factor that have influenced the CJEU when deciding whether such a breach can be proven on the facts of a particular case.

E. Compensation on an Ex Gratia Basis

A fourth direction for reform would be to grant compensation on an ex gratia basis.[352] This standard expresses a conclusion but does not tell us when it should be applied. The conclusion is that compensation should be granted even though there may be no formal legal entitlement to it as such. A person who is injured by the action of a public body may not be able to recover because no established tort has been committed and because no statute gives any legal entitlement. 30–075

The public body may nonetheless decide to grant compensation without formally admitting any legal liability, as has occurred in certain instances.[353] The reasons for preferring ex gratia payments to one of the other grounds for giving compensation vary, but include: the difficulty of devising an adequate principle of liability, flexibility, and an unwillingness to accept that the individual has an entitlement to monetary recovery. The fact that the payment is ex gratia should

---

[352] For a valuable account, see C. Harlow, *Compensation and Government Torts* (1982), Pt 4.

[353] C. Harlow and R. Rawlings, *Law and Administration*, 2nd edn (London: Butterworths, 1997), pp.607–610.

not lead one to conclude either that decisions are wholly "open textured", or that the courts play no role in the process. Guidelines of some specificity will often exist, as was so in the case of the Criminal Injuries Compensation scheme administered by the CICB,[354] and the courts have applied principles of judicial review to its decisions.[355]

F. Conclusion

30–076 The general conclusions to be drawn about tort liability and public bodies are deceptively simple: we either live with what we have or we create something new. The prospects of reform in the short term are not good, given the fate of the Law Commission study. It might be argued that this is a welcome outcome and that any reform should be piecemeal rather than general. It should nonetheless be recognised that any decisions made about a particular area will have broader ramifications. Thus, the decision to grant a novel form of compensation in one area necessarily leads to consideration of whether it is fair or just that it should be absent in a different context. Reform may be piecemeal in practice, but the broader issues outlined above cannot be ignored.

354 C. Harlow and R. Rawlings, *Law and Administration* (1997), pp.610–617. The scheme was given a statutory base, Criminal Justice Act 1988 Pt VII, Criminal Injuries Compensation Act 1995; C. Harlow and R. Rawlings *Law and Administration*, 3rd edn (Cambridge: Cambridge University Press, 2009), pp.777–783.

355 *R. v Criminal Injuries Compensation Board, Ex p. Lain* [1967] 2 Q.B. 864 QBD; *R. v Criminal Injuries Compensation Board, Ex p. Schofield* [1971] 1 W.L.R. 926 DC.

INDEX

This index has been prepared using Sweet and Maxwell's Legal Taxonomy. Main index entries conform to keywords provided by the Legal Taxonomy except where references to specific documents or non-standard terms (denoted by quotation marks) have been included. These keywords provide a means of identifying similar concepts in other Sweet and Maxwell publications and online services to which keywords from the Legal Taxonomy have been applied. Readers may find some minor differences between terms used in the text and those which appear in the index. Suggestions to *sweetandmaxwell.taxonomy@thomson.com.*

All references are to paragraph number